- In nature we can never do just one thing; everything we do creates effects that are often unpredictable (*first law of ecology, or principle of ecological backlash*).

- Everything is connected to and intermingled with everything else; we are all in this together (*second law of ecology, or principle of interdependence*).

- Any chemical that we produce should not interfere with Earth's natural biogeochemical cycles in ways that degrade Earth's life-support systems for us or other species (*third law of ecology*).

- We can't expect to reduce the dangers from most hazards to zero, but the risks can be greatly reduced (*principle of risk-benefit analysis*).

- Any system that depends on fallible humans for its design, operation, and maintenance will sooner or later fail (*limitation-of-risk-benefit-analysis principle*).

- Nature is not only more complex than we think, but also more complex than we can ever think (*principle of complexity*).

Economics and Politics

- The market price of anything should include all present and future costs of any pollution, environmental degradation, or other harmful effects connected with it that are passed on to society and the environment (*principle of internalizing all external costs*).

- Some forms of economic growth are harmful; don't produce harmful goods (*principle of economic cancer*).

- Short-term greed leads to long-term economic and environmental grief; don't deplete Earth's natural capital and mortgage the future (*don't-live-off-Earth-capital principle*).

- The more things you own, the more you are owned by things (*principle of overconsumption and "thing tyranny"*).

- Don't give people subsidies and tax breaks to produce harmful goods and unnecessarily waste resources; either eliminate all resource subsidies or only reward producers who reduce resource waste, pollution, and environmental degradation (*principle of economic and ecological wisdom*).

- Put the poor and their environment first, not last; help the poor sustain themselves and their local environment, and do this with love, not condescension; we cannot have peace, environmental justice, or a sense of pride about our accomplishments as a species as long as anyone still lives in poverty (*eliminate-the-poverty-trap principle*).

- Change Earth-degrading and Earth-depleting manufacturing processes, products, and businesses into Earth-sustaining ones (*break-it-and-fix-it-better principle*).

- We cannot have a healthy economy in a sick environment (*economics-as-if-Earth-mattered principle*).

- Everything we have or will have comes from the sun and the earth; the earth can get along without us, but we can't get along without the earth; an exhausted Earth is an exhausted economy (*respect-your-roots, or Earth-first, principle*).

- Anticipating and preventing problems is cheaper and more effective than reacting to and trying to cure them; an ounce of prevention is worth a pound of cure (*prevention, or input-control, principle*).

- History shows that the most important changes come from the bottom up, not the top down (*individuals-matter principle*).

- Every crisis is an opportunity for change (*bad-news-can-be-good-news principle*).

- Think globally, act locally (*principle of change*).

Worldview and Ethics

- The earth does not belong to us; we belong to the earth (*principle of humility*).

- Our role is to understand and work with the rest of nature, not to conquer it (*principle of cooperation*).

- Every living species has a right to live, or at least to struggle to live, simply because it exists; this right is not dependent on its actual or potential use to us (*respect-for-nature principle*).

- The best things in life aren't things (*principle of love, caring, and joy*).

- Something is right when it tends to maintain the ecological integrity, sustainability, and diversity of Earth's life-support systems for us and other species and wrong when it tends otherwise; the bottom line is that Earth is the bottom line (*principle of sustainability and ecocentrism*).

- It is wrong for humans to cause the premature extinction of any wild species and the elimination and degradation of their habitats (*preservation-of-wildlife-and-biodiversity principle*).

- When we alter nature to meet what we consider to be basic needs or nonbasic wants, we should choose the method that does the least possible harm to other living things; in minimizing harm, it is in general worse to harm a species than an individual organism, and still worse to harm a community of living organisms (*principle of minimum wrong*).

- When we alter nature, we should make such changes at nature's rates and in nature's way (*principle of sustainable change*).

- It is wrong to treat people and other living things primarily as factors of production, whose value is expressed only in economic terms (*economics-is-not-everything principle*).

- We should leave the earth in as good condition as we found it, if not better (*rights-of-the-unborn principle*).

- All people should be held responsible for their own pollution and environmental degradation; dumping our wastes in another area or country is the equivalent of using chemical warfare on the people or other species receiving our wastes (*responsibility-of-the-born principle*).

- No individual, corporation, or nation has a right to an ever-increasing share of the earth's finite resources; don't let need slide into greed (*principle of enoughness*).

- We should protect Earth's remaining wild ecosystems from our activities, rehabilitate or restore ecosystems we have degraded, use ecosystems only on a sustainable basis, and allow many of the ecosystems we have occupied and abused to return to a wild state (*principle of ecosystem protection and healing*).

- In protecting and sustaining nature, go farther than the law requires (*ethics-often-exceeds-legality principle*).

- To prevent excessive deaths of people and other species, people must prevent excessive births (*birth-control-is-better-than-death-control principle*).

- Don't do anything that depletes Earth's physical, chemical, and biological capital, which supports all life and human economic activities; the Earth deficit is the ultimate deficit (*balanced-Earth-budget principle*).

- To love, cherish, and understand the earth and yourself, take time to experience and sense the air, water, soil, plants, animals, bacteria, and other parts of the earth directly (*direct-experience-is-the-best-teacher principle*).

- Learn about, love, care for your local environment, and live gently within that place; walk lightly on the earth (*love-your-neighborhood principle*).

FOUR LEVELS OF ENVIRONMENTAL AWARENESS

First Level of Awareness

Pollution and Environmental Degradation

Environmental problems are seen as pollution problems that threaten human health and welfare. Each environmental problem can be solved in isolation by waiting until it reaches a crisis level and then dealing with it by the use of legal, technological, and economic methods, mostly temporary approaches that attempt to control or clean up pollution instead of preventing it. At this level, it is assumed that growth-oriented, technological societies can continue indefinitely.

There are four major problems with staying at this awareness level. First, it is exclusively a human-centered view, not a life-centered view. Second, individuals see their own impacts as too tiny to matter, not realizing that billions of individual impacts acting together threaten the life-support systems for us and other species. Third, this approach seduces people into thinking that environmental and resource problems can be solved by quick technological solutions. "Have technology fix us up, send me the bill at the end of the month, but don't expect me to change my way of living." Fourth, it attempts to treat the growing symptoms of environmental abuse instead of trying to determine and deal with the causes leading to our environmental and resource problems. It is like trying to use bandages to stop a rapidly spreading cancer.

Second Level of Awareness

Consumption Overpopulation

We recognize that the causes of pollution, environmental degradation, and resource depletion are a combination of people overpopulation in poor countries and consumption overpopulation in affluent countries, with the most environmentally damaging populations living in industrialized societies devoted to very high rates of resource consumption and waste production. At this level, the answers seem obvious. Stabilize and then reduce population sizes in all countries. Reduce wasteful consumption of matter and energy resources—especially in the affluent countries that consume 80% of the world's resources.

At this level, there is little emphasis on transforming political and economic systems in ways that help sustain the earth, and in setting aside or restoring much larger areas of Earth's natural systems as wilderness areas, parks, and wildlife preserves. There is little awareness that most protected natural areas are too small to sustain their natural diversity of organisms and are being rapidly overwhelmed and biologically impoverished by unsustainable use of resources and the pollutants produced by technological, growth-oriented societies. This second level of awareness still views humans as above or outside nature and as more important than other species.

Third Level of Awareness

Spaceship Earth

The goal at this level is to use technology and existing economic and political systems to control population growth, pollution, and resource depletion to prevent environmental overload. Earth is viewed as a spaceship—a machine that we have the capacity and the duty to control and dominate by using advanced technology. If Earth becomes too crowded, we will build stations in space for the excess population. If Earth becomes depleted of mineral resources, we will mine other planets. Genetic engineering will be used to control the evolution of life forms and develop organisms that produce more food, clean up oil spills and toxic wastes, and satisfy more of our unlimited wants. Because of our ingenuity and power over the rest of nature, there will always be more.

This view of the earth as a spaceship is a sophisticated expression of the idea that through technology and human ingenuity we can control nature and create artificial environments and life forms to avoid environmental overload. Instead of novelty, spontaneity, joy, freedom, and biological and cultural diversity, the spaceship model is based on cultural sameness, social regimentation (ground control), artificiality, monotony, and gadgetry. This approach can also cause environmental overload and resource depletion in the long run, because it is based on the false idea that we understand how nature works and that there are no limits to the earth's resources and our ability to overcome any problem with technological innovations.

This view calls for sustainable economic development and sustainable societies for humans. Sustainable has become the buzzword for governments and businesses. Careful analysis reveals that some of the proposals now being made under the guise of sustainability are in the long run unsustainable. The human-centered spaceship worldview is inadequate for dealing with an overpopulated, environmentally stressed, and globally interconnected world based on living by depleting and degrading Earth's natural capital.

Fourth Level of Awareness

Sustainable Earth

The first three levels of understanding are human-centered views, in which we shape the world to meet our needs. They do not recognize that the solution to our problems lies in giving up our destructive fantasies of omnipotence. Instead, we must develop an Earth-centered or life-centered worldview based on the principles summarized on the preceding two pages.

We cannot have sustainable or any form of economic development or sustainable societies unless we help sustain the entire earth by working with Earth's natural processes. We must do this not only because it helps ensure our survival, but also because it is wrong to do otherwise.

SEVENTH EDITION

An Introduction to Environmental Science

Living in the Environment

G. TYLER MILLER, JR.

Wadsworth Publishing Company
Belmont, California
A Division of Wadsworth, Inc.

SCIENCE EDITOR: Jack Carey

EDITORIAL ASSISTANT: Kathy Shea

PRODUCTION EDITOR: Vicki Friedberg

MANAGING DESIGNER: Cynthia Schultz

TEXT DESIGNERS: James Chadwick/Cynthia Schultz

PRINT BUYER: Barbara Britton

ART EDITOR: Donna Kalal

PERMISSIONS EDITOR: Peggy Meehan

COPY EDITOR: Carole Crouse

PAGE MAKE-UP: Wendy Calmenson

PHOTO RESEARCHER: Stephen Forsling

TECHNICAL ILLUSTRATORS: Darwin and Vally Hennings, Tasa Graphic Arts, Inc., John and Judith Waller, Marjorie Leggitt, Guy Magellenes, Susan Breitbard, Joan Carol, Raychel Ciemma, Florence Fujimoto, Linda Harris, Victor Royer, Jeanne M. Schreiber, and Kathryn W. Werhane.

COMPOSITOR: Thompson Type/San Diego, CA

COLOR SEPARATOR: Accu-color/St. Louis, MO

PRINTER: Arcata Graphics/Kingsport, TN

COVER DESIGN: Cynthia Schultz

PART OPENING PHOTOGRAPHS:

Part 1: Brian Parker/Tom Stack & Associates

Part 2: Los Angeles Convention & Visitors Bureau

Part 3: United Nations

Part 4: Errol Andrew/FPG International

Part 5: California Energy Commission

Part 6: Thomas Kitchin/Tom Stack & Associates

Part 7: Sam Kittner/SIPA Press

COVER PHOTOGRAPH: Short-tailed weasel (ermine) in winter, Grand Teton National Park, Wyoming, © 1985 Tom Mangelsen. The ermine, which helps control rodent population, was selected as the cover image for this book not only because of its striking beauty but also because it is a part of Earth's vital biodiversity, which we are severely reducing. The ermine symbolizes the ecological and ethical issues we face every day. As you look into the eyes of this animal, ask yourself: Would you kill this animal or have it killed to make a fur coat?

3 4 5 6 7 8 9 10 — 96 95 94 93 92

Library of Congress Cataloging-in-Publication Data

Miller, G. Tyler (George Tyler), 1931–

    Living in the environment : an introduction to environmental science / G. Tyler Miller, Jr. — 7th ed.

      p. cm.

    Includes bibliographical references and index.

    ISBN 0-534-16560-5

    1. Human ecology. 2. Environmental policy. I. Title.

GF41.M54 1992

363.7 — dc20   91-35584

PREFACE

TO THE INSTRUCTOR

GOALS This book is designed for introductory courses in environmental science. The basic goal of environmental science is to learn how everything is interconnected, and this book summarizes what I have learned after spending 26 years trying to understand how the various parts of the earth are connected. My goals for the book are to

- provide an introduction to environmental science in an accurate, balanced, and interesting way without the use of mathematics or complex scientific information

- help your students discover that dealing with environmental and resource issues is fun, interesting, and important to their lives

- allow you to use the material in a flexible way, depending on course length and what you believe are the important topics

- introduce students to the key concepts and principles that govern how nature works and apply those concepts and principles to possible solutions to environmental and resource problems

- show how environmental and resource problems are interrelated and to emphasize that they must be understood and responded to in an integrated way, locally, regionally, nationally, and globally

- give a realistic but hopeful view of how much has been done and what remains to be done in sustaining the earth for us and other species

- indicate what individuals can do in their personal lives to help sustain rather than degrade Earth's life-support systems

A WELL-TESTED BOOK The material in this textbook has been used and class-tested by more than 2 million students at over two-thirds of the country's colleges and universities. It has been the most widely used environmental science textbook in the United States and throughout the world since 1975, when the first edition was published. In 1990 it was selected by *The Ecologist* as one of the 20 best environmental books published between 1970 and 1990—the only textbook to make the list. Also in 1990 it and its briefer version, *Environmental Science*, were selected as the official textbooks to accompany the Annenberg/CPB Project television series, *Race to Save the Planet*, broadcast on PBS.

THREE DIFFERENT TEXTBOOKS AVAILABLE This book is one of a series of three textbooks designed for different introductory courses on environmental science and resource conservation.

- This book, *Living in the Environment* (7th ed., Wadsworth, 1992, 706 pages, 514 illustrations), gives broad and fairly detailed discussions of environmental and resource issues.

- *Resource Conservation and Management* (Wadsworth, 1990, 546 pages, 406 illustrations) has a different organization. It provides less detailed discussions of ecological concepts, population, and pollution than does *Living in the Environment*, but offers expanded coverage of renewable resources, including seven separate chapters on the following resources and their management: food, fishery, rangeland, forest (two chapters), and wildlife (two chapters).

- *Environmental Science: Sustaining the Earth* (3rd ed., Wadsworth, 1991, 465 pages, 479 illustrations) is the briefest book and is designed especially for a one-semester course. It has a different organization from *Living in the Environment* and *Resource Conservation and Management* and combines some of the features of those two books.

MAJOR CHANGES IN THIS EDITION *This new edition is a comprehensive revision.* Major changes include

- Updating and revising material throughout the book.

- Improving readability by reducing sentence and paragraph length, omitting unnecessary details, and writing in a more personal style.

- Adding three new chapters: "Geologic Processes: The Dynamic Earth" (Chapter 7), "Deforestation and Loss of Biodiversity" (Chapter 10), and "Climate Change, Ozone Depletion, and Nuclear War" (Chapter 11). Chapters 10 and 11 make up a new part (Part 4) titled "Ultimate Global Problems."

- Adding 42 new *Spotlights*, 20 new *Case Studies*, 10 new *Pro/Con* discussions of controversial issues, 7 new *Guest Essays*, and 25 *Individuals Matter* boxes (summaries of what individuals can do to help sustain the earth).

- Expanding coverage of many topics, including pollution prevention, waste reduction, loss of biodiversity, population dynamics, urban problems, climate, global warming, depletion of the ozone layer, tropical deforestation, deforestation in the United States and Canada (the old-growth controversy), sustainable forestry, hazardous waste, and global poverty.

- Adding many new topics, including vanishing amphibians, coral reefs, mangrove swamps, co-evolution, loss of biodiversity in Madagascar, Japan's global environmental impact, the Aral Sea disaster, junk bonds and deforestation, declining populations of American songbirds, environmental effects of the Persian Gulf war, deep-well disposal, the solar envelope house, and environmental careers.

- Increasing the number of chapters from 24 to 26 and the length of the basic text by 85 pages, mostly to accommodate the new chapters and topics and new Guest Essays plus the 95 additional figures and photos. Those wanting a shorter textbook can use *Environmental Science, 3rd ed.*, or *Resource Conservation and Management*.

- Adding four-color diagrams and color photographs. These 514 illustrations (95 more than in the 6th edition) make this the most graphically exciting and teachable edition of this book.

- Increasing the number of maps from 42 to 56 to give students a better geographic perspective. A new feature is a series of "Where is . . . ?" maps that show students where areas being discussed are located.

- Adding one or more experiments, individual projects, or group projects to the Discussion Topics at the end of most chapters. These items are marked with an asterisk (*).

See the pages that follow for a more detailed summary of major changes for each chapter.

KEY FEATURES

- *Concept centered approach:* Uses basic principles and concepts to help students understand environmental and resource problems and possible solutions to these problems in an integrated manner. This approach gives students a way to tie together and evaluate the tremendous amount of information in an incredibly complex field that uses information and ideas from almost every discipline. I have introduced only the concepts and principles

necessary to understand material in this book and have tried to present them simply but accurately. Key principles are summarized inside the front cover.

- *Global, national, and local treatment of issues and solutions.*

- *Flexibility:* The book is divided into seven major parts (see Brief Contents). After covering all or most of Parts 1 and 2, the rest of the book can be used in almost any order. In addition, most chapters and many sections within these chapters can be moved around or omitted to accommodate courses with different lengths and emphases.

- *Readability:* Students often complain that textbooks are difficult and boring. I have tried to overcome this problem (I hope) by writing in a clear, interesting, and informal way and by relating the information in the book to the real world and to the students' own lives.

- *Comprehensive review of the professional literature:* More than 10,000 research sources have been used; key readings are listed for each chapter at the end of the book.

- *Extensive manuscript review by more than 200 experts and teachers:* Several experts reviewed each chapter, and teachers of environmental science courses reviewed most or all of the manuscript to help make the material accurate and up to date.

- *Guest Essays* (18) to provide more information and expose readers to various points of view.

- *Pro/Con* boxes (28) to present opposing views on controversial environmental and resource issues.

- *Case Studies* (59) to apply concepts and to give in-depth information about key issues.

- *Spotlights* (74) to highlight and offer further insights into environmental and resource problems.

- *Individuals Matter* boxes (25) to give individuals examples of what they can do to help sustain the earth.

- *Four-color diagrams* (287) to illustrate complex ideas simply; carefully selected *color photographs* (227) to show how the book's topics relate to the real world.

- *Maps* (56) to give student a geographic perspective.

- *Summary of key principles* inside the front cover.

- *General questions and issues* summarized at the beginning of each chapter.

- *Numerous cross references* to show how environmental and resource concepts, problems, and solutions are interrelated.

- *Key terms* shown in **boldface type**.

- *Glossary* of all key terms.

- *Discussion Topics* at the end of each chapter, with emphasis on encouraging students to think critically about and apply what they have learned.

- *Experiments, individual projects, and group projects* at the end of most chapters in the Discussion Topics sections. These items are marked with an asterisk (*).

- *Measurements* expressed in metric units, followed with their English equivalents in parentheses.

HELP ME IMPROVE THIS BOOK To minimize errors the manuscript has been reviewed by many teachers and experts, but some errors inevitably creep in during the complex process of publishing a book. If you find any, please write them down and send them to me. Most errors can be corrected in subsequent printings of this edition, rather than waiting for a new edition.

Let me know how you think this book can be improved and encourage your students to evaluate the book and send me their suggestions. Send any errors you find and your suggestions to Jack Carey, Science Editor, Wadsworth Publishing Company, 10 Davis Drive, Belmont, CA 94002. He will forward them to me.

SUPPLEMENTARY MATERIALS David Cotter at Georgia College has written an excellent instructor's manual and test items booklet for use with this text. It contains sample multiple-choice test questions with answers, suggested projects, field trips, experiments, and a list of topics suitable for term papers and reports for each chapter. Master sheets for making overhead transparencies of most key diagrams are also available to adopters.

ANNENBERG/CPB TELEVISION COURSE This textbook is being offered as part of the Annenberg/CPB Project television series *Race to Save the Planet*, broadcast on PBS.

Race to Save the Planet is a ten-part public television series and a college-level television course that examines the major environmental questions facing the world today, ranging from population growth to soil erosion, from the destruction of forests to climate changes induced by human activity. The series takes into account the wide spectrum of opinion about what constitutes an environmental problem, as well as the controversies about appropriate remedial measures. It analyzes problems and emphasizes the successful search for solutions. The course develops a number of key themes that cut across a broad range of environmental issues, including sustainability, the interconnection of the economy and the ecosystem, short-term versus long-term gains, and the tradeoffs involved in balancing problems and solutions.

In addition to my books (*Environmental Science* and *Living in the Environment*) and the video programs, the course includes a study guide and faculty guide available from Wadsworth Publishing Company that integrate the telecourse and my texts. The television program was developed as part of the Annenberg/CPB Collection.

For further information about available television course licenses, duplication licenses, and off-air taping licenses contact: PBS Adult Learning Service, 1320 Braddock Place, Alexandria, VA 22314-1698, 1-800-ALS-ALS-8.

For information about purchasing videocassettes and print materials, contact the Annenberg/CPB Collection, P.O. Box 2284, South Burlington, VT 05407-2284, 1-800-LEARNER.

ACKNOWLEDGMENTS I wish to thank the many students and teachers who responded so favorably to the six editions of *Living in the Environment*, the three editions of *Environmental Science*, and the first edition of *Resource Conservation and Management* and offered many helpful suggestions for improvement.

I am also deeply indebted to the many reviewers who pointed out errors and suggested important improvements to this and earlier editions, and to those who wrote guest essays for this edition. I am especially indebted to Kenneth J. Van Dellen, Macomb Community College, for his detailed and very helpful review of the entire manuscript and for serving as the primary author of Chapter 7, "Geologic Processes: The Dynamic Earth." Any errors and deficiencies left are mine.

The members of Wadsworth's talented production team have also made important contributions. My thanks also go to Wadsworth's dedicated sales staff.

Special thanks to Jack Carey, Science Editor at Wadsworth, for his encouragement, help, friendship, and superb reviewing system. It helps immensely to work with the best and most experienced editor in college textbook publishing.

Finally, I wish to thank Peggy Sue O'Neal, my earthmate, spouse, and best friend, for her love and support of me and the earth. I dedicate this book to her and to the earth that sustains us all.

G. Tyler Miller, Jr.

SOME CHANGES IN

THE SEVENTH EDITION

Ecological Protection and Restoration in Costa Rica, and Greed, Junk Bonds, and Redwood Trees; Pro/Con on How Much of the Amazon Basin Should Be Developed?

Chapter 11 Climate Change, Ozone Depletion, and Nuclear War
New chapter with detailed discussion of the chapter's three main topics; 4 color photos; 10 diagrams; 3 Spotlights on The Nature of Scientific Evidence, The Good News, and The Cancer You Are Most Likely to Get; new Guest Essay by Stephen H. Schneider

PART FIVE
Resources and Resource Management
Chapter 12 Soil Resources
10 color photos; 2 new diagrams

Chapter 13 Water Resources
7 color photos; 3 new diagrams; discussion of the unique physical properties of water (Section 13-1); 1 new Spotlight on Escalating Water Crises in the Middle East; 1 new Case Study on The Aral Sea Ecological Disaster

Chapter 14 Food Resources
7 color photos; 1 new diagram; 4 new Spotlights on Nutritional-Deficiency Diseases, Food Additives, Loss of Genetic Variability, and Drift Net Fishing; 1 new Pro/Con on Should Government Farm Subsidies Be Eliminated?

Chapter 15 Land Resources: Forests, Rangelands, Parks, and Wilderness
9 color photos; 1 new diagram; 2 new Pro/Cons on Responsible Forestry: Monocultures or Mixed Cultures? and How Much Timber Should Be Cut From National Forests?; expanded discussion of sustainable forestry; discussion of national trails system

Chapter 16 Wild Plant and Animal Resources
24 color photos; 1 new diagram; 2 new Spotlights on Declining Populations of North American Songbirds and Poaching in the United States: The New Killing Fields; new Case Study on The Water Hyacinth

Chapter 17 Perpetual and Renewable Energy Resources
12 color photos; 2 new diagrams; 2 new Spotlights on Why Don't We Have Fuel-Efficient Cars? and The Solar Envelope House

Chapter 18 Nonrenewable Energy Resources
5 color photos; new Spotlight on Natural Gas as a Vehicle Fuel; 2 new Case Studies on The Search for a Radioactive Waste Depository and Osage, Iowa: Local Economic Development by Improving Energy Efficiency

Chapter 19 Nonrenewable Mineral Resources and Solid Waste
10 color photos; 4 new diagrams; expanded discussion of solid waste and waste reduction; 5 new Spotlights on Mining with Microbes, What It Means to Live in a Throwaway Society, Comparison of Incineration in Japan and the United States, Mega-Landfills, and The Diaper Dilemma; 2 new Case Studies on Recycling Aluminum and What Should We Do About Plastics?; new Pro/Con on Should Mineral Development Be Allowed in Antarctica?

PART SIX
Pollution
Chapter 20 Risk, Human Health, and Hazardous Waste
5 color photos; 1 new diagram; expanded discussion of hazardous waste and pollution prevention; 4 new Spotlights on Are Chemicals Good or Bad?, Working Can Be Hazardous to Your Health, Implications of Exponential Growth in Synthetic Organic Chemicals, Waste Reduction and Pollution Prevention Pay; 3 new Case Studies on Sexually Transmitted Diseases, Smoking, and Should States Be Allowed to Have Stronger Hazardous-Waste Management Laws Than the Federal Government?; new Pro/Con on Is Deep-Well Disposal of Hazardous Waste a Good Idea?; 2 new Guest Essays by Vincent T. Covello and Lois Marie Gibbs

Chapter 21 Air Pollution
6 color photos; 1 improved diagram; new Spotlight on The Clean Air Act of 1990

Chapter 22 Water Pollution
3 color photos; 2 new Spotlights on Environmental Tragedy in the Persian Gulf and Is Drinking Bottled Water the Answer?; 2 new Case Studies on Groundwater Contamination in Woburn, Massachusetts, and Working with Nature to Purify Sewage

Chapter 23 Pesticides and Pest Control
9 color photos; new Spotlight on Agent Orange Controversy; new Pro/Con on Should Food Be Irradiated?

PART SEVEN
Environment and Society
Chapter 24 Economics and Environment
1 color photo; 1 new diagram; 2 new Spotlights on The Case for Zero Discharge and Assuming Chemicals Are Guilty Until Proven Innocent and Using Free Trade as an Excuse to Restrict Environmental Protection and Sustainable Use of Resources

Chapter 25 Politics and Environment
2 color photos; discussion of strategies of polluters and resource depleters; new Spotlight on Environmental Careers; new Guest Essay by Claudine Schneider

Chapter 26 Worldviews, Ethics, and Environment
1 color photo; discussion of bioregions; new Guest Essay by Hugh Kaufman and Lynn Moorer

GUEST AUTHOR AND GUEST ESSAYISTS

Kenneth J. Van Dellen, Professor of Geology and Environmental Science, Macomb Community College, is the primary author of Chapter 7.

The following are the authors of the Guest Essays:

Kenneth E. Boulding, Research Associate, Program of Research on Political and Economic Change, Institute of Behavioral Science, University of Colorado, Boulder; **Vincent T. Covello**, Professor of Environmental Sciences, School of Public Health, and Director, Center for Risk Communication, Columbia University; **Herman E. Daly**, Senior Environmental Economist, World Bank; **Lois Marie Gibbs**, Director, Citizens' Clearinghouse for Hazardous Wastes; **Garrett Hardin**, Professor Emeritus of Human Ecology, University of California, Santa Barbara; **Hugh Kaufman**, Hazardous Waste Expert, Environmental Protection Agency; **Edward J. Kormondy**, Chancellor and Professor of Biology, University of Hawaii-Hilo/West Oahu College; **Amory B. Lovins**, Energy Policy Consultant and Director of Research, Rocky Mountain Institute; **Jessica Tuchman Mathews**, Vice President, World Resources Institute; **Peter Montague**, Senior Research Analyst, Greenpeace, and Director, Environmental Research Foundation; **Lynn Moorer**, Environmental Grassroots Leader; **Norman Myers**, Consultant in Environment and Development; **David Pimentel**, Professor of Entomology, Cornell University; **Philip R. Pryde**, Department of Geography, San Diego State University; **Claudine Schneider**, former Congresswoman, Rhode Island; **Stephen H. Schneider**, Head, Interdisciplinary Climate Systems Section, National Center for Atmospheric Research; **Julian L. Simon**, Professor of Economics and Business Administration, University of Maryland; **Gus Speth**, President, World Resources Institute; **Alvin M. Weinberg**, Distinguished Fellow, Institute for Energy Analysis for the Oak Ridge Associated Laboratories

REVIEWERS

Barbara J. Abraham, Hampton College; Donald D. Adams, Plattsburgh State University of New York; Larry G. Allen, California State University, Northridge; James R. Anderson, U.S. Geological Survey; Kenneth B. Armitage, University of Kansas; Gary J. Atchison, Iowa State University; Marvin W. Baker, Jr., University of Oklahoma; Virgil R. Baker, Arizona State University; Ian G. Barbour, Carleton College; Albert J. Beck, California State University, Chico; Keith L. Bildstein, Winthrop College; Jeff Bland, University of Puget Sound; Roger G. Bland, Central Michigan University; Georg Borgstrom, Michigan State University; Arthur C. Borror, University of New Hampshire; John H. Bounds, Sam Houston State University; Leon F. Bouvier, Population Reference Bureau; Michael F. Brewer, Resources for the Future, Inc.; Mark M. Brinson, East Carolina University; Patrick E. Brunelle, Contra Costa College; Terrence J. Burgess, Saddleback College North; David Byman, Pennsylvania State University, Worthington-Scranton; Lynton K. Caldwell, Indiana University; Faith Thompson Campbell, Natural Resources Defense Council, Inc.; Ray Canterbery, Florida State University; Ted J. Case, University of San Diego; Ann Causey, Auburn University; Richard A. Cellarius, Evergreen State University; William U. Chandler, Worldwatch Institute; F. Christman, University of North Carolina, Chapel Hill; Preston Cloud, University of California, Santa Barbara; Bernard C. Cohen, University of Pittsburgh; Richard A. Cooley, University of California, Santa Cruz; Dennis J. Corrigan; George Cox, San Diego State University; John D. Cunningham, Keene State College; Herman E. Daly, The World Bank; Raymond F. Dasmann, University of California, Santa Cruz; Kingsley Davis, Hoover Institution; Edward E. DeMartini, University of California, Santa Barbara; Thomas R. Detwyler, University of Wisconsin; Peter H. Diage, University of California, Riverside; Lon D. Drake, University of Iowa; T. Edmonson, University of Washington; Thomas Eisner, Cornell University; David E. Fairbrothers, Rutgers University; Paul P. Feeny, Cornell University; Nancy Field, Bellevue Community College; Allan Fitzsimmons, University of Kentucky; Kenneth O. Fulgham, Humboldt State University; Lowell L. Getz, University of Illinois, Urbana-Champaign; Frederick F. Gilbert, Washington State University; Jay Glassman, Los Angeles Valley College; Harold Goetz, North Dakota State University; Jeffery J. Gordon, Bowling Green State University; Eville Gorham, University of Minnesota; Michael Gough, Resources for the Future; Ernest M. Gould, Jr., Harvard University; Peter Green, Golden West College; Peter Gregs, Golden West College; Katharine B. Gregg, West Virginia Wesleyan College; Paul K. Grogger, University of Colorado, Colorado Springs; L. Guernsey, Indiana State University; Ralph Guzman, University of California, Santa Cruz; Raymond Hames, University of Nebraska, Lincoln; Raymond E. Hampton, Central Michigan University; Ted L. Hanes, California State University, Fullerton; William S. Hardenbergh, Southern Illinois University, Carbondale; John P. Harley, Eastern Kentucky University; Neil A. Harrimam, University of Wisconsin, Oshkosh; Grant A. Harris, Washington State University; Harry S. Hass, San Jose City College; Arthur N. Haupt, Population Reference Bureau; Denis A. Hayes, Environmental Consultant; John G. Hewston, Humboldt State University; David L. Hicks, Whitworth College; Eric Hirst, Oak Ridge National Laboratory; S. Holling, University of British Columbia; Donald Holtgrieve, California State

University, Hayward; Michael H. Horn, California State University, Fullerton; Mark A. Hornberger, Bloomsberg University; Marilyn Houck, Pennsylvania State University; Richard D. Houk, Winthrop College; Robert J. Huggett, College of William and Mary; Donald Huisingh, North Carolina State University; Marlene K. Hutt, IBM; David R. Inglis, University of Massachusetts; Robert Janiskee, University of South Carolina; Hugo H. John, University of Connecticut; Brian A. Johnson, University of Pennsylvania, Bloomsburg; David I. Johnson, Michigan State University; Agnes Kadar, Nassau Community College; Thomas L. Keefe, Eastern Kentucky University; Nathan Keyfitz, Harvard University; David Kidd, University of New Mexico; Edward J. Kormondy, University of Hawaii-Hilo/West Oahu College; Judith Kunofsky, Sierra Club; E. Kurtz; Theodore Kury, State University College at Buffalo; John V. Krutilla, Resources for the Future, Inc.; Steve Ladochy, University of Winnipeg; Mark B. Lapping, Kansas State University; Tom Leege, Idaho Department of Fish and Game; William S. Lindsay, Monterey Peninsula College; E. S. Lindstrom, Pennsylvania State University; M. Lippmann, New York University Medical Center; Valerie A. Liston, University of Minnesota; Dennis Livingston, Rensselaer Polytechnic Institute; James P. Lodge, Air Pollution Consultant; Raymond C. Loehr, University of Texas, Austin; Ruth Logan, Santa Monica City College; Robert D. Loring, DePauw University; Paul F. Love, Angelo State University; Thomas Lovering, University of California, Santa Barbara; Amory B. Lovins, Rocky Mountain Institute; Hunter Lovins, Rocky Mountain Institute; Gene A. Lucas, Drake University; David Lynn; Timothy F. Lyon, Ball State University; Melvin G. Marcus, Arizona State University; Gordon E. Matzke, Oregon State University; Parker Mauldin, Rockefeller Foundation; Theodore R. McDowell, California State University; Vincent E. McKelvey, U.S. Geological Survey; John G. Merriam, Bowling Green State University; A. Steven Messenger, Northern Illinois University; John Meyers, Middlesex Community College; Raymond W. Miller, Utah State University; Rolf Monteen, California Polytechnic State University; Ralph Morris, Brock University, St. Catherines, Ontario, Canada; William W. Murdoch, University of California, Santa Barbara; Brian C. Myers, Cypress College; Norman Myers, Environmental Consultant; A. Neale, Illinois State University; Duane Nellis, Kansas State University; Jan Newhouse, University of Hawaii, Manoa; John E. Oliver, Indiana State University; Eric Pallant, Allegheny College; Charles F. Park, Stanford University; Richard J. Pedersen, U.S. Department of Agriculture, Forest Service; David Pelliam, Bureau of Land Management, U.S. Department of Interior; Rodney Peterson, Colorado State University; William S. Pierce, Case Western Reserve University; David Pimentel, Cornell University; Peter Pizor, Northwest Community College; Mark D. Plunkett, Bellevue Community College; Grace L. Powell, University of Akron; James H. Price, Oklahoma College; Marian E. Reeve, Merritt College; Carl H. Reidel, University of Vermont; Roger Revelle, California State University, San Diego; L. Reynolds, University of Central Arkansas; Ronald R. Rhein, Kutztown University of Pennsylvania; Charles Rhyne, Jackson State University; Robert A. Richardson, University of Wisconsin; Benjamin F. Richason III, St. Cloud State University; Ronald Robberecht, University of Idaho; William Van B. Robertson, School of Medicine, Stanford University; C. Lee Rockett, Bowling Green State University; Terry D. Roelofs, Humboldt State University; Richard G. Rose, West Valley College; Stephen T. Ross, University of Southern Mississippi; Robert E. Roth, The Ohio State University; David Satterthwaite, I.E.E.D., London; Stephen W. Sawyer, University of Maryland; Arnold Schecter, State University of New York, Syracuse; William H. Schlesinger, Ecological Society of America; Stephen H. Schneider, National Center for Atmospheric Research; Clarence A. Schoenfeld, University of Wisconsin, Madison; Henry A. Schroeder, Dartmouth Medical School; Lauren A. Schroeder, Youngstown State University; Norman B. Schwartz, University of Delaware; George Sessions, Sierra College; David J. Severn, Clement Associates; Paul Shepard, Pitzer College and Claremont Graduate School; Frank Shiavo, San Jose State University; Michael P. Shields, Southern Illinois University, Carbondale; Kenneth Shiovitz; F. Siewert, Ball State University; E. K. Silbergold, Environmental Defense Fund; Joseph L. Simon, University of South Florida; William E. Sloey, University of Wisconsin, Oshkosh; Robert L. Smith, West Virginia University; Howard M. Smolkin, U.S. Environmental Protection Agency; Patricia M. Sparks, Glassboro State College; John E. Stanley, University of Virginia; Mel Stanley, California State Polytechnic University, Pomona; Norman R. Stewart, University of Wisconsin, Milwaukee; Frank E. Studnicka, University of Wisconsin, Platteville; William L. Thomas, California State University, Hayward; Kenneth J. Van Dellen, Macomb Community College; Tinco E. A. van Hylckama, Texas Tech University; Robert R. Van Kirk, Humboldt State University; Donald E. Van Meter, Ball State University; John D. Vitek, Oklahoma State University; Lee B. Waian, Saddleback College; Waran C. Walker, Stephen F. Austin State University; Thomas D. Warner, South Dakota State University; Kenneth E. F. Watt, University of California, Davis; Alvin M. Weinberg, Institute of Energy Analysis, Oak Ridge Associated Universities; Brian Weiss; Raymond White, San Francisco City College; Douglas Wickum, University of Wisconsin, Stout; Charles G. Wilber, Colorado State University; Nancy Lee Wilkinson, San Francisco State University; John C. Williams, College of San Mateo; Ray Williams, Rio Hondo College; Samuel J. Williamson, New York University; Ted L. Willrich, Oregon State University; James Winsor, Pennsylvania State University; Fred Witzig, University of Minnesota, Duluth; George M. Woodwell, Woods Hole Research Center; Robert Yoerg, Belmont Hills Hospital; Hideo Yonenaka, San Francisco State University; Malcolm J. Zwolinski, University of Arizona

PREFACE

TO THE STUDENT

WHY STUDY ENVIRONMENTAL AND RESOURCE ISSUES? The course you are taking is an introduction to how nature works, how the environment has been and is being used and abused, and what you can do to protect and improve it for yourself and others, for future generations, and for other living things. I am convinced that nothing else deserves more of your energy, time, concern, and personal involvement.

Studying environmental and resource problems is different from studying most courses like chemistry, biology, economics, or psychology. Why? Because environmental science is an *interdisciplinary* study. It involves combining ideas and information from physical sciences, such as biology, chemistry, and geology, and social sciences, such as economics, politics, and ethics, to form a general idea of how the world works and what our role in the world should be.

WHAT IS THE PURPOSE OF LEARNING? *You may be surprised to learn that the purpose of education is to learn as little as you can.* The goal of education is to learn how to sift through mountains of information and ideas to find the small number that are really useful and worth knowing.

This book is full of facts and numbers, but remember three things: First, they are merely stepping stones to ideas, concepts, and connections. Facts by themselves are useless and confusing. Second, most statistics and facts are human beings with the tears wiped off and living things whose lives we are threatening. Third, this book is about how everything is connected to everything else. Learning about how various parts of the earth are interconnected and thus influence one another directly or indirectly is the primary goal of en-

vironmental science. This book is a summary of what I have learned about such connections during the past 26 years.

Inside the front cover of this book you will find a list of key principles that summarizes what I have learned so far about how the world works and what my role in it should be. In effect, it is a two-page summary of the key ideas in this book. I use these principles to evaluate other ideas and to make decisions about what to buy or not to buy and how to live my life with increased joy. These ideas are the result of more than 40 years of reading books and articles, tens of thousands of conversations with others, letters from students like you, and direct observations of nature.

Learning is a neverending, wonderful adventure, so I am constantly striving to improve this list by modifying or removing some ideas and adding new ones. As you draw up your own list, please send me any ideas you have and suggest modifications to my list. We are all in this together, and we need all the help we can get.

HOW I BECAME INVOLVED In 1966, when what we now know as the environmental movement began in the United States, I heard a scientist give a lecture on the problems of overpopulation and environmental abuse. Afterward I went to him and said, "If even a fraction of what you have said is true, I will feel ethically obligated to give up my present scientific research on the corrosion of metals and devote the rest of my life to environmental issues. Frankly, I don't want to believe a word you have said and change my life around, and I'm going into the literature to try to prove what you have said is either untrue or grossly distorted."

After six months of study I was convinced of the seriousness of these problems. Since then I have been studying, teaching, and writing about them. I have also attempted to live my life in an environmentally sound way — with varying degrees of success — by treading as lightly as possible on the earth (see pp. 470–473 for a summary of my own progress in attempting to work with nature).

READABILITY Students often complain that textbooks are difficult and boring. I have tried to overcome this problem by writing in a clear, interesting, and informal way. My goal is to communicate with you, not confuse you. Let me know how to do this better.

I also relate the information in the book to the real world and to your own lives, in the main text and in the special *Spotlights, Case Studies, Pro/Con* discussions of issues, and *Individuals Matter* boxes (which suggest things you can do to help sustain the earth) sprinkled throughout the book.

A REALISTIC BUT HOPEFUL LOCAL, NATIONAL, AND GLOBAL OUTLOOK In this book I offer a realistic but hopeful view of the future. Much has been done since the mid-1960s, when many people first became aware of the resource and environmental problems we face. But much more needs to be done to protect the earth, which keeps us and other forms of life healthy and alive. The 1960s, 1970s, and 1980s were merely a dress rehearsal for the much more urgent and difficult work we must do in the 1990s and beyond. This book suggests ways that you can help sustain the earth.

You will also learn that most environmental and resource problems and their possible solutions are interrelated. Treating them in isolation is a recipe for disaster. I point out many of these connections and give cross references to page numbers relating ideas discussed in various parts of the book. Environmental and resource problems must also be considered on a local, national, and global scale—as this book does.

HOW THE BOOK IS ORGANIZED Take a look at the Brief Contents on the next page to get an overview of the seven major parts of this book and the major topics covered in each part. Before studying each chapter, I suggest you look over the major headings listed in the Detailed Contents that follows. This gives you a road map of where you will be going. I have designed the book so that it can be used in courses with different lengths, emphases, and ordering of topics, so don't be concerned if your instructor skips around and omits material.

GENERAL QUESTIONS AND ISSUES, VOCABULARY, AND DISCUSSION TOPICS Each chapter begins with a few general questions about what you will be learning. After you finish a chapter, you can go back and try to answer these questions as a general review of what you have learned.

Each chapter will introduce new terms, whose meanings you need to know and understand. When a term is introduced and defined, it is printed in **boldface** type. There is also a glossary of all key terms at the end of the book.

Each chapter ends with a set of discussion questions designed to encourage you to think critically and apply what you have learned to your own life. They also ask you to take sides on controversial issues and to back up your conclusions and beliefs.

I have not provided questions that test your recall of facts. This important, but mechanical, task is left to you and your instructor. You should know how to learn definitions and facts on your own. It is done the old-fashioned way—by reading, marking key passages, making notes and summaries, and writing and studying flash cards.

VISUAL AIDS To make this book graphically exciting, I have developed a number of four-color diagrams to illustrate concepts and complex ideas simply. I have also used a number of carefully selected color photos to give you a better picture of how the book's key topics relate to the real world.

FURTHER READINGS If you become especially interested in some of the topics in this book, a list of suggested readings for the material in each chapter is given in the back of the book. In Appendix 1 you will find a list of publications to help keep up to date on the book's material and a list of some key environmental organizations.

INTERACT WITH THE BOOK When I read something, I interact with it. I mark sentences and paragraphs with a highlighter or pen. I put an asterisk in the margin next to something I think is important and double asterisks next to something that I think is really important. I write comments in the margins, such as *Beautiful, Confusing, Bull, Wrong,* and so on.

I fold down the top corner of pages with highlighted passages and the top and bottom corners of especially important pages. This way, I can flip through a book and quickly review the key passages. I hope you will interact in such ways with this book. You will learn more and have more fun. I hope you will often disagree with what I have written, take the time to think about or write down why, and send your thoughts to me.

SAVE THIS BOOK After you finish this course, you may be tempted to discard this book or resell it to the bookstore. But learning is a lifelong process, and you will have to deal with the vital issues discussed here for the rest of your life. Therefore, I hope you will keep this book in your personal library for future use. Or at least pass it on free to someone whom you want to learn about sustaining the earth.

HELP ME IMPROVE THE BOOK Writing and publishing a book is such an incredibly complex process that this or any other book is likely to have some typographical and factual errors. If you find what you believe to be an error, write it down and send it to me.

I would also appreciate learning from you what you like and dislike about the book. This information helps me make the book better in future editions. Some of the things you will read here were suggested by students like you.

Send any errors you find and any suggestions for improvement to Jack Carey, Science Editor, Wadsworth Publishing Company, 10 Davis Drive, Belmont, CA 94002. He will send them on to me. Your input helps me, students who take this course in the future, and the earth.

AND NOW Relax and enjoy yourself as you learn more about the exciting and challenging issues we all face in sustaining the earth for us and for other forms of life.

G. Tyler Miller, Jr.

BRIEF CONTENTS

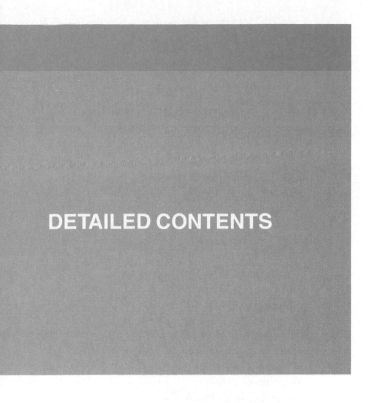

DETAILED CONTENTS

PART ONE

HUMANS

AND NATURE:

AN OVERVIEW

It is only in the most recent, and brief, period of their tenure that human beings have developed in sufficient numbers, and acquired enough power, to become one of the most potentially dangerous organisms that the planet has ever hosted.

JOHN McHALE

The environmental crisis is an outward manifestation of a crisis of mind and spirit. There could be no greater misconception of its meaning than to believe it is concerned only with endangered wildlife, human-made ugliness, and pollution. These are part of it, but more importantly, the crisis is concerned with the kind of creatures we are and what we must become in order to survive.

LYNTON K. CALDWELL

Part of Earth's decreasing biological diversity: A male orangutan in a tropical forest in Sumatra, Southeast Asia.

CHAPTER 1

POPULATION, RESOURCES, ENVIRONMENTAL DEGRADATION, AND POLLUTION

General Questions and Issues

1. How rapidly is the human population increasing?

2. What are Earth's principal types of resources? How can they be depleted or degraded?

3. What are the major types of pollution and how can pollution be controlled?

4. What are the relationships among human population size, resource use, technology, environmental degradation, and pollution?

We must stop mortgaging the future to the present. We must stop destroying the air we breathe, the water we drink, the food we eat, and the forests that inspire awe in our hearts. . . . We need to prevent pollution at the source, not try to clean it up later. . . . It's time to remember that conservation is the cheapest and least polluting form of energy. . . . We need to come together and choose a new direction. We need to transform our society into one in which people live in true harmony — harmony among nations, harmony among the races of humankind, and harmony with nature. . . . We will either reduce, reuse, recycle, and restore — or we will perish.

REV. JESSE JACKSON

W E FACE A COMPLEX MIX of interlocking problems that are reaching crisis levels on the beautiful blue, white, and green planet that is the only home for us and a rich diversity of other life forms. One problem on this oasis in the vastness of space is population growth. World population has more than doubled in only 41 years, from 2.5 billion in 1950 to 5.4 billion in 1991. Unless death rates rise sharply from disease, famine, or global nuclear war, the world's population is projected to double to 10.8 billion by 2045, and could almost triple to 14 billion before levelling off by the end of the next century.

Each year, more of the world's forests, grasslands, and wetlands disappear and deserts grow in size as more people increase their use of the earth's surface and its resources. Vital topsoil is washed or blown away from farmland and cleared forests (Figure 1-1) and clogs streams, lakes, and reservoirs with sediment. Water occurring underground is withdrawn faster than it is replenished in many areas. It is estimated that, every hour, four of Earth's wild species are driven to permanent extinction by our rapidly growing population and agricultural and industrial development.

Forty years ago, most environmental and resource problems were localized. Now our impacts on Earth's natural systems are increasingly regional and global. Burning of one-time deposits of fossil fuels and cutting down and burning forests faster than they are replenished, add carbon dioxide to the lower atmosphere. As we increase the concentrations of carbon dioxide and several other heat-trapping gases in the lower atmosphere, Earth's climate may become warmer through an enhanced *greenhouse effect*, or *heat-trap effect*, within the

Figure 1-1 Severe soil erosion on a hillside in Spain. Removal of forest cover often leads to this type of erosion. Wildlife habitat is lost and eroded, and streams in the land below can be polluted with eroded sediment.

Heather Angel/Biofotos

next 40 years. If such a rapid change in Earth's climate takes place, it will disrupt our ability to grow enough food, alter the distribution of water, and make some densely populated areas uninhabitable either from lack of water or from flooding if average sea levels rise.

Our burning of fossil fuels is also the greatest source of air pollution that threatens trees, lakes, and people, and causes extensive water pollution and land disruption. The oil that runs cars and heats homes and that is used to produce food and most of the products we use will probably be depleted within 50 years. So far, we are doing little to reduce unnecessary waste of this vital resource and to phase in substitutes.

Chemicals we have been adding to the air are drifting into the upper atmosphere and depleting ozone gas, which protects us and most other forms of life by filtering the sun's harmful ultraviolet radiation. In the lower atmosphere, those same chemicals trap heat and help intensify the planet's natural heat-trap effect.

Toxic wastes produced by factories and homes are accumulating and poisoning the air, water, and soil. Agricultural pesticides contaminate the groundwater that many of us drink and some of the food we eat. We pollute the seas, lakes, and streams in virtually every part of the world by overloading them with chemicals and by introducing synthetic chemicals that natural processes cannot break down and recycle.

In other words, we are depleting Earth's natural capital (see Spotlight below) at unprecedented and accelerating rates by living in ways that are eventually

---

Spotlight Don't Squander Your Capital!

Imagine you have inherited $1 million from your parents or won that amount in a sweepstakes. If you invested the entire sum at 10% interest, you would have a sustainable annual income of $100,000 without depleting your capital. You could live quite well on this renewable income indefinitely.

Suppose you want more things than you can afford. Or suppose the size of your family increases so there are more spenders, all with wants that greatly exceed their basic needs. Then you might be tempted to dip into your capital.

Spend $200,000 a year and you will deplete your capital in 10 years. If you spend $150,000 a year, it will take 20 years to use up your capital. Spend $110,000 a year and you will go bankrupt in 40 years.

The lesson to be learned is that you can live comfortably off the interest earned by a large amount of capital indefinitely. Deplete your capital and you change from a sustainable to an unsustainable lifestyle. Get too greedy and you'll soon be needy.

The most important fact of our existence is that the resources keeping us alive, supporting our lifestyles, and driving the world's economies come directly or indirectly from the sun and from Earth's air, water, rocks, fossil fuels, soil, and tens of millions of wild species. With the help of solar energy, Earth's natural processes can dilute, break down, and recycle many of the chemicals we add to the air, water, and soil, as long as we don't overload these natural processes or add synthetic chemicals that nature cannot break down and recycle or cannot recycle fast enough to prevent harm to living organisms. These natural processes, developed over billions of years, can indefinitely renew topsoil, water, air, forests, grasslands, and wildlife, upon which we depend, as long as we don't use these resources faster than they are renewed.

Most of Earth's fixed deposits of nonrenewable minerals can last a long time, if we don't waste them with a throwaway lifestyle. Unlike energy, most of these materials can be recycled or reused, if we don't contaminate them or spread them out so much that recycling and reuse become too costly. History also shows that we can often find substitutes as certain nonrenewable minerals become scarce.

Not wasting energy and living off virtually inexhaustible solar energy in the form of heat, wind, flowing water, and renewable wood and other forms of biomass is a sustainable lifestyle. The "fossil-fuel age" we live in is a brief, unsustainable episode in human history. It is based on rapid depletion of this part of Earth's energy capital and in the process pollution of the atmosphere, water, and soil and destruction of places for wildlife to live. By not wasting so much energy, we could make these fuels last longer, reduce their environmental impacts, and make a less painful transition to a new, renewable-energy age.

The bad news is the growing evidence that much of what we are doing involves unsustainable use of Earth's natural capital at an accelerating rate as more people try to use more of the planet's resources (Figure 1-1). The good news is that we can help sustain Earth for human beings and other species for generations to come by learning how to live off the interest from the natural capital provided for us and other species by the sun and the earth. We can do this if enough of us change the way we view and act in the world, as summarized in the quote that opens this chapter.

This cultural change begins by understanding that we are not in charge of Earth. We can't get along without Earth, but Earth can easily get along without us. Our power to destroy other species and our own species is now so great that we must make peace with the planet, try to understand and cooperate with its magnificent rhythms and cycles, and repair much of the damage we have inflicted on our only home.

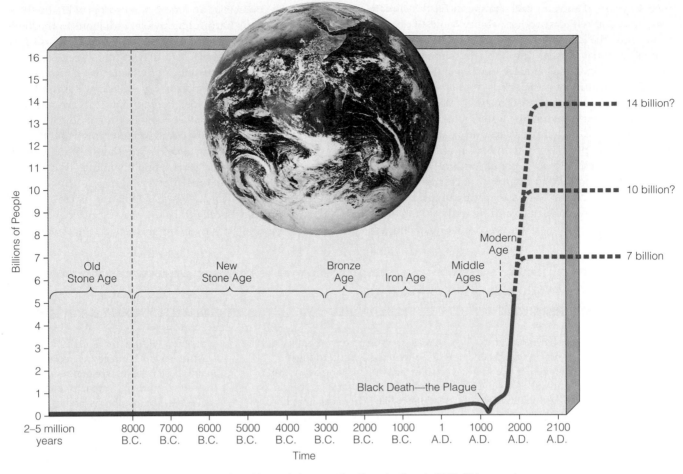

Figure 1-2 J-shaped curve of past exponential world population growth with projections to 2100. This curve is a composite of exponential growth taking place over time at several, mostly increasing, rates. (Data from World Bank and United Nations)

unsustainable. To environmentalists, the increasing number of fishless lakes and streams, dying forests, eroded lands, and extinct species and the millions of environmental refugees, whose homelands can no longer keep them alive, are clear signals that nature's bill for our overexploitation of Earth's resource base is coming due. They believe that we must drastically change our ways now or face serious economic disruption, billions of human deaths, extinction of a million or more of Earth's other species, and perhaps extinction of our own species.

Environment* is a broad term that includes all external conditions and factors, living and nonliving (chemicals and energy), that affect you or any other organism or form of life. This book is an introduction to **environmental science**, the study of how we and other species interact with each other and with the nonliving environment of matter and energy. The two main goals of environmental science are to learn how Earth

works and how to sustain it so we and other species can exist and flourish indefinitely.

1-1 Human Population Growth

RATES OF CHANGE: LINEAR AND EXPONENTIAL GROWTH To understand and deal with a problem, we need to know how fast it is growing. Things such as car speed, population size, resource use, and pollution can increase in two basic ways: linearly (arithmetic growth) or exponentially (geometric growth). With **linear growth**, a quantity increases by some fixed amount during each unit of time. An example is a quantity that increases during each unit of time by one unit: 1, 2, 3, 4, 5, and so on. For example, suppose you start your car and accelerate it by 1.6 kilometers (1 mile) an hour every second. After 60 seconds of such linear growth, you would be travelling at 97 kilometers (60 miles) per hour. After two minutes, your speed would be 193 kilometers (120 miles) per hour.

---

*Boldfaced terms are also defined in the Glossary at the back of the book.

A major shortcoming of the human race is our failure to understand the implications of exponential growth. We can use a fable to help understand this type of growth.

Once there were two kings who enjoyed playing chess, with the loser giving a prize to the winner. After one of their matches, the winner asked the losing king to place a grain of wheat on the first square of the chessboard, two on the second, four on the third, and so on. The number of grains was to double each time until all 64 squares were filled.

The losing king didn't understand the nature of exponential growth and was delighted to get off so easy. He agreed to the proposal. It was the biggest mistake he ever made.

The winning king wanted the losing king to start with one grain of wheat and double it 63 times. This amounts to one less than 2^{64} grains of wheat. This may not seem like much, but it is actually more than 500 times all the wheat harvested in the world this year. It is probably larger than all the wheat that has ever been harvested!

From this example, we can understand some of the properties of exponential growth. It is deceptive because it starts off slowly. However, a few doublings lead quickly to enormous numbers, because after the first doubling, each additional doubling is more than the total of all preceding growth.

Doubling time is the time it takes (usually in years) for the quantity of something growing exponentially to double. We can calculate doubling time in years by using the **rule of 70**. This involves dividing the annual percentage growth rate of a quantity into 70 (70/percentage growth rate = doubling time in years). In 1991, the world's population grew by 1.8%. If that rate continues, Earth's population will double in 39 years (70/1.8 = 39 years) — more growth in this short period than has occurred in all of human history.

Annual exponential growth by only a few percent of any quantity can lead to enormous increases. For example, during a 70-year lifetime, population, solid waste, resource use, or anything growing exponentially at only 2% a year will increase in quantity fourfold. A 5% annual growth leads to a 32-fold increase, and a 10% annual growth rate to a 1,024-fold increase in only 70 years.

With **exponential growth**, a quantity increases by a fixed percentage of the whole in a given time period. With exponential growth, a quantity increases by doubling: 1, 2, 4, 8, 16, 32, and so on. The higher the percentage growth, the less time it takes for the quantity involved to double.

For example, if you doubled the speed of a supercharged car every second, it would take you only five seconds to reach a speed of 103 kilometers (64 miles) per hour, and one second later you would be travelling 206 kilometers (128 miles) per hour. If you had a magic motor, after 30 seconds you would be travelling at 1.6 billion kilometers (1 billion miles) per hour. After 44 seconds, your speed would be 27 trillion kilometers (17 trillion miles) per hour! Another example of exponential growth is given in the Spotlight above.

THE J-SHAPED CURVE OF HUMAN POPULATION GROWTH Plotting the estimated number of people on earth over time gives us a curve with the shape of the letter J (Figure 1-2). This increase in the size of the human population is an example of exponential growth taking place over time at several different rates.

For the first several million years of our existence, the human population grew at a slow average rate of only 0.002% a year. This slow, early phase of exponential growth is represented by the long horizontal part of the composite curve plotted in Figure 1-2.

Since then, the average annual exponential growth rate of the human population has increased. It reached an all-time high of 2.06% in 1970, before dropping to around 1.8% since 1980 — 900 times faster than that of the first several million years of human existence (1.8%/0.002% = 900). As the base of people undergoing growth has increased, the number of people on Earth has risen sharply and the curve of population growth has rounded the bend of the J and headed almost straight up from the horizontal axis (Figure 1-2).

This means that it has taken less time to add each new billion people. It took 2 million years to add the first billion people; 130 years to add the second billion; 30 years to add the third billion; 15 years to add the fourth billion; and only 12 years to add the fifth billion. With present growth rates (see Spotlight on p. 6), the sixth billion will be added during the 10-year period between 1987 and 1997, and the seventh billion is expected to be added during the next 9 years, by 2006.

POPULATION AND ECONOMIC GROWTH IN THE MORE DEVELOPED AND LESS DEVELOPED COUNTRIES Virtually all economies in the world today seek to increase their **economic growth**: an increase in the capacity of the economy to provide goods and services for final use. Such growth is usually measured by an increase in a country's **gross national product (GNP)**: the market value in current dollars of all goods

Figure 1-3 This Brazilian child is one of the estimated 1 billion people on Earth who suffer malnutrition caused by a diet without enough protein and other nutrients needed for good health.

Figure 1-4 One-sixth of the people in the world don't have adequate housing or have no housing. These homeless people in Calcutta, India, are forced to sleep on the street.

In 1991, the world's population of 5.4 billion people grew exponentially at a rate of 1.8%. This meant that by 1992, there were 97 million more people to feed, clothe, and house (5.4 billion people × 0.018 = 97 million). This amounted to an average increase of 1.86 million people a week, 266,000 a day, 11,100 an hour. At that rate, it takes about

- 5 days to add people equal to the number of Americans killed in all U.S. wars

- 4 months to add people equal to the 30 million people killed in all wars fought since 1945

- 9 months to add 75 million people — the number killed in the bubonic plague epidemic of the fourteenth century, the world's greatest disaster

- 1.7 years to add 165 million people — the number of people killed in all wars fought during the past 200 years

- 2.6 years to add 254 million people — the population of the United States in 1991

- 13.2 years to add 1.28 billion people — the population of China in 1991

These figures give you some idea of what it means to go around the bend of the J curve of exponential growth. This enormous increase in population is happening when

- one out of five persons, including one out of three children under the age of five, is hungry or malnourished (Figure 1-3)

- one out of five persons lacks clean drinking water and bathes in water contaminated with deadly, disease-causing organisms

- one out of five persons has inadequate housing and an estimated 150 million people — 100 million of them children — are homeless (Figure 1-4)

- one out of three persons has poor health care and not enough fuel to keep warm and cook food

- more than half of humanity lacks sanitary toilets

- one out of four adults cannot read or write, including one out of three in poor countries and one out of five in the United States

- every day, at least 40,000 children under the age of five die in poor countries of conditions that could be prevented or cured at a cost of about $5 per child a year

and services produced by an economy for final use during a year. To show how the average person's slice of the economic pie in an economy is changing, economists often calculate the **GNP per capita** (per person): the GNP divided by the total population.

The United Nations broadly classifies the world's countries as more developed and less developed according to their degree of economic growth and development. The **more developed countries (MDCs)** are highly industrialized, and most have high GNPs per person. They include the United States, Canada, Japan, the Soviet Union, Australia, New Zealand, and all countries in Europe. These MDCs, with 1.2 billion people (22% of the world's population), command about 80%

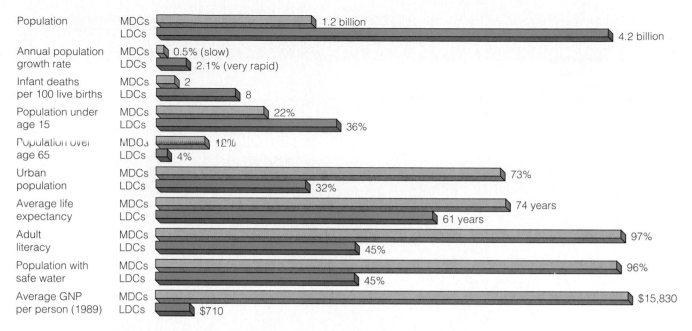

	MDCs	LDCs
Population	1.2 billion	4.2 billion
Annual population growth rate	0.5% (slow)	2.1% (very rapid)
Infant deaths per 100 live births	2	8
Population under age 15	22%	36%
Population over age 65	12%	4%
Urban population	73%	32%
Average life expectancy	74 years	61 years
Adult literacy	97%	45%
Population with safe water	96%	45%
Average GNP per person (1989)	$15,830	$710

Figure 1-5 Some characteristics of more developed countries (MDCs) and less developed countries (LDCs) in 1990. This simple classification does not reveal the considerable variations in GNP per capita among MDCs and LDCs. Also, GNP per capita does not tell us how the wealth of a country is distributed among its population. Most LDCs, such as moderately industrialized Mexico and Brazil, consist of small islands of affluence in a vast ocean of poverty. Another problem is that most governments use GNP and GNP per capita as measures of the well-being of their people when these indicators measure only the speed at which an economy is running. (Data from United Nations and Population Reference Bureau)

of the world's wealth, use about 80% of the world's mineral and energy resources, and generate most of the world's pollution and wastes.

All remaining countries are classified as **less developed countries (LDCs)**, with low to moderate industrialization and low to moderate GNPs per person. Most are located in the Southern Hemisphere in Africa, Asia, and Latin America. The LDCs contain 4.2 billion people, or 78% of the world's population, but have only about 20% of the world's wealth and use only about 20% of the world's mineral and energy resources. Figure 1-5 shows some general differences between MDCs and LDCs.

Most of the projected increase in world population will take place in LDCs, where 1 million people are added every 4.2 days (Figure 1-6). These countries account for nine of every ten babies born and 98% of all infant and childhood deaths.

THE WIDENING GAP BETWEEN THE RICH AND THE POOR Since 1950, the gap between the rich and the poor, as measured by GNP per capita, has grown (Figure 1-7). For decades, economists have talked of wealth produced by economic growth "trickling down" to the poor, but Figure 1-7 shows that little has trickled down. The rich have gotten much richer while the poor have stayed poor and some have gotten even poorer. Today, one in five people on Earth lives in luxury. The next three get by, while the fifth is desperately poor

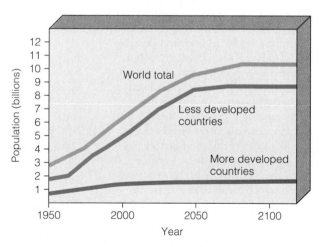

Figure 1-6 Past and projected population size for MDCs, LDCs, and the world, 1950–2120. (Data from United Nations)

and must constantly struggle to survive (see Spotlight on p. 8).

Environmentalists believe that the current forms of economic growth in MDCs, which LDCs seek to emulate, are unsustainable. For example, the total flow of resources worldwide would have to increase sevenfold for the rest of the world to match the current use of resources by the United States. According to environmentalist David Brower, "It is cruel to pretend that the

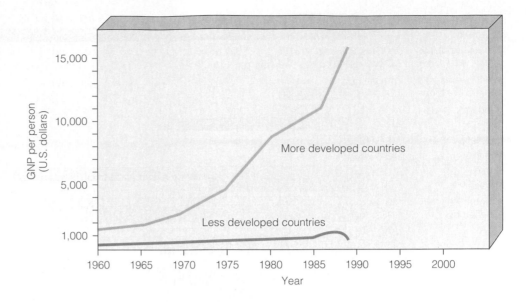

Figure 1-7 The gap in GNP per person in MDCs and LDCs has been widening since 1960 and has accelerated in the 1980s. When adjusted for inflation, this gap is even wider than shown here. (Data from United Nations)

SPOTLIGHT The World's Desperately Poor People

One of every five people on Earth is desperately poor—too poor to grow or buy enough food to maintain good health or perform a job. Each year, at least 20 million (and possibly 40 million) of the world's 1.2 billion desperately poor people die unnecessarily from preventable malnutrition (lack of enough protein and other nutrients needed for good health) and diseases. Half of those who die are children under the age of five (Figure 1-3). Most of these children die from diarrhea and measles, which are deadly diseases for people weakened by malnutrition.

During your lunch hour, at least 2,300 (possibly 4,600) people died prematurely from starvation, malnutrition, and poverty-related diseases. By the time you eat lunch tomorrow, at least 55,000 (possibly 110,000) more will have died. This death toll is equivalent to 137–275 jumbo jet planes, each carrying 400 passengers, crashing every day with no survivors.

This is the most important and disturbing news taking place on the planet every day; yet, this incredibly

tragic news is rarely covered by the media. Because these deaths occur every day, are spread out over the world, and happen mostly in rural areas and urban slums in LDCs away from the glare of TV cameras and reporters, they are not considered major or dramatic news.

Life for the world's poor is a harsh, daily struggle for survival. In typical rural villages or urban slums, groups of malnourished children sit around wood or dung (dried manure) fires eating breakfasts of bread and coffee. The air is filled with the stench of refuse and open sewers.

Children and women carry heavy jars or cans of water, often for long distances, from muddy, microbe-infested streams, canals, or village water faucets. Some people sleep on the street in the open (Figure 1-4) or under makeshift canopies. Others sleep on dirt floors in crowded single-room shacks, often made from straw, cardboard, rusting metal, or drainage pipes.

Parents—some with seven to nine children—are lucky to have an

annual income of $300, an average of 82 cents a day. Some people in affluent countries consider poor people ignorant for having so many children. To most poor parents, however, having many children, especially boys, makes good sense: They need children as a form of economic security to help grow food, tend livestock, work, or beg in the streets. The two or three of their children who typically survive to adulthood are also a form of social security to help their parents survive in old age (typically their forties).

The bad news is that so many of the world's poor are dying every day. The good news is that most of these premature deaths could be prevented at little cost, typically only $5 per child. Such unnecessary deaths will continue until we expand the concept of national and global security to include economic and environmental security for everyone and greatly increase funding for these vital elements of our individual and collective security.

world's developing countries can reach the standard of living of the world's wealthy countries. . . . It is also clear that the wealthy countries can no longer maintain their standards of living. So we have to do something else. We can learn to live lightly on the earth."

1-2 Resources and Environmental Degradation

TYPES OF RESOURCES A **resource** is anything we get from the living and nonliving environment to meet our needs and wants. Resources can be classified as tangible (material) or intangible (nonmaterial). A **material**, or **tangible**, **resource** is one whose quantity can be measured and whose supply is limited. Examples are oil and iron. A **nonmaterial**, or **intangible**, **resource** is one whose quantity cannot be measured. Examples are solitude, beauty, knowledge, security, joy, and love. Although there is no theoretical limit to the amount of these and other nonmaterial resources, their availability can be reduced or destroyed in an increasingly crowded and degraded environment.

Some material resources are directly available for use. Examples are fresh air, fresh water in streams and lakes, fertile soil, and naturally growing edible plants. Most material resources, such as petroleum (oil), iron, groundwater (water occurring underground), and modern crops, aren't directly available. They become resources only when we use our ingenuity to make them available at affordable prices. Petroleum, for example, was a mysterious fluid until we learned how to find it, extract it, and refine it into gasoline, home heating oil, road tar, and other products at affordable prices.

People differ in the material resources they need and want. The material needs of the poor are minimal but represent absolute needs, not merely wants. The affluent use much larger quantities of material resources to satisfy a range of wants far beyond basic survival needs. On our short human time scale, we classify material resources as nonrenewable, perpetual, and renewable (Figure 1-8).

NONRENEWABLE RESOURCES **Nonrenewable**, or **exhaustible**, **resources** exist in a fixed amount (stock) in various places in Earth's crust and have the potential for renewal only by geological, physical, and chemical processes taking place over hundreds of millions to billions of years. Examples are copper, aluminum, coal, and oil. We classify these resources as exhaustible because we are extracting and using them at a much faster

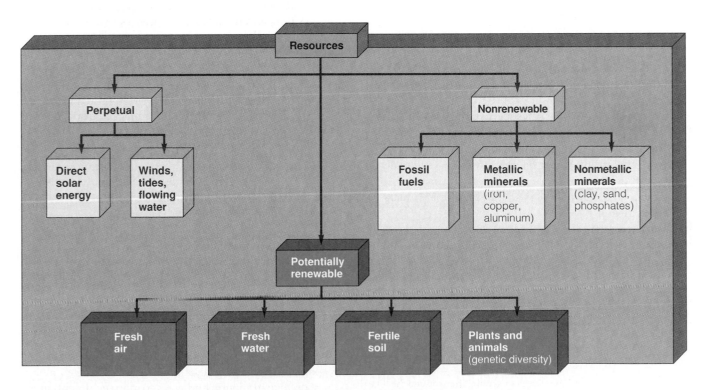

Figure 1-8 Major types of material resources. This scheme isn't fixed; potentially renewable resources can be converted to nonrenewable resources if used for a prolonged time faster than they are renewed by natural processes.

rate than the geological time scale on which they were formed. Instead of being physically exhausted, nonrenewable resources become **economically depleted** to the point where it costs too much to get what is left (typically when 80% of its total estimated supply has been removed and used).

Some nonrenewable resources can be recycled or reused to extend supplies—copper, aluminum, iron, and glass, for example. **Recycling** involves collecting and reprocessing a resource so that it can be made into new products. For example, aluminum beverage cans can be collected, melted, and converted into new beverage cans or other aluminum products. Glass bottles can be crushed and melted to make new glass bottles or other glass items. **Reuse** involves using a resource over and over in the same form. For example, glass bottles can be collected, washed, and refilled many times. If we contaminate materials or spread them out too much, then recycling and reuse can become too costly.

Other nonrenewable resources, such as fossil fuels (mostly coal, oil, and natural gas), can't be recycled or reused. When burned, the useful energy in these fuels is converted to waste heat and exhaust gases that pollute the atmosphere.

Often we can find a substitute or a replacement for a scarce or expensive nonrenewable resource, but substitution isn't always possible. Some materials have properties that can't easily be matched. In other cases, replacements may be inferior, too costly, or too scarce.

PERPETUAL AND POTENTIALLY RENEWABLE RESOURCES A **perpetual resource**, such as solar energy, is virtually inexhaustible on a human time scale. Not wasting energy and living off virtually inexhaustible solar energy in the form of heat, wind, flowing water, and renewable wood and other forms of biomass (tissue from living organisms that can be burned or broken down to provide energy) is a sustainable lifestyle. Depending on indirect solar energy stored in essentially one-time deposits of fossil fuels, or uranium used to fuel nuclear power plants, is sooner or later an unsustainable lifestyle.

A **potentially renewable resource*** is one that theoretically can last indefinitely without reducing the available supply because it is replaced more rapidly through natural processes than are nonrenewable resources. Examples are trees in forests, grasses in grasslands, wild animals, fresh surface water in lakes and streams, most groundwater, fresh air, and fertile soil.

The planet's most valuable resource is its diversity of potentially renewable forms of life (see Spotlight on p. 11).

Classifying something as a potentially renewable resource does not mean that it can't be depleted and that it will always be renewable. The highest rate at which a potentially renewable resource can be used without reducing its available supply throughout the world, or in a particular area, is called its **sustainable yield**. If this natural replacement rate is exceeded, the available supply of a potentially renewable resource begins to shrink—a process known as **environmental degradation**.

Several types of environmental degradation can change potentially renewable resources into nonrenewable or unusable resources:

- Covering productive land with water, concrete, asphalt, or buildings to such an extent that crop growth declines and places for wildlife to live (habitats) are lost.

- Cultivating land without proper soil management, so that crop growth is reduced by soil erosion and depletion of plant nutrients.

- Irrigating cropland without sufficient drainage, so that excessive buildup of water (waterlogging) or salts (salinization) in the soil decreases crop growth.

- Removing water from underground sources (aquifers) and from surface waters (streams and lakes) faster than it is replaced by natural processes. Water scarcity is emerging on every continent.

- Removing trees from large areas (deforestation) without adequate replanting, so that wildlife habitats are destroyed and long-term timber growth is decreased. Every minute, a piece of tropical forest the size of 20 city blocks disappears and another area this size is degraded.

- Depletion of grass by livestock (overgrazing), so that soil is eroded to the extent that productive grasslands are converted into unproductive land and deserts (desertification).

- Eliminating or severely reducing the populations of various wild species through destruction of habitat, commercial hunting, pest control, and pollution.

- Polluting renewable air, water, and soil so that they are unusable for various purposes.

Table 1-1 and Figure 1-10 summarize the status of key life-sustaining resources. One reason for environmental degradation and ways to manage potentially renewable resources are discussed in the Spotlight on page 14.

---

*Most sources use the term *renewable resource*. I have added the word *potentially* to emphasize that these resources can be depleted and converted to nonrenewable resources if we use them faster than they are renewed by natural processes.

Figure 1-9 Two of Earth's incredible diversity of species. On the left is the world's largest flower, called the flesh flower (*Rafflesia*), growing in a tropical rain forest in Sumatra. The flower of this leafless plant can have a diameter as large as 1 meter (3.3 feet). It is the only part of the plant found above the ground. This plant gives off a smell like rotting meat to attract flies that pollinate its flower. On the right is a cottontop tamarin, another resident of a tropical rain forest.

Earth's organisms are classified into different species. A **species** is a group of organisms that resemble one another in appearance, behavior, chemical makeup and processes, and genetic structure. Organisms that reproduce sexually are classified as members of the same species only if they can actually or potentially interbreed with one another and produce fertile offspring.

Over billions of years, the formation of new species and the extinction of species that could not adapt to changing environmental conditions have produced the planet's most valuable resource: **biological diversity**, or **biodiversity**. It is made up of three related concepts: genetic diversity, species diversity, and ecological diversity.

Genetic diversity is variability in the genetic makeup among individuals within a single species. **Species diversity** is the variety of species on Earth and in different parts of the planet such as forests, grasslands, deserts, lakes, and oceans (Photo on p. 1 and Figure 1-9). **Ecological diversity** is the variety of forests, deserts, grasslands, streams, lakes, and other biological communities that interact with one another and with their nonliving environments.

Biologists estimate that Earth's current biodiversity consists of 40 to 80 million different species,

each with variations in its genetic makeup and living in a variety of biological communities. So far, biologists have classified only about 1.5 million species. They know a fair amount about roughly one-third of these species and the detailed roles and interactions of only a few of them.

We are utterly dependent on this biological capital. The priceless diversity within and among species has provided us with food, wood, fibers, energy, raw materials, industrial chemicals, and medicines and contributes hundreds of billions of dollars yearly to the world economy.

Earth's vast genetic library of life forms also helps provide us and other species with free resource recycling and purification services and natural pest control. Every species here today represents stored genetic information that allows the species to adapt to certain changes in environmental conditions. We can think of biodiversity as nature's "insurance policy" against disasters.

Extinction is a natural process, but since agriculture began, about 10,000 years ago, the rate of species extinction has increased sharply as human settlements have expanded worldwide. There is evidence that we are bringing about the greatest mass extinction in 65 million years, since the end of the age of dino-

saurs. Currently, about 100 species per day are becoming extinct because of our activities. By early in the next century, this extinction rate could easily rise severalfold and climb even more for several decades.

Biologists warn that if deforestation (especially of tropical forests), desertification, and destruction of wetlands and coral reefs continue at their present rates, at least 1 million of Earth's estimated 40 to 80 million species are likely to disappear over the next three or four decades.

This catastrophic loss of biological diversity cannot be balanced by formation of new species, because it takes between 2,000 and 100,000 generations for a new species to evolve. Genetic engineering is not a solution to this biological holocaust. Genetic engineers do not create new genes, they transfer genes from one organism to another. Thus, genetic engineering depends on natural biodiversity for its raw material.

Prematurely eliminating many of Earth's species for our own short-term economic gain is not only shortsighted; it is also wrong. It will reduce the ability of our species and other species to survive. What do you think should be done to protect Earth's precious biodiversity from us?

Table 1-1 Health Report for Some of Earth's Vital Resources

Land

Productive Land
About 8.1 million square kilometers (3.1 million square miles) of once-productive land (cropland, forests, grasslands) have become desert in the last 50 years. Each year, almost 61,000 square kilometers (23,500 square miles) of new desert are formed.

Cropland Topsoil
Topsoil is eroding faster than it forms on about 35% of the world's cropland—a loss of about 24 billion metric tons (26 billion tons) of topsoil a year (see Figure 1-1). Crop productivity on one-third of Earth's irrigated cropland has been reduced by salt buildup in topsoil. Waterlogging of topsoil has reduced productivity on at least one-tenth of the world's cropland.

Forest Cover
Almost half of the world's original expanse of tropical forests has been cleared. Each year, about 171,000 square kilometers (66,000 square miles) of tropical forest are destroyed and another 171,000 square kilometers (66,000 square miles) are degraded. Within 30 to 50 years, there may be little of these forests left. One-third of the people on Earth cannot get enough fuelwood to meet their basic needs, and many are forced to meet their needs by cutting trees faster than they are being replenished. In MDCs, 312,000 square kilometers (120,400 square miles) of forest have been damaged by air pollution. Also, many remaining areas of diverse, ancient forests are being cleared and replaced with more vulnerable tree farms that greatly reduce wildlife habitats and biodiversity.

Grasslands
Millions of hectares of grasslands have been overgrazed; some, especially in Africa and the Middle East, have been converted to desert. Almost two-thirds of U.S. rangeland is in fair to poor condition.

Water

Coastal and Inland Wetlands
Between 25% and 50% of the world's wetlands have been drained, built upon, or seriously polluted. Worldwide, millions of hectares of wetlands are lost each year. The United States has lost 56% of its wetlands and loses another 150,000 hectares (371,000 acres) each year.

Oceans
Most of the wastes we dump into the air, water, and land eventually ends up in the oceans. Oil slicks, floating plastic debris, polluted estuaries and beaches, contaminated fish and shellfish are visible signs that we are using the oceans as the world's largest trash dump.

Lakes
Thousands of lakes in eastern North America and in Scandinavia have become so acidic that they contain no fish; thousands of other lakes are dying; thousands are depleted of much of their oxygen because of inputs of various chemicals produced by human activities.

Drinking Water
In LDCs, 61% of the people living in rural areas and 26% of urban dwellers do not have access to safe drinking water. Each year, 5 million die from preventable waterborne diseases. In parts of China, India, Africa, and North America, groundwater is withdrawn faster than it is replenished by precipitation. In the United States, one-fourth of the groundwater withdrawn each year is not replenished. Pesticides contaminate some groundwater deposits in 38 states. In MDCs, hundreds of thousands of industrial and municipal landfills and settling ponds, several million underground storage tanks for gasoline and other chemicals, and thousands of abandoned toxic waste dumps threaten groundwater supplies.

Air

Climate
Emissions of carbon dioxide and other gases into the atmosphere from the burning of fossil fuels and other human activities may raise the average temperature of Earth's lower atmosphere several degrees between now and 2050. This rapid enhancement of Earth's natural heat-trap effect would disrupt food production and water supplies and possibly flood low-lying coastal cities and croplands.

Data from Worldwatch Institute and World Resources Institute

Table 1-1 (continued)

Air (continued)

Atmosphere   Chlorofluorocarbons released into the lower atmosphere are drifting into the upper atmosphere and reacting with and gradually depleting ozone faster than it is being formed. The thinner ozone layer will let in more ultraviolet radiation from the sun. This will cause increases in skin cancer and eye cataracts, and our immune-system defenses against many infectious diseases will be weakened. Levels of eye-burning smog, damaging ozone gas, and acid rain in the lower atmosphere will increase, and yields of some important food crops will decrease.

Biodiversity

Wildlife   An estimated 36,500 species of plants and animals become extinct each year, mostly because of human activities; if deforestation (especially of tropical forests), desertification, and destruction of wetlands and coral reefs continue at present rates, at least 500,000 and perhaps 1 million species will become extinct over the next 20 years.

People

Environmental   Worldwide, an estimated 16 million people have lost their homes and land because
Refugees   of environmental degradation. These people are now the world's largest class of refugees.

Poverty   At least 1.2 billion people — more than one of every four — live in absolute poverty. During the 1980s, this group increased by 200 million people.

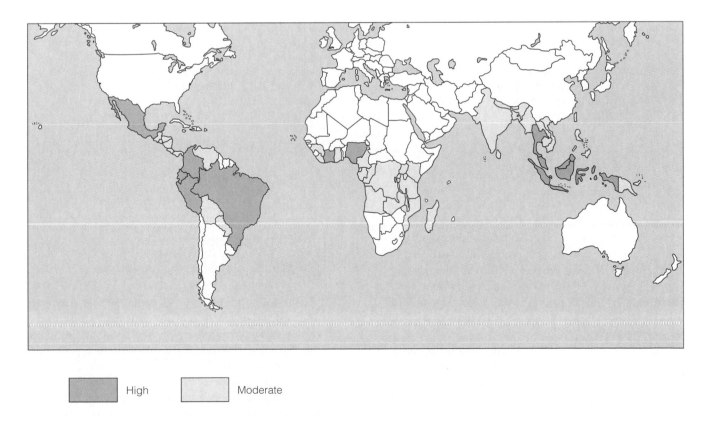

High   Moderate

Figure 1-10   Countries experiencing large annual destruction of tropical forests. (Data from UN Food and Agriculture Organization)

One situation that can cause environmental degradation is the use of **common-property resources**. These are resources that are owned by no one and available for use by everyone. It is difficult to exclude people from using them, and each user depletes or degrades the available supply. Most are potentially renewable. Examples are clean air, fish in parts of the ocean not under the control of a coastal country, migratory birds, Antarctica, gases of the lower atmosphere, and the ozone content of the upper atmosphere.

Abuse or depletion of common-property resources is called the **tragedy of the commons**. It occurs because each user reasons, "If I don't use this resource, someone else will. The little bit I use or the little bit of pollution I create is not enough to matter."

When the number of users is small, there is no problem. Eventually, however, the cumulative effect of many people trying to maximize their use of a common-property resource depletes or degrades the usable supply. Then no one can make a profit or otherwise benefit from the resource. Therein is the tragedy.

One way out of this dilemma is to reduce population size and resource use to the point where potentially renewable common-property resources are not used at rates beyond their estimated sustainable yields. That is difficult to do because people don't like to be told how many children they can have or what types and amounts of resources they can use.

Another approach is to determine what is everyone's fair share of a common-property resource and then regulate access to the resource to ensure that annual sustainable yields are not exceeded. The difficulty is getting the users to agree on what their fair share is. MDCs do not want to give up their use of these resources. LDCs believe they are entitled to a larger share of them and call for MDCs to reduce their use of such resources so that LDCs have a chance of becoming MDCs.

One problem with all these approaches is that it is very difficult and expensive to make reliable estimates of the sustainable yield of a forest, grassland, or the population of a wild animal species. Even if we could do this, sustainable yields can and often do change because of changes in short-term weather, long-term climate, and unpredictable interactions with humans and other species. These uncertainties mean that it is best to use a potentially renewable resource at a rate well below its estimated sustainable yield. This is rarely done because of the strong drive for short-term economic growth and profit.

Another guideline for the management of potentially renewable common-property resources, such as national forests owned jointly by the public, is the **principle of multiple use**. According to this principle, these resources should be used for a variety of purposes, such as timbering, mining, grazing, recreation, wildlife preservation, and soil and water conservation.

The problem with multiple use is that resource managers find it difficult to balance the competing uses because of strong pressures to use these resources for short-term economic gain. Often the result is that one use, such as timber cutting in national forests, becomes dominant. How do you think we should deal with the problem of the "tragedy of the commons"?

TYPES OF RESOURCE SCARCITY Resource scarcity can be absolute or relative. **Absolute resource scarcity** occurs when supplies of a resource are insufficient or too expensive to meet present or future demand. For example, the world's affordable supplies of nonrenewable oil may be used up within the next 50 years. The period of absolute scarcity and increasing cost of oil may begin between 1995 and 2010.

Relative resource scarcity occurs when enough of a resource is still available to meet the demand, but its distribution is unbalanced. For example, between 1973 and 1979, the world had enough oil to meet demand, but not enough oil was produced and distributed to meet the needs and wants of the United States, Japan, and many western European countries. During this period of relative resource scarcity, the price of oil rose from $3 to $35 a barrel (see Case Study on p. 15).

1-3 Pollution

WHAT IS POLLUTION? Any undesirable change in the characteristics of the air, water, soil, or food that can adversely affect the health, survival, or activities of humans or other living organisms is called **pollution**. Most pollutants are unwanted solid, liquid, or gaseous chemicals produced as by-products or wastes when a resource is extracted, processed, made into products, and used. Pollution can also take the form of unwanted energy emissions, such as excessive heat, noise, or radiation.

A major problem is that people differ in what they consider an acceptable level of pollution, especially if

Everything runs on energy. It is the key that unlocks all other natural resources. For most people in MDCs and an increasing number in LDCs, oil is the main source of energy used to help us promote economic growth and dominate the earth. It is used to heat homes, grow food, run vehicles, extract minerals from Earth's crust, and produce most of the products we use. It is also used to find, extract, and process more oil, coal, natural gas, and other sources of energy. When the price of oil rises, so do the prices of other forms of energy and most things we use.

When adjusted for inflation, oil has been cheap since 1950 (Figure 1-11). Its low price has encouraged MDCs and LDCs undergoing economic growth to become heavily dependent on — indeed, addicted to — this important resource. Low prices have also encouraged waste of oil and discouraged the search for other sources of energy.

The relative scarcity of oil between 1973 and 1979 was caused by several factors. One was rapid economic growth during the 1960s, stimulated by low oil prices. Another factor was the growing dependence of the United States and many other MDCs on imported oil (Figure 1-12).

A third factor was that between 1973 and 1979, the Organization of Petroleum Exporting Countries (OPEC)* was able to control the world's supply, distribution, and price of oil. About 63% of the world's known and economically affordable oil deposits (proven reserves) are in the OPEC countries, compared with only 3% in the United States. In 1973, OPEC pro-

*OPEC was formed in 1960 so that LDCs with much of the world's known and projected oil supplies could get a higher price for this resource and stretch remaining supplies by forcing the world to reduce oil use and waste. Today its 13 members are Algeria, Ecuador, Gabon, Indonesia, Iran, Iraq, Kuwait, Libya, Nigeria, Qatar, Saudi Arabia, United Arab Emirates, and Venezuela.

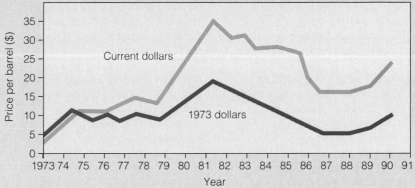

Figure 1-11 Average world crude oil prices between 1973 and 1990. (Data from Department of Energy and Department of Commerce)

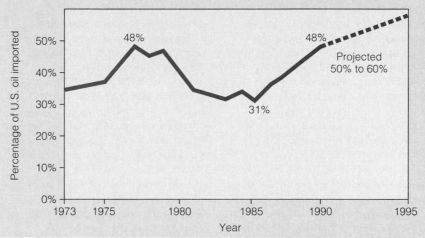

Figure 1-12 Percentage of U.S. oil imported between 1973 and 1990 with projections to 1995. (Data from U.S. Department of Energy and Spears and Associates, Tulsa, Oklahoma)

duced 56% of the world's oil and supplied about 84% of all oil imported by other countries.

This dependence of most MDCs on OPEC countries for oil set the stage for the two phases of the relative oil scarcity crisis of the 1970s. First, in 1973 Arab members of OPEC reduced oil exports to Western industrial countries and banned all shipments of their oil to the United States because of U.S. support of Israel in its 18-day war with Egypt and Syria.

This embargo lasted until March 1974 and caused a fivefold increase in the average world price of crude oil (Figure 1-11). The increase contributed to double-digit inflation in

the United States and many other countries, high interest rates, soaring international debt, and a global economic recession. Americans, accustomed to cheap and plentiful fuel, waited for hours to buy gasoline and turned down thermostats in homes and offices.

Despite the sharp price increase, U.S. dependence on imported oil increased from 30% to 48% between 1973 and 1977. Imports from OPEC increased from 48% to 67% during the same period (Figure 1-12). This increasing dependence was caused mostly by the government's failure to lift controls that kept oil prices

(continued)

artificially low, encouraging energy waste and greatly increasing oil consumption.

The artificially low prices sent a false message to consumers and set the stage for the second phase of the oil distribution crisis. Available world oil supplies decreased when the 1979 revolution in Iran shut down most of that country's production. Waiting lines at gas stations became even longer, and by 1981 the average world price of crude oil had risen to about $35 a barrel.

A combination of energy conservation (using energy more efficiently), substitution of other energy sources for oil, and increased oil production by non-OPEC countries led to a drop in world oil consumption between 1979 and 1989. The drop in demand, and the inability of OPEC countries to reduce their oil production enough to sustain relative resource scarcity and high prices, led to a glut of oil.

Because supply exceeded demand, the price of oil dropped from $35 to around $18 per barrel between 1981 and 1989. This oil glut meant that the price of crude oil in 1989, adjusted for inflation, was about the same as it was in 1974 (Figure 1-11) and had risen only slightly even when oil prices hovered between $25 and $40 in the last half of 1990 because of the invasion of Kuwait by Iraq.

American consumers complain of rises in the price of gasoline and won't elect leaders who propose increasing taxes on gasoline. However, when adjusted for inflation in 1990 dollars, the average price of gasoline has changed little since 1940, and Americans have the least expensive gasoline in the industrialized world. Unlike the United States, the governments of most other MDCs have raised gasoline taxes to encourage oil conservation. Worldwide, gasoline taxes range from 30¢ per gallon in the United States to $3.53 in Italy.

Low gasoline and oil taxes in the United States help explain why the United States is the world's largest waster and importer of oil. As a re-

sult, U.S. dependence on imported oil increased from a low of 31% in 1985 to 48% in 1990 (Figure 1-12), draining over $80 billion a year from the U.S. economy in 1990. Each $1 rise in the price of oil imported into the United States increases the trade deficit by almost $3 billion over the course of a year.

Because of its enormous use and unnecessary waste of oil, the United States has gone from being the world's largest oil exporter to being the world's largest oil importer. The United States will never again be self-sufficient in oil.

In 1990, the world was taught another harsh lesson for being addicted to oil. The invasion of Kuwait by Iraq during the summer of 1990 sent oil prices soaring from around $18 to $40 a barrel within a few months, with the price falling to below $18 in March 1991 after the war ended. Countries relying on oil imports from the volatile Middle East are especially vulnerable to temporary supply disruptions or the threat of such disruptions. These countries include Japan (which got 74% of its oil from the Middle East in 1990), France (46% dependence), and the United States (28% dependence).

This temporary price rise was not due to an actual or a relative shortage of oil. The loss of oil exported from Kuwait and Iraq brought about by an international economic blockade was easily made up by increased production in other oil-producing countries, especially Saudi Arabia. In this case, the price of oil shot up because of the possibility of a future relative shortage of oil should war break out in the Middle East and cause the disruption of oil flows from Saudi Arabia. Such a loss could cause the price of a barrel of oil to reach as high as $100. As Christopher Flavin and Nicholas Lenssen put it, "Not only is the world addicted to cheap oil, but the largest liquor store [oil producer] is in a very dangerous neighborhood."

Most resource analysts expect the price of oil to rise sharply between 1995 and 2010. Sometime dur-

ing this period, we are expected to enter a period of increasing absolute scarcity of oil, when the world's demand for oil is projected to exceed the rate at which remaining supplies can be extracted. During this period, OPEC countries are projected to increase their share of the world's oil market to at least 60%, dominate world oil markets, and raise prices even more than in the 1970s.

The U.S. Department of Energy and most major oil companies project that sometime between 1995 and 2000, the U.S. could be dependent on imported oil for 60% to 70% of its oil consumption—much higher than in 1977 (Fig. 1-12). This would drain the already debt-ridden United States of vast amounts of money, leading to severe inflation and widespread economic recession, perhaps even a major depression.

Because of our rapid exponential growth in oil use, affordable supplies of this nonrenewable resource will probably be gone by 2059. This explains why most analysts believe that over the next 50 years the world must stop wasting so much oil and gradually withdraw from its present oil addiction and find replacements—or face economic turmoil. They also believe that conventional and nuclear wars will become more likely as countries fight for control over the world's dwindling oil supplies to avoid economic collapse.

So far, much too little is being done to stretch the world's remaining supply of oil and to find and phase in substitutes. Experts estimate that the price of oil needs to be between $25 and $30 a barrel to encourage a search for new oil, reduce wasteful uses of oil, and stimulate the phasing in of substitutes for oil.

The first step in dealing with addiction is to admit that we are "oilaholics." The next step is to begin withdrawal and recovery by changing our oil-wasting lifestyles to kick this Earth-degrading addiction.

What do you think should be done to reduce our addiction to oil? What have you done to reduce your own addiction to oil?

they have to choose between pollution control and losing their jobs (see Case Study on p. 18). As philosopher Georg Hegel pointed out, the nature of tragedy is not the conflict between right and wrong, but the conflict between right and right.

SOURCES OF POLLUTION Pollutants can enter the environment naturally (for example, from volcanic eruptions) or through human activities (burning coal). Most natural pollution is dispersed over a large area and is often diluted or broken down to harmless levels by natural processes.

We have been overloading and disrupting this natural dilution, breakdown, and recycling of chemicals essential for life, with the pace picking up sharply during the past 50 years. Most serious pollution from human activities occurs in or near urban and industrial areas, where large amounts of pollutants are concentrated in small volumes of air, water, and soil. Industrialized agriculture is also a major source of pollution. Soil particles, fertilizers, pesticides, animal wastes, and other substances wash into streams. Some of these agricultural chemicals also contaminate groundwater and blow into the air, contaminating faraway land, water, and wildlife.

Some pollutants contaminate the areas where they are produced. Others are carried by winds or flowing water to other areas. Pollution does not respect the state and national boundaries we draw on maps.

Some of the pollutants we add to the environment come from single, identifiable sources, such as the smokestack of a power plant or an industrial plant, the drainpipe of a meat-packing plant, the chimney of a house, or the exhaust pipe of an automobile. These are called **point sources**.

Other pollutants enter the air, water, or soil from dispersed, and often hard-to-identify, sources called **nonpoint sources**. Examples are the runoff of fertilizers and pesticides from farmlands into streams and lakes and pesticides sprayed into the air or blown by the wind into the atmosphere. It is much easier and cheaper to identify and control pollution from fixed point sources than from widely dispersed nonpoint sources.

EFFECTS OF POLLUTION Pollution can have a number of unwanted effects:

- *Nuisance and aesthetic insult* — unpleasant smells and tastes, reduced atmospheric visibility, and soiling of buildings and monuments.

- *Property damage* — corrosion of metals, weathering or dissolution of building and monument materials, and soiling of clothes, buildings, and monuments.

- *Damage to plant and nonhuman animal life* — decreased tree and crop production, harmful health effects on animals, and extinction.

- *Damage to human health* — spread of infectious diseases, irritation and diseases of the respiratory system, genetic and reproductive harm, and cancers.

- *Disruption of natural life-support systems at local, regional, and global levels* — climate change and decreased natural recycling of chemicals and energy inputs and biodiversity needed for good health and survival of people and other forms of life.

Three factors determine how severe the effects of a pollutant will be. One is its *chemical nature* — how active and harmful it is to specific types of living organisms. Another is its *concentration* — the amount per volume unit of air, water, soil, or body weight. One way to reduce the concentration of a pollutant is to dilute it by adding it to a large volume of air or water. Until we started overwhelming the air and waterways with inputs of pollution, dilution was the solution to pollution. Now it is only a partial solution.

A third factor is a pollutant's *persistence* — how long it stays in the air, water, soil, or our bodies. **Degradable**, or **nonpersistent**, **pollutants** are broken down completely or reduced to acceptable levels by natural physical, chemical, and biological processes. Those broken down by living organisms (usually specialized bacteria) are called **biodegradable pollutants**. Human sewage added to a river or the soil is biodegraded fairly quickly by bacteria as long as it is not added faster than it can be broken down.

A major problem is that many of the substances and products we have made and introduced into the environment in large quantities often take decades or longer to degrade. Examples of these **slowly degradable**, or **persistent**, **pollutants**, are the insecticide DDT, most plastics, aluminum cans, and chlorofluorocarbons (CFCs) — chemicals widely used as coolants in refrigerators and air conditioners, spray propellants (in some countries), and foaming agents for making plastics such as Styrofoam.

Nondegradable pollutants are not broken down by natural processes. Examples are the toxic elements lead and mercury. The only ways to deal with pollutants is to not release them into the environment, to recycle them, and to remove them from contaminated air, water, or soil (an expensive process).

A serious problem is that we know little about the potential short- and long-range harmful effects of 80% of the 70,000 synthetic chemicals in commercial use on people and other species. Even our knowledge of the effects of the other 20% of the chemicals we have introduced into the environment is limited.

There are two basic reasons for this lack of knowledge. One is that it is quite difficult, time consuming, and expensive to get this knowledge. The other is that in most cases, we assume that chemicals are innocent until proven guilty and that their benefits will outweigh

I was born and spent the first 14 years of my life in Front Royal, Virginia. It is a small town nestled in a valley at the beginning of the Skyline Drive, which runs through the beautiful mountains of the Shenandoah National Park.

In 1938, the American Viscose Corporation built the world's largest rayon plant a few miles outside the town. The plant provided as many as 3,000 jobs for residents of Front Royal and nearby Warren County. I worked at the plant during two summer vacations while I was in college.

The plant caused problems, however. When the wind blew in a certain direction, the air smelled like rotten eggs because of the toxic hydrogen sulfide and carbon disulfide gases emitted by the plant. Hydrogen sulfide also reacts with metals such as silver and lead to form black metal sulfides. In Front Royal, polished silver usually turned black overnight. It was foolish to paint your house white or a light color using the lead-based paints available in the 1940s. Within a few days, the paint started turning black.

No one paid much attention to those problems in the 1940s. The plant supported the area's economy, and it was not until the 1970s that people in the United States became concerned enough to support effective air pollution laws.

The plant was bought by FMC in 1961 and then sold to Avtex Fibers in 1976. Between 1976 and 1989, air pollution emissions from the plant were sharply reduced in accordance with federal air pollution laws.

In 1980, federal and state environmental officials charged the company with severely polluting the South Fork of the Shenandoah River and groundwater on both sides of the river near the plant with PCBs and other hazardous chemicals. The Shenandoah is a tributary of the Potomac River, a major water source for Washington, D. C. Avtex was forced to spend $750,000 to buy 23 properties with severely polluted wells.

In 1984, the Environmental Protection Agency (EPA) designated the plant's chemical disposal area a Superfund site containing high levels of hazardous waste. Since then, the EPA has sued Avtex and former plant owner FMC for a $9.1 million toxic wastewater cleanup. State agencies have also sued Avtex for $9.3 million for numerous environmental and worker safety violations.

The EPA held a public meeting in September 1988 to discuss ways of cleaning up the plant and contaminated water supplies. The meeting turned into a confrontation between some local residents, who complained about the pollution, and other residents, who worked at the plant and opposed cleanup. "We've got to eat first. We'll die second," said one worker. When one resident, barely holding back tears, urged that the plant be closed "for the sake of our children," a worker stood up and yelled, "What about our jobs and my children who have to eat!"

In November 1988, the state attorney general filed suit against the company for $19.7 million in environmental damage caused by river

and groundwater pollution. In December 1988, Virginia's attorney general charged Avtex with repeated air pollution violations. It was revealed that during 1989, Avtex was at the top of the list in total emissions of toxic materials by American industries.

Avtex laid off 500 of its 1,300 employees in the summer of 1989, citing environmental problems and decreased profitability because of increased competition from other rayon-producing companies. In November 1990, the company was fined $6.15 million for polluting the Shenandoah River and ordered by a state court to pay for the cleanup of PCBs from the river.

In February 1990, Avtex Fibers filed for bankruptcy and closed down its Front Royal plant and its corporate headquarters in Valley Forge, Pennsylvania. Its chairman and principal stockholder retired, and its remaining 800 employees lost their jobs.

Cleanup of the plant site and the contaminated Shenandoah River will cost millions of dollars, taking at least a decade and possibly up to 30 years. Because the company has filed for bankruptcy, federal and state officials may not recover much of the fines and money to be spent on the cleanup.

Suppose enforcement of government pollution control regulations meant that you would lose your job. If you had a choice, would you choose unemployment and a cleaner local and global environment for you and your family or employment and a dirtier environment?

their harmful effects. This means we begin using a chemical with limited knowledge of its possible harmful effects and then, in some cases, learn the hard way that it should never have been introduced.

POLLUTION PREVENTION We can control pollutants by preventing them from entering the environment and by cleaning them up once they have reached the environment. **Pollution prevention**, or **input pollution control**, prevents potential pollutants from enter-

ing the environment or sharply reduces the amounts released. In the United States, the largest drops in pollution have occurred for chemicals such as DDT, PCBs, and airborne lead (from leaded gasoline) because production and use of these chemicals have been banned or sharply reduced.

This approach is summarized in biologist Barry Commoner's **law of pollution prevention**: If you don't put something into the environment, it isn't there. Pollution prevention is achieved by

- evaluating the potential environmental harm of a chemical or technology before it is widely used by assuming it is guilty (potentially harmful) until proven innocent

- recycling and reprocessing hazardous chemicals within industrial processes to keep them from entering the environment

- redesigning technologies so that potential pollutants are not used or produced

- reducing unnecessary and wasteful use of matter and energy resources

- switching from reliance on nonrenewable and potentially polluting fossil fuel and nuclear energy resources to perpetual and renewable energy resources from the sun, wind, flowing water, renewable trees (wood), and heat from Earth's interior (geothermal energy)

- making products that can be recycled or reused, that have long useful lives, and that are easy to repair

This isn't to suggest that all forms of pollution can be prevented. However, the potential for pollution prevention is enormous because we have made so little use of this more effective, and in the long run more cost-effective, approach. The challenge will be to use our economic and political systems to give the greatest tax breaks and rewards to industries and individuals using methods that prevent pollution.

POLLUTION CLEANUP **Output pollution control**, or **pollution cleanup**, deals with wastes after they have entered the environment. Most of the improvements in environmental quality in the United States and other MDCs have been based on using pollution cleanup.

There are several problems with relying mostly on output approaches. One is that as long as population and resource use continue to increase, pollution cleanup is only a temporary bandage. For example, adding catalytic converters to cars has helped reduce air pollution, but as the number of cars has increased, this cleanup approach is being overwhelmed.

A second problem is that cleanup often removes a pollutant from one part of the environment and causes pollution in another part. We can collect garbage, but garbage must be burned (perhaps causing air pollution and leaving a toxic ash that must be put somewhere), dumped into streams, lakes, and oceans (perhaps causing water pollution), buried (perhaps causing soil and groundwater pollution), recycled, or reused.

Another problem is that pollution cleanup relies mostly on pollution control laws administered by government agencies. These agencies must spend enormous amounts of money to draw up and enforce regulations to reduce pollution temporarily. Often these agencies dictate the type of cleanup technology to be used instead of setting standards and allowing pollut-

ers to come up with the best and cheapest ways to meet these standards. This discourages innovation. If most of the current pollution control laws were rewritten to emphasize pollution prevention, pollution levels would decline permanently instead of temporarily and large amounts of money and human creativity would be available to achieve this more desirable goal.

The Soviet Union, many eastern European countries, and most LDCs near the bottom of the economic ladder are far behind in any kind of pollution control (see Case Study on p. 20).

Usually both pollution prevention and pollution cleanup are needed. However, environmentalists urge that we place primary emphasis on pollution prevention because it works better and is cheaper than pollution cleanup. As Benjamin Franklin reminded us long ago: "An ounce of prevention is worth a pound of cure."

As you make decisions about what things to buy and proposed solutions to an environmental or resource problem, ask yourself, "Is this a prevention (input) or a cleanup (output) approach?" Our motto should be: *Pollution cleanup is better than doing nothing, but pollution prevention is the best way to walk more gently on the earth.*

1-4 Relationships Among Population, Resource Use, Technology, Environmental Degradation, and Pollution

ONE MODEL OF ENVIRONMENTAL DEGRADATION AND POLLUTION According to one simple model, the total environmental degradation and pollution—that is, the environmental impact of population—in a given area depends on three factors: the number of people, the average number of units of resources each person uses, and the amount of environmental degradation and pollution generated when each unit of resource is produced and used (Figure 1-15).

Overpopulation occurs when people exceed the **carrying capacity** of an area: the number of people that can be supported in an area given its physical resource base and the way those resources are used. Overpopulation is a result of growing numbers of people, growing affluence (resource consumption), or both.

We know from studying other species that when a population exceeds or *overshoots* the carrying capacity of its environment, it suffers a *dieback* that reduces its population to a sustainable size. So far, we have been able to expand our carrying capacity by using technology to take over much of Earth's surface, extract resources, and crowd out or eliminate other species that compete with us for those resources. The crucial question is, How long will we be able to continue our exponential growth in people and resource use on a finite planet without suffering overshoot and dieback? No one knows the answer to this, but it is a question that

Figure 1-13 Where is Poland?

In 1985, the Polish Academy of Sciences described Poland (Figure 1-13), a heavily industrialized country, as the most polluted country in the world—although Czechoslovakia may be just as polluted. Air, water, and soil pollution are so severe that at least one-third of the country's people are likely to acquire environmentally induced cancers, respiratory illnesses, and a host of other diseases.

Coal supplies Poland with 80% of its energy. Most of the country's coal-burning industrial plants and power plants have no pollution control technology whatsoever, and those that do have fairly ineffective controls. Krakow's location in a river valley that traps pollutants and its concentration of coal-burning steel mills with little air pollution con-

trol (Figure 1-14) make it one of the dirtiest and unhealthiest cities in the world.

Less than half of Poland's 813 cities have sewage treatment plants, and none of its large cities has proper sewage treatment facilities. In the capital city of Warsaw, only 5% of the sewage is treated. The rest is simply dumped into the Vistula River, which flows through the country and empties into the Baltic Sea.

About 90% of the water in the country's rivers is too polluted for use as drinking water. Nearly one-third of the country's water is classified as unfit even for industrial use.

This widespread water pollution has caused a shortage of drinking water in most of Poland's large cities. The Polish Academy of Sciences

projects that by the year 2000, the country will have no safe drinking water.

Twenty-seven areas of the country, containing one-third of the Polish population, have been declared *ecological danger zones* by the Polish parliament. Five of these areas, located in southwestern Poland, where mining and heavy industry are concentrated, have been declared *ecological disaster zones*. By Poland's own lax environmental standards, these regions are so contaminated that the 30% of the country's people living there should be evacuated.

A quarter of Poland's soil is believed to be too contaminated to grow food that is safe for consumption by livestock or people. In 1988, the government declared five vil-

Figure 1-14 The 700 smokestacks of the Nowa Huta Lenin steelworks belch out more than 455,000 metric tons (500,000 tons) of air pollutants a year. These mills, built in the 1950s, sit in a river valley in Krakow, Poland, and are the area's major employer. In 1989, mill officials agreed to reduce emissions of air pollutants from the mills by about one-third by 1992.

Richard Liroff/World Wildlife Fund

lages in the industrial region of Silesia unfit to live in because of high levels of toxic metals in the soil and water and paid the villagers to relocate. Some 60% of the food grown in the Krakow area is considered unfit for human consumption because of soil contamination by toxic heavy metals. The average life span of people living in Silesia is three to four years less than for people in the rest of Poland.

Gdansk's sandy beaches have been closed for years. Many of the fish in the nearby bay contain excessive levels of mercury and have open sores.

Air pollution control is grossly inadequate. Satellite photographs show that the biggest clouds of smoke in Europe hang over southern Poland, partly because large coal-burning power and industrial plants have shut down their air pollution control equipment to save power and money.

Air pollution in nearly every major city is reportedly 50 times above government-set limits. Sometimes air pollution is so thick that motorists must turn on their lights during the day to see. By 1990, 82% of the country's forests showed some signs of damage, and at least 15% had virtually disappeared, after decades of exposure to high levels of air pollutants.

Since the mid-1980s, Polish citizens have organized to demand better environmental protection. About 2,000 environmental groups exist in Poland, and in 1988 the Krakow-based Polish Ecology Club (originally formed in 1980 by the country's Solidarity labor movement) formed the Polish Ecology Party.

Generally, the government has been slow to act to prevent continuing pollution and environmental degradation. Poland is also saddled with a $42 billion debt—64% of its annual GNP—to western MDCs.

Cleaning up the damage already done and minimizing future damage will take at least 15 years and cost about $20 billion, but the costs will be much higher if the government fails to act. Economists estimate that pollution and environmental degradation cost Poland 10% to 20% of its annual GNP.

With its new freedom from So-viet control, Poland is struggling to make the transition to a free-market economy. In 1990, Poland's new Minister of the Environment published a "hit list" of the country's 80 major industrial polluters and announced plans to place them on a cleanup schedule. The ministry has also published new, stricter air pollution emission standards for existing and new sources and outlined a plan to begin building 3,000 new wastewater treatment plants by 1995.

With adequate aid from MDCs, Poland and other eastern European countries could make advances rapidly by implementing modern pollution control, industrial, and energy efficiency technologies developed in MDCs during the past 20 years. Without such aid and without sustained action by its citizens and elected officials, Poland's already serious environmental problems will get worse.

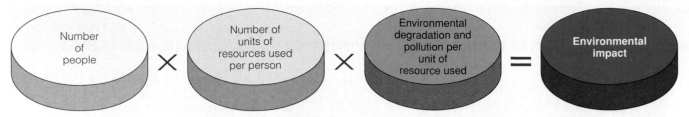

Figure 1-15 Simplified model of how three factors affect overall environmental degradation and pollution, or the environmental impact of population.

warning signals from the earth (Table 1-1 and Figure 1-10) are forcing us to consider seriously.

Differences in the importance of the factors shown in Figure 1-15 lead to two types of overpopulation: people overpopulation and consumption overpopulation (Figure 1-16). **People overpopulation** exists where there are more people than the available supplies of food, water, and other important resources can support at a minimal level (Table 1-1). In this type of overpopulation, population size and the resulting degradation of potentially renewable soil, grasslands, forests, and wildlife resources tend to be the key factors determining total environmental impact (Figure 1-16). In the world's poorest LDCs, people overpopulation causes premature death for at least 20 million, and perhaps 40 million, people each year, and absolute poverty for 1.2 billion people.

Industrialized countries have the second type of overpopulation: **consumption overpopulation**. It exists when a small number of people use resources at such a high rate that significant pollution, environmental degradation, and resource depletion occur. With this type of overpopulation, high rates of resource use per person, and the resulting high levels of pollution and environmental degradation per person, are the key factors determining overall environmental impact (Figure 1-16). **Overconsumption** occurs when some people consume much more than they need at the expense of those who cannot meet their basic needs and at the expense of Earth's present and future life-support systems.

By controlling at least 80% of the world's wealth and material resources, people in MDCs presently enjoy an average standard of living at least 18 times that in LDCs. This high standard of living by the world's 1 billion overconsuming meat eaters, car drivers, and throwaway consumers is the major cause of the world's pollution, environmental degradation, and poverty (or underconsumption). During their lifetime, the 6 million babies added to the population of MDCs in 1991 may do as much damage to Earth's life-support systems as the 91 million babies added in LDCs, and they may do more damage.

Using the model in Figure 1-16, we can conclude that the United States has the world's highest level of consumption overpopulation. With only 4.3% of the world's population, it produces about 21% of all goods and services, uses about one-third of the world's processed mineral resources, uses about one-fourth of the world's nonrenewable energy, and produces at least one-third of the world's pollution and trash. Each year, an additional 19 metric tons (21 tons) of energy and nonfuel mineral resources per American must be obtained just to maintain present standards of living unless the United States shifts from a throwaway, resource-wasting economy to a resource-conserving economy.

According to biologist Paul Ehrlich: "While overpopulation in poor nations tends to keep them poverty stricken, overpopulation in rich nations tends to undermine the life-support capacity of the entire planet. . . . A baby born in the United States will damage the planet 20 to 100 times more in a lifetime than a baby born into a poor family in an LDC. Each rich person in the United States does 1,000 times more damage than a poor person in an LDC."

Based on current exponential increases in population and economic growth (resource consumption), the total stress we are putting on the planet is increasing exponentially at about 5.5% each year. In 1990, the total ecological demand we put on Earth's resources was 448 times larger than in 1880. If present trends continue (which is unlikely), by the year 2000 it will be 776 times as large and by 2020, it will be 2,333 times as large.

MULTIPLE-FACTOR MODEL The three-factor model shown in Figure 1-15, though useful, is too simple. The principal causes of the environmental, resource, and social problems we face are much more complex. They include:

- *Unsustainable population growth resulting in people overpopulation and consumption overpopulation* (Figure 1-16).

- *Population distribution* — the population implosion or urban crisis. The most severe air and water pollution problems occur when large numbers of people and industrial activities are concentrated in an urban area (Figure 1-14). Winds blow many of these pollutants over other cities and rural areas.

- *Overconsumption and wasteful patterns of resource use, especially in industrialized countries* — throw-

People Overpopulation

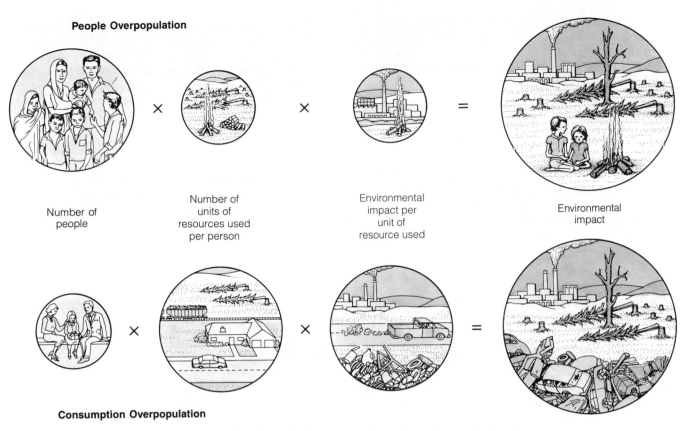

| Number of people | | Number of units of resources used per person | | Environmental impact per unit of resource used | | Environmental impact |

Consumption Overpopulation

Figure 1-16 Two types of overpopulation based on the relative importance of the factors in the model shown in Figure 1-15. Circle size shows relative importance of each factor. People overpopulation is caused mostly by growing numbers of people. Consumption overpopulation is caused mostly by growing affluence (resource consumption).

away mentality, planned obsolescence, producing unnecessary and harmful items, very little recycling and reuse of essential resources, unsustainable industrialized agriculture, and unsustainable industrial production.

■ *Belief that technology will solve our problems* — failure to distinguish between forms of technology that reduce pollution and unnecessary resource waste and help sustain Earth's life-support systems, and those that without proper control can degrade Earth's life-support systems.

■ *Poverty* — failure of the world's economic and political systems to achieve a fairer distribution of the world's land, food, shelter, health care, education, employment, wealth, energy and mineral resources, and political power.

■ *Oversimplification of Earth's life-support systems* — the biodiversity-reduction crisis; excessive reduction of the diversity of plant and animal life in forests, oceans, grasslands, and other parts of Earth's life-support system (see Spotlight on p. 11), resulting in increased soil erosion, flooding, accelerated extinction of wild species, and damage to crops from insects and diseases (Table 1-1 and Figure 1-10).

■ *Crisis in political and economic management* — overemphasizing all types of economic growth instead of encouraging sustainable forms of eco-

nomic growth such as pollution prevention and cleanup, recycling, reuse and resource conservation, and discouraging polluting and resource-wasting forms of economic growth; a short-term outlook that leads governments to go from crisis to crisis instead of trying to anticipate problems and prevent them from reaching crisis levels; emphasis on short-term bandages (output approaches) instead of long-term cures (input approaches); treating problems in isolation rather than as an interacting set.

■ *Failure to have market prices represent the overall environmental cost of an economic good or service to society and to Earth's life-support systems* — not knowing the harmful effects of the products we buy, because most of the costs of pollution, environmental degradation, and resource depletion caused by their production and use are not included in their market prices; using economic systems to reward activities that degrade the earth instead of rewarding activities that help sustain and revitalize the earth.

■ *Human-centered (anthropocentric) worldview and behavior instead of Earth-centered (biocentric) worldview and behavior* — tragedy of the commons (see Spotlight on p. 14); thinking that we are above and in charge of nature; attempting to dominate and alter nature to suit our purposes rather than working with nature by walking gently on the earth; thinking that our cleverness and technology will allow us to escape the physical, chemical, and biological processes that govern the sustainability of Earth's life-support systems.

These and other factors interact in complex and largely unknown ways to produce the serious environmental, resource, and social problems the world faces (Figure 1-17). The population, energy, poverty, pollution, urban, war, and environmental degradation crises we face are interlocking parts of an overall crisis. We can stabilize world population only when poverty is sharply reduced worldwide. As long as LDCs are burdened by enormous debts, they will feel driven to pay the interest on these debts by depleting and degrading their natural resources, mostly for export to MDCs.

We cannot solve pollution problems by continuing to rely mostly on pollution cleanup instead of on pollution prevention. We cannot sustain the earth for us and other species by continuing forms of economic growth based on depleting Earth's natural capital that supports all life and economic activities.

The way out is for us to act together to formulate interdisciplinary, integrated approaches to the problems we face at the local, national, and global levels. Treating each problem in isolation will not work in a world where everything is connected to everything else in a seamless web of life.

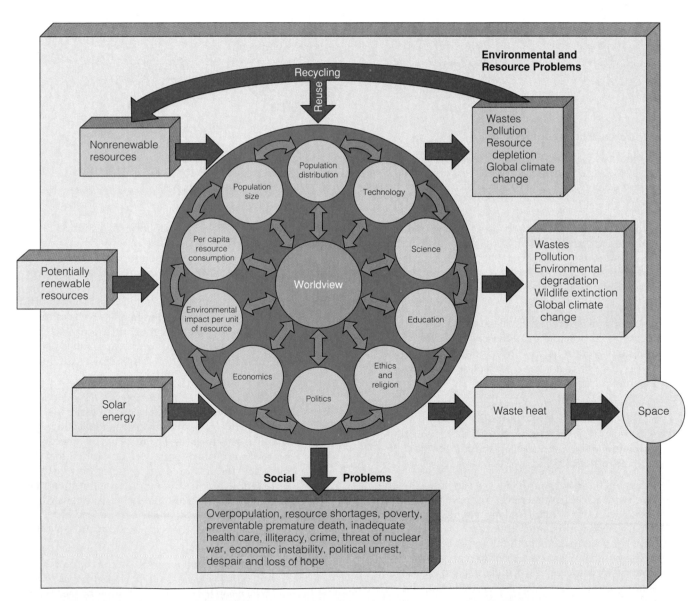

Figure 1-17 Environmental, resource, and social problems are caused by a complex, poorly understood mix of interacting factors, as illustrated by this simplified model.

1-5 What Should Be Done?

WORLDVIEWS There are conflicting views about how serious the world's present and projected environmental and resource problems really are and what should be done about them. These conflicts arise mostly out of differing **worldviews**, how individuals think the world works and what they think our role in the world should be. Our individual decisions and actions are based on the perceptions that make up our worldview. Worldviews are based on the cultures in which people are raised and educated and on their progress through various levels of environmental awareness, summarized on the page after the list of principles found inside the front cover of this book.

People with widely differing worldviews can take the same data and arrive at quite different conclusions because they start with entirely different assumptions. This explains why there is so much controversy over what we should do about our environmental and resource problems.

THROWAWAY AND SPACESHIP-EARTH WORLD-VIEWS Most people, especially in affluent societies, have a **throwaway worldview**, also known as a **frontier worldview**, based on the idea that there will always be more (Figure 1-18). A modified version of this view is the **Spaceship-Earth worldview**, in which Earth is viewed as a spaceship—a machine that we can understand, control, and change at will by using advanced technology.

People with these worldviews see Earth as a place of unlimited resources, where any type of resource conservation or pollution prevention that hampers short-term economic growth is unnecessary. If we deplete or pollute the resources in one area, they believe we will find substitutes and control the pollution through technology. If resources become scarce or a substitute can't be found, we can get materials from the moon and asteroids in the "new frontier" of space. Even if we pollute an area, we can invent a technology to clean it up, dump it into space, move elsewhere, or live in space or on another planet. If we extinguish other species, we can use genetic engineering to create new and better ones.

According to these worldviews, continued economic growth and technological advances will produce a less crowded, less polluted, and more resource-rich world. It will also be a world in which most people will be healthier, will live longer, and will have greater material wealth.

These worldviews are based mostly on two beliefs: We are more important than any other species, and through science and technology we can conquer, control, and change nature to meet our present and future needs and wants.

A SUSTAINABLE-EARTH WORLDVIEW A growing number of people question the usefulness of the throwaway and Spaceship-Earth worldviews. Critics of these worldviews believe we should ask several crucial questions. Is what we are doing really progress? Can we sustain what we are doing? Should we sustain what we are doing? What kinds of growth are useful and sustainable, and what kinds are harmful and unsustainable? If we end up eliminating or killing off large numbers of our own species and millions of other species, is that success?

Figure 1-18 Evidence of the throwaway worldview, based on the premise that the earth plus our technological cleverness will produce a virtually unlimited supply of resources. If we believe that there will always be more, it is not surprising that we dump, burn, or bury the solid wastes we produce instead of seeing them as wasted resources that could be recycled, reused, or in many cases not produced in the first place. This is a sanitary landfill in Prince Georges County, Maryland.

Soil Conservation Service

A small but growing number of people have a **sustainable-Earth worldview**.* They believe that Earth does not have infinite resources, and that ever-increasing production and consumption will put severe stress on the natural processes that renew and maintain the air, water, and soil and support Earth's variety of potentially renewable plant and animal life. They believe that if present trends continue, the world will become more crowded and more polluted, and many resources will be depleted or degraded. They believe that this situation will lead to greater political and economic turmoil and increase the threat of nuclear and conventional wars.

These people see our blind pursuit of exponential economic growth, based on using Earth's resources at ever-increasing rates, and growth in the human population as similar to being on a treadmill that moves faster and faster. They believe that sooner or later we will fall off the treadmill or cause the treadmill motor to break down. Change is a part of all life, but they believe that the rapid rates of change we are imposing on ourselves and the rest of the earth are unsustainable. According to biologist Gerald Durrell, "At the present rate of 'progress,' and unless something is done quickly, disaster faces us in the face. . . . We are bleeding our planet to death. We are led by sabre-rattling politicians who are ignorant of biology . . . and surrounded by powerful commercial interests whose only interest in nature is often to rape it."

People with this worldview believe that the environmental and resource crises we face are seen as different facets of a single crisis—a crisis of perception based on an outdated view of how nature works and what our role in nature should be. People with a sustainable-Earth worldview believe that nature exists for all of Earth's living species, not just for us. This life-centered approach sees human beings as part of nature—not apart from nature and not conquerors of nature. People with this worldview emphasize

- seeing the world as an integrated, interconnected, interdependent whole rather than as a fragmented collection of parts

- seeing our most fundamental value as maintaining the integrity, good functioning, and sustainability of Earth's life-support systems for us and other species now and in the future

- building societies and personal relationships that emphasize cooperation over competition and domination

- protecting Earth's biodiversity by interfering with nonhuman species only to meet important needs

- emphasizing pollution prevention and converting to more environmentally benign technologies

- not wasting nonrenewable minerals, fossil fuels, and water

- greatly increasing our dependence on perpetual solar energy and decreasing our use of fossil fuels and nuclear power

- achieving sustainable use of potentially renewable cropland, forests, and grasslands by using these resources no faster than they can be renewed and by placing primary emphasis on sustaining the fertility of Earth's topsoil

- protecting the world's remaining wild areas from development and pollution and restoring many of the areas we have damaged

- converting the world's existing economic systems, all based on ever-increasing economic growth with little concern over possible long-term consequences, to systems that reward Earth-sustaining forms of growth

- halting human population growth to prevent an enormous dieback; then encouraging a slow population shrinkage toward an optimum level that can allow every person an opportunity for a decent life without impairing the ability of Earth to sustain human and nonhuman life in the future

Major differences between the sustainable-Earth and the throwaway and Spaceship-Earth worldviews are reflected in the two Guest Essays ending this chapter.

There are signs we are beginning to make a gradual transition from the throwaway and Spaceship-Earth worldviews to one closer to a sustainable-Earth worldview. Deep down, most people know that the present political and economic systems are not working and are leading us to unsustainable use of Earth's natural capital. In this unsettling and confusing transition period between worldviews, many people hold a mixture of beliefs from these worldviews.

Eventually, as has happened in the past, a critical mass of people switch to a new worldview as they are overwhelmed by new evidence or catastrophic changes. Then tremendous cultural change, once considered impossible or highly unlikely, can take place rapidly. Once you change your worldview, it simply makes no sense to do things in the old ways based on an outdated worldview, unless you go into a state of denial to avoid reality and the need to change.

EVERYTHING YOU DO MATTERS *The most important message of this book is that we can deal with the problems we face and begin to turn things around within your lifetime. It will not be easy, painless, or without controversy, but it can be done.*

---

*Others have used the terms *sustainable worldview, conserver worldview, holistic worldview,* and *deep ecology worldview* to describe this idea. I add the word *Earth* to make clear that it's all of Earth's life-support systems and life, not just human beings and their societies, that must be sustained.

The key to dealing with these problems is recognizing that *individuals matter*. Billions of individual actions contribute to the environmental and resource problems we face and to the solutions to these problems. Throughout this book you will find a number of boxes, entitled *Individuals Matter*, that suggest what you can do to help sustain the earth.

History shows that significant cultural changes are brought about by individuals from the bottom up. Anthropologist Margaret Mead has summarized our potential for change: "Never doubt that a small group of thoughtful, committed citizens can change the world. Indeed it is the only thing that ever has."

The choice is ours. We can continue to walk hard on the earth and thus on ourselves, or we can learn to walk more gently on the earth.

What's the use of a house if you don't have a decent planet to put it on?

HENRY DAVID THOREAU

GUEST ESSAY The Global Environmental Challenge

Gus Speth

Gus Speth has served as President of the World Resources Institute since it was founded by him and others in 1982. This organization is an important center for policy research and technical assistance on resource and environmental issues of international importance. He served as head of the President's Council on Environmental Quality (CEQ) between 1979 and 1981, after serving as a member of the council from 1977 to 1979. In 1980, he chaired the President's Task Force on Global Resources and Environment. Before his appointment to the CEQ, he was a senior attorney for the Natural Resources Defense Council, an environmental organization he helped found in 1970.

Writing recently in *Foreign Affairs*, George F. Kennan observed that "our world is at present faced with two unprecedented and supreme dangers": any major war at all among great industrial powers and "the devastating effect of modern industrialization and overpopulation on the world's natural environment."

The deterioration of the global environment to which Kennan refers has a scale that encompasses the great life-supporting systems of the planet's biosphere. It includes the alteration of the Earth's climate and biogeochemical cycles, the accumulation of wastes, the exhaustion of soils, loss of forests, and the decline of ecological communities [Table 1-1].

Since World War II, growth in human population and economic activity has been unprecedented. The world's population has more than doubled to 5.4 billion and will reach 6 billion by the end of the century. The gross world product has increased fourfold since 1950. With these increases in population and economic activity have come large increases in both pollution and pressure on natural resources.

Air pollution today poses problems for all countries. As use of fossil fuels has increased, so have emissions of sulfur and nitrogen oxides and other harmful gases. Acid rain, ozone, and other ills born of this pollution are now damaging public health and harming forests, fish, and crops over large areas of the globe.

Another gas emitted when fossil fuels burn is carbon dioxide, the chief culprit among the greenhouse-enhancing gases, which trap heat in the atmosphere. If the buildup of greenhouse gases in the atmosphere is not halted, the global warming now apparently under way will bring about major climate changes. Regional impacts are difficult to predict accurately, but rainfall and monsoon patterns could shift, disrupting agriculture in many areas. Sea levels could rise, flooding coastal areas. Ocean currents could shift, further altering the climate and fisheries. Fewer plant and animal species could survive as favorable habitats are reduced. Heat waves, droughts, hurricanes, and other weather anomalies could harm susceptible people, crops, and forests.

Depletion of the stratosphere's ozone layer also threatens human health and natural systems. In 1987, an international treaty was negotiated to address this problem by reducing the use of chlorofluorocarbons (CFCs). In 1990, this treaty was strengthened to provide for the elimination of CFCs by the year 2000.

These interrelated atmospheric issues constitute the most serious pollution threat in history. Simultaneous and gradual, their effects will be hard to reverse. Because pollutants react with other substances, and with each other, with the utilization of the sun's energy, a well-planned response has to take all these factors into account. These air pollution issues are also linked to the use

(continued)

of fossil fuels. In the future, energy policy and environmental policy should be made together.

The United States can take some pride in actions to improve air quality. But the country still emits about 15% of the world's sulfur dioxide, about 25% of all nitrogen oxides, and 25% of the carbon dioxide, and it still manufactures a major share of all CFCs.

Improvements in U.S. energy efficiency have been considerable. Per capita energy use dropped by 12% between 1973 and 1985—a period when per capita gross domestic product grew 17%. Yet, the United States is still consuming one-fourth of the world's energy annually, and producing only half as much GNP per unit of energy as its world market competitors such as the former West Germany and Japan.

Our national concern for the atmosphere must be matched by a growing awareness of the steady deterioration of forests, soils, and water in much of the developing world. The UN Food and Agriculture Organization predicted in 1985 that without corrective action, rainfed crops in the Third World will become 30% less productive by the end of this century because the soil is depleted or eroded.

In developing countries, 10 trees are cut down for every 1 replanted—30 trees for 1 in Africa—and every minute an average of 38 hectares (94 acres) of tropical forests disappear, as do uncounted species that inhabit them. Fuelwood shortages affect an estimated 1.5 billion people in 63 countries. Most people in developing countries lack access to basic sanitary facilities, and 80% of all illness is due to unsafe water supplies. People in LDCs now rank high among those exposed to toxic chemicals—from lead in Mexico to DDT in China.

In 1988, the World Commission on Environment and Development described a new consensus, supported by industrialized and developing nations. The old notion that environmental loss was the price of economic progress was rejected. Far from bringing about broad-based development, overexploitation or mismanagement of natural resources has contributed to famines and floods, dam reservoirs that fill with silt within a decade, irrigation schemes that salt the soil, and conversion of grasslands and tropical forests into unproductive wastelands. The commission's report, *Our Common Future*, stated: "Many forms of development erode the natural resources upon which they must be based, and environmental degradation can undermine economic development. Poverty is a major cause and effect of global environmental problems."

Fighting poverty requires diffusing the underlying pressures on the world's resource base. While many complex factors are involved, the LDCs must deal with

- *Rapid population growth.* Of the 1 billion people to be added to the world's population between 1987 and 1997, nine out of ten will be born in developing countries.

- *Shortsighted economic policies pursued by governments of both industrial and developing countries.* These include direct and indirect subsidies that encourage the wasteful use of energy, water, and forests, and policies that favor city dwellers over the rural poor.

- *Misguided development and aid programs.* Many large-scale development projects have neglected environmental factors and local needs.

The United States is directly affected by these LDC concerns. Twenty percent of the carbon dioxide contributing to the greenhouse effect is estimated to come from tropical deforestation. A wide range of biological resources—species yet to be analyzed for their agricultural, industrial, or pharmaceutical value—is being lost.

The growth of developing economies expands global U.S. trade and job opportunities at home; already more than a third of U.S. trade is with LDCs. With economic recovery, the developing countries could absorb up to half of all U.S. exports by the year 2000. But sustained growth in much of the developing world requires better management of natural resources.

Sustainable development is the widely accepted answer—development that meets today's needs without compromising the ability of future generations to meet theirs. U.S. leadership in applying this approach requires both vigorous evaluation of environmental consequences of development assistance programs and support for national development strategies that conserve and restore the land's productive capacity.

It means helping developing countries invest in reforestation, agroforestry (growing crops and trees together), water conservation, and energy efficiency. It also means reducing debt and other pressures that force LDCs to cash in their natural resources to earn foreign exchange. Family planning, primary health services, and better sanitation all deserve a high priority since they reduce child mortality and slow birth rates.

In the 1990s, industrialized and developing countries will have to face these challenges together. All nations must act in concert to sustain the earth and its people.

Twenty years ago, the United States responded vigorously to the serious environmental concerns then emerging. New national policies were declared, new agencies created, and major pollution cleanup and resource management initiatives launched.

Today, as we enter the 1990s, the Bush administration and the members of Congress face a new agenda of environmental concerns that are more serious and challenging than the problems of the 1970s.

These concerns are not the ones to which the United States addressed itself when environmental concerns emerged forcefully 20 years ago. They present us with new policy challenges that are more global in scope and international in implication.

The 1990s will be the crucial decade for action on these pressing concerns. If major national and international efforts are not pursued in this period, irreparable damage will be done to the world's environment, and the problems will prove increasingly intractable, expensive, and dominated by crises.

If the United States and other countries do respond, however, tropical deforestation can be arrested and disappearing species saved; poverty can be alleviated and human populations stabilized; soils can be conserved and more food provided; projected climate change can be slowed; regional and global pollution can be reduced.

These and other things can be done with means within our grasp. But success hinges on concerted efforts made with some urgency to change many current policies, to strengthen and multiply successful programs, and to launch bold initiatives where they are needed.

There are ample grounds in the experience of the last two decades for both optimistic and pessimistic assumptions about the future. The gaps between success and failure in addressing resource, environmental, and population problems have been enormous. The good news is that these divergent outcomes are primarily the result of differences in policies and programs pursued by governments, the private sector, and others. In short, leadership and new initiatives can make a world of difference.

Guest Essay Discussion

1. How serious are the problems cited in this essay and throughout this chapter? How do these problems affect your life and lifestyle, now and in the future?

2. Compare the viewpoint in this essay with the one presented by Julian Simon in the essay that follows. Which viewpoint more closely matches your own?

GUEST ESSAY There Is No Environmental, Population, or Resource Crisis

Julian L. Simon

Julian L. Simon is professor of economics and business administration at the University of Maryland. He has effectively presented and defended the position that continued economic growth and technological advances based on the throwaway and Spaceship-Earth worldviews will produce a less crowded, less polluted, and more resource-rich world. His many articles and books on this subject include The Ultimate Resource, The Resourceful Earth, *and* Population Matters *(see Further Readings).*

This book, like most others discussing environmental and resource problems, begins with the proposition that there is an environmental and resource crisis. If this means that the situation of humanity is worse now than in the past, then the idea of a crisis—and all that follows from it—is dead wrong. In almost every respect important to humanity, the trends have been improving, not deteriorating.

Our world now supports 5.4 billion people. In the nineteenth century, the earth could sustain only 1 billion. And 10,000 years ago, only 1 million people could keep themselves alive. People are living more healthily than ever before, too.

One would expect lovers of humanity—people who hate war and worry about famine in Africa—to jump with joy at this extraordinary triumph of the human mind and human organization over the raw forces of nature. Instead, they lament that there are so many human beings and wring their hands about the problems that more people inevitably bring.

The recent extraordinary decrease in the death rate—to my mind, the greatest miracle in history—accounts for the bumper crop of humanity. Recall that it took thousands of years to increase life expectancy at birth from the 20s to the 30s. Then, in just the last 200 years, life expectancy in the advanced countries jumped from the mid-30s to the 70s. And, starting well after World War II, life expectancy at birth in the poor countries, even the very poorest, has leaped upward (averaging 64 in 1990) because of progress in agriculture, sanitation, and medicine. Average life expectancy at birth in China, the world's most populous country, was 68 in 1990, an increase of 24 years since the 1950s. Is this not an astounding triumph?

In the short run, another baby reduces income per person by causing output to be divided among more people.

(continued)

And as the British economist Thomas Malthus argued in 1798, more workers laboring with existing capital results in less output per worker. However, if resources are not fixed, then the Malthusian doctrine of diminishing resources, resurrected by today's doom-and-gloom analysts, does not apply. Given some time to adjust to shortages with known methods and new inventions, free people create additional resources.

It is amazing but true that a resource shortage resulting from population or income growth usually leaves us better off than if the shortage had never arisen. If firewood had not become scarce in seventeenth-century England, coal would not have been developed. If coal and whale oil shortages hadn't loomed, oil wells would not have been dug.

The prices of food, metals, and other raw materials have been declining by every measure since the beginning of the nineteenth century, and as far back as we know. That is, raw materials have been getting less scarce instead of more scarce throughout history, defying the commonsense notion that if one begins with an inventory of a resource and uses some up, there will be less left. This is despite, and indirectly because of, increasing population.

All statistical studies show that population growth doesn't lead to slower economic growth, though this defies common sense. Nor is high population density a drag on economic development. Statistical comparison across nations reveals that higher population density is associated with faster instead of slower growth. Drive around on Hong Kong's smooth-flowing highways for an hour or two. You will then realize that a large concentration of human beings in a small area does not make comfortable existence impossible. It also allows for exciting economic expansion, if the system gives individuals the freedom to exercise their talents and pursue economic opportunities. The experience of densely populated Singapore makes it clear that Hong Kong is not unique, either.

In 1984, a blue-ribbon panel of scientists summarized their wisdom in *The Resourceful Earth*. Among the findings, besides those I have noted above, were these:

- Many people are still hungry, but the food supply has been improving since at least World War II, as measured by grain prices, production per consumer, and the death rate from famine.

- Land availability won't increasingly constrain world agriculture in coming decades.

- In the U.S., the trend is toward higher-quality cropland, suffering less from erosion than in the past.

- The widely published report of increasingly rapid urbanization of U.S. farmland was based on faulty data.

- Trends in world forests are not worrying, though in some places deforestation is troubling.

- There is no statistical evidence for rapid loss of plant and animal wildlife species in the next two decades. An increased rate of extinction cannot be ruled out if tropical deforestation is severe, but no evidence about linkage has yet been demonstrated.

- Water does not pose a problem of physical scarcity or disappearance, although the world and U.S. situations do call for better institutional management through more rational systems of property rights.

DISCUSSION TOPICS

1. Is the world overpopulated? Explain. Is the United States suffering from consumption overpopulation? Explain.

2. Do you favor instituting policies designed to reduce population growth and stabilize **(a)** the size of the world's population as soon as possible and **(b)** the size of the U.S. population as soon as possible? Explain. What policies do you believe should be implemented?

3. Explain why you agree or disagree with the following proposition: High levels of resource use by the United States and other MDCs is beneficial. MDCs stimulate the economic growth of LDCs by buying their raw materials. High levels of resource use also stimulate economic growth in MDCs. Economic growth provides money for more financial aid to LDCs and for reducing pollution, environmental degradation, and poverty.

4. Explain why you agree or disagree with the following proposition: The world will never run out of resources because technological innovations will produce substitutes or allow use of lower grades of scarce resources.

5. Does your own worldview more closely resemble the throwaway, Spaceship-Earth, or sustainable-Earth worldview? If you have a mixed worldview, classify your beliefs that fit into these three categories. What worldview is reflected in your lifestyle? Compare your views with those of others in your class.

6. What are the major resource and environmental problems in **(a)** the city, town, or rural area where you live and **(b)** the state where you live? Which of these problems affect you directly?

7. Would you support a sharp increase in local, state, and federal taxes if you could be sure the money was used to help improve environmental quality?

- There is no persuasive reason to believe that the world oil price will rise in coming decades. The price may fall well below what it has been.

- Compared with coal, nuclear power is no more expensive and is probably much cheaper under most circumstances. It is also much cheaper than oil.

- Nuclear power gives every evidence of costing fewer lives per unit of energy produced than does coal or oil.

- Solar energy sources (including wind and wave power) are too dilute to compete economically for much of humankind's energy needs, though for specialized uses and certain climates they can make a valuable contribution.

- Threats of air and water pollution have been vastly overblown. The air and water in the United States have been getting cleaner, rather than dirtier.

We don't say that all is well everywhere, and we don't predict that all will be rosy in the future. Children are hungry and sick; people live out lives of physical or intellectual poverty and lack of opportunity; war or some other pollution may do us in. *The Resourceful Earth* does show that for most relevant matters we've examined, total global and U.S. trends are improving instead of deteriorating.

Also, we do not say that a better future happens automatically or without effect. It will happen because men and women — sometimes as individuals, sometimes as enterprises working for profit, sometimes as voluntary nonprofit-making groups, and sometimes as governmental agencies — will address problems with muscle and mind, and will probably overcome, as has been usual through history.

We are confident that the nature of the physical world permits continued improvement in humankind's economic lot in the long run, indefinitely. Of course, there are always newly arising local problems, shortages, and pollutions, resulting from climate or increased population and income and new technologies. Sometimes temporary large-scale problems arise. But the world's physical conditions and the resilience in a well-functioning economic and social system enable us to overcome such problems, and the solutions usually leave us better off than if the problem had never arisen. That is the great lesson to be learned from human history.

Guest Essay Discussion

1. Do you agree with the author's contention that there is no environmental, population, or resource crisis? Explain. How is it compatible with the data presented in Table 1-1 and in Gus Speth's essay? After you've finished this course, come back and answer this question again to see if your views have changed.

2. In effect, the authors of this essay and the one that preceded it have taken the same general trends, projected them into the future, and come to quite different conclusions. How can this happen? What criteria can we use to decide who's more likely to be correct?

8. Would you support greatly increasing the amount of land protected from development as wilderness, even if the land contained valuable minerals, oil, natural gas, timber, or other resources?

*9. Make a list of the resources you truly need. Then make another list of the resources that you use each day only because you want them. Then make a third list of resources you want and hope to use in the future.

---

*Discussion Topic items preceded by an asterisk are either laboratory exercises or individual or class projects.

CHAPTER 2

BRIEF HISTORY OF RESOURCE USE, RESOURCE CONSERVATION, AND ENVIRONMENTAL PROTECTION

General Questions and Issues

1. How did early and advanced hunter-gatherer societies affect the environment, and what was their relationship to nature?

2. What major impacts have early agricultural societies and today's nonindustrialized agricultural societies had on the environment, and what is the relationship of these societies to nature?

3. How do present-day industrialized societies affect the environment, and what is their relationship to nature?

4. What are the principal phases in the history of resource use, resource conservation, and environmental protection in the United States?

5. How can we deal with the environmental and resource problems we face during the 1990s and beyond?

A continent ages quickly once we come.

ERNEST HEMINGWAY

OSSIL EVIDENCE SUGGESTS that the most recent form of our species, *Homo sapiens sapiens*, has lived on Earth for only about 40,000 years, a brief instant in the planet's estimated 4.6-billion-year existence. During 30,000 of the 40,000 years our current species has been around, we survived as mostly nomadic hunter-gatherers. Since then there have been two major cultural shifts, the *Agricultural Revolution*, which began 10,000 to 12,000 years ago, and the *Industrial Revolution*, which began about 275 years ago.

These cultural revolutions have given us much more energy (Figure 2-1) and many new technologies with which to alter and control increasingly larger parts of the earth to meet our basic needs and a rapidly expanding list of wants. By expanding food supplies, increasing average life spans, and improving average living standards, each of these shifts led to sharp increases in the size of the human population (Figure 2-2). These cultural shifts also led to the J-shaped curves of exponentially increasing resource use, pollution, and environmental degradation we are experiencing today (Table 1-1).

During the past 25 years, a global environmental movement that began in the United States in the 1960s has questioned whether we can continue expanding in numbers and present forms of economic growth without disrupting Earth's life-support systems for us and other species. Members of this rapidly growing movement believe there is an urgent need to make a new cultural change before we are overwhelmed by rapid exponential growth in people, pollution, and environmental degradation.

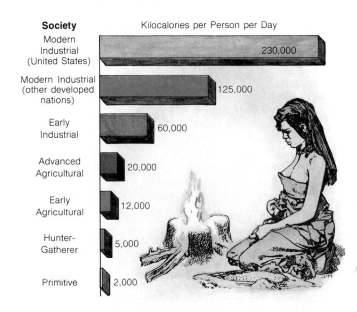

Figure 2-1 Average direct and indirect daily energy use per person at various stages of human cultural development. A *calorie* is the amount of energy needed to raise the temperature of 1 gram of water 1°C (1.8°F). A *kilocalorie* is 1,000 calories.

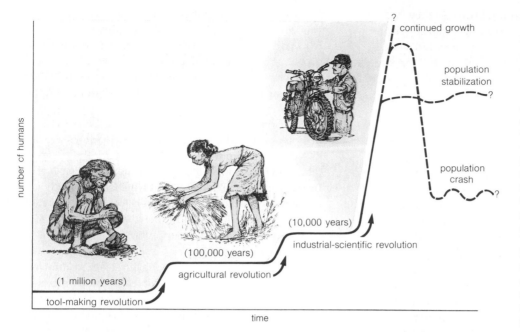

number of humans

time

tool-making revolution

(1 million years)

agricultural revolution

(100,000 years)

industrial-scientific revolution

(10,000 years)

? continued growth

population stabilization ?

population crash ?

Figure 2-2 Humans have expanded Earth's carrying capacity for their species through technological innovation, leading to several major cultural changes, and by displacing and reducing the populations of other species that compete with us for food, space, or other resources and that provide us with such resources as furs, ivory, and food. Dashed lines represent possible future changes in human population size: continued growth, population stabilization, and continued growth followed by a crash and stabilization at a much lower level. This generalized curve is plotted by a different mathematical method from the one used in Figure 1-2. It is a plot of the logarithm of population size versus the logarithm of time. Figure 1-2 is a plot of population size versus time.

2-1 Hunting-and-Gathering Societies

Archaeological evidence suggests that during about three-fourths of our 40,000-year existence, we were **hunter-gatherers**, who survived by gathering edible wild plants and by hunting and killing wild animals (including seafood) from the nearby environment (Figure 2-3). Evidence indicates that our hunter-gatherer ancestors lived in small groups of rarely more than 50 people who worked together to get enough food to survive. If food became scarce, they picked up their few possessions and moved to another area.

Our hunter-gatherer ancestors (and those still living this way today) survived only by having expert knowledge about their natural surroundings. They learned to anticipate the seasons, when the fish would run, when animals would emerge from hibernation, when edible berries would ripen, and when migrating animals would come and go. They learned how to find water, even in the desert. They discovered a variety of plants and animals that could be eaten and used as medicines. By using stones to sharpen and shape sticks, other stones, and animal bones, they made primitive weapons for killing animals, and tools for cutting plants and scraping hides for clothing and shelter. These dwellers in nature had only two energy sources: sunlight captured by plants, which also served as food for the wild animals they hunted, and their own muscular power (Figure 2-1).

In most cases, males and females shared work, food, and power in these social groups based on cooperation. Men did the hunting and women did most of

Figure 2-3 Most people who have lived on Earth have survived by hunting wild game and gathering wild plants. These !Kung bushmen (top) in Africa are going hunting. The man (bottom) is digging for roots in a tropical forest in the Amazon Basin of Brazil.

Simon Trevor/Bruce Coleman Ltd.

Hutchison Library

the gathering. Women could not hunt because they had to carry their nursing infants and young children with them. Thus, cooperation with one another and with nature has been the dominant force during three-fourths of the time our current species has existed.

Groups made conscious efforts to keep their population size in balance with available food supplies. Population control practices varied with different cultures, but they included abstention from sexual intercourse, infanticide, abortion, late marriage, and feeding infants with breast milk as long as possible (a practice that provides some degree of birth control). Infant deaths from infectious diseases and infanticide (killing the newborn) led to an average life expectancy of about 30 years. This prevented the world's hunter-gatherers from undergoing rapid population growth (Figure 2-2).

Archaeological evidence indicates that hunter-gatherers gradually developed improved tools and hunting weapons. Some people learned to work together to hunt herds of reindeer, woolly mammoths, European bison, and other big game. They used fire to flush game from thickets toward hunters lying in wait and to stampede herds of animals into traps or over cliffs. Some also learned to burn vegetation to promote the growth of food plants and plants favored by the animals they hunted.

Advanced hunter-gatherers had a greater impact on their environment than early hunter-gatherers, especially in using fire to convert forests into grasslands. There is also evidence that they contributed to, and perhaps even caused, the extinction of some large game animals in different parts of the world.

Because of their small numbers, nomadic behavior, and dependence on their own muscle power to modify the environment, their environmental impact was fairly small and localized. Both early and advanced hunter-gatherers were examples of *people in nature*, who trod lightly on the earth because they were not capable of doing more. These dwellers in the land survived by being keenly aware of their intimate dependence on nature and by learning to work with nature and with one another.

2-2 Agricultural Societies

THE AGRICULTURAL REVOLUTION About 10,000 years ago, a cultural shift, known as the **Agricultural Revolution**, began at several places in the world. It involved a gradual shift from small mobile hunting-and-gathering bands to settled agricultural communities, where people survived by learning how to breed and raise wild animals and how to cultivate wild plants near where they lived.

Archaeological evidence indicates that plant cultivation, which we call horticulture, probably began in tropical forest areas. People discovered that they could grow various wild food plants by digging holes with a stick (a primitive hoe) and placing roots or tubers (fleshy stems of plants usually found underground) of these plants in the holes.

To prepare for planting, they cleared small patches of forests by **slash-and-burn cultivation**—cutting down trees and other vegetation, leaving the cut vegetation on the ground to dry, and then burning it (Figures 2-4 and 2-5). The ashes that were left replaced plant nutrients in the nutrient-poor soils found in most tropical forest areas. Roots and tubers were then planted in holes dug between tree stumps.

These early growers also used **shifting cultivation** (Figure 2-4). After a plot had been planted and harvested for a few years, few if any crops could be grown. By then, either the soil had been depleted of nutrients or the patch had been invaded by a dense growth of vegetation from the surrounding forest. When yields dropped, the growers shifted to a new area of forest and cleared a new plot. The growers learned that each abandoned patch had to be left fallow (unplanted) for 10 to 30 years before the soil became fertile enough to grow crops again. By doing this, they practiced sustainable agriculture.

These growers practiced **subsistence farming**, growing only enough food to feed their families. Their dependence on human muscle power and crude stone or stick tools meant that they could cultivate only small plots; thus, they had relatively little impact on their environment.

About 7,000 years ago, the use of agriculture increased with the invention of the metal plow, pulled by domesticated animals and steered by the farmer. Animal-pulled plows allowed farmers to cultivate larger plots of land and to break up fertile grassland soils, which previously couldn't be cultivated because of their thick and widespread root systems. In some arid (dry) regions, early farmers further increased crop output by diverting water from nearby streams into hand-dug ditches and canals to irrigate crops.

EMERGENCE OF AGRICULTURE-BASED URBAN SOCIETIES The gradual shift from hunting and gathering to farming had a number of significant effects:

- Using domesticated animals to haul loads and do other tasks increased the average energy use per person (Figure 2-1).

- Population increased, mostly because of a larger, more reliable supply of food (Figure 2-2).

- People controlled and shaped more of Earth's surface to meet their needs by clearing increasingly larger areas of land and by building irrigation systems to transfer water from one place to another.

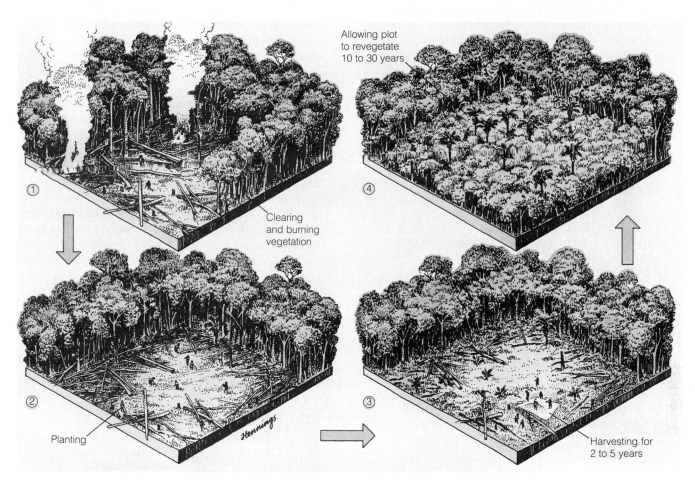

Figure 2-4 Probably the first crop-growing technique was a combination of slash-and-burn and shifting cultivation in tropical forests. This is a sustainable method if only a small portion of the forest is cleared. Soil fertility will not be restored unless each abandoned plot is left unplanted for 10 to 30 years. This form of agriculture can be sustained indefinitely if population levels are low.

Figure 2-5 Slash-and-burn subsistence farming in a small patch of cleared tropical rain forest in Costa Rica. This family will be able to grow crops on this patch for a few years before the plant nutrients in the nutrient-poor soil are depleted. Then the family will move to another part of the forest and repeat this process. This shifting cultivation can be sustained indefinitely if population levels in the forest are low and if the farmers allow each depleted patch to renew its soil fertility for several decades.

- People began accumulating material goods. By necessity, nomadic hunter-gatherers had to travel with few possessions, but farmers living in one place could accumulate as much as they could afford.

- Urbanization—the formation of villages, towns, and cities—began because a small number of farmers could produce enough food to feed their families, plus a surplus that could be traded to other people. Many former farmers moved into permanent villages. Some villages gradually grew into towns and cities, which served as centers for trade, government, and religion.

- Specialized occupations and long-distance trade developed as former farmers in villages and towns learned crafts such as weaving, toolmaking, and pottery to produce handmade goods that could be exchanged for food.

- Conflict increased as ownership of land and water rights became a valuable economic resource and as human numbers grew and societies confronted one another. Armies and their leaders rose to power and took over large areas of land. These rulers forced powerless people—slaves and landless peasants—to do the hard, disagreeable work of producing food and constructing irrigation systems, temples, and other projects.

- Competition between people for land, water, and power led to male-dominated societies still in existence today. To survive, females had to give up the shared power they had in most cooperative hunter-gatherer societies to male warriors who could protect them and their children from aggressors. Men were taught not to show their emotions and inner feelings, since this would make them seem weak and ineffective.

- The war against the rest of nature began. The survival of wild plants and animals, once vital to humanity, no longer seemed to matter. Wild animals, competing with livestock for grass and feeding on crops, were killed or driven from their habitats. Wild plants invading cropfields were a threat to be eliminated.

ENVIRONMENTAL IMPACT The growing populations of these emerging civilizations needed more food and more wood for fuel and buildings. To meet these needs, people cut down vast areas of forest and plowed up large areas of grasslands. Such extensive land clearing destroyed and degraded the habitats of many forms of plant and animal wildlife, causing or hastening their extinction.

Many of these cleared lands were poorly managed. This led to greatly increased deforestation, soil erosion, salt buildup in irrigated soils, and overgrazing of grasslands by huge herds of sheep, cattle, and other livestock. These unsustainable practices helped convert fertile land to desert. The topsoil that washed off these barren areas polluted streams, lakes, and irrigation canals, making them useless. The gradual degradation of the vital resource base of soil, water, forests, grazing land, and wildlife was a major factor in the downfall of many great civilizations (see Spotlight on p. 37).

The gradual spread of agriculture meant that most of the world's human population shifted from hunter-gatherers *in nature* to shepherds, farmers, and urban dwellers *against nature*, who viewed their role as learning to tame and control wild nature and to gain power and wealth by controlling other humans. When people settled down to till the soil, they started on the road to cities, wars, overpopulation, male-dominated societies, environmental degradation, air and water pollution, and nuclear weapons.

Many analysts believe that this cultural change in how people viewed their relationship to nature and each other is a major cause of today's resource and environmental problems. They consider the frontier and throwaway worldviews that agriculture helped shape as the root causes of our escalating war against nature and each other.

2-3 Industrial Societies: The Industrial Revolution

EARLY INDUSTRIAL SOCIETIES The next great cultural change, known as the **Industrial Revolution**, began in England in the mid-1700s and spread to the United States in the 1800s. It greatly increased the average per capita energy consumption and thus our power to alter and shape the earth to meet our needs and wants and fuel economic growth (Figure 2-1). This led to greatly increased production, trade, and distribution of goods.

The Industrial Revolution arose as a response to absolute resource scarcity in England caused by the overuse and depletion of wood for fuel and construction. People began burning surface deposits of coal as a substitute for wood. The availability of coal led to the invention of coal-powered steam engines to pump water and perform other tasks.

People invented an increasing array of new machines powered by coal and later by oil and natural gas. Thus, the Industrial Revolution represented a shift from dependence on renewable wood and flowing water as principal sources of energy to dependence on nonrenewable fossil fuels (first coal, then oil and natural gas).

These new fuels and machines led to a switch from small-scale, localized production of goods by hand to large-scale production of goods by machines in centralized factories. The use of coal as an energy source meant that manufacturing plants could be located in cities rather than dispersed throughout the country-side as they had been to take advantage of wood supplies and power sources such as flowing water. Fossil-fuel-powered farm machines, commercial fertilizers, and new plant-breeding techniques greatly increased the crop yields per area of cultivated land.

Increased agricultural production, plus the concentration of factories in cities, freed farm workers to move to the cities for work. Many found jobs in the growing number of mechanized factories. There they worked long hours for low pay in boring assembly-line jobs. Most factories were noisy, dirty, and dangerous places to work. Other workers toiled in dangerous and unhealthy coal mines. In 1840, the average life expectancy for workers in the coal mines around Manchester, England, was only 17 years, compared with 34 years for people in surrounding rural areas. With more income and a more reliable supply of food, the size of the human population began the sharp exponential increase we are still experiencing today (Figures 1-2 and 2-2).

ADVANCED INDUSTRIAL SOCIETIES After World War I (1914–18), more efficient machines and mass-production techniques were developed, forming the basis of today's advanced industrial societies in the United States, Canada, Japan, and western Europe (Figure 1-5). These societies are characterized by

- greatly increased production and consumption of goods, stimulated by mass advertising to create artificial wants (the consumer society) and encourage economic growth and the creation of more jobs

- greatly increased dependence on nonrenewable resources such as oil, natural gas, coal, and various metals

- a shift from dependence on natural materials, which are environmentally harmless or are broken down and recycled by natural processes, to dependence on synthetic materials that break down slowly in the environment and many of which are toxic to humans and wildlife

- a sharp rise in the amount of energy used per person for transportation, manufacturing, agriculture, lighting, and heating and cooling (Figure 2-1)

Advanced industrial societies benefit most people living in them. These benefits include

- creation and mass production of many useful and economically affordable products

- a sharp increase in average agricultural productivity per person because of advanced industrialized agriculture, in which a small number of farmers produce large amounts of food

- a sharp rise in birth control and average life expectancy from improvements in sanitation, hygiene,

---

SPOTLIGHT **Environmental Abuse and the Fall of Civilizations**

As late as 7000 B.C., sites of the great Sumerian and Babylonian civilizations were covered with productive forests and grasslands. With each generation, however, the elaborate network of irrigation canals that supported these civilizations became filled with more sediment from deforestation, soil erosion, salt buildup in irrigated soils, and overgrazing. More and more slaves and laborers were needed to keep the irrigation channels free of sediment.

By 3000 B.C., much of this once-productive land had been turned into the barren desert that makes up much of Iran and Iraq today. A combination of environmental degradation, climate change, drought, and a series of invading armies eventually led to the downfall of the Sumerian and Babylonian civilizations.

Severe environmental degradation also took place in other areas around the Mediterranean Sea and in Saharan Africa, where the remains of great cities are now buried in the sand. In Central America, the great Mayan civilization, which had peaked in A.D. 800, collapsed when its agricultural base failed.

These people squandered the natural capital they inherited by gradually depleting the soil that supported their civilizations. There is evidence that we may be repeating this mistake on a much larger scale (see Table 1-1 and Figure 1-10).

---

nutrition, and medicine, taking place first in MDCs and, to a lesser extent, more recently in most LDCs

- a gradual decline in the exponential rate of population growth in MDCs because of improvements in health, birth control, education, average income, and old-age security (Figure 1-6)

ENVIRONMENTAL IMPACT Along with their many benefits, industrialized societies have intensified many existing resource and environmental problems and created new ones (Table 1-1 and Figure 1-10) — the same problems that contributed to the downfall of earlier civilizations (see Spotlight above). The key factor responsible for rapid economic growth and today's environmental problems is the greatly increased use of relatively cheap fossil fuels that supports industrialization, modern agriculture, and urbanization. Burning these fuels gives us enormous amounts of energy to alter Earth's surface to provide large quantities of resources for people with affluent lifestyles. Burning fossil fuels is also responsible for most of the world's air pollution and much of its water pollution. There is growing evidence that burning these fuels is changing the content of the atmosphere in ways that could bring about rapid and highly disruptive changes in global and regional climates over the next 50 years.

Industrialization has greatly intensified the view that our role is to conquer nature, a worldview that began to take hold with the invention of agriculture. Domination of Earth is viewed as progress. Many analysts believe that as long as we have this worldview, we will continue to abuse Earth's life-support systems.

2-4 Historical Overview of Resource Use, Resource Conservation, and Environmental Protection in the United States

AMERICA'S FIRST CONSERVATIONISTS When Europeans discovered North America in the fifteenth and sixteenth centuries, they found it populated with diverse groups of indigenous (aboriginal) people—called Indians by the Europeans and now often referred to as Native Americans. For at least 10,000 years, these people practiced mostly hunting and gathering and survived by being immersed in and learning to work with nature.

Although there were exceptions, the cultures of most Native Americans were based on a deep respect for the land and its animals. This way of viewing the earth is revealed by a medicine woman in California's Wintu tribe:*

The white people never cared for the land or deer or bear. When the Indians kill meat, we eat it all up. When we dig roots, we make little holes. When we build houses, we make little holes. . . . We don't chop down trees. We only use dead wood. But the white people plow up the ground, pull down the trees, kill everything. The tree says: "Don't. I am sore. Don't hurt me." But they chop it down and cut it up. The spirit of the land hates them. . . . The white people destroy all. They blast rocks and scatter them on the ground. The rock says: "Don't. You are hurting me." But the white people pay no attention. . . . How can the spirit of the Earth like the white man? . . . Everywhere the white man has touched the Earth it is sore.

FRONTIER EXPANSION AND RESOURCE USE (1607–1900) When European colonists began settling in North America in 1607, they found a vast continent.

---

*Many environmental textbooks and articles illustrate Native American views about land and nature by quoting from a letter that Chief Seattle of the Dwamish tribe of the state of Washington allegedly wrote to President Franklin Pierce in 1865. Historical research, however has revealed that he never wrote a letter to President Pierce. The famous and inspiring letter that is often published and attributed to Chief Seattle was written in the winter of 1971–72 by Ted Perry, a screenwriter, for a film called *Home*, shown on U.S. national television in 1972. While some of the ideas in this speech were based on Chief Seattle's speeches, its content should be viewed as closer to a summary of the more modern sustainable-Earth worldview.

Chris Caldwell/NRDC

Figure 2-6 Sunlight filtering through a redwood forest in the Muir Woods near the coast of northern California. At one time, large areas of these and other ancient forests covered much of the United States. Now most redwood forests have been cleared or have been eliminated by climate shifts. Many of the country's few remaining ancient forests, especially in the northwest, are also being cleared rapidly for timber. This is happening at the same time that the U.S. government is urging tropical LDCs not to cut down most of their remaining ancient forests in order to protect Earth's biodiversity and to help delay projected global warming.

It had abundant and seemingly inexhaustible supplies of timber, fertile soil, wildlife, water, minerals, and other resources for their own use and for export to Europe. Enormous flocks of geese, ducks, and passenger pigeons blotted out the sun. Remarkably diverse forests seemed to stretch endlessly from the Atlantic coast to the Great Plains. Forests beyond the Great Plains were even more dramatic (Figure 2-6).

American settlers viewed the continent as a hostile wilderness to be conquered, opened up, cleared, and used as quickly as possible. This frontier attitude led to enormous resource waste and little regard for future resource needs.

After the Civil War, the federal government turned its attention to expanding the frontier westward. That meant displacing the Native Americans—mostly Apaches, Comanches, Arapahos, Kiowas, and Sioux—who were obstacles to settling the plains. This involved the mass killing of these indigenous peoples and of the

American bison, which served as a major source of food and other resources for these dwellers in the land (see Case Study on p. 40).

In 1850, about 80% of the total land area of the United States was government owned. Most of this land had been taken from indigenous Native Americans, who had lived on it sustainably for thousands of years. By 1840, Native Americans had been killed in battle or by disease (especially smallpox) or expelled from most of the eastern half of the United States. As the West was settled, they were killed or displaced from most of the land in that area. The government signed and then broke dozens of treaties giving various nations and tribes of Native Americans ownership of large tracts of land.

By 1876, remaining Native Americans—a defeated and broken people—had been pushed onto a few government-managed reservations. In 1891, an old Sioux Indian summarized the behavior of the American government: "They made us many promises, more than I can remember, but they never kept but one; they promised to take our land and they took it."

By 1900, more than half of the public land had been given away or sold at low cost to railroad, timber, and mining companies, land developers, states, schools, universities, and homesteaders. By artificially lowering the prices of resources, these land transfers encouraged widespread waste, and degradation of much of the country's forests, grasslands, and minerals. Most of this land was obtained by speculators and large corporations.

EARLY CONSERVATION WARNINGS (1832–70) Between 1832 and 1870, some individuals warned that America's forest, grassland, and wildlife resources were being depleted and degraded at an alarming rate. These early conservationists included George Catlin, Horace Greeley, Ralph Waldo Emerson, Frederick Law Olmsted, Charles W. Eliot, Henry David Thoreau, and George Perkins Marsh. They proposed that part of the unspoiled wilderness owned by the government be protected from resource use and left untouched as a heritage to future generations.

These warnings were either ignored or vigorously opposed by many citizens and politicians. They believed that the country's forests and wildlife would last forever and that people had the right to do with private and public land as they pleased.

BEGINNINGS OF THE FEDERAL GOVERNMENT'S ROLE IN RESOURCE CONSERVATION (1870–1916)
In the late 1800s, the American conservation movement emerged as a number of citizens and government officials began to realize the extent of deforestation and wildlife depletion throughout the country. The federal role in forest and wildlife resource conservation began in 1872, when the government set aside over 809,000 hectares (2 million acres) of forest, mostly in northwestern Wyoming, as Yellowstone National Park, and banned all hunting in the area.

Congress protected this land mostly because it was viewed as essentially useless as a source of resources. However, this action marked the beginning of the *first wave of resource conservation* in the United States.

In 1891, Congress passed the Forest Reserve Act. It set aside Yellowstone Timberland Reserve as the first federal forest reserve. The act also authorized the president to set aside additional federal lands to ensure future supplies of timber and to protect water resources. This was a turning point in establishing the federal government's responsibility to protect public lands from unsustainable resource use.

Between 1891 and 1897, Presidents Benjamin Harrison and Grover Cleveland withdrew large areas of public land, located mostly in the West, from timber cutting. Powerful and wealthy political foes—especially Westerners accustomed to using these public lands as they pleased—called these actions undemocratic and un-American.

The Lacey Act of 1900 made it illegal to transport live or dead wild animals, or their parts, across state borders without a federal permit. It also made it illegal to import foreign wildlife without a government permit. Although this federal law reduced commercial hunting, it did not end the excessive slaughter of wildlife.

More effective protection of forests and wildlife didn't occur until Theodore Roosevelt, an ardent conservationist, became president. The period of his presidency, from 1901 to 1909, is regarded by many as the country's golden age of conservation.

Roosevelt's first step was to persuade Congress to grant him executive powers to establish federal wildlife refuges. In 1903, he established the first federal refuge, at Pelican Island off the east coast of Florida, for preservation of the endangered brown pelican (Figure 2-7). Roosevelt also tripled the size of the forest reserves and transferred administration of them from the Department of the Interior, which had a reputation for lax enforcement, to the Department of Agriculture.

In 1905, Congress created the U.S. Forest Service to manage and protect the forest reserves. Roosevelt appointed Gifford Pinchot as its first chief. Pinchot pioneered efforts to manage potentially renewable forest resources scientifically, using the principles of sustainable yield and multiple use (see Spotlight on p. 14).

In 1907, Congress, upset over Roosevelt's addition of vast tracts to the forest reserves, amended the Forest Reserve Act of 1891 to ban further withdrawals of public forests by the president. This amendment also changed the name of the reserves to national forests, implying that these lands should not be preserved from all types of development. On the day before the amendment became law, Roosevelt defiantly reserved another 6.5 million hectares (16 million acres) of national forests.

Early in this century, conservationists disagreed over how the beautiful Hetch Hetchy Valley in what is now Yosemite National Park was to be used. This controversy split the American conservation movement into two schools of thought (see Spotlight on p. 42). One group, called *preservationists*, believed that wilderness areas should be left untouched. The other group, made up of *utilitarian resource managers*, believed that wilderness and other public lands should be managed wisely to provide resources for the people.

Figure 2-7 The first national wildlife refuge was set up off the coast of Florida in 1903 to protect the brown pelican from extinction. In the 1960s, this species was threatened with extinction when exposure to DDT and other persistent pesticides in the fish it eats caused reproductive losses. Now it is making a comeback.

E. R. Degginger

CASE STUDY The Near Extinction of the American Bison Through Overhunting

When European explorers discovered North America in the late 1400s, various tribes of Native Americans depended heavily on bison for survival. The meat was their staple diet. The skin was used for tepees, moccasins, and clothes. The gut made their bowstrings, and the horns their spoons. Even the dried feces, called buffalo chips by English-speaking settlers, were used for fuel.

In 1500, before European settlers came to North America, between 60 million and 125 million grass-eating American bison roamed the plains, prairies, and woodlands over most of the continent (Figure 2-8). Single herds covered thousands of square kilometers of land. Their numbers were so large they were thought to be inexhaustible. By 1906, however, the once-extensive range of the American bison was reduced to a tiny area, and the species was nearly driven to extinction, mostly because of overhunting and loss of habitat.

As settlers moved west after the Civil War, the sustainable balance between Native Americans and bison was upset. Native Americans of the plains traded bison skins to settlers for steel knives and firearms, and began killing bison in larger numbers.

Much greater depletion of this potentially renewable resource was caused by other factors. First, as railroads spread westward in the late 1860s, railroad companies hired professional bison hunters to supply construction crews with meat. The well-known bison hunter "Buffalo Bill" Cody killed an estimated 4,280 bison in only 18 months—surely a world record. Passengers also gunned down bison from train windows, purely for the "joy" of killing, leaving the carcasses to rot.

As farmers settled the plains, they shot bison because the animals destroyed crops. Ranchers killed them because they competed with cattle and sheep for grass and knocked over fences, telegraph poles, and sod houses.

An army of commercial hunters shot millions of bison for their hides and for their tongues, which were considered a delicacy. Instead of being eaten, however, most of the meat was left to rot. "Bone pickers" then collected the bleached bones that whitened the prairies, and shipped them east for use as fertilizer.

Finally, after the Civil War, the U.S. Army began to subdue plains tribes of Native Americans and take over their lands by killing off their primary source of food. At least 2.5 million bison were slaughtered each year between 1870 and 1875 in this form of biological warfare.

By 1890, only one herd of about 1 million bison was left. Commercial hunters and skinners descended on this herd, and by 1892, only 85 bison were left. They were given refuge in Yellowstone National Park and were protected by an 1893 law against the killing of wild animals in national parks.

In 1905, sixteen people formed the American Bison Society to protect and rebuild the captive population of the animal. In the early 1900s, the federal government established the National Bison Range near Missoula, Montana. Since then, captive herds on this federal land and other herds mostly on privately owned land scattered throughout the West have been protected by law.

Today, there are about 100,000 bison in the United States—one-fifth of them on the National Bison Range. Some captive bison are crossbred with cattle to produce hybrids, called beefalo. Their meat is tasty, and they grow faster and are easier to raise than cattle, with no need for expensive grain feed.

In 1912, Congress created the U.S. National Park System, and in 1916, it passed the National Park System Organic Act. This law declared that national parks are to be set aside to conserve and preserve scenery, wildlife, and natural and historic objects for the use, observation, health, and pleasure of people. The parks are to be maintained in a manner that leaves them unimpaired for future generations.

The law also established the National Park Service within the Department of the Interior to manage the system. The Park Service's first director, Stephen Mather, recruited a corps of professional park rangers to manage the parks.

During the Republican administrations of 1921–33, the government increased emphasis on using public resources to favor big business and promote economic growth. Indeed, while Herbert Hoover was president, between 1929 and 1933, he proposed that the federal government return all remaining federal lands to the states or sell them to private interests so they could make money out of them. The economic depression of the 1930s, however, made the financial burden of owning such lands unattractive to state governments and private interests.

EXPANDING FEDERAL ROLE IN WILDLIFE AND PUBLIC LAND MANAGEMENT (1933–60) The *second wave of national resource conservation* began in the early 1930s, as President Franklin D. Roosevelt attempted to get the country out of the Great Depression (1929–41). Conservation of resources benefited because

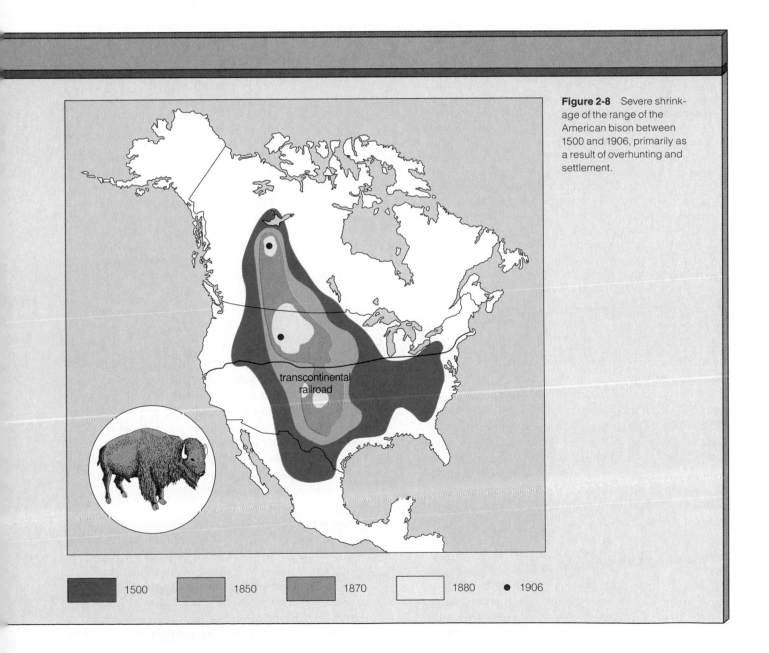

Figure 2-8 Severe shrinkage of the range of the American bison between 1500 and 1906, primarily as a result of overhunting and settlement.

transcontinental railroad

| 1500 | 1850 | 1870 | 1880 | • 1906 |

In 1901, resource managers, led by Gifford Pinchot and San Francisco mayor James D. Phelan, proposed to build a dam and flood the Hetch Hetchy Valley to create a reservoir to supply drinking water for San Francisco. Preservationists, led by naturalist John Muir, wanted to keep this beautiful spot from being flooded.

After a highly publicized, 12-year battle, the dam was built and the valley was flooded. The controversy between these two schools of thought continues today, with preservationists pressing to have the dam removed.

Past and present preservationists emphasize protecting large areas of untouched public lands from mining, timbering, and other forms of resource extraction so they can be enjoyed by present generations and passed on unspoiled to future generations. After Muir's death in 1914, preservationists were led by forester Aldo Leopold. According to Leopold, the role of the human species should be that of a member and protector of nature — not that of a conqueror of nature.

Another effective supporter of wilderness preservation was Robert Marshall, an officer in the U.S. Forest Service. In 1935, he and Leopold founded the Wilderness Society. Others who have led preservationist efforts in recent years include David Brower (former head of the Sierra Club and founder of Friends of the Earth and Earth Island Institute), Ernest Swift, and Stewart L. Udall.

In contrast, utilitarian resource managers see wilderness and other public lands as resources to be managed wisely to enhance economic growth and national strength and to provide the greatest benefit to the greatest number of people. To them, the government's role should be to protect these lands from degradation by managing them efficiently and scientifically for sustainable yield and multiple use. Early resource managers were led by Theodore Roosevelt, Gifford Pinchot, John Wesley Powell, Charles Van Hise, and others.

According to Roosevelt and Pinchot, conservation experts would form an elite corps of resource managers in the federal bureaucracy. They would be protected from excessive political pressure and could design and implement management strategies based on scientific criteria. Pinchot angered Muir and other preservationists, who had been active allies in Roosevelt's conservation efforts, when he stated his principle of the wise use of resources:

The first great fact about conservation is that it stands for development. There has been a fundamental misconception that conservation means nothing but the husbanding of resources for future generations. There could be no more serious mistake. . . . The first principle of conservation is the use of the natural resources now existing on this continent for the benefit of the people who live here now.

Although they differed on how resources should be used, both schools were against letting these public resources fall into the hands of a few for private profit. This goal of equity has not been achieved. Since 1910, the rights to much of the forest and mineral resources on public lands and the water resources, supplied by federally financed dam and irrigation projects in the West, have gone to large, privately owned farms, ranching operations, mining companies, and timber companies. Often the resource rights on public lands have been sold to these influential private interests at below normal market prices.

financially strapped landowners were eager to sell vast tracts of land at low prices to the government.

To provide jobs for 2 million unemployed young men, Roosevelt established the Civilian Conservation Corps (CCC). The CCC planted trees, developed parks and recreation areas, restored silted waterways, provided flood control, controlled soil erosion, protected wildlife, and carried out other conservation projects.

During the Depression, the federal government built and operated many large dams in the arid western states, such as Hoover Dam on the Colorado River. These projects stimulated the economy by providing jobs, cheap irrigation water, flood control, and cheap electricity.

In 1933, the Soil Erosion Service under the Department of Agriculture was created. Its mission was to correct some of the enormous erosion problems that had ruined many of the farms of the Great Plains states.

This erosion, brought about by prolonged drought and lack of soil conservation, contributed to the Great Depression. It forced large numbers of bankrupt farmers in the Midwest to migrate to eastern and western cities in search of nonexistent jobs, as described in John Steinbeck's novel *The Grapes of Wrath*. In 1935, the Soil Erosion Service was renamed the Soil Conservation Service, and Hugh H. Bennett became its first director.

The Migratory Bird Hunting Stamp Act, enacted in 1934, requires waterfowl hunters to buy a federal duck stamp, which they have to attach to their state hunting licenses. Since 1934, the sale of these permits has brought in over $300 million for use in waterfowl research and the purchase of waterfowl refuge lands.

The passage of the Taylor Grazing Act in 1934 marked the beginning of the regulation of grazing of domesticated livestock on public lands, especially in the West, which for many decades had been overgrazed by ranchers. This law required permits and fees for the use of federal grazing lands and placed limits on the number of animals that could be grazed.

From the start, ranchers resented government interference with their long-established, unregulated use of public land. Since 1934, they have led repeated efforts, called *sagebrush rebellions*, to have these lands removed from government ownership and turned over to private ranching, mining, timber, and development interests.

In 1935, Paul B. Sears wrote *Deserts on the March*. In this book, he warned that continuing abuse of western rangeland could convert much of it to desert, as earlier civilizations had learned the hard way. This warning was largely ignored.

Until passage of the Federal Land Policy and Management Act in 1976, western congressional delegations kept the Grazing Service (which in 1946 became the Bureau of Land Management, or BLM) poorly funded, understaffed, and without enforcement authority. This allowed many ranchers and mining and timber companies to continue abusing western public lands.

In 1937, the Federal Aid in Wildlife Restoration Act (also known as the Pittman-Robertson Act) levied a federal tax on all sales of guns and ammunition. This tax and matching state funds have provided more than $2.1 billion for states to buy land for wildlife conservation (mostly for game species), to support wildlife research, and to reintroduce wildlife in depleted areas. A similar law, the Federal Aid in Fish Restoration Act, was enacted in 1950 to help state fisheries supply and conserve game fish by providing federal funds raised from a tax on fishing equipment.

In 1940, the Bureau of Sport Fisheries in the Department of Commerce and the Bureau of Biological Survey in the Department of Agriculture were merged to form what is now called the U.S. Fish and Wildlife Service. This new agency was placed in the Department of the Interior and given the roles of managing the National Wildlife Refuge System and protecting wild species in danger of becoming extinct.

Between 1940 and 1960, there were few new developments in federal resource conservation policy because of preoccupation with World War II (1941–45) and economic recovery after the war. In 1948, the United States had its first major air pollution disaster, when pollutants from a steel mill, a zinc smelter, and a sulfuric acid plant stagnated over the town of Donora, Pennsylvania. About 6,000 of the town's 14,000 inhabitants fell ill, and 20 died from breathing the polluted air. The incident caused some people to question the sight of belching smokestacks as an acceptable nuisance and a sign of economic progress.

In 1948, William Voight warned about the dangers of rapid population growth and overpopulation in his book *The Road to Survival*. The same year, Fairfield Osborn wrote about the need to increase efforts to protect and conserve the country's natural resources during the period of rapid economic growth after World War II. Few people took either of these warnings seriously until the 1960s.

RISE OF THE ENVIRONMENTAL MOVEMENT

(1960–80) The *third wave of national resource conservation* began during the short administration of John F. Kennedy (1961–63). These efforts were expanded under the administration of Lyndon B. Johnson (1963–68).

In 1962, biologist Rachel Carson published *Silent Spring* (see Further Readings). This book described the pollution of air, water, and wildlife from the widespread use of slowly degradable pesticides such as DDT. It helped broaden the concept of resource conservation to include the preservation of the *quality* of the air, water, and soil, which were under assault by a country experiencing rapid economic growth. She pointed out that "For the first time in the history of the world, every human being is now subjected to dangerous chemicals, from the moment of conception until death." The public's unprecedented response to Carson's book was the beginning of what is now known as the environmental movement in the United States. She died in 1964 without knowing that her efforts were a key in starting today's environmental movement.

In 1964, Congress passed the Wilderness Act. It authorized the government to protect undeveloped tracts of public land as part of the National Wilderness System unless Congress later decides they are needed for the national good. Land in this system is to be protected from development and used only for nondestructive forms of recreation, such as hiking and camping.

Between 1965 and 1970, the emerging science of ecology received widespread media coverage. At the same time, the popular writings of biologists such as Paul Ehrlich, Barry Commoner, and Garrett Hardin helped the public become aware of the interlocking relationships between population growth, resource use, and pollution (Figure 1-16).

During that period, a number of events covered by the media increased public awareness of pollution:

- In 1963, high concentrations of pollutants accumulated in the air above New York City, killing about 300 people and injuring thousands.

- In the mid-1960s, foam caused by widespread use of nonbiodegradable substances in synthetic laundry and cleaning detergents began appearing on creeks and rivers (Figure 2-9).

- In 1969, the oil-polluted Cuyahoga River, running through Cleveland, Ohio, caught fire and burned for eight days. Two bridges were burned by the five-story-high flames.

- In 1969, oil leaking from an offshore well near Santa Barbara, California, coated beaches and wildlife.

Figure 2-9 Foam on a creek caused by nondegradable components in synthetic laundry detergents in 1966.

Soil Conservation Service

■ By the late 1960s, Lake Erie had become severely polluted. Large numbers of fish died, numbers of desirable species of commercial and game fish dropped sharply, and many bathing beaches had to be closed.

■ During the late 1960s and early 1970s, several well-known species of wildlife, including the American bald eagle (Figure 2-10), the grizzly bear, the whooping crane, and the peregrine falcon were threatened with extinction from pollution and loss of habitat.

On April 22, 1970, the first annual Earth Day took place in the United States. About 20 million people in more than 2,000 communities took to the streets to demand better environmental quality. Elected officials got the message. Between 1969 and 1980, Congress passed more than 24 pieces of legislation to help protect the air, water, land, and wildlife (see page before the inside back cover). The accomplishments during this period by government and by citizen-supported, private environmental and conservation groups were the *fourth wave of national resource conservation*.

The 1973 OPEC oil embargo and the shutdown of oil production in Iran in 1979 led to oil shortages and sharp rises in the price of oil between 1973 and 1981 (see Case Study on p. 15). This period of relative oil scarcity showed the need for not wasting energy resources, especially oil.

In 1977, President Jimmy Carter created the Department of Energy to help the country deal with short-ages of oil. He, along with most conservationists, realized that the United States and other industrialized countries must develop a long-range energy strategy.

Most efforts to make the United States face up to the end of the cheap oil era were undermined by Carter's political defeat and the temporary oil glut of the 1980s. These events sent a false message to many consumers and elected officials that energy conservation and a search for oil substitutes were no longer high priorities.

During his term, Carter appointed a number of competent and experienced administrators to key posts in the Environmental Protection Agency, the Department of the Interior, and the Department of Energy. He drew heavily on established environmental and conservation organizations for such appointees and for advice on environmental and resource policy. He also created the Superfund to clean up abandoned hazardous waste sites, such as the Love Canal suburb in Niagara Falls, New York.

Just before leaving office, Carter used the Antiquities Act of 1906 to increase the amount of public land protected from development. He tripled the amount of land in the National Wilderness System, primarily by adding vast tracts of public land in Alaska. This also doubled the area administered by the National Park Service.

CONTINUING CONTROVERSY AND SOME RETRENCHMENT (THE 1980s) The Federal Land Policy and Management Act of 1976 gave the Bureau of Land

Figure 2-10 An estimated 250,000 American bald eagles were found in the United States when this bird became the national symbol in 1782. During the late 1960s and early 1970s, the number of American bald eagles in the lower 48 states declined because of loss of habitat, illegal hunting, and reproductive failure caused by pesticides in fish, their primary diet. Federal protection has led to recovery in many areas. In 1989, there were about 35,300 bald eagles in the wild, with 5,300 in the lower 48 states and about 30,000 in Alaska. In 1989, the U.S. Fish and Wildlife Service spent $3.9 million on this recovery program.

Management its first real authority to manage the public lands, mostly in the West, under its control. This angered ranchers, farmers, miners, users of off-road motorized vehicles, and others, who had been doing pretty much as they pleased on these public lands.

In the late 1970s, western ranchers, who had been paying low fees for grazing rights that encouraged overgrazing, launched a political campaign known as the *sagebrush rebellion*. Its primary goal, like that of earlier efforts, was to remove most western public lands from public ownership and turn them over to the states. Then these campaigners planned to persuade state legislatures to sell or lease the resource-rich lands at low prices to ranching, mining, timber, land development, and other private interests.

In 1981, Ronald Reagan, a self-declared sagebrush rebel, became president, having won the election by a large margin. He had campaigned as a champion of strong national defense, less federal government control, and reduced government spending to lower the national debt and combat the economic recession that had followed the sharp rises in oil prices during the 1970s.

During his eight years in office, Reagan mounted an attack on the country's major conservation and environmental laws. He

- Appointed people who came from industries or legal firms that opposed existing federal environmental, resource conservation, and land use legislation and policies to key positions in the Interior Department, BLM, and EPA.

- Barred established environmental and conservation organizations and leaders from giving advice on such appointments and on the administration's environmental and resource policies.

- Made the enforcement of existing environmental and resource conservation laws difficult by encouraging drastic budget and staff cuts in enforcement agencies.

- Greatly increased energy and mineral development and timber cutting by private enterprise on public lands. Often the government sold these resources at giveaway prices to private corporations, shortchanging the citizens, who jointly own the resources.

- Increased the federal budget for nuclear power. This way of producing electricity is still not economically competitive with most other energy alternatives, even though U.S. taxpayers have given the nuclear industry over $40 billion in subsidies.

- Cut federal funding for energy conservation by 70%, lowered automobile gas mileage standards, and relaxed air- and water-quality standards.

- Eliminated tax incentives for encouraging residential solar energy and energy conservation.

- Drastically cut federal funding for energy conservation.

- Reduced funding for research and development on perpetual and renewable energy resources by 85%.

Although Reagan was an immensely popular president, many people strongly opposed his environmental and resource policies. These policies were blunted by strong opposition in Congress, public outrage, and legal challenges by environmental and conservation organizations, whose memberships soared in this period.

The net effect of the Reagan years was to slow down the momentum of environmental protection and resource conservation built up in the 1970s. Instead of moving forward, environmental and conservation organizations spent much of their time and money fighting off a vigorous attempt to move backward.

THE 1990s: MORE FOOT-DRAGGING OR A NEW ENVIRONMENTAL AWAKENING? Environmentalists warn that we must make the 1990s a new decade of the environment — a green decade — that will go further than the 1970s and make up for lost momentum in the 1980s. Such an environmental awakening will require strong national and global leadership by the United States, the world's richest country and largest polluter and user and waster of resources.

In 1989, George Bush became president, promising to be an environmental president. By 1992, Bush's environmental record was mixed, often lacking the much-needed strong action and national and global leadership he had promised. In March 1990, *U.S. News and*

World Report asked leaders of 10 conservation groups and 10 business and trade groups to grade the Bush administration's environmental efforts. The conservation leaders gave him a grade of D; the business leaders gave him a C+.

Environmentalists have been especially disappointed by his failure to provide leadership in reducing energy waste and to phase in solar and other perpetual and renewable forms of energy as a way to withdraw from our wasteful addiction to oil and other fossil fuels and to reduce our emissions of greenhouse gases. Instead of leading the global effort to deal with projected global warming, he has undermined international efforts and willingness to begin dealing with this urgent problem by calling for more research instead of action. He has also not taken the lead in halting tropical deforestation or the clear-cutting of ancient forests in the national forests of the Pacific Northwest, both of which are major causes of the rapid loss of Earth's precious biodiversity.

On April 22, 1990, the twentieth Earth Day took place. An estimated 200 million people in 141 nations on all 7 continents participated—the largest global

Guest Essay A New Environmentalism for the 1990s and Beyond

Peter Montague

Peter Montague is senior research analyst for Greenpeace and director of the Environmental Research Foundation in Washington, D.C. The Foundation conducts studies of environmental problems and provides the general public with information about environmental problems and the technologies and policies that might contribute to their solution. Montague has served as manager of a technology computer information center and project administrator of a hazardous waste research program at Princeton University. Prior to that he taught undergraduate and graduate courses in environmental impact analysis at the School of Architecture and Planning at the University of New Mexico. He has coauthored two books on toxic heavy metals in the natural environment and is editor of Rachel, *a highly informative and readable newsletter on environmental problems, with an emphasis on hazardous waste.*

Environmentalism as we have known it for the past 20 years is dead. The environmentalism of the 1970s advocated strict numerical controls on releases of *dangerous wastes* (any unwanted or uncontrolled materials that can harm living things or disrupt ecosystems) into the environment. Industry's ability to create new hazards, however, quickly outstripped government's ability to establish adequate controls and enforcement programs.

After 20 years of effort by government and by concerned citizens (the environmental movement), the overwhelming majority of dangerous chemicals are still not regulated in any way. Even those few that *are* covered by regulations have not been adequately controlled.

In sum, the *pollution management* approach to environmental protection has failed and stands discredited; *pollution prevention* is the way of the future and is our only hope. An ounce of prevention really *is* worth a pound of cure.

Here, in outline form, is the new environmentalism that is emerging:

1. All waste disposal—landfilling, incineration, deep well injection—is intrinsically polluting because disposal means dispersal into the environment. Once wastes are created they cannot be contained or controlled because of the scientific laws of matter and energy [Chapter 3]. The old environmentalism failed to recognize this important truth, and thus squandered enormous resources trying to achieve the impossible. We in the United States presently spend about $90 billion per year on pollution control. Yet, the global environment is increasingly threatened by a buildup of heat because of heat-trapping gases we emit into the atmosphere. At least half the surface of the planet is being subjected to an influx of damaging ultraviolet radiation from the sun as a result of ozone depleting chemicals we have discharged into the atmosphere, and vast regions of the United States, Canada, and Europe are suffering from loss of forests, crop productivity, and fish as a result of acid rain (caused by releases of sulfur and nitrogen compounds, chiefly by power plants and automobiles) and other air pollutants. Soil and water are dangerously polluted at thousands of locales where municipal garbage and industrial wastes have been (and continue to be) dumped or incinerated; thousands of such sites remain to be discovered, according to U.S. government estimates.

2. The inevitable result of our reliance on waste treatment and disposal systems has been an unrelenting buildup of exotic synthetic toxic materials in humans and in other forms of life worldwide. For example, breast milk of women in industrialized countries like the United

demonstration in history. Its main goals were to reach out to minorities and the poor struggling daily for survival throughout the world; make people everywhere aware of the difference their actions could make in sustaining the earth by acting locally and thinking globally (summarized in its slogan: Who Says You Can't Change the World?); and get people involved in making every day Earth Day. If only 5% of the people who took part in Earth Day 1990 stay actively involved in the race to sustain the earth, that would be 10 million people—an enormous force for change.

AN EARTH-SUSTAINING AGENDA FOR THE 1990s AND BEYOND Dealing with the environmental and resource problems we face will not be easy or cheap. It will involve much controversy and require us to make some trade-offs and significant changes in our worldview, economic and political systems, and lifestyles.

Specific actions environmentalists believe are needed to help sustain the earth are presented throughout this book.

Emphasis will have to shift from pollution cleanup to pollution prevention (see Guest Essay on p. 46), from

States is so contaminated with pesticides and industrial hydrocarbons that if human milk were bottled and sold commercially, it would be subject to ban by the Food and Drug Administration (FDA) as unsafe for human consumption. Another illustrative example: If a whale today beaches itself on the shores of the United States and dies, legally, its body must be treated as a "hazardous waste" because whales contain PCBs (polychlorinated biphenyls—a class of industrial toxins) at levels that exceed threshold concentrations for classifying a waste as legally "hazardous." Soon polar bears in their natural habitat are likely to join whales in the "hazardous waste" category because their PCB levels are steadily rising.

3. The ability of humans and other forms of life to adapt to changes in their chemical environment is strictly limited by the genetic code each form of life inherits. Continued contamination occurring hundreds of times faster than we can adapt will drive humans to increasingly widespread sickness, to degradation of the species, and ultimately to extinction.

4. Damage to humans (and to other forms of life) is abundantly documented. Birds, fish, and humans in industrialized countries like the United States are enduring steadily rising levels of cancer and other serious disorders attributable to pollution. An astonishing 88% of children under six years old in the United States have sufficient toxic lead in their blood to cause them to perform below par on standardized tests of physical, mental, and emotional development. If we will but look, the handwriting is on the wall everywhere.

To deal with these problems, industrial societies must abandon their reliance on waste treatment and disposal and on the regulatory system of numerical standards created by government to manage the damage that results from relying on waste disposal instead of waste prevention. We must quickly move the industrialized and industrializing countries to new technical approaches

accompanied by new industrial goals—namely clean production or zero discharge systems.

"Clean production" involves industrial systems that avoid or eliminate dangerous wastes and dangerous products and minimize the use of raw materials, water, and energy. Goods manufactured in a clean production process must not damage natural ecosystems throughout their entire life cycle, including (a) raw materials selection, extraction, and processing; (b) product conceptualization, design, manufacture, and assemblage; (c) materials transport during all phases; (d) industrial and household usage; and (e) reintroduction of the product into industrial systems or into the environment when it no longer serves a useful function.

Clean production does not include "end-of-pipe" pollution controls such as filters or scrubbers or chemical, physical, or biological treatment. Measures that pretend to reduce the volume of waste by incineration or concentration, mask the hazard by dilution, or transfer pollutants from one environmental medium to another are also excluded from the concept of "clean production."

A new industrial pattern, and a new environmentalism, is thus emerging. It insists that the long-term well-being of humans and other species must be factored into our production and consumption plans. These new requirements are not optional; human survival depends on our willingness to make, and pay for, the necessary changes.

Guest Essay Discussion

1. Do you agree with the author that the *pollution management* approach to environmental protection practiced during the past 20 years has failed and must be replaced with a *pollution prevention* approach? Explain.

2. List key economic, health, consumption, and lifestyle changes you might experience as a consequence of switching from pollution management to pollution prevention. What changes might the next generation experience?

Jessica Tuchman Mathews

Jessica Tuchman Mathews is currently vice president of the World Resources Institute, a highly respected center for policy research on global resource and environmental issues. Dr. Mathews has served as director of the Office of Global Issues on the president's National Security Council and on the editorial board of The Washington Post. *In 1989, she published an influential article in* Foreign Affairs *calling for nations to redefine national security in terms of national and global environmental security.*

National security and *national sovereignty* must be redefined during the 1990s to accommodate new global environmental realities, just as they were during the 1970s to accommodate global economic realities.

Intricately interconnected effects of the way we live—the buildup of greenhouse gases, the depletion of the ozone layer, and the loss of tropical forests and species—are shifting the center of gravity in international relations. These phenomena threaten national securities, defy solution by one or a few countries, and render national borders irrelevant. By definition, then, they pose a major challenge to national sovereignty.

They also compound the difficulty of ensuring security in an international order already in flux as the bipolar order that emerged from World War II gives way to multipolarity. One of the few things that is clear about the post–cold war era we're entering is that national security will increasingly depend on how resource, environmental, and demographic issues are resolved. It is no coincidence that control of Persian Gulf oil was central to this era's first international crisis.

Regional environmental decline is already threatening well-being and thereby political stability in many parts of the world. Eastern Europe's horrendous environmental degradation is undercutting attempts to rebuild shattered economies: for instance, 95% of the water in Poland's rivers is unfit for human consumption, land is being withdrawn from cultivation because of contamination with toxic heavy metals, and air pollution causes heavy economic losses due to health costs and lost productivity. In the developing world, natural resources such as farmland, forests, and fisheries are being laid waste while the number of people these resources must sustain is expected to grow by nearly 1 billion during the 1990s.

The fallout from global environmental trends goes far beyond economic and political arrangements. Unless the community of nations finds ways to reverse these trends, they will eventually shake not just the security of states, but the foundations of life.

Ozone Depletion

People living in South America and Australia are already exposed to dangerous levels of ultraviolet radiation as the Antarctic ozone hole breaks up each spring. The U.S. Environmental Protection Agency announced in 1991 that the ozone layer is thinning much faster than expected, by as much as 5% since 1978 over the northern hemisphere's middle latitudes, where most of the industrial world's population lives. Increased exposure to ultraviolet radiation from ozone depletion in the upper atmosphere is expected to increase skin cancer, cataracts, and immune system damage, and to damage terrestrial and marine

waste disposal to waste prevention and reduction, from species protection to habitat protection, and from increased resource use to increased resource conservation.

Existing economic and political systems will need to be used to reward Earth-sustaining economic activities and discourage those that harm the earth. We must recognize that short-term economic greed eventually leads to long-term economic and environmental grief.

We will have to allow parts of the world we have damaged to heal, help restore severely damaged areas, and protect remaining wild areas from any form of destructive development. Governments will have to cooperate to deal with a host of global and regional environmental and resource problems (see Guest Essay above).

We found our house—the planet—with drinkable, potable water, with good soil to grow food, with clean air to breathe. We at least must leave it in as good a shape as we found it, if not better.

REV. JESSE JACKSON

DISCUSSION TOPICS

1. Explain how in one sense the roots of our present environmental and resource problems, and our escalating war against the rest of nature, began with the invention of agriculture 10,000 to 12,000 years ago.

2. Do you think we would be better off if agriculture had never been discovered and we were still hunters and gatherers today? Explain.

ecosystems, thereby threatening the world's food supplies.

Climate Change

Despite remaining uncertainties about the extent and timing of enhanced greenhouse warming, most scientists agree that it will usher in adverse changes the world over in the next century. The rate of change is critical, and unless nations can substantially slow the present rate of greenhouse gas emissions, change could be catastrophic for some. If climate models are correct, nations will have to adapt to rising sea levels, changing rainfall patterns, and temperatures higher than the world has seen for 2 million years. Adaptive mechanisms will be costly, and the gap between rich and poor countries will almost certainly widen. Sea-level rise calls into question some nations' very existence. Most wildlife and their habitats will adapt or perish on their own, beyond the reach of human intervention.

Tropical Forest and Species Loss

Tropical forests are being cleared at the rate of about 17 million hectares (42 million acres) a year, or 50% faster than only a decade ago. Since these forests are home for more than half of Earth's species, tropical deforestation is the main force behind a species extinction rate that is unmatched in 65 million years. These interlocking losses are eroding tropical countries' economic prospects and shredding the planet's biological heritage. Deforestation in the tropics, and elsewhere, also contributes to an enhanced greenhouse effect, though far less than fossil-fuel use. In turn, greenhouse warming is expected to amplify species loss over the coming decades.

Dealing with these global environmental problems will require a higher and higher level of collective international cooperation and management. Fortunately, nations are beginning to act as though they understand their mutual interest in cooperation, as demonstrated most spectacularly by the agreement to phase out emissions of ozone-destroying chemicals that was reached by 93 nations meeting in London in June 1990 to update the Montreal treaty developed in 1987.

Turning this mutual interest into effective international management remains an elusive goal. Progress does not lie in a vain attempt to apply uniform environmental standards to nations whose members differ by 100-fold in per capita income and have vastly different cultures, climates, religions, resources, and attitudes toward nature. Instead, it lies in institutional innovations as sweeping as those that inaugurated the post–World War II period we're now emerging from.

The new international system must be designed to catalyze cooperation. Instead of the glacial pace required to negotiate treaties that set particular performance standards, we need fluid international processes that respond quickly to changes in scientific understanding and that set all nations moving in the same direction at whatever pace is realistic for each nation's circumstances.

Scientific theory and economic, political, and environmental concerns are all in a constant state of flux. Only a new institutional agility can keep international environmental governance closely attuned to these changing realities and ensure the best possible outcome.

Guest Essay Discussion

1. Do you agree that national security and national sovereignty must be redefined to include national and global environmental security? Explain.

2. What changes in the current international interactions between nations do you believe must be made to catalyze cooperation between nations on global environmental problems? How would you bring about these changes?

3. Make a list of the most important benefits and drawbacks of an advanced industrial society such as the United States. Do you feel that the benefits outweigh the drawbacks? Explain. What are the alternatives?

4. Public forests, grasslands, wildlife reserves, and wilderness areas are owned by all citizens and managed for them by federal and state governments. In terms of the management policies for most of these lands, would you classify yourself as a preservationist or a utilitarian resource manager? Explain.

5. Many observers argue that the world's remaining hunter-gatherer societies should be given title to the land they and their ancestors have lived on for centuries and the right to be left alone by modern civilization. We have created protected reserves for endangered wild species, so why not create reserves for these endangered human cultures? What do you think?

6. Do you believe that a cultural change to a sustainable-Earth society over the next 50 years is desirable? Explain. What beneficial and harmful effects do you believe such a change would have on your life? On any children you choose to have? On the poor in LDCs and MDCs?

7. Do you believe that a cultural change to a sustainable-Earth society is possible over the next 50 years or so? What changes, if any, have you made, and what changes do you plan to make in your lifestyle to help bring about such a change?

PART TWO

SCIENTIFIC

PRINCIPLES

AND CONCEPTS

*Animal and vegetable life is too compli-
cated a problem for human intelligence to
solve, and we can never know how wide a
circle of disturbance we produce in the
harmonies of nature when we throw
the smallest pebble into the ocean of
organic life.*

GEORGE PERKINS MARSH

Los Angeles, California, and other cities
survive by using resources from around
the world and by producing enormous
amounts of wastes.

CHAPTER 3

MATTER AND ENERGY RESOURCES: TYPES AND CONCEPTS

General Questions and Issues

1. What is science and how does it differ from technology?

2. What are the principal forms of matter? What is matter made of? What makes matter useful to us as a resource?

3. What are the principal forms of energy? What energy resources do we rely on? What makes energy useful to us as a resource?

4. What are physical and chemical changes? What scientific law governs changes of matter from one physical or chemical form to another?

5. What are the three principal types of nuclear changes that matter can undergo?

6. What two scientific laws govern changes of energy from one form to another?

7. How can we waste less energy? How much net useful energy is available from different energy resources?

8. How are the scientific laws governing changes of matter and energy from one form to another related to resource use and environmental disruption?

The laws of thermodynamics control the rise and fall of political systems, the freedom or bondage of nations, the movements of commerce and industry, the origins of wealth and poverty, and the general physical welfare of the human race.

FREDERICK SODDY
(NOBEL LAUREATE, CHEMISTRY)

 HAT KEEPS YOU alive and healthy? From a chemical and physical standpoint, it is a balanced flow of certain types of matter and energy resources through your body.

This chapter is a brief introduction to what is going on in the world from a physical and chemical standpoint. It describes the principal types of matter and energy and the scientific laws governing changes of matter and energy from one form to another. Chapters 4–6 are an introduction to what is going on in the world from an ecological standpoint, based on how key physical and chemical processes are integrated into the biological systems we call life.

 3-1 ### Science and Technology

WHAT IS SCIENCE? Which of the following statements are true?

- Science emphasizes facts or data.
- Science has a method — a how-to scheme — for learning about nature.
- Science establishes absolute truth or proof about nature.
- Science emphasizes the use of logic, not creativity, imagination, and intuition.

The answer is that they are all false or mostly false. Let's see why.

Science is an attempt to discover order in nature and then use that knowledge to make predictions about what will happen in nature. In this search for order, scientists try to answer two basic questions: *What happens in nature over and over with the same results? How or why do things happen this way?*

WHAT DO SCIENTISTS DO? To find out what is happening, scientists collect **scientific data**, or facts, by making observations and taking measurements. Collecting data, however, is not the main purpose of science. As the French scientist Henri Poincaré put it, "Science is built up of facts, but a collection of facts is no more science than a heap of stones is a house."

Data are the stepping stones to **scientific laws**, which summarize what happens in nature over and over in the same way. Examples are the law of conservation of matter and the two energy laws discussed in this chapter.

Once a scientific law has been formulated, scientists try to explain how or why things happen this way. They make a **scientific hypothesis**, an educated guess that attempts to explain a scientific law or certain scientific facts.

Then they test the hypothesis by making more observations and taking more measurements. If many experiments by different scientists support the hypothesis, it can become a scientific theory. In other words, a **scientific theory** is a well-tested and widely accepted scientific hypothesis. The *atomic theory*, the idea that all matter is composed of atoms, is an example.

ARE SCIENTIFIC THEORIES AND LAWS TRUE?

A favorite debating and advertising trick is to claim that something "has not been scientifically proved." But scientists don't establish absolute proof or truth.

Scientists are concerned only with how useful a theory or a law is in describing, explaining, and predicting what happens in nature. Science is the acceptance of what works and the rejection of what does not. That is why scientific theories may be modified, or even discarded, because of new data or more useful explanations of the data. It is also why advances in scientific knowledge are often based on vigorous disagreement, speculation, and controversy.

Scientific laws and theories are based on statistical probabilities, not on certainties. Scientists trying to find out how oak trees grow cannot study any more than a minute fraction of Earth's oak trees. The growth of oak trees is affected by numerous variables—factors that vary from site to site. Examples are climate, soil, genetic composition, competition from other plants, insect damage, diseases, and pollution. Scientists can study only a small number of the thousands, perhaps millions, of possible interactions of these and other variables.

SCIENTIFIC METHODS

The ways scientists gather data and formulate and test scientific laws and theories are called **scientific methods**. A scientific method is a set of questions with no particular rules for answering them. The questions a scientist attempts to answer are these:

- What question about nature should I try to answer? This is the most difficult and important question to answer. One could spend a lot of time and money trying to answer a trivial question.

- What is already known and what new data should I collect?

- How should I collect these data?

- How can I organize and analyze the data I have collected to develop a scientific law?

- How can I come up with a hypothesis to explain the data and the law and use it to predict some new facts?

- Is this the best or most useful hypothesis?

- What new experiments should I run to test the hypothesis (and modify it if necessary) so it can become a scientific theory?

Trying to answer such questions may require logical reasoning, but it also requires imagination and intuition. Albert Einstein, the famous physicist, once said, "Imagination is more important than knowledge, and there is no completely logical way to a new scientific idea."

Thus, intuition, imagination, and creativity are as important in science as in poetry, art, music, and other great adventures of the human spirit. There are only a few truly creative or great scientists, however, just as there are only a few great artists or poets. Science, at its best, is an adventure that helps awaken us to the wonder, mystery, and beauty of the universe, the earth, and life.

IS SCIENCE VALUE- AND INFLUENCE-FREE? Science is often held up as being value-free and neutral. Scientists are supposed to be coldly rational and objective and not allow their personal beliefs and biases or outside pressures to influence their work.

That is an impossible dream because scientists are ordinary human beings. They have conscious and unconscious biases, values, opinions, and financial and other needs that can influence what questions they ask of nature, how they design experiments, and how they interpret the results. Sometimes they also resist new ideas, like most people, and hold on to a pet theory longer than they should. Open publishing of results and mutual criticism among scientists help to control for biases more than in other professions, but they do not remove them. Most science today is so expensive to do that few scientists can finance their own research. That explains why 51% of the world's scientists work on military-related research and 36% work for large corporations. Much of this work is not published and thus is not open to evaluation and correction. Scientists who do not support or publicly challenge the positions of organizations they depend on for a living face unemployment or loss of research grants.

Holding up science as being value-free and neutral is dangerous. It allows scientists to avoid responsibility for choosing their line of inquiry, or for not trying to project and publish some of the environmental and social implications of the results of their research.

WHAT IS TECHNOLOGY? **Technology** is the creation of new products and processes that are supposed to improve our survival, comfort, and quality of life. In many cases, technology develops from known scientific laws and theories. Scientists invented the laser, for example, by applying knowledge about the internal structure of atoms. Applied scientific knowledge about chemistry has given us nylon, pesticides, laundry detergents, ways to control some types of pollution, and countless other products. Scientific knowledge of genetics has been used to develop new strains of crops and livestock, and genetic engineering is expected to accelerate this process.

Some technologies were developed long before anyone understood the scientific principles upon which they were based. Aspirin, originally derived from a chemical found in the bark of a tropical willow tree, relieved pain and fever long before anyone found out how it did so. Photography was invented by people who had no knowledge of its chemistry.

Science and technology differ in the way the information and ideas they produce are shared. Much of the results of scientific research are published and passed around freely so they can be evaluated, verified, and perhaps challenged. This process strengthens the validity of scientific knowledge and helps expose cheaters. In contrast, technological discoveries are often kept secret until the inventor or the company can get a patent for the new process or product.

ENVIRONMENTAL SCIENCE: A HOLISTIC SCIENCE For the past 250 years, scientists have studied nature most by examining increasingly lower levels of organization of matter (Figure 3-1). This approach is called *reductionism*. It is based on the belief that if we can understand subatomic particles, then we can go back up the ladder of organizational levels and understand atoms, then molecules, and so on to organisms, communities, ecosystems, the ecosphere, and eventually the universe.

The reductionist approach has been useful in learning much about nature, but in the last few decades, we have learned that it has a basic flaw. Each higher level of organization of matter has properties that cannot be predicted or understood merely by understanding the lower levels that make up its structure. Even if you learn all there is to know about a particular tree, you will know only a small part of how a forest works.

The science of ecology has shown the need for combining reductionism with *holism* (sometimes spelled *wholism*) — an attempt to describe all properties of a level of organization, not merely those based on the lower levels of organization that make up its underlying structure. This approach also attempts to understand and describe how the various levels of organization interact with one another and with their constantly changing environments. This challenging and incredibly difficult task requires interdisciplinary research and cooperation. Unfortunately, such research is rare, because most of the jobs and grants reward those who do specialized research.

Environmental science is a holistic science that uses and integrates knowledge from physics, chemistry, biology (especially ecology), geology, resource technology and engineering, resource conservation and management, demography (the study of population dynamics), economics, politics, and ethics.

SCIENCE, TECHNOLOGY, AND THE FUTURE Advances in science and technology have clearly improved the lives of many people. This progress, however, has also produced many unforeseen effects, such as pollution, that diminish the quality of our lives and threaten some of Earth's life-support systems.

Our challenge is to learn how to use scientific knowledge and technology to sustain the earth for humans and other species and to improve the quality of life for all people — not to plunder the planet for short-term economic gain. This means that scientists and technologists need to consider the possible short- and long-range implications of their research, air these thoughts, and engage the public and decision makers in an ongoing debate about the ends that science should serve. To help achieve this goal, the education of all scientists and engineers should include courses on holistic and integrative thinking and value analysis.

It's also important for nonscientists to have a basic knowledge of how nature works, because most decisions about how to use science and technology are made by nonscientists, usually with advice from scientists. Decision makers in business and government must have enough general knowledge of science and technology to ask tough questions of scientists and engineers, evaluate the answers, and make difficult decisions without having enough information.

3-2 Matter: Forms, Structure, and Quality

NATURE'S BUILDING BLOCKS: CHEMICAL AND PHYSICAL FORMS OF MATTER **Matter** is anything that has mass (the amount of material in an object) and takes up space. On Earth, where gravity is present, we weigh an object to determine its mass.

Matter is found in three *chemical forms:* **elements** (the distinctive building blocks of matter that make up every material substance), **compounds** (two or more elements held together in fixed proportions by attractive forces called *chemical bonds*), and **mixtures of elements and compounds**. Collectively, elements and compounds are called *chemicals*, some of them natural and some of them made by humans.

All matter is built from the 109 known chemical elements. Ninety-two of them occur naturally and the other 17 have been synthesized in laboratories. Each of these elements has a size, an internal structure, and other properties uniquely different from the others, just as each of the 26 letters in the English alphabet is different from the others. Examples of these basic building blocks of all matter include hydrogen (represented by the symbol H), carbon (C), oxygen (O), nitrogen

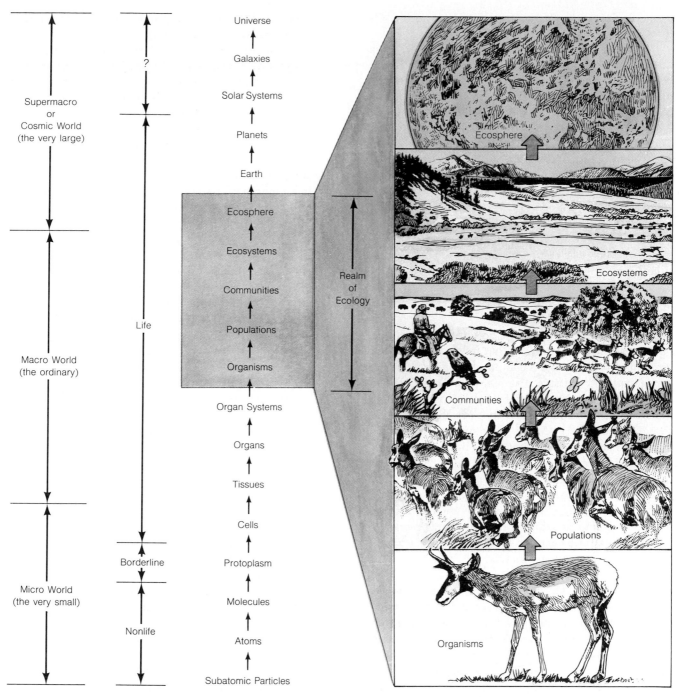

Figure 3-1 Levels of organization of matter, according to size and function. This is one way scientists classify patterns of matter found in nature. Part of this chapter is devoted to a discussion of the three lowest levels of organization of matter — subatomic particles, atoms, and molecules — which make up the basic components of all higher levels. Chapter 4 discusses the five higher levels of organization of matter — organisms, populations, communities, ecosystems, and the ecosphere — the primary concerns of ecology.

(N), phosphorus (P), sulfur (S), chlorine (Cl), fluorine (F), bromine (Br), sodium (Na), calcium (Ca), and uranium (U).

Some elements are found in nature as molecules, or combinations of their atoms. Examples are the nitrogen and oxygen gases, making up about 99% of the volume of air we breathe. Two atoms of nitrogen (N) combine to form a nitrogen gas molecule with the shorthand formula N_2 (read as "N-two"). The subscript after the symbol of the element gives the number of atoms of that element in a molecule. Similarly, most of the oxygen gas in the atmosphere exists as O_2 (read as "O-two") molecules. A small amount of oxygen, found mostly in the second layer of the atmosphere (stratosphere), exists as ozone molecules with the formula O_3 (read as "O-three").

Elements can combine to form an almost limitless number of compounds, just as the letters of our alphabet can be combined to form the almost 1 million words in the English language. So far, chemists have identified more than 10 million compounds. Chemists have made many of these compounds by putting the 109 known elements together in various combinations, but the majority of the compounds we know about occur naturally.

If you had a supermicroscope with which to look at the world's elements and compounds, you would discover that they are made up of three types of building blocks: **atoms** (the smallest unit of an element that can exist and still have the unique characteristics of that element), **ions** (electrically charged atoms), and **molecules** (combinations of atoms held together by chemical bonds). Since ions and molecules are formed from atoms, atoms are the ultimate building blocks for all matter.

If you increased the magnification of your supermicroscope, you would find that each of the world's different types of atoms is composed of a certain number of *subatomic particles*. The main building blocks of an atom are positively charged **protons** (represented by the symbol p), uncharged **neutrons** (n), and negatively charged **electrons** (e). Many other subatomic particles have been identified in recent years, but they need not concern us at this introductory level.

Matter is also found in three *physical forms:* solid, liquid, and gas. Water, for example, exists as ice, liquid water, and water vapor. The differences among the three physical states of a sample of matter are the relative degree of ordering between the atoms, ions, or molecules that make up their structure.

ATOMS AND IONS Your supermicroscope would show that each atom of an element consists of a relatively small center, or **nucleus**, containing protons and neutrons, and one or more electrons in rapid motion somewhere around the nucleus. We can describe electrons only in terms of the probability that they might be at various locations outside the nucleus.

The distinguishing feature of an atom of any given element is the number of protons in its nucleus, called its **atomic number**. The simplest element, hydrogen (H), has only 1 proton in its nucleus, and its atomic number is 1. Carbon (C), with 6 protons in its nucleus, has an atomic number of 6. Uranium (U), a much more complex atom, has 92 protons in its nucleus and an atomic number of 92 (Figure 3-2).

Atoms normally have the same number of positively charged protons and negatively charged electrons, and thus do not carry an electrical charge. For example, an uncharged atom of hydrogen has one positively charged proton in its nucleus and one negatively charged electron outside its nucleus. Similarly, each

atom of uranium has 92 protons in its nucleus and 92 electrons outside (Figure 3-2).

Protons and neutrons have essentially the same mass and are assigned a relative mass of 1. Each electron outside the nucleus is assigned a relative mass of 0 because its mass is almost negligible compared with the mass of a proton or a neutron. This means that the approximate relative mass of an atom is determined by the number of neutrons plus the number of protons in its nucleus. This number is called its **mass number**. An atom of hydrogen with 1 proton and no neutrons has a mass number of 1, and an atom of uranium with 92 protons and 143 neutrons has a mass number of 235 (Figure 3-2).

Although uncharged atoms of an element must have the same number of protons and electrons, they may have different numbers of uncharged neutrons in their nuclei, and thus different mass numbers. These different forms of an element are called **isotopes** of that element and are identified by attaching their mass numbers to the name or symbol of the element. A natural sample of an element contains a mixture of its isotopes in a fixed proportion or percent abundance by weight (Figure 3-2).

Atoms of some elements can lose or gain one or more electrons to form **ions**: atoms or groups of atoms with one or more net positive ($+$) or negative ($-$) electrical charges. Each electron lost by an atom increases its net charge by $+1$, and each electron gained by an atom increases its charge by -1. For example, an atom of sodium (Na) can lose one of its electrons and become a sodium ion with a positive charge of one (Na^+). An atom of chlorine (Cl) can gain an electron and become an ion of chlorine with a negative charge of one (Cl^-). The number of positive or negative charges on an ion is shown as a superscript after the symbol for an atom or a group of atoms. Examples of other positive ions are calcium ions (Ca^{2+}) and ammonium ions (NH_4^+). Other common negative ions are nitrate ions (NO_3^-), sulfate ions (SO_4^{2-}), and phosphate ions (PO_4^{3-}).

COMPOUNDS Most matter exists as **compounds** — combinations of atoms, or oppositely charged ions, of two or more elements held together by chemical bonds. Water, for example, is a *molecular compound* made up of H_2O (read as "H-two-O") molecules, each consisting of two hydrogen atoms chemically bonded to an oxygen atom. Sodium chloride, or table salt, is an *ionic compound*, consisting of a network of oppositely charged ions (Na^+ and Cl^-) held together by the forces of attraction that exist between opposite electric charges.

Compounds can be classified as organic or inorganic. Table sugar, vitamins, plastics, aspirin, penicillin, and many other materials important to you and your lifestyle have one thing in common. They are *organic compounds*, containing atoms of the element carbon, usually combined with each other and with atoms of

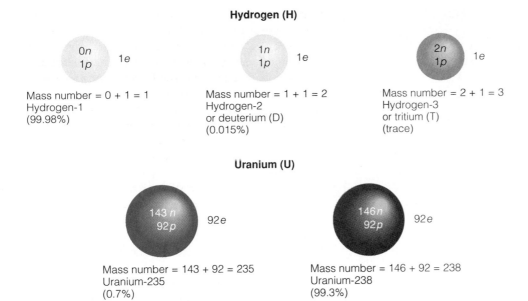

Hydrogen (H)

Mass number = 0 + 1 = 1
Hydrogen-1
(99.98%)

Mass number = 1 + 1 = 2
Hydrogen-2
or deuterium (D)
(0.015%)

Mass number = 2 + 1 = 3
Hydrogen-3
or tritium (T)
(trace)

Uranium (U)

Mass number = 143 + 92 = 235
Uranium-235
(0.7%)

Mass number = 146 + 92 = 238
Uranium-238
(99.3%)

Figure 3-2 Isotopes of hydrogen and uranium. Note that all isotopes of hydrogen have an atomic number (number of protons in their nuclei) of 1 and those of uranium an atomic number of 92. However, the isotopes of each of these elements have different mass numbers because their nuclei contain different numbers of neutrons. Figures in parentheses show the percent abundance by weight of each isotope in a natural sample of each element. A natural sample of hydrogen is a mixture of three isotopes: hydrogen-1, or H-1; hydrogen-2, or H-2 (common name, deuterium); and hydrogen-3, or H-3 (common name, tritium), with most of the sample made up of hydrogen-1. A sample of uranium consists of two isotopes: uranium-235, or U-235, and uranium-238, or U-238, with most of the sample consisting of uranium-238.

one or more other elements such as hydrogen, oxygen, nitrogen, sulfur, phosphorus, chlorine, and fluorine.

The following are examples of the more than 10 million known organic compounds:

- *Hydrocarbons* — compounds of carbon and hydrogen atoms. An example is methane (CH_4), the principal component of natural gas.

- *Chlorinated hydrocarbons* — compounds of carbon, hydrogen, and chlorine atoms. Examples are DDT ($C_{14}H_9Cl_5$), an insecticide, and toxic PCBs (such as $C_{12}H_5Cl_5$), used as insulating materials in electric transformers.

- *Chlorofluorocarbons* (CFCs) — compounds of carbon, chlorine, and fluorine atoms. An example is Freon-12 (CCl_2F_2), used as a coolant in refrigerators and air conditioners, as aerosol propellants, and as foaming agents for making some plastics.

- *Carbohydrates* (simple sugars) — certain types of compounds of carbon, hydrogen, and oxygen atoms. An example is glucose ($C_6H_{12}O_6$), which most plants and animals break down in their cells to obtain energy.

All other compounds are called *inorganic compounds*. Some of the inorganic compounds you will encounter in this book are sodium chloride (NaCl), water (H_2O), nitrous oxide (N_2O), nitric oxide (NO), carbon monoxide (CO), carbon dioxide (CO_2), nitrogen dioxide (NO_2), sulfur dioxide (SO_2), ammonia (NH_3), sulfuric acid (H_2SO_4), and nitric acid (HNO_3).

Since 1945 the production of synthetic chemicals in the United States has increased almost a million-fold. Worldwide, about 70,000 synthetic chemicals are in everyday use. About 1,000 new ones are added each year.

MATTER QUALITY **Matter quality** is a measure of how useful a matter resource is, based on its availability and concentration (Figure 3-3). **High-quality matter** is organized, concentrated, and usually found near the earth's surface. It has great potential for use as a matter resource. **Low-quality matter** is disorganized, diluted, or dispersed, and is often found deep underground or dispersed in the ocean or in the atmosphere. It usually has little potential for use as a matter resource.

An aluminum can is a more concentrated, higher quality form of aluminum than aluminum ore with the same amount of aluminum. That is why it takes less energy, water, and money to recycle an aluminum can than to get aluminum from ore and make a new can.

Scientists use the term **entropy** as a measure of disorder or randomness in a system. The greater the disorder of a sample of matter, the higher its entropy; the greater its order, the lower its entropy. Thus, an aluminum can has a lower entropy (more order) than aluminum ore with the same amount of aluminum

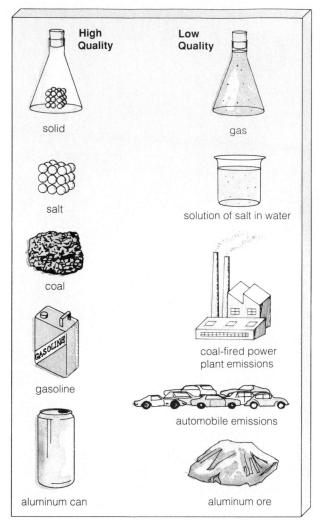

High Quality · Low Quality

solid

salt

coal

gasoline

aluminum can

gas

solution of salt in water

coal-fired power plant emissions

automobile emissions

aluminum ore

Figure 3-3 Examples of differences in matter quality. High-quality matter is fairly easy to get and is concentrated. It is ordered and thus has low entropy. Low-quality matter is hard to get and is dispersed. It is more disorganized and has a higher entropy than high-quality matter.

mixed with other materials. Similarly, a piece of ice in which the water molecules are held in an ordered solid structure has a lower entropy (more order) than the highly dispersed water molecules in water vapor.

3-3 Energy: Types, Forms, and Quality

TYPES OF ENERGY Energy, not money, is the real "currency" of the world. We depend on it to grow our food, run factories, keep us and other organisms alive, and warm and cool our bodies and the buildings where we work and live. We also use it to move people and objects from one place to another, change matter from one physical or chemical form to another, and raise the temperature of a sample of matter.

Energy is defined as the capacity to do work by performing mechanical, physical, chemical, or electrical tasks or to cause a heat transfer between two objects at different temperatures. Forms of energy include light (a form of radiant energy), heat, chemical energy stored in the chemical bonds holding elements and compounds together, moving matter, and electricity.

Scientists classify energy as either kinetic or potential. **Kinetic energy** is the energy that matter has because of its motion and mass. Examples include a moving car, a falling rock, a speeding bullet, heat, and the flow of water or charged particles (electrical energy).

Heat refers to the total kinetic energy of all the randomly moving atoms, ions, or molecules within a given substance, excluding the overall motion of the whole object. **Temperature** is a measure of the average speed of motion of the atoms, ions, or molecules in a sample of matter at a given moment. A substance can have a high heat content (much mass and many moving atoms, ions, or molecules) but a low temperature (low average molecular speed). For example, the total heat content of a lake or an ocean is enormous, but its average temperature is low. Other samples of matter can have a low heat content and a high temperature. For example, a cup of hot coffee or a burning match has a much lower heat content than an ocean or a lake, but it has a much higher temperature.

Radio waves, TV waves, microwaves, infrared radiation, visible light, ultraviolet radiation, X rays, and gamma rays are forms of kinetic energy travelling as electromagnetic waves and known as **electromagnetic radiation**. These forms of radiant energy make up a wide band or spectrum of electromagnetic waves that differ in their wavelength (distance between each peak or trough) and energy content (Figure 3-4).

Potential energy is stored energy that is potentially available for use. A rock held in your hand, a stick of dynamite, still water stored in a reservoir behind a dam, and nuclear energy stored in the nuclei of atoms all have potential energy. Other examples are the chemical energy stored in molecules of gasoline and in the carbohydrates, proteins, and fats of the food you eat.

ENERGY RESOURCES USED BY PEOPLE *The direct input of perpetual solar energy alone supplies 99% of the energy used to heat Earth and all the buildings we have constructed.* Were it not for this direct input of energy from the sun, the average temperature would be −240°C (−400°F), and life as we know it would not have arisen. This input of solar energy also helps recycle the carbon, oxygen, water, and other chemicals we and other organisms need to stay alive and healthy and to reproduce.

Broadly defined, **solar energy** includes perpetual *direct* energy from the sun and a number of *indirect*

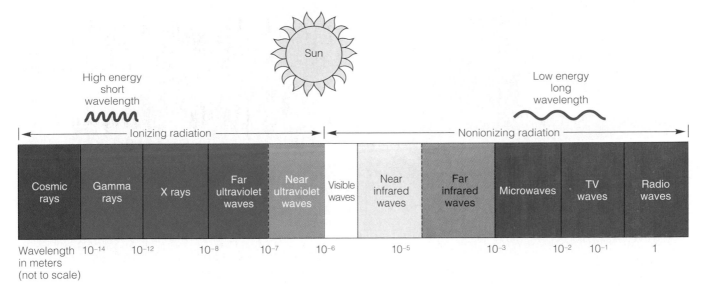

Figure 3-4 Electromagnetic spectrum of different types of kinetic energy travelling as electromagnetic waves that differ in their wavelength (distance between each peak or trough) and energy content. Cosmic rays, gamma rays, X rays, and ultraviolet radiation have a high enough energy content to knock electrons from atoms and change the atoms to positively charged ions. The resulting highly reactive electrons and ions disrupt millions of organic compounds in living cells, interfere with body processes, and cause many types of sickness, including various cancers. These potentially harmful forms of electromagnetic radiation are called **ionizing radiation**. The other forms of electromagnetic radiation do not have enough energy content to form ions and are called **nonionizing radiation**. There is now some controversial evidence that long-term exposure to nonionizing radiation emitted by radios, TV sets, the video display terminals of computers, overhead electric-power lines, electrically heated water beds, electric blankets, and other electrical devices may also damage living cells.

forms of energy produced by the direct input. Indirect forms of solar energy include wind, falling and flowing water (hydropower), and biomass (solar energy converted to chemical energy stored in the chemical bonds of organic compounds in trees and other plants).

Passive solar energy systems capture and store direct solar energy and use it to heat buildings and water without the use of mechanical devices. Examples are a well-insulated, airtight house with large insulating windows that face the sun and the use of rock, concrete, or water to store and release heat slowly.

Direct solar energy can also be captured by *active* solar energy systems. For example, specially designed roof-mounted collectors concentrate direct solar energy; pumps transfer this heat to water, to the interior of a building, or to insulated storage tanks of stone or water to store and release heat slowly. We have also learned how to make solar cells that convert solar energy directly into electricity in one simple, nonpolluting step. We also use wind turbines and hydroelectric power plants to convert indirect solar energy in the form of wind and falling or flowing water into electricity.

The sun's input of 99% of the energy used to heat the earth and make it livable is not sold in the marketplace. The remaining 1% of the energy we use on Earth to supplement solar input is *commercial energy* sold in the marketplace (Figure 3-5). Most of this commercial energy is produced by the burning of nonrenewable fossil fuels. It is also a form of indirect solar energy stored in the chemical bonds of the organic compounds of ancient dead plants and animals whose tissues have decomposed and have been buried and subjected to intense pressures and high temperatures for millions of years.

Since 1800, the annual use of commercial energy produced by fossil fuels throughout the world has been growing exponentially, with the annual rate of growth rising sharply since 1900. MDCs and LDCs differ greatly in their sources of energy (Figure 3-5), the total amount used, and the average energy used per person. The most important supplemental source of energy for LDCs is potentially renewable biomass—especially fuelwood—the main source of energy for heating and cooking for roughly half the world's population (Figure 3-5). One-fourth of the world's population in MDCs may soon face shortages of oil, but half the world's population in LDCs already face a fuelwood shortage.

The United States is the world's largest user of energy. With only 4.7% of the world's population, it uses 25% of the world's commercial energy. In contrast, India, with about 16% of the world's people, uses only about 1.5% of the world's commercial energy. In 1991, 254 million Americans used more energy for air conditioning alone than 1.1 billion Chinese used for all purposes.

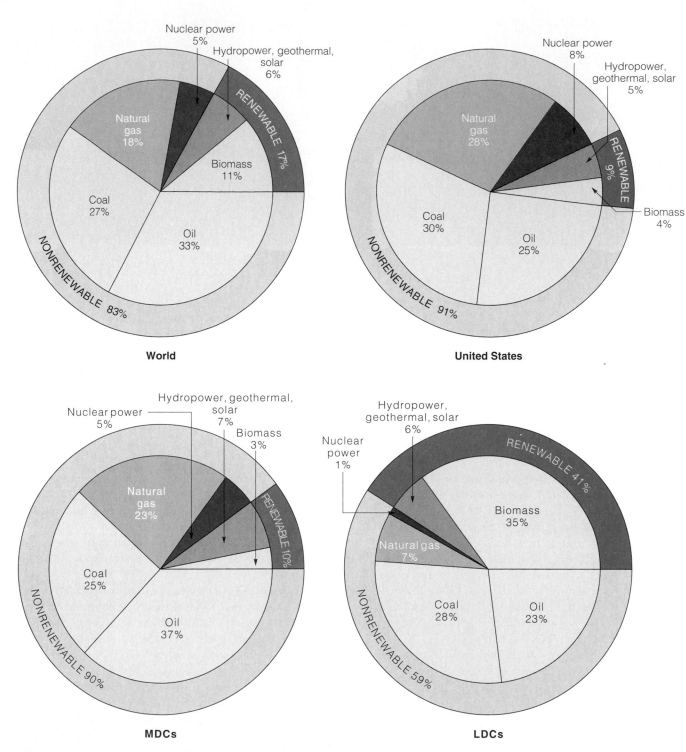

Figure 3-5 Commercial energy use by source in 1988 in the world, MDCs, LDCs, and the United States. This amounts to only 1% of the energy used in the world. The other 99% of the energy used to heat Earth comes from the sun and is not sold in the marketplace. (Data from U.S. Department of Energy, British Petroleum, and Worldwatch Institute)

The United States is also the world's largest waster of energy. Average per capita energy use in the United States is about twice that of Japan and most western European countries with average standards of living similar to those in the United States (Figure 2-1).

In 1850, the United States and most other MDCs had a decentralized energy system based on locally available renewable resources, primarily wood. Today, they have a centralized energy system based on nonrenewable fossil fuels (Figure 3-6), increasingly produced in one part of the world and transported to and used in another part. By 1988, about 83% of the commercial energy used in the United States was provided by burning oil, coal, and natural gas (Figure 3-5).

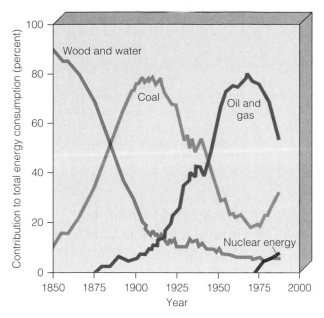

Figure 3-6 Shifts in the use of commercial energy resources in the United States since 1850. Shifts from wood to coal and then from coal to oil and natural gas have each taken about 50 years. Affordable oil is running out, and burning fossil fuels is the primary cause of air pollution and projected warming of the atmosphere, which could change climate patterns and disrupt food production. For these reasons, most analysts believe we must make a new shift in energy resources over the next 50 years. Some believe we should use more nuclear energy, convert coal to a gas for use as a fuel, and install pollution control devices to sharply reduce air pollution emissions from burning coal and other remaining fossil fuels. Others believe we should depend more on renewable energy from the sun, wind, flowing water, and plant matter (biomass), and greatly reduce our present unnecessary waste of large amounts of energy. (Data from U.S. Department of Energy)

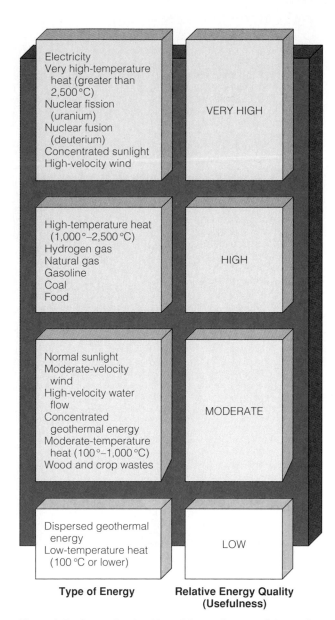

Type of Energy   **Relative Energy Quality (Usefulness)**

Figure 3-7 Generalized ranking of the quality or usefulness of different types of energy. *High-quality energy* is organized (low-entropy) or concentrated and has great ability to perform useful work. *Low-quality energy* is disorganized (high entropy) or dispersed and has little ability to do useful work.

To bring the energy use of LDCs up to levels currently used by MDCs by the year 2025 would require a fivefold increase in present global commercial energy use. Many scientists believe that even a doubling of energy use based mostly on nonrenewable fossil fuels will seriously disrupt Earth's already damaged life-sustaining processes. This explains why our top priorities should be to waste less energy by greatly improving energy efficiency and to greatly increase our use of perpetual and renewable forms of energy.

ENERGY QUALITY Energy varies in its quality, or ability to do useful work. **Energy quality** is a measure of energy usefulness (Figure 3-7). **High-quality energy** is organized or concentrated and has great ability to perform useful work. It has low entropy. Examples of these useful forms of energy are electricity, coal, gasoline, concentrated sunlight, nuclei of uranium-235, and heat concentrated in a fairly small sample of matter, so that its temperature is high.

By contrast, **low-quality energy** is disorganized or dispersed and has little ability to do useful work. It has high entropy. An example is heat dispersed in the moving molecules of a large sample of matter such as the atmosphere or a large body of water, so that its temperature is relatively low. For instance, the total amount of heat stored at a relatively low temperature in the Atlantic Ocean is greater than the amount of high-quality chemical energy stored in all the oil deposits in Saudi Arabia. However, this heat is so widely dispersed in the ocean that we can't do much with it. This dispersed heat, like that in the air around us, can't be used to move things or to heat things to high temperatures.

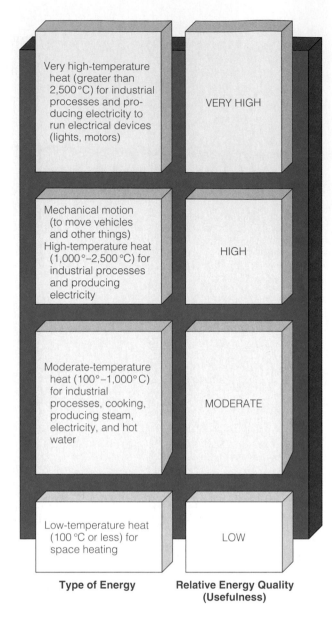

Type of Energy   **Relative Energy Quality (Usefulness)**

Figure 3-8 General quality of energy needed to perform various energy tasks. To avoid unnecessary energy waste, it is best to match the quality of an energy source (Figure 3-7) to the quality of energy needed to perform a task—that is, not to use energy of a higher quality than necessary. This saves energy and usually saves money.

We use energy to accomplish certain tasks, each requiring a certain minimum energy quality (Figure 3-8). Electrical energy, which is very high-quality energy, is needed to run lights, electric motors, and electronic devices. We need high-quality mechanical energy to move a car, but we need only air at a low temperature (less than 100°C) to heat homes and other buildings. It makes sense to match the quality of an energy source (Figure 3-7) to the quality of energy needed to perform a particular task (Figure 3-8). This saves energy and usually saves money (see Guest Essay on p. 75).

Unfortunately, many forms of high-quality energy do not occur naturally. These include a sample of matter at a high temperature, electricity, gasoline, hydrogen gas (a useful and clean-burning fuel that can be produced by passing electricity through water), and concentrated sunlight. We must use other forms of high-quality energy, such as fossil, wood, and nuclear fuels, or devices such as solar collectors or solar cells, to produce, concentrate, and store them, or to upgrade their quality so they can be used to perform certain tasks.

3-4 Physical and Chemical Changes and the Law of Conservation of Matter

PHYSICAL AND CHEMICAL CHANGES Elements and compounds can undergo physical and chemical changes; each change either gives off or requires energy, usually in the form of heat. A **physical change** is one that involves no change in chemical composition. For example, cutting a piece of aluminum foil into small pieces is a physical change. Each cut piece is still aluminum.

Changing a substance from one physical state to another is also a physical change. For example, when solid water, or ice, is melted or liquid water is boiled, none of the H_2O molecules involved is altered; instead, the molecules are organized in different spatial patterns.

In a **chemical change**, or **chemical reaction**, there is a change in the chemical composition of the elements or compounds involved. For example, when coal burns completely, the carbon (C) it contains combines with oxygen gas (O_2) from the atmosphere to form the gaseous compound carbon dioxide (CO_2). In this case, energy is given off, making coal a useful fuel.

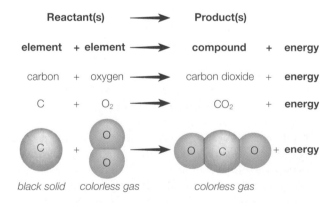

This reaction shows how the burning of coal or any carbon-containing compounds, such as those in wood, natural gas, oil, and gasoline, adds carbon dioxide gas to the atmosphere. It is projected that as the concentration of carbon dioxide in the lower atmosphere increases, this heat-trapping gas could warm the lower atmosphere, enhance Earth's natural greenhouse effect, and possibly bring about changes in global climate, water distribution, and food production.

THE LAW OF CONSERVATION OF MATTER: THERE IS NO AWAY Earth loses some gaseous molecules to space, and it gains small amounts of matter from space, mostly in the form of occasional stony or metallic bodies (meteorites) and the fallout of small amounts of cosmic dust. These losses and gains of matter are minute compared with Earth's total mass—somewhat like the world's beaches losing or adding a few grains of sand.

This means that *Earth has essentially all the matter it will ever have*. In terms of matter, Earth is essentially a closed system. Fortunately, over billions of years, natural processes have evolved for continuously cycling key chemicals back and forth between the nonliving environment (soil, air, and water) and the living environment.

You, like most people, probably talk about consuming or using up material resources, but the truth is that we don't consume any matter. We only use some of Earth's resources for a while. We take materials from the earth, carry them to another part of the globe, and process them into products. These products are used and then discarded, reused, or recycled.

In making and using products, we may change various elements and compounds from one physical or chemical form to another, but we neither create from nothing nor destroy to nothingness any measurable amount of matter.* This fact, based on many thousands of measurements of matter undergoing physical and chemical changes, is known as the **law of conservation of matter:** *In all physical and chemical changes, we can't create or destroy any of the atoms involved. All we can do is rearrange them into different spatial patterns (physical changes) or different combinations (chemical changes).*

The law of conservation of matter means that there is no "away." *Everything we think we have thrown away is still here with us in one form or another*. We can collect dust and soot from the smokestacks of industrial plants, but these solid wastes must then go somewhere. We can remove substances from polluted water at a sewage treatment plant, but this produces a gooey, often toxic, sludge. The sludge must be burned (producing some air pollution), buried (possibly contaminating underground water supplies used for drinking water), or cleaned up and applied to the land as fertilizer (dangerous if the sludge contains toxic metals, such as lead and mercury).

---

*According to modern physics, we may be converting a tiny amount of matter into energy when a chemical reaction takes place. However, the amount is so minute that it cannot be detected by even the most sensitive measuring devices.

We can make the environment cleaner and convert some potentially harmful chemicals into less harmful, or even harmless, physical or chemical forms. Nevertheless, the law of conservation of matter means that we will always be faced with the problem of what to do with some quantity of wastes. By placing much greater emphasis on pollution prevention (input control), however, we can greatly reduce the amount of wastes we add to the environment.

3-5 Nuclear Changes

NATURAL RADIOACTIVITY In addition to physical and chemical changes, matter can undergo a third type of change, known as a **nuclear change**. It occurs when nuclei of certain isotopes spontaneously change or are forced to change into one or more different isotopes. The three principal types of nuclear change are natural radioactivity, nuclear fission, and nuclear fusion.

The law of conservation of matter does not apply to nuclear changes because they involve conversion of a small but measurable amount of the mass in a nucleus into energy. This type of change is governed by the **law of conservation of matter and energy:** *In any nuclear change, the total amount of matter and energy involved remains the same*.

Natural radioactivity is a nuclear change in which unstable nuclei spontaneously shoot out particles (usually alpha or beta particles), energy (gamma rays), or both at a fixed rate. An isotope of an atom that spontaneously emits fast-moving particles, high-energy radiation, or both from its unstable nucleus is called a **radioactive isotope**, or **radioisotope**.

Radiation emitted by radioisotopes is damaging ionizing radiation. The most common form of ionizing energy released from radioisotopes is **gamma rays**, a form of electromagnetic radiation with a high energy content (Figure 3-4). High-speed particles emitted from the nuclei are a different form of ionizing radiation, with enough energy to hit other atoms and dislodge one or more of their electrons to form positively charged ions. The two most common types of ionizing particles emitted by radioactive isotopes are high-speed **alpha particles** (positively charged chunks of matter that consist of two protons and two neutrons) and **beta particles** (high-speed electrons). Figure 3-9 shows the relative penetrating power of alpha, beta, and gamma ionizing radiation. You are exposed to small amounts of harmful ionizing radiation from natural sources and from human sources.

NUCLEAR FISSION: SPLITTING NUCLEI **Nuclear fission** is a nuclear change in which nuclei of certain

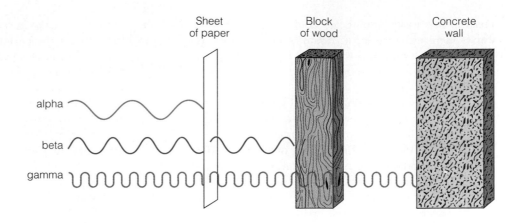

Figure 3-9 The three principal types of ionizing radiation emitted by radioactive isotopes vary considerably in their penetrating power.

Sheet of paper

Block of wood

Concrete wall

alpha

beta

gamma

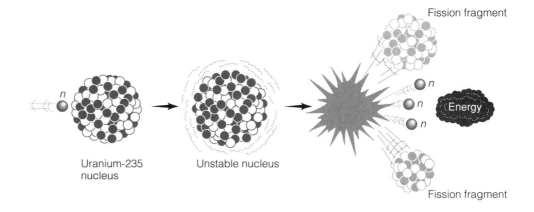

Figure 3-10 Fission of a uranium-235 nucleus by a slow-moving neutron.

Fission fragment

Uranium-235 nucleus

Unstable nucleus

Energy

Fission fragment

isotopes with large mass numbers (such as uranium-235, Figure 3-2) are split apart into lighter nuclei when struck by neutrons; this process releases more neutrons and energy (Figure 3-10). Each fission produces two or three neutrons. Each of these neutrons, in turn, can cause an additional fission. For these multiple fissions to take place, there must be enough fissionable nuclei present to provide the **critical mass** needed for efficient capture of these neutrons.

These multiple fissions taking place within the critical mass represent a **chain reaction** that releases an enormous amount of energy (Figure 3-11). Living cells can be damaged by the ionizing radiation released by the radioactive lighter nuclei and by high-speed neutrons produced by nuclear fission.

In an atomic or nuclear fission bomb, an enormous amount of energy is released in a fraction of a second in an uncontrolled nuclear fission chain reaction. This reaction is initiated by an explosive charge, which suddenly pushes two masses of fissionable fuel together from all sides, causing the fuel to reach the critical mass needed for a chain reaction.

In the nuclear reactor of a nuclear electric power plant, the rate at which the nuclear fission chain reaction takes place is controlled, so that under normal op-

eration, only one of each two or three neutrons released is used to split another nucleus. In conventional nuclear fission reactors, nuclei of uranium-235 are split apart and release energy. The heat released is used to produce high-pressure steam. It is used to spin turbines, which run generators that produce electricity.

NUCLEAR FUSION: FORCING NUCLEI TO COMBINE **Nuclear fusion** is a nuclear change in which two nuclei of isotopes of light elements, such as hydrogen (Figure 3-2), are forced together at extremely high temperatures until they fuse to form a heavier nucleus, releasing energy in the process (Figure 3-12). Temperatures of at least 100 million°C are needed to force the positively charged nuclei (which strongly repel one another) to join together.

High-temperature fusion is much harder to initiate than fission, but once started, it releases far more energy per unit of fuel than fission. Fusion of hydrogen nuclei to form helium nuclei is the source of energy in the sun and other stars.

After World War II, the principle of *uncontrolled nuclear fusion* was used to develop extremely powerful hydrogen, or thermonuclear, bombs and missile warheads. These weapons use the D-T fusion reaction,

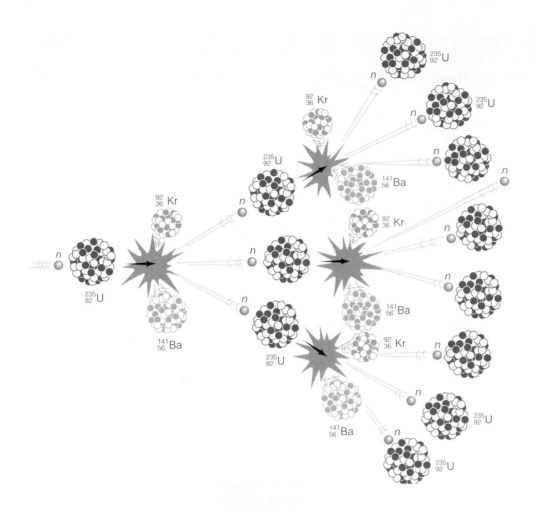

in which a hydrogen-2, or deuterium (D), nucleus and a hydrogen-3, or tritium (T), nucleus are fused to form a larger, helium-4 nucleus, a neutron, and energy (Figure 3-12).

Scientists have also tried to develop *controlled nuclear fusion*, in which the D-T reaction would be used to produce heat that could be converted into electricity. Despite more than 40 years of research, however, this process is still at the laboratory stage. Even if it were to become technologically and economically feasible, it probably would not be a practical source of energy until 2050 or later, if ever.

3-6 The First and Second Laws of Energy

FIRST LAW OF ENERGY: YOU CAN'T GET SOMETHING FOR NOTHING After making millions of measurements, scientists have observed energy being changed from one form to another in physical and chemical changes, but they have never been able to detect any creation or destruction of energy.

This information is summarized in the **law of conservation of energy**, also known as the **first law of energy** or the **first law of thermodynamics**: In physical and chemical changes, no detectable amount of energy is created or destroyed, but in these processes, energy can be changed from one form to another. This law does not apply to nuclear changes, where energy can be produced from small amounts of matter. This law means that *energy input always equals energy output: We can't get something for nothing in terms of energy quantity.*

SECOND LAW OF ENERGY: YOU CAN'T BREAK EVEN Because the first law of energy states that energy can be neither created nor destroyed, you might think that there will always be enough energy; yet, if you fill a car's tank with gasoline and drive around, or if you use a flashlight battery until it is dead, you have lost something. If it isn't energy, what is it? The answer is energy quality (Figure 3-7).

Millions of measurements by scientists have shown that in any conversion of energy from one form to another, there is always a decrease in energy quality or the amount of useful energy. This summary of what we always find occurring in nature is known as the **second law of energy** or the **second law of thermodynamics**:

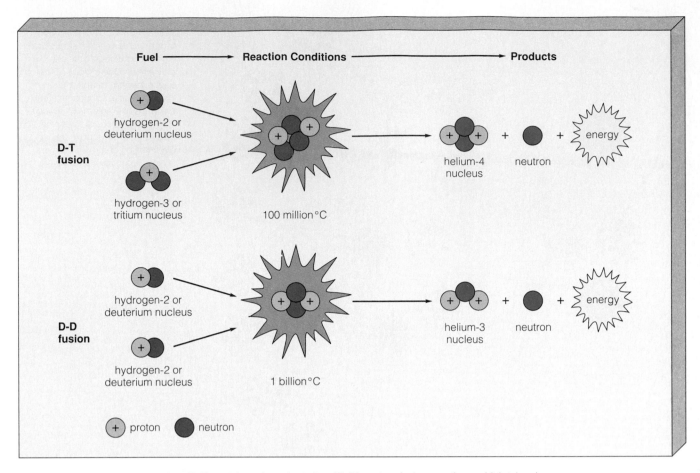

Figure 3-12 The deuterium-tritium (D-T) and deuterium-deuterium (D-D) nuclear fusion reactions, which take place at extremely high temperatures.

When energy is changed from one form to another, some of the useful energy is always degraded to lower-quality, more dispersed (higher entropy), less-useful energy. This degraded energy is usually in the form of heat that flows into the environment and is dispersed in the random motion of air or water molecules at a relatively low temperature. In other words, according to this law of degradation of energy quality, *we can't break even in terms of energy quality*. The more energy we use, the more disordered, low-grade energy (heat), or entropy, we add to the environment. No one has ever found a violation of this fundamental scientific law.

Consider three examples of the second energy law in action. First, when a car is driven, only about 10% of the high-quality chemical energy available in its gasoline fuel is converted into mechanical energy to propel the vehicle and into electrical energy to run its electrical systems. The remaining 90% is degraded to low-quality heat that is released into the environment and eventually lost into space. Second, when electrical energy flows through filament wires in an incandescent light bulb, it is changed into a mixture of about 5% useful radiant energy, or light, and 95% low-quality heat that flows into the environment. What we call a light bulb is

really a heat bulb. A third example of the degradation of energy quality in living systems is illustrated in Figure 3-13.

The second energy law also means that *we can never recycle or reuse high-quality energy to perform useful work*. Once the concentrated, high-quality energy in a piece of food, a gallon of gasoline, a lump of coal, or a piece of uranium is released, its degraded, low-quality heat becomes dispersed in the environment. We can heat air or water at a low temperature and upgrade it to high-quality energy, but the second energy law tells us that it will take more high-quality energy to do this than we get.

LIFE AND THE SECOND ENERGY LAW Life represents a creation and maintenance of ordered (low-entropy) structures. Thus, you might be tempted to think that life is not governed by the second law of thermodynamics.

However, to form and preserve the highly ordered arrangement of molecules and the organized network of chemical changes in your body, you must continually get and use high-quality matter resources and energy resources from your surroundings. As you use these

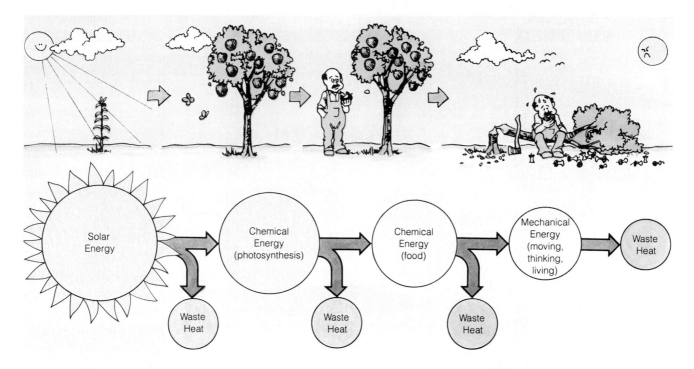

Figure 3-13 The second energy law in action in living systems. When energy is changed from one form to another, some of the initial input of high-quality energy is degraded, usually to low-quality heat, which is added to the environment.

resources, you add disordered, low-quality (high-entropy) heat and waste matter to your surroundings.

For example, your body continuously gives off heat equal to that of a 100-watt light bulb; this is the reason a closed room full of people gets warm. You also continuously give off molecules of carbon dioxide gas and water vapor, which become dispersed in the atmosphere.

Planting, growing, processing, and cooking the foods you eat, all require high-quality energy and matter resources that add low-quality (high-entropy) heat and waste materials to the environment. In addition, enormous amounts of low-quality heat and waste matter are added to the environment when concentrated deposits of minerals and fuels are extracted from the earth's crust, processed, and used or burned to heat and cool the buildings you occupy, to transport you, and to make roads, clothes, shelter, and other items you use.

Measurements show that the total amount of entropy, in the form of dispersed, low-quality heat and dispersed, low-quality matter, added to the environment to keep you (or any organism living) alive and to provide the items you use is much greater than the order maintained in your body. Thus, *all forms of life are tiny pockets of order (low entropy) maintained by creating a sea of disorder (high entropy) in their environment. The primary characteristic of any advanced industrial society is an ever-increasing flow of high-quality energy and matter re-*

sources to maintain the order in human bodies and the larger pockets of order we call civilization.

As a result, today's advanced industrial societies are increasing the entropy of the environment at a faster rate than any other society in human history. The second energy law tells us that we can't avoid this *entropy trap*, but we can reduce or minimize our production of entropy.

3-7 Energy Efficiency and Net Useful Energy

INCREASING ENERGY EFFICIENCY You may be surprised to learn that only 16% of all commercially produced energy that flows through the U.S. economy performs useful work or is used to make petrochemicals, which are used to produce plastics, medicines, and many other products (Figure 3-14). This means that *84% of all commercial energy used in the United States is wasted.* About 41% of this energy is wasted automatically because of the energy-quality tax (degradation of energy quality) imposed by the second energy law, but 43% of the commercial energy used in the United States is unnecessarily wasted.

One way to cut much of this energy waste and save money is to increase **energy efficiency** (see Guest Essay

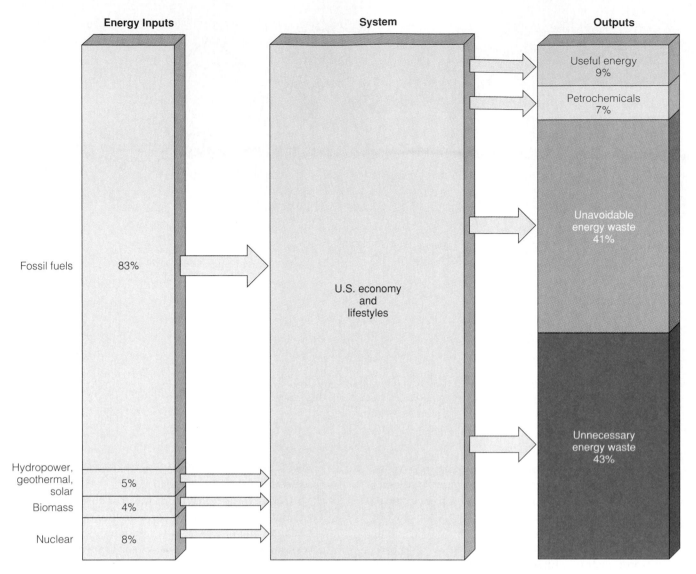

Figure 3-14 Flow of commercial supplemental energy through the U.S. economy. Note that only 16% of all commercial energy used in the United States ends up performing useful tasks, or is converted to petrochemicals. The rest either is automatically and unavoidably wasted because of the second law of energy (41%) or is wasted unnecessarily (43%).

on p. 75). This is the percentage of total energy input that does useful work and is not converted to low-quality, essentially useless heat in an energy conversion system. The energy conversion devices we use vary considerably in their energy efficiencies (Figure 3-15).

We can save energy and money by buying the most energy-efficient home heating systems, water heaters, cars, air conditioners, refrigerators, and other household appliances available. The initial cost of the most energy-efficient models is usually higher, but in the long run, they usually save money by having a lower **life-cycle cost**: the initial cost plus lifetime operating costs.

The net efficiency of the entire energy delivery process of a heating system, water heater, or car is determined by finding the efficiency of each energy conversion step in the process. These steps include extracting the fuel, purifying and upgrading it to a useful form, transporting it, and then using it.

Figure 3-16 shows how net energy efficiencies are determined for heating a well-insulated home **(1)** passively with an input of direct solar energy through windows facing the sun and storing this heat in rocks or water for slow release, and **(2)** with electricity produced at a nuclear power plant, transported by wire to the home, and converted to heat (electric resistance heating). This analysis shows that the process of converting the high-quality nuclear energy in nuclear fuel to high-quality heat at several thousand degrees, converting this heat to high-quality electricity, and then using the electricity to provide low-quality heat for warming a house to only about 20°C (68°F) is extremely wasteful of high-quality energy. Burning coal, or any fossil fuel, at

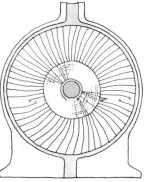

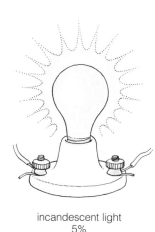

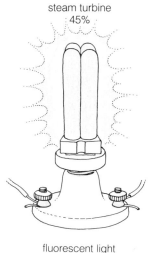

Figure 3-15 Energy efficiency of some common energy conversion devices.

human body
20 to 25%

internal combustion engine
(gasoline) 10%

steam turbine
45%

fuel cell
60%

incandescent light
5%

fluorescent light
22%

a power plant to supply electricity for space heating is also inefficient. By contrast, it is much less wasteful to use a passive or active solar heating system to obtain low-quality heat from the environment, store it in stone or water, and, if necessary, raise its temperature slightly to supply space heating.

Using high-quality electrical energy to provide low-quality heat for heating space or household water is like using a chain saw to cut butter or a sledgehammer to kill a fly. A general rule of energy use is the *principle of matching energy quality to energy tasks:* Don't use high-quality energy to do something that can be done with lower-quality energy (Figures 3-7 and 3-8).

Figure 3-17 lists the net energy efficiencies for a variety of space heating systems. It shows that the two most wasteful (least efficient) and most expensive ways to heat a house are with electricity produced by nuclear power plants and with electricity produced by coal-fired power plants. A heat pump is an efficient way to heat a house as long as the outside temperature does not fall below −15°C (4.5°F), but when it does, these devices begin using electric resistance heating, the most expensive, energy-wasting way to heat any space. Heat pumps are useful for spacing heating in areas with

warm climates, but in such areas, their main use is for air conditioning. The air conditioning units with most heat pumps are much less energy-efficient than many stand-alone units. Most heat pumps also require expensive repair every few years.

A similar analysis of net energy efficiency shows that the least efficient and most expensive way to heat water for washing and bathing is to use electricity produced by nuclear power plants. Indeed, we save money and waste less energy by not using high-quality electricity produced by any type of power plant to heat water for washing and bathing.

The most efficient method is to use a tankless instant water heater fired by natural gas or liquefied petroleum gas (LPG) (Figure 3-18). Such heaters fit under a sink or in a small closet and burn fuel only when the hot-water faucet is turned on. They heat the water instantly as it flows through a small burner chamber and provide hot water only when, and as long as, it is needed. In contrast, conventional natural gas and electric resistance heaters keep a large tank of water hot all day and night, and can run out after a long shower or two. Tankless heaters are widely used in many parts of Europe and are slowly beginning to appear in the

Figure 3-16 Comparison of net energy efficiency for two types of space heating. The cumulative net efficiency is obtained by multiplying the percentage for each step (shown inside the circle) by the energy efficiency for that step (shown in parentheses). Usually, the greater the number of steps in an energy conversion process, the lower its net energy efficiency. With passive solar heating, only about 10% of the incoming solar energy is wasted. By contrast, about 86% of the energy used to provide space heating by electricity produced at a nuclear power plant is wasted.

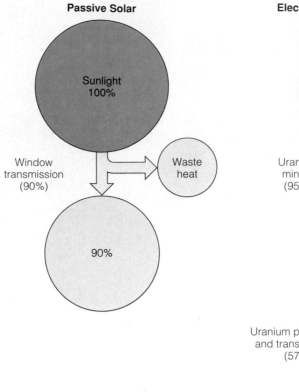

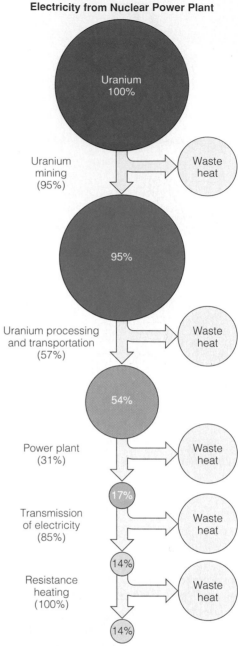

United States. A well-insulated, conventional natural gas or LPG water heater is also efficient.

Using electricity to heat space or water by any method is extremely wasteful of energy and money because it involves using high-quality heat produced at a power plant to provide moderate-quality heat (Figure 3-8). In 1990, the average price of obtaining 250,000 kilocalories for heating space or water in the United States was $5.50 using natural gas, $9 using fuel oil, and $23 using electricity. If you like to throw away money, then use electricity to heat your house and bath water.

If engineers were asked to invent three devices that would waste enormous amounts of energy, they would probably come up with these:

- The incandescent light bulb (which wastes 95% of its energy input)

- A car or truck with an internal combustion engine (which wastes 90% of the energy in its fuel)

- A nuclear power plant producing electricity to heat space or water for washing and bathing (which wastes 86% of the energy in its nuclear fuel, Figure 3-16)

These devices were developed and widely used during a time when energy was cheap and plentiful. As this era draws to a close, we will have to replace or greatly improve the energy efficiency of these and other energy conversion items (see Guest Essay on p. 75).

Net Energy Efficiency

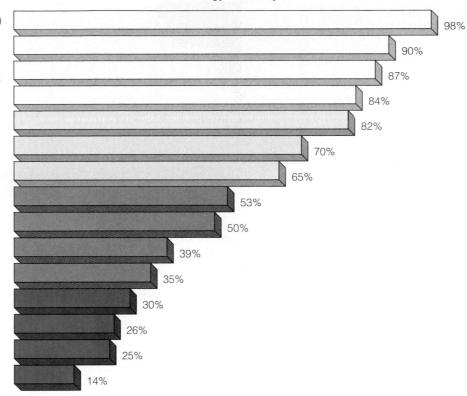

Superinsulated house (100% of heat) (R-43)	98%
Passive solar (100% of heat)	90%
Passive solar (50% of heat) plus high-efficiency natural gas furnace (50% of heat)	87%
Natural gas with high-efficiency furnace	84%
Electric resistance heating (electricity from hydroelectric power plant)	82%
Natural gas with typical furnace	70%
Passive solar (50% of heat) plus high-efficiency wood stove (50% of heat)	65%
Oil furnace	53%
Electric heat pump (electricity from coal-fired power plant)	50%
High-efficiency wood stove	39%
Active solar	35%
Electric heat pump (electricity from nuclear plant)	30%
Typical wood stove	26%
Electric resistance heating (electricity from coal-fired power plant)	25%
Electric resistance heating (electricity from nuclear plant)	14%

Figure 3-17 Net energy efficiencies for various ways to heat an enclosed space such as a house. From this information, we see that the most energy-efficient way to heat space is to build a *superinsulated house*. Such a house is so heavily insulated and airtight that even in areas where winter temperatures fall to − 40°C (− 40°F), all of its space heating can usually be supplied by a combination of passive solar gain (about 59%), waste heat from appliances (33%), and body heat from occupants (8%). Passive solar heating is the next most efficient and next cheapest method of heating a house, followed by one of the new, high-efficiency, natural gas furnaces. The most wasteful way to heat an enclosed space is to use electric resistance heating with the electricity provided by coal-burning or nuclear power plants.

Figure 3-18 Two LPG tankless instant water heaters that I use to provide backup hot water and space heating in my office (see Spotlight on p. 470). The unit on the right provides hot water for washing and bathing. Roof-mounted solar collectors (Figure 17-26) preheat water stored in an insulated tank—a discarded conventional water heater wrapped in extra insulation. When I turn on a hot-water faucet, the solar-heated water flows through the instant heater. If a sensor indicates that the water is below 49°C (120°F), the instant heater comes on to raise the water temperature to that level. About 50% to 60% of my space heat is provided passively by solar energy (Figure 17-26). The rest is provided by a combination of active solar collectors and the tankless water heater shown on the left. Roof-mounted solar collectors store heat in a well-insulated tank—another discarded conventional water heater wrapped in extra insulation. When the thermostat calls for heat, this solar-heated water is pumped through the instant heater and then through a coil and back to the tank it came from. A fan blows air over the coil and transfers hot air through heating ducts, as with a conventional forced-air space-heating system. Any heat not extracted from the hot water by the coil is returned to the insulated tank for reuse in this closed-loop system.

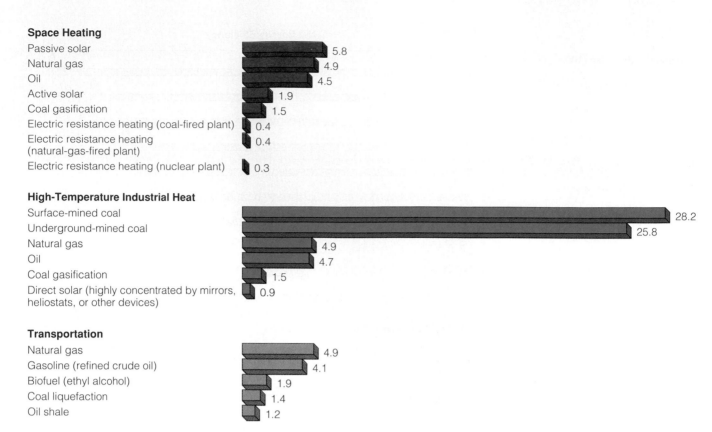

Figure 3-19 Net useful energy ratios for various energy systems over their estimated lifetimes. (Data from Colorado Energy Research Institute, *Net Energy Analysis*, 1976; and Howard T. Odum and Elisabeth C. Odum, *Energy Basis for Man and Nature*, 3rd ed., New York: McGraw-Hill, 1981)

USING WASTE HEAT We cannot recycle high-quality energy, but we can slow the rate at which waste heat flows into the environment when high-quality energy is degraded. For instance, in cold weather, an uninsulated, leaky house loses heat almost as fast as it is produced. By contrast, a well-insulated, airtight house can retain most of its heat for five to ten hours, and a well-designed, superinsulated house can retain most of its heat up to four days.

In some office buildings and stores, waste heat from lights, computers, and other machines is collected and distributed to reduce heating bills during cold weather and is exhausted to reduce cooling bills during hot weather. Waste heat from industrial plants and electrical power plants can be distributed through insulated pipes and used as a district heating system for nearby buildings, greenhouses, and fish ponds, as is done in some parts of Europe.

Another way to use waste heat produced by industrial plants burning coal or other fuels to produce heat or steam is **cogeneration**, the production of two useful forms of energy, such as steam and electricity, from the same fuel source. Waste heat from coal-fired and other industrial boilers can be used to produce steam to spin turbines and generate electricity at half the cost of buying it from a utility company. The electricity can be used

by the plant or sold to the local power company for general use. Cogeneration is used in many industrial plants throughout Europe. If all large industrial boilers in the United States used cogeneration, there would be no need to build any electric power plants through the year 2020.

NET USEFUL ENERGY: IT TAKES ENERGY TO GET ENERGY The usable amount of high-quality energy obtainable from a given quantity of an energy resource is its **net useful energy**. It is the total useful energy available from the resource over its lifetime minus the amount of energy used (the first energy law), automatically wasted (the second energy law), and unnecessarily wasted in finding, processing, concentrating, and transporting it to users. For example, if nine units of fossil-fuel energy are needed to supply ten units of nuclear, solar, or additional fossil-fuel energy (perhaps from a deep well at sea), the net useful energy gain is only one unit of energy.

We can express this relationship as the ratio of useful energy produced to the useful energy used to produce it. In the example just given, the net energy ratio would be 10/9, or 1.1. The higher the ratio, the greater the net useful energy yield. When the ratio is less than 1, there is a net energy loss over the lifetime of the

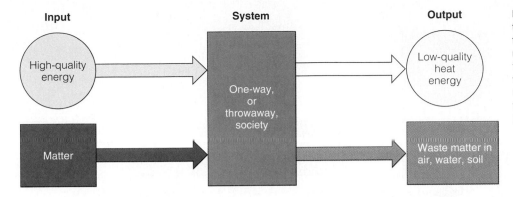

Figure 3-20 The one-way, or throwaway, society of most industrialized countries is based on maximizing the rates of energy flow and matter flow, rapidly converting the world's high-quality matter and energy resources into trash, pollution, and low-quality heat (entropy).

system. Figure 3-19 lists estimated net useful energy ratios for various alternatives to space heating, high-temperature heat for industrial processes, and gaseous and liquid fuels for vehicles.

Currently, oil has a relatively high net useful energy ratio because much of it comes from large, accessible deposits such as those in Saudi Arabia and other parts of the Middle East. When those sources are depleted, however, the net useful energy ratio of oil will decline and prices will rise. Then more money and high-quality fossil fuel will be needed to find, process, and deliver new oil from widely dispersed small deposits and deposits found deeper in the earth's crust and in remote, hostile areas like Alaska, the Arctic, and the North Sea — far from where the energy is to be used.

Conventional nuclear fission energy has a low net energy ratio because large amounts of energy are required to extract and process uranium ore, to convert it into a usable nuclear fuel, and to build and operate power plants. Additional energy is needed to take nuclear plants apart after their 25 to 30 years of useful life and to store the resulting highly radioactive wastes for thousands of years.

 3-8 **Matter and Energy Laws and Environmental and Resource Problems**

THROWAWAY SOCIETIES Because of the law of conservation of matter and the second law of energy, resource use by each of us automatically adds some waste heat and waste matter to the environment, thus increasing its entropy. The more energy and matter resources we use, the faster and the greater the entropy increase in the environment (the entropy trap).

Your individual use of matter and energy resources and your addition of waste heat, waste matter, and entropy to the environment may seem small and insignificant. But you are only one of the 1.2 billion individuals in industrialized countries using large quantities of Earth's matter and energy resources at a rapid rate.

Meanwhile, the 4.2 billion people in less developed countries hope to be able to use more of these resources. Each year, there are 97 million more consumers of Earth's energy and matter resources.

Today's advanced industrialized countries are **throwaway societies**, sustaining ever-increasing economic growth by maximizing the rate at which matter and energy resources are used and wasted (Figure 3-20). The scientific laws of matter and energy tell us that if more and more people continue to use and waste more and more energy and matter resources at an increasing rate, sooner or later the capacity of the local, regional, and global environments to dilute and degrade waste matter and absorb waste heat will be exceeded.

MATTER-RECYCLING SOCIETIES A stopgap solution to this problem is to convert from a throwaway society to a **matter-recycling society**. The goal of such a shift would be to allow economic growth to continue without depleting matter resources and without producing excessive pollution and environmental degradation. As we have learned, however, there is no free lunch when it comes to energy.

The two laws of energy tell us that *recycling matter resources always requires high-quality energy, which cannot be recycled*. In the long run, a matter-recycling society based on indefinitely increasing economic growth must have an inexhaustible supply of affordable high-quality energy. The environment must also have an infinite capacity to absorb and disperse waste heat and to dilute and degrade waste matter. There is also usually a physical limit to the number of times a material, such as paper fibers, can be recycled before it becomes unusable.

Shifting from a throwaway society to a matter-recycling society is only a temporary solution to our problems in a world built on the goal of ever-increasing economic growth. We should recognize that the main purpose of the shift to a matter-recycling society is to give us more time to shift to a sustainable-Earth society.

Experts disagree on how much high-quality energy we have, mostly in the form of fossil and nuclear fuels. However, supplies of coal, oil, natural gas, and uranium

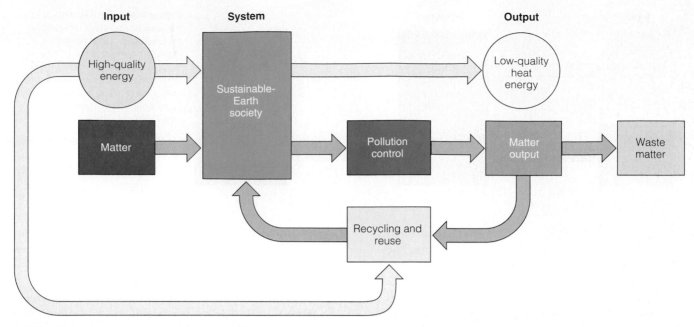

Figure 3-21 A sustainable-Earth society, based on energy flow and matter recycling, reuses and recycles renewable matter resources, wastes less matter and energy, reduces unnecessary consumption, emphasizes pollution prevention and waste reduction, and controls population growth.

are clearly finite. Affordable supplies of oil, the most widely used supplementary energy resource, may be used up in several decades.

"Ah," you say, "but don't we have a virtually inexhaustible supply of solar energy flowing to Earth?" The problem is that the amount of solar energy reaching a particular small area of the earth's surface each minute or hour is low, and it is nonexistent at night.

With a proper collection and storage system, using passive and active systems to concentrate solar energy slightly to provide hot water and to heat a house to moderate temperatures makes good thermodynamic and economic sense. But to provide the high temperatures needed to melt metals or to produce electricity in a power plant, solar energy may not be cost-effective. Why? Because it has a very low net useful energy ratio (Figure 3-19). It takes a lot of energy to concentrate and raise its quality to a high level.

Suppose that affordable solar cells, nuclear fusion at room temperature, or some other breakthrough were to supply an essentially infinite supply of affordable useful energy. Would that solve our environmental and resource problems? No!

Such a breakthrough would be important and useful, but the second energy law tells us that the faster we use more energy to transform more matter into products and to recycle those products, the faster large amounts of low-quality heat and waste matter are dumped into the environment. Thus, the more we attempt to "conquer" Earth, the more stress we put on the environment. Experts argue over how close we are

to reaching overload limits, but the scientific laws of matter and energy indicate that such limits do exist.

SUSTAINABLE-EARTH SOCIETIES The three scientific laws governing matter and energy changes indicate that the best long-term solution to our environmental and resource problems is to shift from a throwaway society, based on maximizing matter and energy flow (and, in the process, wasting an unnecessarily large portion of Earth's natural resources), to a **sustainable-Earth society** (Figure 3-21).

A sustainable-Earth society would do the following:

- Use energy more efficiently and not use high-quality energy to do things that require moderate-quality energy (Figure 3-8). This is an important first step that buys us time, saves us money, and reduces pollution. Unless we lower the rate at which we use matter and energy resources, however, we'll eventually be back where we started as long as more people use more energy.

- Use matter and energy resources at optimum rates designed to sustain Earth's life-support systems.

- Shift from exhaustible and potentially polluting fossil and nuclear fuels to less harmful perpetual and renewable energy obtained from the sun and from Earth's natural cycles and flows.

- Recycle and reuse most (at least 80%) of the matter we now discard as trash.

- Reduce use and waste of matter resources by making things that last longer and are easier to recycle, reuse, and repair. Our lifestyle motto should be: *Throwaway no, recycle yes, reuse is better, and reduced use is best*.

- Bring human population growth to a halt to reduce stress on Earth's life support systems.

- Emphasize pollution prevention and waste reduction instead of pollution cleanup and waste management.

The matter and energy laws show us why pollution prevention makes more sense thermodynamically and economically (in the long run) than pollution cleanup. For example, preventing a toxic chemical from reaching underground supplies of drinking water is much easier and cheaper than trying to remove the chemical once it has contaminated groundwater. Until we make this shift to prevention approaches, we are merely treating the undesirable symptoms of unsustainable, throw-away societies instead of transforming them into sustainable-Earth societies.

Because of the three basic scientific laws of matter and energy, we are all dependent on each other and on the other living and nonliving parts of nature for our survival. Everything is connected to everything else, and we are all in it together. In the next chapter, we will apply these laws to living systems and look at some biological principles that can teach us how to work with the rest of nature.

The second law of thermodynamics holds, I think, the supreme position among laws of nature. . . . If your theory is found to be against the second law of thermodynamics, I can give you no hope.

ARTHUR S. EDDINGTON

GUEST ESSAY Technology Is the Answer (But What Was the Question?)

Amory B. Lovins

Physicist and energy consultant Amory B. Lovins is one of the world's most recognized and articulate experts on energy strategy. In 1989, he was the first recipient of the Delphi Prize for environmental work; in 1990, The Wall Street Journal *named him as one of the 39 people in the world most likely to change the course of business in the 1990s. He is director of research at Rocky Mountain Institute in Old Snowmass, Colorado, a nonprofit resource policy center, which he and his wife, Hunter, founded in 1982. He has briefed eight heads of state and served as a consultant to 190 utilities, private industries, and international organizations, and many national, state, and local governments. He is active in energy affairs in 31 countries and has published several hundred papers and a dozen books, including* Soft Energy Paths *(New York: Harper Colophon, 1979) and the nontechnical version of that work with senior coauthor L. Hunter Lovins,* Energy Unbound: Your Invitation to Energy Abundance *(San Francisco: Sierra Club Books, 1986).*

The answers you get depend on the questions you ask. But sometimes it seems so important to resolve a crisis that we forget to ask what problem we're trying to solve.

It is fashionable to suppose that we're running out of energy and that the solution is obviously to get lots more of it. But asking how to get more energy begs the question of how much we need. That depends not on how much we used in the past but on what we want to do in the future and how much energy it will take to do those things.

How much energy it takes to make steel, run a sewing machine, or keep you comfortable in your house depends on how cleverly we use energy, and the more it costs, the smarter we seem to get. It is now cheaper, for example, to double the efficiency of most industrial electric motor drive systems than to fuel existing power plants to make electricity. (Just this one saving can more than replace the entire U.S. nuclear power program.) We know how to make lights five times as efficient as those presently in use and how to make household appliances that give us the same work as now, using one-fifth as much energy (saving money in the process).

Ten automakers have made good-sized, peppy, safe prototype cars averaging 29 to 59 kilometers per liter (62 to 138 miles per gallon). We know today how to make new buildings and many old ones so heat-tight (but still well ventilated) that they need essentially no energy to maintain comfort year-round, even in severe climates. (In fact, I live in one.)

These energy-saving measures are uniformly cheaper than going out and getting more energy. Detailed studies in over a dozen countries have shown that supplying energy services in the cheapest way — by wringing more

(continued)

CHAPTER 3   Matter and Energy Resources   **75**

work from the energy we already have — would let us increase our standard of living while using several times less total energy (and electricity) than we do now. Those savings cost less than finding new domestic oil or operating existing power plants.

However, the old view of the energy problem included a worse mistake than forgetting to ask how much energy we needed: It sought more energy, in any form, from any source, at any price — as if all kinds of energy were alike. This is like saying, "All kinds of food are alike; we're running short of potatoes and turnips and cheese, but that's okay, we can substitute sirloin steak and oysters Rockefeller."

Some of us have to be more discriminating than that. Just as there are different kinds of food, so there are many different forms of energy, whose different prices and qualities suit them to different uses [Figure 3-7]. There is, after all, no demand for energy as such; nobody wants raw kilowatt-hours or barrels of sticky black goo. People instead want energy services: comfort, light, mobility, ability to bake bread, ability to make cement, hot showers, and cold beverages. We ought therefore to start at that end of the energy problem and ask, "What are the many different tasks we want energy for, and what is the amount, type, and source of energy that will do each task the cheapest?"

Electricity is a particularly special, high-quality, expensive form of energy. An average kilowatt-hour delivered in the United States in 1990 was priced at about 7 cents, equivalent to buying the heat content of oil costing $116 per barrel — over six times the average world price in early 1990. The average cost of electricity from nuclear plants (including fuel and operating expenses) beginning operation in 1988 was 13.5 cents per kilowatt-hour, equivalent on a heat basis to buying oil at about $216 per barrel.

Such costly energy might be worthwhile if it were used only for the premium tasks that require it, such as lights, motors, electronics, and smelters. But those special uses, only 8% of all delivered U.S. energy needs, are already met twice over by today's power stations. Two-fifths of our electricity is already spilling over into uneconomic, low-grade uses such as water heating, space heating, and air conditioning; yet, no matter how efficiently we use electricity (even with heat pumps), we can never get our money's worth on these applications.

Thus, *supplying more electricity is irrelevant to the energy problem that we have*. Even though electricity accounts for almost all of the federal energy research and development budget and for at least half of national energy investment, it is the wrong kind of energy to meet our needs economi-cally. Arguing about what kind of new power station to build — coal, nuclear, solar — is like shopping for the best buy in antique Chippendale chairs to burn in your stove or brandy to put in your car's gas tank. *It is the wrong question*.

Indeed, *any kind of new power station is so uneconomical that if you have just built one, you will save the country money by writing it off and never operating it*. Why? Because its additional electricity can be used only for low-temperature heating and cooling (the premium "electricity-specific" uses being already filled up) and is the most expensive way of supplying those services. Saving electricity is much cheaper than making it.

The real question is, What is the cheapest way to do low-temperature heating and cooling? That means weatherstripping, insulation, heat exchangers, greenhouses, superwindows (which have as much insulating value as an outside wall of a typical house), window shades and overhangs, trees, and so on. These measures generally cost about half a penny per kilowatt-hour; the running costs *alone* for a new nuclear plant will be nearly four cents per kilowatt-hour, so it is cheaper not to run it. In fact, under the crazy U.S. tax laws, the extra saving from not having to pay the plant's future subsidies is probably so big that by shutting the plant down society can also recover the capital cost of having built it!

If we want more electricity, we should get it from the cheapest sources first. In approximate order of increasing price, these include

1. Converting to efficient lighting equipment. This would save the U.S. electricity equal to the output of 120 large power plants plus $30 billion a year in fuel and maintenance costs.

2. Using more efficient motors to save half the energy used by motor systems. This would save electricity equal to the output of another 150 large power plants and repay the cost in about a year.

3. Eliminating pure waste of electricity, such as lighting empty offices at headache level. Each kilowatt-hour saved can be resold without having to generate it anew.

4. Displacing with good architecture, and with passive and some active solar techniques, the electricity now used for water heating and space heating and cooling. Some U.S. utilities now give low- or zero-interest weatherization loans, which you need not start repaying for ten years or until you sell your house — because it saves the utility millions of dollars to get electricity that way compared with building new power plants.

Most utilities also offer rebates for buying efficient appliances.

5. Making appliances, smelters, and the like cost-effectively efficient.

Just these five measures can quadruple U.S. electrical efficiency, making it possible to run today's economy, with no changes in lifestyles, using no thermal power plants, whether old or new and whether fueled with oil, gas, coal, or uranium. We would need only the present hydroelectric capacity, readily available small-scale hydroelectric projects, and a modest amount of wind power. If we still wanted more electricity, the next cheapest sources would include

6. Industrial cogeneration, combined-heat-and-power plants, low-temperature heat engines run by industrial waste heat or by solar ponds, filling empty turbine bays and upgrading equipment in existing big dams, modern wind machines or small-scale hydroelectric turbines in good sites, steam-injected natural gas turbines, and perhaps recent developments in solar cells with waste heat recovery.

It is only after we had clearly exhausted all these cheaper opportunities that we would even consider

7. Building a new central power station of any kind — the slowest and costliest known way to get more electricity (or to save oil).

To emphasize the importance of starting with energy end uses rather than energy sources, consider a sad little story from France, involving a "spaghetti chart" (or energy flowchart) — a device energy planners often use to show how energy flows from primary sources via conversion processes to final forms and uses. In the mid-1970s, energy conservation planners in the French government started, wisely, on the right-hand side of the spaghetti chart. They found that their biggest need for energy was to heat buildings, and that even with good heat pumps, electricity would be the most uneconomic way to do this. So they had a fight with their nationalized utility; they won, and electric heating was supposed to be discouraged or even phased out because it was so wasteful of money and fuel.

Meanwhile, down the street, the energy supply planners (who were far more numerous and influential in the French government) were starting on the left-hand side of the spaghetti chart. They said: "Look at all that nasty imported oil coming into our country! We must replace that

oil. Oil is energy. . . . We need some other source of energy. Voilà! Reactors can give us energy; we'll build nuclear reactors all over the country." But they paid little attention to what would happen to that extra energy, and no attention to relative prices.

Thus, the two sides of the French energy establishment went on with their respective solutions to two different, indeed contradictory, French energy problems: *more energy of any kind* versus *the right kind to do each task cheapest*. It was only in 1979 that these conflicting perceptions collided. The supply-side planners suddenly realized that the only thing they would be able to *sell* all that nuclear electricity for would be electric heating, which they had just agreed not to do.

Every industrial country is in this embarrassing position (especially if we include "heating" air conditioning, which just means heating the outdoors instead of the indoors). Which end of the spaghetti chart we start on, or *what we think the energy problem is*, is not an academic abstraction: It *determines what we buy*. It is the most fundamental source of disagreement about energy policy.

People starting on the left side of the spaghetti chart think the problem boils down to whether to build coal or nuclear power stations (or both). People starting on the right realize that *no* kind of new power station can be an economic way to meet the needs for low- and high-temperature heat and for vehicular liquid fuels that are 92% of our energy problem.

So if we want to provide our energy services at a price we can afford, let's get straight what question our technologies are supposed to provide the answer to. Before we argue about the meatballs, let's untangle the strands of spaghetti, see where they're supposed to lead, and find out what we really need the energy *for*!

Guest Essay Discussion

1. List the energy services you would like to have, and note which of these must be furnished by electricity.

2. The author argues that building more nuclear, coal, or other electrical power plants to supply electricity for the United States is unnecessary and wasteful. Summarize the reasons for this conclusion and give your reasons for agreeing or disagreeing with this viewpoint.

3. Do you agree or disagree that increasing the supply of energy, instead of concentrating on improving energy efficiency, is the wrong answer to U.S. energy problems? Explain.

DISCUSSION TOPICS

1. Explain why we don't really consume anything and why we can never really throw matter away.

2. A tree grows and increases its mass. Explain why this isn't a violation of the law of conservation of matter.

3. If there is no "away," why isn't the world filled with waste matter?

4. Use the second energy law to explain why a barrel of oil can be used only once as a fuel.

5. Explain why most energy analysts urge that improving energy efficiency forms the basis of any individual, corporate, or national energy plan. Is it an important part of your personal energy plan or lifestyle? Why or why not?

6. Explain why using electricity to heat a house and to supply household hot water by resistance heating is expensive and wasteful of energy. What energy tasks can be done best by electricity?

7. a. Use the law of conservation of matter to explain why a matter-recycling society will sooner or later be necessary.
   b. Use the first and second laws of energy to explain why, in the long run, a sustainable-Earth society, not just a matter-recycling society, will be necessary.

*8. You are about to build a house. What energy supply (oil, gas, coal, or other) would you use for space heating, cooking food, refrigerating food, and heating water? Consider the long-term economic and environmental impact. Would you decide differently if you planned to live in the house for only 5 years instead of 25 years? If so, how?

*9. As a class project, determine the following information about your school.
   a. What energy sources are used for heating and cooling? How do these vary with the ages and types of buildings?
   b. How much money is spent on heating and cooling? How do these costs vary on a monthly basis throughout the year? How do they vary with the ages and types of buildings?
   c. What is the rough energy efficiency of the devices used for heating, cooling, and lighting?
   d. What efforts have been made to improve the energy efficiency of heating, cooling, and lighting devices and to increase insulation and reduce air infiltration during the past ten years? How much money has been saved by such actions during this time?
   e. Use this information to draw up an energy-saving and money-saving plan for your school, and submit the results to appropriate officials.

CHAPTER 4

ECOSYSTEMS: WHAT ARE THEY AND HOW DO THEY WORK?

General Questions and Issues

1. What two fundamental natural processes keep us and other organisms alive?

2. What is an ecosystem, and what are its most important living and nonliving components?

3. What happens to energy in an ecosystem?

4. What happens to matter in an ecosystem?

5. What roles do different organisms play in an ecosystem, and how do organisms interact?

If we love our children, we must love the earth with tender care and pass it on, diverse and beautiful, so that on a warm spring day 10,000 years hence they can feel peace in a sea of grass, can watch a bee visit a flower, can hear a sandpiper call in the sky, and can find joy in being alive.

HUGH H. ILTIS

WHAT ORGANISMS LIVE in a field or a pond? How do they get enough matter and energy resources to stay alive? How do these organisms interact with one another and with their physical and chemical environment? What changes might this field or pond undergo through time?

Ecology is the science that attempts to answer such questions about how nature works. In 1869, German biologist Ernst Haeckel coined the term *ecology* from two Greek words: *oikos*, meaning "house" or "place to live," and *logos*, meaning "study of."

Ecology is the study of how organisms interact with one another and with their nonliving environment of energy and matter (Figure 4-1). The key word is *interact*. Scientists usually carry out this study by examining different **ecosystems**: communities with groups of different species interacting with one another and with their nonliving physical and chemical environment.

This chapter will consider the principal nonliving and living components of ecosystems and how they interact. The next two chapters will consider principal types of life zones and ecosystems and the changes they can undergo because of natural events and human activities.

4-1 Earth's Life-Support Systems: An Overview

EARTH: A DYNAMIC PLANET Several important, interacting parts play a role in sustaining life on Earth (Figure 4-2). They are

- The **atmosphere**—a thin, gaseous envelope that surrounds the planet (Figure 4-3). About 95% of

Figure 4-1 Ecology is a study of how organisms interact with other living things and with nonliving things such as sunlight, air, water, and soil. This arctic fox, with its winter coat that helps hide it in the snow, and other animals depend on sunlight, water, plants, and decomposers (mostly bacteria and fungi) for their survival. When the snow melts during the brief arctic summer, the fox's coat turns brown so it can blend into its environment.

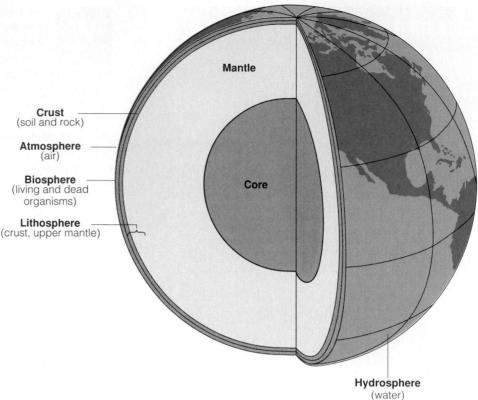

Figure 4-2 Our life-support system: the general structure of the earth.

Crust
(soil and rock)

Atmosphere
(air)

Biosphere
(living and dead
organisms)

Lithosphere
(crust, upper mantle)

Mantle

Core

Hydrosphere
(water)

the mass of the planet's air is found in the atmosphere's innermost layer, known as the **troposphere**, extending about 17 kilometers (11 miles) above sea level. The atmosphere's second layer, extending from about 17 to 48 kilometers (11 to 30 miles) above the earth's surface, is called the **stratosphere**.

- The **hydrosphere**—liquid water (oceans, lakes, and other bodies of surface water, and underground water), frozen water (polar ice caps, floating ice caps, and ice in soil known as permafrost), and small amounts of water vapor in the atmosphere.

- The **geosphere**—interior core, mantle, and crust (containing soil and rock). Fossil fuels and the minerals we use are found in Earth's crust and upper mantle, known as the **lithosphere**. The lithosphere consists of several gigantic plates that have been moving very slowly over hundreds of millions of years.

- The **biosphere**—the entire realm where life is found. It consists of parts of the atmosphere (the troposphere), hydrosphere (mostly surface water and groundwater), and lithosphere (mostly soil and surface rocks and sediments on the bottoms of oceans and other bodies of water) where life is found. The biosphere is a relatively thin, 20-kilometer (12-mile) zone of life extending from the deepest ocean floor to the tops of the highest mountains.

We speak of Earth as a dynamic planet because these principal spheres of the planet undergo short- and long-term changes in response to changing environmental conditions caused by natural processes and by our activities.

Earth's collection of living organisms (found in the biosphere) interacting with one another and their nonliving environment (energy and matter) throughout the world is called the **ecosphere**.* If Earth were an apple, the ecosphere would be no thicker than the apple's skin, existing between the molten heat of Earth's interior and the lifeless cold of space. *The goal of ecology is to learn how this thin global skin of air, water, soil, and organisms works and how it sustains itself.*

ENERGY FLOW AND MATTER CYCLING Life on Earth depends largely on two fundamental processes (Figure 4-4):

- The *one-way flow of high-quality (usable) energy* from the sun, through materials and living things on or near the earth's surface, then into the environment (mostly as low-quality heat dispersed into air or water molecules at a low temperature), and eventually into space as infrared radiation

---

*Many sources use the term *biosphere* in this way. I use the term *biosphere* to indicate where Earth's life is found and the term *ecosphere* to represent the interaction of the biosphere (life) with the energy and matter in the surrounding nonliving environment.

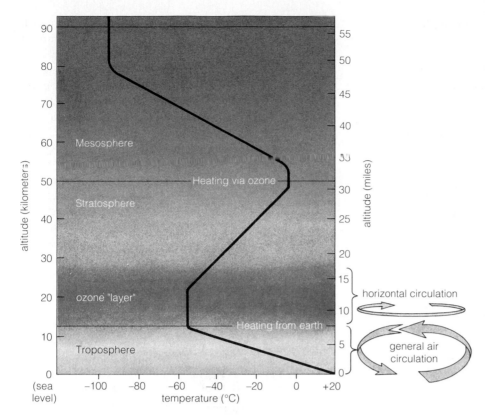

Figure 4-3 Earth's atmosphere. About 95% of the planet's mass of air circulates in the troposphere, where temperatures decrease rapidly with altitude. About 99% of the volume of clean, dry air in the troposphere consists of two gases: nitrogen (78%) and oxygen (21%). The remaining volume of air in the troposphere has slightly less than 1% argon and about 0.035% carbon dioxide. Air in the troposphere also holds water vapor in amounts varying from 0.01% by volume at the frigid poles to 5% in the humid tropics. Most ultraviolet radiation from the sun is absorbed by small amounts of gaseous ozone (O_3) in the stratosphere, where temperatures rise with increasing altitude. Most of this ozone is found in what is called the ozone layer, between 17 and 26 kilometers (11 and 16 miles) above sea level. This filtering action by the thin gauze of ozone in the stratosphere protects us from increased sunburn, skin cancer, eye cancer, and eye cataracts. This global sunscreen also prevents damage to some plants and aquatic organisms. (Used by permission from Cecie Starr, *Biology: Concepts and Applications*, Belmont, Calif.: Wadsworth, 1991)

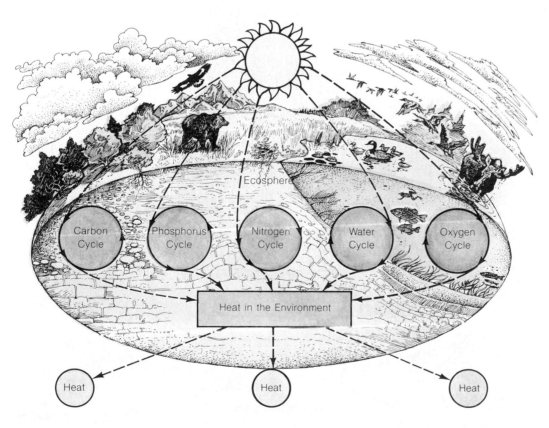

Figure 4-4 Life on Earth depends on the cycling of critical elements (solid lines around the circles) and the one-way flow of energy from the sun through the ecosphere (dashed lines). This greatly simplified overview shows only a few of the many elements that are recycled.

- The *cycling of matter* required by living organisms through parts of the ecosphere

THE SUN: SOURCE OF ENERGY FOR LIFE The source of the energy that sustains life on Earth is the sun. It lights and warms Earth and supplies the energy used by green plants and some bacteria to synthesize the compounds that keep them alive and serve as food for almost all other organisms. Solar energy also powers the recycling of key forms of matter and drives the climate and weather systems that distribute heat and fresh water over the earth's surface.

The sun is a gigantic fireball composed mostly of hydrogen (72%) and helium (28%) gases. Temperatures and pressures in its inner core are high enough for the hydrogen nuclei found there to undergo nuclear fusion to form helium nuclei (Figure 3-12) and constantly release enormous amounts of energy.

This gigantic, faraway nuclear fusion reactor radiates energy into space as a spectrum of electromagnetic radiation (Figure 3-4). These forms of radiant energy travel outward in all directions through space and make the 150-million-kilometer (93-million-mile) trip to Earth in about eight minutes.

Earth, a tiny target in the vastness of space, receives only about one-billionth of the sun's total energy output. When this spectrum of electromagnetic energy reaches Earth, much of it is either reflected or absorbed by chemicals in parts of the atmosphere. This prevents most of the harmful, high-energy cosmic rays, gamma rays, X rays, and ultraviolet ionizing radiation from reaching the planet's surface. The radiant energy reaching the troposphere is mostly in the form of roughly equal amounts of visible light and infrared radiation (which most organisms experience as heat), plus a small amount of ultraviolet radiation not absorbed by ozone molecules in the stratosphere.

About 34% of the solar energy reaching the troposphere is immediately reflected back to space by clouds, chemicals, and dust and by the earth's surface of land and water (Figure 4-5). Most of the remaining 66% warms the troposphere and land, evaporates water and cycles it through the ecosphere, and generates winds. A tiny fraction (0.023%) is captured, mostly by green plants and by some bacteria, and is used in the process of photosynthesis to make organic compounds that many plants and organisms feed on to survive.

Most of the 66% of solar radiation not reflected away is degraded into lower-quality infrared radiation (which we experience as heat) as it interacts with the earth (Figure 4-5). The rate at which this heat flows through the troposphere and eventually into space is affected by the presence of heat-trapping gases, such as water vapor, carbon dioxide, methane, nitrous oxide, and ozone, in the troposphere.

Our activities are adding large quantities of carbon

Figure 4-5 The flow of energy to and from Earth.

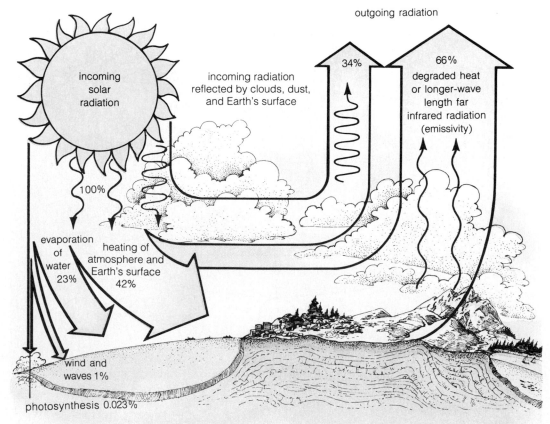

dioxide and several other heat-trapping gases to the troposphere. Scientists are concerned that this could enhance Earth's natural greenhouse effect. Computer models of Earth's climate systems suggest that this could alter the planet's climate patterns, disrupt food growing patterns and wildlife habitats, and possibly raise average sea levels.

BIOGEOCHEMICAL CYCLES Any element an organism needs to live, grow, and reproduce is called a **nutrient**. About 40 elements are essential to organisms, although the number and types of these elements can vary with different organisms. Usually these nutrient elements are found in various compounds.

Elements required by organisms in large amounts are called **macronutrients**. Examples are carbon, oxygen, hydrogen, nitrogen, phosphorus, sulfur, calcium, magnesium, and potassium. These elements and their compounds make up 97% of the mass of your body and more than 95% of the mass of all organisms. The 30 or so other elements required by organisms in small, or trace, amounts are called **micronutrients**. Examples are iron, copper, zinc, chlorine, and iodine.

Most of Earth's chemicals do not occur in forms useful to the planet's living organisms. Fortunately, elements and their compounds required as nutrients for life on Earth are continuously cycled in complex paths through the living and nonliving parts of the ecosphere and converted into useful forms by a combination of biological, geological, and chemical processes.

This cycling of nutrients from the nonliving environment (reservoirs in the atmosphere, the hydrosphere, and Earth's crust) to living organisms, and back to the nonliving environment, takes place in **biogeochemical cycles** (literally, "life [*bio*]- earth [*geo*]- chemical cycles). These cycles, driven directly or indirectly by incoming energy from the sun, include the carbon, oxygen, nitrogen, phosphorus, sulfur, and hydrologic (water) cycles (Figure 4-4).

Thus, a chemical may be part of an organism at one moment and part of the organism's environment at another moment. For example, one of the oxygen molecules you just inhaled may be one inhaled previously by you, your grandmother, King Tut thousands of years ago, or a dinosaur millions of years ago. Similarly, some of the carbon atoms in the skin covering your right hand may once have been part of a leaf, a dinosaur skin, or a layer of limestone rock.

<table>
<tr><td>**4-2**</td><td>**Ecosystems: Types and Components**</td></tr>
</table>

THE REALM OF ECOLOGY Ecology is concerned primarily with interactions among five of the levels of organization of matter shown in Figure 3-1: organisms, populations, communities, ecosystems, and the ecosphere. An **organism** is any form of life. All organisms are classified into species that make up the planet's biodiversity (see Spotlight on p. 11). Biologists have classified only about 1.5 million of Earth's estimated 40 to 80 million species.

The smallest living unit of an organism is the **cell**. All cells are encased in an outer membrane or wall. Each cell contains genetic material in the form of DNA and other components that perform specialized functions necessary for life. Organisms such as bacteria consist of only one cell, but most organisms contain many cells.

Cells are classified as eukaryotic or prokaryotic on the basis of their internal structure. All cells, except bacteria, are **eukaryotic**. They have a *nucleus*, a region of genetic material surrounded by a membrane. Membranes also enclose several other internal parts of a eukaryotic cell. Bacterial cells are said to be **prokaryotic** because they don't have a distinct nucleus. Other internal parts are also not enclosed by membranes.

In this book, Earth's organisms are classified into five major kingdoms:

- **Bacteria** are prokaryotic, single-cell organisms. Many are **decomposers**, which get the nutrients they need by breaking down complex organic compounds in the tissues of living or dead organisms into simpler, inorganic nutrient compounds. Others, such as cyanobacteria (formerly called blue-green algae), use sunlight to combine inorganic chemicals to make the organic nutrient compounds they need (*photosynthesis*). Some combine inorganic chemicals without the presence of light to make the organic nutrients they need (*chemosynthesis*).

- **Protists** are eukaryotic, mostly single-cell organisms such as diatoms, amoebas, some algae (golden brown and yellow-green), protozoans, and slime molds. Some protists produce their own organic nutrients through photosynthesis. Others are decomposers, and some feed on bacteria, other protists, or cells of multicellular organisms.

- **Fungi** are eukaryotic, mostly multicelled organisms such as mushrooms, molds, and yeasts. They are decomposers that get the nutrients they need by secreting enzymes that break down the organic matter in the tissue of other living or dead organisms. Then they absorb the resulting nutrients.

- **Plants** are eukaryotic, mostly multicelled organisms such as algae (red, brown, and green), mosses, ferns, flowers, cacti, grasses, beans, wheat, rice, and trees (see Spotlight on p. 84). These organisms use photosynthesis to produce organic nutrients for themselves and for other organisms feeding on them. Water and other inorganic nutrients are obtained from the soil by terrestrial plants and from the water by aquatic plants.

- **Animals** are eukaryotic, multicelled organisms such as sponges, jellyfishes, arthropods (insects,

Earth contains a variety of plants with structures that enhance their survival and growth under various environmental conditions. Three principal types of land plants are trees, shrubs, and grasses.

Some plants have large leaves to capture sunlight in dense forests or to evaporate water in areas with abundant moisture. Others have small leaves, needles, or thin stems (grasses) with waxy, waterproof coatings to minimize loss of water by evaporation in areas where moisture is limited.

Some plants are **evergreens**, which retain some of their leaves or needles throughout the year. Examples are ferns, tall broadleaf trees that thrive in warm-moist rain forests, and cone-bearing trees (conifers) such as firs, spruces, pines, redwoods, and sequoias (Figure 4-6). The leaves or needles of these plants enable them to carry out photosynthesis all year long in warm, tropical climates or to take maximum advantage of a short growing season in colder climates.

Losing water by evaporation through leaves is a disadvantage during a dry season or drought. During cold seasons, plants with leaves or needles can lose large amounts of heat, making them more susceptible to the cold. **Deciduous plants**, such as oak and maple trees, survive during dry seasons or cold seasons by shedding their leaves.

Succulent plants, such as desert cacti (Figure 4-7), survive in dry climates by having no leaves, thus reducing the loss of scarce water. They store water and use sunlight to produce the food they need in the thick fleshy tissue of their green stems and branches.

Plants have different root systems to anchor them in the soil and to supply water and soil nutrients in areas with different climatic conditions. Some plants, such as grasses and most cacti, have fairly shallow roots with multiple branches that spread out to hold them in the soil and to quickly absorb water in areas

National Park Service

where rainfall is infrequent. Other plants, such as dandelions, oak, hickory, and mesquite trees, have deep roots to anchor them and get moisture from deep underground. Some plants have a combination of shallow and deep roots.

Other land plants survive without having roots extending into the soil. These plants, called **epiphytes**, use their roots to attach themselves to branches high in trees, especially in tropical forests (Figure 4-8). These plants have small seeds that are carried to tree limbs by birds and other animals or by the wind. They include mosses, ferns, lichens, and flowering plants. These flowering plants, sometimes called "air

plants," include various orchids, cacti, and pineapple-shaped bromeliads.

Aquatic plants are also adapted to various environmental conditions. Some live in fresh water (water lilies) and others in saltwater (eelgrass). Some emerge from the water's surface (bulrushes), while others live underwater (kelp). Some aquatic plants found near the shore have leaves, stems, and roots (cattails), and others are rootless and float or drift on the water (water hyacinths and red, brown, and green algae). Some plants maintain their position in rapidly flowing water by being attached to surfaces such as stream bottoms or rocks (mosses).

Figure 4-6 Giant sequoia trees are evergreen conifers found in 75, mostly small, groves along the western slopes of the Sierra Nevada of east central California. Although coastal redwoods can grow taller, giant sequoias are Earth's largest and most massive species. The General Sherman Tree, shown at left, is found in California's Sequoia National Park. This 2,500- to 3,000-year-old tree is about 84 meters (275 feet) high, and the diameter of its trunk is 11 meters (36 feet) — about the size of a large classroom. Notice the relative sizes of the tree and the people near its base. Its bark, which is more than 61 centimeters (2 feet) thick, helps protect it from fire, predators, and disease. Midway up the tree is a single branch that is larger than the typical tree of any species east of the Mississippi River. The average giant sequoia requires at least 1,132 liters (300 gallons) of water a day. The energy involved in the capillary action used to draw this amount of water from the tree's roots to its top leaves equals the energy needed to place a can of soda into a low Earth orbit.

François Gohier/Ardea London

Figure 4-7 These saguaro (pronounced sa-WA-ro) cacti in Arizona are succulent green plants that store water and produce food in the fleshy tissue of their stems and branches. They reduce water loss in the hot desert climate by having no leaves and by having pores (stomata) that open only at night. Their thorns help keep predators away.

Kenneth W. Fink/Ardea Landon

Figure 4-8 The white orchid epiphyte growing in the fork of a tree in this tropical forest in Latin America survives by using its roots to attach itself to the tree rather than soil. Epiphytes use their foliage and root systems to get water from the humid air and falling drops and trap nutrients from bits of organic matter falling from the heavily populated canopy of leaves above. Epiphytes provide many hiding and breeding sites for entire communities of small animals — frogs, birds, rodents, snakes, and insects — some of which live their entire lives in these aerial gardens. In this interaction between the epiphytes and their host tree, the epiphytes gain access to water and other nutrients and the tree is apparently unharmed.

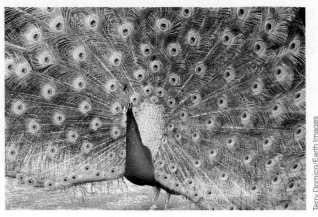

Figure 4-9 This peacock with its courtship display is a vertebrate because it has a backbone. This display can also be used to scare off predators.

Figure 4-10 This cobalt blue sea star found on a barrier coral reef in Indonesia has no backbone and is classified as an invertebrate. Other invertebrates are insects, crabs, jellyfish, sponges, and mollusks.

shrimp, lobsters), mollusks (snails, clams, oysters, octopuses), fishes, amphibians (frogs, toads, salamanders), reptiles (turtles, lizards, alligators, crocodiles, snakes), birds, and mammals (kangaroos, bats, cats, rabbits, elephants, whales, porpoises, monkeys, apes, humans). They get their organic nutrients by feeding on plants (**herbivores**), other animals (**carnivores**), or both (**omnivores**). Some animals, called **vertebrates**, have backbones (Figure 4-9), and others, called **invertebrates**, have no backbones (Figure 4-10). Some are cold blooded (invertebrates, fish, amphibians, and reptiles), and others are warm blooded (birds and mammals).

A **population** is a group of individuals of the same species occupying a given area at the same time (Figure 4-11). The place where a population (or an individual organism) lives is its **habitat**. Examples of populations are all sunfish in a pond, gray squirrels in a forest, white oak trees in a forest, people in a country, or people in the world.

Populations of all species occupying a particular place make up what is called a **community** or **biological community**. What constitutes a community depends on the size of the place on which we wish to focus. For example, we could study an entire forest, a patch of the forest, or a single tree or log as a community.

An **ecosystem** is a community of different species interacting with one another and with the chemical and physical factors making up its nonliving environment. An ecosystem is an ever-changing (dynamic) network of biological, chemical, and physical interactions that sustain a community and allow it to respond to changes in environmental conditions. Like that of a community, the size of an ecosystem is arbitrary and is defined in terms of what system we wish to study. All of Earth's ecosystems together make up the **ecosphere**.

Figure 4-11 Population of monarch butterflies hibernating during winter in Michoacán, Mexico. Each fall, monarchs on the west and east coasts fly south for the winter. Those on the west coast hibernate in a few spots along the coast of southern California, with many of these habitats being threatened by expanding cities. Those on the east coast migrate to the slopes of volcanic mountains near Mexico City, which have been designated as ecological reserves by the Mexican government. Before they become butterflies, the caterpillars of this species eat milkweed, which contains chemicals that poison some of the milkweed's predators, but not monarch caterpillars. These poisons are incorporated into the caterpillar's body, and after metamorphosis, the adult monarch butterfly is foul-tasting and poisonous to some of its predators. The bright colors of the monarch butterfly warn such predators to stay away. Other butterfly species, such as the viceroy, are protected by looking like the monarch butterfly. This protective device is called mimicry.

Large areas of Earth's land (terrestrial) surface have the same general **climate**, the average weather conditions of an area over a long time. The general climate of an area is the primary factor determining the types and abundance of life, especially plants, found in a particu-

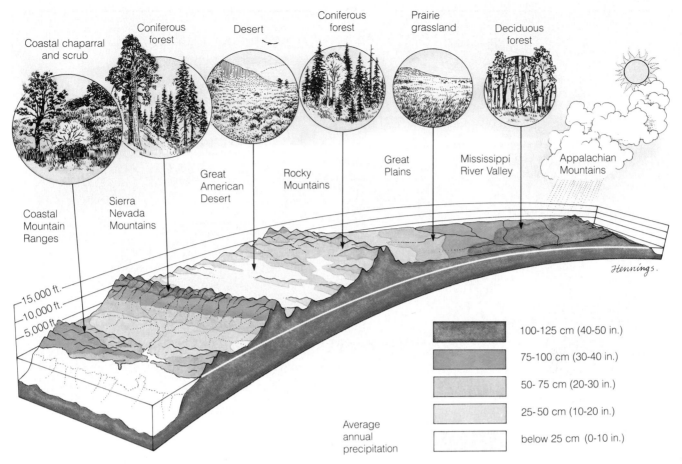

Figure 4-12 Gradual transition from one major biome to another along the 39th parallel crossing the United States. These transitions are caused primarily by changes in climate, which are due mainly to differences in average temperature and average precipitation.

Average annual precipitation

	100-125 cm (40-50 in.)
	75-100 cm (30-40 in.)
	50- 75 cm (20-30 in.)
	25- 50 cm (10-20 in.)
	below 25 cm (0-10 in.)

lar land area. Biologists have divided the terrestrial portion of the biosphere into **biomes**, large ecological regions inhabited by certain types of life, especially vegetation (Figure 4-12).* Examples of these large-scale vegetational zones are forests, deserts, and grasslands.

Each biome consists of large numbers of ecosystems whose communities have adapted to smaller differences in climate, soil, and other environmental factors within the biome. Marine and freshwater portions of the biosphere can also be divided into life zones, each made up of numerous ecosystems. Principal terrestrial and aquatic life zones and ecosystems are discussed in more detail in Chapter 5.

ABIOTIC COMPONENTS OF ECOSYSTEMS Ecosystems consist of various nonliving (abiotic) and living (biotic) components. Figures 4-13 and 4-14 are greatly

simplified diagrams showing a few of the components of ecosystems in a freshwater pond and in a field.

The nonliving, or **abiotic**, components of an ecosystem include various physical and chemical factors. The physical factors having the greatest effect on ecosystems are

- sunlight and shade
- average temperature and temperature range
- average precipitation and its distribution throughout each year
- wind
- latitude (distance from the equator)
- altitude (distance above sea level)
- nature of soil (for terrestrial ecosystems)
- fire (for terrestrial ecosystems)
- water currents (in aquatic ecosystems)
- amount of suspended solid material (for aquatic ecosystems)

---

*Some sources call biomes major terrestrial ecosystems, but most classify them as large life or vegetation zones made up of many different smaller ecosystems.

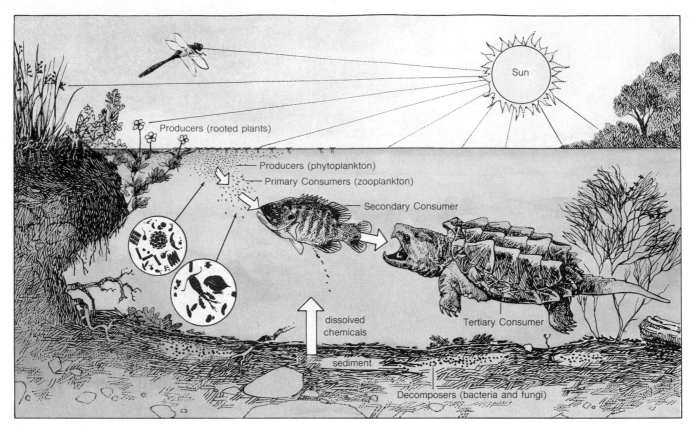

Figure 4-13 Some principal components of a freshwater-pond ecosystem.

Figure 4-14 Some principal components of an ecosystem in a field.

The chemical factors having the greatest effect on ecosystems are

- level of water and air in soil
- level of plant nutrients dissolved in soil moisture in terrestrial ecosystems and in water in aquatic ecosystems
- level of natural or artificial toxic substances dissolved in soil moisture in terrestrial ecosystems and in water in aquatic ecosystems
- salinity of water for aquatic ecosystems
- level of dissolved oxygen in aquatic ecosystems

BIOTIC COMPONENTS OF ECOSYSTEMS Organisms that make up the living, or **biotic**, components of an ecosystem are usually classified as *producers* and *consumers*, based on how they get the food or organic nutrients they need to survive (Figures 4-13 and 4-14).

Producers — sometimes called **autotrophs** (self-feeders) — are organisms that can manufacture the organic compounds they need as nutrients from simple inorganic compounds obtained from their environment. In most terrestrial ecosystems, green plants are the producers. In aquatic ecosystems, most of the producers are phytoplankton, consisting of various species of floating and drifting bacteria and protists. Only producers make their own food. All other organisms are consumers and live, directly or indirectly, on the food provided by producers.

Most producers make the organic nutrients they need through **photosynthesis**. In this complicated process, producers absorb energy from the sun and use it to combine carbon dioxide (which land producers get from the atmosphere and aquatic producers get from water) with water (which they get from the soil or aquatic surroundings) to make carbohydrates (such as glucose) and other organic nutrient compounds. Oxygen gas is given off as a by-product of photosynthesis. Although hundreds of chemical changes take place in sequence during photosynthesis, the overall net chemical change can be summarized as follows:

carbon dioxide + water + **solar energy** $\longrightarrow$ glucose + oxygen

$6\,CO_2 + 6\,H_2O +$ **solar energy** $\longrightarrow C_6H_{12}O_6 + 6\,O_2$

In essence, this complex process converts radiant energy from the sun into chemical energy stored in the chemical bonds that hold glucose and other organic nutrient compounds together. Producers secure other nutrients, including nitrogen and phosphorus, from compounds dissolved in the water they obtain from their environment.

Some producer organisms, mostly specialized bacteria, can extract inorganic compounds from their environment and convert them into organic nutrient compounds without the presence of sunlight. This process is called **chemosynthesis**. For example, in the pitch-dark environment around hydrothermal vents in some parts of the deep ocean, specialized producer bacteria carry out chemosynthesis by converting inorganic hydrogen sulfide to organic nutrients used by the bacteria and organisms feeding on them.

All other organisms in ecosystems are **consumers**, or **heterotrophs** (other-feeders), which cannot synthesize the organic nutrients they need and which get their organic nutrients by feeding on the tissues of producers or of other consumers. There are several classes of consumers, depending on their food sources.

- **Primary consumers** (*herbivores*) feed directly on plants or other producers.
- **Secondary consumers** (*carnivores*) feed only on primary consumers. Most secondary consumers are animals, but some are plants, such as the Venus flytrap, which traps and digests insect prey.
- **Tertiary or higher-level consumers** (*carnivores*) feed only on animal-eating animals.
- **Omnivores** ("everything eaters") can eat both plants and animals. Examples are pigs, rats, foxes, cockroaches, and humans.
- **Detritivores** (decomposers and detritus feeders) live off **detritus**, parts of dead organisms and cast-off fragments and wastes of living organisms (Figure 4-15). **Decomposers** digest detritus by breaking down the complex organic molecules in these materials into simpler, inorganic compounds and absorbing the soluble nutrients. Decomposers consist of various bacteria and fungi (mostly molds and mushrooms) (Figure 4-16). Bacteria and fungi decomposers in turn are an important source of food for organisms such as worms and insects living in the soil and water. **Detritus feeders**, such as crabs, carpenter ants, termites, and earthworms, extract nutrients from partly decomposed particles of organic matter.

The chemical energy stored in glucose and other organic nutrient compounds is used by producers and consumers to drive their life processes. This energy is released by the process of **aerobic respiration**, in which aerobic organisms use oxygen produced in their cells or transferred to their cells from their environment to break down the glucose and organic nutrient compounds they synthesize (producers) or eat (consumers) back into carbon dioxide and water. The hundreds of chemical changes taking place in sequence during this complex process can be summarized by the following overall net chemical change:

glucose + oxygen $\longrightarrow$ carbon dioxide + water + **energy**

$C_6H_{12}O_6 + 6\,O_2 \longrightarrow 6\,CO_2 + 6\,H_2O +$ **energy**

Aerobic respiration (not the same as the breathing process called respiration) is a slow "burning process"

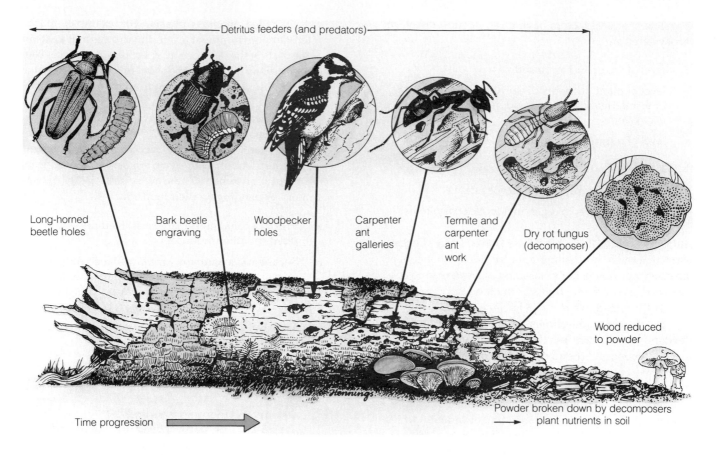

Detritus feeders (and predators)

Long-horned beetle holes

Bark beetle engraving

Woodpecker holes

Carpenter ant galleries

Termite and carpenter ant work

Dry rot fungus (decomposer)

Wood reduced to powder

Powder broken down by decomposers plant nutrients in soil

Time progression

Figure 4-15 Some detritivores, called *detritus feeders*, directly consume fragments of this log. The woodpecker shown in this diagram is not a detritivore. In its search for insects, it pecks out fragments of organic matter that are consumed by detritivores. Other detritivores, called *decomposers* (mostly fungi and bacteria), digest and break down complex organic chemicals in fragments of the log into simpler, inorganic nutrient chemicals, absorbing the soluble nutrients. If these inorganic chemicals are not washed away or otherwise removed from the system, they can be used again as nutrients by producers.

S. Flegler/Visuals Unlimited

Hans Reinhard/Bruce Coleman Ltd.

Figure 4-16 Two types of decomposers are shelf fungi (left) and *Boletus luridus* mushrooms (right).

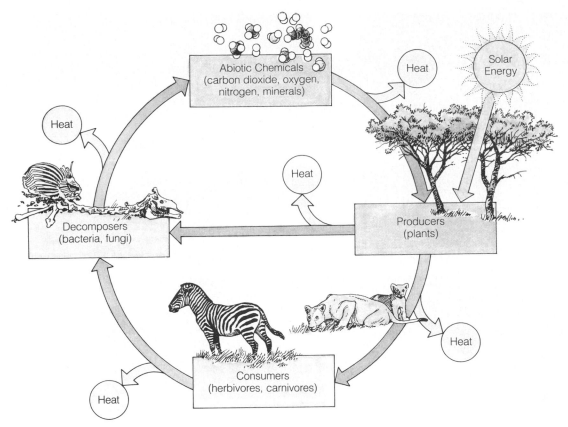

Figure 4-17 The principal structural components (energy, chemicals, and organisms) of an ecosystem are connected through the functions of energy flow and matter recycling. There is a one-way flow of energy from the sun through the living components of an ecosystem and back into the environment as heat. Because of the second energy law, the quality of this energy is degraded as it flows through the ecosystem (Figure 3-13). Nutrients are transferred from one organism to another and modified as needed. Decomposers break down the complex organic matter accumulated in organisms into simpler, inorganic compounds, which may be used by producers to begin the cycle again.

in which oxygen is used to release the energy stored in the chemical bonds of carbohydrates and other organic nutrient compounds. Although the detailed steps in the complex processes of photosynthesis and aerobic respiration differ, the net chemical change for aerobic respiration is the opposite of that for photosynthesis.

The survival of any individual organism depends on *matter flow and energy flow* through its body. However, the community of organisms in an ecosystem survives primarily by a combination of *matter recycling and a one-way flow of energy* (Figure 4-17).

If there were no death in ecosystems, there could be no life, because all organisms, in one way or another, live by the death of organisms. Ecosystems are sustained by this constant cycling of life and death.

Figure 4-17 shows that decomposers are responsible for completing the cycle of matter in this life-and-death cycle by breaking down organic compounds in detritus into inorganic nutrients that can be used by producers. Without decomposers, the entire world would soon be knee-deep in plant litter, dead animal bodies, animal wastes, and garbage. Figure 4-17 also shows that the ecosphere and its ecosystems need only

producers and decomposers to exist. This means that we and all other consumers, except decomposers, are an unnecessary part of the ecosphere.

TOLERANCE RANGES OF SPECIES TO ABIOTIC FACTORS The reason that organisms don't spread everywhere is that populations of species have a particular **range of tolerance** to variations in chemical and physical factors, such as temperature, in their environment (Figure 4-18). Individual organisms within a large population of a species may have slightly different tolerance ranges because of small differences in their genetic makeup, health, and age. For example, it may take a little more heat or a little more of a poisonous chemical to kill one fish or one person than another.

The tolerance range includes an optimum range of values within which populations of a species thrive and operate most efficiently (Figure 4-18). This range also includes values slightly above or below the optimum level of each abiotic factor — values that usually support a smaller population size. When values exceed the upper or lower limits of tolerance, few if any organisms of a particular species survive.

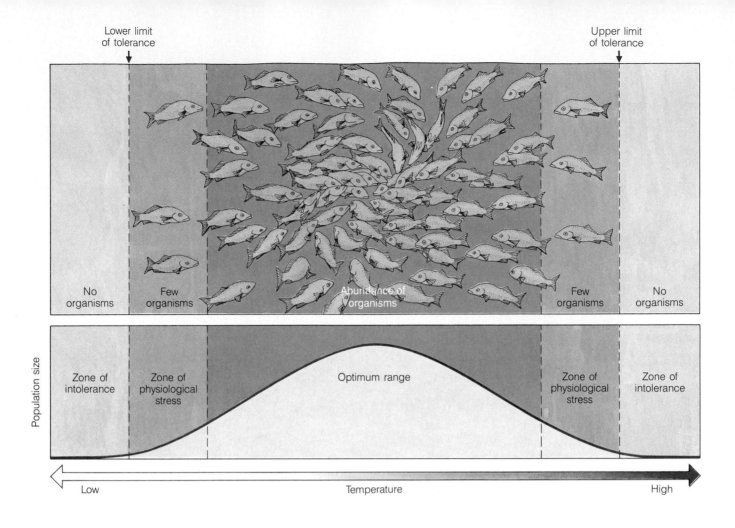

Figure 4-18 Range of tolerance for a population of organisms of the same species to an abiotic environmental factor—in this case, temperature.

These observations are summarized in the **law of tolerance:** *The existence, abundance, and distribution of a species in an ecosystem are determined by whether the levels of one or more physical or chemical factors fall within the range tolerated by the species.* A species may have a wide range of tolerance to some factors and a narrow range of tolerance to others. Most organisms in a species are least tolerant during juvenile or reproductive stages of the life cycle. Highly tolerant species are likely to be able to live in a range of habitats with different conditions.

For example, goldfish can survive in temperatures ranging from about −2°C (28°F) to 34°C (93°F). Neon tetras and angelfish, often kept in an aquarium, will die if the water temperature drops below 16°C (60°F) or so. In contrast, trout will not breed if the water in their streams gets that warm.

Some species can adjust their tolerance to physical factors such as temperature if exposed to gradually changing conditions. For example, you can tolerate a higher water temperature by getting into a tub of fairly hot water and then slowly adding hotter and hotter water.

This adjustment to slowly changing new conditions, or **acclimation**, is a useful protective device. However, there are limits to acclimation and it can be dangerous. With each change, the species comes closer to its limit of tolerance. Suddenly, without any warning signals, the next small change triggers a **threshold effect**, a harmful or even fatal reaction as the tolerance limit is exceeded—much like adding the single straw that breaks an already overloaded camel's back. Acclimation, unlike evolutionary adaptation, cannot be passed on to the next generation.

The threshold effect partly explains why many environmental problems seem to arise suddenly even though they have been building for a long time. For example, one or more tree species in certain forests begin dying in large numbers after prolonged exposure to numerous air pollutants. We usually notice the problem only when entire forests die, as is happening in parts of Europe and North America. By then, we are 10 to 20 years too late to prevent the damage. The threshold effect also explains why we must emphasize input approaches to prevent pollution thresholds from being exceeded.

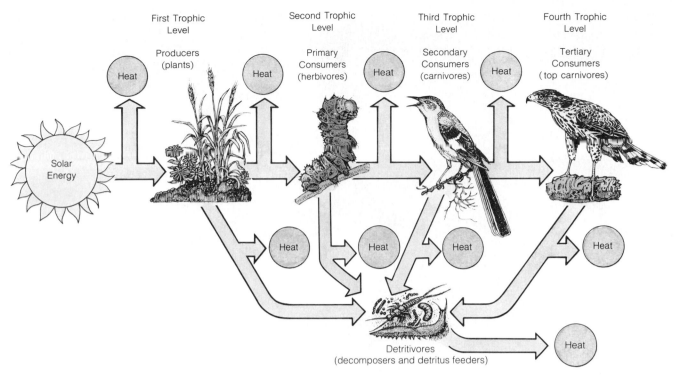

First Trophic Level — Producers (plants) — Heat

Second Trophic Level — Primary Consumers (herbivores) — Heat

Third Trophic Level — Secondary Consumers (carnivores) — Heat

Fourth Trophic Level — Tertiary Consumers (top carnivores) — Heat

Solar Energy

Heat · Heat · Heat · Heat · Heat

Detritivores (decomposers and detritus feeders) — Heat

Figure 4-19 A food chain. The arrows show how chemical energy in food flows through various trophic levels, with most of the high-quality chemical energy being degraded to low-quality heat in accordance with the second law of energy.

LIMITING FACTORS IN ECOSYSTEMS Another ecological principle related to the law of tolerance is the **limiting factor principle:** *Too much or too little of any abiotic factor can limit or prevent growth of a population of a species in an ecosystem even if all other factors are at or near the optimum range of tolerance for the species.* A single factor found to be limiting the population growth of a species in an ecosystem is called the **limiting factor**.

Examples of limiting factors in biomes and terrestrial ecosystems are temperature, water, light, and soil nutrients. For example, suppose a farmer plants corn in a field where the soil has too little phosphorus. Even if the corn's needs for water, nitrogen, potassium, and other nutrients are met, the corn will stop growing when it has used up the available phosphorus. In this case, availability of phosphorus is the limiting factor that determines how much corn will grow in the field. Growth can also be limited by the presence of too much of a particular abiotic factor. For example, plants can be killed by too much water or by too much fertilizer.

In aquatic ecosystems, **salinity** (the amounts of various salts dissolved in a given volume of water) is a limiting factor. It determines the species found in marine ecosystems, such as oceans, and in freshwater ecosystems, such as streams and lakes. Aquatic ecosystems can also be divided into surface, middle, and bottom layers or life zones. Three important limiting factors determining the numbers and types of organisms found in these different layers are temperature,

sunlight, and **dissolved oxygen content** (the amount of oxygen gas dissolved in a given volume of water at a particular temperature and pressure).

4-3   Energy Flow in Ecosystems

FOOD CHAINS AND FOOD WEBS *There is no waste in functioning natural ecosystems.* All organisms, dead or alive, are potential sources of food for other organisms. A caterpillar eats a leaf; a robin eats the caterpillar; a hawk eats the robin. When the plant, caterpillar, robin, and hawk die, they are in turn consumed by decomposers.

The general sequence of who eats or decomposes whom in an ecosystem is called a **food chain** (Figure 4-19). These relationships show how energy is transferred from one organism to another as it flows through an ecosystem.

Ecologists assign every organism in an ecosystem to a **trophic**, or feeding, **level** (from the Greek *trophos,* "nourishment"), depending on whether it is a producer or a consumer and depending on what it eats or decomposes (Figure 4-19). Producers belong to the first trophic level; primary consumers, whether feeding on living or dead producers, belong to the second trophic level; secondary consumers (meat eaters) are assigned to the

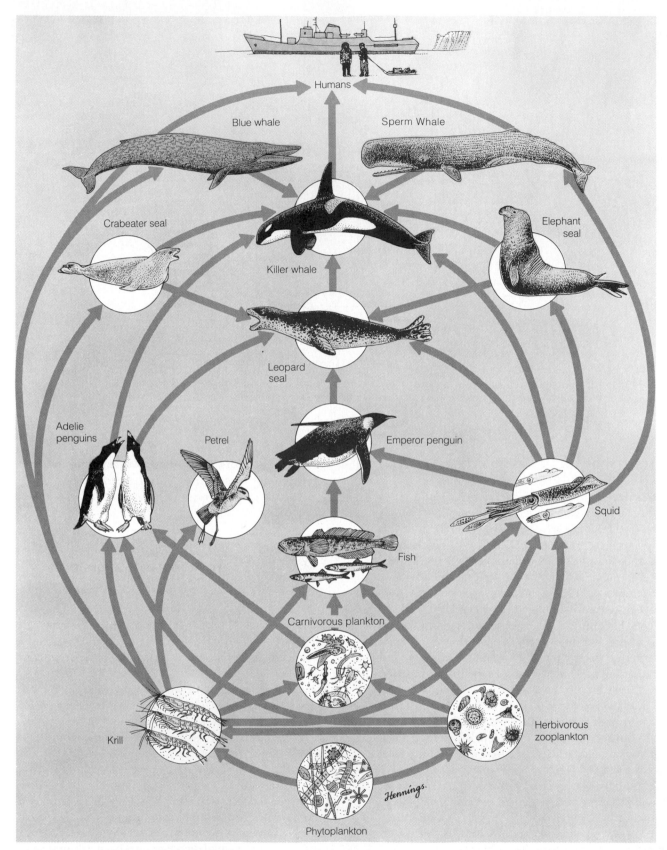

Figure 4-20 Greatly simplified food web in the Antarctic. There are many more participants, including an array of decomposer organisms.

third trophic level, and so on. A special class of consumers, detritivores, obtains energy and materials from detritus accumulated from all trophic levels.

You will have a hard time finding simple food chains like the one shown in Figure 4-19 in ecosystems. Most consumers feed on two or more types of organisms and, in turn, are fed on by several other types of organisms. Some animals feed at several trophic levels. This means that the organisms in most ecosystems are involved in a complex network of many interlinked feeding relationships, called a **food web**. A simplified food web in the Antarctic is diagrammed in Figure 4-20. Trophic levels can be assigned in food webs just as in food chains.

ENERGY FLOW PYRAMIDS **Biomass** is the organic matter produced by plants and other photosynthetic producers. Large amounts of high-quality chemical energy are stored in the chemical bonds holding the organic compounds in biomass together. This potential energy can be released when this organic matter is broken down by aerobic respiration in the cells of organisms. In a food chain or web, biomass is transferred from one trophic level to another.

A food chain or web begins by transferring some of the biomass created by producers to primary consumers. Before it is transferred, some of this biomass is broken down and used by the producers, with some of the energy released as heat to the environment. This means that the amount of high-quality energy available to primary consumers is less than that available to the producers. Also, some of the biomass available to organisms at the next trophic level is not eaten or is not digested or absorbed.

An additional loss of high-quality energy in biomass occurs at each successive trophic level. This reduction in high-quality energy available to organisms at each successive trophic level in a food chain or web is mostly the result of the inevitable energy-quality tax imposed by the second law of energy.

The percentage of available high-quality energy transferred from one trophic level to another varies from 5% to 20%, depending on the types of species involved and the ecosystem in which the transfer takes place. The pyramid-shaped diagram in Figure 4-21 illustrates this loss of usable high-quality energy at each step in a simple food chain, assuming a 90% loss in usable energy with each transfer from one trophic level

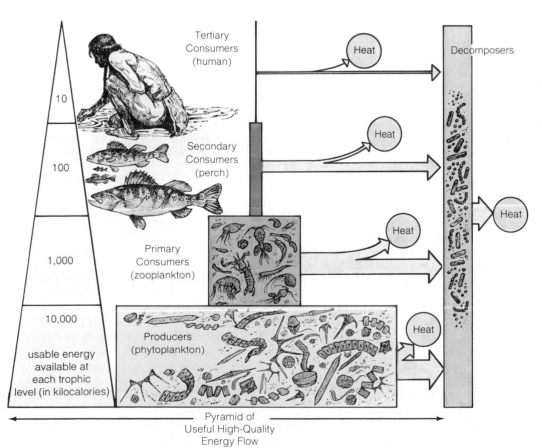

Figure 4-21 Generalized pyramid of energy flow, showing the decrease in usable high-quality energy available at each succeeding trophic level in a food chain or web. In this diagram, it is assumed that there is a 90% loss in usable energy with each transfer from one trophic level to another. In nature, such losses vary from 80% to 95%.

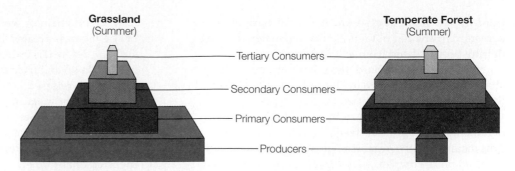

Figure 4-22 Generalized pyramids of numbers in ecosystems. Pyramids of numbers for a grassland and many other ecosystems taper off in going from the producer level to the higher trophic levels (left). For some ecosystems, however, the number pyramids have different shapes and can take an inverted form (right). For example, a redwood forest has a small number of large producers (the trees) that support a much larger number of small primary consumers (insects) that feed on the trees.

to another. The **pyramid of energy flow** in Figure 4-21 shows that the greater the number of trophic levels or steps in a food chain or web, the greater the cumulative loss of usable high-quality energy.

The energy flow pyramid explains why a larger population of people can be supported if people eat at lower trophic levels by consuming grains directly (for example, rice → human) rather than eating animals that feed on grains (grain → steer → human).

PYRAMIDS OF NUMBERS AND BIOMASS We can collect samples of organisms in ecosystems and count the number of each type found at each trophic level. This information can then be used to construct **pyramids of numbers** for ecosystems (Figure 4-22). For example, a million phytoplankton in a small pond may support 10,000 zooplankton, which in turn may support 100 perch, which might feed 1 person for a month or so.

Each trophic level in a food chain or web contains a certain amount of biomass, the dried weight of all organic matter contained in its organisms. This can be estimated by harvesting several randomly selected patches or narrow strips in an ecosystem. The organisms in the samples are then sorted according to known trophic levels, dried, and weighed. These data are then used to plot a **pyramid of biomass** for the ecosystem (Figure 4-23).

PRODUCTIVITY OF PRODUCERS The *rate* at which an ecosystem's producers capture and store a given amount of chemical energy as biomass in a given length of time is called the ecosystem's **primary productivity**. The actual amount of energy depends on the balance between the rate at which biomass is produced by an ecosystem's producers and the rate at which the producers use some of this biomass (usually by aerobic

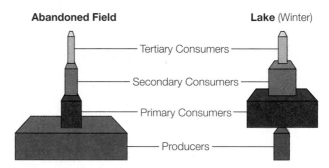

Figure 4-23 Generalized pyramids of biomass in ecosystems. The size of each tier represents the dry weight per square meter of all organisms at that trophic level. For most land ecosystems, the total biomass at each successive trophic level of a food chain or web usually decreases. This yields a pyramid of biomass with a large base of producers, topped by a series of increasingly smaller trophic levels of consumers (left). In aquatic ecosystems, the pyramid of biomass can be upside down, with the biomass of consumers exceeding that of producers (right). In aquatic ecosystems, the producers are microscopic phytoplankton that grow and reproduce rapidly, not large plants that grow and reproduce slowly.

respiration) to stay alive. The difference in these two rates is an ecosystem's **net primary productivity**.

| net primary productivity | = rate at which producers produce chemical energy stored in biomass through photosynthesis | − rate at which producers use chemical energy stored in their biomass through aerobic respiration |

Net primary productivity is usually reported as the energy output of a specified area of producers over a given period of time (Figures 4-24 and 4-25).

Type of Ecosystem

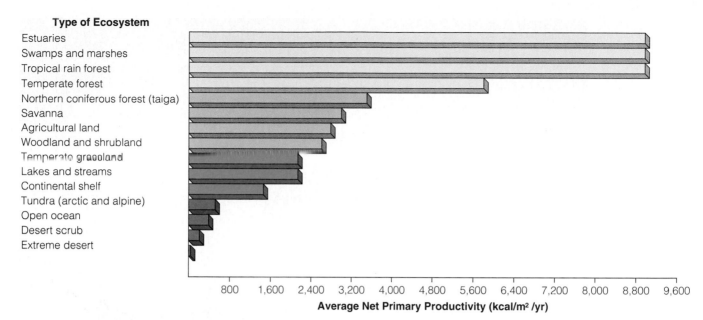

Estuaries
Swamps and marshes
Tropical rain forest
Temperate forest
Northern coniferous forest (taiga)
Savanna
Agricultural land
Woodland and shrubland
Temperate grassland
Lakes and streams
Continental shelf
Tundra (arctic and alpine)
Open ocean
Desert scrub
Extreme desert

800   1,600   2,400   3,200   4,000   4,800   5,600   6,400   7,200   8,000   8,800   9,600

Average Net Primary Productivity (kcal/m² /yr)

Figure 4-24 Estimated annual average net productivity of producers per unit of area in principal types of life zones and ecosystems. Values are given in kilocalories of energy produced per square meter per year.

Type of Ecosystem

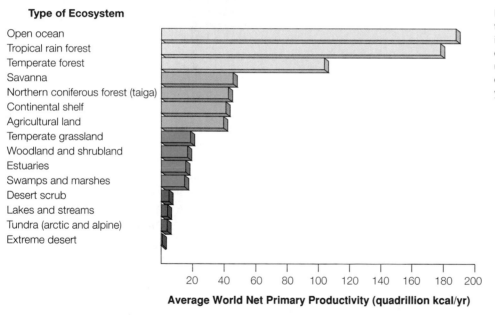

Open ocean
Tropical rain forest
Temperate forest
Savanna
Northern coniferous forest (taiga)
Continental shelf
Agricultural land
Temperate grassland
Woodland and shrubland
Estuaries
Swamps and marshes
Desert scrub
Lakes and streams
Tundra (arctic and alpine)
Extreme desert

20   40   60   80   100   120   140   160   180   200

Average World Net Primary Productivity (quadrillion kcal/yr)

Figure 4-25 Estimated annual total world net primary productivity of producers in principal types of life zones and ecosystems. Values are given in billions of kilocalories of energy produced per year.

Net primary productivity can be thought of as the basic food source or "income" of the consumers in an ecosystem. Ecologists have estimated the average annual net primary production per square meter of producers for the principal terrestrial and aquatic ecosystems. Figure 4-24 shows that ecosystems with the highest average net primary productivities are estuaries, swamps and marshes, and tropical rain forests;

the lowest are tundra (arctic grasslands), open ocean, and desert.

You might conclude that we should clear tropical forests to grow crops and that we should harvest plants growing in estuaries, swamps, and marshes to help feed the growing human population. That conclusion would be incorrect. One reason is that the plants — mostly grasses — in estuaries, swamps, and marshes

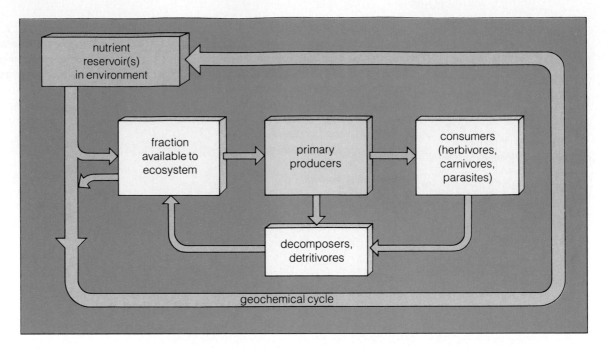

Figure 4-26 Generalized model of nutrient cycling in a mature ecosystem. Nutrients move from the environment, through organisms, and back to the environment in biogeochemical cycles. Some nutrients are lost in mature ecosystems, but most are recycled. Younger, developing ecosystems gain many of their nutrients from other ecosystems and lose many of their nutrients to other ecosystems. (Used by permission from Cecie Starr, *Biology: Concepts and Applications*, Belmont, Calif.: Wadsworth, 1991)

cannot be eaten by people, though they are extremely important as food sources and spawning areas for fish, shrimp, and other forms of aquatic life that provide us and other consumers with protein. So we should protect, not harvest or destroy, these plants.

In tropical forests, most of the nutrients are stored in the trees and other vegetation rather than in the soil. When the trees are cleared, the low levels of nutrients in the exposed soil are rapidly depleted by frequent rains and by growing crops. Thus, food crops can be grown only for a short time without enormous, expensive inputs of commercial fertilizers. So we should protect, not cut down, these forests.

Figure 4-25 shows the total world net primary productivity of producers per year for principal types of ecosystems. An estimated 59% of Earth's annual net primary productivity takes place on land and the remaining 41% in oceans and other aquatic systems. Because their total area is small, estuaries are low on the list. On the other hand, because about 71% of the world's surface is covered by oceans, the world's open-ocean ecosystems head the list.

This can be misleading. The world's net primary productivity is high for oceans because they cover so much of the globe, not because they have a high average

productivity per square meter of producers per year. Also, harvesting widely dispersed algae and seaweeds from the ocean requires enormous amounts of energy — more than the chemical energy available from the food that would be harvested.

We are already consuming, diverting, and wasting about 27% of the world's potential net primary productivity and about 40% of that produced on land. What will happen if we double the human population within the next 40 years?

4-4 Matter Cycling in Ecosystems

BIOGEOCHEMICAL CYCLES Nutrients, the chemicals essential for life, are cycled in the ecosphere (Figure 4-4) and in mature ecosystems in biogeochemical cycles (Figure 4-26). In these cycles, nutrients move from the environment, through organisms, and back to the environment. All are driven, directly or indirectly, by energy from the sun and by gravity.

There are three types of interconnected biogeochemical cycles. In *gaseous cycles*, nutrients circulate

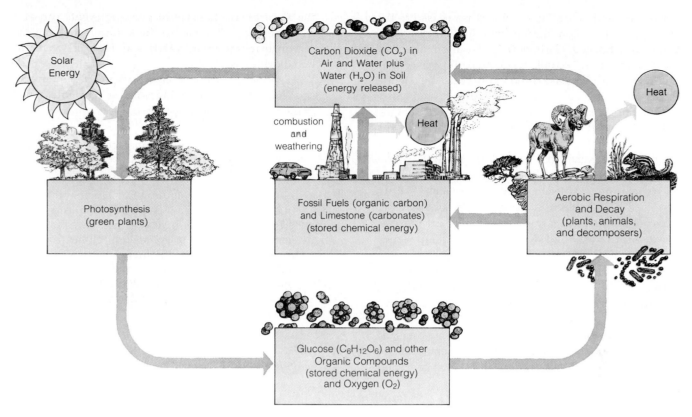

Figure 4-27 Simplified diagram of a portion of the gaseous carbon cycle, showing matter cycling and one-way energy flow through the processes of photosynthesis and aerobic respiration. Photosynthesis takes in carbon dioxide and releases oxygen, and aerobic respiration takes in oxygen and releases carbon dioxide. This cyclical movement of matter through ecosystems and the ecosphere is also an important part of the oxygen and hydrogen cycles.

mostly among the atmosphere, the hydrosphere (water), and living organisms. In most of these cycles, elements are recycled rapidly, often within hours or days. The principal gaseous cycles are the carbon, oxygen, hydrogen, and nitrogen cycles.

In *sedimentary cycles*, nutrients circulate mostly among the earth's crust (soil, rocks, and sediments on land and on the seafloor), the hydrosphere, and living organisms. Elements in these cycles are usually recycled much more slowly than those in atmospheric cycles because the elements are tied up in sedimentary rocks for long periods of time, often thousands to millions of years, and some don't have a gaseous phase. Phosphorus and sulfur are two of the 36 or so elements recycled in this manner. In the *hydrologic cycle*, water circulates among the ocean, the air, the land, and living organisms. This cycle also distributes heat from the sun over the planet's surface.

CARBON CYCLE Carbon is the basic building block of the carbohydrates, fats, proteins, nucleic acids such as DNA and RNA, and other organic compounds necessary for life. The carbon cycle is based on carbon dioxide gas, which makes up only about 0.03% by volume of the troposphere and is also dissolved in water.

Producers absorb carbon dioxide from the atmosphere (terrestrial producers) or water (aquatic producers) and use *photosynthesis* to convert the carbon in carbon dioxide into carbon in complex organic compounds such as glucose. Then the cells in oxygen-consuming producers and consumers carry out *aerobic respiration*, which breaks down glucose and other complex organic compounds and converts the carbon back to carbon dioxide in the atmosphere or water for reuse by producers. Photosynthesis takes place during the day shift, when sunlight is available. Aerobic respiration takes place during the day shift and the night shift.

This linkage between photosynthesis in producers and aerobic respiration in producers and consumers circulates carbon in the ecosphere and is an important part of the global carbon cycle (Figure 4-27). Oxygen and hydrogen, the other elements in glucose and other organic nutrients, cycle almost in step with carbon. Each year, about half of the carbon entering the atmosphere (as CO_2) is taken up by producers (as biomass) and the oceans.

Figure 4-28 shows other parts of the global carbon cycle in terrestrial ecosystems and marine ecosystems. It reveals that some of Earth's carbon is tied up deep in the earth for long periods in fossil fuels—mostly coal, petroleum, and natural gas—until it is released to the atmosphere as carbon dioxide when fossil fuels are extracted and burned. Carbon dioxide is also released to the atmosphere by aerobic respiration and by volcanic eruptions, which release carbon from rocks deep in the earth's crust.

Carbon dioxide gas is readily soluble in water. Some of this dissolved CO_2 remains in the sea, and some is removed by photosynthesizing producers. The warmer the water, the greater the amount of dissolved carbon dioxide and oxygen gases returning to the atmosphere.

In marine ecosystems, some organisms take up dissolved CO_2 molecules or carbonate ions (CO_3^{2-}) from ocean water and form slightly soluble calcium carbonate ($CaCO_3$) to build shells and rocks and the skeletons of marine organisms from tiny protozoans to corals. When the shelled organisms die, tiny particles of their shells and bone fall slowly to the ocean depths and are buried over eons of time in bottom sediments (Figure 4-28).

Carbon in these deep ocean sediments reenters the cycle very slowly when some of the sediments dissolve and form dissolved carbon dioxide gas that can enter the atmosphere. Long-term geologic events can also bring bottom sediments to the surface, exposing the carbonate rock to chemical attack and conversion to carbon dioxide gas.

Especially since 1950, as world population and resource use have increased rapidly, we have intervened in the carbon cycle mainly in two ways:

- Removal of forests and other vegetation without sufficient replanting, which leaves less vegetation to absorb CO_2.

- Burning carbon-containing fossil fuels and burning wood faster than it is regrown (Figure 4-28). This produces carbon dioxide that flows into the atmosphere. Some scientists project that this carbon dioxide, along with other chemicals we are adding to the atmosphere, could enhance Earth's natural greenhouse effect, alter climate patterns, and disrupt global food production and wildlife habitats.

NITROGEN CYCLE   Organisms require nitrogen in various chemical forms to synthesize proteins, nucleic

Figure 4-28   Simplified diagram of the global gaseous carbon cycle. The left portion shows the movement of carbon through marine ecosystems, and the right portion its movement through terrestrial ecosystems. (Used by permission from Cecie Starr, *Biology: Concepts and Applications*, Belmont, Calif.: Wadsworth, 1991)

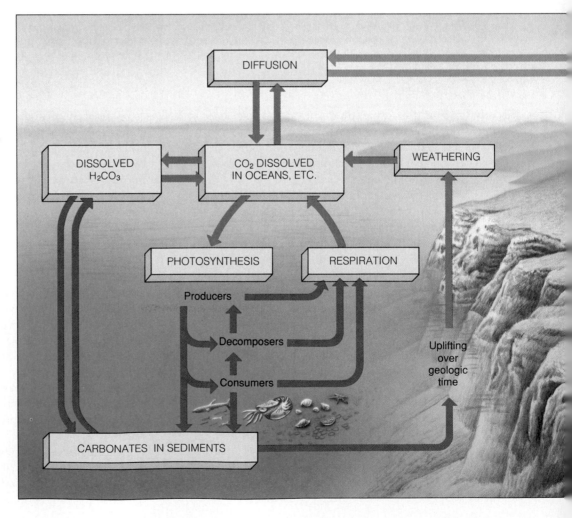

acids such as DNA and RNA, and other nitrogen-containing organic compounds. Earth's largest reservoir of nitrogen is the troposphere, with about 78% of its volume made up of nitrogen gas (N_2).

This abundant form of nitrogen, however, cannot be used directly as a nutrient by multicellular plants or animals. Fortunately, nitrogen gas is converted into water-soluble ionic compounds containing nitrate ions (NO_3^-) and ammonium ions (NH_4^+), which are taken up by plant roots as part of the **nitrogen cycle**. This gaseous cycle is shown in simplified form in Figure 4-29.

The conversion of atmospheric nitrogen gas into other chemical forms useful to plants is called **nitrogen fixation**. It is carried out mostly by certain kinds of bacteria (mostly cyanobacteria) in soil and water and by rhizobium bacteria living in small swellings, called nodules, on the roots of alfalfa, clover, peas, beans, and other legume plants (Figure 4-30). Lightning also plays a role in nitrogen fixation by converting nitrogen gas and oxygen gas in the atmosphere into nitric oxide (NO). Some of this gas combines with oxygen in the atmosphere to form nitrogen dioxide (NO_2). These gases react with water vapor in the atmosphere and are converted into nitrate ions that return to Earth as nitric acid (HNO_3) dissolved in precipitation and as particles of solid nitrate compounds.

Plants convert inorganic nitrate ions and ammonium ions obtained from soil water into proteins, DNA, and other large, nitrogen-containing organic compounds they require. Animals get their nitrogen-containing nutrients by eating plants or other animals that have eaten plants.

After nitrogen has served its purpose in living organisms, armies of specialized decomposer bacteria convert the nitrogen-containing organic compounds found in the wastes, cast-off particles, and dead bodies of organisms into simpler inorganic compounds, such as ammonia gas (NH_3) and water-soluble salts containing ammonium ions (NH_4^+). Other specialized groups of bacteria then convert these inorganic forms of nitrogen back into nitrite (NO_2^-) and nitrate (NO_3^-) ions in the soil and then into nitrogen gas, which is released to the atmosphere to begin the cycle again.

Despite this cycling of nitrogen, soil nitrogen needed by plants is often scarce. The fact that ammonium, nitrate, and nitrite ions are soluble in water

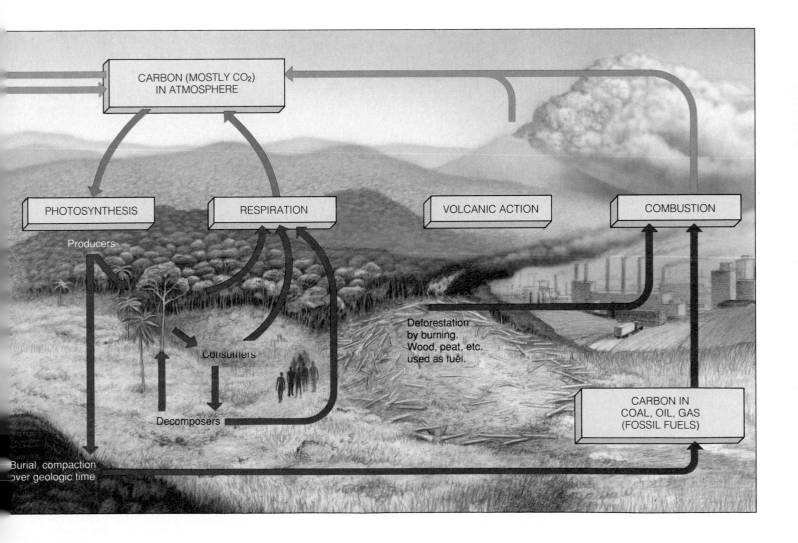

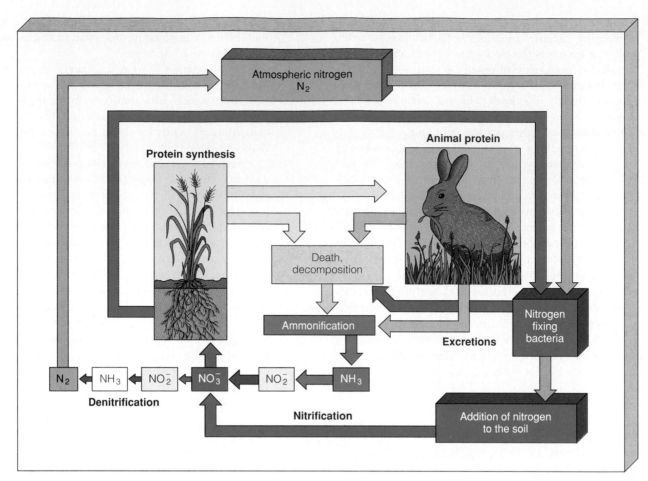

Figure 4-29 Simplified diagram of the gaseous nitrogen cycle. (Used by permission from Carolina Biological Supply Company)

Figure 4-30 Plants in the legume family have root nodules where rhizobium bacteria fix nitrogen by converting nitrogen (N_2) in the atmosphere into ammonia (NH_3), which in soil water forms ammonium ions (NH_4^+) that are taken up by the roots of plants. This mutualistic interaction between these plants and bacteria benefits both species. The bacteria capture atmospheric nitrogen and convert it into a form usable by the plants, and the legume provides the bacteria with sugar.

means they can be taken up by plant roots, but it also means they can be leached deep into the soil. Also, some of this soil nitrogen is converted back to N_2 gases by bacteria. Some is also transferred from one ecosystem to another by erosion caused by wind or flowing water. In addition, crops take up soil nitrogen, which is lost when the crops are harvested.

Nitrogen is also scarce near the surface waters of the open ocean and deep lakes because most of it is in bottom sediments. This explains why the highest net primary productivity per area of producers in the oceans is in shallow estuaries, where nitrogen and other bottom nutrients are readily available (Figure 4-24) or where ocean currents sweep nutrients up from the bottom (upwellings).

We intervene in the nitrogen cycle in several ways:

- Emission of large quantities of nitric oxide into the atmosphere when wood or any fuel is burned. Most of this NO is produced when nitrogen and oxygen molecules in the air combine

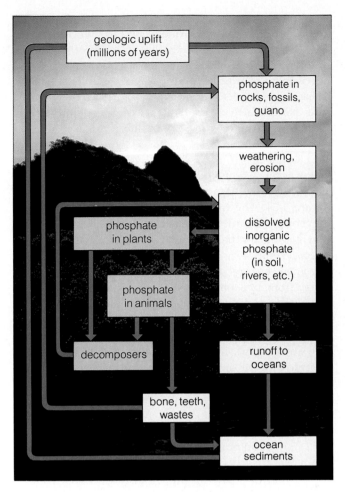

Figure 4-31 Simplified diagram of the sedimentary phosphorus cycle. (Used by permission from Cecie Starr, *Biology: The Unity and Diversity of Life*, 5th ed., Belmont, Calif.: Wadsworth, 1989)

at the high temperatures involved when fuels are burned in air. The nitric oxide then combines with oxygen gas in the atmosphere to form nitrogen dioxide (NO_2) gas, which can react with water vapor in the atmosphere to form nitric acid (HNO_3). This acid is a component of acid deposition, which is damaging trees and killing fish in parts of the world.

- Emission of the heat-trapping gas nitrous oxide (N_2O) into the atmosphere by the action of certain bacteria on commercial inorganic fertilizers and livestock wastes.

- Mining mineral deposits of compounds containing nitrate and ammonium ions for use as commercial inorganic fertilizers.

- Depleting nitrate ions and ammonium ions from soil by harvesting nitrogen-rich crops.

- Adding excess nitrate ions and ammonium ions to aquatic ecosystems in runoff of animal wastes from livestock feedlots, runoff of commercial ni-

trate fertilizers from cropland, and discharge of untreated and treated municipal sewage. This excess supply of plant nutrients stimulates rapid growth of algae and other aquatic plants. The breakdown of dead algae by aerobic decomposers depletes the water of dissolved oxygen gas, killing great numbers of fish.

PHOSPHORUS CYCLE Phosphorus, mainly in the form of certain types of phosphate ions (PO_4^{3-} and HPO_4^{2-}), is an essential nutrient of both plants and animals. It is a part of DNA molecules, which carry genetic information; ATP and ADP molecules, which store chemical energy for use by organisms in cellular respiration; certain fats in the membranes that encase plant and animal cells; and bones and teeth in animals.

Various forms of phosphorus are cycled mostly through the water, Earth's crust, and living organisms by the sedimentary **phosphorus cycle**, shown in simplified form in Figure 4-31. In this cycle, phosphorus moves slowly from phosphate deposits on land and shallow ocean sediments to living organisms and back to the land and ocean. Bacteria are less important in the phosphorus cycle than in the nitrogen cycle.

Phosphorus released by the slow breakdown, or weathering, of phosphate rock deposits is dissolved in soil water and taken up by plant roots. Wind can also transport phosphate particles long distances. Most soils contain only small amounts of phosphorus because phosphate compounds are only slightly soluble in water and are found in few kinds of rocks. Thus, phosphorus is the limiting factor for plant growth in many soils and aquatic ecosystems.

Animals get their phosphorus by eating producers or by eating animals that have eaten producers. Animal wastes and the decay products of dead animals and producers return much of this phosphorus to the soil, to streams, and eventually to the ocean bottom as deposits of slightly soluble phosphate rock.

Some phosphate is returned to the land as guano — the phosphate-rich manure produced by fish-eating birds such as pelicans, gannets, and cormorants. This return is small, though, compared with the much larger amounts of phosphate transferred from the land to the oceans each year by natural processes and human activities.

Over millions of years, geologic processes may push up and expose the seafloor. Weathering then slowly releases phosphorus from the exposed rocks and allows the cycle to begin again.

We intervene in the phosphorus cycle chiefly in two ways:

- Mining large quantities of phosphate rock (Figure 4-32) to produce commercial inorganic fertilizers and detergent compounds.

Figure 4-32 Surface mining of phosphate rock in Illinois. Because phosphorus is recycled so slowly to the land, it is the principal plant nutrient likely to be in short supply for use as a commercial fertilizer to grow more food for the world's rapidly increasing population.

- Adding excess phosphate ions to aquatic ecosystems in runoff of animal wastes from livestock feedlots, runoff of commercial phosphate fertilizers from cropland, and discharge of untreated and treated municipal sewage. As with nitrate and ammonium ions, an excessive supply of this nutrient causes explosive growth of cyanobacteria, algae, and various aquatic plants that disrupt life in aquatic ecosystems.

SULFUR CYCLE   Sulfur is transformed into various compounds and circulated through the ecosphere in the mostly sedimentary **sulfur cycle** (Figure 4-33). It enters the atmosphere from natural sources as

- hydrogen sulfide (H_2S), a colorless, highly poisonous gas with a rotten-egg smell, from active volcanoes and the decay of organic matter in swamps, bogs, and tidal flats by anaerobic decomposers

- sulfur dioxide (SO_2), a colorless, suffocating gas, from active volcanoes

- particles of sulfate (SO_4^{2-}) salts, such as ammonium sulfate, from sea spray

About one-third of all sulfur compounds and 99% percent of the sulfur dioxide reaching the atmosphere from all sources come from human activities. Burning sulfur-containing coal and oil to produce electric power accounts for about two-thirds of the human-related input of sulfur dioxide into the atmosphere. The remaining third comes from industrial processes such as petroleum refining and the conversion (smelting) of sulfur compounds of metallic minerals into free metals such as copper, lead, and zinc.

In the atmosphere, sulfur dioxide reacts with oxygen to produce sulfur trioxide gas (SO_3), which reacts with water vapor to produce tiny droplets of sulfuric acid (H_2SO_4). It also reacts with other chemicals in the atmosphere to produce tiny particles of sulfate salts. These droplets of sulfuric acid and particles of sulfate salts fall to Earth as components of acid deposition, which can harm trees and aquatic life.

HYDROLOGIC CYCLE   The **hydrologic cycle**, or **water cycle**, which collects, purifies, and distributes Earth's fixed supply of water, is shown simplified in Figure 4-34. The hydrologic cycle is linked with the other biogeochemical cycles, because water is an important medium for the movement of nutrients into and out of ecosystems.

Solar energy and gravity continuously convert water from one physical state to another and move water among the ocean, the air, the land, and living organisms. The main processes in this water recycling and purifying cycle are *evaporation* (conversion of water into water vapor), *condensation* (conversion of water vapor into droplets of liquid water), *transpiration* (the process in which water is absorbed by the root systems of plants and passes through pores [stomata] in their leaves or other parts and then evaporates into the atmosphere as water vapor), *precipitation* (dew, rain, sleet, hail, snow), and *runoff* back to the sea to begin the cycle again.

Incoming solar energy evaporates water from oceans, streams, lakes, soil, and vegetation into the atmosphere. Winds and air masses transport this water vapor over various parts of Earth's surface. Decreases in temperature in parts of the atmosphere cause the water vapor to condense and form tiny droplets of water in the form of clouds or fog. Eventually these droplets combine and become heavy enough to fall to the land and into bodies of water as precipitation.

Some of the fresh water returning to Earth's surface as precipitation becomes locked in glaciers. Much of it collects in puddles and ditches and runs off into nearby lakes and into streams, which carry water back to the oceans, completing the cycle. This runoff of surface water from the land helps replenish streams and lakes and also causes soil erosion, which moves various chemicals through portions of other biogeochemical cycles.

A large portion of the water returning to the land seeps into or infiltrates surface soil layers, and some percolates downward into the ground. There it is stored as groundwater in the pores and cracks of rocks. This underground water, like surface water, flows downhill and seeps out into streams and lakes or comes out in springs. Eventually, this water, like surface water, evaporates or reaches the sea to begin the cycle again. The average rate of circulation of underground water in the hydrologic cycle is extremely slow (hundreds of years)

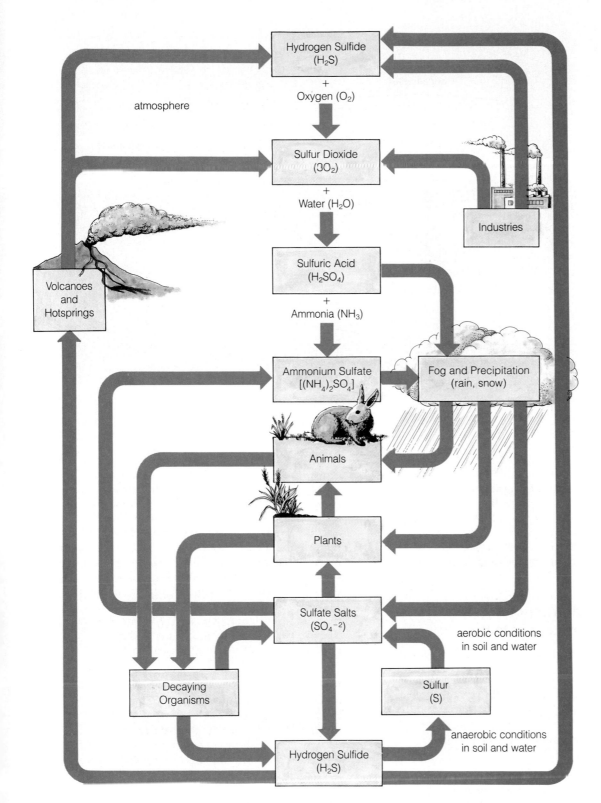

Figure 4-33 Simplified diagram of the mostly sedimentary sulfur cycle. This cycle also has a shorter, less pronounced gaseous phase.

Hydrogen Sulfide (H_2S)
+
Oxygen (O_2)

atmosphere

Sulfur Dioxide (SO_2)
+
Water (H_2O)

Industries

Volcanoes and Hotsprings

Sulfuric Acid (H_2SO_4)
+
Ammonia (NH_3)

Ammonium Sulfate $[(NH_4)_2SO_4]$

Fog and Precipitation (rain, snow)

Animals

Plants

Sulfate Salts (SO_4^{-2})

aerobic conditions in soil and water

Decaying Organisms

Sulfur (S)

Hydrogen Sulfide (H_2S)

anaerobic conditions in soil and water

compared with that on the surface (10 to 120 days) and in the atmosphere (10 to 12 days).

In some cases, nutrients are transported when they dissolve in flowing water. In other cases, slightly soluble or insoluble nutrient compounds in the soil or on the seafloor are moved from one place to another by the flow of water.

We intervene in the water cycle in two main ways:

■ Withdrawing large quantities of fresh water from streams, lakes, and aquifers. In heavily populated or heavily irrigated areas, withdrawals have led to groundwater depletion or intrusion of ocean salt water into underground water supplies.

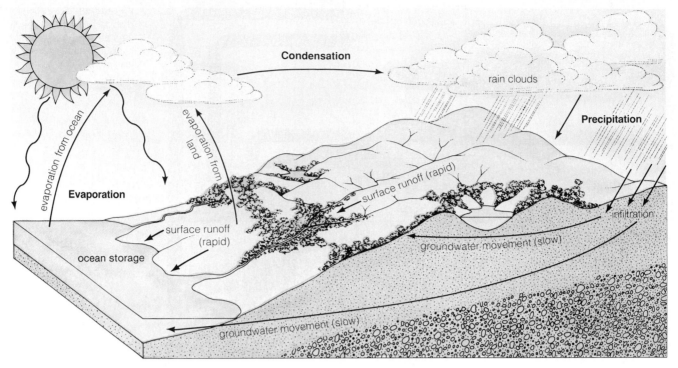

Figure 4-34 Simplified diagram of the hydrologic cycle.

- Clearing vegetation from land for agriculture, mining, roads, parking lots, construction, and other activities. This reduces seepage that recharges groundwater supplies, increases the risk of flooding, and increases the rate of surface runoff, which increases soil erosion and landslides.

4-5 Roles and Interactions of Species in Ecosystems

TYPES OF SPECIES FOUND IN ECOSYSTEMS If you observe various ecosystems you will find that they can have four types of species:

- **Native species**, which normally live and thrive in a particular ecosystem.

- **Immigrant**, or **alien species**, which migrate into an ecosystem or which are deliberately or accidently introduced into an ecosystem by humans. Some of these species are beneficial, while others can take over and eliminate many native species.

- **Indicator species**, which serve as early warnings that a community or an ecosystem is being degraded. For example, the present decline of migratory, insect-eating songbirds in North America indicates a loss of habitat in their summer homes in North America and in their winter homes in

the rapidly disappearing tropical forests in Latin America and the Caribbean Islands. Some indicator species, such as the brown pelican (Figure 2-7) and the American bald eagle (Figure 2-10), feed at high trophic levels in food chains and webs. This makes them vulnerable to high levels of fat-soluble toxic chemicals such as DDT, whose concentrations are increased in the tissues of organisms at each successive trophic level. Some species of frogs, toads, salamanders, and other amphibians that live part of their lives in water and part on land can serve as indicator species (see Spotlight on p. 107).

- **Keystone species**, which play roles affecting many other organisms in an ecosystem. The loss of a keystone species can lead to sharp population drops and extinctions of other species that depend on it for certain services. An example is the alligator (see Case Study on p. 108). Other examples are gopher tortoises found in Florida and other southern states, sea otters off the west coast of the United States from California to Washington, and various species of bats that pollinate flowers and disperse the seed of plants in tropical forests.

NICHE The **ecological niche** (pronounced "nitch") of a species is its total way of life or its role in an ecosystem. It includes all physical, chemical, and biological conditions a species needs to live and reproduce in an ecosystem. Physical and chemical factors that deter-

Amphibians first appeared about 350 million years ago. Fossil records suggest that frogs and toads, the oldest of today's amphibians, were living as long as 150 million years ago. Such long-term endurance is testimony to the adaptability of these organisms to changes in environmental conditions.

Recently, however, hundreds of the world's estimated 5,100 amphibian species have been vanishing or experiencing sharp drops in their populations in a variety of habitats in at least 16 countries (Figure 4-35). Disappearances and declines have been occurring even in protected wildlife reserves and parks. Scientists have not identified any single reason for this decline, but they believe that the numerous causes involved result mostly from environmental degradation caused by humans.

The fact that amphibians live part of their lives in water and part on land means they are exposed to pollutants in the water, soil, and air. Their soft, permeable skin allows them to absorb oxygen from water, but it also makes them extremely sensitive to pollutants in the water. Some scientists speculate that the amphibians' skin also makes them susceptible to harm from small increases in ultraviolet radiation caused by depletion of ozone in the stratosphere. Their diet of insects guarantees them abundant food, but it also means they ingest insecticides.

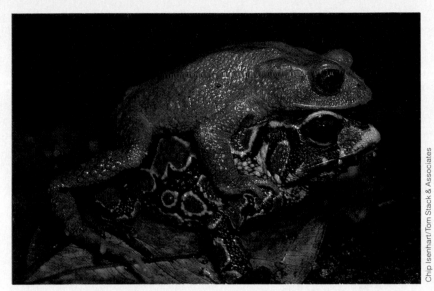

Figure 4-35 Populations of golden toads have dropped sharply in recent years, even in protected tropical forest areas such as the Monteverde Cloud Forest Reserve in the mountains of Costa Rica. The female of this species is multicolored. The male's dazzling carrot orange to red color helps it attract a mate. This photo shows a pair of these toads mating. Golden toads have glands that excrete a poison that kills some of their predators. Scientists believe that greatly increased extinction and population declines of hundreds of species of toads and other amphibians in many parts of the world indicate a deterioration of the environment brought about mostly by human activities.

Chip Isenhart/Tom Stack & Associates

In addition to pollution, possible causes of the decline in amphibians are loss of habitat as forests have been cleared and drainage of wetlands and ponds to provide cropland and to build shopping centers and housing developments. In Asia, where frog legs are a delicacy, overhunting may play a part in the decline of many frog species.

Scientists are concerned about the disappearance and decline of many amphibians for two reasons. First, it suggests that the world's environmental health is poor and is deteriorating rapidly. Second, amphibians, which outnumber and eat more insects than birds, play an important role in the world's ecosystems.

mine the niche of a species include the amount of light, carbon dioxide, water, oxygen, and other nutrients it needs and the ranges of temperature, acidity, salinity, and other factors it can tolerate (Figure 4-18). Biological factors include the kinds of food it needs, the places it finds food, the diseases it tends to contract, the predators that feed on it, and the competitors that vie for the same limited resources it needs.

Species can be broadly classified as specialists or generalists, according to their niches. Some species, called **specialists**, have narrow niches. They may be able to live in only one type of habitat, tolerate only a

narrow range of climatic and other environmental conditions, or use only one or a few types of food.

Examples of specialists are Tiger salamanders, which can breed only in ponds that are fishless to prevent their larvae from being eaten, and red-cockaded woodpeckers, which build their nesting cavities primarily in longleaf pines that must be at least 75 years old. Another highly specialized species is the giant panda, which gets 99% of its food by consuming bamboo plants. The destruction of several species of bamboo in parts of China, where the panda is found, has led to the animal's near extinction.

People tend to divide plants and animals into "good" and "bad" species and to assume that we have a duty to wipe out the villains, or to use them up to satisfy our needs and wants. One species that we drove to near extinction in many of its marsh and swamp habitats is the American alligator (Figure 4-36).

Alligators have no natural predators except people. Hunters once killed large numbers of these animals for their exotic meat and supple belly skin used to make shoes, belts, and other items. Between 1950 and 1960, hunters wiped out 90% of the alligators in Louisiana. The alligator population in the Florida Everglades also was threatened.

People who say "So what?" are overlooking the key role the alligator plays in subtropical, wetland ecosystems such as the Everglades. Alligators dig deep depressions, or "gator holes," which collect fresh water during dry spells. These holes are refuges for aquatic life and supply fresh water and food for birds and other animals.

Large alligator nesting mounds also serve as nest sites for birds such as herons and egrets. As alligators move from gator holes to nesting mounds, they help keep waterways open. They also eat large numbers of gar, a fish that preys on other fish. This means that alligators help maintain populations of game fish such as bass and bream.

In 1967, the U.S. government placed the American alligator on the

Figure 4-36 The American alligator is a keystone species in its marsh and swamp habitats in the southeastern United States. In 1967, it was classified as an endangered species in the United States. This protection allowed the population of the species to recover to the point that its status has been changed from endangered to threatened. Because of its thick skin, speed in the water, and powerful jaws, this species has no natural predators except humans.

Luther C. Goldman/U.S. Fish and Wildlife Service

endangered species list. Averaging about 40 eggs per nest and protected from hunters, by 1975 the alligator population had made a strong comeback in many areas — too strong, according to some people who found alligators in their backyards and swimming pools.

The problem is that both human and alligator populations are increasing rapidly, and people are taking over the natural habitats of the alligator. A gator's main diet is snails, apples, sick fish, ducks, raccoons, and turtles, but a pet or a person who falls into or swims in a canal, a pond, or some other area where a gator lives is subject to being attacked.

In 1977, the U.S. Fish and Wildlife Service reclassified the American alligator from endangered to threatened in Florida, Louisiana, and Texas, where 90% of the animals live. In 1987, this reclassification was extended to seven other states.

As a threatened species, alligators are still protected from excessive harvesting by hunters, but limited hunting is allowed in some areas to keep the population from growing too large. Florida, with at least 1 million alligators, permits 7,000 kills a year. The comeback of the American alligator is an important success story in wildlife conservation.

In a tropical rain forest, an incredibly diverse array of species survive by occupying a variety of specialized ecological niches in distinct layers of the forest's vegetation (Figure 4-37). The widespread clearing and degradation of such forests is dooming millions of specialized species to extinction. Figure 4-38 shows the various feeding niches of different bird species in a wetland.

Other species, called **generalists**, have a broad niche. They can live in many different places, eat a variety of foods, and tolerate a wide range of environmental conditions. Examples of generalist species are flies, cockroaches, mice, rats, white-tailed deer, raccoons, and human beings.

Is it better to be a generalist than a specialist? It depends. When environments have fairly constant conditions, such as in a tropical rain forest, specialists have an advantage because they have fewer competitors (Figures 4-37 and 4-38). But when environments are changing rapidly, the adaptable generalist is usually better off than the unadaptable specialist.

THE PRINCIPAL WAYS SPECIES INTERACT When any two species in an ecosystem have some activities or

Figure 4-37 Stratification of specialized plant and animal niches in various layers of a tropical rain forest. These specialized niches allow species to avoid or minimize competition for resources with other species and lead to the coexistence of a great diversity of species. This niche specialization has been promoted by adaptation of plants to different levels of light available in the forest's layers and hundreds of thousands of years of adaptation and evolution in a fairly constant climate.

requirements in common, they may interact to some degree. Any two species can interact in ways that can benefit, harm, or not affect either or both species. If they do not interact, their relationship is neutral. The principal types of species interactions are *interspecific competition, predation, parasitism, mutualism*, and *commensalism*. In mutualism and commensalism, neither species is harmed by the interaction. Three of these interactions—parasitism, mutualism, and commensalism—are **symbiotic relationships**, in which two kinds of organisms live together in an intimate association, with members of one or both species benefiting from the association.

COMPETITION BETWEEN SPECIES FOR LIMITED RESOURCES As long as commonly used resources are abundant, different species can share them. This allows each species to come closer to occupying its **fundamental niche**: the full potential range of the physical,

chemical, and biological factors it could use, if there is no competition from other species.

In most ecosystems, each species faces competition from one or more other species for one or more of the limited resources (such as food, sunlight, water, soil nutrients, or space) it needs. Because of such **interspecific competition**, parts of the fundamental niches of different species overlap significantly. However, experiments have shown that no two species can occupy exactly the same fundamental niche indefinitely in a habitat where there is not enough of a particular resource to meet the needs of both species. This is called the **competitive exclusion principle**.

When the fundamental niches of two competing species overlap, one species may occupy more of its fundamental niche than the other species by producing more young, getting more food or solar energy, defending itself better, or limiting or preventing the other species from using a resource. This may cause a species to

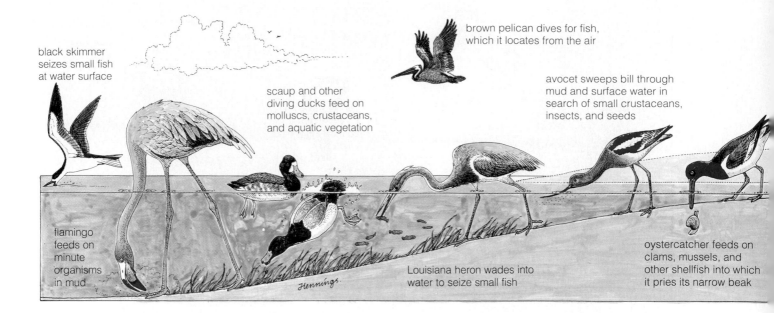

black skimmer seizes small fish at water surface

scaup and other diving ducks feed on molluscs, crustaceans, and aquatic vegetation

brown pelican dives for fish, which it locates from the air

avocet sweeps bill through mud and surface water in search of small crustaceans, insects, and seeds

flamingo feeds on minute organisms in mud

Louisiana heron wades into water to seize small fish

oystercatcher feeds on clams, mussels, and other shellfish into which it pries its narrow beak

Hennings

be eliminated from an area or force an animal species to migrate to another area.

Another way in which the degree of fundamental niche overlap is reduced is by **resource partitioning**, the process of dividing up resources so that species with similar requirements use the same scarce resources at different times, in different ways, or in different places. In effect, they "share the wealth," with each competing species occupying a **realized niche**, which is only a part of its fundamental niche.

For example, hawks and owls feed on similar prey, but hawks hunt during the day and owls hunt at night. Where lions and leopards occur together, lions take mostly larger animals as prey and leopards take smaller ones. Different species of birds, such as warblers in New England forests, avoid competition for food by hunting for insects in different parts of the same coniferous trees.

PREDATION AND PARASITISM: CONSUMER-VICTIM INTERACTIONS The most obvious form of species interaction in food chains and webs is **predation**: An individual organism of one species, known as the **predator**, feeds on parts or all of an organism of another species, the **prey**, but does not live on or in the prey. Together, the two kinds of organisms involved, such as lions and zebras, are said to have a **predator-prey relationship**. Defined broadly, predator-prey relationships include carnivore-prey, herbivore-plant, and parasite-host interactions. Examples of predators and their preys are shown in Figures 4-13, 4-14, 4-19, and 4-20.

Some predators hunt and kill live prey. Other predators, called **scavengers**, feed on dead organisms that either were killed by other organisms or died naturally.

Vultures, flies, and crows are examples of scavengers. Sharks are one of the most important predators in the world's oceans (see Case Study on p. 112).

Prey species have various protective mechanisms. Otherwise, they would easily be captured and eaten. Some can run, swim, or fly fast, and others have highly developed sight or sense of smell that alerts them to the presence of a predator. Some have thick or tough skins (alligator, Figure 4-36), shells (turtles), or bark (giant sequoia, Figure 4-6), and others have spines (porcupines) or thorns (cacti, Figure 4-7). Still others have camouflage coloring (stone plant that looks like a gray stone) or the ability to change color (chameleon) so that they can hide by blending into their environment.

Some prey species give off chemicals that smell (skunks and skunk cabbages) or taste bad to their predators (buttercup) or irritate (bombardier beetles) or poison them (poison arrow frogs and golden toads, Figure 4-35). The bright colors of some prey species warn predators that they are poisonous (monarch butterfly, Figure 4-11, and golden toad). Some prey species attempt to scare off predators by puffing up or spreading their wings (peacock, Figure 4-9), or by looking like (mimicking) poisonous species (the viceroy butterfly that looks like the poisonous monarch butterfly, Figure 4-11) or like predators of some prey species (snake caterpillar). Other prey gain some protection by living in large groups (schools of fishes, herds of antelope).

Predators also have a variety of methods that help them capture prey. Some carnivores, such as the cheetah, catch prey by being able to run fast, and others have keen eyesight (American bald eagle, Figure 2-10). Other carnivores cooperate in capturing their prey by hunting in packs, as spotted hyenas, African lions, wolves, jackals, and Cape hunting dogs do. Like prey species, some

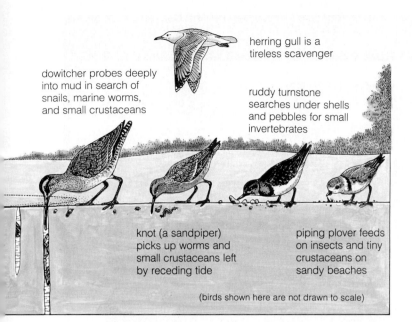

Figure 4-38 Specialized feeding niches of various species of birds in a wetland. This allows them to share limited resources.

dowitcher probes deeply into mud in search of snails, marine worms, and small crustaceans

herring gull is a tireless scavenger

ruddy turnstone searches under shells and pebbles for small invertebrates

knot (a sandpiper) picks up worms and small crustaceans left by receding tide

piping plover feeds on insects and tiny crustaceans on sandy beaches

(birds shown here are not drawn to scale)

predators use camouflage to hide and wait for unsuspecting prey or to blend into their environment (arctic fox, Figure 4-1). Many predators attack prey that is young, old, weak, sick, crippled, or in some way disabled. This natural weeding out of diseased and weak individuals also benefits the prey species by preventing the spread of disease and leaving stronger and healthier individuals for breeding. Other predators, such as humans, have invented weapons and traps to capture prey.

Another type of predator-prey interaction is parasitism. A **parasite** is a consumer that feeds on another living organism (its **host**) by living on or in its host organism for all or most of the host's life. Parasitism is a special form of predation in which the predator (parasite) is much smaller than its prey (host) and either lives on or within its living prey. The parasite draws nourishment from and gradually weakens its host. This may or may not kill the host. Tapeworms, disease-causing organisms (pathogens), and other parasites live inside their hosts. Lice, ticks, mosquitoes, mistletoe plants, and lampreys (Figure 4-40) attach themselves to the outside of their hosts.

Some parasites can move from one host to another, as dog fleas do. Others may spend their adult lives attached to a single host. Examples are mistletoe, which feeds on oak tree branches, and tapeworms, which feed in the intestines of humans and other animals.

MUTUALISM AND COMMENSALISM **Mutualism** is a type of species interaction in which both participating species generally benefit. The honeybee and certain flowers have a mutualistic relationship. The honeybee feeds on the flower's nectar and in the process picks up pollen and pollinates female flowers when it feeds on

them. Other examples are the mutualistic relationships between rhinos and oxpeckers (Figure 4-41) and between legume plants and rhizobium bacteria that live in nodules on the roots of these plants (Figure 4-30).

Another mutualistic relationship takes place between giant sequoia trees (Figure 4-6) and a fungus species that infects their roots. The roots of these massive trees are usually only 0.9 to 1.8 meters (3 to 6 feet) deep and extend outward only about 15 meters (50 feet). How can such a shallow and relatively small root system take in enough water and nutrients to support its growth? The answer lies in the minute fungus that infects the roots of the sequoia and sends out billions of tiny hairlike extensions into the soil around the tree's roots. The fungus gets the nutrition it needs from the tree and in turn helps the sequoia absorb much more water and many more nutrients than the tree's roots could on their own.

In another type of species interaction, called **commensalism**, one species benefits, while the other is neither helped nor harmed to any great degree. In the open sea, certain types of barnacles live on the jawbones and outer coverings of whales. The barnacles benefit by having a safe place to live and a steady supply of the plankton on which they feed. The whale apparently gets no benefit from this relationship, but it suffers no harm from it, either.

This chapter has shown that the essential feature of the living and nonliving parts of individual terrestrial and aquatic ecosystems and of the global ecosystem, or ecosphere, is interdependence and connectedness. Without the services performed by diverse communities of species, we would be starving, gasping for breath, and drowning in our own wastes. We have also seen how some species survive by avoiding competi-

Sharks have lived in the oceans for over 450 million years, long before dinosaurs appeared. There are now about 360 species of sharks, whose size, behavior, and other characteristics differ widely (Figure 4-39).

Sharks range in size from the 0.1-meter (6-inch) long dwarf-dog shark to the 18-meter (60-foot) long whale shark—the world's biggest fish. The whale shark, like two other large shark species—the basking shark and the megamouth shark—are harmless to people because they feed on microscopic diatoms and plants and small aquatic animals such as zooplankton and shrimp.

Sharks have extremely sensitive sense organs. Some sharks can detect the scent of decaying fish or blood even when it is diluted to only one part per million parts of seawater. They can probably hear underwater sounds that originate as far as 3 kilometers (2 miles) away and can tell the direction from which underwater sounds are coming. They also sense weak electrical impulses radiated by the muscles and hearts of fish, making it difficult for their prey to escape detection.

Sharks are key predators in the world's oceans, helping control the numbers of many other ocean predators. Without sharks, the oceans would be overcrowded with dead and dying fish and depleted of many healthy ones that we rely on for food. Recently, greatly increased commercial shark fishing in the Gulf of Mexico has sharply reduced populations of some shark species. One result is an increase in bathers stepping on stingrays, which some sharks feed upon.

Every year, we catch and kill over 100 million sharks, mostly for food and for their fins. Dried shark fins, which sell for $117 per kilogram ($53 per pound) in Asian markets, are used to make shark fin soup, which sells for as much as $50 a bowl in fine Hong Kong restaurants. Other sharks are killed for sport and out of fear. Sharks are vulnerable to overfishing because it takes most spe-

Figure 4-39 This blue shark and other types of sharks are key predators in the world's oceans. This is one of only a small number of shark species that occasionally attack swimmers. These sharks prefer deep water and are a threat only to people swimming from boats in deep water.

cies 10 to 15 years to begin reproducing and they produce only a few offspring.

Influenced by movies and popular novels, most people see sharks as people-eating monsters. This is far from the truth. Every year, a few types of shark—mostly great white, bull, tiger, gray reef, blue, and oceanic whitetip—injure about 100 people worldwide and kill about 25. Most attacks are by great white sharks, which often feed on sea lions and other marine mammals and sometimes mistake human swimmers for their normal prey, especially if they are wearing black wet suits. In a typical year, only about 10 or 12 shark attacks occur in U.S. waters (most off Florida and southern California), with only one or two of those attacks being fatal.

If you are a typical ocean-goer, your chances of being killed by an unprovoked attack by a shark are about 1 in 100 million. You are more likely to be killed by a pig than a shark and thousands of times more likely to get killed when you drive a car.

Sharks help save human lives. In addition to providing people with food, they are helping us learn how to fight cancer, bacteria, and viruses. Sharks are very healthy and have aging processes similar to ours. Their highly effective immune system allows wounds to heal quickly without becoming infected, and their blood is being studied in connection with AIDS research. A chemical extracted from shark cartilage is being used as an artificial skin for burn victims.

Sharks are among the few animals in the world that almost never get cancer and eye cataracts. Understanding why can help us improve human health. Chemicals extracted from shark cartilage have killed cancerous tumors in laboratory animals, research that someday could help prolong your life or the life of a loved one.

Sharks are needed in the world's ocean ecosystems. Although they don't need us, we need them. We are much more dangerous to sharks than they are to us. For every shark that bites a person, we kill 1 million sharks.

Figure 4-40 Parasitism. Sea lampreys are parasites that use their suckerlike mouths to attach themselves to the sides of fishes on which they prey. Then they bore a hole in the fish with their teeth and feed on its blood.

Tom Stack

Joe McDonald/Tom Stack & Associates

Figure 4-41 Mutualism. These oxpeckers are feeding on the ticks that infest this endangered black rhinoceros in Kenya, Africa. The rhino benefits by having these parasites removed from its body, and oxpeckers benefit by having a dependable source of food. Only about 3,500 black rhinos are left in Africa. This and other species of rhinoceros face extinction because they are illegally killed for their horns, which can sell for as much as $44,000 a kilogram ($20,000 a pound), and because of a loss of habitat. Private and government conservationists are trying to protect rhinos from further poaching by creating fenced or heavily guarded sanctuaries and private ranches, relocating some animals to protected areas, and building up captive breeding populations for all species. These efforts have led to a slow increase in numbers in protected areas and in captivity, but it is an expensive and dangerous uphill fight. Wildlife officials are also cutting off the horns of surviving rhinos and burning the horns to protect the animals from being killed.

tion and by entering into nondestructive relationships (mutualism and commensalism) with other species — lessons that the human species could learn from. The next chapter shows how this interdependence is the key to understanding the earth's principal types of life zones and ecosystems.

We sang the songs that carried in their melodies all the sounds of nature — the running waters, the sighing of winds, and the calls of the animals. Teach these to your children that they may come to love nature as we love it.

GRAND COUNCIL FIRE OF AMERICAN INDIANS

DISCUSSION TOPICS

1. **a.** A bumper sticker asks, "Have you thanked a green plant today?" Give two reasons for appreciating a green plant.

    b. Trace the sources of the materials that make up the sticker and see whether the sticker itself is a sound application of the slogan.

    c. Explain how decomposers help keep you alive.

2. **a.** How would you set up a self-sustaining aquarium for tropical fish?

    b. Suppose you have a balanced aquarium sealed with a clear glass top. Can life continue in the aquarium indefinitely as long as the sun shines regularly on it?

    c. A friend cleans out your aquarium and removes all the soil and plants, leaving only the fish and water. What will happen?

3. Using the second law of energy, explain why there is such a sharp decrease in high-quality energy as energy flows through a food chain or web. Doesn't an energy loss at each step violate the first law of energy? Explain.

4. Using the second law of energy, explain why many poor people in less developed countries exist mostly on a vegetarian diet.

5. Using the second law of energy, explain why on a per weight basis steak costs more than corn.

6. Why are there fewer lions than mice in an African ecosystem supporting both types of animals?

CHAPTER 5

CLIMATE, TERRESTRIAL LIFE, AND AQUATIC LIFE

General Questions and Issues

1. What are the most important factors determining variations in climate?

2. What are the principal types of biomes, and how does climate influence the type found in a given area?

3. What are the basic types of aquatic life zones and ecosystems, and what main factors influence the kinds of life they contain?

When we try to pick out anything by itself, we find it hitched to everything else in the universe.

JOHN MUIR

THE BIOSPHERE CONTAINS an astonishing variety of life zones and ecosystems, some found on land and others in Earth's waters. Each realm of life contains characteristic communities of species adapted to certain environmental conditions. Each varies in the average productivity of its producers, which directly or indirectly support other forms of life (Figures 4-24 and 5-1).

Climate is the primary factor determining the forms of life, especially plants, found in the deserts, grasslands, and forests that are the planet's principal terrestrial ecological regions, or biomes. Climate also influences the life found in Earth's lakes, ponds, streams, wetlands, oceans, and other aquatic life zones and ecosystems, except for some remote areas in the deep oceans. This chapter is an overview of climate and how it and other factors affect the diverse realms of terrestrial and aquatic life found in the biosphere.

5-1 Climate: A Brief Introduction

WEATHER AND CLIMATE Every moment, there are changes in temperature, barometric pressure, humidity, precipitation, sunshine (solar radiation), cloud cover, wind direction and speed, and other conditions in the troposphere (Figure 4-3). These short-term changes in the properties of the troposphere at a given place and time are what we call **weather**.

Climate is the average weather of an area. It is the general pattern of atmospheric or weather conditions, seasonal variations, and weather extremes in a region over a long period—at least 30 years. The two most important factors determining the climate of an area are its temperature with its seasonal variations and the quantity and distribution of precipitation over each year (Figure 5-2). Variations in these factors are in turn caused by the uneven way in which sunlight heats the planet, the behavior of air at different temperatures, the rotation of the earth on a tilted axis, ocean currents, chemical composition of the atmosphere, and topography.

CLIMATE AND GLOBAL AIR CIRCULATION The uneven patterns of average temperature and average precipitation that lead to different climates throughout the world (Figure 5-2) are caused mostly by the way air circulates over Earth's surface. Several factors determine these patterns of global air circulation:

- *Long-term variations in the amount of incoming solar energy striking Earth.* These happen because of occasional changes in solar output, slight changes in the way in which Earth's axis wobbles (22,000-year cycle) and tilts (44,000-year cycle) as it revolves

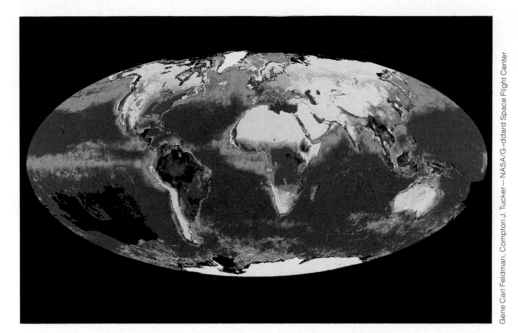

Gene Carl Feldman, Compton J. Tucker—NASA/G–ddard Space Flight Center

Figure 5-1 The biosphere. Three years of satellite data were combined to produce this picture of Earth's biological productivity. Rain forests and other highly productive areas appear as dark green, deserts as yellow. The concentration of phytoplankton, a primary indicator of ocean productivity, is represented by a scale that runs from red (highest) to orange, yellow, green, and blue (lowest).

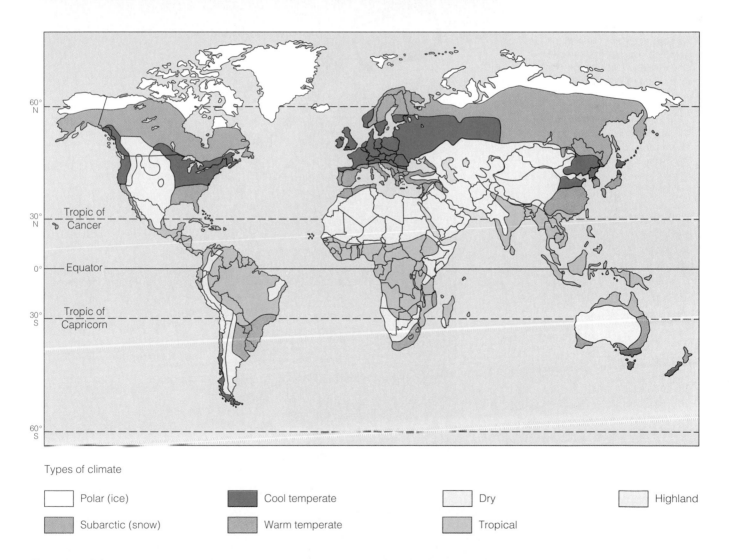

Types of climate

Polar (ice)	Cool temperate	Dry	Highland
Subarctic (snow)	Warm temperate	Tropical	

Figure 5-2 Generalized map of global climates. These climates are dictated mainly by two variables: the temperature, with its seasonal variations, and the quantity and distribution of precipitation over each year.

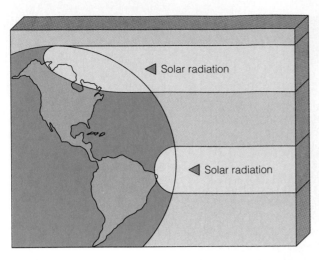

Figure 5-3 Solar energy doesn't strike all parts of Earth equally.

around the sun, and minute changes in the shape of Earth's orbit around the sun (100,000-year cycle).

- *Differences in the amount of solar energy striking different parts of Earth's surface, so that air is heated much more at the equator than at the poles* (Figure 5-3). These differences help explain why equatorial regions are hot, polar regions are cold, and areas in the latitudes between these two regions generally have less-extreme temperatures.

- *Properties of air.* Changes in temperature cause air to expand or contract, rise or fall, and retain or release some of its moisture evaporated from Earth's surface. This causes air to move in giant convection cells that circulate air in the troposphere and distribute heat and moisture around the globe (Figure 5-4).

Figure 5-4 Global air circulation and biomes. Heat and moisture are distributed over Earth's surface by convection currents taking place in large cells found at different latitudes. The direction of air flow and the ascent and descent of air masses in six giant convection cells determine Earth's general climatic zones. This uneven distribution of heat and moisture over different parts of the planet's surface leads to the forests, grasslands, and deserts that make up the planet's biomes.

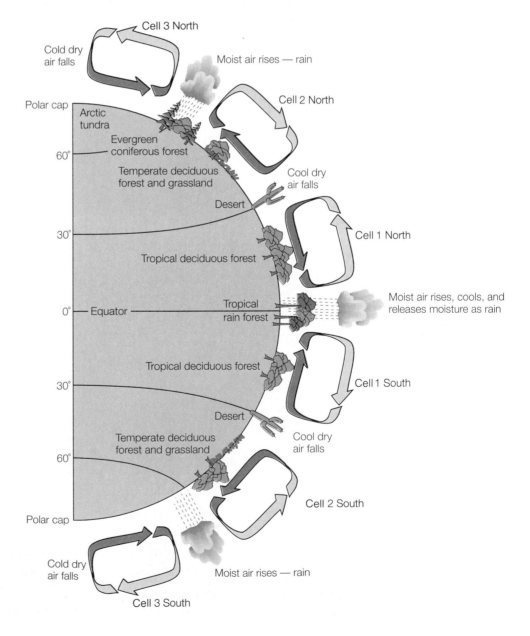

■ *Rotation of the earth on a tilted axis.* If Earth were a smooth sphere and did not rotate on its tilted axis (the imaginary line connecting the North and South Poles), hot, moist air would rise at the equator, move north and south to the poles, cool and sink, and flow back near the surface to the equator. Winds (movements of air masses) would then blow largely in a north-south direction. However, this general north-south circulation is broken up into six huge cells of swirling air masses (three north of the equator and three south of the equator) because of forces created in the atmosphere as Earth rotates on its axis (Figure 5-5). The movement of large air masses through these cells establishes the direction of prevailing east and west winds that distribute air and moisture over Earth's surface. This affects the climate of various areas, which is the primary factor determining the general types of vegetation found at different latitudes (Figure 5-4). Seasonal variations in climate in parts of the world away from the equator are caused by Earth's annual revolution around the sun and its daily rotation on its tilted axis (Figure 5-6), which tip parts of Earth toward or away from the sun.

CLIMATE AND OCEAN CURRENTS Earth's rotation, the inclination of its axis, prevailing winds, and differences in water density cause ocean currents and surface drifts that generally move parallel with the equator (Figure 5-7). Trade winds blowing almost continuously from the east toward the equator push surface ocean waters westward in the Atlantic, Pacific, and Indian oceans until these waters bounce off the nearest continent. This causes several large circular water movements, called *gyres*, that turn clockwise in the Northern Hemisphere and counterclockwise in the Southern Hemisphere. These gyres move warm waters to the north and to the south of the equator.

Ocean currents and surface drifts, like air currents, redistribute heat and thus influence climate and the types of terrestrial vegetation that can be supported, especially near coastal areas. Without the warm Gulf Stream, which transports 25 times more water than all the world's rivers, the climate of northwestern Europe would be more like that of the subarctic. The mild, wet climate of the Pacific Northwest is largely a result of the California Current.

Ocean currents and drifts also help mix ocean waters and distribute nutrients and dissolved oxygen needed by aquatic organisms. Recurring short-term changes in global climate and weather can change water temperatures and currents (Figure 5-8).

CLIMATE AND THE CHEMICAL COMPOSITION OF THE ATMOSPHERE: THE GREENHOUSE EFFECT AND THE OZONE LAYER Fairly small amounts of carbon dioxide and water vapor (mostly in clouds) and trace amounts of ozone, methane, nitrous

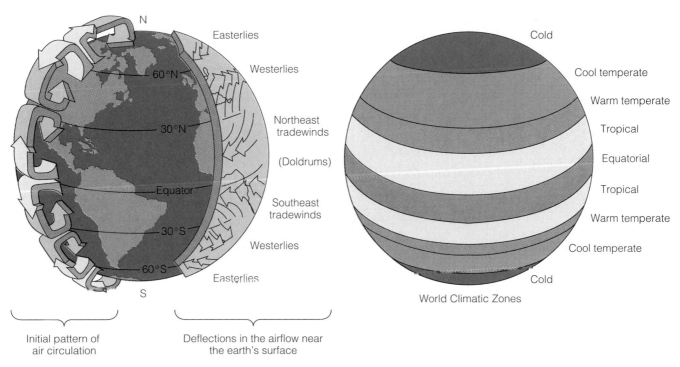

Figure 5-5 Formation of prevailing surface winds that disrupt the general flow of air from the equator, north and south to the poles, and back to the equator. As Earth rotates, its surface turns faster beneath air masses at the equator and slower below those at the poles. This deflects air masses moving north and south to the west or east. This creates six huge cells in which air swirls upward through a corkscrew pathway and down toward Earth's surface at different latitudes. The direction of air movement in these cells sets up belts of prevailing winds that distribute air and moisture over Earth's surface and affect the general types of climate found in different areas.

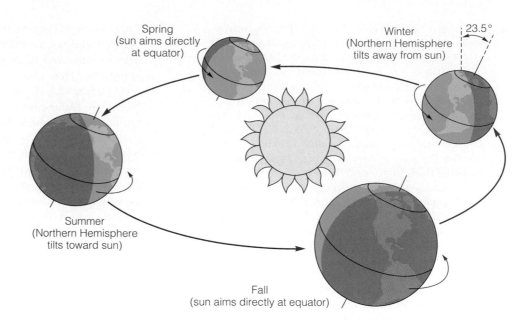

Figure 5-6 Seasonal changes in climate (shown here for the Northern Hemisphere only) are caused by variations in the amount of solar energy reaching various areas as Earth makes its annual revolution around the sun on an axis tilted about 23.5 degrees. As Earth revolves around the sun, various regions are tipped toward or away from the sun. In summer, the North Pole is tilted toward the sun, so that the sun's rays strike the Northern Hemisphere more directly and bring longer days and warmer weather. At the same time, the South Pole is angled away from the sun; thus, winter conditions prevail over the Southern Hemisphere. As Earth makes its annual revolution around the sun, these conditions shift and cause seasonal changes.

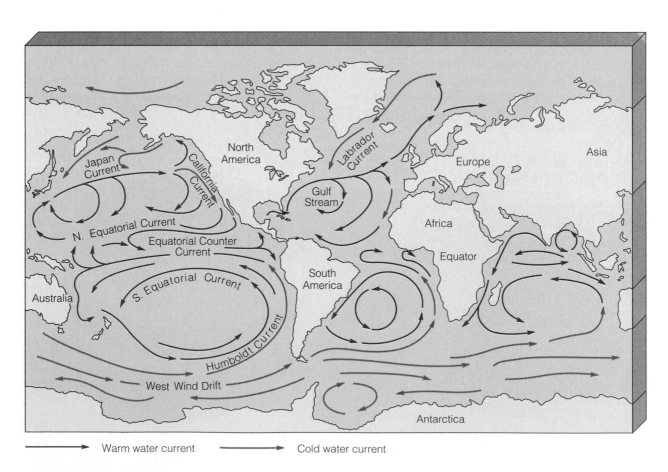

Figure 5-7 The principal warm and cold surface currents of the world's oceans. These water movements are produced by Earth's winds and modified by its rotational forces (Figure 5-5). They circulate water in the oceans in great surface gyres and have profound effects on the climate of adjacent lands.

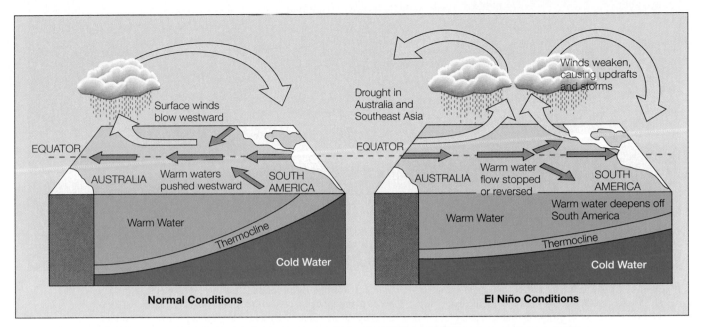

Figure 5-8 Normal surface water temperature and currents in *upwellings* of nutrient-rich bottom water near the coast of Peru (left) and warming of these surface waters by a periodic change in climate patterns called the *El Niño–Southern Oscillation (ENSO)* (right). ENSOs occur every three to seven years, but typically recur every three to four years. When an ENSO lasts 12 to 15 months, it severely disrupts populations of plankton, fish, and seabirds in upwelling areas. A strong ENSO can also trigger extreme weather changes over at least two-thirds of the globe, especially in the countries along the Pacific and Indian oceans. Some areas receive abnormally high rainfall; others experience severe droughts.

oxide, chlorofluorocarbons, and other gases in the troposphere play a key role in determining Earth's average temperature and thus its climates.

These gases, known as **greenhouse gases**, act somewhat like the glass panes of a greenhouse or of a car parked in the sun with its windows rolled up. They allow light, infrared radiation, and some ultraviolet radiation from the sun to pass through the troposphere. Earth's surface then absorbs much of this solar energy and degrades it to infrared radiation, which rises into the troposphere (Figure 4-5). Some of this heat escapes into space, and some is absorbed by molecules of greenhouse gases, which warms the air. This heat is then radiated back toward the earth's surface. This trapping of heat in the troposphere is called the **greenhouse effect** (Figure 5-9).

Without our current heat-trapping blanket of gases, Earth's average surface temperature would be −18°C (0°F) instead of its current 15°C (59°F). Much of the planet would be frozen, like Mars, and life as we know it would not exist. With too much of these gases, Earth, like Venus, would be too hot to support life. Thus, we and other species benefit from the right level of the greenhouse or heat-trap effect, with only minor and slow fluctuations. However, too much warming or cooling, especially if it occurs over a few decades instead of the normal hundreds to thousands of years, would be disastrous for us and many other species.

Ozone (O_3) is formed in the stratosphere as a result of the interaction between the sun's ultraviolet rays and regular oxygen molecules (O_2). In addition to filtering out harmful ultraviolet radiation, ozone in the stratosphere affects climate. Absorption of UV radiation by ozone creates warm layers of air high in the stratosphere that prevent churning gases in the troposphere from entering the stratosphere (Figure 4-3). This thermal cap is an important factor in determining the average temperature of the troposphere and thus Earth's current climates.

Any human activities that decrease the amount of ozone in the stratosphere and increase the amount of greenhouse gases in the troposphere can have far-reaching effects on climate, human health, economic and social systems, and the health and existence of other species. Numerous measurements reveal that we are depleting ozone in the stratosphere and increasing the concentrations of various greenhouse gases in the troposphere.

CLIMATE AND TOPOGRAPHY Mountains, valleys, and other topographical features of Earth's surface also influence regional climates. Because of their higher elevation, mountain highlands tend to be cooler, windier, and wetter than bordering valleys.

Mountains interrupt the flow of prevailing surface winds and the movement of storms. When prevailing winds blowing inland from an ocean reach a mountain range, the moist air cools as it is forced to rise and expand. This causes the air to lose most of its moisture as rain and snow on the windward (wind-facing)

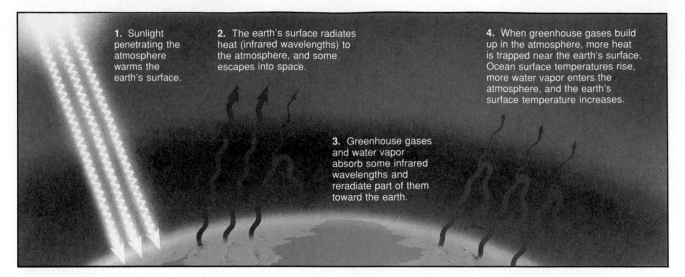

Figure 5-9 The greenhouse effect. Without the atmospheric warming provided by this effect, Earth would be a cold and mostly lifeless planet. However, we are adding such large quantities of greenhouse, or heat-trapping, gases to the atmosphere that computer models of Earth's climate project that we could bring about significant warming of the troposphere in only about 50 years—many times the rate at which rises and falls of Earth's average atmospheric temperature have taken place during its long history. If warming (or cooling) of the planet's atmosphere should take place in such a relatively short time, places where we could grow food and have adequate water supplies would shift faster than our ability to adapt and develop new systems of food production and water distribution. Many analysts consider this the most serious environmental problem we face. (Used by permission from Cecie Starr, *Biology: Concepts and Applications*, Belmont, Calif.: Wadsworth, 1991)

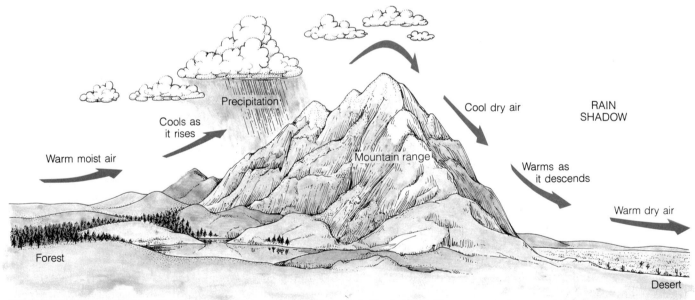

Figure 5-10 The rain shadow effect. The moist air in prevailing surface winds blowing inland from an ocean loses most of its moisture as rain and snow on the windward (wind-facing) slopes of mountains. This leads to semiarid and arid conditions on the leeward side of the mountain range and the land beyond. The Mojave Desert, east of the Sierra Nevada (a range of snow-capped mountains parallel to the coast of California), in the United States is produced by this effect.

slopes. As the drier air mass flows down the leeward (not facing the wind) slopes, it is compressed, becomes warmer, and can hold more moisture. This air draws moisture out of plants and soil it passes over rather than giving up moisture as precipitation. This reduction in precipitation and the resulting semiarid and arid conditions on the leeward side of high mountains and the land beyond is called the **rain shadow effect** (Figure 5-10).

5-2 ## Biomes: Life on Land

EFFECTS OF CLIMATE ON THE DISTRIBUTION OF TERRESTRIAL PLANTS Why is one area of Earth's land surface a desert, another a grassland, and another a forest? Why are there different types of deserts, grass-

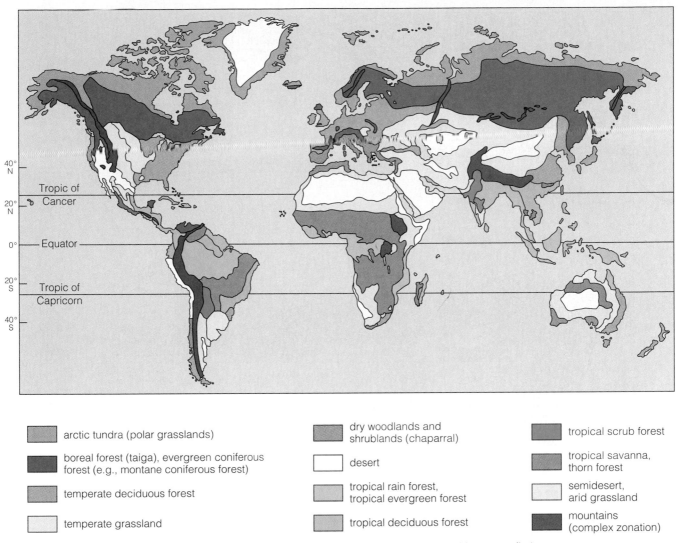

arctic tundra (polar grasslands)	dry woodlands and shrublands (chaparral)	tropical scrub forest
boreal forest (taiga), evergreen coniferous forest (e.g., montane coniferous forest)	desert	tropical savanna, thorn forest
temperate deciduous forest	tropical rain forest, tropical evergreen forest	semidesert, arid grassland
temperate grassland	tropical deciduous forest	mountains (complex zonation)

Figure 5-11 Earth's principal biomes. This is a map of the main types of natural vegetation we would expect to find in different land areas, mostly because of differences in climate. Each biome consists of large numbers of ecosystems whose communities have adapted to smaller differences in climate, soil, and other environmental factors within the biome. This is not a map of what we actually find in different parts of the world, because people have removed or altered much of this natural vegetation to grow food, provide lumber and fuelwood, mine minerals, transfer water resources, and build villages and cities.

lands, and forests? What determines the types of life you would expect to find in these biomes if they were undisturbed by human activities?

The general answer to these questions is differences in climate—caused mostly by differences in average temperature and average precipitation throughout the world as a result of global air circulation (Figure 5-4). Figure 5-2 shows the global distribution of the main types of climate based on these two factors. Figure 5-11 shows the distribution of eleven principal *biomes*—ecological regions with characteristic types of natural vegetation we would expect to find if the land in these areas has not been disturbed by human activities. By comparing these two figures, you can see how the world's principal biomes vary with climate.

With respect to plants, *precipitation generally is the limiting factor that determines whether most of the world's land areas are desert, grassland, or forest.* A **desert** is an area where evaporation exceeds precipitation and the average amount of precipitation is less than 25 centimeters (10 inches) a year. Such areas have little vegetation or have widely spaced, mostly low vegetation.

Grasslands are regions where the average annual precipitation is great enough to allow grass, and in some areas a few trees, to prosper, yet is so erratic that drought and fire prevent large stands of trees from growing. Grasses in these biomes are renewable resources if not overgrazed. They grow out from the bottom instead of at the top, and their stems can grow again after being nibbled off by grazing animals. Graz-

Figure 5-12 Average precipitation and average temperature act together over a period of 30 years or more as limiting factors that determine the type of desert, grassland, or forest biome found in a particular area. Although the actual situation is much more complex than that, this simplified diagram gives you a general idea of how climate determines the types and amounts of natural vegetation you would expect to find in an area that has not been disturbed by human activities.

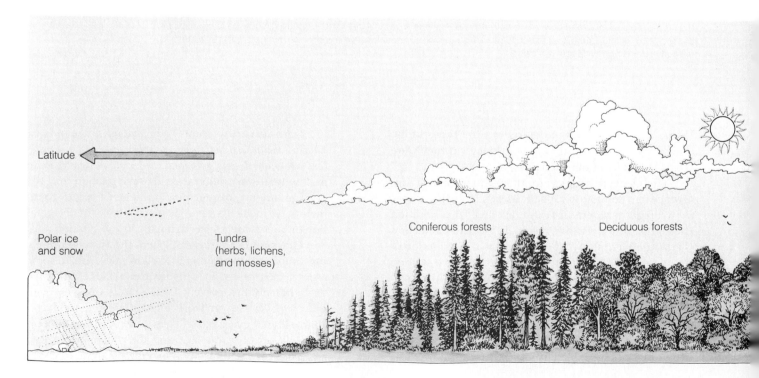

ing by herbivores enhances primary productivity by stimulating growth of grasses, as long as the density of animals is not too high. Undisturbed areas with moderate to high average annual precipitation tend to be covered with **forest**, containing various species of trees and smaller forms of vegetation.

Average precipitation and average temperature, along with soil type, are the most important factors determining the particular type of desert, grassland, or forest in a particular area. Acting together, these factors lead to tropical, temperate, and polar deserts, grasslands, and forests (Figures 5-12 and 4-12).

Climate and vegetation both vary with **latitude** (distance from the equator) and **altitude** (height above sea level). If you travel from the equator toward either of Earth's poles, you will encounter increasingly cold and wet climates (Figure 5-2) and zones of vegetation adapted to each climate (Figure 5-13). Similarly, as elevation or height above sea level increases, the climate becomes colder and is often wetter. If you climb a tall mountain from its base to its summit, you will find changes in plant life similar to those you would find in travelling from the equator to one of Earth's poles (Figure 5-13).

DESERTS   In general, three types of deserts occur because of combinations of low average precipitation and different average temperatures: tropical, temperate, and cold (Figure 5-12). *Tropical deserts*, such as the southern Sahara and the Namib in Africa, make up about one-fifth of the world's desert area (Figure 5-14). They typically have few plants and a hard, windblown surface strewn with rocks and some sand. In *temperate deserts*

(Figure 5-15), such as the Mojave in southern California, daytime temperatures are hot in summer and cool in winter. In *cold deserts*, such as the Gobi lying beyond the Himalaya south of Siberia, winters are cold and summers are warm or hot. In mostly semiarid zones between deserts and grasslands we find *semidesert*, dominated by thorn trees and shrubs adapted to a long dry season followed by brief, sometimes heavy rains.

Plants and animals in all deserts are adapted to capture and conserve scarce water. Some are evergreens with wax-coated leaves that reduce the amount of water lost by evaporation (creosote bush). Certain desert plants get water through roots that reach deep into the soil to tap groundwater (mesquite), while fleshy-stemmed, short (prickly pear) and tall (saguaro, Figure 4-7) cacti have widespread shallow roots to collect water that is stored in the succulent tissues of these plants.

Most desert animals escape the daytime heat by staying underground in burrows or under rocks or in crevices during the day and being active at night. Desert animals also have special adaptations to help them conserve water (Figure 5-16). Insects and reptiles have thick outer coverings to minimize water loss through evaporation. Some desert animals become dormant during periods of extreme heat or drought.

The slow growth rate of plants, low species diversity, and shortages of water make deserts quite fragile. For example, vegetation destroyed by human activities such as livestock grazing and driving of motorcycles and other off-road vehicles may take decades to grow back. Vehicles can also collapse some underground burrows that are habitats for many desert animals. Deserts are spreading (desertification) at an alarming rate because of a combination of prolonged drought from climatic change and conversion of large areas of grassland and other biomes into desert, mostly because of over-grazing by domestic livestock and poor irrigation processes.

The lack of water in deserts also makes them very attractive for dumping nuclear and other hazardous wastes. China, for example, has offered to dump Germany's nuclear waste in the Gobi Desert, and some West African countries have offered to dump hazardous wastes produced in Europe in their desert regions. Because of their ample sunlight, deserts are also potential sites for large concentrations of solar collectors or solar cells used to produce electricity.

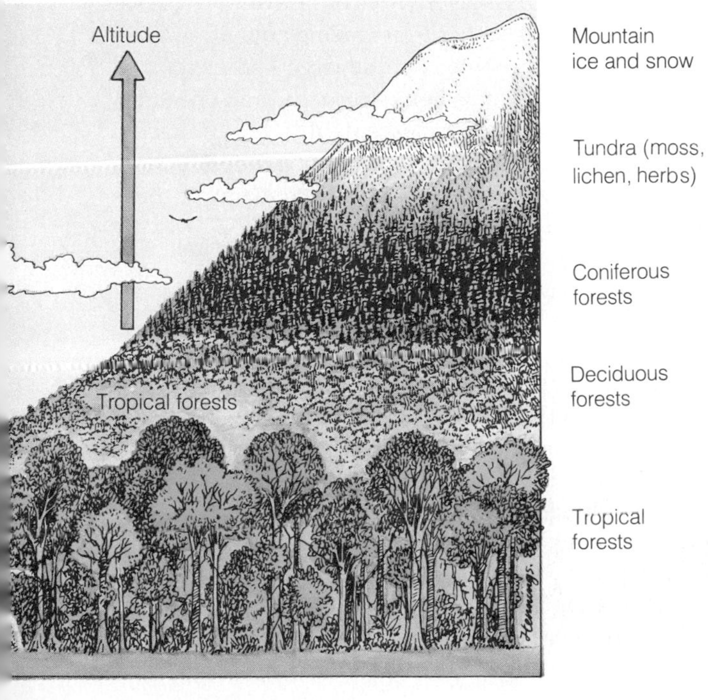

Altitude

Mountain ice and snow

Tundra (moss, lichen, herbs)

Coniferous forests

Deciduous forests

Tropical forests

Tropical forests

Figure 5-13 Generalized effects of latitude and altitude on climate and biomes. Different biomes with similar types of vegetation occur primarily as a result of changes in climate in travelling from the equator toward Earth's poles or up mountain slopes on land undisturbed by human activities. Similar types of animals live in each of these vegetation belts or life zones by adapting to similar environmental conditions.

Figure 5-14 Tropical desert. The Namib Desert of southwest Africa. Few of the world's deserts are covered with vast expanses of sand and dunes as shown in this photograph. Most deserts are covered with rock or small stones.

Figure 5-15 Temperate desert in Arizona. The vegetation includes creosote bushes, ocotillo, saguaro cacti, and prickly pear cacti. After a brief and infrequent rain, the ground is covered with a variety of wildflowers. Most animals escape the hot days by living underground and coming out at night.

GRASSLANDS The three principal types of grasslands — tropical, temperate, and polar — occur because of combinations of low average precipitation and different average temperatures (Figure 5-12). *Tropical grasslands* are found in areas with high average temperatures and low to moderate average precipitation. They occur in a wide belt on either side of the equator beyond the borders of tropical rain forests (Figures 5-4 and 5-11).

A grassland that has scattered trees is called a *savanna* (Figure 5-17). Most are tropical savannas, found between deserts and tropical forests, although some temperate savannas do occur. Tropical savannas are found in areas with warm temperatures year-round, no winter, two prolonged dry seasons, and abundant rain the rest of the year.

Figure 5-16 This nocturnal kangaroo rat in a California desert is a master of water conservation. It comes out of its burrow only at night, when the air is cool and water evaporation is slow. This animal stores dry seeds in its burrow, and these absorb some of the moisture lost in the animal's exhaled breath. Instead of drinking water, it gets the water it needs from recycled moisture in the seeds it eats and from metabolic water produced by aerobic respiration of the sugars in the seeds. It also conserves water by excreting hard, dry feces and thick, nearly solid urine.

African tropical savannas are grazed by vast herds of wildebeests, gazelles, zebras, giraffes, antelope, and other large herbivores with specialized eating habits that allow them to minimize competition for scarce resources in these biomes. Giraffes eat leaves and shoots found high up on the scattered trees, and elephants eat leaves and branches farther down. Elands and Grant's gazelles eat mostly leaves and shoots on bushes. Thompson's gazelles and wildebeests prefer short grass, while zebras graze on longer grass and stems.

During the dry season, fires often sweep these savannas, and the great herds of grazing animals migrate in search of food. Some of these large herbivores and their predators, such as lions, leopards, and cheetahs, are disappearing rapidly, except in a few protected areas, because of ranching, farming, hunting, poaching, and other human activities. The remains of these herbivores and their predators are picked over by hyenas, jackals, vultures, and other scavengers.

Tropical savannas are very efficient at converting carbon dioxide into carbohydrates through photosynthesis, equaling or even exceeding the net primary productivity of tropical rain forests. Much of the carbon removed from the atmosphere is locked up in the soil, in dead plant matter, and in roots and underground stems. Thus, deliberately burning savanna, plowing up its grasses, and converting it into cropland release large quantities of carbon dioxide into the atmosphere, contributing to an enhanced greenhouse effect (Figure 5-9). Although it receives little publicity, current burning and conversion of savanna to cropland may contrib-

Figure 5-17 African elephant on the Serengeti Plain in Tanzania. This is an example of one type of tropical grassland, called a tropical savanna. Most savannas consist of open plains covered with low or high grasses and occasional small, mostly deciduous trees or shrubs, such as palm, acacia, and baobab. These plants shed their leaves during the dry season and thus avoid excessive water loss. Many savanna animal species are threatened with extinction because people kill them for their beautiful coats (cheetah), ivory tusks (elephant), or horns (rhinoceros, Figure 4-41), which command high prices on the black market.

Figure 5-18 A patch of tall-grass prairie temperate grassland in Mason County, Illinois, in early September. Grasses on this type of biome may be more than 2 meters (6.5 feet) high. Only 1% of the original area of tall-grass prairies that once thrived in the midwestern United States and Canada remain. Because of their highly fertile soils, most have been cleared for crops such as corn, wheat, and soybeans, and for hog farming.

Figure 5-19 Sheep grazing on a temperate grassland (short-grass prairie) in Idaho. Grasses on this biome are less than 0.6 meter (2 feet) high. Precipitation is too light and soils are too low in some plant nutrients to support taller grasses. These grasslands are widely used to graze unfenced cattle and, in some areas, to grow wheat and irrigated crops.

ute as much as, or even more than, the clearing and burning of tropical rain forests, to the projected enhanced greenhouse effect.

Temperate grasslands are found in the large, interior areas of continents, especially North America, South America, Europe, and Asia (Figure 5-11), where winters are bitterly cold with hard frosts and summers are hot and dry. Tall or short grasses cover the flat land or gently rolling hills in these biomes. Summer drought, occasional fires, and intense grazing help prevent the growth of trees and bushes, except near rivers where they can obtain some water during the hot, dry summers.

Types of temperate grasslands are the *tall-grass prairies* (Figure 5-18) and *short-grass prairies* (Figure 5-19) of the midwestern and western United States and Canada, the *pampas* of South America, the *veld* of southern Africa, and the *steppes* that stretch from central Europe into Siberia. In these biomes, winds blow almost continuously and evaporation is rapid. As long as it is not plowed up, the soil is held in place by a thick network of grass roots, but because of their highly fertile soils, many of the world's temperate grasslands have been cleared of their native grasses and used for growing crops (Figure 5-20). Overgrazing, mismanagement, and occasional prolonged droughts lead to severe wind

erosion and loss of topsoil, which can convert these fertile grasslands into desert or semidesert.

Polar grassland, or *arctic tundra*, is found in areas south of the Arctic polar ice cap (Figure 5-11). During most of the year, this treeless plain is bitterly cold, with icy, strong winds, and is covered with ice and snow. Winters are long and dark, and average annual precipitation is low and occurs mostly as snow.

Figure 5-20 Replacement of a temperate grassland with a monoculture cropland near Blythe, California. When the tangled network of natural grasses is removed, the fertile topsoil is subject to severe wind erosion unless it is kept covered with some type of vegetation. If global warming accelerates as projected over the next 50 years, many of these grasslands are expected to become too hot and dry for farming, thus threatening the world's food supply.

Figure 5-22 Arctic tundra is a fragile ecosystem, as shown by this degradation of tundra soil on Victoria Island, Northwest Territories, Canada. Vehicles have broken the thin layer of vegetation and soil that covers the permafrost (ice) and shields it from the sun. Some of the permafrost melts, and the tire tracks turn into thin ribbons of water and ice. Such tracks can mar the terrain for decades.

Figure 5-21 Polar grassland (arctic tundra) in Alaska in summer. During the long, dark, cold winter, this land is covered with snow and ice. Its low-growing plants are adapted to the lack of sunlight and water, to freezing temperatures, and to constant high winds in this harsh environment. Below the surface layer of soil is a thick layer of ice, called permafrost, which remains frozen year-round.

Although this biome covers one-fifth of Earth's land surface, it supports less than 1% of the planet's vegetation. It is carpeted with a thick, spongy mat of low-growing plants such as lichens (symbiotic associations of algae and fungi), sedges (grasslike plants often growing in dense tufts in marshy places), mosses, grasses, and low shrubs (Figure 5-21). Most of the an-

nual growth of these plants occurs during the three to four months of summer, when there is sunlight almost around the clock. Because of the cold temperatures, decomposition is slow, and partially decomposed organic matter accumulates as soggy masses of peat (bogs), which contain about 95% of this biome's carbon.

Another effect of the extreme cold is **permafrost** — a thick layer of ice beneath the soil surface that remains frozen year-round. During the summer, water in the surface layer of soil thaws, but the permafrost layer below remains frozen and prevents water melted at the surface from seeping into the ground. During this period, the largely flat tundra turns into a soggy landscape dotted with shallow lakes, marshes, bogs, and ponds. Hordes of mosquitoes, deerflies, blackflies, and other insects thrive in the shallow surface pools. They serve as food for large colonies of migratory birds, especially waterfowl, which migrate from the south to nest and breed in the bogs and ponds. The underground layer of permafrost and the cold, icy winter weather prevent the establishment of trees in this biome.

Most of the tundra's permanent animal residents are small herbivores such as lemmings, hares, voles, and ground squirrels, which burrow under the ground to escape the cold. Their numbers are regulated by predators, such as the lynx, arctic wolf, weasel, snowy owl, and arctic fox (Figure 4-1). Few species are present in large numbers.

The low rate of decomposition, the shallow soil, and the slow growth rate of plants make the arctic tundra perhaps Earth's most fragile biome. Wheel ruts left by a single wagon crossing tundra soil 100 years ago are

Figure 5-23 Tropical rain forest in Monteverde Cloud Forest Reserve in Costa Rica. Life in these storehouses of biodiversity exists in several layers, populated mostly by species with specialized niches (Figure 4-37). The broadleaf evergreen trees that dominate these biomes keep most of their leaves throughout the year and can grow to enormous heights. Some of the tallest trees emerge above the surrounding vegetation and capture direct sunlight. Beneath this *emergent layer* lies the *canopy*, where the leaves and branches at tops of shorter trees overlap and allow only dim light to reach the *understory* of smaller trees. Even less light reaches the *shrub layer* near the ground, and only about 2% of the incoming sunlight reaches the dark *ground layer*, where there is relatively little vegetation. The popular image of the floor of a tropical rain forest as a tangled, almost impenetrable jungle is accurate only along river banks, near the edges of cleared areas, or where a large tree has fallen and allows sunlight to reach the ground. Although tropical forests cover only about 7% of Earth's land surface, they contain almost half of the world's growing wood and a third of its plant matter. They are also habitats for 50% to 80% of Earth's species.

still visible. Vegetation destroyed by this and other human activities can take decades to grow back (Figure 5-22).

Discoveries of oil and gas have led to the building of pipelines through the North American tundra. Buildings, roads, oil and natural gas pipelines, and railroads must be built over bedrock, on insulating layers of gravel, or on deep-seated pilings. Otherwise, the structures melt the upper layer of permafrost and tilt or crack as the land beneath them shifts and settles.

Another type of tundra, called *alpine tundra*, occurs above the limit of tree growth but below the snow line on high mountains (Figure 5-13). The vegetation there is similar to that found in arctic tundra, but there is no permafrost layer below the soil surface.

FORESTS *Tropical rain forests* are a type of evergreen broadleaf forest (Figure 5-23) found in areas near the equator (Figure 5-11), where hot, moisture-laden air rises and then dumps its moisture (Figure 5-4). They have a warm annual mean temperature that varies little

daily or seasonally, high humidity, and heavy rainfall almost daily.

The almost unchanging climate in rain forests means that water and temperature are not limiting factors as they are in other biomes. In this biome, nutrients from the often nutrient-poor soils are the principal limiting factors.

A mature rain forest has a greater diversity of plant and animal species per unit of area than any other biome. More species of animals can be found in a single tree in a tropical forest than in an entire forest at higher latitudes.

These diverse forms of plant and animal life occupy a variety of mostly specialized niches in distinct layers, based mostly on their ability to thrive with different levels of sunlight (Figure 4-37). Vines, also called *lianas*, with their roots in the soil grow up tree trunks until their leaves reach the canopy, where sunlight is available. Orchids and other epiphytes are attached to the trunks and limbs of canopy trees and catch water and nutrients falling from above in their specially shaped leaves. Philodendrons and other plants have huge, dark green leaves that can capture the maximum amount of sunlight in the understory's dim light. Many of the house and office plants we use that don't need much sunlight come from the understory and lower layers of tropical rain forests.

Much of the animal life, particularly insects, bats, and birds, is found in the sunny canopy layer, with its abundance of shelter, flowers, fruits, and other foods. Monkeys (Figure 1-9), apes (see photo on p. 1), toads (Figure 4-35), geckos, sloths, snakes, chameleons, and other animals move up and down the trunks and vines to feed on insects, fruits, or leaves. A great variety of tiny animals live on the ground, where there are also vast populations of termites and decomposers. Because of the warm, moist conditions, decomposition of dropped leaves and dead animals is very rapid; this rapid recycling of scarce soil nutrients is why there is little litter on the ground. Because the air in a tropical rain forest is still, plant pollination by wind is not possible. Instead, many of the plants have evolved elaborate flowers (Figure 1-9) that attract insects, birds, or bats as pollinators.

Left to themselves, tropical rain forests can sustain themselves indefinitely, but if you clear large areas, you end up with patches of grassland, and eventually, desert. The reason for this fragility is that most of the nutrients in this biome are in the vegetation, not in the upper layers of soil as in most other biomes. Once the vegetation is removed, the few nutrients in these soils are quickly leached out and the runoff carries them away in solution. As a result, these nutrient-poor soils can be used to grow crops for only a few years without large-scale use of commercial fertilizers. Furthermore, when vegetation is cleared, the heavy daily rainfall washes away most of the thin layer of topsoil. Thus regenerating a mature rain forest on large cleared areas is almost impossible on a human time scale.

These forested storehouses of Earth's precious biodiversity (see Spotlight on p. 11) are being cleared or degraded at an alarming rate to harvest timber, to mine minerals, and to plant crops and graze livestock on unsustainable soils (Figure 1-10). If the clearing and degradation of tropical rain forests continue at the present rate, within 50 years only a few scattered fragments of these diverse biomes will remain. Also gone will be hundreds of thousands of animal and plant species with highly specialized niches in these forests.

Burning and clearing the vegetation from large areas of these forests also releases enormous quantities of carbon dioxide into the atmosphere and decreases the number of plants removing this gas from the atmosphere as part of the global carbon cycle (Figure 4-28). This could enhance Earth's natural greenhouse effect (Figure 5-9), cause rapid warming of the troposphere, and disrupt global water and food supplies.

As we move a little farther from the equator, we find *tropical deciduous forests* (sometimes called tropical monsoon forests or tropical seasonal forests), usually located between tropical rain forests and tropical savannas (Figures 5-4 and 5-11). These forests are warm year-round. Although they have plentiful rainfall, most of this rainfall occurs during a wet (monsoon) season that is followed by a long dry season.

These forests are less complex than tropical rain forests and contain a mixture of drought-tolerant evergreen trees and deciduous trees, which lose their leaves to help survive the dry season. Many tropical seasonal forests are being cleared for timber, grazing land, and agriculture.

Most soils in tropical deciduous forests, like those in tropical rain forests, are nutrient poor. Thus, clearing them subjects the soil to nutrient loss and erosion, which can lead to desertification. In areas where the dry season in tropical areas is even longer, we find *tropical scrub forests* (Figure 5-11), which contain mostly smaller deciduous trees and shrubs.

In scattered temperate areas with ample rainfall or moisture from ocean fogs, we find another type of evergreen broadleaf forest, known as *temperate rain forests*. Some are found along the west coast of North America from Canada to northern California (Figure 5-11). These North American temperate rain forests are dominated by large conifers such as Douglas firs, Sitka spruce, and redwoods (Figure 2-6). These forests depend on the frequent rains and the summer fog that rolls in from the Pacific. Other temperate rain forests are dominated by broadleaf evergreens or contain a mixture of conifers and broadleaf evergreens. Because they contain stands of large, valuable trees that have been growing for hundreds of years, many of these ancient forests are being clear-cut for their lumber and replaced by tree plantations. The result is further loss of Earth's priceless biodiversity.

Temperate deciduous forests grow in areas with moderate average temperatures that change significantly during four distinct seasons (Figure 5-11). These areas have long summers, cold but not too severe winters, and abundant precipitation, often spread fairly evenly throughout the year.

This biome is dominated by a few species of broadleaf deciduous trees, such as oak, hickory, maple, poplar, sycamore, and beech. These plants survive during winter by dropping their leaves and going into an inactive state. Each spring, they sprout buds that grow into deep green leaves that change in the fall into a beautiful array of colors before dropping (Figure 5-24).

Mature temperate deciduous forests usually have a simpler structure than tropical rain forests, with more sunlight penetrating to the ground. Normally, vegetation in these forests is found in a partially open canopy of leaves in the tops of the tallest trees, an understory

Paul W. Johnson/Biological Photo Service

Paul W. Johnson/Biological Photo Service

Paul W. Johnson/Biological Photo Service

Paul W. Johnson/Biological Photo Service

Figure 5-24 Temperate deciduous forest in Rhode Island during winter, spring, summer, and fall.

Figure 5-25 Tree farm, or plantation, of southern pine in North Carolina. Converting a diverse temperate deciduous forest to an even-aged stand of a single species (monoculture) increases the production of wood for timber or pulpwood but results in a loss of biological diversity. Such monocultures are more vulnerable to attacks by pests, disease, and air pollution than the more diverse forests they replaced.

Figure 5-26 Evergreen coniferous forest (taiga or boreal forest) in Washington. Many of these ancient forests and the temperate rain forests found along the west coast from Canada to northern California have been clear-cut and replaced with tree plantations. There is intense pressure to clear-cut many of the remaining stands of these forests located on publicly owned land in the national forests.

of shorter, shade-tolerant trees and shrubs, and a layer of ferns, mosses, and other low-growing plants on the forest floor. Compared with tropical rain forests, temperate deciduous forests contain relatively few tree species. However, the penetration of sunlight supports a richer diversity of plant life at the ground level.

This layering of vegetation supplies a diversity of niches for animal life. Hawks and owls nest in the canopy. They play an important ecological role by keeping down populations of mice and other small rodents, which would otherwise destroy much of the vegetation on the forest floor. Woodcocks and black bears nest and feed on the ground, and squirrels regularly commute between the canopy and the forest floor.

Once, the temperate deciduous forests in the eastern United States were home for many large predators such as bears, badgers, wolves, foxes, wildcats, and mountain lions. Today, most of the predators have been killed or displaced, and large numbers of plant-eating whitetail deer live in these forests. Warblers, robins, and other bird species migrate to the forests during the summer to feed and breed, although many of these species are declining in numbers because of loss of their winter habitats in Central and South America and their summer habitats in North America.

Temperate deciduous forests have nutrient-rich soil (helped by decomposition of the annual fall of leaves) and valuable timber. This biome now includes some of the most densely populated areas of the world. All but

about 0.1% of the original stands of temperate deciduous forests in North America have been cleared for farms, orchards, timber, and urban development. Some have been converted to intensely managed *tree farms* or *plantations*, where a single species is grown for timber or pulpwood (Figure 5-25).

Evergreen coniferous forests, also called *boreal forests* (meaning "northern forests") and *taigas* (meaning "swamp forests"), are found in northern regions with a subarctic climate (Figures 5-2 and 5-4). Winters are long and dry, with light snowfall. Sunlight is available only 6 to 8 hours a day, and temperatures range from cool to extremely cold. Summers are short, with mild to warm temperatures, and the sun typically shines 19 hours each day. These biomes form an almost unbroken belt just south of the Arctic tundra across North America, Asia, and Europe (Figure 5-11).

These forests are dominated by a few species of coniferous evergreen trees, such as spruce, fir, cedar, hemlock, and pine (Figure 5-26). The tiny, needle-shaped, waxy-coated leaves of these trees can withstand the intense cold and drought of winter. Plant diversity is low in these forests because few species can survive the winters, when soil moisture is frozen. A few broadleaf deciduous species, such as aspens, birch, willow, and larch, are hardy enough to survive the short growing seasons in parts of these biomes.

The crowded needles of the evergreen trees block out much of the light. Beneath the dense stands of trees,

Figure 5-27 The ocean planet. About 97% of the volume of Earth's water is in the interconnected oceans that cover 90% of the surface of the planet's mostly ocean hemisphere (left) and 50% of the surface of its land-ocean hemisphere (right).

Ocean hemisphere   Land-ocean hemisphere

a carpet of fallen needles and leaf litter covers the nutrient-poor soil, making the soil acidic and preventing most other plants from growing on the dim forest floor. During the brief summer, the soil becomes waterlogged. Wet bogs, or muskegs, are found in low-lying areas of these forests. Insects thrive during the warm summer months. They are fed upon by birds that migrate from the south for the breeding season.

In settled areas of this biome in North America, farmers and ranchers have essentially eliminated large predators, such as timber wolves, which can prey on livestock. As a result, populations of moose, caribou, and mule deer have increased, devastating taiga vegetation. In the long run, this reduces the ability of the land to support grazing livestock.

Loggers have cut the trees from large areas of taiga in North America. Much fur trapping has also taken place in this biome. Most of the vast boreal forests that once covered Finland and Sweden have been cut and replaced with even-aged tree plantations.

Boreal forests are especially vulnerable to acid deposition and other forms of air pollution. Because they keep most of their needles, the trees are exposed to air pollution year-round, especially at high altitudes, where they can be almost continuously bathed in clouds and fogs. The naturally acidic soils of these forests cannot neutralize the acid compounds in acid deposition, which weakens the trees. Most life in nearby lakes and streams can be killed from runoff of water containing acids leached from the soil.

5-3   Life in Water Environments

WHY ARE THE OCEANS IMPORTANT? As landlubbers, we tend to think of Earth in terms of land, but Earth is largely a water planet. A more accurate name

for the planet would be Ocean, because oceans cover more than 70% of its surface (Figure 5-27).

The oceans play key roles in the survival of virtually all life on Earth. Because of their size and currents, the oceans mix and dilute many human-produced wastes flowing or dumped into them to less harmful or even harmless levels, as long as they are not overloaded. Oceans also play a major role in regulating Earth's climate by distributing solar heat through ocean currents (Figure 5-7) and by evaporation as part of the global hydrologic cycle (Figure 4-34). They also participate in other important biogeochemical cycles.

By serving as a gigantic reservoir for carbon dioxide (Figure 4-28), oceans help regulate the temperature of the troposphere through the greenhouse effect (Figure 5-9). Oceans provide habitats for about 250,000 species of marine plants and animals, which are food for many organisms, including human beings. They also serve as a source of iron, sand, gravel, phosphates, magnesium, oil, natural gas, and many other valuable resources.

PRINCIPAL OCEAN ZONES Oceans have two principal life zones: coastal and open sea (Figure 5-28). The **coastal zone** is the relatively warm, nutrient-rich, shallow water that extends from the high-tide mark on land to the gently sloping, relatively shallow edge of the *continental shelf*, the submerged part of the continents. The coastal zone, representing less than 10% of the world's ocean area, contains 90% of all ocean species and is the site of most of the large commercial marine fisheries.

Along coasts, nutrients wash from the land and are deposited by rivers into shallow coastal waters. Surface winds and ocean currents stir up the resulting deposits of nutrient-rich sediments from the ocean bottom. This ample supply of nutrients, plus the sunlight penetrating these shallow waters, supports huge populations of photosynthetic marine producers, which in turn support oceanic animal life. This explains why the thin

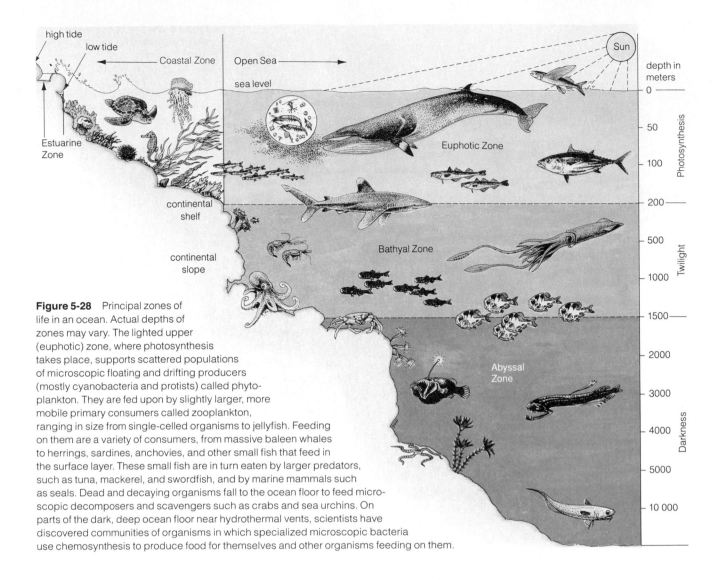

high tide
low tide
Coastal Zone
Open Sea
sea level
Sun
depth in meters
0
50
Euphotic Zone
100
Estuarine Zone
200
continental shelf
500
Bathyal Zone
continental slope
1000
1500
2000
Abyssal Zone
3000
4000
5000
10 000

Photosynthesis
Twilight
Darkness

Figure 5-28 Principal zones of life in an ocean. Actual depths of zones may vary. The lighted upper (euphotic) zone, where photosynthesis takes place, supports scattered populations of microscopic floating and drifting producers (mostly cyanobacteria and protists) called phytoplankton. They are fed upon by slightly larger, more mobile primary consumers called zooplankton, ranging in size from single-celled organisms to jellyfish. Feeding on them are a variety of consumers, from massive baleen whales to herrings, sardines, anchovies, and other small fish that feed in the surface layer. These small fish are in turn eaten by larger predators, such as tuna, mackerel, and swordfish, and by marine mammals such as seals. Dead and decaying organisms fall to the ocean floor to feed microscopic decomposers and scavengers such as crabs and sea urchins. On parts of the dark, deep ocean floor near hydrothermal vents, scientists have discovered communities of organisms in which specialized microscopic bacteria use chemosynthesis to produce food for themselves and other organisms feeding on them.

coastal zone is the source of most of the oceans' net primary productivity per unit of area (Figure 5-1).

The sharp increase in water depth at the edge of the continental shelf marks the separation of the coastal zone from the **open sea**, which is divided into three zones, based primarily on the ability of sunlight to penetrate to various depths (Figure 5-28). This vast zone contains about 90% of the world's ocean area but has only about 10% of all ocean species.

Average net primary productivity per unit of area in the open ocean—sometimes referred to as a wet desert—is quite low. This is due to a lack of sunlight in the lower layers (Figure 5-28) and low levels of nutrients in the surface layer for the microscopic floating and drifting phytoplankton that are the main photosynthetic producers of the open ocean. Exceptions occur in a few areas of open ocean near the equator where different water movements to the north and south come

together and push deep waters plus nutrients to the surface to form *equatorial upwellings*.

THE COASTAL ZONE: A CLOSER LOOK The coastal zone includes a number of different ecosystems with the world's highest net primary productivities per unit of area (Figure 4-24). An **estuary** is a partially enclosed coastal area at the mouth of a river where fresh river water, carrying fertile silt and runoff from the land, mixes with salty seawater. Often this results in the formation of a **delta**—a built-up deposit of river-borne sediments (Figure 5-29). In these areas, temperature and salinity levels vary widely because of seasonal variations in stream flow and the daily rhythms of the tides.

A **wetland** is an area of land covered all or part of the year with salt water (called a **coastal wetland**) or fresh water (called an **inland wetland**, excluding lakes, ponds, and streams). About 5% of all wetlands in the

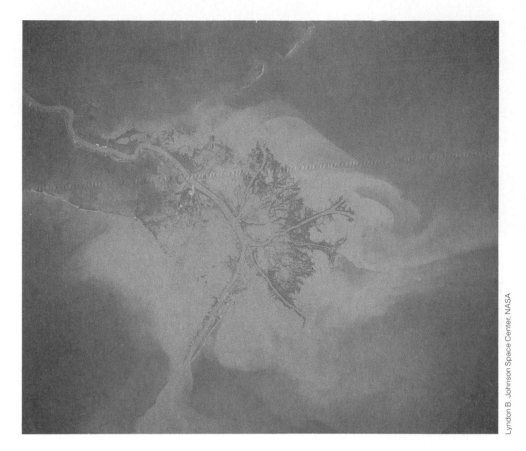

Figure 5-29 Mississippi Delta and surrounding estuaries and coastal wetlands where sediment-loaded fresh water from the Mississippi River flows into the Gulf of Mexico and mixes with salty seawater, resulting in deposits of nutrient-rich silts. The cloud of mud and silt delivered to the ocean gives the water a lighter color around the mouth of the river. This material is deposited as banks of mud, sand, and clay as the delta grows seaward. Constant water movements from tidal flows in the delta and surrounding estuaries and coastal wetlands stir up these abundant nutrients, such as nitrates and phosphates, needed by producers. This makes estuaries and coastal wetlands among Earth's most productive ecosystems per unit of area (Figure 4-24). They are also nursery grounds for many species of fish and shellfish and support many types of waterfowl, such as ducks and migratory geese.

United States are coastal wetlands. The other 95% are inland wetlands.

Coastal wetlands extend inland from estuaries. In temperate areas, coastal wetlands usually consist of a mix of bays, lagoons, salt flats, mud flats, and salt marshes (Figure 5-30), where grasses are the dominant vegetation. In coastal areas with warm tropical climates, we find saltwater swamps dominated by mangrove trees, any of about 55 species of trees and shrubs that can live partly submerged in the relatively salty environment of coastal swamps (Figure 5-31). These swamps have the highest net primary productivity per unit of area of any terrestrial or aquatic ecosystem. Indonesia, Brazil, Australia, and Nigeria have the world's largest areas of mangrove swamps.

Mangrove trees and shrubs get the oxygen they need in the oxygen-deficient silt bed of these swamps through stilt ("breathing") roots, which protrude above the water at low tide and funnel oxygen down to the rest of their silt-covered roots. Mangrove swamps stem the flow of tidal and estuarine waters and trap silt, allowing it to accumulate and build up mud banks. Mangroves also help protect the coastline from erosion and reduce damage from typhoons, cyclones, and hurricanes.

Figure 5-30 Salt marsh on Cape Cod off the coast of Massachusetts. These and other temperate coastal wetlands trap nutrients and sediment flowing in from rivers and nearby land and thus have a high net primary productivity. They also filter out and degrade some of the pollutants deposited by rivers and land runoff.

The coastal zones of warm tropical and subtropical oceans often contain *coral reefs* (Figure 5-32). They are formed by massive colonies containing billions of tiny coral animals, called polyps, which secrete a stony sub-

Figure 5-31 Mangrove swamp in Gambia, Africa. Since the mid-1960s, some tropical coastal countries have lost half or more of their mangrove forests because of industrial logging for timber and fuelwood, conversion to ponds for raising fish and shellfish (aquaculture), conversion to rice fields and other agricultural land, and urban development. The worst destruction has taken place in Asia, especially in the Philippines, Indonesia, and Java.

Figure 5-32 Coral reef in the Red Sea. These incredibly diverse and productive ecosystems are being destroyed and degraded at an alarming rate.

Figure 5-33 Rocky shore beach in Acadia National Park, Maine. Organisms of most seashores must be able to withstand the tremendous force of incoming waves and the pull of the outgoing tide. Rocky coasts like this one provide rocks to which organisms can attach themselves.

stance (calcium carbonate) around themselves for protection. When the corals die, their empty outer skeletons form layers that cause the reef to grow. Thus, most of the reef is dead but is covered by a thin, living skin of coral. The resulting maze of cracks, crevices, and caves provides shelter for huge numbers of various marine plants and animals, including many colorful fishes (Figure 5-32). Human activities are a major cause of the widespread destruction and degradation of these vital ecosystems, making them the most threatened ecosystems in the coastal zone (see Case Study on p. 135).

Some coasts have steep *rocky shores* pounded by waves (Figure 5-33). Many organisms live in the numerous intertidal pools in the rocks. Other coasts have gently sloping *barrier beaches* at the water's edge. If not destroyed by human activities, one or more rows of natural sand dunes on such beaches (with the sand held in place by the roots of grasses) serve as the first line of defense against the ravages of the sea (Figure 5-34). Such beaches, however, are prime sites for human developments (Figure 5-35).

Along some coasts (such as most of North America's Atlantic and Gulf coasts), we find *barrier islands*: long, thin, low offshore islands of sediment that generally run parallel to the shore. These islands help protect the mainland, estuaries, lagoons, and coastal wetlands by dispersing the energy of approaching storm waves.

People build cottages, hotels, casinos (Atlantic City), and other structures on barrier islands (Figure 5-36) and barrier beaches (Figure 5-35), even though they are the most dynamic places on Earth. Their low-lying beaches are constantly shifting, with gentle waves

building them up and storms flattening and eroding them. Longshore currents running parallel to the beaches are also constantly removing sand from one area and depositing it in another. Sooner or later, many of the structures we build on low-lying barrier islands

Coral reefs form as a result of mutualism. Tiny single-celled, photosynthesizing protists (dinoflagellates) living in or between the cells of coral animals synthesize organic food compounds for the polyps. In this symbiotic partnership, the protists gain a protected habitat in which to live and some minerals from the polyps' body fluids and wastes. Algae and other producers, which give corals their bright coloration, grow on the outside surfaces of coral animals and provide plentiful food for fish (Figure 5-32), starfish (Figure 4-10), and other marine animals.

Coral reefs are among the world's oldest (5,000 to 10,000 years old) and most diverse and productive ecosystems—often described as the marine equivalent of tropical rain forests. A single reef may contain 3,000 species of corals. They support at least one-third of all marine fish species, as well as numerous other marine organisms.

The reefs reduce the energy of incoming waves and help protect the shores against storms. When a coral reef in Sri Lanka was destroyed, the shoreline was pushed back some 300 meters (984 feet) by erosion from waves.

By forming limestone shells, coral polyps remove carbon dioxide from the atmosphere as part of the carbon cycle (Figure 4-28) and thus play an important role in reducing the impact of greenhouse gases we are adding to the troposphere (Figure 5-9). Destruction of large areas of these ecosystems could accelerate our enhancement of Earth's natural greenhouse effect. This could make the surface waters of tropical oceans too warm for coral animals to survive.

Despite their importance, these ecosystems are being destroyed or damaged in 93 of the 109 countries with significant coral reefs. Part of the problem is that these ecosystems are fragile and grow slowly; to grow a coral colony the size of your head takes at least 20 years. They thrive only in water that is clear, clean, warm but not too hot, and fairly shallow, and that has a constant high salinity. There must also be ample sunlight and enough wave action to provide sufficient dissolved oxygen and nutrients.

The greatest threats to these delicate ecosystems come from deforestation, construction, crop growing, and poor land management, often on land far away from tropical coastlines. These activities allow more eroded soil to flow down rivers and eventually into the ocean, killing coral polyps by blocking off sunlight and smothering them. Other threats include coastal development, chemical pollution, anchor damage, dredging, overfishing (which may contribute to increases in populations of coral-eating crown-of-thorns starfish), the use of dynamite to kill fish, oil spills, the mining of coral (limestone) for use as building material, the testing of nuclear weapons by France, and the collection of coral for sale to local tourists and for export.

Natural threats include devastation by hurricanes, predation by crown-of-thorns starfish, and ocean warming from El Niño–Southern Oscillations (Figure 5-8). Normally, reefs gradually recover from the ravages of nature, but human activities are upsetting this healing process.

Some 300 areas of coral reefs in 65 countries are protected as reserves or parks, and another 600 have been recommended for protection. That is an important step, but protecting these reefs is quite difficult and expensive, and only half the countries with coral reefs have set aside such reserves. These important forms of Earth's natural capital will continue to disappear until we deal with the human actions that are the root causes of most of the reefs' destruction and degradation.

and gently sloping barrier beaches are damaged or destroyed by flooding, severe beach erosion, and wind from major storms (including hurricanes).

Each year, U.S. taxpayers provide people building along highly vulnerable shorelines—the country's most hazardous land—with an insurance subsidy of $138 billion. Greatly reducing the risk to homeowners and developers encourages unsustainable development of coastal areas.

When coastal developers remove the dunes or build behind the first set of dunes, minor hurricanes and sea storms can flood and even sweep away houses and other buildings. Coastal dwellers mistakenly call these human-assisted disasters natural disasters and expect federally supported insurance and disaster aid to allow them to rebuild in these highly vulnerable areas and await the next disaster.

Along some steep, western coasts of continents, almost-constant trade winds blow offshore and push surface water away from the shore. This outwardly moving surface water is replaced by an **upwelling** of cold, nutrient-rich bottom water (Figure 5-8, left). An upwelling brings plant nutrients from the deeper parts of the ocean to the surface and supports large populations of plankton, fish, and fish-eating seabirds. Although they make up only about 0.1% of the world's total ocean area, upwellings are highly productive (Figure 5-1). However, changes in climate and ocean currents that take place every few years, coupled with overfishing, can reduce their high productivity and

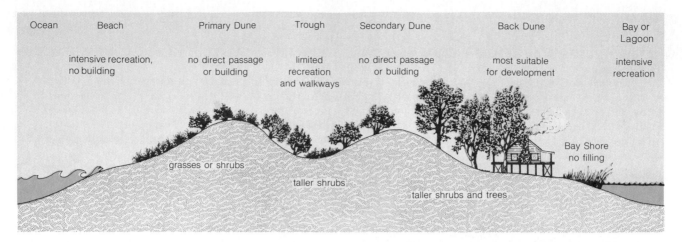

Ocean | Beach | Primary Dune | Trough | Secondary Dune | Back Dune | Bay or Lagoon

intensive recreation, no building | no direct passage or building | limited recreation and walkways | no direct passage or building | most suitable for development | intensive recreation

grasses or shrubs

taller shrubs

taller shrubs and trees

Bay Shore no filling

Figure 5-34 Primary and secondary dunes on a gently sloping beach play an important role in protecting the land from erosion by the sea. The roots of various grasses that colonize the dunes help hold the sand in place. Ideally, construction and development should be allowed only behind the second strip of dunes, with walkways to the beach built over the dunes to keep them intact. This helps protect structures from being damaged and washed away by wind, high tides, beach erosion, and flooding from storm surges. This type of protection, however, is rare, because the short-term economic value of limited oceanfront land is considered to be much higher than its long-term ecological and economic values.

Myrtle Beach Area Chamber of Commerce

Figure 5-35 Developed beach, Myrtle Beach, South Carolina. Note that the protective dunes have been eliminated.

G. H. Demetrakas/O. C. Camera

Figure 5-36 Developed barrier island, Ocean City, Maryland (Fenwick Island), is host to 8 million visitors a year. There is no effective protection against flooding and damage from severe storms, as residents on barrier islands in South Carolina learned when a devastating hurricane hit in 1989. If global warming raises average sea levels as projected sometime in the next century, most of these valuable pieces of real estate will be underwater.

cause sharp drops in the annual catch of some important marine fish species, such as anchovies (used mostly as livestock feed) (see Case Study on p. 379). Because of their immense value to us and other species, coastal zones need to be protected and managed in ways that sustain their productivity (see Case Study on p. 137).

FRESHWATER LAKES AND RESERVOIRS Freshwater habitats are very limited in area, with inland lakes covering about 1.8% of Earth's surface and running water (streams) covering about 0.3%. **Lakes** are large natural bodies of standing fresh water formed when precipitation, land runoff, or flowing groundwater fills depressions in the earth. Causes of such depressions include glaciation (the Great Lakes of North America), crustal displacement accompanied by or resulting in earthquakes (Lake Nyasa in East Africa), and volcanic activity (Lake Kivu in Africa). Lakes normally consist of four distinct zones (Figure 5-38), which provide a variety of habitats and ecological niches for different species.

A lake with a large or excessive supply of nutrients needed by producers is called a **eutrophic** ("well-nourished") **lake** (Figure 5-39). These lakes have a high net primary productivity and are often shallow. This type of lake has large populations of phytoplankton (especially cyanobacteria) and zooplankton and diverse populations of fish, such as bass, sunfish, and yellow perch. In warm summer months, the bottom layer of a eutrophic lake is often depleted of dissolved oxygen.

A lake with a small supply of nutrients (mostly nitrates and phosphates) needed by producers is called

CASE STUDY Value, Use, and Protection of Coastal Zones

Many people view estuaries (Figure 5-29) and coastal wetlands (Figures 5-30 and 5-31) as desolate, mosquito-infested, worthless lands. They believe these ecosystems should be drained, dredged, filled in, built on, or used as dumps for human-generated pollutants and waste materials.

Nothing could be further from the truth. These highly productive areas supply food and serve as spawning and nursery grounds for many species of marine fish and shellfish. In the United States, estuaries and coastal wetlands are spawning grounds for more than 70% of the country's commercial fish and shellfish, generating $5.5 billion a year and employing 330,000 people.

Tens of millions of people, mostly in fishing villages in coastal LDCs, depend on the coastal zone to get enough food to survive. Tens of millions of other people in LDCs survive by growing crops on the deep layers of nutrient-rich silt deposited in estuaries and deltas near the mouths of major rivers.

Estuaries and coastal wetlands are also breeding grounds and habitats for waterfowl and other wildlife, including many endangered species. Each year, millions of people visit coastal zones for whale or bird watching, waterfowl hunting, and other recreational activities.

Coastal wetlands also serve as natural filters, much like the kidneys in our bodies. They dilute and filter out large amounts of nutrients and waterborne pollutants, helping protect the quality of waters used for swimming, fishing, and wildlife

habitats. It is estimated that 0.4 hectare (1 acre) of tidal estuary substitutes for a $75,000 waste treatment plant and has a total land value of $83,000 when its production of fish for food and recreation is included. By comparison, 0.4 hectare (1 acre) of prime farmland in Kansas has a top value of $1,200 and an annual production value of $600.

Estuaries, coastal wetlands, barrier islands, and the natural sand dunes found on most gently sloping beaches help protect coastlines and land behind them from storms and flooding. They absorb damaging waves caused by violent storms and hurricanes, and coastal wetlands serve as giant sponges to absorb floodwaters.

They are also among our most densely populated and most intensely used and polluted ecosystems. Nearly 55% of the area of estuaries and coastal wetlands in the United States has been destroyed or damaged, primarily by conversion to cropland and from contamination by wastes from upstream sources and highly developed coastal areas. California has lost 90% of its original coastal wetlands.

These ecosystems are particularly vulnerable to toxic contamination because they trap pesticides, heavy metals, and other pollutants, concentrating them to very high levels. Among America's most polluted estuaries are Boston's Massachusetts Bay, New York's Long Island Sound, Maryland's Chesapeake Bay, California's San Francisco Bay, and Washington's Puget Sound. On any given day, one-third of U.S. shellfish beds

are closed to commercial or sport fishing because of contamination.

In 1990, about 54% of the U.S. population lived within 80 kilometers (50 miles) of coastal waters (61% in California and 71% in Florida). Nine of the country's largest cities, most major ports, about 40% of the manufacturing plants, and two out of three nuclear and coal-fired power plants are located in coastal counties. The coasts are also the sites of large numbers of motels, hotels, condominiums, beach cottages, and other developments (Figures 5-35 and 36).

Fortunately, about 45% of the area of estuaries and coastal wetlands in the United States remains undeveloped. Each year, however, additional areas are developed or severely degraded, especially in the southeastern United States, where 83% of the remaining wetlands in the lower 48 states are found.

Some coastal areas have been purchased by federal and state governments and by private conservation agencies to help protect key areas from development and to allow most of them to be used as parks and wildlife habitats. However, many ecologically important, undeveloped estuarine areas, coastal wetlands, and barrier islands will be developed before enough funds can be raised to protect them.

The National Coastal Zone Management Acts of 1972 and 1980 gave federal aid to the 37 coastal and Great Lakes states and territories to help them develop programs for protecting and managing coastlines not under federal protection. These
(continued)

programs, however, are voluntary, and many are vague and don't provide enough enforcement authority. Since 1981, their implementation has also been hindered by cuts in the federal budget. California and North Carolina are considered to have the strongest programs, but developers and other interests make continuing efforts to weaken them.

A major problem is that more than 70% of the length of the country's shoreline (excluding Alaska) is privately owned. Unless they are given much larger tax breaks for preserving undeveloped coastal areas, most private owners find it hard to resist lucrative offers from developers.

The Water Quality Act of 1987 established the National Estuary Program with the goals of identifying nationally significant estuaries, protecting and improving their water quality, and sustaining their living resources. It also identified 11 estuaries for "priority consideration" by the EPA. The EPA's role is to provide technical assistance and an organizational umbrella under which federal, state, and local interests work together to develop long-term protection and management plans.

Beach erosion is a serious problem along most of the gently sloping beaches of barrier islands and mainland shores. The main cause of this problem is that sea levels have been rising gradually ever since the last ice age ended, about 12,000 years ago. The warmer climate since then has melted much of the ice and expanded the volume of seawater. Also, a shoreline is a dynamic system. Sediment supplied mostly by rivers and by cliff erosion is continually being removed from one area by waves and currents and deposited in another. Thus, beach erosion in one place and beach buildup in another place is a natural process that we can do little to control.

Many states require that oceanfront structures be elevated and built of concrete. However, such structures can still be toppled by beach erosion and wind and wave damage as the average high-tide mark gradually moves inland. Several methods have been tried to halt or reduce beach erosion (Figure 5-37), but they either make matters worse or are only temporary solutions.

The best solution is to prevent development on remaining beach areas or to allow such development only behind protective dunes (Figure 5-34). Construction of seawalls, breakwaters, groins, and jetties should also be banned or severely limited. Structures built too close to eroding beaches should be moved back from the water's edge, and any that are destroyed by storms or erosion should only be rebuilt farther inland. Eliminating federal flood insurance subsidies would help protect beaches and save taxpayers money by making individuals and corporations responsible for the risks they incur when they build in highly risky areas. This would also start us on the path of working with the dynamics of nature along shorelines by making it cheaper in the long run to move vulnerable structures back from the water's edge and not erect new buildings in such areas.

In our desire to live near the coast and use coastal resources, we are destroying the values that make coastal areas so enjoyable and valuable. An urgent environmental priority should be to protect remaining unspoiled estuaries, coastal wetlands, beaches, and coral reefs throughout the world from destruction and degradation and to manage those we have developed in sustainable ways. According to ocean expert G. Ray Carleton: *"The coastal zone may be the single most important portion of our planet. The loss of its biodiversity may have repercussions far beyond our worst fears."*

---

an **oligotrophic** ("poorly-nourished") **lake** (Figure 5-39). Because of its relatively low net primary productivity, such a lake usually has crystal-clear blue or green water. This type of lake is often deep, with steep banks. It has small populations of both phytoplankton and fish, such as smallmouth bass and lake trout. Many lakes fall somewhere between the two extremes of nutrient enrichment and are called **mesotrophic lakes**.

Eutrophication (pronounced yoo-TRO-fuh-KAY-shun) refers to the physical, chemical, and biological changes that take place after a lake receives inputs of nutrients and silt from the surrounding land basin as a result of natural erosion and runoff over a long period of time. Some lakes naturally become more eutrophic over time, but others do not because of differences in the surrounding waterbasin.

Near urban or agricultural centers, the input of nutrients to a lake can be greatly accelerated by human activities, a process known as **cultural eutrophication**. It is caused mostly by nitrate- and phosphate-containing effluents from sewage treatment plants, runoff of fertilizers and animal wastes, and accelerated erosion of nutrient-rich topsoil.

Reservoirs are normally large, deep, human-created bodies of standing fresh water. Large reservoirs

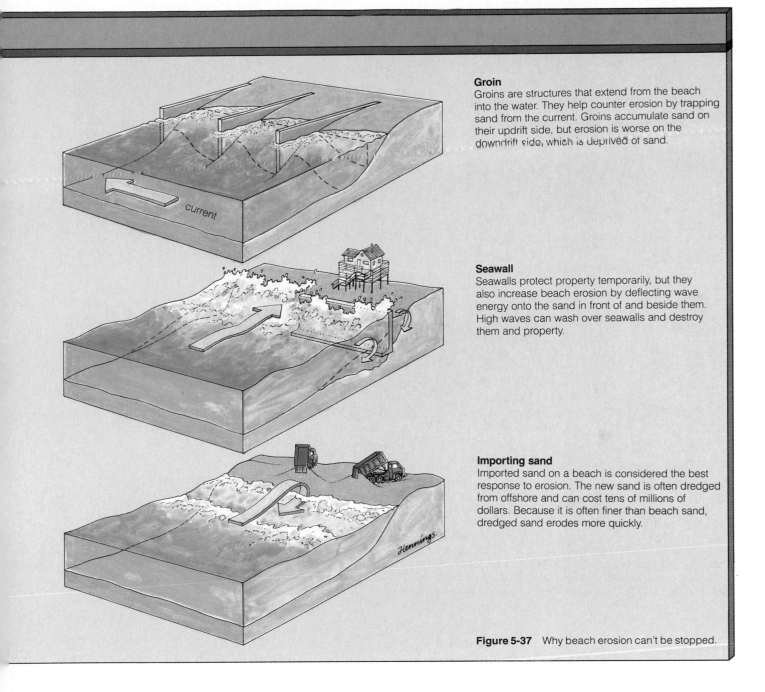

Groin
Groins are structures that extend from the beach into the water. They help counter erosion by trapping sand from the current. Groins accumulate sand on their updrift side, but erosion is worse on the downdrift side, which is deprived of sand.

Seawall
Seawalls protect property temporarily, but they also increase beach erosion by deflecting wave energy onto the sand in front of and beside them. High waves can wash over seawalls and destroy them and property.

Importing sand
Imported sand on a beach is considered the best response to erosion. The new sand is often dredged from offshore and can cost tens of millions of dollars. Because it is often finer than beach sand, dredged sand erodes more quickly.

current

Hennings.

Figure 5-37 Why beach erosion can't be stopped.

are frequently created by building dams to collect water running down from mountains in streams (Figure 5-40). Often artificial reservoirs are incorrectly called lakes. For example, I live not too far from a huge reservoir in central North Carolina called Jordan Lake.

Reservoirs store water, which can be released in a controlled manner to produce hydroelectric power at the dam site, provide irrigation water on dry land found below the dam, prevent or reduce flooding in land below the reservoir, and provide water carried by aqueduct to towns and cities. Reservoirs are also used for recreation such as swimming, fishing, and boating.

FRESHWATER STREAMS Precipitation that doesn't infiltrate the ground or evaporate remains on the earth's surface as **surface water**. This water becomes **runoff**, which flows into streams and eventually downhill to the oceans to continue circulating in the hydrologic cycle (Figure 4-34). The entire land area that delivers the water, sediment, and dissolved substances via small streams to a major stream (river), and ultimately to the sea, is called a **watershed**, or **drainage basin**.

The downward flow of water from mountain highlands to the sea takes place in three phases in a *river system* (Figure 5-41). Because of differences in environmental conditions in each phase, a river system consists

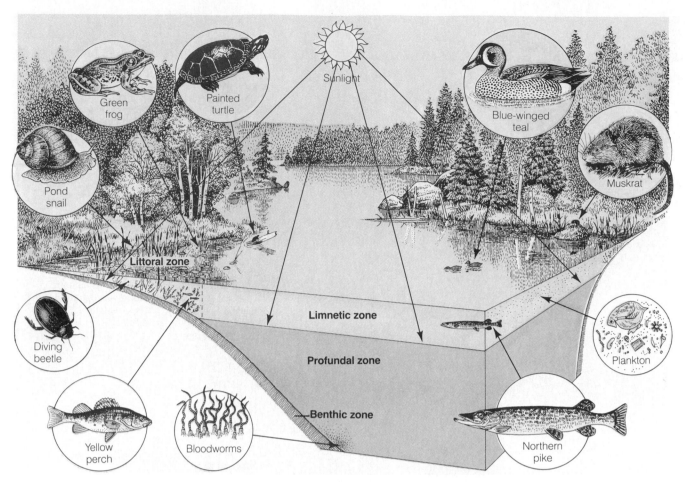

Figure 5-38 The four distinct zones of life in a lake. The *littoral zone* includes the shore and the shallow, nutrient-rich waters near the shore, in which sunlight reaches the bottom. It contains a variety of floating and drifting producers (phytoplankton), rooted aquatic plants, and other forms of aquatic life, such as frogs, snails, and snakes. The *limnetic zone*, like the euphotic zone of the ocean (Figure 5-28), is the open-water surface layer that gets enough sunlight for photosynthesis. It contains varying amounts of phytoplankton, plant-eating zooplankton, and fish, depending on the supply of nutrients available to producers. The *profundal zone* is the deep, open water where it is too dark for photosynthesis. It is inhabited by fish adapted to its cooler, darker water. The *benthic zone*, at the bottom of a lake, is inhabited mostly by large numbers of decomposers (bacteria and fungi), detritus-feeding clams, and wormlike insect larvae. They feed mostly on plant debris, animal remains, and animal wastes that descend from above.

of a series of different ecosystems. First, narrow headwater or mountain highland streams with cold, clear water rush down steep slopes. As this turbulent water flows and tumbles downward over waterfalls and rapids, it dissolves large amounts of oxygen from the air. Most plants in this flow survive because they are attached to rocks. Fish that thrive in this environment are usually cold-water fish, such as trout, which require a high level of dissolved oxygen.

In the second phase, the headwater streams merge to form wider, deeper, lower-elevation streams that flow down gentler slopes and meander through wider valleys. Here the stream channel is wider and deeper and there are fewer obstacles. As a result, the flow of water is less turbulent, but its velocity is higher. The warmer water and other conditions found in this phase can sup-

port a variety of cold-water and warm-water fish species with slightly lower oxygen requirements.

Gradually, these streams coalesce into wider and deeper rivers that meander across broad, flat valleys. The main channels of these rivers support a distinctive variety of fish, whereas their backwaters support species similar to those found in lakes. Meandering streams are sometimes straightened, deepened, and widened to improve navigation and to help reduce flooding and bank erosion, but such *stream channelization* is controversial. At its mouth, a river may divide into many channels as it flows across a delta and coastal wetlands and estuaries, where river water mixes with ocean water (Figure 5-29).

As streams flow downhill, they become powerful shapers of land. Over millions of years, the friction of

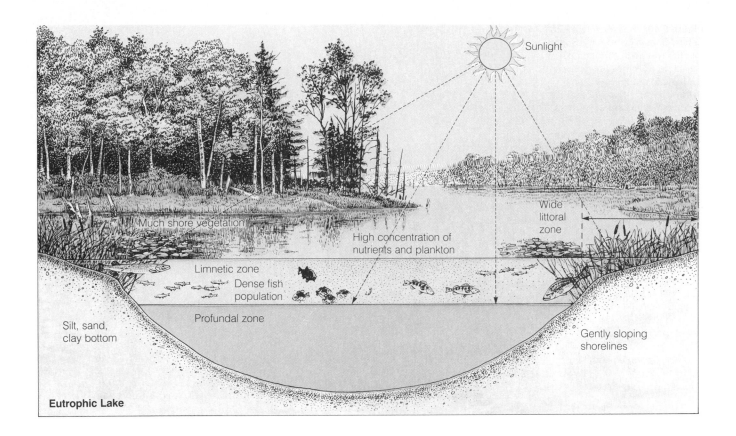

Eutrophic Lake

- Much shore vegetation
- High concentration of nutrients and plankton
- Wide littoral zone
- Limnetic zone
- Dense fish population
- Profundal zone
- Silt, sand, clay bottom
- Gently sloping shorelines

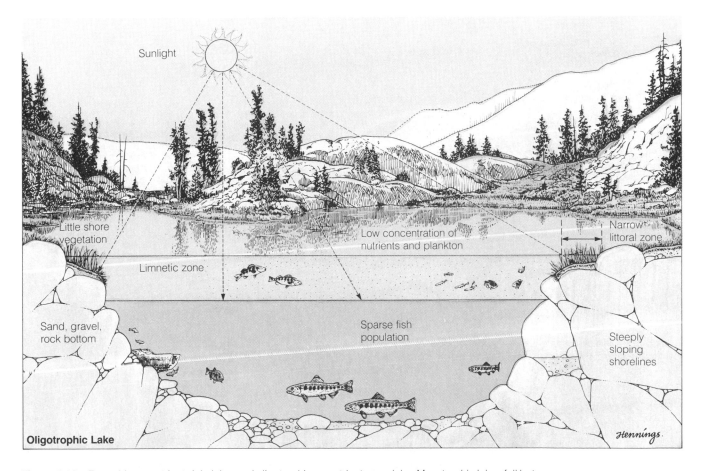

Oligotrophic Lake

- Sunlight
- Little shore vegetation
- Low concentration of nutrients and plankton
- Narrow littoral zone
- Limnetic zone
- Sand, gravel, rock bottom
- Sparse fish population
- Steeply sloping shorelines

Hennings

Figure 5-39 Eutrophic, or nutrient-rich, lake, and oligotrophic, or nutrient-poor, lake. Mesotrophic lakes fall between these two extremes of nutrient enrichment.

Figure 5-40 Reservoir formed behind Shasta Dam on the Sacramento River north of Redding, California. This reservoir and dam are used to produce electricity (hydropower) and to help control flooding in areas below the dam by storing and releasing water slowly. Water flowing through the base of the dam drives turbines that spin generators and produce electricity. About 13.5% of the electrical power used in the United States is produced by large hydroelectric power plants like this one. This is a potentially renewable source of energy as long as short-term drought or long-term changes in climate don't reduce water flow in the water basin where reservoirs are located. While they can help reduce flooding at lower elevations below a dam, large reservoirs flood huge areas of land behind the dam, displace people from those areas, and destroy wildlife habitats in the flooded area.

U.S. Department of Interior/Bureau of Reclamation

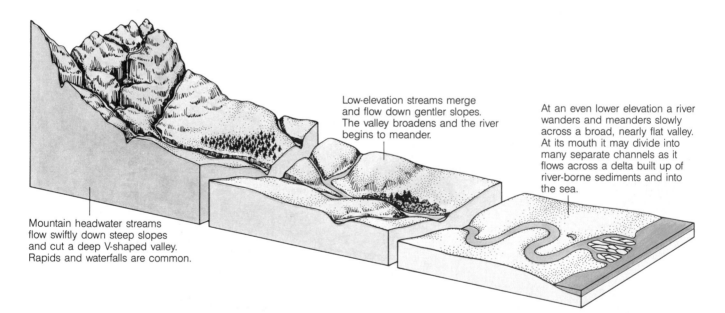

Low-elevation streams merge and flow down gentler slopes. The valley broadens and the river begins to meander.

At an even lower elevation a river wanders and meanders slowly across a broad, nearly flat valley. At its mouth it may divide into many separate channels as it flows across a delta built up of river-borne sediments and into the sea.

Mountain headwater streams flow swiftly down steep slopes and cut a deep V-shaped valley. Rapids and waterfalls are common.

Figure 5-41 The three phases in the flow of water downhill from mountain headwater streams to wider, lower-elevation streams to rivers, which empty into the ocean.

Inland wetlands provide habitats for a variety of fish, waterfowl, and other wildlife, including many rare and endangered species. Wetlands near rivers help regulate stream flow by storing water during periods of heavy rainfall and releasing it slowly. This helps reduce riverbank erosion and flood damage. These inland wetlands also improve water quality by filtering, diluting, and degrading various sediments and pollutants as water flows through.

By storing water, many wetlands allow increased infiltration, thus helping recharge groundwater supplies. Inland wetlands are used for recreation, especially waterfowl hunting, and to grow crops such as blueberries, cranberries, and rice (which feeds half the world's people). They also play significant roles in the global cycles of carbon, nitrogen, and sulfur. Wetlands — particularly the huge tracts of peat-bogs in the Northern Hemisphere — contain the planet's second-largest pool of carbon, exceeded only by that found in tropical forests. These peaceful oases in an increasingly hectic world are also great places to visit.

Because people are unaware of their ecological importance, inland wetlands often are dredged or filled in and used as croplands, garbage dumps, and sites for urban and industrial development. They are viewed as wastelands and threats to public health.

Altogether, about 56% of the area of coastal and inland wetlands that existed in the lower 48 states when the first Europeans arrived has been destroyed — enough to cover an area four times the size of Ohio. About

80% of this loss was due to draining and clearing of wetlands for agriculture. Most of the rest was used for mining, forestry, oil and gas extraction, highways, and urban development. Iowa has lost 99% of its inland wetlands and Nebraska 91%. Other countries have similar losses, with the former West Germany having lost 57% of its inland wetlands since 1950 and the Netherlands, 55%.

About 95% of remaining U.S. wetlands are inland wetlands, usually on or adjacent to agricultural property. Each year about 121,000 hectares (300,000 acres) are destroyed. About 80% of this loss involves draining and clearing for agricultural purposes.

Attempts have been made to reduce loss of inland wetlands in the United States. The Tax Reform Act of 1985 eliminated the deduction for most wetland drainage expenses and removed the capital gains benefits on the appreciation of the value of land created by destroying wetlands.

The Farm Act of 1985 has a "swampbuster" provision that denies agricultural subsidies for farmers who drain wetlands and plant crops on them. A big loophole in this law is that it does not penalize farmers who merely drain wetlands. Also, enforcement of this law is difficult and limited. Even if it were fully enforced, it would apply to only about one-third of the country's vulnerable inland wetlands.

In 1990, Congress passed the North American Wetlands Conservation Act. It will provide approximately $25 million a year for implementing the North American

Waterfowl Management Plan, by which the Canadian and American governments and conservation organizations plan to acquire and restore large areas of wetlands in the next 15 years.

A serious problem is that only about 8% of the area of remaining inland wetlands is under federal protection, and federal, state, and local protection of wetlands is weak. A federal permit is now required by a person wanting to fill wetlands or deposit dredged or fill material in them, but this law is poorly enforced. Also, this law does prohibit excavation, drainage, clearing, and flooding of wetlands not used for dredged or fill material or for agricultural purposes.

Current federal policy has the goal of no net loss of the function and value of wetlands, but this is deceptive because it allows destruction of existing wetlands as long as an equal area of the same type of wetland is restored or created. Exceptions are also allowed. Wetland restoration and creation is desirable but cannot duplicate the complex ecological services supplied by natural wetland ecosystems with any scientific certainty.

The United States urgently needs a better system for protecting and managing its wetlands, both coastal and inland. The immediate goal of such a program should be to prevent further loss of the country's natural wetlands. The long-term goal should be to restore the quantity and quality of the country's wetlands.

moving water levels mountains and cuts deep canyons. The rock and soil the water removes is then deposited as sediment in low-lying areas (Figure 5-29).

INLAND WETLANDS Lands covered with fresh water all or part of the year (excluding lakes, reservoirs, and streams) and located away from coastal areas are called **inland wetlands**. They include inland bogs,

marshes, prairie potholes (Figure 5-42), swamps, mud flats, bogs, floodplains, moors, wet meadows, and the wet arctic tundra (Figure 5-22) during summer. Shallow marshes and swamps are among the world's most productive ecosystems per unit of area (Figure 4-24). Inland wetlands are very important ecosystems that are being rapidly destroyed and degraded (see Spotlight above).

Figure 5-42 Prairie potholes in Minnesota. This type of inland wetland stores water for groundwater recharge and provides nesting areas for migratory birds. Many of these wetlands have been drained and converted into cropland. The pothole on the right has been partially drained for conversion to cropland.

CONNECTIONS BETWEEN TERRESTRIAL AND AQUATIC ENVIRONMENTS Distinguishing between land and water environments is useful, but we also need to understand how these realms of life are linked together. One important connection is the runoff of plant nutrients, mostly as nitrates and phosphates, from the land into aquatic environments. These nutrients help support plant life in streams, lakes, and estuaries, which in turn support aquatic animal life. When soil erodes into lakes and slow-moving streams, it builds up bottom sediments. These sediments gradually change the types of aquatic life that can thrive; eventually they can convert an aquatic ecosystem into a terrestrial ecosystem.

This movement of nutrients and sediment from the land to aquatic environments is a natural process. However, natural events (such as landslides, earthquakes, and hurricanes) and human activities can greatly increase the rate at which these materials are transferred from land to water.

Matter resources also flow from aquatic to terrestrial environments. Fish and shellfish are sources of food for many land-dwelling animals, such as seabirds, bears, eagles, and people. When seabirds deposit their wastes on land, they return some of these nutrients from the sea to the land as part of the nitrogen and phosphorous cycles.

The lesson to be learned from the overview of climate and Earth's terrestrial and aquatic habitats given in this chapter is that everything is interconnected, as expressed in the quote at the beginning of this chapter. Trying to deal with the problems we have created or intensified in the ecosphere's realms of air, water, land, and life without recognizing their interdependence is a blueprint for failure.

Earth and water, if not too blatantly abused, can produce again and again for the benefit of all.

STEWART L. UDALL

DISCUSSION TOPICS

1. List a limiting factor for each of the following ecosystems: **(a)** a desert, **(b)** the surface layer of the open sea, **(c)** the Arctic tundra, **(d)** the floor of a tropical rain forest, and **(e)** the bottom of a deep lake.

2. Since the deep oceans are vast and located far away from human habitats, why not use them as a depository for essentially all of our radioactive and other hazardous wastes? Give your reasons for agreeing or disagreeing with this proposal.

3. Why are coastal and inland wetlands and coral reefs considered to be some of the planet's most important ecosystems? Why have so many of these vital ecosystems been destroyed by human activities? What factors in your lifestyle contribute to the destruction and degradation of wetlands?

4. Suppose you buy coral for use in an aquarium, take samples of coral from a reef on a diving trip, damage a coral reef when you drop the anchor of the boat you are using, or discharge sewage from the boat. Explain how each of these actions can reduce Earth's biodiversity, possibly enhance global warming, and mean that sometime in the future you or any children you might have could not have enough food or water.

*5. What type of biome do you live in or near? What effects have human activities had on the characteristic vegetation and animal life normally found in this biome? How is your own lifestyle affecting this biome?

*6. If possible, visit a nearby lake. Would you classify it as oligotrophic, mesotrophic, or eutrophic? What are the primary factors contributing to its nutrient enrichment? Which of these are related to human activities?

CHAPTER 6

CHANGES IN POPULATIONS, COMMUNITIES, AND ECOSYSTEMS

General Questions and Issues

1. What are the principal effects of environmental stress on living systems?

2. How can populations of species change and adapt to natural and human-induced stresses?

3. How can populations of plant and animal species adapt to natural and human-induced stresses to preserve their stability and sustainability?

4. How can communities and ecosystems change and adapt to small- and large-scale natural and human-induced stresses?

5. What impacts do human activities have on populations, communities, and ecosystems?

6. What efforts are being made to restore ecosystems damaged by human activities?

We cannot command nature except by obeying her.

SIR FRANCIS BACON

ORGANISMS, POPULATIONS, COMMUNITIES, and ecosystems are dynamic, not static. They are always changing and adapting in response to major and minor changes in environmental conditions caused by interactions between organisms (Section 4-5), disruptions such as climate change and floods, and human actions such as land clearing and emissions of various pollutants. Understanding how organisms, populations, communities, and ecosystems adapt to stress and the limits of those adaptations can help us in sustaining these living systems rather than continuing to degrade and destroy them.

6-1 Responses of Living Systems to Environmental Stress

HOMEOSTASIS AND INFORMATION FEEDBACK

To survive, you must maintain various internal conditions, such as temperature and blood pressure, within certain tolerable ranges (Figure 4-18) in the face of a harsh and often fluctuating external environment. This state of dynamic balance is called **homeostasis**: the maintenance of constant internal conditions despite fluctuations in the external environment. Homeostasis is not a static, unchanging condition. It is a *dynamic steady state* in which internal processes change continuously in response to changes in external environmental conditions.

Homeostasis is maintained through a flow of information along a network of interconnected parts in the system. Homeostatic systems have three essential elements: a *receptor*, or *sensor*, to detect the environmental conditions; a *comparator* to evaluate information from the receptor and make decisions; and an *effector*, which executes commands from the comparator. These systems operate through **information feedback**, in which information is fed back into a system and causes it to change. This circuit of sensing, evaluating, and reacting to changes in environmental conditions is called a **feedback loop**.

There are two types of information feedback: negative and positive. **Negative feedback** is a flow of information into a system that counteracts the effects of change in external conditions to maintain a particular dynamic steady state. In effect, a *negative feedback loop* "says no" to a change in external conditions. The thermostat on a home furnace is an example of control of temperature by negative feedback of information. If the temperature of a room drops below the temperature set on the thermostat, that information (in the form of an electrical signal) is fed back into the system to turn the furnace on and raise the air temperature. When the desired temperature is reached, information is fed back to cut the furnace off.

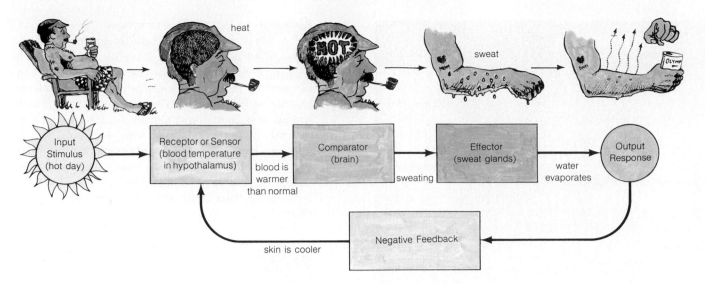

Figure 6-1 Keeping cool on a hot day — a human temperature-control system based on negative feedback of information to counteract a change in environmental conditions (arrows show flow of information). This is the principal way organisms maintain a state of fluctuating dynamic balance, or homeostasis, in which internal conditions are maintained within tolerable ranges by continuous responses to changes in environmental conditions.

Negative feedback also keeps your body temperature around 37°C (98°F), as shown in Figure 6-1. If you go outdoors on a hot day, *sensors* in your skin detect the high temperature and send that information as a nerve signal to the hypothalamus of your brain (*comparator*). Your brain then sends information as a nerve impulse to sweat glands in your skin (*effectors*) to activate sweating, a cooling mechanism. Evaporation requires energy. Thus, as sweat evaporates, it removes heat from your skin. When your body has cooled down, this new information (output response) is fed back to your skin sensors. Then your brain sends a new message to your skin effectors to slow or stop the sweating process. *You and other animals are self-regulating homeostatic systems maintained at the dynamic steady state we call life mostly by negative feedback.*

Positive feedback — also known as *runaway feedback* — occurs when a change in the system in one direction provides information that causes the system to change further in the same direction. In effect, a *positive feedback loop* "says yes" to a change in external conditions. For example, suppose the wires connecting the thermostat and a furnace were accidentally hooked up backwards. Then a positive feedback of information from the thermostat would turn the furnace on when the room got too hot. The room would then get hotter and hotter — the opposite of the desired goal.

Negative feedback generally contributes to homeostasis and tends to keep a system in a dynamic steady state, while positive feedback tends to disrupt a system's stability. In social systems, the arms race is an example of positive feedback. When country A produces more weapons, country B produces more weap-

ons, which causes country A to make more weapons, which leads country B to increase its weapons, and so on. Such a process may help prevent war through mutual deterrence. On the other hand, this runaway feedback process can continue until one or both countries go bankrupt or blow each other (and a lot of other countries and organisms) up.

Positive feedback is not always harmful. Falling in love is an example of positive feedback that amplifies beneficial feelings and actions. You take an interest in, and do something nice for, your partner, and then your partner reciprocates. This leads you to do more, your partner to do more, and so on.

Some scientists have proposed that the entire earth is a gigantic living organism, or homeostatic system, that uses complex feedback systems to regulate environmental conditions over millions of years so that life can continue. This hypothesis, proposed in the early 1970s by British chemist and inventor James Lovelock and American biologist Lynn Margulis, is called the **Gaia** (pronounced GUY-uh) **hypothesis**. According to this idea, the biosphere is an interactive, interconnected living system — a self-regulating system in which living organisms interact with nonliving chemical and geophysical processes to maintain conditions, such as atmospheric temperature and the chemical compositions of the atmosphere and oceans, that allow most existing forms of life to exist and evolve.

TIME DELAYS A characteristic of systems regulated by information feedback is **time delay**: the lapse between the time a stimulus is received and the time the system makes a corrective action by negative feedback.

Time delays can protect a system from information overload and prevent hasty responses until more information is received; however, a long delay between a cause and its effect often means that corrective action is not effective by the time symptoms of harm appear. For example, cigarette smoking is a time-delay trap. A smoker exposed to cancer-causing (carcinogenic) chemicals in inhaled cigarette smoke may not get lung cancer for 20 or 30 years. By then, it is too late for a corrective response (not to smoke) through negative feedback.

The longer the time between an action and the harmful effects of an action, the less likely we are to respond before serious damage occurs. Most of the world's economic systems and our individual economic behavior are based on maximum short-term economic gain, even though that can lead to long-term economic and environmental pain. The pleasurable effects (more money, more things) of borrowing money and depleting Earth's natural capital show up now. The ultimate financial and environmental bankruptcy from borrowing too much money and depleting nature's capital don't show up until much later. By then, the harm has been done, and correcting the situation is very expensive and painful, if it is possible at all.

Additional examples of the harmful effects of prolonged time delays are toxic dumps that have been lying around as chemical time bombs for decades, depletion of the ozone layer, projected global warming and climate change from an enhanced greenhouse effect, and degradation and destruction of forests from prolonged exposure to air pollutants. Also, by the time we discover that our actions have reduced the population of a species to the point where it is in danger of becoming extinct, it is often too late to protect and restore the species.

Similarly, if rapid exponential growth of the human population (Figure 1-2) overshoots the carrying capacity of a particular area or of most of the earth, the result is a tremendous dieback of people, mostly through disease and famine, or possibly through war as nations compete for scarce resources. The way to avoid the time-delay trap is to use input approaches to prevent long-term harm instead of relying on output (cleanup) approaches to deal with harm after the symptoms appear.

SYNERGISTIC INTERACTIONS You were taught that 1 plus 1 always equals 2, but in nature 1 plus 1 may sometimes be greater than 2, because of synergistic interactions. A **synergistic interaction** occurs when two or more processes interact so that the net effect is greater than the sum of their separate effects (1 plus 1 is greater than 2).

Acting separately, either cigarette smoke or tiny particles of asbestos fibers inhaled into the lungs over a prolonged period can cause lung cancer and death.

However, workers who are exposed to asbestos and who smoke are ten times more likely to die of lung cancer than asbestos workers who do not smoke because of a synergistic interaction between these two health risks.

Environmental problems can become worse than we project, if we fail to consider the destructive synergistic interactions between various natural processes and these environmental problems. For example, ozone-destroying chlorofluorocarbons we emit into the atmosphere synergistically link the problems of an enhanced greenhouse effect in the troposphere (Figure 5-9) and ozone depletion in the stratosphere. Marine phytoplankton, which are important absorbers of CO_2 from the troposphere, can be harmed by an increase in ultraviolet-B (UV-B) ionizing radiation resulting from a decrease in stratospheric ozone. If the quantity of marine phytoplankton should be significantly reduced by increased UV-B radiation, the ability of Earth's oceans to serve as a major sink for atmospheric carbon dioxide would be greatly reduced. The result of this harmful synergistic interaction would be an intensification and acceleration of global warming, unless other, currently unknown factors or interactions counteracted this effect.

Beneficial synergistic interactions can be used to counteract or reduce the severity of some environmental problems. For example, widespread tree planting in the tropics would produce a larger sink for removing carbon dioxide from the atmosphere to help counteract an enhanced greenhouse effect. If much of this planting consisted of tree plantations on already degraded land, it could lessen the need to cut tropical forests for lumber, reduce soil erosion and excessive flows of sediment into aquatic ecosystems, and help rehabilitate degraded land. It would also help preserve biodiversity, reduce inputs of heat-trapping CO_2 into the atmosphere when tropical forests are cut and burned without being replanted, help regulate water flow, and reduce flooding caused by deforestation.

We need much more research on harmful and beneficial environmental synergistic interactions. With such information, we will be better able to anticipate, counteract, and even prevent some of the environmental problems we face.

TYPES AND EFFECTS OF ENVIRONMENTAL STRESS Ecosystems are affected by a number of natural and human-caused changes, which are summarized in Table 6-1. Some of these changes are gradual, and some are sudden or catastrophic.

Table 6-2 summarizes what can happen to organisms, populations, communities, and ecosystems as a result of environmental stress in which one or more environmental factors fall above or below the levels tolerated by various species (Figure 4-18). The stresses that

Table 6-1 Changes Affecting Ecosystems

Natural Changes

Catastrophic	Drought
	Flood
	Fire
	Volcanic eruption
	Earthquake
	Hurricane
	Disease
Gradual	Changes in climate
	Immigration and emigration of species
	Adaptation and evolution of species as a response to environmental stress
	Changes in plant and animal life (ecological succession)

Human-Caused Changes

Catastrophic	Deforestation
	Overgrazing of grasslands
	Plowing of grasslands
	Soil erosion
	Using pesticides
	Excessive or inappropriate use of fire
	Release of toxic substances into the air, water, or soil
	Urbanization
	Mining
Gradual	Salt buildup in soil from irrigation (salinization)
	Waterlogging of soil from irrigation
	Compaction of soil from agricultural equipment
	Pollution of surface waters (streams, lakes, reservoirs, wetlands, oceans)
	Depletion and pollution of underground aquifers
	Air pollution (can also be catastrophic)
	Loss and degradation of wildlife habitat (can also be catastrophic)
	Killing of undesirable predator and pest species
	Introduction of alien species
	Release of toxic substances into the air, water, and soil
	Overhunting
	Overfishing
	Excessive tourism

Table 6-2 Some Effects of Environmental Stress

Organism Level

Physiological and biochemical changes

Psychological disorders

Behavioral changes

Fewer or no offspring

Genetic defects in offspring (mutagenic effects)

Birth defects (teratogenic effects)

Cancers (carcinogenic effects)

Death

Population Level

Population increase or decrease

Change in age structure (old, young, and weak may die)

Survival of strains genetically resistant to stress

Loss of genetic diversity and adaptability

Extinction

Community and Ecosystem Levels

Disruption of energy flow
  Decrease or increase in solar energy input
  Changes in heat output
  Changes in trophic structure in food chains and food webs

Disruption of chemical cycles
  Depletion of essential nutrients
  Excessive addition of nutrients

Simplification
  Reduction in species diversity
  Reduction or elimination of habitats and filled ecological niches
  Less complex food webs
  Possibility of lowered stability
  Possibility of ecosystem collapse

can cause the changes shown in Table 6-2 may result from natural hazards (such as earthquakes, volcanic eruptions, hurricanes, droughts, floods, and fires) or from human activities (industrialization, warfare, transportation, urbanization, and agriculture).

A population of a species that is well adapted to its environment has four basic ways to deal with an environmental stress:

- decrease its birth rate (number of births over a period of time) or suffer an increase in its death rate (number of deaths over a period of time)

- migrate to another area with a similar but less stressful environment (slow or very difficult for most plants)

- adapt to changed environmental conditions through natural selection (very slow for species that reproduce slowly and have few offspring and unlikely for a population whose members have little genetic diversity)

- become extinct

6-2 Population Responses to Stress: Population Dynamics

CHARACTERISTICS OF POPULATIONS Populations as a whole have certain characteristics, including size, density, dispersion, and age structure.

Population size is the number of individuals making up a population's gene pool. Population size affects the ability of a given population to survive. Very small populations can easily become extinct. More individuals may die naturally than are born because of the inability of individuals of reproductive age to find mates. Such populations can also become extinct when all or most remaining individuals are killed by disease, predation, or some catastrophic event such as flooding, rapid climate change, or land clearing. Genetically close individuals in small populations may also inbreed, which can lead to weakened or malformed individuals and a reduction in genetic diversity needed to adapt to changes in environmental conditions. On the other hand, when population size becomes too large, many individuals may not be able to get enough resources to survive or may be easier targets for predators.

Population density is the number of individuals of a population found in a certain amount of space at a given time. This may vary with time for some populations because of social characteristics, mating behavior, changes in seasons, or other factors. Population density also affects the ability of a population to survive. High population densities may make individuals more susceptible to disease. On the other hand, high population densities, such as those found in schools of fish and large herds of grazing animals, may provide protection for some individuals through safety in numbers.

Population dispersion refers to the general pattern in which the members of a population are arranged through its habitat. The most common dispersion pattern is clumping—for example, a herd of elephants, a flock of birds, a school of fish, or a stand of pines. Less often, individuals in a population may be randomly or rather evenly dispersed over their habitat. Population dispersion also varies with time, often in response to changing seasons or during mating seasons.

Age structure is the relative proportion of individuals of each age found in a population. These are often divided into the prereproductive, reproductive, and postreproductive age categories. A population with a large proportion of individuals in the prereproductive and reproductive categories has a high potential for rapid population growth, especially if most of the individuals in the prereproductive age group survive long enough to reproduce.

Populations undergo changes in their size, density, dispersion, and age distribution in response to changes in environmental conditions, such as an excess or a shortage of food or other critical nutrients. These changes in the properties of populations are called **population dynamics**.

CHANGES IN POPULATION SIZE: EXPONENTIAL GROWTH, BIOTIC POTENTIAL, AND CARRYING CAPACITY Changes in the birth rate (number of live births in a population per unit of time), the death rate (number of deaths in a population per unit of time), or both, are the principal ways that populations of most species respond (usually involuntarily) to changes in resource availability or other environmental changes (Figure 6-2). Favorable changes usually cause an increase in population size through more births than deaths. Unfavorable changes usually cause a drop in population size through more deaths than births.

Suppose we have a population with 1,000 members ($N = 1,000$) and that during a particular year, 30 individuals are born and 10 die. The **growth rate (r)** of the initial population (N) in percent per unit of time (such as a year) would be:

$$\text{growth rate, r (\%)} = \frac{\text{births} - \text{deaths}}{\text{initial population size (N)}} \times 100$$
$$= \frac{30 - 10}{1,000} \times 100 = 2\%$$

As long as r remains positive (births exceed deaths), the population size will increase exponentially by ever larger amounts per unit of time. Each year in which deaths exceed births results in a negative r and an exponential decrease in population size.

Populations vary in their capacity to grow exponentially. The **biotic potential** of a population is the *maximum* rate (r_{max}) at which the population of a given species can increase when there are no limits of any sort on its rate of growth. Species have different biotic potentials because of variations in **(1)** how soon reproduction starts and lasts (reproductive age span), **(2)** how often reproduction occurs, **(3)** how many live offspring are born each time, and **(4)** how many of the offspring survive to reproductive age. For many bacteria, biotic potential is 100% every half hour; for humans and other large mammals, it is between 2% and 5% per year.

With unlimited resources and ideal environmental conditions, a species can produce offspring at its maximum rate. Such growth starts slowly and then increases

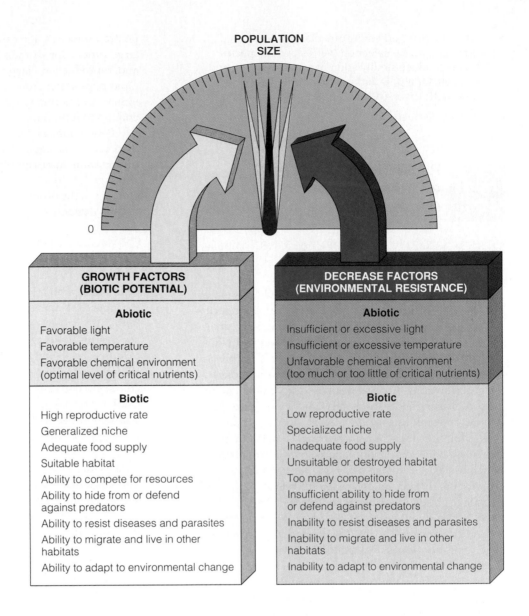

Figure 6-2 Population size is a balance between factors that increase numbers and factors that decrease numbers.

POPULATION SIZE

0

GROWTH FACTORS (BIOTIC POTENTIAL)	DECREASE FACTORS (ENVIRONMENTAL RESISTANCE)
Abiotic	**Abiotic**
Favorable light	Insufficient or excessive light
Favorable temperature	Insufficient or excessive temperature
Favorable chemical environment (optimal level of critical nutrients)	Unfavorable chemical environment (too much or too little of critical nutrients)
Biotic	**Biotic**
High reproductive rate	Low reproductive rate
Generalized niche	Specialized niche
Adequate food supply	Inadequate food supply
Suitable habitat	Unsuitable or destroyed habitat
Ability to compete for resources	Too many competitors
Ability to hide from or defend against predators	Insufficient ability to hide from or defend against predators
Ability to resist diseases and parasites	Inability to resist diseases and parasites
Ability to migrate and live in other habitats	Inability to migrate and live in other habitats
Ability to adapt to environmental change	Inability to adapt to environmental change

rapidly to produce an *exponential growth curve*, or J-shaped curve of population growth that grows steeper with time (Figure 1-2).

No matter how rapidly a population may grow, it will eventually reach some size limit imposed by shortages of one or more limiting factors, such as light, water, space, and nutrients. Infinite growth cannot be sustained indefinitely in an environment with a finite size and finite resources.

Environmental resistance consists of all the limiting factors jointly acting to limit the growth of a population. They determine the **carrying capacity (K)**, the number of individuals of a given species that can be sustained indefinitely in a given area. The carrying capacity for a population is not fixed and can vary over time because of changes in seasons and other environmental conditions.

Because of environmental resistance, any population growing exponentially at, or below, its biotic poten-

tial starts out slowly, goes through a rapid growth phase, and then levels off once the carrying capacity is reached. In most cases, the size of a population undergoing this type of growth fluctuates slightly above and below its carrying capacity. A plot of this type of growth yields an *S-shaped curve* (Figure 6-3a).

Sometimes a population undergoing rapid growth overshoots its carrying capacity and suffers a dieback or population crash (Figure 6-3b), unless large numbers can migrate to an area with more favorable conditions. When resource limits are approached, time is required for the birth rate to fall and the death rate to rise. This *reproductive time lag* allows a population to temporarily overshoot its carrying capacity. The population may then fall back to a size that typically fluctuates around the area's carrying capacity, or to a lower level if the area's carrying capacity was lowered because of resource destruction and degradation during the overshoot period.

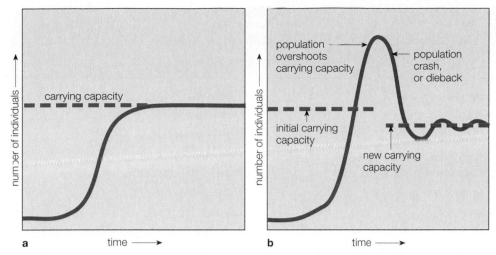

Figure 6-3 (**a**) Idealized S-shaped curve of population growth. (**b**) Overshoot and dieback occur when a rapidly expanding population temporarily overshoots the carrying capacity of its environment, or when a change in environmental conditions lowers that carrying capacity. The population size may fall roughly to the size supported by the area's carrying capacity. If the excess population destroyed or degraded vegetation, soil, or other resources, the carrying capacity of an area may be lowered. Then the population dieback or crash is more severe. These idealized curves only approximate what goes on in nature.

Crashes have occurred in the human populations of various countries throughout history. Ireland, for example, experienced a population crash after a fungus infection destroyed the potato crop in 1845. Because of this prolonged disaster, about 1 million people died and 3 million people emigrated to other countries.

In spite of such local and regional disasters, the overall human population on Earth has continued to grow (Figure 1-2). Humans have made technological, social, and other cultural changes that have extended Earth's carrying capacity for their species (Figure 2-2). These changes include developing methods of increasing food production, controlling disease, and using large amounts of energy and matter resources to make normally uninhabitable areas of Earth inhabitable. A crucial question is how long we will be able to keep doing this on a planet with finite resources, which we are depleting and degrading at a rapid rate.

REPRODUCTIVE STRATEGIES: r-STRATEGISTS AND K-STRATEGISTS Each species has a characteristic mode of reproduction. At one extreme are species, called **r-strategists**, that reproduce early and produce large numbers of usually small and short-lived offspring in a short period of time. These offspring are small, mature rapidly, and receive little or no parental care. Typically, large numbers of these competitively inferior and vulnerable offspring die before reaching reproductive age, but some survive long enough to reproduce.

This reproductive mode is based on a species having the capacity for a high rate of population growth (r), explaining why these species are called r-strategists.

Examples of r-strategists are algae, bacteria, rodents, annual plants, many fish, and most insects.

Such species tend to be *opportunists* that can reproduce rapidly when conditions are favorable, or when a new habitat or niche becomes available—a cleared forest or a newly plowed field, for example. Unfavorable environmental conditions, however, can cause such populations to crash. Hence, populations of most r-strategists exhibit large fluctuations in size as they go through "boom-and-bust" cycles.

At the other extreme are **K-strategists**, species that produce a few, often fairly large offspring but invest a great deal of time and energy to ensure that most of those offspring will reach reproductive age. These species typically live in fairly stable environments and tend to maintain their population size near their habitat's carrying capacity (K), explaining why they are called K-strategists. Their populations typically follow an S-shaped growth curve (Figure 6-3). Examples are humans, elephants, rhinoceroses, whales, sharks, most other moderate to large mammals, and most large, long-lived plants, such as the saguaro cactus (Figure 4-7).

Table 6-3 summarizes the characteristics of r-strategists and K-strategists. In reality, most species have reproductive strategies that fall somewhere between these two extremes.

MIGRATION AND CHANGES IN AGE STRUCTURE Members of some animal species can avoid, or reduce the effects of, an environmental stress by leaving one area (emigration) and migrating to an area (immigration) with more favorable environmental conditions and

Table 6-3 Characteristics of r-Strategists and K-Strategists

r-strategists	K-strategists
Many, small young	Fewer, larger young
Little or no care of young	More care of young
Rapid development	Slower development
Early reproductive age	Later reproductive age
Limited competitive ability	Greater competitive ability
Short life (less than 1 year)	Longer life
Small adults	Larger adults
Live in areas with variable or unpredictable climates and other environmental conditions	Live in areas with moderately stable climates and other environmental conditions
Emphasis on productivity	Emphasis on efficiency
Population size fluctuates wildly, usually far below carrying capacity	Population size remains fairly stable, usually close to its carrying capacity

resource supplies. Plants can migrate to other areas, but that often takes decades or centuries. Thus, four variables—births, deaths, immigration, and emigration—determine the rate of change in the number of individuals in a population over a period of time:

$$\text{population change rate} = \left(\begin{array}{c}\text{births} \\ + \\ \text{immigration}\end{array}\right) - \left(\begin{array}{c}\text{deaths} \\ + \\ \text{emigration}\end{array}\right)$$

There also may be a change in the age structure of the population; that is, the numbers of individuals of different ages and sex may change. Old, very young, and weak members may die when exposed to an environmental stress.

6-3 Population Responses to Stress Through Adaptation

NATURAL SELECTION A population of a particular species can undergo changes in its genetic composition, or gene pool, that enable it to adapt better to changes in environmental conditions. This can happen because not all individuals of a population have exactly the same genes. Each has a unique combination of such traits as size, shape, color, and ability to withstand temperature extremes and exposure to certain toxic substances.

This *genetic diversity* helps protect a species from extinction. Individuals with a genetic composition that allows them to survive changes in environmental conditions generally produce more offspring than those that don't have these traits, and they pass these traits on to their offspring, a process known as **differential reproduction**.

The process by which some genes and gene combinations in a population are reproduced more than others is called **natural selection**. Charles Darwin, who proposed this idea in 1858, described natural selection as "survival of the fittest." That phrase has often been misinterpreted to mean survival of the strongest, biggest, or most aggressive. Instead, *fittest* means that individuals in a population with the genetic traits best able to survive and reproduce under existing environmental conditions tend to outreproduce and replace less successful individuals (Figure 6-4). If individuals in a population with one kind of genetic endowment regularly outreproduce those with another, then natural selection is taking place.

EVOLUTION The change in the genetic composition of a population exposed to new environmental conditions resulting from differential reproduction of genetic types (genotypes) and natural selection is called **biological evolution**, or simply **evolution**.

Species differ widely in how rapidly they can undergo evolution through natural selection. The primary requirement is that some individuals in a population must be able to survive and reproduce when there is an environmental change. Ability to do that depends on the amount of genetic diversity in the gene pool of the species, the degree of the environmental change, and how rapidly the change takes place.

A population of species with a high degree of genetic diversity is more likely to have some members that

J. A. Bishop and L. M. Cook

J. A. Bishop and L. M. Cook

Figure 6-4 Two varieties of peppered moths found in England in the 1800s. In the mid-1800s, before the Industrial Revolution, the speckled light gray form of this moth was prevalent. These moths, active at night, rested on light gray speckled lichens on tree trunks during the day. Their color helped camouflage them from their bird predators. A dark gray form also existed but was quite rare. However, as the Industrial Revolution proceeded during the last half of the 1800s, the dark form of this moth sharply increased in frequency, especially near industrial cities. Soot and other pollutants from factory smokestacks began killing lichens and darkening tree trunks. In this new environment, the dark form blended in with the blackened trees and the light form was highly visible to its bird predators. Through natural selection, the dark form began to survive and reproduce at a greater rate than its light-colored kin. (Both varieties appear in each photo. Can you spot them?)

can tolerate a low to moderate environmental change, or one that takes place gradually. Conversely, a species with little genetic diversity is subject to extinction from even a small change in environmental conditions. As the degree of environmental change or the rate at which it occurs increases, greater genetic diversity is required for survival. That is why it is so important for us not to destroy the existing genetic diversity within each species (see Spotlight on p. 11). Of course, cataclysmic environmental changes, such as nuclear war, rapid climate change (within a few decades), or the clearing of a tropical rain forest containing highly specialized species, cause the extinction of large numbers of species.

Species that are r-strategists (Table 6-3) that can quickly produce a large number of tiny offspring with short average life spans (weeds, insects, rodents, bacteria) and that have a fairly high genetic diversity can adapt to a change in environmental conditions through natural selection in a relatively short time. For example, when a chemical is used as a pesticide to reduce the insect population in an area, a small number of resistant individuals usually survive. They can then rapidly breed new populations with a larger number of individuals genetically resistant to the toxic effects of the chemical. Thus, in the long run, our present chemical approach to pest control usually increases, not decreases, the populations of species we consider pests. It is an example of a harmful or runaway positive feedback system that eventually worsens the situation we are trying to correct. As one observer put it, "I hope that when the insects take over the world, they will remember that we always took them along on our picnics."

K-strategist species—elephants, tigers, sharks, and humans—have long generation times and a small number in each litter, and may have only low to moderate genetic diversity. This means that they cannot reproduce a large number of offspring rapidly. For such species, adaptation to an environmental stress by natural selection typically takes thousands to millions of years. If they cannot adapt or evolve into a new species because of lack of time or low genetic diversity, they become extinct.

COEVOLUTION Over a long period of time, interacting species in an ecosystem exert selective pressures on each other that can lead each to undergo various adaptations. Evolution resulting from such interactions between species is called **coevolution**. For example, a carnivore species may become increasingly efficient at hunting and capturing its prey. If certain individuals in the prey population have traits that allow them to elude the predator species, they pass these adaptive traits on to their offspring. Then the predator species may evolve ways to overcome this new trait, leading the prey to new adaptations, and so on.

Similarly, plants may evolve defenses, such as camouflage or unpleasant or poisonous chemicals, against efficient herbivores. This, in turn, can lead their herbivore consumers to evolve ways to counteract those defenses. Animals may also evolve adaptations such as poisons (Figure 4-35) to help protect them from their predators. Through coevolution, animals may also develop camouflage for protection or to make them more effective predators.

Coevolution enhances or leads to mutualism (Figure 4-41), commensalism, and other relationships between species. An example is the mutual dependence of flowering plants on animal pollinators and seed dispersers and of these animal species on those same plants for their nutrition. For example, various species of pollinating hummingbirds with different beak lengths have coevolved with flowering plants of different colors and sizes adapted to their beak sizes (Figure 6-5).

SPECIATION AND EXTINCTION Earth's estimated 40 to 80 million species are believed to be the result of a combination of two processes taking place over billions of years (Figure 6-6). One is **speciation**: the formation of two species from one species as a result of divergent natural selection in response to changes in environmental conditions. The other is **extinction**: A species ceases to exist because it cannot genetically adapt and successfully reproduce under new environmental conditions. It may no longer exist in any form, or it may evolve into a new, genetically modified species better adapted to new environmental conditions. Most of the evidence we have about speciation and extinction comes from the discovery of fossils.

Biologists estimate that 98% to 99% of all the species that have ever lived are now extinct. However, the fact that we have 40 to 80 million species on Earth today means that speciation, on average, has kept ahead of extinction. Speciation can occur from changes within a single genetic line over a long period of time, often because of long-term changes in climate (Figure 6-7). It can also take place by the gradual splitting of lines of descent into two or more new species in response to new environmental conditions. This type of speciation is believed to occur when members of a particular species become distributed over geographical areas with different climates, food sources, soils, and other environmental conditions for long periods — typically for 1,000 to 100,000 generations.

Populations of some animal species may split up and live in areas with quite different environmental conditions when part of the group migrates in search of food (Figure 6-8). Populations may also become separated by physical barriers caused by earthquakes, continental drift, and other geological events, or by accidental or deliberate transplantation of a few individuals to new areas by humans. Winds can transport the seeds of plant species to new areas with different environmental conditions.

Long-term geographic separation of members of a particular sexually reproducing species is called **reproductive isolation**. If the isolated populations remain separated under different conditions long enough, they may diverge in their genetic makeup because of differences in selection pressure. If this happens, members of the two populations may become so different that even if they were united, they would no longer be capable of interbreeding and producing fertile offspring. Members of the isolated populations may have devel-

Figure 6-5 Coevolution. Many flowering plants have co-evolved with animals such as hummingbirds, which transfer pollen from one flower to another so the plant species can reproduce. Through coevolution, the flowers of the plant shown here have a distinct color and depth that attract certain species of hummingbirds. In turn, species of hummingbirds have evolved beak lengths and responses to specific flower colors and shapes that enable them to feed on certain flower species. This helps reduce competition and niche overlap between various hummingbird species.

oped different courtship signals and may no longer respond to each other's signals. Or the genetic makeup of the two populations may have become so different that any hybrid offspring they produce are sterile (like mules) or are so weak and malformed that they die before reaching reproductive age. As a result of such reproductive isolation, one species has become two different species.

In some rapidly producing organisms (mostly r-strategists), speciation may take place in thousands or even hundreds of years. With most species (especially K-strategists), however, it takes from tens of thousands to millions of years.

Over billions of years, the combination of speciation and extinction operating through natural selection has produced the planet's most valuable resource: *biological diversity*, or *biodiversity*. One of our goals should be not to reduce by our actions the *genetic diversity, species diversity, and ecological diversity* that make up this biological part of Earth's natural capital.

6-4 Community and Ecosystem Responses to Stress

ECOLOGICAL SUCCESSION One characteristic of most communities and ecosystems is that the types of species present in a given area are usually changing. The process by which gradual changes occur in the composition of species making up a community or ecosystem is called **ecological succession**, or **community development**.

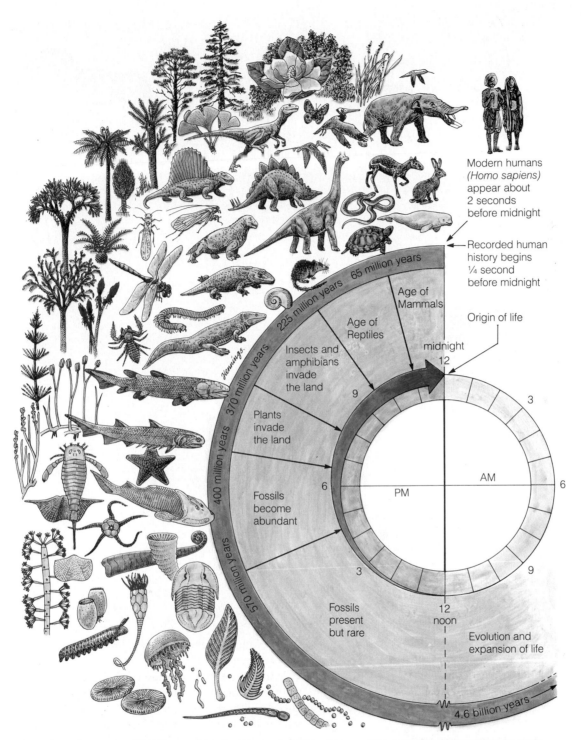

Figure 6-6 Greatly simplified history of the development of different forms of life on Earth through biological evolution. If we compress the development of different forms of life on Earth through biological evolution to a 24-hour time scale, our closest human ancestors (*Homo sapiens*) appeared about 2 seconds before midnight, and our species (*Homo sapiens sapiens*) appeared less than 1 second before midnight. Agriculture began only ¼ second before midnight, and the Industrial Revolution has been around for only seven thousandths of a second. Despite our brief time on Earth, we are now in the process of hastening the extinction of more of the planet's species in a shorter time than at any other time in Earth's 4.6-billion-year history. (Adapted from George Gaylord Simpson and William S. Beck, *Life: An Introduction to Biology*, 2nd ed., New York: Harcourt Brace Jovanovich, 1965.)

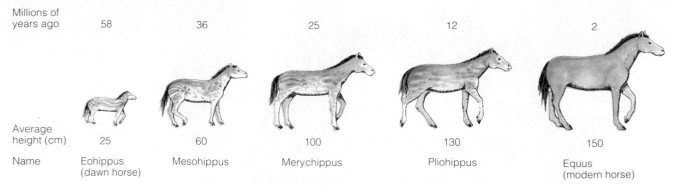

Figure 6-7 Speciation of the horse through natural selection along the same genetic line into different equine species in response to changing environmental conditions, especially long-term changes in climate.

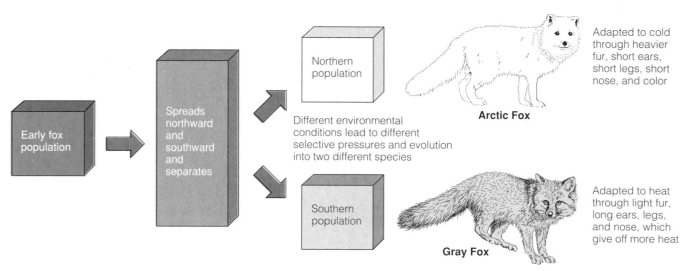

Figure 6-8 Speciation of an early species of fox into two different species as a result of migration of portions of the original fox population into areas with different climates. See Figure 4-1 for a photograph of an arctic fox with its white winter coat.

Succession is a normal process in nature. It reflects the results of the continuing struggle between various species with different adaptations to obtain the food, light, space, nutrients, and other resources each needs to survive and reproduce under changing environmental conditions.

Ecologists recognize two types of ecological succession: primary and secondary. Which type takes place depends on the conditions at a particular site at the beginning of the process. **Primary succession** involves the development of biotic communities in an area with no true soil. Examples of such areas include the rock or mud exposed by a retreating glacier or a mudslide, cooled lava, a new sandbar deposited by a shift in ocean currents, and surface-mined areas from which all topsoil has been removed.

After such a large-scale disturbance, life usually begins to recolonize a site. First, a few hardy **pioneer species**, often microbes, mosses, and lichens, invade the environment (Figure 6-9). They are usually r-strategists with the ability to quickly establish large populations in a new area. Sometimes, the species that make up this pioneer community change environmental conditions so much that the area is more suitable for other species with different niche requirements, a process called *facilitation*. More common is *inhibition*, in which early species create conditions that hinder invasions and growth by other species. Then succession can proceed only when a fire, extensive grazing, bulldozing, or some other disturbance removes most of the early-successional species and paves the way for other species. In other cases, later species are largely unaffected by the presence of earlier species, a phenomenon known as *tolerance*.

Newly created ponds may also undergo primary succession. When a pond is created, it is a nutrient-poor

Figure 6-9 Colorful red and yellow lichens growing on bare slate rocks in the foothills of the Sierra Nevada near Merced, California. Lichens are formed by a mutualistic relationship in which fungi and algae live together, resulting in perhaps nature's simplest community. The fungus absorbs moisture that the alga needs, secretes acids that help the lichen remain attached to the rock, and dissolves minerals from the rock that are used by the fungus and the alga. The alga, in turn, carries out photosynthesis and supplies itself and the fungus with carbohydrates. These symbiotic communities produce acid compounds, which dissolve parts of the rocky surfaces, contributing mineral matter needed for gradual soil development.

(oligotrophic) body of water (Figure 5-39). As plant nutrients enter the pond from the surrounding land, the pond supports rooted and floating plants. Eventually the floating plants are replaced by invading rooted plants, which may convert the pond to a swamp or bog. Continuing buildup of sediment allows shrubs and trees to colonize the area.

The more common type of succession is **secondary succession**, which begins in an area where the natural vegetation has been removed or destroyed but where the soil or bottom sediment has not been covered or removed. Examples of areas that can undergo secondary succession include abandoned farmlands, burned or cut forests, heavily polluted streams, and land that has been flooded naturally or to produce a reservoir or pond. Because some soil or sediment is present, new vegetation can usually sprout within only a few weeks.

In the central (Piedmont) region of North Carolina, European settlers cleared away the native mature oak and hickory forests and planted the land in crops. Figure 6-10 shows how abandoned farmland there, covered with a thick layer of soil, has undergone secondary succession over a period of about 150 years until the area is again covered with a mature oak and hickory forest.

Ecological succession can result in a progression from immature, rapidly changing, unstable communities to more mature, self-sustaining communities when this process is not disrupted by large-scale natural events or human actions. It is tempting to conclude that succession proceeds in an orderly, predictable sequence, with each successional stage leading predictably to the next, more stable stage until an area is occupied by a stable, mature, or climax, community.

Research has shown that this is not necessarily the case. The exact sequence of species and community types that appear during primary or secondary succession can be highly variable. Thus, we cannot safely predict what the course of a given succession will be or view it as some preordained progress toward an ideally adapted climax community. Nor can we consider the so-called climax species that dominate an ecosystem at a mature stage of succession to be "superior" to species that have preceded them in earlier stages of succession.

COMPARISON OF IMMATURE AND MATURE ECOSYSTEMS Immature ecosystems and mature ecosystems have strikingly different characteristics, as summarized in Table 6-4. Immature communities at the early stages of succession have only a few species (low species diversity) and fairly simple food webs, made up mostly of producers fed upon by herbivores, with relatively few decomposers.

Most of the plants in a pioneer community are small annuals that grow close to the ground. They are r-strategists that use most of their energy to produce large numbers of small seeds for reproduction rather than to develop large root, stem, and leaf systems. They receive some matter resources from other ecosystems because they are too simple to hold and recycle many of the nutrient elements they need.

In contrast, the community in a mature ecosystem has high species diversity, relatively stable populations, and complex food webs dominated by decomposers. Most plants in mature ecosystems are larger herbs and trees that produce a small number of large seeds. They use most of their energy and matter resources to maintain their large root, trunk, and leaf systems rather than to produce large numbers of new plants. They also have the complexity necessary to entrap, hold, and recycle most of the nutrients they need.

DOES DIVERSITY LEAD TO STABILITY? Organisms, populations, communities, and ecosystems have some ability to withstand or recover from externally imposed changes or stresses (Table 6-1)—provided those stresses are not too severe. In other words, they have some degree of *stability*.

This stability, however, is maintained only by constant dynamic change. Although an organism maintains a fairly stable structure over its life span, it is continually gaining and losing matter and energy. Similarly, in a mature tropical rain forest, some trees will die, and others will take their place. Some species may disappear, and the number of individual species in the forest may change. Unless it is cut, burned, or blown

Table 6-4 Ecosystem Characteristics at Immature and Mature Stages of Ecological Succession

Characteristic	Immature Ecosystem	Mature Ecosystem
Ecosystem Structure		
Plant size	Small	Large
Species diversity	Low	High
Trophic structure	Mostly producers, few decomposers	Mixture of producers, consumers, and decomposers
Ecological niches	Few, mostly generalized	Many, mostly specialized
Community organization (number of interconnecting links)	Low	High
Ecosystem Function		
Food chains and webs	Simple, mostly plant → herbivore with few decomposers	Complex, dominated by decomposers
Efficiency of nutrient recycling	Low	High
Efficiency of energy use	Low	High

Figure 6-10 Secondary ecological succession of plant communities in an abandoned farm field in North Carolina over about 150 years. Succession of animal communities is not shown.

down, however, you will recognize it as a tropical rain forest 50 years from now.

It is useful to distinguish between three aspects of stability in living systems. **Inertia**, or **persistence**, is the ability of a living system to resist being disturbed or altered. **Constancy** is the ability of a living system, such as a population, to maintain a certain size or keep its numbers within certain limits. **Resilience** is the ability of a living system to restore itself close to an original condition after being exposed to an outside disturbance that is not too drastic.

Communities and ecosystems are so complex and variable that ecologists have little understanding of how they maintain some degree of inertia and resilience and also undergo continual change in response to changes in environmental conditions. A major problem is the difficulty of conducting controlled experiments. Identifying and observing even a tiny fraction of the interacting variables in simple communities and ecosystems is virtually impossible. Greatly simplified ecosystems can be set up and observed under laboratory conditions, but extrapolating the results of such experiments to much more complex, natural communities and ecosystems is difficult, if not impossible.

At one time, it was believed that the higher the species diversity in an ecosystem, the greater its stability. According to this idea, an ecosystem with a diversity of species has more ways to respond to most environmental stresses because it does not "have all its eggs in one basket." Research indicates that there are numerous exceptions to this intuitively appealing idea. The relationship between species diversity and stability is at best rather loose, and in some cases it does not exist.

Part of the problem is that there are different ways to define stability and diversity. Does an ecosystem need both high inertia and high resilience to be considered stable? Evidence indicates that some ecosystems have one of these properties but not the other. For example, California redwood forests (Figure 2-6) and tropical rain forests (Figure 5-23) have high species diversity and high inertia. This means they are hard to alter significantly or to destroy. However, once large tracts of these diverse ecosystems are cleared or severely degraded, they have such low resilience that they may never become such forests again—the soil nutrients and other environmental conditions needed for recovery are no longer present.

On the other hand, grasslands, with a much lower species diversity than most forests, burn easily and thus have low inertia. However, because most of their plant matter consists of roots beneath the ground surface, these ecosystems have high resilience, which allows them to recover quickly. A grassland can be destroyed only if its roots are plowed up and wheat or some other crop is planted in its soil (Figure 5-20).

Another difficulty is that until recently most ecologists have assumed that the normal condition of a population, a community, or an ecosystem is a fairly stable state of natural dynamic equilibrium. Populations of predator and prey populations were believed to remain in an essentially stable balance. Populations of fish and wildlife were thought to grow to the maximum size, the carrying capacity, that could be sustained by their environment. Populations will tend to remain at or near this level, if the species is not harvested at a rate that exceeds it—the concept of sustainable yield widely used in wildlife management. A forest grows to a diverse, mature climax stage that becomes its naturally permanent condition. When populations and communities are disturbed they have a built-in tendency to return their former states of dynamic equilibrium.

However, recent research casts doubt on this intuitively appealing concept of natural equilibrium or balance of nature. Populations, communities, and ecosystems are rarely, if ever, at equilibrium. Instead, nature is in a continuing state of disturbance and fluctuation. Change and turmoil, more than constancy and balance, is the rule. The size and other properties of undisturbed populations and communities vary between some limits but rarely remain at some constant level. When disturbed, these systems may change and operate within a new set of limits, rather than returning to some "perfect" equilibrium state.

Clearly, we have a long way to go in understanding how the factors involved in natural communities and ecosystems interact and change in response to changes in environmental conditions. Because of our limited understanding of how nature works, we are often unable to predict the short- and long-term beneficial and harmful effects of simplifying an ecosystem by the intentional or accidental removal or addition of a species (see Spotlight on p. 160).

| 6-5 | ## Human Impacts on Ecosystems |

HUMAN BEINGS AND ECOSYSTEMS In modifying ecosystems for our use, we simplify them. For example, we plow grasslands and clear forests. Then we replace the thousands of interrelated plant and animal species in those ecosystems with greatly simplified, single-crop ecosystems (Figures 5-20 and 5-25), or monocultures, or with structures, such as buildings, highways, and parking lots. A monoculture of plants is an unstable and vulnerable system that lacks the checks and balances of a natural diverse ecosystem.

Modern agriculture is based on the practice of deliberately keeping ecosystems in early stages of succes-

Table 6-5 Comparison of a Natural Ecosystem and a Simplified Human System

Natural Ecosystem (marsh, grassland, forest)	Simplified Human System (cornfield, factory, house)
Captures, converts, and stores energy from the sun	Consumes energy from fossil or nuclear fuels
Produces oxygen and consumes carbon dioxide	Consumes oxygen and produces carbon dioxide from the burning of fossil fuels
Creates fertile soil	Depletes or covers fertile soil
Stores, purifies, and releases water gradually	Often uses and contaminates water and releases it rapidly
Provides wildlife habitats	Destroys some wildlife habitats
Filters and detoxifies pollutants and waste products free of charge	Produces pollutants and waste, which must be cleaned up at our expense
Usually capable of self-maintenance and self-renewal	Requires continual maintenance and renewal at great cost

sion, in which the biomass productivity of one or a few plant species (such as corn or wheat) is high. Such simplified ecosystems are highly vulnerable.

A serious problem is the continual invasion of crop fields by unwanted pioneer species, which we call *weeds* if they are plants, *pests* if they are insects or other animals, and *pathogens* if they are harmful microorganisms such as bacteria, fungi, and viruses. Weeds, pests, or pathogens can wipe out an entire monoculture crop unless it is artificially protected with pesticides such as insecticides (insect-killing chemicals) and herbicides (plant-killing chemicals) or by some form of biological control.

When rapidly breeding insect species develop genetic resistance to certain chemicals in pesticides, farmers must use ever-stronger doses or switch to a new product. This increases the rate of natural selection of the pests to the point that eventually the chemicals become ineffective. This illustrates biologist Garrett Har-

din's **first law of ecology**: We can never do merely one thing. Any intrusion into nature has numerous effects, many of which are unpredictable.

Cultivation is not the only way people simplify ecosystems. Ranchers, who don't want bison or prairie dogs competing with sheep for grass, eradicate those species, as well as wolves, coyotes, eagles, and other predators that occasionally kill sheep. Far too often, ranchers allow livestock to overgraze grasslands until excessive soil erosion converts these ecosystems to simpler and less productive deserts.

The cutting of vast areas of diverse tropical rain forests is causing the irreversible loss of many plant and animal species. People also tend to overfish and overhunt some species to extinction or near extinction, another way of simplifying ecosystems. The burning of fossil fuels in industrial plants, homes, and vehicles creates atmospheric pollutants that return to Earth as acidic compounds in fog, rain, and solid particles. These chemicals simplify forest ecosystems by killing or weakening trees and aquatic ecosystems by killing fish.

It is becoming increasingly clear that the price we pay for simplifying, maintaining, and protecting such stripped-down ecosystems is high: It includes time, money, increased use of matter and energy resources, reduced biodiversity, and loss of natural landscape (Table 6-5). There is also the danger that, as the human population grows, we will convert too many of the world's mature ecosystems to simple, young, productive, but highly vulnerable forms. The challenge is to maintain a balance between simplified, human ecosystems and the neighboring, more complex (mature), natural ecosystems on which our simplified systems and other forms of life depend.

During the last 40,000 years or so, the human species has used its intelligence to develop technologies and cultural mechanisms to gain increasing control over Earth's nonliving and living resources and thus greatly expand the apparent carrying capacity of the planet for humans (Figure 2-2). We have also learned to speed up genetic change in other species—first through crossbreeding and recently through genetic engineering (see Pro/Con below).

PRO/CON Do the Benefits of Genetic Engineering Outweigh the Risks?

For many decades, humans have selected and crossbred genetic varieties of plants and animals to develop new varieties with certain desired qualities. Today, "genetic engineers" have learned how to splice genes and recombine sequences of existing DNA molecules in organisms to produce DNA with new genetic characteristics (recombinant DNA).

In other words, they use laboratory techniques to transfer traits from one species to another to make new genetic combinations (Figure 6-11) instead of waiting for nature to evolve new genetic combinations through natural selection. We are already using this biotechnology to produce new forms of life that are then patented and sold in the marketplace. Genetic engineering may give us greatly increased control over the course of evolution of Earth's living species.

This developing technology excites some scientists and many investors. They see it as a way to increase crop and livestock yields and to produce, patent, and sell plant and livestock varieties that have greater resistance to diseases, pests, frost, and drought and that provide greater quantities of nutrients such as proteins. They hope to develop and sell bacteria that can destroy oil spills, degrade toxic wastes, and concentrate metals found in low-grade ores, and to develop new vaccines, drugs, and therapeutic hormones. Gene therapy would also

Figure 6-11 Genetic engineering. The six-month-old mouse on the left is normal. The other mouse of the same age contains a human-growth hormone gene in the chromosomes of all its cells. In general, mice with the human-growth hormone gene grow two to three times as fast and grow twice as large as mice without the gene. The transference of this trait can be used to study possible effects of using this form of genetic engineering on individuals whose growth is stunted. Basketball coaches might hope to use it to grow taller players.

R. L. Brinster and R. E. Hammer/School of Veterinary Medicine, University of Pennsylvania

be used to eliminate certain genetic diseases and other genetic afflictions.

Already, genetic engineering has produced a drug to arrest heart attacks and agents to fight diabetes, hemophilia, and some forms of cancer. It has also been used to diagnose AIDS and cancer. Genetically altered viruses have been used to manufacture more effective vaccines and human-growth hormones.

In agriculture, gene transfer has been used to develop strawberries that resist frost and smaller cows that produce more milk. Toxin-producing genes have been transferred from bacteria to plants, increasing the plants' immunity to insect attack. Genetic technology has also produced edible fish that grow faster and bigger than conventional varieties.

(continued)

Some people are horrified by the prospect of biotechnology running amok. Most of these critics recognize that it is essentially impossible to stop the development of genetic engineering, which is already well under way, but they believe that this technology should be kept under strict control.

They are particularly concerned that it may be used to reduce the natural genetic diversity among individuals of a single species. It could also reduce the biological diversity represented by the world's variety of species. Genetic diversity and species diversity are essential to the long-term functioning and adaptability of ecosystems and the ecosphere. These critics do not believe that people have enough understanding of how nature works to be trusted with such great control over the genetic characteristics of humans and other species.

Critics also fear that unregulated biotechnology could lead to the development of "superorganisms." If such organisms were released deliberately or accidentally into the environment, they could cause unpredictable, possibly harmful effects. Most would probably be safe, but some would almost certainly turn out to be dangerous.

Critics are especially concerned with increasing military control over the development of biotechnology in the United States and other countries. These highly secret activities are not subject to the normal scientific review. Also, the military is likely to use genetic engineering to develop harmful organisms for use in biological warfare. The history of grossly inadequate control over the safety of nuclear weapons facilities in the United States and in the Soviet Union over the past 45 years heightens public fears about safety in government biological warfare facilities.

Since many organisms, especially bacteria, are capable of rapidly reproducing and spreading to new locations, any problems they cause would be widespread. For example, genetically altered bacteria designed to clean up ocean oil spills by degrading the oil might multiply rapidly and eventually degrade the world's remaining oil supplies—including the oil in cars and trucks.

Genetically engineered organisms might also mutate and change their form and behavior. Unlike defective cars and other products, living organisms can't be recalled once they are in the environment.

The risks of this or other catastrophic events resulting from biotechnology are small. Nevertheless, critics fear that biotechnology is a potential source of such enormous profits that without strict controls, greed—not ecological wisdom and restraint—will take over. They contend that rules proposed by the EPA in 1988 for regulation of biotechnology are wholly inadequate. A serious problem is that regulatory authority would be delegated to committees dominated, if not fully controlled, by the industries proposing releases of bioengineered organisms into the environment.

Genetic scientists answer that it is highly unlikely that the release of genetically engineered species would cause serious and widespread ecological problems. To have a serious effect, such organisms would have to be outstanding competitors and resistant to predation. In addition, they would have to be capable of becoming dominant in ecosystems and in the ecosphere. Critics point out that this has happened many times when we have accidentally or deliberately introduced alien organisms into biological communities.

In 1989, a committee of prominent ecologists appointed by the Ecological Society of America released a report stating that many of the assertions about the inherent safety of genetically engineered organisms are not true. They point out that the risk posed by a bioengi-neered organism released or escaping into the environment depends on whether it survives and reproduces, its potential for spread, its interactions with other organisms, and its effects on the physical environment. No sweeping statements about safety can be valid until there are answers to these important questions.

Generally, adding a gene or genes tends to reduce the fitness of an organism to survive and thrive in the environment. However, the committee warns that it might take hundreds of thousands of generations before the trait is eliminated. Meanwhile, natural selection will tend to increase the fitness of the organism. If the organism passes on the new gene to other organisms in the environment, that trait could persist even after the original modified organism has died out.

The committee also pointed out that genetic engineering techniques provide the ability to transfer traits among very different species, creating combinations that could not rise from traditional crossbreeding. The ecological impacts of these new combinations would be difficult to predict.

This report calls for a case-by-case review of any proposed environmental releases. It also calls for carefully regulated, small-scale field tests before any bioengineered organism is put into commercial use.

This controversy illustrates the difficulty of balancing the actual and potential benefits of a technology with its actual and potential risks of harm.

What restrictions, if any, do you believe should be placed on genetic engineering research and use? How would you enforce such restrictions?

SOME ENVIRONMENTAL LESSONS It should be clear from the brief discussion of principles in this chapter and in Chapters 4 and 5 that living systems have six key features: *interdependence, diversity, resilience, adaptability, unpredictability,* and *limits* (see Spotlight below).

In addition to the first law of ecology, our actions should take into account the **second law of ecology** or principle of interrelatedness: *Everything is connected to and intermingled with everything else; we are all in it together.* Another cardinal rule is the **third law of ecology**: *Any substance that we produce should not interfere with any of Earth's natural biogeochemical cycles.*

6-6 Ecosystem Rehabilitation and Restoration

REHABILITATION VERSUS RESTORATION Researchers are creating a new discipline of *rehabilitation and restoration ecology*, devoted to renewing damaged areas and ecosystems. When a degraded ecosystem is abandoned, in most cases it will eventually restore itself, at least partially, through ecological succession (Figure 6-10).

Usually, such *natural restoration* takes a long time. It typically takes more than a century for a slash-and-burn site in a tropical forest (Figure 2-5) to be fully reforested. If such a site is cleared by bulldozer, natural recovery will take at least 1,000 years. Large cleared areas of tropical rain forests may become grasslands or deserts.

By studying how natural ecosystems respond to and recover from severe stresses, scientists are learning how to speed up the repair of environments that have been damaged by our actions. Environmentally degraded ecosystems can be either rehabilitated or restored, at least partially, by our active involvement. *Rehabilitation* involves trying to make degraded land useful for humans again on a sustainable basis. It is particularly useful for stopping soil erosion and desertification and allowing degraded land to be used again to produce food or fuel.

Active restoration is more ambitious. Its goal is to take a degraded site and reestablish a community of organisms close to what would be found naturally. Instead of trying to restore an ecosystem to a particular state, it attempts to restore the process of natural ecological succession and evolution in wild ecosystems of the same type. It is used mostly to reestablish unique or rare ecosystems in parts of the world where most ecosystems have been degraded or destroyed. Often, you don't have to plant anything. Instead, you find the strongest types of natural growth, protect them, and remove all plant and animal species not native to the area being restored.

SPOTLIGHT Nature's Secrets for Sustainable Living

Nature is sustained by several processes:

- Relying on abundant, nonpolluting, and inexhaustible solar energy by using plants to capture solar energy and convert it to chemical energy used to keep plants and plant-eating animals alive.

- Using biological, chemical, and geological processes to gain resources and dispose of waste by recycling vital nutrients.

- Relying on renewable resources by having soil, water, air, plants, and animals that are renewed through natural processes.

- Biodiversity — evolving a variety of species (species diversity), genetic variety within species (ge-

netic diversity), and ecosystems (ecological diversity) in response to environmental changes over billions of years and as a mechanism for responding to future changes.

- Adaptation in which natural populations can change their genetic makeup in response to changes in environmental conditions.

- Population control in which the birth rates, death rates, age distribution, and migration patterns of natural populations respond to changes in environmental conditions.

- Resource conservation in which there is little waste. Organisms generally use only what they

need to survive, stay healthy, and reproduce.

These are the secrets of nature that we must understand and mimic as we alter nature. Understanding these secrets does not mean that we should stop growing food, building cities, and making other changes that affect Earth's biological communities. We do need to recognize, however, that such human induced changes have far-reaching and unpredictable consequences. We need to use wisdom, care, and restraint as we alter the ecosphere (see Guest Essay on p. 165).

One of the most extensive restoration projects has focused on restoring areas of tall-grass prairie that once blanketed the midwestern United States. Since 1936, scientists at the Aboretum of the University of Wisconsin-Madison have worked to restore the Curtis Prairie, a project conceived by Aldo Leopold in 1934. After over 50 years of painstaking work and research, parts of the Curtis Prairie are now almost comparable to the native prairie once found on the site.

Another pioneering example of prairie restoration is near Chicago. In 1962, Ray Schulenberg, curator of Plant Collections for the arboretum at Lisle, Illinois, began reestablishing a prairie on a plot of land at the Morton Arboretum. He collected seeds from remnants of prairie in the area, raised seedlings in a greenhouse, and then broadcast them on the plot.

For two years, teams of workers removed weeds by hand. After the prairie grasses became established, they used controlled burning each spring to remove weeds and encourage the growth of perennial prairie plants. Today, this site is covered with healthy prairie plants. It is used for educational purposes and as a refuge for endangered species of local plants and insects.

The largest prairie restoration project is being carried out at the Fermi National Accelerator Laboratory in Illinois by Schulenberg and Robert Betz, a biology professor at Northeastern Illinois University in Chicago. Schulenberg and Betz found remnants of virgin Illinois prairie in old cemeteries, on embankments, and on other patches of land. In 1972, they transplanted these by hand on a 4-hectare (10-acre) patch at the Fermi Laboratory site.

Each year, volunteers carefully prepared more land, sowed it with virgin prairie plants, and weeded it manually. Today, more than 180 hectares (445 acres) of the plot have been restored with prairie plants. New species are introduced each year, with the goal of eventually establishing the 150 to 200 species that once flourished on the entire 240-hectare (593-acre) site.

A number of scientists, with the aid of dedicated volunteers, have been successful in restoring or rehabilitating various types of damaged ecosystems to reasonably good health (see Spotlight above). Ecosystem restoration isn't easy. It takes lots of money and decades of hard work, but the long-term costs of doing nothing are much higher. Also, restored ecosystems are ecologically different from and less complex than the natural systems that were destroyed or degraded.

THE VALUES OF EARTH HEALING Sometimes government agencies allow developers to destroy one ecosystem if they protect or restore another, similar one of roughly the same size. Although that is better than wanton destruction of ecosystems, this trade-off approach defeats the main purpose of ecosystem restoration, which is to repair previous damage, not to legitimize further destruction.

The dedicated scientists who are carrying out ecological restoration projects and the many volunteers who help them are important and inspiring examples of people caring for the earth. Expanding and supporting this emerging field designed to heal rather than hurt the earth must become a top priority.

It is arrogant to think that we can rebuild damaged systems completely, but we can repair some of the damage we have done. Anyone can become involved in such Earth-healing. Volunteers can get together and revitalize a creek or revegetate a small abandoned plot of land in a city.

Active ecological restoration or rehabilitation is a useful way for people of all ages to learn more about how nature works, improve their local environment, and gain a sense of accomplishment that can lead to other Earth-sustaining activities. Repairing parts of Earth's damaged fabric will also help show that it is easier and cheaper not to hurt the earth in the first place. To do this, we must tune our senses to how nature works and sustains itself, sensing in nature fundamental rhythms we can trust and cooperate with, even though we will never fully understand them.

What has gone wrong, probably, is that we have failed to see ourselves as part of a large and indivisible whole. For too long we have based our lives on a primitive feeling that our "God-given" role was to have "dominion over the fish of the sea and over the fowl of the air and over every living thing that moveth upon the earth." We have failed to understand that the earth does not belong to us, but we to the earth.

ROLF EDBERG

Edward J. Kormondy

Edward J. Kormondy is chancellor and professor of biology at the University of Hawaii-Hilo/West Oahu College. He has taught at the California State University at Los Angeles, the University of Southern Maine, the University of Michigan, Oberlin College, and Evergreen State College. Among his many research articles and books are Concepts of Ecology *and* Readings in Ecology *(both published by Prentice-Hall). He has been a major force in biological education and for several years was director of the Commission on Undergraduate Education in the Biological Sciences.*

Energy flows—but downhill only in terms of its quality; chemical nutrients circulate—but some stagnate; populations stabilize—but some go wild; communities age—but some age faster. These dynamic and relentless processes are as characteristic of ecosystems as are thermonuclear fusion reactions in the sun.

Thinking one can escape the operation of these and other laws of nature is like thinking one can stop Earth from revolving or make rain fall up. Yet, we have peopled Earth only for hundreds of millions to endure starvation and malnutrition; deliberately dumped wastes only to ensure contamination; purposefully simplified agricultural systems only to cause widespread crop losses from pest invasions. Such actions suggest that we believe energy and food automatically increase as people multiply, that things stay where they are put, that simplification of ecosystems aids in their productivity. Such actions indicate that we have ignored basic, inexorable, and unbreakable laws of ecosystems. We have proposed, but nature has disposed, often in unexpected ways counter to our intent.

We proposed more people, more mouths to be fed, more space to be occupied. Nature disposed by placing an upper limit on the rate at which plants can produce organic nutrients for themselves and for the people and other animals that feed on them. It also disposed by using and degrading energy quality at and between all trophic levels in the biosphere's intricate food webs and by imposing an upper limit on the total space that is available and can be occupied by humans and other species.

Ultimately, the only way there can be more and more people is for each person to have less and less food and fuel energy and less and less physical space. Absolute limits to growth are imposed both by thermodynamics and by space. We may argue about what these limits are and when they will be reached, but there are limits and, if present trends continue, they will be reached. The more timely question then becomes a qualitative one. What quality of life will we have within these limits? What kind of life do you want? What quality of life will future generations have?

We proposed exploitative use of resources and indiscriminate disposal of human and technological wastes. Nature disposed, and, like a boomerang, the consequences of our acts came back to hit us. On the one hand, finite oil, coal, and mineral resource supplies are significantly depleted—some nearing exhaustion. On the other hand, air, water, and land are contaminated, perhaps beyond restoring.

Nature's laws limit each resource; some limits are more confining than others, some more critical than others. Earth is finite, and its resources are therefore finite.

Yet another of nature's laws is that fundamental resources—elements and compounds—circulate, some fully and some partially. They don't stay where they are put. They move from the land to the water and the air, just as they move from the air and water to the land. Must not our proposals for using resources and discharging wastes be mindful of ultimate limits and Earth's chemical recycling processes? What about your own patterns of resource use and waste disposal?

We proposed simplification of our agricultural systems to ease the admittedly heavy burden of cultivation and harvest. Nature has disposed otherwise, however. Simple ecosystems such as a cornfield are youthful ones and, like our own youth, are volatile, unpredictable, and unstable. Young ecosystems do not conserve nutrients, and agricultural systems in such a stage must have their nutrients replaced artificially and expensively by adding commercial inorganic fertilizers. Young agricultural systems essentially lack resistance to pests and disease and have to be protected artificially and expensively by pesticides and other chemicals. These systems are also more subject to the whims of climate and often have to be expensively irrigated. Must not our proposals for managing agricultural systems be mindful of nature's managerial strategy of providing biological diversity to help sustain most complex ecosystems? What of your own manicured lawn?

The take-home lesson is a rather straightforward one: We cannot propose without recognizing how nature disposes of our attempts to manage Earth's resources for human use. We are shackled by basic ecological laws of

(continued)

energy flow, chemical recycling, population growth, and community aging processes. We have plenty of freedom within these laws, but like it or not we are bounded by them. You are bounded by them. What do you propose to do? And what might nature dispose in return?

Guest Essay Discussion

1. List the patterns of your life that are in harmony with the laws of energy flow and chemical recycling and those that are not.

2. Can you think of other examples of "we propose" and "nature disposes"?

3. Set up a chart with examples of "we propose" and "nature disposes," but add a third column titled "we re-propose," based on using ecological principles to work with nature.

DISCUSSION TOPICS

1. Explain how 1 plus 1 does not always equal 2 in an organism or ecosystem.

2. Give two examples of time delays not discussed in this chapter. How can time delays be harmful? How can they be helpful?

3. Someone tells you not to worry about air pollution because through natural selection the human species will develop lungs that can detoxify pollutants. How would you reply?

4. Are human beings or insects such as flies and mosquitoes better able to adapt to environmental change? Defend your choice and give the primary way each of these species can adapt to environmental change.

5. Explain how a species might bring about changes in local conditions so that the species becomes extinct in a given ecosystem. Could human beings do this to themselves? Explain.

6. Explain why a simplified ecosystem such as a cornfield is much more vulnerable to harm from insects, plant diseases, and fungi than a more complex, natural ecosystem such as a grassland. Why are natural ecosystems less vulnerable?

7. Do you believe that genetic engineering should be widely used? Explain. What restrictions, if any, would you place on its use? How would you enforce such restrictions, especially in secret biological warfare facilities?

*8. Visit a nearby land area or pond and look for signs of ecological succession. If possible, compare the types of species found on an abandoned farm field or lot with another nearby area that is at a more mature stage of ecological succession.

CHAPTER 7

GEOLOGIC
PROCESSES:
THE DYNAMIC
EARTH

General Questions and Issues

1. What are the principal structural and chemical components of Earth?

2. What are the major processes occurring on and in Earth?

3. How does the rock cycle recycle earth materials and concentrate resources?

4. What natural hazards are of special concern?

5. In what time frames do geologic processes take place?

Resources are like air — of no great importance until you are not getting any.

ANONYMOUS

 E LIVE ON A DYNAMIC planet that has a continually changing internal structure and external form. Over billions of years, Earth's interior has separated into three major, concentric zones which geologists identify as the core, the mantle, and the crust (Figure 4-2). It is from Earth's crust, which is still forming in various places, that mineral resources and soil come, as well as the elements that make up our bodies and those of other living organisms.

However, Earth also presents a variety of natural hazards: earthquakes, volcanic eruptions, floods, landslides, and subsidence (sinking or collapse) of parts of Earth's surface. We can best avoid or minimize harm from such hazards by not living in places where they pose a serious risk; however, many people continue to live in and move to such areas because they have no other choice or because they believe the benefits outweigh the risks.

7-1 Earth Structure and Composition

CORE So far, mines and drillholes have penetrated less than 15 kilometers (9 miles) into Earth. What we know of Earth's much deeper interior comes from indirect evidence of various kinds, such as density measurements, seismic (earthquake) wave studies, measurements of heat flow from the interior, analyses of lava, and research on meteorite composition.

The distance from the surface of Earth to its center is 6,400 kilometers (4,000 miles). Earth's central zone, the **core**, begins a little less than halfway from the surface to the center. The *inner core* is a solid ball about 1,200 kilometers (745 miles) in diameter, made mostly of iron with perhaps some nickel. Its temperature may be as high as 4,300°C (7,800°F) or more, but the inner core is not liquid, because the extreme pressure there prevents melting.

The *outer core*, surrounding the inner core, is liquid, with a temperature of 3,700°C to 4,300°C (6,700°F to 7,800°F). At these depths, the pressure is low enough to permit melting. Earth's magnetic field originates from flow in this liquid. The outer core currently extends from 2,900 to about 5,200 kilometers of depth (1,800 to 3,200 miles), but its base is gradually rising as more of it changes to inner core by solidification. The outer and inner core make up 31% of the mass and 16% of the volume of Earth (Figure 7.1).

Note: **Kenneth J. Van Dellen**, professor of geology and environmental science, Macomb Community College, is the primary author of this chapter, with assistance provided by G. Tyler Miller, Jr.

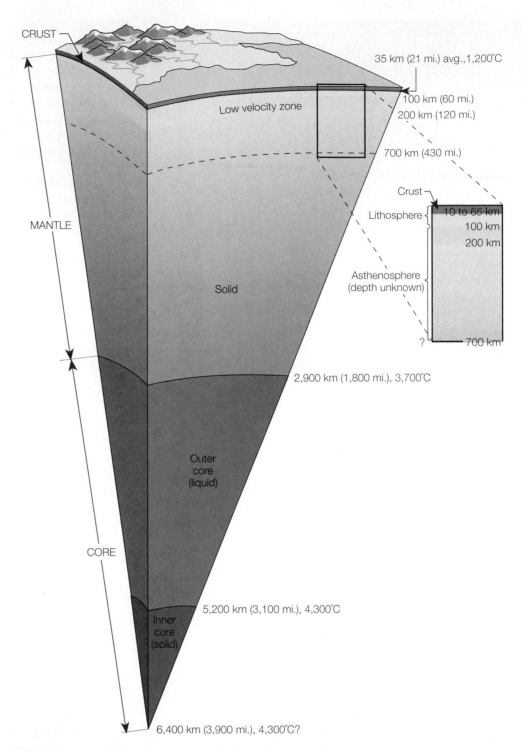

Figure 7-1 Earth's internal zones. (Surface features are not to scale.)

CRUST

35 km (21 mi.) avg.,1,200°C

100 km (60 mi.)

200 km (120 mi.)

700 km (430 mi.)

Low velocity zone

MANTLE

Solid

Crust

Lithosphere { 10 to 65 km

100 km

200 km

Asthenosphere (depth unknown)

? 700 km

2,900 km (1,800 mi.), 3,700°C

Outer core (liquid)

CORE

5,200 km (3,100 mi.), 4,300°C

Inner core (solid)

6,400 km (3,900 mi.), 4,300°C?

MANTLE Earth's core is surrounded by a thick, solid zone called the **mantle**, which begins at a depth of 7 to 65 kilometers (4 to 40 miles) (Figure 7-1). This largest zone makes up 82% of Earth's volume and 68% of its mass. Iron is a major constituent, as in the core, but oxygen, silicon, and magnesium are also present in large proportions. More than 90% of Earth's mass is due to these four elements.

The outermost part of the mantle is rigid and strong, but apparently temperature and pressure conditions between 100 and 200 kilometers (62 and 124 miles) are such that rock is able to melt and is perhaps 1% to 10% liquid. Because earthquake waves slow when they reach this zone, like a car hitting a deep puddle of water, it is called the *low-velocity zone*. Below this zone the mantle is apparently completely solid again.

CRUST The **crust** (Figure 7-1) is the zone of Earth that we know best because we have direct evidence about it. It is the thinnest of Earth's zones and makes up only 2% of the planet's volume and 1% of its mass.

Only eight elements make up 98.5% of the weight of Earth's crust (Figure 7-2). These are, in order of abundance, oxygen (combined with other elements to form solid materials), silicon, aluminum, iron, calcium, sodium, potassium, and magnesium. All other elements make up only 1.5% of the weight of Earth's crust.

Earth's crust is made of two categories of material—oceanic crust and continental crust—which differ in composition, density, and thickness (Figures 7-1 and 7-3). These differences account for the two distinct surface elevations.

About 71% of Earth's surface is *oceanic crust*, low regions with 7-kilometer (4-mile) thick, relatively dense crust that have provided a place for a large part of Earth's water to collect as oceans (Figure 5-27). Three prominent features of oceanic crust are the oceanic ridge system, the abyssal floor, and the trenches (Figure 7-3).

The *oceanic ridge* system extends into all of Earth's oceans. With a total length of more than 80,000 kilometers (50,000 miles), it is 1,500 to 2,500 kilometers (930 to 1,550 miles) wide and rises 2 to 3 kilometers (1.2 to 1.9 miles) above the abyssal floor. The *abyssal floor* consists of deep-ocean basins, usually found on both sides of oceanic ridges. Part of it consists of numerous abyssal hills, found also on the oceanic ridge system, and part is flat abyssal plains, where abyssal hills have been buried by sediment. It generally lies at depths of about 5 kilometers (3 miles). *Trenches*, the lowest areas of Earth's surface, are typically about 8 kilometers (5 miles) below sea level. The deepest one, in the Pacific Ocean, is 11 kilometers (7 miles) below sea level. They occur along mountainous continental margins and volcanic island arcs.

Continental crust is higher and thicker than oceanic crust, as much as 65 kilometers (40 miles) thick under high mountain ranges, and averaging 35 kilometers (22 miles) thick (Figure 7-3). It has rock with a lower density than does the oceanic crust. Its lower density and greater thickness cause it to "float" much higher on the denser mantle. Continents consist of *folded mountain belts* and *cratons*. In folded mountain belts, such as the Appalachians, the Alps, the Andes, and the Himalaya, the rocks have been severely deformed and fractured,

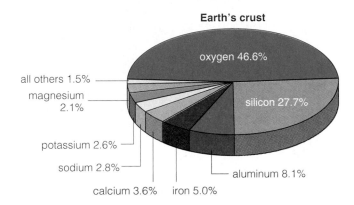

Earth's crust

Figure 7-2 Composition by weight of Earth's crust. Various combinations of only eight elements make up the bulk of most minerals. Because of separation processes that occurred as the interior of Earth cooled, the crust is richer in the lighter elements than is the rest of the planet.

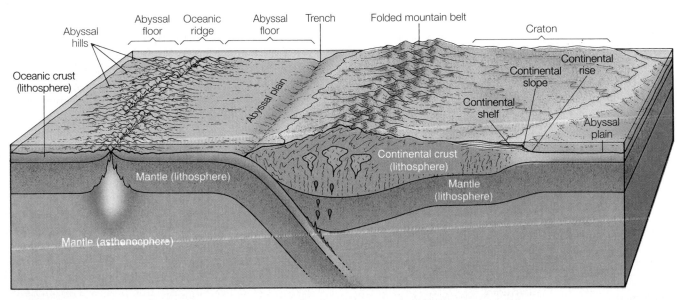

Figure 7-3 Major features of Earth's crust and upper mantle. The rigid, brittle outer part of Earth, composed of the crust and outermost mantle, is called the *lithosphere*. It is made up of many pieces, called *plates*, of various sizes. The asthenosphere is a plastic zone (capable of solid flow) in the mantle. The relatively thin *oceanic crust* has an almost uniform thickness. The *continental crust* is thicker overall, much thicker under high mountains, and slightly less dense than the oceanic crust. Major topographic features of oceans are oceanic ridges, trenches, and abyssal plains. The continents' major topographic features are folded mountain belts and cratons.

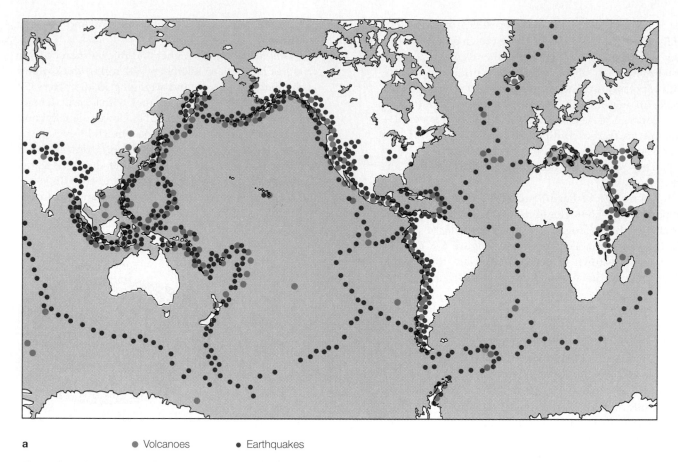

a   ● Volcanoes   ● Earthquakes

Figure 7-4 Earthquakes and volcanoes occur mostly along lithospheric plate boundaries (**a**). According to the *theory of plate tectonics*, the rigid lithosphere consists of various-size plates that move apart (diverge), move toward one another (converge), and slide past one another with parallel motion at transform faults (**b**). Divergent plate

and intruded by molten rock material. A craton is a nonmountainous part of a continent, where earlier mountains have been eroded away. Over much of a craton, the remains of earlier mountains are covered with layers of rock that are essentially horizontal except in a few areas where they have been gently warped up or down.

The *continental shelf* is the part of a craton that is flooded by the sea (Figure 7-3). The continental shelf has extended over much of North America and other continents at various times in Earth's history, depending on how extensive the seas were. Ecologically, the edge of the ocean is at the shoreline, but geologically, it is at the *continental slope*.

7-2   Internal and External Earth Processes

INTERNAL PROCESSES: CONVECTION CELLS AND MANTLE PLUMES Geologic changes originating from within Earth are called *internal processes*. Generally, they build up the planet's surface. The energy for

these processes comes from the heat in Earth's interior, but gravity also plays an important role.

Residual heat from the formation of Earth is still being given off as the inner core cools and the outer core both cools and solidifies. Continued decay of radioactive elements in the crust, especially continental crust, adds to the flow of heat from within Earth.

The deep heat causes much of the mantle to behave plastically, in the same way that a red-hot iron horseshoe behaves plastically, from the top of the low-velocity zone to an undefined depth. Some researchers place the base of this plastic region, known as the *asthenosphere*, at a depth of 200 kilometers (120 miles) at the base of the low-velocity zone, while others place it at 700 kilometers (430 miles) and still others think it may extend all the way to the core. Although there is obviously some degree of uncertainty about what is going on inside Earth, indirect evidence suggests that at least two kinds of movement are occurring in the asthenosphere: convection cells and mantle plumes.

There are indications that the solid rock of the mantle moves in huge *convection cells*, following a pattern resembling convection in the atmosphere or in a pot of boiling soup. Measurements of heat flow from the inte-

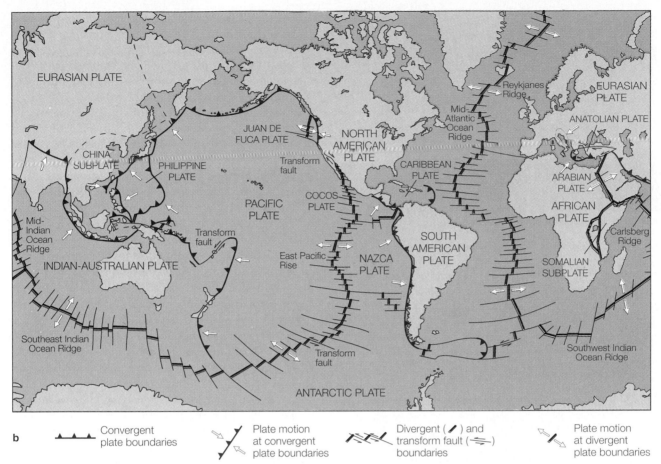

b

‖▲‖▲‖▲ Convergent
          plate boundaries

⟩⟩ Plate motion
     at convergent
     plate boundaries

Divergent (⟋) and
transform fault (⇌)
boundaries

⟩⟩ Plate motion
     at divergent
     plate boundaries

boundaries are marked by oceanic ridge segments and rift valleys. Convergent plate boundaries are marked by volcanic island chains or folded mountain belts and usually trenches. Transform faults connect the other two types of plate boundaries. (A few are marked with black arrows as examples.)

rior and observations of other phenomena support this model.

Another type of movement occurs at a *mantle plume*. There, mantle rock flows slowly upward in a column, presumably beginning at the top of the core, like smoke from a chimney on a cold, calm morning. When it reaches the top of the plume, it moves in a radial pattern, as if the material were flowing up an umbrella through the handle and then moving out in all directions from the tip of the umbrella to the rim.

Both convection currents and mantle plumes move upward as the heated material is displaced by heavier, cooler material that sinks under the influence of gravity. At various depths, different groups of minerals have formed from apparently the same set of chemical elements as a result of temperature and pressure differences.

INTERNAL PROCESSES: PLATE TECTONICS A map of Earth's earthquakes and volcanoes shows that most of these phenomena are not random but occur along certain lines or belts on Earth's surface (Figure 7-4a). The several, various-size areas of Earth outlined by these major belts are called plates (Figure 7-4b). They

are composed of the crust and the rigid, outermost part of the mantle outside the asthenosphere, a combination called the **lithosphere**. They slowly move, carried around on the flowing asthenosphere like large pieces of ice floating on the surface of a lake during the spring breakup. Some plates move faster than others, but a typical speed is about as fast as fingernails grow.

The theory that explains the movements of the plates and the processes that occur at their boundaries is called **plate tectonics**. The concept, which became widely accepted by geologists in the mid-1960s, is a more complex version of an earlier idea called *continental drift*. Throughout Earth's history, continents have split and joined, as plates have drifted thousands of kilometers back and forth across Earth's surface (see Figure 7-27 later in this chapter).

Lithospheric plates have three types of boundaries: divergent, convergent, and transform fault (Figure 7-5). At a **divergent plate boundary**, the plates move apart in opposite directions; for example, one plate might go east and the other west (←|→). Because many divergent plate boundaries are along the oceanic ridge system, geologists often refer to those as oceanic spreading centers (Figure 7-5).

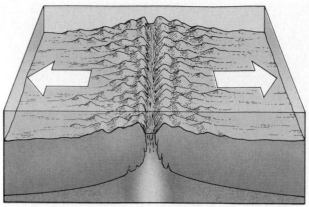

Oceanic ridge at divergent plate boundary

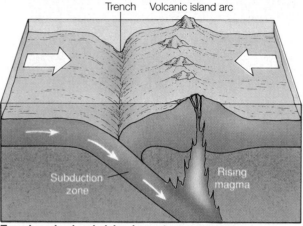

Trench   Volcanic island arc

Subduction zone   Rising magma

Trench and volcanic island arc at a convergent plate boundary

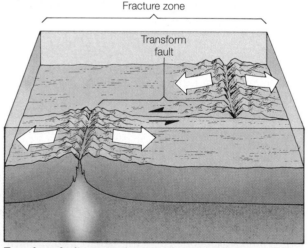

Fracture zone

Transform fault

Transform fault connecting two divergent plate boundaries

Figure 7-5 Types of boundaries between Earth's lithospheric plates. All three boundaries occur both in oceans and on continents.

Divergent plate boundaries can also occur on continents. A good example is found at the East African rift valleys. If divergence were to continue there, a new ocean would develop. The Red Sea is in a slightly later stage of this process, and the Atlantic Ocean has advanced beyond that.

As the plates move apart, the lowering of pressure causes already hot and partially molten rock in the low-velocity zone to undergo further melting, producing still more liquid. The liquid rock moves upward into the rift, some of it flowing out on the surface and some cooling underground. When this material solidifies, it adds to the separating plates, both underground and on the surface, and produces new lithosphere. The rifting or spreading is thought to be usually caused by side-by-side convection cells in the asthenosphere with their tops flowing away from each other, dragging the litho-spheric plates apart. In some cases, however, it may also be due to radial flow at mantle plumes.

Volcanoes and lava flows along the East African rift valleys are associated with rifting, as is the volcanism along the oceanic spreading centers. Iceland, which is on the mid-Atlantic ridge, is the site of a mantle plume that has produced a *hot spot* in the lithosphere above it at this spreading center. Another current site of a hot spot, this one not involved with rifting, is at the big island of Hawaii. Earthquakes also result from the separation of Earth's plates, but most have relatively little effect on people because they often occur in the marine environment (Figure 7-4a).

Where the tops of adjacent convection cells flow toward each other, the lithospheric plates are pushed together ($\rightarrow$|$\leftarrow$). This produces a **convergent plate boundary** (Figure 7-5). Folded mountains are developing where these boundaries occur. Some of these boundaries are found next to a *volcanic island arc*, such as Japan, the Aleutian Islands, or the West Indies. Others are adjacent to a continental margin, such as the Andes Mountains of South America (Figure 7-4b) or the Cascade Range in the northwestern United States.

At most convergent plate boundaries, oceanic lithosphere is carried downward (subducted) under the island arc or the continent at a **subduction zone**. A trench ordinarily forms at the boundary between the two converging plates (Figure 7-3). Both earthquakes and volcanoes occur at subduction zones (Figure 7-4).

Only oceanic lithosphere is dense enough to subduct. If a continent is part of a subducting plate, it will not subduct when it reaches the subduction zone. Instead it will collide with the island arc or the other continent that is there. That is what happened when India collided with the rest of Asia about 10 million years ago, producing the Tibetan Plateau and the Himalaya. Convergence continues there today.

The third type of plate boundary, called a **transform fault**, occurs where plates move in opposite but parallel directions ($\rightleftharpoons$) along a fracture (fault) in the lithosphere (Figure 7-5). Like the other types of plate boundaries, most transform faults are on the ocean floor. They are the sites of earthquakes, most of which do not affect people. Transform faults on land do pose a risk, however, as demonstrated by California's San Andreas Fault (Figure 7-6). Ordinarily, volcanism does not occur at transform faults, but some may be "leaky."

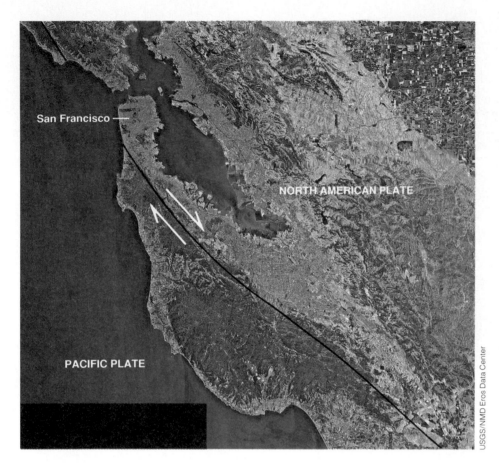

Figure 7-6 The San Andreas Fault in California is a *transform fault* on a continent. It connects an oceanic ridge segment in the Gulf of California with one off the coast of northern California and is the boundary between the North American Plate and the Pacific Plate in that region. The relative movement is indicated by the arrows. When part of the fault locks, strain builds until the fault ruptures and movement occurs along the fault. The sudden release of strain produces an earthquake. The 1989 earthquake near San Francisco, which killed 67 people, involved part of the San Andreas Fault. The popular conception that California is going to fall into the ocean is wrong. That would require a different kind of fault and much different conditions from those that currently exist there. Instead, as long as the San Andreas Fault is active, Los Angeles will slowly move northward toward San Francisco.

USGS/NMD Eros Data Center

The movement of the lithospheric plates is important to us for several reasons. Plate motion is responsible for producing mountains (including most volcanoes), the oceanic ridge system, trenches, and other features of Earth's surface (Figure 7-3). Certain natural hazards are likely to be found at places where plates interact (Figure 7-4a). Perhaps most importantly, plate movements and interactions concentrate many of the minerals we extract and use.

EXTERNAL PROCESSES: EROSION AND MASS WASTING Geological changes based directly or indirectly on energy from the sun and on gravity, instead of on heat in Earth's interior, are called *external processes*. While internal processes generally build up Earth's surface, external processes tend to lower it.

The sun causes water to evaporate from Earth, as part of the water cycle (Figure 4-34). Precipitation that falls as rain can run off in streams, percolate into the ground as groundwater, and collect in lakes and oceans. That which falls as snow may soon melt and do the same, or it may accumulate as snowfields that may, in turn, develop into glacial ice. Groundwater, streams, and glaciers remove earth material from various places, transport it, and deposit it as *sediment* in other places. Waves and currents, generated by winds resulting from solar energy, do the same along the shores of lakes and oceans, and so does the wind itself (Figure 7-7).

Gravity plays an important role in these processes. It is involved in causing the convection of the atmosphere that leads to precipitation and in causing the downslope flow of water and the movement of glaciers. In addition, it causes sliding, flowing, and falling of rock and soil. In general, these processes have a levelling effect on Earth's surface.

Erosion is the process or group of processes by which earth materials, loose or consolidated, are dissolved, loosened, or worn away, and removed from one place and deposited in another. One of the subprocesses of erosion is **weathering**, in which solid rock exposed at Earth's surface is changed to separate solid particles and dissolved material that can then be moved to another place and deposited as *sediment*.

Weathering can occur as a result of mechanical processes, chemical processes, or both. In *mechanical weathering*, a large rock mass is broken into smaller pieces of the original material, similar to the results you would get by breaking a rock into small fragments. The most important agent of mechanical weathering is *frost action*, in which ice forms in pores and cracks of rock, expands (because a given mass of ice has a larger volume than the water from which it forms), and breaks pieces of the rock off. Another important agent of mechanical weathering is fracturing in rocks from stress caused by the slow erosional removal of the weight of overlying masses of rock.

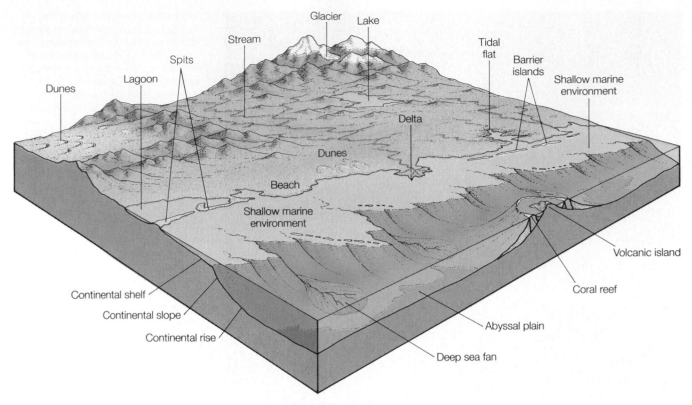

Figure 7-7 Solar energy (through the hydrologic cycle and wind), the force of gravity, and the activities of organisms such as reef-building corals (Figure 5-32) have produced a variety of landforms and sedimentary environments.

In *chemical weathering*, a mass of rock is decomposed by one or more chemical reactions, producing materials that are chemically different from the original material. The products usually include both solid and dissolved components. Most chemical weathering involves reaction of rock material with oxygen, carbon dioxide, and moisture in the atmosphere and the ground.

Some rocks, such as rock salt and gypsum, dissolve in plain water. Limestone dissolves in water containing carbonic acid that forms naturally when carbon dioxide in the atmosphere or the soil combines with water. Carbonic acid also reacts with certain minerals in various rocks, changing them to clay and dissolved materials.

Iron, aluminum, and other metals that are part of some minerals are made vulnerable to attack by oxygen through some of the reactions in chemical weathering. The resulting metal oxides may be carried away in water solutions, but some may form a solid residue that is merely a stain or may accumulate as a resource (Figure 7-8).

Disintegration of rock by mechanical weathering accelerates chemical weathering by increasing the surface area that can be attacked by agents of chemical weathering. This is similar to the way granulated sugar dissolves much faster than a large solid chunk of sugar

crystal. Chemical weathering is also aided by higher temperatures and precipitation, occurring most rapidly in the tropics and second most rapidly in temperate climates.

Weathering is responsible for the development of the world's soils, without which nonmarine life would probably not exist. *Bed rock*, the solid rock mass of Earth, is sometimes exposed. Usually, however, it is under a blanket of unconsolidated material called *regolith*. If the regolith results from mechanical and chemical weathering, as most does, it is *residual regolith*. If it is deposited by wind, water, or ice, it is *transported regolith*.

Regolith or rock masses newly detached from underlying material may move downslope in various ways under the influence of gravity, without being carried in, on, or under a glacier, a stream, or some other agent of erosion. This transport of material is called **mass wasting**. The names used to classify the types of mass wasting, such as rockfall, rockslide, slump, creep, earthflow, and mudflow, often give clues to their characteristics.

Mass wasting is most common on sides of mountains above valleys and on coasts of oceans and large lakes. Whenever streams, glaciers, or waves erode the landscape, producing cliffs or steep slopes, there is a potential for mass wasting. However, under the right conditions, it can occur even on quite gentle slopes.

Figure 7-8 Chemical weathering. This granitelike rock is a part of some glacially deposited material. Air and water weathered it around the outside, producing a shell of weathering products that surrounds it like a rind on an orange, except on the front where the products have washed off. Weathering also happened in a zone through the rock where there was a fracture. The quartz grains of the parent rock are still present in the weathering rind, but some of the silicates have reacted with oxygen and carbonic acid to form clay, brown iron oxide, and soluble products. In this way, soil is formed and some trace elements are added to soil and groundwater. (The camera lens cap in the photo is used to show the relative size of the rock.)

Figure 7-9 This view of a portion of the Grand Canyon in Arizona, illustrates several geologic phenomena. The canyon was eroded by the Colorado River, which is brown with a suspended load of sediment. A sequence of sedimentary rocks deposited over an interval of more than 300 million years is exposed here. These stratified sedimentary rocks are mostly limestone, sandstone, and shale. Mechanical weathering loosens rock on the sides of the canyon and causes rockfalls, a type of mass wasting. Analyses of such exposed layers of sedimentary rock, with the fossils they include, give geologists information about Earth's geological and biological history.

Groundwater erodes by solution, transports its load in solution, and deposits its load by precipitation from solution. The effects of these processes are evident underground in limestone caverns and on the surface in sinkholes and solution valleys.

Streams also erode by solution, as well as by abrasion from the sand and gravel they carry and by hydraulic action as the force of water washes away regolith or weak bedrock. They transport part of their load in solution; the rest is carried as sediment in suspension or is carried along the channel floor by rolling, sliding, and bouncing. As the stream velocity decreases, coarser particles are laid down at high stream velocities and finer particles at lower stream velocities. Streams are the most important agent of erosion, operating everywhere on Earth except in the polar regions. They produce ordinary valleys, canyons (Figure 7-9), and deltas (Figure 5 29).

A **glacier** is a flowing body of ice, formed in a region where snowfall exceeds melting. Under the influence of gravity, glaciers move slowly down a valley on a mountainside, as in the Alps, or over a wide area, as in Antarctica. Glaciers erode by abrasion and by their own unique process called *plucking*, in which glacial ice freezes to rock and pulls fragments out when the glacier flows. Glaciers transport most of their eroded sediment within the ice, at or near the underside of the glacier.

During the last ice age, which ended about 10,000 years ago, ice sheets called continental glaciers covered vast areas of North America, Europe, and Asia (Figure 7-10). In North America, ice scoured and gouged the rock of the Canadian shield and New England and wrapped Lakes Michigan, Huron, and Erie with *moraines*, ridges of sediment of assorted sizes, like multi strand necklaces. The Great Lakes, the largest mass of fresh water in the world, occupy glacially eroded stream valleys that filled with water as glaciers melted back. The last major meltback began about 16,000 years ago. Niagara Falls originated about 12,000 years ago when the glacier melted back from that area, and about 10,000 years ago the entire Great Lakes area was ice-free. The beautiful glacial valley found in Glacier National Park, Montana, also formed during the last ice age.

Figure 7-10 The Pleistocene epoch of Earth's long geologic history began about 99.94% of the way from the beginning of Earth's history. (It was originally thought to coincide with the ice age, but we now know that that began 2 to 2.5 million years ago.) It ended about 10,000 years ago when the current epoch, the Holocene (and agriculture), began. During this period, much of the Northern Hemisphere was covered several times with thick sheets of ice. The glacial stages alternated with warmer interglacials. The moving ice modified large areas of Earth's surface by erosion and deposition as ice sheets, up to 3 kilometers (2 miles) thick in the north and 1.6 kilometers (1 mile) thick in the Great Lakes area, moved over the surface and melted.

Figure 7-11 A few minerals consist of a single element. One such example is gold, shown here in a rock crevice in Colorado.

Figure 7-12 Most minerals consist of various combinations of the eight elements that make up most of the weight of Earth's crust (Figure 7-2). This is a sample of quartz, a form of silica (silicon dioxide, SiO_2).

Wind is not a significant agent of erosion except in areas of sparse vegetation, particularly deserts, beaches, and some valleys of major streams. It erodes by removing loose particles of fine sand and dust (silt and clay), leaving coarser sand and pebbles. Wind also erodes by abrasion, producing flat sides on stones. Much of the fertile farmland of Iowa, Illinois, and other midwestern states is in loess (dust) blown out of meltwater deposits from the continental glacier during the last ice age.

Along the shores of the oceans and large lakes, waves erode in the same ways that streams do, by solution, abrasion, and hydraulic action. This produces wave-cut cliffs, sea caves, sea arches, and other erosional features (Figure 5-33). The resulting sediments, along with those brought into the coastal environment by streams, are transported along the shore by wave action and by currents that are caused by the waves. Eventually, the sediments are deposited, forming beaches (Figure 5-34), barrier islands (Figure 5-36), a variety of sandbars, and other coastal features (Figure 7-7).

Human activities, particularly those that destroy the vegetation, accelerate erosion. Overgrazing by cattle, agricultural activities, timbering, surface mining, construction, use of off-road vehicles, and other activities often contribute to erosion. Soils and soil erosion are discussed in more detail in Chapter 12.

7-3 Mineral Resources and the Rock Cycle

MINERALS AND ROCKS A **mineral** is an element or an inorganic compound that occurs naturally and is solid. It is usually defined as having a crystalline internal structure made up of an orderly, three-dimensional arrangement of atoms or ions. All of Earth's crust, except the rather small proportion of the crust that contains organic material, is made of minerals.

Some minerals consist of a single element, such as gold (Figure 7-11), silver, diamond (carbon), and sulfur. However, most of the over 2,000 identified minerals oc-

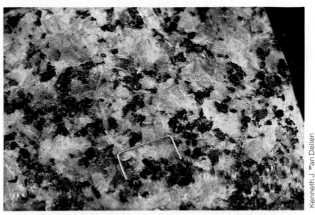

Figure 7-13 Igneous rock forms when magma (molten material below Earth's surface) intrudes into rock or extrudes onto Earth's surface, cools, and hardens. This close-up view of granite shows that it consists of four types of mineral grains or crystals. The magma from which it formed cooled very slowly, so large crystals developed from the melt.

cur as inorganic compounds formed by various combinations of the eight elements that make up 98.5% by weight of Earth's crust (Figure 7-2). Examples are salt, mica, and quartz (Figure 7-12), all of which, along with many others, have economic importance. Other minerals are important mainly as rock formers.

To a geologist, **rock** is any material that makes up a large, natural, continuous part of Earth's crust. Rock usually consists of two or more minerals; sometimes, however, it consists of only one, and a few rocks are made of nonmineral material.

ROCK TYPES AND THE ROCK CYCLE   Based on its origin and formation, a rock is placed in one of three broad classes: igneous, sedimentary, or metamorphic. **Igneous rock** forms when molten rock material (magma) wells up from Earth's upper mantle or deep crust, cools, and hardens into rock. Igneous rock masses that form underground are called *igneous intrusions*. These generally form at sites of volcanic activity, which are mostly at convergent and divergent plate boundaries (Figures 7-4 and 7-5).

Because rock is a good heat insulator, igneous intrusions usually cool very slowly, allowing enough time for mineral grains or crystals to grow by crystallization until they are large enough to be distinguished easily without magnification. Granite is a familiar example of an intrusive igneous rock (Figure 7-13).

Extrusive igneous rocks are formed when lava erupts from volcanoes or cracks in the earth's surface, cools rapidly, and hardens. **Lava** is the term used for magma that has been extruded onto Earth's surface, and is also a general name for the igneous rocks that form from it. The rapid cooling always produces either a fine-grained or a glassy texture, because crystals do not have time to form. Basalt, obsidian, and pumice are examples.

Igneous rocks are the most abundant type of rock and are the main source of many nonfuel mineral resources we use. Granite and its relatives are used for monuments and as decorative stone in buildings, basalt as crushed stone where gravel is scarce, and volcanic rocks in landscaping. Many of the popular gemstones, such as diamonds, tourmaline, garnet, ruby, and sapphire, are found in igneous rocks.

Sedimentary rock forms from the accumulated products of erosion and, in some cases, from the compacted shells, skeletons, and other remains of dead organisms. Gravel, sand, silt, and clay are the results of chemical weathering, abrasion, and other erosional processes. When transported and deposited by water, ice, and wind, they may become compacted and cemented into layers of solid rock: conglomerate, sandstone, siltstone, and shale (Figure 7-9).

Other sedimentary rocks are precipitated from solution. Rock salt, gypsum, and several limestones form this way. Some limestones are composed of essentially nothing but the skeletons of corals, clams, or other organisms. Lignite and bituminous coal are sedimentary rocks derived from plant remains (Figure 7-14).

In most places, sedimentary rocks are not more than 100 meters (330 feet) thick, but they cover nearly three-fourths of Earth's land surface. Consequently, they make up much of the scenic landscape. Some types are important resources. Limestone, for example, is used as crushed stone, as building stone, as flux in blast furnaces for smelting iron ore, and with shale in making portland cement.

Metamorphic rock is produced when a preexisting rock is subjected to high temperature (which may cause it to melt partially), high pressure, chemically active fluids, or a combination of those agents. Slate (Figure 7-15), marble, and anthracite (Figure 7-14) are important metamorphic rocks.

Slate, used for roofs and floors of buildings, and marble, also used in buildings and in sculptures and monuments, are economically important metamorphic rocks. Some gem minerals, talc, minerals of the asbestos group, graphite, and titanium are also found in metamorphic rocks.

Earth's rocks are constantly being exposed to various physical and chemical conditions that over time can change them from one type of rock to another. This happens because a particular mineral is stable under only a certain range of conditions. Thus, a change in the pressure, temperature, or chemical environment may be sufficient to cause a mineral to change to a different mineral and so change one type of rock to another.

The interaction of processes that change rocks of Earth from one type to another is called the **rock cycle** (Figure 7-16). Recycling material over millions of years,

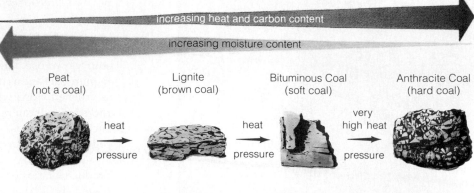

Figure 7-14 Stages in the formation of coal over millions of years. Peat is a soil material made of moist, partially decomposed organic matter. Lignite and bituminous coal are sedimentary rocks, and anthracite is a metamorphic rock.

increasing heat and carbon content

increasing moisture content

Peat
(not a coal)

heat
pressure

Lignite
(brown coal)

heat
pressure

Bituminous Coal
(soft coal)

very
high heat
pressure

Anthracite Coal
(hard coal)

partially decayed plant and animal matter in swamps and bogs; low heat content

low heat content; low sulfur content; limited supplies in most areas

extensively used as a fuel because of its high heat content and large supplies; normally has a high sulfur content

highly desirable fuel because of its high heat content and low sulfur content; supplies are limited in most areas

this slowest of Earth's cyclic processes is responsible for concentrating mineral resources on which humans depend.

MINERAL RESOURCES A **mineral resource** is a concentration of naturally occurring solid, liquid, or gaseous material, in or on Earth's crust, in such form and amount that its extraction and its conversion into useful materials or items are currently or potentially profitable. Internal and external Earth processes have produced numerous mineral resources, which are mostly essentially nonrenewable because of the slowness of the rock cycle. They include *energy resources* (coal, oil, natural gas, uranium, and geothermal energy) (Figure 7-17), *metallic mineral resources* (iron, copper, and aluminum), and *nonmetallic mineral resources* (salt, gypsum, clay, sand, phosphates, water, and soil) (Figure 1-8).

The U.S. Geological Survey divides mineral resources into two broad categories, identified and undiscovered, based on degree of geologic understanding and certainty that the resource exists (Figure 7-18). **Identified resources** are deposits of a particular mineral-bearing material that have location, quantity, and quality that are known or are estimated from direct geological evidence and measurements. **Reserves** are identified resources from which a usable mineral can be extracted profitably at present prices with current mining technology (Figure 7-18).

Undiscovered resources are potential supplies of a particular mineral. They are believed to exist on the basis of geologic knowledge and theory, though specific locations, quality, and amounts are unknown.

The term **ore** refers to that part of a metal-yielding material that can be economically and legally extracted at a given time. Ore may be either identified or undiscovered.

Kenneth J. Van Dellen

Figure 7-15 Metamorphic rock is formed from a preexisting rock as a result of exposure to high temperatures, high pressures, chemically active fluids, or a combination of those factors. These rocks, near Negaunee, Michigan, were once layers of mud that included some layers of sand. They then became shale with sandstone beds. As a result of a mountain-building event about 1.75 billion years ago, they have been tilted nearly vertically, and metamorphosed to slate (dark) with quartzite (light).

Most published estimates of particular mineral resources refer only to reserves. Reserves can be increased when exploration finds undiscovered, economic resources. They can also be increased when identified, subeconomic resources become economic because of new technology or higher prices (which can encourage development of new technology).

Once they are burned, supplies of fossil-fuel mineral resources are gone forever. The high-quality energy they contain cannot be recovered and recycled because of the second law of thermodynamics (Section 3-6). Supplies of nonfuel mineral resources are also finite and nonrenewable on a human time scale. However, supplies can be extended by recycling and reuse if the items

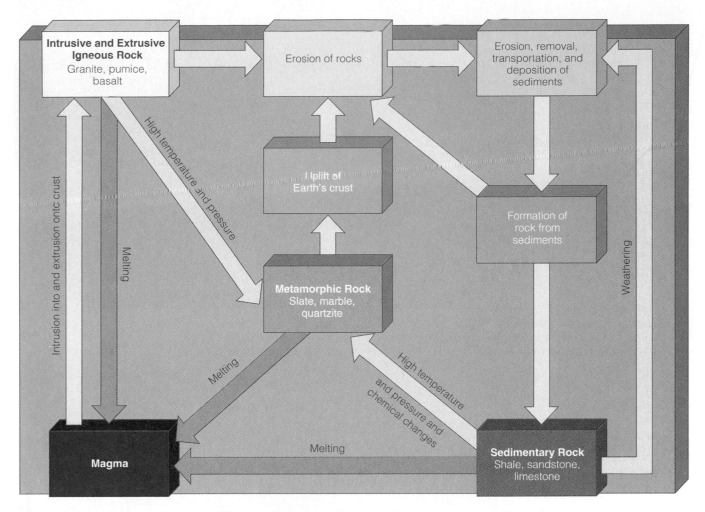

Figure 7-16 The rock cycle, the slowest of Earth's cyclic processes. Earth materials are recycled over millions of years by three processes: melting, erosion, and metamorphism. These processes produce igneous, sedimentary, and metamorphic rocks, respectively. Rock of any of the three classes can be converted to rock of either of the other two classes, or can even be recycled within its own class.

they are used to make are not so widely dispersed that it is too expensive to collect them.

FORMATION AND CONCENTRATION OF MINERAL RESOURCES The reason some elements seem more abundant than they really are in Earth's crust is that slow-acting, infrequent, or localized processes have selectively concentrated them. Copper, for example, makes up 0.0058% by weight of the crust, and ore must contain 0.5% copper, so the ore must have a concentration of copper that is 86 times (0.5/.0058) its average crustal abundance. Aluminum ore must have only 3.7 times the average crustal abundance of that metal, and iron 5 times. However, the gold in gold ore must be concentrated 1,600 times its crustal average, and mercury an astonishing 100,000 times.

This limited and uneven concentration of nonrenewable metal resources raises serious questions about the wisdom of extracting concentrated deposits, and scattering them all over the countryside in landfills (Figure 1-18), junkyards, or in other forms. Instead, we should think of discarded items made of these nonrenewable metallic and nonmetallic materials as potential resources that we should be recycling and reusing to reduce energy use, extraction of virgin minerals, pollution, and volume of waste.

Many mineral resources — rocks or important mineral components of rocks — have been concentrated by the processes directly involved in the rock cycle (Figure 7-16). We will now consider some of those that were not mentioned in the discussion of the rock cycle and others concentrated by processes less directly related to that cycle.

Groundwater that circulates down to depths of high temperature and pressure beneath developing mountains at subduction zones (Figure 7-5) can dissolve materials from rocks there and form mineral deposits elsewhere. Water with dissolved mineral material

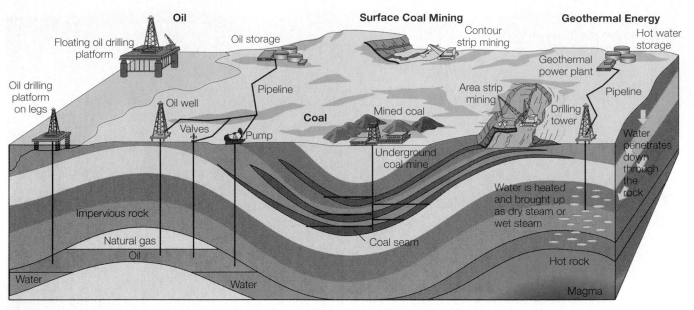

Figure 7-17 Important energy resources we obtain from Earth's crust are geothermal energy, coal, oil, and natural gas. Uranium ore is also extracted from the crust, and then processed to increase the concentration of uranium-235 (Figure 3-2), which can undergo nuclear fission (Figure 3-11) in nuclear reactors used to produce electricity.

Figure 7-18 General classification of mineral resources by the U.S. Geological Survey. *Reserves* are resources that are both identified and economic. Other resources are either undiscovered, subeconomic, or both. This is *not* an area graph depicting abundance of reserves relative to other resources.

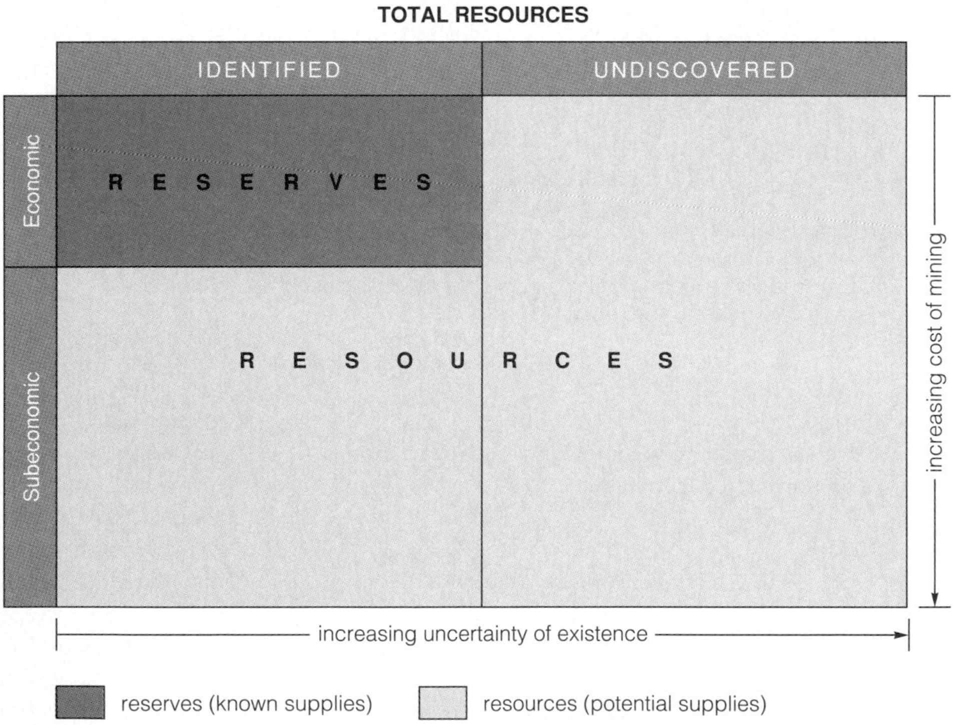

TOTAL RESOURCES

	IDENTIFIED	UNDISCOVERED
Economic	R E S E R V E S	
Subeconomic	R E S O U R C E S	

increasing cost of mining

increasing uncertainty of existence

■ reserves (known supplies)   ▢ resources (potential supplies)

can also be released in the late stages of the cooling of magma. These waters, called *hydrothermal solutions*, can be injected into fissures and pores, forming veins and other types of ore deposits. Lead, zinc, copper, tin, gold, silver, mercury, tungsten, and molybdenum are some of the metals found in such deposits.

Sulfide ores of several of these same metals are produced by hydrothermal solutions at hot springs, called *black smokers* or *chimneys*, at divergent plate boundaries on the seafloor, which also support marine organisms that produce organic nutrients by chemosynthesis. These deposits are mined in places where

Figure 7-19 This rock, known as Lake Superior Banded Iron Formation (or BIF), consists of alternating layers, or bands, of shiny gray hematite, an iron oxide, and red jasper, a flint-like rock that is colored red by an iron oxide. This outcrop is near Ishpeming, Michigan. Most of our iron comes from rock similar to this that was deposited in many parts of the world between 3.2 billion and 1.8 billion years ago.

the seafloor has been shoved up above sea level, such as Cyprus, for which copper is named, and Japan.

Erosion of igneous, metamorphic, and sedimentary rocks is responsible for the concentration of several kinds of mineral resources. Seawater contains many soluble weathering products brought in from the land, but the only mineral materials we currently get from the sea are salt, bromine, and magnesium.

Weathering in the tropics produces residual soils known as *laterite*. They are red from the iron oxide they contain and are usually rather hard. All of our aluminum and some iron, manganese, and nickel come from laterites.

Solid grains and fragments of economic minerals that have been eroded from rocks are carried by streams and deposited at places along the stream channel or in beach and nearshore sands, a type of deposit called a *placer* (pronounced plasser). Minerals found in placer deposits include titanium, gold, diamond, platinum, tin, niobium, tantalum, and uranium. The gold the forty-niners panned for in the California gold rush was in placers eroded from veins, the "mother lode," on the west slope of the Sierra Nevada.

Mineral resources have also been concentrated when sedimentary rock has formed by consolidation of sediment or by precipitation of material from solution. Examples include banded iron formations (the greatest iron ore deposits in the world) (Figure 7-19), and sandstone, the sediments of former sand dunes, beaches, and stream deposits. Analyses of such deposits give us evidence about interactions between Earth's crust, life, and the atmosphere during the planet's long history (see Spotlight on p. 182).

When water in marine lagoons or in desert lakes evaporated partly or completely, with nearly constant replacement of lost water, various minerals, called *evaporites*, were deposited in both ancient and modern times. Examples are salt, gypsum (used in drywall and plaster of Paris), potassium minerals (potash, used in commercial inorganic fertilizers), soda ash and sodium sulfate (used in glass, insecticides, paper, and other products), and boron minerals (used in detergents, glass, ceramics, and other products).

Organisms have also contributed to sedimentary mineral resources (Figure 7-20). Certain bacteria extract sulfur from gypsum and anhydrite (calcium sulfate minerals), producing rich deposits of pure sulfur underground in places along the Gulf Coast of the United States. Phosphate rock deposits that occur as part of the phosphorous cycle (Figure 4-31) are phosphatic bones and teeth of fish and other organisms or chemically precipitated phosphate or sometimes both. Peat, lignite, and bituminous coal result from the transformation of accumulated plant remains. Petroleum and natural gas are indirectly the result of sedimentary processes involving the remains of organisms.

ENVIRONMENTAL IMPACTS OF EXTRACTING, PROCESSING, AND USING MINERAL RESOURCES The extracting, processing, and use of any fuel or nonfuel mineral resource can cause land disturbance, erosion, air pollution, and water pollution (Figure 7-21). After profitable deposits of minerals are located, they are extracted by *surface mining* if they are located at or near the earth's surface or by *subsurface mining* if they are located deeper in the earth's crust, as discussed in more detail in Chapters 18 and 19.

Subsurface mining disturbs less than one-tenth as much land as surface mining and usually produces less waste material. However, it leaves much of the resource in the ground and is more dangerous and expensive than surface mining. Roofs and walls of underground mines collapse, trapping and killing miners. Explosions of dust and natural gas kill and injure them. Prolonged inhalation of mining dust causes lung diseases. Much energy is needed for ventilation and sometimes for pumping water.

Some mineral resources are used just as they come from the ground, so relatively little solid waste and air and water pollution are generated in extracting them. Quarrying stone, for example, requires only that the **overburden** and waste rock, if any, be removed and discarded as **spoil**, a type of waste produced by almost every type of resource extraction.

Many resources, after extraction from the ground, must be separated from other matter. This processing has potential for air and water pollution (Figure 7-21). Ore, for example, typically contains two parts: the ore mineral, which contains the desired metal, and the

The rocks of Earth and the fossils in them tell the story of Earth's history, a history that is still being deciphered. The oldest known indication of life is found in northwestern Australia in 3.5 billion-year-old rocks that contain peculiar limestone structures called stromatolites, produced by and including fossilized cyanobacteria (Figure 7-20). Chemical evidence in rocks shows that photosynthesis, which releases oxygen to the atmosphere, was occurring at that time.

This photosynthesis resulted in the gradual accumulation of dissolved oxygen in the seawater. As the oxygen level increased, the gas eventually began to escape into the atmosphere, leading to the modern oxygen-rich atmosphere. This also resulted in the formation of the ozone layer (Figure 4-3), making possible the existence of life in shallow water and on the land. Some of the evidence for these changes in the atmosphere's oxygen content is based on sediments with a red color caused by strongly oxidized iron in rocks as old as 2.5 billion to 2.8 billion years.

At about the same place in the rock sequence that this strongly oxidized iron in rocks was discovered, we also find the first occurrence of a type of economically important iron deposit known as the Lake Superior Banded Iron Formation (Figure 7-19). These iron ores may have been laid down as long as 3.2 billion years ago, but are found most abundantly in rocks between 2.6 billion and 1.8 billion years old. No banded iron formations are found in rocks younger than that. This example shows that the history of life, of the atmosphere, and of Earth's crust were all intertwined at that time in a uniquely important way.

C. A. Henley/Biofotos

Figure 7-20 Sedimentary rock forms from the accumulated products of erosion, the remains of organisms, or in this case, from material deposited by organisms. These limestone structures, called *stromatolites*, are similar to those deposited as much as 3.5 billion years ago by photosynthetic cyanobacteria (formerly known as blue-green algae). During the Proterozoic era (1.5 million to 2 million years ago), stromatolites probably were a common feature on Earth. These rocks are composed of numerous layers, each a former microbiological community. Modern cyanobacteria also produce stromatolites in a few places in the world, such as Shark's Bay, Australia, shown here.

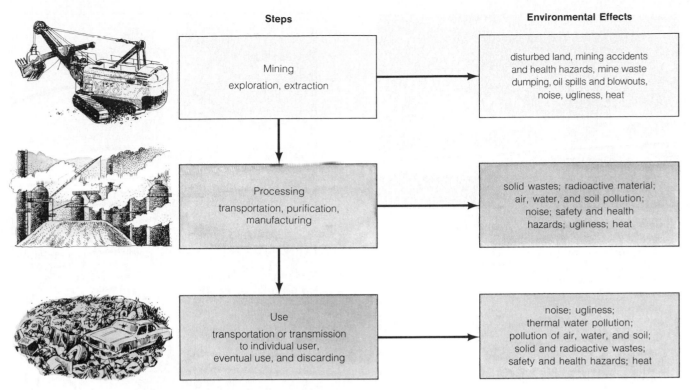

Steps		Environmental Effects
Mining exploration, extraction	→	disturbed land, mining accidents and health hazards, mine waste dumping, oil spills and blowouts, noise, ugliness, heat
Processing transportation, purification, manufacturing	→	solid wastes; radioactive material; air, water, and soil pollution; noise; safety and health hazards; ugliness; heat
Use transportation or transmission to individual user, eventual use, and discarding	→	noise; ugliness; thermal water pollution; pollution of air, water, and soil; solid and radioactive wastes; safety and health hazards; heat

Figure 7-21 Some harmful environmental effects of resource extraction, processing, and use. The energy produced and used in carrying out each step causes further pollution and environmental degradation. Most of the harm results from not requiring that the full costs of the pollution and environmental degradation caused by mining, processing, and manufacturing companies be included in the price of their products. Many of these "external" costs are still passed on to society in the form of poorer health, increased costs of health care and insurance, and increased taxes to pay for the problems caused by pollution and environmental degradation. If these external costs were internalized and included in the market cost of raw materials and manufactured goods, most of these harmful effects would be eliminated or reduced to more acceptable levels.

gangue, which is the waste mineral material. **Beneficiation**, or separation of the ore mineral from the gangue in a mill, produces waste called **tailings**.

Mining can affect the environment in several ways. Most noticeable are scarring and disruption of the land surface and the ugliness of spoil heaps and tailings. Underground fires in coal mines sometimes cannot be put out. Land above underground mines collapses or subsides, causing roads to buckle, houses to tilt, railroad tracks to bend, sewer lines to crack, gas mains to break, and groundwater systems to be disrupted. Spoil heaps and tailings can be eroded by wind and water. The air can be contaminated with dust and toxic substances, and water pollution is a serious concern associated with mining.

Sediment pollution may occur, and hazardous materials may be carried away in solution. *Acid mine drainage* occurs when aerobic bacteria produce sulfuric acid from iron sulfide minerals in spoils from coal mines and some ore mines. Rainwater seeping through the mine or mine wastes may carry the acid to nearby streams, destroying aquatic life and contaminating water supplies. It may also infiltrate the ground. Other harmful materials running off, or dissolved from underground mines or aboveground mining wastes, are radioactive uranium compounds and compounds of toxic metals such as lead, arsenic, or cadmium.

Most ore minerals do not consist of pure metal, so **smelting** is done to separate the metal from the other elements in the ore mineral. Without effective pollution control equipment, smelters emit enormous quantities of air pollutants that damage vegetation and soils in the surrounding area. Pollutants include sulfur dioxide, soot, and tiny particles of arsenic, cadmium, lead, and other toxic elements and compounds found in many ores. Decades of uncontrolled sulfur dioxide emissions from copper-smelting operations near Copperhill and Ducktown, Tennessee, killed all vegetation over a large area around the smelter (Figure 7-22). Smelters also cause water pollution and produce liquid and solid hazardous wastes that must be disposed of safely.

The burning of fossil fuels, the manufacture of items from mineral resources, and the use and discarding of many of these items produce solid waste (Chapter 19), hazardous waste (Chapter 20), air pollution (Chapter 21), and water pollution (Chapter 22).

Figure 7-22 Sulfur dioxide and other fumes from a copper smelter that operated for 52 years near Ducktown and Copperhill, Tennessee, killed the forest once found on this land and left a desert in its place. After decades of replanting, some vegetation has returned to the area, but recovery has been slow because of severe soil erosion.

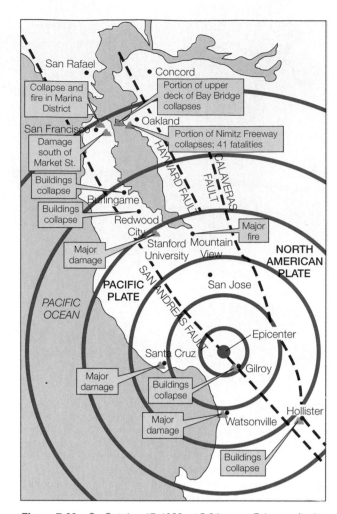

Figure 7-23 On October 17, 1989, at 5:04 P.M., a 7.1-magnitude earthquake occurred in northern California along the San Andreas Fault. It was the largest earthquake in northern California since 1906, when the "Great San Francisco Quake" and the resulting fires destroyed much of San Francisco. In 1989, the most extensive damage was within a 32-kilometer (20-mile) radius of the epicenter, although seismic waves caused serious damage as far away as San Francisco and Oakland. Sixty-seven people were killed, and official damage estimates were as high as $10 billion. This was North America's costliest natural disaster.

7-4 Natural Hazards

EARTHQUAKES Earth's internal and external processes cause **natural hazards**, events that destroy or damage wildlife habitats and kill or harm humans and damage property. Earthquakes and volcanoes are the result of internal Earth processes. Floods and mass wasting are the result of external Earth processes.

Stress can cause solid rock to deform elastically until it suddenly fractures and is displaced along the fracture, producing a *fault* (Figure 7-5). The faulting or a later abrupt movement on an existing fault causes an **earthquake**. An existing fault may rupture repeatedly at irregular intervals that may be many years apart, resulting in more and more displacement along the fault as long as it is active.

Three kinds of human activities have caused or increased earthquake activity, also called seismic activity. The added load of water in Lake Mead behind Hoover Dam caused numerous tremors in the early years after the dam was completed, and this has also happened elsewhere. Underground nuclear testing has been another cause of earthquakes, as has deep-well disposal of liquid wastes.

Reports of an earthquake commonly mention the *focus* and the *epicenter*. The *focus* is the point of initial movement, and the *epicenter* is the point on the surface directly above the focus. The epicenter may not be on the fault, either because the fault does not reach the surface or because the fault is not vertical and, therefore, surfaces some distance away from the epicenter.

One way the severity of an earthquake is measured is by its *magnitude* on the Richter scale. The magnitude

is a measure of the amount of energy released in the earthquake, as indicated by the amplitude (size) of the vibrations when they reach the recording instrument. Using this scale, seismologists rate earthquakes as *insignificant* (less than 4 on the Richter scale), *minor* (4 to 4.9), *damaging* (5 to 5.9), *destructive* (6 to 6.9), *major* (7 to 7.9), and *great* (8 to 8.9). The northern California earthquake of 1989 had a Richter magnitude of 7.1 and caused damage within a radius of 97 kilometers (60 miles) from its epicenter (Figure 7-23).

Each higher step on the Richter scale represents an amplitude that is 10 times greater than the step below, so a magnitude 5 is 10 times a magnitude 4, and a magnitude 6 is 100 times a magnitude 4. The amount of energy released is approximately 30 times greater for

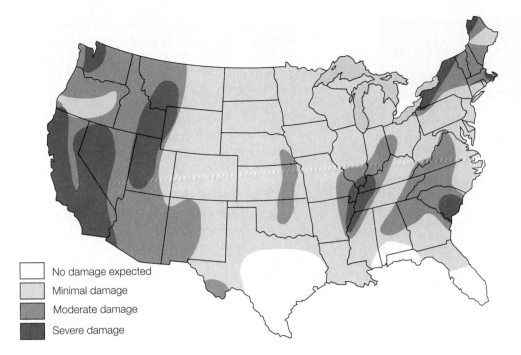

Figure 7-24 Maps have been prepared that can help to determine the general earthquake risk in a particular region, but they do not predict earthquakes. Except for a few regions along the Atlantic and the Gulf, virtually every part of the continental United States is subject to some risk, but several areas are at risk of moderate to major damage from earthquakes. Earthquakes occur along fault zones such as the San Andreas (Figure 7-6) or in intraplate areas such as the New Madrid zone south of the tip of Illinois. This latter zone is now considered by some to be the area of highest risk of a major earthquake in the lower 48 states. (Data from U.S. Geological Survey)

Legend:
- ☐ No damage expected
- ☐ Minimal damage
- ☐ Moderate damage
- ☐ Severe damage

each higher step on the Richter scale. A destructive earthquake with a magnitude of 6 releases energy equal to that from exploding a hydrogen (nuclear fusion) bomb, equivalent to that from detonating 0.9 million metric tons (1 million tons or 1 megaton) of TNT. A great earthquake with an intensity of 8 releases energy equal to that from exploding 60,000 hydrogen bombs.

A rupture in the rock, essentially a tear in the crust, can extend as a fault develops or an existing fault reactivates. As a result, earthquakes often have *aftershocks* that gradually decrease in frequency over a period of up to several months, and some have *foreshocks* from seconds to weeks before the main shock.

A map of earthquake epicenters shows that earthquakes are most common at the three types of plate boundaries, clearly outlining the lithospheric plates (Figure 7-4a), but they also occur at many intraplate sites away from plate boundaries. Shallow-focus earthquakes, those with a focal depth less than 70 kilometers (43 miles), occur in all earthquake zones and are generally more damaging than deeper ones. Intermediate- and deep-focus earthquakes, those with a focal depth between 70 kilometers (43 miles) and 700 kilometers (430 miles), occur only at convergent plate boundaries (Figure 7-5).

Intraplate seismicity (as in Hawaii) may be related to the movement of magma at mantle plumes or to settling over a magma chamber. At other intraplate sites, such as the New Madrid fault zone in the region south of the southern tip of Illinois, it is the result of movement on old faults. Many of the intraplate earthquakes that have occurred in historic times in the eastern United States have been due to unknown causes.

The primary effects of earthquakes include shaking and sometimes permanent vertical or horizontal displacement of the ground. They may have serious effects on people and structures, such as buildings, bridges, freeway overpasses, dams, and pipelines. Secondary effects of earthquakes include various types of mass wasting (such as rockfalls and rockslides, see Case Study on p. 186), urban fires, and flooding due to subsidence of land. Coastal areas can also be severely damaged by large waves, called *tsunamis* (misnamed "tidal waves," although they have nothing to do with tides), that travel as fast as 950 kilometers (590 miles) per hour. Two of the worst earthquakes, in terms of lives lost, happened in China, with about 830,000 killed in 1556 and 500,000 in 1976.

Loss of life and property from earthquakes can be reduced. This requires identification of active fault zones and of earth materials that are more subject to shaking, establishment of building codes that regulate the placement and design of buildings in areas of high risk, and, ultimately, earthquake prediction.

Because movement on a fault may be infrequent, it is sometimes difficult to determine whether a fault is active. Thus, it is important to look at historical records of earthquakes and to do geologic field research that can indicate how recently a fault has moved. Maps indicating earthquake risk, based on both of these kinds of research have been compiled and are continually revised (Figure 7-24).

As geologists study faults more, they can draw maps that indicate which parts of a fault system have been seismically quiet for a long time while other parts have been moving, indicating that stress has been

On May 31, 1970, a major disaster occurred on Nevado Huascaran, a mountain in the Cordillera Blanca region of the Peruvian Andes. It began with a 7.7 Richter magnitude earthquake in the subduction zone near the Pacific coast, about 100 kilometers (60 miles) west of the mountain.

This turned out to be the deadliest earthquake ever recorded in the Western Hemisphere. It shook down the adobe homes of villagers and triggered thousands of small landslides.

It also dislodged a mass of overhanging rock and glacial ice, weighing millions of metric tons, from near the top of the 6,768-meter- (22,200-foot-) high mountain. This material fell about 900 meters (3,000 feet), partially melted on impact, and picked up rock debris. Then the mixture of water, mud, rock, and ice swept down on the village of Yungay at speeds that approached 500 kilometers (310 miles) per hour.

At Yungay, at least 20,000 people were killed, mostly from the debris avalanche, and throughout the region the death toll reached about 70,000. There were three main causes of this tremendous loss of life and property: the earthquake itself, the avalanche, and floods sent downstream when the avalanche reached the Rio Santa river. This shows how one geologic event can trigger a chain of events.

It was not the first natural disaster in this area. In 1870, Yungay was wiped out by a debris avalanche, and several other villages were destroyed by another in 1941. Still another, demolished several villages and killed at least 3,500 people in 1962.

building. Along the San Andreas Fault (Figure 7-6), for example, there are sections that experience almost continuous movement as the fault moves slowly by tectonic creep. Other sections have small earthquakes every few years, and still other sections have been menacingly quiet for many years.

Actual prediction of earthquakes will have to be based primarily on *precursor phenomena*, events that precede an earthquake, as well as on the pattern and frequency of earthquakes in an area. Precursor phenomena include such characteristics of earth materials as slight tilting of rock and changes in electrical and magnetic properties, the amount of radon (a radioactive gas) dissolved in groundwater, the speed of seismic waves passing through the area from nearby quakes, and even the unusual behavior of animals that apparently are able to sense an imminent earthquake.

Seismologists are collecting data on precursor phenomena on active faults in many places around the world. The San Andreas Fault (Figure 7-6) is the most heavily instrumented fault anywhere. Until reliable prediction techniques are established, there might be legitimate concern about the disruptive effects of false alarms and, on the other side of the coin, the possible ignoring of accurate predictions.

Some geologists believe that some damaging earthquakes can be prevented by releasing fault pressure before it becomes so strong that it causes a violent earthquake. The discovery that the occurrence of earthquakes coincided with deep-well disposal of liquid wastes led to experiments with injection of water in a Colorado oil field that indicated the water was in fact relieving pressure. Some have suggested this might work on locked sections of the San Andreas Fault. Although it would be expensive, it could avoid the loss of lives and property. Others have suggested the use of underground explosions, including nuclear ones, to relieve strain.

VOLCANOES   Volcanic activity occurs where magma reaches Earth's surface through a central vent or a long crack (fissure). Such activity can release ejecta (debris ranging from large chunks of lava rock to ash, which may be glowing hot), liquid lava, and gases (water vapor, carbon dioxide, sulfur dioxide, nitrogen, and others) into the surrounding environment.

Volcanic activity is concentrated, for the most part, in the same areas as seismic activity (Figure 7-4a). It usually occurs at divergent and convergent plate boundaries (Figure 7-4b), sometimes at intraplate sites, and perhaps at a few transform faults.

The volcanoes at convergent plate boundaries include Fujiyama (part of the volcanic island arc in Japan) and Mt. St. Helens in Washington (see Case Study on p. 188). All have the steep cone shape that is characteristic of that type of volcano, and all usually erupt explosively.

Those at divergent boundaries, such as the East African rift valleys and the islands of Iceland are ordinarily quieter in their eruptions. The lava typically just flows, or sprays into the air in a steady stream, from fissures.

Intraplate volcanoes have an eruptive style related to their location. Those in the ocean, as on Hawaii, erupt very quietly like those at divergent boundaries, but from the summit or flanks of cones. This produces a broad, gently sloping cone, down which the lava flows in a stream. The main hazard from the Hawaiian volcanoes is lava flows. Lava flows from quiet eruptions are very fluid and can cover roads and villages, igniting brush, trees, and homes in the process. In contrast to that, intraplate volcanoes on continents have erupted very explosively at Yellowstone and other places in the western United States.

Prediction of volcanic activity is being studied, and

it has improved considerably during this century. As with earthquake maps, the eruptive history of a volcano or volcanic center gives some indication of where the risks are. Much experience has been gained at the Hawaii Volcano Observatory on Kilauea in predicting eruptions there, and research is currently being done at Mt. St. Helens and in other places, such as Japan, which has 10% of the world's active volcanoes.

It takes time, though, to accumulate the data necessary to detect patterns of behavior, and every volcano has its own personality. Volcanologists are now looking at such precursor phenomena as tilting or swelling of the cone, changes in magnetic and thermal properties of the volcano, changes in gas composition, and increased seismic activity.

Control of volcanic eruptions would seem impossible, but there has been some success with it. Experimental techniques include damming lava flows, mudflows, and debris flows; bombing lava flows; and spraying lava flows with water, all of which have helped in at least some cases.

We tend to think of volcanic activity in negative terms, but it also provides several benefits. One is outstanding scenery in the form of majestic mountains, some lakes (such as Crater Lake in Oregon), and other landforms. Others are geothermal phenomena, such as geysers and hot springs, which have aesthetic value and economic value in the tourist and travel industry. Geothermal energy is also an important source of energy in some areas (Figure 7-17) and may be more widely used in the future (Section 17-7). Perhaps the most important benefit of volcanism is the highly fertile soils produced by the weathering of lava.

STREAM FLOODS, HURRICANES, AND TYPHOONS Natural flooding by streams, the most common type of flooding, is due primarily to heavy rain or rapid melting of snow, which causes water in the stream to overflow the channel in which it normally flows and to cover the adjacent area. Geologically, the flat valley floor next to a channel is called a **floodplain**. However, for legal purposes, the term is often applied to any low area that has the potential for flooding, including certain coastal areas.

Valleys with geological (and legal) floodplains are popular places for human habitation. In some cases, the wide floor slopes gently down away from the channel, and the channel usually has a ridge, called a *natural levee*, on both sides. The levees are made of fine sand and coarse silt, sediment the stream carried in suspension and deposited when it overflowed the channel. A flood here can easily inundate the entire floodplain because the stream is higher than most of it.

In other areas, a flat-floored valley has a floodplain that slopes toward the stream. It is the result of a stream widening its valley by meandering from one side to the other (Figure 5-41). This type of stream usually lacks levees. In this case, a low-discharge flood will affect only the part of the floodplain near the channel, and a larger one will affect areas farther away from the channel.

People have settled on floodplains since the beginnings of agriculture. The soil is fertile, what farmers in the midwestern United States call bottomland, and there is water for irrigation, if necessary. Communities have access to the water for transportation of people or goods. The beauty of the stream may be an attraction, and floodplains are flat surfaces, ideal sites, in many ways, for buildings, highways, and railroads. People may decide that all of these benefits outweigh the risk of flooding, if they are even aware of the risk.

On marine coasts, flooding is due most often to the wind-driven storm surges and rain-swollen streams associated with tropical cyclones, in which intense winds blow in a circular pattern and internal air currents draw up large amounts of water and dump it on surrounding areas. Tropical cyclones in the Atlantic are known as *hurricanes* and those in the Pacific are called *typhoons*. The greatest risk from hurricanes in the lower 48 states is along the Atlantic and Gulf coasts.

Flooding can also occur on the shorelines of large inland lakes. For example, occasionally the low ground around the west end of Lake Erie is flooded when strong east winds blow the water inland.

In spite of the drama and severity of earthquakes, volcanic eruptions, and major storms, flooding has been the most common type of natural disaster because areas susceptible to flooding are so numerous. Each year, flooding kills thousands of people and causes tens of billions of dollars in property damage, as discussed in Section 13-3.

The main way humans increase the probability of flooding is by removing vegetation—through timbering operations, overgrazing by cattle, construction, forest fires that are accidentally or deliberately set, and certain mining activities. Vegetation retards surface runoff, increasing infiltration; when that vegetation is removed by human activities or natural occurrences, precipitation reaches streams more directly, often with a large load of sediment, increasing the chance of flooding. The practice of putting drain tiles in farm fields accelerates the movement of water from the fields to the stream system and may also contribute to flooding, as may urbanization.

FLOOD CONTROL STRATEGIES The first step in designing a flood control strategy is to construct a *flood-frequency curve*, which illustrates the average recurrence interval between various levels of discharge. This means estimating how often, on average, a flood of a certain size occurs. If the average interval between floods of a certain level in an area is 7 years, this does not mean that a discharge of that amount will occur every 7 years. Instead, the time between floods with such a discharge might be 4 years one time and 10 years the next, giving an average interval of 7 years.

Because the United States is a relatively young country, and because volcanic eruptions may be infrequent even in areas of active volcanism, the public is likely to be unaware of, and unconcerned about, the risks. Public awareness was increased when, after a 123-year dormancy, there was an explosive eruption of Mt. St. Helens in the Cascade Range on May 18, 1980 (Figure 7-25).

This eruption has been described as the worst volcanic disaster in the history of the United States. Its blast had the explosive force of a 30-megaton bomb, 1,500 times as powerful as the one that demolished Hiroshima.

Devastation from the blast occurred in three semicircular zones north of the volcano. In the direct blast zone (the "tree-removal zone"), extending about 13 kilometers (8 miles), everything was obliterated or carried away. Beyond the direct blast zone (in the "tree-down zone") to 30 kilometers (19 miles) out, the blast travelled like a flood through the low areas, blowing down all trees like matchsticks so their tops pointed away from the blast. In the "seared zone," 1 to 2 kilometers (0.6 to 1.2 miles) beyond the second zone, trees were left standing but were scorched brown.

The explosion also threw ash more than 7 kilometers (4 miles) up into the atmosphere. Most of the huge cloud of ash travelled eastward, and several hours after the explosion caused enough darkness to trigger automatic streetlights during

Figure 7-25 Mt. St. Helens, a composite volcano in Washington, near the Washington–Oregon border, before (above), during (near right), and after (far right) its major eruption in May of 1980. It is one in a chain of volcanoes less than 1 million years old that stretches 1,500 kilometers (930 miles) from Lassen Peak in northern California to Mt. Garibaldi in British Columbia. A composite volcano typically has a steep conical shape. It develops adjacent to a subduction zone at a convergent plate boundary and erupts explosively. As a result of this eruption, much of the northern side of the volcano was blown away and the altitude of the summit was reduced by about 450 meters (1,475 feet).

the day in Yakima and Spokane, Washington. Within two weeks, the ash had travelled around the globe. The ash eventually circled the globe several times before most settled out.

The heat of the eruption rapidly melted snow and glacial ice on the mountain and caused mudflows, made of mixtures of volcanic debris and water. They flowed down the stream valleys, clogging the Toutle, Cowlitz, and Columbia Rivers. Such

mudflows commonly flow down steep slopes at speeds of 30 to 70 kilometers (19 to 43 miles) per hour, so you can't outrun one and you may not be able to outdrive some, especially if you are in heavy traffic. The Mt. St. Helens eruption did not produce a lava flow, although, like many volcanoes, it can.

Compared with other volcanic eruptions, the one at Mt. St. Helens ejected a relatively small amount of

---

Various strategies have been developed for reducing the hazard of stream flooding, each with a mix of advantages and disadvantages. *Channelization* deepens, widens, or straightens a section of a stream, sometimes including lining the channel with concrete, to accommodate a higher discharge through that section. This, in turn, increases the discharge downstream and may cause increased erosion upstream.

A *flood control dam* retains floodwater, releasing it downstream over an extended time. Such a dam may

have such secondary benefits as hydroelectric power, water for irrigation, and recreational facilities (Figure 5-40). The reservoir of the dam will accumulate sediment, however, which gradually fills it until it is useless. Also, the weight of the water in the reservoir may put stress on the rocks in the area, causing earthquakes. Tragically, some flood control dams have failed for one reason or another, causing flooding more severe than that which they were constructed to prevent.

Artificial levees are sometimes built where there are

U.S. Geological Survey

U.S. Geological Survey

ash and other materials. When Tambora in Indonesia erupted in 1815 and killed 50,000 to 90,000 people, it threw out so much ash (30 to 80 times as much as Mt. St. Helens) that sunlight was partially blocked out and so much cooling resulted that 1816 became known as "the year without a summer."

Although this most recent eruption of Mt. St. Helens was not a major one, it still had serious consequences:

- Deaths of about 60 people, including a geologist who was gathering data.

- Destruction of more than 200 cabins and homes and damage to many more.

- Obliteration of tens of thousands of hectares of forest, along with campgrounds and bridges.

- Deaths of an estimated 7,000 big game animals (bear, deer, and elk), all birds, and most small mammals in the blast area.

- Damage to salmon hatcheries, causing the deaths of 12 million salmon fingerlings, about 360,000 of which would have survived to adulthood.

- Loss of crops, including alfalfa, apples, potatoes, and wheat, but addition of trace elements from the ash to the soil may benefit agriculture in the long run.

- Unemployment for people living in the area, but establishment of

volcano visitor centers and other promotions may have more than made up for this loss of jobs and income.

In the years since 1980, some volcanic activity has continued, and there remains the risk of further eruptions. There is also some risk of flooding if debris dams holding back drainage were to fail.

Mt. St. Helens is the most studied volcano in history. The information gained from these investigations should help save lives and increase our knowledge of this type of event. By 1990, many biologists were surprised at how fast various forms of life had begun colonizing many of the most devastated areas.

no natural ones and sometimes on top of the natural ones. They may be permanent, or temporary in the form of sandbags placed when a flood is imminent. A serious problem with this approach is that if the levee breaks or the flood spills over it, floodwater may be held between the levee and the valley wall for a long time after the stream discharge has decreased.

From an environmental viewpoint, *floodplain management* is the best approach. Using a flood-frequency curve, a plan is developed to prohibit certain types of

buildings or activities in the high-risk zone, to elevate or otherwise flood-proof buildings that are allowed on the legally defined floodplain, and to construct a floodway that allows floodwater to flow through the community with minimal damage.

A good example of floodway use is in Scottsdale, Arizona, where a floodway forms a beautiful greenbelt, 11 kilometers (7 miles) long, through the city. The floodway contains five parks, bike paths, tennis courts, golf courses, and other features.

The Federal Flood Disaster Protection Act passed by the U.S. Congress in 1973 requires that to be eligible for federal flood insurance, local governments must adopt such floodplain development regulations. It also denies federal funding to proposed construction projects in localities designated as flood hazard areas.

Despite these efforts, in 1990 more than 16.8 million households and $758 billion in property were located on floodplains in the United States. On the average, floods kill more than 200 people and cause over $4 billion in property losses per year in the United States, with California, Florida, Texas, and Louisiana being the four most flood-prone states.

The federal flood-insurance program underwrites $185 billion in policies because private insurance companies are unwilling to fully insure people who live in flood-prone areas from damages. Thus, the federal flood-insurance program encourages many people to build on floodplains and low-lying coastal areas subject to high risks of flooding. People getting this protection pay a premium, but it is not enough to cover the losses. It would make more economic sense and save taxpayers money if the federal government would buy the 2% of the country's land that repeatedly floods instead of continuing to make disaster payments.

MASS WASTING Frost action forces rock apart on the face of a cliff and causes a *rockfall*. Regolith on a mountainside outside Los Angeles becomes saturated by an infrequent rain and, having lost its vegetative cover in a recent brushfire, becomes a *mudflow*. A large mass of rock is jarred loose by an earthquake and creates a *rockslide*. Frost heaving, burrowing animals, and grazing cattle cause the regolith on a hillside to slowly move downhill in a process called *creep*. These are some of the kinds of mass wasting.

Several factors affect whether mass wasting is likely to occur and, if it does, what kind it will be. The earth material (regolith or bedrock) in a region is an important factor. In the case of bedrock, the strength of the rock, the presence of fractures, and the orientation of layering or other zones of weakness may all play a role.

Water frequently contributes to mass wasting. A small amount of water in the pores of earth material may actually improve the stability of regolith, as anyone who has built a sand castle knows, but the weight it adds will contribute to instability. Saturation with water forces soil particles apart, and a mudflow of water-saturated regolith can occur on even a moderate slope where the water table rises and intersects the land surface. Saturation and mudflows can also occur as a result of high precipitation during a storm or rapid melting of ice and snow.

The effect of vegetation on mass wasting varies from case to case. In some cases, vegetation contributes to mass wasting by slowing the fall of rain on slopes, which helps water to infiltrate and saturate the soil. In

other cases, it inhibits mass wasting by removing water from the ground and putting it into the air through transpiration and by holding the regolith together with its roots.

One of the most important factors in mass wasting is the steepness of the slope of the land. Sooner or later, some type of mass wasting is likely to occur on any steep slope.

Human activities may contribute to mass wasting, often in places where it causes loss of property and maybe even injury and death. An example is the building of homes on terraces cut into hillsides, which oversteepens the slope and overloads the surface, greatly increasing the chances of mass wasting. Roadcuts through mountain ridges and along slopes are sometimes unstable, as well.

Utilization of resources can also contribute to mass wasting. In 1972, a 180-meter (590-foot) high spoil pile from a coal mine that had been built over springs on a fairly steep slope just outside Aberfan, Wales, flowed into the town. It killed more than 150 people, mostly children in a school that was destroyed. Mass wasting caused by clear-cutting of timber and building of logging roads is a serious problem in the Cascade Range in Oregon.

The first step in coping with mass wasting is to identify areas of risk. People proposing to build on a potentially unstable site should get professional help during the planning stage, something that is required by building codes in southern California. It would be best to avoid construction on an unstable site, but if there are strong reasons for going ahead with it, there might be ways to reduce the risk in individual cases.

Some factors contributing to mass wasting, such as an earthquake, are unavoidable. It is possible, however, to install drainage to remove water from a slope, and certain types of vegetation can be planted to increase stability. Well-designed retention walls may be effective in some, but not all, cases.

SUBSIDENCE **Subsidence** is a vertical movement of large rock masses that is not slope-related. Collapse can occur in volcanic regions (when magma underlying a large part of the region withdraws and the unsupported rock drops, producing a caldera), in limestone regions (when the roof of a cavern, formed by solution, collapses to make a sinkhole) (Figure 7-26), and in other cases.

Subsidence may involve only a sinking of the ground, without significant fracturing, as a result of thawing or very slow downward warping of the crust over a broad area, such as the Michigan basin. Subsidence that happens rapidly, such as in sinkhole formation, may be especially hazardous, but slow warping can also cause serious structural damage to buildings.

Removal of water, oil, coal, and other resources has caused subsidence of various kinds. For example, parts

Figure 7-26 Subsidence in Winter Park, Florida, in May 1981. This large sinkhole developed rapidly one evening and caused $2 million in damage. By morning, it was about 80 meters (260 feet) across and had swallowed a house, parts of two businesses, portions of pavement on two streets, a large part of a municipal swimming pool, and several cars.

George Remaine

of Houston, Texas, have subsided as much as 3 meters (10 feet) and some areas of Mexico City have subsided as much as 8.5 meters (28 feet) because of excessive withdrawal of groundwater. At some places, artificial recharge of groundwater by the injection of storm water or used water has helped restore the pressure and has slowed the subsidence.

Underground coal mines have collapsed in Wyoming and Pennsylvania, and iron mines have collapsed in Michigan. Some of these incidents resulted in loss of homes and lives.

An important thing to remember about natural hazards is that, although humans contribute to some of them, they would happen, to a great extent, even if there were no humans on Earth. However, we could greatly reduce the loss of life and property damage by not building houses on wave-cut cliffs next to the ocean, on floodplains along streams, or on other hazardous sites. We cannot expect natural processes to come to a screeching halt for us.

<table>
<tr><td>7-5</td><td>**Geologic and Other Time Frames**</td></tr>
</table>

Earth is constantly changing. Throughout Earth's history, the atmosphere has changed (see Spotlight on p. 182), the climate has changed, the geography has changed, the types and numbers of organisms have changed, and some kinds of geologic processes have slowed or accelerated (Figure 7-27). Some of these changes are so slow that we are unaware of them; others are much faster.

Weather changes in a matter of minutes or hours and climate over years to centuries. Populations can change their size and age distribution in response to changes in environmental conditions within hours to decades (Figure 6-3). Earth's species that have become extinct have done so either because they were unable to survive environmental changes or because they changed over the generations into new species (Figures 6-7 and 6-8). This biological evolution of new species usually takes thousands to millions of years, depending mostly on the reproductive ability of each species.

Some geological changes in the earth's interior and crust have taken place on a time scale of millions to billions of years (Figure 7-27). Changes from mass wasting, erosion, volcanic eruption, and some subsidence can happen very rapidly. We and other species who inhabit Earth today are the beneficiaries of processes such as landscape development, biological change, and resource concentration, acting over eons of time.

In the short time we have been on Earth, we have had a powerful impact on the environment. We have the potential to do great harm to Earth. Already, we have accelerated natural processes and introduced processes and changes that would not have occurred without us. We have the ability and the responsibility to be stewards of Earth, to tend it and care for it. In order to do that, we must synchronize the rate at which we affect Earth with the rate at which it responds to us.

A civilization writes its record on the land.

WALTER CLAY LOWDERMILK

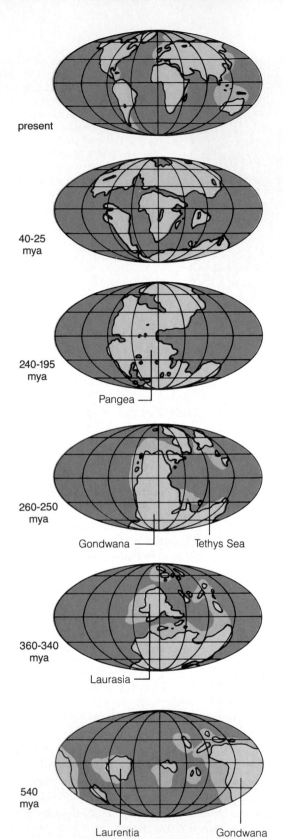

	present
	40-25 mya
	240-195 mya
	Pangea
	260-250 mya
	Gondwana — Tethys Sea
	360-340 mya
	Laurasia
	540 mya
	Laurentia Gondwana

Figure 7-27 Major geological and biological events in the evolution of the earth and its organisms. Many of these geological and biological changes took place over millions to billions of years. The time spans of the different eras are not to scale. These changes make those occurring in the 40,000 years in which our species has existed seem like an eyeblink. (Used with permission from Cecie Starr, *Biology: Concepts and Applications*, Wadsworth, Belmont, Calif., 1990)

Era	Period	Epoch	Millions of Years Ago (mya)
CENOZOIC	Quaternary	Recent	0.01-
		Pleistocene	1.65
	Tertiary	Pliocene	5
		Miocene	25
		Oligocene	38
		Eocene	54
		Paleocene	65
MESOZOIC	Cretaceous	Late	100
		Early	
	Jurassic		138
	Triassic		205
PALEOZOIC	Permian		240
	Carboniferous		290
	Devonian		360
	Silurian		410
	Ordovician		435
	Cambrian		505
PROTEROZOIC			550
ARCHEAN			2,500

1.65 mya to present. Major glaciations. Modern humans emerge and begin what may be greatest **mass extinction** of all time on land, starting with Ice Age hunters.

65-1.65 mya. Unprecedented mountain building as continents rupture, drift, collide. Major climatic shifts; vast grasslands emerge. Major **radiations** of flowering plants, insects, birds, mammals. Origins of earliest human forms.

65 mya. Asteroid impact? **Mass extinction** of all dinosaurs and many marine organisms.

135-65 mya. Pangea breakup continues, broad inland seas form. Major **radiations** of marine invertebrates, fishes, insects, dinosaurs. Origin of angiosperms (flowering plants).

181-135 mya. Pangea breakup begins. Rich marine communities. Major **radiations** of dinosaurs.

205 mya. Asteroid impact? Mass extinction of many organisms in seas, some on land; dinosaurs, mammals survive.

240-205 mya. Recovery, **radiations** of marine invertebrates, fishes, dinosaurs. Gymnosperms the dominant land plants. Origin of mammals.

240 mya. **Mass extinction.** Nearly all species in seas and on land perish.

280-240 mya. Pangea, worldwide ocean form; shallow seas squeezed out. Major **radiations** of reptiles, gymnosperms.

360-280 mya. Tethys Sea forms. Recurring glaciations. Major **radiations** of insects, amphibians. Spore-bearing plants dominate; gymnosperms present. Origin of reptiles.

370 mya. **Mass extinction** of many marine invertebrates, most fishes.

435-360 mya. Laurasia forms, Gondwana moves north. Vast swamplands, early vascular plants. **Radiations** of fishes continue. Origin of amphibians.

435 mya. Glaciations as Gondwana crosses South Pole. **Mass extinction** of many marine organisms.

500-435 mya. Gondwana moves south. Major **radiations** of marine invertebrates, early fishes.

550-500 mya. Land masses dispersed near equator. Simple marine communities. Origin of animals with hard parts.

700-550 mya. Supercontinent Laurentia breaks up; widespread glaciations.

2,500-570 mya. Oxygen present in atmosphere. Origin of aerobic metabolism. Origin of protistans, algae, fungi, animals.

3,800-2,500 mya. Origin of photosynthetic bacteria.

4,600-3,800 mya. Formation of earth's crust, early atmosphere, oceans. Chemical evolution leading to origin of life (anaerobic bacteria).

4,600 mya. Origin of earth.

DISCUSSION TOPICS

1. What might life for us be like if the materials of Earth were in reverse order, with the crust having the composition of the core and vice versa, or if Earth had the same composition throughout?

2. In what important ways would conditions on Earth's surface be different if the outer core were not liquid?

3. Give some of the ways, positive and negative, that plate tectonics is important to you.

4. Discuss the ways, positive and negative, that external Earth processes (mass wasting, weathering, stream erosion, and so on) are important to you.

5. Explain what would happen if plate tectonics stopped. Explain what would happen if erosion and mass wasting stopped. If you were "in charge," would you eliminate either group of processes? Explain.

6. What crustal resources do you use every day? Make a table to show materials used and how they are used.

7. Describe how your life would be different if we did not use crustal resources. Consider food, shelter, health care, transportation, and any other area you can think of.

8. Discuss how both geologic processes and earlier organisms have produced environmental conditions that allow the present variety of life to exist.

*9. On a map of your state
   a. Indicate where various types of crustal resources are extracted, distinguishing each type with a symbol or a colored spot.
   b. Mark where igneous, sedimentary, and metamorphic rocks occur. (You may have to combine two types in certain areas.)
   c. Show what natural hazards exist. Describe what is being done to reduce the risk from those hazards.

PART THREE

THE HUMAN

POPULATION

We need the size of population in which human beings can fulfill their potentialities; in my opinion we are already overpopulated from that point of view; not just in places like India and China and Puerto Rico, but also in the United States and Western Europe.

GEORGE WALD
(NOBEL LAUREATE, BIOLOGY)

Illegal squatter settlements in Rio de Janeiro, Brazil.

CHAPTER 8

POPULATION

DYNAMICS AND

POPULATION

REGULATION

General Questions and Issues

1. How is population size affected by birth rates, death rates, fertility rates, and migration rates?

2. How is population size affected by the percentage of males and females at each age level?

3. What methods can be used to regulate the size and the rate of change of the human population?

4. What success have various countries had in trying to control the rate of growth of their populations?

We shouldn't delude ourselves: the population explosion will come to an end before very long. The only remaining question is whether it will be halted through the humane method of birth control, or by nature wiping out our surplus.

PAUL H. EHRLICH

VERY TIME YOUR HEART BEATS, three more persons are added to the world's population. By this time tomorrow, there will be about 266,000 more people on our only home, 248,000 of them in LDCs and 18,000 in MDCs (Figure 8-1). We are now adding more people each day than at any other time in human history.

The reason that the world's population continues to grow exponentially by 1 billion people every ten years is simple. There are about 3 births for each death, with 1.6 births for each death in MDCs and 3.3 births for each death in LDCs.

We have brought death rates and birth rates down, but death rates have fallen more sharply than birth rates. If this continues, one of two things will probably happen during your lifetime: the number of people on Earth will at least double before population growth comes to a halt or the world will experience an unprecedented population crash, with hundreds of millions, perhaps billions, of people dying prematurely.

Some say that such talk is alarmist and that the world can support billions more people (see Guest Essay on p. 29). They call for countries, especially MDCs, to increase their population size to maintain their economic growth and military security.

Critics of that view point out that we are not adequately supporting one of five people here today (see

Figure 8-1 City pool in Tokyo, Japan. Between 1950 and 1955, Japan cut its population growth rate in half. Japan's population of 124 million is projected to increase to 135 million by 2025. Japanese women have an average of only 1.5 children during their reproductive years — one of the world's lowest fertility rates. Average life expectancy at birth is 79 years — the highest in the world. Japan also has one of the world's lowest rates of deaths among infants under one year of age. Japan's population is aging faster than that of any other country. Because Japan must import most of its timber, mineral, and energy resources, its population has a severe impact on tropical forests, oceans, and other ecosystems worldwide. A 1989 study by the United Nations Environment Programme showed that the Japanese were among the least concerned about a range of global environmental problems (see Case Study on p. 268).

Spotlight on p. 8). They believe that the world is already overpopulated and that slowing world population growth is one of the most urgent issues we face (see Guest Essay on p. 219). Many analysts argue that we are faced with two population problems: people overpopulation in LDCs and consumption overpopulation in MDCs (Figure 1-16). Those who believe that the world is overpopulated argue that if we don't sharply lower birth rates, we are deciding by default to raise death rates. Not to decide is to decide.

The study of population characteristics and changes in the world and parts of the world is called **demography**, the subject of this chapter. In Chapter 9, you will learn how the world's people are distributed between urban and rural areas and about urban problems.

8-1 Factors Affecting Human Population Size

BIRTH RATES AND DEATH RATES Demographers, or population specialists, normally use the annual crude birth rate and crude death rate rather than total live births and deaths to describe population change. The **birth rate**, or **crude birth rate**, is the number of live births per 1,000 persons in a population in a given year. The **death rate**, or **crude death rate**, is the number of deaths per 1,000 persons in a population in a given year. Figure 8-2 shows the crude birth rates and death rates of various groups of countries in 1990.

When the birth rate of an area is greater than the death rate, its population grows (assuming no net migration in or out of the area). When the death rate equals the crude birth rate, population size remains stable. This condition is known as **zero population growth (ZPG)**. When the death rate is higher than the birth rate, population size decreases.

The annual rate at which the size of a population changes is called the **annual rate of natural population change**. It is usually expressed as a percentage.

$$\text{annual rate of population change (\%)} = \frac{\text{birth rate} - \text{death rate}}{1{,}000 \text{ persons}} \times 100$$
$$= \frac{\text{birth rate} - \text{death rate}}{10}$$

In 1991, the crude birth rate for the world was 27, and the death rate was 9. Thus, the world's population grew exponentially in 1991 at a rate of 1.8%: (27 − 9)/10 = 18/10 = 1.8%.

The annual rate at which the world's population was growing decreased from a high of 2% in the mid-1960s to 1.8% in 1991, but the base of the population undergoing this exponential growth increased by more than 2 billion during this period (Figure 1-2). This 10%

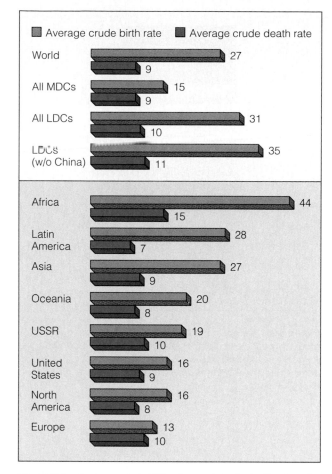

Figure 8-2 Average crude birth rates and crude death rates of various groups of countries in 1990. (Data from Population Reference Bureau)

drop in the annual exponential growth rate is good news; however, it is like learning that a truck heading straight at you has slowed down from 161 kilometers (100 miles) per hour to 145 kilometers (90 miles) per hour while its weight has increased by two-thirds.

Figure 8-3 gives the annual population change rates in major parts of the world. An annual population growth rate of 1% to 3% may seem small, but such exponential rates lead to enormous increases in population size over a 100-year period (see Spotlight on p. 5).

The impact of exponential population growth on population size is much greater in countries with a large existing population base. In sheer numbers, China and India dwarf all other countries, making up 37% of the world's population (Figure 8-4).

FERTILITY RATES Two types of fertility rates affect a country's population size and growth rate. **Replacement-level fertility** is the number of children a couple must have to replace themselves. You might think that two parents need have only two children to replace

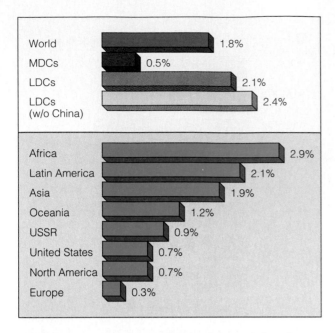

Figure 8-3 Average annual population change rate in various groups of countries in 1990. Population change rates in 1990 ranged from a growth rate of 4.31% in Gaza in western Asia to a decline rate of −0.2% in Hungary. (Data from Population Reference Bureau)

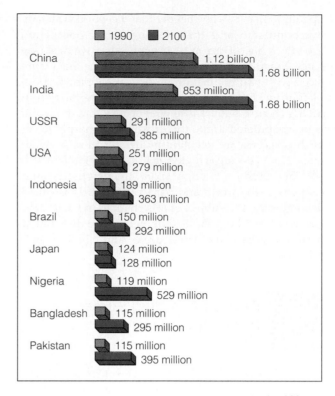

Figure 8-4 The world's ten most populous countries in 1990, with projections of their population size in 2100. (Data from World Bank)

themselves. The actual average replacement-level fertility rate is slightly higher, mostly because some female children die before reaching their reproductive years. In MDCs, the average replacement-level fertility is 2.1 children per couple or woman. In LDCs with high infant mortality rates (deaths of children under the age of one), the replacement level may be as high as 2.5 children per couple or woman.

The most useful measure of fertility for projecting future population change is the **total fertility rate (TFR)**: an estimate of the average number of children that would be born alive to a woman during her lifetime if she passes through all her childbearing years (ages 15–44) conforming to age-specific fertility rates of a given year. In simpler terms, it is an estimate of the average number of children a woman will have during her childbearing years.

In 1991, the average total fertility rate was 3.4 children per woman for the world as a whole, 1.9 in MDCs, and 3.9 in LDCs (4.4 if China is excluded). These rates ranged from a low of 1.2 in Hong Kong to a high of 8.1 in Rwanda in eastern Africa. Population experts expect TFRs in MDCs to remain around 1.9 and those in LDCs to drop to around 2.3 by 2025. That is good news, but it will still lead to a projected population of around 9 billion by then.

Since 1972, the United States has had a total fertility rate at or below the replacement level (Figure 8-5). A total fertility rate below replacement level doesn't necessarily mean that a country's population has stabilized or is declining (see Case Study on p. 199).

Canada's population of 27 million in 1991 was growing at a rate of 0.7%. Its total fertility rate was 1.7 children per woman. If this low fertility rate continues and net immigration averages about 50,000 a year, the country's population will grow to about 34 million by 2025 and then start a slow decline.

FACTORS AFFECTING BIRTH RATES AND FERTILITY RATES The following are the most significant factors affecting a country's average birth rate and total fertility rate:

- *Average levels of education and affluence*. Rates are usually lower in MDCs, where both of these factors are high.

- *Importance of children as a part of the family labor force*. Rates tend to be low in MDCs and high in LDCs (especially in rural areas). They are lower in countries where a compulsory mass education system removes children from the family labor force during most of the year.

- *Urbanization*. People living in urban areas tend to have fewer children than those living in rural areas, where children are needed to help in growing food, collecting firewood and water, and other

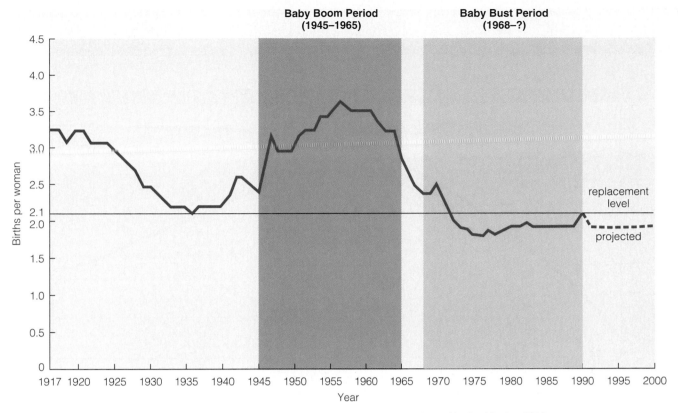

Figure 8-5 Total fertility rate for the United States between 1917 and 1990 and projected rate (dashed line) to 2000. (Data from Population Reference Bureau and U.S. Census Bureau)

CASE STUDY U.S. Population Stabilization

The population of the United States has grown from 4 million in 1790 to 254 million in 1991—a 62-fold increase. Between 1928 and 1991, the country's population more than doubled, from 120 million to 254 million.

The total fertility rate in the United States has oscillated wildly (Figure 8-5). At the peak of the post-World War II baby boom (1945–65) in 1957, the TFR reached 3.7 children per woman. Since then, it has generally declined and has been at or below replacement level since 1972.

Various factors contributed to this decline:

- Widespread use of effective birth control methods.
- Availability of legal abortions.

- Social attitudes favoring smaller families.

- Greater social acceptance of childless couples.

- Rising costs of raising a family. It will cost about $160,000 to raise a child born in 1991 to age 18.

- Increases in the average marriage age between 1958 and 1989 from 20.1 to 23.9 for women and from 22.8 to 26.2 for men.

- An increasing number of women working outside the home. By 1991, more than 70% of American women of childbearing age worked outside the home and had a childbearing rate one-third the rate of those not in the paid labor force.

The drop in the total fertility rate since 1969 has led to a decline in

the annual rate of population growth in the United States. The United States has not reached zero population growth (ZPG) in spite of the dramatic drop in the average total fertility rate to below the replacement level. The main reasons for this are

- The large number of women (58 million) born during the baby-boom period (Figure 8-5) still moving through their childbearing years. Even though the total fertility rate remained at or below the replacement rate between 1973 and 1991, the large number of women moving into childbearing years during that period led to an increase in live births from about 3.2 million in 1973 to 4.2 million in 1991.

(continued)

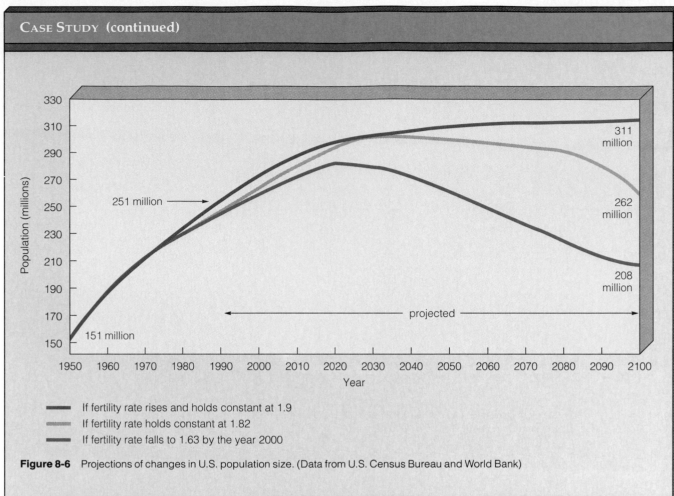

Figure 8-6 Projections of changes in U.S. population size. (Data from U.S. Census Bureau and World Bank)

- High levels of legal and illegal immigration.

- An increase in the number of unmarried young women (including teenagers) having children.

In 1991, the U.S. population grew by 1.1%. This added 2.7 million people: 2.0 million more births than deaths, 0.5 million legal immigrants, and an estimated 0.2 million illegal immigrants.

Given the erratic history of the U.S. total fertility rate, no one knows whether or how long it will remain below replacement level. The Census Bureau and the World Bank have made various projections of U.S. population growth, assuming different average total fertility rates, life expectancies, and net legal immigration rates (Figure 8-6).

All Americans will play a role in determining which of these and other demographic possibilities becomes a reality. What role do you intend to play in determining your country's future demographic history?

survival tasks. People living in urban areas also often have better access to family planning.

- *High costs of raising and educating children.* Rates tend to be low in MDCs, where raising children is much more costly because they don't enter the labor force until their late teens or early twenties.

- *Educational and employment opportunities for women.* Rates tend to be low when women have access to education and to paid employment outside the home.

- *Infant mortality rates.* In areas with low infant mortality rates, people tend to have fewer children because they don't need to replace children who have died.

- *Average marriage age* (or more precisely, the average age at which women give birth to their first child). People have fewer children when the average marriage age of women is 25 or higher. This reduces the typical childbearing years (ages 15–44) by ten or more years and cuts the prime reproductive period (ages 20–29), when most women have children, by half or more.

- *Availability of private and public pension systems:* Pensions eliminate the need for parents to have many children to support them in old age.

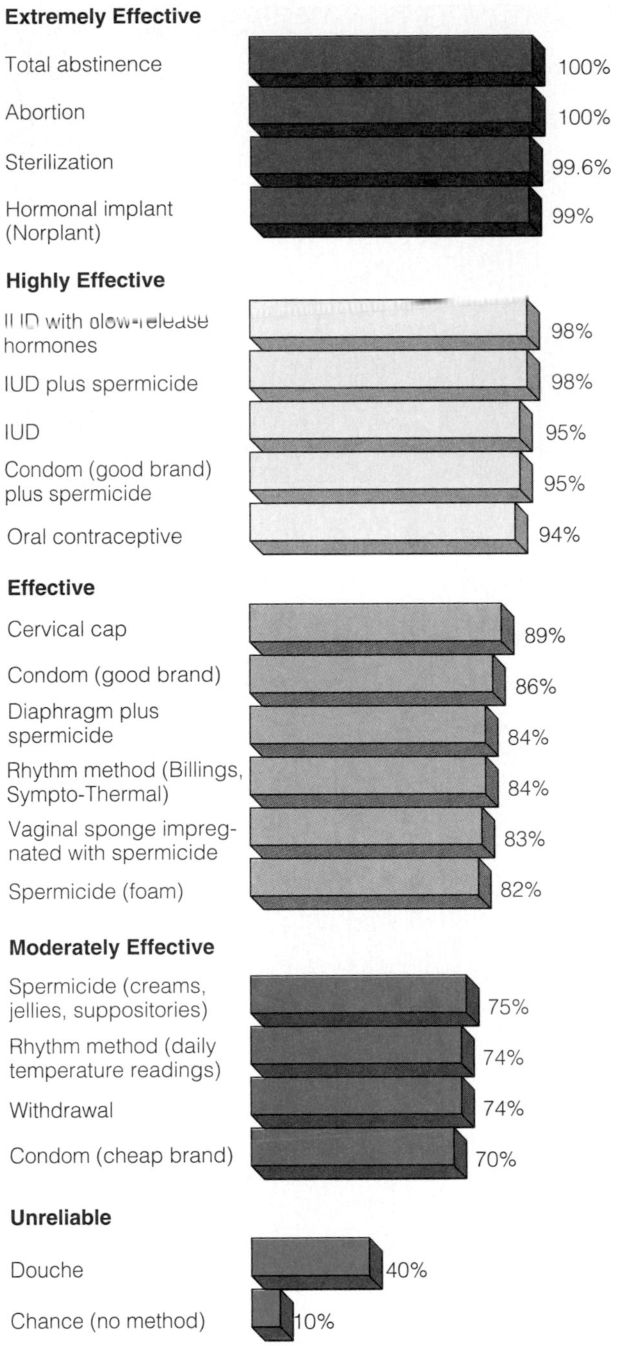

Extremely Effective
Total abstinence
100%
Abortion
100%
Sterilization
99.6%
Hormonal implant (Norplant)
99%
Highly Effective
IUD with slow-release hormones
98%
IUD plus spermicide
98%
IUD
95%
Condom (good brand) plus spermicide
95%
Oral contraceptive
94%
Effective
Cervical cap
89%
Condom (good brand)
86%
Diaphragm plus spermicide
84%
Rhythm method (Billings, Sympto-Thermal)
84%
Vaginal sponge impregnated with spermicide
83%
Spermicide (foam)
82%
Moderately Effective
Spermicide (creams, jellies, suppositories)
75%
Rhythm method (daily temperature readings)
74%
Withdrawal
74%
Condom (cheap brand)
70%
Unreliable
Douche
40%
Chance (no method)
10%

Figure 8-7 Typical effectiveness of birth control methods in the United States. Percent effectiveness is based on the number of undesired pregnancies per 100 couples using a method as their sole form of birth control for a year. For example, a 94% effectiveness for oral contraceptives means that for every 100 women using the pill regularly for one year, 6 will get pregnant. The failure rates shown are for the United States. Failure rates tend to be higher in LDCs because of human error and lack of education. (Data from Alan Guttmacher Institute)

- *Availability of reliable methods of birth control.* Widespread availability tends to reduce birth and fertility rates (Figures 8-7 and 8-8). New methods of birth control are also being developed (see Spotlight on p. 203).

World
Sterilization 37%
IUD 19%
Pill 15%
Abortion 13%
Condom 11%
Other 5%
United States
Sterilization 31% (female 18%, male 13%)
Pill 30%
Condom 16%
Diaphragm 6%
Abortion 5%
Rhythm 4%
IUD 3%
Sponge 3%
Spermicides 2%

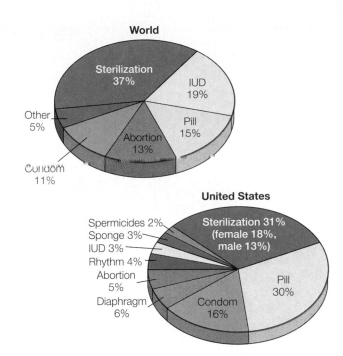

Figure 8-8 Estimated percentage of couples of reproductive age in the world and in the United States using various birth control methods in 1989. (Data from UN Population Division, Population Crisis Committee, U.S. National Center for Health Statistics, and National Academy of Sciences)

- *Religious beliefs, tradition, and cultural norms that influence the number of children couples want to have.*

Figure 1-2 shows three projections of world population growth through the next century. Each projection is based on a different set of assumptions about fertility rates, death rates, and international migration patterns.

No one really knows whether any of these projections will prove accurate. Demographic projections are not predictions of what will necessarily take place. Instead, they represent possibilities based on present trends and certain assumptions about people's future reproductive behavior. Despite their uncertainty, demographic projections help us focus our energies on converting the most desirable possibilities into reality.

FACTORS AFFECTING DEATH RATES The rapid growth of the world's population over the past 100 years was not caused by a rise in crude birth rates. Rather, it is due largely to a decline in crude death rates, especially in the LDCs (Figure 8-9).

The principal interrelated reasons for this general drop in death rates are

- better nutrition because of increased food production and better distribution
- fewer infant deaths and increased average life expectancy because of a reduction in the incidence

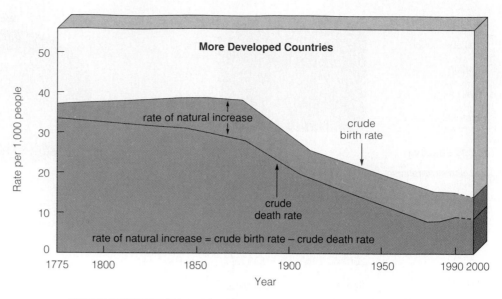

Figure 8-9 Changes in crude birth and death rates for MDCs and LDCs between 1775 and 1990, with projected rates (dashed lines) to 2000. (Data from Population Reference Bureau and United Nations)

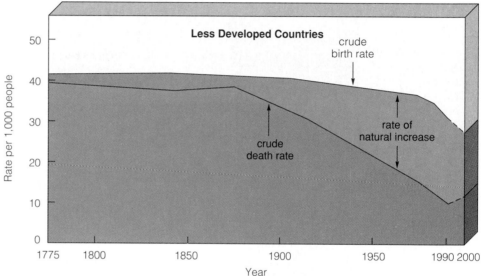

and spread of infectious diseases from improved personal hygiene, sanitation, and water supplies

- improvements in medical and public-health technology, including antibiotics, immunization, and insecticides

Two useful indicators of overall health in a country or region are **life expectancy**—the average number of years a newborn infant can be expected to live—and the **infant mortality rate**—the number of babies out of every 1,000 born each year that die before their first birthday (Figure 8-10).

In 1991, average life expectancy at birth ranged from a low of 41 years in Afghanistan in southern Asia to a high of 79 years in Japan, followed by Sweden (78 years). In the world's 41 poorest countries, mainly in Asia and Africa, average life expectancy is only 47 years.

Between 1900 and 1991, average life expectancy at birth rose sharply in the United States from 42 to 75 (78.3 for females and 71.3 for males); yet, in 1991, people in 25 countries and colonies had an average life expectancy at birth one to three years higher than people in the United States. The average life expectancy for blacks in the United States is 69 years, six years less than that for whites. Reasons for this difference include the perils of living in poor neighborhoods, second-rate education, and inadequate access to health care.

A high infant mortality rate usually indicates insufficient food (undernutrition), poor nutrition (malnutrition), and a high incidence of infectious disease (usually from contaminated drinking water). In 1991, infant mortality rates ranged from a low of 2.7 deaths per 1,000 live births in Liechtenstein to a high of 182 deaths per 1,000 live births in Afghanistan in southern Asia.

In 1991, the U.S. infant mortality rate was 9.1

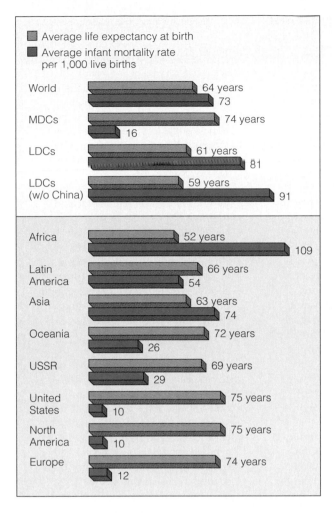

Figure 8-10 Average life expectancy at birth and average infant mortality rate for various groups of countries in 1990. (Data from Population Reference Bureau)

deaths per 1,000. Largely because of poor prenatal care, infant mortality for blacks in the United States (18 deaths per 1,000) was twice as high as for whites (9 deaths per 1,000).

Although the infant mortality rate in the United States is low by world standards, it is among the highest in the developed world, with 22 other countries having lower rates. Several factors keeping the U.S. infant mortality rate higher than it could be are

- Lack of adequate health care for poor women during pregnancy and for their babies after birth.

- Drug addiction among pregnant women. Infant mortality in some major cities, such as Detroit, Washington, and Baltimore, averages 19 to 20 deaths per 1,000.

- The high birth rate for teenage women in the United States (see Case Study on p. 204).

(see Case Study on p. 204)

SPOTLIGHT Future Methods of Birth Control

Researchers throughout the world are at work trying to develop new and better methods of fertility control. Examples include biodegradable implants that don't require surgical removal, a two-year pregnancy vaccine, a contraceptive for men that reduces sperm count, and chemicals for nonsurgical sterilization. Attempts are also being made to develop female and male sterilization techniques that can be more easily reversed.

How soon these methods become available depends mostly on the amount of money invested in research and development and in safety testing. To develop, test, and evaluate the safety of a new contraceptive takes 15 years or more and $50 million or more. Despite the importance of population control, annual worldwide expenditures on reproductive research and contraceptive development have declined from a high of $250 million a year to $200 million a year today—an average of only 25 cents per person.

In the United States, contraceptive research and development by private drug firms has virtually stopped, mostly because of the difficulty and expense of getting FDA approval of a new contraceptive. Other factors are changes in patent protection laws that have reduced company profits, fear of liability suits, and the high cost of liability insurance. Drug companies also make more money by selling birth control pills that have to be taken daily than in selling a contraceptive pill, vaccine, or implant that prevents conception for a month to five years.

Since 1979, federal funding for research has decreased by 25% (adjusted for inflation) because of budget cuts and political pressure from pro-life groups. Most population experts fear that unless government and private funding of contraceptive research is at least doubled, few if any of the possible improved forms of birth control will be available in the United States. For Americans, this will probably mean more sterilizations, more abortions (including illegal ones if abortion is outlawed or restricted), and more unwanted children.

MIGRATION The annual rate of population change for a particular country, city, or other area is also affected by movement of people into (immigration) and out of (emigration) that area:

$$\text{population change rate} = \left(\begin{array}{c}\text{births}\\+\\\text{immigration}\end{array}\right) - \left(\begin{array}{c}\text{deaths}\\+\\\text{emigration}\end{array}\right)$$

The United States has the highest teenage pregnancy rate of any industrialized country, ten times higher than Japan's, two times higher than Canada's, and two to five times higher than in most European countries. Every year in the United States approximately 1 million teenage women—one in every nine between ages 15 and 19—become pregnant. About 83% of these pregnancies are not planned. About 600,000 of these young women give birth. The remaining 400,000 have abortions, accounting for almost one of every four abortions performed in the United States.

Teenage pregnancies cost state and federal governments at least $21 billion a year. Almost half of the babies born to teenage mothers in the United States depend on welfare to survive. Each of these babies costs taxpayers an average of $16,000 over the 20 years following its birth.

Babies born to teenagers are more likely to have a low birth weight—the most important factor in infant deaths—thus increasing the country's infant mortality rate. The United States has developed the medical technology for saving low-weight babies, but babies of poor teenage women with no health insurance often do not have access to these expensive, life-saving procedures.

Why are teenage pregnancy rates in the United States so high? UN studies show that U.S. teenagers aren't more sexually active than those in other MDCs, but they are less likely to take precautions to prevent pregnancy. Surveys indicate that 53% of sexually active teenage women did not use any form of birth control at first intercourse and that one-third do not use any method during their teen years.

In Sweden, which has a much lower teenage pregnancy rate than the United States, every child receives a thorough grounding in basic reproductive biology by age 7. By age 12, each child has been told about the various types of contraceptives.

Polls show that 85% of Americans favor sex education in the schools, including information about birth control, and school clinics that dispense contraceptives with parental consent. A 1990 survey by the Alan Guttmacher Institute showed that 93% of U.S. schools offer some form of sex education. About 86% of the teachers in such courses recommended abstinence as the best alternative to pregnancy, but at least half of teenagers are sexually active. Fewer than half of the teachers said they discussed where to get birth control.

In 1990, 162 schools in 33 states had health clinics, usually located within a high school or in an adjacent building. These clinics offer comprehensive health services, including family planning. Students are given prescriptions for contraceptives or are referred to a separate birth control clinic. Studies show that in cities with school-based clinics, teens are more likely to use birth control.

Many analysts urge that effective sex education programs be developed in which U.S. children are made aware of the values of abstinence and the various types of contraceptives by age 12 and that school-based health clinics be opened in all junior and senior high schools. These proposals are vigorously opposed by groups who fear that early sex education will lead to increased sexual activity. What do you think should be done about sex education and teenage pregnancy?

Most countries control their rates of population growth to some extent by restricting immigration. Only a few countries annually accept a large number of immigrants or refugees. This means that population change for most countries is determined mainly by the differences between their birth rates and death rates.

Migration within countries, however, especially from rural to urban areas, plays an important role in the population dynamics of cities, towns, and rural areas. This migration affects the way population is distributed within countries, as discussed in Chapter 9.

8-2 Population Age Structure

AGE STRUCTURE DIAGRAMS Why will world population probably keep growing for at least 60 years after the average world total fertility rate has reached or dropped below the replacement-level fertility of 2.1? The answer to this question lies in an understanding of the **age structure**, or age distribution, of a population: the percentage of the population, or the number of people of each sex, at each age level.

Demographers make a population age structure diagram by plotting the percentages or numbers of males and females in the total population in three age categories: *prereproductive* (ages 0–14), *reproductive* (ages 15–44), and *postreproductive* (ages 45–85+). Figure 8-11 shows the age structure diagrams for countries with rapid, slow, and zero growth rates.

Mexico and most LDCs with rapidly growing populations have pyramid-shaped age structure diagrams (Figure 8-11, left). This means that these countries have a high ratio of children under age 15 to adults over age 65. In contrast, the diagrams for the United States, Sweden, and most MDCs undergoing slow or no population growth have a narrower base (Figure 8-11, middle). This shows that such countries have a much smaller

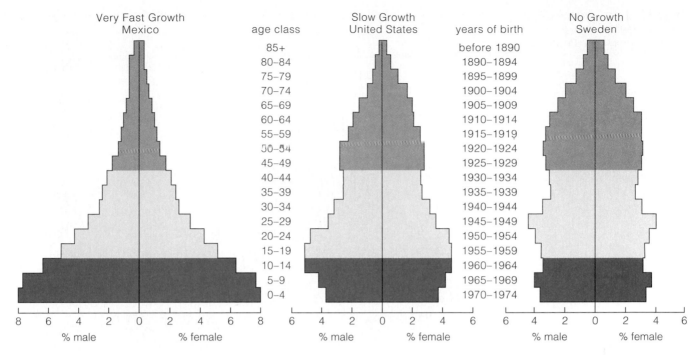

Figure 8-11 Population age structure diagrams for countries with rapid, slow, and zero population growth rates. Bottom portions represent prereproductive years (0–14), middle portions represent reproductive years (15–44), and top portions represent postreproductive years (45–85 +). (Data from Population Reference Bureau)

percentage of population under age 15 and a larger percentage above age 65 than countries experiencing rapid population growth.

MDCs, such as Sweden and Denmark, that have achieved or nearly achieved zero population growth have roughly equal numbers of people at each age level (Figure 8-11, right). Hungary and Monaco, which are experiencing a slow population decline, have roughly equal numbers of people at most age levels but lower numbers under age 5.

AGE STRUCTURE AND POPULATION GROWTH MOMENTUM Any country with a large number of people below age 15 has a powerful built-in momentum to increase its population size unless death rates rise sharply. The number of births rises even if women have only one or two children, because the number of women who can have children increases greatly as females reach their reproductive years. The population of a country with a large number of people under 15 continues to grow for one average lifetime—roughly 60 to 70 years—after the total fertility rate of its women has dropped to replacement level or lower.

In 1991, one of every three persons on this planet was under 15 years old. In LDCs, the number is even higher—36% compared with 21% in MDCs. Figure 8-12 shows the powerful momentum for population growth in LDCs because of their large numbers of people under age 15 who will be moving into their reproductive years. If each female in this group has only two children, world population will still grow for 60 years

unless deaths rise sharply. Instead of having two children, women in LDCs now have an average of 3.9 children (4.4 children excluding China).

This explains why population experts project that the world's population will not level off until around the middle of the next century and perhaps not until the end of the next century. The key question is whether it will peak at 7 billion, 10 billion, or 14 billion (Figure 1-2).

The powerful force for continued population growth, mostly in LDCs, will be slowed only by an effective program to reduce birth rates or a catastrophic rise in death rates. Greatly increasing efforts to reduce birth rates now could bring the projected peak population down to 7 billion instead of 10 billion, or even 14 billion. Many analysts consider this one of our most urgent challenges.

MAKING PROJECTIONS FROM AGE STRUCTURE DIAGRAMS A baby boom took place in the United States between 1945 and 1965. This 75-million-person bulge, called the *baby-boom generation*, will move upward through the country's age structure during the 80-year period between 1945 and 2025 as baby boomers move through their youth, young adulthood, middle age, and old age (Figure 8-13).

In 1970, the median age of the U.S. population was about 29. By 1991, it was almost 33, and it is projected to reach 39 by 2010 and 43 by 2050. By 2030, when all living members of the baby-boom generation are senior citizens, about 21% of the projected population will

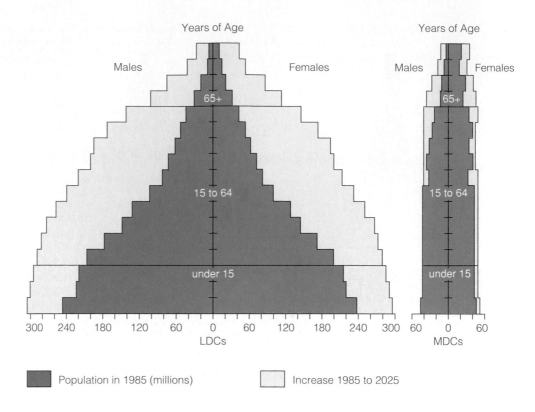

Figure 8-12 Age structure of LDCs and MDCs, 1985–2025. (Data from Population Reference Bureau)

Years of Age — Males / Females

65+

15 to 64

under 15

300 240 180 120 60 0 60 120 180 240 300
LDCs

Years of Age — Males / Females

65+

15 to 64

under 15

60 0 60
MDCs

Population in 1985 (millions)   Increase 1985 to 2025

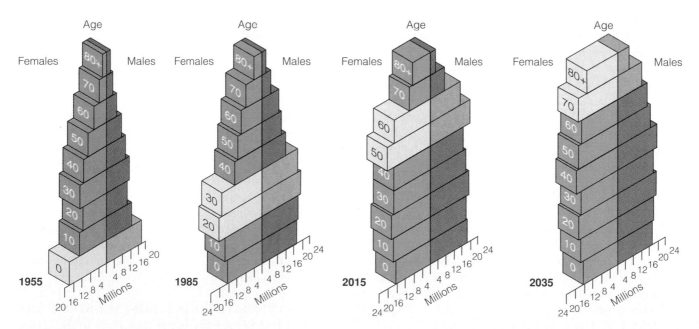

Figure 8-13 Tracking the baby-boom generation. Age structure of the U.S. population in 1955, 1985, 2015, and 2035. (Data from Population Reference Bureau and U.S. Census Bureau)

consist of people 65 and older, compared with 12% in 1985.

Today, baby boomers make up nearly half of all adult Americans. In sheer numbers, they dominate the population's demand for goods and services. Compa-

nies not providing products and services for this aging bulge in the population can go bankrupt. Young people making career choices should also consider these demographic facts of life. Baby boomers, who made up an estimated 60% of registered voters in 1991, will play an increasingly important role in deciding who gets elected and what laws are passed between now and 2030.

During their working years, baby boomers will create a large surplus of money in the Social Security trust fund. However, even if elected officials resist the temptation to pass laws allowing them to dip into these funds for balancing the budget or other purposes, the large number of retired baby boomers will quickly use up this surplus. Unless changes in funding are made, the Social Security fund will be depleted by 2048. Elderly baby boomers will also put severe strains on health care services.

The economic burden of helping support so many retired baby boomers will be on the *baby-bust generation*, the much smaller group of people born between 1968 and 1991, when total fertility rates fell sharply (Figure 8-5). Retired baby boomers may use their political clout to force members of the baby-bust generation to pay greatly increased income, health care, and Social Security taxes.

In many respects, the baby-bust generation should have an easier time than the baby-boom generation. Much smaller numbers of people will be competing for education, jobs, and services. Labor shortages should also drive up their wages, but three out of four new jobs available between now and 2010 will require education or technical training beyond high school. People without such training may face economic hard times.

Although they will probably have no trouble getting entry-level jobs, the baby-bust group may find it hard to get job promotions as they reach middle age because most upper-level positions will be occupied by the much larger baby-boom group. Many baby boomers may delay retirement because of improved health and the need to build up adequate retirement funds. From these few projections, we see that any baby-boom bulge or baby-bust indentation in the age structure of a population creates a number of social and economic changes that ripple through a society for decades.

8-3 Methods for Regulating Population Change

CONTROLLING MIGRATION A government can influence the size and rate of growth or decline of its population by encouraging a change in any of the three basic demographic variables: births, deaths, and migration. The governments of most countries achieve some degree of population regulation by allowing little immigration from other countries. Some governments also encourage emigration to other countries to reduce population pressures. Only a few countries, chiefly Canada, Australia, and the United States (see Case Study below), allow large annual increases in their population from immigration.

CASE STUDY Immigration and Population Growth in the United States

The United States, founded by immigrants and their children, has admitted more immigrants and refugees than any other country in the world. Between 1820 and 1991, the United States admitted almost twice as many immigrants as all other countries combined.

Immigrants add cultural diversity to the United States. Also, a typical working immigrant will add about $3,000 a year to the Social Security trust fund. As workers and consumers, trained immigrants also contribute to economic growth.

The number of legal immigrants entering the United States since 1820 has varied during different periods because of changes in immigration laws and economic growth

(Figure 8-14). Between 1820 and 1960, most legal immigrants came from Europe. Since then, most have come from Asia and Latin America.

Between 1960 and 1990, the number of legal immigrants admitted per year almost doubled, from 250,000 to 495,000. In 1990, Congress passed a law raising the annual legal immigration level from 490,000 in 1990 to 675,000 by 1995. These limits do not include refugees, who are admitted under other regulations.

Each year, an additional 200,000 to 500,000 people enter the United States illegally, most from Mexico and other Latin American countries. This means that in 1991, legal and illegal immigrants increased the U.S.

population by 695,000 to 995,000 people, accounting for 28% to 38% of the country's population growth. Soon, immigration is expected to be the primary factor increasing the population of the United States.

Some have called for an annual ceiling of no more than 450,000 for all categories of legal immigration, including refugees, to reduce the intensity of some of the country's social, economic, and environmental problems and reach zero population growth sooner. Some opponents of the country's open-door policy often portray immigrants as either job stealers or welfare recipients, but recent studies indicate the opposite is true. Immigrants tend to be energetic and talented people who draw

(continued)

very lightly on Social Security and medicare, and virtually the same as other Americans do on other kinds of welfare spending.

Studies also show that immigrants do not deprive Americans of work. In fact, they create jobs, sometimes helping ailing businesses stay alive.

Other analysts favor increasing the number of immigrants and changing immigration law to give much more preference to those with valuable professional skills, high levels of education, and a knowledge of English. This could help offset the projected decrease in skilled younger workers as U.S. population growth slows (Figure 8-6) and the U.S. median age increases. In 1990, Congress voted to increase the number of immigrants admitted each year because of their skills and talents from 54,000 to 140,000.

Some people, however, oppose a policy of immigration based primarily on skills. They argue that it amounts to a brain drain of educated and talented people from LDCs that need these important human resources. It would also diminish the historic role of the United States in serving as a place of opportunity for the world's poor and oppressed.

In 1986, Congress passed a new immigration law designed to help control illegal immigration. This law included an amnesty program for some illegal immigrants and allowed them to become temporary residents and apply for citizenship after 6.5 years. By the May 4, 1988, deadline, about 2.1 million of the estimated 5 million illegal aliens had signed up for the amnesty program.

The 1986 law also prohibits the hiring of illegal immigrants. Em-

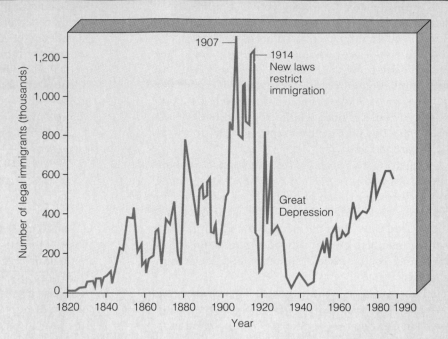

Figure 8-14 Legal immigration to the United States: 1820–1990. (Data from U.S. Immigration and Naturalization Service)

ployers must examine the identity documents of all new employees. Employers who knowingly hire illegal aliens are subject to fines of $250 to $10,000 per violation, and repeat offenders can be sentenced to prison for up to six months. The bill also authorized funds to increase the border patrol staff by 50%, to increase efforts to detect employers violating the new law, and to deport illegal aliens.

Critics charge that illegal immigrants can get around the law with readily available fake documents. Employers are not responsible for verifying the authenticity of documents or for keeping copies. Besides, the Immigration and Naturalization Service does not have

enough money or staff to check most employers, prosecute repeated violators, or effectively patrol more than a small fraction of the 3,140-kilometer (1,950-mile) U.S.–Mexico border.

With nearly 60% of Mexico's labor force unemployed or underemployed, many Mexicans and immigrants from other Latin American countries think being caught and sent back is a minor risk compared with remaining in poverty. What, if anything, do you think should be done about legal and illegal immigration into the United States?

CONTROLLING BIRTHS Increasing the death rate is not an acceptable alternative for regulating population size. Thus, decreasing the birth rate is the focus of most efforts to slow population growth. Today, about 93% of the world's population and 91% of the people in LDCs live in countries with fertility reduction programs. Three general approaches to decreasing birth rates are *economic development, family planning,* and *socioeconomic change.*

The effectiveness and funding of these programs vary widely from country to country. Few governments spend more than 1% of the national budget on them. There is also controversy over whether population growth is good or bad (see Pro/Con on p. 209).

Overpopulation is often defined as the condition of having more people than can live on Earth in comfort, happiness, and health and still leave the planet a fit place for future generations (Figure 1-16). To most environmentalists, the data in Table 1-1 suggest that the planet is already overpopulated. Because of differing concepts of carrying capacity, however, experts differ widely over what level of population is considered too high.

Some project that if everyone existed at a minimum survival level, the earth could support 20 to 48 billion people. This anthill existence would require that everyone exist only on a diet of grain, cultivating all arable land, and mining much of the earth's crust to a depth of 1.6 kilometers (1 mile). Other analysts believe the earth could support 7 to 12 billion people at a decent standard of living by distributing the world's land and food supply more equitably and shifting from less abundant resources (such as lead, tin, uranium, oil, and natural gas) to more abundant resources (such as aluminum, glass, and various forms of solar energy).

Let's assume that these optimistic estimates of sustainable populations are possible from a technological and environmental viewpoint. Even so, many analysts believe that it is unlikely that our social and political structures could adapt to such a crowded and stressful world without resorting to mass destruction through nuclear, chemical, and biological warfare.

Others believe that asking how many people the world can support is the wrong question. Asking what the **maximum sustainable population** might be is like asking how many cigarettes one can smoke before getting lung cancer. Instead, we should be asking what the **optimum sustainable population** of Earth might be. Such an optimum level would allow most, if not all, of the world's people to live with reasonable comfort and freedom and without impairing the ability of the earth to support such a population in the future.

Again, no one knows what this optimum population might be. Some consider it a meaningless question; some put it at 20 billion, others at 8 billion, and others at a level below today's population size.

Critics of the view that Earth is overpopulated point out that the world now supports 5.4 billion people and the average life span of these people is longer than at any time in the past. Things are getting better, not worse, for many of the world's people.

Many of these analysts call for more population growth. They argue that people are the world's most valuable resource for finding solutions to our problems, not drains on the wealth and resources of a country. An increase in the number of people leads to increased economic productivity by creating and applying new knowledge. These analysts are confident that the nature of the physical world combined with human ingenuity permits continued improvement in humanity's lot in the long run, indefinitely (see Guest Essay on p. 29).

Some believe that a "birth dearth" eventually leading to a population decline in MDCs will decrease their economic growth and power. They argue that without more babies, MDCs with declining populations will face a shortage of workers, taxpayers, scientists and engineers, consumers, and soldiers needed to maintain healthy economic growth, national security, and global power and influence.

They also contend that the aging societies in MDCs will be less innovative and dynamic. These analysts urge the governments of the United States and other MDCs to prevent this by giving tax breaks and other economic incentives to couples who have more than two children.

To these analysts, the primary cause of poverty and despair for one out of five people on Earth is not population growth. Instead, it is a lack of free and productive economic systems in LDCs.

Others opposed to population regulation feel that all people should have the freedom to have as many children as they want. To some, population regulation is a violation of their deep religious beliefs. To others, it is an intrusion into their personal privacy and freedom. To minorities, population regulation is sometimes seen as a form of genocide to keep their numbers and power from rising.

Proponents of population regulation point to the fact that we are not providing adequate basic necessities for one out of five people on Earth today who don't have the opportunity to be a net economic gain for their country. They see people overpopulation in LDCs and consumption overpopulation in MDCs (Figure 1-16) as threats to Earth's life support systems for us and other species (Table 1-1).

These analysts recognize that population growth is not the only cause of our environmental and resource problems. They believe, however, that adding several hundred million more people in MDCs and several billion more in LDCs will intensify many environmental and social problems by increasing resource use and waste, environmental degradation, rapid climate change, and pollution. To proponents of population regulation, it is unethical for us not to encourage a sharp drop in birth rates and unsustainable forms of resource use to prevent a sharp rise in death rates and human misery and a decrease in Earth's biodiversity in the future (see Guest Essay on p. 219).

Despite promises about sharing the world's wealth, the gap between the rich and the poor has been getting larger since 1960 (Figure 1-7). Proponents of population regulation believe this is caused by a combination of population growth and unwillingness of the wealthy to share

(continued)

the world's wealth and resources more fairly. They call for MDCs to use their economic systems to reward population regulation and sustainable forms of economic growth instead of continuing their unsustainable forms of economic growth and encouraging LDCs to follow this eventually unsustainable and disastrous path for the planet.

Recently, the Population Crisis Committee compiled a human-suffering index for each of 130 countries based on ten measures of human welfare. They found a high correlation between the level of human suffering and the rate of population increase in countries. The 30 countries falling in the *extreme* human-suffering range—all in Africa and Asia—averaged a high annual rate of population increase of 2.8%. The 44 countries with a *high* human-suffering rate—all in Africa, Asia, and Latin America—also had an average annual population increase of 2.8%.

Those favoring population regulation point out that technological innovation, not sheer numbers of people, is the key to military and economic power in today's world. Otherwise, England, Germany, Japan, and Taiwan, with fairly small populations, should have little global economic and military power, and China and India should rule the world. Also, as world military tensions ease, people are becoming aware that environmental security is now the key to economic and national security.

History does not show that an older society is necessarily more conservative and less innovative than one dominated by younger people. A society with a higher average age tends to have a larger pool of collective wisdom based on experience. Indeed, the most conservative and least innovative societies in the world today are LDCs with a large portion of their populations under age 29.

Instead of encouraging births, these analysts believe that the United States and other MDCs should establish an official goal of stabilizing their populations by 2025. This would help reduce the severe environmental impact of these MDCs on the biosphere. It would also set a good example for LDCs to reduce their population growth more rapidly and adopt sustainable forms of economic development.

Proponents of population regulation believe that we should have the freedom to produce as many children as we want only as long as this does not reduce the quality of other people's lives now and in the future by impairing the ability of Earth to sustain life. Limiting individual freedom to protect the freedom of other individuals is the basis of most laws in modern societies. What do you think?

ECONOMIC DEVELOPMENT AND THE DEMOGRAPHIC TRANSITION Demographers examined the birth and death rates of western European countries that industrialized during the nineteenth century. On the basis of these data, they developed a hypothesis of population change known as the **demographic transition**. Its basic idea is that as countries become industrialized, they have declines in death rates followed by declines in birth rates. As a result, they move from fast growth, to slow growth, to zero growth, and eventually to a slow decline in population.

This transition takes place in four distinct phases (Figure 8-15). In the *preindustrial stage*, harsh living conditions lead to a high birth rate (to compensate for high infant mortality) and a high death rate, and the population grows slowly, if at all. The *transitional stage* begins shortly after industrialization begins. In this phase, the death rate drops, mostly because of increased food production and improved sanitation and health. However, the birth rate remains high, and the population grows rapidly (typically 2.5% to 3% a year).

In the *industrial stage*, industrialization is widespread. The birth rate drops and eventually approaches the death rate. The main reason for this is that couples in cities realize that children are expensive to raise and that having too many children hinders them from taking advantage of job opportunities in an expanding economy. Population growth continues, but at a slower and perhaps fluctuating rate, depending on economic conditions. Most MDCs are now in this third phase.

A fourth phase, the *postindustrial stage*, takes place when the birth rate declines even further to equal the death rate, thus reaching zero population growth. Then the birth rate falls below the death rate and total population size slowly decreases.

By 1991, 18 European countries had reached or were close to ZPG. Two of these countries—Hungary and Germany—were experiencing population declines. When the number of people under age 15 in a population is less than the number at higher age levels, we can expect the population to decline for 60 years or so. The only way to prevent this is for the women in their child-

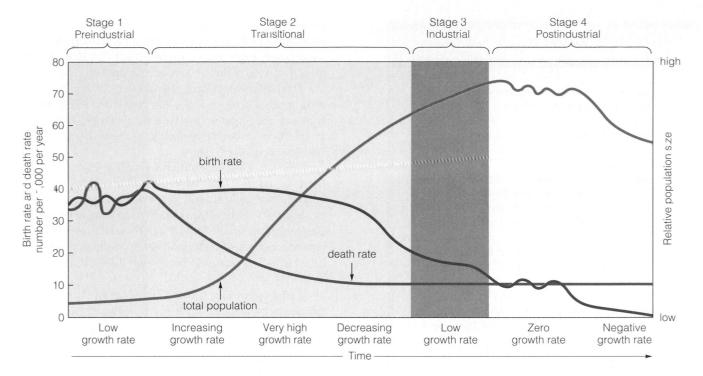

Figure 8-15 Generalized model of the demographic transition.

bearing years to have more children or for the number of immigrants to increase.

CAN MOST OF TODAY'S LDCs MAKE THE DEMOGRAPHIC TRANSITION? In most LDCs today, death rates have fallen much more than birth rates (Figure 8-9). In other words, these LDCs are still in the transitional phase, halfway up the economic ladder, with high population growth rates. Some economists believe that LDCs will make the demographic transition over the next few decades without increased family planning efforts.

Many population analysts fear that the rate of economic growth in many LDCs will never exceed their high rates of population growth. Without rapid and sustained economic growth, LDCs could become stuck in the transitional stage of the demographic transition.

Furthermore, some of the conditions that allowed today's MDCs to develop are not available to today's LDCs. Even with large and growing populations, many LDCs do not have enough skilled workers to produce the high-technology products needed to compete in today's economic environment. Most low- and middle-income LDCs also lack the capital and resources needed for rapid economic development. Also, the amount of money being given or lent to LDCs—struggling under tremendous debt burdens—has been decreasing since 1980.

LDCs also face stiff competition from MDCs and recently industrialized LDCs in selling the products on which their economic growth depends, and many LDCs with the fastest rates of population growth do not have enough natural resources to support economic development similar to that in Europe and North America.

FAMILY PLANNING? Recent evidence suggests that improved and expanded family planning programs may bring about a more rapid decline in the birth rate, and at a lower cost, than economic development alone. **Family planning** programs provide educational and clinical services that help couples choose how many children to have and when to have them.

Such programs vary from culture to culture, but most provide information on birth spacing, birth control (Figures 8-7 and 8-8), breastfeeding (see Spotlight on p. 212), and prenatal care, and distribute contraceptives. In some cases, they also perform abortions and sterilizations, often without charge or at low rates. For religious and cultural reasons, most of these efforts focus on married couples. With the exception of China (discussed in Section 8-4), family planning programs in most countries have not tried to persuade or coerce couples to have fewer children.

In MDCs, about 71% of women in their reproductive period use some form of birth control. In LDCs, only about 52% of women in their reproductive period practice birth control, with the figure dropping to 44% if China is excluded.

Family planning services were first introduced in LDCs in the 1940s and 1950s by private physicians and

Breastfeeding can play a role in controlling fertility. Some women who regularly nurse a baby do not ovulate and thus cannot conceive for at least a year. Although regular breastfeeding helps reduce a woman's chances of becoming pregnant, it is not a reliable method of birth control. Breastfeeding also helps reduce infant mortality rates because mother's milk provides a baby with antibodies to help prevent disease, and breast milk is usually the most nutritious food available for infants in poor families.

Unfortunately, breastfeeding is declining in many LDCs, mostly because large U.S.–based international companies have promoted the use of infant formulas instead of mother's milk. Buying infant formula when free breast milk is available is an unnecessary expense for a poor family struggling to survive. Using formula can lead to infant illnesses and deaths. Poor people, lacking fuel, often prepare formula with unboiled, contaminated water and use unsterilized bottles.

women's groups. Since then, the International Planned Parenthood Federation, the Planned Parenthood Federation of America, the United Nations Fund for Population Activities, the U.S. Agency for International Development, the Ford Foundation, the World Bank, and other organizations have been helping countries carry out family planning by providing technical assistance, funding, or both.

Family planning saves a government money by reducing the need for various social services. It also has health benefits. In LDCs, about 1 million women die from pregnancy-related causes. Half of these deaths could be prevented by effective family planning and health care programs. Family planning programs also help control the spread of AIDS and other sexually transmitted diseases.

HOW SUCCESSFUL HAS FAMILY PLANNING BEEN?
Family planning has been a significant factor in reducing birth and fertility rates in highly populous China and in Indonesia (see Case Study on p. 213), in Brazil (see Case Study on p. 225), and several other LDCs with moderate to small populations. These successful programs have been based on committed leadership, local implementation, and wide availability of contraceptive services.

Family planning has had moderate to poor results in more populous LDCs such as India, Egypt, Bangladesh, Pakistan, and Nigeria. Results have also been poor in 79 less populous LDCs—especially in Africa and Latin America—where population growth rates are usually very high. For example, only 3% to 10% of couples in African countries use contraception.

Despite these efforts, the delivery of family planning services in much of the less developed world is still woefully inadequate, particularly in rural areas. The momentum of family planning in many major LDCs has slowed in recent years.

An estimated 400 million women in LDCs want to limit the number and determine the spacing of their children but lack access to services that would help them do so. Extending family planning services to these women and those who will soon be entering their reproductive years could prevent an estimated 5.8 million births a year and more than 130,000 abortions a day.

Family planning could be provided in LDCs to all couples who want it for about $8 billion a year—less than four days of world military spending. Currently, only about $3.2 billion is being spent. If MDCs provided half of the $8 billion, each person in the MDCs would spend only $3.33 a year (compared with 3 cents now) to help reduce world population by 2.7 billion.

Even the present inadequate level of expenditure for family planning is decreasing. The United States has sharply curtailed its funding of international family planning agencies since 1985, mostly as a result of political pressure by pro-life activists. The Reagan administration slashed aid to international family planning, and the Bush administration has not restored it. In 1989, President Bush vetoed a foreign aid bill because it contained a tiny $15 million targeted for the UN Population Fund. Critics believe that unless the United States reverses this policy, it sends a message to the world that the United States considers mass starvation preferable to helping people prevent unwanted pregnancies.

Some analysts believe that family planning and effective sex education must be expanded to include teenagers, who make up almost half of the world's population. In most LDCs and MDCs, pregnancy rates among unmarried teenagers have been increasing and threaten to overcome family planning efforts focused mostly on married couples (see Case Study on p. 204).

Increased teenage pregnancy also contributes to higher legal and illegal abortion rates and the spread of sexually transmitted diseases, including AIDS. However, teaching effective sex education in schools and extending family planning to teenagers are highly controversial issues that often go against religious and cultural taboos.

ECONOMIC REWARDS AND PENALTIES Some population experts argue that family planning, even coupled with economic development, cannot lower birth and fertility rates fast enough to avoid a sharp rise in death rates in many LDCs. The main reason for this

Indonesia is the world's fifth most populous country, with a population of 181 million in 1990 (Figure 8-16). It also has one of the world's most successful family planning programs. Between 1970 and 1990, its birth rate dropped from 44 to 25 per 1,000, and the number of couples using contraceptives jumped from around 0 to 48%.

Even with this tremendous effort, the country's population is growing exponentially at 1.7% a year, adding 3.1 million people in 1990. Mostly because 37% of its population is under age 15, Indonesia's population is projected to reach almost 283 million by 2025.

Indonesia, like most LDCs and MDCs, is faced with increasing pregnancy among unmarried teenagers. In 1987, the government began family planning education for out-of-school teenagers. Sometime in the 1990s, government officials expect to have a required population education course in grades 4 through 12, where students will learn about the economic and environmental implications of population growth.

However, the government has held back from including sex education in the public school curriculum. In a country where 90% of the population is Muslim, the government is fearful that doing so would provoke political instability by alienating powerful Muslim religious leaders.

Figure 8-16 Where is Indonesia?

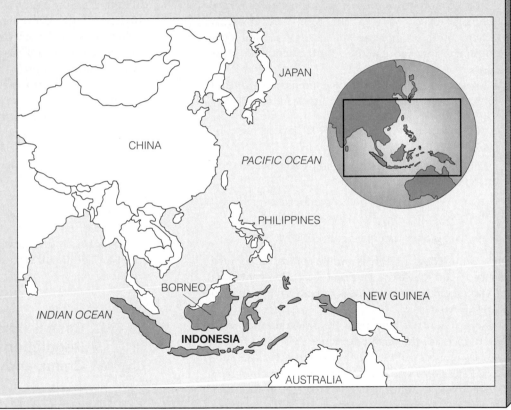

is that most couples in LDCs want three or four children—well above the 2.1 fertility rate needed to bring about eventual population stabilization.

These experts call for increased emphasis on bringing about socioeconomic change to help regulate population size. The key is improving the quality of life, especially in rural areas of LDCs, so that people don't feel they have to have large families because some of their children are sure to die or because many children are needed to support elderly family members. They call for better basic health care and education, expanded women's rights, increased equity in land ownership, and fair prices for agricultural products.

Governments can discourage births by using economic rewards and penalties. Also, increased rights, education, and work opportunities for women would reduce fertility rates.

About 20 countries offer small payments to individuals who agree to use contraceptives or to be sterilized. They also pay doctors and family planning workers for each sterilization they perform and each IUD they insert. In India, for example, a person receives about $15 for being sterilized, the equivalent of about two weeks' pay for an agricultural worker.

Such payments, however, are most likely to attract people who already have all the children they want. In some cases, the poor feel they have to accept them in order to survive.

Some countries, such as China, penalize couples who have more than a certain number of children—usually one or two. Penalties may be extra taxes and other costs, or not allowing income tax deductions for a couple's third child (as in Singapore, Hong Kong, Ghana, and Malaysia). Families who have more children than the desired limit may also suffer reduced free health care, decreased food allotments, and loss of job choice.

Like economic rewards, economic penalties can be psychologically coercive for the poor. Programs that withhold food or increase the cost of raising children punish innocent children for the actions of their parents.

Experience has shown that economic rewards and penalties designed to reduce fertility work best if they

- nudge rather than push people to have fewer children

- reinforce existing customs and trends toward smaller families

- do not penalize people who produced large families before the programs were established

- increase a poor family's income or land

Once population growth is out of control, a country may be forced to use coercive methods to prevent mass starvation and hardship. This is what China has had to do (Section 8-4).

Some countries have tried to use economic incentives to increase the birth rate. Since the 1930s, France has had vigorous pro-birth policies. All parents get substantial subsidies and services to help with child raising. Despite these efforts, France's total fertility rate has fallen from 2.7 children per woman in 1960 to 1.8 today.

CHANGES IN WOMEN'S ROLES Another socioeconomic method of population regulation is to improve the condition of women. Today, women do almost all of the world's domestic work and child care, mostly without pay. They also do more than half the work associated with growing food, gathering fuelwood, and hauling water. Women also provide more health care with little or no pay than all the world's organized health services put together. As one Brazilian woman put it, "For poor women, the only holiday is when you are asleep."

The worldwide economic value of women's work at home is estimated at $4 trillion annually. This unpaid work is not included in the GNP of countries, so the central role of women in an economy is unrecognized and unrewarded.

Despite their vital economic and social contributions, most women in LDCs don't have a legal right to own land or to borrow money to increase agricultural productivity. Although women work two-thirds of all hours worked in the world, they get only one-tenth of the world's income and own a mere 1% of the world's land. Many are abused or beaten by their husbands, who, in effect, own them as slaves.

At the same time, women make up about 60% of the world's almost 900 million adults who can neither read nor write. Women also suffer the most malnutrition, because men and children are usually fed first where food supplies are limited.

Numerous studies have shown that increased education is a strong factor leading women to have fewer children. Educated women are more likely than uneducated women to be employed outside the home rather than to stay home and raise children. They marry later, thus reducing their prime reproductive years, and lose fewer infants to death, a significant factor in reducing fertility rates.

Giving more of the world's women the opportunity to become educated and to express their lives in meaningful, paid work and social roles outside the home will require some major social changes. Making these changes will be difficult because of the long-standing political and economic domination of society by men throughout the world. In addition, in many countries, competition between men and women for already scarce jobs should become even more intense by 2000, when an additional billion people will be looking for work.

8-4 Case Studies: Population Regulation in India, China, and Thailand

INDIA India (Figure 8-17) started the world's first national family planning program in 1952, when its population was nearly 400 million. In 1991, after 39 years of population control effort, India was the world's second most populous country, with a population of 859 million. This is larger than the combined populations of the Soviet Union, the United States, and Indonesia, the world's third, fourth, and fifth most populous countries (Figure 8-4). About three-fourths of India's people try to survive by working the land and tending livestock animals in rural areas.

In 1952, India was adding 5 million people to its population each year. In 1991, it added 17 million. According to UN projections, India's population should reach 1 billion by the year 2000, 1.4 billion by 2025, and

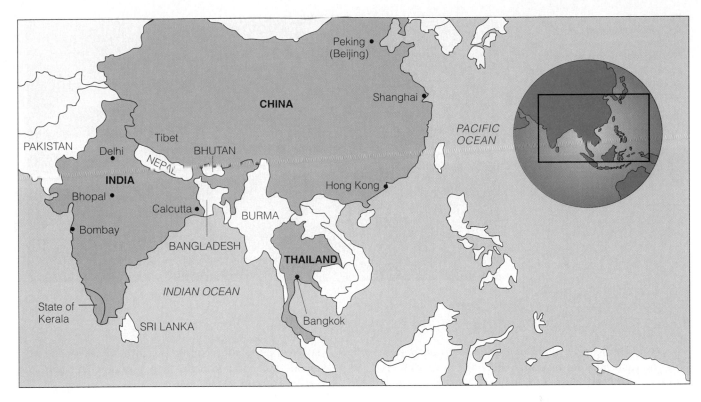

Figure 8-17 Where are India, China, and Thailand?

1.6 billion before levelling off early in the twenty-second century.

India's people are among the poorest in the world, with average income per person equivalent to less than $350 a year. At least one-third of its population has an annual income per person of less than $100 a year, and 10 out of every 100 babies born die before their first birthday. To add to the problem, nearly half of India's labor force is unemployed or can find only occasional work. An Indian government report indicated that at least 2.5 million Indians live their entire lives on the streets and that, of the urban poor, 65% have no tap water, 37% have no electricity, and 50% must defecate in vacant lots and fields.

Currently, India produces enough food to give its population an adequate survival diet, but widespread poverty means that many people don't have enough land to grow the food they need or enough money to buy sufficient food (Figure 8-18). Life expectancy is only 57 years, and the infant mortality rate is 91 deaths per 1,000 live births. Some analysts fear that hunger and malnutrition will increase in India as its population continues to grow rapidly. About 40% of India's cropland is degraded as a result of soil erosion, waterlogging, salinization, overgrazing, and deforestation, and roughly 80% of the country's land is subject to repeated droughts—often lasting two to five years.

Without its long-standing family planning program, India's numbers would be growing even faster.

However, the results of the program have been disappointing. Factors contributing to this failure have been poor planning, bureaucratic inefficiency, the low status of women (despite constitutional guarantees of equality), extreme poverty, and too little administrative and financial support.

The roots of the problem are deeper. About three out of every four people in India live in 560,000 rural villages, where birth rates tend to be higher than in urban areas and where the illiteracy rate for women is typically 80% to 90%.

For years, the government has provided information about the advantages of small families; yet, Indian women still have an average of 3.9 children because most couples believe they need many children as a source of cheap labor and old-age survival insurance. Almost one-third of Indian children die before age 5, reinforcing that belief. Thus, although 90% of Indian couples report knowing of at least one method of birth control, only 49% actually use one.

In 1976, Indira Gandhi's government started a mass sterilization program, primarily for men in the civil service who already had two or more children. The program was supposed to be voluntary, with financial incentives given to those who volunteered to be sterilized. Officials allegedly used coercion to meet sterilization quotas in a few rural areas. The resulting backlash played a role in Gandhi's election defeat in 1977.

Figure 8-18 A camp for starving refugees in New Delhi, India. There is fear that hunger and malnutrition will increase in India as more of its rapidly growing, mostly poverty-stricken population become unable to grow or buy enough food.

R. Koch/Contrasto/Picture Group

In 1978, the government took a new approach, raising the legal minimum age for marriage from 18 to 21 for men and from 15 to 18 for women. The 1981 census, however, showed that there was no drop in the population growth rate between 1971 and 1981. Since then, the government has increased family planning efforts and funding, with the goal of achieving 60% contraceptive use and replacement-level fertility by 2000.

The government is also considering adopting an incentive program in jobs and housing for couples who agree to meet family planning goals. In addition, the government is pushing to raise the legal average age at marriage farther, increase female literacy and employment opportunities for women, and decrease infant mortality, all of which could help reduce fertility levels. Whether these efforts will succeed remains to be seen.

CHINA Between 1958 and 1962, an estimated 30 million people died from famine in China. Since 1970, however, China has made impressive efforts to feed its people and bring its population growth under control. Since 1990, however, the number of homeless and hungry people in China has been rising. As in India, the average income in China is equivalent to about $360 a year.

Today, China has enough grain both to export and to feed its population of 1.1 billion. Between 1972 and 1985, China achieved a remarkable drop in its crude birth rate, from 32 to 18 per 1,000 people, and its average total fertility rate dropped from 5.7 to 2.1 children per woman. Since 1985, China's infant mortality rate has been less than one-half the rate in India. Life expectancy in China is 69 years—twelve years higher than in India.

To accomplish a sharp drop in fertility, China has established the most extensive, and intrusive, and the strictest population control program in the world, with an outlay of about $1 per person annually. The following are its most important features:

- Strongly encouraging couples to postpone marriage (age 28 for men and 25 for women).

- Expanding educational opportunities.

- Providing married couples with easy access to free sterilization, contraceptives, and abortion. The vacuum technique for abortion, now widely used around the world, was developed by the Chinese in the 1960s.

- Urging couples to have no more than one child (Figure 8-19).

- Giving couples who sign pledges to have no more than one child economic rewards, such as salary bonuses, extra food, larger pensions, better housing, free medical care and school tuition for their child, and preferential treatment in employment when the child grows up.

- Requiring those who break the pledge to return all benefits.

- Exerting pressure on women pregnant with a third child to have abortions.

- Requiring one of the parents in a two-child family to be sterilized.

- Using mobile units and paramedics to bring sterilization, family planning, health care, abortion, and education to rural areas. The goal has been to bring basic health care and family planning services to the entire population, with emphasis on maximizing infant survival and maternal health. More than 71% of couples of reproductive age use some form of birth control, compared with 74% of reproductive-age couples in the United States.

Figure 8-19 Poster encouraging couples in China to have no more than one child. Couples who do this are given economic rewards, and those who do not suffer economic penalties.

United Nations

IT IS BETTER TO HAVE ONE CHILD ONLY　只生一个孩子好

- Training local people to carry on the family planning program.
- Expecting all leaders to set an example with their own family size.

China is a dictatorship. Thus, unlike India, which is a democracy, China has been able to impose a unified policy from the top down. Moreover, Chinese society is fairly homogeneous and has a widespread common written language. India, by contrast, has over 1,600 languages and dialects and numerous major religions that make it difficult to educate people about family planning and to institute population regulation policies.

Despite these efforts, there have been reversals in China's population control programs since 1985. Between 1985 and 1991, China has had a birth rate of 21 (compared with 17 in 1984), an average total fertility rate of 2.3 (compared with 2.1 in 1984), and an annual population growth rate of 1.4% (compared with 1% in 1984).

The primary reasons for these increases were the large number of women moving into their childbearing years, some relaxation of the government's stringent policies, and a strong preference for male children. Most couples who have a female child are eager to try again for a son, who by custom helps support his parents as they grow old. The desire to have a son within the one-child limit has also led to an increase in female infanticide, which has been a long-standing tradition in the Chinese culture.

China's leaders have a goal of reaching zero population growth by 2000 with a population at 1.2 billion, followed by a slow decline to a population of 0.6 billion to 1.0 billion by 2100. Achieving this goal will be very difficult, because 27% of the Chinese people are under age 15. As a result, the United Nations projects that the population of China may be around 1.2 billion by the year 2000, 1.6 billion by 2025, and 1.7 billion before reaching ZPG perhaps around the year 2100.

Most countries cannot or do not want to use the coercive elements of China's program. Other parts of this program, however, could be used in many LDCs. Especially useful is the practice of localizing the program, rather than asking the people to go to distant centers. Perhaps the best lesson that other countries can learn from China's experience is not to wait to curb population growth until the choice is between mass starvation and coercive measures. Even harshly coercive measures can fail if a country starts too late. The lesson of China also shows how rapid population growth can help lead to severe limitations on individual freedom.

THAILAND　Thailand (Figure 8-17), with a population of 59 million in 1991, is undergoing rapid industrializing, with an economy growing at 10% a year. Much of this increase in prosperity has been made possible by a government policy that cut the country's population growth rate in half, from 3% in 1975 to 1.3% in 1991, and in the process preventing 9 million births.

Emphasis was on public education designed to persuade people to reduce the average number of children they had from six to three or fewer. Much of the program's success was due to leadership by a government economist, Mechai Viravaidya. He used humor and imaginative ways to greatly increase the use of condoms throughout the country to the point where a condom is now known as a "mechai" in the Thai language. Today, 95% of the Thai people want only two children and 68% use birth control—almost the same as in Europe.

Some of these techniques included proclaiming one day a year as "Cops and Rubbers Day" and paying

There is controversy over whether population growth is good or bad (see Pro/Con on p. 209). If you believe that population growth in MDCs and LDCs is harmful to the biosphere, push for

- the United States and other MDCs to establish policies designed to reach zero population growth by 2025
- worldwide family planning, with generous assistance from the United States and other MDCs to raise the level of spending to $8 billion a year
- making birth control information and devices available to every man and woman at little or no cost
- forgiving the debts of LDCs that institute effective programs to regulate population growth and agree to protect unspoiled areas from unsustainable development
- compulsory education on population dynamics and the implications of rapid population growth in MDCs and LDCs from the third grade through college
- greatly expanded sex education for the world's teenagers, unless this is against your religious beliefs
- policies that will slow the flow of the rural poor to urban areas by placing more emphasis on sustainable economic development in rural areas
- giving the world's women the opportunity to become educated, to own property, and to express their lives in meaningful, paid work and social roles outside the home
- shifting from unsustainable to sustainable development in MDCs to reduce consumption overpopulation, which is undermining the planet's life-support capacity (Figure 1-16)
- sharply reducing poverty to lessen unnecessary human suffering and to diminish the need for people to have a large number of children as a form of social security

Finally, on a more personal level, you should carefully consider whether to have children or not, and if so, how many children you want. Some people have the capacity to be good parents and to raise emotionally and physically healthy children. Others do not. Our goal should be to provide every child with a high-quality childhood that is nurturing, not damaging.

the insurance for taxi drivers willing to dispense condoms and birth control pills from inside their cabs.

Demonstrations and ads were widely used to familiarize children and adults with condoms and see them as normal and useful household products. Viravaidya told people to touch a condom, not be embarrassed by it, and blow it up like a balloon, with school children having condom-blowing championships. He also showed how condoms could be used as a tourniquet for deep cuts and snake bites and to carry coins or a beverage. People were also advised to use the ring at the end of a condom as a hair band. Humorous and informative songs were written with messages about condom use and the need to have no more than two children as a way to promote economic growth and jobs.

Thailand's population is still growing, but at half its previous rate. Although the country also has some serious pollution and environmental degradation problems, those problems would be much worse today without the government program that prevented 9 million births in 15 years.

CUTTING GLOBAL POPULATION GROWTH Regulating population growth will not solve the world's resource, environmental, and social problems, but most analysts believe that reducing population growth will reduce the intensity of those problems.

Lester Brown, president of the Worldwatch Institute, urges the leaders of countries to adopt a goal of cutting world population growth in half between 1990 and 2000. Assuming that the average world death rate remains at 9 per 1,000 people, this would require reducing the average global birth rate from 28 to 18 per 1,000 people.

The experience of some countries indicates that this is a possible goal. Japan cut its birth rate and population growth rate in half between 1949 and 1956 by legalizing abortion and by creating a national family planning program. Between 1970 and 1976, China was able to cut its birth rate and population growth rate in half.

Cutting the global birth rate in half as soon as possible will require a combination of family planning, sustainable economic development, economic rewards and penalties, and changes in women's roles. The mix of these factors must be carefully designed to work with the culture of each country. Each of us plays an important role in controlling global population growth (see Individuals Matter at left).

Short of thermonuclear war itself, rampant population growth is the gravest issue the world faces over the decades immediately ahead.

ROBERT S. MCNAMARA

Garrett Hardin

As professor of human ecology at the University of California at Santa Barbara for many years, Garrett Hardin made important contributions to the joining of ethics and biology. He has raised hard ethical questions, sometimes taken unpopular stands, and forced people to think deeply about environmental problems and their possible solutions. He is best known for his 1968 essay, "The Tragedy of the Commons," which has had significant impacts on economics, political science, and the management of potentially renewable resources. His many books include Promethean Ethics *and* Filters Against Folly: How to Survive Despite Economists, Ecologists, and the Merely Eloquent.

For many years, Angel Island in San Francisco Bay was plagued with too many deer. A few animals transplanted there early in this century lacked predators and rapidly increased to nearly 300 deer — far beyond the carrying capacity of the island. Scrawny, underfed animals tugged at the heartstrings of Californians, who carried extra plant food from the mainland to the island.

Such charity worsened the plight of the deer. Excess animals trampled the soil, ate the bark off small trees, and destroyed seedlings of all kinds. The net effect was a lowering of the carrying capacity, year by year, as the deer continued to multiply in a deteriorating habitat.

State game managers proposed that the excess deer be shot by skilled hunters. "How cruel! " some people protested. Then the managers proposed that coyotes be imported to the island. Though not big enough to kill adult deer, coyotes can kill defenseless young fawns, thus reducing the size of the herd. However, the Society for the Prevention of Cruelty to Animals was adamantly opposed to such human introduction of predators.

In the end, it was agreed to export deer to some other area suitable for deer life. A total of 203 animals were caught and trucked many miles away. From the fate of a sample of animals fitted with radiocollars, it was estimated that 85% of the transported deer died within a year (most of them within two months) from various causes: predation by coyotes, bobcats, and domestic dogs; shooting by poachers and legal hunters; and being run over by automobiles.

The net cost (in 1982 dollars) for relocating each animal that survived for a year was $2,876. The state refused to finance the continuation of the program, and no volunteers stepped forward to pay future bills. Even if funding had been forthcoming, managers would soon have run out of areas suitable for deer life. Organisms reproduce exponentially like compound interest [see Spotlight on p. 5], but the environment doesn't increase at all. The moral is a simple ecological commandment: *Thou shalt not transgress the carrying capacity*.

Now let's look at the human situation. A competent physicist has placed the human carrying capacity of the globe at 50 billion — about ten times the present world population. Before you are tempted to urge women to have more babies, consider what Robert Malthus said nearly 200 years ago: "There should be no more people in a country than could enjoy daily a glass of wine and piece of beef for dinner."

A diet of grain or bread is symbolic of minimum living standards; wine and beef are symbolic of all forms of higher living standards that make greater demands on the environment. When land used for the direct production of plants for human consumption is converted into land for growing crops for wine or corn for cattle, fewer calories get to the human population. Since carrying capacity is defined as the *maximum* number of animals (humans) an area can support, using part of the area to support such cultural luxuries as wine and beef reduces the carrying capacity. This reduced capacity is called the *cultural carrying capacity*. Cultural carrying capacity is always less than simple carrying capacity.

Energy is the common coin in which all competing demands on the environment can be measured. Energy saved by giving up a luxury can be used to produce more bread and support more people. We could increase the simple carrying capacity of the earth by giving up any (or all) of the following "luxuries": street lighting; vacations; most private cars; air conditioning; and artistic performances of all sorts — drama, dancing, music, and lectures. Since the heating of buildings is not as efficient as multiple layers of clothing, space heating would be forbidden.

Is that all? By no means: To come closer to home, look at this book. The production and distribution of such an expensive treatise consume a great deal of energy. In fact, the energy bill for the whole of higher education is very high (which is one reason tuition costs so much). By giving up all education beyond the eighth grade, we could free enough energy to sustain millions more human lives.

At this point a skeptic might well ask: "Does God give a prize for the maximum population?" From this brief analysis we can see that there are two choices. We can maximize the number of human beings living at the lowest possible level of comfort, or we can try to optimize the quality of life for a much smaller population.

(continued)

What is the carrying capacity of the earth? is a scientific question. Scientifically, it may be possible to support 50 billion people at a "bread" level. Is that what we want? What is the cultural carrying capacity? requires that we debate questions of value, about which opinions differ.

An even greater difficulty must be faced. So far, we have been treating the capacity question as a *global* question, as if there were a global sovereignty to enforce a solution on all people. However, there is no global sovereignty ("one world"), nor is there any prospect of one in the foreseeable future. We must make do with nearly 200 national sovereignties. That means, as concerns the capacity problem, that we must ask how nations are to coexist in a finite global environment if different sovereignties adopt different standards of living.

Consider a redwood forest [Figure 2-6]. It produces no human food. Protected in a park, the trees do not even produce lumber for houses. Because people have to travel many kilometers to visit it, the forest is a net loss in the national energy budget. However, those who are fortunate enough to wander quietly through the cathedral-like aisles of soaring trees report that the forest does something precious for the human spirit.

Now comes an appeal from a distant land where millions are starving because their population has overshot the carrying capacity. We are asked to save lives by sending food. So long as we have surpluses, we may safely indulge in the pleasures of philanthropy. But the typical population in such poor countries increases by 2.5% a year—*or more*; that is, the country's population doubles every 28 years—*or less*. After we have run out of our surpluses, then what?

A spokesperson for the needy makes a proposal: "If you would only cut down your redwood forests, you could use the lumber to build houses and then grow potatoes on the land, shipping the food to us. Since we are all passengers together on Spaceship Earth, are you not duty bound to do so? Which is more precious, trees or human beings?"

The last question may sound ethically compelling, but let's look at the consequences of assigning a preemptive and supreme value to human lives. There are at least 2 billion people in the world who are poorer than the 32 million legally "poor" in America, and they are increasing by about 40 million per year. Unless this increase is brought to a halt, sharing food and energy on the basis of need would require the sacrifice of one amenity after another in rich countries. The final result of sharing would be complete poverty everywhere on the face of the earth to maintain the earth's simple carrying capacity. Is that the best humanity can do?

To date, there has been overwhelmingly negative reaction to all proposals to make international philanthropy conditional upon the stopping of population growth by the poor, overpopulated recipient nations. Foreign aid is governed by two apparently inflexible assumptions:

- The right to produce children is a universal, irrevocable right of every nation, no matter how hard it presses against the carrying capacity of its territory.

- When lives are in danger, the moral obligations of rich countries to save human lives is absolute and undeniable.

Considered separately, each of these two well-meaning doctrines might be defended; together, they constitute a fatal recipe. If humanity gives maximum carrying capacity questions precedence over problems of cultural carrying capacity, the result will be universal poverty and environmental ruin.

Or do you see an escape from this harsh dilemma?

Guest Essay Discussion

1. What population size do you believe would allow the world's people to have a good quality of life? What do you believe is the cultural carrying capacity of the United States? Should the United States have a national policy to establish this population size as soon as possible? Explain.

2. Do you agree with the two principles the author of this essay says are the basis of foreign aid to needy countries? If not, what changes would you make in the requirements for receiving such aid?

DISCUSSION TOPICS

1. Why are falling birth rates not necessarily a reliable indicator of future population growth trends?

*2. How many children do you plan to have? Why? Conduct a survey of members of your class to determine the number of children they plan to have and tally the results. Then make a random survey of at least 100 other students to determine the number of children they plan to have. Compare the results from this group with those from your class.

3. Why is it rational for a poor couple in India to have six or seven children? What changes might induce such a couple to think of their behavior as irrational?

4. Project what your own life may be like at ages 25, 45, and 65 on the basis of the present population age structure of the country in which you live. What changes, if any, do such projections make in your career choice and in your plans for children?

5. Do you believe that all U.S. high schools and colleges should have health clinics that make contraceptives available to students and provide prenatal care for pregnant teenage women? Explain. Should such services be available at the junior high school age level, when many teenagers first become sexually active? Explain.

6. a. Should the number of legal immigrants and refugees allowed into the United States each year be sharply reduced? Explain.
   b. Should illegal immigration into the United States be sharply decreased? Explain. If so, how would you go about achieving this?

7. Should families in the United States be given financial incentives and persuaded to have more children to prevent population decline? Explain.

8. Debate the following resolution: The United States has a serious consumption overpopulation problem and should adopt an official policy to stabilize its population and reduce unnecessary resource waste and consumption as rapidly as possible.

9. What are some ways in which women are discriminated against in the United States? On your campus? In what ways, if any, do these forms of discrimination contribute to fertility?

10. Why has China been more successful than India in reducing its rate of population growth? Do you agree with China's present population control policies? Explain. What alternatives, if any, would you suggest?

CHAPTER 9

POPULATION DISTRIBUTION: URBANIZATION, URBAN PROBLEMS, AND URBAN LAND USE

General Questions and Issues

1. How is the world's population distributed between rural and urban areas?

2. What factors determine how urban areas develop?

3. What are the principal benefits and problems associated with living in an urban area?

4. How do transportation systems affect population distribution and urban growth?

5. What methods are used to decide and regulate how different parcels of land in urban areas are used?

6. How can cities be made more livable and sustainable?

The test of the quality of life in an advanced economic society is now largely in the quality of urban life. Romance may still belong to the countryside — but the present reality of life abides in the city.

JOHN KENNETH GALBRAITH

CONOMIC, ENVIRONMENTAL, AND SOCIAL conditions are affected not only by population growth and age structure but also by how population is distributed geographically in rural or urban areas. Since 1800, there have been two *urban revolutions*, involving the mass migration of people from rural areas to cities and towns. The *first urban revolution*, now largely over, occurred between 1800 and 1991, when the urban population in MDCs rose from 5% to 73%. The *second urban revolution* is taking place in LDCs, where the number of people living in towns and cities increased from 3% to 34% between 1940 and 1991 and could rise to 58% by the year 2020.

Supplying resources to support urban areas is a principal cause of degradation of forests, farmlands, rangelands, watersheds, and other nonurban areas. Urban areas also concentrate pollutants, some of which are transported by wind and flowing water to rural and other urban areas. How we deal with the problems of urban growth and the resulting resource use, pollution, and environmental degradation will be the primary factor determining the well-being and health of urban and rural dwellers and the environment upon which all people and other species depend.

9-1 Urbanization and Urban Growth

THE WORLD SITUATION An **urban area** is often defined as a town or a city with a population of more than 2,500 people, although some countries set the minimum at 10,000 to 50,000. A country's **urbanization** is the percentage of its population living in an urban area. **Urban growth** is the rate of growth of urban populations.

Urban populations grow in two ways: by natural increase (more births than deaths) and by immigration (mostly from rural areas). Generally, economic development tends to *pull* rural people looking for jobs and a better life into urban areas. Rapid population growth and poverty in rural areas tend to *push* people into urban areas.

Several trends are important in understanding the problems and challenges of urbanization and urban growth:

- The percentage of the population living in urban areas increased from 14% to 43% (73% in MDCs and 34% in LDCs) between 1900 and 1991 (Figure 9-1). It is projected that by 2020, almost two out of three people will be living in urban areas.

- Urbanization varies in different parts of the world (Figure 9-2).

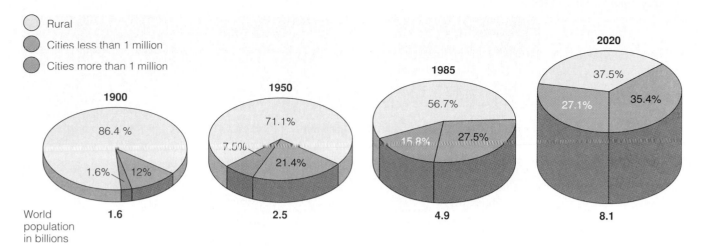

Rural

Cities less than 1 million

Cities more than 1 million

1900

86.4 %

1.6% 12%

1.6

1950

71.1%

7.5% 21.4%

2.5

1985

56.7%

15.8% 27.5%

4.9

2020

37.5% 35.4%

27.1%

8.1

World population in billions

Figure 9-1 Patterns of world urbanization from 1900 to 1985, with projections to 2020. (Data from United Nations and Population Reference Bureau)

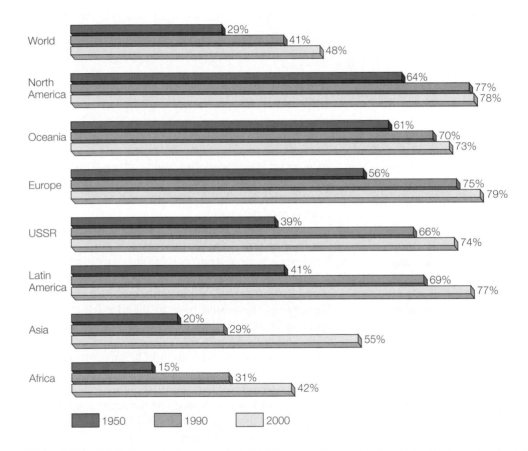

World	29%	41%	48%
North America	64%	77%	78%
Oceania	61%	70%	73%
Europe	56%	75%	79%
USSR	39%	66%	74%
Latin America	41%	69%	77%
Asia	20%	29%	55%
Africa	15%	31%	42%

1950   1990   2000

Figure 9-2 Urbanization of various groups of countries, 1950–2000. (Data from United Nations and Population Reference Bureau)

- The number of large cities is increasing rapidly. Today, one of every ten persons lives in a city with a million or more inhabitants, and many of these live in *megacities* with 10 million or more people. The United Nations projects that by 2000, there will be 26 megacities, more than two-thirds of them in LDCs (Table 9-1).

- LDCs, with 34% urbanization, are simultaneously experiencing high rates of natural population increase and rapid and increasing urban growth, four and a half times as fast as in MDCs. LDCs are projected to reach 58% urbanization by the year 2020, with their urban populations tripling from 1.3 billion to 3.9 billion between 1990 and 2020 — the greatest mass migration in history.

Table 9-1 The Ten Largest Megacity Urban Areas in the World in 1985 and 2000

1985		2000	
Urban Area	**Population (millions)**	**Urban Area**	**Projected Population (millions)**
Tokyo–Yokohama	18.8	Mexico City	25.8
Mexico City	17.3	São Paulo	24.0
São Paulo	15.9	Tokyo–Yokohama	20.2
New York–N.E. New Jersey	15.6	Calcutta	16.5
Shanghai	12.0	Greater Bombay	16.0
Calcutta	11.0	New York–N.E. New Jersey	15.8
Greater Buenos Aires	10.9	Shanghai	14.3
Rio de Janeiro	10.4	Seoul	13.8
London	10.4	Tehran	13.6
Seoul	10.2	Rio de Janeiro	13.3

Data from United Nations

- In MDCs, with 73% urbanization, urban growth is increasing at lower rates than in LDCs. Between 1990 and 2020, the urban population in MDCs is projected to rise from 890 million to 1 billion.

THE WORSENING SITUATION IN LDCs The second urban revolution, now under way at an accelerating pace, is taking place mostly in LDCs, which can't provide adequate services, shelter, and jobs for a third to a half of their present urban populations (see Case Study on p. 225). Just to maintain present inadequate standards, LDCs will need to increase housing, food, jobs, and other basic needs for their projected urban dwellers by two-thirds between 1990 and 2000 and threefold between 1990 and 2020.

People are pulled to urban areas mostly in search of jobs and a better life. Other factors push rural people into urban areas. Modern mechanized agriculture decreases the need for farm labor and allows large landowners to buy out small-scale, subsistence farmers who cannot afford to modernize. Without jobs or land, these people are forced to move to cities.

Urban growth in LDCs is also caused by government policies that distribute most income and social services to urban dwellers at the expense of rural dwellers—policies that both push and pull people into the cities. For example, in many LDCs where 70% of the population is rural, only about 20% of the national budget goes to the rural sector. This means that the major cities in LDCs are the source of most of a country's jobs, housing, lower food prices (often made cheaper than in rural areas by government policies), and other opportunities, all of which bring in rural people hoping for a better life.

For most of the rural poor migrating to urban areas in LDCs, as well as for the urban poor in MDCs, the city becomes a poverty trap, not an oasis of economic opportunity (see Case Study on p. 226). Those fortunate enough to get a job must work long hours for low wages. To survive, they often have to take jobs that expose them to dust, hazardous chemicals, excessive noise, and dangerous machinery.

Many of the urban poor in LDCs are forced to live on the streets (Figure 1-4). Worldwide, an estimated 150 million are homeless. In Bombay, India, about half a million homeless people sleep on the streets, sidewalks, or any place they can find. In São Paulo, Brazil, there are at least 3 million homeless children.

The United Nations estimates that at least 1 billion people — 20% of the world's population — live in crowded, often wretched, inhumane conditions in slums of central cities and in the vast squatter settlements that ring the outskirts of most cities in LDCs. In squatter settlements (see photo on p. 195), people generally live illegally on public or private land that no one else wants to live on because it is too wet, too dry, too steep, too hazardous (subject to landslides, flooding, or fumes from industrial plants), or too polluted (city dumps). Most of the squatters live in shacks made from corrugated metal, plastic sheets, cardboard, discarded

Brazil, the largest country in South America, ranks fifth in land area in the world and eighth in population (Figure 9-3). In 1991, its population of about 153 million was expanding by 1.9%, adding 2.9 million people a year. It is encouraging that between 1965 and 1991, Brazil's total fertility rate fell from 6.8 to 3.3. As in most LDCs, however, a large share of Brazil's population (35%) is under age 15. This explains why the country's population is projected to reach 246 million by 2025.

Brazil's gross national product averages almost $2,550 per person, making it a middle-income developing country. This average is deceiving because most of the country's wealth is concentrated in the hands of a small fraction of the population. Most other people are poor and must survive on an average income of only several hundred dollars a year. About 70% of the country's rural families are landless.

Brazil has fueled much of its recent economic growth by borrowing abroad. In 1989, its foreign debt was over $115 billion, the largest of any LDC. Of every $100 Brazil earns from exports of minerals, timber, beef, soybeans, and manufactured products, $41 is paid out in interest to its creditors.

This heavy burden of debt pushes the country to expand its exports of timber, minerals, and other resources to pay the interest on its debt, and in the process deplete and degrade its natural resource base. This is leading to widespread deforestation and degradation of Brazil's tropical forests in the Amazon basin (Figure 9-3).

In effect, the country is mortgaging its environmental and economic future for short-term economic gain by the wealthy few in Brazil and the affluent in Japan, the United States, and other MDCs who buy its exported resources. Brazil is like a family giving the appearance of affluence by living off credit cards and having to use much of its capital and income to finance its debt.

Brazil is divided geographically into a largely impoverished tropical north and a temperate south, where most industry and wealth are concentrated. The Amazon basin, which covers about one-third of the country's territory, remains largely unsettled. This is changing as landless poor migrate there, hoping to grow enough food to survive, and as its tropical forests are cut down for grazing livestock, timber, and mining or are flooded to create large reservoirs for hydroelectric dams.

With 75% of its population living in urban areas, Brazil is more than twice as urbanized as most LDCs. Attracted by the prospect of jobs, many of the rural poor in the north and northeast have flooded into Rio de Janeiro and São Paulo in the south. These modern cosmopolitan

(continued)

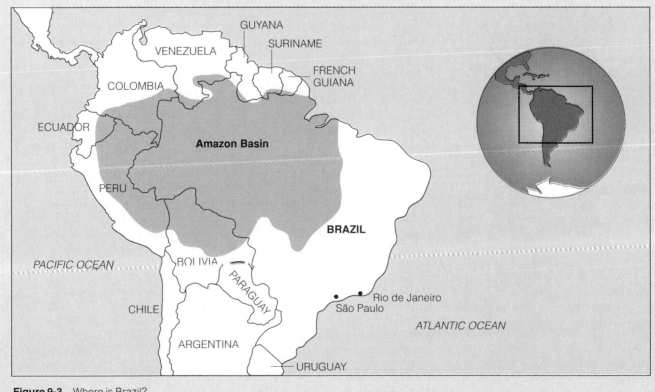

Figure 9-3 Where is Brazil?

centers are surrounded by mostly illegal squatter settlements where the poor try to survive (see photo on p. 195) and by widespread poverty in rural areas. By the year 2000, São Paulo is expected to be the world's second most populous city (Table 9-1).

Overpopulation is one factor increasing the ranks of the unemployed and underemployed in rural and urban Brazil. Many poor people have also been displaced from the land by the conversion of small farms in the south into industrialized agriculture for export crops. Deforestation and desertification in the extremely poor northeast have also helped push environmental refugees to southern cities and to development projects in the tropical forests of the Amazon basin.

As a safety valve for its exploding population, the Brazilian government has encouraged migration to the Amazon basin, with economic aid from international lending agencies, such as the World Bank. This policy is supported by wealthy Brazilians, who want to diffuse pressures for more equitable land distribution, and by wealthy ranchers, who until 1990 received government subsidies to establish cattle ranches by clearing tropical forests.

CASE STUDY Mexico City, Mexico

In 1991, Mexico's (Figure 9-4) population was 86 million and was growing exponentially at 2.3% a year. Between 1965 and 1991, Mexico's average total fertility rate dropped from 6.7 to 3.8, but because 39% of Mexico's population is under age 15 (Figure 8-11), its population is projected to reach 143 million by 2025. Annual per capita income is $1,990, but this gives a distorted view because much of the wealth is in the hands of a few.

Economic growth has slowed mostly because of falling oil prices in the 1980s and a huge foreign debt of $100 billion. Each year, over 1 million people enter the labor force looking for jobs, but only 100,000 to 200,0000 new jobs are created. Because of the high levels of unemployment and underemployment, hundreds of thousands of Mexicans emigrate legally and illegally to the United States in search of work.

In 1990, the population of Mexico City, the capital of Mexico (Figure 9-4), was 22 million—the most populous city that has ever existed. Every day, an additional 2,000 poverty-stricken rural peasants pour into the city, hoping to find a better life. Each year, the city's population increases by an amount equal to that of San Francisco or Baltimore.

The city suffers from severe air pollution, high unemployment (close to 50%), deafening noise, congestion, and a soaring crime rate. One-third of the city's people live in crowded slums (called barrios) or squatter settlements, without running water or electricity.

With at least 5 million people living without sewer facilities, huge amounts of human waste are left in gutters and vacant lots every day. When the winds pick up dried excrement, a "fecal snow" often falls on parts of the city. About half of the city's garbage is left in the open to rot, attracting armies of rats and swarms of flies.

Over 3 million cars, 15,000 buses, 40,000 taxis, and 130,000 factories (making up half of the country's industry) spew pollutants into the atmosphere. Air pollution is intensified because the city lies in a basin surrounded by mountains and has frequent thermal inversions that trap pollutants near ground level (Figure 9-5). Between 1982 and 1990, the amount of contamination in the city's air more than tripled.

Breathing the city's air is like smoking two packs of cigarettes a day from birth. The city's air and water pollution cause an estimated 100,000 premature deaths a year. According to a World Health Organization study, 7 out of 10 babies born in Mexico City have unsafe levels of lead in their blood—threatening an entire generation of children with intellectual stunting. These problems, already at crisis levels, will become even worse if this urban area, as projected, grows to 26.3 million people by the end of this century.

The Mexican government is industrializing other parts of the country in an attempt to stop or at least slow migration to Mexico City. In 1990, a 12.5% tax on all fossil fuels was established to fund much-needed air pollution control for Mexico City. All motor vehicles must stay off the streets one day a week.

In 1991, Mexico's president announced a $1.3 billion program to replace outmoded taxis and buses and shut down a giagantic oil refinery in northwestern Mexico City. By 1993, all new cars in Mexico must have catalytic converters (output devices for reducing pollution emissions), but new cars represent only about 5% of the cars on the road each year. If you were in charge of Mexico City, what would you do?

(continued)

Figure 9-4 Where is Mexico City?

United Nations

Figure 9-5 The air in Mexico City ranks with the dirtiest in the world. This is due to a combination of topography, a large population, industrialization, large numbers of motor vehicles, and too little emphasis on reducing rural-to-urban migration and preventing and controlling pollution. Breathing the city's air has been compared to smoking two packs of cigarettes a day. This photo was taken in the morning on a bright, sunny day.

A few squatter communities have organized to improve their living conditions. They gradually turn flimsy shacks into solid buildings, and work together to lay out streets, build schools, and bring in water and electricity lines.

One example is Rio de Janeiro's Santa Marta slum, home for 11,500 of the city's 2 million squatters. Residents organized to establish a day-care program and to bring in water lines, electricity, health clinics, and drainage systems to prevent mud slides.

In Villa El Salvador, a squatter settlement outside of Lima, Peru, a network of women's groups and neighborhood associations planted half a million trees, trained hundreds of door-to-door health workers, and built 300 community kitchens, 150 day-care centers, and 26 schools. Through their own efforts, the people now have homes with electricity, over half have water and sewers, and trees and gardens flourish in what was once desert. In this town of 300,000 people, illiteracy has fallen to 3% — one of the lowest rates in Latin America — and infant mortality is 40% below the national average.

Such self-help success stories are rare, but they show what can be done. Governments can encourage this self-help process by giving squatters ownership of the land that they have usually occupied illegally. This gives them great incentive to make improvements they know won't be taken away.

packing crates, or whatever building materials they can come up with.

In most large cities in LDCs, squatter populations double every five to seven years — four to five times the population growth rate of the entire city. Currently, an estimated 850 million people are urban squatters, and the number could grow to 2 billion by the year 2000. Squatters are rarely included in urban population estimates such as those given in Table 9-1.

People in these illegal settlements live in constant fear of eviction by police or of having their makeshift shelters destroyed by bulldozers. When this happens, the people either move back in, relocate to another existing squatter settlement, or create a new one.

Most cities refuse to provide these settlements with adequate drinking water, sanitation, electricity, food, health care, housing, schools, and jobs. Not only do they lack the money, officials also fear that improving services will attract even more of the rural poor. Officials, with urging from business owners, sometimes allow illegal settlements because they provide a source

of cheap labor without costing the city money for services.

Despite joblessness, squalor, overcrowding, and rampant disease, squatter and slum residents cling to life with resourcefulness, tenacity, and hope. Most urban migrants do have more opportunities and are better off than the rural poor they left behind. With better access to family planning programs, they tend to have fewer children, and the children in most cities have better access to schools than do rural dwellers. Even so, nearly half of all school-age children in urban areas of LDCs drop out before they finish the fourth grade, to work or take care of younger children.

Many squatter settlements provide a sense of community and a vital survival safety net for the poor. Families can share child care, health care, and money or goods during hard times, and can organize to improve their conditions (see Spotlight at left).

THE SITUATION IN THE UNITED STATES AND OTHER MDCs In most MDCs in North America and Europe, the rapid migration of people from rural areas to central cities that accompanied industrialization during the 1800s and the early 1900s had slowed down. In some cases, this trend has been reversed as people have moved from the central city to suburbs and smaller cities.

In 1800, only 5% of Americans lived in cities. Since then, three major internal population shifts have taken place in the United States:

- *Migration from rural to mostly large central cities.* Currently, about 74% of Americans live in the nation's 284 *metropolitan areas* — cities and towns with at least 50,000 people that are linked socially or economically. Two out of three Americans live in the country's 28 largest urban regions (Figure 9-6). Nearly half (48%) of the American people live in *consolidated metropolitan areas* with 1 million or more people. Of the 24% of the U.S. population who live in rural areas, most work in small towns, commute to work in a nearby city, or are unemployed or retired. Only 0.8% of the population are farmers living in rural areas and only 0.25% now engage in full-time farming. It is projected that by 1995, 83% of the U.S. population will live in urban areas.

- *Migration from large central cities to suburbs and smaller cities.* Since 1970, this type of migration has taken place mostly because of the large numbers of new jobs in such areas. Today, about 41% of the country's urban dwellers live in central cities and 59% live in suburbs.

- *Migration from the North and East to the South and West.* Since 1980, about 80% of the population increase in the United States has occurred in the

1 **Bosman** (Boston–Manchester)
2 **Mega York** (New York–Philadelphia)
3 **Philwil** (Philadelphia–Wilmington)
4 **Washbalt** (Washington–Baltimore)
5 **Pittyoung** (Pittsburgh–Youngstown)
6 **Miamilaud** (Miami–Fort Lauderdale)
7 **Hougalbeau** (Houston–Galveston–Beaumont)
8 **Dalworth** (Dallas–Fort Worth)

9 **Denboul** (Denver–Boulder)
10 **San Angeles** (Los Angeles–San Diego)
11 **San Franjose** (San Francisco–San Jose)
12 **Seatac** (Seattle–Tacoma)
13 **Chimilgar** (Chicago–Milwaukee–Gary)
14 **Detanntol** (Detroit–Ann Arbor–Toledo)
15 **Clevak** (Cleveland–Akron)

Figure 9-6 Major urban regions in the United States. (Data from U.S. Census Bureau)

South and West, particularly near the coasts. Most of this growth is due to migration from the North and East. This shift is projected to continue, with the South having the largest population increase between 1987 and 2010, followed by the West. Each day 900 people migrate to Florida.

Since 1920, many of the worst urban environmental problems in MDCs have been significantly reduced. Most people have better working and housing conditions. Air and water quality have improved. Better sanitation, public water supplies, and medical care have sharply reduced death rates and sickness from malnutrition and from transmissible diseases such as measles, diphtheria, typhoid fever, pneumonia, and tuberculosis.

The biggest problems facing numerous cities in the United States and in other industrialized countries are deteriorating services, aging and decaying infrastructure (such as streets, schools, housing, sewers), budget crunches from a loss in tax revenue and rising costs, environmental degradation, inner-city decay, and neighborhood collapse. Many jobs, many businesses, and many people in the middle and upper classes have moved to the suburbs. This has caused a drop in the tax base needed to provide money for health care, social services, mass transportation, police protection, and other services, and to repair and maintain city infrastructures.

The result is usually an increase in violence, drug traffic, drug abuse, crime, decay, and blight in parts of central cities. In these areas, the poor, the elderly, the unemployed (typically 50% or higher in economically depressed inner-city areas), the homeless (an estimated 3.5 million in the United States), the handicapped, and other people who cannot afford to leave the city are trapped in downward spiral of poverty and degradation. Jobs that are available usually involve menial, minimum-wage work, with little chance for the advancement needed to escape the poverty trap.

SPATIAL PATTERNS OF URBAN DEVELOPMENT
Three generalized models of urban structure are shown in Figure 9-7. A city resembling the *concentric-circle*

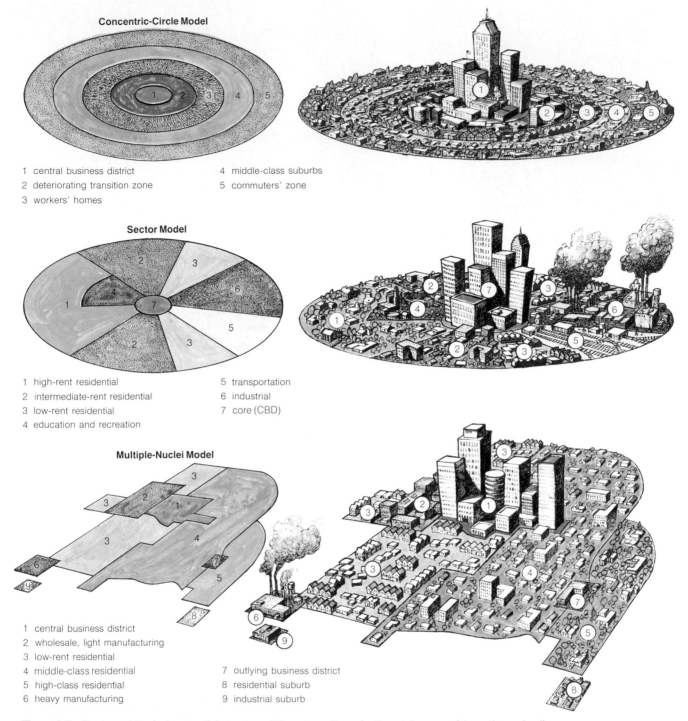

Concentric-Circle Model

1 central business district
2 deteriorating transition zone
3 workers' homes
4 middle-class suburbs
5 commuters' zone

Sector Model

1 high-rent residential
2 intermediate-rent residential
3 low-rent residential
4 education and recreation
5 transportation
6 industrial
7 core (CBD)

Multiple-Nuclei Model

1 central business district
2 wholesale, light manufacturing
3 low-rent residential
4 middle-class residential
5 high-class residential
6 heavy manufacturing
7 outlying business district
8 residential suburb
9 industrial suburb

Figure 9-7 Three models of urban spatial structure. Although no city perfectly matches any of them, these simplified models can be used to identify general patterns of urban development. (Modified with permission from Harm J. deBlij, *Human Geography*, New York: John Wiley, 1977)

model develops outward from its central business district (CBD) in a series of rings as the area grows in population and size. For example, metropolitan New York City now extends over a generally circular area of suburbanized existing towns and villages and newly created ones more than 80 kilometers (50 miles) from the central business district in downtown Manhattan.

Typically, industries and businesses in the CBD are surrounded by circular zones of housing that become more affluent as one moves outward into the suburbs. In many LDCs, however, the affluent live mostly in the central city and many of the poor live in squatter settlements that spring up around the central core (see photo on p. 195).

Figure 9-8 Because it is built on an island, downtown Manhattan in New York City has had to expand upward. However, many of the middle- and upper-income people who work in the central city live in nearby and distant suburbs and satellite cities. Some of these suburban residents spend three to four hours a day commuting to and from jobs in the city center.

Figure 9-9 Aigues-Mortes, France. For security, walls were built around the city between the fourteenth and sixteenth centuries. Today, most of the city's population still lives within the walls of this compact city.

A city resembling the *sector model* grows in a system of pie-shaped wedges, or ribbons. These growth sectors develop when commercial, industrial, and housing districts push outward from the central business district along major transportation routes. An example is the large urban area stretching from San Francisco to San Jose.

In the *multiple-nuclei model*, a large city develops around a number of independent centers, or satellite cities, rather than a single center. Los Angeles comes fairly close to this pattern. Some cities develop in a combination of these patterns.

As they grow, many urban areas spread out and merge with other urban areas to form a large urban area, or *megalopolis*. For example, the remaining open space between Boston and Washington, D.C., is being rapidly urbanized and merged. This giant urban area, sometimes called *Bowash*, is becoming a sprawling megalopolis with almost 50 million people. This and other megalopolises are forming as major U.S. cities spread out and merge (Figure 9-6).

If suitable rural land is not available for conversion to urban land, a city grows upward, not outward; it occupies a relatively small area and develops a high population density. Upward expansion is the only way that cities such as New York, Tokyo, and Hong Kong, without room to expand outward, can increase in population size (Figure 9-8).

Most people living in such compact cities walk, ride bicycles, or use energy-efficient mass transit. Residents often live in multistory apartment buildings with fewer outside walls, reducing heating and cooling costs. Because of the lack of land, many European cities are compact (Figure 9-9) and tend to be more energy-efficient than the dispersed cities of the United States and Aus-

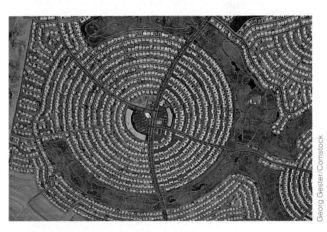

Figure 9-10 Sun City, Arizona, is typical of urban sprawl that has taken place in the United States because of the widespread use of automobiles and the development of highways to carry people and goods. This retirement community of more than 60,000 people is nearly totally dependent on the outside for its resources. It is also built in an area with an arid climate, where demands for water are beginning to exceed the available supply.

tralia, where there is often ample land for outward expansion.

A combination of cheap gasoline, a large supply of rural land suitable for urban development, and a network of highways usually results in a dispersed, car-culture city with a low population density—often called *urban sprawl* (Figure 9-10). Most people living in such a city rely on cars with low energy efficiencies for transportation and live in single-family houses, with unshared walls that lose and gain heat rapidly unless they are well insulated and airtight.

9-2 Resource and Environmental Problems of Urban Areas

EFFECTS OF URBAN AREAS ON RESOURCES AND ENVIRONMENT Although cities give the illusion of self-sufficiency, efficiency, and independence from natural processes, they are not self-sustaining. To support its people and economic activities, an urban area takes in air, water, energy (see photo on p. 51), food, and other resources, and produces wastes (Figure 9-11).

Most modern cities use resources fairly inefficiently, wasting much more energy than necessary (Figure 3-14) and producing air and water pollution and hazardous and solid waste (Figure 1-18). This results mostly from placing primary emphasis on increasing short-term economic growth, with too little concern for the long-term environmental and economic consequences of such growth.

As urban areas grow, their resource input needs and pollution outputs place increasing stress on distant sources of water, wetlands, estuaries, forests, crop-lands, rangelands, wilderness, and other ecosystems. In the words of Theodore Roszak:

The supercity . . . stretches out tentacles of influence that reach thousands of miles beyond its already sprawling parameters. It sucks every hinterland and wilderness into its technological metabolism. It forces rural populations off the land and replaces them with vast agroindustrial combines. Its investments and technicians bring the roar of the bulldozer and oil derrick into the most uncharted quarters. It runs its conduits of transport and communication, its lines of supply and distribution through the wildest landscapes. It flushes its wastes into every nearby river, lake, and ocean or trucks them away into desert areas. The world becomes its garbage can.

VEGETATION Urban areas generally have a scarcity of trees, shrubs, and other natural vegetation. As one observer remarked, "Cities are places where they cut down the trees and then name the streets after them." This is unfortunate, because urban plants give off oxygen, help cool the air as water evaporates from their leaves, muffle noise, provide wildlife habitats, and give aesthetic pleasure.

Figure 9-11 Typical daily input and output of matter and energy for a major U.S. city of 1 million people.

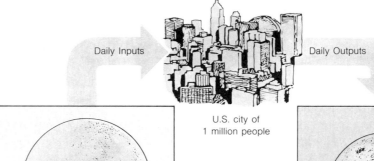

Daily Inputs   U.S. city of 1 million people   Daily Outputs

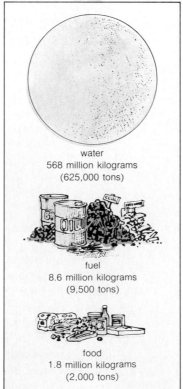

water
568 million kilograms
(625,000 tons)

fuel
8.6 million kilograms
(9,500 tons)

food
1.8 million kilograms
(2,000 tons)

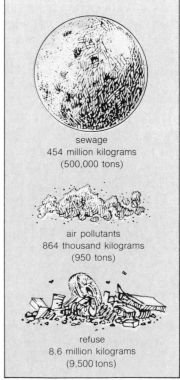

sewage
454 million kilograms
(500,000 tons)

air pollutants
864 thousand kilograms
(950 tons)

refuse
8.6 million kilograms
(9,500 tons)

Cities also produce little of the food they consume. However, individuals can meet some of their food needs by planting community gardens in unused lots and by using window-box and balcony planters and gardens or greenhouses built on the roofs of apartment buildings.

URBAN MICROCLIMATE Urbanization alters local, and sometimes, regional climate. Average temperatures, precipitation, fog, and cloudiness are generally higher in urban areas than in suburbs and nearby rural areas.

The cars, factories, furnaces, lights, and people in cities generate enormous amounts of heat. In the United States, for example, energy use is so high that each of the 254 million Americans is directly and indirectly injecting heat into the atmosphere equal to the heat of one hundred 100-watt light bulbs. The tall buildings, paved streets, and parking areas in cities absorb heat and obstruct cooling winds. Rainfall runs off quickly, so that little standing water is available to cool the air through evaporation.

The effect of this atmospheric heating is felt in large cities, which are typically like islands of heat surrounded by cooler suburban and rural areas. This microclimatic effect is known as an **urban heat island**. This dome of heat also traps pollutants, especially tiny solid particles (suspended particulate matter), creating a **dust dome** above urban areas (Figure 9-12). As a result, concentrations of suspended particulate matter over urban-industrial areas may be 10 to 1,000 times higher than those over rural areas.

If wind speeds increase, the dust dome elongates downwind to form a dust plume, which spreads the city's pollutants to rural areas and other urban areas up to hundreds of miles away. As cities grow and merge into vast urban regions, the heat from the cities forms regional heat islands, which affect regional climates and prevent polluted air from being adequately diluted and cleansed.

WATER, RUNOFF, AND FLOODING As cities grow and their water demands increase, expensive reservoirs and canals must be built and deeper wells must be drilled. This huge transfer of water to urban areas decreases supplies of surface water in rural and wild areas and sometimes depletes underground water faster than it is replenished.

Covering land with buildings, asphalt, and concrete means that precipitation cannot soak into the earth. Instead, it runs off quickly and can overload sewers and storm drains, contributing to water pollution and flooding in cities and downstream areas. Moreover, many cities are built on floodplains, areas subject to natural flooding. Floodplains are considered prime land for urbanization because they are flat, accessible, near rivers, and easy to develop. Because they have greater concentrations of people and buildings, urban areas generally suffer more flood damage than rural areas.

Many of the world's largest cities are in coastal areas. If an enhanced greenhouse effect increases the average atmospheric temperature as projected, a rise in average sea level of even a meter or so could flood many of these cities sometime during the next century.

SOLID WASTE AND AIR AND WATER POLLUTION Urban residents are generally subjected to much higher concentrations of pollutants than people in rural

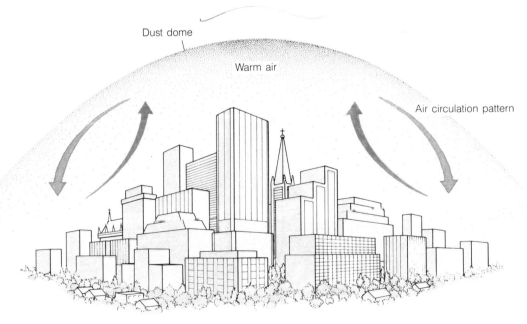

Dust dome

Warm air

Air circulation pattern

Figure 9-12 An urban heat island causes patterns of air circulation that create a dust dome over the city. Winds elongate the dome toward downwind areas. A strong cold front can blow the dome away and lower urban pollution levels.

areas. However, some of the air and water pollutants produced in urban areas are transported by winds and flowing water to other cities and to rural and wild areas.

Litter and garbage are abundant in slums and squatter villages, where solid waste pickup services often don't exist. This invites disease-carrying rodents. An estimated 60% to 80% of rat bites occur in inner-city areas and squatter settlements.

From 50% to 85% by weight of urban air pollution is caused by motor vehicles, depending on the city. Smog is now a virtually unavoidable aspect of urban life in most of the world (Figure 9-5). Other major sources of air pollution, especially in LDCs, are smoky factories and the burning of wood, charcoal, and coal for cooking and heating. In 1988, the World Health Organization warned that nearly 1 billion city dwellers are being exposed to health hazards from air pollutants. Lead is present in paint, plaster, and caulking of the older buildings found in slums. Many children suffer from lead poisoning after ingesting or inhaling particles of these toxic materials.

Air pollution control since 1970 has helped keep levels of some air pollutants from rising in many urban areas in MDCs, but these output controls are now beginning to be overwhelmed by more people, more cars, more factories, and other activities that burn fossil fuels. Air pollution control in most cities in LDCs is lax because of lenient pollution laws, lack of enforcement, corrupt officials, inadequate testing equipment, and a shortage of funds.

Water purification and waste treatment plants and fairly strict pollution control laws have reduced water pollution from some pollutants in most MDCs. In LDCs, however, few cities can afford to build, upgrade, or maintain such systems for their rapidly growing urban populations. For example, most of the 50-year-old sewer system in Cairo, Egypt, was built to serve 2 million, but it is now overwhelmed by almost 12 million people. Less than 16% of India's urban residents are served by even partial sewer systems and water treatment facilities.

About 200 million people in cities in LDCs do not have safe drinking water. Where the poor are forced to use contaminated water, diarrhea, dysentery, typhoid, and cholera are widespread and infant mortality is high. Inner-city dwellers are exposed to much higher than average amounts of lead in their drinking water because water pipes in inner-city housing often contain lead-based pipe or joint cementing compounds. Air pollution is discussed in more detail in Chapter 21, water pollution in Chapter 22, solid waste in Chapter 19, and hazardous waste in Chapter 20.

NOISE POLLUTION   As sound passes through your fluid-filled inner ear, it moves tiny projections (called microvilli) on the surfaces of millions of sensory cells

suspended in the fluid. This motion sets off chemical reactions in your sensory cells that produce electrical impulses, which are sent through the auditory nerve to your brain, where the incoming signal is analyzed and interpreted as sound.

With normal hearing, you can hear sounds with frequencies ranging from 16 to 20,000 cycles per second (20,000 Hertz or Hz). The resilient microvilli lining the surface of your sensory cells can repeatedly bend and then spring back up. However, they can be permanently damaged if loud sounds smash them down too hard or too often or rip them out. Then there is a permanent loss in the ability to hear sounds above a certain frequency. Continued exposure to excessive noise can lead to deafness.

According to the Environmental Protection Agency, nearly half of all Americans, mostly urban residents, are regularly exposed in their neighborhoods and jobs to **noise pollution**—any unwanted, disturbing, or harmful sound that impairs or interferes with hearing, causes stress, hampers concentration and work efficiency, or causes accidents. Every day, 1 of every 10 Americans (25 million people) lives, works, or plays around noise of sufficient duration and intensity to cause some permanent loss of hearing, and that number is rising rapidly. The lives of 40 million more Americans, mostly urban dwellers, are significantly disrupted by noise pollution from cars, trucks, buses, jackhammers, construction equipment, motorcycles, power lawn mowers, vacuum cleaners, sirens, and unwanted loud music.

Industrial workers head the list, with 19 million hearing-damaged people in an industrial work force of 75 million. Millions of people who listen to music at loud levels using home and car stereos, portable stereos ("boom boxes") held close to the ear, and earphones are also damaging their hearing.

To determine harmful levels of noise, sound pressure is measured in decibels (db) with a decibel meter. Sounds also have pitch (frequency), and high-pitched sounds seem louder and more annoying than low-pitched sounds at the same intensity. Normally, sound pressure is weighted for high-pitched sounds to which people are more sensitive and expressed in the decibel-A (dbA) scale, in dbA units, as shown in Table 9-2.

Sound pressure becomes damaging at about 75 dbA and painful at around 120 dbA, and can kill at 180 dbA. Extremely loud sounds above 120 dbA—the level of a loud rock band or earphones at a loud level—can rip out the sound-producing projections (microvilli) on the ear's sensory cells. This can cause nerve signals that the brain interprets as a high-pitched whine or ringing in the ears. A persistent ringing in the ears is called tinnitus, a distressing disorder for which there is no treatment.

Because the db and dbA sound pressure scales are logarithmic, a 10-fold increase in sound pressure occurs with each 10-decibel rise. Thus, a rise from 30 dbA

Table 9-2 Effects of Common Sounds

Example	Sound Pressure (dbA)	Effect from Prolonged Exposure
Jet takeoff (25 meters away*)	150	Eardrum rupture
Aircraft carrier deck	140	
Armored personnel carrier, jet takeoff (100 meters away), earphones at loud level	130	
Thunderclap, textile loom, live rock music, jet takeoff (161 meters away), siren (close range), chain saw, boom stereo systems in cars	120	Human pain threshold
Steel mill, riveting, automobile horn at 1 meter, "boom box" stereo held close to ear	110	
Jet takeoff (305 meters away), subway, outboard motor, power lawn mower, motorcycle at 8 meters, farm tractor, printing plant, jackhammer, garbage truck	100	
Busy urban street, diesel truck, food blender, cotton spinning machine	90	Hearing damage (8 hours), speech interference
Garbage disposal, clothes washer, average factory, freight train at 15 meters, dishwasher, blender	80	Possible hearing damage
Freeway traffic at 15 meters, vacuum cleaner, noisy office or party, TV audio	70	Annoying
Conversation in restaurant, average office, background music, chirping bird	60	Intrusive
Quiet suburb (daytime), conversation in living room	50	Quiet
Library, soft background music	40	
Quiet rural area (nighttime)	30	
Whisper, rustling leaves	20	Very quiet
Breathing	10	
	0	Threshold of hearing

*To convert meters to feet, multiply by 3.3.

(quiet rural area) to 60 dbA (normal restaurant conversation) represents a 1,000-fold increase in sound pressure on the ear.

Studies have shown that by age 30, most Americans have been exposed to enough noise to lose 5 db of their hearing sensitivity and can't hear anything above 16,000 cycles per second (Hz). By age 65, most people have a 40 dbA reduction in hearing sensitivity and can't hear sounds above 8,000 cycles per second (Hz).

Increasing exposure to noise in the United States and in most urban areas throughout the world over the past 40 years has accelerated this normal pattern of hearing loss. Studies have shown that 60% of the incoming students at the University of Tennessee have significant hearing loss in the high frequency range. In effect, these and many other young people are entering their twenties with the hearing capability of people in their sixties. In downtown Cairo, Egypt, noise levels are ten times the limit set by health and safety standards.

Annoyance is usually the first response to excessive noise. When a person is exposed to a sudden noise or a persistent loud noise, adrenaline is released, the heart beats faster, blood pressure rises, and muscles tense. Harmful effects from prolonged exposure to excessive noise include permanent hearing loss, high blood pressure (hypertension), tense muscles, migraine headaches, an increase in cholesterol levels, gastric ulcers, irritability, insomnia, and psychological disorders.

Basically, there are four ways to control noise:

- Modify the way things are made or done so that they produce less noise.

- Shield noise-producing devices or processes.

- Shield workers or other receivers from the noise.

- Move noisy operations or things away from people.

Modern urban societies can reduce excessive noise by building and using quieter industrial machinery, jackhammers, airplane and vehicle motors, vacuum cleaners (which are deliberately made loud because people think quiet models are not picking up much dirt), and other noisy machines. Normally operating newer automobiles today are quieter than older ones. Commercial airliners are 50% to 70% quieter than those of the 1960s and 1970s, but they could be made much quieter.

Noisy factory operations can be totally or partially enclosed by walls. Houses and other buildings can be insulated to reduce sound transfer (and energy waste). Workers can wear protective devices to reduce the amount of noise entering their ears or can work in booths. New airports and flight patterns can be located to minimize people's exposure to noise. Governments can set noise control standards for equipment, and cities can enact and strictly enforce noise control laws.

The control of noise pollution in the United States has lagged behind that in the Soviet Union and many western European and Scandinavian countries. Noise is not effectively controlled in the United States because of industry pressure against establishing stricter workplace noise standards, the virtual elimination of the EPA's budget for noise pollution control since 1981, and lax enforcement of noise control laws.

Federal laws require U.S. employers to use engineering or other controls to adhere to certain noise standards (said to be too high by most hearing specialists), but *only to the extent feasible*. Compliance and enforcement are lax because the law does not specify what is or is not feasible.

Europeans have developed quieter jackhammers, pile drivers, and air compressors that do not cost much more than their noisy counterparts. Most European countries also require that small sheds and tents be used to muffle construction noise.

Some countries reduce the clanging associated with garbage collection by using rubberized collection trucks. Subway systems in Montreal and Mexico City have rubberized wheels to reduce noise. In France, cars are required to have separate highway and city horns, the latter much quieter than the former. What do you think should be done to reduce noise pollution?

Figure 9-13 A typical suburban housing tract in McHenry County, Illinois. Each year, about 526,000 hectares (1.3 million acres) of rural land — mostly cropland — are converted into urban development, rights-of-way, highways, and airports in the United States. This is equivalent in area to building a 1-kilometer (0.6-mile) wide highway stretching from New York City to Los Angeles each year.

Soil Conservation Service

A 1988 research study found that the combination of noise and carbon monoxide may worsen the health effects of noise exposure. This possible synergistic interaction (Section 6-1) means that smokers, commuters, and workers exposed to fairly high levels of carbon monoxide are especially vulnerable to the harmful effects of exposure to excessive noise.

You are being exposed to a sound level high enough to cause permanent hearing damage if you need to raise your voice to be heard above the racket, a noise causes your ears to ring, or nearby speech seems muffled. Prolonged exposure to lower noise levels and occasional loud sounds may not damage your hearing but can greatly increase internal stress. Noise can be reduced in several ways (see Spotlight above).

LAND CONVERSION AND DISRUPTION OF SMALL TOWNS AND RURAL AREAS As urban areas expand, they swallow up rural land, especially flat or gently rolling cropland with well-drained, fertile soil (Figure 9-13). Once farmland is paved over or built upon, it is lost for food production.

The outward expansion of cities creates numerous problems for the once-rural counties, villages, and towns that are disrupted and severely altered in the process. Narrow country roads and town streets become congested with traffic. Town and county health, school, police, fire, water, sanitation, and other services are overwhelmed, and air pollution, crime, noise, congestion, and water pollution increase.

Suburbanized towns and counties must raise taxes to meet the greatly increased demand of new roads, schools, and other public services. This causes land values and property taxes to escalate rapidly. Farmers and others sell their land to developers, for high profits or because they can't pay their higher property taxes.

Some earlier residents and business people profit from the increased jobs and economic growth, and new migrants from central cities escape some of the crime, crowding, high costs, and other problems they faced. However, other long-time residents are forced out because of rising prices, higher property taxes, decreased environmental quality, and disruption of their way of life. If growth is not carefully controlled, which is rare, eventually residents experience the central-city problems they were hoping to avoid.

Uncontrolled urban growth also reduces biological diversity in the name of economic growth. This was summarized by songwriter and singer Joni Mitchell, "They paved paradise and put up a parking lot. They took all the trees and put them in a tree museum. And they charged all the people a dollar and a half just to see them."

9-3 Transportation and Urban Development

TRANSPORTATION OPTIONS The decision to build highways between cities and freeways and beltways within urban areas is probably the most far-reaching land-use, energy policy, and environmental decision a country, state, or city makes. These ways to move people and goods by cars and trucks profoundly shape where we live and work, how we get from place to place, how urban areas can grow (Figure 9-7), how much energy we waste, and how much pollution we produce.

People in urban areas move from one place to another primarily by three types of transportation:

- *individual transit* by private automobile, taxi, motorcycle, motor scooter, bicycle, and walking

- *mass transit* by bus and rail systems (subway, train, and trolley)

- *paratransit* involving car pools, van pools, jitneys or van taxis travelling along fixed routes, and dial-a-ride systems

MOTOR VEHICLES Worldwide, there are about 550 million motor vehicles, consisting of 440 million cars and 110 million trucks—more than a tenfold increase since 1950. If this rate continues, the global motor vehicle population will reach 740 million by the year 2000 and 1.2 billion by 2030.

About 89% of the world's cars are in MDCs, especially in the United States, Australia, Canada, and other affluent countries with large land areas. With only 4.8% of the world's people, the United States has 36% of the world's cars. In America's dispersed cities cars are not just a necessity, they are a way of life. In the United States, the car is now used for about 98% of all urban transportation, 85% of all travel between cities, and 84% of all travel to and from work. Most cars carry only one passenger (Figure 9-14). No wonder British author J. B. Priestley remarked, "In America, the cars have become the people."

By contrast, China and India, with 37% of the world's people, have less than 0.5% of its cars. In LDCs, most people cannot afford a car and travel mostly by foot, bicycle, or motor scooter (Figure 9-15). Only 8% of the people in the world own cars.

The original interstate highway system in the United States was designed primarily to carry motorists

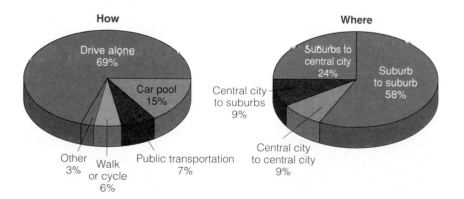

Figure 9-14 How people in the United States go to and from work. Every day, about 86 million Americans drive to and from work alone. In Denver, Houston, Phoenix, and Los Angeles, 90% of the people commute to work by car. (Data from U.S. Census Bureau)

Figure 9-15 Most urban residents in LDCs cannot afford a car and travel by foot, bicycle, motor scooter, or bicycle-powered or horse-drawn rickshaw, as shown in this crowded street in Agra, India. Cycle rickshaws are the taxis of Southeast Asia, and sturdy tricycles serve as light trucks. However, car fleets in LDCs are increasing in size twice as fast as those in MDCs, as people begin making enough money to pursue their dream of owning a car. Death rates from car accidents are high in MDCs, but in LDCs they are 20 times higher, mostly because people walking or riding bicycles in crowded streets are often killed by cars.

from city to city, and its beltways and freeways were built mainly as city bypasses for long-distance travellers. Instead, these highways allowed the rapid growth of suburban areas. The result was the jamming of the beltways by commuters driving within or between suburbs and into the central city, a problem not anticipated by most urban planners. Shopping malls usually located near beltway exchanges have largely replaced most downtown stores in numerous cities and have intensified inner-city decay.

Cars have many advantages and promise us a world of speed, freedom, and convenience. However, societies that have built their transport systems and urban areas around the automobile are learning that the problems created by too much reliance on the car often outweigh its benefits (see Pro/Con on p. 240).

CYCLING AND WALKING Worldwide, there are twice as many bicycles as cars, and annual bicycle sales exceed automobile sales. A bicycle is an inexpensive form of transportation, burns no fossil fuels, produces no pollution (including heat-trapping carbon dioxide), takes few resources to make, and is the most energy-efficient form of transportation (including walking).

In urban traffic, cars and bicycles move at about the same average speed. Using separate bike paths or lanes

running along roads, bicycle riders can make most trips under 8 kilometers (5 miles) faster than a car. Such trips make up 43% of all urban trips in the United States and 75% of the trips in the United Kingdom.

Bicycle accidents can cause injuries, but they are unlikely to kill people unless motor vehicles are involved. Separate bike and pedestrian paths or lanes that are smooth and wide enough, bike and pedestrian overpasses and underpasses at intersections, stoplights at intersections that allow cyclists and pedestrians to proceed before motor vehicles, low speed limits, and speed bumps, trees, or other barriers to slow down motor traffic greatly improve safety for cyclists and pedestrians.

Chinese cities often provide exclusive pedestrian/bicycle lanes and bridges for the country's 300 million cyclists. Many cities in the Netherlands, the former West Germany, Sweden, Denmark, other western European countries, and Japan have taken back the streets for pedestrians, cyclists, and children's play by banning cars in city centers and certain neighborhoods and by traffic calming, in which lower speed limits, bumps, and barriers are used to slow motor traffic in residential and shopping areas. These programs, which treat automobiles as uninvited or slow-moving guests instead of fast-moving bullies in certain areas, have met with great success and are rapidly multiplying. Studies in the United States, the United Kingdom, and the former West Germany have shown that creating automobile-free pedestrian zones in city centers increases local business sales by 25% or more.

For longer trips, secure bike parking spaces can be provided at mass transit stations or buses and trains can be equipped to carry bicycles. Such bike-and-ride systems are widely used in Japan, Germany, the Netherlands (with more bicycle paths than any other country), and Denmark.

In most MDCs, bicycles are used mainly for recreation. They are, however, the principal means of short-distance transportation in Asia, where bicycles transport more people than do automobiles in all other countries combined (Figure 9-15). Some city governments in China have relieved pressure on overcrowded buses by paying workers a monthly allowance for cycling to work. In India, Ghana, and several other countries, city workers receive low-cost loans for buying bicycles.

The bicycle won't replace cars in the dispersed urban areas of the United States, but bicycle use could be significantly increased. (It's ironic that many people in the United States drive their cars to health clubs to ride exercise bicycles.) Between 1977 and 1988, the number of Americans using bicycles to commute to and from work (called the "no-pollute commute") regularly rose from approximately 500,000 to 2.7 million. This is an encouraging trend, but it still represents only 2% of all commuters.

Contrast that with the Netherlands, where bicycle travel makes up 30% of all urban trips and 50% in some Dutch cities. In Japan, 15% of all commuters ride bicycles to work or to commuter-rail stations.

Bicycle use in the United States, especially in areas with a warm climate and flat terrain, could be increased by building well-maintained and well-lit bike paths along major streets and wide shoulders on major highways, providing bicycle lockers and racks at mass transit stations, and establishing bike-carrying buses and trains. Businesses could reduce car use, congestion, air pollution, and the need for parking space by providing secure bike parking areas and showers for employees and shoppers (as required in Palo Alto, California). Motorized tricycles could also be widely used for commuting and shopping.

So far, only a handful of U.S. cities, such as Davis, California (see Case Study on p. 242), and Palo Alto, California, have extensive bike paths and secure bike parking facilities. In Palo Alto, an estimated 14% of the residents who work in town use a bicycle to commute to and from work. New commercial and residential developments must provide secure bicycle storage areas, and new stores must have bike parking racks. New businesses and industries must provide showers so bike commuters can freshen up. City workers get per kilometer cash reimbursements for using bicycles. By 1992, a 27-kilometer (17-mile) bicycle freeway from suburban St. Paul to downtown St. Paul, Minnesota is scheduled to be completed.

MASS TRANSIT Mass transit consists of rail systems (subways, trains, and trolleys) and buses. Although the total population has increased, the number of riders on all forms of mass transit in the United States has dropped drastically: from 24 million in 1945 to about 8 million since 1980, about the same as in 1900. This decline generally parallels the increased use of the automobile and the resulting development of increasingly dispersed cities. These interrelated social changes were stimulated by takeover and dismantlement of the country's efficient trolley system by automobile, oil, and tire companies; cheap gasoline and affordable cars; and use of funds from federal gasoline taxes to build highways. In the United States, mass transit accounts for only 7% of all passenger travel, compared with 15% in the former West Germany and 47% in Japan.

In 1917, all major U.S. cities had efficient and well-functioning trolley or streetcar systems run by electricity. Together with bus systems, they attracted 20 million riders in the 1920s and 24 million in 1945. When I was a high school student in Richmond, Virginia, in the 1940s, I could get to school or anywhere in the city on a streetcar quickly, easily, and cheaply.

By 1950, privately owned streetcar systems in 100 major cities were purchased by a holding company (Na-

tional City Lines) formed by General Motors, Firestone Tire, Standard Oil, Phillips Petroleum, and Mack Truck (which also made buses) and were dismantled to increase sales of buses and cars. The courts found the companies guilty of conspiracy to eliminate about 90% of the country's light-rail system, but the damage had already been done. The corporate executive officers responsible were fined $1 each, and each company paid a fine of $5,000, less than the profit returned from replacing a single street car with a bus. General Motors alone had made $25 million in additional bus and car sales by the time the case was tried.

Another factor helping create the car culture in the United States was the huge government investment in 4.8 million kilometers (3 million miles) of roads and a 64,400-kilometer (40,000-mile) interstate highway system. Only one-tenth of the federal gasoline tax goes to mass transit, with the rest going to building highways. This encourages states and cities to invest in highways instead of in mass transit.

The federal tax code also discriminates against mass transit and those who cycle or walk to work. In the United States, only 10% of commuting employees pay for parking, mainly because employers can deduct the expense of providing parking for workers from their taxes. This gives auto commuters a tax-free fringe benefit worth $200 to $400 a month in major cities. On the other hand, employers get only a $15 a month tax write-off for employees who use public transit and nothing for those who walk or ride a bicycle to work. As long as automobile owners are given such inducements, they stay in their cars instead of using mass transit, cycling, or walking to get to and from work.

Tax benefits for company cars is another common subsidy that encourages auto use. Much-higher government subsidies for big trucks also help discourage the hauling of freight by more energy-efficient railroads.

The key to breaking out of this cycle is to make drivers pay directly for most of the true costs of auto use. Federal, state, and local government auto subsidies in the United States amount to $300 billion to $500 billion a year, an average of $2,000 to $3,300 per vehicle. Taxpayers (drivers and nondrivers) foot this bill but don't relate higher federal, state, and local taxes to car use by themselves or others. If automobile users had to pay these costs of driving cars directly in the form of a gasoline tax, they would be paying $4.50 to $7.50 in taxes for each gallon of gasoline. Direct costs of cars could also be made more visible by greatly increasing registration and license fees and by levying taxes based on fuel economy and on emission of pollutants. Making people pay directly for these and other costs of automobile use — estimated at about $1 a mile — would lead to a dramatic increase in the use of fuel-efficient cars, mass transit (funded by the increased tax revenue), and bicycles and would make cities more compact, energy-efficient, and livable.

The automobile has many advantages. Above all, it offers people freedom to go where they want to go, when they want to go there. The basic purpose of a motor vehicle is to get one from point A to point B as cheaply, quickly, and safely as possible. However, to most people, cars are also personal fantasy machines that serve as symbols of power, success, speed, excitement, sexiness, spontaneity, and adventure.

In addition, much of the world's economy is built on producing motor vehicles and supplying roads, services, and repairs for those vehicles. Half of the world's paychecks and resource use are auto related.

In the United States, one of every six dollars spent and one of every six nonfarm jobs are connected to the automobile or related industries, such as oil, steel, rubber, plastics, automobile services, and highway construction. This industrial complex accounts for 20% of the annual GNP and provides about 18% of all federal taxes. It also is the world's largest consumer of energy and raw materials.

In spite of their advantages, motor vehicles have many harmful effects on human lives and on air, water, land, and wildlife resources. The automobile may be the most destructive machine ever invented. Though we tend to deny it, riding in cars is one of the most dangerous things we do in our daily lives.

Since 1885, when Karl Benz built the first automobile, almost 18 million people have been killed by motor vehicles. Every year, cars and trucks worldwide kill an average of 250,000 people—as many as were killed in the atomic bomb attacks on Hiroshima and Nagasaki—and injure or permanently disable 10 million more. Half of the world's people will be involved in an auto accident at some time during their lives.

Each year in the United States, motor vehicle accidents kill around 49,000 people—more than from all other accidental deaths combined—and seriously injure at least 300,000. Since the automobile was introduced, almost 3 million Americans have been killed on the highways—about twice the number of Americans killed on the battlefield in all U.S. wars. In addition to the tragic loss of life, these accidents cost American society about $60 billion annually in lost income and in insurance, administrative, and legal expenses.

By providing almost unlimited mobility, automobiles and highways have been the biggest factor leading to urban sprawl in the United States and other countries with large livable land areas. This dispersal of cities has made it increasingly difficult for subways, trolleys, and buses to be economically feasible alternatives to the private car.

Worldwide, at least a third of urban land is devoted to roads and parking. Half the land in an average American city is used for cars, prompting urban expert Lewis Mumford to suggest that the U.S. national flower should be the concrete cloverleaf.

Los Angeles is a global symbol of urban sprawl built around a vast network of freeways. An estimated one-third of the city's total metropolitan area and two-thirds of its downtown area are devoted to roads, parking lots, gasoline stations, and other automobile-related uses. Each day, its network of streets and freeways is crowded with more than 5 million vehicles, which are

RAIL SYSTEMS   Rail systems are usually operated by electric engines and fall into four categories:

- *rapid rail* (also called the underground, tube, metro, or subway), which operates on exclusive rights-of-way in tunnels or on elevated tracks

- *suburban or regional trains*, which connect the central city with surrounding areas or provide transportation between major cities in a region (see Spotlight on p. 243)

- *streetcars (or trams)*, which move on regular streets with other traffic

- *light rail (or trolleys)* — more modern versions of streetcars, which can run either with other traffic or on exclusive rights-of way.

Rapid-rail and suburban train systems have the greatest capacity to transport large numbers of people at high speed, but they are useful only where many people live along a narrow corridor and can easily reach properly spaced stations.

In recent years, some U.S. cities have built successful rapid-rail systems. Since Atlanta's system opened in 1979, it has steadily added riders and opened new stations. Pittsburgh has cleaner air and renewed business vitality, partly because of its new subway system, which opened in 1985.

The Metro heavy-rail system in Washington, D.C., carries almost 500,000 riders a day. However, this very expensive system doesn't reach far enough into the suburbs to allow many people this option instead of driving to work on the city's heavily congested streets. Congress provides an annual $250 million subsidy for operation of the system, equal to nearly half the mass transit budget for the entire country. Without this subsidy, fares would probably double and the system might lose riders.

One of the world's most successful new subway

responsible for 85% of both the air pollution and the noise in this urban area. At peak traffic periods, it can take three hours to drive only 32 kilometers (20 miles). If current trends continue, the average speed on its freeway system is expected to fall to 18 kilometers (11 miles) per hour by 2010.

Instead of reducing automobile congestion, the construction of roads has encouraged more automobiles and travel, causing even more congestion or gridlock. As economist Robert Samuelson put it, "Cars expand to fill available concrete." In 1975, some 40% of U.S. rush hour traffic was rated as congested. By 1990, that figure had risen to 77%.

If present trends continue, U.S. motorists will spend an average of two years of their lifetimes in traffic jams. Companies are losing billions of dollars because many of their employees can't get to work on time or arrive at work tired and irritated.

In 1907, the average speed of horse-drawn vehicles through the borough of Manhattan was 18.5 kilometers (11.5 miles) per hour. Today, cars and trucks with the potential power of 100 to 300 horses creep along Manhattan streets at an average speed of 8 kilometers (5 miles) per hour. In London, average auto speeds are about 13 kilometers (8 miles) per hour, and they are even lower in Paris and in Tokyo, where everyday traffic is called *tsukin jigoku*, or commuting hell.

Streets that used to be for people are now for cars. Pedestrians and people riding bicycles in the streets are subjected to noise, pollution, stress, and danger (Figure 9-15).

Motor vehicles are the largest source of air pollution, producing a haze of smog over the world's cities (Figure 9-5). In the United States, they produce at least 50% of the country's air pollution, even though U.S. emission standards are as strict as any in the world.

Worldwide, motor vehicles account for 13% of the input of the primary greenhouse gas, carbon dioxide, into the atmosphere. In the United States, they account for almost 25% of the country's CO_2 emissions (the highest in the world) and 13% of the emissions of chlorofluorocarbons that act as greenhouse gases and also deplete life-sustaining ozone in the stratosphere.

Motor vehicle use is also responsible for water pollution from oil spills, gasoline spills, leakage and dumping of used engine oil, and contamination of underground drinking water from leaking underground oil and gasoline storage tanks. Highway runoff of oil, gasoline, and salt (used to deice roads) also pollutes waterways.

Motor vehicles are the biggest cause of oil addiction in MDCs, and to a growing extent in LDCs (see Case Study on p. 15). Motor vehicles account for 63% of the oil used in the United States (up from 50% in 1973), 51% in the Soviet Union, 50% in LDCs, 40% in western Europe, and 25% in Japan. This makes the economies of countries dependent on oil imports vulnerable to oil price hikes and increases their foreign trade deficits.

Oil addiction, based mostly on addiction to energy-inefficient gasoline-powered vehicles, also increases chances of wars as the United States and other countries attempt to protect oil supplies in the oil-rich but volatile Middle East. What do you think should be done?

systems is in Hong Kong. Fare revenues on this $4.2-billion system exceed operating costs by 50%, even though fares for most trips range from 25 cents to 65 cents. Several factors contribute to the success of this system. Hong Kong is a narrow, densely packed city located between the ocean and nearby mountains, making it ideal for a heavy-rail system running through a heavily populated corridor. Most people live in high-rise apartment buildings, and half of the population can walk to a subway station in five minutes. Also, most people are dependent on public transportation because only 1 in 30 owns a car.

Over the past two decades, 21 large cities in LDCs, including Cairo, Shanghai, and Mexico City, have built metro systems. These systems, which are often used as showcases of modernization, have improved transport service in dense city centers, but often at at great cost. Critics believe that this money could have been better spent to expand and modernize bus systems that could carry many more people at a much lower cost.

In recent years, American cities such as San Diego (see Case Study on p. 243), Sacramento, San Jose, Buffalo, and Portland (Oregon), and Canadian cities such as Toronto, Edmonton, and Calgary have built light-rail systems. A light-rail line costs about one-tenth as much to build per kilometer as a highway or a heavy-rail system.

Although the start-up cost of a light-rail system is higher than for a bus system carrying a comparable number of passengers, a trolley system's operating costs are much lower. By linking cars together, a light-rail system can carry up to 400 people with one driver, compared with 40 to 50 passengers on a bus. Trolleys are also cleaner and quieter than buses.

BUSES AND PARATRANSIT Buses are cheaper and more flexible than rail systems. They can be routed to almost any area in widely dispersed cities and rerouted overnight to meet changing transportation patterns.

Davis, California (Figure 9-16) has ample sunshine, a flat terrain, and about 38,000 people. Its citizens and elected officials have committed themselves to making it an ecologically sustainable city.

The city's building codes encourage the use of solar energy to provide space heating and hot water, and require all new homes to meet high standards of energy efficiency. When any existing home is sold, it must be inspected and the buyer must bring it up to the energy conservation standards for new homes. The community also has a master plan for planting deciduous trees, which provide shade and reduce heat gain in the summer and allow solar gain during the winter.

The city has adopted several policies that discourage the use of automobiles and encourage the use of bicycles. Some streets are closed to automobiles, and people are encouraged to work at home.

A number of bicycle paths and lanes have been built, and some city employees are given bikes (Figure 9-17). Any new housing tract must have a separate bicycle lane. As a result, 28,000 bikes account for 40% of all in-city transportation and much less land is needed for parking spaces. This heavy dependence on the bicycle is made possible by the city's warm climate and flat terrain.

Davis also limits the type and rate of growth and development and maintains a mix of homes for people with low, medium, and high incomes. Development of the fertile farmland surrounding the city for residential or commercial use is restricted. What things are being done to make the area where you live more sustainable?

Figure 9-17 Bicyclists in Davis, California.

University of California, Davis

Figure 9-16 Where is Davis, California?

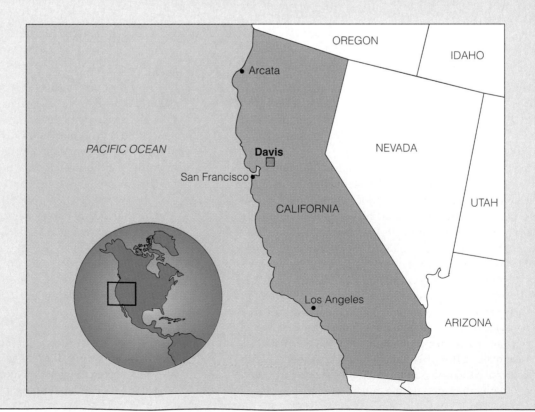

SPOTLIGHT **High-Speed Regional Train Systems**

Throughout much of western Europe and Japan, a new generation of streamlined, comfortable, and low-polluting bullet-train, or high-speed rail (HSR), lines are being developed for medium-distance travel between cities within a region. These regional trains run on new or upgraded existing tracks and can travel at speeds up to 300 kilometers (186 miles) per hour. Journeys between major cities within a region on these supertrains are smooth and cheaper than an airplane.

In Japan, such trains, which began operating in 1964, have helped build the Tokyo-to-Osaka stretch into the world's largest megalopolis. These trains have carried over 2.5 billion passengers without a single injury or fatality and depart and arrive on schedule 99% of the time. However, these systems are expensive to run and maintain and must operate along heavily used transportation routes to be profitable.

A future alternative to the automobile and the airplane for medium-distance travel between cities is the magnetic-levitation (MAGLEV) train, which uses powerful superconducting electromagnets to suspend the train on a cushion of air slightly above a guideline. Such trains zoom along without friction at speeds up to 499 kilometers (310 miles) per hour and can carry 150 to 1,000 passengers, depending on the number of cars used. Germany and Japan have prototypes in operation that can travel more than 322 kilometers (200 miles) per hour.

If a network regional MAGLEV system was developed in the United States over the next 30 years, it could replace the airplane, bus, and private car for most medium-distance travel between major American cities. Such systems could use the airport of a major metropolitan area as a hub to provide rapid transportation to regional cities.

CASE STUDY **San Diego's Successful Trolley System**

In the United States, the light-rail approach got its biggest boost in recent years from the remarkable success of San Diego's "Tijuana Trolley," running between downtown San Diego and the Mexican border city of Tijuana. Two new routes have been added since the system opened in 1981, and a 182-kilometer (113-mile) system is envisioned by the year 2000.

This system was funded by California state sales tax revenue and built at a cost per kilometer less than one-fourth that of San Francisco's subway system (BART). Ridership has increased at an average annual rate of more than 12% since 1983.

Fares pay 92% of the system's operating costs, compared with an average of 48% for all public transportation. System managers keep operating costs low by hiring a nonunion work force (possible because no federal funds were involved) and reducing the number of workers by collecting fares on the honor system. More than 12 other U.S. cities are building trolley systems.

Bus systems also require less capital and have lower operating costs than heavy-rail systems.

The best and most energy-efficient approach is the use of express buses that run in lanes restricted to buses, van pools, and car pools. Coupling express buses with park-and-ride stops in suburban areas is the cheapest and most energy-efficient mass transportation system for getting people to and from work and major shopping and entertainment centers.

However, by offering low fares to attract riders, bus systems usually lose money. To make up for losses, bus companies tend to cut service and maintenance and seek federal, state, and local subsidies. Unless they operate in separate express lanes, buses get caught up in traffic congestion.

Diesel buses, especially in LDCs, emit large quan-

tities of pollutants, although the number of cars needed to carry an equivalent number of passengers would create more air pollution. The technology exists to sharply reduce such emissions, and buses can also run on less-polluting fuels, such as natural gas (used in China and Brazil) and propane (used in parts of Europe).

Because full-sized buses are cost-effective only when full, they are sometimes supplemented by car pools, van pools, jitneys, and dial-a-ride systems. These paratransit systems are a practical solution to some of the transportation problems of today's dispersed urban areas.

Dial-a-ride systems operate in an increasing number of American cities. Passengers call for a van, minibus, or tax-subsidized taxi, which comes by to pick them up at their doorstep, usually in 20 to 50 minutes. Two-way radios and computerized routing can increase the efficiency of these systems. Dial-a-ride systems are fairly expensive to operate and are the most inefficient transportation system in terms of total energy costs per passenger kilometer, explaining why they are not in widespread use.

In cities such as Mexico City, Caracas, and Cairo, large fleets of jitneys—small vans or minibuses that travel relatively fixed routes but stop on demand—carry millions of passengers each day. Laws banning jitney service in the United States were repealed in 1979, despite objections by taxi and transit companies. Since then, privately owned jitney service has flourished in San Diego, San Francisco, and Los Angeles and may spread to other cities.

9-4 Urban Land-Use Planning and Control

CONVENTIONAL LAND-USE PLANNING AND URBAN DECAY Most urban areas and some rural areas use some form of **land-use planning** to decide the best present and future use of each parcel of land in the area. Land-use planning involves mapping out suitable locations for houses, industries, businesses, open space, parks, roads, water lines, sewer lines, reservoirs, hospitals, schools, waste treatment plants, and so on. Then zoning regulations or other devices are used to control how land is used.

Because land is such a valuable economic resource, land-use planning is a complex and controversial process involving competing values and intense power struggles. Most land-use planning is based on the assumption that substantial future growth in population and economic development in an area is good and should be encouraged, regardless of the environmental and other consequences. Typically, this leads to uncontrolled or poorly controlled urban growth and sprawl, which lies at the root of many urban and environmental problems.

A major reason for allowing this usually destructive process is that 90% of the revenue that local governments use to provide schools, roads, police and fire protection, public water and sewer systems, welfare services, and other obligations comes from *property taxes*, taxes on all buildings and property proportional to their economic values. When an area is economically developed, property values and local tax revenues go up.

However, the costs of providing more services to accommodate population and economic growth often exceed the revenue from increased property values. Because local governments can rarely raise property taxes enough to meet expanding needs, they often try to raise more money by promoting further economic growth. Typically, the long-term result is a treadmill of economic growth eventually leading to environmental decay. Then, businesses and residents move away, decreasing the tax base, reducing tax income, and causing further environmental and social decay as governments are forced to cut the quantity and quality of services or raise the tax rate (which drives more people away and worsens the situation).

ECOLOGICAL LAND-USE PLANNING Environmentalists challenge the "all-growth-is-good" dogma that is the basis of most land-use planning. They urge communities to use comprehensive, regional *ecological land-use planning*, in which all major variables are considered and integrated into a model designed to anticipate present and future needs and problems and propose solutions for an entire region (see Spotlight on p. 245). Emphasis is placed on blending economics and ecology to control the nature and speed of urban and suburban growth in ways that can minimize environmental degradation, pollution, and social decay.

Ecological land-use planning sounds good on paper, but it is not widely used for several reasons:

- Land is a valuable economic resource and a potential source of increased tax revenue from rising property taxes, so there is intense pressure by economically and politically powerful people to develop urban land for short-term economic gain, with little regard for long-term ecological and economic losses.

- Local officials seeking election every few years usually focus on short-term rather than long-term problems and can often be influenced by economically powerful developers.

- Officials are unwilling to pay for costly ecological land-use planning and implementation, even though a well-designed plan can prevent or ease many urban problems and save money in the long run.

- It's difficult to get municipalities in the same general area to cooperate in planning efforts. Thus, an ecologically sound development plan in one area may be disrupted by unsound development in nearby areas.

METHODS OF LAND-USE CONTROL Once a plan is developed, governments control the uses of various parcels of land by legal and economic methods. The most widely used approach is **zoning**, in which various parcels of land are designated for certain uses. Principal categories include commercial (various categories), residential (various categories), industrial, utilities, transport, recreation (parks and forest preserves), bodies of water, floodplains, and wildlife preserves. Zoning can be used to protect areas from certain types of development and to control growth.

Zoning is useful, but it can be influenced or modified by developers because local governments depend on property taxes for revenue. Thus, zoning often favors high-priced housing and factories, hotels, and other businesses. Zoning can also be too strict and discourage use of innovative approaches to solving urban problems.

In addition to zoning, local governments can control the rate of growth and development of urban areas by limiting the number of building permits, sewer hookups, roads, and other services. State and federal governments can take any of the following measures to protect cropland, forestland, wetlands, and other nonurban lands near expanding urban areas from degradation and ecologically unsound development:

- Give tax breaks to landowners who agree to use land only for specified purposes, such as agriculture, wilderness, wildlife habitat, or nondestructive forms of recreation. Such agreements are called *conservation easements*.

- Tax land on the basis of its use as agricultural land or forestland rather than its fair market value based on its economically highest potential use. This prevents farmers and other landowners from being forced to sell land to pay their tax bills.

- Use *land trusts* to buy and protect ecologically valuable land. A group raises money to buy a certain plot of land and put it into an open space trust, a legal designation that prevents the land from being developed. Such purchases can be made by private groups such as the Nature Conservancy, the Audubon Society, and local and regional nonprofit, tax-exempt, charitable organizations, as well as by public agencies.

- Purchase land development rights that restrict the way land can be used (for example, to preserve prime farmland near cities).

- Require environmental impact analysis for proposed private and public projects such as roads, industrial parks, shopping centers, and suburban developments; cancel harmful projects unless they are revised to minimize harmful environmental impacts.

- Give subsidies to farmers for taking highly erodible cropland out of production, or eliminate subsidies for farmers who farm such land or who convert wetlands to cropland.

9-5 Making Urban Areas More Livable and Sustainable

TAKING BACK THE CITIES FOR PEOPLE Most current patterns of urban development are unnecessarily stressful to natural systems and to people. Instead of being developed primarily to meet the physical needs of cars, urban areas should be designed to meet the basic needs of people: diversity, pleasant surroundings, and economic and physical security.

These needs are most likely to be met when citizens participate in planning and design. Emphasis needs to be placed on giving pedestrians and cyclists safe access to points throughout cities and integrating cycling and walking with efficient public transport.

REPAIRING EXISTING CITIES As philosopher-longshoreman Eric Hoffer observed, "History shows that the level achieved by a civilization can be measured by the degree to which it performs maintenance." America's older cities have enormous maintenance and

---

SPOTLIGHT Steps in Ecological Land-Use Planning

1. *Make an environmental and social inventory.* Experts make a survey of geologic factors (such as soil type, fault lines, floodplains, and water availability), ecological factors (forest types and quality, wildlife habitats, stream quality, and pollution), economic factors (housing, transportation, utilities, and industrial development), and health and social factors (disease and crime rates, ethnic distribution, and illiteracy).

2. *Determine goals and their relative importance.* Experts, public officials, and the general public decide on goals and rank them in order of importance. For example, is the primary goal to encourage or to discourage further economic development and population growth? To preserve prime cropland from development? To reduce soil erosion?

3. *Develop individual and composite maps.* Data for each factor obtained in step 1 are plotted on separate transparent plastic maps. The transparencies are then superimposed on one another or combined by computer to give three composite maps — one each for geological, ecological, and socioeconomic factors.

4. *Develop a master composite.* The three composite maps are combined to form a master composite, which shows how the variables interact and indicates the suitability of various areas for different types of land use.

5. *Develop a master plan.* The master composite (or a series of alternative master composites) is evaluated by experts, public officials, and the general public, and a final master plan is drawn up and approved.

6. *Implement the master plan.* The plan is set in motion and monitored by the appropriate governmental, legal, environmental, and social agencies.

---

repair problems — most of them aggravated by decades of neglect.

Most of the sewers in New Orleans, some of which were purchased secondhand from Philadelphia in 1896, need replacement. When it rains in Chicago, sewage backs up into basements of about one-fourth of the homes. An estimated 46% of Boston's water supply and 25% of Pittsburgh's are lost through leaky pipes.

Thirty-eight percent of America's bridges (55% to 68% in 11 states) are in unsafe condition because of structural problems or designs that no longer meet safety standards for the heavy traffic loads they receive.

Figure 9-18 The Riverwalk area in downtown San Antonio, Texas, which took 30 years to develop, is popular with the city's tourists and convention-goers.

About 62% of the paved highways in the United States need repairs, and 13% are in very poor condition.

Maintenance, repair, and replacement of existing U.S. bridges, roads, mass transit systems, water supply systems, sewers, and sewage treatment plants during the 1990s could cost a staggering $1.2 trillion or more—an average expenditure of $1.4 million a minute during the next ten years. These huge bills from neglect are coming due in a time of record budget deficits, cutbacks in federal funds for building and maintaining public works, and strong citizen opposition to increases in federal, state, and local taxes.

REVITALIZING EXISTING CITIES Billions of dollars have been spent in decaying downtown areas to build new civic centers, museums, office buildings, parking garages, high-rise luxury hotels, and shopping centers. Montreal, Canada, has built a large underground mall or "minicity" serviced by its subway system. Pittsburgh has rejuvenated its central-city area. Boston, Baltimore, San Francisco, Long Beach (California), Norfolk (Virginia), and New Orleans have revitalized their urban waterfront areas. San Antonio, Texas, has improved its environment by planting trees and building shops along a river canal (Figure 9-18).

These projects add beauty, preserve and reuse historic buildings, and help revive downtown areas. They provide white-collar jobs for suburbanites and generally safe and secure shopping and cultural facilities for urban residents and tourists. Downtown revitalization can indirectly benefit the poor by providing additional tax revenues. However, such projects are of little direct benefit to the poor and sometimes displace much-needed low-cost housing.

In many U.S. cities, older neighborhoods are being revitalized by middle- and high-income residents who buy run-down houses at low prices, renovate them, and either live in them or sell them at high prices—a process called *gentrification*. This benefits the city economically by increasing property tax values and slowing the flight of businesses and people to the suburbs, but it also displaces low-income residents.

A number of cities have set up *urban homesteading* programs to help middle- and low-income people purchase houses and apartment buildings abandoned by their owners or acquired by a city because of failure to pay taxes. The city sells these buildings to individuals or to cooperatives of low-income renters for $1 to $100 or provides buyers with low-interest, long-term loans. The new owners must agree to renovate the buildings and live in them for at least three years. This approach has been particularly successful in Wilmington (Delaware), Detroit, and Baltimore.

REVITALIZING PUBLIC HOUSING America is increasingly becoming a nation of housing haves and have-nots. Of the 13 million families with incomes under $10,000 a year, nearly half pay more than 50% of their income for housing. Many middle-income families cannot afford to buy a home.

Federal support for subsidized low-income housing was slashed 85% between 1981 and 1990. During that period, 2.5 million units of low-income housing and single-room occupancy hotels were torn down, abandoned, or converted into high-rent apartments, luxury condominiums, and office buildings. By 2003, the gap between the number of people needing low-income housing and the number of available units is expected to be 7.8 million.

One way to help some of the poor would be to provide aid for low-income tenants to renovate and manage many of the country's 1.3 million public housing units and the 70,000 abandoned units (see Individuals Matter at right). The government could also provide more aid and lower interest rates to help first-time low- and middle-income families buy homes.

CREATING URBAN ENTERPRISE ZONES Some analysts call for increased federal aid to help revitalize poor urban areas. Others argue that federal aid is often wasted because it is controlled by distant bureaucrats who have little knowledge of the needs of local people. These analysts favor a program in which federal, state, and local tax breaks and other benefits are given to private companies that locate or expand in economically depressed urban areas, hire the unemployed or disadvantaged, or build or rehabilitate low-income housing. Neighborhoods that qualify for such tax breaks are called *urban enterprise zones*.

Since 1978, urban enterprise zones have been established in 80 American cities. Results have been mixed. Some zones have been successful and some have not. In most cases, it is difficult to tell whether an increase in jobs is due to normal economic growth or the lure of the zone. Some companies lay off workers in one part of an urban area and hire new ones in an enterprise zone to qualify for tax breaks. Moreover, tax breaks rarely are enough to attract businesses to the worst urban neighborhoods with high crime rates and few trained workers.

PRESERVING URBAN OPEN SPACE Some cities have had the foresight to preserve moderate amounts of open space in the form of municipal parks. Central Park in New York City (Figure 9-19), Golden Gate Park in San Francisco, Fairmont Park in Philadelphia, and Lake Front Park in Chicago are examples of large urban parks in the United States.

Unfortunately, older cities that did not plan for such parks early in their development have little or no chance of getting them now. However, as newer cities expand, they can develop large and medium-size parks.

Another way to provide open space and control urban growth is to surround a large city with a *greenbelt*—an open area used for recreation, sustainable forestry, or other nondestructive uses (Figure 9-20). Satellite towns can be built outside the belt.

Since World War II, the typical pattern of suburban housing development in the United States has been to bulldoze a tract of woods or farmland and build rows

INDIVIDUALS MATTER Tenant-Owned Public Housing

In 1981, the 3,500 tenants of the Kenilworth-Parkside public housing project in Washington, D.C., lived in a crime-ridden, drug-infested neighborhood. For three years, they had no heat or hot water and the roofs of their apartments were caving in. Today, residents have turned the once-squalid project into safe, well-kept buildings.

Things began turning around in 1982, when Kimi Gray, an unemployed welfare mother of five, persuaded housing authorities to let her and other tenants run the project. Gray was also able to get $23 million in federal aid for renovation of all 464 units. Under her leadership, the tenants evicted drug dealers, and at least one member of each family was required to take six weeks of training in home repairs, pest control, and personal budgeting. Residents took turns as hall and building captains.

Within a few years, residents had cleaned up the area, made repairs, and restored utilities. Crime dropped sharply, rent collections rose 77%, administrative costs were reduced by 66%, welfare dependency fell from 85% to 2%, and teenage pregnancies were cut in half.

With aid from the federal government, the tenants have established a day-care center (only for tenants who are working or actively looking for work), several businesses, a treatment center for residents addicted to alcohol or other drugs, and a van shuttle that takes residents to jobs in the suburbs. The tenant-run management corporation now employs more than 100 people, 80% of them residents.

The government sold the project to the management corporation for $1. In 1990, tenants were allowed to apply money they formerly paid in rent to buy their units at discounted prices.

This project required $23 million in federal aid. In the long run, the money will be recovered by the lower administrative costs (already saving the government $5.7 million in operating expenses), elimination of most welfare payments, and taxes paid by tenants who now have jobs. Kimi Gray, who now has a college degree, has successfully trained tenant leaders in St. Louis, in Montgomery County, Maryland, and in other urban areas.

of houses, usually standard houses on standard lots (Figure 9-10). Many of these developments and their streets are named after the trees and wildlife they displaced: Oak Lane, Cedar Drive, Pheasant Run, Fox Fields. In recent years, builders have made increased use of a new pattern, known as *cluster development*,

Figure 9-19 Central Park in New York City.

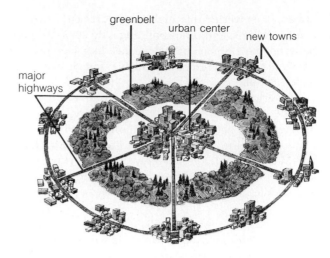

Figure 9-20 Use of a greenbelt around a large city to control urban growth and provide open space for recreation and other nondestructive uses. Satellite towns are sometimes built outside the belt. This approach has been used in London, England. American cities attempting to preserve greenbelts, with varying degrees of success, include Seattle, Boston, San Francisco, Cincinnati, and Boulder, Colorado. Stockholm, Sweden, is ringed with satellite communities of 25,000 to 50,000 people each, with shops, apartments, and offices from which people have quick access to train stations. Rail systems transport people around the periphery or into the central city.

which provides areas of open space within housing developments (Figure 9-21).

The most overlooked open spaces are the small strips and odd-shaped patches of unused land that dot urban areas. Some cities have converted abandoned railroad track lines and dry creek beds into bicycle, hiking, and jogging paths (Figure 9-22).

Abandoned lots can be developed as community gardens, small plazas, and vest-pocket parks. Research by William H. Whyte, director of the Street Life Project in New York City, has shown that the most widely used small urban plazas and miniparks are located just a few steps from busy streets so that people can easily see and enter them. Ideally, the people who will use these spaces should be involved in their design, construction, and management. Even for the smallest parks, systems must be set up for daily maintenance and security.

BUILDING NEW CITIES AND TOWNS Most urban problems will have to be solved in existing cities. However, we could ease some of these problems by building new cities and towns to take the pressure off overpopulated and stressed urban areas.

Great Britain has built 16 new towns and is building 15 more. New towns have also been built in Singapore, Hong Kong, Finland, Sweden, France, the Netherlands, Venezuela, Brazil, and the United States. There are three types: *satellite towns*, located fairly close to an existing large city (Figure 9-20); *freestanding new towns*, located far from any major city; and *in-town new towns*, located in existing urban areas. Typically, new towns are designed for populations of 20,000 to 100,000 people (see Case Study on p. 249).

New towns rarely succeed without enormous financial support from the government. Some don't succeed even then, primarily because of poor planning and management. In 1971, the Department of Housing and Urban Development (HUD) provided more than $300 million in federally guaranteed loans for developers to build 13 new towns in the United States. By 1980, HUD had to take title to 9 of those projects, which had gone bankrupt, and HUD no longer funds new towns.

Private developers of new towns must put up large amounts of money to buy the land and install facilities, and must pay heavy taxes and interest charges for decades before they see profit. In the United States, two privately developed new towns—Reston, Virginia, and Columbia, Maryland—have been in financial difficulty since they were established about two decades ago. However, their situations are gradually improving.

Recently, a successful new town called Las Colinas has been built 8 kilometers (5 miles) from the Dallas–Fort Worth Airport on land that was once a ranch. The community is built around an urban center, with a lake and water taxis to carry passengers between buildings. The town is laced with greenbelts and open spaces to separate high-rise office buildings, warehouses, and residential buildings. People working in high-rise buildings park their cars outside the core and take a computer-controlled personal transit system to their offices.

MAKING URBAN AREAS MORE LIVABLE AND SUSTAINABLE An important goal in coming decades should be to make existing and new urban areas more self-reliant, sustainable, and enjoyable places to live (see Case Study on p. 249). Four principal forces will

Figure 9-21 Conventional and cluster developments as they would appear if constructed on the same land area. With cluster development, houses, town houses, condominiums, and two-to-six-story apartments are built on only part of the tract. The rest, typically 30% of the area, is left as open space, parks, and cycling and walking paths. Parking spaces and garages can also be clustered so that cars are not used within residential areas, with access only by walking and bike paths or small electric or methane-powered golf carts.

Figure 9-22 Joggers, walkers, and cyclists using the Sugar River Trail in central Wisconsin, which at one time was a railroad track. U.S. railroad companies are now abandoning nearly 6,400 kilometers (4,000 miles) of track a year. In Seattle, 8,000 people walk, bike, roller-skate, and run every day on one of the 150 "rail trails" in the United States.

CASE STUDY Tapiola, Finland

Tapiola, Finland, a satellite new town not far from Helsinki, has an international reputation for ecological design, beauty, and a high quality of life for its residents. Designed in 1951, it is being built gradually in seven sections, with an ultimate projected population of 80,000. Today, many of its 50,000 residents work in Helsinki, but the long-range goal is industrial and commercial independence.

Tapiola is divided into several villages separated by greenbelts. Each village consists of several neighborhoods clustered around a shopping and cultural center that can be reached by foot. Playgrounds and parks radiate from this center, and walkways lead to the various residential neighborhoods.

Each neighborhood has a social center and contains a mix of about 20% high-rise apartments and 80% single-family houses nestled among lush evergreen forests and rocky hills. Housing is not segregated by income. Because housing is clustered, more land is available for open space, recreation areas, and parks.

Industrial building and factories, with strict pollution controls, are sited away from residential areas and screened by vegetation to reduce noise and visual pollution, but they are close enough so people can walk or bicycle to work. Finland plans to build six more satellite towns around Helsinki.

shape the future of "ecocity" or "green" urban areas: improvements in energy efficiency, less reliance on the automobile, reduction of the environmental impacts of urban life, and more emphasis on improving life in rural areas and small towns as the best way to reduce the current rapid rural-to-urban migration in LDCs and the resulting degradation of urban life.

As the era of cheap oil and gasoline comes to a close over the next few decades, urban sprawl and car culture cities are likely to become unaffordable and unsustainable luxuries. Cities are likely to become more compact and less dependent on the automobile. In ecologically sustainable cities, people would walk or use a bicycle or tricycle for most short trips and walk or bike to bus, metro, or trolley stops for longer urban trips. Rapid rail transport between cities would replace many long drives and short airplane flights. In a few decades, it is likely that people in today's car-dominated cities and countries will be wondering why they allowed cars to dominate their lives and degrade the environment for so long.

Toronto and several other cities have shown that it is not too late for well-established cities to change their auto-based land-use patterns and make their cities more compact and transit oriented. Toronto has used zoning and incentives for developers to concentrate projects in areas near subway stops. As a result, 77% of downtown workers commute by public transport. Other older cities making similar uses of land-use controls include Paris, Hamburg, Tokyo, Copenhagen, and Stockholm.

Even dispersed cities in the United States, such as Portland, Oregon, and Davis, California (see Case Study on p. 242) are beginning to rethink and reshape their use of land and cars. Each of us has an important role to play in making cities more enjoyable, affordable, and sustainable places to live (see Individuals Matter on p. 251).

Urban areas that fail to become more ecologically sustainable are inviting economic depression and increased unemployment, pollution, and social tension. We can make urban areas better places to live and work, with less stress on natural systems and people. Each of us has a vital role in converting this dream into reality.

The city is not an ecological monstrosity. It is rather the place where both the problems and the opportunities of modern technological civilization are most potent and visible.

PETER SELF

DISCUSSION TOPICS

1. What conditions, if any, would encourage you to rely less on the automobile? Would you regularly travel to school or work by bicycle or motor scooter, on foot, by mass transit, or by a car or van pool? Explain.

2. Do you believe that cities should continue expanding into agricultural land? If not, how would you control this?

3. How is land use decided in your community? What roles do citizens have in this process?

4. Should squatters around cities of LDCs be given title to the land they don't own or rent? Explain. What are the alternatives?

*5. Consult local officials to identify any floodplain areas in your community. How are these areas used?

*6. As a class or group project, try to borrow one or more sound pressure decibel meters from the physics or engineering department or from a local stereo or electronics repair shop. Make a survey of sound pressure levels at various times of day and at several locations and plot the results on a map. Also measure sound levels in a room with a stereo and from earphones at several different volume settings. If possible, measure sound levels at an indoor concert or a nightclub at various distances from the sound system speakers. Correlate your findings with those in Table 9-2.

*7. As a class project, evaluate land use and land-use planning by your school, draw up an improved plan based on ecological principles, and submit the plan to school officials.

*8. As a class project, try to estimate the number of homeless people in your community. Find out what is being done to help them and to provide better housing for the poor.

*9. List the advantages and disadvantages of living in (**a**) the downtown area of a large city, (**b**) suburbia, (**c**) a small town in a rural area, (**d**) a small town near a large city, and (**e**) a rural area. Which would you prefer to live in? Why? Which will you probably end up living in? Why? Tally and analyze the answers to these questions for your entire class. As a class project, ask 200 randomly selected students these questions, tally the results, and compare them with those from your class.

*10. As a class or group project, evaluate the transportation system in your community. Are there enough buses, subways, and trolleys to help people get around easily, especially those who don't have cars? Could routes be changed to accommodate more people? Do major streets have bicycle lanes? Is car or van pooling encouraged?

Since most people now live, or will live, in urban areas, improving the quality of urban life must be one of our most urgent priorities. Ways to do this include:

Economic Development and Population Regulation

- Reduce the flow of people from rural to urban areas by increasing investments and social services in rural areas and by not giving higher food, energy, and other subsidies to urban dwellers than to rural dwellers. In LDCs, this is the most important way to slow the flight of the poor to cities, reduce poverty, and increase food production.

- Reduce national population growth rates (Section 8-3).

- Emphasize development of existing economic resources instead of trying to attract new industries. Plug dollar drains from local economies by setting up "buy local" programs, greatly improving energy efficiency, and instituting extensive recycling programs.

- Recruit only new businesses that meet unfulfilled community and business needs and that won't compete with existing local businesses.

Land Use and Maintenance

- Rely on comprehensive, regional ecological land-use planning and control to regulate the speed and nature of economic development in urban areas and to protect rural and natural areas from unsustainable development.

- Give squatters legal title to land they have lived on, and provide them with support and low-cost loans to develop housing, water, sanitation, and utility systems and to plant community gardens and trees for fruit, shade, and fuel.

- Repair and revitalize existing cities.

- Stimulate the development of ecologically and economically sustainable new towns.

- Allow existing suburban areas and small towns to grow to medium-size cities with populations between 30,000 and 50,000, large enough to support a diversity of urban services, but small enough to provide a manageable community.

- Ease urban crowding by building underground cities, which would also increase energy efficiency and provide better protection against earthquakes. Some of Japan's largest construction companies are now planning such cities.

- Use regulations and tax incentives to encourage cluster-developed communities, surrounded by open or low-density areas (Figure 9-21). Emphasis should be on locating homes, shops, and workplaces within walking or cycling distance or near efficient public transport.

- Plant lawns and public areas with wildflowers and natural ground cover vegetation instead of lawns that must be drenched with water, fertilizer, and pesticides.

- Restore shorefronts, marshes, springs, and streams.

- Establish greenbelts of undeveloped forestland and open space within and around urban areas (Figure 9-20), and preserve nearby wetlands and agricultural land.

- Plant large numbers of trees in greenbelts, on unused lots, and along streets to reduce air pollution and noise and to provide recreational areas and wildlife habitats.

Transportation

- Raise gasoline taxes and car registration fees, and add sizable taxes based on fuel economy and pollutant emissions so that car owners pay the full costs of driving directly instead of paying these costs indirectly in higher income, sales, and other taxes and higher insurance and health costs. If phased in over a decade to avoid economic disruption, this is the most effective way to make cities more compact and livable, reduce noise and pollution (including ozone depletion and projected global warming), greatly increase the energy efficiency of motor vehicles, and make public transport, cycling, and walking more appealing.

- Provide efficient bus and trolley service, including park-and-ride systems.

- Establish express lanes solely for cars and vans with three or more people and for buses.

- Reduce road building (which only increases car use and congestion) and concentrate on maintaining existing roads and highways.

- Charge commuters with fewer than three passengers per vehicle high fees to enter cities and to park their vehicles.

- Provide tax incentives for individuals and businesses using car and van pooling.

- Use zoning laws to prevent commercial and residential construction in places not near public transport terminals.

- Require separate well-maintained and well-lit paths or lanes on all major streets and roads for use by cyclists and pedestrians.

- Eliminate tax subsidies for employers who provide workers with car parking spaces, or provide equally attractive subsidies

(continued)

for those who use mass transit or who walk or bicycle to work.

- Provide secure bicycle parking at mass transit stations and establish bike-carrying trains and buses.

- Require businesses to provide secure bike parking and showers for workers and protected bike parking for shoppers.

- Establish car-free zones in some parts of downtown areas, with mass transit systems carrying people to and from the edges of these zones. Several European cities are using this approach with great success.

- Discourage or prevent through traffic in residential areas by using signs, setting low speed limits, and installing speed bumps or other barriers.

- Use at least half of the revenue from gasoline taxes for mass transit, bike and pedestrian paths and parking facilities, and improving the energy efficiency of motor vehicles.

- Use tax incentives to encourage the use of high-speed trains or rental cars for travel between cities in a region, and bicycles, powered tricycles, motor scooters, motorcycles, small cars (powered by electricity, natural gas, or alcohol) for most trips within urban areas.

Improving Energy Efficiency

- Get more energy from locally available resources. Many cities can increase the energy they get from perpetual and renewable energy resources by relying more on firewood (with adequate reforestation and pollution control for efficient wood stoves), solar energy collectors and solar cells

mounted on rooftops, small-scale hydroelectric plants, farms of wind turbines, geothermal sources, methane gas from landfills, and cogeneration of electricity and heat at industrial plants (Chapter 17).

- Bring home, workplace, and services closer together to cut down on energy use, transportation, and the land devoted to accommodating cars.

- Enact laws that require all new cars to have fuel efficiencies of at least 17 kilometers per liter (40 miles per gallon) by the year 2000 and 21 kilometers per liter (50 miles per gallon) by 2010.

- Give tax rebates to businesses and individuals who use gas-sipping vehicles, and impose heavy taxes on those using gas guzzlers.

- Enact building codes that require new and existing buildings to be energy-efficient and responsive to climate.

- Retrofit public buildings to obtain all or most of their energy from renewable sources.

Water

- Encourage water conservation by installing water meters in all buildings and raising the price of water to reflect its true cost.

- Establish small, neighborhood water-recycling plants.

- Enact building codes that require water conservation in new and existing buildings and businesses.

Food

- Grow food (with emphasis on sustainable organic methods) in abandoned lots, community gar-

den plots, small fruit-tree orchards, rooftop gardens and greenhouses, apartment window boxes, school yards, and solar-heated fish ponds and tanks, and on some of the land in greenbelts (with careful controls).

- Lower meat consumption (especially beef) to reduce deforestation, overgrazing, and health problems.

Pollution and Wastes

- Discourage industries that produce large quantities of pollution and that use large amounts of water or energy.

- Enact and enforce strict noise control laws to reduce stress from rising levels of urban noise.

- Give tax breaks and other economic incentives to businesses that recycle and reuse resources and that emphasize pollution prevention (input approaches) instead of relying mostly on output methods for cleaning up pollution.

- Establish urban composting centers to convert yard and food wastes into soil conditioner for use on parks, highway medians, and other public lands.

- Recycle food wastes and effluents and sludge from sewage treatment plants as fertilizer for parks, roadsides, flower gardens, parks, and forests.

- Recycle or reuse at least 80% of urban solid waste and some types of hazardous waste instead of dumping it or burning it.

- Give tax breaks and other subsidies to business and industries that emphasize pollution prevention and waste reduction.

PART FOUR

ULTIMATE GLOBAL
PROBLEMS

If we don't address the issues of global ecology, we won't have to worry about the other issues.

CARLOS SALINAS DE GORTARI
(PRESIDENT OF MEXICO)

Cutting of a 200-year-old Douglas fir in an old-growth forest in Oregon.

CHAPTER 10

DEFORESTATION AND LOSS OF BIODIVERSITY

General Questions and Issues

1. What are the principal types of forests, and why are they such important ecosystems?

2. How fast is tropical deforestation taking place, and why should we care about this problem?

3. What are the principal causes of tropical deforestation and fuelwood shortages?

4. What can be done to reduce tropical deforestation and fuelwood shortages?

5. Why are remaining virgin, old-growth forests in the United States important, and what can be done to prevent their destruction?

What do forests bear? Soil, water, and pure air.
CHIPKO TREE-PROTECTION MOVEMENT

INCE AGRICULTURE BEGAN, about 10,000 years ago, our activities have reduced Earth's forest cover by at least one-third. Forests, especially tropical forests, are disappearing faster than any other biome as they are cleared for timber, fuelwood, food growing, livestock grazing, mining, dam reservoirs, and urbanization.

During the second it takes for you to snap your fingers, an area of tropical forest almost the size of two football fields was destroyed, and roughly the same area of these incredibly diverse and important biomes was degraded. Such extensive tropical deforestation—taking place ten times faster than these forests are being replaced by natural regrowth and human replanting—is happening every second of every day (Figure 1-10). This explains why most of world's remaining tropical forests, as well as the few remaining virgin, ancient forests in the northwestern United States (Figure 2-6 and photo on p. 253) and southwestern Canada, will be gone within the next 30 to 40 years.

Forests are potentially renewable resources if they are used sustainably. They are also home to from 50% to 90% of the species that make up the planet's precious biodiversity. Preventing further destruction and degradation of these vital forms of Earth capital is an urgent global priority.

10-1 Forests: Types and Importance

TYPES OF FORESTS   A forest where the crowns of trees touch and form a closed canopy during all or part of the year is called a **closed forest** (Figure 4-37). Closed forests make up about 62% of Earth's forested area. An area where trees are abundant but their crowns don't form a closed canopy is known as an **open forest** or **woodland**.

Today, about 34% of the world's land area is covered with open and closed forests (Figure 5-11). Four countries have 58% of the world's closed forests: the USSR (28%), Brazil (13%), Canada (9%), and the United States (7%). Most of Africa and Asia, and some parts of Central and South America, have little forest.

It's also useful to distinguish between secondary and old-growth forests. **Secondary forests** are stands of trees resulting from secondary ecological succession (Figure 6-10). Most forests in the United States and other temperate areas are secondary forests that developed after the logging of virgin forests (forests not altered by human activity) or the abandonment of agricultural lands. About 40% of the forests in tropical areas are secondary forests.

Old-growth forests are virgin forests containing

massive trees that are often hundreds, sometimes thousands, of years old. Examples include forests of Douglas fir, western hemlock, giant sequoia (Figure 4-6), and coastal redwoods (Figure 2-6) in the western United States; loblolly pine in the Southeast; and 60% of the world's tropical forests.

Generally, old-growth forests have a greater diversity of plant and animal life than secondary forests. The various understory zones and other vegetation in old-growth forests provide a variety of ecological niches for different plants and animals (Figure 4-37). These forests also have large numbers of standing dead trees (snags) and fallen logs (boles), which are habitats for a variety of plants, animals, and microorganisms. Their decay returns nutrients to the soil.

The type of forest that can grow in a particular area is determined mostly by its climate and its soil (Figures 5-11, 5-12, and 5-13). Principal types of these biomes include tropical rain forests, tropical deciduous forests, temperate deciduous forests, and evergreen coniferous forests.

COMMERCIAL IMPORTANCE Forests supply us with lumber for housing, biomass for fuelwood, pulp for paper, medicines, and many other products, worth over $150 billion a year (Figure 10-1). Many forestlands are also used for mining, grazing livestock, and recreation. Some are flooded to provide reservoirs for hydropower dams and flood control (Figure 5-40).

Worldwide, about one-half of the timber cut each year is used as fuel for heating and cooking, especially in LDCs. Some of this is burned directly as firewood, and some is converted into charcoal, widely used as a fuel by urban dwellers in LDCs and by some industries. One-third of the world's annual harvest is sawlogs that are converted to lumber, veneer, panels, plywood, hardboard, particleboard, and chipboard. One-sixth is converted into pulp used in a variety of paper products. Sawlogs and wood pulp are the primary uses of timber in MDCs.

ECOLOGICAL IMPORTANCE Forests have many vital ecological functions. As biologist René Dubos reminds us, "Trees are the great healers of nature."

Forested watersheds act as giant sponges, slowing down runoff and absorbing and holding water that recharges springs, streams, and aquifers. Thus, they regulate the flow of water from mountain highlands to croplands and urban areas and help control soil erosion. This reduces the severity of flooding and the amount of sediment washing into streams, lakes, and artificial reservoirs.

Forests also play an important role in local, regional, and global climate. For example, about 50% to 80% of the moisture in the air above tropical forests comes from trees by transpiration and evaporation. If large areas of these forests are cleared, average annual precipitation decreases and the region's climate gets hotter and drier. Rain that does fall runs off the bare soil rapidly instead of being absorbed and slowly released by vegetation. As the climate gets even hotter and drier, soil moisture and fertility drop further. Eventually, these changes can convert a diverse tropical forest into a sparse grassland or even a desert. Regeneration of a tropical forest on such areas may not be possible or, where it can occur, may take hundreds of years.

Forests also play an important role in the global carbon cycle (Figure 4-28) and act as an important defense against projected global warming from an enhanced greenhouse effect (Figure 5-9). Through photosynthesis, trees help remove carbon dioxide from and add oxygen to the air, explaining why the world's forests have been called a key part of Earth's "lungs." Eliminating vast areas of CO_2-absorbing trees and other vegetation faster than they are replanted naturally or artificially contributes to projected global warming, as discussed in more detail in Section 11-1.

Forests provide habitats for a larger number of wildlife species than any other biome, making them the planet's principal reservoir of biological diversity (see Spotlight on p. 11). They also help buffer us against noise, absorb some air pollutants, and nourish the human spirit by providing solitude and beauty.

On a human time scale, all of Earth's remaining virgin forests should be considered nonrenewable resources. They should not be cut down, because their long-term ecological services are far more important than the short-term economic gain from removing them. According to one calculation, a typical tree provides $196,250 worth of ecological benefits in the form of oxygen, reduction of air pollution, soil fertility and erosion control, water recycling and humidity control, wildlife habitat, and protein for wildlife. Sold as timber, the same tree is worth only about $590.

Ecologists recognize that some forests have to be cut. However, they oppose the widespread destruction of the world's rapidly dwindling virgin forests because of the loss of ecological services these essentially nonrenewable, diverse communities of life provide.

Economists, managers of timber companies, and farmers rarely consider the ecological benefits of forests in helping sustain the biosphere. They see the ancient virgin forests and diverse secondary forests primarily as a commodity to be cut, used as timber, replanted with plantations of fast-growing trees (Figure 5-25), or converted into cropland, grazing land, or urban developments. To them, the trees in a protected virgin forest are wasted resources that shouldn't be left to die and rot away. As long as the lasting and renewable ecological benefits of forests are assigned little or no value, we will continue to destroy and degrade these vital ecosystems.

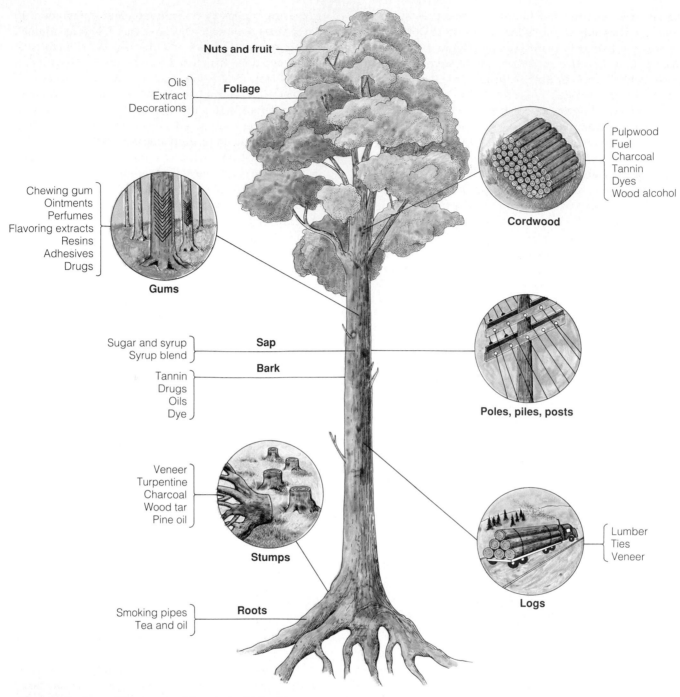

Nuts and fruit

Oils
Extract
Decorations
— **Foliage**

Cordwood
Pulpwood
Fuel
Charcoal
Tannin
Dyes
Wood alcohol

Chewing gum
Ointments
Perfumes
Flavoring extracts
Resins
Adhesives
Drugs

Gums

Sugar and syrup
Syrup blend
— **Sap**

Bark

Tannin
Drugs
Oils
Dye

Poles, piles, posts

Veneer
Turpentine
Charcoal
Wood tar
Pine oil

Stumps

Lumber
Ties
Veneer

Logs

Smoking pipes
Tea and oil
— **Roots**

Figure 10-1 Some of the many useful products obtained from trees.

10-2

Tropical Deforestation and the Biodiversity Crisis

DEFORESTATION AND DEGRADATION OF TROP-ICAL FORESTS Tropical forests are found near the equator in Latin America, Africa, and Asia and cover 6% to 7% of Earth's total land area (Figure 5-11). They include *tropical rain (evergreen) forests* (Figure 5-23) and *tropical deciduous forests*. Brazil contains almost 33% of the total area of these forests, mostly in the Amazon

basin (Figure 9-3). Zaire and Indonesia (Figure 8-16) each have 10%.

These irreplaceable storehouses of Earth's precious biodiversity are being cleared and degraded for timber, cattle grazing, fuelwood, mining, and farming (Figure 10-2) at an alarming rate (Figure 1-10). The area of land now covered by tropical forests is about half what it once was, and the area of these forests cleared per year more than doubled in the 1980s. All but about 2% of the once-extensive biome of the world's original tropical deciduous forests has been cut, and we are now in the

Figure 10-2 The cutting and burning of an area of tropical forest in Brazil's Amazon basin for growing crops.

R. Ian Lloyd

Figure 10-3 Photo taken from the space shuttle *Discovery* in September 1988 shows smoke from fires set to burn cleared areas of tropical rain forests in South America's Amazon River basin. The white areas that look like clouds are plumes of smoke. The smoke shown in this photograph covers an area about three times the size of Texas. These fires may have accounted for as much as 10% of the global input of carbon dioxide to the atmosphere during 1988. Because of international pressure and elimination of new government subsidies to cattle ranchers, the amount of forest land cleared in Brazil dropped by about 30% between 1988 and 1990.

NASA

process of eliminating most of the planet's virgin rain forests.

About half of all tropical deforestation is taking place in the vast Amazon basin, mostly in Brazil. Three countries—Brazil (Figures 10-2 and 10-3), Indonesia, and Zaire—account for 44% of the current annual loss.

According to the UN Food and Agriculture Organization and the World Resources Institute, satellite sensing shows that the world's tropical forests are vanishing at a rate of 171,000 square kilometers (66,000 square miles) a year. As a result, each year we are destroying tropical forests covering an area equal to that of Oklahoma or Syria—or about 37 city blocks every minute. Tropical forest expert Norman Myers (see Guest Essay on p. 282) estimates that 214,400 square kilometers (82,800 square miles) of tropical moist and tropical dry forest were cleared in 1989, with most of this deforestation taking place in tropical dry forests and the rest in tropical moist forests.

It is estimated that an equal area of these forests is degraded every minute. For example, selective cutting of prize trees in these dense forests is highly destructive—typically, 17 or more other trees are knocked down by logging equipment and road building for each tree removed. Reforestation in the tropics is proceeding at a snail's pace, with 10 trees cut for every 1 planted. In Africa, 29 are cut for each 1 planted.

Many tropical countries have already lost most of their original forest cover. Examples are Haiti (98% loss), the Philippines (97% loss), and Madagascar (93% loss). If the current exponential rate of loss continues, all remaining tropical forests (except for a few preserved and vulnerable patches) will be gone within 40 to 50 years, and much sooner in some areas.

Tropical forest expert Norman Myers (see Guest Essay on p. 282) estimates that at current deforestation rates, tropical forests in West Africa (except for Cameroon) will probably be gone by the year 2000, and most in Latin America and Southeast Asia will disappear by 2010. In southeastern Mexico, the largest tropical rain forest in North America (the Lacondona) is being burned and cleared even more rapidly than the tropical forests of the Amazon. Since 1970, 60% of this forest has been cleared and is likely to be gone by the year 2000 unless the Mexican government takes immediate steps to halt its destruction.

WHY SHOULD WE CARE ABOUT TROPICAL FORESTS? Conservationists and ecologists consider the present destruction and degradation of tropical forests one of the world's most serious environmental and resource problems (see Guest Essay on p. 282). Tropical forests are the world's key storehouse of biological diversity developed by 100 million years of evolutionary activity—an irreplaceable genetic treasure that our

Roy P. Fontaine/Photo Researchers

William Grenfell/Visuals Unlimited

Figure 10-4 The world's tropical forests are the planet's largest storehouse of biological diversity and contain between 50% and 90% of Earth's 40 to 80 million species. Two of these species are the red uakari monkey (left) in the Peruvian portion of the Amazon basin (Figure 9-3) and the keel-billed toucan in Belize, Central America (right). Most tropical forest species have specialized niches. This makes them highly vulnerable to extinction when their forest habitats are cleared or severely degraded.

present activities will destroy within a few decades unless we come to our senses. To biologist Thomas Lovejoy, permitting the loss of these forests is "one of the greatest acts of desecration in human history."

Although tropical rain forests cover only about 6% to 7% of the world's dry land area, they provide homes for at least 50% (some estimate as much as 90%) of Earth's total stock of species (Figure 10-4). So far, biologists have identified about 500,000 species of tropical organisms.

This genetic heritage includes disappearing amphibians (Figure 4-35), two-thirds of all known plants (Figure 1-9), 90% of nonhuman primates (Figures 1-9 and 10-4 and photo on p. 1), 40% of birds of prey, and 80% of the world's insect species. A single tree in a tropical forest may support 400 insect species.

Most tropical forest species have highly specialized niches in which resources in the various stratified layers of such forests (Figure 4-37) are shared by resource partitioning. Coevolution also plays a role in the continual development and modification of the niches in these ecosystems (Figure 6-5).

If the current rate of tropical forest destruction and degradation continues, at least 1 million species will become prematurely extinct because of our activities in the next 15 years. No rate of extinction of this magnitude has occurred since the end of the Cretaceous period (Figure 7-27), 65 million years ago (see Case Study on p. 259).

Tropical forests supply half of the world's annual harvest of hardwood. They also supply hundreds of food products, including coffee, spices, nuts, chocolate, and tropical fruits; industrial materials such as natural latex rubber (see Spotlight on p. 261), resins, dyes, and essential oils; and plants that provide ingredients for one-fourth of the world's prescription and nonprescription medicines.

The raw materials in one-fourth of the prescription and nonprescription medicines and drugs we use come from plants growing in tropical rain forests. These include life-saving drugs that are used to treat cancer, malaria, leukemia and Hodgkin's disease (Figure 10-10), heart disease, high blood pressure, and multiple sclerosis.

Almost three-fourths of the 3,000 plants identified by the National Cancer Institute as having chemicals that fight cancer come from tropical rain forests. While you are reading this page, a plant species that can cure a type of cancer, AIDS, or some other deadly disease could be wiped out forever.

Most of the original strains of rice, wheat, and corn that supply more than half of the world's food were

Madagascar, the world's fourth largest island, lies in the Indian Ocean off the East African coast (Figure 10-5). Because of its astounding biological diversity, this island, slightly smaller than Texas, is considered a crown jewel among Earth's ecosystems—a "biological superpower."

Through the process of continental drift (Figure 7-27), Madagascar broke away from mainland Africa at least 150 million years ago. Most of its plants, animals, and microorganisms have evolved in relative isolation for at least 40 million years after the separation between the island and Africa became large enough to prevent migration of most forms of life from the mainland.

The result is an estimated 160,000 species that are unique to this island, with most found in its rapidly disappearing eastern rain forests (Figure 10-5). Species unique to the island include 85% of its 8,000 or more species of plants (including 1,000 orchid species), 60% of the world's species of chameleons (Figure 10-6), 800 butterfly species, half of the island's bird species, and all of the island's reptiles and mammals (Figure 10-7).

The island's plant and animal species are also among the world's most endangered, mostly because of loss of habitat. Since humans arrived on this biological jewel about 1,500 years ago, 93% of its tropical forests and over 66% of its rain forests have been chopped down for cropland, fuelwood, and hardwoods, leaving blood-red gullies and streams and endless fields and hillsides of eroded and degraded land. Because of such widespread loss of vegetation, Madagascar is the most eroded country in the world, with much of the resulting sediment ending up in the Indian Ocean (Figure 10-8).

Most of the forest destruction and species extinction has been the result of rapid population growth, poverty, and small-scale farming in increasingly densely populated rural areas. In 1991, Madagascar's

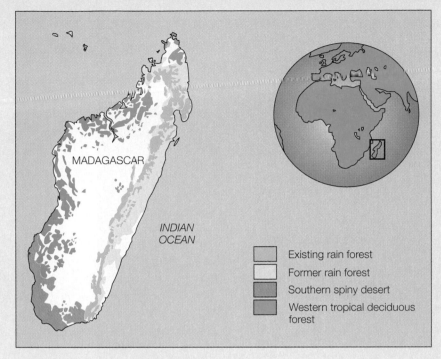

Figure 10-5 Where is Madagascar?

MADAGASCAR

INDIAN OCEAN

Existing rain forest
Former rain forest
Southern spiny desert
Western tropical deciduous forest

Figure 10-6 Parson's giant chameleon in a tropical forest in Madagascar. The largest of the chameleons, an adult Parson's can reach 70 centimeters (28 inches) in length. Among its prey are small birds. Madagascar is the only home for 60% of the world's known species of chameleons, some as small as the size of a thumbnail.

Gérard Lacz/NHPA

Figure 10-7 Endangered ring-tailed lemur in Madagascar. Lemurs are the oldest distant relative of our species. The 29 species of lemurs existing on this island are found nowhere else in the wild. Half of these species are endangered.

Robert and Linda Mitchell

(continued)

Figure 10-8 Sediment entering the Indian Ocean from the mouth of the Betsiboka River, Madagascar. Most of this sediment is the result of deforestation.

NASA

population was 12.4 million, more than twice as many people as there were in 1960. Its population is growing rapidly, at 3.2% a year, and is projected to more than double, to 34 million, by 2025. Madagascar is one of the world's poorest countries, with an annual per capita income of about $230.

The 78% of its people who live in the island's rural areas try to survive mostly by slash-and-burn and shifting cultivation (especially of rice) in the island's rapidly vanishing forests. Trees are also cut for fuelwood and for conversion into charcoal, sold mostly as a fuel for large numbers of the rural poor who are migrating to its cities in a desperate attempt to survive.

Since 1984, the government of Madagascar, conservation agencies (such as the World Wildlife Fund and Conservation International), the World Bank, the Agency for International Development, and scientists around the world have united in efforts to slow the island's rapid slide

into an environmental wasteland. These groups consider stemming the destruction in Madagascar the world's number one environmental priority.

With a $90 million grant from the World Bank—the first such effort for this agency long criticized for its environmental insensitivity—the country has developed and begun implementing a 15-year Environmental Action Plan. It involves surveying its remaining biodiversity, protecting some areas from development, and sustainably using remaining fragments of forests and biodiversity.

For this ambitious plan to be successful, population growth will have to be slowed drastically and the people will have to be taught how to carry out sustainable agriculture and agroforestry (combined planting of crops and trees). Living standards in rural areas must also be improved with emphasis on family planning, health care, and education.

Local people must be involved in the planning and management of conservation areas, given ownership of land and trees they plant, and allowed to make a living from reforestation, tourism, and sustainable use of forest, wildlife, and soil resources. If we look after the people who live in forests and give them sustainable alternatives, we look after the forests.

The hour is late, but if fully supported and implemented, the efforts to prevent Madagascar from becoming a biological wasteland can serve as a test case and a model for other areas. Even then, an estimated half of the island's plant and animal species will be lost, but doing nothing is much worse. If Madagascar's environmental descent can't be stabilized by this internationally funded program within the next 10 years, there is little hope of efforts being successful elsewhere.

Rubber tapping is one way to use tropical forests without destroying them. A rubber tapper cuts a diagonal groove through the bark of a live rubber tree and lets milky liquid latex trickle into a collecting cup (Figure 10-9). When the cut has stopped producing, another cut is made next to it. The latex, which is about 30% rubber, is processed to make rubber. The scars heal without killing the tree.

About 300,000 rubber tappers make their living in the Amazon basin by harvesting latex from rubber trees spread throughout the region. They also gather Brazil nuts, fruits, and fibers in the forests and cultivate small plots near their homes.

A 1988 study by a team of scientists showed that sustainable harvesting of such nonwood products as nuts, fruits, and latex rubber over 50 years would generate twice as much revenue per hectare as timber production and three times as much as cattle ranching. Although the wholesale clearing and degradation of tropical forests is a long-term economic and ecological disaster, it continues.

In the western Amazon basin, the livelihood of rubber tappers is being threatened as tropical forests are cleared. Some who have opposed the destruction of rain forests by ranchers, farmers, and miners have been beaten or murdered.

Chico Mendes, the rubber tapper shown in Figure 10-9, proposed that parts of the rain forest be set aside as *extractive reserves* — parcels of land that would be used only for harvesting renewable resources like rubber and nuts without removing the trees. He was one of 1,000 rubber tappers, priests, lawyers, union officials, and other activists against rain forest destruction who were killed between 1985 and 1990. Most of those homicides have not been investigated by Brazilian officials.

Because of the international outcry over Mendes's murder, Brazilian

Randall Hyman

Figure 10-9 Rubber tapping is a way to use tropical forests without destroying them. This photo, taken in 1987, shows Chico Mendes, leader of 70,000 Amazon rubber tappers in his Brazilian home state of Acre, making a cut on a rubber tree near the village of Xapuri. On December 22, 1988, he was murdered near his home in Xapuri by ranchers who opposed his internationally known efforts to protect Brazil's rain forests from unsustainable land clearing, colonization, and other destructive forms of development.

officials have vowed to preserve some areas of Amazon rain forest from destruction and degradation. A state agency has established a $1-million program to help rubber tappers develop four extractive reserves in the state where Chico Mendes was murdered. The government has plans to establish 15 other extractive reserves throughout Brazil.

Funding and implementing these plans, which is not assured, will be a small step in the right direction, but it will put only a small dent in the rapid legal and illegal destruction of forests throughout Brazil.

Patches of tropical forest can also be cleared and used sustainably to raise crops by slash-and-burn and shifting cultivation (Figure 2-4). However, this is sustainable only for low-density populations of people and only if these plots are not cultivated or grazed for 10 to 30 years after their nutrient-poor soils are depleted (Figure 2-5). As more of the landless poor move into tropical forests, the large-scale use of this type of agriculture and subsequent grazing by livestock are primary factors leading to the destruction of these ecosystems.

Figure 10-10 Rosy periwinkle found in the threatened tropical forests of Madagascar. A compound extracted from this plant has been used to increase the survival rate of children suffering from leukemia and to treat Hodgkin's disease. Mostly because of coevolution, highly specialized tropical plants have developed an astonishing variety of compounds that reduce their chances of being eaten. Many of these compounds can be used as medicines and natural pesticides. Only a tiny fraction of tropical plants has been studied for such potential uses. Many will become extinct because of our activities before we can learn of their potential uses.

developed from wild strains grown in the tropics. Wild tropical strains have also been used by plant breeders, and, more recently, by genetic engineers to provide improved varieties of these vital food plants. Scientists believe that undiscovered strains of these and tens of thousands of other plants that could be used as sources of new foods and genetically engineered varieties exist mostly in tropical forests.

Despite their immense potential, less than 1% of tropical forest species have been examined for their possible use as human resources. Destroying these forests and many of the species they contain for short-term economic gain is like throwing away an unwrapped present or burning down an ancient library before you read the books.

Tropical forests are also home for 250 million people, many of whom survive by hunting and gathering (Figure 2-3) or by slash-and-burn and shifting cultivation (Figure 2-4). Indigenous tribespeople are seeing their land bulldozed, burned, and flooded and are disappearing as rapidly as the forests themselves. They are being driven illegally from their homelands and forced to adopt new ways that subject them to disease (against which they have little immunity because of their isolation from modern civilization), hunger, and cultural shock. Those who resist are often killed by ranchers, miners, and settlers.

Eliminating these people who are living gently on the earth involves a tragic loss of ecological wisdom and cultural diversity that the rest of the world needs. These tribal people have more ecological knowledge about how to live sustainably in tropical forests and what plants can be used as foods and medicines than anyone, including the world's foremost tropical biologists.

Tropical forests also protect watersheds and regulate water flow for farmers, who grow food for over 1 billion people in LDCs. The Environmental Policy Institute estimates that unless the destruction of tropical forests stops, the resulting loss of water and topsoil, along with flooding, will cause as many as 1 billion people to starve to death during the next 30 years.

Regardless of the economic, health, and ecological importance of tropical forests to us, people with a sustainable-Earth worldview (Section 1-5 and Chapter 26) believe that this destruction must be stopped because it is *wrong*. Over the next few decades, it could cause the premature extinction of at least 1 million plant and animal species who have as much right to exist, or struggle to exist, as we do.

10-3 Causes of Tropical Deforestation

RESOURCE EXTRACTION FOR MDCs Tropical forests are not being destroyed and degraded because of ignorance but largely because of affluence, greed, and poverty. Much of the destruction and degradation of the world's tropical forests is caused by gigantic projects of multinational corporations and international lending agencies that finance resource extraction, mostly to support the affluent lifestyles of people in MDCs. These projects include

- Cattle ranches used mostly to produce raw and canned beef for export to MDCs (see Pro/Con on p. 263).

- Inefficient commercial logging and paper mills, with most of the logs and paper exported to MDCs.

- Immense plantations of sugar cane and cash crops such as bananas and coffee, mostly for export to MDCs.

- Growing of marijuana and cocaine-yielding coca, with most of these drugs smuggled into MDCs to supply the rapidly growing and highly profitable illegal drug trade. In Peru, the annual earnings from coca produced by 200,000 growers are $1 billion, which is 25% of the country's GNP.

- Mining operations, with much of the extracted minerals exported to MDCs.

- Dams, often used as sources of electric power for mining and smelting operations for minerals exported to MDCs.

Between 1965 and 1983, satellite photos showed that cattle ranches raising beef mostly for export to MDCs in Europe were responsible for 30% of the total deforestation in Brazil's portion of the Amazon basin (Figure 9-3). Tropical forests in Latin America are also being cleared and used to grow soybeans that are exported to feed cattle in western Europe.

During the past 25 years, Central America has lost two-thirds of its tropical forests (Figure 1-10). Much of this land has been cleared and used as rangeland to raise beef for export to the United States, Canada, and western Europe (Figure 10-11). This imported beef is sold mostly to fast-food chains and food-processing companies for use in hamburgers, hot dogs, luncheon meats, chilis, stews, frozen dinners, and pet food.

As one rancher puts it: "It boils down to $95 per cow in Montana versus $25 in Costa Rica." So tropical forests are felled and cheaper beef is produced and imported to meet consumer demand and reduce the cost of a pound of hamburger by a nickel. American and other consumers need to realize that when they bite into a fast-food hamburger or hot dog or feed their dogs or cats, they indirectly have their hands on the chain saws, bulldozers, and matches that are bringing about the current biological holocaust in the world's tropical forests.

The true cost of a quarter-pound hamburger made from cattle grazing on land that was once tropical forest is the destruction of half a metric ton (1,100 pounds) of the forest occupying an area roughly the size of a small kitchen (5 square meters or 54 square feet). This irreplaceable chunk of the planet's natural wealth was destroyed to save five cents on the price of a quick snack that doctors tell us is unhealthy for our hearts.

After being grazed for five to ten years, tropical pastures can no longer be used for cattle. Often, torrential rains and overgrazing turn the nutrient-poor soils into eroded wastelands. Ranchers then move to another area and repeat the process. This destructive *shifting ranching* is often encouraged by government tax subsidies.

Environmental and consumer groups (especially the Rainforest Action Network in San Francisco) have organized boycotts of hamburger chains buying beef imported from Central America and other tropical countries. Because of these efforts, many large chains claim they no longer buy beef from tropical countries. However, such claims are quite difficult to verify. In some cases, cattle raised in a tropical country are imported to the United States or other MDCs and slaughtered there. This allows hamburger chains and other meat processors to claim they are using American beef.

Environmentalists call for a ban on all beef or beef products raised on cleared land in tropical forest. This would encourage tropical countries to raise beef on existing rangeland and to stop giving ranchers the subsidies needed to make raising beef on cleared tropical forestland profitable. However, banning beef imports deprives exporting LDCs of much-needed income.

Numerous studies have shown that with improved management, the sustainable output of beef from a typical existing Central American and South American ranch could be doubled or tripled. This solution would provide low-cost beef for export to other countries without causing further deforestation. What do you think should be done?

Figure 10-11 The hamburger connection. Large areas of tropical forests have been cleared in Central America and South America and converted into rangeland for grazing cattle. This rangeland in Brazil's Amazon basin was once covered with trees. Some of the beef raised on Central American rangeland is exported to the United States to cut the cost of hamburgers by about a nickel. Much of the beef raised on cleared areas of tropical forests in Brazil is exported as raw beef to western Europe or as canned beef to the United States.

R. Azoury/SIPA-Press

One-third of the world's tropical forests are found in South America's Amazon basin (Figure 9-3), which occupies an area equal in size to almost 90% of the land area of the continental United States. Although only about 10% of the tropical forests in this vast area has been destroyed so far, 80% of this deforestation has taken place since 1980 (Figures 10-2 and 10-3).

The Brazilian government's solution to widespread rural and urban poverty (see Case Study on p. 225) has been to send the landless poor off to chop down tropical forests in the Amazon basin, giving them title to the land they clear. These policies are supported and encouraged by wealthy landowners to help counteract political pressures for more equitable land distribution. A $1.5-billion regional development project in the Amazon basin, which began with the paving of a preexisting road, brought in 500,000 new people in less than 10 years.

Much of this development is financed with loans from the World Bank and other international lending agencies (controlled by MDCs) and from MDCs, mostly for building roads and large dams. These roads open up the forests for logging, farming (Figure 10-2), ranching (Figure 10-11), mining (Figure 10-12), and other forms of development that destroy and degrade once-inaccessible biomes. For example, a gold rush in the Amazon brought in 30,000 illegal miners, who use toxic mercury to extract the gold, thereby poisoning the soil and the water.

The poor who move to the Amazon in a desperate search for enough land to survive rarely improve their lives. Most contract malaria. They must clear new plots

Figure 10-12 During the early 1980s, up to 50,000 mining workers toiled at this mine in the Amazon basin of Brazil. Once the gold was extracted, miners moved to other gold-rich areas of the Amazon basin. The hole shown here is now flooded with water. Toxic mercury used to extract the gold here and at other mining sites has poisoned nearby soil and water.

Serra Pelada/SIPA-Press

every two to three years as the soil in earlier plots is depleted. In some areas, there are violent clashes between the new immigrants and indigenous tribes, who resent being driven from land they have lived on sustainably for centuries. Rubber tappers also lose their livelihood as the forests are cleared (see Spotlight on p. 261). Some of the new settlers are illegally driven off their land or killed by gunmen working for wealthy ranchers and cash-crop farmers trying to amass large land holdings. (The average price for a settler's life is $25.)

The lands abandoned by agricultural squatters usually end up in the hands of ranchers and cash-crop farmers. Thanks to government tax breaks and subsidies, these groups can profit from the land even though their operations lose money. After several years of further over-exploitation, most of these lands are left in a severely degraded state.

This destruction is hastened by land speculation. Wealthy investors buy up enormous tracts of land and protect their ownership by clearing the land and putting out a few cattle to graze. Once good roads reach the area, they resell the land for up to ten times the original price. Low taxes on such land and on the resulting profits encourage this destructive practice.

Conservationists have mounted a global campaign to preserve 70% of the forests in the Amazon basin.

Governments of tropical countries feel driven to sell cash crops, timber, and minerals to MDCs at low prices to help finance economic growth and to pay interest on loans made by MDCs and international lending agencies controlled by MDCs (see Pro/Con above).

TIMBER HARVESTING Since 1950, the consumption of tropical lumber has risen 15-fold, with Japan now accounting for 60% of the annual consumption. Although 68% of Japan is covered with forests, it prefers to deplete the forests of other countries (see Case Study

This is an uphill fight against powerful economic forces that want short-term economic gain from depleting this treasure house of potentially renewable Earth capital.

Brazilian officials argue that they must exploit the resources in these forests to help finance economic development and to help pay the interest on their huge foreign debt. They claim they are doing the same thing that the United States and other MDCs did to help finance their economic growth, including cutting down most of their native forests. The United States is still encouraging rapid destruction of its own remaining old-growth forests on public lands in the northwest by offering government subsidies. Sweden, Finland, and the USSR are doing the same thing to their virgin northern coniferous forests.

The Brazilian government is going ahead with plans to build internationally financed highways to open up larger areas of the Amazon for development, despite objections by environmentalists and other governments. The key to greatly increased development of the currently inaccessible regions of the Amazon basin is completion of the last 805-kilometer (500-mile) stretch of a major road (BR-364) linking the Brazilian state of Acre, which borders Peru, with the road that now runs through the rest of the Amazon basin (Figure 9-3).

The Japanese are particularly interested in developing this road, since it would give them access to hardwoods in the last wilderness of the Amazon and allow mass shipments of timber to Japan from ports in Peru. Brazilian government leaders ask, "How would Americans feel if the British or some other government told them that they should not build a highway from New York to California because it would destroy their forests? We have as much right to clear our wilderness as Americans did when they cleared most of theirs."

They point out that much of the timber, beef, and mineral resources removed from tropical forests in the Amazon basin are exported to support throwaway lifestyles in MDCs. Brazilian officials also argue that the world's MDCs are the biggest culprits behind global warming, ozone depletion, and the threat of nuclear war.

In 1988, the Brazilian government temporarily suspended new subsidies and tax breaks for agricultural and ranching operations in the Amazon basin, but old subsidies remain for existing ranches and have already cost the debt-ridden government more than $2.5 billion in lost revenue. Brazil's president has declared his intention to maintain these incentive programs indefinitely.

The government has also established two forest reserves and three new national parks in the Amazon region and in 1989 announced a $100-million, five-year program to zone the Amazon basin for both economic use and ecological protection. Environmentalists applaud these actions but fear that they are mostly window dressing to help defuse international pressures to protect much larger areas of the Amazon basin from development.

Since 1980, the Washington-based World Bank and the Inter-American Development Bank (both controlled by MDCs) have lent Brazil more than $82 billion for development of 166 hydropower dams and

reservoirs, over half of them in the Amazon basin. Most of this power will be used to support mining, smelting, and other resource extraction industries, with most of the extracted resources exported to MDCs. These dams and reservoirs will displace about 500,000 people and flood vast areas of tropical rain forests.

With funding and technical advice from the World Bank, Japan, and the European community, Brazil seeks to exploit mineral deposits and encourage settlements in a mineral-rich area of the eastern Amazon twice the size of the state of California. Smelters that will convert iron ore into pig iron will be powered by charcoal produced from wood. The cheapest way to get the charcoal is to chop down the surrounding forests and burn the trees. Environmentalists fear that this project will repeat the ecological disaster of a similar project in southeastern Brazil, where pig-iron production consumed nearly two-thirds of the area's forests.

Although tropical forests in the Amazon basin receive most of the attention, forests on Brazil's Atlantic coast are even more threatened. As the populations of the nearby urban centers of Rio de Janeiro and São Paulo (Figure 9-3,) have skyrocketed, the area of these forests has shrunk by 90%, with only a few fragments left. Conservationists urge that preserving the remaining fragments should be the top priority in all of South America. What do you think should be done about economic development and forest preservation in the Amazon basin and in the rest of Brazil?

on p. 266). Other leading importers of tropical hardwoods are the United States and Great Britain.

In 1960, Nigeria was a leading exporter of tropical logs. By 1985, its forests were so depleted that it now imports 100 times more wood than it exports. Southeast Asia's exports of raw logs to Japan — by far the world's biggest importer of tropical wood — were dominated by the Philipines during the 1960s, Indonesia during much of the 1970s, and Malaysia during the 1980s. Malaysia, currently the world's leading exporter of tropical logs, is

Until recently, environmentalists focused most of their attention on the United States and countries in western Europe, which are by far Earth's biggest resource users and polluters. However, as Japan (see map, Figure 8-16) has developed into a leading economic power, its impact on the global environment has grown rapidly.

Japan's control of industrial pollution is one of the best in the world. Its control of urban air pollution is better than that in the United States. Because of its lack of domestic resources, Japan has one of the highest resource recycling rates in the world, using a sophisticated resource recovery system. During the 1960s, Japan sharply cut its rate of population growth and now has an annual population growth rate half that of the United States.

Japan has preserved most of its forests, and reverence for nature infuses Japanese art, literature, and religion. Like most other MDCs, however, Japan has not shown a high regard for nature outside its boundaries. Japan is the world's largest importer of low-cost tropical hardwoods, resulting in the deforestation of vast tracts in Asian forests. Most of this wood is used to make throwaway plywood forms for molding concrete, furniture, buildings, and about 25 billion pairs of throwaway chopsticks a year.

Because Asian tropical forests will be stripped of timber within 15 years, Japan is now shifting its operations to tropical forests in Brazil and other parts of South America. Diverse, old-growth stands of timber in U.S. national forests in the states of Washington, Oregon, and Alaska have also been clear-cut and sold to Japan at bargain prices.

Japan is also the world's largest consumer of many threatened wild species. Over the years, thousands of elephants have been slaughtered for their valuable ivory. Wedding ornaments, hair combs, and jewelry are made from the shells of endangered hawksbill turtles. Recently, Japan has moved to reduce or ban imports of ivory and 3 endangered species. However, its government has used a provision in the Convention on International Trade of Endangered Species to exempt itself from bans on imports of 11 endangered species.

Until commercial whaling was banned from 1987 to 1992, Japan was the world's leading whaling nation. It still takes several hundred Minke whales for "scientific" purposes. Although the International Whaling Commission says this killing does not qualify for research, Japan has refused to stop the practice and works to have the ban on commercial whaling lifted. They view whales as an important source of food, the same way Americans see cattle.

Japan's huge fishing industry has also been severely criticized for its use of large drift nets across great expanses of the Pacific Ocean. While these nets — called "curtains of death" by environmentalists — are intended to catch mostly tuna and squid, they also catch and kill hundreds of thousands of dolphins, porpoises, seals, and seabirds. Their use can also deplete stocks of commercially valuable fish.

Since 1990, Japan has been the world's largest donor of aid to LDCs.

However, most of this aid is commercially oriented, favoring trading partners in Asia, low-interest loans rather than grants, and support of large-scale projects such as roads, dams, power plants, and mines, which have severe environmental impacts. The Japanese government has been unwilling to require that environmental impact assessments be made before these projects are approved.

Conservationists are concerned that Japan may hide its support of environmentally destructive projects to avoid international criticism. One method would be to make unrestricted loans to foreign banks, with the understanding that the banks would then lend the money to finance controversial projects.

A 1989 study by the United Nations Environment Programme showed that the Japanese were among the least concerned about a range of global environmental problems. The environmental movement, an increasingly powerful force in Europe and the United States, has only a small (but growing) following in Japan.

On the positive side, Japan has ratified the international treaty to protect the ozone layer and has supported international efforts to slow global warming. Japan has also shown the capacity to move forcefully and quickly to change its policies when subjected to intense international scrutiny and criticism. If Japan should decide to accept its responsibility and use its economic power to become a major force in helping to sustain the global environment, it could turn its critics into admirers.

cutting down trees four times faster than they are being replenished and has lost 85% of its primary forest area during the past 20 years. Within a decade, the nation could become a net importer of wood.

As the remaining supply of tropical timber in Asia is depleted in the 1990s, timber cutting in tropical forests will shift to Latin America and Africa. The World Bank estimates that of the 33 countries that are currently net exporters of tropical timber, only 10 will have any timber left to export by the year 2000.

Sustainable harvesting of trees in tropical forests involves removing only about four large trees per 0.4

hectare (1 acre), leaving behind medium-sized trees, so that a new crop is ready for selective harvesting in about 30 years. However, most logging in tropical countries is unsupervised and is based on the get-all-you-can-fast philosophy of greed. Less than 0.1% is done on a sustained-yield basis. Careful selective cutting is costly and time-consuming. The loggers do not own the land they are cutting timber from, and they are under pressure to cut as much wood as quickly as possible. Typically, they remove the best large and medium trees and topple up to 17 other trees for every 1 they remove.

Unfortunately, I recently had to witness this grossly irresponsible type of forestry on a large plot of land next to where I live. The owners viewed the land primarily as a commodity and could not be bothered to see that the job was done in a way that helped sustain rather than degrade this unique piece of the earth. As John Muir wrote in 1900: "Any fool can destroy trees. They cannot defend themselves or run away."

POVERTY Tropical forests are also destroyed by the landless poor who migrate there, hoping to get enough land to survive. They are driven to tropical forests by a combination of rapid population growth, poverty, and lack of access to arable land, much of which is owned by a few wealthy people. Small-scale farming is the largest single cause of tropical deforestation, accounting for about 60%, followed by commercial logging and cattle ranching.

Some destruction occurs because there are too many people to support sustainable slash-and-burn and shifting cultivation (Figure 2-4). Out of necessity or ignorance, some of the new forest dwellers clear and replant abandoned plots after only a few years instead of waiting the 10 to 25 years needed for restoration of soil fertility. This exhausts soil nutrients and eventually converts the land into shrubland, often used by wealthy ranchers to graze livestock (Figure 10-11) until the land is severely degraded.

This mass migration of poor people to tropical forests would not be possible without the internationally financed projects that build roads and open up these usually inaccessible areas.

THE FUELWOOD CRISIS IN LDCs In some areas, tropical and other types of forests are depleted by extensive gathering of fuelwood faster than it is replenished naturally or by replanting (Figure 10-13). Almost 70% of the people in LDCs rely on biomass as their primary fuel for heating and cooking. About half of this comes from burning wood or charcoal produced from wood, 33% from crop residues, and 17% from dung.

City dwellers rely more on charcoal than on wood because charcoal's light weight makes it easier to transport from the countryside to the city. When wood is converted into charcoal, more than half the original energy content is lost. This means that villagers who

move to a city and switch from wood to charcoal double their consumption of wood—if they can afford it.

By 1985, about 1.5 billion people—almost one out of every three persons on earth—in 63 LDCs either could not get enough fuelwood to meet their basic needs or were forced to meet their needs by consuming wood faster than it was being replenished (Figure 10-13). The UN Food and Agriculture Organization projects that by the end of this century, 3 billion people in 77 LDCs will experience a fuelwood crisis.

Fuelwood scarcity leads to several harmful effects in addition to deforestation and accelerated soil erosion (Figures 1-1 and 10-8). It places an additional burden on the poor, especially women. Often, they must walk long distances to find and carry home large bundles of fuelwood. Buying fuelwood or charcoal can take 40% of a poor family's meager income. Poor families who can't get enough fuelwood often burn dried animal dung and crop residues for cooking and heating (Figure 10-14). This keeps these natural fertilizers from reaching the soil and reduces cropland productivity, creating a vicious circle of land degradation that helps lock the poor in the poverty trap.

10-4 Reducing Tropical Deforestation and Fuelwood Shortages

REDUCING THE DESTRUCTION AND DEGRADATION OF TROPICAL FORESTS From a scientific, ecological, aesthetic, economic, or ethical point of view, destruction of most of the world's remaining virgin tropical forests (and other virgin forests) and much of their biodiversity is a tragedy of horrendous proportions. It is a devastating global biological war against ourselves, our children and grandchildren, and other species.

To slow this destruction, we must recognize several things:

- Virgin tropical forests and all other virgin, old-growth forests are nonrenewable resources on our accelerated time scale.

- In our interconnected global markets, we are all involved in the destruction of rain forests, whether we like it or not.

- We all have a responsibility to correct this situation in tropical countries and in MDCs where rapid deforestation is also occurring (Section 10-5). This involves carefully considering what we buy and promoting and supporting government policies such as those suggested in the remainder of this section.

- It must be done now or never. We have only about ten years to turn things around.

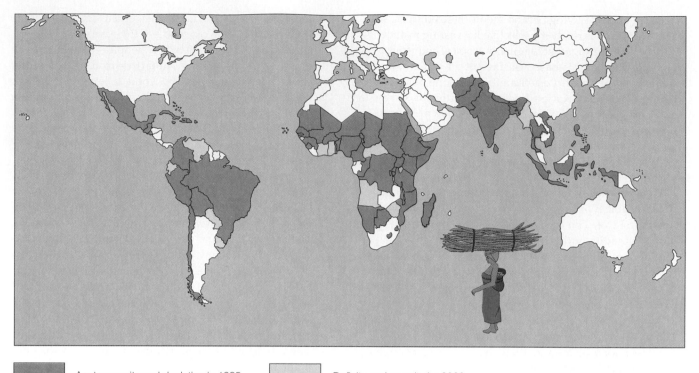

■ Acute scarcity and depletion in 1985   ▢ Deficits and scarcity by 2000

Figure 10-13 Generalized areas of the world experiencing fuelwood scarcity and deficits, 1985 and 2000 (projected). (Data from UN Food and Agriculture Organization)

Pierre A. Pittet/UN Food and Agriculture Organization

Figure 10-14 Making fuel briquettes from cow dung in India. As fuelwood becomes scarce, more people collect and burn dung, depriving the soil of an important source of plant nutrients.

To reduce the severity of this unnecessary catastrophe, environmentalists believe that over the next ten years we need to do a number of things:

Prevention (Input) Approaches

- Establish an international ban on imports of timber, wood products, beef, and other goods that directly or indirectly destroy or degrade existing virgin tropical forests.

- Fully fund the Rapid Assessment Program (RAP), which sends teams of highly qualified tropical biologists to gather ecological data rapidly on "hot spots," imperiled tracts of tropical forests that are the most deserving of protection. By 1990, Norman Myers (see Guest Essay on p. 282) and Conservation International biologists had identified 15 hot spots in danger of being cleared by the year 2000 and had evaluated two of these tracts.

- Provide aid and debt relief for tropical countries that ban commercial logging, cattle ranching, and other destructive uses of virgin tropical forests and that emphasize economically and ecologically sustainable harvesting of rubber, nuts, fruits, and other renewable resources (see Spotlight on p. 261). So far, only 0.1% of the world's tropical forests is managed sustainably.

- Set aside large areas of the world's tropical forests as reserves and parks protected from unsustainable development. Establishing such areas is one thing, but keeping the hungry and the greedy out of them is quite another thing. The key is to get local people involved in the protection of such areas by showing them how to profit from using these areas sustainably (see Case Study on p. 270).

- Use debt-for-nature swaps and conservation easements to encourage countries to protect areas of tropical forests or other valuable natural systems. In a *debt-for-nature swap*, participating tropical countries act as custodians for protected forest reserves in return for foreign aid or relief from some of their debt (see Case Study on p. 270). With *conservation easements*, a country, a private organization, or a consortium of countries compensates individual countries for protecting specific natural habitats selected on a priority basis. These legally binding agreements specify what can and cannot be done with the designated land, establish a mechanism for enforcement, and set appropriate penalties for violations.

- Phase out and halt funding for dams, tree and crop plantations, ranches, roads, colonization programs, and destructive types of tourism on any land now covered by virgin tropical forests.

- Require responsible and well-supervised logging practices and reforestation on all tropical forestlands approved for timber cutting (secondary forests and existing tree plantations), and ban all logging of virgin tropical forests.

- Include indigenous tribal peoples, women, and private local conservation organizations in the planning and execution of tropical forestry plans.

- Give indigenous people title to tropical forest lands that they and their ancestors have lived on sustainably for centuries, with the stipulations that these lands cannot be developed in unsustainable ways and cannot be sold. The Colombian government is giving indigenous tribes complete control of two-thirds of the country's land area in the Amazon basin, with the requirement that they must never sell the land.

- Require an extensive environmental impact evaluation for any proposed development project in tropical forests, and use internationally accepted standards for such studies.

- Prevent banks and international lending agencies from lending money for environmentally destructive projects involving tropical forests. The key is to regulate road building, because a road is the first and most important step leading to the disappearance of an untouched forest area.

- Carefully monitor funded projects, and halt further funding when abuse occurs.

- Exert political and consumer pressure (boycotts) on large U.S., Japanese, and British timber, paper, meat-processing, and food companies now involved in destructive development projects in tropical forests. Coca-Cola recently abandoned a plan to develop a large citrus fruit plantation in Belize after pressure from the environmental organization Friends of the Earth.

- Support effective family planning and programs that attack the root causes of poverty, including unequal distribution of farmland.

Output Approaches

- Rehabilitate degraded tropical forests and watersheds (see Case Study on p. 272).

- Provide financial incentives to villagers and village organizations to establish fuelwood trees and tree plantations for growing fuelwood and timber on abandoned and degraded land with suitable soil.

REDUCING THE FUELWOOD CRISIS LDCs can reduce the severity of the fuelwood crisis by planting more fast growing fuelwood trees, such as the leucaenas and acacias, burning wood more efficiently, and switching to other fuels. Experience has shown that planting projects are most successful when local people, especially women, are involved in their planning and implementation. Programs work best when village farmers own the land or are given ownership of any trees grown on land owned by a village. This gives them a strong incentive to plant and protect trees for their own use and for sale.

Bolivia is a tropical South American country (Figure 10-15). Its population of 7.5 million is growing rapidly at 2.6% a year, mostly because the average fertility rate is 4.9 children per woman, and is projected to reach 14.3 million by 2025.

Annual per capita income is $600. Because of widespread poverty, the country's infant mortality rate is high, with 1 out of every 9 babies dying before reaching their first birthday. The country is also saddled with a $5.7-billion foreign debt.

In 1984, biologist Thomas Lovejoy suggested that debtor nations willing to protect some of their natural resources should be eligible for discounts or credits against some of their debts. With such **debt-for-nature swaps**, a certain amount of foreign debt is cancelled in exchange for local currency investments that will improve natural resource management in the debtor country. Typically, a conservation or other organization buys a certain amount of a country's debt from a bank at a discount rate and negotiates a debt-for-nature swap.

In 1987, Conservation International, a private U.S. banking consortium, paid $100,000 to a Swiss bank to buy up $650,000 of Bolivia's national debt. In exchange for forgiveness of this part of its debt, Bolivia agreed to protect 1.5 million hectares (3.7 million acres) of tropical forest around its existing Beni Biosphere Reserve in the Amazon basin from harmful forms of development. The government was to establish maximum legal protection for the reserve and create a $250,000 fund, with the interest to be used to manage the reserve.

This land is supposed to be a model of how conservation of forest and wildlife resources can be mixed with sustainable economic development (Figure 10-15). The core of this land is a virgin tropical forest to be set aside as a biological reserve. It will be surrounded by a protective buffer of savanna to be used for sustainable grazing of livestock.

Controlled commercial logging, as well as hunting and fishing by local natives, will be permitted in some of the forest in the tract. Logging will not be allowed in the mountain area above the tract, to protect the area's watershed and to prevent erosion.

However, by 1991, four years after the agreement was signed, the Bolivian government had not provided legal protection for the reserve. It also waited until April 1989 to contribute only $100,000 to the reserve management fund. Meanwhile, with approval from the Bolivian government, timber companies have cut thousands of mahogany trees from the area, with most of this lumber exported to the United States.

One lesson learned from this first debt-for-nature swap is that the legislative and budget requirements should be established before the swap is made. Another is that such swaps need to be carefully monitored by environmental organizations to be sure that paper proposals labelled as models of sustainable development are not ways to disguise eventually unsustainable development. Debt-for-nature swaps are an excellent idea if they lead to true protection or restoration of some of Earth's remaining natural areas.

Since 1987, an increasing number of these arrangements have been made. This method will not solve the problem of the destruction and degradation of tropical forests and other natural systems, but it is an important tool for protecting priority areas.

Figure 10-15 Mixing economic development and conservation in a 1.5-million-hectare (3.7-million-acre) tract in Bolivia. A U.S. conservation organization arranged a debt-for-nature swap to help protect this land from harmful forms of development.

The governments of China, Nepal, Senegal, and South Korea have established successful tree-planting programs at the village level in selected areas. Typically, these are joint ventures by the government and village forestry associations, consisting of locally elected bodies managed by villagers. Government foresters supply villagers with seed or seedlings of fast-growing fuelwood trees and shrubs and provide advice on the planting and care of the trees; villagers do the planting. They are encouraged to plant these species in fields along

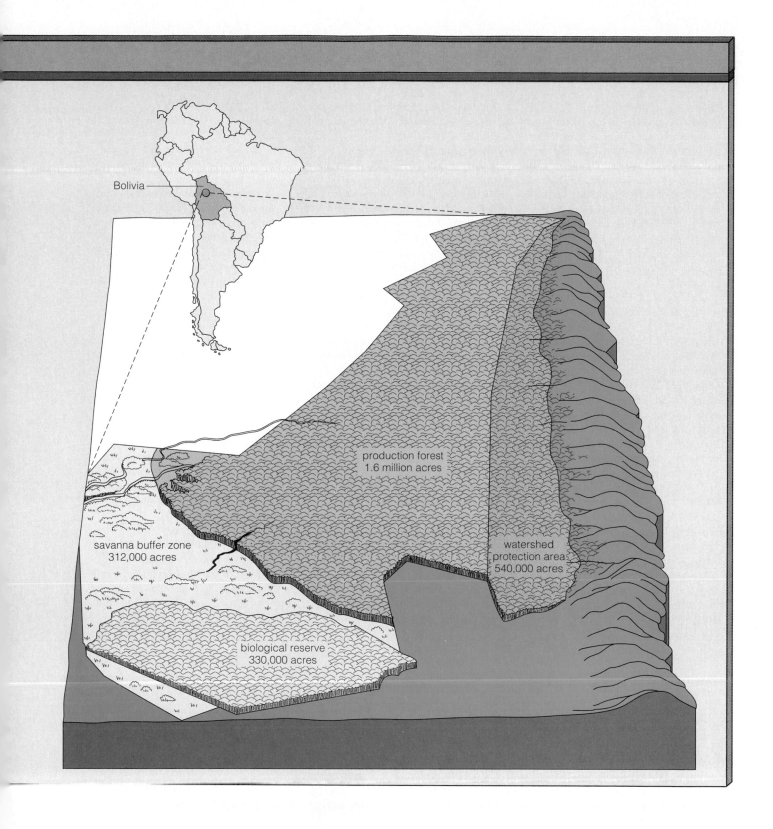

Bolivia

production forest
1.6 million acres

savanna buffer zone
312,000 acres

watershed
protection area
540,000 acres

biological reserve
330,000 acres

with crops (agroforestry), on unused patches of land around homes and farmland, and along roads and waterways. However, fast-growing tree species used to establish fuelwood plantations must be selected carefully to prevent harm to local ecosystems.

Another promising method is to encourage villagers to use the sun-dried roots of common gourds and squashes as cooking fuel. These rootfuel plants produce large quantities of burnable biomass per unit of area on dry deforested lands. These plants, which re-

Once, Costa Rica (Figure 10-16) was almost completely covered with tropical forests (Figure 2-5). Between 1963 and 1983, politically powerful ranching families cleared much of the country's forests to graze cattle, with most of the beef exported to the United States and western Europe (see Pro/Con on p. 263). By 1983, only 17% of the country's original tropical forest remained and soil erosion was rampant.

This pushed large numbers of the country's rural poor deeper into the jaws of the poverty trap. Many small landholders lost their land to ranchers, and rural jobs dried up because ranching requires much less labor than growing crops. Large numbers of landless poor migrated to expanding cities or were forced to farm fragile slopes or to clear forests in ways that accelerated the country's deforestation and soil erosion.

The bright note is that Costa Rica now leads all tropical countries in efforts to protect its remaining tropical forests and restore degraded areas. In the mid-1970s, Costa Rica established a system of national parks and reserves that presently protects 12% of the country's land area. Despite widespread degradation, tiny Costa Rica, like Madagascar (see Case Study on p. 259), is a "superpower" of biological diversity, with an estimated 500,000 species of plants and animals living on a land mass twice the size of Vermont.

Since Oscar Arias was elected president of the country in 1986, these conservation efforts have increased sharply. The country's plan is to combine conservation and sustainable economic development and to expand protected areas to 25% of the country's land by the end of this century. Even with this farsighted program, the country's forests are disappearing at the rate of 4% a year as the poor clear forests to survive.

A rugged mountainous region with a tropical rain forest contains the Guanacaste National Park, which has been designated an international biosphere reserve. One of the country's most visible projects is the restoration of the tropical deciduous forest in this park, the world's first project of this kind.

Daniel Janzen, professor of biology at the University of Pennsylvania in Philadelphia, has helped galvanize international support for this restoration project. Janzen is a leader in the growing field of rehabilitation and restoration of degraded ecosystems. His vision is to make the nearly 40,000 local people who live near the park an essential part of the restoration of 70,000 hectares (270 square miles) of degraded forest—a concept he calls *biocultural restoration*.

By actively participating in the project, local residents will reap enormous educational, economic, and environmental benefits. Local farmers have been hired to plant large areas with tree seeds and with seedlings started in Janzen's lab.

The essence of the program is to make the park a living classroom. Students in grade schools, high schools, and universities will study the ecology of the park in the classroom and go on annual field trips in the park itself. There will also be educational programs for civic groups and tourists from Costa Rica and elsewhere. These visitors and activities will stimulate the local economy.

The project will also serve as a training ground in tropical forest restoration for scientists throughout the world. Research scientists working on the project will give guest lectures in classrooms and lead some of the field trips.

Janzen recognizes that in 20 to 40 years, these children will be running the park and the local political system. If they understand the importance of their local environment, they are more likely to protect and sustain its biological resources.

---

generate themselves each year, help reduce soil erosion and also produce an edible seed that is high in protein.

Several countries have started programs to encourage rural and urban people to switch from energy-wasting open fires to more-efficient cook stoves and to other fuels. New types of stoves must be designed to make use of locally available materials and to provide both heat and light like the open fires they replace. Villagers in Burkina Faso in West Africa have been shown how to make a stove from mud and dung that cuts wood use by 30% to 70%. It can be made by villagers in half a day at virtually no cost.

Despite encouraging success in some countries, most LDCs suffering from fuelwood shortages have inadequate forestry policies and budgets and lack trained foresters. Such countries are cutting trees for fuelwood and forest products 10 to 20 times faster than new trees are being planted.

10-5 Deforestation in the United States and Canada

ANCIENT FORESTS: A DISAPPEARING NATIONAL AND GLOBAL HERITAGE Tropical deforestation is clearly a serious global environmental problem, but the same thing is happening to much of the remaining old-growth (virgin) forests in the United States. Untouched, old-growth forests once covered much of what is now

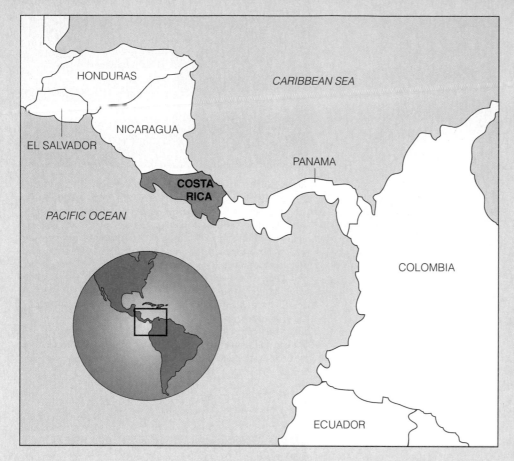

Figure 10-16 Where is Costa Rica? This country, smaller than West Virginia, has a population of 3 million and an annual population growth rate of 2.4%. Average total fertility is 3.3 children per woman, and population size is projected to reach 5.6 million by 2025. Annual per capita GNP is $1,790.

Costa Rica is making a dedicated effort to protect and sustain much of its remaining storehouse of the planet's biodiversity. However, it is waging an uphill fight against the highest rate of deforestation in Latin America, rapid population growth, air and water pollution, pesticide contamination, and the ever-present pressure of wealthy individual and multinational interests to overexploit its resources for short-term profit. At the present rate of deforestation, the country's forests could disappear in less than 15 years.

the lower 48 states (Figure 10-17). Today, an estimated 95% to 97% of these virgin forests have been cleared away, and most of what is left is found in the Pacific Northwest (Figure 10-18).

These virgin forests are dominated by a diversity of huge conifers, such as western red cedar, western hemlock, Sitka spruce, and Douglas fir (see photo on p. 253). Some tiny, scattered stands and strips of the once-vast forests of coastal redwood (Figure 2-6) and giant sequoia (Figure 4-6) remain, but most are gone. The tree species that dominate much of this region often live for 500 years and can survive for as long as 3,500 years — over 37 times longer than the United States has been in existence. Ecologist Elliot Norse calls these threatened giant trees "the whales of the forests."

What's left of these ancient forests, often referred to as the crown jewels of America's forests, is being destroyed and fragmented at a rapid rate — much higher than the rate of destruction of the rain forests in Brazil. Almost 90% are already gone, a far greater loss than that of tropical forests, coral reefs (see Case Study on p. 135), and wetlands (see Case Study on p. 137 and Spotlight on p. 143), which receive much well-deserved attention.

Each year, enough old-growth trees are taken from the Pacific Northwest to fill a convoy of logging trucks 32,000 kilometers (20,000 miles) long — almost enough to circle the entire planet. A single 500-year-old Douglas fir from this region can provide enough timber to build the average U.S. home. At current rates of logging, all

Virgin Forests, 1620

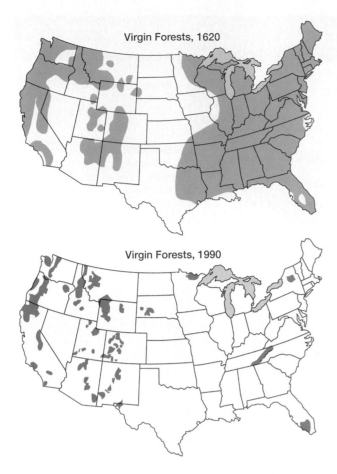

Virgin Forests, 1990

Figure 10-17 Vanishing primeval forests in the United States. Since 1620, an estimated 95% to 97% of the virgin forests that once covered much of America's lower 48 states have been cleared away. Most of the fragments that have not been cut are in public lands in the northwestern United States. About 80% of the area of the remaining old-growth forest in 12 national forests in this area is slated for logging. This has led to an intense struggle — a "war in the woods" over the fate of these irreplaceable ecosystems that are nonrenewable on a human time scale. Politically powerful officials of timber companies want to cut these trees for short-term profit and replace them with plantations of fast-growing trees that can be harvested every 45 to 65 years instead of the at least 200 years required for growth of a less diverse secondary forest after a virgin forest has been cut. Loggers and their families generally side with the timber companies because of fear of losing their livelihood. Environmentalists believe that most of these diverse and irreplaceable ecosystems, owned by the entire American public, should not be destroyed to serve the interests of timber company owners and loggers whose jobs will soon be gone anyway because of over-exploitation of this resource. (Data from the Wilderness Society and the U.S. Forest Service).

Figure 10-18 An evergreen coniferous old-growth forest in the Salmon Huckleberry Wilderness near Mt. Hood, Oregon. This forest, like other remaining old-growth forests of the Pacific Northwest, has more species of giant conifers, such as Douglas fir, western hemlock, and western red cedars, than any other place on Earth. In addition to a diversity of trees and other forms of wildlife, snags (standing dead trees) and boles (fallen dead trees) play crucial roles in providing habitats for numerous species that recycle key nutrients through the soil and back to the trees in these complex ecosystems. Attached to the ancient trees are a variety of mosses, lichens, liverworts, and other epiphytes that draw most of their nutrients from rainfall and from particles of organic matter falling from the trees and animals. Some of these plants provide nutrients for the trees — short-circuiting the usual soil-root-tree nutrient cycle.

Figure 10-19 Patch clear-cutting and logging roads in Gifford Pinchot National Forest, Washington. This destroys diverse ancient forests and fragments what remains into patches or islands that are often too small and too isolated to support some of the species that live in these biomes. After an area is clear-cut, the debris is burned, leaving a blackened soil, studded with tombstonelike stumps. A Forest Service ranger conceded that the clear-cut area looks "as if it had been nuked."

The growth of the conifers in old-growth forests depends on a mutualistic relationship between the tree roots and a class of fungi, known as mycorrhizae, that infect their roots. Unable to carry out photosynthesis, these underground fungi attach themselves to tree roots to get the sugars they need. In return, the fungi absorb water, nutrients, and oxygen from the soil and pass them along to the tree.

Antibiotic compounds in the fungi protect the tree from root-rot pathogens, and the sheath of fungus around the roots acts as a barrier to keep out some parasites. The fungi also produce chemicals that speed the growth of new root tips.

This root-fungus mutualistic relationship is, in turn, dependent upon symbiotic relationships with a number of the forest's small mammals, such as flying squirrels, voles, and mice. To reproduce, the fungus produces a fleshy collection of spores and other material—called

truffles—which are important sources of food for these mammals. The animals detect the truffles by their strong, cheesy smell, dig them up, and eat them. The spores themselves are not digested and are excreted in the animals' feces, thus spreading this important fungus throughout the forest.

Many of these animals, in turn, need large decaying logs for protection from predators. Spotted owls and other predators also play a key role in the forest's complex ballet of interactions by controlling the populations of the small mammals so they won't dig up too many truffles.

Fragmenting these forests into small patches and clearing and replacing them with tree plantations and second-growth forests destroys or severely reduces the vital network of symbiotic relationships that help sustain the complex, old-growth forest communities. Without snags, an estimated 10% of the wildlife species (excluding birds) would be

eliminated. Without snags and boles, about 29% of the wildlife found in old-growth forests would be eliminated.

Within 45 to 65 years, a clear-cut old-growth forest may be replaced with a tree farm, which can be harvested. But such farms, called managed forests, are intensively managed young-growth tree crops, not forests. They have little diversity and lack the large dead logs, snags, big trees, and diversity of wildlife that make up an old-growth forest.

Thus, the ancient forests that we are cutting down are not renewable on a human time scale, despite the boast of the owner of a logging company that he could "replicate the forest, redo it like a farmer growing a crop and do it better than nature." No amount of crossbreeding, genetic engineering, or boasting is going to replace old-growth forests or a 1,000-year-old Douglas fir.

---

unprotected ancient forests in western Washington and Oregon will be gone by the year 2023. In Olympic, Siskiyou, and Gifford Pinchot (Figure 10-19) national forests, the last stands will be gone by 2008, and could be irreparably fragmented by 1995.

ECOLOGY OF OLD-GROWTH FORESTS IN THE PACIFIC NORTHWEST In the Pacific Northwest, it typically takes 175 to 250 years for old-growth forest characteristics to develop and at least 350 years for the forest to reach its prime state of growth and diversity (Figure 10-18). These forests

- Store more carbon as organic matter than any other biome—twice as much per unit of area as tropical rain forests.

- Accumulate biomass more efficiently than any ecosystem on Earth.

- Hold enough moisture to help protect against fires and floods. Their complex natural filtration produces some of the world's purest water.

- Have the world's largest accumulation of dead standing trees (snags) and fallen dead trees

(boles), which decompose slowly over 200 to 400 years and recycle nutrients in the forest ecosystem.

- Are unusually rich in wildlife species (biodiversity) for their latitude.

- Help support some of the world's richest fisheries by providing spawning grounds for Pacific salmon.

We know relatively little about how these complex old-growth forests work, but research has revealed that they survive by a complex network of cooperative or symbiotic relationships between their species (see Spotlight above)

CONTROVERSY OVER OLD-GROWTH DEFORESTATION To timber cutters, the giant living trees and rotting dead trees in old-growth forests are valuable resources going to waste. They argue that they do the earth a favor by clearing away the living and decaying trees and allowing new ones to grow.

To them, these forests are resources that should be harvested for timber, profits, and jobs, not locked up to

About 96% of California's original coastal redwood forests have been cut. The philosophy of such overexploitation was summed up by Ronald Reagan when he was governor of California: "When you've seen one redwood tree, you've seen them all." Of the 4% of these forests left, about 3% is protected in parks (Figure 2-6).

Almost half of the remaining 1% is owned by one company, Pacific Lumber. Until 1985, it was a highly profitable, debt-free, model logging company, with a $60-million surplus in its employee pension fund. To make its redwood forests last indefinitely, it had for decades selectively cut individual trees by harvesting them no faster than they grew back.

That changed in 1985 when the company was taken over by Charles Hurwitz, a corporate raider and head of a financial empire worth an estimated $8.5 billion, in a leveraged buyout. In a leveraged buyout, investors borrow huge sums of money, usually through the sale of high-risk, or "junk," bonds, to purchase a company they think is undervalued in the stock market. They use the company's assets as collateral for the borrowed funds. Then they get the cash to pay off the interest on the debt and the junk bonds

by selling off the company's undervalued assets.

If the target is chosen correctly, the takeover can lead to huge profits for the investors. Timber companies are often attractive takeover targets because their forest assets can be cut and converted quickly into cash that can be invested in the takeover of other companies — a cut-and-git strategy of greed.

In 1986, Hurwitz raised $750 million to buy up Pacific Lumber's stock with a short-term bank loan and high-interest corporate (junk) bonds. Overnight, Pacific Lumber was burdened with a $750-million debt.

Hurwitz drained the $60-million excess from the pension fund and sold off the company's welding division and office building for $417 million. This gave him back almost two-thirds of what he paid for the company and plenty of money to make his interest payments, and he began paying off the junk bonds.

Then he began the rapid liquidation of the company's timberlands, estimated to be worth more than $1.4 billion. This included doubling (some say tripling) the rate of logging and switching from selective cutting to extensive clear-cutting of the company's old-growth red-

woods. At the current rate of cutting, these once indefinitely sustainable redwoods will be gone in about 17 years and the highest-value old-growth stands before 1995. Many employees are working overtime now to bring in larger harvests, but they fear that when the old redwoods and other holdings are gone, their jobs will be gone, too.

Critics have labelled this high-stakes game of leveraged buyout and corporate greed the California chain-saw massacre. But Hurwitz and others pat themselves on the back for being so clever in making a large profit by depleting chunks of Earth's natural capital. He likes to tell his critics and scared employees of companies he takes over about his version of the Golden Rule: "Those who have the gold rule."

Other timber companies that had been sustaining their forests are being forced to liquidate (clear-cut) their timber assets to ward off being taken over. Environmentalists call for changes in tax laws and lending regulations to halt such rapid depletion of nonrenewable or slowly renewable natural resources for short-term economic gain. What do you think should be done?

please environmentalists. Timber companies call forests renewable resources and point out that in the Northwest, they plant six young healthy trees for each one they cut.

They also note that the timber industry brings millions of dollars annually into the Northwest's economy and provides jobs for about 168,000 loggers and millworkers. Timber officials argue that protecting large areas of remaining old-growth forests on public lands will cause a loss of at least 26,000 jobs and hurt the economy of logging and milling towns throughout the Pacific Northwest.

The situation, however, is not that simple. The biggest reason for past and projected job losses in the timber industry in this region is not that some of the old-growth forests on public lands have been or will be

saved from chain saws and bulldozers. It is that the timber companies have already cut 90% of these irreplaceable ancient trees on unprotected lands and want to cut the rest. Then they will move on to other parts of the country or the world or invest their profits in other businesses.

Between 1983 and 1989, the timber cut in the Northwest increased 40% while employment in the timber industry per board foot cut decreased by 33%. This loss of more than 26,000 jobs was the result of automation and the exporting of large volumes of unprocessed logs overseas, where millworkers in Japan, China, and South Korea, rather than in the United States, turned them into lumber, plywood, and other wood products. Since 1980, about one out of four raw logs cut in the Northwest has been sent overseas for processing. The

Wilderness Society estimates that another 20,800 timber-related jobs will be lost, mostly for these same reasons, during the 1990s.

Current federal law makes it illegal to export unprocessed logs from federal lands west of the 100th meridian. Timber companies get around this ban, however, by a combination of legal loopholes and lax enforcement that enables them to export logs cut from their own private lands and then cut timber from publicly owned national forests for domestic sale. Technically, this practice, known as substitution, is illegal. However, reporting of exports is done on the honor system, and federal agencies rarely check the accuracy of such reports and don't have the personnel to police the situation. Even when violations are detected, the penalties are minute compared with the profits from violating the law. The result is that loggers and millworkers are mostly pawns in a high-stakes game of corporate profit and greed, and the nation and the world are losing irreplaceable forests.

Environmentalists charge that the Forest Service also plays a key role in the destruction of old-growth forests on public lands. The forests of the Northwest provide 60% of the revenue generated by the Forest Service's timber sales. This helps make up for the loss of millions of dollars of tax revenue from timber sales in many other national forests. Forest rangers who speak out against timber sales are likely to find themselves transferred. Those who build big timber sales programs are the ones who tend to get promoted. Some dynamics of the U.S. economic system also stimulate timber companies to liquidate old-growth timber on their lands and then turn to public lands (see Case Study on p. 276).

Environmentalists seek to protect remaining old-growth forests because of their rich, irreplaceable biodiversity. To ecologists, the living and dead trees in these forest represent not waste but vital nutrients being recycled in an incredibly complex ecosystem. These forests are living laboratories and treasuries of information for increasing our understanding of nature.

To environmentalists, America's remaining ancient forests are a national and global treasure whose true value can never be estimated in dollars or in board feet of timber. The fate of these forests is a national issue because these forests are owned by all the American people, not just the timber industry or the residents of a region. It is a global issue because these forests are important reservoirs of threatened global biodiversity and because what the United States does with its remaining virgin forests sets a precedent for other nations who have been asked not to destroy their own virgin forests, wetlands, coral reefs, and other vital parts of Earth's natural capital for short-term economic gain.

The majestic beauty of old-growth forests in the Pacific Northwest, and elsewhere, attract growing numbers of visitors who seek connections with a wild world that is already gone or is going fast. Environmentalists contend that the long-term aesthetic, recreational, and tourist values of the country's remaining old-growth forests far exceed the economic value of cutting them down. The spotted owl has become a symbol in the struggle between environmentalists and timber company owners over the fate of unprotected old-growth forests on public lands in the Pacific Northwest (see Spotlight on p. 278).

REDUCING OLD-GROWTH FOREST DESTRUCTION Ways to reduce the destruction of remaining old growth forests in the United States include

- Reducing the annual sale and harvesting of timber from federal public lands by about 50%.

- Sharply raising the price of timber sold from national forests and other public lands. The bargain-basement sales of public timber discourage private owners from managing their forests more intensively.

- Providing aid to help retain loggers and millworkers, whose jobs are being threatened by automation, exports of raw logs, forest depletion, and forest protection.

- Giving logging and milling towns grants and interest-free loans to spur economic diversification.

- Closing loopholes in and strictly enforcing the law that bans the export of unprocessed logs from the Pacific Northwest, and expanding this ban to the entire United States.

- Taxing exports of raw logs heavily, but leaving exports of lumber, plywood, and other finished wood products untaxed.

- Providing tax breaks and interest-free loans for revamping mills to cut smaller secondary-growth logs instead of large old-growth trees.

- Providing funds for extensive reforestation and restoration on denuded lands to furnish alternative jobs for unemployed loggers and millworkers.

- Using the revenue from higher prices on timber cut from public lands and from taxes on exported logs to add productive second-growth timberland to the national forest system, while leaving remaining virgin forests as reservoirs of biological diversity. Some of this revenue could also be used to rehabilitate degraded forestland.

- Allowing individuals, conservation organizations, or other groups to buy conservation easements that prevent harvesting of the timber on designated areas of old-growth forests on public lands. In such *conservation-for-tax-relief swaps*, purchasers would be allowed tax breaks for the funds they put up.

If we don't do things like this, we won't save the jobs or remaining old-growth forests.

The spotted owl (Figure 10-20) is a monogamous, territorial bird that lives almost exclusively in at least 200-year-old-growth forests dominated by Douglas fir in the Pacific Northwest. These nocturnal owls hunt flying squirrels, red-backed voles, and mice and nest only in standing dead trees. To get enough food to survive, each nesting pair of these predators needs between 931 and 1,800 hectares (2,300 and 4,500 acres) of old-growth forest.

This species is vulnerable to extinction because of its low reproductive rates and the low survival rate of juveniles through their first five years. Because the owl feeds at the top trophic levels in old-growth forest food webs, it is what ecologists call an *indicator species*, which can be used as a measure of the health of the ancient forests where it lives. If the owl's survival is threatened, probably dozens of other species are just as threatened.

An estimated 1,700 breeding pairs of these owls live in the mid- to low-elevation virgin forests dominated by Douglas fir in the Pacific Northwest. However, estimates range from 1,000 to 3,000 breeding pairs because these nocturnal and secretive birds are hard to count. Because of their slow breeding potential, it would take 1,700 breeding pairs in a protected habitat about 100 years to grow to 2,200 breeding pairs.

In July 1990, the U.S. Fish and Wildlife Service added the spotted owl to the federal list of threatened species. This requires that its estimated 1.2-million-hectare (3-million-acre) habitat be protected from logging or other practices that would decrease its chances of survival.

Listing of the spotted owl as a threatened species, however, does not affect existing logging contracts on federal land in its habitat, and timber companies are looking for ways to get around the decision. For instance, they are trying to persuade the president and the Congress to revise the Endangered Species Act to allow economic considerations, or to declare some or most of the spotted owl's protected habitat an exception to this law.

A team of scientists asked by the federal government to study the situation recommended that the spotted owl be protected by banning logging on federal lands where it lives. To accomplish this, the scientists recommended that the annual harvest of old-growth timber on federal lands in the Pacific Northwest be reduced by 47%. However, President Bush rejected this recommendation and proposed that the harvest be cut by only 21%, a compromise that angered both environmentalists and timber company representatives.

Despite simplistic media coverage, this isn't an owl issue. The owl is merely a symbol of the broader clash between timber company owners who want to cut most remaining old-growth stands in the national forests and environmentalists who want to protect them. The threatened owl is the best tool environmentalists have available to help them achieve this broader goal.

Recently, another rare species, the Pacific yew, has opened up a new front in the battle to preserve old-growth forests in the Pacific Northwest. An extract (taxol) from this tree's bark can be used to effectively treat ovarian cancer, which each year kills about 12,000 women in the United States. Taxol may also be used in the treatment of malignant melamona (an often fatal form of skin cancer) and breast cancer.

Yew trees are frequently found in the same forests as old-growth species, such as Douglas fir. These slow-growing trees, which have little commercial value as timber and so are often burned by loggers, take nearly 100 years to grow large enough to be a useful source of taxol.

Figure 10-20 The endangered northern spotted owl lives mostly out of sight in old-growth forests of the Pacific Northwest. Two decades ago, it was one of the least-known birds of North America. Now, it is one of the best known because of its role in the controversy over protecting many of the remaining old-growth forests on public lands in the Pacific Northwest from being cut. Using the Endangered Species Act to protect the spotted owl is a way to reach the much wider goal of preserving biodiversity by preventing further destruction of America's rapidly dwindling old-growth forests.

The American Cancer Society, cancer researchers, and ten leading environmental organizations petitioned the Department of the Interior to list the tree as a threatened species but in 1991 were turned down. Environmental groups are now seeking other means of protection for the tree.

Figure 10-21 Wangari Maathai, the first Kenyan woman to earn a Ph.D., organized the Green Belt movement in 1977. The goal of this widely regarded women's self-help community action group is to plant a tree for each of Kenya's 25 million people. She recruited 50,000 women to establish tree nurseries and to help farmers raise tree seedlings. Members of the group get a small fee for each tree that survives. By 1990, more than 10 million trees had been planted. She and members of this group are true Earth heroes.

DESTRUCTION OF OLD-GROWTH FORESTS IN WESTERN CANADA In 1990, Canada ranked third in the world in producing softwood timber. One out of every ten jobs in Canada is related directly to forestry.

In 1989, timber companies in British Columbia alone cut more timber than was cut from all of the U.S. national forests. In British Columbia, there are no limits on the size of clear-cut areas, which sometimes extend for kilometers. Each year, timber companies clear-cut about 270,000 hectares (667,000 acres) of old-growth forest in British Cloumbia, and they hold government licenses to harvest almost all of what remains.

In Canada, a timber company receives a free license to cut but must pay a small tax on each tree cut down. If the Canadian government wants to withdraw part of the land covered by a timber cutting license, it must pay the company the current value of the standing timber, usually millions of dollars.

Such generous concessions to timber companies explain why so little (5%) of British Columbia's old-growth forests are protected as parks and reserves. Environmentalists have called for the Canadian government to protect 12% of the remaining old-growth forests in western Canada before most of what is worth saving is gone. One tool in this struggle may be to declare certain areas off limits to logging to protect the

endangered marbled murrelet, a rare and secretive bird that nests in the treetops of some forest areas in British Columbia.

10-6 What Can Individuals Do?

CHANGE BEGINS FROM THE BOTTOM UP People throughout the world have engaged in efforts to reduce deforestation and forest degradation. In Malaysia, Penan tribesmen have joined forces with environmentalists in an effort to halt destructive logging. In Brazil, 500 conservation organizations have organized a coalition to preserve the country's remaining tropical forests. In the United States, members of Earth First! have perched in the tops of giant Douglas firs and put their bodies in front of logging trucks and bulldozers to prevent the felling of trees in national forests (see Figure 25-5).

Today, up to 25,000 women's self-help groups are active in Earth-sustaining activities, especially soil conservation and tree planting. In Kenya, Wangari Maathai started the Green Belt movement, a national effort by 50,000 women farmers and half a million school children to plant trees for firewood and to help hold the soil in place (Figure 10-21). This inspiring leader has said:

I don't really know why I care so much. I just have something inside me that tells me that there is a problem and I have got to do something about it. And I'm sure it's the same voice that is speaking to everyone on this planet, at least everybody who seems to be concerned about the fate of the world, the fate of this planet.

For two decades, women and children in parts of India have gone into nearby forests, joined hands, and encircled trees to prevent commercial loggers from cutting them down (see Individuals Matter on p. 280).

WHAT YOU CAN DO Each of us has an important role to play (see Individuals Matter on p. 281).* Worldwide, during the 1990s, we need to plant and take care of trees on about 1.2 million square kilometers (463,000 square miles) of land (especially in LDCs) to reduce erosion on deforested areas, provide fuelwood, and help slow projected global warming. This is roughly equal to the land area of South Africa or the combined

---

*Printing this textbook on recycled paper has not been possible because of high costs, unreliable supplies, and problems with paper quality and inking requirements for the use of color. As an alternative, for each tree used to produce this book, Wadsworth Publishing Company and I donate money to plant and care for a tree in a tropical forest. In addition, I plant 50 trees for each tree I use as paper in preparing this book.

In the late fifteenth century, Jambeshwar, the son of the leader of a village in northern India, renounced his inheritance and set out to teach people to care for their health and the environment. He developed 29 principles for living and founded a Hindu sect, called the Bishnois, based on a religious duty to protect trees and wild animals.

In 1730, when the Maharajah of Jodhpur in northern India ordered that the few trees left in the area be cut down, the Bishnois forbade it. Women rushed in and hugged the trees to protect them, but the Maharajah's minister ordered the work to proceed anyway. According to legend, 363 Bishnois women died on that day.

In the 1960s, people in the villages located in the foothills of the Himalaya mountain ranges of northern India faced disaster from severe deforestation, torrential floods, and landslides. Over two decades, the slopes of many of the mountains had been cleared of most trees.

This deforestation occurred because of intensive commercial logging combined with the needs of a growing population for firewood and land for cultivation. Men were being forced to leave the villages to find work in other parts of the country. Women were having to travel further every day in search of firewood.

In 1973, some women in the Himalaya village of Gopeshwar started the modern Chipko (an Indian word for "hug" or "cling to") movement to protect the remaining trees in a nearby forest from being cut down to make tennis rackets for export. It began when Chandi Prasad Bhatt, a village leader, urged villagers to run into the forest ahead of loggers and "hold fast," or "chipko," to protect the trees (Figure 10-22), thus carrying on the tradition started several hundred years earlier by the Bishnois.

Robert Hutchison

Figure 10-22 Leader of the Chipko movement protecting a tree in northern India from being cut down for export to industrialized countries. This is another example of a successful grassroots group dedicated to helping sustain the earth. Although the Chipko leader shown here is a man, women are actually the driving force of this movement.

When the loggers came, local women, children, and men rushed into the forests, flung their arms around trees, and dared the loggers to let the axes fall on their backs. This successful movement spread rapidly as their action inspired the women of other Himalaya villages to protect their forests. As a result, the commercial cutting of timber in the hills of the Indian state of Uttar Pradesh has been banned.

Since 1973, the Chipko movement, whose slogan is given in the quote that opens this chapter, has widened its efforts. Now the women who still guard trees from loggers also plant trees, prepare village forestry plans, and build walls to stop soil erosion. This inspired Ghanshyam "Shaliana," a Chipko poet, to write: *Embrace the life of living trees and streams to your hearts. Resist the digging of mountains which kill our forests and streams.*

The spreading actions of such Earth citizens should inspire us to help protect the earth. Sustaining the earth will come mostly from the bottom up, not from the top down. It will happen because of the daily actions of ordinary people who collectively force leaders to get on the bandwagon or lose their power.

- If you or your loved ones own forested land, develop a management and conservation plan for the sustainable use of those resources.

- Plant trees on a regular basis in your yard and in your town.* Take care of trees you plant so they survive. Select species adapted for growth under local climate and soil conditions.

- Join or form a neighborhood or block association devoted mainly to tree planting and care.

- Get local officials to involve school children in planting and caring for trees around schools and on other public lands.

- Get local businesses, utilities, and land developers to plant and care for trees on their property and to donate funds to local tree-planting groups.

- Develop and implement a tree-planting and care program for your school.

- Cut down on the use of wood and paper products you don't really need, recycle paper products, and buy recycled paper products. Pressure your office or school to start a paper-recycling program.

- Recycle aluminum cans, or better yet, switch to reusable glass beverage containers. Recognize that using aluminum cans or other throwaway aluminum products encourages the development of more aluminum mines and smelters in the Amazon basin, powered by dams. These dams flood large areas of tropical forests and displace indigenous people from their lands.

- Reduce your consumption of beef, some of which is produced by clearing tropical and other forests (Figure 10-11).

- Don't buy furniture or other items made from tropical hardwoods, such as teak, mahogany, and plywood containing mahogany. Claims that wood products do not use tropical hardwoods are almost impossible to verify. If you must buy such hardwoods, look for the Good-Wood Seal given by Friends of the Earth.

- Don't buy a tropical plant or animal (including fish). If you must do this, buy one that was raised in the United States.

- Contribute time, money, or both to organizations devoted to forest conservation, especially of the world's rapidly disappearing tropical forests, and tree planting.†

- Engage in protests and physically help protect virgin forests from being cleared or degraded.

- Don't use plastic or cut trees at Christmas. Instead, buy a living tree in a tub for later planting outdoors.

- Help rehabilitate or restore a degraded area of forest or grassland near where you live.

- Don't buy products produced by companies involved in destructive development projects in tropical forests. Information on such companies can be obtained from the Rainforest Action Network and Friends of the Earth (see Appendix 1).

- Lobby elected officials to protect all remaining virgin forests on public lands in the United States. American citizens own these lands and have an obligation to see that they are used responsibly and that their biodiversity is handed on to future generations of humans and other species.

- Support and push for implementation of proposals such as those listed on pages 267 and 269 to reduce tropical deforestation and those on page 277 to reduce deforestation of old-growth forests in the United States.

*Sources of information for tree planting are Treepeople, *The Simple Act of Planting a Tree* (Los Angeles: Tarcher, 1990); Global Releaf (American Forestry Association, P.O. Box 2000, Washington, DC 20013); and the 1990 *Green Front Report* (available from Friends of the Trees, P.O. Box 1466, Chelan, WA 98816). You can also get technical assistance on species and tree planting from county cooperative extension services, state forestry or conservation departments, or local parks and public works departments.

†Examples are the American Forestry Association (which has a campaign to plant 100 million trees throughout the United States between 1989 and 1992), Environmental Defense Fund, Friends of the Trees, Greenpeace, Nature Conservancy, Programme for Belize (each $50 donation is used to buy and protect an acre of endangered tropical forestland in Belize, a small country in Central America), Rainforest Action Network, Rainforest Alliance (each $55 donation is used to buy and protect one acre of rain forest in Costa Rica's Monteverde Cloud Forest Reserve, Figure 5-23), Trees for Life, and Treepeople. Addresses and other organizations are given in Appendix 1.

Norman Myers

Norman Myers is an international consultant in environment and development with emphasis on conservation of wildlife species and tropical forests. He has served as a consultant for many development agencies and research organizations, including the U.S. National Academy of Sciences, the World Bank, the Organization for Economic Cooperation and Development, various UN agencies, and the World Resources Institute. Among his recent publications (see Further Readings) are The Sinking Ark *(1979),* Conversion of Tropical Moist Forests *(1980), A* Wealth of Wild Species *(1983),* The Primary Source *(1984),* The Gaia Atlas of Planet Management *(1985), and* The Gaia Atlas of Future Worlds *(1990).*

Tropical forests still cover an area roughly equivalent to the "lower 48" United States. Climatic and biological data suggest they could have once covered an area at least twice as large. So we have already lost half of them, mostly in the recent past.

Worse, remote-sensing surveys show that we are now destroying the forests at a rate of at least 1.25% a year, and we are grossly degrading them at a rate of at least another 1.25% a year — and both rates are accelerating rapidly. Unless we act now to halt this loss, within just another few decades at most, there could be little left, except perhaps a block in central Africa and another in the western part of the Amazon basin. Even those remnants may not survive the combined pressures of population growth and land hunger beyond the middle of the next century.

This means that we are imposing one of the most broad-scale and impoverishing impacts on the biosphere that it has ever suffered throughout its 4 billion years of existence. Tropical forests are the greatest celebration of nature to appear on the face of the planet since the first flickerings of life. They are exceptionally complex ecologically, and they are remarkably rich biotically. Although they now account for 6% to 7% of the earth's land surface, they still are home for half, and perhaps three-quarters or more, of all the planet's species of plant and animal life. Thus, elimination of these forests is by far the leading factor in the mass extinction of species that appears likely over the next few decades.

Already, we are certainly losing several species every day because of clearing and degradation of tropical forests. The time will surely come, and come soon, when we shall be losing many thousands every year. The implications are profound, whether they be scientific, aesthetic, ethical — or simply economic. In medicine alone, we benefit from myriad drugs and pharmaceuticals derived from tropical forest plants. The commercial value of these products worldwide can be reckoned at $20 billion each year.

By way of example, the rosy periwinkle [Figure 10-10] from Madagascar's tropical forests has produced two potent drugs against Hodgkin's disease, leukemia, and other blood cancers. Madagascar has — or used to have — at

areas of Texas, California, and Pennsylvania. Most of these trees need to be planted and cared for on eroded hillsides and next to dwellings, and sometimes planted with crops (agroforestry). The estimated annual cost runs from $2.6 billion in 1990 to $6.8 billion in the year 2000.

The task is enormous, but deforestation can be stopped and degraded forestlands can be restored — if you and enough other people care. Ours is the last generation that has the opportunity to save Earth's remaining virgin forests in the tropics and elsewhere. Act — starting now!

Forests precede civilizations, deserts follow them.

FRANÇOIS-AUGUSTE-RENÉ
DE CHATEAUBRIAND

DISCUSSION TOPICS

1. What difference could the loss of essentially all the remaining virgin tropical forests and old-growth forests in the United States have on your life and on the life of any child you might have?

2. Explain how eating a hamburger in some U.S. fast-food chains indirectly contributes to the destruction of vir-

least 8,000 plant species, of which more than 7,000 could be found nowhere else. Today, Madagascar has lost 93% of its virgin tropical forest [Figure 10-5]. The U.S. National Cancer Institute estimates that there could be many plants in tropical forests with potential against various cancers, provided pharmacologists can get to them before they are eliminated by chain saws and bulldozers.

We benefit in still other ways from tropical forests. One critical environmental service is the famous "sponge effect," by which the forests soak up rainfall during the wet season and then release it in regular amounts throughout the dry season. When tree cover is removed and this watershed function is impaired, the result is a yearly regime of floods followed by droughts, which destroys property and reduces agricultural production. There is also concern that if tropical deforestation becomes wide enough, it could trigger local, regional, or even global changes in climate. Such climatic upheavals would affect the lives of billions of people, if not the whole of humankind.

All this raises important questions about our role in the biosphere and our relations with the natural world around us. As we proceed on our disruptive way in tropical forests, we—political leaders and the general public alike—give scarcely a moment's thought to what we are doing. We are deciding the fate of the world's tropical forests unwittingly, yet effectively and increasingly.

The resulting shift in evolution's course, stemming from the elimination of tropical forests, will rank as one of the greatest biological upheavals since the dawn of life. It will equal, in scale and significance, the development of aerobic respiration, the emergence of flowering plants, and the arrival of limbed animals, taking place over eons of time [Figures 6-6 and 7-27].

Whereas those were enriching disruptions in the course of life on this planet, the loss of biotic diversity associated with the destruction of tropical forests will be almost entirely an impoverishing phenomenon brought about entirely by human actions. And it will all have occurred within the twinkling of a geologic eye.

In short, our intervention in tropical forests should be viewed as one of the most challenging problems that humankind has ever encountered. After all, we are the first species ever to be able to look upon nature's work and to decide whether we should consciously eliminate it or leave much of it untouched.

So the decline of tropical forest is one of the great sleeper issues of our time. Yet, we can still save much of these forests and the species they contain. Should we not consider ourselves fortunate that we alone among all generations are being given the chance to preserve tropical forests as the most exuberant expression of nature in the biosphere—and thereby to support the right to life of many of our fellow species and their capacity to undergo further evolution without human interference?

Guest Essay Discussion

1. What obligation, if any, do you as an individual have to preserve a significant portion of the world's remaining tropical forests?

2. Should MDCs provide most of the money to preserve remaining tropical forests in LDCs? Explain.

3. What can you do to help preserve some of the world's tropical forests? Which, if any, of these actions do you plan to carry out?

gin tropical forests? What, if anything, do you believe should be done about this?

3. Explain why you agree or disagree with each of the proposals listed on pages 267 and 269 concerning protection of the world's tropical forests.

4. Governments are in the process of virtually eliminating the world's remaining hunter gatherers and other indigenous peoples, who have lived gently on the land for centuries and who can teach us much about how to live sustainably. This cultural extinction is being done in the name of "progress" by taking over their lands. Some believe that the world's remaining tribal and indigenous people should be given title to the land they and their

ancestors have lived on for centuries, a decisive voice in formulating policies about resource development in their areas, and the right to be left alone by modern civilization. We have created protected reserves for endangered wild species, so why not create reserves for these endangered human cultures? What do you think? Explain.

5. Should all cutting on remaining ancient forests in U.S. national forestlands be banned? Explain.

6. Explain why you agree or disagree with each of the proposals listed on page 277 concerning protection of remaining old-growth forests in the United States.

CHAPTER 11

CLIMATE CHANGE, OZONE DEPLETION, AND NUCLEAR WAR

General Questions and Issues

1. How can our activities cause global warming, and what are some possible effects from doing this?

2. What can we do to delay and reduce possible global warming and adjust to its effects?

3. How are we depleting ozone in the stratosphere, and what are some possible effects from doing this?

4. What can we do to slow down ozone depletion?

5. What effects might even limited nuclear war have on Earth's life-support systems for humans and many other species?

We, humanity, have finally done it: disturbed the environment on a global scale.

THOMAS E. LOVEJOY

LTHOUGH OUR SPECIES has been on Earth for only an eyeblink of Earth's overall existence, we are now altering the chemical content of Earth's entire atmosphere 10 to 100 times faster than its natural rate of change over the past 100,000 years (see cartoon). Projected global warming brought about by our one-time binge of fossil-fuel burning (Figure 3-5) and tropical deforestation (Figure 1-10), depletion of life-sustaining ozone in the stratosphere (Figure 4-3) caused by our widespread use of chlorofluorocarbons and other chemicals that we could learn to do without, and the buildup of nuclear weapons are now frightening global environmental threats.

Largely invisible and silent, these ultimate problems will continue building until they trigger significant thresholds of change. When those thresholds are crossed, it will be too late to prevent the drastic, lasting, and unpredictable effects they have on the ecosphere that supports us and other species. There will be no place for us to escape to and no place to hide from the effects of these global changes. Dealing with these planetary emergencies to prevent the ultimate tragedy of the commons for our species and many other species will require significant changes in the way we think and act and international cooperation on an unprecedented scale.

11-1 Global Warming from an Enhanced Greenhouse Effect

PAST CLIMATE CHANGES   Earth's average surface temperatures and climate are the result of a number of interacting factors, which we only partially understand (Section 5-1). Throughout Earth's 4.6 billion years of existence, there have been pronounced changes in the composition of the atmosphere, geosphere, hydrosphere, and biosphere and in the nature of the interactions between these portions of the ecosphere

A CENTURY OF ABUSE RISES TO HAUNT AN OBLIVIOUS, DECADENT SOCIETY!

REVENGE OF THE ENVIRONMENT

WITH INDUSTRIAL POLLUTERS, SELF-SERVING POLITICIANS, GREEDY DEVELOPERS, AND AN APATHETIC PUBLIC   COMING SOON!

(Figure 4-2). By examining the fossil evidence of climate-sensitive organisms and the composition of rock strata and ice cores, scientists have tried to piece together a crude picture of Earth's past climatic history.

This scientific detective work—which is preliminary and often speculative—suggests that the estimated average surface temperature of the earth has fluctuated considerably over geologic time. It indicates that over the past 800,000 years, there have been several great ice ages, during which much of the planet was covered with thick ice sheets (Figure 7-10). Each glacial period lasted about 100,000 years and was followed by a warmer interglacial period lasting 10,000 to 12,500 years.

The last great ice age ended about 10,000 years ago. At the coldest point of that ice age, the mean temperature of Earth's surface was only about 5°C (9°F) cooler than it is today. Thus, a fluctuation of this magnitude, up or down, is considered a significant temperature change and leads to drastic changes in climate throughout the world.

For the past 10,000 years, we have been enjoying the warmer temperatures (compared with those of the last ice age) of the latest interglacial period (Figure 11-1). During this period of favorable climate, Earth's mean surface temperature has risen about 5°C (9°F). Agriculture began and spread rapidly throughout the world to support the exponential increase in world population (Figure 2-2) that this generally warmer climate allowed.

During the warm period we now live in, Earth's mean surface temperatures have fluctuated only moderately, typically up or down 0.5°C to 1°C (0.9°F to 1.8°F), over 100- to 200-year periods. These moderate and relatively slow fluctuations in climate have not led to drastic changes in the nature of soils and vegetation patterns throughout the world, thus allowing large increases in food production.

The greatest threat to human food production and economic systems and to wildlife habitats is rapid climate change involving only a few degrees in Earth's mean surface temperature, taking place over a few decades. This would drastically alter the places where certain biomes and thus certain species could exist (Figure 5-11) and would change conditions faster than some species, especially vegetation that supports animal species, could adapt and migrate to other areas. Such rapid changes in climate would shift the areas where we could grow food. Some areas would become uninhabitable because of lack of water or because of flooding from a rise in average sea levels.

TEMPERATURE, CLIMATE, AND THE CHEMICAL COMPOSITION OF THE ATMOSPHERE The chemical composition of the troposphere and the stratosphere (Figure 4-3) is an important factor determining the mean temperature of the planet's surface and thus

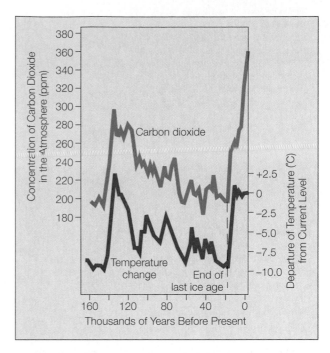

Figure 11-1 Long-term variations of mean global surface temperature and average tropospheric carbon dioxide levels over the last 160,000 years. Since the last great ice age ended, about 10,000 years ago, we have been living in a warm interglacial period. One factor determining Earth's mean surface temperature is the greenhouse effect, caused by the presence of heat-trapping gases in the troposphere (Figure 5-9). Carbon dioxide is the principal greenhouse gas, and its levels in the troposphere vary as a result of changes in the global carbon cycle (Figure 4-28). Changes in carbon dioxide levels in the troposphere correlate fairly closely with changes in Earth's mean surface temperature and thus its climate, although other factors may also influence global climate.

its climate. Heat is trapped in the troposphere by a natural process called the *greenhouse effect* (Figure 5-9).

The amount of heat trapped depends mostly on the concentrations of various heat-trapping gases, known as *greenhouse gases*, in the troposphere. The principal greenhouse gases are carbon dioxide, water vapor (mostly in clouds), ozone, methane, nitrous oxide, and chlorofluorocarbons. Increase the concentrations of these gases faster than they are removed from the troposphere and Earth's mean surface temperature increases. Decrease their concentrations faster than they are emitted and Earth's mean surface temperature drops.

The two greenhouse gases with the largest concentrations in the troposphere are carbon dioxide and water vapor. Addition of carbon dioxide to the troposphere and removal from it are controlled mostly by the global gaseous carbon cycle (Figure 4-28), and the level of water vapor is controlled by the hydrologic cycle (Figure 4-34). Over the past 160,000 years, estimated levels of water vapor in the troposphere have remained fairly constant while those of carbon dioxide have fluctuated.

Figure 11-2 Increases in average concentrations of greenhouse gases in the troposphere, mostly because of human activities. (Data from Electric Power Research Institute. Adapted by permission from Cecie Starr and Ralph Taggart, *Biology: The Unity and Diversity of Life*, 5th ed., Belmont, Calif.: Wadsworth, 1989)

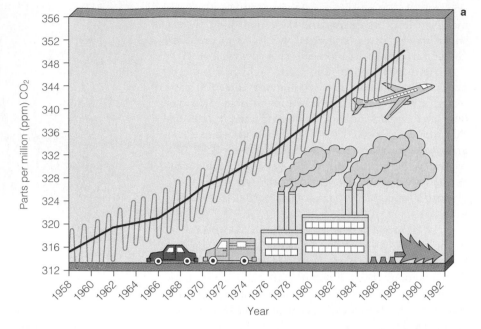

a. Carbon dioxide (CO₂) This gas is responsible for 49% of the human-caused input of greenhouse gases. The main sources are fossil-fuel burning (67%) and deforestation (33%). CO₂ remains in the atmosphere for about 500 years. Industrial countries account for about 76% of annual emissions.

b. Chlorofluorocarbons (CFCs) These gases are responsible for 14% of the human input of greenhouse gases and by 2020 will probably be responsible for about 25% of the input. CFCs also deplete ozone in the stratosphere. The main sources are leaking air conditioners and refrigerators, evaporation of industrial solvents, production of plastic foams, and propellants in aerosol spray cans (in some countries). CFCs remain in the atmosphere for 60 to 400 years, depending on the type, and generally have 10,000 to 20,000 times the impact per molecule on global warming that each molecule of CO₂ has.

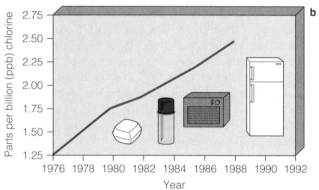

c. Methane (CH₄) This gas is responsible for about 18% of the human input of greenhouse gases. It is produced by bacteria that decompose organic matter in oxygen-poor environments. About 40% of global methane emissions come from oxygen-poor environments such as waterlogged soils, bogs, marshes, and rice paddies. A 1°C (1.8°F) warming may increase methane emissions from these sources by 20% to 30% and amplify global warming. Other sources of methane are landfills, burning of forests and grasslands, the guts of termites, whose populations are expanding to digest the dead woody materials left after deforestation, and the digestive tracts of billions of cattle, sheep, pigs, goats, horses, and other livestock. Some methane also leaks from coal seams, natural gas wells, pipelines, storage tanks, furnaces, dryers, and stoves. Natural sources produce an estimated one-third of the methane in the atmosphere, and human activities produce the rest. CH₄ remains in the troposphere for 7 to 10 years, and each molecule is about 25 times more effective in warming the troposphere than a molecule of carbon dioxide.

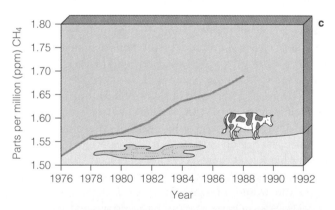

d. Nitrous oxide (N₂O) This gas is responsible for 6% of the global warming. It is released from the breakdown of nitrogen fertilizers in soil, livestock wastes, and nitrate-contaminated groundwater, and by biomass burning. Its average stay in the troposphere is 150 years. It also depletes ozone in the stratosphere. The global warming from each molecule of this gas is about 230 times that of a CO₂ molecule.

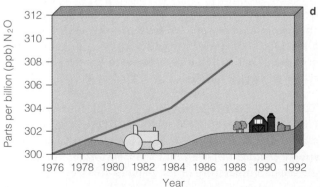

Estimated changes in the carbon dioxide content of the troposphere during this period correlate fairly closely with variations in Earth's mean surface temperature (Figure 11-1).

RISING LEVELS OF GREENHOUSE GASES Until recently, most greenhouse gases were emitted and removed from the troposphere by Earth's major biogeochemical cycles without disruptive interferences from human activities. However, since the Industrial Revolution, and especially since 1950, we have been putting enormous quantities of greenhouse gases into the atmosphere (Figure 11-2), primarily from the burning of fossil fuels (57%), the use of chlorofluorocarbons (17%), agriculture (15%), and deforestation (8%). There is growing concern that these gases can amplify the natural greenhouse effect and turn up the planet's thermostat fairly rapidly.

Satellite and other measurements indicate that currently carbon dioxide accounts for about 49% of the annual human-caused input of greenhouse gases, chlorofluorocarbons (CFCs) for 14%, methane for 18%, and nitrous oxide for 6%. However, the last three gases have a much greater warming effect per molecule than carbon dioxide (Figure 11-2). Overall, the United States is responsible for the largest emissions of greenhouse gases (17%), followed by the Soviet Union (14%), European countries (12%), China (8%), Brazil (6%), India (5%), Japan (4%), and Indonesia (3%). Countries with the highest per capita emissions in 1988 were, in order, the United States, Australia, Canada, Myamar (Burma), Germany, and the Soviet Union.

Carbon dioxide is released when carbon or any carbon-containing compound is burned. Fossil fuels provide almost 80% of the world's energy (Figure 3-5), cause about 75% of current CO_2 emissions, and produce most of the world's air pollution. The carbon dioxide level in the troposphere is now the highest it has been in at least 130,000 years, and the level is rising. The United States is by far the largest emitter of CO_2 (20% of the world's emissions), followed by the Soviet Union. Thus, the projected global warming crisis, along with greatly increased air pollution, is largely an *energy crisis* caused mostly by rapid, large scale, and wasteful burning of the world's fossil fuels.

To make matters worse, we are reducing Earth's ability to remove carbon dioxide through photosynthesis by deforestation around the globe (Chapter 10). Deforestation, especially the wholesale clearing and burning of tropical forests, is believed to account for about 20% of the increase in carbon dioxide levels. The EPA projects that unless action is taken to reduce fossil-fuel burning and deforestation, global emissions of carbon dioxide, the principal greenhouse gas, will more than double between 1985 and 2025, with emissions doubling in MDCs and quadrupling in LDCs.

Modern farming, forestry, industries, and motor vehicles are also releasing other greenhouse gases — mostly chlorofluorocarbons, methane, nitrous oxide, and ozone formed in smog — into the troposphere at an accelerating rate (Figure 11-2b, c, and d).

PROJECTED GLOBAL WARMING The greenhouse effect is one of the most widely accepted scientific theories. Scientists disagree, however, on how much average global temperature might rise as a result of our increasing inputs of greenhouse gases into the atmosphere, whether other factors in the climate system will counteract or amplify a temperature rise, how fast temperatures might climb, and what the effects will be on various areas. The reasons for these disagreements are uncertainty about the accuracy of the mathematical models and geological evidence used to project changes in climate and assumptions about how rapidly we will consume fossil fuels and clear forests. Such controversy is a normal part of science (see Spotlight on p. 288).

Since 1880, when reliable measurements began, mean global temperatures have risen about 0.5°C (0.9°F) (Figure 11-3). However, there is no strong evidence linking this recent warming to an enhanced greenhouse effect. The reason we don't have a smoking gun is that, so far, any temperature changes caused by an enhanced greenhouse effect have been too small to exceed normal short-term swings in mean atmospheric temperatures.

The more pressing question, however, is what kind of climate is likely to develop over the next 50 to 60 years. Circumstantial evidence from the past and climatic modeling have convinced many climate experts that global warming will begin accelerating in the 1990s or in the first decade of the next century, rising above the background temperature changes (climatic noise) that presently mask such an effect.

Five of the ten years between 1981 and 1990 were the hottest in the 130-year record of global temperature measurement and 1990 was the hottest year during that period. We can't be certain that the warmer weather was caused by an enhanced greenhouse effect, but such years give us a glimpse of what we can expect in a warmer greenhouse world.

Current climatic models project that Earth's mean surface temperature will rise 1.5°C to 5.5°C (2.7°F to 9.9°F) over the next 60 years (by 2050) if inputs of greenhouse gases continue to rise at the current rate (Figure 11-3). By way of comparison, the typical natural variation in Earth's mean surface temperature over periods of 100 to 200 years during the interglacial period we live in has been at most 0.5°C to 1°C (0.9°F to 1.8°F).

Because of the many uncertainties in these global climate models (see Spotlight on p. 288), their developers believe their projections are accurate within a factor of two. This means that projected global warming

The main way scientists, economists, and others project (not predict) behavior of climate, ecological, economic, and other complex systems is to develop mathematical models that simulate such systems. Then the models are run on high-speed computers. Various data and assumptions are fed into the models to make a series of projections of behavior and effects. How well the results correspond to the real world depends on the design of the model and on the accuracy of the data and assumptions used.

Another way to project how climate might change is to see how it has changed in the past (Figure 11-1). Evidence about past climate change has been gathered by analyzing the chemical content and fossil evidence of climate-sensitive forms of life found in deeply buried samples of rock, sediments on the bottoms of oceans and lakes, and deep cores removed from ice sheets. Such limited and often speculative evidence can be used to test and improve computer models of Earth's climate systems.

Scientists recognize that their models of Earth's climate are crude approximations at best. Present models do not adequately include the role of cloud formation and cover on climate, interactions between the atmosphere and the oceans (which contain 50 times more CO_2 than the atmosphere), how the Greenland and Antarctic ice sheets affect climate, and how soils, forests, and other ecosystems respond to changes in atmospheric temperature. Each factor could dampen or amplify global warming.

For example, global warming will increase the average surface temperatures of the world's oceans, which will increase the rate of evaporation of water into the atmosphere to form clouds. If there is a net increase in thick, low-level clouds that reflect sunlight into space, the rate of global warming will slow. On the other hand, if winds and other factors lead to a net increase in thin, high-level clouds, which act as a blanket to trap heat in the lower atmosphere, the rate of global warming will increase. We don't know the net effects of such factors or how long they take to act.

We must mount a crash research program to greatly improve our understanding of Earth's climate. Even so, we will never have the scientific certainty that decision makers want before making highly controversial decisions, such as greatly slowing down the use of fossil fuels upon which much of the world's present economy depends.

Often, those opposing change or wishing to delay decision making say that something should not be done until it has been scientifically "proved." This, however, misrepresents the results of science.

Scientific theories, models, and forecasts are based on mostly circumstantial and incomplete evidence and on statistical probabilities, not on certainties (Section 3-1). All scientists can do is project that there is a low, medium, high, or very high chance of something happening. Such information is quite useful, but the only way to get conclusive, direct proof about a possible future event is to wait and see if it happens.

Many climate experts believe there is already enough circumstantial evidence to warrant immediate action to slow this warming down to a more manageable rate. This will buy us precious time to do more research, shift to less harmful practices, and adapt to a warmer Earth.

They argue that if we wait for Earth's mean temperature to rise to the point where it exceeds normal climatic fluctuations, it will be too late to prevent lasting and highly disruptive social, economic, and environmental changes. Waiting to act amounts to performing a gigantic experiment on ourselves and other species—a form of global Russian roulette.

Besides, since fossil fuels (especially oil) are running out and are the leading causes of air pollution, water pollution, and land disruption, we need to drastically improve energy efficiency and shift to other energy sources as fast as possible, even if there is no threat from global warming. Similarly, since deforestation is one of the greatest threats to Earth's biodiversity, we should halt and reverse this form of environmental degradation whether the threat of global warming is serious or not.

Since 1945, the world's countries, mostly MDCs, have spent over $12 trillion to protect us from the possibility of nuclear war. Global warming is a much more likely and an equally serious threat to national, economic, and individual security; yet, we have spent only a pittance to deal with this potentially devastating threat. The time to act is rapidly running out. What do you think should be done?

during the next century could be as low as 0.7°C (1.3°F) or as high as 11°C (20°F). There is about a 50% chance either way. If we keep pumping greenhouse gases into the atmosphere and continue cutting down much of the world's forests, we are flipping a coin and gambling with life as we know it on this planet.

You might be wondering why we should worry about a rise of a few degrees in the mean temperature of Earth's surface. After all, we often have that much change between June and July, or between yesterday and today. The key point is that we are not talking about the normal swings in weather from place to place. We

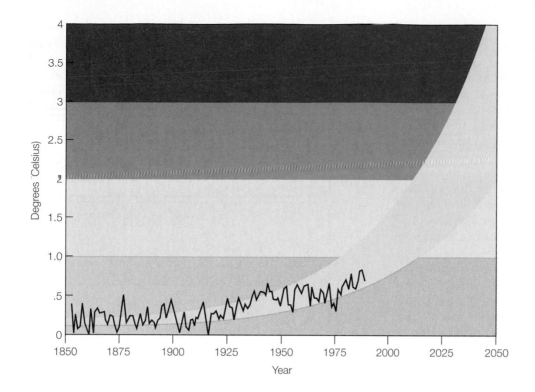

Figure 11-3 Changes in Earth's mean surface temperature between 1855 and 1990 (dark line). The yellow region shows the range of global warming predicted by various computer models of Earth's climate systems. Note that the results of the computer models roughly match the historically recorded changes in Earth's mean surface temperature between 1855 and 1990. All current models project that global warming will increase significantly between now and 2050, a larger and more rapid change in mean surface temperature than those taking place over 100 to 200 years during the 10,000 years since agriculture began. Scientists estimate that projections from current models could underestimate or overestimate the amount of warming by a factor of two. (Data from National Academy of Sciences and National Center for Atmospheric Research)

are talking about a projected global change in average climate in your lifetime, with much larger changes in various parts of the world. Global warming will alter not only temperature and precipitation, but winds, humidity, and cloud cover.

Current models indicate that the Northern Hemisphere will warm more and faster than the Southern Hemisphere, mostly because there is so much more ocean in the Southern Hemisphere (Figure 5-27) and water takes longer to warm than land. Temperatures at middle and high latitudes are projected to rise two to three times the average increase, while temperature increases in tropical areas near the equator would be less than the global average. The United States, the Mediterranean, and much of China—the world's heavily populated mid-latitudes—could be hard-hit by such climate changes.

Projecting changes in mean global temperature is difficult enough, but it is easy compared with projecting climate changes in specific regions of the world. About all we can hope for is a series of scenarios of regional climate change based on feeding different assumptions into current and improved climatic models. Current climate models generally project the same results on a global basis (Figure 11-3) but disagree widely on projected climate changes in different geographic regions.

One thing is clear, however. We now have the potential to bring about disruptive climate change at a rate 10 to 100 times faster than has occurred during the past 10,000 years. By the end of the next century, the world could be warmer than at any time since the dinosaurs disappeared 65 million years ago, when alligators were found in what is now Canada and Antarctica was ice-free.

Such rapid global warming would be comparable to global nuclear war (Section 11-5) in its potential to cause sudden, unpredictable, and widespread disruption of ecological, economic, and social systems. The faster the change, the more unpredictable the results, and the harder it will be for society and the natural environment to cope with the consequences.

POSSIBLE EFFECTS ON CROP PRODUCTION, ECOSYSTEMS, AND BIODIVERSITY At first glance, a warmer average climate might seem desirable. It could lead to lower heating bills and longer growing seasons in middle and high latitudes. Crop yields might increase 60% to 80% in some areas because more carbon dioxide in the atmosphere can increase the rate of plant photosynthesis. Increased warming of the troposphere might cause some cooling in the stratosphere, thereby slowing down reactions that destroy ozone.

However, other factors could offset those effects. Use of air conditioning would increase and contribute more heat to the troposphere. That would intensify and spread urban heat islands (Figure 9-12), causing people to use even more air conditioning. Using fossil fuels to produce more electricity to run air conditioners would add more carbon dioxide and chlorofluorocarbons (used as coolants in air conditioners) to the atmosphere, accelerating global warming and ozone depletion. That would also add more nitrogen oxides and sulfur dioxide to the troposphere, increasing ground-level ozone, photochemical smog, and acid deposition (Chapter 21).

Potential gains in crop yields from increased CO_2 levels could be wiped out by increased damage from insect pests, which breed more rapidly in warmer temperatures. Higher temperatures would also increase aerobic respiration rates of plants and reduce availability of water. Recent evidence suggests that many plants have responded to past CO_2 increases by developing fewer of the pores they use to take in CO_2 and thus reducing their rate of photosynthesis. Potential increases in crop yields could also be cancelled out by decreased yields as a result of ultraviolet radiation from depletion of ozone in the stratosphere.

Regional climate changes shift the ecological tolerance of species hundreds of kilometers horizontally and hundreds of meters vertically (Figure 5-13), with unpredictable consequences for natural systems and crops. Past evidence and computer models indicate that climate belts would shift northward by about 161 kilometers (100 miles) for each 1°C (1.8°F) rise in the global atmospheric temperature. In other words, the wheatbelt climate that feeds much of the world would move northward.

Current and even improved climatic models won't be able to accurately project where such changes might occur, but the point is that there would be pronounced and unpredictable shifts in where we could grow food (see cartoon). The main reason we can grow so much food today is that global and regional climates have not changed much during the past 200 years.

Having to shift the location of much of our agricultural production in only a few decades would create great disruptions in food supplies and could lead to as many as 1 billion environmental refugees and mass starvation in some areas. Shifting crop production would also require huge investments in new dams, irrigation systems, water supply distribution systems, fertilizer plants, and other parts of our agricultural systems.

However, since the effects of rapid climate change would be largely unpredictable, we might do all that only to find that food-growing areas shift again if global warming accelerates or starts to drop. As millions of people are forced to migrate and then move again and as food and other resources are stretched to the limit, conflicts would erupt over what remains.

Current models indicate that food production could drop in many of the world's major agricultural regions, including the U.S. midwestern grain belt (Figure 11-4), the Canadian prairie provinces, the Ukraine, and northern China, because of reduced soil moisture in the summer growing season. Computer models suggest that by 2030, 10% to 30% of existing irrigated cropland in the western United States would be pulled out of production because of projected climatic changes. Parts of Af-

rica and India and the northern reaches of the Soviet Union and Canada may get climates that could increase food production. However, soils in some of these potential new food-growing areas, such as Canada and Siberia, are poor and would take centuries to reach the productivity of current agricultural land. Meanwhile, food prices would skyrocket.

In some areas lakes, streams, and aquifers that have nourished ecosystems, cropfields, and cities for centuries could shrink or dry up altogether, forcing entire communities and populations to migrate to areas with adequate water supplies. The Gulf Stream (Figure 5-7) might stop flowing northeastward as far as Europe, leading to a much colder climate in that part of the world.

Global warming might also speed up the bacterial decay of dead organic matter in the soil. That could lead to a rapid release of vast amounts of carbon dioxide from dry soils and methane from waterlogged wetlands and rice paddies. Huge amounts of methane tied up in hydrates in soils of the arctic tundra (Figure 5-21) and in muds on the bottom of the Arctic Ocean could also be released if the blanket of permafrost covering tundra soils melts and the oceans warm. Because methane is such a potent greenhouse gas (Figure 11-2c), this could greatly amplify global warming.

The spread of tropical climates from the equator would bring malaria, encephalitis, and other insect-borne diseases to formerly temperate zones. Tropical skin diseases would also spread to many areas that now have a temperate climate.

In a warmer world, the frequency and intensity of highly damaging weather extremes, such as prolonged heat waves and droughts, would increase in many parts of the world. As the upper layers of seawater warm, the

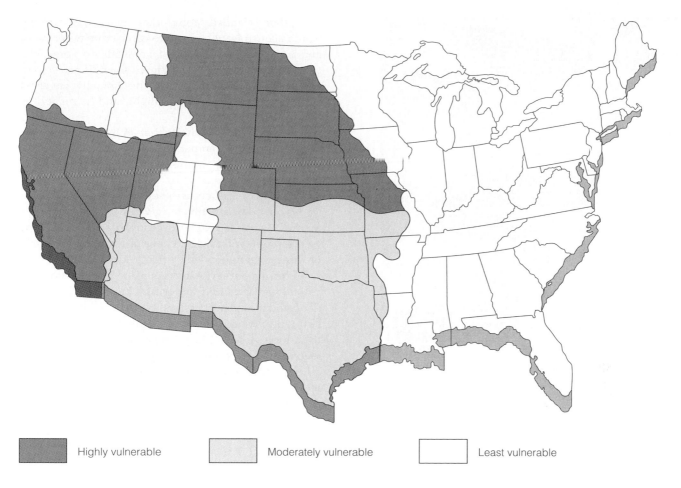

| | Highly vulnerable | | Moderately vulnerable | | Least vulnerable |

Figure 11-4 Areas in the United States where water supplies may be reduced as the world's climate warms up from the greenhouse effect. This is only one of many possibilities projected by computer models of the effects of global warming on Earth's climate. (Data from American Association for the Advancement of Science)

severity of hurricanes and typhoons would increase in some parts of the world. For example, computer models project that giant hurricanes, with 50% more destructive potential than those of today, would hit farther north and during more months of the year. Cities such as Miami, Galveston, Atlantic City, Charleston, and Myrtle Beach (Figure 5-35) could be devastated by the impact of such superhurricanes. Even a very slight warming of surface waters could increase the intensity of hurricanes in partially enclosed ocean basins like the Gulf of Mexico and the Bay of Bengal.

Changes in regional climate brought about by global warming would be a great threat to forests, especially those in temperate climates and the northern coniferous forests in regions with a subarctic climate. Least affected would probably be tropical rain forests, if we haven't cut most of them down.

As Earth warms, forest growth in temperate regions will move toward the poles and replace open tundra and some snow and ice. However, tree species in such forests can move only through the slow growth of new trees along their edges — typically about 0.9 kilometer (0.5 mile) a year or 9 kilometers (5 miles) per

decade. If climate belts move faster than this very slow migration or if migration is blocked by cities, cropfields, highways, and other human barriers, then entire forests will wither and die (Figure 11-5). These diebacks could amplify the greenhouse effect when the decaying trees release carbon dioxide into the air. Then the increased bacterial decay of organic matter in the warmer exposed soil would release even more CO_2.

Large-scale forest diebacks would also cause mass extinction of plant and animal species that couldn't migrate to new areas. Fish would die as temperatures soared in streams and lakes and as lower water levels concentrated pesticides.

There would be increased stress to trees from pests and disease microorganisms, which are able to adapt to climate change faster than trees are. The number of devastating fires in drier forest areas and grasslands would increase, adding more carbon dioxide to the atmosphere. Costly efforts to plant trees may fail when many of the new trees die.

Any shifts in regional climate caused by an enhanced greenhouse effect would pose severe threats to many of the world's parks, wildlife reserves, wilderness

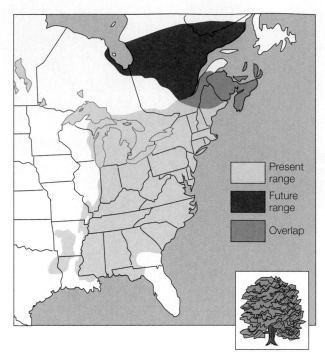

Figure 11-5 Climate model projection of how beech trees now widely distributed throughout the eastern United States would die out if carbon dioxide emissions were doubled between 1990 and 2090. In this case, the trees would be able to survive only in a greatly shrunken range in southeast Canada (shown in orange and red). (Data from Margaret B. Davis and Catherine Zabinski, University of Minnesota)

Present range

Future range

Overlap

areas, and wetlands (Chapter 15) and would accelerate the already-serious and increasing loss of Earth's biodiversity. Biologist Thomas Lovejoy of the Smithsonian Institution warns: "There will be no winners in this game of ecological chairs, for it will be fundamentally disruptive and destabilizing, and we can anticipate hordes of environmental refugees."

POSSIBLE EFFECTS ON SEA LEVELS Water expands slightly when it is heated. This explains why global sea levels would rise if the oceans warm, like heating the fluid in a thermometer. Additional rises would occur if the higher-than-average heating at the poles causes some, or even complete, melting of ice sheets and glaciers.

The Greenland and Antarctic ice sheets act like enormous mirrors to cool the earth by reflecting sunlight back into space. Some scientists fear that even a small temperature rise would shrink these glaciers, allowing more sunlight to hit the earth. Global warming would amplify and cause a larger rise in average sea levels than that from the thermal expansion of water. If most of the Greenland and West Antarctic ice sheets melted, as happened during a warm period 150,000 years ago, sea levels would gradually rise as much as 6 meters (20 feet) over several hundred years.

Other scientists argue that increased warming would allow the atmosphere to carry more water vapor and increase the amount of snowfall on some glaciers, particularly the Antarctic ice sheet. If snow accumulates faster than ice is lost, the Antarctic ice sheet would grow, reflect more sunlight, and help cool the atmosphere.

Current models indicate that an increase in the average atmospheric temperature of 3°C (5°F) would raise the average global sea level by 0.2 to 1.5 meters (1 to 5 feet) over the next 50 to 100 years. If the Antarctic ice sheet grows in size because snow accumulation exceeds ice loss, the lower estimate (give or take 0.4 meter) is more likely by the year 2050. Approximately half of the world's population lives in coastal regions that would be threatened or flooded by rising seas.

Even a modest rise in average sea level would flood coastal wetlands and low-lying cities and croplands, flood and move barrier islands (Figure 5-36) further inland, and contaminate coastal aquifers with salt. A one-third-meter rise would push shorelines back about 30 meters (98 feet) compared with 136 meters (445 feet) for a 1.5-meter (5-foot) rise in the average sea level. Only a few of the most intensively developed resort areas along the U.S. coast have beaches wider than 30 meters at high tide. Especially hard-hit would be North and South Carolina (Figure 5-35), where the slope of the shoreline is so gradual that a 0.3-meter (1-foot) rise in sea level would push the coastline back several kilometers.

A modest 1-meter (3-foot) rise would flood low-lying areas of major cities such as Shanghai, Cairo, Bangkok, and Venice and large areas of agricultural lowlands and deltas in Egypt, Bangladesh, India, and China, where much of the world's rice is grown. With a 1.5-meter (5-foot) rise, many small low-lying islands like the Marshall Islands in the Pacific, the Maldives (a series of about 1,200 islands off the west coast of India that are home to 200,000 people), and some Caribbean nations would cease to exist, creating a multitude of environmental refugees.

Large areas of the wetlands that nourish the world's fisheries would also be destroyed (see Case Study on p. 137). The EPA projects that a rise in sea level of 1 meter (3 feet) would result in 26% to 65% less coastal wetlands in the United States. That would flood all of Florida's Everglades National Park, making it the first national park to be lost. Even a 0.5-meter (1.6-foot) rise would result in the loss of about one-third of U.S. coastal wetlands. The salinity of streams, bays, and coastal aquifers would increase. Tanks storing hazardous chemicals along the Gulf and Atlantic coasts would be flooded. Places such as the low-lying Florida Keys and the present beaches of Malibu, California, would be covered with water.

Low-lying areas in U.S. cities such as New Orleans, New York, Atlantic City, Boston, Washington, D.C., Galveston, Charleston, Savannah, and Miami (which lies at or just above sea level on swampland reclaimed from the Everglades) would be threatened by flooding unless billions of dollars were spent to build and maintain extensive systems of dikes and levees. Even dikes and levees wouldn't save Miami because it sits on a porous bed of limestone. This means that the ocean will seep in underneath the city, contaminating all freshwater supplies and making the entire area uninhabitable. A comedian has joked that he was planning to buy land in Kansas because it would probably become valuable beachfront property.

11-2 Dealing with Global Warming

SLOWING DOWN GLOBAL WARMING We have two options for dealing with the global warming many scientists believe we have set in motion: slow it or adjust to its effects. Many experts believe that we must do both, with no time to lose.

The cures for this planetary crisis we have caused are controversial, difficult, and painful. If the models are correct, we are in the position of a long-time alcoholic whose doctor tells him that if he doesn't stop drinking now he will die. Mostafa Tolba, Executive Director of the United Nations Economic Program, warns that "no one should have any illusions about the difficulty of containing climate change. It will require a new global ethic based on economic growth which does not threaten nature."

We and many other species can learn to live under different climatic conditions, if we are given time to make the necessary changes. That explains why slowing down any significant climate change — warming or cooling — caused by our activities must become the top priority of our species worldwide (see Guest Essay on p. 305). Otherwise, environmental and economic security could be threatened everywhere within a single generation.

The general guidelines for slowing global warming and deforestation are to reduce our use of the five deadly C's — cars, coal, cattle, chlorofluorocarbons, and chain saws — and increase our use of the Earth-saving C's — contraceptives and conservation. Ways to do this include:

Prevention (Input) Approaches

■ Banning all production and uses of chlorofluorocarbons and halons by 1995. This is the easiest thing we can do because we can either do without these chemicals or phase in substitutes for their essential uses. It is also the best early test of worldwide commitment to protecting the atmosphere from both global warming and ozone depletion.

■ Cutting current fossil-fuel use by 20% by 2000, 50% by 2010, and 70% by 2030. The largest users of fossil fuels, such as the United States and the Soviet Union, should cut their use by about 35% by the year 2000.

■ Greatly improving energy efficiency. This is the quickest, cheapest, and most effective method to reduce emissions of CO_2 and other air pollutants during the next two to three decades (see Spotlight on p. 294).

■ Shifting, over the next 30 years, to perpetual and renewable energy resources that do not emit CO_2 (Chapter 17). Increased use of perpetual and renewable energy resources can cut projected U.S. CO_2 emissions 8% to 15% by the year 2000, and virtually eliminate them by 2010.

■ Transferring energy efficiency and renewable energy technology and pollution prevention and waste reduction technology to LDCs so they can leapfrog into a new sustainable-Earth age instead of following the energy- and matter-wasting and Earth-degrading path of today's MDCs.

■ Increasing the use of nuclear power to produce electricity *if* a new generation of much safer reactors can be developed and the problem of how to store nuclear waste safely for thousands of years can be solved (Section 18-3). However, improving energy efficiency is much quicker and safer and reduces emissions of CO_2 2.5 to 10 times more than nuclear power per dollar invested (see Pro/Con on p. 500).

■ Placing heavy taxes on gasoline and emissions fees on each unit of carbon in fossil fuels (especially coal) burned to reduce emissions of CO_2 and other air pollutants. This tax revenue should to be used to improve the energy efficiency of dwellings and heating systems for the poor in MDCs and LDCs and to provide them with enough energy to offset higher fuel prices and to subsidize the transition to perpetual and renewable energy resources. At the same time, current large taxpayer subsidies for fossil fuels and nuclear power should be withdrawn over a 10-year period. Finland, Sweden, and the Netherlands have instituted such carbon taxes. A $100 per ton carbon tax on fossil fuels in the United States, phased in over 10 years, would generate an estimated $130 billion a year, equal to almost one-third of the revenue from individual federal income taxes in 1988. This would improve the nation's energy efficiency by 23% and lower projected carbon emissions by 37%.

■ Sharply reducing the use of coal, which emits 60% more carbon dioxide per unit of energy produced than any other fossil fuel. Using the world's estimated coal supplies would produce at least a sixfold or eightfold increase in atmospheric carbon dioxide. To power its industrialization program, China plans to nearly double coal use in the next decade, and India plans to triple its use. MDCs

Energy expert Amory Lovins (see Guest Essay on p. 75) says that arguments over whether global warming is happening, will happen, may not happen, or may not be as severe as projected and over what its impacts will be are largely irrelevant and divert us from doing what needs to be done anyway. The reason is that the remedies listed in the text for slowing global warming are things we need to do *now* even if there were no threat of global warming or any other type of climate change.

Lovins also argues that getting countries to sign treaties and agree to cut back their use of fossil fuels in time to reduce serious environmental effects is difficult, if not almost impossible, and very costly. Evidence for this appeared in November 1989, when representatives from 70 nations couldn't even agree to freeze their emissions of greenhouse gases at 1988 levels by the year 2005, mainly because of opposition by the United States, the Soviet Union, Japan, and China—which together account for 58% of the world's output of these gases.

In 1990, at the Second World Climate Conference, 22 countries including 12 western European countries, Sweden, Norway, Finland, Switzerland, Australia, and Japan agreed to freeze their CO_2 emissions at their 1990 levels by the year 2000. Even this small step in the right direction was opposed and watered down by opposition from the United States.

Instead of providing the much-needed global environmental leadership he promised during his election campaign, President George Bush mainly called for more research rather than action to delay global warming. Claudine Schneider, a member of the U.S. House of Representatives (see Guest Essay on p. 691), calls this the "let's wait until the ship hits the rocks, and then figure out what to do" approach so

prevalent in public policy-making today.

Australia, Canada, and most countries in western Europe have announced plans to cut their emissions of CO_2 by 20% (Canada) to 57% (Portugal) between 1988 and 2005. Policy proposed by the Bush administration will lead to at least a 20% increase during this same period. President Bush claims that the costs of reducing greenhouse gases is too high. Environmentalists and several economists point out, however, that the administration's projected costs do not include the large savings from increases in energy efficiency and reduced air pollution and greatly underestimate or leave out the costs of reduced biodiversity and crop yields and the costs of shifting and retooling much of the country's agriculture, forestry, and wildlife programs.

According to Lovins and climate expert Stephen H. Schneider (see Guest Essay on p. 305), the good news, among all the gloom-and-doom about global warming, is that improving energy efficiency is the fastest, cheapest, and surest way to sharply cut emissions of carbon dioxide and most other air pollutants within two decades using existing technology. This approach should also be immensely profitable, saving the world as much as a trillion dollars a year—as much as the annual global military budget. According to a 1991 report by the National Academy of Sciences, improvements in energy efficiency could cut U.S. emissions of greenhouse gases by up to 40% from 1990 levels at little or no expense.

Moreover, reducing use of fossil fuels by improving energy efficiency reduces all forms of pollution, helps protect biodiversity, and avoids arguments among governments about how CO_2 reductions should be divided up and enforced. This approach will also make the world's supplies of fossil fuel last longer, re-

duce international tensions over who gets the world's dwindling oil supplies, and give us more time to phase in alternatives to fossil fuels.

Industrialized countries will have to set a better example by committing themselves to a crash program to improve energy efficiency (Section 17-2). They will also have to lead the shift from nonrenewable fossil fuels and nuclear energy (Chapter 18) to perpetual and renewable energy sources (Chapter 17).

Existing and new technologies for improving energy efficiency and using perpetual and renewable energy must also be transferred to LDCs, which on average are nearly three times less energy-efficient than the average MDC. According to Lovins, this in principle could allow LDCs to expand their economies by about tenfold with no increase in energy use and avoid the dirtiest stage of the industrialization process. Instead of doing this, the United States and some other industrialized countries are now exporting their least efficient energy technologies—the ones too obsolete and costly to sell at home—to LDCs.

Greatly improving energy efficiency *now* is a money-saving , life-saving, and Earth-saving offer that we must not refuse. So far, however, no government has made this approach much more than a token part of its national strategy for slowing greenhouse warming, reducing dependence on oil, and reducing air and water pollution.

must try to prevent this by helping these and other LDCs greatly improve their energy efficiency and shift from coal to perpetual and renewable energy sources.

- Switching from coal to natural gas for producing electricity and high-temperature heat in countries, such as the United States and the Soviet Union, that have ample supplies of natural gas, which emits only half as much CO_2 per unit of energy as coal. Switching to natural gas also sharply reduces emissions of other air pollutants. Because burning natural gas still emits CO_2, this is only a short-term method that helps buy time to switch to an age of energy efficiency and renewable energy. Also, a recent study indicates that methane leaking from natural gas distribution systems has such a powerful greenhouse effect that it could offset the benefits of switching from coal to natural gas.

- Capturing methane gas emitted by landfills and using it as a fuel. Burning this methane gas produces carbon dioxide, but each molecule of methane reaching the atmosphere causes about 25 times more global warming than each molecule of CO_2.

- Sharply reducing beef production to reduce the fossil-fuel inputs into agriculture, carbon dioxide released because of deforestation for grazing land (Figure 10-11), and methane produced by the animals themselves. Producing the beef in only 20 hamburgers is responsible for the release of more carbon dioxide than 0.4 hectare (1 acre) of trees can absorb in a year.

- Halting unsustainable deforestation everywhere by the year 2000 (Sections 10-4 and 10-5).

- Switching from unsustainable to sustainable agriculture (Section 14-6). Worldwide, agriculture is responsible for about 15% of the greenhouse gases we emit into the atmosphere. If LDCs increase their use of unsustainable, industrialized agriculture, that percentage could rise.

- Slowing population growth (Section 8-3). If we cut greenhouse-gas emissions in half and population more than doubles, we are back where we started.

- Dismantling the global poverty trap to reduce unnecessary deaths, human suffering, and environmental degradation and to help LDCs help themselves and not follow the present throwaway industrial path of today's MDCs (Section 24-6).

Cleanup (Output) Approaches

- Developing better methods to remove carbon dioxide from the smokestack emissions of coal-burning power and industrial plants and from vehicle exhausts. If used, currently available methods would remove only about 30% of the CO_2 and would at least double the cost of electricity. Even-

tually, this approach would be overwhelmed by increased use of fossil fuels. Also, the recovered CO_2 must be kept out of the atmosphere, presumably by putting it in the deep ocean, spent oil and gas wells, and excavated salt caverns, or by reacting it with other substances to convert it to a solid such as limestone. The effectiveness and cost of these methods are unknown.

- Planting trees. Each of us should plant and care for at least one tree every six months. This is an important form of Earth care, especially in restoring deforested and degraded cropland and rangeland. However, we should recognize that tree planting is only a stopgap measure for slowing CO_2 emissions. To absorb the carbon dioxide we are now putting into the atmosphere each year, we would have to plant and tend an average of 1,000 trees per person every year and 4,500 trees annually for each American citizen — 18,000 trees a year for a family of four.

- Recycling CO_2 released in industrial processes.

- Removing CO_2 by photosynthesis by using tanks and ponds of marine algae or by fertilizing the oceans with iron to stimulate the growth of marine algae.

ADJUSTING TO GLOBAL WARMING Even if all the things just listed are done, we are still likely to experience some global warming, although at a more manageable rate. If we stopped adding greenhouse gases to the atmosphere now, current models indicate that what we have already added could warm the earth by 0.5°C to 1.8°C (0.9°F to 3.2°F). Since there is a good chance that many of the things we should do will either not be done or be done too slowly, some analysts suggest that we should also begin preparing for the effects of long-term global warming. Their suggestions include

- increasing research on the breeding of food plants that need less water and plants that can thrive in water too salty for ordinary crops

- building dikes to protect coastal areas from flooding, as the Dutch have done for hundreds of years

- moving storage tanks of hazardous materials away from coastal areas

- banning new construction on low-lying coastal areas

- storing large supplies of key foods throughout the world as insurance against disruptions in food production

- expanding existing wilderness areas, parks, and wildlife refuges northward in the Northern Hemisphere and southward in the Southern Hemisphere and creating new wildlife reserves in these areas

- developing management plans for existing parks and reserves that take into account possible climate changes

- connecting existing and new wildlife reserves by corridors that would allow mobile species to change their geographic distributions and transplanting endangered species to new areas

- wasting less water (see Individuals Matter inside the back cover)

We have known about the possibility of an enhanced greenhouse effect and its possible consequences for decades. We also know what needs to be done at the international, national, local, and individual levels (see Individuals Matter on p. 297). Research must be expanded to help clear up the uncertainties that continue to exist, but to most environmentalists and many climatologists that is no excuse for doing nothing or very little now.

11-3 Depletion of Ozone in the Stratosphere

THE VITAL OZONE LAYER About 2 billion years ago, microorganisms living under water evolved with the ability to carry out photosynthesis. Gradually over millions of years, those organisms began adding oxygen to the atmosphere. As some of that oxygen drifted upward it reacted with incoming ultraviolet radiation and was converted to ozone in the stratosphere. Before this *oxygen revolution* began, life on Earth could exist only under water, where it was protected from the sun's intense ultraviolet rays.

Today, we and many types of plants and other animals survive because this thin gauze of ozone in the stratosphere (Figure 4-3) keeps much of the harmful ultraviolet radiation (specifically ultraviolet-B, or UV-B) given off by the sun from reaching Earth's surface.

USES OF CHLOROFLUOROCARBONS AND HALONS In 1974, chemists Sherwood Roland and Mario Molina theorized that human-made chlorofluorocarbons (CFCs), also known by their Du Pont trademark, Freons, were lowering the average concentration of ozone in the stratosphere and creating a global time bomb. No one suspected such a possibility when CFCs were developed in 1930.

The two most widely used CFCs are CFC-11 (trichlorofluoromethane) and CFC-12 (dichlorofluoromethane). When they were developed, these stable, odorless, nonflammable, nontoxic, and noncorrosive chemicals were a chemist's dream. Soon they were widely used as coolants in air conditioners and refrigerators and as propellants in aerosol spray cans. Now they are also used to clean electronic parts such as computer chips, as hospital sterilants, as fumigants for granaries and cargo holds, and to create the bubbles in polystyrene plastic foam (often called by its Du Pont trade name, Styrofoam), used for insulation and packaging.

Bromine-containing compounds, called *halons*, are also widely used, mostly in fire extinguishers. Other widely used ozone-destroying chemicals are carbon tetrachloride (used mostly as a solvent) and methyl chloroform, or 1,1,1,-trichloroethane (used as a cleaning solvent for metals and in more than 160 consumer products, such as correction fluid, dry-cleaning sprays, spray adhesives, and other aerosols).

Industrial countries account for 84% of CFC production, with the United States being the top producer followed by western European countries and Japan. Worldwide, aerosols account for 25% of global CFC use. Since 1978, however, most uses of CFCs in aerosol cans have been banned in the United States, Canada, and most Scandinavian countries, mostly because of consumer boycotts. In the United States, CFCs are still legally used as aerosol propellants in asthma and other medication sprays and cleaning sprays for VCRs and sewing machines, and in products such as canned confetti.

The United States accounts for about 25% of the global consumption of CFCs, and per capita use of CFCs in the United States is six times greater than global per capita use. Vehicle air conditioners account for about three-quarters of annual CFC emissions in the United States.

DEPLETION OF THE OZONE LAYER Ozone is destroyed and replenished in the stratosphere by natural atmospheric chemical reactions and is maintained at a fairly stable level. However, there is much evidence that we are upsetting this balance and reducing the levels of life-saving ozone in the stratosphere.

Spray cans, discarded or leaking refrigeration and air conditioning equipment, and the production and burning of plastic foam products release CFCs into the atmosphere. Depending on the type, CFCs are so unreactive that they stay intact in the atmosphere for 60 to 400 years. This gives them plenty of time to rise slowly through the troposphere until they reach the stratosphere. There, under the influence of high-energy UV radiation from the sun, they break down and release chlorine atoms, which speed up the breakdown of ozone (O_3) into O_2 and O.

Over time, a single chlorine atom can convert as many as 100,000 molecules of O_3 to O_2. A single polystyrene cup contains over 1 billion molecules of CFCs. Although this effect was proposed in 1974, it took 15 years of interaction between science and politics be-

While waiting for the world's governments to adopt strategies for slowing global warming, we can take matters into our own hands.

- Be aware of your CO_2 emissions and reduce them. Average per capita emission of CO_2 in the United States is 16.7 metric tons (18.4 tons) a year, six times more than the average citizen in an LDC. Using one kilowatt-hour of electricity generated at a coal-fired power plant emits 0.9 kilogram (2 pounds) of CO_2, and burning 3.8 liters (1 gallon) of gasoline emits 9.8 kilograms (21.5 pounds) of CO_2. A 12 kilometer-per-liter (28 mile-per-gallon) car, driven 16,000 kilometers (10,000 miles) releases 3.8 metric tons (4.2 tons) of carbon dioxide into the atmosphere.

- Reduce your use and unnecessary waste of energy (see Individuals Matter inside the back cover). Since use and waste of fossil fuels is the primary cause of projected global warming and most other forms of pollution and environmental degradation, this is the most important thing you can do. Driving a car that gets at least 15 kilometers per liter (35 miles per gallon), using a car pool and mass transit, and walking or bicycling where possible are the best ways you can reduce your emissions of CO_2 and other air pollutants and save money.

- Don't use electricity to heat space or water (Section 3-6), and use energy-efficient fluorescent light bulbs, refrigerators, and other appliances.

- Make your house energy-efficient and heat it and household water by using as much perpetual energy from the sun as possible. Cool it by using shade trees and available winds.

- If you can't use perpetual and renewable energy to heat your house and water, use natural gas. When burned, it produces much less carbon dioxide and other air pollutants than burning oil or using electricty produced by burning coal at a power plant.

- Plant and care for trees and help cool the globe and your house. Ask your employer to sponsor a tree-planting program by buying seedlings to be planted by children in a local school.

- Use the following priorities for all items: No use unless necessary; reuse, recycle, and throw away only as a last resort. Also, buy products made from recycled materials. It is encouraging that so many people have begun recycling, but it is merely the first baby step in the right direction. The emphasis must now shift to reuse and no use (of throwaway and hazardous items).

- Urge state and national legislators to sponsor bills aimed at greatly improving energy efficiency, halting the harvesting of stands of ancient forests in national forests (Section 10-5), and curbing emissions of greenhouse gases and other air pollutants.

- Don't support highly unpredictable schemes such as covering the oceans with white Styrofoam chips to help reflect more energy away from Earth's surface, dumping iron into oceans to stimulate the growth of marine algae to remove CO_2 from the atmosphere (costing about $1 billion per year), unfurling a gigantic foil-faced sun shield in space, or injecting sunlight-reflecting particulate matter into the stratosphere to cool it by exploding nuclear bombs near Earth's surface or by using aircraft or rocket systems. Some of these large-scale technological solutions may be possible in the future, but they can have harmful side effects that we can't anticipate because of our poor understanding of how the earth works.

---

fore countries took action to begin slowly phasing out CFCs.*

Several other stable, chlorine-containing compounds, including widely used solvents such as methyl chloroform (1,1,1-trichloroethane) and carbon tetrachloride, also rise into the stratosphere and destroy ozone molecules. When fire extinguishers are used, their unreactive bromine-containing halon compounds enter the air and eventually reach the stratosphere, where they are broken apart by UV radiation. Each of their bromine atoms destroys hundreds of times more ozone molecules than a chlorine atom. All these compounds, especially CFCs, are also greenhouse gases that contribute to global warming during their trip through the troposphere (Figure 11-2b).

In the 1980s, researchers were surprised to find that up to 50% of the ozone in the upper stratosphere over the Antarctic is destroyed during the antarctic spring from September through mid-October — something not predicted by computer models of the stratosphere. During these two months of 1987, 1989, and

---

*For a fascinating account of how corporate stalling, politics, economics, and science interact, see Sharon Roan's *Ozone Crisis: The 15-Year Evolution of a Sudden Global Emergency* (New York: John Wiley, 1989).

Figure 11-6 The pink and darker pink shades in these images taken by the NIMBUS-7 satellite show the annual ozone hole (area with extremely low ozone concentrations) that appeared in the upper stratosphere over the Antarctic on October 3, 1987, 1988, 1989, and 1990. In 1987, 1988, and 1990, this hole, where the normal ozone level has been cut in half, was ten times larger than the area of the continental United States. It is caused by ozone-destroying chlorofluorocarbons we have put into the atmosphere. The lower the Dobson units, shown in the scale on the right, the greater the depletion of ozone. Normal Dobson units for the stratosphere are around 350; on October 3, 1990, the level over the Antarctic fell to an all-time low of 125.

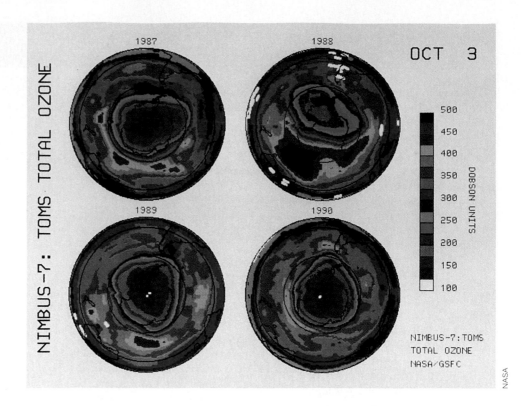

1990, this antarctic ozone hole covered an area larger than the continental United States (Figure 11-6). Depletion in 1990 was the largest recorded. A new analysis in 1991 suggests that this already-serious seasonal loss of ozone could double in size by 2001.

Measurements indicate that this large annual decrease in ozone over the South Pole is caused when water droplets in clouds form tiny ice crystals as they enter large streams of air, called polar vortices, that circle the poles in wintertime in both the Antarctic and the Arctic. The surfaces of these ice crystals absorb CFCs and other ozone-depleting chemicals. This greatly increases the rate at which these chemicals destroy ozone and leads to the sharp seasonal drop in ozone over the Antarctic.

After about two months, the vortex breaks up and great clumps of ozone-depleted air flow northward and linger over parts of Australia, New Zealand, and the southern tips of South America and Africa for a few weeks. During this period, ultraviolet levels in these areas may increase as much as 20%. In Australia, which has the world's highest rate of skin cancer, television stations air daily reports on ultraviolet radiation levels and issue warnings for people to stay indoors during bad spells.

Since 1988, scientists have discovered that a similar but smaller ozone hole forms over the Arctic during the two-month arctic spring, with an annual ozone loss of 15% to 25%. When this hole breaks up, clumps of ozone-depleted air flow southward and linger over parts of Europe and North America. This can produce a 5% winter loss of ozone over much of the Northern Hemisphere.

In 1988, the National Aeronautics and Space Administration (NASA) released a study showing that the stratospheric ozone-depletion average over the whole year has decreased by as much as 3% over heavily populated regions of North America, Europe, and Asia since 1969 (Figure 11-7). A 1991 NASA study revealed that ozone losses between 1978 and mid-1990 were about twice those shown in Figure 11-7. Unless emissions of ozone-depleting chemicals are cut drastically, average levels of ozone in the stratosphere could drop by 10% to 25% by 2050 or sooner, with much higher drops in certain areas (Figure 11-6).

In 1990, two Soviet rocket scientists warned that the motors in U.S. space shuttles are contributing to depletion of the ozone layer, with each launch adding 170 metric tons (187 tons) of ozone-destroying chlorine molecules to the atmosphere. Soviet rocket engines use a fuel mixture that is 7,000 times less damaging than the fuel used in American shuttle engines. However, Soviet shuttles still destroy 1,400 metric tons (1,500 tons) of ozone per launch.

EFFECTS OF OZONE DEPLETION With less ozone in the stratosphere, more biologically harmful ultraviolet-B radiation will reach Earth's surface. This form of UV radiation damages DNA molecules and can cause genetic defects on the outer surfaces of plants and animals, including your skin. Each 1% loss of ozone leads to a 2% increase in the ultraviolet radiation striking

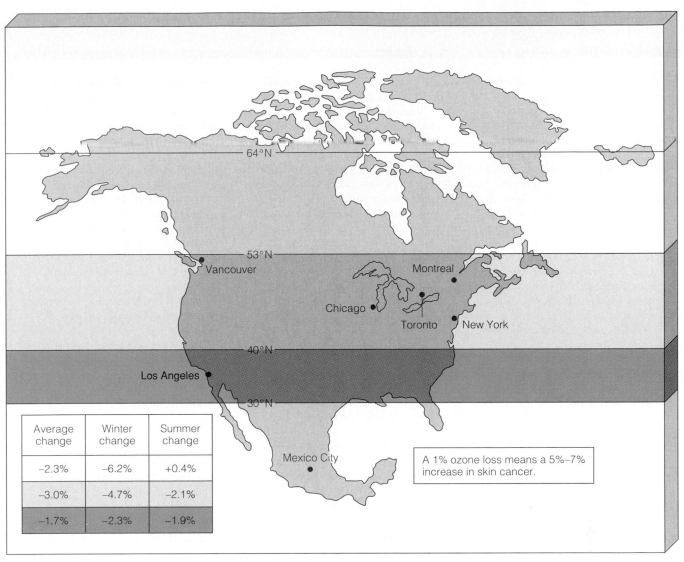

Average change	Winter change	Summer change
–2.3%	–6.2%	+0.4%
–3.0%	–4.7%	–2.1%
–1.7%	–2.3%	–1.9%

A 1% ozone loss means a 5%–7% increase in skin cancer.

Figure 11-7 Average drops in ozone levels in the stratosphere above parts of the earth between 1969 and 1986, based on data gathered from satellites and ground stations. A 1991 NASA study showed that between 1978 and mid-1990 the drops in ozone were about twice the percentages shown in this figure. (Data from NASA)

Earth's surface and a 5% to 7% increase in skin cancer, including a 1% increase in deadly malignant melanoma (see Spotlight on p. 300).

The EPA estimates that a 5% ozone depletion would cause the following effects in the United States:

- An extra 170 million cases of skin cancer by the year 2075. This includes an average of 2 million extra cases of basal-cell and squamous-cell skin cancers a year (Figures 11-8a and b) and an additional 30,000 cases annually of often-fatal melanoma skin cancer (Figure 11-8c), which now kills almost 9,000 Americans each year.

- A sharp increase in eye cataracts (a clouding of the eye that causes blurred vision and eventual blindness) and severe sunburn in people, and eye cancer in cattle.

- Suppression of the human immune system, which would reduce our defenses against a variety of infectious diseases, an effect similar to that of the AIDS virus.

- Health-care costs in the United States totalling $3.5 billion.

- An increase in eye-burning photochemical smog, highly damaging ozone, and acid deposition in the troposphere (Chapter 21). According to the EPA, each 1% decrease in stratospheric ozone may cause a 2% increase in ozone near the ground.

- Decreased yields of important food crops such as corn, rice, soybeans, and wheat.

- Reduction in the growth of ocean phytoplankton that form the base of ocean food chains and webs and that help remove carbon dioxide from the atmosphere. Especially vulnerable are UV-sensitive

Normally nonfatal skin cancer is by far the most common form of cancer; about one in seven Americans get it sooner or later. Cumulative exposure to ultraviolet ionizing radiation in sunlight over a number of years is the primary cause of basal-cell and squamous-cell skin cancers (Figure 11-8a and 11-8b). These two types of cancer can be cured if detected early enough, although their removal may leave disfiguring scars. I have had three basal-cell cancers on my face because of too much exposure to the sun in my younger years. I wish I had known what I know now.

Evidence suggests that just one severe, blistering burn as a child or teenager is enough to double a person's risk of contracting deadly malignant melanoma (Figure 11-8c) later in life, regardless of the skin type or the amount of cumulative exposure to the sun. This cancer of the cells that produce the skin's pigment spreads rapidly to other organs and can kill its victims. Each year, it kills about 9,000 Americans and 100,000 people worldwide. The number of cases of this type of cancer is increasing at a rapid rate, with whites seven to ten times more susceptible than blacks. Depletion of

the ozone layer will lead to a sharp increase in all types of skin cancers.

Virtually anyone can get skin cancer, but those with very fair and freckled skin run the highest risk. People who spend long hours in the sun or in tanning booths (which are even more hazardous than direct exposure to the sun) greatly increase their chances of developing skin cancer. They also tend to have wrinkled, dry skin by age 40. Blacks are almost immune to sunburn but do get skin cancer, although at a rate one tenth that of whites. A dark suntan also doesn't prevent skin cancer. Outdoor workers are particularly susceptible to cancer of the exposed skin on the face, hands, and arms.

The safest thing to do is to stay out of the sun and tanning booths. Avoid direct exposure between 10:00 A.M. and 3:00 P.M., when the sun's ultraviolet rays are strongest. Sitting under an umbrella does not protect against the sun because sunlight is reflected from sand, concrete, and water. Clouds are deceptive because as much as 80% of the sun's harmful ultraviolet radiation passes through them.

When you are in the sun, wear tightly woven protective clothing

and a wide-brimmed hat, and apply a sunscreen with a protection factor of 15 or more (25 if you have light skin) to all exposed skin. Reapply sunscreen after swimming or excessive perspiration. Children using a sunscreen with a protection factor of 15 anytime they are in the sun from birth to age 18 decrease their chance of skin cancer by 80%.

Get to know your moles, and examine your skin surface at least once a month for any changes. The warning signs of skin cancer are a change in the size, shape, or color of a mole or wart (the major sign of malignant melanoma, which needs to be treated quickly), sudden appearance of dark spots on the skin, and a sore that keeps oozing, bleeding, and crusting over but does not heal. You should also be on the watch for precancerous growths that appear as reddish brown spots with a scaly crust. If any of these signs are observed, you should immediately consult a doctor. What are you doing to protect your skin and your life?

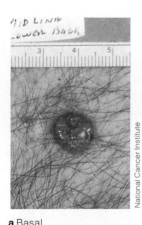

a Basal

b Squamous

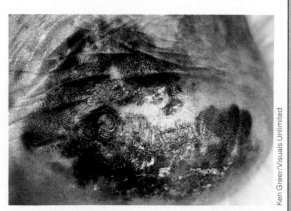

c Malignant melanoma

Figure 11-8   Three types of skin cancer: basal (**a**), squamous (**b**), and malignant melanoma (**c**). The occurrence of these types of cancer is rising because of increased exposure to ultraviolet-B radiation. This is being caused by depletion of ozone gas in the stratosphere by chlorofluorocarbons (CFCs) and other chemicals containing chlorine or bromine atoms.

phytoplankton which are the base of the principal food web in the Antarctic (Figure 4-20).

- A loss of perhaps $2 billion a year from degradation of paints, plastics, and other polymer materials.

- Increased global warming from an enhanced greenhouse effect.

In a worst-case scenario, people would not be able to expose themselves to the sun (see cartoon). Cattle could graze only at dusk without eye damage. Farmers might measure their exposure to the sun in minutes.

" I MISS THE OZONE LAYER...."

11-4   Protecting the Ozone Layer

A PLAN OF ACTION Models of atmospheric processes indicate that just to keep CFCs at 1987 levels would require an immediate 85% drop in total CFC emissions throughout the world. Analysts believe that the first step toward this goal should be an immediate worldwide ban on the use of CFCs in aerosol spray cans and in producing plastic foam products. Cost-effective substitutes are already available for those uses. Automotive service shops should be required to recycle CFCs from automotive air conditioners, and by 1992, the sale of small cans of CFCs used by consumers to charge leaky air conditioners should be banned. Nissan, Toyota, and Honda have announced that by 1995, air conditioners in their cars will no longer use CFCs.

The next step would be to phase out all other uses of CFCs, halons, carbon tetrachloride (a highly toxic but cheap chemical), and methyl chloroform by 1995. Substitute coolants in refrigeration and air conditioning will probably cost more, but compared with the potential economic and health consequences of ozone depletion, such cost increases would be minor. For example, the estimated harmful costs of releasing the CFCs in a single aerosol can total $12,000. The harmful costs of CFCs released from a single car air conditioner during use and repair are many times that figure.

Although they receive little publicity compared with CFCs, the widely used solvents carbon tetrachloride and methyl chloroform (1,1,1-trichloroethane) contribute more to ozone-threatening chlorine levels than all but two of the eight CFCs and halons now partially controlled by an international treaty. Substitutes are available for virtually all uses of these two chemicals.

Water-based cleaning can be used to replace most uses of CFCs, methyl chloroform, and carbon tetrachloride as cleaning solvents. A researcher has found that orange peels and other citrus rinds contain oils called terpenes that can be used to clean electronic circuit boards.

However, we must be sure that substitutes don't contribute to atmospheric warming or cause other harmful effects. Currently, there are three principal types of substitutes. One consists of chemicals outside the fluorocarbon family that can be used as cleaning and blowing agents. The other two types, useful mainly as cooling agents in refrigerators and air conditioners, are hydrofluorocarbons (HFCs), which contain no chlorine or bromine atoms and hydrochlorofluorocarbons (HCFCs), which contain fewer atoms of chlorine per molecule than conventional CFCs.

HFCs and HCFCs are decomposed more rapidly than conventional CFCs and have lower atmospheric lifetimes of 2 to 20 years depending on the compound. But HCFCs contain some ozone-destroying chlorine atoms, and both HFCs and HCFCs are still greenhouse gases. However, their ozone-depletion potential is only 2% to 10% of conventional CFCs, and they would contribute about 90% less per kilogram to greenhouse warming than currently used CFCs.

One HCFC, called Dymel, is being marketed by Du Pont as an aerosol propellant in hair sprays, deodorants, colognes, and other products. Sometimes this unnecessary use of an HCFC is incorrectly labelled as being "environmentally friendly." HFC and HCFC substitutes may help make the transition away from CFCs for essential uses such as refrigeration, but eventually these new chemicals will also have to be banned to halt ozone depletion.

HOPEFUL BUT INADEQUATE PROGRESS Some progress has been made since the discovery of the antarctic ozone hole (Figure 11-6). That event and public pressure forced political leaders in MDCs to begin taking action after over a decade of corporate stalling and political "foot dragging," with repeated calls for more research instead of action. This same pattern is now being used to delay action on slowing potential global warming, improving energy efficiency, and reducing ground-level air pollution.

In 1987, 24 nations meeting in Montreal, Canada, developed a treaty — commonly known as the Montreal Protocol — to reduce production of the eight most widely used and most damaging CFCs. By early 1990, 49 countries had signed this historic treaty. If carried out, it will reduce total emissions of CFCs into the atmosphere by about 35% between 1989 and 2000. According to the EPA, this would prevent about 137 million cases of skin cancer, 27 million deaths from skin cancer, and 1.2 million eye cataracts.

Most scientists agree that the treaty is an important symbol of global cooperation but that it does not go far enough in preventing significant depletion of the ozone layer and global warming. Indeed, by 1989, new evidence showed we had already destroyed as much ozone as the treaty makers assumed we would lose by 2050.

Since some of these chemicals are unnecessary and substitutes exist, most scientists call for phasing out all uses of ozone-depleting chemicals by 1995, as Sweden has agreed to do. Environmentalists also call for all products that contain or require CFCs, halons, or other ozone-depleting chemicals for their manufacture to be clearly labelled so that consumers can consciously choose whether to use such products.

In June 1990, delegates from 93 countries meeting in London, England, expanded the Montreal Protocol and pledged to phase out all production of CFCs and halons by the year 2000, if substitutes are available by then. They also agreed on the need to phase out or reduce the use of other ozone-depleting substances, such as carbon tetrachloride, methyl chloroform, and the HCFCs now being used as substitutes for some CFCs, but set no deadlines for such actions. According to the EPA, overall concentrations of chlorine from these ozone-destroying chemicals in the stratosphere could double, triple, or quadruple in the next century even if CFCs are completely phased out. Also, the effectiveness of any ban on ozone-depleting chemicals will depend on the willingness of LDCs such as China and India to participate.

Even if all ozone-depleting substances were banned tomorrow, it would take about 100 years for the planet to recover from the present ozone depletion and that which will come from those already in the atmosphere. The key question is whether MDCs and LDCs can agree to sacrifice short-term economic gain by eliminating their use of *all* ozone-depleting chemicals within the next decade to protect life on Earth in coming decades.

Perhaps the challenges posed by global warming and ozone depletion can be a catalyst for worldwide awareness of the urgent need to get serious about sustaining the earth and learning how to deal with long-term problems that build up slowly and invisibly until they exceed threshold levels. Let's hope so and begin by sharply reducing our individual impacts on the ozone layer (see Individuals Matter on p. 303).

11-5 Climate, Biodiversity, and Nuclear War

THE ULTIMATE ECOLOGICAL CATASTROPHE
Most people believe that global nuclear war is the greatest threat to the human species and Earth's life-support systems for most species. The nuclear age began in August 1945, when the United States exploded a single nuclear fission atomic bomb over Hiroshima and another over Nagasaki. These blasts killed an estimated 110,000 to 140,000 people and injured tens of thousands more.

By the end of that year, 100,000 more had died, mostly from exposure to high levels of ionizing radiation from neutrons emitted by the nuclear fission chain reaction (Figure 3-11) and by radioactive isotopes (Figure 3-9) in the resulting fallout: dirt and debris sucked up and made radioactive by the blast, and dropped back to Earth's surface near ground zero and on downwind areas hundreds and even thousands of kilometers away. Other people, exposed to nonlethal doses of ionizing radiation, developed cataracts, leukemia, and other forms of lethal cancer decades later. Some are still dying today. This shows us what a small nuclear bomb can do.

Today, the world's nuclear arsenals have an explosive power equal to more than 952,000 Hiroshima-type bombs or 3,333 times all the explosives detonated during World War II. Each Trident II submarine that began coming on line in 1989 carries nuclear warheads with the explosive power of 4,570 Hiroshima bombs or over 30 times all the explosives detonated in World War II. *Today, we live in a world with enough nuclear weapons to kill everyone on Earth 60 times*. By the end of this century, 60 countries — 1 of every 3 in the world — will have either nuclear weapons or the knowledge and capability to build them.

In addition to the health and environmental threats, the buildup of nuclear and conventional weapons drains funds and creativity that could be used to solve most of the world's population, food, health, resource, and environmental problems. For example, about 40% of the world's research and development expenditures and 50% of its physical scientists and engineers are devoted to developing weapons to improve our ability to kill one another.

NUCLEAR WINTER AND NUCLEAR AUTUMN EFFECTS
Some U.S. and Soviet military strategists have talked about the concept of "limited nuclear war," wherein combatants would direct nuclear weapons only at military targets rather than launching an all-out nuclear attack on both military targets and major cities. According to these strategists, most people in the United States and the Soviet Union could survive a lim-

- Avoid purchasing products containing chlorofluorocarbons, carbon tetrachloride, and methyl chloroform (1,1,1-trichloroethane on most ingredient labels). Such products include cleaning sprays for sewing machines, VCRs, and electronic equipment, spray-on cleaners and spot removers, bug killers and foggers, shoe polish sprays and other aerosols, and polystyrene foam insulation and packaging. Seek out the substitutes that are or will soon be available for these products.

- Don't buy CFC-containing polystyrene foam insulation. Types of insulation that don't contain CFCs are extended polystyrene (commonly called EPS or beadboard), fiberglass, rock wool, cellulose, and perlite.

- Don't buy halon or carbon dioxide fire extinguishers for home use. Instead, buy those using dry chemicals.

- Stop using all aerosol spray products, except in some medical sprays. Even those not using

CFCs and HCFCs (such as Dymel) emit hydrocarbon or other propellant chemicals into the air. Use roll-on and hand-pump products instead.

- Pressure legislators to ban all uses of CFCs and halons by 1995, carbon tetrachloride and methyl chloroform by 2000, and HCFC and HFC substitutes by the year 2010.

- Pressure legislators to tax the billions of dollars in windfall profits that CFC and halon manufacturers will get from phasing out their use and to use these tax revenues for climate research, improving energy efficiency, and switching to perpetual and renewable energy resources. Pressure legislators to use the revenue from taxes on the sale of CFCs, instituted in 1989, for these purposes rather than using them as general revenue.

- As they become available, buy new refrigerators and freezers that use vacuum insulation (as in Thermos bottles) instead of rigid-foam insulation and that use he-

lium as a coolant instead of CFCs or HCFCs (such refrigerators are available from Cryodynamics, 1101 Bristol Road, Mountainside, NJ 07092).

- Pressure legislators to require that all products containing or requiring CFCs, halons, or other ozone-depleting chemicals for their manufacture be clearly labelled and to require recovery of CFCs when refrigerators, freezers, and home and auto air conditioners are junked.

- Since leaky air conditioners in cars are the largest source of CFC emissions in the United States, make sure your auto air conditioner is not leaking. If it needs to be recharged, take it to a shop that has the equipment to recycle its CFCs.

- Don't fall for highly unpredictable and money-wasting schemes such as using lasers to blast CFCs out of the sky and building more supersonic commercial airplanes (SSTs), whose emissions could further deplete ozone in the stratosphere.

ited nuclear war, and the effects on most other countries not involved in the exchange would not be drastic.

Since 1982, however, evaluation of previously overlooked calculations has suggested that even a limited nuclear war could kill 1 billion to 4 billion people—20% to 80% of the world's current population. Such an exchange would probably take place in the Northern Hemisphere, presumably between the United States and the Soviet Union, either because of a direct confrontation between these two superpowers or because conflicts between other countries with nuclear weapons escalate into a global conflict involving the superpowers. If that happened, the direct effects of the explosions would kill an estimated 1 billion people, mostly in the Northern Hemisphere. Tens of millions more would suffer injuries.

Computer models indicate that within the next two years, another 1 billion to 3 billion people might die

from starvation caused by disruption of world agricultural production, first in the Northern Hemisphere and later in the Southern Hemisphere, because of what is called the *nuclear winter* or *nuclear autumn effect*.

Depending on the extent, time, and location of the explosions, average atmospheric temperatures in temperate areas would probably drop rapidly to temperatures typical of fall or early winter. This atmospheric cooling would happen because of a reverse greenhouse effect. Enormous amounts of smoke, soot, dust, and other debris, lifted into the atmosphere as a result of the nuclear explosions and subsequent fires, would coalesce into huge smoke clouds. Within two weeks, these dense clouds would cover large portions of the Northern Hemisphere and prevent 20% to 90% of all sunlight from reaching large areas (Figure 11-9).

The abnormally cold temperatures and reduction of sunlight would cause a sharp drop in food production

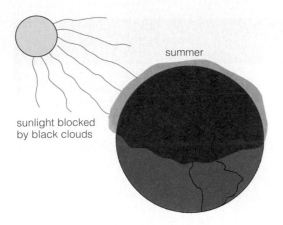

Figure 11-9 The nuclear winter or autumn effect caused by a limited nuclear war in the Northern Hemisphere.

in the growing season following the war. This would cause widespread starvation in the Northern Hemisphere and in African and Asian countries dependent on food imports from countries such as the United States and Canada.

Food production in the Southern Hemisphere might also be affected as the smoke clouds gradually became less dense and spread southward. Drops in temperature and sunlight there would be less severe than in the Northern Hemisphere. However, even a slight reduction in temperature could be disastrous to agriculture in tropical and subtropical forest areas and could lead to the extinction of numerous plant and animal species. Subtropical grasslands and savannas in Africa (Figure 5-17) and South America might be the least affected of the world's ecosystems because their plants are more cold tolerant and drought resistant.

A cold and dark nuclear winter or autumn would not be the only cause of food scarcity. Plagues of rapidly producing insects and rodents—the life forms best equipped to survive nuclear war—would damage stored food and spread disease. In areas where crops could still be grown, farmers would be isolated from supplies of seeds, fertilizer, pesticides, and fuel. People hoping to subsist on seafood would find many surviving aquatic species contaminated with radioactivity, runoff from ruptured tanks of industrial liquids, and oil pouring out of damaged offshore rigs.

A limited nuclear war would also destroy 30% to 70% of the ozone layer, leading to a deadly *ultraviolet summer*. This would sharply decrease the ability to grow crops and harvest fish. It would also cause a huge increase in skin cancers and eye cataracts and impair immune systems so that already-weakened survivors would die from infectious diseases.

Incineration of oil in tanks and refineries, storage tanks of hazardous chemicals, rubber tires, and other materials would produce toxic smog, which would

cover much of the Northern Hemisphere. Large areas might also be assaulted with extremely acid rains. High levels of radioactivity from fallout would contaminate most remaining supplies of food and water and would kill many people and other warm-blooded animals, some crops, and certain coniferous trees, especially pines. Thus, people not killed outright by the nuclear explosions would find themselves choking and freezing in a smoggy, radioactive darkness with contaminated water supplies and little chance of growing food for a year or perhaps several years.

The computer models of the atmosphere used to make these calculations are crude and may overestimate or underestimate the effects of nuclear explosions. Scientists agree, however, that even if the effects are less than the models suggest, they would still cause serious disruptions in regional and global climate and thus disrupt food and water supplies.

It is encouraging that there is some thawing in the cold war tensions between the United States and the Soviet Union and that these countries have destroyed a small number of their nuclear missiles. However, most people are unaware that only the delivery systems have been destroyed. The fissionable bomb material has merely been removed and stored for possible future use. Also, changing conditions and leadership in the Soviet Union could lead to a renewal of cold war tensions that have severely damaged the U.S. and Soviet economies.

We must go much further and abolish war, something that Kenneth Boulding thinks is now within our grasp (see Guest Essay on p. 306). War is fatally obsolete in a world where much more explosive power can be carried in one submarine than has been detonated in all wars on Earth so far. A start would be to reduce the combined U.S. and Soviet arsenals of nuclear weapons to no more than 12,000 (6,000 apiece).

Some people have wondered whether there is intelligent life in other parts of the universe. Perhaps the real question we should ask is whether there is intelligent life on Earth? If we can seriously deal with the four planetary emergencies discussed in this chapter and with deforestation, discussed in Chapter 10, *now*—not after decades more of discussion, research, delay, and wasteful depletion of Earth's natural capital—then the answer is a hopeful yes. Otherwise, it is a tragic no, and our species may bring about its own extinction and take several million more species with it. The choice is ours. Not to decide is to decide.

The atmosphere is the key symbol of global interdependence. If we can't solve some of our problems in the face of threats to this global commons, then I can't be very optimistic about the future of the world.

MARGARET MEAD

Stephen H. Schneider

Stephen H. Schneider is a widely respected expert on climate modelling, climatic change, and global warming. He is currently head of the Interdisciplinary Climate Systems Section at the National Center for Atmospheric Research. He is the author of Global Warming: Are We Entering the Greenhouse Century? *(1989),* The Coevolution of Climate and Life *(with R. Londer, 1984), and* Climate and Global Survival *(with L. Meisrow, 1979), and is the author or coauthor of over 160 scientific papers and other publications. He is editor of the scientific journal* Climatic Change, *a frequent witness at Congressional hearings, and an effective communicator in the print and broadcast media about climatic change. In 1984, he was selected by* Science Digest *as one of the "One Hundred Outstanding Young Scientists in America."*

It is my personal view that it will take a decade or two before research will begin to narrow the wide range of uncertainties surrounding the possible climatic future to which natural and human systems will have to adapt in the decades ahead. It is possible, with luck, that we may experience only a degree or so of warming over the next century, an amount that most species could adapt to.

On the other hand, uncertainties are just as likely to make present estimates (which project a few degrees' warming by the middle of the next century) underestimates as much as overestimates. In that case, we would be unlucky and committed to catastrophic magnitudes of change well before the end of the next century. Since some developing countries are counting on the use of cheap fossil fuels to power industrialization and since developed countries have from 3 to 20 times the per capita consumption levels of energy and materials that poor developing countries have, international negotiations for limiting emissions of greenhouse gases will be very difficult.

---

*Any opinions, findings, conclusions, or recommendations expressed in this essay are those of its author and do not necessarily reflect the views of the National Science Foundation, which is the sponsor of the National Center for Atmospheric Research.

It is my belief, however, that solutions can be found that do not require big unacceptable concessions from either side, at least for a period of a decade or so. Fortunately, since 1985, engineering and economic analyses have conclusively demonstrated that previous assertions that cost-effective investment in efficient lighting, housing, machinery, transportation, farming, and other activities can cut developed countries' greenhouse-gas emissions by some 20% before the end of this century are correct. Further, they have shown that this can be done at zero to negative net costs. In other words, our current energy, housing, agricultural, and industrial practices are well behind the "best" practices already available with state-of-the-art technology.

Although such technology sometimes involves substantial initial capital investment, that investment will pay back enough dividends over the next ten years to make the return on investment better than average for investments made by individuals, corporations, or governments (for example, better than 7% per year return). In that sense, these investments are negative costs that pay for themselves in about a decade and save money after that.

Moreover, energy efficiency will not only reduce the magnitude of gaseous emissions that can affect global warming but also reduce acid deposition (acid rain), health- and plant-damaging air pollutants, dependence on unreliable foreign supplies of energy (especially oil), balance-of-payments deficits for energy-importing countries, and so forth. These multiple benefits — what has been referred to as "a tie-in strategy" are essentially "free" additional benefits we receive for investing in reduction of greenhouse-gas emissions.

Another tie-in strategy is to reduce rates of tropical deforestation [Section 10-4]. This will reduce the emissions and increase the absorption of some greenhouse gases and at the same time help to preserve the vast number of wild species being driven to extinction through indiscriminate deforestation in the tropics and elsewhere.

Banning fluorocarbons [Section 11-4] is another tie-in action, since it eliminates the prime source of stratospheric ozone reduction in addition to reducing the potential for global warming. Another tie-in is curtailing population growth [Section 8-3]. This would reduce the principal cause of pressure on land, settlements, and natural resources to provide the doubling of food and the more than doubling of economic standards projected to be needed over the next 40 years to deal with the near-doubling of population in that time.

Clearly, any of these tie-in actions make sense on their own merits, and the fact that they also reduce the risk of climate warming by reducing the injection of greenhouse gases into the atmosphere gives them urgent priority. The tough questions are not whether to carry out such policy actions, but how much they should be extended beyond negative costs and who should pay.

(continued)

Developing countries argue that they created less than half the projected global warming problem and do not have the resources to deal with it anyway. They argue that developed countries should both transfer modern technology to LDCs and pay the net extra costs associated with their use of state-of-the-art technologies in comparison with their use of inefficient and environmentally less benign old technologies. I understand their views, but it will be politically controversial to get developed countries faced with high budget deficits and pressures to improve standards of living of their own least advantaged citizens to both cut their wasteful consumption and, at the same time, transfer significant resources to developing countries.

However, it is my belief that increasing population pressure in the developing world and the growing gap in the equitable distribution of resources between developed and developing countries [Figure 1-7] can only heighten world tensions in the 21st century. This will threaten not only the environment but also global security. Therefore, investments in environmentally sustainable development are urgent with or without global warming. Furthermore, the fact that reduction of global warming is a dividend that we get for making such investments puts them at the top of my environmental priority list for the 1990s and beyond.

The magnitude of the investment needed to achieve environmentally sustainable development that can slow population growth rates, reduce pressure on forests, stabilize and then curtail greenhouse-gas emissions, and so forth, will probably take on the order of tens to hundreds of billions invested annually for decades. While that

GUEST ESSAY   The Abolition of War as a Condition for Human Survival

Kenneth E. Boulding

Kenneth E. Boulding is Distinguished Professor of Economics Emeritus and a research associate of the Program of Research on Political and Economic Change at the Institute of Behavioral Sciences, University of Colorado at Boulder. During his long and distinguished career as an economist and social thinker, he has served as president of the American Economic Association and the American Association for the Advancement of Science. He has engaged in research on peace, systems analysis, economic theory, economics and ethics, and economics and environment. He was the first leading economist to propose in the late 1960s that we move from our present throwaway or frontier economy to a sustainable-Earth economy.

Perhaps the most profound change in the state of the Planet Earth in the last 100 years has been the development of more destructive forms of warfare. The first major development was aerial warfare and the bombing of cities. The second was the development of the nuclear weapon, especially the hydrogen bomb with its enormous destructive power, and the long-range missile that can deliver it to virtually any point on the earth's surface.

Something like this, however, has happened before in human history, though on a much smaller scale. A good example is the development of gunpowder and the effective cannon in the 15th and 16th centuries, which really brought the feudal system to an end and created national states the size of England or France.

As long as the means of destruction were spears and arrows, there was some sense in having a castle or a city wall. With the coming of the effective cannon, these made no sense. The baron who stayed in his castle got blown up. Some attempt was made to save the city wall by building longer triangular projections from them, with cannons on them, a little reminiscent of the Strategic Defense Initiative (SDI), or "Star Wars," defense now being pursued by the United States. This turned out to be ineffective. Most city walls were torn down and became boulevards, and castles became tourist attractions.

The nuclear weapon and the long-range missile have done for unilateral national defense precisely what the cannon did for the feudal baron and the city wall, but we

seems like a staggering sum on a global basis, some perspective can be gained by recognizing that the world currently spends some trillion dollars annually in armaments, an order of a tenth of the investments needed to provide environmentally sustainable development and environmental security.

If the world declared war on poverty, overpopulation, overaffluence, and environmental damage, it could cut back substantially its investments in armaments and divert perhaps half of those savings to environmentally sustainable development. Governments could use the other half of those savings to satisfy the demand for improved living conditions by the disadvantaged in their own countries.

Fundamentally, dealing with global warming is like dealing with many other global issues of environmental development and security. It involves a shift away from short-term national interests and toward long-term global survival.

Guest Essay Discussion

1. Do you agree with the author that reducing the threat of global warming and the other dividends this provides should be the top environmental priority for the 1990s and beyond? Explain.

2. The author argues that we need to make a shift from emphasis on short-term national interest toward long-term global survival. Do you agree or disagree? Explain. What things do you believe should be done to make this transition?

---

haven't caught on to this, yet. We delude ourselves by thinking that we have a stable deterrence. Deterrence says, "You do something nasty to me and I'll do something nasty to you."

Deterrence can work over short periods and in specific places, but it cannot be stable in the long run; otherwise, it would not deter in the short run. If the probability of nuclear weapons going off were zero, that would be the same as not having them. They would deter nobody.

Deterrence always has a positive probability of breaking down. It is a fundamental principle that if there is a positive probability of anything, it will happen if we wait long enough. When one reflects that the Chernobyl nuclear power plant was carefully designed not to go off and that nuclear weapons are carefully designed to go off, the possibility of even accidental nuclear war may be alarmingly high.

For the first time in human history, the fate of the planet is in the hands of a very few decision makers. There is always a positive probability that one or more of them will make a fatal decision.

There is some uncertainty about the consequences of nuclear war. There is some probability it might create a nuclear winter or autumn [Figure 11-9], which could cause at least a billion, perhaps several billion, human beings to starve to death. We know very little about the long-run effects of enormous radiation fallout from a major nuclear war, and there may even be some small probability that it would bring the whole evolutionary process on Earth to an end.

What is more probable is that it would be a disaster that would distort and in some sense cripple the whole process of evolutionary development on Earth for a very long time to come. This is also a threat to the environment that exceeds anything else that the human race is doing, whether in terms of an enhanced "greenhouse effect," depletion of the ozone layer, tropical forest destruction, or chemical pollution.

The only way to remove this dire threat to the planet is through the abolition of war. This, too, has a noticeable probability. Again, there are historical parallels. We abolished dueling when it went from swords to pistols and often both parties were getting killed. We abolished slavery when it became economically and morally unacceptable.

Now the great task of the human race is to abolish national defense and transform the military into a means of production rather than a means of destruction. We have to learn that military victory is something that has disappeared from the earth, that we have to live without enemies.

The great problem of the military is that they have to have enemies in order to justify their budgets. Hence, they are designed to be very ineffective at conflict management, the most important skill we need on this planet

(continued)

today. Somehow, we must catch onto this and recognize that the greatest conflict in the world at the moment is between the united military of the world and the human race, which of course includes those in the military system. Once we recognize that, things can happen.

Peace is not something exotic and improbable. In the last 150 years, we have seen the rise of stable peace among many nations, beginning perhaps in Scandinavia, spreading to North America by about 1870. More recently, it has spread to western Europe and the Pacific, where we now have perhaps 18 nations in a great triangle from Australia to Japan to Finland, who have no plans whatever to go to war with each other.

We now seem close to stable peace around the whole temperate zone, with the extraordinary changes that have taken place in the communist countries. The United States is still dragging its feet a little. The tragic confrontation in the Middle East suggests that the illusions of military power are still strong, deterrence is still unstable, and the prospect of a major catastrophe is appallingly high. Nevertheless, if the learning process can go on, stable peace may spread to both Islam and tropical LDCs.

It is a fundamental principle that what exists must be possible. Stable peace has existed now in many nations

for at least 150 years. It must clearly be possible. In that, there is great hope for the human race and this incredibly beautiful planet.

Guest Essay Discussion

1. Do you think or talk about the possibility of nuclear war? Why or why not? What causes most people to largely ignore this greatest threat to their survival and the survival of their children and grandchildren?

2. The history of warfare has shown that any advance in military technology is countered by another advance in military technology and that the pace of this process is increasing. In light of this, do you believe that the United States should pour hundreds of billions of dollars into a "Star Wars" defense system against nuclear attack? Explain.

3. Do you agree that the most urgent task on this planet is to abolish war? Why? Do you believe that this is possible? Explain. If you agree that it is the most urgent task, then what are you doing as an individual to convert this possibility into reality?

DISCUSSION TOPICS

1. What consumption patterns and other features of your lifestyle directly add greenhouse gases to the atmosphere? Which, if any, of those things would you be willing to give up to slow projected global warming and reduce other forms of air pollution?

2. Explain why you agree or disagree with each of the proposals for (a) slowing down emissions of greenhouse gases into the atmosphere listed on pp. 293 and 295 and (b) adjusting to the effects of global warming listed on pp. 295–296. Explain. What effects would carrying out these proposals have on your lifestyle and those of any children you might choose to have? What effects might not carrying out these actions have?

3. Should MDCs set up a world food bank to store several years' supply of food to reduce the harmful effects of a loss in food production caused by a change in climate? How would you decide who gets this food in times of need?

4. What consumption patterns and other features of your lifestyle directly and indirectly add ozone-depleting chemicals to the atmosphere? Which, if any, of those things would you be willing to give up to slow ozone depletion?

5. Should all uses of CFCs, halons, and other ozone-depleting chemicals be banned in the United States and worldwide? Explain. Suppose this meant that air conditioning (especially in cars and perhaps in buildings) had to be banned or became fives times as expensive. Would you still support such a ban?

6. In 1989, U.S. Senator Albert Gore introduced a legislative package he calls the Strategic Environment Initiative (SEI), an ecological version of Ronald Reagan's Strategic Defense Initiative (SDI). Domestically, the SEI would focus on improving energy efficiency, developing alternative fuels, reforestation, comprehensive recycling, and drastic cuts in ozone-depleting chemicals. It would also help LDCs obtain energy-efficient technology and develop environmentally sustainable industries and agriculture. Do you support such a bill? What things, if any, would you add? What has happened to this proposal since it was first introduced in 1989?

7. Do you believe that most of the survivors of a global nuclear war would envy the dead? Why? Would you want to be one of the survivors? Why or why not?

8. Do you think that nuclear war is preventable? How?

PART FIVE

RESOURCES AND RESOURCE MANAGEMENT

Our entire society rests upon — and is dependent upon — our water, our land, our forests, and our minerals. How we use these resources influences our health, security, economy, and well-being.

JOHN F. KENNEDY

Wind farm in a mountain pass in California.

CHAPTER 12

SOIL RESOURCES

General Questions and Issues

1. What are the principal components and types of soil, and what properties make a soil best suited for growing crops?

2. How serious is the problem of soil erosion in the world and in the United States?

3. How can we reduce erosion and nutrient depletion in topsoil?

4. How is soil degraded by excessive salt buildup (salinization) and waterlogging?

Below that thin layer comprising the delicate organism known as the soil is a planet as lifeless as the moon.

G. Y. JACKS AND R. O. WHYTE

NLESS YOU ARE A FARMER, you probably think of soil as dirt—something you don't want on your hands, clothes, or carpet. You are acutely aware of your need for air and water, but you may be unaware that your life and that of other organisms depend on soil, especially the upper portion known as topsoil.

The nutrients in the food we eat come from soil. To a large extent, all flesh is soil nutrients. Soil also provides you with wood, paper, cotton, and many other vital materials and helps purify the water you drink.

As long as soil is held in place by vegetation, it stores water and releases it in a nourishing trickle instead of a devastating flood. Soil's decomposer organisms recycle the key chemicals we and most other forms of life need. Bacteria in soil decompose degradable forms of garbage you throw away, although this process takes decades to hundreds of years in today's compacted, oxygen-deficient landfills. Soil is truly the base of life and civilization.

Yet, since the beginning of agriculture, we have abused this vital, potentially renewable resource. Entire civilizations have collapsed because they mismanaged the topsoil that supported their populations (see Spotlight on p. 37).

Today, we are abusing soil more than ever. Each of us must become involved in protecting the life-giving resource we call soil. In saving the soil, we save ourselves and other forms of life.

12-1 Soil: Components, Types, and Properties

SOIL LAYERS AND COMPONENTS Pick up a handful of soil and notice how it feels and looks. The **soil** you hold in your hand is a complex mixture of inorganic materials (clay, silt, pebbles, and sand), decaying organic matter, water, air, and billions of living organisms. Processes leading to the formation of various types of soils are mechanical and chemical weathering of solid rock (Figure 7-8), the buildup of sediments deposited by erosion, and interactions of weathered materials and sediments with various forms of life.

The components of mature soils are arranged in a series of zones called **soil horizons** (Figure 12-1). Each horizon has a distinct texture and a distinct composition that vary with different types of soils. A cross-sectional view of the horizons in a soil is called a *soil profile*. Most mature soils have at least three of the possible horizons, but some new or poorly developed soils don't have horizons.

The top layer, *surface-litter layer*, or *O-horizon*, consists mostly of freshly fallen and partially decomposed leaves, twigs, animal waste, fungi, and other organic

O–Horizon

A–Horizon

E–Horizon

B–Horizon

C–Horizon

R

Surface litter:
Freshly fallen leaves and organic debris
and partially decomposed organic matter

Topsoil:
Partially decomposed organic matter (humus), plant
roots, living organisms, and some inorganic minerals

Zone of leaching:
Area through which dissolved or suspended
materials move downward

Subsoil:
Unique colors and often an accumulation of iron,
aluminum, and humic compounds, and clay leached
down from above layers

Parent material:
Partially broken-down
inorganic materials

Bedrock:
Impenetrable layer, except for fractures

materials. Most often, it is brown to black in color. The underlying *topsoil layer*, or *A-horizon*, is usually a porous mixture of partially decomposed organic matter (humus), living organisms, and some inorganic mineral particles. Normally, it is darker and looser than deeper layers. The roots of most plants and most of a soil's organic matter are concentrated in these two upper soil layers (Figure 12-1).

The two top layers of most well-developed soils are also teeming with bacteria, fungi, earthworms, and small insects. These layers are also home for larger, burrowing animals such as moles and gophers. All these soil organisms interact in complex food webs (Figure 12-2). Most are bacteria and other decomposer microorganisms, with billions found in every handful of soil. They partially or completely break down some of the complex compounds in the upper layers of soil into simpler, nutrient compounds that dissolve in soil water. Soil moisture carrying these dissolved nutrients is drawn up by the roots of plants and transported through stems and into leaves (Figure 12-3). When soil is eroded, it is the vital surface litter and topsoil layers that are lost.

These two top layers usually contain dead leaves and stems of plants, dead roots, and the waste products and dead bodies of animals (Figure 12-1). Decomposers such as fungi and bacteria produce a slimy substance

that contains enzymes that speed up the partial breakdown of this detritus. This leaves a sticky, brown, slightly soluble residue of undigested or partially decomposed organic material called **humus**. The more plants and animals that lived in the soil, the more humus the soil will contain. Because humus is only slightly soluble in water, most of it remains in the topsoil layer. A fertile soil, useful for growing high yields of crops, has a thick topsoil layer containing a high content of humus.

Humus is a very important soil material. It coats the sand, silt, and clay particles in topsoil and binds them together into clumps, giving a soil its *structure*. That explains why soils with a high humus content (5% or more by weight) have a spongy feeling. Humus also helps topsoil hold water and nutrients taken up by plant roots. Particles of humus and of clay tend to have a negative electrical charge on their surfaces. This allows them to attract and hold positively charged nutrient ions such as potassium (K^+), calcium (Ca^{2+}), and ammonium (NH_4^+) strongly enough to prevent them from being detached as water percolates downward through the topsoil.

Humus also provides spaces for the growth of nutrient-absorbing root hairs and a class of fungi, known as mycorrhizae fungi, that are the mutualistic partners

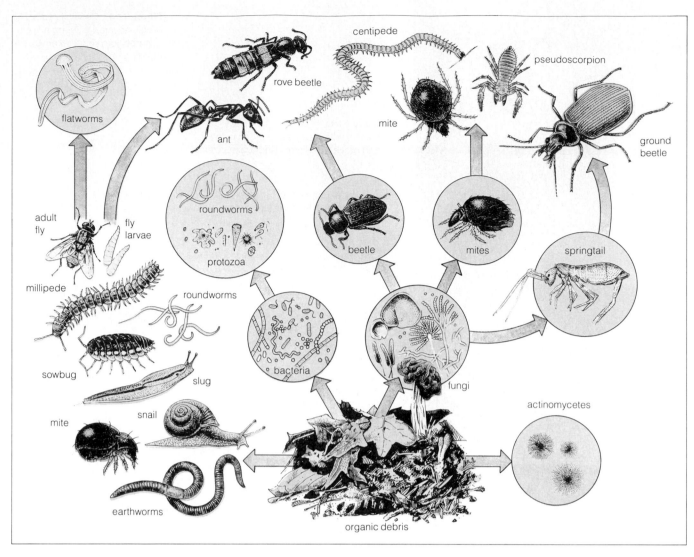

Labels within the figure:
centipede
pseudoscorpion
rove beetle
flatworms
mite
ground beetle
ant
roundworms
adult fly
fly larvae
protozoa
beetle
mites
springtail
millipede
roundworms
sowbug
bacteria
fungi
slug
actinomycetes
mite
snail
earthworms
organic debris

Figure 12-2 Greatly simplified food web of living organisms found in soil.

of some trees and other plants (see Spotlight on p. 275). The burrowing activity of mice, earthworms, and other organisms keeps the clumps loose.

The color of the topsoil layer tells us a lot about how useful a soil is for growing crops. For example, dark brown or black topsoil has a large amount of organic matter and is nitrogen rich. Gray, bright yellow, or red topsoils are low in organic matter and will require nitrogen fertilizer to increase their fertility.

The B-horizon (subsoil) and the C-horizon (parent material) contain most of a soil's inorganic matter. Most of this is broken-down rock in the form of varying mixtures of sand, silt, clay, and gravel. The C-horizon lies on a base of bedrock (Figure 12-1).

The spaces, or pores, between the solid organic and inorganic particles in the upper and lower soil layers contain varying amounts of two other key inorganic components: air (mostly nitrogen and oxygen gas) and

water. The oxygen gas, highly concentrated in the topsoil, is used by the cells in plant roots to carry out aerobic respiration.

Some of the rain falling on the soil surface percolates downward through the soil layers and occupies many of the pores. This downward movement of water through soil is called **infiltration**. As the water seeps downward, it dissolves and picks up various soil components in upper layers and carries them to lower layers—a process called **leaching**. Most materials leached from the topsoil layer (sometimes called the *zone of leaching*) accumulate in the B-horizon (sometimes referred to as the *zone of deposition*), if one has developed.

TYPES OF SOIL Soils develop and mature slowly. One maturation process is **humification**, in which organic matter in the upper soil layers is reduced to finely divided pieces of humus or partially decomposed organic

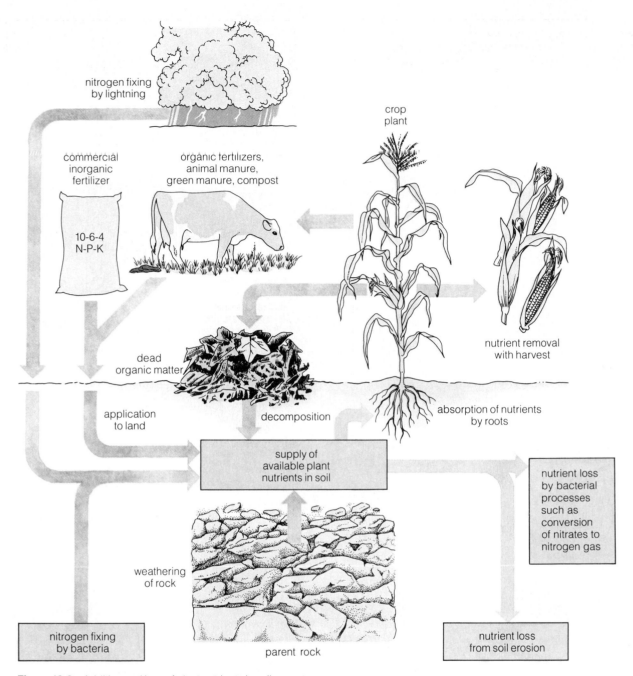

Figure 12-3 Addition and loss of plant nutrients in soils.

matter. In lower layers, a soil matures through **mineralization**, in which decomposers turn organic materials into inorganic ones.

Mature soils in different major biomes (Figure 5-11) vary widely in color, content, pore space, acidity (pH), and depth. These differences can be used to classify soils throughout the world into ten principal types, or orders. Five important soil types, each with a distinct soil profile, are shown in Figure 12-4. Most of the world's crops are grown on grassland soils and on soils exposed when deciduous forests are cleared.

SOIL TEXTURE AND POROSITY Soils vary in their content of clay (very fine particles), silt (fine particles), sand (medium-size particles), and gravel (coarse to very coarse particles). The relative amounts of the different sizes and types of mineral particles determine **soil texture**. Figure 12-5 shows how soils can be grouped into textural classes according to clay, silt, and sand content. Soils containing a mixture of clay, sand, silt, and humus are called **loams**.

To get a general idea of a soil's texture, take a small amount of topsoil, moisten it, and rub it between your

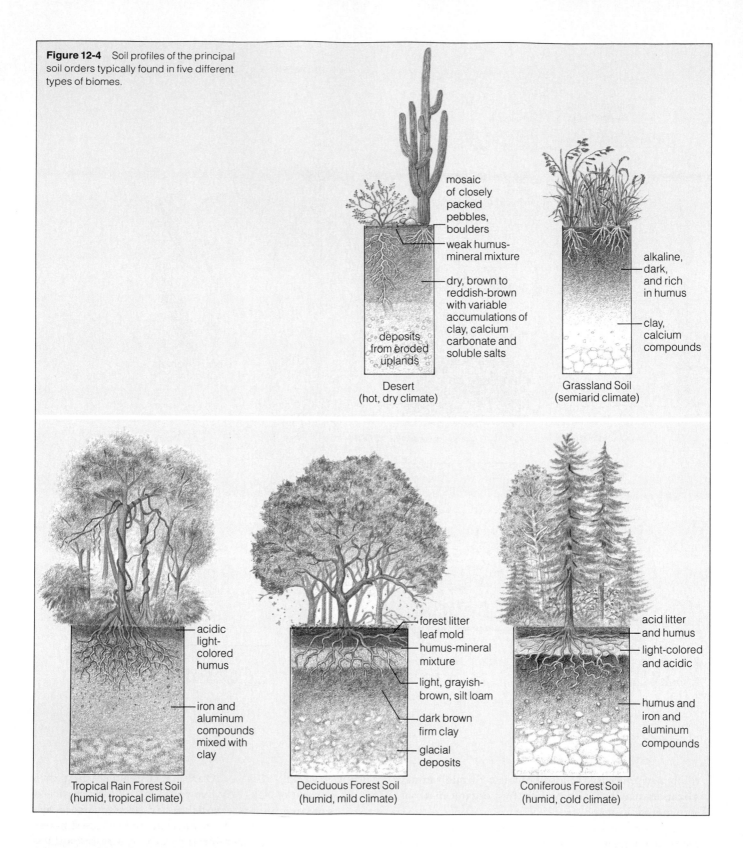

Figure 12-4 Soil profiles of the principal soil orders typically found in five different types of biomes.

mosaic of closely packed pebbles, boulders

weak humus-mineral mixture

dry, brown to reddish-brown with variable accumulations of clay, calcium carbonate and soluble salts

deposits from eroded uplands

Desert
(hot, dry climate)

alkaline, dark, and rich in humus

clay, calcium compounds

Grassland Soil
(semiarid climate)

acidic light-colored humus

iron and aluminum compounds mixed with clay

Tropical Rain Forest Soil
(humid, tropical climate)

forest litter leaf mold

humus-mineral mixture

light, grayish-brown, silt loam

dark brown firm clay

glacial deposits

Deciduous Forest Soil
(humid, mild climate)

acid litter and humus

light-colored and acidic

humus and iron and aluminum compounds

Coniferous Forest Soil
(humid, cold climate)

fingers and thumb. A gritty feel means that it contains a lot of sand. A sticky feel means that it has a high clay content, and you should be able to role it into a clump. Silt-laden soil feels smooth like flour. A loam topsoil (Figure 12-5), best suited for plant growth, has a texture between these extremes. It has a crumbly, spongy feel-

ing, and many of its particles are clumped loosely together.

Soil texture helps determine **soil porosity**: a measure of the volume of pores per volume of soil, and the average distances between those spaces. Forty to sixty percent of the volume of soil is normally pore space.

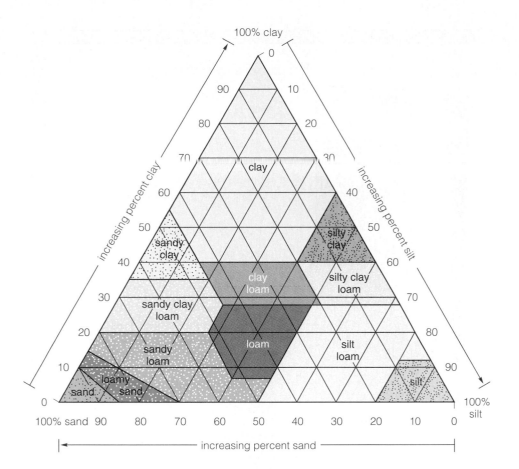

Figure 12-5 Soil texture depends on the percentages of clay, silt, and sand particles in the soil. Soil texture affects soil porosity — the average number and spacing of pores in a volume of soil. Loams, made up of roughly equal mixtures of clay, sand, and silt, are the best soils for growing most crops. (Data from Soil Conservation Service)

Table 12-1 Physical and Chemical Properties of Soils with Different Textures

Soil Texture	Nutrient-Holding Capacity	Water Infiltration	Water-Holding Capacity	Aeration	Workability
Clay	Good	Poor	Good	Poor	Poor
Silt	Medium	Medium	Medium	Medium	Medium
Sand	Poor	Good	Poor	Good	Good
Loam	Medium	Medium	Medium	Medium	Medium

The spaces allow air and water to travel through the soil. If there are few, or no spaces, plant roots cannot get the air and water they need. If the spaces are too big, water will quickly drain through the soil.

The average size of the spaces or pores in a soil determines **soil permeability**: the rate at which water and air move from upper to lower soil layers. Soil porosity is also influenced by **soil structure**: how the particles that make up a soil are organized and clumped together.

Soil texture, porosity, and permeability determine a soil's **water-holding capacity** (the ability of the soil to store water), **aeration** (the ability of air to move through the soil), and **workability** (the ability to be cultivated easily). Table 12-1 compares the main physical and chemical properties of clay, silt, sand, and loam soils.

Loams (Figure 12-5) are the best soils for growing most crops because they retain a large amount of water that is not held too tightly for plant roots to absorb. Soils with a high sand content are easy to work and have less pore space per volume of soil (lower porosity) than other soils. However, sandy soils have a high permeability because their pores are larger than those in most other soils. This is why water flows rapidly

Figure 12-6 Scale of pH, used to measure acidity and alkalinity of water solutions. Values shown are approximate. A neutral solution has a pH of 7; one with a pH greater than 7 is basic, or alkaline; one with a pH less than 7 is acidic. The lower the pH below 7, the more acidic the solution. Each whole-number decrease in pH represents a tenfold increase in acidity.

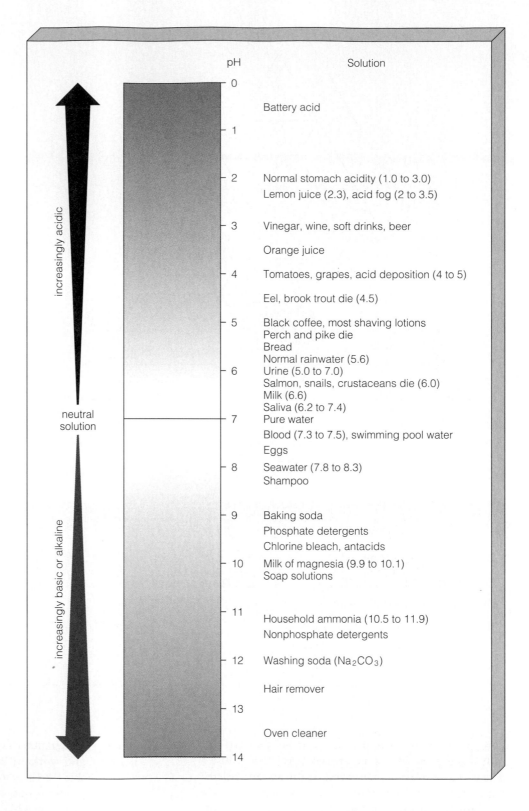

pH	Solution
0	
	Battery acid
1	
2	Normal stomach acidity (1.0 to 3.0)
	Lemon juice (2.3), acid fog (2 to 3.5)
3	Vinegar, wine, soft drinks, beer
	Orange juice
4	Tomatoes, grapes, acid deposition (4 to 5)
	Eel, brook trout die (4.5)
5	Black coffee, most shaving lotions
	Perch and pike die
	Bread
	Normal rainwater (5.6)
6	Urine (5.0 to 7.0)
	Salmon, snails, crustaceans die (6.0)
	Milk (6.6)
	Saliva (6.2 to 7.4)
7	Pure water
	Blood (7.3 to 7.5), swimming pool water
	Eggs
8	Seawater (7.8 to 8.3)
	Shampoo
9	Baking soda
	Phosphate detergents
	Chlorine bleach, antacids
10	Milk of magnesia (9.9 to 10.1)
	Soap solutions
11	Household ammonia (10.5 to 11.9)
	Nonphosphate detergents
12	Washing soda (Na_2CO_3)
	Hair remover
13	
	Oven cleaner
14	

increasingly acidic

neutral solution

increasingly basic or alkaline

through sandy soils. They are useful for growing irrigated crops or those without large water requirements, such as peanuts and strawberries.

The particles in clay soils are very small and easily compacted. When these soils get wet, they form large, dense clumps, explaining why wet clay is so easy to mold into bricks and pottery. Clay soils have more pore space per volume and a greater water-holding capacity than sandy soils, but the pore spaces are so small that these soils have a low permeability. Because little water can infiltrate to lower levels, the upper layers can easily become too waterlogged to grow most crops.

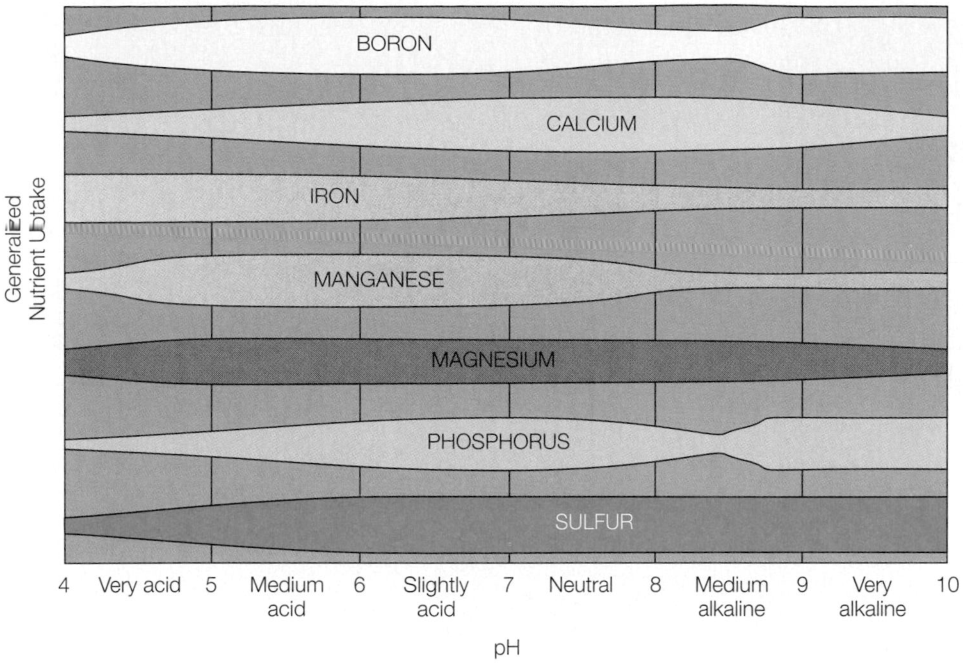

Figure 12-7 Effect of soil pH on availability of plant nutrients.

BORON

CALCIUM

IRON

MANGANESE

MAGNESIUM

PHOSPHORUS

SULFUR

Generalized Nutrient Uptake

| 4 | Very acid | 5 | Medium acid | 6 | Slightly acid | 7 | Neutral | 8 | Medium alkaline | 9 | Very alkaline | 10 |

pH

SOIL ACIDITY (pH) The acidity or basicity (alkalinity) of a soil is another factor determining the types of crops it can support. Different levels of acidity and basicity of water solutions of substances are commonly expressed in terms of **pH** (Figure 12-6).

Soils vary in acidity, and the pH of a soil influences the uptake of soil nutrients by plants (Figure 12-7). Crops vary in the pH ranges they can tolerate. For example, wheat, spinach, peas, corn, and tomatoes grow best in slightly acidic soils; potatoes and berries do best in very acidic soils; and alfalfa and asparagus do best in neutral soils. Rhododendrons and azaleas of the northwestern and southeastern conifer forests also thrive in acidic soils.

When soils are too acidic for the desired crops, the acids can be partially neutralized by an alkaline substance such as lime. Because lime speeds up the undesirable decomposition of organic matter in the soil, manure or another organic fertilizer should also be added to maintain soil fertility.

In areas of low rainfall, such as the semiarid regions in the western and southwestern United States, calcium and other alkaline compounds are not leached away. Soils in the region may be too alkaline (pH above 7.5) for some crops. If drainage is good, irrigation can reduce the alkalinity by leaching the alkaline compounds away. Adding sulfur, which is gradually converted into sulfuric acid by soil bacteria, is another way to reduce soil alkalinity. Soils in areas affected by acid deposition are becoming increasingly acidic.

The burning of fossil fuels, especially coal, releases sulfur dioxide and nitrogen oxides, which form acidic compounds in the atmosphere. These compounds fall back to the earth as *acid deposition* (Section 21-2). As acidic rain or melted acidic snow infiltrates the soil, the hydrogen ions (H^+) in the acids become attached to particles of minerals and humus in the topsoil layer and displace some of the potassium (K^+), calcium (Ca^{2+}), magnesium (Mg^{2+}), and ammonium (NH_4^+) ions attached to those particles. This results in a loss of soil fertility that can kill crops and trees or weaken them and make them more vulnerable to drought, disease, and pests.

12-2 Soil Erosion

NATURAL AND HUMAN-ACCELERATED SOIL EROSION Soil does not stay in one place indefinitely. **Soil erosion** is the movement of soil components, especially topsoil, from one place to another. The two main forces causing soil erosion are flowing water (Figures 12-8 and 10-8) and wind (Figure 12-9).

Some soil erosion always takes place because of natural water flow and winds (Section 7-2), but the roots of plants generally protect soil from excessive erosion. Agriculture, logging, construction, off-road vehicles, and other human activities that remove plant cover increase the rate at which soil erodes.

Although wind causes some erosion, most is caused by the force of moving water. Soil scientists distinguish between three types of erosion by water:

Figure 12-8 Rill and gully erosion of vital topsoil from this irrigated cropland in Arizona.

Figure 12-9 Wind eroding soil from farmland in Stevens County, Kansas.

sheet, rill, and gully. **Sheet erosion** occurs when surface water moves down a slope or across a field in a wide flow and peels off uniform layers or sheets of soil. Because it erodes topsoil evenly, sheet erosion may not be noticeable until much damage has been done. In **rill erosion**, the surface water forms little rivulets that flow at high velocities and cut small channels or ditches in the soil (Figure 12-8). In **gully erosion**, rivulets of fast-flowing water join together and with each succeeding rain cut the ditches wider and deeper until they become large ditches or gullies (Figure 12-8). Gully erosion can become severe on steep slopes where all or most of the vegetation has been removed (Figure 1-1).

Excessive erosion of topsoil reduces both the fertility and the water-holding capacity of a soil. The resulting sediment, the largest source of water pollution, clogs irrigation ditches, navigable waterways, reservoirs, lakes, and oceans (Figures 5-29 and 10-8).

Soil, especially the topsoil, is classified as a slowly renewable resource because it is continually regenerated by natural processes. However, in tropical and temperate areas, the renewal of 2.54 centimeters (1 inch) of soil takes from 200 to 1,000 years, depending on climate and soil type. If the average rate of topsoil erosion exceeds the rate of topsoil formation on a piece of land, the topsoil on that land becomes a nonrenewable resource being depleted. Annual erosion rates for agricultural land throughout the world are about 20 to 100 times the natural renewal rate (see Guest Essay on p. 330). Table 12-2 compares the main properties that affect accumulation of soil nutrients and soil renewability in natural and cultivated ecosystems.

Soil erosion on forestland and rangeland is not as severe as erosion on cropland, but forest soil takes two to three times longer to restore itself than cropland soil.

Table 12-2 Characteristics That Affect Soil Nutrient Content and Soil Erosion in Natural and Cultivated Terrestrial Ecosystems

Factor	Natural	Cultivated
Abiotic		
Water infiltration rate	High	Low
Water runoff rate	Low	High
Soil erosion rate	Low	High
Leaching losses	Low	High
Mineral loss rate	Low	High
Soil organic matter	High	Low
Soil temperature	Low	High
Biotic		
Structural diversity of plants	High	Low
Plant and animal species diversity	High	Low
Plant reproductive potential	High	Low

Construction sites usually have the highest erosion rates by far.

THE WORLD SITUATION Today, topsoil is eroding faster than it forms on about one-third of the world's cropland. In some countries, more than half the land is affected by soil erosion. They include Nepal (95%), Peru (95%), Turkey (95%) Lesotho (88%), Madagascar (79%), and Ethiopia (53%). In Africa, soil erosion has increased 20-fold in the last three decades.

Figure 12-10 Terracing of rice fields in Bali, Indonesia, reduces soil erosion. Terraces also increase the amount of usable land in steep terrain.

Prato/Bruce Coleman Ltd.

Worldwide, the estimated amount of topsoil washing and blowing into the world's streams, lakes, and oceans each year would fill a train of freight cars long enough to encircle the planet 150 times. At that rate, the world is losing about 7% of its topsoil from potential cropland each decade. The situation is worsening as farmers in MDCs and LDCs cultivate areas unsuited for agriculture to feed themselves and the world's growing population.

In mountainous areas, such as the Himalaya on the border between India and Tibet and the Andes near the west coast of South America, farmers have traditionally built elaborate systems of terraces (Figure 12-10). Terracing allowed them to cultivate steeply sloping land that would otherwise rapidly lose its topsoil.

Today, farmers in some areas cultivate steep slopes without terraces, causing a total loss of topsoil in 10 to 40 years. Although most poor farmers know that cultivating a steep slope without terracing causes a rapid loss of topsoil, they often have too little time and too few workers to build terraces. They engage in destructive cultivation practices to ward off starvation. The resultant loss of protective vegetation and topsoil also greatly increases the intensity of flooding in the lowland areas of watersheds, as has happened in Bangladesh (see Case Study on p. 342).

Since the beginning of agriculture, people in tropical forests have successfully used slash-and-burn, shifting cultivation (Figure 2-4) to provide food for relatively small populations. In recent decades, however, growing population and poverty have caused farmers in many tropical forest areas to reduce the fallow period of their fields to as little as 2 years, instead of the 10 to 30 years needed to allow the soil to regain its fertility. The result

has been a sharp increase in the rate of topsoil erosion and nutrient depletion.

Once-forested hills in many LDCs, such as Madagascar (see Case Study on p. 259), have been stripped bare of trees by poor people for firewood and by timber companies for use in MDCs. Because new trees are seldom planted in LDCs, the topsoil quickly erodes away (Figure 10-8).

Overgrazing and poor logging practices also cause heavy losses of topsoil. Intense grazing has turned many areas of North Africa and other arid and semi-arid areas from grassland to desert (see Case Study on p. 320).

In MDCs, where large-scale industrialized agriculture is practiced, many farmers have replaced traditional soil conservation practices with enormous inputs of commercial inorganic fertilizers and irrigation water. But the 17-fold increase in the use of fertilizer and the tripling of the world's irrigated cropland between 1950 and 1991 have only temporarily masked the effects of erosion and nutrient depletion.

Commercial inorganic fertilizer is not a complete substitute for naturally fertile topsoil; it merely hides for a time the gradual depletion of this vital resource. Nor is irrigation a long-term solution. Repeated irrigation of cropland without sufficient drainage eventually decreases or destroys its crop productivity as a result of waterlogging and salt buildup. Even with drainage, repeated irrigation removes soil nutrients by leaching.

Severe erosion accelerated by human activities is most widespread in India, China, the Soviet Union, and the United States, which together account for over half the world's food production and contain almost half the world's people.

According to the UN Environment Programme, about 35% of Earth's land surface — on which about 1 billion people try to survive — is classified as arid or semiarid desert (Figure 5-11). The world's deserts are spreading at an alarming rate in drier parts of every continent from a combination of natural processes and human activities (Figure 12-11).

The conversion of productive rangeland (uncultivated land used for animal grazing), rain-fed cropland, or irrigated cropland into desertlike land with a drop in agricultural productivity of 10% or more is called **desertification**.

Moderate desertification causes a 10% to 25% drop in productivity, and *severe desertification* causes a 25% to 50% drop. *Very severe desertification* causes a drop of 50% or more and usually results in formation of large gullies and sand dunes. Moderate, severe, and very severe desertification is a serious and growing problem in many parts of the world (Figure 12-11).

Instead of advancing on a broad front, desertification often begins with small patches and then spreads outward like a skin disease. Eventually, the land can completely lose its ability to support vegetation as its topsoil is washed or blown away and the sun bakes the subsoil rock-hard (Figure 12-12).

Moderate desertification can go unrecognized. For example, overgrazing has reduced the productivity of much of the grassland of the western United States. Yet, most citizens living in many of those areas do not realize they live in an area moderately desertified by human action.

Most desertification occurs naturally near the edges of existing deserts. It is caused by dehydration of the top layers of soil during prolonged drought and increased evaporation because of hot temperatures and high winds.

However, natural desertification is greatly accelerated by practices that leave topsoil vulnerable to erosion by water and wind:

- overgrazing of rangeland as a result of too many livestock on too little land area (the biggest cause of desertification, Figure 12-12)
- improper management of soil and water resources, which leads to increased erosion, salinization (salt buildup), and waterlogging of soil
- cultivation of land with unsuitable terrain or soils
- deforestation and surface mining without adequate replanting (Figure 10-12)
- soil compaction by farm machinery, cattle hoofs, and the impact of raindrops on denuded soil surfaces

These destructive practices are intensified by rapid population growth, high population densities, poverty, and poor land management. The consequences of desertification include intensified drought and famine, declining living standards, and swelling numbers of environmental refugees whose degraded land can no longer keep them alive.

It is estimated that 810 million hectares (2 billion acres) — an area the size of Brazil and 12 times the size of Texas — have become desertified during the past 50 years. The United Nations Environment Programme estimates that worldwide 63% of rangelands, 60% of the rain-fed cropland, and 30% of the irrigated cropland are threatened by loss of productivity because of desertification. The total area of this threatened land is 33 million square kilometers (13 million square miles) — about the size of North and South America combined. If present trends continue, desertification could threaten the livelihoods of 1.2 billion people worldwide by the year 2000.

Every year, an estimated 60,000 square kilometers (23,000 square miles) — an area the size of West Virginia — of new desert are formed, and an additional 210,000 square kilometers (81,000 square miles) of land — an area the size of Kansas — are degraded by soil and nutrient loss to the point where they are no longer worth farming or grazing. The areas most affected by current and projected future desertification are sub-Saharan Africa (between North Africa's barren Sahara and the plant-rich land to its south), eastern and southern Africa, the Middle East, western Asia (from Iran to Bangladesh), South Asia, Australia, the western United States, southern South America, and parts of Mexico (Figure 12-11).

In 1977, government representatives from around the world gathered at Nairobi for the United Nations Conference on Desertification. Out of that conference came a plan of action to halt or sharply reduce the spread of desertification and to reclaim desertified land.

The only effective way to slow the march of desertification is to sharply reduce the overgrazing, deforestation (Section 10-4), and destructive forms of crop planting, irrigation, and mining that accelerate the process. In addition to these prevention or input approaches, we can mount extensive reforestation programs to slow the advance of desertification and at the same time provide fuelwood and reduce the threat of global warming.

The total cost of such prevention and rehabilitation would be about $141 billion, only five and one-half times the estimated $26 billion annual loss in agricultural productivity from desertified land. Thus, once this potential productivity is restored, the costs of the program could be recouped in 5 to 10 years.

However, by 1991, little had been done because of inadequate efforts and funding; only about one-tenth of the amount needed had been provided. What do you think should be done?

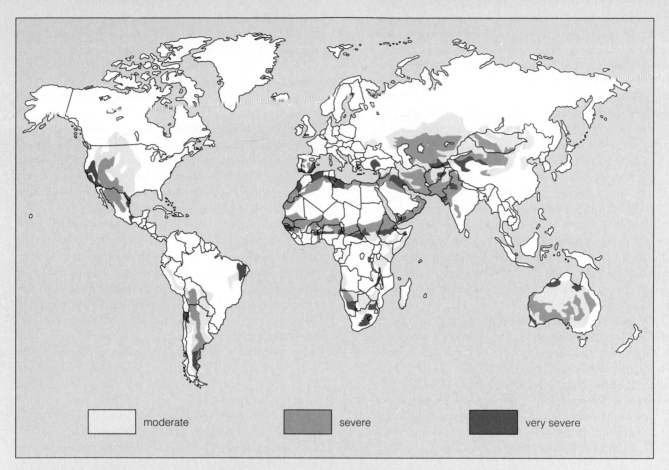

moderate   severe   very severe

Figure 12-11 Desertification of arid and semiarid lands. (Data from UN Environmental Programme and Harold E. Dregnue)

Figure 12-12 Desertification in this arid outback region of Australia was caused by cattle overgrazing the vegetation. Livestock cropped plants so severely that the vegetation died; trampling prevented the establishment of seedlings.

THE U.S. SITUATION According to surveys by the Soil Conservation Service, about one-third of the original topsoil on U.S. croplands in use today has been washed or blown into streams, lakes, and oceans. Surveys also show that the average rate of erosion on cultivated land in the United States is about seven times the rate of natural soil formation.

This average national rate of soil erosion masks much higher erosion in heavily farmed regions, especially the corn belt and the Great Plains. Some of the country's most productive agricultural lands, such as those in Iowa, have lost about half their topsoil. In California, the erosion rate is 80 times faster than the natural rate of soil formation.

Enough topsoil erodes away each day in the United States to fill a line of dump trucks 5,600 kilometers (3,500 miles) long. Two-thirds of this soil comes from less than one-fourth of the country's cropland. The losses of plant nutrients from this erosion of Earth capital are worth at least $18 billion a year. Erosion also causes at least $4 billion a year in damages when silt, plant nutrients, and pesticides are carried into streams, lakes, and reservoirs.

Of the world's major food-producing countries, only the United States is effectively reducing some of it soil losses. Even so, effective soil conservation is practiced on only about half of all U.S. farmland and on less than half of the country's most erodible cropland. Increased soil conservation is particularly important in the fertile midwestern plains, which are subject to high rates of erosion from high winds and occasional prolonged drought (see Case Study on p. 323).

12-3 Soil Conservation and Land-Use Control

CONSERVATION TILLAGE The practice of **soil conservation** involves using various methods to reduce soil erosion, to prevent depletion of soil nutrients, and to restore nutrients already lost by erosion, leaching, and excessive crop harvesting (Figure 12-3). Most methods used to control soil erosion involve keeping the soil covered with vegetation.

In **conventional-tillage farming**, the land is plowed, disked several times, and smoothed to make a planting surface. In areas such as the midwestern United States, severe winters prevent plowing of the soil in time for the beginning of the spring growing season. Thus, cropfields are often plowed in the fall so that crops can be planted in the spring. This leaves the soil bare during the winter and early spring months, a practice that makes it vulnerable to erosion.

To lower labor costs, save energy, and reduce erosion, an increasing number of U.S. farmers are using **conservation-tillage farming**, also known as *minimum-tillage* or *no-till farming*, depending on the degree to which the soil is disturbed. Farmers using this method disturb the soil as little as possible in planting crops.

For the minimum-tillage method, special tillers break up and loosen the subsurface soil without turning over the topsoil, previous crop residues, and any cover vegetation. Forms of low-tillage cultivation include *mulch-till* (whereby crop residue is left over the entire surface), *ridge-till* (whereby crop residue is placed in valleys between ridges where seeds are planted to leave less residue to interfere with planting), and *strip-till* (whereby clean strips of ground are cultivated with a strip of crop residue left between each planted strip). In no-till farming, special planting machines inject seeds, fertilizers, and weed killers (herbicides) into slits made in the unplowed soil (Figure 12-14).

In addition to reducing soil erosion, conservation tillage reduces fuel and tillage costs, water loss from the soil, and soil compaction. It also increases the number of crops that can be grown during a season (multiple cropping). Yields are as high as or higher than yields from conventional tillage. Depending on the soil type, this approach can be used for three to seven years before more extensive soil cultivation is needed to prevent crop yields from declining. However, conservation tillage is no cure-all. It requires increased use of herbicides to control weeds that compete with crops for soil nutrients (Chapter 23).

Conservation tillage is now used on about one-third of U.S. croplands and is projected to be used on over half by 2000. The USDA estimates that using conservation tillage on 80% of U.S. cropland would reduce soil erosion by at least half. So far, the practice is not widely used in other parts of the world.

Sometimes, *emergency tillage* is used to reduce wind erosion. This is done by tilling dry, flat, and highly erodible land into large chunks to reduce the removal of soil particles by harsh winds.

CONTOUR FARMING, TERRACING, STRIP CROPPING, AND ALLEY CROPPING Soil erosion can be reduced 30% to 50% on gently sloping land by means of **contour farming**: plowing and planting crops in rows across, rather than up and down, the sloped contour of the land (Figure 12-15). Each row planted horizontally along the the slope of the land acts as a small dam to help hold soil and slow the runoff of water. If crops were planted in rows that ran up and down a hillside, rain would carry topsoil from the top down the rows to the bottom of the hill, and the top rows would get little water.

Terracing can be used on steeper slopes. The slope is converted into a series of broad, nearly level terraces with short vertical drops from one to another that run along the contour of the land (Figure 12-10). Some of

The Great Plains of the United States stretch through ten states, from Texas through Montana and the Dakotas. The region is normally dry and very windy and occasionally experiences long, severe droughts.

Before settlers began grazing livestock and planting crops in the 1870s, the extensive root systems of prairie grasses held the topsoil of these soils in place (Figure 12-4). When the land was planted in crops, the perennial grasses were replaced by annual crops with less-extensive root systems.

In addition, the land was plowed up after each harvest and left bare part of the year. Overgrazing also destroyed large areas of grass, leaving the ground bare. The stage was set for crop failures during prolonged droughts, followed by severe wind erosion.

The droughts arrived in 1890 and in 1910 and again, with even greater severity, between 1926 and 1934. In 1934, hot, dry windstorms created dust clouds thick enough to cause darkness at midday in some areas. The danger of breathing this dust-laden air was revealed by the dead rabbits and birds left in its wake.

During May 1934, the entire eastern half of the United States was blanketed with a huge dust cloud of topsoil blown off the Great Plains from as far as 2,400 kilometers (1,500 miles) away. Ships 322 kilometers (200 miles) out in the Atlantic Ocean received deposits of midwestern topsoil. These events

gave a portion of the Great Plains a tragic new name: the Dust Bowl (Figure 12-13).

An area of cropland equal in size to the combined areas of Connecticut and Maryland was destroyed, and additional cropland equal in area to New Mexico was severely damaged. Thousands of displaced farm families from Oklahoma, Texas, Kansas, and other states migrated to California or to the industrial cities of the Midwest and East. Most found no jobs because the country was in the midst of the Great Depression.

In May 1934, Hugh Bennett of the U.S. Department of Agriculture (USDA) addressed a congressional hearing in Washington, pleading for new programs to protect the country's topsoil. Lawmakers took action when dust blown from the Great Plains began seeping into the hearing room.

In 1935, the United States established the Soil Conservation Service (SCS) as part of the Department of Agriculture. With Bennett as its first head, the SCS began promoting good conservation practices, first in the Great Plains and later in every state. Soil conservation districts were established throughout the country, and farmers and ranchers were given technical assistance in setting up soil conservation programs.

These efforts, however, did not completely stop human-accelerated erosion in the Great Plains. The basic problem is that the climate of

Figure 12-13 The Dust Bowl of the Great Plains, where a combination of periodic severe drought and poor soil conservation practices led to severe erosion of topsoil by wind in the 1930s.

much of the region makes it better suited for grazing than for farming.

In 1975, the Council of Agricultural Science and Technology warned that severe drought could again create a dust bowl in the Great Plains. So far, those warnings have been ignored.

Great Plains farmers, many of them debt-ridden, have continued to stave off bankruptcy by minimizing expenditures for soil conservation. Depletion of the Ogallala Aquifer is also threatening crop production and cattle raising in parts of the Dust Bowl area (see Case Study on p. 352). If projected global warming makes this region even drier (Figure 11-4), farming will have to be abandoned. What do you think should be done about this situation?

---

the water running down the vegetated slope is retained by each terrace. Thus, terracing provides water for crops at all levels and decreases soil erosion by reducing the amount and speed of water runoff. In areas of high rainfall, diversion ditches must be built behind each terrace to permit adequate drainage.

In **strip cropping**, a series of rows of one crop, such as corn or soybeans, is planted in a wide strip; then the next strip is planted with a soil-conserving cover crop, such as a grass or a grass-legume mixture, which com-

pletely covers the soil and thus reduces erosion (Figure 12-15). The alternating rows of cover crop trap soil that erodes from the row crop and catch and reduce water runoff. The alternating rows of different types of crops also help prevent the spread of pests and plant diseases from one strip to another. They also help restore soil fertility if nitrogen-rich legumes, such as soybeans or alfalfa, are planted in some of the strips.

Erosion can also be reduced by **alley cropping**, in which crops are planted in alleys between hedgerows

Figure 12-14 No-till farming in Lancaster County, Pennsylvania. This is one form of conservation-tillage farming that greatly reduces soil erosion because the soil is not plowed before planting. A specially designed machine plants seeds and adds fertilizers and weed killers at the same time, with almost no disturbance of the soil.

Figure 12-15 On this gently sloping land in Illinois, contoured rows planted with alternating crops (strip cropping) reduce soil erosion.

Figure 12-16 Alley cropping in Peru. Several crops are planted together in strips or alleys between trees and shrubs. The trees provide shade (which reduces water loss by evaporation) and help retain soil moisture and release it slowly.

Figure 12-17 Windbreaks, or shelterbelts, reduce erosion on this farm in South Dakota. They also reduce wind damage and evaporation and help hold soil moisture in place, supply some wood for fuel, and provide a habitat for wildlife.

of trees or shrubs that can be used as sources of fruits and fuelwood (Figure 12-16). The hedgerow trimmings can be used as mulch (green manure) for the crops and fodder for livestock.

GULLY RECLAMATION AND WINDBREAKS
Water runoff quickly creates gullies in sloping land not covered by vegetation (Figures 12-8 and 1-1). Such land can be restored by **gully reclamation**. Small gullies can be seeded with quick-growing plants, such as oats, barley, and wheat, to reduce erosion. In deeper gullies, small dams can be built to collect silt and gradually fill in the channels. Rapidly growing shrubs, vines, and trees can also be planted to stabilize the soil. Channels can be built to divert water from the gully and prevent further erosion.

Erosion caused by exposure of cultivated lands to high winds can be reduced by **windbreaks**, or **shelterbelts**: long rows of trees planted to partially block wind (Figure 12-17). They are especially effective if land that is not under cultivation is kept covered with vegetation. Windbreaks also provide habitats for birds, pest-eating and pollinating insects, and other animals. Unfortunately, many of the windbreaks planted in the upper Great Plains following the Dust Bowl disaster of the 1930s have been destroyed to make way for large irrigation systems and farm machinery (Figure 5-20).

LAND-USE CLASSIFICATION AND CONTROL To encourage wise land use and reduce erosion, the U.S. Soil Conservation Service has set up the classification

The 1985 Farm Act established a strategy designed first to take highly erodible land out of production and put it into a conservation reserve and then to require farmers to use soil-conserving techniques to reduce erosion on farmland still in cultivation. In the first phase of this program, farmers are given a subsidy of about $121 per hectare ($49 per acre) for highly erodible land they take out of production and replant with soil-saving grass or trees for ten years. During this period, the land in this conservation reserve cannot be farmed, grazed, or cut for hay. Farmers who violate their contracts must pay back all government payments with interest.

By 1990, about 14 million hectares (34 million acres) of highly erodible cropland had been placed in the conservation reserve. This helped cut soil erosion on U.S. cropland by almost one-third. If the pro-gram is expanded and adequately enforced, it could reduce excessive soil loss from U.S. cropland by 80%.

The second phase of the program required all farmers with highly erodible land to develop SCS-approved five-year soil conservation plans for their entire farms by the end of 1990. By 1995, these farms have to implement their plans or they lose their eligibility for federal agricultural subsidies and loans.

A third provision of the Farm Act authorizes the government to forgive all or part of debts farmers owe the Farmers Home Administration if they agree not to farm highly erodible cropland or wetlands for 50 years. Farmers are required to plant trees or grass on this land or convert it back into wetland.

Since 1987 the Soil Conservation Service has eased the standards that farmers' soil conservation plans must meet to keep farmers eligible for other subsidies. Conservationists have also accused the Soil Conservation Service of laxity in enforcing the farm bill's "swampbuster" provisions, which deny federal funds to farmers who drain or destroy wetlands on their property.

A rising demand for grain could cause farmers to break their agreements and put all or some of their highly erodible land back into production, because the short-term profits from farming such lands could exceed the loss of government subsidies. This could lead to a return of the record erosion levels seen in the 1970s.

Despite some weaknesses, the 1985 Farm Act is a landmark piece of legislation. It has allowed the United States to become the first major food-producing country to make soil conservation a national priority.

---

system summarized in Table 12-3 and illustrated in Figure 12-18. An obvious land-use approach to reducing erosion is to prohibit the planting of crops or the clearing of vegetation on marginal land (classes V through VIII in Table 12-3 and Figure 12-18).

The Soil Conservation Service has also established almost 3,000 soil and water conservation districts throughout the United States. It surveys soil in these districts and classifies soils according to type and quality.

The SCS basically relies on voluntary compliance with its guidelines through the local and state soil and water conservation districts and provides technical and economic assistance through the local district offices. This means that American soil conservation policy lacks teeth. The soil conservation associations that regulate the districts are made up of officials who mostly represent the private interests of local farmers and ranchers. They are under intense peer pressure to make land-use decisions based on short-term economic gains that can have harmful long-term environmental and economic impacts.

According to the General Accounting Office, this voluntary compliance and the lack of an integrated re-gional and national program help to explain the fact that although the federal government has spent about $18 billion on soil erosion control efforts, these programs have had only minimal success in reducing soil erosion. The National Wildlife Federation observes that despite four decades of soil erosion control, the United States experienced 35% more soil erosion in 1981 than in the Dust Bowl days of the 1930s.

Since 1985, U.S. farmers who take highly erodible cropland out of production have been given government subsidies (see Spotlight above).

MAINTAINING AND RESTORING SOIL FERTILITY Organic fertilizers and commercial inorganic fertilizers can be applied to soil to partially restore and maintain plant nutrients lost by erosion, leaching, and crop harvesting and to increase crop yields (Figure 12-3). Three basic types of **organic fertilizer** are animal manure, green manure, and compost. **Animal manure** includes the dung and urine of cattle, horses, poultry, and other farm animals. In China and South Korea, human manure, sometimes called night soil, is used to fertilize crops in vegetable-growing greenbelts around cities.

Table 12-3 Land Capability Classification According to the Soil Conservation Service

Class	Land Class Characteristics	Primary Uses	Secondary Uses	Conservation Measures
Land Suitable for Cultivation				
I	Excellent flat, well-drained land	Agriculture	Recreation Wildlife Pasture	None
II	Good land with minor limitations such as slight slope, sandy soil, or poor drainage	Agriculture Pasture	Recreation Wildlife	Strip cropping Contour farming
III	Moderately good land with important limitations of soil, slope, or drainage	Agriculture Pasture Watershed	Recreation Wildlife Urban industry	Contour farming Strip cropping Waterways Terraces
IV	Fair land, severe limitations of soil, slope, or drainage	Pasture Orchards Limited agriculture Urban industry	Pasture Wildlife	Farming on a limited basis Contour farming Strip cropping Waterways Terraces
Land Not Suitable for Cultivation				
V	Rockiness; shallow soil, wetness, or slope prevents farming	Grazing Forestry Watershed	Recreation Wildlife	No special precautions if properly grazed or logged; must not be plowed
VI	Moderate limitations for grazing and forestry	Grazing Forestry Watershed Urban industry	Recreation Wildlife	Grazing or logging should be limited at times
VII	Severe limitations for grazing and forestry	Grazing Forestry Watershed Recreation Aesthetics Wildlife Urban industry		Careful management required when used for grazing or logging
VIII	Unsuitable for grazing and forestry because of steep slope, shallow soil, lack of water, too much water	Recreation Aesthetics Watershed Wildlife Urban industry		Not to be used for grazing or logging

Application of animal manure improves soil structure, increases organic nitrogen content, and stimulates the growth and reproduction of soil bacteria and fungi. It is particularly useful on crops of corn, cotton, potatoes, and cabbage.

Despite its effectiveness, the use of animal manure in the United States has decreased. One reason is that separate farms for growing crops and animals have replaced most mixed animal- and crop-farming operations. Animal manure is available at feedlots near urban areas, but transporting it to distant rural crop-growing areas usually costs too much. Thus, much of this valuable resource is wasted and can end up polluting nearby bodies of water. In addition, tractors and other motorized farm machinery have replaced horses and other draft animals that naturally added manure to the soil.

Green manure is fresh or growing green vegetation plowed into the soil to increase the organic matter and humus available to the next crop. It may consist of weeds in an uncultivated field, grasses and clover in a field previously used for pasture, or legumes such as alfalfa or soybeans grown for use as fertilizer to build up soil nitrogen.

Compost is a rich natural fertilizer and soil conditioner. Farmers and homeowners produce it by piling up alternating layers of carbohydrate-rich plant wastes (such as cuttings and leaves), animal manure, and topsoil (Figure 12-19). This mixture provides a home for

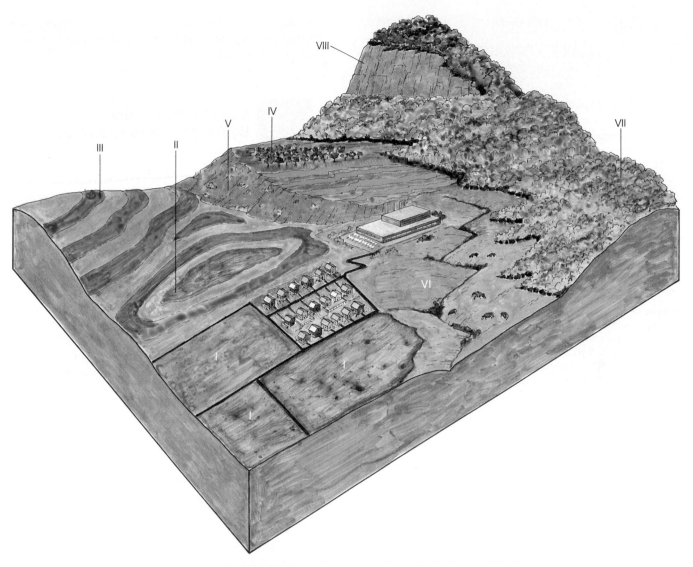

Figure 12-18 Classification of land by the U.S. Soil Conservation Service according to the land's capability for various uses. See Table 12-3 for a description of each class.

microorganisms that aid the decomposition of the plant and manure layers.

Today, especially in the United States and other industrialized countries, farmers partially restore and maintain soil fertility by applying **commercial inorganic fertilizers**. The most common plant nutrients in these products are nitrogen (as ammonium ions, nitrate ions, or urea), phosphorus (as phosphate ions), and potassium (as potassium ions). Other plant nutrients may also be present in low or trace amounts. Farmers can have their soil and harvested crops chemically analyzed to determine the mix of nutrients that should be added.

Inorganic commercial fertilizers are easily transported, stored, and applied. Throughout the world, their use increased about 17-fold between 1950 and 1991. By 1991, the additional food they helped produce fed one of every three persons in the world. Without this input, world food output would plummet by an estimated 40%.

Commercial inorganic fertilizers, however, have some disadvantages. They do not add humus to the soil. Unless animal manure and green manure are added to the soil along with commercial inorganic fertilizers, the soil's content of organic matter and thus its ability to hold water will decrease. If not supplemented by organic fertilizers, inorganic fertilizers cause the soil to become compacted and less suitable for crop growth. By decreasing its porosity, inorganic fertilizers also lower the oxygen content of soil and prevent added fertilizer from being taken up as efficiently. In addition, most commercial fertilizers do not contain many of the nutrients needed in trace amounts by plants.

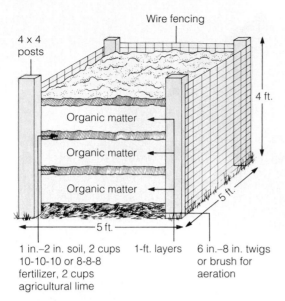

Wire fencing

4 x 4 posts

4 ft.

Organic matter

Organic matter

Organic matter

5 ft.

5 ft.

1 in.–2 in. soil, 2 cups 10-10-10 or 8-8-8 fertilizer, 2 cups agricultural lime

1-ft. layers

6 in.–8 in. twigs or brush for aeration

Figure 12-19 A simple home compost bin can be used to produce a mulch for garden and yard plants. A layer or two of cat litter or alfalfa meal can be used to cut down on odors. Leave a depression at the top center of the pile to collect rainwater. Turn the pile over every month or so, and cover it with a tarp during winter months. Small compost bins have been developed for use indoors in apartments and houses.

Water pollution is another problem caused by the widespread use of commercial inorganic fertilizers, especially on sloped land near streams and lakes. Some of the plant nutrients in the fertilizers are washed into nearby bodies of surface water, where the resulting cultural eutrophication causes excessive growth of algae, oxygen depletion, and fish to die off. Rainwater seeping through soil can leach nitrates in commercial fertilizers into groundwater. High levels of nitrate ions make drinking water drawn from wells toxic, especially for infants.

A third method for preventing depletion of soil nutrients is **crop rotation**. Crops such as corn, tobacco, and cotton remove large amounts of nutrients (especially nitrogen) from the soil and can deplete the topsoil of nutrients if planted on the same land several years in a row. Farmers using crop rotation plant areas or strips with corn, tobacco, and cotton one year. The next year they plant the same areas with legumes, whose root nodules (Figure 4-30) add nitrogen to the soil, or with crops such as oats, barley, rye, or sorghum. This method helps restore soil nutrients and reduces erosion by keeping the soil covered with vegetation. Varying the types of crops planted from year to year also reduces infestation by insects, weeds (especially if the land is planted in sorghum, which releases natural herbicides), and plant diseases.

Concern about soil erosion should not be limited to farmers. At least 40% of soil erosion in the United States

is caused by timber cutting, overgrazing, mining, and urban development carried out without proper regard for soil conservation.

<table>
<tr><td>**12-4**</td><td>**Soil Contamination by Excess Salts and Water**</td></tr>
</table>

SALINIZATION   About 18% of the world's cropland is now irrigated, producing about one-third of the world's food. Irrigated cropland is projected to at least double by 2020.

Irrigation can increase crop yields two to three times the yields on the same area of land watered only by rain, but it also has some harmful side effects. Irrigation water contains various dissolved salts. In dry climates, much of the water in this saline solution is lost to the atmosphere by evaporation, leaving behind high concentrations of salts, such as sodium chloride, in the topsoil. The accumulation of salts in soils is called **salinization** (Figure 12-20). Salt buildup stunts crop growth, decreases yields, and eventually kills crop plants and makes the land unproductive (Figure 12-21).

It is estimated that salinization is reducing yields on one-fourth of the world's irrigated cropland. In Egypt, where virtually all cropland is irrigated, half is salinized enough to reduce yields. Worldwide, it is projected that 50% to 65% of all currently irrigated cropland will suffer reduced productivity from excess soil salinity by the year 2000.

When irrigation water is repeatedly withdrawn from and returned to a stream as it flows from its mountain headwaters to the ocean (Figure 5-41), the salinity of the water increases in downstream areas. Using this more-saline water for irrigation accelerates the rate of soil salinization. Eventually, the water can become so saline that it is useless for irrigation.

For example, by the time the Colorado River makes its way from its headwaters in the Rocky Mountains and reaches Mexico, its salt concentration has increased 20-fold, making it essentially useless for crop irrigation. This has led to a long-standing dispute between Mexico and the United States, which may be partially resolved by the recent opening of the Yuma Desalting Plant in Arizona. Economic and political policies will be needed that require upstream users to take account of their harmful effects on downstream users of irrigation water.

One way to reduce salinization is to flush salts out of the soil by applying much more irrigation water than is needed for crop growth, but that increases pumping and crop-production costs and wastes enormous amounts of water. Another method is to pump groundwater from a central well and apply it with a sprinkler system that pivots around the well. This method main-

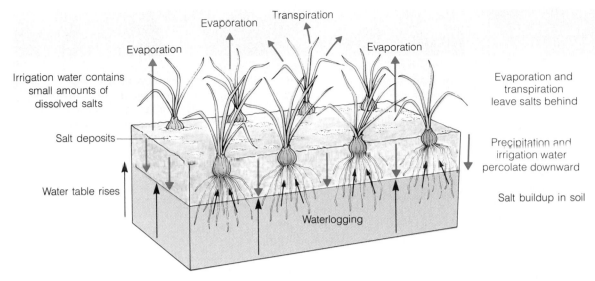

Figure 12-20 Salinization and waterlogging of soil on irrigated land without adequate drainage lead to decreased crop yields.

Soil Conservation Service

Figure 12-21 Because of high evaporation, poor drainage, and severe salinization, white alkaline salts have replaced crops that once grew in this heavily irrigated land in Colorado.

tains downward drainage and is especially effective at preventing salinization, but at least 30% of the water is lost by evaporation. Also, groundwater in unconfined aquifers eventually becomes too saline for irrigation and other human uses unless expensive drainage systems are installed.

Once topsoil has become heavily salinized, the farmer can renew it by taking the land out of production for two to five years, installing an underground network of perforated drainage pipes, and flushing the soil with large quantities of low-salt water. This scheme is very expensive and only slows down the buildup of soil salinity; it does not stop the process. Flushing salts from the soil also increases the salinity of irrigation water delivered to farmers further downstream, unless the saline water can be drained into evaporation ponds rather than returned to the stream or canal.

In the Indian state of Ultar Pradesh, farmers are rehabilitating tracts of salinized land by planting a saline-tolerant tree that lowers the water table by taking up water through its roots. Tube wells can also be used to lower water tables, but they are useful only in areas with an adequate groundwater supply.

WATERLOGGING A problem often accompanying soil salinity in dry regions is **waterlogging** (Figure 12-20). To keep salts from accumulating and destroying fragile root systems, farmers often apply heavy amounts of irrigation water to leach salts deeper into the soil. If drainage isn't provided, water accumulating underground gradually raises the water table. Saline water envelops the roots of plants and kills them.

Waterlogging is a particularly serious problem in the heavily irrigated San Joaquin Valley in California, where soils contain a clay layer with a low permeability to water. Worldwide, at least one-tenth of all irrigated land suffers from waterlogging, and the problem is getting worse.

Because soil is the base of life, we must demand that soil abuse be halted and be replaced with soil healing and soil protection so that these vital, slowly renewable resources are used sustainably. Each of us has a role to play (see Individuals Matter on p. 330).

Civilization can survive the exhaustion of oil reserves, but not the continuing wholesale loss of topsoil.

LESTER R. BROWN

Here are some ways you can help protect the soil.

- Establish a soil conservation program for the land around your home.

- If you are building a home, save all the trees possible, and have the contractor set up barriers to catch any soil eroded during construction. Require the contractor to disturb as little soil as possible and to save and replace any topsoil removed instead of hauling it off and selling it. Plant any disturbed area with fast-growing native ground cover (preferably not grass) immediately after construction is completed.

- Landscape the area not used for gardening with a mix of wildflowers, herbs (for cooking and to repel insects), low-growing ground cover, small bushes, and other forms of vegetation natural to the area. This biologically diverse type of yard saves water, energy, and money and reduces infestation of mosquitoes and other damaging insects by providing a diversity of habitats for their natural predators.

- Set up a compost bin (Figure 12-19) and use it to produce mulch and soil conditioner for yard and garden plants.

- Use organic methods (no commercial fertilizers or pesticides) for growing vegetables and maintaining your yard. This involves using organic fertilizers (mulch, green manure, and animal manure) and biological and cultural control of pests.

- Insist that local, state, and federal elected officials establish and strictly enforce laws and policies that sharply reduce soil erosion, salinization, and waterlogging.

GUEST ESSAY Land Degradation and Environmental Resources

David Pimentel

David Pimentel is professor of insect ecology and agricultural sciences in the College of Agriculture and Life Sciences at Cornell University. He has chaired the Board on Environmental Studies (1979–1981) and the Malaria Prevention and Control Panel (1990–) in the National Academy of Sciences, and the Panel on Soil and Land Degradation, Office of Technology Assessment (1978–1981). He has published over 350 scientific papers and 12 books on environmental topics, including land degradation, agricultural pollution and energy use, biomass energy, and pesticides. He was one of the first ecologists to employ an interdisciplinary, holistic approach in investigating complex environmental problems.

At a time when the world's human population is rapidly expanding and its need for more land to produce food, fiber, and fuelwood is also escalating, valuable land is being degraded through erosion and other means at an alarming rate. Soil degradation is of great concern because soil reformation is extremely slow. Under tropical and temperate agricultural conditions, an average of 500 years (with a range of 220 to 1,000 years) is required for the renewal of 2.5 cm (1 inch) of soil—a renewal rate of about 1 metric ton (t) of topsoil per hectare (ha) of land per year (1t/ha per year). Worldwide annual erosion rates for agricultural land are about 20 to 100 times this natural renewal rate.

Erosion rates vary in different regions because of topography, rainfall, wind intensity, and the type of agricultural practices used. In China, for example, the average annual soil loss is reported to be about 40t/ha while the U.S. average is 18t/ha. In states like Iowa and Missouri, however, annual soil erosion averages are greater than 35t/ha.

Worldwide, about 10 million hectares (about the size of Virginia) of land are abandoned for crop production each year because of high erosion rates plus waterlogging of soils, salinization, and other forms of soil degradation. In addition, according to the UN Environment Programme, crop productivity becomes uneconomical on about 20 million hectares each year because soil quality has been severely degraded.

Soil erosion also occurs in forestland but is not as severe as that in the more exposed soil of agricultural land. However, soil erosion in managed forests is a primary concern because the soil reformation rate in forests is about two to three times longer than that in agricultural land. To compound this erosion problem, at least 24 million hectares of forest are being cleared each year throughout the world [Section 10-2]. About 80% of this is being cleared and planted with crops to compensate for loss of agricultural land caused by erosion and population growth. Average soil erosion per hectare increases when trees are removed and the land is planted with crops.

The effects of agriculture and forestry are interrelated in many other ways. Large-scale removal of forests without adequate replanting reduces fuelwood supplies and forces the poor in LDCs to substitute crop residue and manure for fuelwood. When these plant and animal wastes are burned instead of being returned to the land as ground cover and organic fertilizer, erosion is intensified and productivity of the land is decreased. These factors, in turn, increase pressure to convert more forestland into agricultural land, further intensifying soil erosion.

One reason that soil erosion does not receive high priority among many governments and farmers is that it usually occurs at such a slow rate that its cumulative effects may take decades to become apparent. For example, the removal of 1 millimeter (1/25 inch) of soil is so small that it goes undetected. But the accumulated soil loss at this rate over a 25-year period would amount to 25 mm (1 inch) — an amount that would take about 500 years to replace by natural processes.

Although reduced soil depth is a serious concern because it is cumulative, other factors associated with erosion also reduce productivity. These are losses of water, organic matter, and soil nutrients. Water is the primary limiting factor for all natural and agricultural plants and trees. When some of the vegetation on land is removed, most water is lost to remaining plants because it runs off rapidly and does not penetrate the soil. In addition, soil erosion reduces the water-holding capacity of soil because it removes organic matter and fine soil particles that hold water. When this happens, water infiltration into the soil can be reduced as much as 90%.

Organic matter in soil plays an important role in holding water and in decreasing removal of plant nutrients. Thus, it is not surprising that a 50% reduction of soil organic matter on a plot of land has been found to reduce corn yields as much as 25%. When soil erodes, there is also a loss of vital plant nutrients such as nitrogen, phosphorus, potassium, and calcium. With U.S. annual cropland erosion rates of about 18t/ha, estimates are that $18 billion of fertilizer nutrients are lost annually by erosion.

This loss of fertilizers substantially adds to the cost of crop production.

Some analysts who are unaware of the numerous and complex effects of soil erosion have falsely concluded that the damages are relatively minor. For example, they report that an average soil loss in the United States of 18t/ha per year causes an annual reduction in crop productivity of only 0.1% to 0.5%. However, we need to consider all the ecological effects caused by erosion, including a reduction in soil depth, reduced water availability for crops, and reduction in soil organic matter and nutrients. When this is done, agronomists and ecologists report a 15% to 30% reduction in crop productivity — a key factor in increased levels of costly fertilizer and declining yields on some land despite high levels of fertilization. Because fertilizers are not a substitute for fertile soil, they can only be applied up to certain levels before crop yields begin to decline.

Reduced agricultural productivity is only one of the effects and costs of soil erosion. In the United States, water runoff is responsible for transporting about 3 billion metric tons (3.3 billion tons) of sediment each year to waterways in the 48 contiguous states. About 60% of these sediments come from agricultural lands. Estimates show that off-site damages to U.S. water-storage capacity, wildlife, and navigable waterways from these sediments cost an estimated $6 billion each year. Dredging sediments from U.S. streams, harbors, and reservoirs alone costs about $570 million each year. About 25% of new water storage capacity in U.S. reservoirs is built solely to compensate for sediment buildup.

When soil sediments that include pesticides and other agricultural chemicals are carried into streams, lakes, and reservoirs, fish production is adversely affected. These contaminated sediments interfere with fish spawning, increase predation on fish, and destroy fisheries in estuarine and coastal areas.

Increased erosion and water runoff on mountain slopes flood agricultural land in the valleys below, further decreasing agricultural productivity. Eroded land also does not hold water very well, further decreasing crop productivity. This effect is magnified in the 80 countries (with nearly 40% of the world's population) that experience frequent droughts. The rapid growth in the world's population, accompanied by the need for more crops and a projected doubling of water needs in the next 20 years, will only intensify water shortages, particularly if soil erosion is not contained.

Thus, soil erosion is one of the world's critical problems and if not slowed will seriously reduce agricultural and forestry production and degrade the quality of aquatic ecosystems. Solutions are not particularly difficult but are often not implemented because erosion occurs so gradually that we fail to acknowledge its

(continued)

cumulative impact until damage is irreversible. Many farmers have also been conditioned to believe that losses in soil fertility can be remedied by applying increasingly higher levels of fertilizer or the use of fossil-fuel energy.

The principal method of controlling soil erosion and its accompanying runoff of sediment is to maintain adequate vegetative coverage on soils by various methods discussed in Section 12-3. These methods are also cost-effective in preventing erosion, especially when off-site costs of erosion are included. Scientists, policymakers, and agriculturists need to work together to implement soil and water conservation practices before world soils lose most of their productivity.

Guest Essay Discussion

1. Some analysts contend that average soil erosion rates in the United States and the world are low and that this problem has been overblown by environmentalists and can easily be solved by improved agricultural technology such as no-till cultivation and increased use of commercial inorganic fertilizers. Do you agree or disagree with this position? Explain.

2. What specific things do you believe elected officials should do to decrease soil erosion and the resulting sediment water pollution in the United States?

DISCUSSION TOPICS

1. Why should everyone, not just farmers, be concerned with soil conservation?

2. Explain how a plant can have ample supplies of nitrogen, phosphorus, potassium, and other essential nutrients and still have stunted growth.

3. Describe briefly the Dust Bowl phenomenon of the 1930s, and explain how and where it could happen again. How would you try to prevent a recurrence?

4. What are the main advantages and disadvantages of using commercial inorganic fertilizers to help restore and maintain soil fertility? Why should organic fertilizers also be used on land treated with inorganic fertilizers?

*5. Visit rural or mostly undeveloped areas near your school, and classify the lands according to the system shown in Figure 12-18 and Table 12-3. Look for examples of land being used for purposes to which it is not best suited.

*6. Visit several homesites in your community, and evaluate their use of natural vegetation to reduce soil erosion and enhance natural biological diversity. Also, evaluate the planting of your own homesite and various areas found around your school.

*7. As a class project, examine the land around your school to evaluate the use of natural vegetation and other methods to reduce soil erosion. Use this information to develop a soil conservation plan for your school and present it to school officials.

CHAPTER 13

WATER RESOURCES

General Questions and Issues

1. How is the existence of life on Earth related to liquid water's unique physical properties?

2. How much usable fresh water is available for human use, and how much of this supply are we using?

3. What are the most serious water resource problems in the world and in the United States?

4. How can water resources be managed to increase the supply and reduce unnecessary waste?

If there is magic on this planet, it is in water.

LOREN EISLEY

 E LIVE ON the water planet, with this life-giving resource covering about 71% of Earth's surface (Figure 5-27). This precious film of water—most of it salt water and the remainder fresh water—helps maintain Earth's climate, dilutes pollutants, and is essential to all life because most living things are made up mostly of water molecules (H_2O). A tree is about 60% water by weight, you and most animals are about 65% water, and a jellyfish is more than 90% water.

Earth's relatively small amount of fresh water is constantly recycled and purified by the hydrologic cycle (Figure 4-34). This fresh water is a vital resource for agriculture, manufacturing, transportation, and countless other human activities.

Despite its importance, water is one of the most poorly managed resources on earth. We waste it and pollute it. We also charge too little for making it available, encouraging even greater waste and pollution of this vital renewable resource.

 ## 13-1 Water as a Unique Liquid

Most of water's usefulness is due to liquid water's many unique properties compared with those of other molecules of similar weight.

1. *Water is a liquid within the range of temperature most suited for life processes because of liquid water's high boiling point of 100°C (212°F) and low freezing point 0°C (32°F).* Without these properties, liquid water in the earth's surface waters and in the tissues of living organisms would be in the gaseous or solid state at the normal temperature range found on Earth, and life as we know it would not exist.

2. *Liquid water changes temperature very slowly because of its extremely high heat capacity—the ability to store a large amount of heat without a large change in temperature.* This property prevents large bodies of water from warming or cooling rapidly, helps protect living organisms from the shock of abrupt temperature changes, aids in keeping Earth's climate moderate, and makes water an effective coolant for car engines, power plants, and other heat-producing industrial processes.

3. *Liquid water has a very high heat of vaporization—the amount of heat needed to evaporate liquid water.* This ability to absorb large amounts of heat when liquid water is converted into water vapor and release this heat when the vapor condenses back to liquid water is a primary factor in distributing heat throughout the world (Figure 5-4). This property also means that evaporation of water is an effective cooling process for plants and animals, explaining

why you feel cooler when perspiration evaporates from your skin.

4. *Liquid water is a superior solvent, able to dissolve large amounts of a variety of compounds.* This enables water to carry dissolved nutrients throughout the tissues of living organisms, to flush waste products out of those tissues, to be a good all-purpose cleanser, and to remove and dilute the water-soluble wastes of civilization, if aquatic systems are not overloaded. However, this ability of water to act as a solvent also means that it is easily polluted by water-soluble wastes.

5. *Liquid water has an extremely high surface tension (attractive forces between molecules that cause the surface of a liquid to contract) and an even higher wetting ability (the capability to adhere to and coat a solid).* Together, these properties are responsible for liquid water's capillarity — the ability to rise from tiny pores in the soil into thin, hollow tubes, called capillaries, in the stems of plants. These properties, along with water's solvent ability, allow plants to receive nutrients from the soil, thus supporting their own growth and the animals that feed on them.

6. *Liquid water is the only common substance that expands rather than contracts when it freezes.* Consequently, ice has a lower density (mass per unit of volume) than liquid water. Thus, ice floats on water, and bodies of water freeze from the top down instead of from the bottom up. Without this property, lakes and streams in cold climates would freeze solid and most current forms of aquatic life would not exist. Because water expands on freezing, it can also break pipes, crack engine blocks (which is why we use antifreeze), and fracture streets and rocks.

Water is truly a wondrous substance that connects us to each other, to other forms of life, and to the entire planet.

13-2 Supply, Renewal, and Use of Water Resources

WORLDWIDE SUPPLY, RENEWAL, AND DISTRIBUTION The world's fixed supply of water in all forms (vapor, liquid, and solid) is enormous. If this water were spread evenly over Earth's surface in liquid form, it would form a layer nearly 3,000 meters (9,800 feet) deep.

However, only a tiny fraction of the planet's supply is available to us as fresh water, and that is distributed very unevenly. About 97% of Earth's volume of water is found in the oceans and is too salty for drinking, growing crops, and most industrial uses except cooling.

The remaining 3% is fresh water. About 2.997% of this is locked up as ice at the poles and in glaciers or is groundwater that is too deep and too expensive for us to extract. This means that only about 0.003% of Earth's total volume of water is easily available to us in lakes, soil moisture, exploitable groundwater, atmospheric water vapor, and streams. If the world's water supply were only 100 liters (26 gallons), our usable supply of fresh water would be only about 0.003 liter (one-half teaspoon) (Figure 13-1).

Fortunately, this supply of fresh water is continually collected, purified, and distributed in the *hydrologic cycle* (Figure 4-34). The global average for replacement of water in streams is 18 to 20 years, while water in the atmosphere is replaced every 12 days. Deep groundwater requires several hundred years or more for renewal, except for deep fossil aquifers, which are nonrenewable on a human time scale.

This natural recycling and purification process works and provides plenty of fresh water as long as we don't pollute the water faster than it is replenished, overload it with slowly degradable and nondegradable wastes, or withdraw it from slowly renewable underground supplies faster than it is replenished. Unfortunately, we are disrupting the water cycle by doing all of those things.

Earth's usable fresh water is very unevenly distributed around the world. Because of differences in average annual precipitation, the world is divided into water "haves" in tropical and temperate climate zones and water "have-nots" in arid and semiarid climate zones.

As population and industrialization increase, water supply crises in already-water-short regions will intensify. Unpredictable changes in rainfall patterns brought about by a possible enhanced greenhouse effect (Section 11-1) are likely to cause great disruption in these and other areas. It's hard to predict where such shifts in annual precipitation will occur, but one study suggests that most of the entire western United States — much of which is already short of water — could experience a 40% to 76% drop in levels of precipitation (Figure 11-4).

SURFACE WATER The fresh water we use comes from two sources: surface water and groundwater (Figure 13-2). Precipitation that does not infiltrate the ground or return to the atmosphere by evaporation or transpiration is called **surface water**. It is the fresh water that is on Earth's surface in streams, lakes, wetlands, and artificial reservoirs. **Watersheds**, also called **drainage basins**, are those areas of land that drain runoff water into bodies of surface water.

Water flowing off the land into bodies of surface water is called **surface runoff**, and water flowing in rivers to the ocean is called **river runoff**. About 69% of the water reaching the world's rivers comes from rain and melted snow in their watersheds, with the rest coming

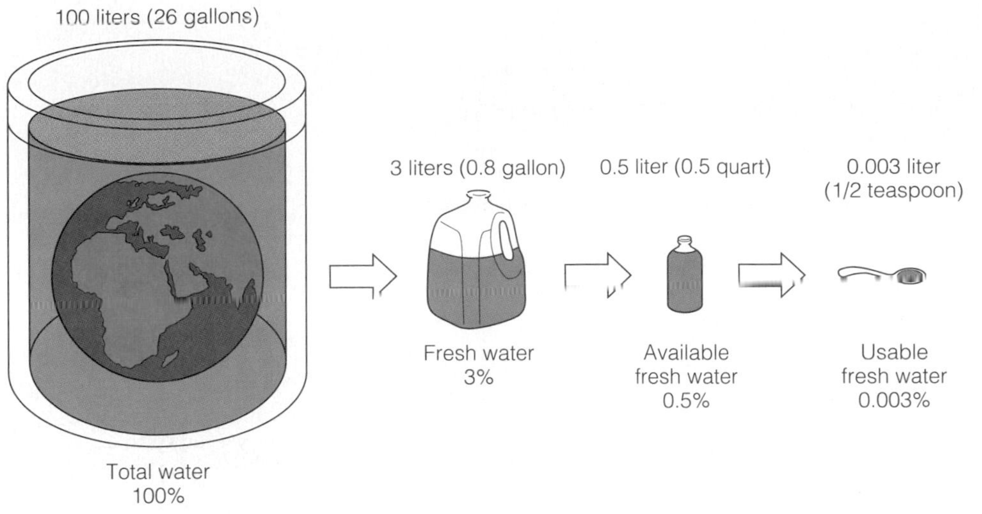

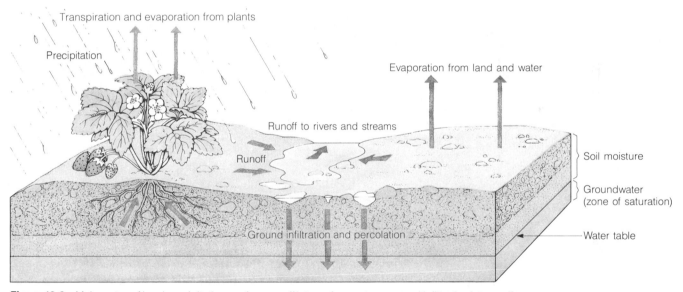

100 liters (26 gallons)

Figure 13-1 Only a tiny fraction of the world's water supply is available as fresh water for human use.

3 liters (0.8 gallon)   0.5 liter (0.5 quart)   0.003 liter (1/2 teaspoon)

Fresh water
3%

Available
fresh water
0.5%

Usable
fresh water
0.003%

Total water
100%

Transpiration and evaporation from plants

Precipitation

Evaporation from land and water

Runoff to rivers and streams

Runoff

Soil moisture

Groundwater
(zone of saturation)

Ground infiltration and percolation

Water table

Figure 13-2   Main routes of local precipitation: surface runoff into surface waters, ground infiltration into aquifers, and evaporation and transpiration into the atmosphere.

from groundwater discharge. South America has the largest river runoff (26% of the world total) of any continent — twice the runoff of all other continents taken together. River basins fed mainly by rainfall occupy 60% of the planet's land area and support 90% of the world's population.

Deforestation (Section 10-2) can cause significant changes in seasonal patterns of river runoff. This can result in higher surface runoff rates and flooding in wet seasons and a greater chance of dried-up rivers in dry seasons.

GROUNDWATER   Some precipitation infiltrates the ground and fills pores (spaces or cracks) in soil and rock in the earth's crust. The below-ground area where all available soil and rock are filled by water is called the **zone of saturation**, and the water in these pores is called

groundwater (Figure 13-3). The **water table** is the upper surface of the zone of saturation. It is the dividing line between saturated soil and rock, where every available pore has been filled, and unsaturated rock and soil, where the pores can still absorb more water.

There is 40 times as much groundwater below Earth's surface as there is in all the world's streams and lakes. However, this groundwater is unequally distributed, and only a small amount of it is economically exploitable. Mining deep groundwater faster than it is recharged by the hydrologic cycle consumes potentially renewable liquid Earth capital.

The ability of soil or rock to hold water is dependent on its porosity and permeability (Table 12-1). Porous, water-saturated layers of sand, gravel, or bedrock that can yield an economically significant amount of water are called **aquifers**. Some aquifers are enormous. The

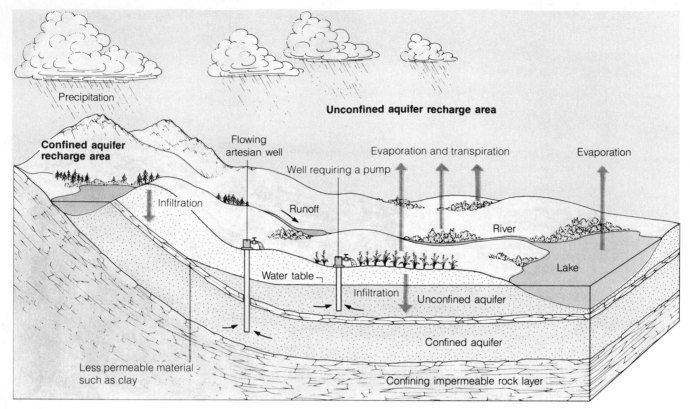

Figure 13-3 The groundwater system. An *unconfined*, or *water table*, *aquifer* forms when groundwater collects above a layer of rock or compacted clay through which water flows very slowly (low permeability). A *confined aquifer* is sandwiched between layers such as clay or shale that have a low permeability. Groundwater in this type of aquifer is confined and under pressure.

largest in the world is the Ogallala Aquifer, which stretches from southern South Dakota to northwestern Texas.

Most aquifers are recharged or replenished naturally by precipitation, which percolates downward through soil and rock in what is called **natural recharge** (Figure 13-3). Any area of land allowing water to pass through it and into an aquifer is called a **recharge area** (Figure 13-3). Groundwater moves from the recharge area through an aquifer and out to a discharge area as part of the hydrologic cycle. Discharge areas can be wells, springs, lakes, geysers, streams, and oceans.

The direction of flow of groundwater from recharge areas to discharge areas is dependent on gravity, pressure, and friction. Normally, groundwater moves from points of high elevation and pressure to points of lower elevation and pressure. This movement is quite slow, typically only a meter or so (about 3 feet) a year and rarely more than 0.3 meter (1 foot) a day. Thus, most aquifers are like huge, slow-moving underground lakes.

If the withdrawal rate of an aquifer exceeds its natural recharge rate, the water table around the withdrawal well is lowered, creating a waterless volume known as a *cone of depression* (Figure 13-4). Any pollutant discharged within the land area above the cone of

depression will be pulled directly into the well and can have a devastating effect on the quality of water withdrawn from that well.

Some aquifers, called *fossil aquifers*, are often found deep underground, get very little recharge, and are nonrenewable resources on a human time scale. Withdrawals from these deposits amount to "water mining," eventually depleting these one-time deposits of liquid Earth capital.

WORLD AND U.S. WATER USE Two common measures of human water use are withdrawal and consumption. **Water withdrawal** involves taking water from a groundwater or surface-water source and transporting it to a place of use. **Water consumption** occurs when water that has been withdrawn is not returned to the surface water or groundwater from which it came so that it may be used again in that area.

In a particular area, most water is consumed by evaporation and transpiration. In arid areas, such as much of the western United States, the biggest consumptive uses of water are irrigation and lawn watering. Worldwide, about 60% of the water withdrawn is consumed.

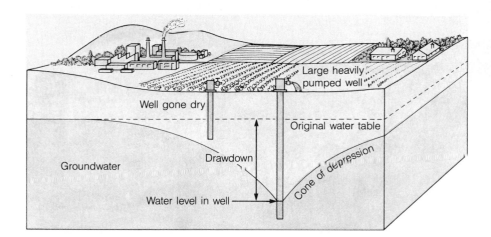

Figure 13-4 Drawdown of water table and cone of depression.

Since 1950, global water withdrawal has increased three and a half times and per capita use has trebled, largely in response to the rapid growth in population, agriculture, and industrialization. Water withdrawals are projected to at least double in the next two decades to meet the food and other resource needs of the world's rapidly growing population.

Annual total water withdrawal varies considerably among various MDCs and LDCs, with the largest volumes drawn, in decreasing order, by the United States, China, India, and the Soviet Union. The United States also has the highest per capita water withdrawal in the world, followed by Canada, Australia, the Soviet Union, Japan, and Mexico. Per capita water withdrawal in LDCs is typically 1% to 2% of that in the United States. If everyone on Earth had the same average per capita water withdrawal as in the United States, we would be trying to withdraw more fresh water than is available worldwide.

Uses of withdrawn water vary widely from one country to another (Figure 13-5). Averaged globally, about 63% of the water withdrawn each year is used to irrigate 18% of the world's cropland. That is projected to decline to 55% by the year 2000, mostly because of increased withdrawals for industrial use in Asia, Africa, and Latin America.

The largest areas of irrigated land are found in the United States, the Soviet Union, and Mexico. The percentage of withdrawn water used for irrigation can reach 80% or more in some areas, such as Egypt, where all cropland must be irrigated, and Pakistan, where 77% of the cropland is irrigated.

In the western United States, irrigation accounts for about 85% of all water use. Irrigation to grow food (such as hay, corn, grass, and sorghum) for livestock accounts for about 50% of that use and irrigated crops for the remaining 35%. Much of the water used for irrigation in western states is wasted, mainly because the cost of water to most farmers is heavily subsidized by the federal government.

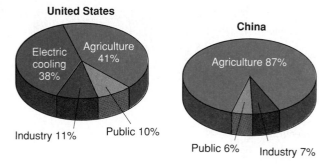

Figure 13-5 Use of water in the United States and China. (Data from Worldwatch Institute and World Resources Institute)

Worldwide, about 23% of the water withdrawn is used for energy production (oil and gas production and power-plant cooling) and industrial processing, cleaning, and removal of wastes. Water withdrawal for energy production and industrial use is highest in the United States (Figure 13-5) and the Soviet Union. Growing food and manufacturing various products require large amounts of water (Figure 13-6), although in most cases, much of that water could be used more efficiently and reused.

Domestic and municipal use accounts for about 7% of worldwide withdrawals and 13% to 16% in industrialized countries. Domestic and municipal use is highest in the United States, followed by Canada and Switzerland. Although the quantity of water required for domestic and municipal needs is not large, the quality must be high.

Increases in domestic and municipal water use and industrial use are usually accompanied by an increase in wastewater. As population and industrialization grow in LDCs, the volume of wastewater needing treatment will increase enormously in areas where most of the wastewater produced today is treated only partially or not at all.

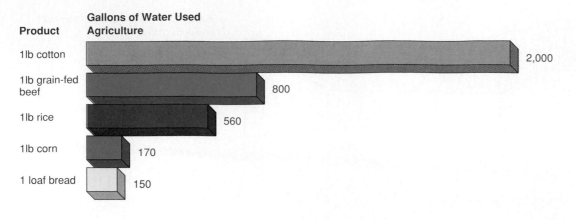

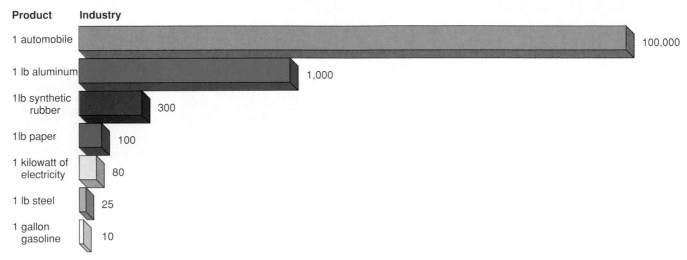

Figure 13-6 Amount of water typically used to produce various foods and products in the United States. (Data from U.S. Geological Survey)

13-3 Water Resource Problems

TOO LITTLE WATER According to the International Red Cross, droughts do more economic damage and harm more people worldwide than any other natural hazard. At any given time, up to one-fifth of the world's land area is gripped by severe drought.

During the 1970s, severe droughts affected an average of 24.4 million people per year, killed over 23,000 a year, and created large numbers of environmental refugees—a trend that continued in the 1980s and into the 1990s (Figure 13-7). At least 80 arid and semiarid countries, where nearly 40% of the world's people live, experience cycles of droughts that can last several years. In water-short areas, many women and children must walk long distances each day, carrying heavy jars or cans, to get a meager supply of sometimes-contaminated water for their families (Figure 13-8).

Areas likely to face increased water shortages in the 1990s and beyond include northern Africa, parts of In-

dia, northern China, much of the Middle East, Mexico, and parts of the western United States, Poland, and the central Soviet Union. A prolonged drought affected much of Africa between 1982 and 1986. It led to widespread starvation and disease, affected at least 55 million people, and forced at least 10 million people to abandon their homes in a desperate search for food and water (Figure 13-7).

Reduced precipitation, higher than normal temperatures, or both usually trigger a drought, but rapid population growth and poor land use intensify its effects. The effects of drought are made worse by trying to support too many people and livestock in areas that normally have prolonged droughts and by local and regional climate changes brought about by severe loss of vegetation from deforestation (Section 10-2), overgrazing grasslands (Figure 12-11), plowing prairies, and irrigating fields. In many LDCs, large numbers of poor people have no choice but to try to survive on drought-prone land.

Unless we take action now to slow down projected global warming (Section 11-2), severe droughts may occur more frequently in some areas of the world (Figure 11-4).

Figure 13-7 Camp of drought refugees in Burkino Faso, West Africa, depicts the plight of some of the estimated 10 million people driven from their homes world-wide by environmental degradation.

International Development Research Centar/ Ottawa, Canada

World Bank

Figure 13-8 In West Africa's Burkino Faso, women sometimes must walk 32 kilometers (20 miles) just to get a jar of water for their families. Sometimes, they are forced to take water from contaminated sources. (One out of five people in the world do not have access to clean water.) This situation occurs in many water-poor countries.

It is also likely that irrigation systems will be poorly matched to altered rainfall patterns. That will jeopardize our ability to produce enough food for the world's growing population and could lead to virtual abandonment of many water starved cities—including Los Angeles, San Diego, and Cairo—built in desert areas.

Water will be the foremost foreign-policy issue for water-short countries in the 1990s and beyond. Almost 150 of the world's 214 largest river systems are shared by two countries and 50 by three to ten countries. Together, these countries contain 40% of the world's population, and they often clash over water rights (see Spotlight on p. 340).

Competition between cities and farmers for scarce water within countries is also escalating in areas such as California and northern China, where dozens of cities, including Beijing, already face acute water shortages. Water shortages are expected in 450 of China's 644 cities by the turn of this century. In most cases, the only way to lessen these problems is to shift more of a region's water from farmers, who use the most, to city dwellers, whose water use is less and generally produces much greater economic benefits.

A new type of water pump, invented by Arthur Bentley, may help provide water in water-short areas by tapping into deep deposits of groundwater. Conventional pumps require large amounts of expensive electricity or diesel fuel to pump water from deep underground. Bentley's invention sends sonic waves down a well to drive a piston up and down and push water up, and becomes more efficient the deeper you go. It uses a little motor that draws practically no electricity and can easily be powered by solar cells. Its initial cost is about half that of conventional systems and one-third that of a wind turbine. It is an excellent example of appropriate technology.

TOO MUCH WATER Some countries have enough annual precipitation but get most of it at one time of the year. In India, for example, 90% of the annual precipitation falls between June and September, the monsoon season. This downpour can cause flooding, waterlogging of soils, nutrient depletion of soils, and the washing away of topsoil and crops.

Hurricanes and typhoons can flood low-lying coastal areas (Section 7-4). Prolonged rains anywhere can cause streams and lakes to overflow and flood surrounding land areas, but low-lying river basins are

Nowhere are conflicts over water supplies more serious than in the water-short Middle East. There, precious water is supplied by three shared river basins: the Jordan, the Tigris-Euphrates, and the Nile (Figure 13-9).

Arguments between Egypt, Ethiopia, and the Sudan over access to the water from the Nile River basin (Figure 13-9) are escalating rapidly. Ethiopia, which controls the headwaters of 80% of the Nile's flow, has plans to divert more of this water; so does Sudan.

Egypt, where it hardly ever rains, is almost completely desert except for a thin strip of productive land along the Nile and its delta. Most of its 56 million people crowd on the less than 4% of its land where irrigated crops can be grown. Its population is projected to double to 102 million by 2020. During the 1990s, Egypt's per capita water supply is expected to drop by one-third.

Any drop in the water available to Egypt, which is already having serious problems growing enough

food, could lead to a dire situation. In 1989, Egypt's foreign minister warned: "The next war in our region will be over the waters of the Nile." Egypt's only practical course is to sharply reduce population growth, which increases by 1 million every nine months, and reduce the enormous amount of water wasted through inefficient irrigation techniques.

Competition for water is also fierce between Jordan, Israel, and Syria, which get most of their water from the Jordan River basin (Figure 13-9). The 1967 Arab-Israeli war was fought in part over access to water from this river basin. Many towns in Jordan receive water only twice a week, and the country must double its supply over the next 20 years just to keep up with projected population growth.

Syria expects water shortages by the year 2000. If it uses more of the water from the Jordan River basin, the plight of Jordan, its downstream neighbor, could worsen.

Israel has been more effective at

water conservation than any country in the world. Despite that success, Israel is now using 95% of its renewable supplies of fresh water, and supplies are projected to fall 30% short of demand by the year 2000 because of the expected immigration of 750,000 people from the Soviet Union. Also, 750,000 Palestinians in the Gaza Strip face catastrophe because of overpumping and contamination of groundwater by seawater intrusion. This area has been described as a sewage time bomb waiting to explode.

Turkey is building a vast complex of dams on the Euphrates River. That project will drastically reduce the flow of water to Syria and Iraq, which lie downstream. These three countries have traded threats over access to this water. Indeed, the greatest threat to Iraq is a cutoff of its water supply by Turkey and Syria. Clearly, distribution of water resources will be a key issue in any future peace processes in this highly volatile region.

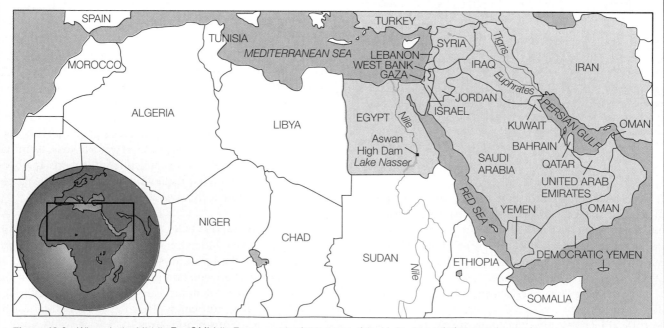

Figure 13-9 Where is the Middle East? Middle East countries have some of the highest population growth rates in the world. Because of their dry climate, food production depends on irrigation. In the 1990s and beyond, conflicts between countries over access to water supplies in this region may overshadow conflicts over ownership of oil supplies and long-standing religious and ethnic clashes.

especially vulnerable to flooding. An example is the low-lying plain of the Ganges River basin in India and Bangladesh. This area now supports 500 million mostly poor people, and the number of people living there is projected to reach 1 billion by the year 2020. In terms of the number of people involved, flooding in this basin is the greatest ecological hazard on Earth. Because of destruction of tree cover in the mountainous Himalayan watersheds, the area prone to flooding in India has more than quadrupled since 1960.

During the 1970s, disastrous floods affected 15.4 million people annually, killed an average of 4,700 people a year, and caused tens of billions of dollars in property damages. This trend continued throughout the 1980s. In India, for example, losses from flooding doubled in the 1980s.

Floods, like droughts, are usually called natural disasters, but human activities have contributed to the sharp rise in flood deaths and damages since the 1960s. Cultivation of land, deforestation (Figure 1-1), overgrazing (Figure 12-12), and mining (Figure 10-12) have removed water-absorbing vegetation and soil (see Case Study on p. 342). In Thailand, loggers have been banned from forests after catastrophic floods in 1988 buried entire villages in mud and logs from cutover hillsides.

Urbanization also increases flooding, even with moderate rainfall. It replaces vegetation and soil with highways, parking lots, shopping centers, office buildings, homes, and other structures that lead to rapid runoff of rainwater. If sea levels rise during the next century as a result of projected global warming, flooding of low-lying coastal cities, wetlands, and croplands will increase dramatically.

Flood damage can be prevented or reduced by reforestation, channelization, dams, artifical levees, and floodplain management (Section 7-4).

WATER NOT WHERE IT IS NEEDED In some countries, the largest rivers, which carry most of the runoff, are far from agricultural and population centers where the water is needed. For example, South America has the largest average annual runoff of any continent, but 60% of the runoff flows through the Amazon, the world's largest river, in areas far from where most people live (Figure 9-3).

CONTAMINATED DRINKING WATER Not only is water becoming more scarce in many parts of the world, its quality is also being degraded. Rivers in Poland (see Case Study on p. 20), Latin America, and Asia are severely polluted, as are some in MDCs. Aquifers used as sources of drinking water in many MDCs and LDCs are becoming contaminated with pesticides, fertilizers, and hazardous organic chemicals. In China, for example, 41 large cities get their drinking water from polluted groundwater.

In its passage through the hydrologic cycle, water is polluted primarily by three kinds of waste. One is the sediment washed from the land into surface waters by natural erosion and by greatly accelerated erosion of soil from agriculture, forestry, mining, construction, and other land-clearing and disturbing activities (Section 12-2 and Figure 10-8). Another is organic waste from human and animal excreta and the discarded parts of harvested plants. The third is the rapidly increasing volume of a variety of hazardous chemicals produced by industrialized societies. All three categories of waste are increasing because of rapid population growth, poverty, and industrialization. These forms of water pollution are discussed in Chapter 22.

According to the World Health Organization, 1.5 billion people do not have a safe supply of drinking water and 1.7 billion do not have adequate sanitation facilities. At least 5 million people, mostly children under age 5, die every year from waterborne diseases that could be prevented by improvements in supplies of drinking water and in sanitation. This amounts to an average death rate of 13,700 people a day.

In 1980, the United Nations called for MDCs and LDCs to spend $300 billion to supply all the world's people with clean drinking water and adequate sanitation by 1990. The $30-billion-a-year cost of this program would be roughly equal to what the world spends every ten days for military purposes, but the actual amount spent during the 1990s was only about $1.5 billion a year. Some progress has been made in several countries, including Indonesia, Mexico, and Ghana. However, by 1990, the program had fallen far short of its goal because of lack of funding, lack of commitment by MDCs and LDCs, and increased population.

THE U.S. SITUATION Overall, the United States has plenty of fresh water, but much of the country's annual runoff is not in the desired place, occurs at the wrong time, or is contaminated from agricultural and industrial activities. Most of the eastern half of the country usually has ample precipitation, while much of the western half has too little. In the East, the largest uses for water are energy production and cooling and manufacturing. In the West, the largest use by far is for irrigation.

Many major urban centers in the United States are located in areas that don't have enough water or are projected to have water shortages by 2000, especially in the West and Midwest (Figure 13-11). These shortages could worsen if the world's climate warms up as a result of an enhanced greenhouse effect (Figure 11-4). Because water is such a vital resource, you might find Figures 11-4 and 13-11 useful in deciding where to live in coming decades.

In many parts of the eastern United States, the most serious water problems are flooding, inability to supply enough water to some large urban areas, and

Bangladesh (Figure 8-17) is located on a vast, low-lying delta of shifting islands of silt at the mouth of the Ganges, Brahmaputra, and Meghna rivers. It is one of the world's most densely populated countries, with 117 million people—almost half the population of the United States—packed into an area roughly the size of Wisconsin. Women average 4.9 children, and the country's population is projected to reach 226 million by the year 2025. Bangladesh is also one of the world's poorest countries, with an average per capita income of about $180. Eighty percent of its population can't read or write.

Its people are accustomed to flooding after water from annual monsoon rains in the Himalaya of India, Nepal, Bhutan, and China flows downward through rivers to Bangladesh and into the Bay of Bengal. Bangladesh depends on this annual flooding to grow rice, its primary source of food. The annual deposit of Himalayan soil in the delta basin also helps maintain soil fertility. Thus, the people of this country are used to moderate annual flooding and need it for their survival. However, severe flooding from excessive runoff from the Himalaya and from storm surges caused by cyclones in the Bay of Bengal is disastrous.

In the past, great floods occurred only once every 50 years or so, but since 1950, the number of large-scale floods has increased sharply. During the 1970s and 1980s, the average interval between major floods in Bangladesh was only four years. After a flood in 1974, an estimated 300,000 people died in a famine.

In 1988, a disastrous flood covered two-thirds of the country's land mass for several days and levelled 2 million homes after the heaviest monsoon rains in 70 years (Figure 13-10). At least 2,000 people drowned, and 30 million people—1 out of 4—were left homeless. Hundreds of thousands more contracted diseases such as cholera and typhoid fever from contaminated

Figure 13-10 Some annual flooding in Bangladesh is necessary for growing rice, but the country now experiences more disastrous floods because of forest clearing in other countries in the watershed of the Himalaya.

water and food supplies. At least a quarter of the country's crops were destroyed, costing this impoverished nation at least $1.5 billion and causing the premature deaths of thousands from starvation.

Bangladesh's flooding problems begin in the Himalayan watershed. There, a combination of rapid population growth, deforestation, overgrazing, and unsustainable farming on easily erodible steep mountain slopes has greatly diminished the ability of soil in this mountain watershed to absorb water. Instead of being absorbed and released slowly, water from the annual monsoon rain runs off the denuded foothills of the Himalaya north of Bangladesh's border. Then, heavier than normal monsoon rains cause severe flooding in Bangladesh. This deluge of water also carries with it the topsoil vital to the survival of people in the Himalaya. This demonstrates that what happens in the world's mountain highlands affects a third of the people on Earth.

In their struggle to survive, the poor in Bangladesh have cleared many of the country's coastal mangrove forests (Figure 5-31) for fuelwood and for growing food. This has increased the severity of flooding because these coastal wetlands help protect the low-lying coastal areas from storm surges generated

by cyclones in the Bay of Bengal. In 1970, between 200,000 and 1 million people drowned in one of these storms. Flood damages and deaths in areas where protective mangrove forests still exist are much lower than in areas where they have been cleared. Another cyclone killed at least 100,000 people in 1991.

This human-caused environmental disaster, which is likely to be repeated, causes as much damage as that wrought by a war. Rising sea levels from an enhanced greenhouse effect would put the heavily populated portion of Bangladesh that juts into the Bay of Bengal under water. This illustrates the folly of not placing at least as much emphasis on environmental security as on military security. The severity of this problem can only be reduced if Bangladesh, Bhutan, China, India, and Nepal all agree to cooperate in reforestation efforts and flood control measures.

MDCs also have an important role to play. They must provide aid for reforestation and flood control. Equally important, they must do their part in dismantling the global poverty trap that forces the poor into unsustainable land use and makes them highly vulnerable to environmental change by having to survive on unprotected floodplains.

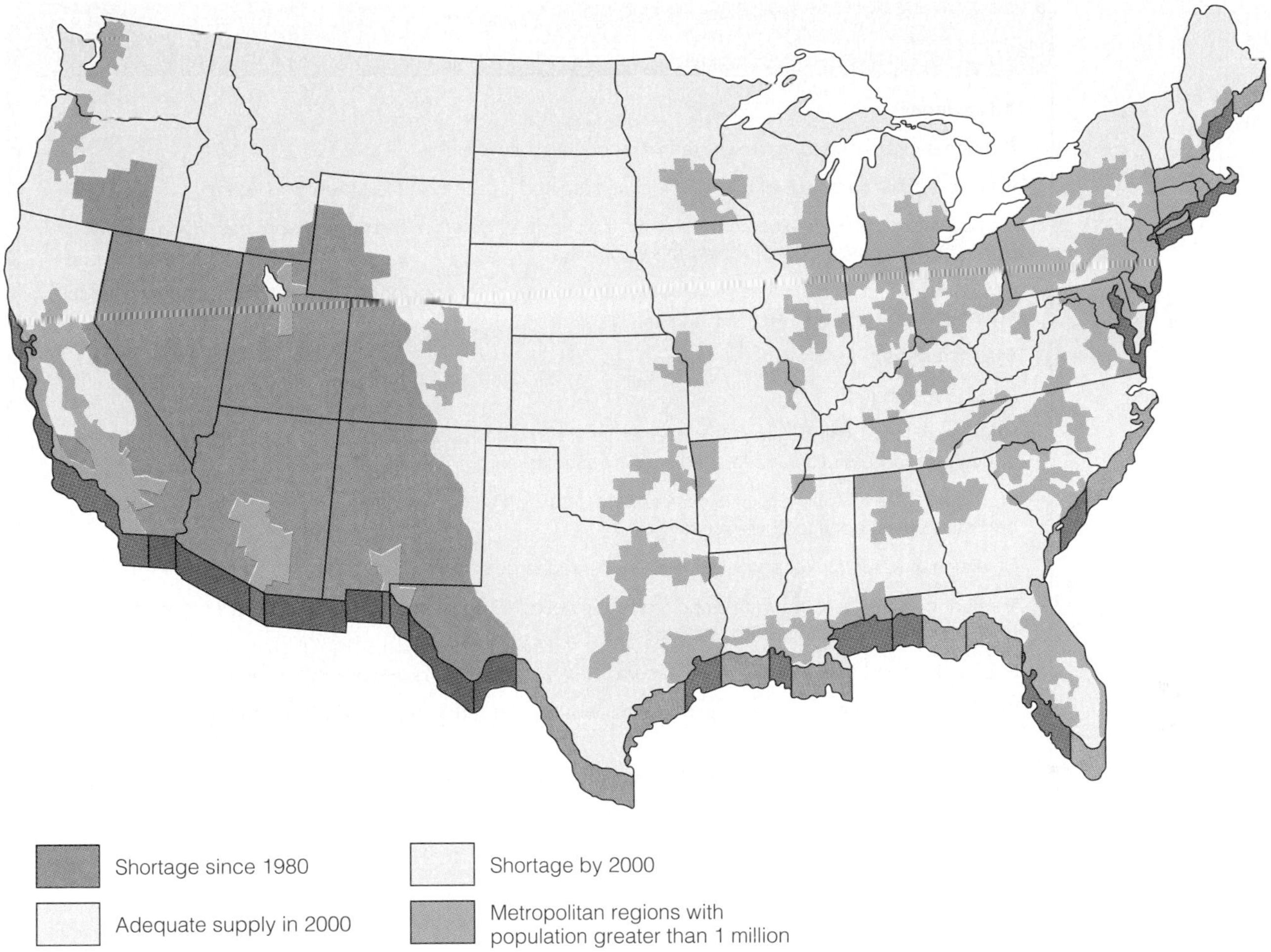

Shortage since 1980
Shortage by 2000
Adequate supply in 2000
Metropolitan regions with population greater than 1 million

Figure 13-11 Present and projected water deficit regions in the United States compared with present metropolitan regions with populations greater than 1 million. (Data from U.S. Water Resources Council and U.S. Geological Survey)

pollution of streams, lakes, and groundwater. For example, 3 million residents of Long Island, New York, must draw all their water from an aquifer. This aquifer is becoming severely contaminated by industrial wastes, leaking septic tanks and landfills, and ocean salt water, which is drawn into the aquifer when fresh water is withdrawn faster than it is naturally recharged.

The most serious water problem in the arid and semiarid areas of the western half of the country is a shortage of runoff caused by low precipitation, high rates of evaporation, and recurring prolonged drought. About 85% of western water is used to irrigate crops. As a result, water tables are dropping rapidly as farmers and cities deplete groundwater aquifers faster than they are recharged. Experts project that present shortages and conflicts over water supplies will become much worse as more industries and people migrate west (Figure 9-6) and compete with farmers for scarce water resources.

13-4 Water Resource Management

METHODS FOR MANAGING WATER RESOURCES

One way to manage water resources is to increase the supply in a particular area, mostly by building dams and reservoirs, bringing in surface water from another area, and tapping groundwater. The other approach is to improve the efficiency of water use by decreasing unnecessary use and waste.

LDCs may or may not have enough water, but they rarely have the money needed to develop the water storage and distribution systems needed to increase their supply. Their people must settle where the water is.

In MDCs, people tend to live where the climate is favorable and bring in water through expensive transfers of water from one watershed to another. Some settle in a desert and expect water to be brought to them at a

Table 13-1 Advantages and Disadvantages of Large Dams and Reservoirs

Advantages

Reduce danger of flooding downstream by controlling stream flow.

Provide a controllable supply of water for irrigating arid and semiarid land below the dam.

Can be used to provide electric power from the energy of water flowing through turbines. Hydroelectric power plants provide 20% of the world's electricity.

Reservoirs behind large dams can also be used for outdoor recreation such as swimming, boating, and fishing.

Disadvantages

Expensive to build.

Flooding of land behind dam to form the reservoir displaces people and destroys vast areas of valuable agricultural land, wildlife habitat, and scenic natural beauty.

Storage of water behind a dam raises the water table, which often waterlogs the soil on nearby land, decreasing its crop or forest productivity.

Diversion of water into reservoir reduces aquifer recharge in the watershed above the dam.

Tremendous weight of the water impounded in reservoirs increases the likelihood of fault movement, which causes subsidence and earthquakes (Section 7-4).

Evaporation increases the salinity of reservoir water, decreasing its usefulness for irrigation.

Reservoirs fill up with silt and become useless in 40 to 200 years, depending on local climate and land-use practices.

Can give developers and residents in a floodplain below the dam a false sense of safety from major floods, which can overwhelm the ability of a dam to control floodwaters.

Danger of collapse.

Disrupts the migration and spawning of fish, such as salmon.

Deprives downstream croplands and estuaries of vital nutrients from silt deposited by annual flooding and decreases their productivity.

---

low price. Others settle on a floodplain and expect the government to keep floodwaters away.

Increasing the water supply in some areas is important, but this approach is eventually overwhelmed by increasing population, food production, industrialization, and unpredictable shifts in water supplies from projected global warming. Thus, it makes much more sense economically and environmentally to put the primary emphasis on prevention (input) methods that increase the efficiency of the ways we use water in agriculture and industry and in homes and thus help prevent unnecessary waste of this precious resource in an increasingly thirsty world.

CONSTRUCTING DAMS AND RESERVOIRS Rainwater and water from melting snow that would otherwise be lost can be captured and stored in large reservoirs behind dams built across streams (Figure 5-40). Large dams and reservoirs have benefits and drawbacks (see Table 13-1 and Case Study on p. 345).

Studies have shown that large-scale dams in LDCs often tend to benefit a small minority of the well-to-do while flooding the lands and often destroying floodwater farming and fisheries that are vital to the poor majority. Building small dams, which can avoid most of the destructive effects of large dams and reservoirs (Table 13-1), is a useful way to trap more water for irrigation. China built 90,000 small dams between 1950 and 1980 but is now building or planning a number of large-scale projects.

Despite protests by more than 50,000 villagers, the Indian government is going ahead with plans to build 30 large-scale dams and thousands of smaller ones along the Namada River and 41 of its tributaries. The project will flood an estimated 4,000 square kilometers (1,500 square miles) of forests and farms and displace 1 million people. In Brazil, the $1 billion Balbina dam in the Amazon (Figure 9-3) destroyed 2,400 square kilometers (930 square miles) of virgin tropical forest, displaced thousands of indigenous people, and killed millions of wild animals—all to supply only 80 megawatts of electricity.

Faulty construction, earthquakes, floods, landslides, sabotage, or war can cause dams to fail, taking a

The billion-dollar Aswan High Dam on the Nile River in Egypt (Figure 13-9) shows what can happen when a large-scale dam and reservoir project is built without adequate consideration of long-term environmental effects and costs. The dam was built in the 1960s to provide flood control and irrigation water for the lower Nile basin and electricity for Cairo and other parts of Egypt.

Today, the dam supplies about one-third of Egypt's electrical power, and it saved Egypt's rice and cotton crops during the droughts of 1972 and 1973. Year-round irrigation in the lower Nile basin has increased food production and allows farmers there to harvest crops three times a year on land that was previously harvested only once a year. Irrigation has also brought about 405,000 hectares (1 million acres) of desert land under cultivation.

Since the dam opened in 1964, it has also had a number of harmful ecological effects. It ended the yearly flooding that had fertilized the Nile Delta with silt, had flushed mineral salts from the soil, and had swept away snails that infect humans with schistosomiasis, a disease that causes pain, weakness, and premature death. Now the river's silt accumulates behind the dam, filling up Lake Nasser.

Cropland in the Nile Delta basin now has to be treated with commercial fertilizer at a cost of over $100 million a year to make up for plant nutrients once available at no cost. The country's new fertilizer plants use up much of the electrical power produced by the dam. Because salts are no longer flushed from the soil, salinization (Figure 12-20) has offset three-fourths of the gain in food production from new, less productive land irrigated by water from the reservoir.

Because it contains less sediment, the Nile has eroded its bed and has undermined numerous bridges and smaller dams downstream. To remedy this problem, the government proposes to build ten barrier dams. The projected cost is $250 million — one-fourth of what the original dam cost.

Without the Nile's annual discharge of sediment, the sea is eroding the delta and advancing inland, reducing productivity on large areas of agricultural land. This loss of productive land by erosion and saltwater intrusion is increased by subsidence in Egypt's Nile Delta from a rise in sea level and centuries of deposited sediments.

Now that the nutrient-rich silt no longer reaches the waters at the river's mouth, Egypt's sardine, mackerel, shrimp, and lobster industries have all but disappeared. This has led to losses of approximately 30,000 jobs, millions of dollars annually, and an important source of protein for Egyptians. Eventually, these losses are expected to be recovered by a new fishing industry based on taking bass, catfish, and carp from Lake Nasser behind the dam.

Flooding to create Lake Nasser uprooted 125,000 people. It was supposed to be full by 1970 and to have enough water to meet the needs of Egypt and the Sudan during a prolonged drought, but evaporation and seepage of water into the underlying sandstone have been much greater than projected. Today, the reservoir is only about half full. Most authorities believe that the level will not rise much more in the next 100 years. In addition, about 80% of the water flowing into Lake Nasser comes from the Nile River basin from Ethiopia. This vital source of water may be reduced by dams being built along the Nile by Ethiopia as well as by severe drought (see Spotlight on p. 340).

Although it is a low-risk area, the area around the dam suffered a fairly severe earthquake in 1981. Scientists believe the quake was triggered by the weight of the water in Lake Nasser.

Some analysts believe that in the long run, the benefits of the Aswan High Dam will outweigh its costs. Others consider it an economic and ecological disaster. What do you think?

---

terrible toll in lives and property. According to the Federal Emergency Management Agency, the United States has about 1,300 unsafe dams in populated areas. The agency reported that the dam safety programs of most states are inadequate because of weak laws and budget cuts. In 1986, Congress authorized $15 million annually for state dam safety, but the money never was appropriated. A bright spot is Pennsylvania, which since 1986 has cut its number of unsafe dams from 203 to 40.

WATERSHED TRANSFERS People have been moving water around for thousands of years. This is done by building dams and reservoirs to collect river runoff and then using tunnels, canals, and underground pipes to transfer water from water-rich watersheds to water-poor areas. Currently, the world's largest watershed transfer project is the controversial California Water Plan (see Case Study on p. 346).

In 1971, construction began on a much larger, $50-billion, 50-year scheme, known as the James Bay project, to harness the wild rivers that flow into the James and Hudson bays in Canada's Quebec province to produce 26,000 megawatts of electric power for use by Canadian and U.S. consumers. The basic idea of the plan is to divert fresh water from northern Quebec before it can mingle with the salty Hudson Bay. When completed, the project will involve reversing or altering the flow of 19 major rivers, reshaping a territory the size of

In California, the basic water problem is that 75% of the population lives south of Sacramento, but 75% of the rain falls north of there. The California Water Plan uses a maze of giant dams, pumps, and aqueducts to transport water from water-rich parts of northern California to heavily populated parts of northern California and to mostly arid and semiarid, heavily populated southern California (Figure 13-12). Southern California gets roughly half of its water from a single aqueduct system, the California Aqueduct (Figure 13-13). For decades, northern and southern Californians have been feuding over how the state's water should be allocated under this plan.

People in arid southern California say they need more water from the north for growing crops and supporting Los Angeles, San Diego, and other large and growing urban areas. Opponents in the north say that sending more water south would degrade the Sacramento River, threaten fishing, and reduce the flushing action that helps clean San Francisco Bay of pollutants.

They also argue that much of the water already sent south is wasted and that an increase of only 10% in irrigation efficiency would provide enough water for domestic and industrial uses in southern California. Pointing out that agriculture accounts for only 2.5% of the state's economy while using 83% of the water withdrawn, they contend that water used in other ways contributes more to economic growth.

Conservationists believe that the government should not award new long-term water contracts that give many farmers and ranchers cheap, federally subsidized water for irrigating crops — especially grass for cows, rice, alfalfa, and cotton — that could be grown more cheaply in

Figure 13-12 California Water Plan and Central Arizona Project for large-scale transfer of water from one watershed to another. Arrows show general direction of water flow.

rain-fed areas. The amount of water used to irrigate pasture for livestock, which could be raised elsewhere without irrigation, is more than that used by all 30 million Californians.

In California's giant Central Valley irrigation project, farmers have had to pay only 5% of what it cost American taxpayers to supply them with this water over the last 40 years. To supply agribusiness with such cheap water, the Bureau of Reclamation has drained major rivers and lakes and large areas of prime wetlands, destroyed thousands of kilometers of salmon habitat, and contaminated rivers and groundwater with pesticides and fertilizers. A five-year drought between 1986 and 1991 cut irrigation water from the Central Valley Project by 75%, caus-

ing thousands of hectares to be abandoned as cropland.

One example of the environmental consequences of the California Water Plan is the shrinkage of Mono Lake, a salty desert lake east of Yosemite National Park, by one-third. This has threatened populations of resident and migratory birds that use the lake as a source of food and shelter. In 1985, the California Supreme Court ordered the state to reserve enough water to protect the wildlife and other environmental values of this lake.

Conservationists propose that cities wanting more water should also be required to pay farmers to install water-saving irrigation technology and then have the right to use the water saved. Bringing about these changes is difficult because

Figure 13-13 The California Aqueduct provides southern California with about half of its water. It carries water from the Sacramento River Delta 800 kilometers (500 miles) south to Los Angeles. A major earthquake on the nearby Hayward Fault could destroy levees that protect this precious and fragile system, which is the water lifeline for almost 20 million people. (Note the wind farm windmills at left, which are used to generate electricity.)

the political power of California's farmers greatly exceeds their contribution to the state's economy.

A related project is the federally financed $3.9 billion Central Arizona Project, which pumps water from the Colorado River uphill to Phoenix and Tucson (Figure 13-12). When the first part of this project was completed in 1985, southern California, especially the arid and booming San Diego region, began losing up to one-fifth of its water, which Arizona has a legal right to divert. Because of this project, Arizona has been able to reduce its dependence on groundwater from over 90% to about 65%.

If water supplies in California should drop sharply because of projected global warming (Figure 11-4), water delivered by this huge distribution system would drop sharply. Most irrigated agriculture in California would have to be abandoned, and much of the population of southern California might have to move to areas with more water. The five-year drought that northern and southern California experienced between 1986 and 1991 was a small taste of what might be normal or worse conditions in the future.

Groundwater is no answer. It is already being withdrawn faster than it is replenished throughout most of California. Santa Barbara, Los Angeles, and several other southern California cities are planning to build experimental desalination plants—an option that is five times more costly than state-provided water. Improving irrigation efficiency is a much quicker and cheaper solution.

Another example of large-scale watershed transfer is in Soviet Central Asia, which has the driest climate in the Soviet Union. Ninety percent of the cropland is irrigated. Since 1960, enormous amounts of irrigation water have been diverted from the inland Aral Sea (Figure 13-14) and the two rivers that replenish its water, to grow cotton and food crops.

However, the irrigation water that made the desert bloom and incomes rise has caused a regional ecological disaster that is eliminating the Aral Sea and affecting the livelihood and health of 35 million people in this semiarid region. This catastrophe has been described by one Russian official "as ten times worse than the 1986 accident at the Chernobyl nuclear power plant."

Since 1960, the flow of the two rivers into the Aral Sea has been reduced to a trickle. As a result, the volume of the Aral Sea — once the world's fourth largest freshwater lake — has dropped by 69%, salinity levels have risen threefold, and its surface area has shrunk by 46% (Figure 13-14). About 30,000 square kilometers (11,600 square miles) of its former sea bottom has turned into desert, which continues to spread as more of the sea evaporates. Without drastic measures, this once gigantic freshwater lake will become a small brine lake surrounded by desert.

All native fish species have disappeared, devastating the area's fishing industry, which once provided work for more than 60,000 people. Two major fishing towns are now in a desert containing graveyards of stranded fishing boats and rusting commercial ships. Roughly half of the area's species of birds and mammals have disappeared.

Salt, dust, and dried pesticide residues have also been carried by winds and deposited on towns and cropfields as far as 300 kilometers (190 miles) away. People outside feel salt on their lips and in their eyes all the time. Rains have deposited Aral salt as far west as the Black Sea and as far north as the Soviet Arctic. As the salt spreads, it kills crops and trees, wildlife, and pastureland. This has added a new term to the planet's vocabulary of environmental ills: *salt rain*.

Irrigation water infiltrating the soil has raised the water table, causing waterlogging and salinization (Figure 12-20). Data indicate that the Aral Sea basin may be experiencing some of the worst salinization in the world.

These changes have also affected the area's already semiarid climate. The once-huge Aral Sea acted as a thermal buffer, moderating the heat of summer and the extreme cold of winter. Now there is less rain, summers are hotter, winters are colder, and the growing season has shortened. The result of this plus salinization is a dramatic drop in cotton and crop yields.

Local farmers have turned to herbicides, insecticides, and fertilizers to keep growing some crops. Since the basin has no drainage to the outside, some of the pesticides and fertilizers applied to the fields percolate downward and accumulate to dangerous levels in the groundwater used as the source of most drinking water.

Soviet newspapers and the local medical literature report soaring rates of hepatitis (up 7-fold since 1960), typhoid fever (up 30-fold since 1960), kidney disease, birth deformities, intestinal infections, throat and other cancers, and respiratory and eye diseases. The area also has the highest infant mortality rate in the Soviet Union. Inhabitants now call it the "salty sea of death" and charge the government with trying to commit cultural genocide on the area's mostly Muslim population.

Ways to deal with this problem include charging farmers more for irrigation water to reduce waste and encourage a shift to less-water-intensive crops, decreasing irrigation-water quotas by 15% to 20%, introducing water-saving technologies such as drip irrigation, developing a regional integrated water management plan, planting protective forest belts, improving health services,

France with hundreds of dams and dikes, flooding 176,000 square kilometers (68,000 square miles, equal to the area of the state of Washington) of boreal forest and tundra, and displacing thousands of members of the Cree Indian nation.

Its proponents call it "the engineering project of the century," while its opponents call it the "ecological and economic folly of the century." Opponents say it involves taking a huge territory notable for its running water and converting it into a vast area of stagnant reservoirs that will become toxic sinks for pollutants entering them from the atmosphere. They also point out that

the project has proceeded without a full environmental impact assessment and public review.

Most of the work on the first phase of the project — building three enormous dams along the La Grande River — has been completed. These dams supply 10,000 megawatts of power for use in southern Quebec and the United States.

The second phase, which involves damming the Great Whale River, is scheduled to begin soon but is being opposed in court by the Cree Indians, whose ancestral hunting grounds would be flooded and whose fishing grounds have already been polluted with

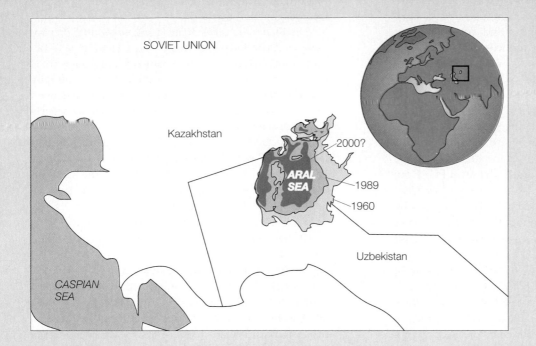

Figure 13-14 Where is the Aral Sea? Actually, it is a lake, and was at one time the world's fourth largest lake. Since 1960 it has been shrinking and getting saltier because most of the water from the rivers that replenish it has been diverted to grow cotton and food crops. As the sea shrinks, it leaves a desert of sand and salt.

and instituting a serious family planning effort to slow the area's rapid population growth (3% a year). Underground water could be used to supplement irrigation water, lower the water table to reduce waterlogging and salinization, and free river water to flow into the Aral Sea.

One gigantic scheme to save the Aral Sea involves reversing the current flow into the Arctic Ocean of the Ob and Irtysh rivers in Siberia and channelling it 2,400 kilometers (1,500 miles) south to refill the sea and provide more irrigation water

for the area. This project, with a start-up cost of $40 billion, has already been rejected three times because of the cost and possible environmental side effects.

Some scientists fear that diverting such large amounts of relatively warm water from Siberia and the Arctic Ocean could lower the temperature and increase salt levels in the Arctic Ocean. This, in turn, could cause regional climate changes that could affect the global climate system. This solution would also do nothing about the waterlog-

ging and salinization now undermining the productivity of the farmland in this region.

In 1990, the Soviet Union and the United Nations Environment Programme signed an agreement to save the Aral Sea. However, with the Soviet economy in crisis, the huge sums of money needed to do this will probably not be available.

toxic mercury released by severe flooding in the project's first phase. In 1990, the federal court of Canada ordered a full environmental impact assessment for this project, including public hearings.

An immense diversion of water from rivers feeding the Aral Sea in the Soviet Union to irrigate cropland has almost destroyed this sea, decreased crop productivity, and threatened the health of many of the people in this area (see Case Study on 348).

There have been proposals to tow massive icebergs to arid coastal areas (such as Saudi Arabia and southern California) and pump the fresh water from the melting

bergs ashore. However, the technology for doing this is not available, and the costs may be too high, especially for water-short LDCs.

TAPPING GROUNDWATER In the United States, about half of the drinking water (96% in rural areas and 20% in urban areas), 40% of the irrigation water, and 23% of all fresh water used is withdrawn from groundwater. In Florida, Hawaii, Idaho, Mississippi, Nebraska, and New Mexico, more than 90% of the population depends on groundwater for supplies of drinking water.

Overuse of groundwater can cause or intensify several problems: *aquifer depletion, subsidence* (sinking of land when groundwater is withdrawn), and *intrusion of salt water into aquifers* (Figure 13-15). Groundwater can also become contaminated from industrial and agricultural activities, septic tanks, and other sources. Groundwater depletion also reduces streamflow because groundwater is the source of about 40% of the river runoff in the United States.

Currently, about one-fourth of the groundwater withdrawn in the United States is not replenished. Although 35 states are withdrawing groundwater faster than it is being replenished by nature, the most serious groundwater overdraft problem is in parts of the huge Ogallala Aquifer, extending under the farm belt from southern South Dakota to northwestern Texas (see Case Study on p. 352). Aquifer depletion is also worsened by dams and reservoirs, which reduce the amount of water available for aquifer recharge in the watershed above the dam.

Aquifer depletion is also a serious problem in northern China, Mexico City, Bangkok (Thailand), and parts of India. In Beijing, one-third of the city's wells have gone dry, and the water table drops by as much as 2 meters (6.6 feet) a year. The demands of Mexico City's 22 million people (see Case Study on p. 226) are causing the water table of their main aquifer to drop as much as 3.4 meters (11 feet) annually.

Saudi Arabia's remarkable success in increasing its agricultural production is based on withdrawing 90% of the water used for irrigating crops in the desert from groundwater resources. Virtually all of that water comes from fossil aquifer storage that accumulated thousands of years ago with an essentially negligible recharge rate. At the current rate of depletion, the country's nonrenewable fossil groundwater will be exhausted by 2007.

Ways to slow groundwater depletion include reducing the amount withdrawn by wasting less irrigation water, not growing water-thirsty crops in dry areas, developing crop strains that require less water and that are more resistant to heat stress, and controlling population growth.

When groundwater in an unconfined aquifer (Figure 13-3) is withdrawn faster than it is replenished, relatively unconsolidated land overlying the aquifer can sink, or subside. This can damage pipelines, highways, railroad beds, and buildings (Figure 7-26).

When fresh water is withdrawn from an aquifer near a coast faster than it is recharged, salt water intrudes into the aquifer (Figure 13-17). Saltwater intrusion threatens to contaminate the drinking water of many towns and cities along the Atlantic and Gulf coasts (Figure 13-15) and in the coastal areas of Israel, Syria, and the Arabian Gulf states. Another growing problem in the United States and many other countries is groundwater contamination, discussed in Section 22-4.

DESALINATION Removing dissolved salts from ocean water or brackish (slightly salty) groundwater is an appealing way to increase freshwater supplies. Distillation and reverse osmosis are the two most widely used desalination methods.

Distillation involves heating salt water until it evaporates and condenses as fresh water, leaving salts behind in solid form. In reverse osmosis, high pressure is used to force salt water through a thin membrane whose pores allow water molecules but not dissolved salts to pass through. Desalination plants in arid parts of the Middle East (especially Saudi Arabia) and North Africa produce about two-thirds of the world's desalinated water. Saudi Arabia alone has 800 plants and Florida has more than 100 plants. Soon, some cities in southern California may begin to use this expensive method to supplement their water supplies.

The basic problem with these desalination methods is that they use large amounts of energy and therefore are expensive. Desalination can provide fresh water for coastal cities in arid regions, such as sparsely populated and oil-rich Saudi Arabia, where the cost of getting fresh water by any method is high. However, desalinated water will probably never be cheap enough to irrigate conventional crops or to meet much of the world's demand for fresh water, unless efficient solar-powered methods can be developed.

Another problem is that even more energy and money would be needed to pump desalinated water uphill and inland from coastal desalination plants. Also, a vast network of desalination plants would produce mountains of salt to be disposed of. The easiest and cheapest solution would be to dump the salt in the ocean near the plants, but this would increase the salt concentration and threaten food resources in estuarine waters.

CLOUD SEEDING Several countries, particularly the United States, have been experimenting for years with seeding clouds with chemicals to produce more rain over dry regions and snow over mountains. Cloud seeding involves finding a large, suitable cloud and injecting it with a powdered chemical such as silver iodide from a plane or from ground-mounted burners. Small water droplets in the cloud clump together around tiny particles of the chemical and form drops or ice particles large enough to fall to the earth as precipitation.

Cloud seeding, however, is not useful in very dry areas, where it is most needed, because rain clouds are rarely available. Large-scale use could also change snowfall and rainfall patterns and alter regional or even global climate patterns in unknown and perhaps undesirable ways. Widespread cloud seeding would also introduce large amounts of silver iodide (or other cloud-seeding chemicals) into soil and water systems, possibly with harmful effects on people, wildlife, and agricultural productivity.

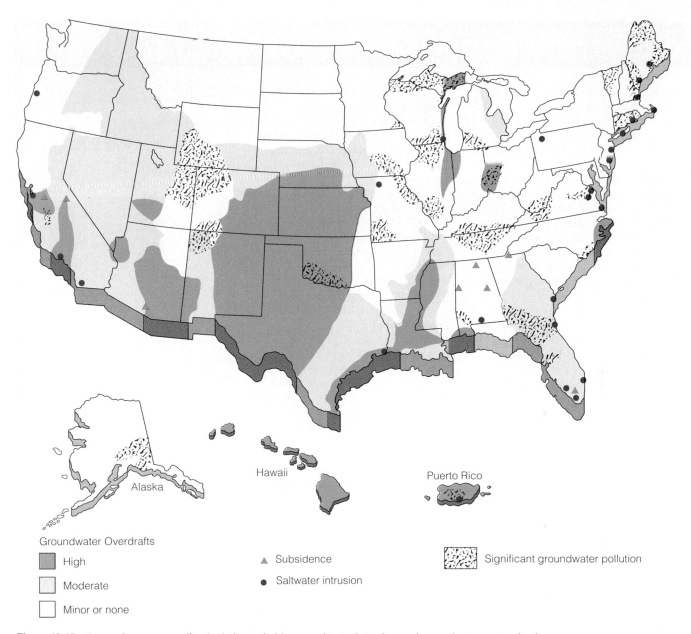

Figure 13-15 Areas of greatest aquifer depletion, subsidence, saltwater intrusion, and groundwater contamination in the United States. (Data from U.S. Water Resources Council and U.S. Geological Survey)

Groundwater Overdrafts

- ■ High
- ▨ Moderate
- □ Minor or none

- ▲ Subsidence
- ● Saltwater intrusion

- ▨ Significant groundwater pollution

Another obstacle to cloud seeding is legal disputes over the ownership of water in clouds. For example, during the 1977 drought in the western United States, the attorney general of Idaho accused officials in neighboring Washington of "cloud rustling" and threatened to file suit in federal court.

UNNECESSARY WATER WASTE Mohamed El-Ashry of the World Resources Institute estimates that 65% to 70% of the water people use throughout the world is unnecessarily wasted through evaporation, leaks, and other losses. The United States—the world's largest user of water—does slightly better but still unnecessarily wastes 50% of the water it withdraws. El-Ashry believes that it is economically and technically feasible to reduce water waste to 15%, which would meet most of the world's current and projected water needs.

A prime cause of water waste in the United States (and in most countries) is artificially low water prices, which discourage users from conserving water and installing water-conserving devices and processes. Low-cost water is the only reason that farmers in Arizona and southern California can grow water-thirsty crops like alfalfa in the middle of the desert. It also allows people in Palm Springs, California, to keep their lawns and 74 golf courses green in a desert area.

These and other water subsidies are paid for by all taxpayers in the form of higher taxes. Because these external costs don't show up on monthly water bills,

Water withdrawn from the vast Ogallala Aquifer (Figure 13-16), which underlies the arid Great Plains, is used to irrigate one-fifth of all U.S. cropland in an area too dry for rainfall farming. The aquifer supports $32 billion of agricultural production a year—mostly wheat, sorghum, cotton, and corn and 40% of the country's grain-fed beef cattle.

The Ogallala Aquifer contains a huge amount of water, but it is essentially a nonrenewable fossil aquifer with an extremely slow recharge rate. Today, the overall rate of withdrawal from this aquifer is eight times its natural recharge rate.

Even higher withdrawal rates, sometimes 100 times the recharge rate, are taking place in parts of the aquifer that lie beneath Texas, New Mexico, Oklahoma, and Colorado. Water resource experts project that at the present rate of withdrawal, much of this aquifer will be dry by 2020, and much sooner in areas where it is shallow.

When this water is gone, it will take thousands of years to replenish itself. Then the area would become the Great American Desert, with tumbleweeds as its largest crop.

Long before that happens, however, the high cost of pumping water from a rapidly dropping water table will force many farmers to grow crops that need much less water, such as wheat and cotton, instead of profitable but thirsty crops such as corn and sugar beets. Some farmers will have to go out of business. The amount of irrigated land already is declining in five of the seven states using this aquifer because of the high cost of pumping water from depths as great as 1,830 meters (6,000 feet).

If farmers in the Ogallala region began using water conservation measures and switched to crops with low water needs, depletion of the aquifer would be delayed. Since water is being depleted from this one-time deposit to provide 40% of the beef produced in the United States, each time Americans eat hamburgers or other forms of beef, they contribute to this loss of Earth capital. What do you think should be done?

Ogallala Aquifer

Figure 13-16 Ogallala Aquifer.

---

consumers have little incentive to conserve. Raising the price of water to reflect its true cost would provide powerful incentives for reducing water waste.

In the United States, the federal Bureau of Reclamation supplies one-fourth of the water used to irrigate land in the West under long-term contracts (typically 40 years) at greatly subsidized prices. For example, farmers getting subsidized water in the Central Valley Project of California have had to pay only $50 million, or 5%, of the project's $931-million cost over the last 40 years. A 1982 law says that cheap federal water should go only to farms of 389 hectares (960 acres) or less. The big growers have gotten around this by reorganizing their holdings into smaller tracts. In 1987, a single 389-hectare (960-acre) farm in the Central Valley of California received a water subsidy worth $1.8 million.

During the 1990s, hundreds of these long-term water contracts will be coming up for renewal. If Congress requires the Bureau of Reclamation to sharply raise the price of federally subsidized water to encourage investments in improving water efficiency, many of the water supply problems in the West could be eased.

Otherwise, water waste used to support unsustainable short-term economic growth will continue until the new contracts run out.

Outdated laws governing access and use of water resources also encourage unnecessary water waste (see Spotlight on p. 354).

Another reason that water waste in the United States is greater than necessary is that the responsibility for water resource management in a particular watershed is divided among many state and local governments rather than being handled by one authority. For example, the Chicago metropolitan area has 349 water supply systems, divided among some 2,000 local units of government over a six-county area.

In sharp contrast is the regional approach to water management used in England and Wales. The British Water Act of 1973 replaced more than 1,600 agencies with 10 regional water authorities based on natural watershed boundaries. In this integrated approach, each water authority owns, finances, and manages all water supply and waste treatment facilities in its region. The responsibilities of each authority include water pollu-

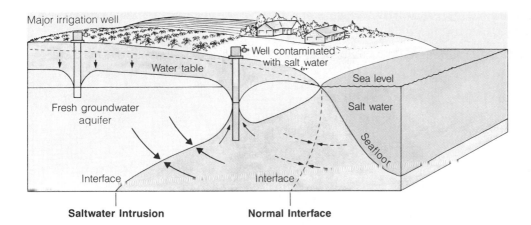

Major irrigation well

Water table

Well contaminated with salt water

Sea level

Fresh groundwater aquifer

Salt water

Seafloor

Interface

Interface

Saltwater Intrusion

Normal Interface

Figure 13-17 Saltwater intrusion along a coastal region. When the water table is lowered, the normal interface (dotted line) between fresh and saline groundwater moves inland (solid line).

tion control, water-based recreation, land drainage and flood control, inland navigation, and inland fisheries. Each water authority is managed by a group of elected local officials and a smaller number of officials appointed by the national government.

REDUCING IRRIGATION LOSSES Since irrigation accounts for 70% of water use and since almost two-thirds of that water is wasted, more efficient use of even a small amount of irrigation water frees water for other uses. Most irrigation systems distribute water from a groundwater well or a surface canal by downslope or gravity flow through unlined field ditches (Figure 13-19). This method is cheap as long as farmers in water-short areas don't have to pay the real cost of making this water available. However, it provides far more water than needed for crop growth, and at least 50% of the water is lost by evaporation and seepage. Such overwatering without adequate drainage also decreases crop yields by waterlogging and the buildup of salts in the soil (Figure 12-20).

Farmers could prevent seepage by placing plastic, concrete, or tile liners in irrigation canals. Lasers can also be used as a surveying aid to help level fields so that water gets distributed more evenly. Small check dams of earth and stone can be used to capture runoff from hillsides and channel this water to fields. Holding ponds can be used to store rainfall or to capture irrigation water for recycling to crops. Restoring deforested watersheds also leads to a more manageable flow of irrigation water, instead of a devastating flood (see Case Study on p. 342).

Farmers in LDCs can use inexpensive tube wells to withdraw groundwater for irrigation, watering livestock, and household use, as long as withdrawals don't exceed the natural recharge rate. In rural areas where there is no electricity, new energy-efficient Bentley pumps for these wells can be run by photovoltaic cells powered by the sun.

Many farmers served by the dwindling Ogallala Aquifer have switched from gravity flow canal sys-

tems to center-pivot sprinkler systems (Figure 13-20), which reduce water waste from 50% or more to 30%. Some farmers are switching to low-energy precision-application (LEPA) sprinkler systems. These systems cut water waste to about 25% by spraying water closer to the ground and in larger droplets than the conventional center-pivot system. They also reduce energy use and costs by 20% to 30%. However, because of the high initial costs, sprinklers are used on only about 1% of the world's irrigated land.

In the 1960s, highly efficient trickle or drip irrigation systems were developed in arid Israel. A network of perforated piping, installed at or below the ground surface, releases a small volume of water close to the roots of plants (Figure 13-21). This minimizes evaporation and seepage and cuts water waste to 10% to 20%. These systems are expensive to install but are economically feasible for high-profit fruit, vegetable, and orchard crops and for home gardens. They would become cost-effective in most areas if water prices were raised to reflect the true cost of this resource.

Irrigation efficiency can also be improved by computer-controlled systems that monitor soil moisture and irrigate only when necessary. Farmers can switch to crop varieties that are more water efficient, drought resistant, and salt tolerant. Also, organic farming techniques produce higher crop yields per hectare and require only one-quarter of the water and fertilizer used by conventional farming. Since 1950, Israel has used many of these techniques to decrease waste of irrigation water by about 84%, while expanding the country's irrigated land by 44%.

As supplies of fresh water become more scarce and cities take over much of the water formerly used for irrigation, carefully treated urban wastewater could be used for irrigation. Effluents from sewage treatment plants are rich in plant nutrients, mostly nitrates and phosphates. Presently, these nutrients are often dumped into waterways where they overfertilize aquatic plant life, deplete dissolved oxygen, kill fish, and disrupt aquatic ecosystems. It makes more sense

Laws regulating water access and use differ in the eastern and western parts of the United States (Figure 13-18). In most of the East, water use is based on the doctrine of **riparian rights**. Basically, this system of water law gives anyone whose land adjoins a flowing stream the right to use water from the stream as long as some is left for downstream landowners. However, as population and water-intensive land uses grow, there is often not enough water to meet the needs of all the people along a stream.

In the arid and semiarid West, the riparian system does not work, because large amounts of water are needed in areas far from major sources of surface water. In most of this region, the principle of **prior appropriation** regulates water use. In this first-come, first-served approach, the first user of water from a stream establishes a legal right for continued use of the amount originally withdrawn. If there is a shortage, later users are cut off in order, one by one, until there is enough water to satisfy the shares of the earlier users. Some areas of the United States have a combination of riparian and prior appropriation water rights (Figure 13-18).

To hold on to their prior appropriation rights, users within a particular state must keep on withdrawing and using a certain amount of water even if they don't need it—a use-it-or-lose-it approach. This discourages farmers from using water-conserving irrigation methods.

This use-it-or-lose-it rule does not apply to water bodies shared by

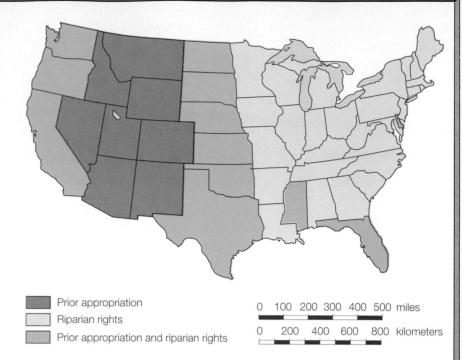

Prior appropriation

Riparian rights

Prior appropriation and riparian rights

0 100 200 300 400 500 miles

0   200   400   600   800 kilometers

Figure 13-18 Legal systems governing access to and use of water from rivers and streams in the continental United States.

two or more states. Water allocation between states is determined by interstate compacts and court decrees.

Most groundwater use is based on common law, which holds that subsurface water belongs to whoever owns the land above such water. This means that landowners can withdraw as much as they want to use on their land.

When many users tap the same aquifer, that aquifer becomes a common-property resource. Because of the tragedy of the commons (see Spotlight on p. 14), the multiple users may remove water at a faster rate than it is replaced by natural re-

charge. The largest users have little incentive to conserve and can deplete the aquifer for everyone.

Conservationists and many economists call for a change in laws allocating rights to surface and groundwater supplies, with emphasis on *water marketing*. They believe that farmers and other users who save water through conservation or switching to less-thirsty crops should be able to sell or lease the water they save to industries and cities rather than losing their rights to this water. What do you think should be done?

to return these nutrients to the land to fertilize trees, crops, and other vegetation. Israel is now using 35% of its municipal wastewater, mostly for irrigation, and plans to reuse 80% of this flow by the year 2000.

However, as long as government-subsidized water is available at low cost, farmers have little incentive to conserve it. Farmers in many parts of the world also have little incentive to conserve because they are charged according to the amount of land they irrigate,

regardless of how much water they use. In most parts of the world, water is our most underpriced resource.

WASTING LESS WATER IN INDUSTRY Manufacturing processes either can use recycled water or can be redesigned to use and waste less water. Japan and Israel lead the world in reducing water use and waste and recycling water in industry. For example, to produce 0.9 metric ton (1 ton) of paper, a paper mill in Hadera,

Figure 13-19 Gravity flow systems like this one in California irrigate most of the world's irrigated cropland, but only about 40% to 50% of the water actually gets to the crops.

Figure 13-20 Center-pivot irrigation systems like this one in Texas can reduce water consumed by seepage and evaporation to about 30%. Turbine pumps remove water from deep wells and feed it through huge water-propelled sprinklers that move in a huge circle and spray water on the land.

Figure 13-21 Drip irrigation greatly reduces water use and waste. A perforated pipe delivers a small volume of water close to the roots of plants in Rancho, California. For about $250, homeowners can install such a system to irrigate gardens and also add fertilizer. Plastic tubing is run to the plants, and a pressure regulator is used to reduce the flow rate. For another $50, a timer run by a computer chip and soil moisture sensor can be used to operate the system.

Israel, uses one-tenth as much water as most paper mills. Manufacturing aluminum from recycled scrap rather than virgin ores can reduce water needs by 97% percent.

Industry is the largest conserver of water. However, the potential for water recycling in U.S. manufacturing has hardly been tapped because the cost of water to many industries is subsidized by taxpayers through federally financed water projects. A higher, more realistic price would greatly stimulate water reuse and conservation in industry.

WASTING LESS WATER IN HOMES AND BUSINESSES Flushing toilets, washing hands, and bathing account for about 78% of the water used in a typical home in the United States. However, in the arid western United States and in dry Australia, watering lawns and gardens can use up to 80% of a household's daily water expenditure. Much of this water is unnecessarily wasted (Figure 13-22).

Leaks in pipes, water mains, toilets, bathtubs, and faucets waste an estimated 20% to 35% of water withdrawn from public supplies. Because water costs so little, in most places leaking water faucets are not repaired and large quantities of water are used to clean sidewalks and streets and to irrigate lawns and golf courses. Instead of being a status symbol, a green lawn in an arid or semiarid area should be viewed as a major ecological wrong and should be replaced with types of natural vegetation adapted to a dry climate.

Many cities offer no incentive to reduce leaks and waste. In New York City, for example, 95% of the residential units don't have water meters. Users are charged flat rates, with the average family paying less than $100 a year for virtually unlimited use of high-quality water. In Boulder, Colorado, the introduction of water meters reduced water use by more than one-third.

Commercially available systems can be used to purify and completely recycle wastewater from houses, apartments, and office buildings. Such a system can be leased and installed in a small shed outside a residence or building and can be serviced for a monthly fee about equal to that charged by most city water and sewer systems. In Tokyo, all the water used in Mitsubishi's 60-story office building is purified for reuse by an automated recycling system. In Michigan, a hotel saved about $750,000 in construction costs and water and sewer bills over a period of eight years by installing water-efficient toilets, faucets, and shower heads when it was built.

The University of Arizona's Casa del Agua (House of Water) is a demonstration project in which a house has been relandscaped and redesigned with water-

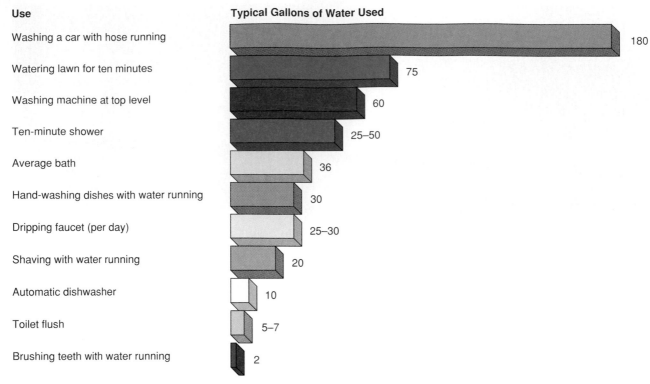

Use	Typical Gallons of Water Used
Washing a car with hose running	180
Watering lawn for ten minutes	75
Washing machine at top level	60
Ten-minute shower	25–50
Average bath	36
Hand-washing dishes with water running	30
Dripping faucet (per day)	25–30
Shaving with water running	20
Automatic dishwasher	10
Toilet flush	5–7
Brushing teeth with water running	2

Figure 13-22 Some ways domestic water is wasted in the United States. (Data from American Water Works Association)

saving and water-recycling devices. Rainfall is captured and used to irrigate plants and to provide water for some household uses. Gray water, generated from bath, shower, sinks, and the clothes washer, is stored, carefully treated, and reused for irrigation and other purposes.

FUTURE WATER MANAGEMENT GOALS Sustainable use of Earth's water resources involves developing an integrated approach to managing water resources and water pollution throughout each watershed and reducing or eliminating water subsidies so that its market price more closely reflects its true cost.

Doing this will require us to truly accept the fact that the environment that we now treat as separate parts — air, water, soil, life — is an interconnected whole. This will require unprecedented cooperation between communities, states, and countries. Each of us can contribute to bringing about this drastic change in the way we view and act in the world by reducing unnecessary water waste (see Individuals Matter inside the back cover). Trend is not destiny.

Water is more critical than energy. We have alternative sources of energy. But with water, there is no other choice.

EUGENE ODUM

DISCUSSION TOPICS

1. How do human activities increase the harmful effects of prolonged drought? How can those effects be reduced?

2. How do human activities contribute to flooding? How can those effects be reduced?

3. Explain why dams and reservoirs may lead to more flood damage than would have occurred if they had not been built. Should all proposed large dam and reservoir projects be scrapped? What criteria would you use in determining desirable projects?

4. Should the price of water for all uses in the United States be increased sharply to encourage water conservation? Explain. What effects might this have on the economy, on you, on the poor, on the environment?

5. List ten effective ways to conserve water on a personal level. Which, if any, of these practices do you now use or intend to use (see Individuals Matter inside the back cover)?

*6. In your community:
   a. What are the major sources of the water supply?
   b. How is water use divided among agricultural, industrial, power-plant cooling, and public uses? Who are the biggest consumers of water?
   c. What has happened to water prices during the past 20 years? Are they too low to encourage water conservation and reuse?
   d. What water supply problems are projected?
   e. How is water being wasted?

CHAPTER 14

FOOD RESOURCES

General Questions and Issues

1. How is food produced throughout the world?

2. What are the world's food problems?

3. Can increasing crop yields and cultivating more land solve the world's food problems?

4. How much food can we get from catching more fish and cultivating fish in aquaculture farms and ranches?

5. What can government policies, giving food aid, and redistributing land to the poor do to help solve the world's food problems?

6. How can agricultural systems in MDCs and LDCs be designed to be ecologically and economically sustainable?

Hunger is a curious thing: At first it is with you all the time, working and sleeping and in your dreams, and your belly cries out insistently, and there is a gnawing and a pain as if your very vitals were being devoured, and you must stop it at any cost. . . . Then the pain is no longer sharp, but dull, and this too is with you always.

KAMALA MARKANDAYA

GRICULTURE USES MORE of Earth's soil, water, plant, animal, and energy resources and causes more pollution and environmental degradation than any other human activity. By 2025, the world's population is expected to reach at least 8.6 billion. To feed these people, we must produce as much food during the next 30 years as was produced over the last 10,000 years since the dawn of agriculture.

Producing enough food to feed the world's population, however, is only one of a number of complex, interrelated food resource problems. Another serious problem is *food quality*—whether the food has enough proteins, vitamins, and minerals to prevent malnutrition. We must also have enough storage facilities to keep food from rotting or being eaten by pests after it is harvested. An adequate transportation and retail outlet system must be available to distribute and sell food throughout each country and the world.

There are more hungry people in the world today than at any time in human history, and their numbers are growing. Poverty is the leading cause of hunger and of premature death from lack of food and from poor food quality. Making sure the poor have enough land or income to grow or buy enough food is the key to reducing deaths from malnutrition and to helping the poor escape the poverty trap. Farmers must also have economic incentives to grow enough food to meet the world's needs.

Finally, the world's agricultural systems must be managed in sustainable ways to minimize the harm done to soil, air, water, and wildlife by the production and distribution of food. This means that we must not deplete or degrade the soil, water, and genetic resources or alter the fairly stable climate that supports the entire agricultural system.

14-1 World Agricultural Systems: How Is Food Produced?

PLANTS AND ANIMALS THAT FEED THE WORLD
Although about 80,000 species of plants are edible, only about 30 crops feed the world, and fewer than 20 produce 90% of our food. Four crops—wheat, rice, corn, and potato—make up more of the world's total food production than all others combined. Those four and most other crops we depend upon are annuals. That means that each year we must disturb the soil and plant new seeds. The rest of the food people eat is mainly fish, meat, and animal products such as milk, eggs, and cheese, obtained largely from 8 species of domesticated livestock.

Grain production provides about half the world's calories, with two out of three people in the world surviving on a primarily vegetarian diet. Meat and animal products are too expensive for most people, because of the loss of usable energy when an animal trophic level is added to a food chain (Figure 4-21).

As incomes rise, people consume more grain *indirectly*, in the form of meat, milk, eggs, cheese, and other products from grain-fed domesticated animals. In MDCs, almost half of the world's annual grain production (especially corn and soybeans) is fed to livestock. Thus, indirectly, the meat-eating third of humanity consumes nearly 40% of the world's grain. About one-third of the world's annual fish catch is converted into fish meal and fed to livestock.

PRINCIPAL TYPES OF AGRICULTURE Two types of agricultural systems are used most widely throughout the world to grow crops and raise livestock: industrialized agriculture and traditional subsistence and intensive agriculture (see Spotlight on p. 360).

Industrialized agriculture produces large quantities of a single type of crop or livestock for sale both within the country where it is grown and to other countries. Industrialized agriculture involves supplementing solar energy with large inputs of energy from fossil fuels, mostly oil and natural gas (used for crop drying and to produce fertilizer), water, commercial inorganic fertilizers, and pesticides. It is sometimes called *high-input agriculture*.

Industrialized agriculture, which is practiced on about 25% of all cropland, is widely used in MDCs and since the mid-1960s has spread to parts of some LDCs (Figure 14-1). It is supplemented by **plantation agriculture**, in which specialized cash crops, such as bananas, coffee, and cacao, are grown in tropical LDCs mostly for sale to MDCs.

Traditional subsistence agriculture produces enough crops or livestock for a farm family's survival and, in good years, a surplus to sell or put aside for hard times. Subsistence farmers supplement solar energy with energy from human labor and draft animals. Examples are shifting cultivation of small plots in tropical forests (Figure 2-4) and nomadic herding of livestock. With **traditional intensive agriculture**, farmers increase their inputs of labor, fertilizer, and water to produce enough food to feed their families and perhaps a surplus that can be sold (Figure 14-2). These forms of traditional agriculture are practiced by about 2.7 billion

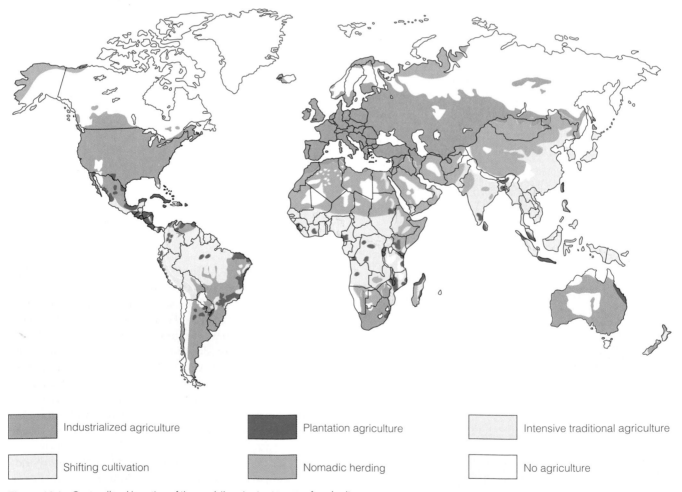

Industrialized agriculture   Plantation agriculture   Intensive traditional agriculture

Shifting cultivation   Nomadic herding   No agriculture

Figure 14-1 Generalized location of the world's principal types of agriculture.

Figure 14-2 Labor-intensive cultivation of rice in the Guan Kong province of China. Use of biological pest control and hand weeding has made expensive and harmful spraying with insecticides and pesticides unnecessary. Despite China's success, intensive farming of much of its land has caused extensive soil erosion, depletion of soil nutrients, falling water tables, and water pollution from widespread use of commercial inorganic fertilizers. If China cannot bring its population under control (Section 8-4), widespread famine may return.

Terry Qing/FPG International

people — half the people on Earth — who live in rural areas in LDCs.

The relative inputs of land, human and animal labor, fossil-fuel energy, and capital (money) needed to produce one unit of food energy by industrialized agriculture and the three types of traditional agriculture are shown in Figure 14-5.

INDUSTRIALIZED AGRICULTURE AND GREEN REVOLUTIONS Crop production is increased either by cultivating more land or by getting higher yields from existing cropland. Since 1950, most of the increase in world food production has come from increasing the yield per hectare in what is called a **green revolution**. This involves planting monocultures of scientifically bred plant varieties and applying large amounts of inorganic fertilizer, irrigation water, and pesticides (Figure 5-20).

Between 1950 and 1970, this approach led to dramatic increases in yields of major crops in the United States and most other industrialized countries, a phenomenon sometimes known as the *first green revolution* (Figure 14-6). In 1967, after 30 years of genetic research and trials, a modified version of the first green revolution began spreading to many LDCs. High-yield, fast-growing, dwarf varieties of rice and wheat, specially bred for tropical and subtropical climates, were introduced into several LDCs in what is known as the *second green revolution* (Figure 14-6).

The shorter, stronger, and stiffer stalks of the new varieties allow them to support larger heads of grain without toppling over (Figure 14-7). With large inputs of fertilizer, water, and pesticides, the wheat and rice yields of these varieties can be two to five times those of traditional varieties. The fast-growing varieties allow farmers to grow two, and even three, consecutive crops a year (multiple cropping) on the same parcel of land.

Nearly 90% of the increase in world grain output in the 1960s and about 70% of that in the 1970s were the result of the second green revolution. In the 1980s and 1990s, at least 80% of the additional production of grains is expected to be based on improved yields of existing cropland through the use of green revolution techniques.

These increases, however, depend heavily on fossil-fuel inputs to run machinery, produce and apply inorganic fertilizers and pesticides, and pump water for irrigation. Since 1950, agriculture's use of fossil fuels has increased 4-fold, the number of tractors has quadrupled, irrigated area has tripled, use of commercial fertilizer use has risen 17-fold, and use of pesticides has risen 32-fold. Green revolution agriculture, like other parts of industrialized societies, has become addicted to oil and now uses about 1/12 of the world's oil output.

These high inputs of energy, water, and pesticides can increase yields dramatically for a while. But plants are unable to use more than a certain amount of water and fertilizer, so at some point, further inputs produce no significant increases in yield and cost more than they are worth. Experience has shown that yields also decrease because of increased soil erosion, loss of soil fertility, aquifer depletion, salinization and waterlogging, desertification, pollution of surface water and groundwater, and genetic resistance of pests to pesticides.

Despite the successes of industrialized agriculture, its impressive productivity is at the mercy of oil prices and, like any form of agriculture, depends on favorable weather and a stable climate. Projected increases in the price of oil, changes in global climate, or both could disrupt agricultural production, cause sharp rises in food prices, and lead to mass starvation and disease.

INDUSTRIAL FARMERS	TRADITIONAL FARMERS	INDUSTRIAL FARMERS	TRADITIONAL FARMERS
Crop Production		**Meat and Animal Product Production**	
Grow large quantities of food for sale by investing a large amount of money, usually borrowed.	Grow enough food to feed their families, investing little, if any, money.	Produce large quantities of a single type of meat or animal product for sale by investing a large amount of money, often borrowed.	Produce enough meat and animal products to feed their families, investing little money. Usually have a surplus for sale or storage.
Buy scientifically bred hybrid seeds of a single crop variety and plant as a monoculture on a large field (Figure 5-20).	Plant a diversity of naturally available crop seeds on a small plot (Figure 2-4).	Use animal feedlots to raise hundreds to thousands of domesticated livestock in a small space (Figure 14-3). Give animals antibiotics and growth hormones to encourage rapid weight gain and to achieve efficient, factorylike production (Figure 14-4).	Use natural grassland and forests as sources of food and water for small groups of livestock. Often move from one place to another to provide enough food and water.
Buy equipment that is costly to purchase, operate, repair, or replace.	Make or buy simple equipment that costs little to run, repair, or replace.		
Often farm on flat, easily cultivated fields with fertile soil.	Often farm on easily erodible, hard-to-cultivate, mountainous highlands, drylands with fragile soils, and tropical forests with low-fertility soils.	Produce fatty meat that most consumers like but is considered unhealthful in large amounts.	Produce lean meat that is more healthful than fatty meat.
Increase crop yields by using irrigation and commercial inorganic fertilizers.	Increase crop yields by making efficient use of natural inputs of water and organic fertilizers.	Use enormous inputs of energy by burning fossil fuels for heating, cooling, pumping water, producing feed, and transporting supplies and livestock.	Use human and animal labor with no or low inputs of fossil fuels.
Plant one crop and use chemicals to kill pest species along with a variety of predators of pest species.	Plant a diversity of crops to provide numerous habitats for natural predators of pest species.		
Work against nature by using large amounts of fossil-fuel energy to keep a monoculture at an early stage of ecological succession.	Work with nature by allowing a diversity of crops to imitate natural ecological succession.	Produce large concentrations of animal wastes, which can wash into nearby surface water and contaminate it with disease-causing bacteria and excess plant nutrients (cultural eutrophication) and contaminate groundwater with nitrates.	Return nutrient-rich animal wastes to the soil where animals roam, or collect it and use it as organic fertilizer for growing crops, or dry it and burn it as a fuel for heating and cooking.
Do most work with farm machinery powered by fossil fuels (Figure 5-20).	Do work by hand (Figure 14-2) or with help from draft animals.		

INDUSTRIALIZED AGRICULTURE IN THE UNITED STATES Since 1940, U.S. farmers have more than doubled crop production while cultivating about the same amount of land. They have done this through industrialized agriculture coupled with a favorable climate and some of the world's most fertile and productive soils.

Farming has become *agribusiness* as large companies and increasingly larger family-owned farms have taken control of most of U.S. food production. About 56% of the country's food production comes from only 7% of its farms, and the U.S. Department of Agriculture projects that 1% of U.S. farms will account for 50% of all food production by the year 2000. Only 15 companies provide 60% of all farm supplies, and 6 companies buy up and sell about 95% of U.S. corn and wheat exports. Three corporations supply about 80% of U.S. beef.

Only about 2% of the U.S. population lives on the country's 2.1 million farms, and only about 650,000 Americans work full-time at farming. Yet, these people produce enough food to feed most of their fellow citi-

Figure 14-3 Feedlots like this huge one for cattle near Coalinga, California, increase production efficiency. However, they concentrate enormous amounts of animal wastes, which, without proper controls, can pollute groundwater with excessive levels of nitrates, and contribute to cultural eutrophication of nearby lakes and slow-moving streams. Beef cattle are usually moved to feedlots to be fattened a few weeks before slaughter. Other types of livestock, such as chickens, pigs, and calves raised for veal, are kept in automated feedlots from birth to death.

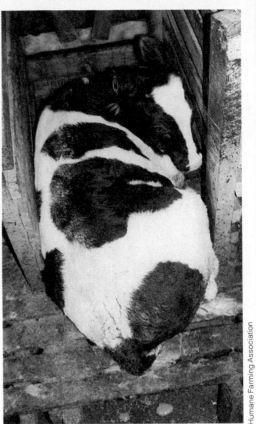

Figure 14-4 From shortly after birth until slaughter, this and other veal calves in Petaluma, California, are confined in small enclosures to ensure the tenderness of their meat. The reason that veal is so tender is that calves are never allowed to take a step.

zens better and at a lower percentage of their income than do farmers in any other country. Americans spend an average of 11% to 15% of their disposable income on food.

By contrast, people in much of the world spend 40% or more of their disposable income on food. The 1 billion people making up the poorest fifth of humankind typically spend 60% to 80% of their meager income on food and still don't have an adequate diet.

In addition, U.S. farmland, called the "breadbasket" of the world, produces enough grain to supply half the world's grain exports. In 1990, one U.S. farmer fed and clothed 120 persons at home and abroad, up from 58 persons in 1976. Only 0.08% of the world's population working on U.S. farms produces about 25% of the world's food and fiber.

About 23 million people—9% of the population—are involved in the U.S. agricultural system in activities ranging from growing and processing food to selling it at the supermarket. In total annual sales, the agricultural system is the biggest industry in the United States—bigger than the automotive, steel, and hous-

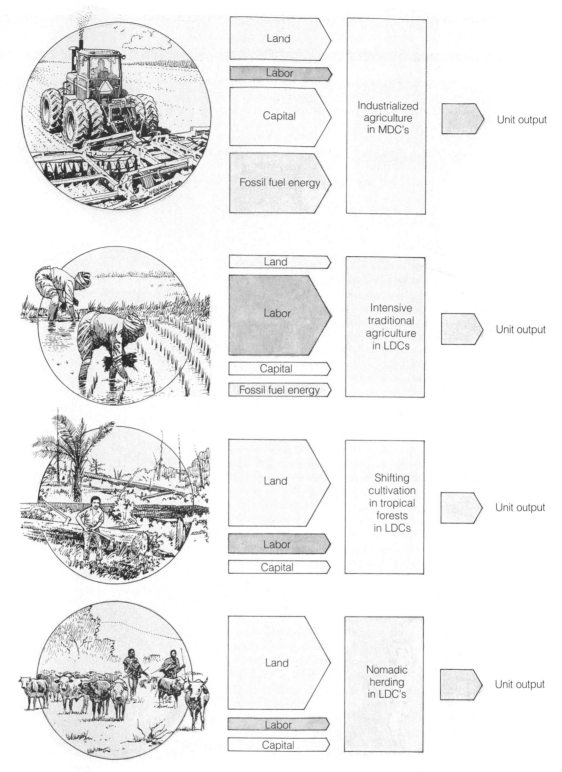

Figure 14-5 Relative inputs of land, labor, capital (money), and fossil-fuel energy to principal types of agricultural systems. The bottom three systems are labor-intensive types of traditional agriculture. An average of 60% of the people in LDCs are involved directly in producing food, compared with only 8% in MDCs (2% in the United States).

ing industries combined. It generates about 18% of the country's GNP (2% from farming, 2% from agricultural chemicals, and 14% from processing, marketing, and retail sales) and 19% of all jobs in the private sector, employing more people than any other industry.

U.S. farmers get an average of only 25 cents of every dollar spent on food in the United States, compared with 41 cents in 1950, but this return varies with different products. For each retail dollar spent, U.S. farmers receive about 64 cents for eggs, 58 cents for choice beef, 54 cents for chicken, 52 cents for milk, 9 cents for white bread, and 5 cents for lettuce.

The amount of agricultural chemicals used to support industrialized agriculture in the United States is

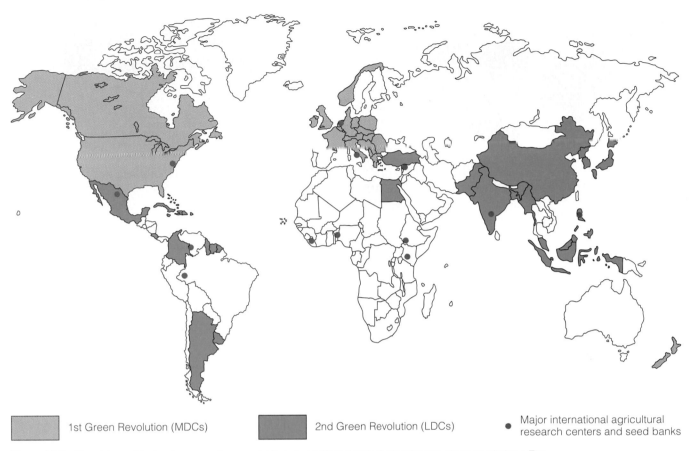

1st Green Revolution (MDCs)	2nd Green Revolution (LDCs)

● Major international agricultural research centers and seed banks

Figure 14-6 Countries achieving increases in crop yields per unit of land area during the two green revolutions. The first took place in MDCs between 1950 and 1970, and the second between 1967 and 1988 in LDCs with enough rainfall or irrigation capacity. Thirteen agricultural research centers and gene storage banks play a key role in developing high-yield crop varieties.

Figure 14-7 Two older parent strains of rice, PETA from Indonesia (center) and DGWG from China (right), were crossbred to yield IR-8 (left), a new, high-yield, semidwarf variety of rice used in the second green revolution.

phenomenal. Currently, the country uses about 18% of the commercial inorganic fertilizers and 45% of the pesticides produced worldwide each year.

The industrialization of agriculture in the United States and elsewhere was made possible by the low cost of energy, particularly oil (Figure 1-11). The gigantic American agricultural system consumes about 17% of all commercial energy used in the United States each year (Figure 14-8).

Most of this energy comes from oil, followed by natural gas used for drying and producing inorganic fertilizers. The prices of these crucial inputs are expected to rise sharply over the next two or three decades (see Case Study on p. 15 and Section 18-1).

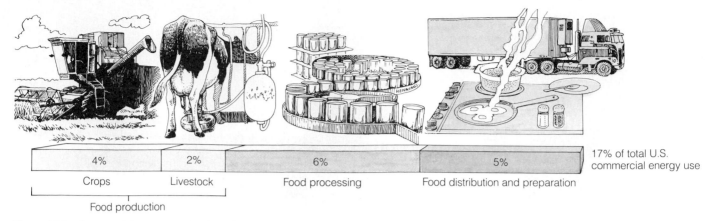

| 4% | 2% | 6% | 5% | 17% of total U.S. commercial energy use |
| Crops | Livestock | Food processing | Food distribution and preparation | |

Food production

Figure 14-8 Commercial energy use by the U.S. industrialized agriculture system. About 20% of the total energy used directly on farms to produce crops is for pumping irrigation water. On average, a piece of food eaten in the United States travelled 2,100 kilometers (1,300 miles). Processing food also requires large amounts of energy. For example, supplying orange juice takes four times more energy than providing fresh oranges that contain the same amount of juice.

Most plant crops in the United States provide more food energy than the energy (mostly from fossil fuels) used to grow them. However, raising animals for food requires much more fossil-fuel energy than the animals provide as food energy (Figure 14-9).

Energy efficiency is much worse if we look at the entire U.S. food system. Counting fossil-fuel energy inputs used to grow, store, process, package, transport, refrigerate, and cook all plant and animal food, *an average of about ten units of nonrenewable fossil-fuel energy is needed to put one unit of food energy on the table—an energy loss of nine units per unit of food energy produced*. By comparison, every unit of energy from the human labor of subsistence farmers provides at least one unit of food energy, and with traditional intensive farming, up to ten units of food energy.

Suppose everyone in the world ate a typical American diet consisting of food produced by industrialized agriculture. If the world's known oil reserves were used only for producing this food, those reserves would be depleted in less than 12 years. This indicates that the present world population already exceeds the capacity of known supplies of cultivatable land and petroleum to provide everyone with a U.S.-type diet using industrialized agriculture.

Suppose that fossil fuel, especially oil, suddenly becomes and remains scarce or much more expensive, as most energy experts believe will happen sometime between 1995 and 2010. The present industrialized agricultural system in MDCs would collapse, with a sharp drop in world food production and a rise in food prices, malnutrition, and famine.

Industrialized farming in the United States is truly big business and has made remarkable gains in food production and short-term economic gain. However, to environmentalists, it is an environmentally and economically unsustainable way to produce food. They call it *high-input unsustainable agriculture (HIUA)*, built upon depleting and degrading the soil and water Earth capital upon which the entire system depends.

EXAMPLES OF TRADITIONAL AGRICULTURE

Farmers in LDCs use various forms of traditional subsistence and intensive agriculture to grow crops on about 75% of the world's cultivated land (Figure 14-1). Many traditional farmers imitate nature by simultaneously growing a variety of crops on the same plot, a strategy called **interplanting**. This biological diversity reduces their chances of losing most or all of their year's food supply to pests, flooding, drought, or other disasters. Common interplanting strategies include

- **Polyvarietal cultivation**, in which a plot of land is planted with several varieties of the same crop.

- **Intercropping**, in which two or several different crops are grown at the same time on a plot—for example, a carbohydrate-rich grain that depletes soil nitrogen and a protein-rich legume that adds nitrogen to the soil. In Central America, farmers have interplanted squash, beans, and maize for centuries. The squash provides ground cover that reduces erosion and weed growth, the beans enrich the soil with nitrogen, and the maize provides stalks for the beans to grow on.

- **Agroforestry**, a variation of intercropping in which crops and trees are planted together—for example, a grain or legume crop planted around fruit-bearing orchard trees or in rows between fast-growing trees or shrubs that can be used for fuelwood or to add nitrogen to the soil.

- **Polyculture**, a more complex form of intercropping in which a large number of different plants maturing at different times are planted together (see Case Study on p. 365). If cultivated properly, these "natural supermarkets and drugstores" can provide food, medicines, fuel, and natural pesticides and fertilizers on a sustainable basis.

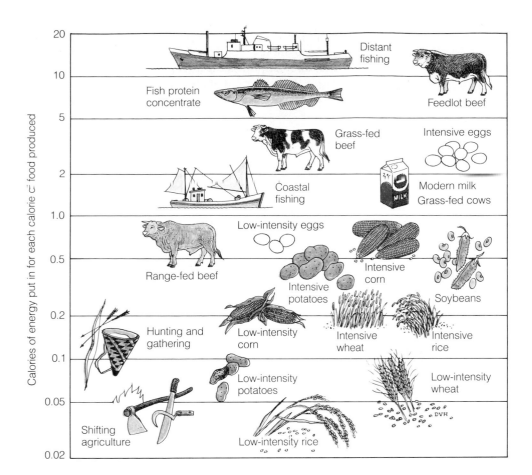

Figure 14-9 Energy input needed to produce one unit of food energy in different types of food production.

CASE STUDY Small-Scale, Ecologically Sustainable Polyculture in the Philippines

In the Philippines, many subsistence-farming families use small-scale polyculture to feed themselves. Typically, they harvest crops throughout the year by planting a small plot with a mixture of fast-maturing grains and vegetables, slow-maturing perennials such as papayas and bananas, and slow-maturing tubers such as cassavas, taros, and sweet potatoes.

The diverse root systems at different depths beneath the ground capture soil nutrients and soil moisture efficiently and reduce the need for supplemental organic fertilizer

Note: The information in this case study is based on research carried out by geographer David L. Clawson at the University of New Orleans (see Further Readings).

(usually home-generated chicken manure) and irrigation water. Year-round coverage with plants protects the soil from wind and water erosion.

The diversity of habitats for natural predators means that crops don't need to be sprayed with insecticides to control pests. Weeds have difficulty in competing for plant nutrients with the multitude of crop plants. As a result, weeds can be removed fairly easily by hand with no herbicide use.

Various crops are harvested throughout year, so there is always something to eat or perhaps to sell. Crop diversity also provides insurance against unexpected weather changes. If one crop fails because of too much or too little rain, another crop may survive or even thrive.

This approach also spreads the need for labor throughout the year.

Most of the crops produced in this particular system have little market value because they are high in starch and low in protein. Nevertheless, using their own hand labor, a typical Filipino farming family can supply most of the food they need with this system without borrowing any money.

Although small-scale farmers using mechanized, green revolution agriculture can produce enough to sell some of their their crops, many of them have such large debts that they go bankrupt. They then lose their land and can no longer feed their families by farming.

14-2 World Food Problems

THE GOOD NEWS ABOUT FOOD PRODUCTION
World grain production expanded 2.6-fold between 1950 and 1984, and per capita production rose by almost 40%. During the same period, average food prices, adjusted for inflation, dropped by 25%, and the amount of food traded in the world market quadrupled. Most of the increase in food production since 1950 came from increases in crop yields per hectare by means of improved labor-intensive traditional agriculture in many LDCs (Figure 14-2) and energy-intensive industrialized agriculture in MDCs and some LDCs (Figure 14-6).

THE BAD NEWS ABOUT FOOD PRODUCTION
The impressive improvements in world food production disguise the fact that per capita grain production declined between 1950 and 1990 in 43 LDCs (22 in Africa) containing one of every seven persons on Earth. In Africa, per capita food production dropped 28% between 1960 and 1990 and is projected to drop another 30% during the next 25 years (see Case Study on p. 367). In Latin America, it has declined 16% since 1981 and in India 24% since 1983.

Thus, population growth is outstripping food production in areas in which 2 billion people live (Figure 14-10). For the world as a whole, the annual growth in grain production from 1984 to 1990 was 1%, while that of population was 1.8%. Most of the world's 183 countries now require food imports from other countries, primarily the United States, Canada, Australia, Argentina, and France.

Excess grain reserves set aside each year for future shortfalls are considered the best short-term measure of food security. To avoid volatile changes in food prices, these reserves must be able to supply food for at least 60 days. Between 1987 and 1991, grain reserves fell from a 102-day supply to only a 66-day supply, precariously close to the danger point.

Another disturbing trend is that the rate of increase in world per capita food production declined during each of the past three decades. It rose 15% between 1950 and 1960, 7% between 1960 and 1970, and only 4% between 1970 and 1980. Between 1984 and 1989, per capita food production fell by 14%. This trend is caused by a combination of population increase, a decrease in yields per unit of land area for some crops cultivated by industrialized agriculture, a levelling off or a drop in food production in some countries, unsustainable use of soil and water, and widespread drought in 1987 and 1988.

FOOD QUANTITY AND QUALITY: UNDERNUTRITION, MALNUTRITION, AND OVERNUTRITION
Poor people who cannot grow or buy enough food to provide them with the basic minimum of calories (2,700

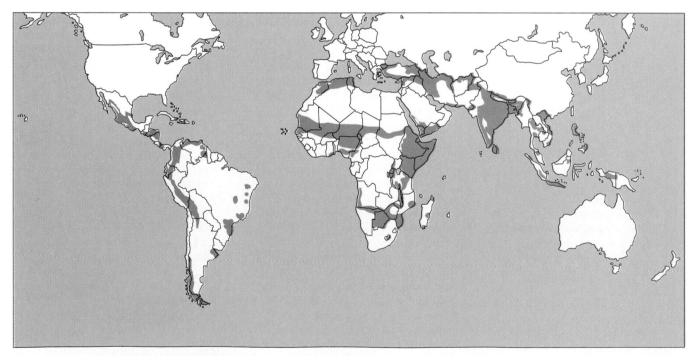

Figure 14-10 Areas where population may exceed the capacity of the land to provide enough food to meet minimum needs. (Data from United Nations and World Resources Institute)

In 1970, Africa was essentially self-sufficient in food. Since then, rapid population growth and other factors have led to a tragic breakdown of life-support systems in Africa, where thousands die each day from malnutrition or hunger-related diseases — making it the world's nutritional "basket case." Since 1985, one of every four Africans has been fed with grain imported from abroad — a dependence likely to increase.

Average per capita food production is lowest in most of the 47 African countries south of the Sahara, an area known as *sub-Saharan Africa*, where 76% of the continent's people live (Figure 14-11). Famine has been especially severe in a zone known as the *Sahel* (an Arabic word meaning edge of desert), which runs horizontally through the seven countries nearest the desert. In sub-Saharan Africa, about 160 million people — 30% of the population — suffer from chronic hunger and malnutrition, both of which are spreading and intensifying each year.

This worsening situation in much of Africa is caused by a number of interacting factors:

- The fastest population growth rate of any continent (Figure 8-3), with 1 million more mouths to feed every three weeks and its population projected to more than double between 1990 and 2020.

- A 17-year drought. Rainfall can vary by as much as 40% from year to year, and prolonged droughts are common. Rainfall is seasonal, and when it comes, it is heavy and can cause extensive soil erosion and leaching of soil nutrients.

- Poor natural endowment of productive soils in many areas. Three-tenths of the continent is covered by desert or is too sandy for crops.

- Little use of the green revolution in Africa (Figure 14-6), where both money and water are in short supply. Also, most of the green revolution research involved wheat and rice (Figure

(continued)

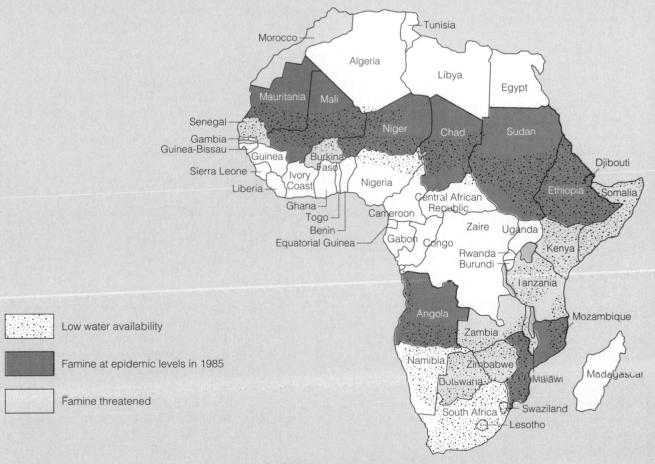

Figure 14-11 African countries suffering from low per capita food production, famine, and poor water availability. These conditions are caused by a combination of rapid population growth, prolonged drought, land misuse, war, and ineffective water and soil resource management. (Data from UN Food and Agriculture Organization)

14-7), which are not major crops in Africa.

- Overgrazing, deforestation, soil erosion, and desertification in many areas. The result is a dust bowl in the Sahel, which has some of the most severe wind erosion on Earth.

- Depletion of fuelwood, which provides 80% of Africa's energy (Figure 10-13). In Africa, 29 trees are cut for each 1 that is replanted.

- Poor food distribution systems.

- Governments that often keep food prices low to prevent urban unrest, giving rural farmers little incentive to grow more crops.

- Social unrest and frequent wars within and between some countries.

- Increasing dependence on food imports that has helped raise Africa's foreign debt eightfold between 1974 and 1990 to $210 billion — equal to nearly half the continent's annual income. The region's interest bill is $9 billion a year. Financial assistance to sub-Saharan Africa on a per person basis is the highest in the world, but heavy foreign debt cancels out many of the benefits from such aid.

- Severe underinvestment and lack of interest by African governments, MDCs, and international aid agencies in rural agriculture and family planning. Only a few countries, including Botswana, Mauritius, and Zimbabwe, have active family-planning policies.

- Government policies designed to subsidize urban dwellers at the expense of the rural poor, who make up 71% of Africa's population.

- Lack of legal rights to land or access to credit for women, who produce at least 70% (some say 85%) of Africa's food and manage half of the farms, thus giving them little incentive or ability to increase food productivity.

- Poor use of foreign aid, with funds traditionally used to raise cash crops on irrigated land, mostly for export, rather than for improving dryland farming, growing food for domestic use, conserving soil and water resources, and replanting trees.

Unless African governments and donors of foreign aid address this complex mix of environmental, political, and economic problems, the likelihood of reducing environmental degradation and famine is slight.

This will require investments in population regulation, debt forgiveness, sustainable agriculture involving alley cropping (Figure 12-16) and agroforestry, soil and water conservation, use of fertilizers to build up deficient soil nutrients, sustainable forestry, rural development, improvement of conditions for women, and allowing local people to participate in the planning and execution of aid projects.

Projects in some of the sub-Saharan countries show that food and fuel production can be greatly increased by such changes, which can be spread rapidly through networks of village self-help cooperatives with active participation and leadership by women (Figure 10-21). In 30 of the 47 countries of the sub-Saharan region, government controls and ownership are being loosened and farmers are being allowed to get higher prices for food.

There is hope for Africa, but time for action is running out. It has already run out for many of its people who die prematurely or who become environmental refugees (Figure 13-7) because population has outstripped the carrying capacity of the land (Figure 14-10).

---

calories per day for men and 2,000 calories per day for women) suffer from **undernutrition**. On average, people in the richest countries eat 30% to 40% more calories than they need and those in the poorest countries get 10% less than they need.

For good health and immunity to infectious diseases, people need not only a certain number of calories but also food quality that provides them with the proper amounts of protein (41 grams per adult a day), carbohydrates, fats, vitamins, and minerals. Because most poor people are forced to live on a low-protein, high-starch diet of grains such as wheat, rice, or corn, they often suffer from **malnutrition**, or deficiencies of protein and other key nutrients.

Many of the world's desperately poor people suffer from both undernutrition (insufficient food quantity) and malnutrition (poor food quality). Chronic malnutrition and undernutrition causes people to become weak, confused, and listless. It can also stunt growth, impair mental functions (especially in children under age 3), damage the immune system, and increase susceptibility to and death from infectious diseases, such as diarrhea, measles, flu, diphtheria, pneumonia, and tuberculosis that rarely kill well-nourished people. Malnutrition can also cause various nutritional-deficiency diseases (see Spotlight on p. 370).

According to the World Health Organization, about 1.3 billion people — one of every four on Earth — are

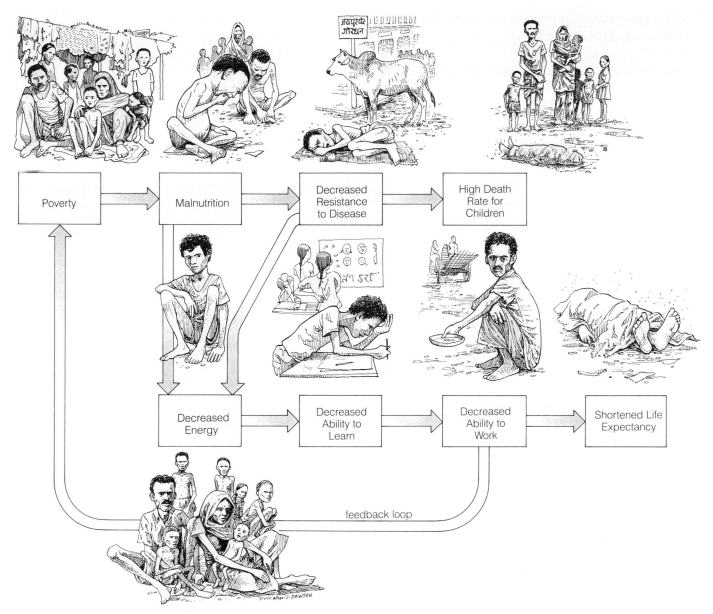

Figure 14-12 Interactions among poverty, malnutrition, and disease form a tragic cycle that tends to perpetuate such conditions in succeeding generations of families.

underfed and undernourished because they are too poor to grow or buy the quantity and quality of food they need. According to the World Bank, 630 million people get less than 80% of their basic needs of calories, nutrients, or both.

Each year, 20 to 40 million people (some say 60 million)—half of them children under age 5—die prematurely from undernutrition, malnutrition, or normally nonfatal infections and diseases worsened by malnutrition. *Every two to five days, hunger-related causes kill as many people as the atomic bomb killed at Hiroshima.* The World Health Organization estimates that diarrhea alone kills at least 5 million children under age 5 each year. Many malnourished children who survive

to adulthood become locked in a tragic *malnutrition-poverty cycle* that continues these conditions in each succeeding generation (Figure 14-12).

Officials of the United Nations Children's Fund (UNICEF) estimate that between half and two-thirds of the worldwide annual childhood deaths from undernutrition, malnutrition, and associated infections and diseases could be prevented at an average annual cost of only $5 to $10 per child—10 to 19 cents a week. This life-saving program would involve the following simple measures:

- immunizing against childhood diseases such as measles

The two most widespread nutritional-deficiency diseases are marasmus and kwashiorkor. **Marasmus** (from the Greek, "to waste away") occurs when a diet is low in both total energy (calories) and protein. Most victims of marasmus are infants in poor families in which children are not breastfed or in which food quantity and quality are insufficient after the children are weaned.

A child suffering from marasmus typically has a bloated belly, a thin body, shriveled skin, wide eyes, and an old-looking face (Figure 1-3). If the child is treated in time with a balanced diet, most of these effects can be reversed.

Kwashiorkor (meaning "displaced child" in a West African dialect) occurs in infants and children one to three years old who suffer from severe protein deficiency, usually after the arrival of a new baby deprives them of breast milk. The displaced child's diet changes from highly nutritious breast milk to grain or sweet potatoes, which provide enough calories but not enough protein.

Children suffering from kwashiorkor have skin swollen with fluids, bloated abdomens, lethargy, liver damage, hair loss, diarrhea, stunted growth, possible mental retardation, and irritability. If such malnutrition is not prolonged, most of the effects can be cured with a balanced diet.

Each of us must have a daily intake of small amounts of vitamins that cannot be made in the human body. Although balanced diets, vitamin-fortified foods, and vitamin supplements have greatly reduced the number of vitamin-deficiency diseases in MDCs, millions of cases occur each year in LDCs. For example, each year more than 500,000 children in LDCs are partially or totally blinded because their diet lacks vitamin A.

Other nutritional-deficiency diseases are caused by the lack of certain minerals, such as iron and iodine. Too little iron causes anemia. Anemia causes fatigue, makes infection more likely, increases a woman's chances of dying in childbirth, and increases an infant's chances of dying from infection during its first year of life. In tropical regions of Asia, Africa, and Latin America, iron-deficiency anemia affects about 10% of the men, more than half of the children, two-thirds of the pregnant women, and about half of the other women.

Too little iodine in the diet can cause goiter, an abnormal enlargement of the thyroid gland in the neck, which leads to deafness if untreated. It affects up to 80% of the population in the mountainous areas of Latin America, Asia, and Africa, where soils are deficient in iodine and there is no access to seafood.

- encouraging breastfeeding
- preventing dehydration from diarrhea by giving infants a solution of a fistful of sugar and a pinch of salt in a glass of water
- preventing blindness by giving people a small vitamin A capsule twice a year at a cost of about 75 cents per person
- providing family planning services to help mothers space births at least two years apart
- increasing education of women, with emphasis on nutrition, sterilization of drinking water, and child care

While 15% of the people in LDCs suffer from severe undernutrition and malnutrition, about 15% of the people in MDCs suffer from **overnutrition**, an excessive intake of food (especially fats) that can cause obesity, or excess body fat, in people who do not suffer from glandular or other disorders that promote obesity.

Overnourished people exist on diets high in calories, cholesterol-containing saturated fats (especially from red meat), salt, sugar, and processed foods, and low in unprocessed fresh vegetables, fruits, and fiber. Partly because of these dietary choices, overweight people have significantly higher than normal risks of diabetes, high blood pressure, stroke, heart disease, kidney disease, arthritis, and some types of cancer.

Overnutrition is associated with at least two-thirds of the deaths in the United States each year. While 20 to 40 million people die each year from hunger or hunger-related diseases and 1.6 billion people suffer from chronic hunger, at least 38 million overweight Americans spend $5 billion a year on diet books, diet foods, and diet programs.

Thousands of Chinese villagers have been monitored in the world's largest study of diet and health. Early results indicate that the healthiest diet for humans is nearly vegetarian, with only 10% to 15% of calories coming from fat. Such a diet is gentler to the earth and to the body than the typical meat-based diet with 40% of the calories coming from fats.

There is also concern over possible harmful effects from some of the chemicals, called **food additives**, that are added to processed foods for sale in grocery stores and restaurants to retard spoilage, to enhance flavor, color, and texture, and to provide missing vitamins or other nutrients (see Spotlight on p. 371).

HUNGER AND POVERTY The world produces more than enough food to meet the basic calorie needs of every person on Earth. Indeed, if distributed equally, the grain currently produced in the world would provide enough calories to give 6 billion people — the projected world population for the year 1998 — a subsistence diet. The world's supply of food, however, is not now produced or distributed equally among the world's people, nor will it be, because of differences in soil, climate, political and economic power, and average income throughout the world.

In contrast, if the world's food were used to give everyone the typical diet of a person in a developed country with 30% of the calories coming from meat, it would support only 2.5 billion people. That is less than half the present world population and only one-fourth of the 10 billion people projected sometime in the next century (Figure 1-2). *Thus, poverty — not lack of food production — is the chief cause of hunger, malnutrition, and premature death from hunger-related diseases throughout the world.*

Increases in worldwide total food production and food production per person often hide widespread differences in food supply and quality between and within countries. For example, about one-third of the world's hungry live in India, even though it is self-sufficient in food production. Nearly half of its population is too poor to buy or grow enough food to meet basic needs, and India's population increases by 17 million each year. Also, India's increase in food production since 1970 has been based on mining much of its soils and groundwater. An estimated two-thirds of its land is threatened by erosion, water shortages, and salinization. This, coupled with population growth, may mean that India will again suffer from famine in the 1990s and beyond.

In more fertile and urbanized southern Brazil, the average daily food supply per person is high. However, in Brazil's semiarid, less fertile northeastern interior, many people are severely underfed. Overall, almost two out of three Brazilians suffer from malnutrition (see Case Study on p. 225 and Figure 1-3).

Food is also unevenly distributed within families. In poor families, the largest part of the food supply goes to men working outside the home. Children (ages 1–5) and women (especially pregnant women and nursing mothers) are the most likely to be underfed and malnourished.

MDCs also have pockets of poverty and hunger. A 1985 report by a task force of doctors estimated that at least 20 million people (12 million children and 8 million adults) — 1 out of every 11 Americans — were hungry, mostly because of cuts in food stamps and other forms of government aid since 1980. A 1991 study revealed that 1 out of 8 U.S. families with children under the age of 12 experience hunger due to poverty. The highest percentage of hunger was found in Mississippi, the District of Columbia, Arkansas, Alabama, and New Mexico.

In 1989, the UN World Food Commission reported that progress in fighting hunger, malnutrition, and poverty came to a halt or was reversed in many parts of the world during the 1980s. Without a widespread increase in income and access to land, the number of chronically hungry and malnourished people in the world could increase in the 1990s and beyond.

SPOTLIGHT Food Additives

In the United States, at least 2,800 chemicals are deliberately added to processed foods, with sales of these food additives amounting to $4.5 billion a year. Some of these food additives are useful in extending shelf life and preventing food poisoning, but most are added to improve appearance and sales.

The presence of synthetic chemical additives does not necessarily mean that a food is harmful, and the fact that a food is completely natural is no guarantee it is safe. A number of natural or totally unprocessed foods contain potentially harmful toxic substances.

It was not until 1958 that federal laws required that the safety of any new food additive be established by the manufacturer and approved by the Food and Drug Administration (FDA) before the additive could be put into common use. Today, the manufacturer of a new additive must carry out extensive toxicity testing, costing up to $1 million per item, and submit the results to the FDA for evaluation.

However, these federal laws did not apply to the hundreds of additives in use before 1958. Instead of making expensive, time-consuming tests, the FDA drew up a list of the food additives in use in 1958, and asked several hundred experts for their professional opinions on the safety of these substances. A few substances were removed, and in 1959 a list of the remaining 415 substances was published as the "generally recognized as safe," or GRAS (pronounced "grass"), list. Since 1959, further testing has led the FDA to ban several substances on the original GRAS list.

Since 1958, federal law has prohibited the deliberate use of any food additive that has been shown in tests to cause cancer in laboratory animals or in people. This requirement is absolute, allowing for no extenuating circumstances or consideration of benefits versus risks. However, between 1958 and 1990, the FDA used this amendment to ban only nine chemicals.

The food industry would like to see this requirement removed, and some scientists and politicians want it modified to allow a consideration of benefits versus risks. Instead of revoking this requirement, some scientists feel it should be strengthened and expanded to include additives that cause birth defects or genetic mutations in test animals or in people. These critics cite the FDA's infrequent use of the clause as evidence that the law is too weak.

ENVIRONMENTAL EFFECTS OF PRODUCING FOOD Both industrialized agriculture and traditional agriculture have a number of harmful impacts on the air, soil, and water resources that sustain all life (see Spotlight on p. 372).

Industrialized Agriculture

- Soil erosion and loss of soil fertility through poor land use, failure to practice soil conservation techniques, and too little use of organic fertilizers (Section 12-3).

- Salinization and waterlogging of heavily irrigated soils (Figure 12-20).

- Reduction in the number and diversity of nutrient-recycling soil microorganisms from heavy use of pesticides and commercial inorganic fertilizers and soil compaction by large tractors and other farm machinery.

- Air pollution caused by dust blown off cropland that is not kept covered with vegetation (Figure 12-9) and from overgrazed rangeland (Figure 12-12). The 1.4 billion metric tons (1.5 billion tons) of particulate soil air pollutants that blow off agricultural fields and overgrazed land dwarf particulate air pollution from all other sources.

- Air pollution from droplets of pesticide sprayed from planes or by ground sprayers and blown into the air from plants and soil.

- Air pollution caused by the extraction, processing, transportation, and combustion of enormous amounts of fossil fuels used in industrialized agriculture (Figures 14-8 and 7-17).

- Pollution of estuaries and deep ocean zones with oil from offshore wells and tankers and from improper disposal of oil, the main fossil fuel used in industrialized agriculture.

- Pollution of streams, lakes, and estuaries and killing of fish and shellfish from pesticide runoff.

- Depletion of groundwater aquifers by excessive withdrawals for irrigation (Figure 13-15).

- Pollution of groundwater caused by leaching of water-soluble pesticides, nitrates from commercial inorganic fertilizers, and salts from irrigation water.

- Overfertilization of lakes and slow-moving rivers caused by runoff of nitrates and phosphates in commercial inorganic fertilizers, livestock animal wastes, and food-processing wastes.

- Sediment pollution of surface waters caused by erosion and runoff from farm fields and animal feedlots (Figure 5-29).

- Loss of genetic diversity of plants caused by clearing biologically diverse grasslands and forests and replacing them with monocultures of single crop varieties (Figure 5-20). Expansion of agriculture accounts for about 85% of the worldwide destruction of forests each year (Chapter 10).

- Endangerment and extinction of animal wildlife from loss of habitat when grasslands and forests are cleared and wetlands are drained for farming.

- Depletion and extinction of commercially important species of fish caused by overfishing.

- Threats to human health from nitrates in drinking water and pesticides in drinking water, food, and the atmosphere.

Traditional Subsistence and Intensive Agriculture

- Soil erosion and rapid loss of soil fertility caused by clearing and cultivating steep mountain highlands without terracing (Figure 12-10), using shifting cultivation in tropical forests without leaving the land fallow long enough to restore soil fertility (Figure 2-4), overgrazing of rangeland (Figure 12-12) and deforestation to provide cropland or fuelwood (Figure 10-2).

- Increased frequency and severity of flooding in lowlands when mountainsides are deforested (see Case Study on p. 342).

- Desertification caused by cultivation of marginal land with unsuitable soil or terrain, overgrazing, deforestation, and failure to use soil conservation techniques (see Case Study on p. 320).

- Air pollution caused by dust blown from cropland not kept covered with vegetation and from overgrazed rangeland (Figure 12-12).

- Sediment pollution of surface waters caused by erosion and runoff from farm fields, overgrazed rangeland, and deforested land.

- Endangerment and extinction of animal wildlife caused by loss of habitat when grasslands and forests are cleared for farming.

- Threats to human health from flooding intensified by poor land use and from human and animal wastes discharged or washed into irrigation ditches and sources of drinking water.

14-3 Methods of Increasing World Food Production

INCREASING CROP YIELDS Agricultural experts expect most future increases in crop production to come from increased yields per hectare on existing cropland and from expansion of green revolution technology to other parts of the world. One promising development, after over 40 years of research, is triticale, a new cereal grain produced by crossbreeding wheat and rye. This grain can flourish under a variety of conditions, including poor soils and cold and hot climates, and by 1990 was being grown on more than 1.5 million hectares (3.7 million acres) in 32 countries. But triticale is subject to some diseases, and its genetic resistance to various diseases could be broken down if it is grown over large areas.

Agricultural scientists are working to create new green revolutions—or *gene revolutions*—by using genetic engineering and other forms of biotechnology (see Pro/Con on p. 161). Over the next 20 to 40 years, they hope to breed high-yield plant strains that have greater resistance to insects and disease, thrive on less fertilizer, make their own nitrogen fertilizer like legumes (Figure 4-30), do well in slightly salty soils, withstand drought, and make more efficient use of solar energy during photosynthesis.

If even a small fraction of the research and development of genetically engineered crops and livestock is successful, the world could experience rapid and enormous increases in crop production before the middle of the next century. However, some analysts point to several factors that have limited the spread and long-term success of the green revolutions:

- Without huge doses of fertilizer and water, green revolution crop varieties produce yields no higher and often lower than those from traditional strains. Without good soil, water, and weather, new genetically engineered crop strains will fail.

- So far, plants have been far less responsive to genetic engineering than animals. The entire process, from gene transfer to widespread planting of a new crop variety, can take as long as conventional crossbreeding (typically, 5 to 15 years).

- Areas without enough rainfall or irrigation water or with poor soils cannot benefit from the new varieties; that is why the second green revolution has not spread to many arid and semiarid areas (Figure 14-6).

- Increasingly larger and thus more expensive inputs of fertilizer, water, and pesticides eventually produce little or no increase in crop yields as the J-shaped curve of crop productivity reaches limits and is converted into an S-shaped curve.

- Without careful land use and environmental controls (Section 9-4), degradation of water and soil can limit the long-term ecological and economic sustainability of green revolutions.

- The cost of genetically engineered crop strains is too high for most of the world's subsistence farmers in LDCs. Also, LDCs are not being compensated adequately for the genetic strains that scientists collect from their countries and use to produce patented seed varieties.

- The severe and increasing loss of Earth's biological diversity from deforestation and destruction and degradation of other ecosystems, and replacement of a diverse mixture of natural crop varieties with monoculture crops, limit the future success of crossbreeding and genetic engineering (see Spotlight on p. 374).

CULTIVATING MORE LAND Despite our technological cleverness, only about 11% of Earth's land area is suitable for growing crops. The rest is covered by ice, is too dry or too wet, is too hot or too cold, is too steep, or has unsuitable soils for growing crops. Currently, we are growing crops on about half of the world's potential cropland. The other half is used for grazing land or is covered by forests.

Some agricultural experts have suggested that farmers could more than double the world's cropland by clearing tropical forests and irrigating arid lands, mostly in Africa, South America, and Australia (Figure 14-13). Others believe only a small portion of these lands can be cultivated because most are too dry or too remote or lack productive soils.

Even if more cropland were developed, much of it would be on marginal land that would require large and expensive inputs of fertilizer, water, and energy. Also, these possible increases in cropland would not offset the projected loss of almost one-third of today's cultivated cropland from erosion, overgrazing, waterlogging, salinization, mining, and urbanization. Since 1979, China, India, and the Soviet Union—three of the world's largest food producers—have each lost about 13% of their grain-producing cropland to erosion, soil degradation, and nonagricultural uses.

Pollution is also reducing crop yields on existing cropland. In the United States, air pollution by ozone formed in the troposphere reduced harvests of crops by at least 5% during the 1980s. Other air pollutants, such as sulfur dioxide and nitrogen oxides, have also damaged crops in the United States and other MDCs. Yields of some crops and populations of marine phytoplankton that support fish and shellfish used as food have been reduced by depletion of ozone in the stratosphere (Figures 11-6 and 11-7).

Scientists can crossbreed varieties of plant and animal life (Figure 14-7), and genetic engineers can move genes from one organism to another, but they need the genetic materials found in Earth's existing plants and animals to do so. By the year 2000, the Food and Agriculture Organization estimates that two-thirds of all seed planted in LDCs will be of uniform strains. This genetic uniformity increases the vulnerability of food crops to pests and diseases. This, plus widespread species extinction, severely limits the potential of future green and gene revolutions.

In the mid-1970s, for example, a valuable wild corn species was barely saved from extinction. When this strain was discovered, only a few thousand stalks were surviving in three tiny patches in South Central Mexico that were about to be cleared by squatter cultivators and commercial loggers. This wild species is the only known perennial strain of corn. Crossbreeding it with commercial varieties of corn could reduce the need for yearly plowing and sowing, which would reduce

soil erosion, water use, and energy use.

Even more important, this strain of wild corn has built-in genetic resistance to four of the eight major viruses that affect corn; corn breeders have not been able to breed such resistance to these diseases into commercial corn strains. Using this strain to add immunity to commercial corn strains could save $500 million a year in corn lost to these diseases.

This wild corn rescued in the nick of time also grows in habitats that are cooler and damper than established corn lands. Breeding in these genetic traits could expand the types of land used to grow corn by up to 10%. Overall, the genetic benefits supplied by this wild plant could total several billion dollars a year.

In Sri Lanka, farmers grew some 2,000 traditional varieties of rice as recently as 1959. Today, only 5 principal varieties are grown. In India, which once had 30,000 varieties of rice, more than 75% of rice production now comes from fewer than 10 varieties.

Wild varieties of the world's most important plants can be collected and stored in gene banks, agricultural research centers (Figure 14-6), and botanical gardens, but space and money severely limit the number of species that can be preserved in those facilities. Many species, however, cannot be stored successfully in gene banks, and accidents such as power failures, fires, and unintentional disposal of seeds can cause irrecoverable losses. Also, stored plant species do not continue to evolve and thus are less fit for reintroduction to their native habitats, which may have undergone various environmental changes.

Because of these limitations, ecologists and plant scientists warn that the only effective way to preserve the genetic diversity of most of the world's plant and animal species is to protect large areas of representative ecosystems throughout the world from agriculture and other forms of development.

LOCATION, SOIL, AND INSECTS AS LIMITING FACTORS About 83% of the world's potential new cropland is in the remote rain forests of the Amazon and Orinoco river basins in South America and in Africa's rain forests. Most of this forested land is located in just two countries, Brazil (Figure 9-3) and Zaire (Figure 14-11).

Cultivation would require huge investments of capital and energy to clear the land and to transport the harvested crops to distant populated areas. The resulting deforestation would greatly increase soil erosion and enhance projected global warming through a net release of the greenhouse gases carbon dioxide and nitrous oxide (Section 11-1). It would also reduce the world's biological diversity by eliminating vast numbers of plant and animal species found only in these ecosystems.

Tropical rain forests have plentiful rainfall and long or continuous growing seasons, but their soils often are not suitable for intensive cultivation. About 90% of the plant nutrient supply is in ground litter and vegetation above the ground rather than in the soil (Figure 12-4).

Cleared land has few soil nutrients, most of which are eroded or leached away by heavy tropical rains.

Nearly 75% of the Amazon basin, roughly one-third of the world's potential new cropland, has highly acidic and infertile soils. In addition, 5% to 15% of tropical soils (4% of those in the Amazon basin), if cleared, would bake under the tropical sun into a brick-hard surface called laterite, useless for farming.

Some tropical soils can produce up to three crops of grain per year if enormous quantities of fertilizer are applied at the right time. However, costs are high, and rapid runoff and leaching of soil nutrients from heavy tropical rains limit production. The warm temperatures, high moisture, and year-round growing season also support large populations of pests and diseases that can devastate monoculture crops in the tropics. Huge doses of pesticides could be used, but the same conditions that favor crop growth in the tropics also favor rapid development of genetic resistance in pest species.

In Africa, potential cropland in savanna (Figure 5-17) and other semiarid land, covering an area larger than the continental United States, cannot be used for

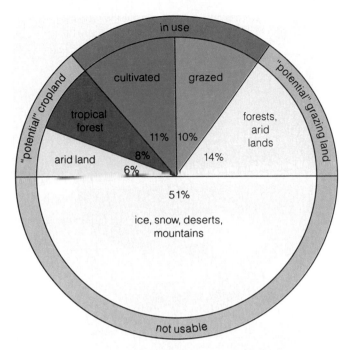

Figure 14-13 Classification of Earth's land. Theoretically, we could double the world's cropland in size by clearing tropical forests and irrigating arid lands. However, converting this marginal land into cropland would destroy valuable forest resources, reduce Earth's biodiversity, cause serious environmental problems, and usually not be cost-effective.

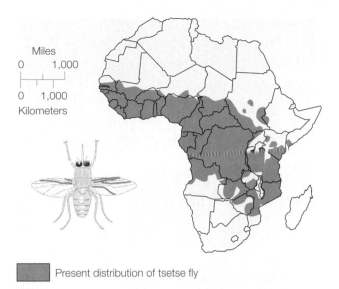

Present distribution of tsetse fly

Figure 14-14 Region of savanna and other semiarid land in Africa infested by the tsetse fly. Its bite can infect people with incurable sleeping sickness and transmit a fatal disease to livestock. According to official records some 20,000 Africans fall victim to sleeping sickness each year, but a much larger number of cases probably go unreported.

farming or livestock grazing because it is infested by 22 species of the tsetse fly (Figure 14-14). The bite of this insect can infect people and livestock with incurable sleeping sickness and transmit the wasting disease nagana to livestock. A $120-million eradication program has been proposed, but many scientists doubt it can succeed. Others point out that if it should succeed, the farming of this land and overgrazing by livestock would cause extinction of many forms of wildlife, thus contributing to the planet's growing biodiversity crisis.

Researchers hope to develop new methods of intensive cultivation in tropical areas. But some scientists argue that it makes more ecological and economic sense not to use intensive cultivation in the tropics. Instead, farmers should use shifting cultivation with fallow periods long enough to restore soil fertility (Figure 2-4) and various forms of interplanting. Scientists also recommend plantation cultivation of rubber trees (Figure 10-9), oil palms, and banana trees, which are adapted to tropical climates and soils.

WATER AS A LIMITING FACTOR Much of the world's potentially cultivatable land lies in dry areas, where water shortages limit crop growth, especially in Africa (Figure 14-11). Large-scale irrigation in these areas would be very expensive, requiring large inputs of fossil fuel to pump water long distances. Irrigation systems would deplete many groundwater supplies

and require constant and expensive maintenance to prevent groundwater contamination, salinization, and waterlogging (Figure 12-20).

There are signs that irrigation limits are being reached in land now under cultivation. Between 1950 and 1980, the world's irrigated cropland almost tripled, increasing the average irrigated area per person by 52%. However, during the 1980s, growth in irrigated area slowed dramatically and fell behind population growth, leading to an 8% drop in the irrigated area per person.

DO THE POOR BENEFIT? Increasing per capita food production is a big task, but making sure that it reaches the hungry is a much greater one. Whether present and future green or gene revolutions reduce hunger among the world's poor depends on how the technology is applied. In LDCs, the resource most available to agriculture is human labor. When green revolution techniques are used to increase yields of traditional labor-intensive agriculture on existing or new cropland in countries with equitable land distribution, the poor benefit, as has occurred in China.

Most poor farmers, however, don't have enough land, money, or credit to buy the seed, fertilizer, irrigation water, pesticides, equipment, and fuel that the new plant varieties need. This means that the second green revolution (Figure 14-6) has bypassed more than 1 billion poor people in LDCs.

Figure 14-15 The winged bean is a protein-rich annual plant from the Philippines. It has edible flowers, seeds, seedpods, tendrils, and tubers. It is only one of many little-known and little-used plants that could become important sources of food and fuel. Other examples are the sugar apple of South America, protein-rich seeds of the grain amaranth, the groundnut (a high-protein tuber eaten by Native Americans), and cocoyam (a native plant of West Africa and Latin America that is as nutritious as the potato).

Figure 14-16 In South Africa, "Mopani"—larvae of a species of emperor moth—is one example of a number of insects that are eaten. In the Kalahari Desert of Africa, cockroaches are consumed as food. Lightly toasted butterflies are a favorite food in Bali. French-fried ants are sold on the streets of Bogotá, Colombia, and Malaysians love deep-fried grasshoppers. Most of these insects are 58% to 78% protein by weight—three to four times that of beef, fish, or eggs.

Switching to industrialized agriculture makes LDCs heavily dependent on large, MDC-based multinational companies for expensive supplies, increasing the LDCs' foreign debts. It also makes their agricultural and economic systems more vulnerable to collapse from increases in oil and fertilizer prices and environmental degradation. In addition, mechanization displaces many farm workers, thus increasing rural-to-urban migration and overburdening the cities.

UNCONVENTIONAL FOODS AND PERENNIAL CROPS Some analysts recommend greatly increased cultivation of various nontraditional plants in LDCs to supplement or replace traditional foods such as wheat, rice, and corn. One of many possibilities is the winged bean, a protein-rich legume presently used extensively only in New Guinea and Southeast Asia (Figure 14-15). Its edible winged pods, leaves, tendrils, and seeds contain as much protein as soybeans, and its edible roots

contain more than four times the protein of potatoes. Indeed, this plant yields so many different edible parts that it has been called a "supermarket on a stalk." Insects are also important potential sources of protein, vitamins, and minerals (Figure 14-16).

Scientists have identified many plants and insects that could be used as sources of food. The problem is getting farmers to cultivate such crops and persuading consumers to try new foods.

Most crops we depend on are tropical annuals. Each year, the land is cleared of all vegetation, dug up, and planted with the seeds of annuals. David Pimentel (see Guest Essay on p. 330) and plant scientists such as Wes and Dana Jackson of the Land Institute in Salina, Kansas, believe we should rely more on polycultures of perennial crops that are more closely adapted to regional soil and climate conditions than most annuals. This would eliminate the need to till soil each year and would greatly reduce the amount of fossil-fuel, draft-animal, and human energy used in agriculture each year. It would also conserve water and reduce soil erosion and sediment water pollution.

Widespread use of perennials would greatly reduce the income of large agribusiness companies that sell annual seeds, fertilizers, and pesticides, explaining why they don't favor this approach. Thus, research and development of such Earth-sustaining crops must be carried out by governments and private groups.

14-4 Catching More Fish and Fish Farming and Ranching

THE WORLD'S FISHERIES Concentrations of particular aquatic species suitable for commercial harvesting in a given ocean area or inland body of water are called **fisheries**. Worldwide, people get an average of 20% of the animal protein in their food directly from fish and shellfish and another 5% indirectly from fish meal fed to livestock. In most Asian coastal and island countries, fish and shellfish supply 30% to 90% of the animal protein eaten by people.

About 87% of the annual commercial catch of fish and shellfish comes from the ocean and the rest from fresh water. Ninety-nine percent of the world marine catch is taken from plankton-rich waters (mostly estuaries and upwellings) within 370 kilometers (200 nautical miles) of the coast. However, this vital coastal zone is being disrupted and polluted at an alarming rate (see Case Study on p. 137).

Only about 40 of the world's 20,000 known species of fish are harvested in large quantities. Just six groups—cods, herrings, jacks, redfishes, mackerels, and tunas—account for nearly two-thirds of the annual commercial marine fish catch. Some of the commercially important species of fish in marine habitats are shown in Figure 14-17. Almost half of the world's commercial marine catch is taken by only five countries: Japan (16% of the catch), the USSR (13%), China (7%), the United States (6%), and Chile (6%). The United States, however, depends on imports for about 50% of its seafood consumption, and that figure may rise to 80% by the year 2000.

More than 90% of the fish and shellfish we consume is obtained by using small and large motorized fishing boats to hunt and gather these resources over a large area. Because 30% to 40% of the operating costs of motorized fishing boats is spent on fuel, energy inputs for each unit of food energy obtained from most marine species are enormous (Figure 14-18). This, plus declining yields from overfishing, explains why the prices of many favorite types of fish and shellfish are high.

TRENDS IN THE WORLD FISH CATCH Between 1950 and 1970, the weight of the annual commercial fish catch grew annually by about 7% and increased more than threefold (Figure 14-19). This increase was larger than that of any other human food source during the same period. Since then, the rate of growth has slowed down, and the marine catch may soon reach the estimated sustainable yield.

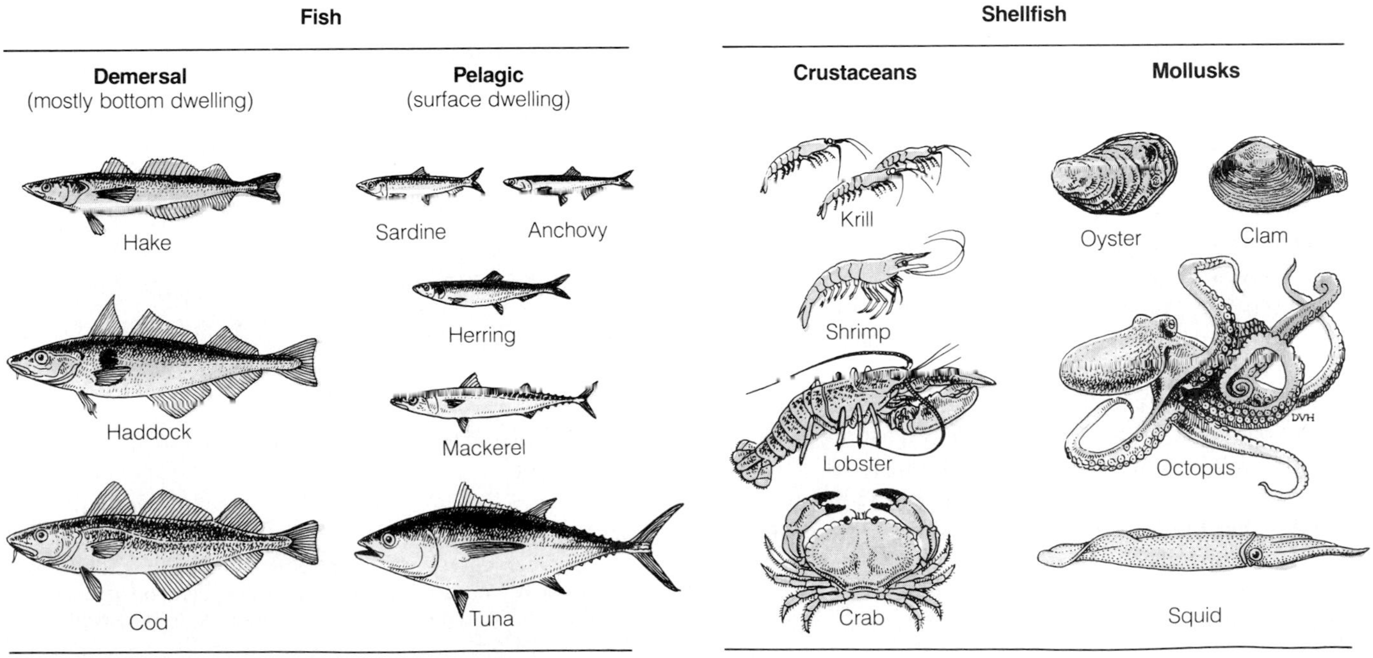

Figure 14-17 Some major types of commercially harvested marine fish and shellfish.

Figure 14-18 Average energy input needed to produce one unit of food energy from some commercially desirable types of fish and shellfish.

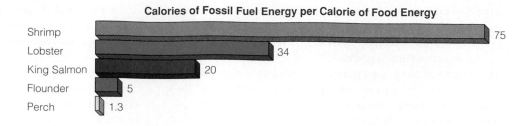

Calories of Fossil Fuel Energy per Calorie of Food Energy

Shrimp — 75
Lobster — 34
King Salmon — 20
Flounder — 5
Perch — 1.3

Figure 14-19 World fish catch. About one-third of the annual marine catch is used to feed animals and fertilize croplands. Scientists estimate that the sustainable yield of the world's marine fishery is 100 million metric tons (110 million tons), which may be reached or exceeded soon. If this yield is exceeded, key fish stocks will be depleted and yields will drop sharply. (Data from UN Food and Agriculture Organization)

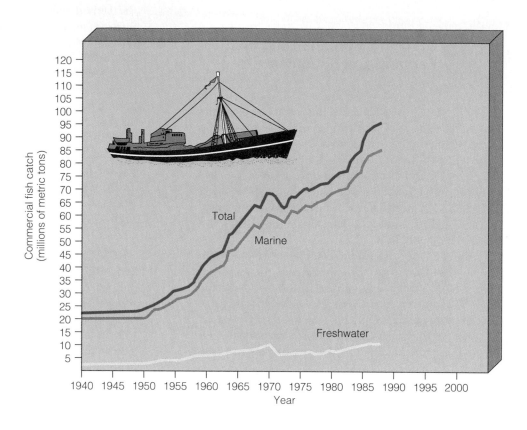

Although the total fish catch has grown, the worldwide per capita fish catch has declined in most years since 1970 because world population has grown at a faster rate than the fish catch (Figure 14-20). Because of overfishing, pollution, population growth, and increased demand, the world catch per person is projected to drop back to the 1960 level by the year 2000.

Overfishing occurs when so many fish are taken that too little breeding stock is left to prevent a drop in numbers. In other words, the sustainable yield is exceeded. Overfishing rarely causes biological extinction because commercial fishing becomes unprofitable before that point. Instead, prolonged overfishing leads to **commercial extinction**, the point at which the stock of a species is so low that it's no longer profitable to hunt and gather the remaining individuals in a specific fishery. Fishing fleets then move to a new species or to a new region, hoping that the overfished species will eventually recover.

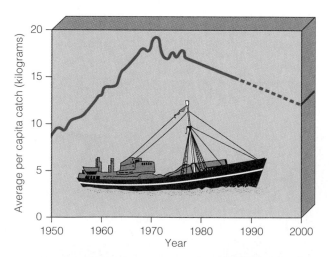

Figure 14-20 Per capita world fish catch has declined in most years since 1970 because population has grown faster than the fish catch. The per capita catch is projected to drop further by the end of this century. (Data from United Nations and Worldwatch Institute)

In 1953, Peru began fishing for anchovy in nutrient-rich upwellings off its western coast. The size of the fishing fleet increased rapidly. Factories were built to convert the small fish into fish meal for sale to MDCs for use as livestock feed. Between 1965 and 1971, harvests of the Peruvian anchovy made up about 20% of the world's annual commercial fish catch (Figure 14-21).

Between 1971 and 1978, however, the Peruvian anchovy became commercially extinct. The collapse of this fishery is an example of how biology, geography, economics, and politics interact, and often clash, in fishery management.

At unpredictable intervals, the productivity of the upwellings off the coast of Peru drops sharply because of a natural weather change called the El Niño-Southern Oscillation, or ENSO, which warms the normally cool water of the Humboldt Current flowing along Peru's coast (Figure 5-8). The numbers of anchovy, other fish, seabirds, and marine mammals in food webs based on phytoplankton then drop sharply.

Biologists with the UN Food and Agriculture Organization warned that during seven of the eight years between 1964 and 1971, the anchovy harvest exceeded the estimated sustainable yield. Peruvian fishery officials ignored those warnings.

Peru's fishing industry was financed largely by short-term loans.

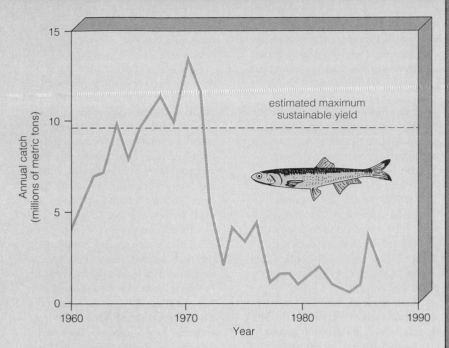

Figure 14-21 Peruvian anchovy catch, showing the combined effects of overfishing and a natural climate change, known as El Niño–Southern Oscillation (Figure 5-8), that occurs every few years. (Data from UN Food and Agriculture Organization)

Government officials decided to risk the collapse of the fishery to pay off the loans and avoid putting thousands of people out of work. They also believed that a slight drop in the anchovy catch would be beneficial because it would cause shortages and raise the price of fish meal.

Disaster struck in 1972, when a strong ENSO arrived. The anchovy population, already at dangerously low levels because of overfishing, could not recover from the effects of the ENSO. By putting short-term economics above biology, Peru lost a major source of income and jobs and had to increase its foreign debt.

The country has made some economic recovery by harvesting the Peruvian sardine, which took over the niche once occupied by the anchovy. The catches of mackerel, bonita, and hake have also increased. Since 1983, the Peruvian anchovy fishery has been making a slight recovery (Figure 14-21).

By the early 1980s, overfishing had caused declines in the yields of numerous fisheries and the collapse of 42 valuable fisheries. Examples of fisheries that have collapsed or sharply declined because of overfishing include cod and herring in the North Atlantic, salmon and the Alaska king crab in the northwest Pacific, pilchard in the Pacific, capelin off the coast of Norway, and Peruvian anchovy in the southeast Pacific (see Case Study above).

A hopeful sign was the signing of the 1982 United Nations Convention on the Law of the Sea by 159 countries. This treaty gives all coastal countries the legal right to control fishing by their own fishing fleets and by foreign ships within 364 kilometers (200 nautical miles) of their coasts.

If enforced, this treaty can reduce overfishing. However, 22 countries, including the Soviet Union, the United States, Germany, and the United Kingdom, have refused to sign or ratify the treaty. Their refusal is based mostly on disagreement with provisions in the treaty that consider mineral and living resources in the open ocean as belonging to the entire world, with MDCs

Since 1980, an estimated 1,800 fishing vessels from Japan, South Korea, and Taiwan have used drift net fishing, mostly in the Pacific Ocean (but also in the Atlantic and the Caribbean), to capture and kill almost anything that comes in contact with the thousands of kilometers of almost invisible nets they set out each night during the fishing season (Figure 14-22).

Each of these almost indestructible nylon-mesh walls of death descends as much as 15 meters (50 feet) deep and is up to 65 kilometers (40 miles) long. During each night of the fishing season, the entire fleet sets out enough nets to more than circle the world.

The intended catches are mostly squid, albacore tuna, marlin, swordfish, sea trout, and salmon (taken illegally, because by international agreement, deep-sea salmon that spend part of their life in fresh water and part in the ocean belong to the country where they spawn). This indiscriminate marine holocaust not only depletes the sea of the intended species but also entangles and kills hundreds of thousands of dolphins, turtles, seals, sharks (see Case Study on p. 112), small whales, and other forms of marine life that become entangled in the fine mesh of the nets (Figure 14-22).

To make matters worse, an estimated 800 kilometers (500 miles) of lost and discarded sections of drift nets — known as ghost nets — are left floating in the ocean each year. They can entangle and kill hundreds

of thousands of fish, marine mammals, and birds year-round for centuries.

This vacuuming of the seas by drift net fishing has brought huge short-term profits to the fishing industries of Japan, South Korea, and Taiwan. However, it is a destructive practice that depletes commercial fisheries, kills large numbers of non-targeted animals, and brings financial ruin and hunger to some of the poor who catch such fish for survival and for a living.

Environmentalists consider drift net fishing to be on an ecological par with deforestation and ozone depletion and have tried to have it banned. Japan, which has over half the world's drift net vessels, has banned small-mesh drift net fleets from its coastal waters but strongly resists a worldwide ban on this practice. Indeed, every country that has used drift nets has eventually banned them in their own waters. Now it's time to ban them in international waters.

In 1990, the UN General Assembly adopted a resolution calling for a moratorium of large-scale drift net fishing in international waters after June 1992 and a phaseout of drift net fishing in the South Pacific by July 1991. However, such a ban is not legally binding, even for countries voting in favor of it. Japan agreed to the ban, but only in the South Pacific, and Taiwan and South Korea (neither of them members of the UN) say they will not observe it.

The ban also has numerous loop-

holes that could allow resumption of drift net fishing and no effective mechanism for monitoring, enforcement, and punishment. Indeed, enforcement over vast ocean areas is impractical.

Environmentalists believe that the only effective way to reduce drift net fishing is to mount U.S. and global boycotts of fish caught by this method. This tactic, led by the Earth Island Institute, caused companies importing or selling tuna in the United States to stop buying tuna caught by purse seine or drift net methods because they killed hundreds of thousands of dolphins each year.

To be sure this voluntary ban is enforced, environmentalists are pushing Congress to pass a law requiring all companies selling tuna in the United States (which consumes 40% of the world's canned tuna) to have labels on their products indicating that purse seine and drift net fishing were not used. They also hope to spread the tuna boycott to other countries so that the unnecessary killing of dolphins by tuna fishing fleets will stop worldwide.

A large-scale boycott of fish or fish products obtained by drift net fishing by U.S. consumers would have a powerful impact because fisheries exports by drift net countries (Japan, South Korea, and Taiwan) into the United States exceed $1.5 billion a year. What do you think should be done?

having to share these resources, or profits made from them, with LDCs. Also, the effectiveness of this treaty in reducing overfishing is being offset by the increased use of techniques such as drift net fishing (see Spotlight above).

AQUACULTURE **Aquaculture**, in which fish and shellfish are raised in enclosed structures for all or part of their lives, supplies about 10% of the world's commercial fish harvest. There are two basic types of aquaculture. **Fish farming** involves cultivating fish in a

controlled environment, usually a pond, and harvesting them when they reach the desired size (Figure 14-23). **Fish ranching** involves holding species in captivity for the first few years of their lives and then harvesting the adults when they return to spawn. Ranching is useful for *anadromous species*, such as salmon and ocean trout, which after birth move from fresh water to the ocean and then back to fresh water to spawn.

Almost three-fourths of the world's annual aquaculture catch comes from 71 LDCs. Species cultivated in LDCs include carp (Figure 14-23), tilapia, milkfish,

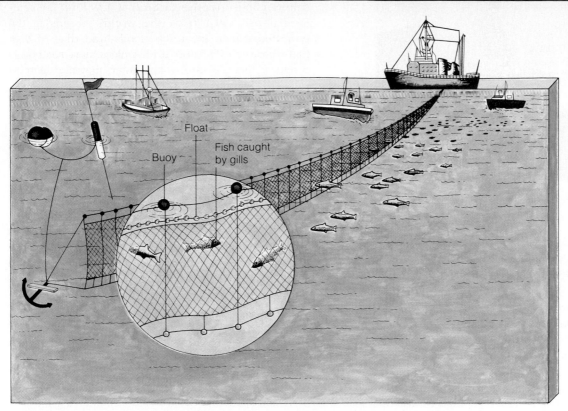

Figure 14-22 Drift net fishing by a distant-water fishing fleet. Typically, such a fleet has several huge factory ships that use sophisticated electronic detection devices, helicopters, and aerial photography to find large schools of fish. Each ship then launches 20 to 50 fast, small catcher boats to set hundreds to thousands of kilometers of drift nets, weighed down to stay at the wanted depth. After drifting overnight, the nets are hauled in by the factory ships. The catch is then processed on the ship by canning or freezing. Because these "curtains of death" can deplete target fish species and large numbers of other, nontarget species, environmentalists have been trying to have a worldwide ban imposed and enforced on this Earth-degrading type of fishing.

clams, and oysters, which feed low in food webs on phytoplankton and other forms of aquatic plants. These are usually raised in small freshwater ponds or underwater cages. Aquaculture supplies 60% of the fish eaten in Israel, 40% in China, and 22% in Indonesia.

In MDCs, aquaculture is used mostly to raise expensive fish and shellfish and to stock lakes and streams with game fish. This benefits anglers who fish for sport and is highly profitable for aquaculture farmers and companies, but it does little to increase food and protein supplies for the poor.

In the United States, a $5-billion-a-year fish farming industry supplies about 15% of U.S. seafood consumption and is projected to supply 25% by the year 2000. About 40% of the oysters and most of the catfish, crayfish, and rainbow trout consumed as food in the United States is supplied by U.S.-based fish farms. Tilapia (similar to sole), raised on U.S. fish farms, is being pushed as the fish of the future.

Aquaculture has a number of advantages. It can produce high yields per unit of area. Large amounts of fuel are not required, so yields and profits are not

Figure 14-23 Harvesting silver carp in an aquaculture farm in China.

closely tied to the price of oil, as they are in commercial hunting-and-gathering fishing (Figure 14-18). Also, aquaculture is usually labor-intensive and can provide much-needed jobs in LDCs.

There are problems, however. Large-scale aquaculture requires considerable capital and scientific knowledge, which are in short supply in LDCs. Scooping out huge ponds for fish and shrimp farming in Ecuador, the Philippines, Panama, Indonesia, Honduras, and other South Pacific LDCs has led to widespread destruction of ecologically important mangrove forests (Figure 5-31). Fish in aquaculture ponds can be killed by pesticide runoff from nearby croplands. Bacterial and viral infections of aquatic species can also limit aquaculture yields. Also, without adequate pollution control, waste outputs from shrimp farming and other large-scale aquaculture operations can contaminate nearby estuaries, surface water, and groundwater.

CAN THE ANNUAL CATCH BE INCREASED SIGNIFICANTLY? Some scientists believe that the world fish catch can be expanded by harvesting more squid, octopus, Antarctic krill, and other unconventional species. However, this could have unpredictable and possibly harmful effects on ocean food webs. Greatly expanded harvesting of shrimplike krill, for example, could lead to sharp declines in the populations of certain whales and other species dependent on krill (Figure 4-20). Also, food scientists have been unable to process krill into foods that taste good enough for people to eat. Currently, krill is used to make livestock feed.

Additional increases could also be brought about by a sharp decrease in the one-fifth of the annual catch now wasted, mainly from throwing back potentially useful fish taken along with desired species. More refrigerated storage at sea to prevent spoilage would also increase the catch. Some experts project that freshwater and saltwater aquaculture production could be doubled during the 1990s.

Other fishery experts believe that further increases in the annual marine catch are limited by overfishing and by pollution and destruction of estuaries and aquaculture ponds. Another factor that may limit the commercial fish catch from the world's oceans is the projected rise in the price of oil—and thus of boat fuel—between 1995 and 2015. Unless more seafood is produced by aquaculture, consumers may find seafood prices too high.

14-5 Making Food Production Profitable, Giving Food Aid, and Distributing Land to the Poor

GOVERNMENT AGRICULTURAL POLICIES Agriculture is an especially risky business. Whether a farmer has a good or a bad year is determined by factors over which the farmer has little control—weather, crop prices, crop pests and disease, interest rates, and the global market. Because of that and the need to have a reliable supply of food to prevent political unrest, most governments provide various forms of assistance to farmers.

Governments can influence crop and livestock prices, and thus the supply of food, in several ways:

- They can keep food prices artificially low. This makes consumers happy but can decrease food production by reducing profits for farmers.

- They can give farmers subsidies to keep them in business and encourage them to increase food production.

- They can eliminate price controls and subsidies, allowing market competition to determine food prices and thus the amount of food produced.

Most governments in LDCs have concentrated their limited financial resources on the cities and on industrial development, neglecting farming and rural areas. Governments in many LDCs keep food prices in cities lower than in the countryside to prevent political unrest.

Low prices, however, discourage farmers from producing enough to feed the country's population, and the government must use limited funds or go into debt to buy imported food. With food prices higher in rural areas than in cities, more rural people migrate to urban areas, aggravating urban problems and unemployment. These conditions increase the chances of political unrest, which the price control policy was supposed to prevent.

Governments can stimulate crop and livestock production by guaranteeing farmers a certain minimum yearly return on their investment. However, if government price supports are too generous and the weather is good, farmers may produce more food than can be sold. Food prices and profits then drop because of the

In MDCs, government price supports and other subsidies for agriculture farmers total more than $300 billion a year. This makes farmers and agribusiness executives happy. They are also popular with most consumers because they make food prices seem low. Politicians favor this approach because it increases their chances of staying in office.

What most consumers don't realize is that they are paying higher prices for their food indirectly in the form of higher taxes to provide the subsidies. There is no free lunch. A 1989 Department of Agriculture study estimated that U.S. shoppers would pay $30 to $35 more each year if federal farm subsidies were eliminated. However, the same study did not point out that those subsidies cost each U.S. taxpayer an average of $200 in 1990.

According to many food experts, the U.S. agricultural system is too successful for its own good. It produces so much food that the government must pay farmers not to produce food on one-fourth of U.S. cropland or must buy up and store unneeded crops. This encourages farmers to produce even more, discourages the use of Earth-sustaining agriculture, wastes taxpayer dollars,

and is a form of welfare for wealthy farmers. In 1989, nearly 60% of the federal farm subsidies went to the wealthiest 25% of U.S. farms.

Some analysts believe that the way out of this dilemma is to gradually wean U.S. farmers from all federal subsidies, say over five years, and let them respond to market demand. Only those who were good farmers and financial managers would be able to stay in business. However, any phaseout of farm subsidies in the United States or any other country should be coupled with increased aid for the poor, who would suffer the most from any increase in food prices.

Eliminating all price controls and agricultural subsidies and allowing market competition to determine food prices and production is not easy to do. Farmers and owners of farm-related businesses usually have enough votes to elect congressional representatives opposed to phasing out all farm subsidies.

Instead of eliminating subsidies, some agricultural experts suggest using them to regulate crop production rather than crop acreage. This would reduce the pressure on growers to increase yields per hectare to qualify for help, thereby reducing

soil erosion and excessive inputs of fertilizers, pesticides, and irrigation water. Regulations should be set up and strictly enforced so that subsidies go only to needier, but competent, small-scale farmers, not, as in the present situation, to large-scale farmers who do not need government payments to be profitable.

Generally, environmentalists favor eliminating most agricultural subsidies, but not those that encourage soil and water conservation, reforestation, and wildlife protection. They warn that the current global General Agreement on Tariffs and Trade (GATT) negotiations to deregulate global trade in agricultural and related products would devastate small farmers around the world and greatly increase the control of big business over the production of and the trade in food and other natural products. This agreement, backed by the Bush administration and corporate interests, would reduce or eliminate all farm subsidies, including those for environmental protection and conservation and deforestation, weaken environmental and health safety standards, and undermine local, state, and national authority. What do you think should be done?

oversupply. The resulting availability of large amounts of food for export or food aid to LDCs depresses world food prices. The low prices reduce the financial incentive for farmers to increase domestic food production. Whether government agricultural subsidies should be maintained, reduced, or eliminated is a controversial issue (see Pro/Con above).

INTERNATIONAL AID Between 1945 and 1985, the United States was the world's largest donor of nonmilitary foreign aid to LDCs. Since 1986, however, Japan has been the largest donor of such aid to LDCs. This aid is used mostly for agriculture and rural development, food relief, population planning, health, and economic development. Private charity organizations, such as CARE and Catholic Relief Services, and funds from benefit music concerts and record sales provide over $3 billion a year of additional foreign aid.

In addition to helping other countries, foreign aid stimulates economic growth and provides jobs in the donor country. For example, 70 cents of every dollar the United States gives directly to other countries is used to purchase American goods and services. Today, 21 of the 50 largest buyers of U.S. farm goods are countries that once received free U.S. food.

Despite the humanitarian benefits and economic returns of such aid, the percentage of the U.S. gross national product used for nonmilitary foreign aid to LDCs has dropped from a high of 1.6% in the 1950s to only 0.20% since 1980—an annual average of only $30 per American. Since 1980, 16 other MDCs used a higher percentage of their GNP for nonmilitary foreign aid to LDCs than the United States. Some people call for greatly increased food relief for starving people from government and private sources, while others question the value of such aid (see Pro/Con on p. 384).

Most people view food relief as a humanitarian effort to prevent people from dying prematurely. However, some analysts contend that giving food to starving people in countries where population growth rates are high does more harm than good in the long run. By encouraging population growth and not helping people grow their own food, food relief condemns even greater numbers to premature death in the future.

Biologist Garrett Hardin (see Guest Essay on p. 219) has suggested that we use the concept of *lifeboat ethics* to decide which countries get food aid. He starts with the belief that there are already too many people in the lifeboat we call Earth. If food aid is given to countries that are not reducing their population, this adds more people to an already-overcrowded lifeboat. Sooner or later the boat will sink and kill most of the passengers.

Large amounts of food aid can also depress local food prices, decrease food production, and stimulate mass migration from farms to already-overburdened cities. It discourages the government from investing in rural agricultural development to enable the country to grow enough food for its population on a sustainable basis.

Another problem is that much food aid does not reach hunger victims. Transportation networks and storage facilities are inadequate, so that some of the food rots or is devoured by pests before it can reach the hungry. Typically, some of the food is stolen by officials and sold for personal profit. Some must often be given to officials as bribes for approving the unloading and transporting of the remaining food to the hungry.

Critics of food relief are not against foreign aid. Instead, they believe that such aid should be given to help countries control population growth, grow enough food to feed their population using sustainable agricultural methods (Section 14-6), or develop export crops to help pay for food they can't grow. Temporary food aid should be given only when there is a complete breakdown of an area's food supply because of natural disaster. What do you think?

DISTRIBUTING LAND TO THE POOR An important step in reducing world hunger, malnutrition, poverty, and land degradation is land reform. Land reform involves giving the landless rural poor in LDCs ownership or free use of enough land to produce the food they need to survive, and ideally to produce a surplus for emergencies and for sale. China and Taiwan have had the most successful land reforms.

Such reform would increase agricultural productivity in LDCs and reduce the need to farm and degrade marginal land. It would also help reduce the flow of poor people to overcrowded urban areas by creating employment in rural areas.

Many of the countries with the most unequal land distribution are in Latin America, especially Guatemala, Bolivia, and Brazil (see Case Study on p. 225). In Latin America, 7% of the population owns 93% of the farmland. Most of this land is used for luxury export crops or beef (see Pro/Con on p. 263) that degrade the land and do little to help the landless poor. Unfortunately, land reform is difficult to institute in countries where government leaders are unduly influenced by wealthy and powerful landowners.

14-6 Sustainable-Earth Agriculture

SUSTAINABLE-EARTH AGRICULTURAL SYSTEMS Industrialized agriculture has undeniably achieved substantial short-term gains in food production. However, to environmentalists, it is based on eventually unsustainable practices. The bills for using Earth's capital resources unsustainably are now coming due in terms of eroded and nutrient-depleted soils (Figure 12-8), desertification (Figures 12-11 and 12-12), waterlogged and salted fields (Figure 12-21), overfertilized and pesticide-poisoned surface waters and groundwater, and drained and contaminated aquifers (Figure 13-15).

To environmentalists, the key to reducing world hunger and the harmful environmental impacts of industrialized and traditional forms of agriculture is to develop a variety of **sustainable-Earth agricultural systems**. This involves combining appropriate parts of existing industrialized and subsistence agricultural systems and new agricultural techniques to take advantage of local climates, soils, resources, and cultural systems.

A sustainable-Earth agricultural system does not require large inputs of fossil fuels, promotes polyculture (see Case Study on p. 365) instead of monoculture, promotes perennial instead of annual crop strains, conserves topsoil and builds new topsoil with organic fertilizer, conserves irrigation water, and controls pests with little or no use of pesticides. This type of agriculture would increase food supplies in ways that minimize erosion, desertification, salinization, water pollution, and loss of biodiversity. It will require devising institutional mechanisms that will reward farmers for valuing the world's precious soil, water, and biodiversity.

The following are general guidelines for sustainable-Earth agriculture:

- *Place primary emphasis on preserving and renewing the soil and on conserving water.* Long-term sustainability of the soil, not short-term agricultural productivity, must always come first.

- *Recognize that the marketplace cannot sustain agriculture because it does not assign an infinite value to the soil and water upon which all agriculture depends.* The marketplace is concerned with increasing short-term crop production even when this decreases the long-term sustainability of agriculture.

- *Stop thinking of and dealing with agriculture as an industry.* Agriculture involves living things and biological processes, whereas the materials of an industry are not alive and the processes are mechanical. A factory has a limited life, while the life of a farm is unlimited if its topsoil is properly used and maintained. Much of the environmental degradation from industrialized agriculture occurs because plants, livestock animals, and workers are regarded as specialized machines supported by technologies that are supposed to provide virtually inexhaustible supplies of fossil fuels, water, and fertile soil.

- *Adapt and design the agricultural system to the environment (soil, water, climate, and pest populations) of the region.* This means not trying to grow water-thirsty crops in arid and semiarid areas, maintaining vegetative cover on cropland, raising water prices to encourage water conservation, increasing the organic content of soils, and limiting livestock grazing on arid and semiarid lands.

- *Emphasize small- to medium-scale intensive production of a diverse mix of fruit, vegetable, and fuelwood crops and livestock animals, rather than large-scale monoculture production of a single crop or livestock animal.* This means we must halt and reverse the replacement of small, diversified, low-input, self-sustaining, family farms with large, monoculture, high-input, unsustainable "agrifactories." Emphasis should be placed on intercropping and integrated crop and livestock production. Decreasing the average size of the U.S. farm from 170 hectares (420 acres) in 1990 to 120 hectares (300 acres) would create over 1 million jobs, and 2 million jobs if the additional farms used low-input organic methods.

- *Whenever possible, matter inputs should be obtained from locally available, renewable biological resources and used in ways that preserve their renewability.* Examples include using organic fertilizers from animal and crop wastes, planting fast-growing trees to supply fuelwood and add nitrogen to the soil, and building simple devices for capturing and storing rainwater for irrigating crops. Commercially produced inputs such as inorganic fertilizers and pesticides should be used only when needed and in the smallest amount possible.

- *Greatly reduce the use of fossil fuel in agriculture by using locally available perpetual and renewable energy resources such as sun, wind, and flowing water to perform as many functions as possible and by increasing the use of animal and crop wastes as organic fertilizer.* These reductions would have several positive synergistic effects. Reducing fossil-fuel consumption in agriculture decreases greenhouse-gas emissions and other forms of air pollution and helps reduce our threatening addiction to oil. Reducing the use of inorganic fertilizers helps curb emissions of nitrous oxide—a powerful greenhouse gas (Figure 11-2)—and decreases pollution of groundwater and surface water with nitrates. The use of manure and compost, along with crop rotation and intercropping, would help improve the quality of soils and restore degraded agricultural land.

- *Emphasize use of biological pest control (Section 23-5), windbreaks (Figure 12-17), crop rotation, green manure, and other methods that reduce soil erosion and nutrient depletion, conserve water, encourage beneficial organisms, and discourage pests.*

- *Governments must develop agricultural development policies that include economic incentives to encourage farmers to grow enough food to meet the demand using sustainable-Earth agricultural systems.* These include greatly enhancing the role of women in agriculture by ensuring their access to land ownership, credit, loans, and information about new agricultural techniques, and significant increases in government-supported research and development and demonstration projects of sustainable-Earth agriculture.

- *Limit population growth (Section 8-3).*

In MDCs, such as the United States, a shift from large-scale industrialized agriculture to small- to medium-scale sustainable-Earth agriculture is difficult. It would be strongly opposed by agribusiness companies, by successful farmers with large investments in industrialized agriculture, and by specialized farmers who are unwilling to learn the demanding managerial skills and agricultural knowledge needed to run a diversified farm.

The shift, however, could be brought about gradually over 10 to 20 years by a combination of methods:

- Greatly increasing government support of research and development of sustainable-Earth agricultural methods and equipment. A 1989 study by the National Academy of Sciences urged U.S. farmers to begin shifting to low-input, sustainable agriculture (LISA), a step toward true sustainable-Earth agriculture. This shift will be hindered, however, as long as only about 3% of the Department of Agriculture's annual research budget continues to be used for this purpose.

- Setting up demonstration projects in each county so that farmers can see how sustainable systems work.

- Look at your lifestyle to find ways to reduce your unnecessary use and waste of food, fertilizers, and pesticides. Recognize that agriculture has a greater environmental impact than any other human activity (see Spotlight on p. 372). Reducing your impact from this activity is a political act that is an important form of planetary patriotism.

- Eat lower on the food chain by eliminating or reducing meat consumption, especially beef. This saves money and energy and can reduce your intake of fats that contribute to heart disease and other disorders. It also reduces air and water pollution, water use, deforestation, soil erosion, overgrazing, species extinction, and emissions of the greenhouse gas methane produced by cattle. In the United states, animal agriculture pollutes more fresh water than all municipal and industrial uses combined. If Americans reduced their meat intake by just 10%, the savings in grain and soybeans

could adequately feed 60 million people. More than half of U.S. cropland is devoted to growing livestock feed. Livestock also use more than half the water withdrawn in the United States, either directly, through water consumption by the animals; or indirectly, through irrigation of feed crops and management of manure. Each time an American switches to a pure vegetarian diet, 0.4 hectare (1 acre) of U.S. trees and 4.2 million liters (1.1 million gallons) of water are saved per year and half as much water is polluted by that individual. John Robbins suggests that we think of hamburgers as "ground-up cows who've had their throats slit by machetes or their brains bashed in by sledgehammers." If you do eat meat, select organically fed, humanely treated, range-fed beef or poultry. Currently, only about 3% of Americans are vegetarians.

- If you have a dog or a cat, don't feed it canned meat products. Balanced grain pet foods are

available and are better for your pet. Each year, Americans spend about $5 billion on dog and cat food compared with $0.7 billion on baby food.

- Use sustainable-Earth cultivation techniques to grow some of your own food in a backyard plot, a window planter, a rooftop garden, or a cooperative community garden. Spending $31 to plant a living-room-size garden can give you vegetables worth about $250 — a better return than almost any financial investment you can make. Currently, about 30% of the U.S. population grows fruits, vegetables, and herbs at home, with 57% of these foods grown organically. In the Soviet Union, 68% of the country's food is grown on private vegetable gardens on only 2% of the land.

- Fertilize your crops primarily with organic fertilizer produced in a compost bin (Figure 12-19). This recycles most of your food and yard wastes instead of adding them to the growing problem of solid waste. Use small

---

- Establishing training programs in sustainable-Earth agriculture for farmers, county farm agents, and most Department of Agriculture personnel.

- Establishing college curricula for sustainable-Earth agriculture. We need a new generation of Earth-sustaining farmers. The average U.S. farmer is 57 years old, and most farmers know only how to grow one or two crops and use resource-inefficient technologies.

- Giving subsidies and tax breaks to farmers using sustainable-Earth agriculture and to agribusiness companies developing products for this type of farming.

Each of us has a role to play in bringing about a shift from unsustainable to sustainable agriculture at the local, national, and global levels (see Individuals Matter above).

The need to bring birthrates well below death rates, increase food production, while protecting the environment, and distribute food to all who need it is the greatest challenge our species has ever faced.

PAUL AND ANNE EHRLICH

DISCUSSION TOPICS

1. What are the biggest advantages and disadvantages of **(a)** labor-intensive subsistence agriculture, **(b)** energy-intensive industrialized agriculture, and **(c)** sustainable-Earth agriculture?

2. Summarize the advantages and limitations of each of the following proposals for increasing world food supplies and reducing hunger over the next 30 years: **(a)** cultivating more land by clearing tropical forests and irrigating arid lands, **(b)** catching more fish in the open

amounts of commercial inorganic fertilizer only when supplies of certain plant nutrients are inadequate.

- Use drip irrigation (Figure 13-21) to water your crops.

- Control pests by a combination of cultivation and biological methods (see Section 23-5). Use carefully selected chemical pesticides in small amounts only when absolutely necessary.

- Help reduce the use of pesticides on agricultural products by asking grocery stores to stock fresh produce and meat produced by organic methods (without the use of commercial fertilizers and pesticides). Insist that such foods have been tested to certify that they were grown by organic methods, and support legislation that will set standards for labelling and certification of organic foods. Currently, about 0.5% of U.S. farmers grow about 3% of the country's crops using organic methods. This $2-billion-a-year business is the fastest-growing sector in U.S. agriculture because of rapidly increasing consumer demand.

- Recognize that organically grown fruits and vegetables may have a few holes, blemishes, or frayed leaves, but they taste just as good and are just as nutritious as more perfect-looking products (on which pesticides were used). Eating organically grown food is also a form of health insurance. You won't be ingesting small amounts of pesticides.

- Reduce unnecessary waste of food. An estimated 25% of all food produced in the United States is wasted; it rots in the supermarket or refrigerator or is thrown away off the plate in households and restaurants. This wasted food is worth at least $50 billion a year. Put no more food on your plate than you intend to eat, ask for smaller portions in restaurants, and support programs that collect excess food from restaurants and school cafeterias and distribute it to the poor and homeless.

- Exert pressure on candidates for public office and elected officials to support policies designed to develop and encourage sustainable-Earth agricultural systems in the United States and throughout the world.

- Support efforts to regulate and slow down population growth (Section 8-3). Ultimately, the size of the world population will determine the need for food and the harmful environmental impacts of producing that food.

sea, (c) producing more fish and shellfish with aquaculture, and (d) increasing the yield per area of cropland.

3. Should price supports and other federal subsidies paid to U.S. farmers out of tax revenues be eliminated? Explain. Try to have one or more farmers discuss this problem with your class.

4. Is sending food to famine victims helpful or harmful? Explain. Are there any conditions you would attach to sending such aid? Explain.

5. Should tax breaks and subsidies be used to encourage more U.S. farmers to switch to sustainable-Earth farming? Explain.

6. Do you eat meat? Would you be willing to go to a slaughterhouse and kill a cow or a pig?

*7. If possible, visit a nearby conventional industrialized farm and an organic farm. Compare soil erosion and other forms of land-degradation, use and costs of energy, use and costs of pesticides and inorganic fertilizer, use and costs of natural pest control and organic fertilizer, yields per hectare for the same crops, and overall profit per hectare for the same crops.

CHAPTER 15

LAND RESOURCES:

FORESTS,

RANGELANDS, PARKS,

AND WILDERNESS

General Questions and Issues

1. What are the principal types of public lands in the United States, and how are they used?

2. How should forest resources be managed and conserved?

3. Why are rangelands important, and how should they be managed?

4. What problems do parks face, and how should parks be managed?

5. Why is wilderness important, and how much should be preserved?

We abuse land because we regard it as a commodity belonging to us. When we see land as a community to which we belong, we may begin to use it with love and respect.

ALDO LEOPOLD

F ORESTS, RANGELANDS, PARKS, AND WILDERNESS are key land and biological resources that are coming under increasing stress (Table 1-1 and Chapter 10) from population growth and economic development. Protecting these vital resources from degradation, using them sustainably, and healing those we have degraded are very important challenges.

The public lands of the United States—lands that belong to all Americans—are under intense pressure to be developed and also face threats from pollution and overuse. Much greater emphasis must be placed on expanding and protecting this unique heritage.

15-1 Public Lands and Forest Resources in the United States

U.S. PUBLIC LANDS: AN OVERVIEW No other nation on Earth has set aside such a large portion of its land for the public's use and enjoyment. About 42% of all U.S. land consists of public lands owned jointly by all citizens and managed for them by federal, state, and local governments. Over one-third (35%) of the country's land is managed by the federal government (Figure 15-1). About 95% of this federal public land is in Alaska (73%) and in the western states (22%).

This remarkable inheritance of publicly owned and federally managed land is found in the country's national forests, national parks and monuments, national wildlife refuges, and lands administered by the Bureau of Land Management. The allowed uses of these lands vary (see Spotlight on p. 390).

Federally administered public lands contain a large portion of the country's commercial timber (40%), grazing land (54%), and energy resources (especially shale oil, uranium, coal, and geothermal energy) and most of its copper, silver, asbestos, lead, molybdenum, beryllium, phosphate, and potash. Through various laws, Congress has allowed private individuals and corporations to harvest or extract many of these resources—often at below-market prices. Because of the economic value of these resources, there has been a long and continuing history of conflict between various groups over management and use of these public lands, as discussed in Section 2-4.

Since 1980, public agencies managing these lands have, little by little, yielded to pressure for more grazing, more roads, more timber cutting, more mining, more resorts in national parks, and more drilling for oil and natural gas. These activities can degrade the public's national land inheritance by soil erosion, air pollution, water pollution, excessive timbering, overgrazing, aircraft noise pollution, habitat destruction and degradation, and loss of biological diversity.

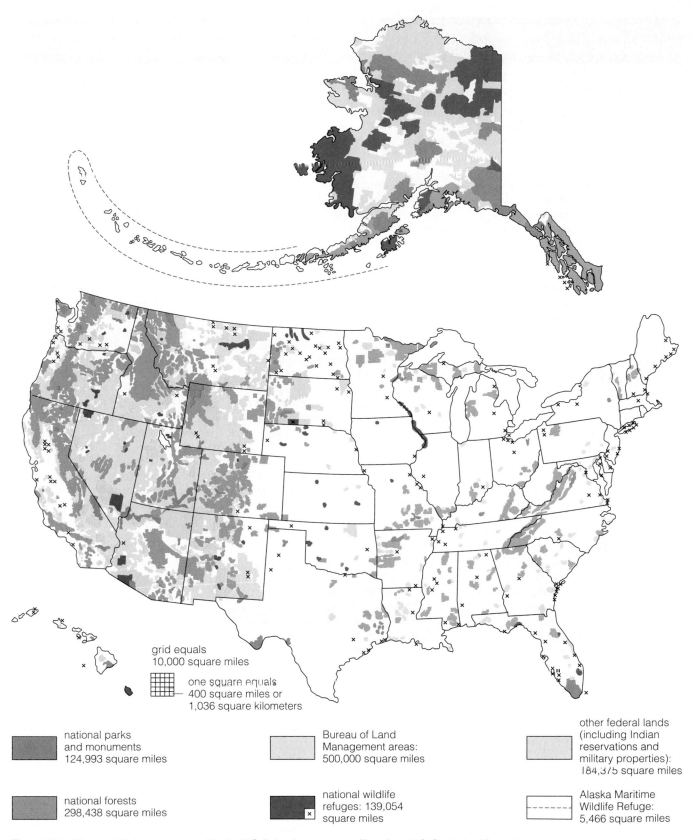

grid equals
10,000 square miles

one square equals
400 square miles or
1,036 square kilometers

national parks
and monuments
124,993 square miles

national forests
298,438 square miles

Bureau of Land
Management areas:
500,000 square miles

national wildlife
refuges: 139,054
square miles

other federal lands
(including Indian
reservations and
military properties):
184,375 square miles

Alaska Maritime
Wildlife Refuge:
5,466 square miles

Figure 15-1   Major public lands managed by the U.S. federal government. (Data from U.S. Geological Survey)

Multiple-Use Lands

National Forests The forest system includes 156 national forests and 19 national grasslands managed by the Forest Service. Excluding the 15% protected as wilderness areas, this land is supposed to be managed according to the principles of sustainable yield and multiple use. According to the *principle of sustainable yield*, a potentially renewable resource should not be harvested or used faster than it is replenished throughout the world or in a particular area. *Multiple use* means that public forests are to be managed to allow a variety of uses *on the same land, at the same time*. Currently, national forests are used for timbering, mining, grazing, agriculture, oil and gas leasing, recreation, sport hunting, sport and commercial fishing, conservation of watershed, soil, and wildlife resources. Off-road vehicles are usually restricted to designated routes.

National Resource Lands These lands are mostly grassland, prairie, desert, scrub forest, and other open spaces located in the western states and Alaska. They are managed by the Bureau of Land Management under the *principle of multiple use*. Emphasis is on providing a secure domestic supply of energy and strategically important nonenergy minerals and on preserving the renewability of rangelands for livestock grazing under a permit system. About 10% of these lands are being evaluated for possible designation as wilderness areas.

Moderately Restricted–Use Lands

National Wildlife Refuges This system includes 452 refuges and various ranges managed by the Fish and Wildlife Service. About 24% of this land is protected as wilderness areas. The purpose of most refuges is to protect habitats and breeding areas for waterfowl and big-game animals to provide a harvestable supply for hunters. A few refuges have been set aside to save specific endangered species from extinction. These lands are not officially managed under the principles of multiple use and sustained yield. Nevertheless, sport hunting, trapping, sport and commercial fishing, oil and gas development, mining (old claims only), timber cutting, livestock grazing, and farming are permitted as long as the Secretary of the Interior finds such uses compatible with the purposes of each unit.

Restricted-Use Lands

National Parks This system consists of 356 units. They include 50 major parks (mostly in the West) and 306 national recreation areas, monuments, memorials, battlefields, historic sites, parkways, trails, rivers, seashores, and lakeshores. All are managed by the National Park Service. Its management goals are to preserve scenic and unique natural landscapes, preserve and interpret the country's historic and cultural heritage, provide protected wildlife habitats, protect wilderness areas within the parks, and provide certain types of recreation. National parks may be used only for camping, hiking, sport fishing, and motorized and nonmotorized boating. Motor vehicles are permitted only on roads, and off-road vehicles are not allowed. National recreation areas can be used for the same activities as national parks plus sport hunting, new mining claims, and new oil and gas leasing. About 49% of the land in the National Park System is protected as wilderness areas.

National Wilderness Preservation System This system includes 474 roadless areas within the national parks, national wildlife refuges, and national forests. They are managed, respectively, by the National Park Service, the Fish and Wildlife Service, and the Forest Service. These areas are to be preserved in their essentially untouched condition "for the use and enjoyment of the American people in such a manner as will leave them unimpaired for future use and enjoyment as wilderness." Wilderness areas are open only for recreational activities such as hiking, sport fishing, camping, nonmotorized boating, and, in some areas, sport hunting and horseback riding. Roads, timber harvesting, grazing, mining, commercial activities, and human-made structures are prohibited, except where such activities occurred before an area's designation as wilderness. Motorized vehicles, boats, and equipment are banned except for emergency uses such as fire control and rescue operations. However, aircraft are allowed to land in Alaskan wilderness areas.

EXTENT OF U.S. FORESTS Today, forests cover about one-third of the land area in the lower 48 states and make up 10% of the world's forested land area. However, most of the country's virgin forests have been cut (Figure 10-17), and what remains is under threat (Section 10-5). U.S. forests provide habitats for more than 80% of the country's wildlife species and are the prime setting for outdoor recreation.

Nearly two-thirds of this land is classified as commercial forestland. About three-fourths of it is privately owned. Much of it consists of small plots that are poorly managed. Most of the remaining one-third of U.S. forestland is not capable of producing commercially valuable timber or is set aside as parks, wildlife refuges, or wilderness. Since 1950, the United States has kept up with the demand for wood and wood products without serious depletion of its commercial forestlands.

15-2 Forest Management and Conservation

TYPES OF FOREST MANAGEMENT Although crops can be harvested annually, trees take 20 to 1,000 years to mature. There are two basic forest management systems: even-aged management and uneven-aged management. With **even-aged management**, trees in a given stand are maintained at about the same age and size, harvested all at once, and replanted naturally or artificially so a new even-aged stand will grow. Growers emphasize mass production of low-quality wood with the goal of maximizing economic return on investment in as short a time as possible.

Even-aged management begins with the cutting of all or most trees from a diverse, old-growth (Figure 10-18) or secondary forest. Then the site is replanted with an even-aged stand, or *tree farm*, of a single species (monoculture) of faster-growing softwoods (Figure 5-25). Tree farms need close supervision and usually require expensive inputs of fertilizers and pesticides to protect the monoculture species from diseases and insects. Once the trees reach maturity, the entire stand is harvested and the area is replanted with seeds or seedlings. Genetic crossbreeding and genetic engineering can be used to improve both the quality and the quantity of wood produced from tree farms.

With **uneven-aged management**, trees in a given stand are maintained at many ages and sizes to permit continuous natural regeneration. Here the goals are to sustain biological diversity, maintain long-term production of high-quality timber, provide a reasonable economic return, and allow multiple use of a forest stand. The emphasis is on selective cutting of mature trees, with clear-cutting used only on small patches of tree species that benefit from this type of harvesting.

THE FOREST MANAGEMENT PROCESS Forest management consists of a cycle of decisions and events (Figure 15-2). Each cycle of management between planting and harvesting is called a *rotation*. The most important steps in this cycle include making an inventory of the site, developing a forest management plan, preparing the site for harvest, harvesting commercially valuable timber, and regenerating and managing the site before the next harvest.

The volume of wood produced by a forest varies as it goes through various stages of growth and ecological succession (Figure 15-3). If the goal is to produce a large quantity of fuelwood or fiber for paper production in the shortest time, the forest is usually harvested on a short rotation cycle before the rate of growth begins to decline (point A of Figure 15-3). Harvesting when the trees reach their peak growth gives the maximum yield of wood (point B of Figure 15-3). If the goal is quality of growth for fine furniture or veneer, managers use longer rotations to take advantage of the high-quality wood in larger, older-growth trees (point C of Figure 15-3).

TREE HARVESTING The method chosen for harvesting depends on whether uneven-aged or even-aged forest management is being used. It also depends on the tree species involved, the nature of the site, and the objectives and resources of the owner.

In **selective cutting**, intermediate-aged or mature trees in an uneven-aged forest are cut singly or in small groups (Figure 15-4). This reduces crowding, encourages the growth of younger trees, maintains an uneven-aged stand with trees of different species, ages, and sizes, and allows natural regeneration of trees. It also decreases the fire hazard because the volume of wood debris (slash) left after harvest is reduced. If done properly, selective cutting also helps protect the site from soil erosion and tree damage and blowdown by the wind.

Selective cutting is costly unless the value of the trees removed is high, and maintaining a good mixture of tree ages and sizes takes considerable planning and skill. It's not useful for shade-intolerant species, which require full sunlight for seedling growth. The need to reopen roads and trails periodically for selective harvests can cause erosion of certain soils.

One type of selective cutting, not considered a sound forestry practice, is *high grading*, or *creaming*—removing the most valuable trees without considering the quality or the distribution of the remaining trees needed for regeneration. Many loggers in tropical forests in LDCs use this destructive form of selective cutting. For example, 100 trees may be destroyed just to remove 1 mature mahogany tree in a tropical forest.

Some tree species do best when grown in full or moderate sunlight in forest openings or in large cleared and seeded areas. Even-aged stands or tree farms of such shade-intolerant species are usually harvested by shelterwood cutting, seed-tree cutting, or clear-cutting.

Shelterwood cutting is the removal of all mature trees in an area in a series of cuttings, typically over a period of ten years. This technique can be applied to even-aged or uneven-aged stands. In the first harvest, selected mature trees, unwanted tree species, and dying, defective, and diseased trees are removed. This

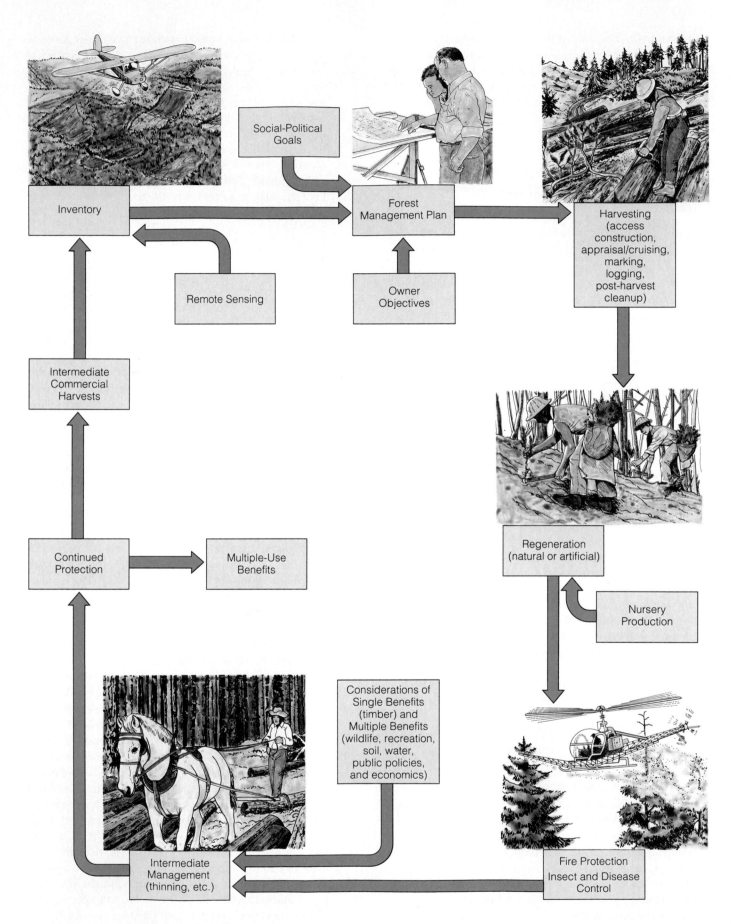

Figure 15-2 The cycle of forest productivity.

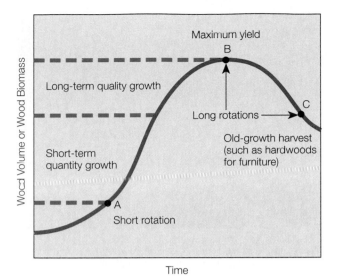

Figure 15-3 Rotation cycle of forest management.

Figure 15-4 Selective cutting of ponderosa pine in Deschutes National Forest, an old-growth forest near Sisters, Oregon.

Pete K. Martin/U.S. Forest Service

Figure 15-5 First stage of shelterwood cutting of a stand of longleaf pine in south Alabama.

J. D. Hodges/University of Mississippi

Figure 15-6 Seed trees left after the seed-tree cutting of a stand of longleaf pine in Alabama. About ten trees per hectare are left to reseed the area.

J. D. Hodges/University of Mississippi

cut opens up the forest floor to light and leaves the best trees to cast seed and provide shelter for growing seedlings (Figure 15-5).

After a number of seedlings have taken hold, a second cutting removes more of the remaining mature trees. Some of the best mature trees are left to provide shelter for the growing young trees. After the young trees are well established, a third cutting removes the remaining mature trees and allows the even-aged stand of young trees to grow to maturity.

This method allows natural seeding from the best seed trees and protects seedlings from being crowded out. It leaves a fairly natural-looking forest that can be used for a variety of purposes. It also helps reduce soil erosion and provides good habitat for wildlife.

Without careful planning and supervision, however, loggers may take too many trees in the initial cut-

ting, especially the most valuable trees. Shelterwood cutting is also more costly and takes more skill and planning than clear-cutting.

Seed-tree cutting harvests nearly all the trees on a site in one cutting, leaving a few seed-producing, wind-resistant trees uniformly distributed as a source of seed to regenerate a new crop of trees (Figure 15-6). After the new trees have become established, the seed trees are sometimes harvested.

By allowing a variety of species to grow at one time, seed-tree cutting leaves an aesthetically pleasing forest, useful for recreation, deer hunting, erosion control, and wildlife conservation. Leaving the best trees for seed can also lead to genetic improvement in the new stand.

Clear-cutting is the removal of all trees from a given area in a single cutting to establish a new, even-aged stand or tree farm. The clear-cut area may consist of a whole stand (Figures 10-2 and 15-7), a group, a strip, or a series of patches (Figure 10-19). After all trees are cut, the site is reforested naturally from seed released by the harvest, or foresters broadcast seed over the site or plant genetically superior seedlings raised in a nursery. If clear-cut areas are kept small enough, seeding may occur from trees in adjacent areas.

Currently, almost two-thirds of the annual U.S. timber production and about one-third of the cutting in national forests is harvested by clear-cutting. Clear-cutting increases the volume of timber harvested per hectare, reduces road building, often permits reforesting with genetically improved stock of fast-growing trees, and shortens the time needed to establish a new stand of trees (Figure 15-3). Timber companies prefer this method because it requires much less skill and planning than other harvesting methods and usually gives them the maximum economic return.

However, large-scale clear-cutting on steeply sloped land leads to severe soil erosion, sediment water pollution, flooding from melting snow and heavy rains (see Case Study on p. 342), and landslides. The heavy logging equipment also compacts the soil and reduces its productivity. As a result, such slopes often remain barren wastelands (Figure 1-1).

Clear-cutting leaves ugly, unnatural forest openings that take decades to regenerate (Figures 15-7 and 10-19) and reduces the recreational value of the forest. It also reduces the number and types of wildlife habitats and thus reduces biological diversity. Trees in stands bordering clear-cut areas are more vulnerable to blowdown by windstorms.

If done properly, clear-cutting can be useful for some shade-intolerant species, such as the Douglas fir. That means not clear-cutting large areas or steeply sloped sites and making sure that the area is reseeded or replanted and protected until the next harvest. The problem is that timber companies have a built-in economic incentive to use large-scale clear-cutting, often on species that could be harvested by less environmentally destructive methods.

A variation of clear-cutting is **whole-tree harvesting**, in which a machine cuts each tree at ground level. In some cases, the entire tree is then transported to a chipping machine, in which huge blades reduce the wood to small chips in about one minute. Some whole-tree harvesting machines pull up the entire tree so that roots are also converted into wood chips. This approach is used primarily to harvest stands for use as pulpwood or fuelwood chips.

Many foresters and ecologists oppose this method because the removal of all tree materials, including standing dead timber and fallen logs, eventually depletes the soil of plant nutrients and removes numerous wildlife habitats (Figure 4-15). Research is under way to determine how whole-tree harvesting methods might be modified to reduce such harmful environmental effects.

Figure 15-7 Forest Service clear-cut in Oregon. All trees in the area are removed and the area is reseeded.

Carolina Biological Supply Company

PROTECTING FORESTS FROM PATHOGENS AND INSECTS In a healthy, diverse forest, tree diseases and insect populations rarely get out of control and seldom destroy many trees. However, a tree farm of one species has few natural defenses and is vulnerable to attack by pathogens and insects.

The most destructive tree diseases are caused by parasitic fungi. In the United States, three highly damaging tree diseases were introduced accidentally from other countries: chestnut blight (from China), Dutch elm disease (from Asia via Europe), and white-pine blister rust (from Europe). Chestnut blight has almost eliminated the once-abundant and valuable chestnut tree from eastern hardwood forests. Dutch elm disease has killed more than two-thirds of the elm trees in the United States.

A few insect species can cause severe damage, especially in tree farms or simplified forests where natural controls don't exist. For example, bark beetles bore channels through the layer beneath the bark of spruce, fir, and pine trees, and the numerous channels loosen the bark. These insects have killed large areas of forest in the western and southern United States. The larvae of leaf eaters, such as spruce budworm and gypsy moth, eat the needles or leaves of trees. Repeated attacks over several years can kill trees by eliminating the foliage they need to carry out photosynthesis and produce food.

The best and cheapest way to prevent excessive damage to trees from diseases and insects is to preserve the biological diversity of the forest. Other methods include

- banning imported timber that might carry harmful parasites

Figure 15-8 Surface fire in Ocala National Forest in Florida. Occasional fires like this burn deadwood, undergrowth, and litter and help prevent more destructive crown fires in some types of forests.

- removing infected trees and vegetation
- clear-cutting infected areas and removing or burning all debris
- treating diseased trees with antibiotics
- developing disease-resistant tree species
- applying insecticides and fungicides (Section 23-1)
- using integrated pest management (Section 23-5)

PROTECTING FORESTS FROM FIRES Scientists now recognize that occasional natural fires set by lightning are an important part of the ecological cycle of many forests. Some species, especially conifers such as pines and redwoods (Figure 2-6), have thick, fire-resistant bark and benefit from occasional fires. For example, the seeds of some conifers, such as the giant sequoia (Figure 4-6) and the jack pine, are released or germinate only after being exposed to intense heat.

In evaluating the effects of fire on forest ecosystems, it's important to distinguish between three kinds of forest fires: surface, crown, and ground. **Surface fires** are low-level fires that usually burn only undergrowth and leaf litter on the forest floor (Figure 15-8). These fires kill seedlings and small trees but don't kill most mature trees. Wildlife can usually escape from these fairly slow-burning fires.

In forests where ground litter accumulates rapidly, a surface fire every five years or so burns away flammable material and helps prevent more destructive crown and ground fires. Surface fires also release and recycle valuable mineral nutrients tied up in slowly decomposing litter and undergrowth, increase the activity of nitrogen-fixing bacteria, stimulate the germination of certain tree seeds, and help control pathogens and in-

Figure 15-9 Destructive crown fire in Yellowstone National Park during the summer of 1988. Wildlife that can't escape are killed, and wildlife habitats are destroyed. Severe erosion can occur. Since 1972, Park Service policy has been to allow most lightning-caused fires to burn themselves out, as long as they don't threaten human lives, park facilities, private property, or endangered wildlife. The Park Service's intention is to allow fire to play its important role in forest succession and regeneration. After fires raged in parts of Yellowstone National Park during the hot, dry summer of 1988, some people called for a reversal of this policy. Biologists oppose this and contend that damage was more widespread than it should have been because the earlier park policy of fighting all fires had allowed the buildup of flammable ground litter and small plants.

sects. Some wildlife species, such as deer, moose, elk, muskrat, woodcock, and quail, depend on occasional surface fires to maintain their habitats and to provide food in the form of vegetation that sprouts after fires.

Crown fires are extremely hot fires that burn ground vegetation and tree tops (Figure 15-9). They usually occur in forests where all fire has been prevented for several decades, allowing the buildup of deadwood, leaves, and other flammable ground litter. In such forests, an intense surface fire driven by a strong wind can spread to treetops. These rapidly burning fires can destroy all vegetation, kill wildlife, and lead to accelerated erosion.

Sometimes, surface fires become **ground fires**, which burn partially decayed leaves, or peat (Figure 7-14), below the ground surface. Such fires, common in northern bogs, may smolder for days or weeks before being detected. They are very difficult to extinguish.

Figure 15-10 The fires that raged in parts of Yellowstone National Park during the summer of 1988 affected less than 0.1% of the park's area so badly that it won't recover. The bulldozers used to fight the fires did more damage to the park's delicate soils than the searing heat. Ash from the fire provided mineral nutrients for new plant growth, and within a few weeks after the fire, grasses and other small pioneer plants, such as fireweed, took over the charred fields. In 1989, park visits rose by about 20%, and business was booming in surrounding towns.

Jim Peaco/National Park Service

The protection of forest resources from fire involves four approaches: *prevention, prescribed burning, presuppression,* and *suppression*. Prevention of forest fires, the most important and the cheapest method, is primarily an educational process. Other methods of fire prevention include requiring burning permits and closing all or parts of a forest to travel and camping during periods of drought and high fire danger.

The Smokey-the-Bear educational campaign of the Forest Service and the National Advertising Council has been successful in preventing many forest fires in the U.S., saving many lives, and avoiding losses of billions of dollars. Ecologists, however, contend that it also has caused harm by allowing litter buildup in some forests, thus increasing the likelihood of highly destructive crown fires (Figure 15-9). For that reason, many fires in national parks and wilderness areas are now allowed to burn as part of the natural ecological cycle of succession and regeneration (Figure 15-10).

Prescribed surface fires in some forests can be an effective method for preventing crown fires, by reducing litter buildup. They are also used to control outbreaks of tree diseases and pests. These fires are started only by well-trained personnel when weather and forest conditions are ideal for control and proper intensity of burning. Prescribed fires are also timed to keep levels of air pollution as low as possible.

Presuppression involves trying to detect a fire at an early stage and reducing its spread and damage. To help confine fires and allow access by fire-fighting equipment, vegetation is cleared to form firebreaks and fire roads, and brush and trees are cleared along existing roads. Helicopters and small airplanes are used to detect small fires before they get out of control. Helicopters are also used to carry fire fighters to remote fires within minutes of detection.

Once a wildfire starts, fire fighters have a number of methods for fire suppression. They use specially designed bulldozers and breaker plows to establish firebreaks. They pump water onto the fire from tank trucks, and they drop water or fire-retardant chemicals from aircraft. Trained personnel use controlled backfires to create burned areas to confine fires.

PROTECTING FORESTS FROM AIR POLLUTION AND GLOBAL WARMING Air pollution is a growing threat to many forests, especially in MDCs. Forests at high elevations and forests downwind from urban and industrial centers are exposed to a variety of air pollutants that can harm trees, especially conifers. In addition to doing direct harm, prolonged exposure to multiple air pollutants makes trees much more vulnerable to drought, diseases, insects, and mosses.

Large-scale forest degradation from air pollution has occurred in Poland, Czechoslovakia, Great Britain, France, Germany, Switzerland, Scandinavia, and eastern North America. The only solution is to sharply reduce emissions of the offending pollutants from coal-burning power plants, industrial plants, and cars (Section 21-4).

In coming decades, an even-greater threat to forests, especially temperate and boreal forests, may be projected changes in regional climate brought about by global warming (Section 11-1). Possible ways to slow down projected global warming are discussed in Section 11-2.

Most commercial foresters believe that tree farms are the best way to meet the increasing demand for wood and wood products and to increase short-term profits for timber companies. They believe that these intensively managed forests can be harvested and regenerated in ways that conserve these potentially renewable resources for future generations.

High yields from tree farms can reduce pressure to clear large areas of old-growth forests. Planting a tree farm is also the quickest way to reforest degraded land and prevent soil erosion and desertification.

Other foresters and many ecologists are concerned that planting vast forest monocultures will lead to environmental degradation of soil and watersheds and to a decline in forest quality and wildlife diversity. These critics are not completely against this form of forest management, but they believe that its use should be limited.

The German experience in forestry between 1840 and 1918 shows the long-term harmful effects of monoculture forestry. Around 1840, German foresters decided to clear-cut diverse natural forests and replace them with pine and spruce plantations to increase the output of wood per hectare. These trees were harvested every 20 to 30 years to provide low-quality timber and pulp. Deciduous hardwood and true fir species became nearly extinct.

Yields of pine and spruce increased for a time, but the monoculture plantations depleted the soil of plant nutrients. After the second or third generation, the yield of the pine and spruce stands declined and the general quality of the wood decreased. Many trees were stunted, and the number killed by pests and diseases and blown down by storms increased.

After 1918, German forestry officials began shifting to a more natural type of forestry management. Monoculture stands were replanted with uneven-aged mixtures of commercially valuable species. Hardwood species were interplanted with softwood species. Instead of cutting all the trees in an area (clear-cutting), loggers harvested only certain economically important trees in a stand (selective cutting).

The result was an increase in timber production and an improvement in soil quality. Today, German foresters are appalled to see the United States and other countries making the same mistakes their predecessors made in sacrificing long-term, sustainable productivity for short-term gain. What do you think?

SUSTAINABLE-EARTH FORESTRY To timber companies, sustainable forestry means getting a sustainable yield of commercial timber in as short a time as possible. This usually means using even-aged management, in which diverse forests are cleared and replaced with intensely managed tree farms.

To environmentalists, this approach is ecologically and economically unsustainable (see Pro/Con above). They call for widespread use of sustainable-Earth forestry, which recognizes that a biologically diverse forest ecosystem is the best protection against soil erosion, flooding, sediment water pollution, and tree loss from fire, wind, insects, and diseases. A diverse ecosystem also provides natural forest regeneration, habitats for a wide variety of fish and wildlife, and many recreational opportunities for people. It is based on the concept that we cannot have a sustainable yield of anything until we first have a sustainable ecosystem to produce the yield.

Sustainable-Earth forest management emphasizes

- growing and harvesting a diversity of high-quality timber, instead of short-term pulpwood production

- growing timber on long rotations, generally from 100 to 200 years depending on the species and the soil quality (Figure 15-3, point c)

- selective cutting of individual trees or small groups of most tree species (Figure 15-4)

- extreme precautions to protect topsoil, upon which all present and future forest productivity depends

- methods of road building and logging that minimize soil erosion and compaction

- use of small, lightweight equipment for logging

- clear-cutting only in small patches of less than 6 hectares (15 acres) and never on steeply sloped land (more than a 15- to 20-degree slope)

- leaving standing dead trees and fallen timber to maintain diverse wildlife habitats and enhance nutrient recycling

- leaving slash, treetops, and branches to help restore soil fertility, unless it causes too much buildup of dry fuel on the ground or hinders seeding of some desirable species

- relying on natural controls to protect the forest from most diseases and pests

- controlling occasional severe pest outbreaks by using natural predators (biological control) and integrated pest management (Section 23-5)

Sustainable-Earth forestry does not mean that tree farms or even-aged management should never be used, but it does mean that their use should be severely limited on public land and especially in old-growth forests (Section 10-5). On private land, they should be regulated to prevent excessive soil erosion and water pollution from runoff of sediment, fertilizers, and pesticides.

MANAGEMENT AND CONSERVATION OF NATIONAL FORESTS IN THE UNITED STATES

About 22% of the country's commercial forest area is located within the 156 national forests managed by the U.S. Forest Service (see Spotlight on p. 390). More than 3 million cattle and sheep graze on national forestlands each year. National forests receive more recreational visits than any other federal public lands—more than twice as many as the National Park System.

Almost half of national forestlands are open to commercial logging. They supply about 20% of the country's total annual timber harvest—enough wood to build about 2 million homes. Each year, private timber companies bid for rights to cut a certain amount of timber from areas designated by the Forest Service.

The Forest Service is required by law to manage national forests according to the principles of sustained yield and multiple use. However, managing a public forest for balanced multiple use is difficult and sometimes impossible. Because of growing and often conflicting demands on national forest resources, the management policies of the Forest Service have been the subject of heated controversy since the 1960s.

Timber company officials complain that they aren't allowed to buy and cut enough timber on public lands, especially in remaining old-growth forests in California and the Pacific Northwest (Section 10-5). Conservationists charge that the Forest Service has made timber harvesting the dominant use in most national forests and has turned multiple use into multiple abuse (see Pro/Con on p. 399).

For example, roughly 74% of the 1990 Forest Service budget was devoted directly or indirectly to the sale of timber. By comparison, 4% of the budget was used for recreation, 2.3% for wildlife and fish conservation, and 1.3% for soil, water, and air management. The Forest Service gets money from Congress and then uses it to make more money for its budget by selling timber. Much of any money the agency makes on a timber sale is kept by the agency, and any losses are passed on to the taxpayer. Since timbering is a way to increase its budget, the Forest Service has a powerful built-in incentive to make timber sales its primary objective.

Congress eased some of the controversy between environmentalists and the Forest Service by passing the National Forest Management Act (NFMA) of 1976, after conservation and environmental groups had won several key court decisions. This law sets certain limitations on clear-cutting and other timber-harvesting methods in national forests. Those restrictions, however, are weakened by numerous exemptions and exceptions written into the law at the urging of timber company interests.

RECYCLING WASTEPAPER

The United States leads the world in the consumption and waste of paper. Annual per capita consumption of paper in the United States is about 318 kilograms (699 pounds), compared with only 2.3 kilograms (5 pounds) per person in India.

Sharply increasing the recycling of paper is a key to reducing clearance and degradation of forests, solid waste, and water and air pollution. Conservationists estimate that at least 50% of the world's wastepaper (mostly newspapers, cardboard, office paper, and computer and copier paper) could be recycled by the end of this century. Only about 25% was recycled in 1989. The percentage was much higher in the Netherlands (53%), Japan (50%, including 90% of its newspapers and 81% of its cardboard products), Mexico (45%), the former West Germany (41%), and Sweden (40%).

During World War II, when paper drives and recycling were national priorities, the United States recycled about 45% of its wastepaper. In 1989, only about 32% was recycled. Countries with the lowest paper recycling rates in 1989 were New Zealand (16%), the Soviet Union (19%), Canada (20%), and China (21%).

Product overpackaging is a major contributor to paper use and waste. Packages inside packages and oversized containers are designed to trick consumers into thinking they're getting more for their money. Nearly $1 of every $10 spent for food in the United States goes for throwaway packaging. Junk mail also wastes enormous amounts of paper.* Each year, the U.S. work force throws away enough office and writing paper to build a 4-meter- (12-foot-) high wall stretching from New York City to Los Angeles.

Recycling the country's Sunday newspapers would save an entire forest of 500,000 trees each week. Recycling paper also saves energy because it takes 30% to 64% less energy to produce the same weight of recycled paper as making the paper from trees. Currently, only about 10% of U.S. newspapers are printed on recycled paper. The U.S. paper industry is the country's third largest consumer of energy and the largest user of fuel oil.

Recycling paper also reduces air pollution from pulp mills by 74% to 95%, lowers water pollution by 35%, conserves large quantities of water, and saves landfill space. Recycling paper also helps prevent

---

*You can reduce your junk mail by about 75% by writing to Mail Preference Service, Direct Marketing Association, 11 West 42nd Street, P.O. Box 3861, New York, NY 10163-3861. They will stop your name from being added to most large mailing-list companies.

Conservationists are alarmed at proposals by the Forest Service to double the timber harvest on national forests between 1986 and 2030 at the urging of the Reagan and Bush administrations and the timber industry.

To accomplish this, the Forest Service has proposed the building of new roads in the national forests over the next 50 years whose overall length will be six times the length of roads in the entire interstate highway system. Conservationists charge that plans to build roads in inaccessible areas (about one-fifth of the proposed new roads) are designed to disqualify those areas from inclusion in the National Wilderness Preservation System.

Conservationists have also accused the Forest Service of poor financial management of public forests. By law, the Forest Service must sell timber for no less than the cost of reforesting the land it was harvested from, but the cost of building roads to make the timber accessible is not included in this price. Most of these roads are built by the timber purchaser, and the road-building costs are deducted from the price of the timber. In essence, the government exchanges timber for roads, with taxpayers paying for the roads used by private timber companies.

Timber sales in some national forests make money, but losses in other areas more than wipe out those gains. In 1990, for example, timber on public lands was sold to private firms at prices so low that sales revenues failed to cover government costs in 98 of the 120 na-

tional forests logged in that year. Studies have shown that between 1978 and 1990, timber sales from national forests lost $3.7 billion. With interest, this addition to the country's tremendous debt cost taxpayers $5.6 billion. This means that taxpayers are providing the timber industry with subsidies that average $343 million a year. Some have suggested that we would be better off if we gave the money to the logging companies and kept them out of the national forests.

One glaring example is the logging operation in Alaska's Tongas National Forest, the world's last remaining largely intact temperate rain forest. During the 1980s, the Forest Service lost as much as $383 million in timber sales in this forest. Congress and the Forest Service gave two timber companies 50-year contracts that allow them to cut giant trees in this old-growth forest. The companies pay the government slightly more than $2 for a tree that sells in Japan for hundreds of dollars.

Conservationists oppose these subsidies for private timber companies at taxpayers' expense. The subsidies encourage the cutting of virgin timber on remaining stands of old-growth forests on public lands (Section 10-5) and discourage the recycling of wastepaper that would sharply reduce the demand for virgin timber.

Representatives of the timber industry argue that such subsidies help taxpayers by keeping lumber prices down. However, conservationists note that each year, taxpayers already give the lumber industry

tax breaks almost equal to the cost of managing the entire National Forest System.

Forestry experts and conservationists have suggested several ways to reduce overexploitation of publicly owned timber resources and provide true multiple use of national forests as required by law:

- Cut the present annual harvest of timber from national forests in half instead of doubling it as proposed by the timber industry. The Forest Service took a step in this direction in 1990 when it unveiled a plan to reduce the annual cut in national forests by 11% between 1990 and 1995.

- Keep at least 50% of remaining old-growth timber in any national forest from being cut.

- Require that timber from national forests be sold at a price that includes the costs of roads, site preparation, and site regeneration.

- Require that *all* timber sales in national forests yield a profit for taxpayers based on the fair market value of any timber harvested.

- Don't allow money from sales of timber in national forests to be used to supplement the Forest Service budget.

- Use a much larger portion of the Forest Service budget to improve management and increase timber yields of the country's privately owned commercial forestland to take pressure off the national forests.

What do you think should be done?

---

groundwater contamination from the toxic ink left after paper eventually biodegrades in landfills over a 30- to 60-year period.

Recycling paper can also save money. In 1988, American Telephone and Telegraph earned more than $485,000 in revenue and saved $1.3 million in disposal costs by collecting and recycling high-grade office paper.

Requiring people to separate paper from other waste materials is a key to increased recycling. Otherwise, paper becomes so contaminated with other trash that wastepaper dealers won't buy it. Slick-paper magazines and glossy newspaper and advertising supplements cause contamination and must not be included.

This textbook, other books, and magazines using slick paper with color cannot be effectively printed on recycled paper because of inking and other problems. That is why the publisher and I donate money each year to tree-planting organizations so that at least 1 tree is planted for each tree used in printing this book. To make up for the additional paper I use in writing this book, I plant 50 trees for each tree that I use.

Tax subsidies and other financial incentives that make it cheaper to produce paper from trees than from recycling hinder wastepaper recycling in the United States. Widely fluctuating prices and a lack of demand for recycled paper products also make recycling wastepaper a risky financial venture.

For example, since 1988, the supply of recycled newspapers has exceeded the capacity of U.S. paper mills to use it and the price for recycled paper has plummeted. The problem is that only 8 of 23 U.S. paper mills (and only 1 of the 40 Canadian mills) have modernized to produce acceptable newsprint from recycled paper, and most of the 11 new mills that will open by 1992 are not designed to make effective use of recycled paper. Loans and tax credits to companies that invest in paper-recycling equipment could help ease this unfortunate situation that is discouraging communities from recycling paper just at a time when consumer interest in doing so has soared.

If the demand for recycled paper products increased, recycled paper would be cheaper and the price paid for wastepaper would rise. One way to increase demand is to require federal and state governments to use recycled paper products as much as possible. Half of the trash the government throws away is paper. A tax can also be added to every metric ton of virgin newsprint that is used, as is now done in Florida.

In the mid-1970s, Congress passed a law calling for federal agencies to buy as many recycled products as practical. That law has failed because it contains so many exemptions that almost nothing has to be recycled.

Simple measures like asking teachers to instruct their students to write on both sides of the paper would also reduce unnecessary paper waste and increase environmental awareness. Conservationists call for national, state, and local policies designed to recycle half of the wastepaper in the United States by the year 2000.

15-3 Rangelands

THE WORLD'S RANGELAND RESOURCES Almost half of Earth's ice-free land is **rangeland**: land that supplies forage or vegetation (grasses, grasslike plants, and shrubs) for grazing and browsing animals and that is not intensively managed. Most rangelands are grasslands in semiarid areas too dry for rain-fed cropland

(Figure 5-19). Other types of rangeland are desert shrublands, shrub woodlands, temperate forests, and tropical forests.

Only about 42% of the world's rangeland is used for grazing livestock. Much of the rest is too dry, cold, or remote from population centers to be grazed by large numbers of livestock animals.

About 34% of the total land area of the United States is rangeland. Most of this is short-grass prairies in the arid and semiarid western half of the country (Figure 5-19). About 52% of the nation's rangeland is privately owned, and 43% of U.S. rangeland is owned by the general public and managed by the federal government, mostly by the Forest Service and the Bureau of Land Management (Figure 15-1). The remaining 5% is owned by state and local governments.

RANGE LIVESTOCK PRODUCTION Some grazing and browsing animals, called **ruminant animals**, have three- or four-chambered stomachs, which digest the cellulose in grasses and other vegetation. The simple food chain, grass → grazing animals → humans, is an important source of the protein we need. Ruminant animals are also sources of a major greenhouse gas—methane (Figure 11-2). Nonruminant livestock animals, such as pigs and chickens, can't feed on rangeland vegetation.

Worldwide, there are about 10 billion ruminant and nonruminant domesticated animals—twice the number of people on Earth. About 3 billion of these animals are cattle (1.5 billion), sheep, and goats. Three-fourths of these ruminants forage on rangeland vegetation. The rest are fed mostly in feedlots (Figure 14-3). Seven billion pigs, chickens, and other nonruminant livestock animals feed mostly on cereal grains grown on cropland.

CHARACTERISTICS OF RANGELAND VEGETATION Most of the grasses on rangelands have deep, complex root systems (Figure 12-4). The multiple branches of their roots make these grasses hard to uproot, helping prevent soil erosion.

When the leaf tip of most plants is eaten, the leaf stops growing, but each leaf of rangeland grass grows from its base, not its tip. When the upper half of the shoot and leaves of grass is eaten, the plant can grow back quickly. However, the lower half of the plant must remain if the plant is to survive and grow new leaves. As long as only the upper half is eaten, rangeland grass is a renewable resource that can be grazed again and again.

RANGELAND CARRYING CAPACITY AND OVERGRAZING Grasslands have a remarkable ability to survive and regenerate as long as they're not severely overgrazed, undergrazed, or plowed up and planted with crops. The Dust Bowl in the Great Plains is a tragic example of what can happen when dry grasslands are plowed up and planted with crops without effective soil conservation (see Case Study on p. 323).

Each type of grassland has a herbivore **carrying capacity**: the maximum number of herbivores a given area can support without consuming the metabolic reserve needed for grass renewal. Carrying capacity is influenced by season, range condition, annual climatic conditions, past grazing use, soil type, kinds of grazing animals, and how long animals graze in an area.

Light to moderate grazing is necessary for the health of grasslands. It maintains water and nutrient cycling needed for healthy grass growth and healthy root systems, hinders soil erosion, and encourages buildup of organic soil matter.

Overgrazing occurs when too many grazing animals feed too long and exceed the carrying capacity of a grassland area. Large populations of wild herbivores can overgraze range in prolonged dry periods, but most overgrazing is caused by excessive numbers of livestock feeding too long in a particular area.

Figure 15-11 compares normally grazed and severely overgrazed grassland. Heavy overgrazing converts continuous grass cover into patches of grass and makes the soil more vulnerable to erosion, especially by wind. Then forbs and woody shrubs such as mesquite and prickly cactus invade and take over.

Severe overgrazing combined with prolonged drought can convert potentially productive rangeland into desert (see Figure 12-12 and Case Study on p. 320). Dune buggies, motorcycles, and other off-road vehicles also damage or destroy rangeland vegetation.

CONDITION OF THE WORLD'S RANGELANDS

An estimate of how close a particular rangeland is to its productive potential for forage vegetation is called **range condition**. Range condition is usually classified as excellent (more than 80% of its potential forage production), good (50% to 80%), fair (21% to 49%), and poor (less than 21%).

Except in North America, no comprehensive survey of rangeland conditions has been made. However, data from surveys in various countries indicate that most of the world's rangelands have been degraded to some degree.

Between 1936 and 1988, public rangeland in the United States in fair and poor condition decreased from 84% to 68%, with 26% in poor condition and 42% in fair condition. Privately owned rangeland showed similar improvements.

Despite this improvement, by 1988 about 68% of the country's public rangeland was in unsatisfactory (poor or fair) condition, 29% was in good condition, and only 3% was in excellent condition. However, livestock agencies and farm organizations look at these

Figure 15-11 Overgrazed (left) and lightly grazed (right) rangeland.

same data and say that 74% of the country's public rangeland is in fair or better condition. This means that by 1988, these lands were in better condition than at any time during this century.

Conservationists argue that overall estimates of rangeland condition greatly underestimate severe degradation of heavily grazed areas. Such areas are mostly *riparian zones* — thin strips of lush vegetation adjacent to streams and springs where livestock get their water. According to Hugh Harper, a former grazing management specialist with the Bureau of Land Management, "98% of the livestock use occurs on 1 or 2% of the land — riparian areas." The basic problem in the western United States is that we insist on raising cattle, which need large amounts of water, in a water-poor environment.

RANGELAND MANAGEMENT The primary goal of range management is to maximize livestock productivity without overgrazing rangeland vegetation. The most widely used way to prevent overgrazing is to control the **stocking rate** — the number of a particular kind of animal grazing on a given area — so it doesn't exceed the carrying capacity.

Determining the carrying capacity of a range site, however, is difficult and costly. Even when the carrying capacity is known, it can change because of drought, invasions by new species, and other environmental factors.

Controlling the distribution of grazing animals over a range is the best way to prevent overgrazing and undergrazing. Ranchers can control distribution by building fences to protect degraded rangeland, rotating livestock from one grazing area to another, providing supplemental feeding at selected sites, and locating water holes and salt blocks in strategic places.

A more expensive and less widely used method of rangeland management is to suppress the growth of unwanted plants by spraying with herbicides, mechanical removal, or controlled burning. A cheaper and more effective way to remove unwanted vegetation is controlled, short-term trampling by large numbers of livestock.

Growth of desirable vegetation can be increased by seeding and applying fertilizer, but this method is usually too costly. On the other hand, reseeding is an excellent way to restore severely degraded rangeland.

For decades, hundreds of thousands of predators, such as coyotes (which sometimes kill sheep and goats), have been shot, trapped, and poisoned by ranchers, farmers, and federal predator control officials. In 1990, $29.4 million in federal funds and $15 million in state funds were spent to kill 250,000 wild animals that farmers and ranchers declared pests—everything from prairie dogs to coyotes to grizzly bears. Several hundred pet dogs and domestic cats were also accidently trapped or poisoned. However, experience has shown that killing predators is an expensive and temporary solution—one that sometimes makes matters worse (see Pro/Con on p. 403).

DOMESTICATING WILD HERBIVORES Recently, there has been renewed interest in wild game ranching in arid and semiarid rangelands, especially in Africa. Some ecologists have suggested that wild herbivores, such as eland, oryx, and Grant's gazelles, should be raised in ranches on these hot, dry grasslands.

Because wild herbivores have a more diversified diet than cattle, they can make more efficient use of the available vegetation. Also, most wild herbivores need less water than cattle and are more resistant than cattle to animal diseases found in savanna grasslands.

Since 1978, David Hopcraft has carried out a highly successful game ranching experiment on the Athi Plains near Nairobi, Kenya. The ranch is stocked with a variety of native grazers and browsers, including antelope, zebras, giraffes, and ostriches. Some cattle are also being raised for comparison, but they are gradually being phased out. The yield of meat from the native herbivores has been rising steadily, the condition of the range has improved, and costs are much lower than those for raising cattle in the same region.

MANAGEMENT OF U.S. PUBLIC RANGELANDS Government agencies are required by law to manage public rangelands according to the principle of multiple use. Yet, federal lands larger in area than the combined acreage of the entire Eastern Seaboard from Maine to Florida are leased to 2% of U.S. ranchers for livestock grazing. For years, ranchers and conservationists have battled over how much ranchers should be charged for the privilege of grazing their livestock on public lands (see Pro/Con on p. 404).

THREATS TO PARKS In 1912, Congress created the U.S. National Park System and declared that national parks are to be set aside to conserve and preserve scenery, wildlife, and natural and historic objects for the use, observation, health, and pleasure of people. The parks are to be maintained in a manner that leaves them unimpaired for future generations.

Today, there are over 1,100 national parks of more than 1,000 hectares (2,500 acres) in more than 120 countries. Together, they cover an area equal to that of Alaska, Texas, and California combined. This is an important achievement in the global conservation movement, spurred by the development of the world's first national park system in the United States. In addition to national parks, the U.S. public has access to state, county, and city parks (Figure 9-19). Most state parks are located near urban areas and thus are used more heavily than national parks.

Throughout the world, parks are increasingly threatened. In MDCs, many national parks are threatened by nearby industrial development, urban growth, air and water pollution, roads, noise, invasion by alien species, and loss of natural species. Some of the most popular national parks are also threatened by overuse.

In LDCs, the problems are worse. Plant life and animal life in national parks are being threatened by local people who desperately need wood, cropland, and other resources. Poachers kill animals and sell their parts, such as rhino horns. Park services in these countries have too little money and staff to fight these invasions, either through enforcement or through public education programs. Also, most national parks in MDCs and LDCs are too small to sustain many of their natural species, especially larger animals.

U.S. NATIONAL AND STATE PARKS The National Park System is dominated by 50 national parks found mostly in the West (Figure 15-1). These geologic repositories of majestic beauty (Figure 7-9) and biological diversity have been called America's crown jewels. They are supplemented by numerous state parks.

Nature walks, guided tours, and other educational services provided by National Park Service employees have provided many Americans with a better understanding of how nature works. Some conservationists urge that this effective educational program be expanded to show citizens ways to work with nature in their own daily lives. They have proposed that all park buildings and other facilities be designed as or converted into systems that demonstrate energy-efficient, low-polluting methods of heating, cooling, water purification, waste handling, transportation, and recycling.

Between 1940 and 1972, a controversial and largely unsuccessful control program was waged by western ranchers and the U.S. Department of the Interior against livestock predators, especially the coyote (Figure 15-12). Because coyotes are too numerous and too crafty to be hunted effectively, emphasis was placed on poisoning them. The most popular poison was sodium fluoroacetate, known as compound 1080.

A 1972 report by the government-appointed Advisory Committee on Predator Control recommended that all poisoning of predators by the federal government be halted because poisons can accidentally kill nontarget animals, including eagles, other endangered species, and people. After receiving the report, President Richard M. Nixon issued an executive order banning predator poisoning on public lands or by government employees anywhere. The Environmental Protection Agency then prohibited the use of several poisons, including 1080, even on private land.

Since 1972, western ranchers have tried to have this ban lifted. In 1985, under pressure from ranchers, western congressional representatives, and the Reagan administration, the EPA approved the use of compound 1080 in livestock collars. These poison-filled rubber collars are placed around the necks of sheep, goats, and other livestock. Coyotes and other predators are poisoned when they bite the neck of their prey.

Environmental groups strongly oppose the use of compound 1080. They argue that the poison dribbling down the neck of a sheep after it has been killed by a coyote could kill golden eagles, vultures, and other scavengers feeding on the sheep carcass. Carcasses of poisoned coyotes could also kill scavengers. Conservationists also fear that some ranchers might illegally extract the poison from collars and use it to bait livestock carcasses.

Because the coyote is so adaptable and prolific, conservationists argue that any poisoning program is doomed to failure and is a waste of tax dollars. It would cost taxpayers much less to pay ranchers for each sheep or goat killed by a coyote.

If poisoning or other programs did succeed in killing most coyotes, the populations of rodents and rabbits they eat and keep under control would explode. These small herbivores then would compete with livestock for rangeland vegetation, reducing livestock productivity and causing rangeland degradation. In the long run, a drastic reduction of coyote populations would cause larger economic losses for ranchers than the losses of livestock killed by these predators.

Conservationists suggest that fences, repellents, and trained guard dogs be used to keep predators away. Using a combination of these methods, sheep producers in Kansas have one of the country's lowest rates of livestock losses to coyotes. The annual cost of their predator control program is only 5% of what neighboring Oklahoma spends on a less effective predator control program of poisoning and trapping.

In 1986, Department of Agriculture researchers reported that predation can be sharply reduced by penning young lambs and cattle together for 30 days and then allowing them to graze together on the same range. When predators attack, cattle butt and kick them and in the process protect themselves and the sheep. Llamas and donkeys, also tough fighters against predators, can be used in the same way to protect sheep.

Conservationists point out that most coyotes and other predators do not prey on livestock. Instead of trying to kill all predators, they suggest concentrating on killing or

Figure 15-12 For decades, ranchers in the western United States have declared war on the coyote because of its reputation for killing livestock, as shown by these coyote carcasses lashed to a fence in California. Each year, thousands of coyotes are poisoned, trapped, or shot in the western United States, with all U.S. taxpayers footing the bill for this predator control program that benefits ranchers. Despite these costly efforts, the coyote's high reproductive rate and adaptability allows its population to remain fairly stable. In 1989, the federal government spent $1.35 million on livestock predator control in Wyoming. The average of $182 spent for each animal killed was more than four times the value of sheep lost to predators.

removing the rogue individuals. Despite strong opposition from conservationists, the $29-million-a-year federal animal-damage control program to kill livestock predators continues to be funded because of the political power of ranchers and farmers. What do you think should be done?

The 23,000 U.S. ranchers (including corporations like Union Oil and Getty Oil) who hold permits to graze livestock on Bureau of Land Management and National Forest Service rangelands in 16 western states pay a grazing fee for this privilege. Since 1981, the Reagan and Bush administrations, backed by Congress, have set grazing fees on public rangeland at about one-seventh to one-fifth of the fees charged for grazing on comparable private and state lands.

This means that U.S. taxpayers give the 2% of ranchers (17% of the ranchers in the western United States) with federal grazing permits subsidies amounting to about $100 million a year—the difference between the fees collected and the actual value of the grazing on this land. Each year, the government also spends millions of dollars to manage these rangelands. Overall, the government collects only about $1 from ranchers in grazing fees for every $10 spent on range management.

Conservationists call for grazing fees on public rangeland to be raised to a fair market value for use of this land. Higher fees would reduce incentives for overgrazing and would provide more money for improvement of range conditions, wildlife conservation, and watershed management. So far, repeated attempts to get Congress to sharply raise grazing fees have failed.

Because it is an ecological failure and an economic failure (for taxpayers), conservationists also call for the current grazing permit system to be replaced with a competitive bidding system. Livestock grazing would be allowed only on range in good or excellent condition under strictly controlled conditions to prevent overgrazing. If the bids did not reflect the current market value of the forage, no permit would be issued. Permits would last for only three to five years. Failure to live up to the permit requirements would lead to automatic cancellation. Ranchers with permits would share 50-50 with the government the cost of capital improvements related to livestock grazing.

Ranchers with permits fiercely oppose higher grazing fees and competitive bidding. Grazing rights on public land raise the value of their livestock animals by $1,000 to $1,500 per head. That means that a permit to graze 500 cattle on public land can be worth $500,000 to $750,000 a year to the rancher. The economic value of a permit is included in the overall worth of the ranches and can be used as collateral for a loan.

Ranchers also argue that they must put up fences on the government land and provide water, which also benefits wildlife. Under the federal multiple-use land policy, they must also share the land with hunters, hikers, off-road vehicle enthusiasts, and others seeking outdoor recreation.

Many of the 98% of U.S. ranchers who can't get a grazing permit favor open bidding for grazing rights on public land. They believe that the permit system gives politically influential ranchers an unfair economic advantage at the expense of taxpayers.

Some conservationists believe that all commercial grazing of livestock on public lands should be phased out over a 10- to 15-year period. Despite the huge acreage involved, federal lands provide forage for less than 3% of the domestic cattle and sheep produced annually in the United States. To do this, Americans spend about $2 billion to produce about half a billion dollars' worth of livestock. This makes no economic sense, except to the 2% of U.S. ranchers receiving taxpayer subsidies. Thus, phasing out livestock grazing on public lands would have little effect on the overall production and price of beef and lamb, would save taxpayers money, and would allow restoration of degraded public rangeland. What do you think should be done?

STRESSES ON PARKS The biggest problems of national and state parks stem from their spectacular success. Because of more roads, cars, and affluence, annual recreational visits to National Park System units increased 12-fold and visits to state parks 7-fold between 1950 and 1990. The recreational use of state and national parks and other public lands is expected to increase even more in the future, putting additional stress on many already-overburdened parks.

Under the onslaught of people during the peak summer season, the most popular national and state parks are often overcrowded with cars and trailers and are plagued by noise, traffic jams, litter, vandalism, deteriorating trails, polluted water, drugs, and crime. At Grand Canyon National Park (Figure 7-9), 50,000 small-plane and helicopter flights per year for tourists have turned the area into a noisy flying circus. Park Service rangers now spend an increasing amount of their time on law enforcement instead of on resource conservation and management.

Populations of wolves, bears, and other large predators in and near various parks have dropped sharply or disappeared because of excessive hunting, poisoning by ranchers and federal officials (see Pro/Con on p. 403), and the limited size of most parks. This decline has allowed populations of remaining prey species to increase sharply, destroy vegetation, and crowd out other native animal species.

The movement of alien species into parks is also a threat. Wild boars (descendants of animals imported to

North Carolina in 1912 for hunting) are a great threat to vegetation in part of the Great Smoky Mountains National Park. The Brazilian pepper tree has invaded Florida's Everglades National Park. Mountain goats in Washington's Olympic National Park trample native vegetation and accelerate soil erosion.

The greatest danger to many parks today is from human activities in nearby areas. Wildlife and recreational values are threatened by mining, timber harvesting, grazing, coal-burning power plants, water diversion, and urban development. Florida's Everglades, including the Everglades National Park, is drying up as water is diverted for cities and agriculture. Efforts are being made to divert more water to the Everglades, but it is too early to tell whether those efforts will be successful. According to the National Park Service, human-generated air pollution impairs the visibility of scenic park views more than 90% of the time.

Over the next 50 years, the greatest threat to many of the world's parks may be shifts in regional climate caused by a projected enhanced greenhouse effect (Section 11-1).

PARK MANAGEMENT: COMBINING CONSERVATION AND SUSTAINABLE DEVELOPMENT Some park managers, especially in LDCs, are developing integrated management plans that combine conservation and sustainable development of the park and surrounding areas (Figure 10-15). In such a plan, the inner core and particularly vulnerable areas of the park are protected from development and treated as wilderness. Controlled numbers of people are allowed to use these areas for hiking, nature study, ecological research, and other nondestructive recreational and educational activities.

In other areas, controlled commercial logging, sustainable grazing by livestock, and sustainable hunting and fishing by local people are allowed. Money spent by park visitors adds to local income. By involving local people in developing park management plans, managers help them see the park as a vital resource they need to protect and sustain rather than degrade (see Case Study on p. 272).

Park managers can also survey the land surrounding a park to identify areas that threaten the park's wildlife. Sometimes, these areas can be added to the park. If not, managers may be able to persuade developers or local people to use less-critical areas for certain types of development.

In most cases, however, the protected inner core is too small to sustain many of its natural species. Such plans look good on paper, but often they cannot be carried out because of a lack of funds for land acquisition, enforcement, and maintenance.

AN AGENDA FOR U.S. NATIONAL PARKS The National Park Service has two goals that increasingly conflict. One is to preserve nature in parks. The other is to make nature more available to the public. The Park Service must accomplish these goals with a small budget at a time when park usage and external threats to the parks are increasing.

In 1988, the Wilderness Society and the National Parks and Conservation Association suggested a blueprint for the future of the U.S. National Park System that included the following proposals:

- Educate the public about the urgent need to protect, mend, and expand the system.

- Establish the National Park Service as an independent agency responsible to the president and Congress. This would make it less vulnerable to the shifting political winds of the Department of the Interior.

- Block the mining, timbering, and other threats that are taking place near park boundaries on land managed by the Forest Service and the Bureau of Land Management.

- Acquire new parkland near threatened areas, and add at least 75 new parks within the next decade. About half of the most important types of ecosystems in the United States are not protected in national parks.

- Locate most commercial park facilities (such as restaurants and shops) *outside* park boundaries.

- Raise the fees charged to private concessionaires who operate restaurants and camping, food, and recreation services inside national parks to at least 22% of their gross receipts. The present maximum return for taxpayers is only 5% and the average is only 2.5% of the $1.5 billion the concessionaires take in annually. Many of the large concessionaire companies have worked out up to 30-year contracts with national park officials in which they pay the government as little as 0.75% of their gross receipts.

- Halt ownership by concessionaires of facilities in national parks because such ownership makes buying buildings back from them very expensive.

- Wherever feasible, place visitor parking areas outside the park areas. Use low-polluting vehicles to carry visitors to and from parking areas and for transportation within the park.

- Greatly expand the Park Service budget for maintenance and science and conservation programs.

- Make buildings and vehicles in national and state parks educational showcases for improvements in energy efficiency and the latest developments in the use of energy from the sun, wind, flowing water, and Earth's interior heat (geothermal energy).

- Require the Park Service and the Forest Service to develop integrated management plans so activities in nearby national forests don't degrade national parklands.

15-5 Wilderness Preservation

HOW MUCH WILD LAND IS LEFT? According to the Wilderness Act of 1964, **wilderness** consists of those areas "where the earth and its community of life are untrammeled by man, where man himself is a visitor who does not remain." The Wilderness Society estimates that a wilderness area should contain at least 400,000 hectares (1 million acres). Otherwise, the area can be degraded by air pollution, water pollution, and noise pollution from nearby mining, oil and natural gas drilling, timber cutting, industry, and urban development.

A 1987 survey sponsored by the Sierra Club revealed that only about 34% of Earth's land area is undeveloped wilderness in blocks of at least 400,000 hectares (Figure 15-13). About 30% of these remaining wildlands are forests. Many are in tropical forests, which are being rapidly cleared and degraded (Section 10-2). Tundra and desert make up most of the world's remaining wildlands. Only about 20% of the undeveloped lands identified in this survey are protected by law from exploitation.

WHY PRESERVE WILDERNESS? There are many reasons. We need wild places where we can experience majestic beauty and natural biological diversity. We need places where we can enhance our mental health by getting away from noise, stress, and large numbers of people. Wilderness preservationist John Muir advised:

Climb the mountains and get their good tidings. Nature's peace will flow into you as the sunshine into the trees. The winds will blow their freshness into you, and the storms their energy, while cares will drop off like autumn leaves.

Even if individuals do not use the wilderness, many want to know it is there, a feeling expressed by the writer Wallace Stegner:

Save a piece of country . . . and it does not matter in the slightest that only a few people every year will go into it. This is precisely its value. . . . We simply need that wild country available to us, even if we never do more than drive to its edge and look in. For it can be a means of reassuring ourselves of our sanity as creatures, a part of the geography of hope.

Wilderness areas provide recreation for growing numbers of people. Wilderness also has important ecological values. It provides undisturbed habitats for wild plants and animals, maintains diverse biological reserves protected from degradation, and provides a laboratory in which we can discover more about how

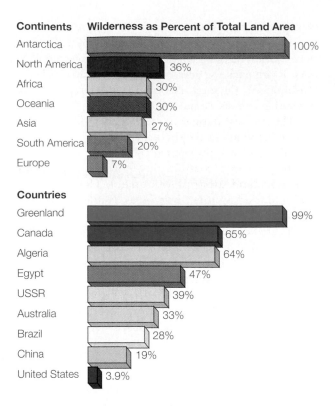

Figure 15-13 Wilderness areas by major geographical areas. (Data from J. Michael McCloskey and Heather Spalding, "A Reconnaissance-Level Inventory of the Wilderness Remaining in the World," Sierra Club, 1987)

nature works. It is an ecological insurance policy against eliminating too much of Earth's natural biological diversity. In the words of Henry David Thoreau: "In wildness is the preservation of the world."

To sustainable-Earth conservationists, the most important reason for protecting and expanding the world's wilderness areas is an ethical one: Wilderness should be preserved because the wild species it contains have a right to exist without human interference.

U.S. WILDERNESS PRESERVATION SYSTEM In the United States, preservationists have been trying to keep wild areas from being developed since 1900. Mostly they have fought a losing battle (Section 2-4). It was not until 1964 that Congress passed the Wilderness Act. It allows the government to protect undeveloped tracts of public land from development as part of the National Wilderness Preservation System.

Only 4% of U.S. land area is protected as wilderness, with almost two-thirds of this in Alaska. Most of the rest is in the West. Only 1.8% of the land area of the lower 48 states is protected in the wilderness system. Almost half of the wilderness east of the Mississippi is in the threatened Florida Everglades National Park and Minnesota's Boundary Waters Canoe Area. Of the 413 wilderness areas in the lower 48 states, only 4 consist of more than 400,000 hectares. Also, the present wilderness preservation system includes only 81 of the country's 233 distinct ecosystems.

There remain almost 40 million hectares (100 million acres) of public lands that could qualify for designation as wilderness. Conservationists believe all of this land should be protected as wilderness and that a vigorous effort should be mounted to rehabilitate other lands to enlarge existing wilderness areas. The long-term goal would be to have 30% of the country's land area protected as wilderness. This would require that virtually all Forest Service and Bureau of Land Management public lands be reclassified as wilderness and restored as natural wildlife habitat. However, resource developers lobby elected officials and government agencies to build roads in areas being evaluated for inclusion in the wilderness system so that those areas can't be designated as wilderness.

USE AND ABUSE OF WILDERNESS AREAS Popular wilderness areas, especially in California, North Carolina, and Minnesota, are visited by so many people that their wildness is threatened. Fragile vegetation is damaged, soil is eroded from trails and campsites, water is polluted from bathing and dishwashing, and litter is scattered along trails. Instead of quiet and solitude, visitors sometimes face the noise and congestion they are trying to escape.

Wilderness areas are also being degraded by air, water, and noise pollution from nearby grazing, logging, oil and gas drilling, factories, power plants, and urban areas. In 1985, the National Park Service reported that scenic views in 64 wilderness areas within national parks were obscured by haze from air pollutants at least 90% of the time. Projected global warming from an enhanced greenhouse effect is expected to be the biggest threat to wilderness, parks, forests, rangelands, croplands, estuaries, and inland wetlands over the next few decades (Section 11-1).

WILDERNESS MANAGEMENT To protect the most popular areas from damage, wilderness managers have had to limit the number of people hiking or camping at any one time. They have also designated areas where camping is allowed. Managers have increased the number of wilderness rangers to patrol vulnerable areas and enlisted volunteers to pick up trash discarded by thoughtless users.

Historian and wilderness expert Roderick Nash suggests wilderness areas be divided into three categories. The easily accessible, popular areas would be intensively managed and have trails, bridges, hiker's huts, outhouses, assigned campsites, and extensive ranger patrols. Large, remote wilderness areas would not be intensively managed. They would be used only

by people who would get a permit by demonstrating their wilderness skills. A third category would consist of large, biologically unique areas. They would be left undisturbed as gene pools of plant and animal species, with no human entry allowed.

NATIONAL WILD AND SCENIC RIVERS SYSTEM
In 1968, Congress passed the National Wild and Scenic Rivers Act. It allows rivers and river segments with outstanding scenic, recreational, geological, wildlife, historical, or cultural values to be protected in the National Wild and Scenic Rivers System.

These waterways are to be kept forever free of development. They may not be widened, straightened, dredged, filled, or dammed along the designated lengths. The only activities allowed are camping, swimming, nonmotorized boating, sport hunting, and sport and commercial fishing. New mining claims, however, are permitted in some areas.

Currently, rivers and river systems protected by the Wild and Scenic Rivers System make up only about 0.2% of the country's 6 million kilometers (3.5 million miles) of rivers. Conservationists have urged Congress to add 1,500 additional eligible river segments to the system by the year 2000. If that goal is achieved, about 2% of the country's unique rivers would be protected from further development. During this period, they want none of the candidate rivers to be developed in any way that might affect its ecological integrity. Conservationists also urge that a permanent federal administrative body be established to manage the Wild and Scenic Rivers System and that states develop their own wild and scenic river programs.

NATIONAL TRAILS SYSTEM In 1968, Congress passed the National Trails Act. It protects scenic and historic hiking trails in the National Trails System. However, no designated scenic or historic trail is complete because the Trails System has a low priority and gets little funding. Conservationists propose that the government take the following measures:

- Place the Trails System under the management of a single agency.

- Make a comprehensive study of present and future trail needs.

- Complete the present system within ten years.

- Add new trails to achieve the goal of having a network of trails throughout the country by the year 2000.

Sustaining existing forests, rangelands, wilderness, and parks and rehabilitating those that we have degraded are urgent tasks. They will cost a great deal of money and require strong support from the public and changes in individual lifestyles (see Individuals Matter above). However, it will cost our civilization much more if we do not protect these resources from degradation and destruction and help heal those we have wounded. We could begin by creating an Earth Conservation Corps at the global, national, state, and local levels (see Spotlight above).

Conservationist Aldo Leopold has developed an ethic to guide our use of land or land community, which he expands to include soils, water, plants, and animals. His land ethic "changes the role of *Homo sapiens* from conqueror of the land community to plain member and citizen of it. "

Health is the capacity of the land for self-renewal. Conservation is our effort to understand and preserve this capacity.

ALDO LEOPOLD

DISCUSSION TOPICS

1. Should private companies cutting timber from national forests continue to be subsidized by federal payments for reforestation and for building and maintaining access roads? Explain.

2. Should exports of timber cut from U.S. national forests and other public lands be banned? Explain.

3. Should fees for grazing on public rangelands in the United States be (a) eliminated and replaced with a competitive bidding system, (b) increased to the point where they equal the fair market value estimated by the Bureau of Land Management and the Forest Service? Explain your answers.

4. Should compound 1080 or other poisons be used in livestock collars to poison coyotes that prey on livestock? Explain. What are the alternatives?

5. Should trail bikes, dune buggies, and other off-road vehicles be banned from public rangeland to reduce damage to vegetation and soil? Explain.

6. Explain why you agree or disagree with each of the proposals listed on page 405 concerning the U.S. National Park System.

7. Should more wilderness areas and wild and scenic rivers be preserved in the United States, especially in the lower 48 states? Explain.

8. Should virtually all U.S. Forest Service and Bureau of Land Management public land be reclassified as wilderness and restored as natural wildlife habitat? Explain.

*9. Investigate paper recycling in your community and by your school. Try to find answers to the following questions:
    a. What percentage of the paper used by your school is recycled?
    b. What percentage of the paper used in your community is recycled?
    c. What percentage of the newsprint in local or nearby newspapers is made from recycled materials?
    d. What percentage of the paper products bought by your school contains recycled fibers?
    e. What percentage of the paper products bought by local government agencies contains recycled fibers?

CHAPTER 16

WILD PLANT AND

ANIMAL RESOURCES

General Questions and Issues

1. Why are wild species of plants and animals important to us and to the ecosphere?

2. What human activities and natural traits cause wild species to become depleted, endangered, and extinct?

3. How can endangered and threatened wild species be protected from premature extinction caused by human activities?

4. How can populations of large game be managed to have enough animals available for sport hunting without endangering the long-term survival of the species?

5. How can populations of species of freshwater and marine fish be managed to have enough available for commercial and sport fishing without endangering their long-term survival?

The mass of extinctions which the earth is currently facing is a threat to civilization second only to the threat of thermal nuclear war.

NATIONAL ACADEMY OF SCIENCES

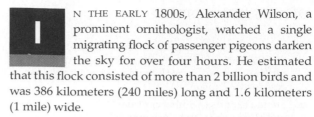

N THE EARLY 1800s, Alexander Wilson, a prominent ornithologist, watched a single migrating flock of passenger pigeons darken the sky for over four hours. He estimated that this flock consisted of more than 2 billion birds and was 386 kilometers (240 miles) long and 1.6 kilometers (1 mile) wide.

By 1914, the passenger pigeon (Figure 16-1) had disappeared forever. How could the species that was once the most numerous bird in North America become extinct in only a few decades?

The answer is people. The main reasons for the extinction of this species were uncontrolled commercial hunting and the loss of habitat and food supplies as forests were cleared for farms and cities.

Passenger pigeons were good to eat, their feathers made good pillows, and they were widely used for fertilizer. They were easy to kill because they flew in gigantic flocks and nested in long, narrow colonies. People captured one pigeon alive, sewed its eyes shut, and tied it to a perch called a stool. Soon a curious flock landed beside this "stool pigeon." They were then shot or trapped by nets that could contain more than 1,000 birds.

Beginning in 1858, the mass killing of passenger pigeons became a big business. Shotguns, fire, traps, artillery, and even dynamite were used. Birds were also suffocated by burning grass or sulfur below their roosts. Live birds were used as targets in shooting galleries. In 1878, one professional pigeon trapper made $60,000 by killing 3 million birds at their nesting grounds near Petoskey, Michigan.

By the early 1880s, commercial hunting ceased because only several thousand birds were left. Recovery of the species was essentially impossible because these birds laid only one egg per nest. Many of the remaining birds died from infectious disease and from severe storms during their annual fall migration to Central and South America.

In 1896, the last major breeding colony of about 250,000 birds was tracked down near Bowling Green, Ohio, not far from Mammoth Cave. Hunters were notified by telegraph and all but about 5,000 birds, which escaped, were killed. In Ohio on March 24, 1900, a young boy shot the last known passenger pigeon in the wild. The last known passenger pigeon on Earth, a hen named Martha after Martha Washington, died in the Cincinnati Zoo in 1914. Her stuffed body is now on view at the National Museum of Natural History in Washington, D.C. (Figure 16-1).

Sooner or later, all species become extinct, but we have become a primary factor in the premature extinction of an increasing number of species as a result of our relentless march across the globe. Every day, at least 11 and probably 100 species become extinct because of our activities, and the loss may soon reach several hundred species a day.

Figure 16-1 The extinct passenger pigeon. The last known passenger pigeon died in the Cincinnati Zoo in 1914.

Figure 16-2 California condor in captivity at the Los Angeles Zoo. None of these birds is left in the wild. As a result of a captive breeding program, there were 52 condors in the Los Angeles Zoo and in the Wild Animal Park in San Diego) by August 1991. In September 1991, scientists returned two captive-born condor chicks to their natural habitat north of Los Angeles, where the species existed for 600,000 years until we began killing them and crowding them out. This species is especially vulnerable to extinction because of its low reproduction rate, long period (7 years) needed to reach reproductive age, failure of parents to hatch chicks when they are scared away from the nest by noise or human activities, and the need for a large, undisturbed habitat.

Many biologists consider the accelerating global epidemic of extinction we are bringing about even more serious than depletion of stratospheric ozone and global warming (Chapter 11) because it is happening more rapidly and is irreversible. Reducing this enormous loss of Earth's biological diversity, protecting wildlife habitats throughout the world, and restoring species that we have helped deplete are planetary emergencies that we must deal with now.

16-1 Why Preserve Wild Plant and Animal Species?

WHY NOT LET THEM DIE? Species extinction over Earth's long history is a natural phenomenon (Figure 7-27), so why should we be concerned about losing a few more? Does it make any difference that the California condor (Figure 16-2), the black rhinoceros (Figure 4-41), or some plant in a tropical forest becomes extinct mostly because of our activities? The answer is yes for a number of reasons.

ECONOMIC AND MEDICAL IMPORTANCE Wild species that are actually or potentially useful to people are called **wildlife resources**. They are potentially renewable resources, if not driven to extinction or near extinction by our activities.

Most of the plants that supply 90% of the world's food today were domesticated from wild plants found in the tropics. Existing wild plant species, most of them still unclassified and unevaluated, will be needed by agricultural scientists and genetic engineers to develop new crop strains (Section 14-3), and many of them may become important sources of food (Figure 14-15). Wild animal species are a largely untapped source of food.

Wild plants and plants domesticated from wild species are also important sources of rubber (Figure 10-9), oils, dyes, fiber, paper, lumber, and other important products (Figure 10-1).

About 75% of the world's population relies on plants or plant extracts as sources of medicines. Roughly half of the prescription and nonprescription drugs used in the world, and 25% of those used in the United States today, have active ingredients extracted from wild organisms (Figure 10-10). Worldwide, medicines from wild species are worth $40 million a year. Only about 5,000 of the world's estimated 250,000 plant species have been studied thoroughly for their possible medical uses. A recent analysis shows that 10% of the U.S. GNP is derived directly from wild resources.

Many wild animal species are used to test drugs, vaccines, chemical toxicity, and surgical procedures and to increase our understanding of human health and disease. Elephants under stress are used to study the causes of heart disease. The nine-banded armadillo (Figure 16-3) is being used to study leprosy and prepare a vaccine for that disease. Mice, rats, chimpanzees, and rhesus monkeys are used to test for possible cancer-causing agents and toxic chemicals. However, animal rights and welfare advocates are protesting the use of animals in medical and biological research and teaching (see Pro/Con on p. 413).

Figure 16-3 The nine-banded armadillo is used in research to find a cure for leprosy.

Figure 16-4 Tourists observing wildlife in a wildlife reserve in Kenya. Wildlife tourism, or eco-tourism, in which tourists visit areas to see and photograph wildlife, is an important source of revenue for LDCs with unique, protected wildlife resources. However, care must be taken to see that eco-tourists do not damage or disturb wildlife and ecosystems, especially in popular areas.

AESTHETIC AND RECREATIONAL IMPORTANCE

Wild plants and animals are a source of beauty, wonder, joy, and recreational pleasure for large numbers of people. Wild **game species** provide recreation in the form of hunting and fishing. Each year, almost 50% of the American population and 84% of the Canadian population participate in bird watching, photographing, and other nondestructive forms of outdoor recreational activity involving wildlife.

Wildlife tourism, sometimes called eco-tourism, is important to the economy of some LDCs, such as Kenya and Tanzania (Figure 16-4). One wildlife economist estimated that one male lion living to seven years of age in Kenya leads to $515,000 of expenditures by tourists. If the lion were killed for its skin, it would be worth only about $1,000. However, too many visitors to favorite eco-tour spots can damage ecosystems and disrupt species. Environmentalists call for strict guidelines governing tours to sensitive areas.

SCIENTIFIC AND ECOLOGICAL IMPORTANCE

Each species has scientific value because it can help scientists understand how life has evolved and will continue to evolve on this planet. Wild species also perform vital ecosystem services. They supply us and other species with food from the soil and the sea, recycle nutrients essential to agriculture, and help produce and maintain fertile soil. They also produce and maintain oxygen and other gases in the atmosphere, moderate Earth's climate, help regulate water supplies, and store solar energy as chemical energy in food, wood, and fossil fuels. Moreover, they detoxify poisonous substances, decompose organic wastes, control potential crop pests and carriers of disease, and make up a vast gene pool of biological diversity from which we and other species can draw.

ETHICAL IMPORTANCE So far, the reasons given for preserving wildlife are based on the actual or potential usefulness of wild species as resources for people. Many ecologists and conservationists believe that wild species will continue to disappear at an alarming rate until we replace this *human-centered (anthropocentric)* view of wildlife and the environment either with a *life-centered (biocentric)* view or with an *ecosystem-centered (ecocentric)* view.

According to the *biocentric worldview*, each wild species has an inherent right to exist, or at least the right to struggle to exist, equal to that of any other species. Thus, it is ethically wrong for us to hasten the extinction of any species. Some go farther and believe that each individual wild creature — not just a species — has a right to survive without human interference, just as each human being has the right to survive.

Some distinguish between the survival rights of plants and those of animals. The poet Alan Watts once commented that he was a vegetarian "because cows scream louder than carrots." Many people make ethical distinctions among various types of animals. For instance, they think little about killing a fly, a mosquito, a cockroach, or a sewer rat, or about catching and killing fish they don't eat. Unless they are strict vegetarians, they also think little about having others kill cattle, calves (Figure 14-4), lambs, and chickens in slaughterhouses to provide them with meat, leather, and other animal products. The same people, however, might deplore the killing of game animals such as deer, squirrels, or rabbits for sport or for food.

The *ecocentric worldview* stresses the importance of preserving biodiversity by preserving, or not degrading, entire ecosystems, rather than focusing only on individual species or on an individual organism. It recognizes that saving wildlife means saving the places

In 1990, about 20 million animals were used in medical research in the United States annually, down 40% since 1968 mostly because of the efforts of animal rights and animal welfare groups. About 90% (18 million) of these animals were rats and mice; 8% (1.6 million) were cows, sheep, and pigs; 1.5% (300,000) were dogs and cats, and 0.5% (100,000) were monkeys and chimpanzees.

The estimated 10 million members in the more than 400 animal rights and animal welfare groups in the United States fall into two categories: "no animal research," and "necessary research yes, cruelty no." Some believe that all use of animals for research and teaching is inhumane and immoral and should be replaced with other methods. To them, animals have as much right to exist as humans.

Others recognize that some use of animals for research and teaching is necessary. But they support efforts to halt the unnecessary use of animals for such purposes and to develop alternative methods. They also call for much stricter laws and better enforcement of existing laws requiring comfortable and considerate treatment for all test animals.

Most scientists favor laws requiring considerate treatment of lab animals, but they contend that some animal experimentation in medicine and science is vital for the welfare of people, pets, and livestock. They point to the crucial roles of test animals in developing vaccines for polio, diphtheria, rabies, and measles; drugs such as insulin, antibiotics, and painkillers; treatment for cancer, diabetes, cystic fibrosis, high blood pressure, and hemophilia; surgical advances such as blood transfusion, coronary bypass, skin graft, and organ transplants; and advances in medical diagnosis, such as angiograms, radiation therapy, artificial joints, and X rays.

Some argue that animals would benefit more if animal rights advocates concentrated on preventing people from abandoning 288,000 dogs and cats *each week* in the United States. Each year, U.S. pounds and animal shelters have to kill about 15 million unwanted cats and dogs because of pet overpopulation and a throwaway mentality. By contrast, about 200,000 dogs and cats—most obtained from shelters and pounds where they would be put to death—are killed each year for research and teaching purposes—less than the number of animals killed in only one week by animal shelters. An additional 100,000 dogs and cats are used in research but are not killed or seriously harmed.

Scientists point out that animals people cherish as pets can now have cataracts removed, undergo open-heart surgery, or wear a pacemaker because of animal research performed to benefit humans. Animals also benefit from vaccines for rabies, distemper, anthrax, tetanus, feline leukemia, and rinderpest (a virus that kills millions of cattle slowly and painfully)—all developed by animal experiments.

Under intense pressure from animal rights groups, scientists are trying to find testing methods that do not cause animals to suffer or, better yet, do not use animals at all. Promising alternatives include the use of cell and tissue cultures, simulated tissues and body fluids, and bacteria. Computer-generated models can also be used to estimate the toxicity of a compound from knowledge of its chemical structure and properties.

Computer simulations of animals under anesthesia can be used to teach veterinary medical students. Videotapes can replace live demonstrations on animals for biology and veterinary medical students.

However, researchers point out that such techniques cannot replace all animal research. Cell cultures, for example, do not have bones and therefore cannot be used to test treatments for arthritis or other bone and joint diseases. Researchers argue that live animals are still needed to help perfect new surgical techniques and to test many lifesaving drugs and vaccines. What do you think?

---

where they live. This view is based on Aldo Leopold's ethical principle that something is right when it tends to maintain Earth's life-support systems for us and other species and wrong when it tends otherwise.

16-2 How Species Become Depleted and Extinct

THE RISE AND FALL OF SPECIES Extinction is a natural process (Section 6-3). As the planet's surface and climate have changed over its 4.6 billion years of existence, species have disappeared and new ones have evolved to take their places (Figure 7-27). It is estimated that throughout Earth's history, roughly 430 million species have existed. The estimate of 40 million to 80 million species (some say 100 million) living on Earth today means that about 370 million to 420 million of the planet's species have become extinct or have evolved into new species in response to changing environmental conditions.

This rise and fall of species has not been smooth. Evidence indicates that over the past 500 million years, there have been several periods when mass extinctions have reduced Earth's biodiversity and other periods, called radiations, when the diversity of life has increased and spread (Figure 7-27). These periods of extinction and radiation were caused by climate change, continental drift, interactions of life with nonliving parts of the ecosphere, and other environmental factors.

EXTINCTION OF SPECIES TODAY Imagine you are driving on an interstate highway at a high speed. You notice that your two passengers are passing the time by using wrenches and screwdrivers to remove various bolts, screws, and parts of your car on a random basis and are throwing them out the window. How long will it be before they remove enough parts to cause a breakdown or a crash?

This urgent question is one that we as a species should be asking ourselves. As we tinker with the only home for us and other species, we are rapidly removing parts of Earth's natural biodiversity upon which we and other species depend in ways we know little about. We are not heeding Aldo Leopold's warning: "To keep every cog and wheel is the first precaution of intelligent tinkering."

Past mass extinctions took place slowly enough to allow new forms of life to arise as adaptations to an ever-changing world (Figure 7-27). This began changing about 40,000 years ago when the latest version of our species came on the scene. Since agriculture began, about 10,000 years ago, the rate of species extinction has increased sharply as human settlements have expanded worldwide. Now we are the primary force in a new mass extinction.

It is hard to document extinctions, since most go unrecorded. Using available data, biologists estimate that during 1991, at least 4,000 and probably 36,000 species became extinct mostly because of our activities; the figure could reach 50,000 by the year 2000. These scientists warn that if deforestation (especially of tropical forests), desertification, and destruction of wetlands and coral reefs continue at their present rates, within the next few decades we could easily cause the loss of at least one-quarter, and conceivably one-half, of Earth's species forever. This will rival some of the great natural mass extinctions of the past (Figure 7-27).

Animal extinctions get the most publicity, but the fate of our species and millions of others is more likely to depend on the survival of numerous known and unknown species of plants, insects that pollinate plants, and decomposers. Plant extinctions are more important ecologically than animal extinctions because most animal species depend directly or indirectly on plants for food. The loss of 1 plant species can cause the loss of as many as 30 species of animals and insects that depend upon it. It is estimated that over the next several decades, 25% of Earth's plant species may become extinct because of our activities, most of them never examined to determine their roles in the ecosphere and their po-

tential usefulness to us as sources of food, fiber, fuel, medicines, and other products.

There are three important differences between the present mass extinction and those in the past:

- The present "extinction spasm" is being brought about by us — the first one to be caused by a single species.

- The current wildlife holocaust is taking place in only a few decades rather than over thousands to millions of years (Figure 7-27). Such rapid extinction cannot be balanced by speciation because it takes between 2,000 and 100,000 generations for new species to evolve.

- Plant species are disappearing as rapidly as animal species, thus threatening many animal species that otherwise would not become extinct at this time.

ENDANGERED AND THREATENED SPECIES TODAY Species heading toward extinction can be classified as either endangered or threatened. An **endangered species** is one having so few individual survivors that the species could soon become extinct over all or most of its natural range. Examples are the white rhinoceros in Africa (100 left), the California condor (Figure 16-2) in the United States (only two in the wild), the giant panda in central China (1,000 left), the snow leopard in central Asia (2,500 left, Figure 16-5), and the rare shallowtail butterfly (Figure 16-6).

A **threatened species** is still abundant in its natural range but is declining in numbers and likely to become endangered. Examples are the bald eagle (Figure 2-10) and the grizzly bear.

Many wild species are not in danger of extinction, but their populations have been sharply reduced locally or regionally. Because such number losses are occurring much faster and more frequently than extinctions, they may be a better sign of the condition of wildlife and entire ecosystems. They can serve as early warnings so that we can prevent species extinction rather than responding mostly to emergencies.

HABITAT LOSS AND DISTURBANCE The greatest threat to most wild species is destruction, fragmentation, and degradation of their habitats. Such disruption of natural communities threatens wild species by destroying migration routes, breeding areas, and food sources. Deforestation, especially of tropical forests (Section 10-2), is the greatest cause of the decline in global biological diversity by habitat loss and degradation, followed by destruction of coral reefs (see Case Study on p. 135) and wetlands and plowing of grasslands (Figure 5-20).

In the United States, tall-grass prairies (Figure 5-18) have been reduced by 98%, virgin forests by 95% (Figure 10-17), wetlands by 50% (see Case Study on

Figure 16-5 The snow leopard, found in Central Asia, is endangered because it has been hunted and killed for its fur.

Figure 16-6 This endangered shallowtail butterfly was almost pushed to extinction in Great Britain but is now hanging on, mostly in protected nature reserves.

Figure 16-7 The whooping crane, shown in its winter refuge in Texas, is an endangered species in North America. Once, it lived throughout most of North America, but its low reproduction rates and fixed migration pattern make it vulnerable to extinction. Mostly because of illegal shooting and loss of habitat, the number of whooping cranes in the wild dropped to only 16 in 1941. Because of a $5-million-a-year habitat protection and captive breeding program directed by the U.S. Fish and Wildlife Service, about 217 birds survive today, including more than 170 in the wild. By the mid-1990s, wildlife officials hope to release 15 to 20 captive birds annually into the wild.

p. 137), and overall forest cover by 33%. Furthermore, much of the remaining wildlife habitat is being fragmented and polluted at an alarming rate. Loss or degradation of habitat is the key factor in the extinction of American bird species such as the heath hen, and the near extinction of Atwater's prairie chicken, the California condor (Figure 16-2), and the whooping crane (Figure 16-7).

Many rare and threatened plant and animal species live in vulnerable, specialized habitats, such as islands (Figure 16-8) or single trees in tropical forests. Madagascar is a prime example of an island where hundreds of species found nowhere else are threatened with extinction (Figure 16-8 and Case Study on p. 259). About 10% of the world's bird species have a range of only one island. Hawaii accounts for two-thirds of the species that became extinct in the 1980s and is fast becoming the world capital of biological extinction because of increasing population and development.

Increasingly, this "island effect" is being experienced within continental land areas. Any ecosystem or habitat surrounded by a different one is, in effect, an island for the species who live there. Human alterations of terrestrial areas fragment wildlife habitats into patches, or "habitat islands," which are often too small to support the minimum number of individuals needed to sustain a population. Most national parks and other protected areas are habitat islands. Habitat destruction for migrating species is also an increasing problem (see Spotlight on p. 416).

COMMERCIAL HUNTING AND POACHING There are three main types of hunting: subsistence, sport, and commercial. The killing of animals to provide enough food for survival is called **subsistence hunting. Sport hunting** is the hunting of animals for recreation and in

Figure 16-8 Island species are especially vulnerable to extinction. The endangered *Symphonia* clings to life on the island of Madagascar, where 90% of the original vegetation has been destroyed.

some cases for food. **Commercial hunting** involves killing animals for profit from sale of their furs or other parts. Illegal commercial hunting or fishing is called **poaching** (see Spotlight on p. 418).

Today, subsistence hunting has declined sharply in most parts of the world because of the decrease in hunting-and-gathering societies. Sport hunting is now closely regulated in most countries. Game species are endangered by sport hunting only when protective regulations do not exist or are not enforced. No animal in the United States, for instance, has become extinct or endangered because of regulated sport hunting.

In the past, legal and illegal commercial hunting has led to the extinction or near extinction of many animal species, such as the American bison (see Case Study on p. 40). This continues today. It's not surprising that Bengal tigers face extinction, since a coat made from their fur sells for $100,000 in Tokyo. A mountain gorilla is worth $150,000; an ocelot skin, $40,000; an Imperial Amazon macaw, $30,000; a snow leopard skin, $14,000 (Figure 16-5); rhinoceros horn, up to $28,600 per kilogram (Figure 16-10); and tiger meat, $286 per kilogram ($130 per pound). Even if the poacher is caught, the economic incentive far outweighs the risk of paying a small fine and the much smaller risk of serving time in jail.

Elephants are slaughtered by poachers for their valuable ivory tusks (Figure 16-11). In 1970, there were about 4.5 million African elephants (Figure 5-17). By 1990, there were only about 610,000 left. If widespread poaching is not halted, the African elephant could be wiped out within ten years. In January 1990, members of a 103-nation convention (CITES) devoted to protecting endangered and threatened species banned all international trade in African elephant products. Although seven countries exempted themselves from the ban, the bottom dropped out of the worldwide ivory market within a short time after the ban. Conservation-

Spotlight Declining Populations of North American Songbirds

Nearly half of the 700 species of birds found in the United States spend two-thirds of the year in the tropical forests of Central America, South America, and the Caribbean islands and return to North America during the summer to breed. This includes some of the country's most popular songbirds, such as thrushes, warblers, vireos, tanagers, and flycatchers.

A U.S. Fish and Wildlife Study showed that between 1978 and 1987, populations of 44 species of insect-eating, migratory songbirds in North America declined, with 20 species showing drops of 25% to 45% (Figure 16-9). The main reasons for these population declines are destruction and fragmentation of tropical forests in the birds' winter habitats in Central and South America (Section 10-2) and fragmentation of their summer habitat in North America, which provides easier access for predators and parasites.

Figure 16-9 Many species of migratory North American songbirds, such as the wood thrush, are suffering serious population declines because of loss of their winter tropical forest habitats in Latin America and the Caribbean islands and fragmentation of their summer habitats in North America. The population of wood thrush, found over most of the eastern United States during the summer, declined by 31% between 1978 and 1987.

ists now fear that poachers will begin killing large numbers of Alaska's population of walrus for their ivory tusks (Figure 16-12).

As more of the world's species become endangered, their economic value and the demand for them on the black market rise sharply, hastening their extinction. Poaching is increasing in the U.S., especially in the western half of the country (see Spotlight on p. 418).

Figure 16-10 All five species of rhinoceros (Figure 4-41), one of the world's oldest mammals, are threatened with extinction because of poachers, who kill them for their horns, and loss of habitat. In parts of the Middle East, such as Yemen, rhino horns are carved into dagger handles. These ornate daggers, which sell for $500 to $12,000, are worn as a sign of masculinity and virility. In the Middle East, Asian rhino horns, the most prized, can fetch as much as $28,600 a kilogram ($13,000 a pound). In China and other parts of Asia, rhino horns are ground into a powder that is used for reducing fever and for other medicinal purposes for which its effectiveness has not been verified by medical science. Some Asians believe the powder is an aphrodisiac. Efforts are being made to protect these species from extinction, but it is an expensive and dangerous uphill fight.

PREDATOR AND PEST CONTROL Extinction or near extinction can also occur when people attempt to exterminate pest and predator species that compete with humans for food and game. Fruit farmers exterminated the Carolina parakeet in the United States around 1914 because it fed on fruit crops. The species was easy to wipe out because when one member of a flock was shot, the rest of the birds hovered over its body, making themselves easy targets.

As animal habitats have shrunk, farmers have killed large numbers of African elephants (Figure 5-17) to keep them from trampling and eating food crops. Since 1929, ranchers and government agencies have poisoned prairie dogs because horses and cattle sometimes step into the burrows and break their legs. This poisoning has killed 99% of the prairie dog population in North America (Figure 16-14). It has also led to the near extinction of the black-footed ferret (Figure 16-15), which preyed on the prairie dog.

Figure 16-11 Vultures feeding on a male elephant carcass in Tanzania. It was killed by a poacher who cut off its ivory tusks. The ivory is used for jewelry, piano keys, ornamental carvings, and art objects. African elephants play several important ecological roles. Through their dung, they spread seeds of fruit they eat. In Central and West Africa, they trample underbrush and uproot small trees, creating open spaces in dense rain forest that allow growth of vegetation favored by gorillas and hoofed plant eaters. In East Africa, these same actions convert woodland into savanna, increasing the habitat for hoofed grazers such as gazelles, wildebeests, and zebras. However, when elephants are forced into a small area of habitat, they can destroy most of the vegetation and also food crops. In 1990, an international ban on the trade of ivory from African elephants was enacted and may help prevent this species from becoming extinct.

Figure 16-12 Increasing numbers of bull walruses found in the Bering Sea off the coast of Alaska are being killed illegally, mostly by Alaska's native Inuits (Eskimos) for their ivory tusks. A pair of these tusks is worth $800 to $1,500 on the black market. Agents for the U.S. Fish and Wildlife Service have found that the tusks are often exchanged for drugs—sometimes for only six joints of marijuana. The ivory-tusked male walruses are easy to kill because they spend the summer on ice floes. Hunters in small boats shoot the slow-moving mammals, use the liver, the heart, and other parts for food (legally allowed if this slaughter is not done in an excessive and wasteful manner), sever the head with a chain saw, and illegally sell the tusks. With an estimated 250,000 walruses remaining in the Pacific, this species is not endangered now, but it may soon be if excessive and wasteful hunting continues.

As wildlife habitats in other parts of the world have disappeared, the United States has become a target for poachers. Officials of the U.S. Fish and Wildlife Service estimate that the trade in illegal animal parts poached from the United States reached $200 million in 1990 — up nearly 100% from 1980. Much of this is taking place in national parks and wilderness areas. The U.S. Fish and Wildlife Service has only 200 special agents, with only 22 agents covering one-third of the country where extensive poaching occurs.

Some of the poaching involves outfitters who charge large fees to help wealthy hunters kill an endangered bighorn sheep or grizzly bear or other prized trophy species and a few renegade hunters who violate hunting laws. Much of the killing and trapping is done by networks of professional poachers tied to markets in China, Japan, Korea, Hong Kong, and Taiwan.

According to the U.S. Fish and Wildlife Service, a poached gyrfalcon sells for $120,000; a bighorn sheep head, $10,000 to $60,000; a large saguaro cactus, $5,000 to

Figure 16-13 The peregrine falcon is endangered in the United States, mostly because of exposure to DDT. The insecticide caused many young birds to die before hatching because their eggshells were too thin to protect them. Only about 1,000 peregrine falcons are left in the lower 48 states. Most of them were bred in captivity and then released into the wild as a result of a $2.7-milion-a-year recovery program. However, some of these birds are illegally shot or captured for sale on the black market. Peregrine falcons can also die during their annual migration to parts of South America and because of loss of habitat in these areas.

$15,000; a peregrine falcon (Figure 16-13), $10,000; a polar bear, $6,000; a grizzly bear, $5,000; an elk head, $5,000 to $10,000; a mountain goat, $3,500; a bald eagle, $2,500; and a bear gallbladder (used in Asia for medicinal purposes), up to $800 a gram (about the same price as heroin).

Most poachers are not caught. There are more police officers in

New York City than wildlife protection officers in the entire United States. Some state and federal judges have begun imposing heavy fines and even prison terms on flagrant violators who are caught, but most poachers get off lightly. What do you think should be done?

PETS AND DECORATIVE PLANTS Each year, large numbers of threatened and endangered animal species are smuggled into the United States, Great Britain, the former West Germany, and other countries (Figure 16-16). Most are sold as pets.

Some species of exotic plants, especially orchids and cacti, are also endangered because they are gathered, often illegally (Figure 16-17). They are then sold to collectors and used to decorate houses, offices, and landscapes. A collector may pay $5,000 for a single rare orchid.

A single prize specimen such as a rare mature crested saguaro cactus can earn cactus rustlers as much as $15,000. To reduce losses from cactus rustlers, Arizona has put 222 species under state protection with penalties of up to $1,000 and jail sentences up to one year. However, only seven people are assigned to enforce this law over the entire state, and the fines are too small to discourage poaching.

POLLUTION AND CLIMATE CHANGE Toxic chemicals degrade wildlife habitats, including wildlife ref-uges, and kill some plants and animals. Slowly degradable pesticides, especially DDT and dieldrin, have caused populations of some bird species to decline (see Spotlight on p. 420).

Wildlife in even the best-protected and best-managed wildlife reserves throughout the world may be depleted in a few decades because of climatic change caused by projected global warming (Section 11-1).

INTRODUCTION OF ALIEN SPECIES As people travel around the world, they sometimes pick up plants and animals intentionally or accidentally and introduce them to new geographical regions. Many of these alien species have provided food, game, and beauty and have helped control pests in their new environments.

Some alien species, however, have no natural predators and competitors in their new habitats. That allows them to dominate their new ecosystem and reduce the populations of many native species (see Case Study on p. 423). Eventually, such alien species can cause the extinction, near extinction, or displacement of native species (Table 16-1).

Figure 16-14 The Utah prairie dog is a threatened species in the United States, mostly because of widespread poisoning by ranchers and government agencies since 1929.

Figure 16-15 The black-footed ferret is one of the most endangered mammals in North America, with none left in the wild. It is nearly extinct because most of the once-abundant prairie dogs (Figure 16-14) that made up 90% or more of its diet have been eliminated. Between 1985 and 1991, the population of black-footed ferrets in captivity grew from 18 to 260. Biologists hope to return about 50 of these captively bred animals a year to a favorable habitat in north-central Wyoming within the next few years.

Figure 16-16 Collectors of exotic birds may pay $10,000 for a threatened hyacinth macaw smuggled out of Brazil. These high prices help doom such species to eventual extinction. Worldwide, more than 3.5 million live birds are captured and sold legally each year, and 2.5 million more are captured and sold illegally. For every bird that reaches a pet shop legally or illegally, at least one other dies in transit. After purchase, many of these animals are mistreated, killed, or abandoned by their owners.

Figure 16-17 The black lace cactus is one of the many U.S. plants that are endangered, mostly because of development and collectors.

One example of an alien species is the kudzu vine, brought in from Japan. In the 1930s, it was planted in many areas of the Southeast to help control soil erosion. It does control erosion, but it is so prolific and hard to kill that it spreads rapidly and covers hills, trees, houses, roadsides, stream banks, utility poles, patches of forest, and anything else in its path (Figure 16-19). Currently, it is confined by climate to the southern United States, but it could spread as far north as the Great Lakes by 2030 if global warming from an enhanced greenhouse effect occurs as projected.

POPULATION GROWTH, AFFLUENCE, AND POVERTY The underlying causes of extinction and population reduction of wildlife are population growth of humans, affluence, and poverty. As the human population grows, it occupies more land and clears and degrades more land to supply food, fuelwood, timber, and other resources.

Increasing affluence leads to greatly increased average resource use per person, which is a prime factor in destruction and degradation of wildlife habitat (Figure 1-16). In LDCs, the combination of rapid popula-

A factor affecting the survival of some individual organisms and populations of organisms is **biological amplification** (also called biological magnification), a condition in which concentrations of certain chemicals in organisms feeding at high trophic levels in a food chain or web are drastically higher than concentrations of those chemicals found in organisms feeding at lower trophic levels.

Chemicals that can be biologically amplified include synthetic organic chemicals (such as the pesticide DDT and PCBs), some radioactive materials, and some toxic mercury and lead compounds. Synthetic organic compounds that can be biologically amplified are insoluble in water, are soluble in fat, and are slowly biodegraded by natural processes. This means that they become more concentrated in the fatty tissues of organisms at successively higher trophic levels in food chains and webs. Radioactive materials and toxic lead and mercury compounds are biologically amplified because they are nondegradable or slowly degradable and concentrate in certain parts of the bodies of animals.

Figure 16-18 shows the biological amplification of DDT in a five-step food chain of an estuary ecosystem. If each phytoplankton organism in such a food chain concentrates one unit of water-insoluble DDT from the water, a small fish eating thousands of phytoplankton will store thousands of units of fat-soluble DDT in its fatty tissue. Then, a large fish that eats ten of the smaller fish will receive and store tens of thousands of units of fat-soluble DDT. A bird or a person that eats several large fish can ingest hundreds of thousands of units of DDT.

High concentrations of DDT or other slowly biodegraded, fat-soluble organic chemicals can reduce populations of species in several ways. They can directly kill the organisms, reduce their ability to reproduce, or weaken them so that they are more vulnerable to diseases, parasites, and predators.

During the 1950s and 1960s, populations of ospreys, cormorants, eastern and California brown pelicans (Figure 2-7), and bald eagles (Figure 2-10) declined drastically. These birds feed mostly on fish at the top of long aquatic food chains and webs and thus ingest large quantities of biologically amplified DDT in their prey.

Populations of predatory birds such as prairie falcons, sparrow hawks, Bermuda petrels, and peregrine falcons (Figure 16-13) also fell when they ate animal prey containing DDT. These birds control populations of rabbits, ground squirrels, and other crop-damaging small mammals.

Research has shown that these population declines occurred because DDE, a chemical produced by the breakdown of DDT, accumulated in the bodies of the affected bird species. This chemical reduces the amount of calcium in the shells of their eggs. As a result, the shells are so thin that many of them break and the unborn chicks die.

Since the U.S. ban on DDT in 1972, populations of most of these bird species have made a comeback. In 1980, however, it was discovered that levels of DDT and other banned pesticides were rising in some areas and in some species, such as the peregrine falcon and the osprey.

These species may be picking up biologically amplified DDT and other chlorinated hydrocarbon insecticides in Latin American countries, where the birds live during winter. In those countries, the use of such chemicals is still legal. Illegal use of DDT and other banned pesticides in the United States may also play a role.

---

tion growth and poverty push the poor to cut forests, grow crops on marginal land, and poach endangered animals.

GENERAL CHARACTERISTICS OF EXTINCTION-PRONE SPECIES Some species have natural traits that make them more vulnerable than others to premature extinction (Table 16-2). One trait that affects the survival of species under different environmental conditions is their reproductive strategy. Generally, in times of stress, r-strategist species have an advantage over many K-strategist species (Table 6-3).

Each animal species has a critical population density and size, below which survival may be impossible because males and females have a hard time finding each other. Once the population reaches its critical size, it continues to decline, even if the species is protected, because its death rate exceeds its birth rate. The remaining small population can easily be wiped out by fire, flood, landslide, disease, or some other catastrophic event.

Some species, such as bats, are vulnerable to extinction for a combination of reasons (see Case Study on p. 426).

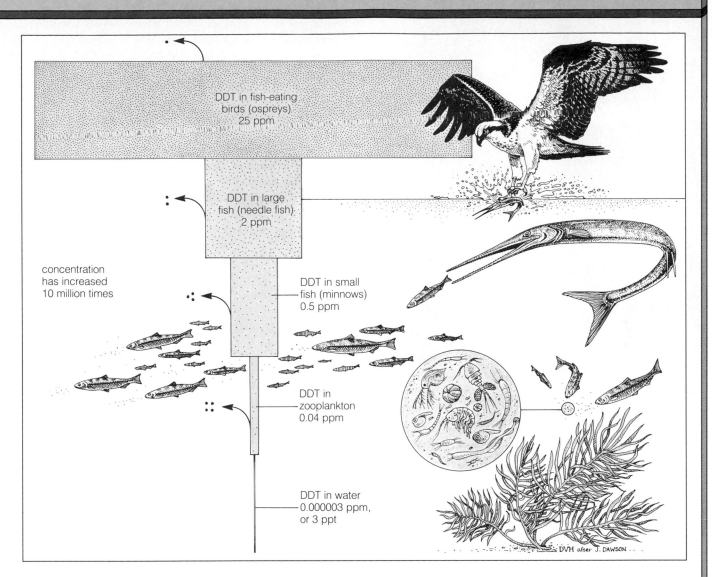

Figure 16-18 The concentration of DDT in the fatty tissues of organisms was biologically amplified about 10 million times in this food chain of an estuary adjacent to Long Island Sound near New York City. Dots represent DDT.

In the figure, labels read:
- DDT in fish-eating birds (ospreys) 25 ppm
- DDT in large fish (needle fish) 2 ppm
- concentration has increased 10 million times
- DDT in small fish (minnows) 0.5 ppm
- DDT in zooplankton 0.04 ppm
- DDT in water 0.000003 ppm, or 3 ppt
- DVH after J. DAWSON

16-3

Protecting Wild Species from Extinction

METHODS FOR PROTECTING AND MANAGING WILDLIFE There are three basic approaches to wildlife conservation and management.

1. *The Species Approach*: Protect endangered species by identifying them, giving them legal protection, preserving and managing their critical habits, propagating species in captivity, and reintroducing species in suitable habitats.

2. *The Ecosystem Approach*: Preserve balanced populations of species in their native habitats, establish legally protected wilderness areas and wildlife reserves, and eliminate alien species from an area.

3. *The Wildlife Management Approach*: Manage species, mostly game species, for sustained yield by using laws to regulate hunting, establishing harvest quotas, developing population management plans, and using international treaties to protect migrating game species, such as waterfowl.

Figure 16-19 Kudzu taking over a field and trees near Lyman, South Carolina. It can grow 0.3 meter (1 foot) a day and is now found throughout the southern United States from East Texas to Florida and as far north as southeastern Pennsylvania. It can't be stopped by being dug up or by burning. Grazing by goats and repeated doses of strong and expensive herbicides can destroy the plant; however, goats and herbicides also destroy other plants, and herbicides can contaminate water supplies. If an enhanced greenhouse effect raises the average minimum winter temperature by 3°C (5.4°F), kudzu could spread as far north as Michigan and southern New England.

THE SPECIES APPROACH: TREATIES AND LAWS
Several international treaties and conventions help protect wild species. One of the most far-reaching treaties is the 1975 Convention on International Trade in Endangered Species (CITES), developed by the World Conservation Union (IUCN) and administered by the UN Environment Programme. This treaty, now signed by 103 countries, lists 675 species that cannot be commercially traded as live specimens or wildlife products because they are endangered or threatened.

However, enforcement of this treaty is spotty, convicted violators often pay only small fines, and member countries can exempt themselves from protection of any listed species. Also, much of the $1- to $2-billion-a-year illegal trade in wildlife and wildlife products goes on in countries that have not signed the treaty.

The United States controls imports and exports of endangered wildlife and wildlife products with two important laws: The Lacey Act of 1900, which prohibits transporting live or dead wild animals or their parts across state borders without a federal permit, and the Endangered Species Act of 1973, including amendments in 1982 and 1988 (see Spotlight on p. 427).

The federal government has the main responsibility for managing migratory species, endangered species, and wildlife on federal lands. States are responsible for the management of all other wildlife.

Funds for state game management programs are provided by the sale of hunting and fishing licenses and federal taxes on hunting and fishing equipment. Two-thirds of the states also have checkoffs on state income tax returns that allow individuals to contribute money to state wildlife programs.

Most of these funds are spent on the management of game species. Only 10% of all federal and state wildlife dollars are spent to study or benefit the nongame species that make up nearly 90% of the country's wildlife species.

THE SPECIES APPROACH: WILDLIFE REFUGES In 1903, President Theodore Roosevelt established the first U.S. federal wildlife refuge at Pelican Island off the east coast of Florida to protect the endangered brown pelican (Figure 2-7). By 1990, the National Wildlife Refuge System had 452 refuges (Figure 15-1). About 85% of the area included in these refuges is in Alaska.

Over three-fourths of the refuges are wetlands for protection of migratory waterfowl. Most of the species on the U.S. endangered list have habitats in the refuge system, and some refuges have been set aside for specific endangered species. These have helped the key deer, the brown pelican of southern Florida (Figure 2-7), and the trumpeter swan to recover. Conservationists complain that there has been too little emphasis on establishing refuges for endangered plants.

Congress has not established guidelines (such as multiple use or sustained yield) for management of the National Wildlife Refuge System, as it has for other public lands. As a result, the Fish and Wildlife Service has allowed many refuges to be used for hunting, fishing, trapping, timber cutting, grazing, farming, oil and gas development, mining, military air exercises, power boating, air boats, and off-road vehicles. By 1990, more than 60% of the refuges were open to hunting and almost 50% were open to fishing.

Development of oil, gas, and mineral resources can destroy or degrade wildlife habitats in refuges through road building, well and pipeline construction, oil and gas leaks, and pits filled with brine or drilling muds (see Pro/Con on p. 428).

The fast-growing water hyacinth is native to Central and South America. In 1884, a woman took one of these plants from an exhibition in New Orleans and planted it in her backyard in Florida. Within ten years, the plant, which can double its population in two weeks, was a public menace.

Unchecked by natural enemies and thriving on Florida's nutrient-rich waters, water hyacinths rapidly displaced native plants. They also clogged boat traffic in many ponds, streams, canals, and rivers in Florida and in other parts of the southeastern United States (Figure 16-20).

Since 1898, mechanical harvesters and a variety of herbicides have been used to keep the plant in check, with little success. Large numbers of Florida manatees, or sea cows (Figure 16-21), can control the growth and spread of water hyacinths in inland waters more effectively than mechanical or chemical methods. However, these gentle and playful herbivores are threatened with extinction, mostly from being slashed by powerboat propellers, becoming entangled in fishing gear, or being hit on the head by oars.

In recent years, scientists have introduced other alien species that feed on water hyacinths to help control its spread. The introduced species include a weevil imported from Argentina, a water snail from Puerto Rico, and the grass carp, a fish brought in from the Soviet Union. These species can help, but the water snail and the grass carp also feed on other, desirable aquatic plants.

There is some good news in this story. Preliminary research indicates that water hyacinths can be used in several beneficial ways. They can be introduced in sewage treatment la-

Figure 16-20   The fast-growing water hyacinth was introduced into Florida from Latin America in 1884. Since then, this plant, which can double its population in only two weeks, has taken over waterways in Florida and other southeastern states.

Heather Angel/Biofotos

Figure 16-21   The endangered Florida manatee, or sea cow, feeds on aquatic weeds and could help control the growth and spread of the water hyacinth in Florida. Only about 1,200 of these animals are left in their habitats in Florida, Georgia, and the Carolinas.

Florida Marine Research Institute/Florida Department of Natural Resources

goons to absorb toxic chemicals. They can be converted by fermentation into a biogas fuel similar to natural gas, added as a mineral and protein supplement to cattle feed, and applied to the soil as fertilizer. They can also be used to clean up polluted ponds and lakes — if their population size can be kept under control.

Table 16-1 Damage Caused by Plants and Animals Imported into the United States

Name	Origin	Mode of Transport	Type of Damage
Mammals			
European wild boar	Russia	Intentionally imported (1912), escaped captivity	Destruction of habitat by rooting; crop damage
Nutria (cat-sized rodent)	Argentina	Intentionally imported, escaped captivity (1940)	Alteration of marsh ecology; damage to levees and earth dams; crop destruction
Birds			
European starling	Europe	Intentionally released (1890)	Competition with native songbirds; crop damage; transmission of swine diseases; airport interference
House sparrow	England	Intentionally released by Brooklyn Institute (1853)	Crop damage; displacement of native songbirds
Fish			
Carp	Germany	Intentionally released (1877)	Displacement of native fish; uprooting of water plants with loss of waterfowl populations
Sea lamprey	North Atlantic Ocean	Entered via Welland Canal (1829)	Destruction of lake trout, lake whitefish, and sturgeon in Great Lakes
Walking catfish	Thailand	Imported into Florida	Destruction of bass, bluegill, and other fish
Insects			
Argentine fire ant	Argentina	Probably entered via coffee shipments from Brazil (1918)	Crop damage; destruction of native ant species
Camphor scale insect	Japan	Accidentally imported on nursery stock (1920s)	Damage to nearly 200 species of plants in Louisiana, Texas, and Alabama
Japanese beetle	Japan	Accidentally imported on irises or azaleas (1911)	Defoliation of more than 250 species of trees and other plants, including many of commercial importance
Plants			
Water hyacinth	Central America	Intentionally introduced (1884)	Clogging waterways; shading out other aquatic vegetation
Chestnut blight (fungus)	Asia	Accidentally imported on nursery plants (1900)	Destruction of nearly all eastern American chestnut trees; disturbance of forest ecology
Dutch elm disease, *Cerastomella ulmi* (fungus)	Europe	Accidentally imported on infected elm timber used for veneers (1930)	Destruction of millions of elms; disturbance of forest ecology

From *Biological Conservation* by David W. Ehrenfeld. Copyright © 1970 by Holt, Rinehart & Winston, Inc. Modified and reprinted by permission.

Table 16-2 Characteristics of Extinction-Prone Species

Characteristic	Examples
Low reproduction rate	Blue whale, polar bear, California condor, Andean condor, passenger pigeon, giant panda, whooping crane
Specialized feeding habits	Everglades kite (eats apple snail of southern Florida), blue whale (krill in polar upwelling areas), black-footed ferret (prairie dogs and pocket gophers), giant panda (bamboo), Australian koala (certain types of eucalyptus leaves)
Feed at high trophic levels	Bengal tiger, bald eagle, Andean condor, timber wolf
Large size	Bengal tiger, African lion, elephant, Javan rhinoceros, American bison, giant panda, grizzly bear
Limited or specialized nesting or breeding areas	Kirtland's warbler (nests only in 6- to 15-year-old jack pine trees), whooping crane (depends on marshes for food and nesting), orangutan (now found only on islands of Sumatra and Borneo), green sea turtle (lays eggs on only a few beaches), bald eagle (prefers habitat of forested shorelines), nightingale wren (nests and breeds only on Barro Colorado Island, Panama)
Found in only one place or region	Woodland caribou, elephant seal, Cooke's kokio, and many unique island species
Fixed migratory patterns	Blue whale, Kirtland's warbler, Bachman's warbler, whooping crane
Preys on livestock or people	Timber wolf, some crocodiles
Certain behavioral patterns	Passenger pigeon and white-crowned pigeon (nest in large colonies), redheaded woodpecker (flies in front of cars), Carolina parakeet (when one bird is shot, rest of flock hovers over body), key deer (forages for cigarette butts along highways—it's a "nicotine addict")

Pollution is also a problem in a number of wildlife refuges. A 1986 study by the Fish and Wildlife Service estimated that one in five federal refuges is contaminated with toxic chemicals. Most of this pollution comes from old toxic-waste dump sites and runoff from nearby agricultural land.

Private groups also play an important role in conserving wildlife in refuges and other protected areas. For example, since 1951, the Nature Conservancy has been able to preserve over 1 million hectares (2.5 million acres) of forests, marshes, prairies, islands, and other areas of unique ecological or aesthetic significance in the United States. The preserved areas are either maintained by the Nature Conservancy and managed by volunteers or donated to government agencies, universities, or other conservation groups.

THE SPECIES APPROACH: GENE BANKS, BOTANICAL GARDENS, AND ZOOS Botanists preserve genetic information and endangered plant species by storing their seeds in gene banks—refrigerated environments with low humidity. Gene banks of most known and many potential varieties of agricultural crops and other plants now exist throughout the world

(Figure 14-6). Scientists have urged that many more be established, especially in LDCs, but some species can't be preserved in gene banks and maintaining gene banks is very expensive.

The world's 1,500 botanical gardens and aboreta hold about 90,000 plant species and also help preserve some of the genetic diversity found in the wild. However, these sanctuaries have too little storage capacity and too little money to preserve most of the world's rare and threatened plants.

Worldwide, zoos house about 540,000 individual animals, many of them from species not threatened or endangered. Zoos and animal research centers are increasingly being used to preserve a representative number of individuals of critically endangered animal species.

Two techniques for preserving such species are egg pulling and captive breeding. *Egg pulling* involves collecting eggs produced in the wild by the remaining breeding pairs of a critically endangered bird species and hatching them in zoos or research centers. For *captive breeding*, some or all of the individuals of a critically endangered species still in the wild are captured and placed in zoos or research centers to breed in captivity.

The world's roughly 950 species of bats (39 species in the United States) make up one-fourth of all mammal species (Figure 16-22). They are the only mammals that truly fly. These night-feeding species range in size from the Kitti hog-nosed bat, smaller than a bumblebee, to the Marianas fruit bat (also known as the flying fox), with a wingspan of 1.3 meters (4.3 feet). Bats are found in all but the most extreme polar and desert areas of the earth.

Despite their variety and distribution, bats have several traits that make them vulnerable to extinction from human activities. They reproduce very slowly compared with other mammals, and many nest in huge breeding colonies in accessible places, such as caves, where people can easily destroy them by blocking the entrances. Once the population level of a bat species falls below a certain level, it has great difficulty in recovering because of its slow reproductive rate.

Bats play important ecological roles and are also of great economic importance to humans. Bats help control many insects that damage human crops and other pest species, such as mosquitoes. About 70% of all bat species feed on various night-flying insects, making them the primary predators of night-flying insects. One brown bat—commonly found in North America—can consume 600 mosquitoes in an hour. One large bat colony in Texas wipes out at least 114 metric tons (125 tons) of insects every night, except during the five winter months when its members hibernate.

Other species of bats feed on certain types of pollen nectar, and still others feed on certain types of fruit. Because of this specialized feeding, these bat species are the chief pollinators for many types of trees, shrubs, and other plants and also disperse plants throughout tropical forests by excreting undigested seeds. If these keystone species are eliminated from an area, dependent plants would disappear. Examples of species pollinated by bats in the United States are the giant saguaro cactus (Figure 4-7) and agaves

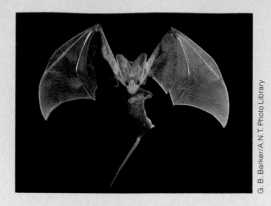

Figure 16-22 Endangered ghost bat carrying a mouse in tropical northern Australia. This carnivorous bat feeds at night and is harmless to people. Bats are considered to be keystone species in many ecosystems because of their roles in pollinating plants, dispersing seeds, and controlling insect and rodent populations.

G. B. Barker/A.N.T. Photo Library

(plants of the desert Southwest used in making fiber rope and tequila).

In Southeast Asia, a cave-dwelling, nectar-eating bat species is the only known pollinator of durian trees, which has fruit crops worth $120 million per year. If you enjoy bananas, cashews, dates, figs, avocados, or mangos, you can thank bats. Likewise, you can thank bats if you have benefited from surgical bandages or life preservers filled with kapok, hemp fibers for rope, and hundreds of other commercially important materials.

Research involving bats has contributed to the development of birth control and artificial insemination methods, drug testing, studies of disease resistance and aging, production of vaccines, and development of navigational aids for the blind.

People kill bats in large numbers because of fears based on misinformation, vampire movies, and folklore and because of lack of knowledge about their important ecological roles. Bats are not dirty, aggressive, rabies-carrying, blood-sucking creatures, and most bat species are harmless to people, livestock, and crops.

Bats clean themselves thoroughly, like cats, and are shy and nonaggressive. Rabies is rare in bats, and individual bats with rabies rarely become aggressive and transmit the disease to wildlife or people. The few people who are bitten are those who foolishly pick up a sick bat, which bites in self-defense, as almost any sick wild animal would.

In all of Asia, Europe, Australia,

and the Pacific islands, only 2 people have been suspected of dying from bat-transmitted rabies. No people in these areas are known to have died of any other bat-transmitted disease. By comparison, in India alone, some 15,000 people die each year from rabies transmitted by other animals, mostly dogs.

In the United States, only 10 people have died of bat-transmitted disease in four decades of record keeping. More Americans die each year from dog attacks or falling coconuts. Only three species of bats (none of them found in the United States) feed on blood, drawn mostly from cattle or wild animals. These bat species can be serious pests to domestic livestock but rarely affect humans.

Because of unwarranted fears of bats and misunderstanding of their vital ecological roles, a number of species have been driven to extinction, and others are threatened. Americans spend millions of dollars annually to have pest control companies exterminate bats. In Europe and the USSR, where there is greater recognition of their benefits, bats receive legal protection.

We need to see bats as valuable allies—not enemies—before we destroy them and lose their important benefits. The extinction of these keystone species can trigger a cascade of extinction of other species dependent on the ecological services bats provide. Educating people about the nature and importance of bats and building barriers to exclude people from bat caves will help.

The Endangered Species Act of 1973 is one of the world's toughest environmental laws. This act makes it illegal for the United States to import or to carry on trade in any product made from an endangered or threatened species unless it is used for an approved scientific purpose or to enhance the survival of the species.

To make control more effective, all commercial shipments of wildlife and wildlife products must enter or leave the country through one of nine designated ports, but many illegal shipments of wildlife slip by. The 60 Fish and Wildlife Service inspectors are able to physically examine only about one-fourth of the 90,000 shipments that enter and leave the United States each year (Figure 16-23). Permits have been falsified, and some government inspectors have been bribed. Even if caught, many violators are not prosecuted, and convicted violators often pay only a small fine.

The law also provides protection for endangered and threatened species in the United States and abroad. It authorizes the National Marine Fisheries Service (NMFS) to identify and list endangered and threatened marine species. The Fish and Wildlife Service (FWS) identifies and lists all other endangered and threatened species. These species cannot be hunted, killed, collected, or injured in the United States.

Any decision by either agency to add or remove a species from the list must be based only on biological grounds, without economic considerations. The act also prohibits federal agencies from carrying out, funding, or authorizing projects that would jeopardize an endangered or threatened species or destroy or modify its critical habitat — the land, air, and water necessary for its survival.

Between 1970 and 1990, the number of species found only in the

Figure 16-23 Confiscated products derived from endangered species. Because of a lack of funds and too few inspectors, probably no more than one-tenth of the illegal wildlife trade in the United States is discovered. The situation is much worse in most other countries.

United States that have been placed on the official endangered and threatened list increased from 92 to 592. Also on the list are 508 species found in other parts of the world.

Once a species is listed as endangered or threatened in the United States, the FWS or the NMFS is supposed to prepare a plan to help it recover. However, because of a lack of funds, recovery plans have been developed and approved for only about 51% of the endangered or threatened species native to the United States, and half of those plans exist only on paper. Only a handful of species have recovered sufficiently to be removed from protection.

The current annual federal budget for endangered species is $8.4 million — equal to the cost of about 25 Army bulldozers. This helps explain why it will take the Fish and Wildlife Service 50 years to evaluate the 3,600 species now under consideration for listing. Many

species will probably disappear before they can be protected, as did 34 species in the 1980s.

In 1990, President Bush's secretary of the interior (who is responsible for wildlife protection) proposed that the Endangered Species Act be weakened. He suggested that economic factors be included in listing endangered and threatened species and in carrying out federally funded projects that threaten the critical habitats of endangered or threatened species. This trial balloon by the Bush administration was vigorously opposed by outraged conservationists and many members of Congress, who argue that we need to make wildlife protection stronger, not weaker, to help protect biological diversity. What do you think should be done?

The Arctic National Wildlife Refuge on Alaska's North Slope is the second largest in the system (Figure 16-24), covering an area the size of South Carolina. This fragile, ecologically valuable area contains more than one-fifth of all the land in the U.S. wildlife refuge system and has been called the crown jewel of the system.

Its coastal plain is the most biologically productive part of the refuge. During all or part of the year, it is home for more than 160 animal species, including the caribou, musk ox, snowy owl, grizzly bear, arctic fox (Figure 4-1), and migratory birds, including as many as 300,000 snow geese. It is also home for about 7,000 Alaskan and Canadian indigenous people who depend on the caribou for a large part of their diet.

The coastal plain in this refuge is the only stretch of Alaska's arctic coastline that has not been opened by Congress to oil and gas development, something the energy companies hope to change because they believe that the area *might* contain oil and natural gas deposits that would increase their profits and reduce U.S. reliance on foreign oil. Since 1985, they have asked Congress to open 607,000 hectares (1.5 million acres) of the coastal plain of the refuge to drilling for oil and natural gas.

In 1987, the Reagan administration supported this proposal, and in 1990, President Bush announced his support of it. He went even further by asking Congress to approve opening all federal land (except national parks) — including national forests, wildlife refuges, and the continental shelf — to oil and gas development whenever oil imports exceed 50% of the country's oil use (Figure 1-12). During and after the Gulf war with Iraq in 1991, administration officials intensified pressure on Congress to approve these proposals.

The Bush administration is also pushing to overturn the law that prohibits export of Alaskan crude oil to other countries. Oil companies favor lifting this ban because they could get a higher price for this American oil by selling it to oil refiners in Japan, Taiwan, and Korea.

Conservationists oppose these proposals and want Congress to designate the entire coastal plain as wilderness. They point to Department of the Interior estimates that there is only a 19% chance of finding oil equal to about as much as the United States consumes every six months. If the oil exists, the earliest it could be developed is the year 2000, and at best it would reduce projected oil imports by only a few percentage points for a short time.

Even if such a deposit of oil is found there, conservationists do not believe that it's worth the potential degradation of this priceless and irreplaceable wilderness area when simple energy conservation measures would save far more oil, faster, and at a much lower cost. For example, boosting auto fuel-efficiency standards 40% in the next decade, a proposal opposed successfully by the Bush administration and the automobile and oil companies in 1990, could save ten times as much oil as the refuge might produce.

Conservationists also oppose allowing oil from Alaska to be sold to other countries so energy companies can make bigger profits. They accuse energy companies of saying we need to develop more oil in Alaska to reduce U.S. oil imports and then asking for permission to export this oil so they can make more money.

Officials of oil companies claim they have developed Alaska's Prudhoe Bay oil fields without significant harm to wildlife. However, the 1989 huge oil spill from the tanker *Exxon Valdez* in Alaska's Prince William Sound cast serious doubt on

---

Many of the facilities use artificial insemination and incubation, and there has been some experimentation with embryo transfer and use of frozen sperm or embryos. Scientists hope that after several decades of captive breeding and egg pulling, the captive population of an endangered species will be large enough that some individuals can be successfully reintroduced into protected wild habitats.

Captive breeding programs at zoos in Phoenix, San Diego, and Los Angeles saved the nearly extinct Arabian oryx (Figure 16-25). This large antelope species once lived throughout the Middle East. However, by the early 1970s, it had disappeared from the wild after being hunted by people using jeeps, helicopters, rifles, and machine guns. Since 1980, small numbers of these animals bred in captivity have been returned to the wild in protected habitats in the Middle East.

Endangered U.S. species now being bred in captivity include the California condor (Figure 16-2), the peregrine falcon (Figure 16-13), and the black-footed ferret (Figure 16-15). Endangered golden lion tamarins bred at the National Zoo in Washington, DC, have been released in Brazilian rain forests.

Keeping populations of endangered animal species in zoos and research centers is limited by lack of space and money. The captive population of each species must number 100 to 500 to avoid extinction through accident, disease, or loss of genetic variability through inbreeding. Moreover, caring for and breeding captive animals is very expensive.

such claims (see Case Study on p. 616). Conservationists also point out that scars left in the fragile arctic tundra soils by drilling pads, airfields, roads, blasting, and mechanized equipment in the Prudhoe Bay area will last for centuries (Figure 5-22).

According to a study leaked from the Fish and Wildlife Service in 1988, oil drilling at Prudhoe Bay has caused much more air and water pollution than was estimated before drilling began in 1972. According to this study, oil development in the coastal plain could cause the loss of 20% to 40% of the area's 180,000-member caribou herd, 25% to 50% of the musk oxen still left, 50% or more of the wolverines, and 50% of the snow geese that winter in this area. A 1988 EPA study found that "violations of state and federal environmental regulations and laws are occurring at an unacceptable rate" in the Prudhoe Bay area.

Do you think that oil and gas development should be allowed in the Arctic National Wildlife Refuge? Do you believe that oil extracted from Alaska should be exported to other countries? Relate your answers to your own use and waste of oil and gasoline.

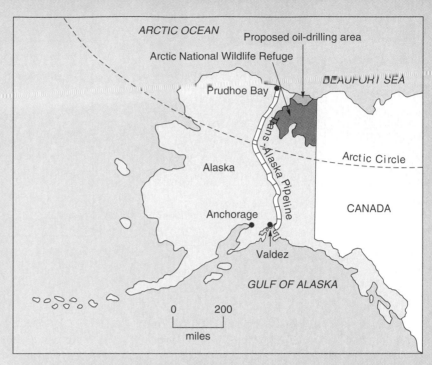

Figure 16-24   Proposed oil-drilling area in Alaska's Arctic National Wildlife Refuge. The Bush administration and the oil companies favor looking for and extracting oil from the coastal plain of this refuge. Conservationists oppose threatening this protected area of precious biodiversity. There is only a one-in-five chance of finding enough oil there to meet all U.S. oil needs for six months. (Data from U.S. Fish and Wildlife Service)

The world's zoos now contain only 20 endangered species of animals with populations of 100 or more individuals. It is estimated that today's zoos and research centers have space to preserve healthy and sustainable populations of only 925 of the 2,000 large vertebrate species that could vanish from the planet. It is doubtful that the more than $6 billion needed to take care of these animals for 20 years will be available.

LIMITATIONS OF THE SPECIES APPROACH   The species approach has been successful in protecting populations of a number of species and allowing them to increase, especially in the United States (Table 16-3).

Because of limited money and trained personnel, however, only a few of the world's endangered and threatened species can be saved by treaties, laws, wildlife refuges, and zoos. That means that wildlife experts must decide which species out of thousands of candidates should be saved. Many experts suggest that the limited funds for preserving threatened and endangered wildlife be concentrated on those species that **(1)** have the best chance for survival, **(2)** have the most ecological value to an ecosystem, and **(3)** are potentially useful for agriculture, medicine, or industry.

THE ECOSYSTEM APPROACH: PROTECTING HABITATS   Most wildlife biologists believe that the best way to prevent the loss of wild species is to establish and maintain a worldwide network of reserves, parks, wildlife sanctuaries, and other protected areas.

Figure 16-25 The Arabian oryx barely escaped extinction in 1969 after being overhunted in the deserts of the Middle East in Oman and Jordan. Captive breeding programs in zoos in Arizona and California have been successful in saving this antelope species from extinction. Some have been reintroduced into the wild in the Middle East, with the wild population now about 120.

Table 16-3 Animal Wildlife Conservation Successes in the United States

Species	Populations 1900	Populations 1988
Trumpeter swan	73	10,000
American bison	1,000	75,000
Sea otters	nearly extinct	100,000
Pronghorn antelope	13,000	1 million
Wild turkey	30,000	3.8 million
Rocky Mountain elk	41,000	1 million
White-tailed deer	500,000	15 million
Canada goose	1 million	2.3 million

Data from U.S. Fish and Wildlife Service

This is based on Aldo Leopold's principle of wildlife conservation "that a species must be saved *in many places* if it is to be saved at all."

By 1990, there were more than 5,000 protected areas throughout the world, occupying about 3.2% of Earth's ice-free land area. That is an important beginning, but it is only one-third of the minimum 10% of the world's land area that conservationists say is needed to protect much of Earth's biodiversity.

These reserves receive varying degrees of protection, and some exist only on paper. Less than 5% of the world's remaining virgin forests are protected within parks and reserves. Furthermore, many of the world's 193 biogeographical types have not been included in reserves, or reserves are too small to protect their populations of wild species.

In 1981, UNESCO proposed that at least one, and ideally five or more, *biosphere reserves* be set up in each of Earth's 193 biogeographical zones. Each reserve should be large enough to prevent gradual species loss as occurs on most isolated islands and should be designed to combine both conservation and sustainable use of natural resources. Currently, more than 70 countries have established some 267 biosphere reserves.

A well-designed biosphere reserve has three interrelated zones: a *core area* containing an important type of ecosystem that has had little, if any, disturbance from human activities; a *buffer zone*, where activities and uses are managed in ways that help protect the core; and a second *buffer or transition zone*, which combines conservation and forestry, grazing, agriculture, and recreation carried out in sustainable ways. Buffer zones can also be used for education and research.

Research indicates that in some areas, several medium-size interconnected reserves may offer more safety from extinction than a single large one. If the population of a species in one of the reserves is lost by a forest fire, an epidemic, or some other disaster, the species might still survive in one or more of the other reserves. Conservation biologists also suggest establishing several protected corridors between reserves to help support more species and allow migrations when environmental conditions in a reserve deteriorate.

Conservationist Norman Myers (see Guest Essay on p. 282) proposes extending all key parks and reserves northward in the northern hemisphere (and southward in the southern hemisphere) and providing a network of corridors, or "green lanes," to allow migration of animal species and some plant species if global warming occurs as projected (Section 11-1). Otherwise, he argues, existing parks and reserves will become death traps instead of sanctuaries.

This ecosystem approach would prevent many species from becoming endangered by human activities and would also be cheaper than managing endangered species one by one. An international fund to help LDCs protect and manage biosphere reserves would cost $100 million a year—about what the world spends on arms every 90 minutes. Since there won't be enough money to protect enough of the world's biodiversity, conservationists believe that efforts should be focused on megadiversity countries, which contain the largest concentrations of Earth's threatened biodiversity (Figure 16-26).

In the United States, conservationists urge Congress to pass an Endangered Ecosystems Act as an

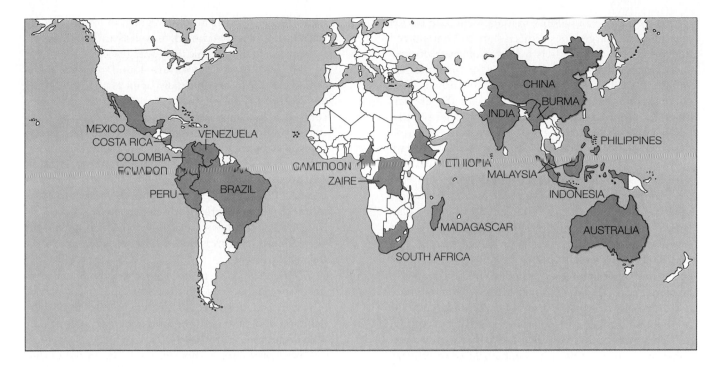

Figure 16-26 Earth's megadiversity countries. These countries are repositories of much of Earth's biodiversity. Conservationists believe that international, national, and local conservation efforts should be concentrated on preserving biodiversity in the remaining wild areas of these countries. For example, Ecuador has more plant species than all of Europe, which is 30 times larger. Tiny Madagascar (see Case Study on p. 259) has five times more tree species than the whole of North America. (Data from Conservation International and the World Wildlife Fund)

important step toward preserving the country's biodiversity. Such an act would also require environmental impact studies to assess the effects of any federal activity on biological diversity.

WORLD CONSERVATION STRATEGY In 1980, the IUCN, the UN Environment Programme, and the World Wildlife Fund developed the *World Conservation Strategy*, a long-range plan for conserving the world's biological resources. The plan was expanded in 1991. Its primary goals are to

- maintain essential ecological processes and life-support systems on which human survival and economic activities depend, mostly by combining wildlife conservation with sustainable development (see Case Study on p. 270)

- preserve species diversity and genetic diversity

- ensure that any use of species and ecosystems is sustainable

- include women in the development of conservation plans

- include indigenous people in the development of conservation plans

- monitor the sustainability of development

- promote an ethic that includes protection of plants and animals as well as people

- encourage the recognition of the harmful environmental effects of armed conflict and economic insecurity

- encourage rehabilitation of degraded ecosystems upon which humans depend for food and fiber

By 1988, 40 countries had planned or established national conservation programs. The United States has not established such a program. If MDCs provide enough money and scientific assistance, this conservation strategy offers hope for slowing the loss of much of the world's biological diversity. Ultimately, however, no system of reserves will be able to protect the planet's biodiversity unless governments act to reduce poverty, control population growth, slow global warming, and reduce the destruction and degradation of tropical and old-growth forests, wetlands, and coral reefs.

 Wildlife Management

MANAGEMENT APPROACHES **Wildlife management** is the manipulation of wildlife populations (especially game species) and habitats for their welfare and for human benefit, the preservation of endangered and threatened wild species, and wildlife law enforcement.

The first step in wildlife management is to decide which species or groups of species are to be managed in a particular area. This is a source of much controversy. Ecologists stress preservation of biological diversity. Wildlife conservationists are concerned about endangered species. Bird watchers want the greatest diversity of bird species. Hunters want large populations of game species for harvest each year during hunting season. In the United States, most wildlife management is devoted to the production of harvestable surpluses of game animals and game birds.

After goals have been set, the wildlife manager must develop a management plan. Ideally, the plan should be based on principles of ecological succession (Section 6-4), wildlife population dynamics (Section 6-2), and an understanding of the cover, food, water, space, and other habitat requirements of each species to be managed. The manager must also consider the number of potential hunters, their success rates, and the regulations available to prevent excessive harvesting.

This information is difficult, expensive, and time-consuming to get. Often it is not available or reliable. That is why wildlife management is as much an art as a science. In practice, it involves much guesswork and trial and error. Management plans must also be adapted to political pressures from conflicting groups and to budget constraints.

MANIPULATION OF HABITAT VEGETATION AND WATER SUPPLIES Wildlife managers can encourage the growth of plant species that are the preferred food and cover for a particular animal species by controlling the ecological succession of vegetation in various areas (Figure 6-10).

Animal wildlife species can be classified into four types according to the stage of ecological succession at which they are most likely to be found: wilderness, late-successional, mid-successional, and early-successional (Figure 16-27). *Early-successional species* find food and cover in weedy pioneer plants. These plants invade an area that has been cleared of vegetation for human activities and then abandoned, as well as areas devastated by mining, fires, volcanic lava, and glaciers.

Mid-successional species are found around abandoned croplands and partially open areas. Such areas are created by the logging of small stands of timber, controlled burning, and clearing of vegetation for roads, firebreaks, oil and gas pipelines, and electrical transmission lines. Such openings of the forest canopy promote the growth of vegetation favored as food by mid-successional mammal and bird species. They also increase the amount of edge habitat, where two communities such as a forest and a field come together. This transition zone allows animals such as deer to feed on vegetation in clearings and quickly escape to cover in the nearby forest.

Late-successional species need old-growth and mature forest habitats to produce the food and cover on which they depend. These animals require the establishment and protection of moderate-size, old-growth forest refuges (Figure 10-18).

Wilderness species flourish only in fairly undisturbed, mature vegetational communities, such as large areas of old-growth forests, tundra, grasslands, and deserts. Their survival depends largely on the establishment of large state and national wilderness areas and wildlife refuges.

Various types of habitat improvement can be used to attract a desired species and encourage its population growth. Improvement techniques include artificial seeding, transplanting certain types of vegetation, building artificial nests, and setting prescribed burns. Wildlife managers often create or improve ponds and lakes in wildlife refuges to provide water, food, and habitat for waterfowl and other wild animals.

POPULATION MANAGEMENT BY CONTROLLED SPORT HUNTING The United States and most MDCs use sport hunting laws to manage populations of game animals. These laws

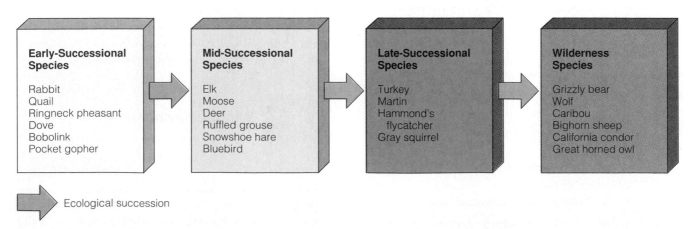

Figure 16-27 Preferences of some wildlife species for habitats at different stages in ecological succession.

Sport hunters, hunting groups, and state game officials believe that Americans should be free to hunt as long as they obey state and local game regulations and don't damage wildlife resources. They argue that carefully regulated sport hunting by human predators is needed because we have eliminated most of the natural predators of deer and other large game animals. Without hunting, populations of game species will exceed the carrying capacity of their habitats and destroy vegetation they and other species need. Hunters also do not believe that hunting and killing a wild animal is unethical.

Sport hunting also provides recreational pleasure for millions of people (16 million in the United States) and stimulates local economies. Defenders of sport hunting also point out that sales of hunting licenses and taxes on firearms and ammunition have provided more than $1.6 billion since 1937. This money has been used to buy, restore, and maintain wildlife habitats and to support wildlife research in

the United States. However, the Council on Environmental Quality observes that "$97 of every $100 spent by federal governments on wildlife management goes to less than three percent of the species; the ones specifically used for hunting, trapping, or fishing."

Conservation groups such as the Sierra Club and Defenders of Wildlife consider hunting an acceptable management tool to keep numbers of game animals in line with the carrying capacity of their habitats. They see it as a way of preserving biological diversity by helping prevent depletion of other native species of plants and animals.

Some individuals and groups, such as the Humane Society, oppose sport hunting. They believe that it inflicts unnecessary pain and suffering on animals, few of which are killed to supply food needed for survival.

The Humane Society also points out that sport hunting tends to reduce the genetic quality of remaining wildlife populations because hunters are most likely to kill the

largest and strongest trophy animals. In contrast, natural predators tend to improve population quality by eliminating weak and sick individuals.

Hunting opponents also argue that game managers deliberately create a surplus of game animals by eliminating their natural predators, such as wolves. Then, having created the surplus, game managers claim that the surplus must be harvested by hunters to prevent habitat degradation or starvation of the game. This increases animal suffering caused by hunters and nature.

Instead of eliminating natural predators, say opponents, wildlife managers should reintroduce them to eliminate the need for sport hunting. However, hunting supporters point out that populations of many game species such as deer are so large that predators like the wolf cannot possibly control them. Also, because most wildlife habitats are fragmented, introduction of predators can lead to the loss of nearby farm animals. What do you think?

- require hunters to have a license
- allow hunting only during certain months of the year to protect animals during mating season
- allow hunters to use only certain types of hunting equipment, such as bows and arrows, shotguns, and rifles, for a particular type of game
- set limits on the size, number, and sex of animals that can be killed and on the number of hunters allowed in a game refuge

However, close control of sport hunting is often not possible. Accurate data on game populations may not exist and may cost too much to get. People in communities near hunting areas, who benefit from money spent by hunters, may push to have hunting quotas raised. On the other hand, some individuals and conservation groups are opposed to sport hunting and exert political pressure to have it banned or sharply curtailed (see Pro/Con above).

MANAGEMENT OF MIGRATORY WATERFOWL In North America, migratory waterfowl such as ducks,

geese, and swans nest in Canada during the summer. During the fall hunting season, they migrate to the United States and Central America along generally fixed routes called **flyways** (Figure 16-28).

Canada, the United States, and Mexico have signed agreements to prevent habitat destruction and overhunting of migratory waterfowl. However, since 1979, the estimated breeding populations of ducks in North America have been declining. The primary reasons for this decrease are prolonged drought in key breeding areas and degradation and destruction of wetland and grassland breeding habitats by farmers.

The remaining wetlands are used by dense flocks of ducks and geese. This crowding makes them more vulnerable to diseases and predators such as skunks, foxes, coyotes, minks, raccoons, and hunters. Waterfowl in wetlands near croplands are also exposed to pollution from pesticides and other chemicals in the irrigation runoff they drink.

Wildlife officials manage waterfowl by regulating hunting, protecting existing habitats, and developing new habitats. More than 75% of the federal wildlife

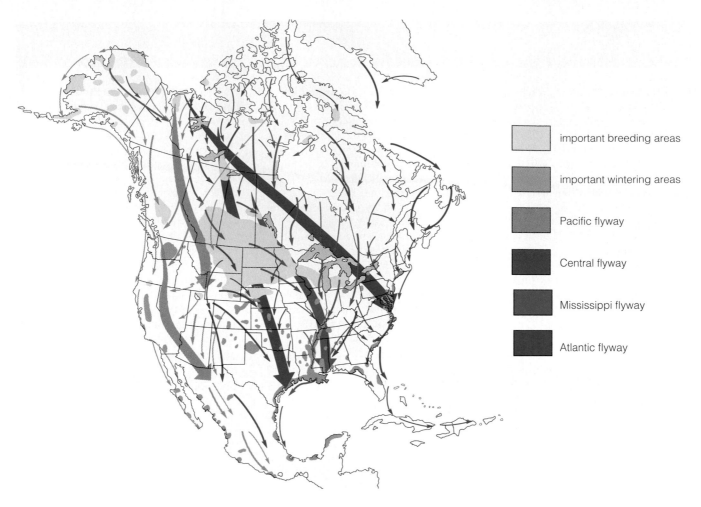

Figure 16-28 Principal breeding and wintering areas and fall migration flyways used by migratory waterfowl in North America.

Legend:
- important breeding areas
- important wintering areas
- Pacific flyway
- Central flyway
- Mississippi flyway
- Atlantic flyway

refuges in the United States are wetlands used by migratory birds. Other waterfowl refuges have been established by local and state agencies and private conservation groups such as Ducks Unlimited, the Audubon Society, and the Nature Conservancy.

Building artificial nesting sites, ponds, and nesting islands is another method of establishing protected habitats for breeding populations of waterfowl. Solar-powered electric fences are being used in some areas to keep predators away from nesting waterfowl.

In 1986, the United States and Canada agreed on a plan to spend $1.5 billion over a 16-year period, with the goal of almost doubling the continental duck breeding population. The key elements in this program will be the purchase, improvement, and protection of an additional waterfowl habitat in five priority areas.

Since 1934, the Migratory Bird Hunting and Conservation Stamp Act has required waterfowl hunters to buy a duck stamp each season they hunt. Revenue from these sales goes into a fund to buy land and easements for the benefit of waterfowl.

16-5 Fishery Management

FRESHWATER FISHERY MANAGEMENT The goals of freshwater fish management are to encourage the growth of populations of desirable commercial and sport fish species and to reduce or eliminate populations of less desirable species. A number of techniques are used:

- regulating the timing and length of fishing seasons
- establishing the minimum-size fish that can be taken
- setting catch quotas
- requiring that commercial fishnets have a large enough mesh to ensure that young fish are not harvested

- building reservoirs and farm ponds and stocking them with game fish

- fertilizing nutrient-poor lakes and ponds with commercial fertilizer, fish meal, and animal wastes

- protecting and creating spawning sites and cover spaces

- protecting habitats from buildup of sediment and other forms of pollution and removing debris

- preventing excessive growth of aquatic plants to prevent oxygen depletion

- using small dams to control water flow

- controlling predators, parasites, and diseases by habitat improvement, breeding genetically resistant fish varieties, and using antibiotics and disinfectants

- using hatcheries to restock ponds, lakes, and streams with species such as trout and salmon

MARINE FISHERY MANAGEMENT The history of the world's commercial marine fishing and whaling industry is an excellent example of the tragedy of the commons—the overexploitation of a potentially renewable resource (see Spotlight on p. 14). As a result, many species of commercially valuable fish (see Case Study on p. 379) and whales in international and coastal waters have been overfished to the point of commercial extinction. At that point, the stock of a species is so low that it's no longer profitable to hunt and gather the remaining individuals in a specific fishery.

Managers of marine fisheries can use several techniques to prevent commercial extinction and allow depleted stocks to recover. Fishery commissions, councils, and advisory bodies with representatives from countries using a fishery can be established. They can set annual quotas for harvesting fish and marine mammals and establish rules for dividing the allowable annual catch among the countries participating in the fishery.

These groups may also limit fishing seasons and regulate the type of fishing gear that can be used to harvest a particular species. Fishing techniques such as dynamiting and poisoning are outlawed. Fishery commissions may also enact size limits that make it illegal to keep fish below a certain size, usually the average length of the particular fish species when it first reproduces.

As voluntary associations, however, fishery commissions don't have any legal authority to compel member states to follow their rules. Nor can they compel all countries fishing in a region to join the commission and submit to its rules.

International and national laws have been used to extend the offshore fishing zone of coastal countries to 370 kilometers (200 nautical miles or 230 statute miles) from their shores. Foreign fishing vessels can take certain quotas of fish within such zones, called *exclusive economic zones*, only with government permission.

Ocean areas beyond the legal jurisdiction of any country are known as the *high seas*. Any limits on the use of the living and mineral common-property resources in these areas are set by international maritime law and international treaties.

Another approach to fishery management is to introduce food and game fish species, such as the striped bass along the Pacific and Atlantic coasts of the United States. Also, artificial reefs can be built from boulders, construction debris, and automobile tires to provide food and cover for commercial and game fish species. About 400 such reefs have been established off U.S. coasts, and Japan has set aside $1 billion to create 2,500 of them.

DECLINE OF THE WHALING INDUSTRY Cetaceans are an order of mammals ranging in size from the 0.9-meter (3-foot) porpoise to the giant 15- to 30-meter (50- to 100-foot) blue whale. They can be divided into two major groups, toothed cetaceans and baleen whales. *Toothed cetaceans*, such as the porpoise, sperm whale, and killer whale, bite and chew their food. They feed mostly on squid, octopus, and other marine animals.

Baleen whales, such as the blue, gray, humpback, and finback, are filter feeders. Instead of teeth, several hundred horny plates made of baleen, or whalebone, extend downward from their upper jaw. These plates filter small plankton organisms, especially shrimplike krill (Figure 4-20) smaller than your thumb, from seawater. Baleen whales are the most abundant group of cetaceans.

The pattern of the whaling industry has been to hunt the most commercially valuable species until it becomes too scarce to be of commercial value and then turn to another species. In 1900, an estimated 4.4 million whales swam the ocean. Today, only about 1 million are left (Figure 16-29). Overharvesting has caused a sharp drop in the populations of almost every whale species of commercial value (Figure 16-30). The populations of 8 of the 11 major species of whales once hunted by the whaling industry have been reduced to commercial extinction. This devastation has happened because of the tragedy of the commons and because whales are more vulnerable to biological extinction than fish species (see Case Study on p. 436).

In 1946, the International Whaling Commission (IWC) was established to regulate the whaling industry. Since 1949, the IWC has set annual quotas to prevent overfishing and commercial extinction. However, these quotas often were based on inadequate scientific information or were ignored by whaling countries. Without any powers of enforcement, the IWC has been unable to stop the decline of most whale species (Figure 16-30).

Figure 16-29 The whaling industry has pushed most of the dozen or so species of great whales to the brink of extinction through overharvesting. This photograph shows pilot whales, which are not now endangered, being butchered in the Faro Islands in the Baltic Sea between the coasts of Sweden and the Soviet Union. After continued protests since the 1960s, the International Whaling Commission banned commercial whaling in 1986, but only until 1992.

In 1970, the United States stopped all commercial whaling and banned all imports of whale products, mostly because of pressure from conservationists and the general public. Since then, conservation groups and the governments of many countries, including the United States, have called for a permanent ban on all commercial whaling.

After years of meetings and delays, the IWC established a five-year halt on commercial whaling, beginning in 1986 and ending in 1991. However, Japan, Norway, and Iceland have continued to harvest several hundred whales each year for "scientific" purposes, despite being refused permits to do this by the IWC. These three countries want to see the moratorium on some species, especially minkes, lifted to allow an annual kill of at least 2,000.

The Western perception of whales as intelligent, beautiful, and therefore worthy of special protection is seen as irrational and sentimental by many Japanese. They note that the Scientific Committee of the IWC has never considered the current blanket moratorium necessary and claim it was put into effect because of pressure from environmentalists. Without continuing worldwide pressure from individuals and conservation organizations and the U.S. government, large-scale

CASE STUDY Near Extinction of the Blue Whale

The blue whale is the world's largest animal and bigger than any dinosaur that once roamed the earth. Fully grown, it's more than 30 meters (100 feet) long—longer than three train boxcars—and weighs 136 metric tons (150 tons)—more than 25 elephants. The adult has a heart as big as a Volkswagen "Beetle" car, and some of its arteries are so big that a child could swim through them. Its brain weighs four times more than yours, its tongue is as large as the size of an adult elephant, and this mammal shows signs of great intelligence.

Blue whales spend about eight months of the year in antarctic waters. There they find an abundant supply of shrimplike krill, which they filter from seawater (Figure 4-20). During the winter months, they migrate to warmer waters, where their young are born.

Once, an estimated 200,000 blue whales roamed the antarctic waters. Today, the species has been hunted to near biological extinction for its oil, meat, and bone (Figure 16-30).

This decline was caused by a combination of prolonged overfishing and certain natural traits of the blue whale. Their huge size made them easy to spot. They were caught in large numbers because they grouped together in their antarctic feeding grounds. Also, they take 25 years to mature sexually and have only one offspring every 2 to 5 years. This low reproduction rate makes it hard for the species to recover once its population has been reduced to a low level.

Blue whales haven't been hunted commercially since 1964 and are classified as an endangered species. Despite this protection, some marine experts believe that not enough blue whales are left for the species to recover. Fewer than 1,000 blue whales may be left today. Within a few decades, the blue whale could disappear forever.

commercial whaling may resume in 1992 when the present moratorium ends.

INDIVIDUAL ACTION We are all involved, at least indirectly, in the destruction of wildlife any time we buy or drive a car, build a house, consume almost anything, and waste electricity, paper, water, or any other resource. All those activities contribute to the destruction or degradation of wildlife habitats or to the killing of one or more individuals of some plant or animal species.

Modifying our consumption habits is a key goal in protecting wildlife, the environment, and ourselves (see Individuals Matter on p. 437). This also involves

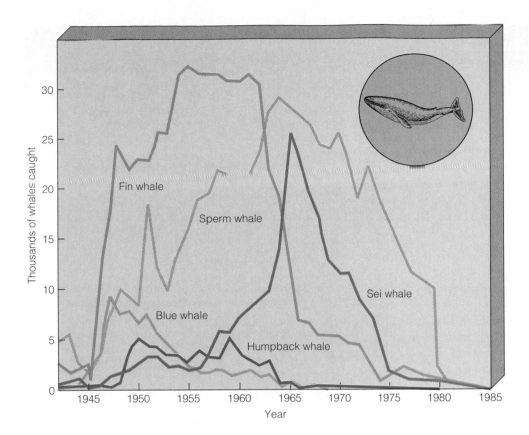

Figure 16-30 Whale harvests, showing the signs of overharvesting. (Data from International Whaling Commission)

Fin whale

Sperm whale

Blue whale

Sei whale

Humpback whale

INDIVIDUALS MATTER What You Can Do

- Improve the habitat on a patch of the earth in your immediate environment, such as backyards, abandoned city lots, campus areas, and streams clogged with debris.

- Develop a wildlife protection and management plan for any land that you own, emphasizing the promotion of biological diversity.

- Develop a backyard wildlife refuge by setting up birdfeeders and birdbaths and establishing plants that attract certain animals.

- Don't buy furs, ivory products, reptile-skin goods, tortoise shell jewelry, rare parrots, or rare orchids or cacti. If enough people did this, the illegal trade in endangered and threatened species would dry up.

- Consider reducing or eliminating your consumption of meat and not using products made from leather or other materials obtained from domesticated animals raised with little regard for their well-being.

- Don't buy brands of tuna fish unless the cans say they were caught by dolphin-safe methods. Support a ban on drift net fishing (Figure 14-22) in international waters.

- Support efforts to ensure that test animals are treated humanely and to reduce their use to a minimum.

- If you have a dog or a cat as a pet, have it spayed or neutered. Each year, U.S. pounds and animal shelters have to kill about 15 million unwanted dogs and cats because of pet overpopulation. That is 75 times the number of dogs and cats killed each year in the United States for research and teaching purposes. Most of these test animals are obtained from animal shelters, where they would have to be killed anyway because of our throwaway attitude toward pets.

- Leave wild animals in the wild. Consider not buying exotic birds, fish, and other pets imported from tropical and other areas. Typically, one or more animals die for each one that reaches a pet shop. Also, most of these pets die prematurely because they are killed, abandoned, or cared for improperly by their owners.

- Learn about endangered species found in or near the area where you live, and work to ensure their protection and recovery.

- Reduce habitat destruction and degradation by recycling paper, cans, plastics, and other household items. Better yet, reuse items and sharply reduce your use of throwaway items.

(continued)

- Support efforts to sharply reduce the destruction and degradation of tropical forests (Section 10-2) and old-growth forests (Section 10-5), slow global warming (Section 11-2), and reduce ozone depletion in the stratosphere (Section 11-4).

- Pressure elected officials to pass laws requiring much larger fines and longer prison sentences for wildlife poachers and to provide more funds and personnel for wildlife protection.

- Pressure Congress to pass a national biological diversity act and to develop a national conservation program as part of the World Conservation Strategy.

- Encourage the development of an international treaty to preserve biological diversity.

---

supporting efforts to reduce deforestation, projected global warming, and ozone depletion—three of the greatest threats to Earth's wildlife and the human species.

During our short time on this planet, we have gained immense power over what species—including our own—live or die. We named ourselves the wise (*sapiens*) species. In the next few decades, we will learn whether we are a wise species. If not, millions of years from now, some new and truly wise species that might take our place may look back and change the name of our extinct species to *Homo unsapiens unsapiens*. If we eliminate ourselves and take millions of other species down with us, we will be mourned by no one, and what's left will go cycling on without us.

Biological diversity must be treated as a global resource to be indexed and used, and above all preserved.

E. O. WILSON

DISCUSSION TOPICS

1. Discuss your gut-level reaction to this statement: "It doesn't really matter that the passenger pigeon is extinct and the blue whale, the whooping crane, the California condor, the rhinoceros, the grizzly bear, and a number of other plant and animal species are endangered mostly because of human activities." Be honest about your reaction, and give arguments for your position.

2. Make a log of your own consumption and use of food and other products for a single day. Relate your consumption to the increased destruction of wildlife and wildlife habitats in the United States, in tropical forests, and in aquatic ecosystems.

3. a. Do you accept the ethical position that each *species* has the inherent right to survive without human interference, regardless of whether it serves any useful purpose for humans? Explain.
   b. Do you believe that *each individual* of an animal species has an inherent right to survive? Explain. Would you extend such rights to individual plants and microorganisms? Explain.

4. Do you believe that the use of animals, mostly mice and rats, to test new drugs and vaccines and the toxicity of chemicals should be banned? Explain. What are the alternatives? Should animals be used to test cosmetics?

5. Are you for or against sport hunting? Explain.

6. You find a young hawk and manage to raise it to maturity. What should you do with it? Offer it to a zoo? Keep it as a pet? Call the local or state fish and wildlife agency and ask for their advice? Release it into a suitable area of the wild? Explain.

*7. Make a survey of your campus and local community to identify examples of habitat destruction or degradation that have had harmful effects on the populations of various wild plant and animal species. Develop a management plan for the rehabilitation of these habitats and wildlife.

CHAPTER 17

PERPETUAL AND RENEWABLE ENERGY RESOURCES

General Questions and Issues

1. How can we evaluate present and future energy alternatives?

2. What are the advantages and disadvantages of improving energy efficiency to reduce unnecessary energy waste?

3. What are the advantages and disadvantages of capturing and using some of the sun's direct input of solar energy for heating buildings and water and for producing electricity?

4. What are the advantages and disadvantages of using flowing water and solar energy stored as heat in water for producing electricity?

5. What are the advantages and disadvantages of using wind to produce electricity?

6. What are the advantages and disadvantages of burning plants and organic waste (biomass) for heating buildings and water, for producing electricity, and for transportation (biofuels)?

7. What are the advantages and disadvantages of using geothermal energy as an energy resource?

8. What are the advantages and disadvantages of using hydrogen gas to produce electricity, to heat buildings and water, and to propel vehicles?

If the United States wants to save a lot of oil and money and increase national security, there are two simple ways to do it: stop driving Petropigs and stop living in energy sieves.

AMORY B. LOVINS

A MAJOR THEME OF THIS BOOK is that energy is the thread sustaining and integrating all life and supporting all economics. That is why it is so important that we understand the nature and the implications of the two energy laws that govern all energy use. I suggest that you review Sections 3-3, 3-6, 3-7, and 3-8 before studying this and the next chapter.

What types of energy we use and how we use them are the principal factors determining how much we abuse the life-support systems for us and other species. Our current dependence on nonrenewable fossil fuels is the primary cause of air and water pollution, land disruption, and projected global warming. In 1973, E. F. Schumacher warned: "A population basing its economic life on nonrenewable fuels is living parasitically, on capital instead of income."

Most analysts agree that the era of cheap oil is coming to an end (see Case Study on p. 15). That means we must find substitutes for the oil that now supports the economies of industrialized countries and many LDCs. Some analysts argue that to reduce the threat of projected global warming (Section 11-1) and air and water pollution, we must reduce our current use of all fossil fuels 50% by 2010, and 70% by 2030 (Section 11-2).

What is our best option for reducing dependence on oil and other fossil fuels? Cut out unnecessary energy waste by improving energy efficiency (see Guest Essay on p. 75). What is our next best energy option? There is disagreement about that.

Some say we should get more of the energy we need from the sun, wind, flowing water, biomass, heat stored in Earth's interior, and hydrogen gas (see Guest Essay on p. 75). These energy choices, based on using Earth's underutilized perpetual and renewable energy resources, are evaluated in this chapter.

Others say we should burn more coal and synthetic liquid and gaseous fuels made from coal. Some believe natural gas is the answer, at least as a transition fuel until a new energy era emerges, built around improved energy efficiency and perpetual and renewable energy. Others think nuclear power is the answer. These choices, based on using more of Earth's nonrenewable energy resources, are evaluated in the next chapter.

17-1 Evaluating Energy Resources

Experience has shown that it takes 50 to 60 years to develop and phase in new supplemental energy resources on a large scale (Figure 3-6). In deciding which combination of energy alternatives we should use in the future, we need to plan for three time periods: the short term (1993 to 2003), the intermediate term (2003 to 2013), and the long term (2013 to 2043).

First, we must decide how much we need, or want, of different kinds of energy, such as low-temperature heat, high-temperature heat, electricity, and fuels for transportation. This involves deciding what type and quality of energy can best perform each energy task (Figure 3-8). Making the wrong decisions, such as using high-quality electricity to heat space and water, wastes energy and money and causes more pollution and environmental degradation than necessary (Figure 3-16). Then, we must decide which energy sources can meet our needs at the lowest cost and with the least environmental impact by answering four questions about each alternative.

1. How much will probably be available during the short term, intermediate term, and long term?

2. What is the estimated net useful energy yield (Figure 3-19)?

3. How much will it cost to develop, phase in, and use?

4. What are its potentially harmful environmental, social, and security impacts, and how can they be reduced?

The most important question decision makers and individuals should ask is, What energy choices will do the most to sustain the earth for us, for future generations, and for the other species living on this planet? Despite its importance, this ethical question is rarely considered by government officials, energy company executives, and most people. Changing this situation is probably the most important and difficult challenge we face.

17-2 Improving Energy Efficiency: Doing More with Less

REDUCING ENERGY WASTE: AN OFFER WE CAN'T AFFORD TO REFUSE The easiest, quickest, and cheapest way to make more energy available with the least environmental impact is to reduce or eliminate unnecessary energy use and waste (Figure 3-14). There are two general ways to do that.

1. *Reduce energy consumption by changing energy-wasting habits.* Examples include walking or riding a bicycle for short trips, using mass transit instead of cars, wearing a sweater indoors in cold weather to allow a lower thermostat setting, turning off unneeded lights, and reducing our use of throw-away items, which require energy for raw materials, manufacture, and disposal.

2. *Improve energy efficiency by using less energy to do the same amount of work.* Examples of doing more with less include adding more insulation to houses and buildings, keeping car engines tuned, and switching to, or developing, more energy-efficient cars, houses, heating and cooling systems, appliances, lights, and industrial processes (Figure 3-15).

Improving energy efficiency has the highest net useful energy yield of all energy alternatives. It reduces the environmental impacts of using energy because less of each energy resource is used to provide the same amount of energy. It adds no carbon dioxide to the atmosphere and is the best, cheapest, and quickest way to slow projected global warming by reducing wasteful use of fossil fuels and the need for costly and politically unacceptable nuclear power. It does not mean freezing in the dark or driving small cars.

Reducing the amount of energy we use and waste makes domestic and world supplies of nonrenewable fossil fuels last longer and buys time for phasing in perpetual and renewable energy resources. It also reduces international tensions and improves national and global military and economic security by decreasing dependence on oil imports (50% in the United States) and the need for military intervention to protect sources of oil, especially in the unstable Middle East, which has 65% of the world's oil reserves (compared with 4% in the United States).

Improving energy efficiency saves money and usually provides more jobs and promotes more economic growth per unit of energy than other energy alternatives. According to energy expert Amory Lovins (see Guest Essay on p. 75), if the world *really* got serious about improving energy efficiency it would save $1 trillion a year. That money, which is now wasted, would be available for other purposes.

The only serious disadvantage of improving energy efficiency is that replacing houses, industrial equipment, and cars, as they wear out, with more energy-efficient ones takes a long time. For example, replacing most buildings and industrial equipment takes several decades, and replacing most older cars on the road with new ones takes 10 to 12 years.

Improvements in energy efficiency have saved the world more than $300 billion worth of energy every year since 1973, but those improvements have only scratched the surface (see Spotlight on p. 441).

IMPROVING INDUSTRIAL ENERGY EFFICIENCY Industrial processes consume 36% of the energy used in the United States. Today, American industry uses 70% less energy to produce the same amount of goods as it did in 1973, but it still wastes enormous amounts of energy. Since 1983, overall U.S. industrial energy efficiency has scarcely improved. Japan has the highest overall industrial energy efficiency in the world, followed closely by the former West Germany.

Industries that use large amounts of both high-temperature heat or steam and electricity can save energy and money by installing *cogeneration units*. They

As the world's largest energy user and waster, the United States has more impact on fossil-fuel depletion, oil pollution, projected global warming, and acid deposition and other forms of air pollution than any other country. At least 43% of all energy used in the U.S. is *unnecessarily* wasted (Figure 3-14). That waste equals all the energy consumed by ⅔ of the world's population.

The largest and cheapest untapped supplies of energy in the U.S. are in energy-wasting buildings, factories, and vehicles, not in Alaska or offshore areas. This vast source of energy is found almost everywhere, can be exploited cheaply and quickly, strengthens rather than weakens the economy and national security, improves rather than damages the environment, and leaves little or no harmful wastes.

The untapped energy available by improving energy efficiency in the United States at a low cost is over three times that from developing remaining nonrenewable energy resources (fossil fuels and nuclear power) at a very high cost (Figure 17-1). Had the United States vigorously pursued a least-cost, high-energy-efficiency energy policy since 1973, instead of its high-cost, mostly fruitless search for significant new domestic deposits of oil, the country would have no need to import any oil today, which would have greatly reduced the need for the United States to engage in any war in the Middle East. Also, enough money would have been saved to pay off the entire national debt.

The good news is that since 1979, the U.S. has gotten more than seven times as much energy from improvements in energy efficiency as from all net increases in the supply of all forms of energy, with little help from federal and state governments. This reduction of energy waste has cut the country's annual energy bill by about $160 billion — about equal to the current annual national deficit. Those savings of $630 per year for each citizen ($2,520 a year for a family of four)

have also reduced emissions of carbon dioxide, sulfur dioxide, and nitrogen oxides 40% below what they otherwise would have been.

Using today's best available technology in transportation, in building, and in industry could save 80% of all the oil used in the United States, while providing the same or better services at lower life-cycle costs. To unhook from Middle East oil, the U.S. would need to capture only 15% of these savings.

The bad news is that energy efficiency in the United States is still half what it could be and has not improved much since 1985. Average gas mileage for new cars and for the entire fleet of cars is below that in most other MDCs. Most U.S. houses and buildings are still underinsulated and leaky. Although electric resistance heating is the most wasteful and expensive way to heat a home (Figure 3-16), it is installed in over half the new homes in the United States, mostly because it saves builders money. Buyers are then left with the high heating bills.

Bringing about a low-cost, energy efficiency revolution by investing about $50 billion a year would stimulate the economy, cut carbon dioxide emissions in half, reduce urban smog and acid deposition, and save $250 billion annually between 1992 and 2002 — enough to pay off the entire national debt. It would also reduce the cost of producing goods and services and make the United States more competitive in the international marketplace.

For example, the United States spends about 11% of its GNP to obtain energy, while Japan uses only 5%. That gives Japanese goods an average 6% cost advantage over American goods. In terms of dollars' worth of goods produced per unit of energy, Japan and the former West Germany are twice as efficient as the United States, France is 2.5 times more efficient, and Sweden is 3.3 times more efficient. If the United States were as energy-efficient as Japan, France, or Sweden, it would need no imported oil.

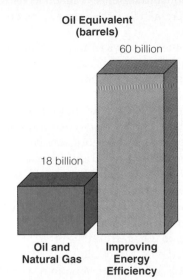

Figure 17-1 Improving energy efficiency in the United States using available technologies would produce over three times as much energy by 2020 at a low cost as would finding and developing at a very high cost all new oil and natural gas deposits believed to exist in the United States. (Data from Natural Resources Defense Council and Rocky Mountain Institute)

Why isn't the United States pursuing an energy strategy that makes economic and environmental sense? There are several reasons. One is the political influence of companies controlling the use of nonrenewable fossil fuels and nuclear power and their emphasis on short-term profits regardless of the long-term economic and environmental consequences. Other reasons include a glut of low-cost fossil fuels, failure of elected officials to require the external costs of using fossil and nuclear fuels to be included in their market prices, and sharp cutbacks in federal support for improvements in energy efficiency and development of perpetual and renewable resources.

Such short-sighted policies will continue until enough citizens demand that elected officials make greatly improving energy efficiency and shifting to renewable energy resources the cornerstones of U.S. energy policy. What do you think should be done?

recover some of the two-thirds of energy in a conventional boiler that is wasted and use it to produce both heat and electricity. By the year 2000, cogeneration has the potential to produce at much lower cost more electricity than all the nuclear power plants in the United States.

Another energy-saving application of cogeneration is to supply energy for district heating and cooling systems — networks of pipes that distribute hot water, chilled water, or steam for space heating and cooling in nearby homes or other buildings. For example, the town of Vesterås, Sweden, uses cogeneration to meet all its electricity and space-heating needs.

About 70% of the electricity used in U.S. industry and half the electricity generated in the United States drives electric motors. Most of those motors run at full speed, and their output is "throttled" to match the task they perform — like driving with one foot pushing the gas pedal to the floor and the other foot on the brake to slow you down. Electronic adjustable speed drives can reduce this waste. According to a study by energy expert Amory Lovins, it would be cost-effective to scrap virtually all standard-efficiency motors now in use and replace them with new high-efficiency motors. Within a year, the extra costs would be paid back.

Switching to high-efficiency lighting is another way to save energy in industry. Industries can also use computer-controlled energy management systems to turn off lighting and equipment in nonproduction areas and make adjustments in periods of low production.

Another significant way to save energy in industry is to greatly reduce the production of throwaway products, which can be done by increasing recycling and reuse and by making products that last longer and are easy to repair and recycle (Section 19-5). Despite the potential for large energy savings, federal support for research and development to improve industrial energy efficiency was cut by almost 60% between 1981 and 1991.

IMPROVING TRANSPORTATION ENERGY EFFICIENCY One-fourth of the commercial energy consumed in the United States is used to transport people and goods. Americans have one-third of the world's automobiles and drive about as many kilometers each year as the rest of the world combined. About one-tenth of the oil consumed in the world each day is used by American motorists on their way to and from work, 69% of them driving alone. California alone uses more gasoline than any country in the world, except the United States and the Soviet Union.

Today, transportation consumes 63% of all oil used in the United States — up from 50% in 1973. Burning gasoline and other transportation fuels accounts for about 33% of total U.S. emissions of carbon dioxide, and the air conditioners in cars and light trucks are responsible for 75% of the country's annual ozone-destroying CFC emissions. Thus, the best way to reduce world oil consumption, to slow ozone depletion in the stratosphere and projected global warming, and to reduce air pollution is to improve the fuel efficiency of vehicles (Figure 17-2), make greater use of mass transit (Figure 17-3), and haul freight more efficiently.

Between 1973 and 1985, the average fuel efficiency of new American cars doubled, and the average fuel efficiency of all the cars on the road increased by 54% (Figure 17-2). During that period, these improvements in fuel efficiency saved American consumers about $285 billion in fuel costs and now save about 5 million barrels of oil a day. That is an important gain, but it is well below what is achievable with existing technology. Also, since 1985, there have been no gains in U.S. fuel efficiency and even a slight decline for new cars (Figure 17-2).

According to the U.S. Office of Technology Assessment, new cars produced in the United States could easily average between 16 and 23 kilometers per liter (kpl) (38 to 55 mpg) within five years and 22 to 33 kpl (52 to 78 mpg) within ten years. The additional cost would be about $500 per car, but the gasoline savings would total at least $2,000 over the life of the car. The fuel efficiency of new light trucks — pickup trucks, minivans, and 4-wheel-drive sport vehicles — could be increased from 8.5 kpl (20 mpg) to 14 kpl (33 mpg) during the 1990s.

Making these improvements in fuel efficiency would raise the fuel efficiency of the entire U.S. automotive fleet from its current 8 kpl (19 mpg) to 14.5 kpl (34 mpg), eliminate the need to import any oil, and save consumers more than $50 billion a year in fuel costs. Within a decade, such improvements would save ten times as much oil as we might get from the Arctic National Wildlife Refuge under the most optimistic projections (see Pro/Con on p. 428) and ten times as much as we are likely to get from more offshore oil leasing in California. Consumers buying new fuel-efficient cars would get back any extra costs involved through fuel savings in about a year. From then on, they would be making money from their cars compared with driving cars that get only 9 to 15 kpl (21 to 35 mpg).

Since 1988, the three leading American car companies have sharply reduced their research and development on small, more fuel-efficient cars and have persuaded elected officials not to raise fuel efficiency standards. The biggest reasons for this are the higher profits to be made on larger cars and declining consumer interest in improved fuel efficiency because of the temporary oil glut of the 1980s and the resulting artificially low oil and gasoline prices (see Case Study on p. 15).

Because the United States is the world's largest market for cars, its fuel efficiency policy and gasoline prices set the standards that the world's automobile manufacturers must meet. Fuel efficiency will not in-

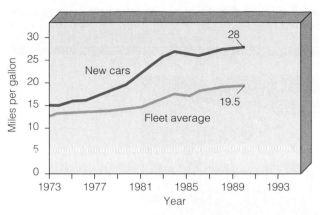

Figure 17-2 Increase in average fuel efficiency of new cars and the entire fleet of cars in the United States between 1973 and 1990. Average fuel efficiency of new cars dropped or stayed about the same between 1984 and 1990 because Congress relaxed standards set in the 1970s and has refused to enact higher standards since then. (Data from U.S. Department of Energy and Environmental Protection Agency)

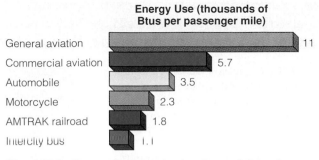

Figure 17-3 Energy efficiency of various types of domestic transportation.

crease in the United States unless elected officials set and enforce greatly increased gas mileage standards. That will not happen unless voters pressure them enough to overcome the political influence of the American automobile industry.

Meanwhile, Japan and some western European countries have increased their research on fuel efficiency. They want to have fuel-efficient cars ready when the oil crisis, expected to occur sometime during the next two decades, replaces the current oil glut. Today, consumers can buy cars such as Chevrolet's Geo Metro, built in Japan by Suzuki with a fuel efficiency of 24 kpl (57 mpg), and the Honda Civic CRX HF, which also gets 24 kpl (57 mpg). However, the technology has existed since the mid-1980s to build cars larger, safer, and much more fuel-efficient than those models (see Spotlight on p. 444).

Electric cars might help out, especially for urban commuting and short trips. All major American car companies have developed prototype electric cars and minivans, some of which might be available by 1995. They are extremely quiet, require little maintenance, and produce no air pollution except that emitted indirectly when the electricity needed to recharge their batteries is produced. Batteries can be recharged each night at off-peak load hours, when rates are lower. If solar cells can be used for recharging, the environmental impacts from producing electricity at coal or nuclear power plants to recharge the batteries would be eliminated.

The Impact prototype built by General Motors has a cruising range of up to 193 kilometers (120 miles) before its batteries need recharging for 8 hours and it accelerates from 0 to 97 kph (0 to 60 mph) in 8 seconds. However, the batteries in this and other electric cars have to be replaced every 40,000 kilometers (25,000

miles) at a cost of about $1,500. This and the electricity costs for recharging mean that current prototypes cost about twice as much to operate as a gasoline-powered car. This could change if new and cost-effective types of batteries that last longer and hold a higher charge density could be developed.

Another way to make the world's diminishing supply of oil last longer is to shift more freight from trucks and airplanes to trains and ships (Figure 17-3). General Motors has developed a new truck trailer that can easily be converted to a railcar and then back to a truck, without having to be unloaded. Using this truck-rail combination would use 80% less fuel than truck transport alone for hauls of more than 322 kilometers (200 miles).

Manufacturers can increase the energy efficiency of new transport trucks 50% by improving their aerodynamic design and using turbocharged diesel engines and radial tires. Truck companies can reduce waste by not allowing trucks to return empty after reaching their destination (but not carrying food on the initial run and garbage or toxic materials on the return run, as has happened in some cases).

The energy efficiency of today's commercial jet aircraft fleet could be doubled by improved designs. Boeing's new 777 jet will use about half the fuel per passenger seat of a 727. Existing advanced diesel engine technology could improve the fuel efficiency of ships by 30% to 40% over the next few decades.

IMPROVING THE ENERGY EFFICIENCY OF COMMERCIAL AND RESIDENTIAL BUILDINGS Commercial and residential buildings are responsible for about 3% of U.S. energy demand at an annual cost of $165 billion. Sweden and South Korea have the world's toughest standards for energy efficiency in homes and other buildings. For example, the average home in Sweden, the world's leader in energy efficiency, consumes about one-third as much energy as an average American home of the same size (Figure 17-5).

A monument to energy waste is the 110-story, twin-towered World Trade Center in Manhattan, which uses as much electricity as a city of 100,000 people. Windows in its walls of glass cannot be opened to take advantage of natural warming and cooling. Its heating

Fuel-efficient cars will take decades to develop, and will be sluggish, small, and unsafe. Wrong! Average fuel economy for new cars produced from 1990 on could have been at least 26 kilometers per liter (61 mpg). The cars could carry four or five people in comfort and be as safe as, or safer than, and at least as peppy as the average new car today.

The main reason this hasn't happened is that elected officials in the United States, influenced by the powerful American automobile companies, did not raise fuel efficiency standards in 1981 to accomplish this goal. Had the higher standards been enacted in 1981, the United States would not have had to import any oil from the Middle East in 1990 when the war with Iraq began with a major goal of protecting U.S. oil imports from Saudi Arabia. After the war with Iraq started in 1991, environmentalists pushed again to have standards enacted that would double the fuel efficiency of new cars by the year 2000, but they were defeated by opposition from the Bush administration and the automobile industry.

Since 1985, at least ten automobile companies, including Volvo, Volkswagen, Renault, Peugeot, and Toyota, have had prototype cars that carry four or five passengers, are nimble and peppy, meet or exceed current safety and pollution standards, and have fuel efficiencies of 29 to 59 kpl (67 to 138 mpg). If they were mass-produced, additional costs to the consumer for such vehi-

Volvo of America Corporation

Figure 17-4 In 1985, Volvo developed this LCP 2000 prototype car, which averages 27 kpl (63 mpg) in city driving and 35 kpl (82 mpg) on the highway. At a speed of 64 kilometers per hour (40 miles per hour), its fuel efficiency is 43 kpl (101 mpg). It accelerates better than the average new car today and can run on various fuels, such as diesel, diesel-gasoline mixture, and vegetable oils. The driver can carry a bottle of vegetable oil along as an emergency source of fuel.

cles would be more than offset by the fuel savings. Because of their improved designs and the use of stronger but lighter materials, some of these prototypes are safer than the cars we have now.

One example of such eco-cars is Volvo's LCP 2000 (Figure 17-4), which could be in production today had there been sufficient consumer demand for fuel-efficient cars. This car averages 28 kpl (65 mpg). Because of better design and use of stronger but lighter materials (such as magnesium, aluminum, and plastics), it exceeds U.S. crash standards. It carries four passengers in comfort, is quiet, is more corrosion resistant than most of today's cars,

and accelerates from 0 to 97 kilometers per hour (0 to 60 miles per hour) in 11 seconds — better than average.

This car also meets California's air pollution emission standards — the most stringent in the world. Over its lifetime, it is estimated that this car would use half the energy of the same size conventional car and add 15 metric tons (17 tons) less carbon dioxide to the atmosphere. It can run on several different fuels, including diesel fuel and vegetable oil. The Volvo LCP 2000 is also designed for easy assembly and for recycling of its materials when it is taken off the road.

and cooling systems must run around the clock, chiefly to take away heat from its inefficient lighting.

By contrast, Atlanta's 17-story Georgia Power Company building uses 60% less energy than conventional office buildings. The largest surface of the building is oriented to capture solar energy. Each floor extends over the one below, allowing heating by the low winter sun and blocking out the higher summer sun to reduce air conditioning costs. Energy-efficient lights focus on desks rather than illuminating entire rooms. Employees

working at unusual hours use an adjoining 3-story building so that the larger structure doesn't have to be heated or cooled when few people are at work.

With existing technology, the United States could save 40% to 60% of the energy used in existing buildings and 70% to 90% of the energy used in new buildings (see Spotlight on p. 446). Building a *superinsulated house* is a superb way to improve the efficiency of residential space heating and cooling by more than 75% and save on lifetime energy costs (Figure 17-6). Such a

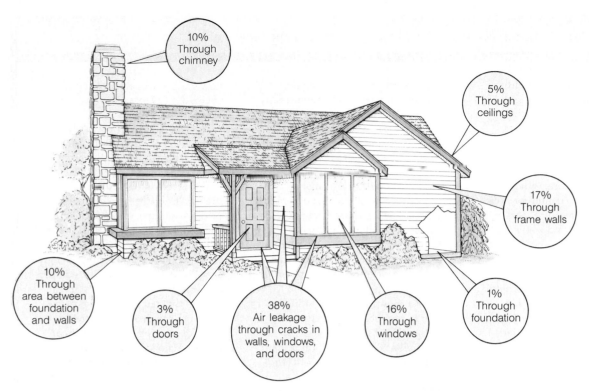

Figure 17-5 Typical ranch-style homes built throughout the United States are heated with energy-wasting electricity and are so full of leaks that up to 85% of this expensive heat is rapidly lost. That is equivalent to having a large, window-size hole in the wall of such houses.

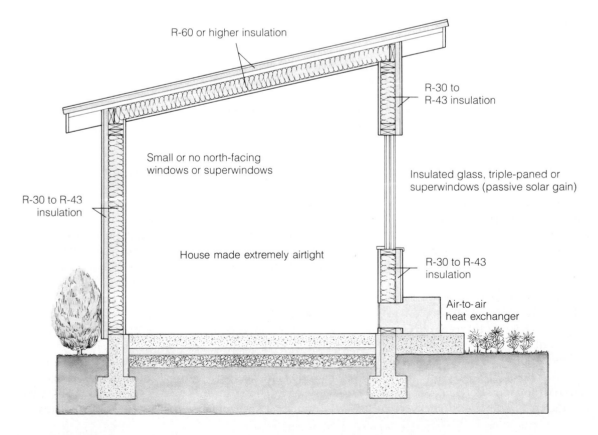

Figure 17-6
Features of a super-insulated house.

Energy experts Amory and Hunter Lovins have built a large, passively heated, superinsulated, partially earth-sheltered home and office (used by 40 people) in Old Snowmass, Colorado, where winter temperatures can drop to $-40°C$ ($-40°F$). This structure, which also houses the research center for the Rocky Mountain Institute, gets 99% of its space heating and water heating and 95% of its daytime lighting (from superwindows) from the sun, uses one-tenth the normal amount of electricity, and uses less than half the normal amount of water for a structure of comparable size. Total energy savings repaid the added cost of its energy-saving features after 10 months and are projected to pay off the cost of the entire facility over about 40 years.

In energy-efficient houses of the near future, microprocessors will monitor indoor temperatures, sunlight angles, and the location of people, and will then send heat or cooled air where it is needed. Some will automatically open and close windows and insulated shutters to take advantage of solar energy and breezes and to reduce heat loss from windows at night and on cloudy days. Sensors can turn off lights in unoccupied rooms or dim lights when sunlight is available.

Researchers are working on "smart windows" that automatically change electronically from clear, which allows sunlight and heat in on cold days, to reflective, which deflects sunlight when the house gets too hot. Superinsulating windows (R-8 to R-10), already available, mean that a house can have as many windows as the owner wants in any climate without much heat loss. Insulating windows with R-12 or better should be available in the near future. Thinner insulation material will allow roofs to be insulated to R-100 and walls to R-43, far higher than today's best superinsulated houses (Figure 17-6).

Small-scale cogeneration units that run on natural gas or LPG (liquefied petroleum gas) are already available. They can supply a home with all its space heat, hot water, and electricity needs. The units are no larger than a refrigerator and make less noise than a dishwasher. Except for an occasional change of filters and spark plugs, they are nearly maintenance-free. Typically, this home-size power and heating plant will pay for itself in four to five years.

Soon, homeowners may be able to get all the electricity they need from rolls of solar cells attached like shingles to a roof or applied to window glass as a coating, already developed by a Japanese and a German firm.

A German firm (Bomin) has developed a solar-powered hydrogen system that can meet all energy needs of a home, an apartment building, or a small village or housing development at an affordable price. A windproof panel of solar collectors automatically tracks the sun, concentrating sunlight at a fixed focus to temperatures as high as 500°C (932°F). The collected heat is stored in metal powders (hydrides) that release hydrogen gas, which burns cleanly to provide energy for cooking, electricity, heating, and cooling. This system, with an energy efficiency greater than that of electric power plants, should be available within a few years.

In 1989, Albers Technologies Corporation of Arizona patented a home air conditioner that uses water, not CFCs or HCFCs, as a coolant, draws half the electricity of a conventional unit, and costs about the same as conventional models with the same cooling capacity. A Saudi Arabian company plans to build 25,000 units every year beginning in 1992, with 20,000 units a year being imported to the United States.

house is heavily insulated and made extremely airtight. Heat from direct solar gain, people, and appliances warms the house, requiring little or no auxiliary heating. An air-to-air heat exchanger prevents buildup of humidity and indoor air pollution.

Most home buyers look only at the initial price, not the more meaningful lifetime cost. A superinsulated house costs about 5% more to build than a conventional house, but this extra cost is paid back by energy savings within five years and can save a homeowner $50,000 to $100,000 over a 40-year period. Sadly, this type of house accounts for less than 1% of new home construction in the United States, mostly because of a lack of consumer demand.

To keep the initial cost for buyers down, developers routinely construct inefficient buildings and stock them with inefficient heating and cooling systems and appliances. When lifetime costs are considered, however, such energy-inefficient houses cost buyers 40% to 50% more. Builders of rental housing have little incentive to pay slightly more to make their units energy-efficient, when renters pay the fuel and electricity bills. Requiring all buildings to meet higher energy-efficiency standards and requiring a building's estimated annual and lifetime energy consumption to be revealed to buyers would help correct these problems.

Many energy-saving features can be added to existing homes, a process called *retrofitting*. Simply increasing insulation above ceilings can drastically reduce heating and cooling loads (Figure 17-5). The homeowner usually recovers initial costs in two to six years and then saves money each year. Caulking and weath-

Figure 17-7 Infrared photo shows heat loss around the windows, doors, roofs, and foundations (red, white, and yellow colors) of houses and stores in Plymouth, Michigan. Because of energy-inefficient design, most existing office buildings and houses in the United States unnecessarily waste about half of the energy used to heat and cool them.

erstripping around windows, doors, pipes, vents, ducts, and wires save energy and money quickly.

Generally, low-income houses and apartments (mostly rental units) are very energy-inefficient, and people with low incomes cannot afford to make improvements in energy efficiency. Since 1973, federal and state aid has been used to improve the energy efficiency of 4 million of the 22 million eligible low-income homes nationwide. Without a significant expansion of such funds, it will take decades to retrofit the eligible units, causing unnecessary energy waste and human suffering.

One-third of the heat in U.S. homes and buildings escapes through closed windows (Figure 17-7)—an energy loss equal to the energy found in all the oil flowing through the Alaskan pipeline every year. During hot weather, these windows also let in large amounts of heat, greatly increasing the use of air conditioning. This loss and gain of heat occurs because a single-pane glass window has an insulating value of only R-1. The R-value of a material is a measure of its resistance to heat flow and thus its insulating ability. Even double-glazed windows have an insulating value of only R-2, and a typical triple-glazed window has an insulating value of R-4 to R-6.

Two U.S. firms now sell "superinsulating" R-8 to R-10 windows, about the insulating value of a normal outside wall (R-11), that pay for themselves in lower fuel bills within in two to four years and then save money every year for decades. If everyone in the United States used these windows, it would save more oil and natural gas each year than Alaska now supplies. The cost of saving this energy is equivalent to buying oil at $2 to $3 a barrel.

Building codes can be changed to require that all new houses use 80% less energy than conventional houses of the same size, as has been done in Davis, California (see Case Study on p. 242). Laws can require that any existing house be insulated and weather-proofed to certain standards before it can be sold, as required in Portland, Oregon. That, plus use of the latest energy-saving designs, could double the energy efficiency of U.S. buildings by 2010, cut carbon emissions in half, and save $100 billion a year.

Using the most energy-efficient appliances available can also save energy and money.* About one-third of the electricity generated in the United States and other industrial countries is used to power household appliances.

One-fourth of the electricity produced in the United States is used for lighting—about equal to the output of 100 large (1,000-megawatt) power plants or half of all coal burned by the nation's electric utilities. Since conventional incandescent bulbs are only 5% efficient, they waste enormous amounts of energy and add to the heat load of houses during hot weather. About half the air conditioning used in a typical U.S. office building is used to remove the internal heat gain from inefficient lighting.

Socket-type fluorescent light bulbs (Figure 3-15) that use one-fourth as much electricity as conventional bulbs are now available. Although they cost about $15 to $20 a bulb, they last 10 to 13 times longer than conventional incandescent bulbs, save 3 times more money than they cost, and emit light indistinguishable from incandescents. Replacing a 75-watt incandescent bulb

---

*Each year, the American Council for an Energy-Efficient Economy (ACEEE) publishes a list of the most energy-efficient major appliances mass-produced for the U.S. market. For a copy, send $3 to the council at 1001 Connecticut Ave., N.W., Suite 530, Washington, DC 20036. Each year, they also publish *A Consumer Guide to Home Energy Savings*, available in bookstores or from ACEEE.

with an 18-watt compact fluorescent bulb reduces electricity consumption by 75% and prevents the generation of 0.9 metric ton (1 ton) of carbon dioxide and 11 kilograms (25 pounds) of sulfur dioxide. Over their lifetime, 15 compact fluorescent bulbs will save a homeowner about $300 to $375. Switching to these bulbs and other improved lighting equipment would save one-third of the electric energy now produced by all U.S. coal-fired plants or eliminate the need for all electricity produced by the country's 113 nuclear power plants. Using energy-efficient lighting could save American businesses $5 billion a year in electricity bills.

Residential refrigerators consume about 7% of the electricity used in the United States — roughly the output of 30 large (1,000-megawatt) power plants. They also account for about 19% of the electricity consumed in the average U.S. household. If all U.S. households had the most efficient typical frost-free refrigerator now available, they would save enough electricity to eliminate the need for 18 existing large nuclear or coal-fired power plants. New prototype refrigerators being built in Denmark and Japan cut electricity use by another 50%.

Most consumers spend $1,000 on a refrigerator and an additional $120 to $180 annually for the electricity it uses, or a total cost of about $4,000 over the machine's 20-year lifetime. A SunFrost refrigerator, now produced by a small California company, costs $1,550 and uses 85% less electricity than the average model. Thus, by spending $550 more on such a refrigerator, a consumer saves about $2,550 in its lifetime cost. Meanwhile, consumers can reduce the energy use of an existing refrigerator by taping about $25 worth of foil-faced rigid insulation to its sides and doors, with a payback time of about one year.

Similar savings are possible with high-efficiency models of other energy appliances, such as stoves, water heaters, and air conditioners. Microwave ovens reduce electricity use for cooking by 25% to 50% (but not if they are used for defrosting food). If the most energy-efficient appliances now available were installed in all U.S. homes over the next 20 years, the savings in energy would equal the energy content of all the oil produced by Alaska's North Slope fields over the appliances' 25-year lifetime.

Department of Energy standards for major household appliances that went into effect in 1990 are likely to save consumers roughly $40 billion by 2015 and eliminate the need to build 8 large power plants. Such standards, however, need to be upgraded every two to three years to reflect advances in technology. They also need to be developed for lighting, windows, and plumbing fixtures.

Energy expert Amory Lovins (see Guest Essay on p. 75) carries around a small briefcase that contains examples of fluorescent light bulbs, a low-flow shower head, superinsulated window glass, and other devices that save energy and money (Figure 17-8). Using these

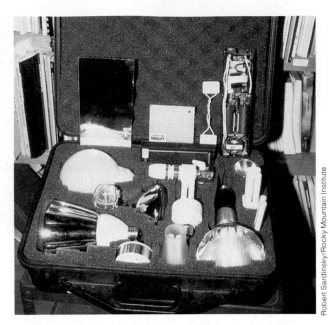

Figure 17-8 Amory Lovins's briefcase of available energy-saving lights, superinsulating window glass, water-flow restrictors, and other devices. Using these throughout the United States would save energy equal to that from 200 large electric power plants, save hundreds of billions of dollars, and sharply reduce pollution and environmental degradation.

devices throughout the United States would save energy equal to the output of 200 large electric power plants and provide better illumination at 10% of the present cost. This would also save enough money to pay off the national debt, eliminate the need to import any oil, sharply reduce pollution and environmental degradation, and slow projected global warming.

DEVELOPING A PERSONAL ENERGY CONSERVATION PLAN Each of us can develop an individual plan for saving energy and money (see Individuals Matter inside the back cover). Here are four basic guidelines.

1. Don't use electricity to heat space or water (Figure 3-8).

2. Insulate new or existing houses heavily, caulk and weatherstrip to reduce air infiltration and heat loss, and use energy-efficient windows.

3. Get as much heat and cooling as possible from natural sources — especially sun, wind, geothermal energy, and trees for windbreaks and natural shading.

4. Buy the most energy-efficient homes, lights, cars, and appliances available, and evaluate them only in terms of lifetime cost.

ENERGY EFFICIENCY DIFFERENCES BETWEEN COUNTRIES Japan, Sweden, and most industrialized western European countries have average standards of living at least equal to, and in some cases greater than, that in the United States. Yet, people in those countries

Table 17-1 Energy Use and Conservation in the United States and Sweden

Use or Method	United States	Sweden
Average per capita use	230,000 kcal/day	150,000 kcal/day
Energy from perpetual and renewable sources	8%	27%
Transportation energy use	High	One-fourth of U.S.
Country size	Large	Small
Cities	Dispersed	Compact
Mass transit use	Low	High
Average car fuel economy	Poor	Good
Gasoline taxes	Low	High to encourage conservation
Tariffs on oil imports	Low	High to encourage conservation
Industrial energy efficiency	Fairly low	High
Nationwide energy-conserving building codes	No	Yes
Municipally owned district heating systems	None	30% of population
Emphasis on electricity for space heating	High (one-half of new homes)	High (one-half of new homes)
Domestic hot water	Most kept hot 24 hours a day in large tanks	Most supplied as needed by instant tankless heaters
Refrigerators	Mostly large, frost-free	Mostly smaller, non-frost-free, using about one-third the electricity of U.S. models
Long-range national energy plan	No	Yes
Government emphasis and expenditures on energy conservation and renewable energy	Low	High
Government emphasis and expenditures on nuclear power	High	Low (to be phased out)

use an average of one-third to two-thirds less energy per person than Americans.

One reason for the difference is that those countries put greater emphasis on improving energy efficiency than the United States does (Table 17-1). Another is that most cities in those countries are more compact than U.S. cities. That means that the average person in Japan, Sweden, or western Europe drives fewer kilometers per year than the average American.

17-3 Direct Solar Energy for Producing Heat and Electricity

THE UNTAPPED POTENTIAL OF PERPETUAL AND RENEWABLE ENERGY RESOURCES The largest, mostly untapped sources of energy for all countries are perpetual and renewable energy from the sun, wind,

flowing water, biomass, and Earth's internal heat (Figure 17-9). Developing these untapped resources could meet 50% to 80% of projected U.S. energy needs by 2030, or sooner, and virtually all energy needs if coupled with improvements in energy efficiency (Figure 17-1).

Doing this would save money, eliminate the need for oil imports, produce less pollution and environmental degradation per unit of energy used, and increase economic, environmental, and military security. In the United States, geothermal power plants, wood-fired (biomass) power plants, wind farms, and solar thermal power plants can produce electricity more cheaply than can new nuclear power plants with far fewer subsidies from the federal government (Figure 17-10). If coal's harmful effects on the biosphere were included as part of its overall price, it would be so expensive that utilities would use it only as a last resort and would replace it with much cheaper perpetual and renewable energy

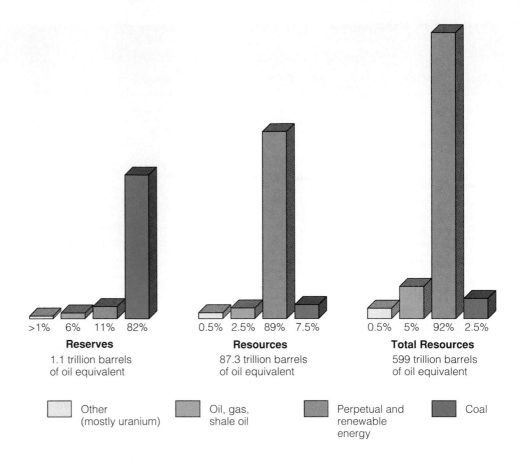

Figure 17-9 U.S. energy resource estimates. The estimated total resources (reserves plus resources) available from perpetual and renewable energy sources are more than ten times those from domestic supplies of coal, oil, natural gas, shale oil, and uranium. Perpetual and renewable energy resources—primarily hydropower and biomass—already supply 20% of the world's energy and 8% of the commercial energy used in the United States. With a worldwide development program, these largely untapped sources of energy could supply 50% to 80% of the world's projected energy needs within a few decades. (Data from U.S. Department of Energy)

>1%	6%	11%	82%

Reserves
1.1 trillion barrels
of oil equivalent

0.5%	2.5%	89%	7.5%

Resources
87.3 trillion barrels
of oil equivalent

0.5%	5%	92%	2.5%

Total Resources
599 trillion barrels
of oil equivalent

Other (mostly uranium) Oil, gas, shale oil Perpetual and renewable energy Coal

resources and even cheaper improvements in energy efficiency.

With an aggressive program to develop perpetual and renewable energy resources, these forms of energy could meet 30% to 45% of the world's projected energy demand by 2050 and bring about enough reduction in greenhouse gases to stabilize projected climate changes. The rest of this chapter evaluates the various perpetual and renewable energy resources available.

PASSIVE SOLAR SYSTEMS FOR SPACE HEATING AND COOLING Solar energy is particularly well suited to supply heat at or below the boiling point of water which can then be used for heating space or water. These uses account for 30% to 50% of energy use in industrial countries and even more in LDCs. Solar energy can be collected, stored, and distributed by passive or active systems.

A **passive solar heating system** captures sunlight directly within a structure and converts it into low-temperature heat for space heating (Figure 17-11). Superwindows, greenhouses, and sunspaces face the sun to collect solar energy by direct gain. Thermal mass (heat-storing capacity), such as walls and floors of concrete, adobe, brick, stone, salt-treated timber, or tile, stores collected solar energy as heat and releases it slowly throughout the day and night. Some designs also store heat in water-filled glass or plastic columns,

black-painted barrels filled with water, and panels or cabinets containing heat-absorbing chemicals.

Besides collecting and storing solar energy as heat, passive systems must also reduce heat loss in cold weather and heat gain in hot weather. Such structures are usually heavily insulated and caulked. Superwindows or movable, insulated shutters or curtains on windows reduce heat loss at night and on days with little sunshine.

Buildup of moisture and indoor air pollutants is minimized by an air-to-air heat exchanger, which supplies fresh air without much heat loss or gain. A small backup heating system may be used, but it is not necessary in a well-designed passively heated and superinsulated house in most climates.

Today, over 250,000 homes and 17,000 nonresidential buildings in the United States have passive solar designs, including earth-sheltered homes (Figure 17-12), and get 30% to 100% of their energy from the sun. However, that is a small number compared with the 80 million homes in the United States and the roughly 3 million new ones built each year.

With technologies already available or under development, passive solar designs could provide at least 80% of a building's heating needs and at least 60% of its cooling needs with an added construction cost of 5% to 10%. Recently, engineer and builder Michael Sykes has developed an Enertia house design that is passively

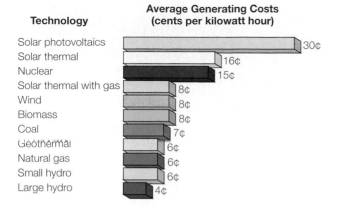

Technology	Average Generating Costs (cents per kilowatt hour)
Solar photovoltaics	30¢
Solar thermal	16¢
Nuclear	15¢
Solar thermal with gas	8¢
Wind	8¢
Biomass	8¢
Coal	7¢
Geothermal	6¢
Natural gas	6¢
Small hydro	6¢
Large hydro	4¢

Figure 17-10 Generating costs of electricity per kilowatt-hour by various technologies in 1989. By the year 2000, costs per kilowatt-hour for wind are expected to fall to five cents, solar thermal with gas assistance to six cents, and solar photovoltaic to ten cents. Costs for other technologies are projected to remain about the same. (Data from U.S. Department of Energy, Council for Renewable Energy Education, and Investor Responsibility Research Center)

heated and cooled by solar energy and the earth beneath it without the need of a conventional heating or cooling system in most areas (see Spotlight on p. 454).

Roof-mounted passive solar water heaters can also supply all or most of the hot water for a typical house (Figure 17-14). The most promising model, called the Copper Cricket, is produced by Sage Advance Company in Eugene, Oregon, and sells for $1,900.

In hot weather, passive cooling can be provided by blocking the high summer sun with deciduous trees, window overhangs, or awnings (Figure 17-11). Windows and fans take advantage of breezes and keep air moving. A reflective foil sheet can be suspended in the attic to block heat from radiating down into the house.

At a depth of 3 to 6 meters (10 to 20 feet), the temperature of the earth stays about 13°C (55°F) all year long in cold northern climates and about 19°C (67°F) in warm southern climates. Earth tubes buried at this depth can pipe cool and partially dehumidified air into an energy-efficient house at a cost of several dollars a summer (Figure 17-11). For a large space, two or three of these geothermal cooling fields running in different directions from the house should be installed. When the added heat degrades the cooling effect from one field, homeowners can switch to another field. During cold months, these geothermal cooling fields are renewed naturally for use during the summer. Initial construction costs (mostly digging) are high, but operating and maintenance costs are extremely low. People allergic to pollen and molds should add an air purification system, but they would also need to do that with a conventional cooling system.

In areas with a dry climate, such as the southwestern United States, evaporative coolers can remove in-

terior heat by evaporating water. Solar-powered air conditioners have been developed but so far are too expensive for residential use. In Reno, Nevada, some buildings stay cool throughout the hot summer without air conditioning; large, insulated tanks of water chilled by cool nighttime air keep indoor temperatures comfortable during the day.

ACTIVE SOLAR SYSTEMS FOR HEATING SPACE AND WATER In an **active solar heating system**, specially designed collectors concentrate solar energy, with a fan or a pump used to supply part of a building's space-heating or water-heating needs. Several connected collectors are usually mounted on a roof with an unobstructed exposure to the sun (Figure 17-14). In middle and high latitudes with cold winter temperatures and moderate levels of sunlight (Figure 17-15), a small backup heating system is needed during prolonged cold or cloudy periods.

Active solar collectors can also supply hot water. Over 1.3 million active solar hot water systems have been installed in the United States, especially in California, Florida, and southwestern states with ample sunshine. The main barrier to their widespread use in the United States is an initial cost of $1,800 to $5,000.

In Cyprus, Jordan, and Israel, active solar water heaters supply 25% to 65% of the hot water for homes. About 12% of the houses in Japan and 37% in Australia use such systems.

PROS AND CONS OF USING SOLAR ENERGY FOR HEATING SPACE AND WATER The energy supply for active or passive systems to collect solar energy for low-temperature heating of buildings is free and is naturally available on sunny days, and the net useful energy yield is moderate (active) to high (passive). The technology is well developed and can be installed quickly. No carbon dioxide is added to the atmosphere, and environmental impacts from air pollution and water pollution are low. Land disturbance is also low because passive systems are built into structures and active solar collectors are usually placed on rooftops.

On a lifetime-cost basis, good passive solar and superinsulated design is the cheapest way to provide 40% to 100% of the space heating for a home or a small building in regions with enough sunlight (Figure 17-15). Such a system usually adds 5% to 10% to the construction cost, but the lifetime cost of operating such a house is 30% to 40% lower than that of conventional houses.

Active systems cost more than passive systems on a lifetime basis because they require more materials to build, they need more maintenance, and eventually they deteriorate and must be replaced. However, retrofitting an existing house with an active solar system is often easier than adding a passive system.

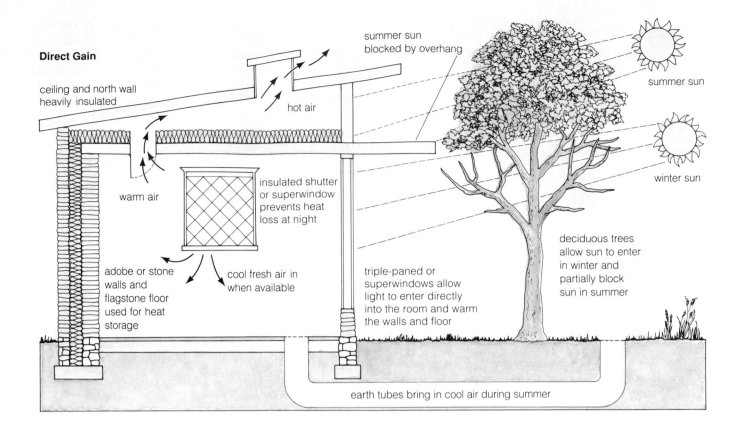

Direct Gain

ceiling and north wall heavily insulated

summer sun blocked by overhang

summer sun

winter sun

hot air

warm air

insulated shutter or superwindow prevents heat loss at night

deciduous trees allow sun to enter in winter and partially block sun in summer

adobe or stone walls and flagstone floor used for heat storage

cool fresh air in when available

triple-paned or superwindows allow light to enter directly into the room and warm the walls and floor

earth tubes bring in cool air during summer

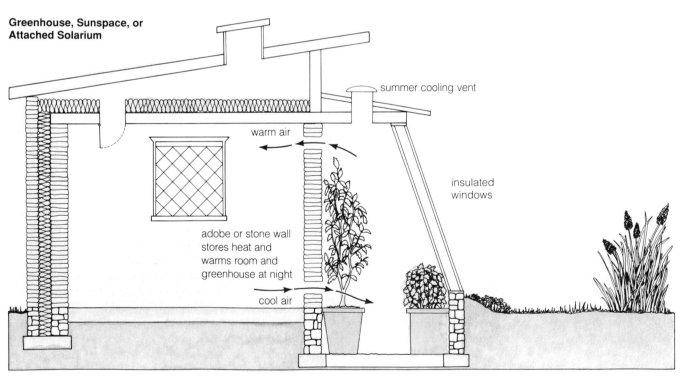

Greenhouse, Sunspace, or Attached Solarium

summer cooling vent

warm air

insulated windows

adobe or stone wall stores heat and warms room and greenhouse at night

cool air

Figure 17-11 Three examples of passive solar design.

(continued)

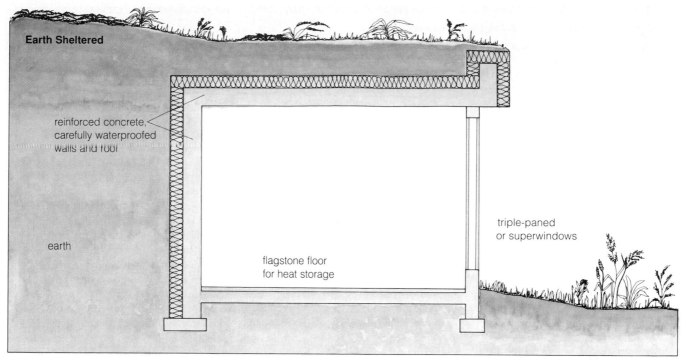

reinforced concrete,
carefully waterproofed
walls and roof

earth

flagstone floor
for heat storage

triple-paned
or superwindows

Earth Sheltered

Figure 17-11 (continued)

Pat Armstrong/Visuals Unlimited

Earth Systems, Inc., Durango, Colorado

Figure 17-12 Exterior of an earth-sheltered house in Will County, Illinois (above). The interior of a dome-shaped earth-sheltered house such as this one in Colorado (right) can look like that of any ordinary house. Passive solar design and skylights can provide more daylight than is found in most conventional houses. On a lifetime-cost basis, earth-sheltered houses are cheaper than conventional aboveground houses of the same size because of reduced heating and cooling costs, no exterior maintenance and painting, and lower fire insurance rates. These structures also provide more privacy, quiet, and security from break-ins, fires, hurricanes, earthquakes, tornadoes, and storms than conventional homes. Across the United States, about 13,000 families have built earth-sheltered houses.

Michael Sykes's solar envelope house is heated and cooled passively by solar energy and the slow storage and release of energy by massive timbers and the earth beneath the house (Figure 17-13). The front and back sides of this house contain two walls of heavy timber impregnated with salt to provide immense thermal storage capacity. The space between these two walls plus the basement form a convection loop or envelope that surrounds the inner shell of the house.

Solar energy entering through windows or a greenhouse on the front side of the house facing the sun circulates around the loop, is stored in the heavy timber, and is released slowly during daylight and at night. In summer, a roof vent re-leases heated air in the convection loop throughout the day. At night, these roof vents, with the aid of a fan, draw air into the loop, which cools the inner shell of the house passively.

The interior temperature of the house typically stays within 2 degrees of 21°C (70°F) year-round, without the need for a conventional cooling or heating system. In areas with a cold climate or a fair number of cloudy days, a small wood stove or vented natural gas heater can be placed in the basement portion of the loop and used as a backup to heat the air in the convection loop.

Because of the large amount of timber involved, the initial costs are high, but they are recovered several-fold by not having to install a con-ventional heating and cooling system and by heating and cooling energy savings over the lifetime of the house. All timber comes precut with a detailed guidebook, which allows quick assembly. Buyers can save money by erecting the inner and outer shells themselves, which requires little experience and few tools. Michael plants 50 trees for each one used in providing builders with his timber kits.

Michael Sykes is 1 of only 13 people who have received a patent in the United States for a concept. For his design, he has received the Department of Energy's Innovation Award and the North Carolina Governor's Energy Achievement Award.

Figure 17-13 Solar envelope house that is heated and cooled passively by solar energy and Earth's thermal energy. In most areas, this patented Enertia design needs no conventional heating or cooling system. It comes in a precut kit engineered and tailored to the buyer's design goals.

Enertia Building Systems, Rt. 1, Box 67, Wake Forest, NC 27587

Active Solar Hot Water Heating System

Figure 17-14 Active and passive solar water heaters.

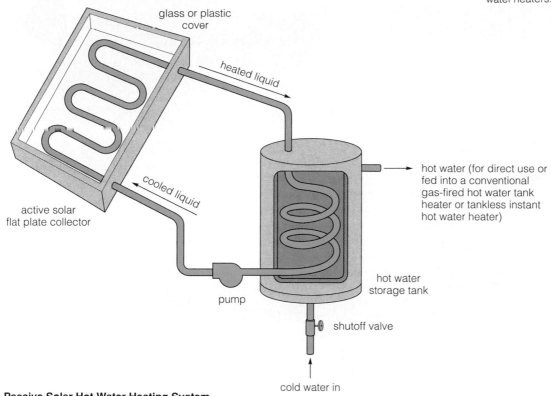

glass or plastic cover

heated liquid

active solar flat plate collector

cooled liquid

hot water (for direct use or fed into a conventional gas-fired hot water tank heater or tankless instant hot water heater)

hot water storage tank

pump

shutoff valve

cold water in

Passive Solar Hot Water Heating System

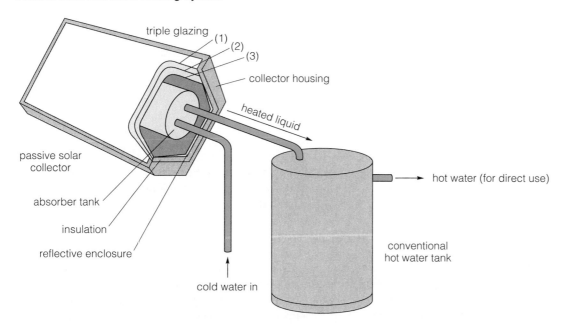

triple glazing (1) (2) (3)

collector housing

heated liquid

passive solar collector

absorber tank

insulation

reflective enclosure

cold water in

hot water (for direct use)

conventional hot water tank

There are disadvantages. Higher initial costs discourage buyers not used to considering lifetime costs and buyers who move every few years. With present technology, active solar systems usually cost too much for heating most homes and small buildings, but better design and mass-production techniques could change that. Some people also believe that active solar collectors sitting on rooftops or in yards are ugly.

Most passive solar systems require that owners open and close windows and shades to regulate heat flow and distribution, but this can be done by cheap microprocessors. Owners of passive and active solar systems also need laws that prevent others from building structures that block a user's access to sunlight. Such legislation is often opposed by builders of high-density developments.

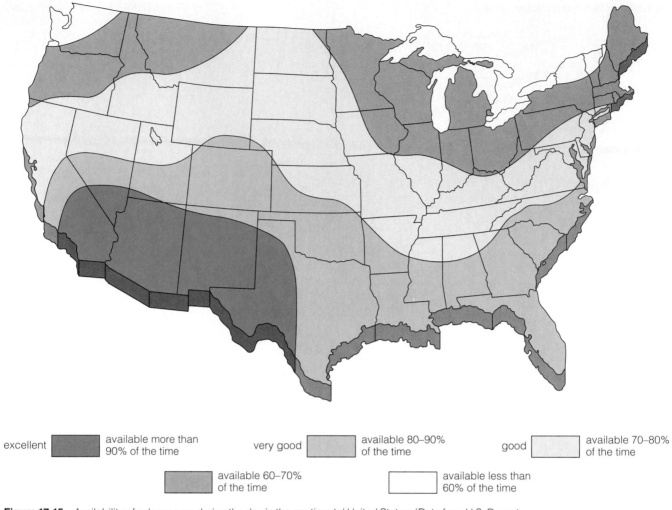

excellent		available more than 90% of the time	very good		available 80–90% of the time	good		available 70–80% of the time

		available 60–70% of the time			available less than 60% of the time

Figure 17-15 Availability of solar energy during the day in the continental United States. (Data from U.S. Department of Energy and National Wildlife Federation)

CONCENTRATING SOLAR ENERGY TO PRODUCE HIGH-TEMPERATURE HEAT AND ELECTRICITY

Huge arrays of computer-controlled mirrors, called heliostats, can track the sun and focus sunlight on a central heat collection point atop a tall tower (Figure 17-16) or on oil-filled pipes running through the middle of curved solar collectors (Figure 17-17). This concentrated sunlight can produce temperatures high enough for industrial processes or for making high-pressure steam to run turbines and produce electricity. By the year 2030, other designs with parabolic dishes (somewhat like TV satellite dishes) that track the sun and focus sunlight onto a single point may produce electricity at about 5 cents per kilowatt-hour.

The main use of these plants is supplying reserve power to meet daytime peak electricity loads, especially in sunny areas with large air conditioning demands. It is estimated that solar-thermal plants occupying less than 1% of the area of the Mojave Desert could supply the electricity needs of Los Angeles. They can be backed up by small turbines burning natural gas. Solar-thermal

power plants could also be used to produce hydrogen gas for use as a fuel (Section 17-8) and to convert hazardous wastes into harmless or less-harmful substances. If the environmental costs of burning coal (about 1.5 cents to 2 cents per kilowatt hour) were considered, solar thermal energy would already be cost competitive (Figure 17-10).

The impact of these solar power plants on air and water is low, and they can be built in only one or two years. They need large areas for solar collection but occupy one-third less land area than a coal-burning plant when the land used to extract coal is included. However, there is concern about building such structures in arid, ecologically fragile desert biomes, where there may not be enough water for use in cooling towers to recondense spent steam.

CONVERTING SOLAR ENERGY DIRECTLY TO ELECTRICITY: PHOTOVOLTAIC CELLS

Solar energy can be converted by **photovoltaic cells**, commonly called *solar cells*, directly into electrical energy. Most so-

Figure 17-16 Solar furnace near Odeillo in the Pyrenees Mountains of southern France produces temperatures high enough to melt metals. A field of curved, computer-driven mirrors not shown in this photo tracks the sun and reflects sunlight onto the giant parabolic collector shown in the photograph.

Figure 17-17 The world's largest solar power facility, in California's Mojave Desert, produces 354 megawatts of electricity by using 810 hectares (2,000 acres) of parabolic collectors to concentrate solar energy. Mirrored troughs focus sunlight on oil-filled tubes that use the concentrated heat absorbed by the oil to produce steam, which is used to run an electricity-generating turbine. Small natural gas turbines are used to run the facility when the sun is not shining. This solar–natural gas fuel mix produces less than one-sixth as much carbon dioxide per kilowatt-hour of electricity as a normal coal-fired plant. This plant, which began operating in 1989, produces enough electricity to meet the residential needs of 750,000 people at a cost lower than that for electricity from a new nuclear power plant (Figure 17-10) and should be cost-competitive with coal by the year 2000.

lar cells consist of layers of purified silicon, which can be made from inexpensive, abundant sand. Trace amounts of other substances (such as gallium arsenide or cadmium sulfide) are added so that the resulting semiconductor emits electrons and produces a small amount of electrical current when struck by sunlight (Figure 17-18).

Today, solar cells supply electricity for at least 30,000 homes worldwide (20,000 in the United States) and for villages in a number of LDCs, including 6,000 villages in India. Most of these homes and villages are in remote areas where it costs too much to bring in electric power lines. Solar cells are also used to switch railroad tracks and to supply power for water wells, irrigation pumping, battery charging, calculators, portable laptop computers, ocean buoys, lighthouses, and offshore oil-drilling platforms in the sunny Persian Gulf.

Because the amount of electricity produced by a single solar cell is very small, many cells must be wired together in a panel to provide 30 to 100 watts of electric power (Figure 17-18). Several panels are wired together and mounted on a roof, or on a rack that tracks the sun, to produce electricity for a home or a building.

Massive banks of such cells can also produce electricity at a small power plant (Figure 17-19). By 2030, the projected price of producing electricity in this way is expected to reach four cents per kilowatt-hour, making it cost-competitive with all other methods of producing electricity.

By the year 2010, solar cells could supply as much of the world's electricity as nuclear power does today at a lower cost and much less risk of environmental harm. The U.S. Solar Energy Research Institute estimates that solar cells are capable of supplying more than half of projected U.S. electricity needs four or five decades from now.

In 1991, Texas Instruments, Inc., and SCE Corporation, a utility company, developed a way to use inexpensive, low purity silicon in photovoltaic cells. This is expected to reduce the cost of generating electricity from solar cells from 30 cents per kilowatt-hour (Figure 17-10) to 14 cents per kilowatt-hour, about what SCE Corporation currently charges residential customers.

Despite their enormous potential, the U.S. federal research and development budget for solar cells was cut by 76% between 1981 and 1990, and the U.S. share of the worldwide solar-cell market fell from 75% to 32%. During that same period, Japanese government expenditures in this area tripled, and Japan's share of the worldwide solar-cell market grew from 15% to 37%. In 1989, a U.S. company (Arco) that was the world's largest manufacturer of solar cells was sold to a German company.

Figure 17-18 Use of photovoltaic (solar) cells to provide DC electricity for an energy-efficient home; any surplus can be sold to the local power company. Prices should be competitive sometime in the 1990s. In 1990, a Florida builder began selling tract houses that get all of their electricity from roof-mounted solar cells. Although the solar-cell systems account for about one-third of the cost of each house, the savings in electric bills will pay this off over a 30-year mortgage period. Sanyo, a Japanese company, has incorporated solar cells into roof shingles.

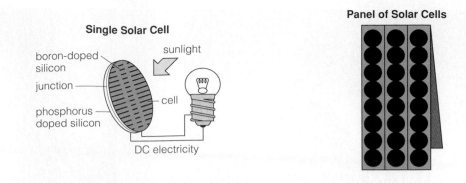

Single Solar Cell

boron-doped silicon

sunlight

junction

cell

phosphorus doped silicon

DC electricity

Panel of Solar Cells

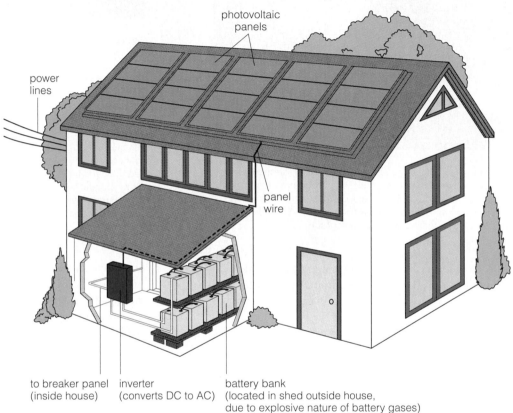

Array of Solar Cell Panels on a Roof

photovoltaic panels

power lines

panel wire

to breaker panel (inside house)

inverter (converts DC to AC)

battery bank (located in shed outside house, due to explosive nature of battery gases)

Federal and private research efforts on photovoltaics in the United States need to be increased sharply. Otherwise, the United States will lose out on a huge global market (at least $100 billion a year) and may find much of its capital being drained to pay for imports of photovoltaic cells from Japan, Germany, Italy, and other countries that are investing heavily in this promising technology.

If the federal government were to order $500 million worth of solar cells, the industry could expand. Because of the assured sales and resulting mass production cost efficiencies, the price of these cells would drop about 90% and become cost-competitive in most parts of the country within a few years. This is a much better investment of taxpayer dollars than searching for more oil, burning more coal, or building new nuclear power plants.

PROS AND CONS OF PHOTOVOLTAIC CELLS If present projections are correct, solar cells could supply 20% to 30% of the world's electricity — half of that in the United States — sometime between 2030 and 2050. That would eliminate the need to build large-scale power plants of any type and would allow many existing nuclear and coal-fired power plants to be phased out.

Solar cells are reliable and quiet, have no moving parts, and should last 30 years or more if encased in glass or plastic. They can be installed quickly and easily and need little maintenance other than occasional washing to prevent dirt from blocking the sun's rays.

Figure 17-19 This power plant in Sacramento, California, uses solar-powered photovoltaic cells to produce electricity. The nuclear power plant in the background has been closed down.

Small or large solar-cell packages can be built, and they can be easily expanded or moved as needed. Suitable locations for solar cells include deserts, marginal lands, alongside interstate highways, yards, and rooftops.

Most solar cells are made from silicon, the second most abundant element by weight in the earth's crust (Figure 7-2). They do not produce carbon dioxide during use. Air and water pollution during operation is low, air pollution from manufacture is low, and land disturbance is very low for roof-mounted systems. The net useful energy yield is fairly high and rising with new designs.

However, solar cells do have some drawbacks. The present costs of solar-cell systems are high but are projected to become competitive in 7 to 15 years. Other problems are that some people feel that racks of solar cells on rooftops or in yards are unsightly; that potential limits could be placed on their use by an insufficient amount of gallium or cadmium; and that absence of effective pollution control could allow production of moderate levels of water pollution from chemical wastes introduced through the manufacturing process.

 17-4

Producing Electricity from Moving Water and from Heat Stored in Water

TYPES OF HYDROELECTRIC POWER In *large-scale hydropower projects*, high dams are built across large rivers to create large reservoirs (Figure 5-40). The stored water is then allowed to flow through huge pipes at controlled rates, spinning turbines and producing electricity.

In *small-scale hydropower projects*, a low dam with no reservoir, or only a small one, is built across a small stream. The renewable natural water flow is used to generate electricity, but electricity production can vary with seasonal changes in stream flow.

Falling water can also be used to produce electricity in *pumped-storage hydropower systems*. Their main use is to supply extra power during times of peak electrical demand. When electricity demand is low, usually at night, pumps using electricity from a conventional power plant pump water uphill from a lake or a reservoir to another reservoir at a higher elevation, usually on top of a mountain. When a power company temporarily needs more electricity than its plants can produce, water in the upper reservoir is released. On its downward trip to the lower reservoir, the water flows through turbines and generates electricity, but this is an expensive way to produce electricity. Much cheaper alternatives, such as natural gas turbines, are available. Another possibility may be the use of solar-powered pumps to raise water to the upper reservoir.

PRESENT AND FUTURE USE OF HYDROPOWER In 1989, hydropower supplied 20% of the world's electricity and 6% of the world's total commercial energy. Hydropower supplies Norway with essentially all its electricity, Switzerland 74%, Austria 67%, and LDCs 50%.

Much of the hydropower potential of North America and Europe has been developed, but Africa has tapped only 5% of its hydropower potential, Latin America 8%, and Asia 9%. Many large-scale hydroelectric dams are being built or planned in Brazil, China, India, and other LDCs. By the year 2000, China, with one-tenth of the world's hydropower potential, is likely to become the world's largest producer of hydroelectricity. China has also built almost 100,000 small dams to produce electricity for villages.

Currently, the United States is the world's largest producer of electricity from hydropower, which supplies 10% to 14% of the electricity and 5% to 8% of all commercial energy used by the United States, with the amount varying with rain and snowfall patterns. However, the era of building large dams is drawing to a close in the United States because of high construction costs, lack of suitable sites, and opposition from conservationists. Any new large supplies of hydroelectric power in the United States will be imported from Canada, which gets more than 70% of its electricity from hydropower.

According to the U.S. Corps of Engineers, retrofitting abandoned small and medium-size hydroelectric sites and building new small-scale hydroelectric plants on suitable sites could supply the United States with electricity equal to that of 47 large power plants. However, since 1985, the development of small-scale hydropower in the United States has fallen off sharply because of low oil prices, loss of federal tax credits, and opposition to some projects from local residents and conservationists.

PROS AND CONS OF HYDROPOWER Many LDCs have large, untapped potential hydropower sites, although many are far from where the electricity is needed. Hydropower has a moderate to high net useful energy yield and fairly low operating and maintenance costs.

Hydroelectric plants rarely need to be shut down, and they produce no emissions of carbon dioxide or other air pollutants during operation. Their reservoirs have life spans two to ten times the life of coal and nuclear plants. Large dams also help control flooding and supply a regulated flow of irrigation water to areas below the dam.

Developing small-scale hydroelectric plants by rehabilitating existing dams has little environmental impact, and once rebuilt, the units have a long life. Only a few people are needed to operate them, and they need little maintenance.

However, hydropower has some drawbacks. Construction costs for new large-scale systems are high, and few suitable sites are left in the United States and Europe. The reservoirs of large-scale projects flood huge areas, destroy wildlife habitats, uproot people, decrease natural fertilization of prime agricultural land in river valleys below the dam, and decrease fish harvests below the dam (see Case Study on p. 345). Without proper land-use control, large-scale projects can greatly increase soil erosion and sediment water pollution near the reservoir above the dam. This reduces the effective life of the reservoir.

By reducing stream flow, small hydroelectric projects threaten recreational activities and aquatic life, disrupt wild and scenic rivers, and destroy wetlands. During drought periods, these plants produce little if any power. Most of the electricity produced by these projects can be supplied at a lower cost and with less environmental impact by industrial cogeneration and by improving the energy efficiency of existing big dams.

TIDAL OR MOON POWER Twice a day, a large volume of water flows in and out of bays and estuaries along the coast as a result of high and low tides caused by gravitational attraction of the moon. In a few places, tides flow in and out of a bay with an opening narrow enough to be obstructed by a dam with turbines to produce electricity.

If the difference in water height between high and low tides is large enough, the kinetic energy in these daily tidal flows based on moon power can be used to spin turbines to produce electricity, but only about two dozen places in the world have these conditions. Currently, only two large tidal energy facilities are operating, one at La Rance, France, and the other in Canada in the Bay of Fundy. The Chinese government has built several small tidal plants.

Using tidal energy to produce electricity has several advantages. The energy source (tides from gravitational attraction) is free, operating costs are low, and the net useful energy yield is moderate. No carbon dioxide is added to the atmosphere, air pollution is low, and little land is disturbed.

Most analysts, however, expect tidal power to make only a tiny contribution to world electricity supplies. There are few suitable sites, and construction costs are high. The output of electricity varies daily with tidal flows, so there must be a backup system. The dam and power plant can be damaged by storms, and metal parts are easily corroded by seawater. The disruption of normal tidal flows may also disturb aquatic life in coastal estuaries.

WAVE POWER The kinetic energy in ocean waves, created primarily by wind, is another potential source of energy. Japan, Norway, Great Britain, Sweden, the United States, and the Soviet Union have built small experimental plants to evaluate this form of hydropower. None of these plants has produced electricity at a competitive price, but some designs show promise.

Most analysts expect wave power to make little contribution to world electricity production, except in a few coastal areas with the right conditions. Construction costs are moderate to high, and the net useful energy yield is moderate. Equipment could be damaged or destroyed by saltwater corrosion and severe storms.

OCEAN THERMAL ENERGY CONVERSION
Ocean water stores huge amounts of heat from the sun, especially in tropical areas. Japan and the United States have been conducting experiments to evaluate the technological and economic feasibility of using the large temperature differences between the cold

deep waters and the sun-warmed surface waters of tropical oceans to produce electricity in *ocean thermal energy conversion* (OTEC) plants anchored to the bottom of tropical oceans in suitable sites. Although scientists have been working on this method for producing electricity for over 50 years, the technology is still in the research and development stage.

The source of energy for OTEC is limitless at suitable sites, and a costly energy storage and backup system is not needed. No air pollution except carbon dioxide is produced during operation, and the floating power plant requires no land area. Nutrients brought up when water is pumped from the ocean bottom might be used to nourish schools of fish and shellfish.

However, most energy analysts believe that the large-scale extraction of energy from ocean thermal gradients may never compete economically with other energy alternatives. Construction costs are high — two to three times those of comparable coal-fired plants. Operating and maintenance costs are also high because of corrosion of metal parts by seawater and fouling of heat exchangers by algae and barnacles. Plants could also be damaged by hurricanes and typhoons.

Other problems include a limited number of sites and a low net useful energy yield; possible disruption of coral reef communities (Figure 5-32) and other aquatic life by pumping large volumes of deep-ocean water to the surface; and the release of large quantities of dissolved carbon dioxide into the atmosphere.

SOLAR PONDS The Israelis have been working on the *solar pond* concept for several decades. *Saline solar ponds* can be used to produce electricity and are usually located near inland saline seas or lakes, in areas with ample sunlight. The bottom layer of water in such ponds stays on the bottom when heated because it has a higher salinity and density (mass per unit volume) than the top layer. Heat accumulated during daylight in the bottom layer can be used to produce steam that spins turbines, generating electricity.

A saline solar pond can be a naturally occurring body of salt water, such as the Dead Sea between Israel and Jordan, the Salton Sea in California, and the Great Salt Lake in Utah. Such ponds can also be built by digging a hole, lining it with black plastic, and filling it with salt and water or brine. An experimental saline solar pond power plant on the Israel side of the Dead Sea has been operating successfully for several years. By 2000, Israel plans to build several plants around the Dead Sea to supply electricity for air conditioning and for desalinating water. Several experimental saline solar ponds have been built in the United States, Australia, India, and Mexico.

Freshwater solar ponds can be used as a source of hot water and space heating. A shallow hole is dug, lined with concrete, and covered with insulation. A number of large, black plastic bags, each filled with several cen-

timeters of water, are placed in the hole. The top of the pond is then covered with fiberglass panels, which let sunlight in and keep most of the heat stored in the water during daylight from being lost to the atmosphere. When the water in the bags has reached its peak temperature in the afternoon, a computer turns on pumps to transfer hot water from the bags to large, insulated tanks for distribution as hot water or for space heating.

Saline and freshwater solar ponds have the same advantages as OTEC systems. In addition, they have a moderate net useful energy yield, have moderate construction and operating costs, and need little maintenance. Freshwater solar ponds can be built in almost any sunny area. They may be useful for supplying hot water and space heating for large buildings and small housing developments.

Saline solar ponds are feasible in areas with moderate to ample sunlight, especially ecologically fragile deserts. Operating costs can be high because of saltwater corrosion of pipes and heat exchangers. Unless lined, the ponds can become ineffective when compounds leached from bottom sediment darken the water and reduce transmission of sunlight. With adequate research-and-development support, solar ponds could supply 3% to 4% of U.S. energy needs by the year 2000.

17-5 Producing Electricity from Wind

WIND POWER Worldwide, by 1990, there were over 20,000 wind turbines, grouped in clusters called wind farms (see photo on p. 309), which feed power to a utility grid. They produced electricity equal to that from 1.6 large (1,000-megawatt) nuclear or coal-burning power plants. Most of these are in California (17,000 machines) and Denmark, located in windy mountain passes and along coastlines. Sweden has installed an offshore wind power plant.

In 1990, California wind farms produced enough electricity to meet the residential power needs of San Francisco. The state has the potential to use wind to produce electricity equal to that from 6 to 31 large power plants by the year 2000 and California is only the 14th windiest state in the country. The island of Hawaii gets about 8% of its electricity from wind, and the use of wind power is spreading to the state's other islands.

The cost of producing electricity with wind farms is about half that of a new nuclear power plant (Figure 17-10) and should be cost-competitive with coal by 1995. Wind power experts project that by the middle of the next century, wind power could supply more than 10% of the world's electricity and 10% to 20% of the electricity used in the United States.

However, the development of this energy resource in the United States has slowed since 1986, when federal tax credits and most state tax credits for wind power were eliminated. Also, the federal budget for research and development of wind power was cut by 90% between 1981 and 1990. Today, Danish companies, with tax incentives and low-interest loans from their government, have taken over the global market for manufacturing wind turbines from the United States.

PROS AND CONS OF WIND POWER Wind power is an unlimited source of energy at favorable sites, and large wind farms can be built in only three to six months. With a moderate to fairly high net useful energy yield, these systems emit no carbon dioxide or other air pollutants during operation, they need no water for cooling, and their manufacture and use produce little water pollution. They operate 80% to 98% of the time the wind is blowing. The land occupied by wind farms can be used for grazing and other purposes (see photo on p. 309), and the leases can provide extra income for farmers and ranchers. Wind power has a significant cost advantage over nuclear power and should become competitive with coal in many areas sometime in the 1990s.

However, wind power can be used only in areas with sufficient winds. Backup electricity from a utility company or from an energy storage system is necessary when the wind dies down, but that is not a problem at sites where the wind blows almost continuously. Backup could also be provided by linking wind farms with a solar-cell or hydropower system or by using efficient turbines fueled by natural gas.

Building wind farms in mountain passes and along shorelines can cause visual pollution. Noise and interference with local television reception have been problems with large turbines, but that can be overcome with improved design and use in isolated areas. Large wind farms might also interfere with the flight patterns of migratory birds in certain areas.

17-6 Energy from Biomass

RENEWABLE BIOMASS AS A VERSATILE FUEL
Biomass is organic plant matter produced by solar energy through photosynthesis. It includes wood, agricultural wastes, and garbage. Some of this plant matter can be burned as solid fuel or converted into more convenient gaseous or liquid *biofuels* (Figure 17-20). In 1989, biomass, mostly from the burning of wood and manure to heat buildings and cook food, supplied about 15% of the world's supplemental energy (4% to 5% in Canada and the United States) and about half of the energy used in LDCs.

Various types of biomass can be used in solid, liquid, and gaseous forms for space heating, water heating, producing electricity, and propelling vehicles. It is a renewable energy resource as long as trees and plants are not harvested faster than they grow back, a requirement that is not being met in most places (Section 10-2).

No net increase in atmospheric levels of carbon dioxide occurs as long as the rate of removal and burning of trees and plants and loss of below-ground organic matter does not exceed the rate of replenishment. Burning of biomass fuels adds much less sulfur dioxide and nitric oxide to the atmosphere per unit of energy produced than the uncontrolled burning of coal, and thus it requires fewer pollution controls.

Biomass energy resources also have some disadvantages. It takes a lot of land to grow biomass fuel. Without effective land-use controls and replanting, widespread removal of trees and plants can deplete soil nutrients and cause excessive soil erosion, water pollution, flooding, and loss of wildlife habitat. Biomass resources also have a high moisture content (15% to 95%), which lowers their net useful energy. The added weight of the moisture makes collecting and hauling wood and other plant material fairly expensive. Each type of biomass fuel has other specific advantages and disadvantages.

BURNING WOOD AND WOOD WASTES About 80% of the people living in LDCs heat their dwellings and cook their food by burning wood or charcoal made from wood. However, at least 1.1 billion people in LDCs cannot find, or are too poor to buy, enough fuelwood to meet their needs, and that number may increase to 2.5 billion by 2000.

In MDCs with adequate forests, the burning of wood, wood pellets, and wood wastes to heat homes and produce steam and electricity in industrial boilers increased rapidly during the 1970s because of price increases in heating oil and electricity. Sweden leads the world in using wood as an energy source, mostly for district heating plants.

In the United States, small wood-burning power plants (Figure 17-21) located near sources of their fuel can produce electricity at about half the price of a new nuclear power plant and almost equal to that produced by burning coal (Figure 17-10). Wood-fired power plants provide 23% of the electricity used in Maine. The National Wood Energy Association estimates that burning the wood wastes from paper and lumber mills, agriculture, urban land clearing, and tree trimming in the United States could provide electricity equal to that from 200 large (1,000-megawatt) power plants.

The forest products industry (mostly paper companies and lumber mills) consumes almost two-thirds of the fuelwood used in the United States. Homes and small businesses burn the rest, with wood providing all the heating needs of 5.6 million U.S. homes and supple-

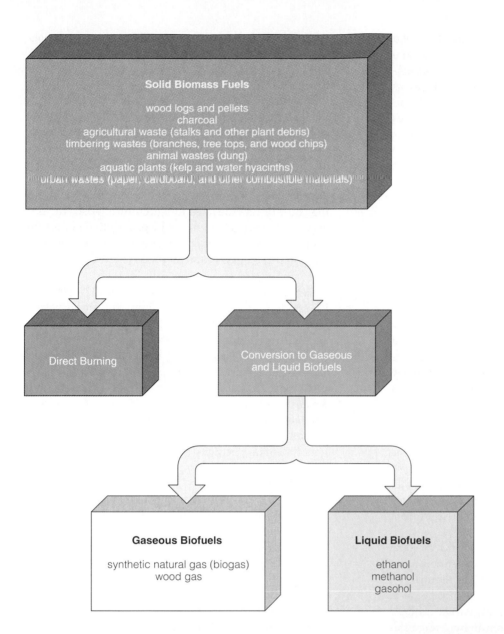

Figure 17-20 Principal types of biomass fuel. Biomass is any plant matter that stores the sun's energy through photosynthesis.

Solid Biomass Fuels

wood logs and pellets
charcoal
agricultural waste (stalks and other plant debris)
timbering wastes (branches, tree tops, and wood chips)
animal wastes (dung)
aquatic plants (kelp and water hyacinths)
urban wastes (paper, cardboard, and other combustible materials)

Direct Burning

Conversion to Gaseous and Liquid Biofuels

Gaseous Biofuels

synthetic natural gas (biogas)
wood gas

Liquid Biofuels

ethanol
methanol
gasohol

mentary heat in an additional 21 million. The largest use of fuelwood is in New England, where wood is plentiful. The amount of firewood used in the United States each year would be enough to build a 30-meter- (100-foot-) high wall from New York City to San Francisco.

Wood has a moderate to high net useful energy yield when collected and burned directly and efficiently near its source. However, in urban areas where wood must be hauled from long distances, it can cost homeowners more per unit of energy produced than oil and electricity. Burning wood produces virtually no emissions of sulfur dioxide.

Harvesting and burning wood can cause accidents. Each year in the United States, over 10,000 people are injured by chain saws, and several hundred people are killed in house fires caused by improperly located or poorly maintained or operated wood stoves.

National Wood Energy Association

Figure 17-21 This small, 16-megawatt biomass power plant in Whitefield, New Hampshire, is operated by Thermo Electron Energy. Nearby forest residue is burned to generate electricity.

Burning fuelwood releases carbon monoxide, solid particulate matter, and unburned residues that pollute indoor and outdoor air. Using typical wood stoves without pollution controls to heat 1 house produces as much particulate matter as heating 300 houses with natural gas. According to the EPA, wood burning causes as many as 820 cancer deaths a year in the United States.

The outdoor air pollution can be reduced 75% by a $100 to $250 catalytic combustion chamber in the stove or stovepipe. These units also increase the energy efficiency of a typical airtight wood stove from 55% to as high as 81% and reduce the need for chimney cleaning and the chance of chimney fires. However, these devices must be replaced every four years at a cost of about $100. Recently, wood stoves have been developed that are 65% efficient, don't use catalytic combustion, and emit 90% less air pollution than conventional wood stoves.

Fireplaces, considered cozy and romantic by many people, can be used for heating but are so inefficient that they result in a net loss of energy from a house. The draft of heat and gases rising up the fireplace chimney exhausts warm air and pulls in cold air from cracks and crevices throughout a house. Fireplace inserts with glass doors and blowers help but still waste energy compared with an efficient wood-burning stove. If you must have a fireplace, shut off the room it is in from the rest of the house. Then crack a window in that room so that the fireplace won't draw much heated air from other rooms, or run a small pipe into the front of the fireplace so it can get the air it needs during combustion from the outside.

In London, in South Korean cities, and in some areas of Colorado, wood fires have been banned to reduce air pollution. Since 1990, the EPA has required all new wood stoves sold in the United States to emit at least 70% less particulate matter than earlier models. Some new stoves meet these standards by using catalytic combustion devices, others by better design or by using cleaner-burning wood pellets for fuel. Anyone owning an older wood stove should add a catalytic converter or replace the stove with a newer model that meets government air-pollution standards.

ENERGY PLANTATIONS One way to produce biomass fuel is to plant large numbers of fast-growing trees (especially cottonwoods, poplars, sycamores, and leucaenas), shrubs, or grasses in *biomass-energy plantations* to supply fuelwood. Plantations of oil palms and varieties of Euphorbia plants, which store energy in hydrocarbon compounds (like those found in oil), can also be established. After these plants are harvested, their oil-like material can be extracted and either refined to produce gasoline or burned directly in diesel engines. Both types of energy plantations can be established on semiarid land not needed to grow crops, although lack of water can limit productivity.

This industrialized approach to biomass production usually requires heavy use of pesticides and fertilizers, which can pollute drinking supplies and harm wildlife. It also requires large areas of land.

Conversion of large forested areas into monoculture energy plantations also reduces biodiversity. In some areas, biomass plantations might compete with food crops for prime farmland. To produce enough liquid fuels to replace all of the gasoline and diesel fuel currently consumed each year in the United States would require planting energy crops on more land than the country now devotes to agriculture. Also, the energy crops are likely to have low or negative net useful energy yields, as do most conventional crops grown by industrialized agricultural methods (Figure 14-9).

BURNING AGRICULTURAL AND URBAN WASTES
In agricultural areas, crop residues (the unharvested parts of food crops) and animal manure can be collected and burned (Figure 17-21) or converted into biofuels. By 1985, Hawaii was burning a residue (called *bagasse*) left after sugarcane harvesting and processing to supply almost 10% of its electricity (58% on the island of Kauai and 33% on the island of Hawaii). Other crop residues that could be burned include coconut shells, peanut and other nut hulls, and cotton stalks. Brazil gets 10% of its electricity by burning bagasse and plans to use this crop residue to produce 35% of its electricity by the year 2000.

This approach makes sense when residues are burned in small power plants located near areas where the residues are produced (Figure 17-21). Otherwise, it takes too much energy to collect, dry, and transport the residues to power plants. Also, ecologists argue that it makes more sense to use crop residues to feed livestock, retard soil erosion, and fertilize the soil.

An increasing number of cities in Japan, western Europe, and the United States have built incinerators that burn trash and use the heat released to produce electricity or to heat nearby buildings (Section 19-4). However, this approach may be limited by opposition from citizens concerned about emissions of toxic gases and what to do with the resulting toxic ash. Some analysts argue that more energy is saved by composting or recycling paper and other organic wastes than by burning them (Section 19-5).

CONVERTING SOLID BIOMASS INTO GASEOUS BIOFUELS Plants, organic wastes, sewage, and other forms of solid biomass can be converted by bacteria and various chemical processes into gaseous and liquid biofuels (Figure 17-20). Examples are *biogas* (a mixture of 60% methane and 40% carbon dioxide), *liquid methanol* (methyl, or wood, alcohol), and *liquid ethanol* (ethyl, or grain, alcohol).

In China, anaerobic bacteria in an estimated 7 million *biogas digesters* convert organic plant and animal

Figure 17-22 This biogas digester converts animal dung into a methane-rich gas that can be burned for cooking, space heating, and other purposes.

World Bank

wastes into methane fuel for heating and cooking. After the biogas has been separated, the solid residue is used as fertilizer on food crops or, if contaminated, on trees. India has about 750,000 biogas digesters in operation, half of them built since 1986 (Figure 17-22).

When they work, biogas digesters are very efficient. However, they are slow and unpredictable. Development of new, more reliable models could change this, and biomass-derived methane could become an affordable alternative to natural gas before the year 2000.

Methane fuel is also produced by underground decomposition of organic matter in the absence of air (anaerobic digestion) in landfills. This gas can be collected by pipes inserted into landfills, separated from other gases, and burned as a fuel. Eighty-two U.S. landfills currently recover methane, but 2,000 to 3,000 large U.S. landfills have the potential for large-scale methane recovery. Burning this gas instead of allowing it to escape into the atmosphere helps slow projected global warming because methane is 25 times more effective in causing atmospheric global warming per molecule than carbon dioxide (Figure 11-2).

Methane can also be produced by anaerobic digestion of manure produced by animal feedlots and sludge produced at sewage treatment plants. It is more economical to digest manure or sludge near sites where it is produced, collect the methane produced, and then burn it at farms, feedlots, or small nearby power plants. In California's Imperial Valley, a private entrepreneur has built a power plant that produces electricity by burning cattle manure bought from nearby feedlot owners. The plant operates at full capacity 85% of the time and produces little air pollution, and its incinerator ash is sold to fertilize soils, pave roads, and soak up toxic waste. The power, which is sold to Southern California Edison, supplies electricity for as many as 20,000 homes.

However, conservationists believe that in most cases, recycling manure to the land instead of using commercial inorganic fertilizer, which requires large amounts of natural gas to produce, would probably save more natural gas than is saved by burning the manure.

CONVERTING SOLID BIOMASS INTO LIQUID BIOFUELS Some analysts believe that methanol and ethanol can be used as liquid fuels to replace gasoline and diesel fuel when oil becomes too scarce and expensive. Both alcohols can be burned directly as fuel without requiring additives to boost octane ratings.

Currently, emphasis is on using ethanol as an automotive fuel. It can be made from sugar and grain crops (sugarcane, sugar beets, sorghum, and corn) by fermentation and distillation. Pure ethanol can be burned in today's cars with little engine modification. Gasoline can also be mixed with 10% to 23% ethanol to make *gasohol*. It burns in conventional gasoline engines and is sold as super unleaded or ethanol-enriched gasoline.

Since 1987, ethanol made by fermentation of surplus sugarcane has accounted for about half the automotive fuel consumption in Brazil. At the height of the program, 90% of all new cars sold in Brazil were powered by pure ethanol or ethanol-gasoline mixtures. Bagasse, a by-product of the production of ethanol from sugarcane, can be burned to produce electricity or steam for industrial processes. The use of ethanol has helped Brazil cut its oil imports and created an estimated 575,000 full-time jobs, but the government has spent $8 billion to subsidize the country's ethanol industry. In recent years, ethanol production has been curtailed because of financial difficulties.

Super unleaded gasoline containing 90% gasoline and 10% ethanol now accounts for about 8% of gasoline sales in the United States — 25% to 35% in Illinois, Iowa, Kentucky, and Nebraska. The ethanol used in gasohol is made mostly by fermenting corn in 150 ethanol production plants built between 1980 and 1985. Excluding federal taxes, it costs about $1.60 to produce a gallon of ethanol, compared with about 50 cents for a gallon of gasoline. However, new, energy-efficient distilleries are lowering the production cost. Soon, this fuel may be able to compete with other forms of unleaded gasoline without federal tax breaks, which are scheduled to expire in 1992.

Ethanol produces 25% less carbon monoxide and 15% less nitrogen oxides per unit of energy than gasoline and is a better antiknock fuel. However, without catalytic converters, cars burning ethanol fuels produce more aldehydes and PANs (peroxyacyl nitrates) that kill plants and cause more eye irritation than do cars burning gasoline. Ethanol also has less energy per liter than gasoline, so cars require larger fuel tanks or more frequent fill-ups. Ethanol produces less carbon dioxide per unit of energy than gasoline, but total carbon dioxide impact depends on the energy source used in the distillation process and whether the crops are grown using energy-intensive industrialized agriculture.

The distillation process to make ethanol produces large volumes of a waste material known as swill, which if allowed to flow into waterways, kills fish and aquatic plants. Another problem is that the net useful energy yield from producing ethanol fuel is low in older distilleries fueled by oil or natural gas. However, the yield is moderate at new distilleries using modern technology and powered by coal, wood, or solar energy.

Some experts are concerned that growing corn or other grains to make alcohol fuel could compete for cropland needed to grow food. It takes nine times more cropland to fuel one average U.S. automobile with ethanol for one year than it does to feed one American per year. About 40% of the entire U.S. annual harvest of corn would be needed to make enough ethanol to meet just 10% of the country's demand for automotive fuel. However, ethanol production uses only the starch portion of the corn, leaving a high-protein by-product that makes an excellent animal feed when supplemented with some carbohydrates. Ethanol's future may depend on learning how to make it economically from wood or agricultural wastes.

Another alcohol, methanol, can be produced from wood, wood wastes, agricultural wastes (such as corncobs), sewage sludge, garbage, coal, or natural gas at a cost of about $1.10 per gallon — almost twice the cost of producing gasoline. High concentrations of methanol corrode some metals and embrittle rubber and some plastics, but in a properly modified engine, methanol burns cleanly without any problems.

A fuel of 85% methanol and 15% unleaded gasoline (called M85) could reduce emissions of ozone-forming hydrocarbons 20% to 50% but may produce more nitrogen oxides than burning gasoline. Running cars on pure methanol would reduce those emissions by 85% to 95% and carbon monoxide emissions by 30% to 90%. However, cars burning pure methanol emit two to five times more formaldehyde, a suspected carcinogen, than those burning gasoline.

Methanol-powered cars emit less carbon dioxide than gasoline-powered cars, but producing the methanol from coal would double carbon dioxide emissions. Methanol also has less energy per liter than gasoline, so cars require larger tanks or more refuelings. It is also more flammable than gasoline and can cause blindness if spilled on the skin or splashed into the eyes. Cars running on methanol would cost about $300 to $500 more than gasoline-powered cars.

17-7 Geothermal Energy

EXTRACTING ENERGY FROM THE EARTH'S INTERIOR Heat contained in underground rocks and fluids is an important source of energy. At various places in the earth's crust, this **geothermal energy** from the earth's interior (Figure 7-1) is transferred over millions of years to underground concentrations of dry steam (steam with no water droplets), wet steam (a mixture of steam and water droplets), and hot water trapped in fractured or porous rock (Figure 7-17).

If these geothermal sites are close enough to the earth's surface, wells can be drilled to extract the dry steam, wet steam (Figure 17-23), or hot water trapped in rocks and fluids beneath Earth's crust. This thermal energy can be used for space heating and to produce electricity or high-temperature heat for industrial processes.

Geothermal reservoirs can be depleted if heat is removed faster than it is renewed by natural processes. Thus, strictly speaking, geothermal resources are nonrenewable on a human time scale, but the potential supply is so vast that it is often classified as a potentially renewable energy resource. However, recent depletion of geothermal sites in California at about twice the expected rate may lead to the classification of some types of geothermal resources as nonrenewable.

Currently, about 20 countries are extracting energy from geothermal sites and supplying enough heat to meet the needs of over 2 million homes in a cold climate and enough electricity for over 1.5 million homes. The United States accounts for 44% of the electricity generated worldwide from geothermal energy. Figure 17-24 shows that most accessible, high-temperature geothermal sites in the United States lie in the West, especially in California and the Rocky Mountain states. Iceland, Japan, and Indonesia are among the countries with the greatest potential for tapping geothermal energy.

Dry-steam reservoirs are the preferred geothermal resource, but they are also the rarest. A large dry-steam well near Larderello, Italy, has been producing electricity since 1904 and is an important source of power for Italy's electric railroads. Two other large dry-steam sites are the Matsukawa field in Japan and the Geysers steam field about 145 kilometers (90 miles) northwest of San Francisco. Currently, 20 plants tapping energy from the Geysers field supply more than 6% of northern California's electricity. Largely without government subsidies, that is enough to meet all the electrical needs of a city the size of San Francisco at less than the cost of electricity from a new coal plant and one-fourth the cost of electricity from a new nuclear plant (Figure 17-10). New units can be added every 2 to 3 years (compared with 6 years for a coal plant and 10 to 12 years for a nuclear plant). By the year 2000, this reservoir may supply one-fourth of California's electricity, if it is not depleted.

Wet-steam reservoirs are more common than dry-steam reservoirs but harder and more expensive to convert into electricity. The world's largest wet-steam power plant is in Wairaki, New Zealand. Others operate in Mexico, Japan, El Salvador, Nicaragua, and the Soviet Union. Four small-scale wet-steam demonstration plants in the western United States are producing electricity at a cost equal to paying $40 a barrel for oil.

Hot-water reservoirs are more common than dry-steam and wet-steam reservoirs. Almost all the homes, buildings, and food-producing greenhouses in Reykjavík, Iceland, a city with a population of about 85,000, are heated by hot water drawn from deep geothermal wells under the city. In Paris, France, the equivalent of 200,000 dwellings are heated by tapping such reservoirs. At 180 locations in the United States, mostly in the West, hot-water reservoirs have been used for years to heat homes and farm buildings and to dry crops.

A fourth potential source of nonrenewable geothermal energy and natural gas is *geopressurized zones*. These are underground reservoirs of water at a high temperature and pressure, usually trapped deep under continental shelf beds of shale or clay. With present drilling technology, they would supply geothermal energy and natural gas at a cost equal to paying $30 to $45 a barrel for oil.

There are also three types of vast, virtually perpetual sources of geothermal energy: *molten rock* (magma) found near the earth's surface; *hot dry-rock zones*, where molten rock that has penetrated Earth's crust from below heats subsurface rock to high temperatures; and low- to moderate-temperature *warm-rock reservoirs deposits*, useful for preheating water and running geothermal heat pumps for space heating and air conditioning. According to the National Academy of Sciences, the amount of potentially recoverable energy from such

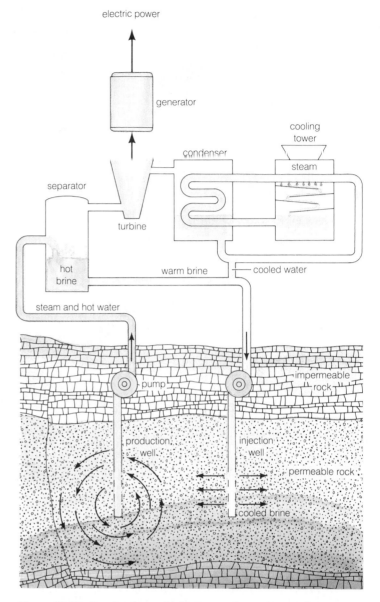

Figure 17-23 Tapping the earth's heat or geothermal energy in the form of wet steam to produce electricity.

reservoirs would meet U.S. energy needs at current consumption levels for 600 to 700 years.

The problem is developing methods to extract this energy economically. Several experimental projects are in progress, but so far, none has been able to produce energy at a cost competitive with other energy sources.

PROS AND CONS The biggest advantages of geothermal energy include a vast and often renewable supply of energy for areas near reservoirs, moderate net useful energy yields for large and easily accessible reservoirs sites, and far less carbon dioxide per unit of energy than fossil fuels. The cost of producing electricity in geothermal plants is cheaper than that from coal-burning plants and much cheaper than from new nuclear plants (Figure 17-10).

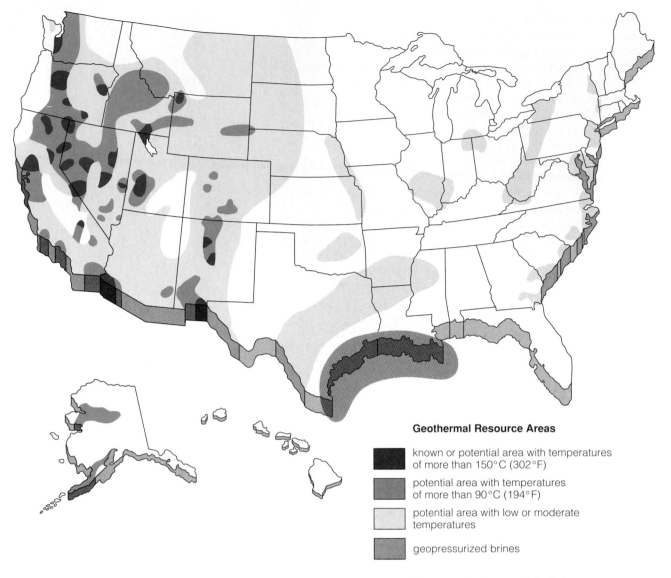

Geothermal Resource Areas

known or potential area with temperatures of more than 150°C (302°F)

potential area with temperatures of more than 90°C (194°F)

potential area with low or moderate temperatures

geopressurized brines

Figure 17-24 Most promising sites of geothermal resources in the United States. (Source: Council on Environmental Quality)

A serious limitation of geothermal energy is the scarcity of easily accessible reservoirs sites. Geothermal reservoirs must also be carefully managed or they can be depleted within a few decades. Geothermal development in some areas can destroy or degrade forests or other ecosystems. In Hawaii, for example, environmentalists are fighting the construction of a large geothermal project, located mostly in the only lowland tropical rain forest left in the United States.

Without pollution control, geothermal energy production causes moderate to high air pollution from hydrogen sulfide, ammonia, mercury, boron, and radioactive materials. It also causes moderate to high water pollution from dissolved solids (salinity) and runoff of toxic compounds of heavy metals such as arsenic and mercury. Noise, odor, and local climate changes can also be problems. Without proper controls, the expansion of geothermal energy could lead to increased water pollution from the hazardous wastes produced. With proper controls, most experts consider the environmental effects of geothermal energy to be less, or no greater, than those of fossil-fuel and nuclear power plants.

17-8 Hydrogen as the Fuel of the Future

THE HYDROGEN REVOLUTION Hydrogen gas (H_2) is an extremely attractive fuel that could be used in place of oil and other fossil fuels and nuclear power. When hydrogen burns, it combines with oxygen gas in the air and produces harmless water vapor clean enough to condense and drink (Figure 17-25). A small

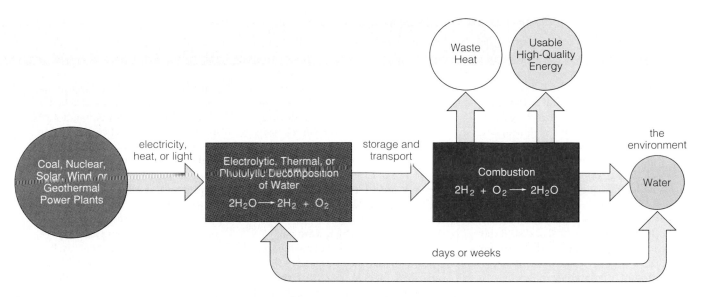

Figure 17-25 The hydrogen energy cycle. The production of hydrogen gas requires electricity, heat, or solar energy to decompose water, thus leading to a negative net useful energy yield. However, hydrogen is a clean-burning fuel that can be used to replace oil and other fossil fuels and nuclear power. Using solar energy to produce hydrogen from water could become an antidote to our fossil-fuel addiction, eliminate most air pollution, and greatly reduce the threat from projected global warming.

amount of nitric oxide (NO) is also produced when the nitrogen and oxygen gases in air combine at the high temperatures reached during the burning of hydrogen (or any other) fuel. Unlike the burning of fossil fuels and biomass fuel, the burning of hydrogen releases no heat-trapping carbon dioxide into the atmosphere. Hydrogen has about 2.5 times the energy by weight of gasoline, making it an especially attractive aviation fuel.

Once hydrogen gas is produced by passing electrical current through water, it can be collected and stored in tanks at high pressures and distributed by pipeline like natural gas or stored in tanks for use in homes, factories, or cars. Hydrogen gas can also be combined with certain reactive metals to form solid metal-hydrogen compounds (hydrides). These solid hydrides can then be heated to release hydrogen gas fuel as it is needed in a car, a furnace, or an electricity-producing fuel cell. Unlike gasoline, the solid metallic hydrogen compounds would not explode or burn if the tank was ruptured in an accident. Several experimental cars have been running on hydrogen fuel for a number of years. The Soviet Union has flown a commercial jet partially fueled by hydrogen.

Switching to hydrogen as our primary fuel—known as the *hydrogen revolution*—would change the world as dramatically as the Agricultural and Industrial revolutions. Burning hydrogen would eliminate most air pollution and water pollution caused by extracting, transporting, and burning fossil fuels and would greatly reduce the threat of projected global warming. It would also reduce the threat of conventional and nuclear wars between countries fighting over dwindling

supplies of oil and faced with economic depression from rapidly escalating oil prices.

Nuclear power could be phased out. We would also have a versatile fuel based on using perpetual energy from the sun and produced from abundant water. Individuals would also be able to produce most, if not all, of their own energy, instead of having to rely on oil and utility companies.

The greatest problem with hydrogen as a fuel is that only trace amounts of the gas occur in nature. Producing it uses high-temperature heat or electricity from another energy source, such as nuclear fission, direct solar power, or wind, to decompose water (Figure 17-25). Currently it would cost about $1.40 to produce hydrogen gas with the energy found in 3.8 liters (1 gallon) of gasoline. However, the current price of gasoline does not include its numerous pollution and health costs, which add at least $1 a gallon to its true cost. Thus, even today, hydrogen is cheaper than gasoline and other fossil fuels when the overall societal costs are considered.

Because of the first and second energy laws (Section 3-6), hydrogen production by any method will take more energy than is released when it is burned. Thus, its net useful energy yield will always be negative. That means that its widespread use depends on having an abundant and affordable supply of some other type of environmentally acceptable energy.

Thus, the key to the spread of the hydrogen revolution is the development of effective and affordable ways of using solar energy to produce electricity that can be passed through water to make hydrogen gas. Using fossil or nuclear fuels to produce hydrogen in

I am writing this book deep in the midst of some beautiful woods in Eco-Lair, a structure that Peggy, my wife and Earthmate, and I designed to work with nature. This ongoing experiment is designed as a low-tech, low-cost example of sustainable-Earth design and living.

First, in 1980 we purchased a 1954 school bus from a nearby school district for $200 and sold the tires for the same price that we paid for the bus. We built an insulated foundation, rented a crane for two hours to lift and set the gutted bus on the foundation, placed heavy insulation around the bus, and added a wooden outside frame. The interior is panelled with wood, some of it obtained from the few trees we carefully selected for removal (Figure 17-26). Most people who visit us don't know the core of the structure is a school bus unless we tell them.

We attached a solar room—a passive solar collector with double-paned conventional sliding glass windows (for ventilation)—to the entire south side of the bus structure (Figure 17-26). Thick concrete floors and filled concrete blocks on the lower half of the interior wall facing the sun absorb and slowly release solar energy collected during the day. The solar room serves as a year-round sitting and work area and contains a small kitchen with a stove and a heavily insulated refrigerator that both run on liquefied petroleum gas (LPG). I plan to replace the windows with new superinsulated windows, which were not available at the time of construction.

The room collects enough solar energy to meet about 60% of the space-heating needs during the cold months. The rest of the heat is provided by a continuous loop system of water preheated by solar collectors and, when necessary, heated further by a tankless instant water heater fueled by LPG (Figure 3-18).

During sunny days, active solar collectors store heat in an insulated tank, which is a discarded conventional hot water tank that is wrapped with thick insulation. A pump connected to the water tank circulates heated water in well-insulated pipes through the instant water heater and from there to a heat exchanger before the water is returned to the tank. A fan transfers the heat in the water to air, which is blown through well-insulated ducts as in a conventional heating system. Some of the heat is recovered for use in the next stage when the heated water returns to the insulated tank. Indoor temperatures are controlled by a conventional thermostat. A valve on the input of the instant water heater senses water temperature and bypasses the heater when the solar heated water has a high enough temperature to provide the necessary space heating.

During the summer, all hot water can be supplied by the roof-mounted active solar collectors (Figure 17-26), which I eventually plan to replace with a Copper Cricket passive collector. In winter, the water heated by these collectors is heated further as needed by a second tankless instant heater fueled by LPG. Our compact fluorescent light bulbs last an average of six years and use about 70% less electricity than conventional bulbs.

For the time being, we are buying electricity from the power company, but we plan to get our

large quantities is too expensive and leaves us with the serious environmental problems associated with those fuels.

Currently, large-scale government funding of such research is generally opposed by powerful fossil-fuel companies, electric utilities, and automobile manufacturers, because a hydrogen revolution is a severe threat to their existence and economic well-being. Earth's people and other species, however, would benefit from an Earth-sustaining hydrogen revolution.

Phasing in the widespread use of hydrogen over several decades would also allow fossil-fuel, utility, car, and other companies to shift to producing and selling hydrogen fuel and the motors, furnaces, and other devices that burn this fuel. Supporting the necessary research and providing the subsidies needed to phase in hydrogen fuel will require considerable political pressure by individuals like you and me to counteract the powerful economic interests temporarily threatened by such a change.

Sometime in the 1990s, a German firm plans to market solar-hydrogen systems that can be used to meet all the heating, cooling, cooking, refrigeration, and electrical needs of a home and also provide hydrogen fuel for one or more cars. Within a few years, BMW plans to introduce hydrogen-powered automobiles, with the hydrogen produced by home generators leased from the company. By the year 2000, a photovoltaic-hydrogen car could be cost-competitive with the gasoline car if gas prices rise to about 53 cents per liter ($2 a gallon).

Scientist John O'M Bockris of Texas A & M University, calculated that energy-related pollution cost the United States $450 billion per year, or $1,800 a person. He estimates phasing in a solar-hydrogen energy base over 25 years, which would eliminate most of this pol-

Evan Kruppenbach

Evan Kruppenbach

Figure 17-26 Eco-Lair is where I work. It is a low-tech, low-cost ongoing experiment in saving energy and money. A south-facing solar room (shown in the photo on the left) collects solar energy passively and distributes it to a well-insulated, recycled 1954 school bus. The solar room also contains a compact, energy-efficient kitchen. Backup heat and hot water are provided by two solar-assisted, tankless instant water heaters fueled by LPG (Figure 3-18). Active solar collectors are shown on the left, and a passive solar water heater is shown near the ground on the right. Cooling is provided by buried tubes (earth tubes) at a cost of about $1 a summer. Water is conserved by the use of a water-saving toilet and shower head and faucet aerators in an attached bathroom behind the large insulated window. The photo on the right shows the interior of the recycled school bus. The computer and desk at the far end are located where the hood and motor of the bus used to be. The large cabinet on the left folds down and serves as a double bed. The bus windows on the right can be opened as needed to allow heat collected in the attached solar room to flow into the bus space.

(continued)

lution, would cost only $120 per person per year. Like improving energy efficiency, it is an undertaking we dare not refuse.

The hydrogen revolution has begun, and with proper support, we could be living in a hydrogen age within two or three decades. However, despite the enormous potential of hydrogen as a fuel, U.S. government research-and-development funding for hydrogen was only a minuscule $3 million in 1989. During that same year, the government of Japan spent $20 million on hydrogen research and development and the government of the former West Germany, $50 million.

TAKING ENERGY MATTERS INTO YOUR OWN HANDS While elected officials, energy company executives, and conservationists argue over the key components of a national energy strategy, many individuals have gotten fed up and have taken energy matters into their own hands. With or without tax credits, they are insulating, weatherizing, and making other improvements to improve energy efficiency and save money.

Some are building passively heated and cooled solar homes. Others are building superinsulated dwellings or are adding passive or active solar heating to existing homes. Each of us can develop a personal energy strategy that improves personal and national security and saves money (see Individuals Matter inside the back cover and Spotlight on p. 470).

Countries that have the vision to change from an unsustainable to a sustainable energy strategy will be rewarded with increased security — not just military security but also economic, energy, and environmental security. Those that do not will experience unnecessary economic and environmental hardships and increased human suffering.

electricity from roof-mounted panels of photovoltaic cells (Figure 17-18) within the next few years. Present electricity bills run around $30 a month (with $18 of this a base charge regardless of how much electricity is used), compared with $100 or more for conventional structures of the same size.

In moderate weather, cooling is provided by opening windows to capture breezes. During the hot and humid North Carolina summers, additional cooling is provided by earth tubes (Figure 17-11).

Four plastic pipes, with a diameter of 10 centimeters (4 inches), were buried about 5.5 meters (18 feet) underground, extending down a gently sloping hillside until their ends emerge some 31 meters (100 feet) away. The other ends of the tubes come up into the foundation of the bus and connect to a duct system containing a small fan with rheostat-controlled speed. When the fan is turned on, outside air at a temperature of 35°C (95°F) is drawn slowly through the buried tubes (which are surrounded by earth at about 16°C or 60°F), entering the structure at about 22°C (72°F). This natural air conditioning costs about $1 per summer for running the fan.

Several large oak trees and other deciduous trees in front of the solar room give us additional passive cooling during summer, and drop their leaves to let the sun in during winter. A used conventional central air conditioning unit (purchased for $200) is used as a backup. It can be turned on for short periods (typically no more than 15 to 30 minutes a day) when excessive pollen or heat and humidity overwhelm our immune systems and the earth tubes. Life always involves some trade-offs.

Eco-Lair is surrounded by natural vegetation, including flowers and low-level ground cover adapted to the climate of the area. This means there is no grass to cut and no lawn mower to repair, feed with gasoline, and listen to. Plants that repel various insects have also been added, so we have few insect pest problems. The surrounding trees and other vegetation also provide habitats for various species of insect-eating birds. When ants, mice, and other creatures find their way inside, we use natural alternatives to repel and control them (see Individuals Matter on p. 648).

Water use has been reduced by installing water-saving faucets, a water-saving shower head, and a low-flush toilet. We have also experimented with a waterless composting toilet that gradually converts waste and garbage scraps into a dry, odorless powder that can be used as a soil conditioner.

Kitchen wastes are composted and recycled to the soil. Paper and bottles are carried to a local recycling center, along with most of the small amounts of plastics we use. We try to never use aluminum cans and throwaway plastic bags. Extra furniture, clothes, and other items we have accumulated or salvaged over the years are stored in three other old school buses and recycled to family, friends, and people in need. For most household chemicals, we use more Earth-friendly substitutes (see Individuals Matter inside the back cover).

Our latest project has been to develop a low-cost, energy-efficient house within the financial reach of most people, which we call Eco-Habitat. We purchased a 130-square meter (1,400-square foot) manufactured home with enough insulation and energy-saving features to qualify for a discount on our electric bill from our electric utility company. The cost of the unit new, which was made in a factory and set up on the lot in two days, was $29,000. Then we added more roof insulation and built a second roof over the original roof to give us a 3-meter- (10-foot-) wide covered porch around the entire house.

Part of the porch on the south side was glassed in to provide a passive solar collector and solar room. Another glassed-in room was added

---

In the long run, humanity has no choice but to rely on renewable energy. No matter how abundant they seem today, eventually coal and uranium will run out. The choice before us is practical: We simply cannot afford to make more than one energy transition within the next generation.

DANIEL DEUDNEY AND CHRISTOPHER FLAVIN

DISCUSSION TOPICS

1. What are the ten most important things an individual can do to save energy in the home and in transportation (see Individuals Matter inside the back cover)? Which, if any, of these do you do? Which, if any, do you plan to do? When?

*2. Make an energy-use study of your school, and use the findings to develop an energy efficiency improvement program.

3. Should the United States institute a crash program to develop solar photovoltaic cells? Explain.

to the north side to provide a useful room during warm weather. Half of the remaining porch was screened and the rest was left open. Any part of the porch could be enclosed in the future to expand the house as needed at little cost.

The gas furnace that came with the house was replaced with a water- and space-heating system like the one shown in Figure 3-18. This project cost $25,000 and gave us 177 square meters (1,900 square feet) of enclosed space, excluding the screened and open porch areas. Thus, we ended up with an energy-efficient house at a cost of $301 per square meter ($28 per square foot), or $54,000 total—at least half the cost per unit of area as a conventional house (excluding the cost of land).

Because I work at home, I do little driving. Our primary car is a Geo Metro that gets 18 kpl (42 mpg). This is backed up by a much less fuel-efficient 4-wheel drive vehicle needed for travel on the 1.6-kilometer (1-mile) dirt road leading to Eco-Lair and Eco-Habitat when the weather is bad. We wish cars like the Volvo LCP 2000 (Figure 17-4) were available. If the technology becomes available and economically feasible in the future, we hope to purchase a vehicle that runs on hydrogen gas produced by solar photovoltaic cells that decompose water into hydrogen and oxygen gas.

We get most of our food from the grocery store rather than growing it ourselves. However, we are planning on growing some of our vegetables using intensive organic gardening techniques on small raised beds. For health and environmental reasons, we have greatly reduced our meat consumption. I have reduced my consumption of beef by 99% and my overall consumption of meat (mostly chicken and fish) by 60%. We should be strict vegetarians, but so far, we have been unwilling to go quite that far.

We feel a part of the piece of land we live on and love. To us, ownership of this land means that we are ethically driven to defend and protect it from degradation. We feel that the trees, flowers, deer, squirrels, hummingbirds, songbirds, and other forms of wildlife we often see are a part of us and we are a part of them. As temporary caretakers of this small portion of the biosphere, we feel obligated to pass it on to future generations with its ecological integrity and sustainability preserved.

Each year, we plant several trees on our land and I donate money to organizations to plant at least 50 trees for each tree I use in writing this and other books. The publisher and I also join together in donating money to tree-planting and land-preserving organizations to offset the paper used in printing this book.

Most of our political activities involve thinking globally but acting locally. They include attempts to prevent an economically unnecessary nuclear power plant from opening about 24 kilometers (15 miles) away (it opened anyway), to prevent an ecologically unsound development along a nearby river that is already badly polluted (we've been successful so far), and to prevent the building of a large, conventional housing development that would double the size of the closest town (successful).

We also financially support numerous environmental and conservation organizations working at the national and global levels. We are not opposed to all forms of development, only those that are ecologically unsound and destructive.

Working with nature gives us great joy and a sense of purpose. It also saves us money. Our attempt to work with nature is in a rural area, but people in cities can also have high-quality lifestyles that conserve resources and protect the environment (see Further Readings).

4. Explain why you agree or disagree with the ideas that the United States can get most of the electricity it needs by (a) developing solar power plants, (b) using direct solar energy to produce electricity in photovoltaic cells, (c) building new, large hydroelectric plants, (d) building ocean thermal electric power plants, (e) building wind farms, (f) building power plants fueled by wood, crop wastes, trash, and other biomass resources, (g) tapping dry-steam, wet-steam, and hot-water geothermal deposits, (h) tapping molten rock (magma) geothermal deposits, and (i) improving energy efficiency by 50%.

5. Explain why you agree or disagree with the following propositions:
   a. The United States should cut average per capita energy use by at least 50% between 1993 and 2013.
   b. A mandatory energy conservation program should form the basis of any U.S. energy policy to provide economic, environmental, and military security.
   c. To solve world and U.S. energy supply problems, all we need do is recycle some or most of the energy we use.

CHAPTER 18

NONRENEWABLE ENERGY RESOURCES

General Questions and Issues

1. What are the advantages and disadvantages of using oil and natural gas as energy resources?

2. What are the advantages and disadvantages of using coal as an energy resource?

3. What are the advantages and disadvantages of using conventional nuclear fission, breeder nuclear fission and nuclear fusion to produce electricity?

4. What are the best present and future energy options for the United States?

We are an interdependent world and if we ever needed a lesson in that, we got it in the oil crisis of the 1970s.

ROBERT S. MCNAMARA

SINCE 1950, OIL, coal, and natural gas have supported most of the world's economic growth. Their use is also responsible for much of the world's pollution and environmental degradation. Nuclear energy was supposed to be providing much of the world's electricity by the year 2000. However, high costs (even with enormous government subsidies), safety concerns, and failure to find an economically and politically acceptable solution for storing its long-lived radioactive wastes have led many countries to sharply scale back or eliminate their plans to build new nuclear power plants.

How long might various fossil fuels last? How can we reduce their environmental impact? What role should nuclear energy play in the future? What should be the energy strategy of the United States? These important and controversial issues are discussed in this chapter.

18-1 Oil and Natural Gas

CONVENTIONAL CRUDE OIL **Petroleum**, or **crude oil**, is a gooey liquid consisting mostly of hydrocarbon compounds and small amounts of compounds containing oxygen, sulfur, and nitrogen. Crude oil and natural gas are often trapped together deep within Earth's crust on land and beneath the seafloor (Figure 7-17). The crude oil is dispersed in pores and cracks in rock formations.

Primary oil recovery involves drilling and pumping out the oil that flows by gravity into the bottom of the well. Thicker, slowly flowing heavy oil is not removed. After the flowing oil has been removed, water can be injected into adjacent wells to force some of the remaining thicker crude oil into the central well and push it to the surface. This is known as **secondary oil recovery**. Usually, primary and secondary recovery remove only one-third of the crude oil in a well.

For each barrel removed by primary and secondary recovery, two barrels of heavy oil are left in a typical well. As oil prices rise, it may become economical to remove about 10% of the heavy oil by **enhanced**, or **tertiary, oil recovery**. One method is to force steam into the well to soften the heavy oil so that it can be pumped to the surface. Carbon dioxide gas can also be pumped into a well to force some of the heavy oil into the well cavity for pumping to the surface.

The problem is that enhanced oil recovery is expensive. The net useful energy yield is low because it takes energy equivalent to that in one-third of a barrel of oil to soften and pump each barrel of heavy oil to the surface. Additional energy is needed to increase the flow rate and to remove sulfur and nitrogen impurities before the heavy oil can be pumped through a pipeline to an oil refinery. Recoverable heavy oil from known U.S. crude oil reserves could supply all U.S. oil needs for only about seven years at current usage rates.

Once it is removed from a well, most crude oil is sent by pipeline to a refinery. There it is heated and distilled to separate it into gasoline, heating oil, diesel oil, asphalt, and other components. Because these components boil at different temperatures, they are removed at different levels of giant distillation columns (Figure 18-1).

Some components and products, called **petrochemicals**, are used as raw materials in industrial chemicals, fertilizers, pesticides, plastics, synthetic fibers, paints, medicines, and many other products. Petrochemical production accounts for about 3% of the crude oil extracted throughout the world and 7% of the oil used in the United States. That explains why the prices of many items we use go up after crude oil prices rise.

HOW LONG WILL SUPPLIES OF CONVENTIONAL CRUDE OIL LAST?

Almost two-thirds of the world's proven oil reserves (Figure 7-18) are in just five countries: Saudi Arabia, Kuwait, Iran, Iraq, and the United Arab Emirates. OPEC countries have 67% of these reserves, with Saudi Arabia having 25%. Geologists believe that the Middle East also contains most of the world's undiscovered oil. Therefore, OPEC is expected to have long-term control over world oil supplies and prices.

The Soviet Union is presently the world's largest oil extractor, with an annual output triple that of Saudi Arabia. The United States, the world's second largest oil extractor, has only 4% of the world's oil reserves but uses nearly 30% of all oil extracted each year. Transportation uses 63% of the 17 million barrels of oil consumed each day in the United States. The rest is used by industry (24%), residences and commercial buildings (8%), and electric utilities (5%).

Most oil occurrences in the Middle East are large and cheap to extract; most in the United States are small and more expensive to tap. Therefore, it has generally been cheaper for the United States to buy oil from other countries than to extract it from its own deposits. In 1990, about 49% of this oil was imported, and dependence on imports is projected to rise (Figure 1-12) unless the country gets serious about improving energy efficiency and phasing in a variety of perpetual and renewable energy resources (Chapter 17).

U.S. oil imports from Arab OPEC countries cost at least $100 a barrel (compared with a market price of around $22 per barrel) when the costs of ensuring the flow of oil from the Persian Gulf are included. That estimate does not include the additional costs of military intervention and presence in the Middle East incurred since 1990 during the Persian Gulf war and its aftermath. Thus, Americans are buying the world's

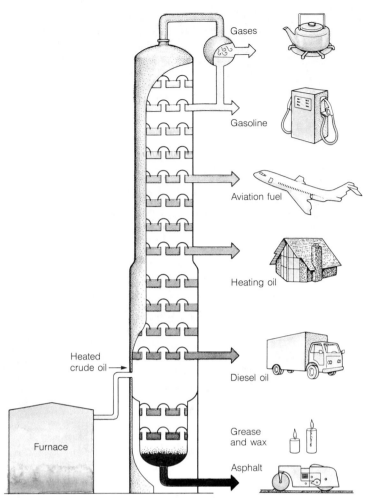

Figure 18-1   Refining of crude oil. Components are removed at various levels, depending on their boiling points, in a giant distillation column.

most expensive oil—to meet about 8% of their consumption.

The Alaska oil pipeline is a much greater threat to U.S. national security than is an inability to move oil by tankers through the Persian Gulf. There are now other oil suppliers and several alternative ways to get oil from the Middle East, but there is only one way to get oil from Alaska. Sabotage of the highly vulnerable Alaska oil pipeline could disrupt the entire American economy. The Department of Defense admits that it is impossible to protect this pipeline.

Figure 18-2 shows the locations of the largest crude oil and natural gas fields in the United States. U.S. oil extraction has declined steadily since 1970 despite greatly increased exploration and test drilling. The net useful energy yield for most new oil is low, and by as early as 1995, it could take more energy to explore for and extract oil in the United States than the wells will produce.

Experts disagree over how long the world's identified and unidentified crude oil resources will last. *Reserves* are identified deposits of a nonrenewable fossil

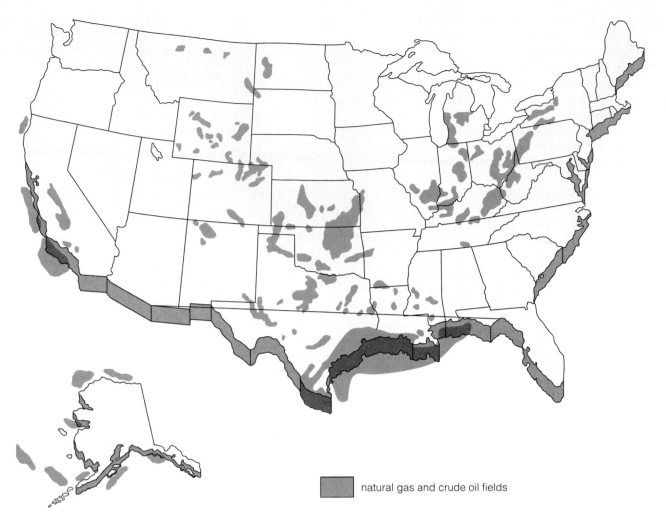

natural gas and crude oil fields

Figure 18-2 Locations of the largest occurrences of natural gas and crude oil in the United States. The oil and natural gas industries have about 15% of the total U.S. land area under lease. Relatively little new oil and natural gas is expected to be found in the United States. For example, even if oil is found by drilling in the Arctic National Wildlife Refuge, the most optimistic projection is that within 10 years it would supply only 300,000 barrels of expensive oil a day for only 20 years. However, increasing the fuel efficiency of new cars to 17 kpl (40 mpg) would reduce U.S. oil consumption by 2.5 million barrels a day within 10 years. (Data from Council on Environmental Quality)

fuel or mineral resource from which the resource can be extracted profitably at present prices with current technology (Figure 7-18). At present consumption rates, world crude oil reserves will be economically depleted in 35 years. U.S. reserves will be economically depleted by 2018 at the current consumption rate and by 2010 if oil use from these reserves increases by 2% a year.

Some analysts argue that higher oil prices will stimulate the discovery and extraction of large new crude oil resources (see Guest Essay on p. 29). They also believe we can extract and upgrade heavy oils from oil shale and tar sands, and by enhanced recovery from existing wells.

Some believe that the earth's crust may contain 100 times more oil than usually thought. Such oil, if it exists, lies 10 kilometers (6 miles) or more below Earth's surface—about twice the depth of today's deepest wells. Most geologists do not believe this oil exists.

Other analysts argue that people who make optimistic projections about future oil supplies don't understand the arithmetic and the consequences of exponential growth in the use of any nonrenewable resource (see Spotlight on p. 5). Consider the following facts about the world's exponential growth in oil use, assuming that we continue to use crude oil at the current rate instead of the projected higher rates. If the following supplies of oil were the only source:

- Saudi Arabia, with the world's largest known crude oil reserves, could supply all the world's oil needs for only 10 years.

- Mexico, with the world's sixth largest crude oil reserves, could supply the world's needs for only about 3 years.

- The estimated crude oil reserves under Alaska's North Slope—the largest ever found in North

America — would meet world demand for only 6 months or U.S. demand for 3 years.

- The oil that oil companies have a one-in-five chance of finding by drilling in Alaska's Arctic Wildlife Refuge could meet world demand for only 1 month and U.S. demand for 6 months (see Pro/Con on p. 428).

- All estimated undiscovered, recoverable deposits of oil in the United States could meet world demand for only 1.7 years and U.S. demand for 10 years.

- Those who believe that new discoveries will solve world oil supply problems must figure out how to discover the equivalent of a new Saudi Arabian supply *every ten years* just to keep on using oil at the current rate.

The ultimately recoverable supply of crude oil is estimated to be three times today's proven reserves. Suppose all that new oil is found and developed — which most oil experts consider unlikely — and sold at a price of $50 to $95 a barrel, compared with the 1990 price of about $22 a barrel. About 80% would be depleted by 2073 at the current usage rate and by 2037 if oil use increased 2% a year.

We can see why most experts expect little of the world's affordable crude oil to be left by the 2059 bicentennial of the world's first oil well. Oil company executives have known this for a long time, which explains why oil companies have become diversified energy companies. To keep making money after oil runs out, these international companies now own much of the world's natural gas, coal, and uranium reserves and have bought many of the companies producing solar collectors and solar cells.

PROS AND CONS OF OIL Oil has been, and still is, cheap (Figure 1-11), can easily be transported within and between countries, and has a high net useful energy yield (Figure 3-19). It is a versatile fuel that can be burned to propel vehicles, heat buildings and water, and supply high-temperature heat for industrial processes and electricity production.

Oil also has some disadvantages. The crucial disadvantage of oil is that affordable supplies are expected to be depleted within 40 to 80 years. Also, its burning releases carbon dioxide gas, which could alter global climate, and other air pollutants such as sulfur oxides and nitrogen oxides, which damage people, crops, trees, fish, and other wild species. Oil spills and leakage of toxic drilling muds cause water pollution, and the brine solution injected into oil wells can contaminate groundwater.

If all the harmful environmental effects of using oil were included in its market price and current government subsidies were removed, oil would be too expensive to use and would be replaced by a variety of less harmful and cheaper perpetual and renewable energy resources. We are addicted to using

Figure 18-3 Sample of oil shale and the shale oil extracted from it. Big oil shale projects have now been cancelled in the United States because of excessive cost.

and wasting oil because governments keep oil's market price artificially low, mostly for political reasons.

HEAVY OIL FROM OIL SHALE **Oil shale** is a fine-grained rock (Figure 18-3) that contains varying amounts of a solid, waxy mixture of hydrocarbon compounds called **kerogen**. After being removed by surface or subsurface mining, the shale is crushed and heated to a high temperature to vaporize the kerogen (Figure 18-4). The kerogen vapor is condensed, forming a slow-flowing, dark brown, heavy oil called **shale oil**. Before shale oil can be sent by pipeline to a refinery, it must be processed to increase its flow rate and heat content and to remove sulfur, nitrogen, and other impurities.

It is estimated that the potentially recoverable heavy oil from oil shale deposits in the United States — mostly on federal lands in Colorado, Utah, and Wyoming — could meet the country's crude oil demand for 41 years if consumption remains at the current level, and for 32 years if consumption rises 2% a year. Large oil shale deposits are also found in Canada, China, and the Soviet Union.

Environmental problems may limit shale oil production. Shale oil processing requires large amounts of water, which is scarce in the semiarid areas where the richest deposits are found. Converting kerogen to processed shale oil and burning the shale oil release more carbon dioxide per unit of energy than processing and burning conventional oil. Nitrogen oxides and sulfur dioxide are also released. If shale is extracted aboveground, there is severe land disruption from the mining and disposal of large volumes of shale rock, which breaks up and expands like popcorn when heated. Various salts, cancer-causing substances, and toxic metal compounds can be leached from the processed shale rock into nearby water supplies.

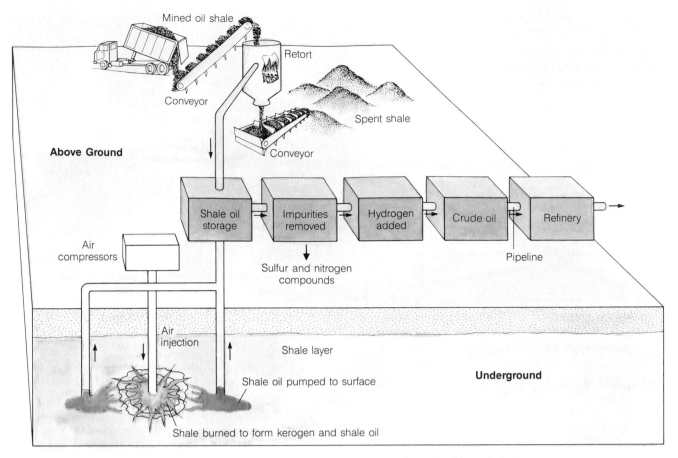

Figure 18-4 Aboveground and underground (*in situ*) methods for producing synthetic crude oil from oil shale.

One way to avoid some of these environmental problems is to extract oil from shale underground, known as *in situ* (in-place) *processing* (Figure 18-4). However, this method is too expensive with present technology and produces more sulfur dioxide emissions than surface processing.

The net useful energy yield of shale oil is much lower than that of conventional oil because the energy equivalent of almost one-half a barrel of conventional crude oil is needed to extract, process, and upgrade one barrel of shale oil (Figure 3-19). Also, shale oil does not refine as well as crude oil and yields fewer useful products.

Some analysts believe that shale oil may never be economically feasible because it takes so much energy (derived mostly from crude oil) to extract, process, upgrade, and refine. If so, each increase in the price of crude oil would also raise the price of shale oil.

HEAVY OIL FROM TAR SAND **Tar sand** (or oil sand) is a deposit of a mixture of clay, sand, water, and varying amounts of **bitumen**, a gooey, black, high-sulfur, heavy oil. Tar sand is usually removed by surface mining and heated with steam at high pressure to make the bitumen fluid enough to float to the top. The bitumen is removed and then purified and chemically upgraded

into a synthetic crude oil suitable for refining (Figure 18-5). So far, it is not technically or economically feasible to remove deeper deposits of tar sand by underground mining or to remove bitumen by underground extraction.

The world's largest known deposits of tar sands lie in a cold, desolate area in northern Alberta, Canada — the famous Athabasca Tar Sands. Heavy oil in these deposits is estimated to exceed the proven oil reserves of Saudi Arabia. Other large deposits are in Venezuela, Colombia, and the Soviet Union. Smaller deposits exist in the United States, mostly in Utah. If all U.S. deposits were developed, they would supply all U.S. oil needs at the current usage rate for only about three months at a price of $48 to $62 a barrel.

Since 1985, two plants have been supplying almost 12% of Canada's oil demand by extracting and processing heavy oil from tar sands at a cost of $12 to $15 a barrel — below the average world oil price between 1986 and 1991. Economically recoverable deposits of heavy oil from tar sands can supply all of Canada's projected oil needs for about 33 years at the current consumption rate. These deposits are an important source of oil for Canada, but they would meet the world's present oil needs for only about 2 years.

Producing synthetic crude oil from tar sands has

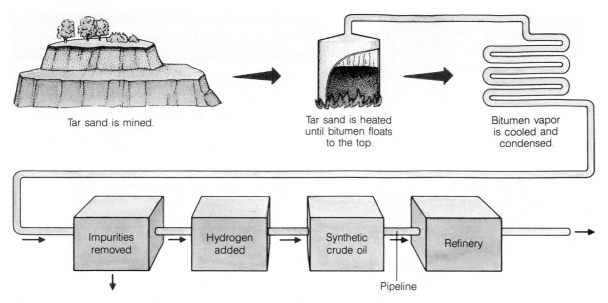

Figure 18-5 Generalized summary of how synthetic crude oil is produced from tar sand.

several disadvantages. The net useful energy yield is low because it takes the energy equivalent of almost one-half a barrel of conventional oil to extract and process one barrel of bitumen and upgrade it to synthetic crude oil before it can be sent to an oil refinery. Other problems include the need for large quantities of water for processing and the release of air and water pollutants. Upgrading bitumen to synthetic crude oil releases sulfur dioxide, hydrogen sulfide, and particulates of toxic metals.

Environmentalists charge that synthetic crude oil is produced from tar sand at a low price in Canada only because the tar sand processing plants are not required to control air pollution emissions. The plants have also created huge waste disposal ponds. Cleaning up these toxic waste dump sites is another external cost not included in the price of crude oil produced from Canadian tar sand.

NATURAL GAS In its underground gaseous state, **natural gas** is a mixture of 50% to 90% by volume of methane gas (CH_4) and smaller amounts of heavier gaseous hydrocarbon compounds such as propane (C_3H_8) and butane (C_4H_{10}). *Conventional natural gas* lies above most occurrences of crude oil (Figure 7-17). Some of this is burned off and wasted when the primary goal is oil extraction (Figure 18-6). *Unconventional natural gas* is found by itself in other underground occurrences.

When a natural gas field is tapped, propane and butane gases are liquefied and removed as **liquefied petroleum gas (LPG)**. LPG is stored in pressurized tanks for use mostly in rural areas not served by natural gas pipelines. The rest of the gas (mostly methane) removed from the field is dried to remove water vapor, cleaned of hydrogen sulfide and other impurities, and pumped into pressurized pipelines for distribution.

At a very low temperature, natural gas can be converted to **liquefied natural gas (LNG)**. This highly flammable liquid form of natural gas can then be shipped to other countries in refrigerated tanker ships.

HOW LONG WILL NATURAL GAS SUPPLIES LAST? The Soviet Union has 40% of the world's proven reserves and is the world's largest extractor of natural gas. Other countries with large proven natural gas reserves are Iran (14%), the United States (6%), Qatar (4%), Algeria (4%), Saudi Arabia (3%), and Nigeria (3%). Geologists expect to find more deposits of conventional natural gas, especially in LDCs that have not been widely explored for this resource.

Most U.S. reserves of natural gas are located with the country's occurrences of crude oil (Figure 18-2). About 95% of the natural gas used in the United States comes from domestic sources; the other 5% is imported by pipeline from Canada. Algeria and the Soviet Union use pipelines to supply many eastern and western European countries with natural gas and are planning more pipelines.

In 1990, about 82% of the natural gas consumed in the United States was used for space heating of residential and commercial buildings and for drying and other purposes in industry. The rest was used to produce electricity (15%) and as a vehicle fuel (3%) (see Spotlight on p. 480).

Conventional supplies of natural gas are better distributed and believed to be larger than those of crude oil. Known reserves and undiscovered, economically recoverable occurrences of conventional natural gas in the United States are projected to last 28 years and world supplies 59 years at present consumption rates.

As the price of natural gas from conventional sources rises, it may become economical to get natural

Figure 18-6 Large quantities of energy are wasted when natural gas that is found with oil is sometimes burned off, as in this oil field in Saudi Arabia. This is done because collecting and using the natural gas cost more than what it can be sold for in the oil-rich Middle East. Burning this high-quality fuel also adds carbon dioxide and other pollutants to the atmosphere, but that causes less projected global warming than allowing the methane to escape into the atmosphere.

gas from unconventional sources. Such sources include coal seams, Devonian shale rock, deep underground deposits of tight sands, and deep geopressurized zones that contain natural gas dissolved in hot water. New technology for extracting gas from these resources is being developed rapidly.

In 1988, the Department of Energy estimated that technically recoverable natural gas from both conventional and unconventional sources in the lower 48 states would meet domestic needs for 50 years at current usage rates. The world's identified reserves of conventional natural gas are projected to last until 2045 at current usage rates and until 2022 if consumption rises 2% a year.

It is estimated that conventional supplies of natural gas and unconventional supplies available at higher prices, would last about 200 years at the current rate and 80 years if usage rose 2% a year. If those estimates are correct, natural gas could become the most widely used fuel for space heating, industrial processes, producing electricity, and transportation, and could serve as a transition fuel to greatly increased dependence on perpetual and renewable energy resources.

SPOTLIGHT Natural Gas as a Vehicle Fuel

Compressed natural gas (CNG) can be used as a fuel in motor vehicles and costs less and burns much cleaner than gasoline. In 1990, about 70 cents' worth of natural gas would provide the same amount of energy as $1.25 worth of unleaded gasoline. However, converting a vehicle to run on this fuel costs about $2,500.

Worldwide, about 700,000 cars and trucks run on compressed natural gas. That includes 300,000 vehicles in Italy, 160,000 in New Zealand, 30,000 in the United States, and 20,000 in Canada.

Because natural gas contains only about one-fourth as much energy as the same volume of gasoline, a tank of CNG must be four times as big as a tank in a gasoline-powered car to cover the same distance. Because of a lack of filling stations selling CNG, it is used mostly by commercial fleets of cars and trucks that return to a central company facility for refueling.

However, one company is making a natural-gas refueling system that can be installed in a driver's own garage. The unit costs $3,000 or can be leased for $50 a month.

PROS AND CONS OF NATURAL GAS Natural gas burns hotter and produces less air pollution than any fossil fuel. Burning it produces virtually no sulfur dioxide and particulate matter, and only about one-sixth as many nitrogen oxides per unit of energy as burning coal, oil, or gasoline. Burning natural gas produces carbon dioxide, but the amount per unit of energy produced is much lower than that of other fossil fuels (Figure 18-7). Methane, the primary component of natural gas, is a greenhouse gas that is 25 times more effective per molecule than carbon dioxide in causing global warming (Figure 11-2). Little of the methane in the atmosphere comes from extraction and use of natural gas.

So far, the price of natural gas has been low. It can be transported easily over land by pipeline and has a high net useful energy yield. It is a versatile fuel that can be burned cleanly and efficiently in furnaces, stoves, water heaters, dryers, boilers, incinerators, motor vehicles, fuel cells, heat pumps, air conditioners, and refrigerators.

New natural gas-burning turbines, working like jet engines, can be used to produce electricity. They cost half as much to build as a coal-fired system, are cheaper to operate, and can be put into operation within 12 to 18 months. Natural gas can also be burned cleanly and efficiently in cogenerators to produce high-temperature heat and electricity, and small amounts can be burned

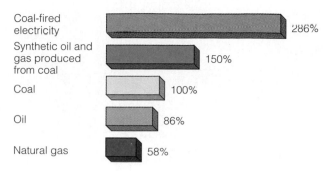

Coal-fired electricity — 286%
Synthetic oil and gas produced from coal — 150%
Coal — 100%
Oil — 86%
Natural gas — 58%

Figure 18-7 Carbon dioxide emissions per unit of energy produced by other fossil fuels as percentages of those produced by coal.

with coal in boilers to reduce emissions of nitrogen oxides by 50% to 75%.

One problem is that natural gas must be converted to liquid natural gas before it can be shipped by tanker from one country to another. Shipping LNG in refrigerated tankers is expensive and dangerous. Huge explosions could kill many people and cause much damage in urban areas near LNG loading and unloading facilities. Conversion of natural gas into LNG also reduces the net useful energy yield by one-fourth.

If large amounts of natural gas can be extracted from nonconventional deposits at affordable prices, natural gas will be a key option for making an acceptable and orderly transition to solar and other energy options as oil is phased out over the next 50 years.

18-2 Coal

TYPES AND DISTRIBUTION **Coal** is a solid formed in several stages as the remains of plants are subjected to intense heat and pressure over millions of years. It is a complex mixture of organic compounds, with 30% to 98% carbon by weight plus varying amounts of water and small amounts of nitrogen and sulfur.

Three types of coal are formed at different stages: lignite, bituminous coal, and anthracite (Figure 7-14). Peat, which is the first stage of coal formation, is not a coal. It is burned in some places but has a low heat content. Low-sulfur coal produces less sulfur dioxide when burned than high-sulfur coal. The most desirable type of coal is anthracite because of its high heat content and low sulfur content.

About 60% of the coal extracted in the world and 70% in the United States is burned in boilers to produce steam to generate electrical power. The rest is converted to coke used to make steel and burned in boilers to produce steam used in various manufacturing pro-

cesses. In 1990, coal was burned to supply 57% of the electricity generated in the United States. The rest was produced by nuclear energy (20%), natural gas (11%), hydropower (9%), and oil (3%).

Coal is the world's most abundant fossil fuel. About 68% of the world's proven coal reserves and 85% of the estimated undiscovered coal deposits are located in three countries: the United States, the USSR, and China.

Most U.S. coal fields are located in 17 states (Figure 18-8). Anthracite, the most desirable form of coal, makes up only 2% of U.S. coal reserves. About 45% is high-sulfur, bituminous coal with a high fuel value. It is found mostly in the East, primarily in Kentucky, West Virginia, Pennsylvania, Ohio, and Illinois.

About 55% of U.S. coal reserves are found west of the Mississippi River. Most of these are deposits of low-sulfur bituminous and lignite coal. Unfortunately, these deposits are far from the heavily industrialized and populated East, where most coal is consumed.

EXTRACTING COAL Surface mining is used to extract almost two-thirds of the coal used in the United States. Most surface-mined coal is removed by area strip mining or contour strip mining, depending on the terrain (Figure 7-17).

Area strip mining is used where the terrain is fairly flat. It involves stripping away the overburden and digging a cut to remove a mineral deposit, in this case, coal (Figure 18-9). After the coal deposit is removed from the cut, the trench is filled with overburden. The power shovel removing coal then digs a cut parallel to the previous one. This process is repeated for the entire deposit. If the land is not restored, this type of mining leaves a wavy series of highly erodible hills of rubble called *spoil banks* (Figure 18-10).

Contour strip mining is a form of surface mining used in hilly or mountainous terrain. A power shovel cuts a series of terraces into the side of a hill or a mountain (Figure 18-11). An earthmover removes the overburden and a power shovel extracts the coal, with the overburden from each new terrace dumped onto the one below. Unless the land is restored, a wall of dirt is left in front of a highly erodible bank of soil and rock called a *highwall*. In the United States, contour strip mining is used mostly for extracting coal in the mountainous Appalachian region. If the land is not restored (Figure 18-12), this type of surface mining has a devastating impact on the land. Sometimes, giant augers are used to drill horizontally into a hillside to extract underground coal.

Subsurface mining is used to remove coal too deep to be extracted by surface mining (Figure 7-17). Miners dig a deep vertical shaft, blast subsurface tunnels and rooms to get to the deposit, and haul the coal or ore to the surface. In the *room-and-pillar method*, as much as half of the coal is left in place as pillars to prevent the

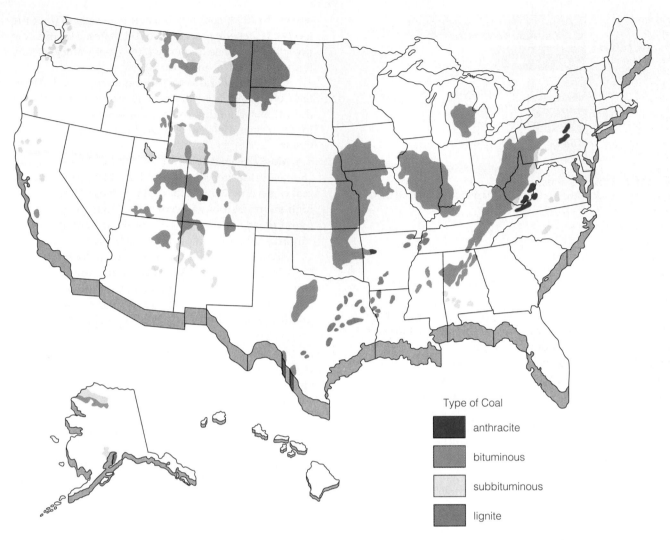

Type of Coal

- anthracite
- bituminous
- subbituminous
- lignite

Figure 18-8 Major coalfields in the United States. (Data from Council on Environmental Quality)

mine from collapsing. In the *longwall method*, a narrow tunnel is created and then supported by movable metal pillars. After a cutting machine has removed the coal or ore from part of the mineral seam, the roof supports are moved forward, allowing the earth behind the supports to collapse. No tunnels are left behind after the mining operation has been completed.

HOW LONG WILL SUPPLIES LAST? Identified world reserves of coal should last about 220 years at current usage and 65 years if usage rises 2% a year. The world's unidentified coal resources are projected to last about 900 years at the current rate and 149 years if usage increases 2% a year.

Identified coal reserves in the United States should last about 300 years at the current usage rate. Unidentified U.S. coal resources could extend those supplies at the current rate for perhaps 100 years, at a much higher average cost.

PROS AND CONS OF SOLID COAL Coal is the most abundant conventional fossil fuel in the world and in the United States. It also has a high net useful energy yield for producing high-temperature heat for industrial processes and for generating electricity (Figure 3-19). In countries with adequate coal supplies, burning solid coal is the cheapest way to produce high-temperature heat and electricity. However, the low costs do not include requiring the best air pollution control equipment on all plants and requiring effective reclamation of all land surface mined for coal (Figure 18-12). *If all of coal's harmful environmental costs were included in its market price and government subsidies were removed, coal would be too expensive to use and would be replaced by cheaper and less environmentally harmful perpetual and renewable energy resources.*

Since 1900, underground mining in the United States has killed more than 100,000 miners and permanently disabled at least 1 million. At least 250,000 retired

Figure 18-9 Area strip mining of coal in Decker, Montana. This type of surface mining is used on flat or gently rolling terrain.

Earl Dotter

National Archives/EPA Documerica

Figure 18-10 Effects of area strip mining of coal near Mulla, Colorado. Restoration of newly strip-mined areas is now required in the United States, but many previously mined areas have not been restored. In arid areas, full restoration isn't possible and enforcement of surface mining laws is often lax.

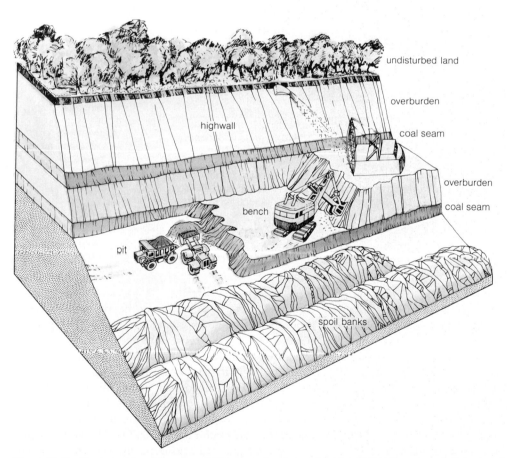

Figure 18-11 Contour strip mining of coal. This type of surface mining is used in hilly or mountainous terrain.

Figure 18-12 With the land returned to its original contour and grass planted to hold the soil in place, it is hard to tell that this was once a surface coal-mining site in Grantsville, Maryland. However, about three-fourths of the coal in the United States that can be surface-mined is in the West, in arid and semiarid regions (Figure 18-8). There the climate and the soil usually prevent full restoration of surface-mined land.

Soil Conservation Service

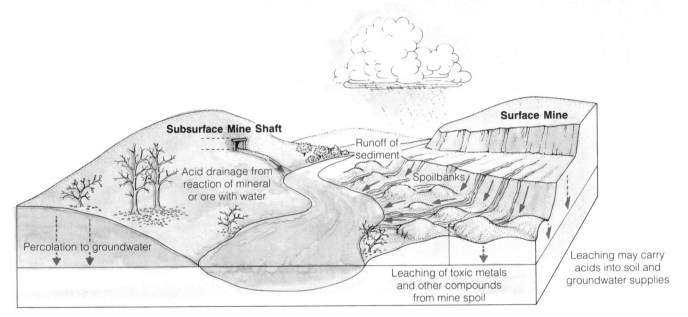

Subsurface Mine Shaft

Surface Mine

Runoff of sediment

Acid drainage from reaction of mineral or ore with water

Spoilbanks

Percolation to groundwater

Leaching of toxic metals and other compounds from mine spoil

Leaching may carry acids into soil and groundwater supplies

Figure 18-13 Degradation and pollution of a stream and groundwater by runoff of acids — called *acid mine drainage* — and toxic chemicals from surface and subsurface mining operations. These substances can kill fish and other forms of aquatic life. In the United States, acid mine drainage has damaged over 26,000 kilometers (16,100 miles) of streams, mostly in Appalachia and in the western states.

U.S. miners suffer from black lung disease, a form of emphysema caused by prolonged breathing of coal dust and other particulate matter. Mining safety laws in most countries are much weaker than those in the United States. Underground mining also causes subsidence when a mine shaft partially collapses during or after mining. Over 800,000 hectares (2 million acres) of land, much of it in central Appalachia, has subsided because of underground coal mining.

Surface mining causes severe land disturbance (Figures 18-10 and 18-11) and soil erosion, and surface-mined land in arid and semiarid areas can be only partially restored. Surface and subsurface mining of coal can cause severe pollution of nearby streams and groundwater from acids and toxic metal compounds (Figure 18-13). Once coal is mined, it is expensive to move from one place to another, and it cannot be used in solid form as a fuel for cars and trucks.

Coal is the dirtiest fossil fuel to burn. Without expensive air pollution control devices, burning coal produces larger amounts of sulfur dioxide, nitrogen oxides, and particulate matter than other fossil fuels. These pollutants contribute to acid deposition, corrode metals, and harm trees, crops, wild animals, and people.

Each year, these and other air pollutants emitted when coal is burned kill about 5,000 people in the

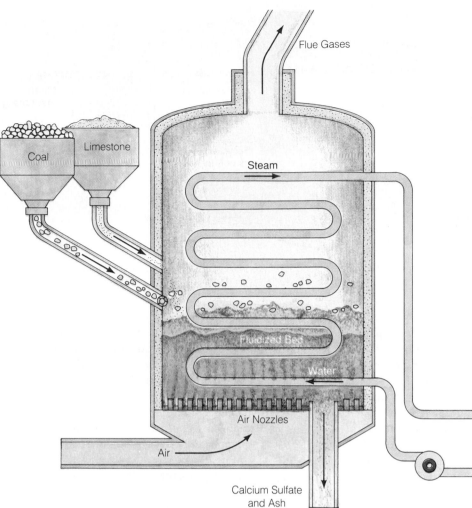

Figure 18-14 Fluidized-bed combustion of coal. A stream of hot air is blown into a boiler to suspend a mixture of powdered coal and crushed limestone. This removes most of the sulfur dioxide, sharply reduces emissions of nitrogen oxides, and burns coal more efficiently and cheaply than conventional combustion methods.

United States. They also cause 50,000 cases of respiratory disease and several billion dollars in property damage each year. Burning coal also produces more carbon dioxide per unit of energy than other fossil fuels (Figure 18-7). That means that burning more coal to meet energy needs can accelerate projected global warming (Section 11-1). This problem by itself may prevent much of the world's coal reserves from being mined and burned.

New ways have been developed to burn coal more cleanly and efficiently. One is *fluidized-bed combustion*, which also sharply reduces emissions of sulfur dioxide and nitrogen oxides (Figure 18-14). Successful small-scale fluidized-bed combustion plants have been built in Great Britain, Sweden, Finland, the Soviet Union, Germany, and China. In the United States, commercial fluidized-bed combustion boilers are expected to begin replacing conventional coal boilers in the mid-1990s.

SYNFUELS: CONVERTING SOLID COAL INTO GASEOUS AND LIQUID FUELS Besides being used in solid form, coal can also be converted into gaseous or liquid fuels, called **synfuels**. They are more useful than solid coal in heating homes and powering vehicles, and burning them produces much less air pollution than burning solid coal.

Coal gasification (Figure 18-15) is the conversion of solid coal into synthetic natural gas (SNG). **Coal liquefaction** is the conversion of solid coal into a liquid hydrocarbon fuel such as methanol or synthetic gasoline. A $2 billion commercial coal liquefaction plant supplies 10% of the liquid fuel used in South Africa at a cost equal to paying $35 a barrel for oil. When two new plants are completed, the country will be able to meet half of its oil needs from this source. Engineers hope to get the cost down to $25 a barrel.

Synfuels can be transported through a pipeline, burn more cleanly than solid coal, and are more versatile than solid coal. Besides being burned to produce high-temperature heat and electricity as solid coal does, synfuels can be burned to heat houses and water and to propel vehicles.

However, a synfuel plant costs much more to build and run than an equivalent coal-fired power plant fully equipped with air pollution control devices. Synfuels also have low net useful energy yields (Figure 3-19). The

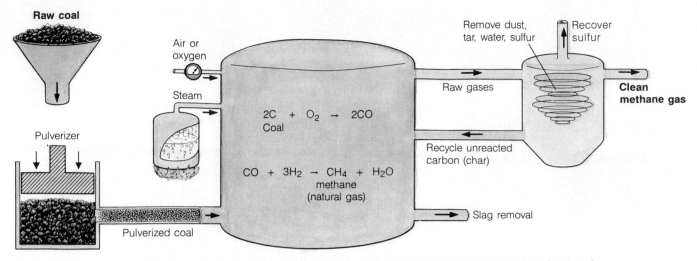

Figure 18-15 Coal gasification. Generalized view of one method for converting solid coal into synthetic natural gas (methane).

widespread use of synfuels would accelerate the depletion of world coal supplies because 30% to 40% of the energy content of coal is lost in the conversion process. It would also lead to greater land disruption from surface mining because producing a unit of energy from synfuels uses more coal than burning solid coal.

Producing synfuels requires huge amounts of water, and burning synfuels releases large amounts of carbon dioxide per unit of energy (Figure 18-7). Converting coal into SNG underground would solve the water problem, but currently, underground coal gasification is not competitive with conventional coal mining and aboveground coal gasification.

The biggest factor holding back large-scale production of synfuels in the United States is their high cost, compared with conventional oil and natural gas. Producing synfuels with current technology is equivalent to buying oil at $38 a barrel. The Department of Energy has a goal of supporting development of new processes that will reduce the cost to $25 per barrel by 1995, but most analysts expect synfuels to play only a minor role as an energy resource in the next 30 to 50 years.

18-3 Conventional Nuclear Fission

A CONTROVERSIAL FADING DREAM By the end of this century, 1,800 nuclear power plants were supposed to supply 21% of the world's supplemental energy and 25% of that used in the United States. Those rosy forecasts turned out to be an example of unrealistic high-tech intoxication.

By 1991, after 44 years of development and enormous government subsidies, about 424 commercial nu-

clear reactors in 25 countries were producing only 19% of the world's electricity — equal to only about 5% of the world's supplemental energy. Little additional construction is expected after the roughly 100 plants still being built are completed.

The percentage of the world's electricity produced by nuclear power will probably drop between 1990 and 2010 as aging nuclear plants are retired faster than new ones are built. By the year 2000, nuclear power will supply less than one-tenth of the electricity it was projected to produce.

Industrialized countries such as Japan and France, which have few fossil-fuel resources, believe that using nuclear power is the best way to reduce their dependence on imported oil. For example, France got 75% of its electricity from nuclear power in 1990 and plans to get 90% sometime during the 1990s.

However, both Japan and France already are producing more electricity than they can use (see Guest Essay on p. 75). France has been forced to sell electricity to neighboring countries at bargain prices and run its plants at partial capacity. In 1989, the French national company that builds and runs the country's plants lost $720 million. The cumulative debt of the utility company is now $46 billion — a sum greater than France's entire income tax receipts in 1988.

Since the Chernobyl nuclear accident in 1986 (see Spotlight on p. 490), many countries have scaled back or eliminated their plans to build nuclear power plants. Since 1975, no new nuclear power plants have been ordered in the United States, and 120 previous orders have been cancelled. In 1991, the 111 licensed commercial nuclear plants in the United States generated about 20% of the country's electricity, and that percentage is expected to decline over the next two decades when more than 60% of the current reactors are scheduled for retirement.

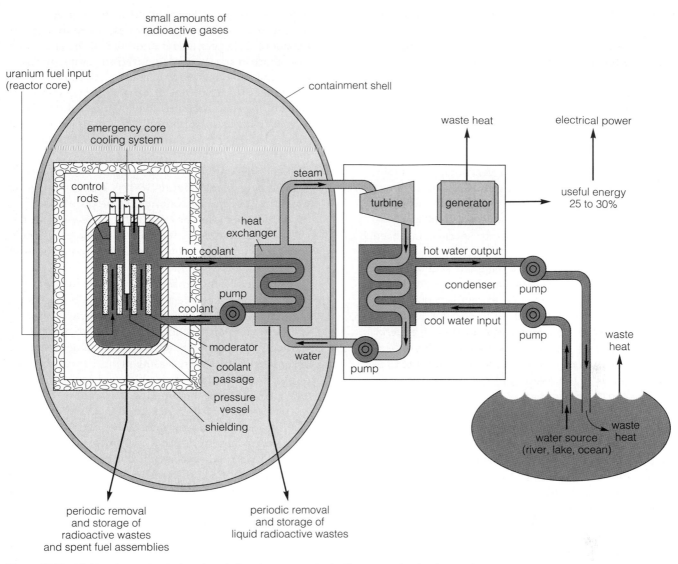

small amounts of
radioactive gases

uranium fuel input
(reactor core)

containment shell

emergency core
cooling system

waste heat   electrical power

steam

control
rods

turbine   generator

useful energy
25 to 30%

heat
exchanger

hot coolant

hot water output

pump

condenser   pump

coolant

cool water input

moderator

pump

coolant
passage

water

waste
heat

pressure
vessel

pump

shielding

waste
heat

water source
(river, lake, ocean)

periodic removal
and storage of
radioactive wastes
and spent fuel assemblies

periodic removal
and storage of
liquid radioactive wastes

Figure 18-16   Light-water-moderated-and-cooled nuclear power plant with a pressurized water reactor.

What happened to nuclear power? The answer is that the nuclear industry has been crippled by high and uncertain costs of building and operating plants, billion-dollar cost overruns, frequent malfunctions, false assurances and cover-ups by government and industry officials, overproduction of electricity in some areas, poor management, and lack of public acceptance because of mistrust and concerns about safety, cost, radioactive waste disposal, and the proliferation of nuclear weapons. To better understand some of the problems with nuclear power, we need to know how a nuclear power plant works.

HOW DOES A NUCLEAR FISSION REACTOR WORK?   When the nuclei of atoms such as uranium-235 and plutonium-239 are split by neutrons, energy is released and converted mostly into high-temperature heat in a nuclear fission chain reaction (Figure 3-11).

The rate at which this happens can be controlled in the nuclear fission reactor in a nuclear power plant, and the heat released can be used to spin a turbine and produce electrical energy.

Light-water reactors (LWRs) now generate about 85% of the electricity generated worldwide (98% in the United States) by nuclear power plants. Key parts of an LWR are the core, fuel assemblies, fuel rods, control rods, moderator, and coolant (Figure 18-16). The core of an LWR typically contains about 40,000 long, thin fuel rods bundled in 180 fuel assemblies of around 200 rods each. Each fuel rod is packed with pencil-eraser-size pellets of uranium oxide fuel.

About 97% of the uranium in each fuel pellet is uranium-238, an isotope that is nonfissionable. The other 3% is uranium-235, which is fissionable. Uranium ore contains 97% uranium-238 by weight and only 0.7% of the fissionable uranium-235 (Figure 3-2).

Enrichment separates some of the uranium-238 from the ore, increasing the concentration of uranium-235 from 0.7% to 3% by weight. This enriched ore can be used as a fuel in a fission reactor. The uranium-235 in each fuel rod produces energy equal to that of three railroad carloads of coal over a lifetime of about three to four years.

When the fuel in the rods can no longer sustain nuclear fission, the intensely radioactive spent fuel rods are removed. If the fuel pellets in the rods are processed to remove plutonium and other very long-lived radioactive isotopes, the remaining radioactive waste must be safely stored for at least 10,000 years. Otherwise, the rods must be stored safely for at least 240,000 years — about six times longer than our species has been around.

Control rods are made of materials such as boron or cadmium that absorb neutrons. The rods are moved in and out of the reactor core to regulate the rate of fission and the amount of power the reactor produces. All reactors place or circulate some type of material between the fuel rods and the fuel assemblies. This material, known as a *moderator*, slows down the neutrons emitted by the fission process so that the chain reaction can be kept going.

Some 75% of the world's commercial reactors use ordinary water, called light water, as a moderator. Thus, the interior of most commercial reactors is somewhat like a swimming pool with a large number of movable vertical fuel rods and control rods hanging in it. The moderator in about 20% of the world's commercial reactors (50% of those in the Soviet Union, including the ill-fated Chernobyl reactor) is solid graphite, a form of carbon. Graphite-moderated reactors can also be used to produce fissionable plutonium-239 for use in nuclear weapons.

A coolant circulates through the reactor's core. It removes heat to keep fuel rods and other materials from melting and to produce steam that spins generators to produce electricity. Most water-moderated and graphite-moderated reactors use water as a coolant; a few gas-cooled reactors use an unreactive gas such as helium or argon for cooling.

A typical light-water reactor has an energy efficiency of only 25% to 30%, compared with 40% for a coal-burning plant. Graphite-moderated, gas-cooled reactors are more expensive to build and operate but are more energy-efficient (38%) than LWRs because they operate at a higher temperature.

Nuclear power plants, each with one or more reactors, are only one part of the nuclear fuel cycle necessary for using nuclear energy to produce electricity (Figure 18-17). *In evaluating the safety and economy of nuclear power, we need to look at the entire cycle, not just the nuclear plant itself.*

After about three to four years in a reactor, the concentration of fissionable uranium-235 in a fuel rod becomes too low to keep the chain reaction going, or the rod becomes damaged from exposure to ionizing radiation. Each year, about one-third of the spent fuel assemblies in a reactor are removed and stored in large, concrete-lined pools of water at the plant site.

After they have cooled for several years and lost some of their radioactivity, the spent fuel rods can be sealed in shielded, supposedly crash-proof casks and transported by truck or train to storage pools away from the reactor or to a nuclear waste repository or dump.

Another option is to send spent fuel to a fuel-reprocessing plant (Figure 18-17). There, remaining uranium-235, and plutonium-239 produced as a by-product of the fission process, are removed and sent to a fuel fabrication plant. Such plants would also handle and ship bomb-grade plutonium-239 that could be used to make nuclear weapons.

Two small commercial fuel-reprocessing plants in operation (one in France and one in Great Britain) have had severe operating and economic problems. Two others are under construction — one in Japan and one in Germany. The United States has delayed development of commercial fuel-reprocessing plants because of technical difficulties, high construction and operating costs, and adequate domestic supplies of uranium.

The fission products produced in a nuclear reactor give off radioactivity by radioactive decay and heat, even after control rods have been inserted to stop all nuclear fission in the reactor core. To prevent a *meltdown* of the fuel rods and the reactor core after a reactor is shut down, huge amounts of water must be kept circulating through the core. A meltdown could release enormous quantities of highly radioactive materials into the environment.

HOW SAFE ARE NUCLEAR POWER PLANTS? To greatly reduce the chances of a meltdown and other serious reactor accidents, commercial reactors in the United States (and most countries) have many safety features:

- thick walls and concrete and steel shields surrounding the reactor vessel

- a system for automatically inserting control rods into the core to stop fission under emergency conditions

- a steel-reinforced concrete containment building to keep radioactive gases and materials from reaching the atmosphere after an accident

- large filter systems and chemical sprayers inside the containment building to remove radioactive dust from the air and further reduce chances of radioactivity reaching the environment

- systems to condense steam released from a ruptured reactor vessel and prevent pressure from rising beyond the holding power of containment building walls

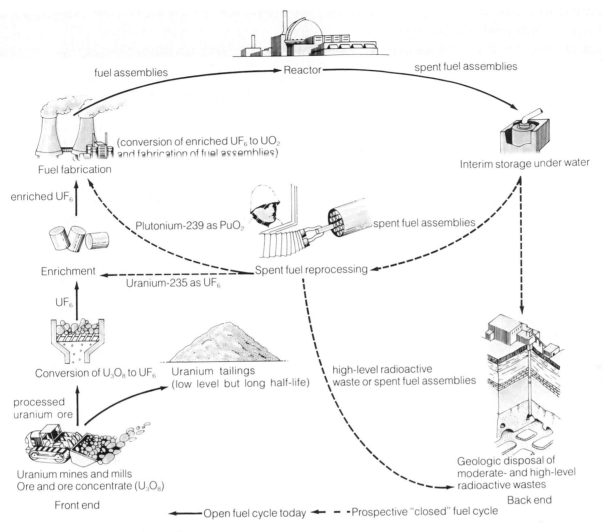

fuel assemblies → Reactor → spent fuel assemblies

(conversion of enriched UF$_6$ to UO$_2$ and fabrication of fuel assemblies)

Fuel fabrication

Interim storage under water

enriched UF$_6$

Plutonium-239 as PuO$_2$

spent fuel assemblies

Enrichment

Uranium-235 as UF$_6$

Spent fuel reprocessing

UF$_6$

Conversion of U$_3$O$_8$ to UF$_6$

Uranium tailings (low level but long half-life)

high-level radioactive waste or spent fuel assemblies

processed uranium ore

Uranium mines and mills
Ore and ore concentrate (U$_3$O$_8$)

Geologic disposal of moderate- and high-level radioactive wastes

Front end

Back end

←—— Open fuel cycle today ←— - -Prospective "closed" fuel cycle

Figure 18-17 The nuclear fuel cycle.

- an emergency core-cooling system to flood the core automatically with huge amounts of water within one minute to prevent meltdown of the reactor core

- two separate power lines servicing the plant, and several diesel generators to supply backup power for the huge pumps in the emergency core-cooling system

- X ray inspection of key metal welds during construction and periodically after the plant goes into operation to detect possible sources of leaks from corrosion

- an automatic backup system to replace each major part of the safety system in the event of a failure

Such elaborate safety systems make a complete reactor core meltdown very unlikely. However, a partial or complete meltdown is possible through a series of equipment failures, operator errors, or both. In 1979, a reactor at the Three Mile Island plant in Penn-

sylvania underwent a partial meltdown because of equipment failures and operator errors (see Spotlight on p. 490).

Many studies of nuclear safety have been made since 1957, when the first commercial nuclear power plant began operating in the United States. However, there is still no officially accepted study of just how safe or unsafe these plants are and no study of the safety of the entire nuclear fuel cycle. Even if engineers can make the hardware 100% reliable, human reliability can never reach 100%.

The Nuclear Regulatory Commission estimated that there is a 15% to 45% chance of a complete core meltdown at a U.S. reactor during the next 20 years. The commission also found that 39 U.S. reactors have an 80% chance of containment failure from a meltdown or a tremendous gas explosion. Scientists in the former West Germany and Sweden project that, worldwide, there is a 70% chance of another serious core-damaging accident within the next 5.4 years.

Winter 1957

Perhaps the worst nuclear disaster in history occurred in the Soviet Union in the southern Ural Mountains near the city of Kyshtym, believed to then be the center of plutonium production for Soviet nuclear weapons. The cause of the accident and the number of people killed and injured remain a secret. However, in 1989, Soviet officials admitted that several hundred square kilometers were contaminated with radioactivity when a tank containing radioactive wastes exploded and that 10,000 people were evacuated. Today, the area is deserted and sealed off, and the names of 30 towns and villages in the region have disappeared from Soviet maps.

October 7, 1957

A water-cooled, graphite-moderated reactor used to produce plutonium for nuclear weapons north of Liverpool, England, caught fire as the Chernobyl nuclear plant did 29 years later. By the time the fire was put out, 516 square kilometers (200 square miles) of countryside had been contaminated with radioactive material. Exposure to high levels of radiation caused an estimated 33 people to die prematurely from cancer.

March 22, 1975

Against regulations, a maintenance worker used a candle to test for air leaks at the Brown's Ferry commercial nuclear reactor near Decatur, Alabama. That set off a fire that knocked out five emergency core-cooling systems. Although the reactor's cooling water dropped to a dangerous level, backup systems prevented any radioactive material from escaping into the environment.

At the same plant, in 1978, a worker's rubber boot fell into a reactor and led to an unsuccessful search costing $2.8 million. Such incidents, caused mostly by unpredictable human errors, are common in most nuclear plants.

March 29, 1979

The worst accident in the history of U.S. commercial nuclear power happened at the Three Mile Island (TMI) nuclear plant near Harrisburg, Pennsylvania (Figure 18-18). One of its two reactors lost its coolant water because of a series of mechanical failures and human operator errors not anticipated in safety studies. The reactor's core became partially uncovered. At least 70% of the core was damaged, and about 50% of it melted and fell to the bottom of the reactor. Unknown amounts of ionizing radiation es-

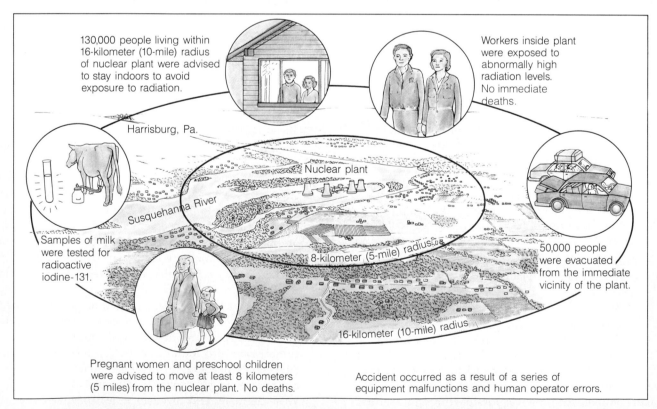

130,000 people living within 16-kilometer (10-mile) radius of nuclear plant were advised to stay indoors to avoid exposure to radiation.

Workers inside plant were exposed to abnormally high radiation levels. No immediate deaths.

Harrisburg, Pa.

Nuclear plant

Susquehanna River

Samples of milk were tested for radioactive iodine-131.

8-kilometer (5-mile) radius

50,000 people were evacuated from the immediate vicinity of the plant.

16-kilometer (10-mile) radius

Pregnant women and preschool children were advised to move at least 8 kilometers (5 miles) from the nuclear plant. No deaths.

Accident occurred as a result of a series of equipment malfunctions and human operator errors.

Figure 18-18   Three Mile Island (TMI) in eastern Pennsylvania, where a nuclear accident occurred on March 29, 1979.

caped into the atmosphere, and 144,000 people were evacuated. Investigators found that if a stuck valve had stayed opened for just another 30 to 60 minutes, there would have been a complete meltdown. No one is known to have died because of the accident, but its long-term health effects on workers and nearby residents are still being debated because data published on the radiation released during the accident are contradictory and incomplete.

Partial cleanup of the damaged TMI reactor will cost more than $1 billion, more than the $700-million construction cost of the reactor. Also, about $187 million of taxpayers' money has been spent by the Department of Energy on the TMI cleanup. Plant owners have also paid out $25 million to over 2,100 people who filed lawsuits for damages. When the partial cleanup is completed, the plant will be sealed and some radioactive debris will be left in the plant for 20 to 90 years.

Confusing and misleading statements about the accident issued by Metropolitan Edison (which owned the plant) and by the Nuclear Regulatory Commission (NRC) eroded public confidence in the safety of nuclear power. Critics of nuclear power contend that it is mostly luck that has prevented the TMI accident and hundreds of serious incidents since then from leading to a complete meltdown and breach of a reactor's containment building. U.S. nuclear industry officials claim that a catastrophic accident has not happened because the industry's multiple-backup safety systems work.

April 26, 1986

At 1:23 A.M., there were two huge explosions inside one of the four graphite-moderated, water-cooled reactors at the Chernobyl nuclear power plant north of Kiev in the Soviet Union. These blasts blew the 909-metric-ton (1,000-ton) roof off the reactor building, set the graphite core on fire, and flung radioactive debris several thousand feet into the air (Figure 18-19). Over the next several days, winds carried some of those radioactive materials over parts of the Soviet Union and much of eastern and western Europe as far as 2,000 kilometers (1,250 miles) from the plant. The accident happened when engineers turned off most of the reactor's automatic safety and warning systems to keep them from interfering with an unauthorized safety experiment (Figure

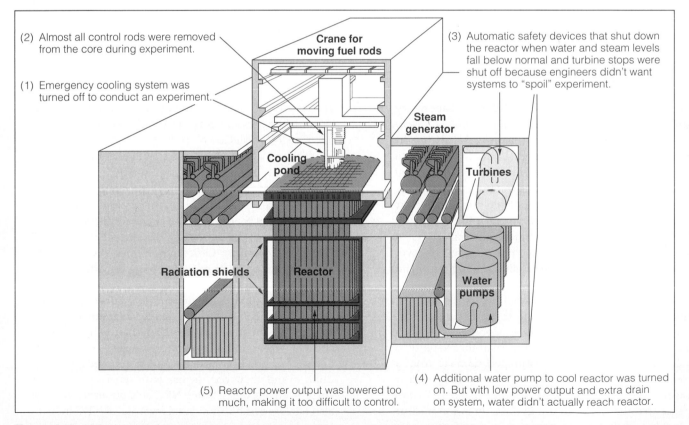

(2) Almost all control rods were removed from the core during experiment.

(1) Emergency cooling system was turned off to conduct an experiment.

Crane for moving fuel rods

(3) Automatic safety devices that shut down the reactor when water and steam levels fall below normal and turbine stops were shut off because engineers didn't want systems to "spoil" experiment.

Steam generator

Cooling pond

Turbines

Radiation shields

Reactor

Water pumps

(5) Reactor power output was lowered too much, making it too difficult to control.

(4) Additional water pump to cool reactor was turned on. But with low power output and extra drain on system, water didn't actually reach reactor.

Figure 18-19 Major events leading to the Chernobyl nuclear power plant accident on April 26, 1986, in the Soviet Union.

18-19). It is likely that little radioactivity would have been released had the reactor been built with a strong containment dome like those found on commercial nuclear reactors in the United States and most other countries (Figure 18-16).

About 135,000 people living within 29 kilometers (18 miles) of the plant were eventually evacuated by an armada of 1,100 buses and trucks. According to Soviet officials, most, if not all, of those people will never be able to return to their contaminated homes and farms.

By 1989, exposure to high levels of ionizing radiation at the accident site had killed 36 plant workers, fire fighters, and rescuers. An additional 237 people were hospitalized with acute radiation sickness. Many of those people will probably die prematurely from cancer in coming years.

The Soviet government has compiled a list of 576,000 potential health victims who may contract cancers, thyroid tumors, eye cataracts, and become sterile. But some top

Soviet officials think exposure to ionizing radiation will affect at least 4 million people, most in the western USSR, but some as distant as Germany and Sweden. The immediate and later death tolls would have been much higher if the accident had happened during the day, when people were not sheltered in houses, and if the wind had been blowing toward Kiev and its 2.4 million people.

A 1990 study by a Soviet governmental organization concluded that the total cost of the accident, including lost electricity production from plants closed down as a result of the incident, will reach $358 billion — almost 90 times the original estimate and about five times larger than the revenues generated in the entire history of the Soviet nuclear industry. The report concluded that the country would have been better off economically if it had not built any nuclear reactors.

Records of radiation levels have been classified top secret, casting doubt on whether the true effects of

the accident will ever be known. Some Soviet politicians and scientists charge that the accident released 20 times more radiation than the government has admitted, with 300 people killed in the explosion, fire, and immediate nuclear fallout.

Because of recent measurements of radioactive contamination, the Soviet government plans to move 200,000 more people to other areas. Some Soviet officials claim that 2.2 million residents need to be moved. Today, the reactor is entombed in concrete and metal.

In 1987, the United States permanently shut down a Chernobyl-type military reactor at Hanford, Washington; 54 serious safety violations had occurred at the plant during 1985 and 1986. The Chernobyl accident eroded public support for nuclear power worldwide and showed people that they need to be concerned about the safety of nuclear plants within and outside the borders of their countries.

A 1982 study by the Sandia National Laboratory estimated that a possible, but highly unlikely, *worst-case accident* in a reactor near a large U.S. city might cause 50,000 to 100,000 immediate deaths, 10,000 to 40,000 later deaths from cancer, and $100 billion to $150 billion in damages. Most citizens and businesses suffering injuries or property damage from a major nuclear accident would get little if any financial reimbursement. Since the beginnings of commercial nuclear power in the 1950s, insurance companies have refused to cover more than a small part of the possible damages from an accident.

In 1957, Congress enacted the Price-Anderson Act, which limited insurance liability from a nuclear accident in the United States. In 1988, Congress extended the law for 20 years and raised the insurance liability to $7 billion — only 7% of the estimated damage from a worst-case accident. Without this law, the U.S. nuclear power industry would never have developed. Critics charge that the law is an unfair subsidy of the nuclear industry and that if nuclear power plants are not safe enough to operate with adequate insurance, then they

are not safe enough to operate at all. Critics also contend that nuclear accident plans in the United States are inadequate (see Pro/Con on p. 493).

There is also widespread lack of confidence in the NRC's ability to enforce nuclear safety. In 1989, NRC documents revealed that four out of five licensed U.S. reactors had failed to make all the new safety changes required in 1979 after the TMI accident. None of those plants was shut down by the NRC. According to a 1987 General Accounting Office report, the NRC has also allowed plants to continue operating even after a record of repeated safety violations.

Congressional hearings in 1987 uncovered evidence that high-level NRC staff members have destroyed documents and obstructed investigations of criminal wrongdoing by utilities, suggested ways utilities can evade commission regulations, and provided utilities and their contractors with advance notice of surprise inspections. Some NRC field supervisors have also harassed and intimidated lower-level NRC inspectors who cite utilities for too many violations. In 1986, U.S. citizens learned that since the mid-1950s, there had

After the TMI accident, 16-kilometer (10-mile) evacuation zones were set up around all U.S. commercial reactors. (Evacuation zones are areas to be evacuated in case of a nuclear accident.) In 1986, critics of nuclear power called for extending the evacuation zone to at least the 30 kilometers (19 miles) Soviet officials found necessary after the Chernobyl accident.

A serious problem is that areas around many U.S. reactors are up to ten times more densely populated than those around most Soviet reactors. For example, whereas 135,000 had to be evacuated because of the Chernobyl accident, about 1.5 million people would have to be evacuated if a similar accident occurred at the Indian Point plant near New York City.

Many urban areas near U.S. reactors would be impossible to evacuate; most Americans would get into their cars and clog exit routes. At Chernobyl, few people had cars.

Instead of increasing the evacuation zone, the U.S. nuclear industry has been pushing the NRC to *reduce* the evacuation area around reactors to as low as 1.6 kilometers (1 mile). Industry officials contend new safety studies show that less radiation would escape in the event of an accident than previously thought.

Environmentalists charge that the industry wants to reduce the size of evacuation zones to prevent state and local governments from blocking the licensing of new nuclear plants with inadequate evacuation plans.

In 1988, just before leaving office, President Reagan issued an executive order allowing the NRC to give operating permits for nuclear power plants without states or localities approving or participating in emergency evacuation plans they believe to be inadequate. Do you agree with that executive decision?

been serious disregard for the safety of workers and nearby residents in the country's nuclear weapons production facilities (see Spotlight on p. 494).

DISPOSAL AND STORAGE OF RADIOACTIVE WASTES Each part of the nuclear fuel cycle (Figure 18-17) for military and commercial nuclear reactors produces solid, liquid, and gaseous radioactive wastes. Some of these, called *low-level radioactive wastes*, give off small amounts of ionizing radiation, usually for a long time. Others are *high-level radioactive wastes*, which give off large amounts of ionizing radiation for a short time and small amounts for a long time.

From the 1940s to 1970, most low-level radioactive waste produced in the United States (and most other countries) was dumped into the ocean in steel drums. Since 1970, low-level radioactive wastes from military activities have been buried at government-run landfills. Three of these have been closed because of leakage.

Low-level waste materials from commercial nuclear power plants, hospitals, universities, industries, and other producers are put in steel drums and shipped to regional landfills run by federal and state governments. By 1990, three of the six commercial landfills had been closed because of radioactive contamination of groundwater and nearby property.

In June 1990, the Nuclear Regulatory Commission caused a shockwave of opposition from environmentalists and the EPA when it proposed that most of the country's low-level radioactive waste be removed from federal regulation. These wastes would then be handled like ordinary trash and dumped in landfills, incinerated, reused, or recycled into consumer products. According to the NRC, exposure to radiation from these unregulated wastes would kill 2,500 Americans — 1 out of every 100,000 citizens. Other estimates show as many as 12,412 more cancer deaths per year.

The NRC contends that this loss of life is acceptable because it would save the nuclear power industry at least $1 billion over the next 20 years. This decision was made despite several recent studies showing that the hazards to humans from exposure to low-level radiation is at least 30 times higher than previously estimated. In 1990, several environmental groups filed a suit to overturn the NRC policy.

Most high-level radioactive wastes are spent fuel rods from commercial nuclear power plants and an assortment of wastes from nuclear weapons plants. After 34 years of research and debate, scientists still don't agree on a safe method of storing these wastes (see Case Study at top of p. 496). Regardless of the storage method, most U.S. citizens strongly oppose the location of a low- or high-level nuclear waste disposal facility anywhere near them (see Case Study at bottom of p. 496).

DECOMMISSIONING NUCLEAR POWER PLANTS AND WEAPONS FACILITIES The useful operating life of today's nuclear power plants is hoped to be 30 to 40 years, but many plants are aging faster than expected. After about 30 years or so of bombardment by neutrons released by nuclear fission (Figure 3-11), the metallic walls of a reactor's pressure vessel become brittle, which can result in cracks that might expose the highly radioactive core (Figure 18-16). Decades of pressure and temperature changes gradually weaken tubes in the reactor's steam generator, which can crack, releasing contaminated water. Corrosion of pipes and valves throughout the system can cause them to crack.

Because the core and many other parts contain large amounts of radioactive materials, a nuclear plant

Since 1986, government studies and once-secret documents have revealed that most of the nuclear weapons production facilities supervised by the Department of Energy have been operated with gross disregard for the safety of their workers and people in nearby areas. Since 1957, these facilities have released huge quantities of radioactive particles into the air and dumped tons of potentially cancer-inducing radioactive waste and toxic substances into flowing creeks and leaking pits without telling local residents.

Between 1945 and 1985, numerous serious incidents were kept secret while government officials repeatedly assured local residents that there was no danger from radioactive contamination. DOE officials also admit that the government ignored repeated requests from private contractors running weapons facilities to provide funds for improving safety and handling procedures at these plants.

In 1990, a federally funded scientific panel found that between 1945 and 1947, an enormous, unreported leak occurred at the Hanford, Washington, nuclear weapons plant, which was shut down in 1988. The scientists estimated that from 1945 to 1947, as many as 13,500 nearby residents of Washington and Oregon received dangerously high doses of radioactive iodine, which can cause thyroid disorders and cancers.

No one will ever know how many workers and innocent people living near weapons facilities have been, or will be, afflicted with cancer, birth defects, and thyroid problems because of releases of radioactive and toxic materials from these plants. Ohio's Senator John Glenn summed up the situation: "We are poisoning our own people in the name of national security."

It is difficult and costly for afflicted individuals to prove in court that their ailments and the deaths of loved ones were caused by radioactivity from weapons facilities. Even if that can be done, contractors running these facilities and the federal government are largely immune from lawsuits to recover damages. No one, it appears, is liable or accountable.

The General Accounting Office and the Department of Energy estimate that it will cost taxpayers $84 billion to $270 billion over 60 years to get these facilities cleaned up and in safe working order. Without loud and constant pressure from citizens, Congress may not appropriate enough money to do the job and ensure that rigid safety standards are required at all government nuclear facilities.

---

cannot be abandoned or demolished by a wrecking ball the way a worn-out coal-fired power plant can be. Most of the radioactivity decays within 50 years, but it takes 3 million years for an abandoned plant to become no more radioactive than its original uranium fuel.

Decommissioning nuclear power plants and nuclear weapons plants is the last step in the nuclear fuel cycle. Three ways have been proposed.

1. *Immediate dismantlement*: removing spent fuel, decontaminating and taking the reactor apart after shutdown, and shipping all radioactive debris to a radioactive-waste burial facility. This promptly rids the plant site of radioactive materials and is the least expensive option, but it exposes work crews to the highest level of radiation and results in the largest volume of radioactive waste.

2. *Mothballing*: removing spent fuel, putting up a barrier, and setting up a 24-hour security guard system to keep out intruders for 30 to 100 years before dismantlement. This permits short-lived radioactive isotopes to decay, which reduces the threat to dismantlement crews and the volume of contaminated waste.

3. *Entombment*: removing spent fuel, covering the reactor with reinforced concrete, and putting up a barrier to keep out intruders. This allows for radioactive decay but passes a dangerous legacy to future generations.

Each method involves shutting down the plant, removing the spent fuel from the reactor core, draining all liquids, flushing all pipes, and sending all radioactive materials to an approved waste storage site yet to be built.

Worldwide, more than 20 commercial reactors (4 in the United States) have been retired and are awaiting decommissioning. Another 229 large commercial reactors (67 in the United States) will need to be retired between 2000 and 2010.

Utility company officials estimate that dismantlement of a typical large reactor should cost about $170 million and mothballing $225 million. Most analysts consider the dismantlement figure too low and estimate that the decommissioning of existing U.S. nuclear power plants could cost $100 billion—about $1 billion per reactor. Since the initial industry estimates for the cost of building nuclear power plants were low by at least 1000%, the higher estimates may also turn out to be low.

So far, utilities have only $3.2 billion set aside for nuclear plant decommissioning. The balance of the cost could be passed along to ratepayers and taxpayers and would add to the already-high cost of electricity produced by nuclear fission. Politicians and nuclear industry officials in the United States and other countries may be tempted to mothball retired plants and pass dismantlement costs and problems on to the next generation.

Some nuclear industry scientists, the NRC, and the Bush administration have proposed renovating existing nuclear plants to extend their useful lives an additional 20 to 40 years. However, this will be difficult, expensive, and highly controversial. Environmentalists call this proposal a wasteful and potentially dangerous financial bailout of the declining nuclear power plant construction industry.

PROLIFERATION OF NUCLEAR WEAPONS Since 1958, the United States has been giving away and selling to other countries various forms of nuclear technology. Today, at least 14 other countries sell nuclear technology in the international marketplace.

For decades, the U.S. government denied that the information, components, and materials used in the nuclear fuel cycle could be used to make nuclear weapons. In 1981, however, a Los Alamos National Laboratory report admitted: "There is no technical demarcation between the military and civilian reactor and there never was one"—something environmentalists had been saying for years.

Today, 134 countries have signed the 1968 Nuclear-Nonproliferation Treaty. They have agreed to forgo building nuclear weapons in return for help with commercial nuclear power. The International Atomic Energy Agency (IAEA) was established to monitor compliance.

However, the system is not tight enough. Nuclear facilities belonging to India, Israel, South Africa, Argentina, Brazil, Pakistan, and other countries that have not signed the treaty are not monitored. Nuclear facilities in countries such as China, France, Great Britain, the Soviet Union, North Korea, and the United States that have signed the treaty are generally not monitored by the IAEA.

There is clear evidence that the governments of Israel, South Africa, Pakistan, and India have made almost 200 nuclear weapons, mostly by diverting weapons-grade fuel from research reactors and commercial power plants. It takes only about 10 kilograms (22 pounds) of plutonium to make a Nagasaki-size nuclear bomb. At least six other countries—Argentina, Brazil, Libya, Syria, Iraq, and Iran—are actively seeking to make nuclear weapons or to buy them from black-market sources. A typical 1,000-megawatt nuclear re-

actor generates about fifteen bombs' worth of plutonium a year.

Sophisticated terrorist groups can also make a small atomic bomb by using about 2.2 kilograms (5 pounds) of plutonium or uranium-233, or about 5 kilograms (11 pounds) of uranium-235. Such a bomb could blow up a large building or a small city block and would contaminate a much larger area with radioactive materials for centuries. For example, a crude 10-kiloton nuclear weapon placed properly and detonated during working hours could topple the World Trade Center in New York City. This could easily kill more people than those killed by the atomic bomb the United States dropped on Hiroshima in 1945.

Spent reactor fuel is so highly radioactive that theft is unlikely, but plutonium separated at commercial and military reprocessing plants (Figure 18-17) is much less radioactive and can be handled fairly easily. Although plutonium shipments are heavily guarded, plutonium could be stolen from nuclear weapons or reprocessing plants, especially by employees. Each year, about 3% of the 142,000 people working in 127 U.S. nuclear weapons facilities in 23 states are fired because of drug use, mental instability, or other security risks. By the mid-1990s, hundreds of shipments of plutonium separated from reprocessing facilities in France, Great Britain, Germany, Japan, and India, will be travelling by land, sea, and air within and between countries.

Those who would steal plutonium need not bother to make atomic bombs. They could simply use a conventional explosive charge to disperse the plutonium into the atmosphere from atop any tall building. Dispersed in that way, 1 kilogram (2.2 pounds) of plutonium oxide powder theoretically would contaminate 8 square kilometers (3 square miles) with dangerous levels of radioactivity for several hundred thousand years.

One way to reduce the diversion of plutonium fuel from the nuclear fuel cycle is to contaminate it with other substances that make it useless as weapons material. So far, no one has come up with a way to do this, and most nuclear experts doubt that it can be done.

The best ways to slow down the spread of bomb grade material are to abandon civilian reprocessing of power plant fuel, develop substitutes for highly enriched uranium in research reactors, and tighten international safeguards.

SOARING COSTS After the United States dropped atomic bombs on Hiroshima and Nagasaki, ending World War II, the scientists who developed the bomb and the elected officials responsible for its use were determined to show the world that the peaceful uses of atomic energy would outweigh the immense harm it had done. One part of this "Atoms for Peace" program was to use nuclear power to produce electricity. American utility companies were skeptical but began ordering nuclear power plants in the late 1950s for four reasons.

Some scientists believe that the long-term safe storage or disposal of high-level radioactive wastes is technically possible. Others disagree, pointing out that it is impossible to show that any method will work for the 10,000 years of fail-safe storage needed for reprocessed wastes and the 240,000 years needed for unreprocessed wastes. The following are some of the proposed methods and their possible drawbacks:

1. *Bury it deep underground.* The currently favored method is to package unreprocessed spent fuel rods and bury them in a deep underground salt, granite, or other stable geological formation that is earthquake resistant and waterproof (Figure 18-20). A better method would be to reprocess the waste to remove very long-lived radioactive isotopes and convert what is left into a dry solid. The solid would then be fused with glass or a ceramic material and sealed in metal canisters for burial. This would reduce burial time from 240,000 years to 10,000 years, but it is expensive. Some geologists question the idea of burying nuclear wastes.

They argue that the drilling and tunnelling to build the repository might cause water leakage and weaken resistance to earthquakes. They also contend that with present geological knowledge, scientists cannot make meaningful 10,000- to 240,000-year projections about earthquake probability and paths of groundwater flows in underground storage areas. According to a 1990 report by the National Academy of Sciences: "Use of geological information — to pretend to be able to make very accurate prediction of long-term site behavior — is scientifically unsound."

2. *Shoot it into space or into the sun.* Costs would be very high, and a launch accident, such as the explosion of the space shuttle *Challenger*, could disperse high-level radioactive wastes over large areas of the earth's surface.

3. *Bury it under the antarctic ice sheets or the Greenland ice caps.* The long-term stability of the ice sheets is not known. They could be destabilized by heat from the wastes, and retrieval of the wastes would

be difficult or impossible if the method failed.

4. *Dump it into descending, subduction zones in the deep ocean* (Figure 7-5). Wastes could eventually be spewed out somewhere else by volcanic activity. Waste containers might leak and contaminate the ocean before being carried downward, and retrieval would be impossible if the method did not work.

5. *Change it into harmless, or less harmful, isotopes.* At this time, there is no way to do this. Even if a method were developed, costs would probably be extremely high. Resulting toxic materials and low-level, but very long-lived, radioactive wastes would have to be disposed of safely.

6. *Use it in shielded batteries to run small electric generators.* Researchers claim that a wastebasket-size battery using spent fuel could produce enough electricity to run five homes for 28 years or longer at about half the current price of electricity. However, leakage could contaminate homes and communities. Dispersing high-

In 1982, Congress passed the Nuclear Waste Policy Act. It set a timetable for the Department of Energy to choose a site and build the country's first deep underground repository for storage of high-level radioactive wastes from commercial nuclear reactors. In 1985, the Department of Energy announced plans to build the first repository, at a cost of at least $10 billion, based on the design shown in Figure 18-20.

The repository is supposed be built in a type of volcanic rock called tuff on federal land in the Yucca

Mountain desert region, 161 kilometers (100 miles) northwest of Las Vegas, Nevada. Construction was to begin in 1998, and the facility was scheduled to open by 2003.

In 1990, the Department of Energy put off the opening date to at least 2010, but it may never open. A young, active volcano is only 11 kilometers (7 miles) away, and according to DOE's own data, there are 32 active earthquake faults on the site itself. Nevada ranks just behind Alaska and California in frequency of earthquakes.

Yucca Mountain's many geologic faults and its large amount of fractured rock also suggest that water flowing through the site could escape through a network of cracks. Some geologists estimate that that water carrying leached radioactive wastes could move 5 kilometers (3.1 miles) or more from the site in 400 to 500 years. This would automatically make it ineligible as a repository under current federal standards.

Since 1988, the state of Nevada has refused to give the Department of Energy permission to study the

level radioactive waste throughout a country would probably be politically unacceptable. Besides, this method would use only a small portion of the nuclear waste.

Critics of nuclear power are appalled that after decades, there has been so little effort to solve the serious problem of what to do with nuclear waste while the industry has plunged ahead and built hundreds of nuclear reactors and weapons facilities. What do you think should be done?

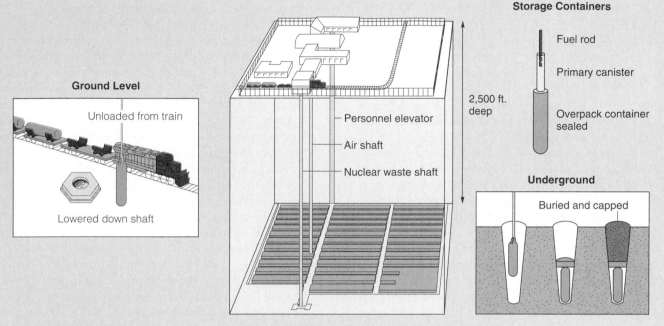

Ground Level

Unloaded from train

Lowered down shaft

2,500 ft. deep

Personnel elevator

Air shaft

Nuclear waste shaft

Storage Containers

Fuel rod

Primary canister

Overpack container sealed

Underground

Buried and capped

Figure 18-20 Proposed general design for deep underground permanent storage of high-level radioactive wastes from commercial nuclear power plants in the United States. (Source: U.S. Department of Energy)

site but was overruled by a federal court in 1991. President Bush's 1991 energy plan calls for states to lose their authority in the selection of radioactive waste sites.

The DOE has also asked Congress to allow it to begin immediate construction of an aboveground interim storage facility for high-level radioactive wastes — a sort of halfway house for wastes awaiting permanent disposal. Critics believe that doing this would seriously undercut efforts to find a permanent storage facility. They fear the temporary fa-

cility could become the permanent site, with DOE declaring the problem solved.

Citizens in cities and states along the proposed routes for transporting these highly radioactive wastes to the Nevada repository are becoming increasingly concerned about the possibility of accidents that would release radioactive materials. Many cities are passing laws to ban shipments of radioactive materials through their areas, but such laws may be overridden by the federal government.

In 1991, the Department of Energy proposed that the handling of nuclear waste be turned over to the private sector, arguing that this would reduce government accountability and regulation and lower budget expenditures. This passing of a political hot potato to the private sector would also limit public access to information about nuclear waste by avoiding disclosure requirements faced by government agencies. What do you think should be done?

1. The Atomic Energy Commission and builders of nuclear reactors projected that nuclear power would produce electricity at a very low cost compared with using coal and other alternatives.

2. The nuclear industry projected that nuclear reactors would have an 88% *capacity factor* — a measure of the time a reactor would operate each year at full power.

3. The first round of commercial reactors was built with the government paying about one-fourth of the cost and with the reactors provided to utilities at a fixed cost with no cost overruns allowed. (The builders lost their shirts but knew they could make big profits on later rounds of plants.)

4. Congress passed the Price-Anderson Act, which protected the nuclear industry and utilities from significant liability to the general public in case of accidents.

It was an offer utility company officials could not resist. Today, many wish they had.

Experience has shown that nuclear power is a very expensive way to produce electricity, even when it is heavily subsidized and enjoys partial protection from free-market competition with other energy sources. According to the Department of Energy, commercial nuclear power received over $1 trillion in research and development and other federal subsidies between 1952 and 1990 — an average of $9 billion per reactor. Yet, after almost four decades of subsidies and development, commercial nuclear reactors in the United States now deliver less of the country's energy than that provided by wood and crop wastes with hardly any subsidies.

New nuclear power plants produce electricity at an average of about 15 cents per kilowatt-hour — equal to buying oil at $247 per barrel. These already-high costs do not include most of the costs of storing radioactive wastes and decommissioning worn-out plants. Nuclear cost analyst, Charles Komanoff, has calculated that including these and other environmental and social costs of nuclear power would add about 9 cents per kilowatt-hour to its already high cost. All other methods of producing electricity in the United States, except solar voltaic and solar thermal, have average costs below those of new nuclear power plants (Figure 17-10). By the year 2000, solar photovoltaics (Figure 17-18) and solar thermal with natural gas backup (Figure 17-17) are expected to be cheaper than nuclear power for producing electricity.

Operating costs of nuclear plants have been higher than projected because U.S. pressurized water reactors (PWRs) operate at an average of only about 60% of their full-time, full-power capacity — far below the 88% capacity projected by proponents of nuclear power in the 1950s. The average capacity factor for PWRs in the United Kingdom is only 51% and those in Sweden 54%. Those in other countries are higher — Japan and Canada (71%), France (74%), the former West Germany (82%), and Switzerland (87%) — mostly because of standardized design and better management.

New nuclear plants in France and Japan cost about half as much per kilowatt of power to build as those in the United States because they are better planned and use standardized designs. However, France ran up an enormous $46-billion debt to finance its nuclear industry, and France and Japan now produce more electricity than they need.

In the United States, where almost every nuclear plant has a different design, poor planning and management and stricter safety regulations since the TMI accident have increased costs and lengthened construction time. Currently, new nuclear power plants cost three times as much to build as equivalent coal-fired plants with the latest air pollution control equipment.

Banks and other lending institutions have become skeptical about financing new U.S. nuclear power plants. The Three Mile Island accident showed that utility companies could lose $1 billion or more of equipment in an hour and at least $1 billion more in cleanup costs, even without any known harmful effects on public health. The business magazine *Forbes* has called the failure of the U.S. nuclear power program "the largest managerial disaster in U.S. business history." It involves perhaps $1 trillion in wasted investments, cost overruns, and unnecessarily high electricity costs, and production of more electricity than the country needs. Abandoned and cost-ineffective nuclear power plants in the United States have generated at least $10 billion of losses for utilities' stockholders. No U.S. utility company is planning the construction of any new nuclear power plants because it is no longer a cost-effective or wise investment.

Is nuclear power dead in the United States and most other MDCs? You might think so because of its high costs and tremendous public opposition, but powerful economic and political forces strive to maintain and expand the world's nuclear power industry (see Pro/Con on p. 500). Also, the U.S. Department of Energy and energy agencies in many other MDCs are heavily staffed with officials who continue to push for nuclear power instead of other, safer, and more cost-effective alternatives.

PROS AND CONS OF CONVENTIONAL NUCLEAR FISSION Using nuclear fission to produce electricity has many advantages. Nuclear plants don't release particulate matter, sulfur dioxide, or nitrogen oxides into the atmosphere, as do coal-fired plants. Water pollution and disruption of land are low to moderate if the entire nuclear fuel cycle operates normally. Multiple safety systems greatly decrease the likelihood of a catastrophic accident releasing deadly radioactive material into the environment.

Nuclear power also has many disadvantages. It produces electricity, which cannot be used to run vehicles without the development of affordable, long-lasting batteries to propel electric cars. Construction and operating costs for nuclear power plants in the United States and most countries are high and rising, even with enormous government subsidies.

Standardized design and mass production can bring costs down, but electricity can still be produced by safer methods at a cost equal to, or lower than, that of nuclear power. Although large-scale accidents are infrequent, a combination of mechanical failure and human errors, sabotage, or shipping accidents could again release deadly radioactive materials into the environment.

The net useful energy yield of nuclear-generated electricity is probably low (Figure 3-19), especially if the entire nuclear fuel cycle (Figure 18-17) is included. Scientists disagree over how high-level radioactive wastes should be stored, and some doubt that an acceptably safe method can ever be developed. Also, some carbon dioxide is released as part of the nuclear fuel cycle.

Today's military and commercial nuclear energy programs commit future generations to storing dangerous radioactive wastes for thousands of years even if nuclear fission power is abandoned tomorrow. The existence of nuclear power technology also helps spread knowledge and materials that can be used to make nuclear weapons. For these reasons, many people feel that it is unethical, uneconomical, and unnecessary to use nuclear power to produce electricity.

18-4 Breeder Nuclear Fission and Nuclear Fusion

NONRENEWABLE BREEDER NUCLEAR FISSION
At the present rate of use, the world's supply of uranium should last for at least 100 years and perhaps 200 years. However, some proponents of nuclear power project a sharp rise in the use of nuclear fission to produce electricity after the year 2000. They urge the development and widespread use of breeder nuclear fission reactors that generate nuclear fuel to start up other breeders (see Guest Essay on p. 507).

Conventional fission reactors use fissionable uranium-235, which makes up only 0.7% of natural uranium ore. **Breeder nuclear fission reactors** convert nonfissionable uranium-238 into fissionable plutonium-239. Since breeders would use over 99% of the uranium in ore deposits, the world's known uranium reserves would last 1,000 years, and perhaps several thousand years.

Under normal operation, a breeder reactor is considered by its proponents to be much safer than a con-

ventional fission reactor. However, if the reactor's safety system should fail, the reactor could lose some of its liquid sodium coolant. This could cause a runaway fission chain reaction and perhaps a small nuclear explosion with the force of several hundred kilograms of TNT. Such an explosion could blast open the containment building, releasing a cloud of highly radioactive gases and particulate matter. Leaks of flammable liquid sodium also can also cause fires, as has happened with all experimental breeder reactors built so far.

Since 1966, small experimental breeder reactors have been built in the the United Kingdom, the Soviet Union, Germany, Japan, and France. In December 1986, France began operating a commercial-size breeder reactor, the Superphenix. It cost three times the original estimate to build. The little electricity it has produced is twice as expensive as that generated by France's conventional fission reactors. In 1987, shortly after the reactor began operating at full power, it began leaking liquid sodium coolant and was shut down. Repairs may be so expensive that the reactor may not be put back into operation.

Tentative plans to build full-size commercial breeders in Germany, the Soviet Union, the United Kingdom, and Japan have been cancelled because of the excessive cost of France's reactor and an excess of electric generating capacity. Also, experimental breeders built so far produce only about one-fourth of the plutonium-239 each year needed to replace their own fissionable material. If this serious problem is not solved, it would take 100 to 200 years at best for breeders to begin producing enough plutonium to fuel a significant number of other breeders. But some nuclear advocates urge us to step up research on breeder reactors because they will be needed sometime during the next century (see Guest Essay on p. 507).

NUCLEAR FUSION Scientists hope someday to use controlled nuclear fusion (Figure 3-12) to provide an almost limitless source of energy for producing high-temperature heat and electricity. For 43 years, research has focused on the D-T nuclear fusion reaction, in which two isotopes of hydrogen—deuterium (D) and tritium (T)—fuse at about 100 million degrees, ten times as hot as the sun's interior.

Another possibility is the D-D fusion reaction, in which the nuclei of two deuterium atoms fuse together at much higher temperatures. If developed, it would run on virtually unlimited heavy water (D_2O) fuel obtained from seawater at a cost of about ten cents a gallon.

After 43 years of research, high-temperature nuclear fusion is still at the laboratory stage. Deuterium and tritium atoms have been forced together by using electromagnetic reactors the size of 12 locomotives, 120-trillion-watt laser beams, and bombardment with high-speed particles. So far, none of those approaches has produced more energy than it uses.

Since the Three Mile Island accident, the U.S. nuclear industry and utility companies have financed a vigorous advertising campaign by the U.S. Council for Energy Awareness. This campaign, with a $340 million budget in 1988, is designed to improve the industry's image, resell nuclear power to the American public, and downgrade the importance of solar energy, conservation, geothermal energy, wind, and hydropower as alternatives to nuclear power.

The campaign's magazine and television ads do not tell readers and viewers that the ads are paid for by the nuclear industry. Most ads use the argument that more nuclear power is needed in the United States to reduce dependence on imported oil.

The truth is that since 1979, only about 5% (3% in 1990) of the electricity in the United States has been produced by burning oil, and 95% of that is residual oil that can't be used for other purposes. Thus, *building more nuclear plants will not save the country any significant amount of domestic or imported oil*.

The nuclear industry also claims that nuclear power, unlike coal burning, does not add any carbon dioxide to the atmosphere. They argue that replacing coal-burning power plants with nuclear plants would help delay projected climate changes from an enhanced greenhouse effect. It is true that nuclear power plants don't release carbon dioxide, but the fuel cycle involved in using nuclear power does produce some carbon dioxide, mainly in the processing of uranium fuel (Figure 18-17). However, the amount of carbon dioxide produced per unit of electricity is only one-sixth that produced by a coal-burning plant.

The nuclear industry hopes to persuade governments and utility companies to build hundreds of new "second-generation" plants using standardized designs. They are supposed to be safer, be quicker to build (3 to 5 years), operate at full power 85% of the time, and last 60 years. Some nuclear experts believe that we can make nuclear power acceptably safe and that we have little choice but to take the risks involved in doing this (see Guest Essay on p. 507).

Nuclear advocates call the new designs, still only on drawing boards, *inherently safe*. However, Robert Pollard, a former safety engineer with the NRC, points out that any scheme for fissioning atoms is inherently dangerous. You can build new reactors that are safer than existing ones, but you can't make them inherently safe.

Scientists disagree about which of the proposed new designs to pursue, and it would take at least 30 years and trillions of dollars for a new type of reactor to begin supplying 10% of U.S. electricity. According to *Nucleonics Week*, an important nuclear industry publication, "experts are flatly unconvinced that safety has been achieved — or even substantially reduced — by the new designs." In addition, construction costs will probably be higher than for conventional nuclear power plants of the same size.

None of the new designs solves the problem of what to do with nuclear waste or the problem of the use of nuclear technology and fuel to build nuclear weapons. Indeed, these problems would become more serious as the number of nuclear

---

If researchers eventually can get more energy out than they put in, the next step is to build a small fusion reactor and then scale it up to commercial size. This task is considered one of the most difficult engineering problems ever undertaken. The estimated cost of a commercial fusion reactor is at least four times that of a comparable conventional fission reactor.

In 1989, two chemists claimed to have brought about some D-D nuclear fusion at room temperature using a simple apparatus. However, subsequent experiments could not substantiate their claims.

If everything goes right, a commercial nuclear fusion power plant might be built as early as 2030. Even if everything goes right, energy experts don't expect nuclear fusion to be a significant source of energy until 2100, if then. Meanwhile, several other, quicker, cheaper, and safer ways can produce and save more electricity than we need.

18-5 Developing an Energy Strategy for the United States

OVERALL EVALUATION OF U.S. ENERGY ALTERNATIVES Table 18-1 summarizes the biggest advantages and disadvantages of the energy alternatives discussed in this and the preceding chapter, with emphasis on their potential in the United States. Energy experts argue over these and other projections, and new data and innovations may change some information in this table, but it does provide a useful framework for making decisions based on presently available information. Four basic conclusions can be drawn.

1. The best short-term, intermediate, and long-term alternatives for the United States and other countries are a combination of improving efficiency of

plants increased from a few hundred to the many thousands needed to slow global warming only a little.

If half of the U.S. use of coal burned to produce electricity was displaced by building 200 large new nuclear plants at a cost of $1.2 trillion or more, the world's greenhouse effect would be reduced by only 2%. Just to make that small dent in the carbon dioxide problem would require completing a new large nuclear reactor in the United States every 3 days for the next 37 years. To do that worldwide, we would have to build *one reactor a day* for 37 years at a total cost of $23 trillion! Already, the United States has spent at least $100 billion on cost overruns and on nuclear power plants that were started but never completed. Imagine what we would have in place today if that money had been spent on solar energy.

Improvements in energy efficiency — especially requiring all new cars to get at least 21 kilometers per liter (50 miles per gallon) of gasoline — would save energy and result in much greater and faster reductions of carbon dioxide emissions at a small fraction of the cost of building new nuclear plants. According to the Rocky Mountain Institute, *if we hope to reduce carbon dioxide emissions using the least-cost methods, then investing in energy efficiency and renewable energy resources are at the top of the list and nuclear power is at the bottom* (see Guest Essay on p. 75 and Spotlight on p. 294).

Indeed, the full costs of heavily subsidized nuclear power are rising while those of perpetual and renewable energy resources, which have received only small subsidies, are decreasing (Figure 17-10). Using the least-cost approach not only is more effective but also frees capital for reforestation and other activities for reducing projected greenhouse warming.

Despite the significant drawbacks of nuclear power compared with other alternatives, President Bush's 1991 energy plan called for building more nuclear power plants and drilling for more oil while providing little emphasis on improving energy efficiency and development of perpetual and renewable energy resources. A major reason for this was the influence of John Sununu, the White House chief of staff. He is a strong proponent of nuclear power and a powerful opponent of most measures proposed by environmentalists as well as by the heads of the Environmental Protection Agency and the Department of Energy.

Bush's energy plan called for the licensing procedure of nuclear plants (involving public hearings) to change from two steps to one step. This would speed up plant construction and help the ailing nuclear industry but would greatly reduce public input. President Bush also proposed that aging nuclear plants be renovated to extend their useful lives another 20 years — a proposal environmentalists believed to be both costly and dangerous. Another proposal cut states out of the approval process in selecting sites for the storage of nuclear waste. What do you think?

---

energy use and greatly increased use of a mix of perpetual and renewable energy resources (Chapter 17).

2. Total systems for future energy alternatives in the world and the United States will probably have low to moderate net useful energy yields and moderate to high development costs. Since there is not enough financial capital to develop all energy alternatives, projects must be chosen carefully. Otherwise, limited capital will be depleted on energy alternatives that yield too little net useful energy or prove to be economically or environmentally unacceptable.

3. We cannot and should not depend mostly on one nonrenewable energy resource like oil, coal, natural gas, or nuclear power. Instead, the world and the United States should rely more on improving energy efficiency and on a mix of perpetual and renewable energy resources.

4. We should decrease dependence on using coal and nuclear power to produce electricity at large, centralized power plants. Individuals, communities, and countries should get more of their heat and electricity from locally available renewable and perpetual energy resources. This would give individuals more control over the energy they use. It would also enhance national security by eliminating large, centralized energy facilities that would be easy to knock out.

ECONOMICS AND NATIONAL ENERGY STRATEGY Cost is the biggest factor determining which commercial energy resources are widely used by consumers. Governments throughout the world use three basic economic and political strategies to stimulate or dampen the short- and long-term use of a particular energy resource (see list at top of p. 504).

Table 18-1 Evaluation of Energy Alternatives for the United States (shading indicates favorable conditions)

Energy Resources	Estimated Availability			Estimated Net Useful Energy of Entire System	Projected Cost of Entire System	Actual or Potential Overall Environmental Impact of Entire System
	Short Term (1993–2003)	Intermediate Term (2003–2013)	Long Term (2013–2043)			
Nonrenewable Resources						
Fossil fuels						
Petroleum	High (with imports)	Moderate (with imports)	Low	High but decreasing	High for new domestic supplies	Moderate
Natural gas	High (with imports)	Moderate (with imports)	Moderate (with imports)	High but decreasing	High for new domestic supplies	Low
Coal	High	High	High	High but decreasing	Moderate but increasing	Very high
Oil shale	Low	Low to moderate	Low to moderate	Low to moderate	Very high	High
Tar sands	Low	Fair? (imports only)	Poor to fair (imports only)	Low	Very high	Moderate to high
Biomass (urban wastes for incineration)	Low	Moderate	Moderate	Low to fairly high	High	Moderate to high
Synthetic natural gas (SNG) from coal	Low	Low to moderate	Low to moderate	Low to moderate	High	High (increases use of coal)
Synthetic oil and alcohols from coal and organic wastes	Low	Moderate	High	Low to moderate	High	High (increases use of coal)
Nuclear energy						
Conventional fission (uranium)	Low to moderate	Low to moderate	Low to moderate	Low to moderate	Very high	Very high
Breeder fission (uranium and thorium)	None	None to low (if developed)	Moderate	Unknown, but probably moderate	Very high	Very high
Fusion (deuterium and tritium)	None	None	None to low (if developed)	Unknown, but may be high	Very high	Unknown (probably moderate to high)
Geothermal energy	Low	Low	Low	Low to moderate	Moderate to high	Moderate to high
Perpetual and Renewable Resources						
Improving energy efficiency	High	High	High	Very high	Low	Decreases impact of other sources

Energy Resources	Estimated Availability			Estimated Net Useful Energy of Entire System	Projected Cost of Entire System	Actual or Potential Overall Environmental Impact of Entire System
	Short Term (1993–2003)	Intermediate Term (2003–2013)	Long Term (2013–2043)			

Perpetual and Renewable Resources (continued)

Energy Resources	Short Term (1993–2003)	Intermediate Term (2003–2013)	Long Term (2013–2043)	Estimated Net Useful Energy of Entire System	Projected Cost of Entire System	Actual or Potential Overall Environmental Impact of Entire System
Water power (hydroelectricity)						
New large-scale dams and plants	Low	Low	Very low	Moderate to high	Moderate to very high	Low to moderate
Reopening abandoned small-scale plants	Moderate	Moderate	Low	High	Moderate	Low
Tidal energy	None	Very low	Very low	Unknown (probably moderate)	High	Low to moderate
Ocean thermal gradients	None	Low	Low to moderate (if developed)	Unknown (probably low to moderate)	Probably high	Unknown (probably moderate)
Solar energy						
Low-temperature heating (for homes and water)	High	High	High	Moderate to high	Moderate	Low
High-temperature heating	Low	Moderate	Moderate to high	Moderate	High initially, but probably declining fairly rapidly	Low to moderate
Photovoltaic production of electricity	Low to moderate	Moderate	High	Fairly high	High initially but declining fairly rapidly	Low
Wind energy						
Neighborhood turbines and wind farms	Low	Moderate	Moderate to high	Fairly high	Moderate	Low
Large-scale power plants	None	Very low	Probably low	Low	High	Low to moderate?
Geothermal energy (low heat flow)	Very low	Very low	Low to moderate	Low to moderate	Moderate to high	Moderate to high
Biomass (burning of wood, crop, food, and animal wastes)	Moderate	Moderate	Moderate to high	Moderate	Moderate	Variable
Biofuels (alcohols and natural gas from plants and organic wastes)	Low to moderate?	Moderate	Moderate to high	Low to fairly high	Moderate to high	Moderate to high
Hydrogen gas (from coal or water)	None	Low to moderate	Moderate to high	Variable	Variable	Variable, but low if produced by using solar energy

1. *Not attempting to control the price*, so that its use depends on open, free-market competition (assuming all other alternatives also compete in the same way)

2. *Keeping prices artificially low* to encourage its use and development

3. *Keeping prices artificially high* to discourage its use and development

Each approach has certain advantages and disadvantages.

FREE-MARKET COMPETITION Leaving it to the marketplace without any government interference is appealing, in principle. However, a free market rarely exists in practice because business people are in favor of it for everyone but their own companies.

Most energy industry executives work hard to get control of supply, demand, and price for their particular energy resource, while urging free-market competition for any competing energy resources. They try to influence elected officials and help elect those who will give their businesses the most favorable tax breaks and other government subsidies. Such favoritism distorts and unbalances the marketplace.

Currently, in the United States and most other countries, the marketplace is greatly distorted by huge government subsidies that make the prices of fossil fuels and nuclear power artificially low. Between 1948 and 1990, 65% of federal energy research and development (R & D) funding in the United States went to nuclear energy, 17% to fossil fuels, 11% to renewable energy (mostly for hydroelectric power), and only 6% for improving energy efficiency. Between 1980 and 1990, federal energy R & D funding for renewable energy and improving efficiency was slashed by 90%.

An equally serious problem with the open marketplace is its emphasis on today's prices to enhance short-term economic gain. This inhibits long-term development of new energy resources, which can rarely compete in their development stages without government support.

KEEPING ENERGY PRICES ARTIFICIALLY LOW: THE U.S. STRATEGY Many governments give tax breaks and other subsidies, pay for long-term research and development, and use price controls to keep prices for particular energy resources artificially low. This is the main approach used by the United States and the Soviet Union.

This approach encourages the development and use of those energy resources getting favorable treatment. It also helps protect consumers (especially the poor) from sharp price increases, and it can help reduce inflation. Because keeping prices low is popular with consumers, this practice often helps leaders in democratic societies get reelected and helps keep leaders in nondemocratic societies from being overthrown.

However, this approach also encourages waste and rapid depletion of an energy resource (such as oil) by making its price lower than it should be, compared with its true value and projected long-term supply. This strategy discourages the development of those energy alternatives not getting at least the same level of subsidies and price control.

Once energy industries, such as the fossil-fuel and nuclear power industries, get government subsidies, they usually have enough clout to maintain that support long after it becomes unproductive. They often successfully fight efforts to provide equal or higher subsidies for the development of new energy alternatives that would allow more nearly equal competition in the marketplace.

According to Harold Hubbard, former director of the Solar Energy Research Institute, government subsidies in 1990 were $26 billion for fossil fuels, $19 billion for nuclear power, and only $5 billion for renewable energy and energy conservation. Furthermore, many of the harmful pollution and health costs of using fossil fuels and nuclear power are not included in their market prices. A 1990 study by the American Solar Energy Society estimated that these hidden costs in the United States amount to at least $109.2 billion a year. Thus, the marketplace is heavily distorted in favor of fossil fuels and nuclear power.

Yet, according to the Department of Energy, reserves and potential supplies of perpetual and renewable energy resources make up 92% of the total energy resources potentially available to the United States and could meet up to 80% of the country's projected energy needs by 2010 (Figure 17-9). If the current short-sighted national energy policy is not corrected during the 1990s, within a few decades the United States will lose out on the huge global market for renewable energy resources and will have to import most of its wind turbines, hydroelectric generators, hydrogen-fuel systems, and solar cells from Japan, Germany, and other countries, including several LDCs. This will drain the country's economic resources, increase the already-enormous national debt, and cause the loss of tens of thousands of jobs—another example of short-term economic gain leading to long-term economic and environmental grief.

Environmentalists are alarmed that an increasing share of the Department of Energy's annual budget is being used to develop nuclear weapons instead of new energy alternatives. Between 1981 and 1990, the share of the DOE's budget used for making nuclear weapons and developing new ones increased from 38% to 69%. Thus, over two-thirds of the DOE's budget is actually an addition to the Department of Defense's budget. Critics call for these activities to be shifted from the Department of Energy to the Department of Defense.

KEEPING ENERGY PRICES ARTIFICIALLY HIGH: THE WESTERN EUROPEAN STRATEGY Governments keep the price of an energy resource artificially high by withdrawing existing tax breaks and other subsidies or by adding taxes on its use. This encourages improvements in energy efficiency, reduces dependence on imported energy, and decreases use of an energy resource (like oil) that has a limited future supply.

Increasing taxes on energy use, however, contributes to inflation and dampens economic growth. It also puts a heavy economic burden on the poor unless some of the energy tax revenues are used to help low-income families offset increased energy prices and to stimulate labor-intensive forms of economic growth, such as improving energy efficiency. High gasoline and oil import taxes have been imposed by many European governments. That is one reason why those countries use about half as much energy per person and have greater energy efficiency than the United States (Table 17-1).

One popular myth is that higher energy prices would wipe out jobs. Actually, low energy prices increase unemployment because farmers and industries find it cheaper to substitute machines run on cheap energy for human labor. On the other hand, raising energy prices stimulates employment because building solar collectors, adding insulation, and carrying out most other forms of improving energy efficiency are labor-intensive activities.

WHY THE UNITED STATES HAS NO COMPREHENSIVE LONG-TERM ENERGY STRATEGY After the 1973 oil embargo, Congress was prodded to pass a number of laws (see page opposite the inside of the back cover) to deal with the country's energy problems. Most energy experts agree, however, that those laws do not represent a comprehensive energy strategy. Indeed, analysis of the U.S. political system reveals why the United States has not been able, and will probably never be able, to develop a coherent energy policy.

One reason is the complexity of energy issues as revealed in this and the preceding chapter, but the biggest problem is that the American political process produces laws, not policies, and is not designed to deal with long-term problems. Each law reflects political pressures of the moment and a maze of compromises between competing groups representing industry, environmentalists, and consumers. Once a law is passed, it is difficult to repeal or modify drastically until its long-term consequences reach crisis proportions.

That means that energy policy in the United States will have to be developed from the bottom up by individuals and communities taking energy matters into their own hands (see Individuals Matter inside the back cover). Local governments in a growing number of towns and cities are developing successful programs to improve energy efficiency and to rely more on locally available energy resources. Across the country, people are realizing that paying for energy is bleeding them to death economically, with 80% to 90% of the money they spend on energy leaving the local economy forever, much of it ending up in the hands of wealthy Saudi Arabians and Texas oil barons (see Case Study on p. 506).

A SUSTAINABLE ENERGY FUTURE FOR THE UNITED STATES Citizens will have to exert intense pressure on elected officials to develop a national energy policy based on improvements in energy efficiency and a transition to a mix of perpetual and sustainable energy resources. The most important components of such a policy are

- Doubling the contribution of perpetual and renewable energy resources to the country's domestic energy production from 10% in 1990 to 20% by the year 2000 and to at least 40% by the year 2010 (Figure 17-9).

- Reducing the use of coal and oil by 50% by 2010 and using natural gas as an interim fuel during the transition toward cleaner, sustainable resources.

- Building no new nuclear reactors and accelerating the retirement of existing plants; funding a modest research and development program for building and testing a few prototype advanced nuclear reactors in case they are needed after the year 2020; and putting off any decision to build commercial versions of such plants until 2010, when the effectiveness of improving energy efficiency and greatly increased reliance on perpetual and renewable energy can be evaluated.

- Phasing out most government subsidies for fossil fuels and nuclear energy and phasing in such subsidies for improvements in energy efficiency and greatly increased use of perpetual and renewable energy resources during the 1990s. Improvements in energy efficiency would serve as the bridge to a renewable-energy economy over the next two to three decades.

- Adding taxes on gasoline and other fossil fuels (carbon taxes) that reflect their true costs to society, with the tax revenues used to improve energy efficiency, encourage use of perpetual and renewable energy resources, and provide energy assistance to poor and lower-middle-class Americans. Giving tax credits or government rebates for purchase of energy-efficient vehicles and adding high taxes on gas guzzlers might also help. Including these costs and eliminating government subsidies for these fuels would make virtually all perpetual and renewable energy resources cheaper ways to produce electricity and would lead to rapid worldwide use of these energy alternatives. This would

Osage, Iowa: Local Economic Development by Improving Energy Efficiency

Simple improvements in energy efficiency can stimulate local economies and save utilities enormous amounts of money. During the last 16 years, Osage, Iowa (population about 4,000), has become the energy efficiency capital of the United States.

It began in 1974 when Wes Birdsall, head of Osage's municipal utility, initiated a program to get the townspeople to save energy and reduce their electric bills and save the utility money by not having to buy more oil and generators. He launched a highly successful nine-year program to weatherize houses, control electricity loads at peak periods, turn down the temperature on water heaters and enclose them in jackets of insulation, and install energy-efficient light bulbs (Figure 17-8), low-flow shower heads, and other devices.

He got people interested in adding insulation, installing energy-saving windows, and plugging air leaks by using an infrared scanner to take a picture of every house in the community (Figure 17-7). When homeowners could see the energy (and money) flowing out of their houses, they took action to waste less energy. The town now uses 25% less energy than the average U.S. town or city.

There were also enormous financial benefits. The outlay saved the utility company enough money to pay off all its debt, accumulate a cash surplus, and cut inflation-adjusted electricity rates by a third. Furthermore, each household received more than $1,000 in savings per year, with this money recirculating in the local economy. Before, this money, amounting to $1.2 million a year, had gone out of town, and usually out of state, to buy energy. What is your local utility and community doing to improve energy efficiency and stimulate the local economy?

greatly reduce air pollution and would reduce projected global warming.

- Requiring all federal and state facilities to meet the highest feasible standards for energy efficiency.

- Having buyers of new cars either get a rebate or pay a fee, depending upon the car's energy efficiency and air pollution emissions. Buyers would receive a government rebate if the rating is high and pay a fee if it is low. The fees would pay for the rebates.

- Greatly increasing fuel efficiency standards for cars and trucks.

- Buying renewable-energy systems for government facilities.

- Strengthening federal energy efficiency standards for commercial and residential appliances and establishing energy-efficient building standards for all new and existing buildings.

- Requiring that all energy systems supported by government funds be based on least-cost analysis, including the harmful environmental costs of each alternative. Such analysis would be based on lifetime costs of each system and would include estimates of all major external costs. Government subsidies would be subtracted from estimated costs so that energy resources would be compared on an equal economic basis. The Bush administration opposes least-cost analysis, arguing that it would interfere in the marketplace. Yet, the administration is continuing (and in some cases expanding) huge federal subsidies for fossil fuels and nuclear power, which represents a severe interference in the marketplace.

- Modifying electric-utility regulations so that the utilities are required to produce electricity on a least-cost basis, can earn money for their shareholders by reducing electricity demand, and are allowed rate increases based primarily on improvements in energy efficiency. Then the goal of utility companies would be to maximize production of what Amory Lovins calls energy- and money-saving "negawatts" instead of megawatts.

Energy experts estimate that implementing these policies now would save oil and money, slow projected global warming, and sharply reduce air and water pollution. This sustainable-energy path would also double the percentage of energy obtained from perpetual and renewable energy resources in the United States to 15% by the year 2000 and to as much as 50% by 2020. This path to a sustainable-energy future will happen only if individuals change their own energy lifestyles and elect or keep in office officials who pledge to support these policies.

Individual and local initiatives are crucial political and economic actions that are bringing about change from the bottom up. Multiplied across the country, such actions can shape a sane national energy strategy with or without help from federal and state governments.

A few countries and states are leading the way in making the transition from the age of oil to the age of energy efficiency and renewable energy. Sweden leads the world in energy efficiency (Table 17-1), followed by

Japan. Brazil and Norway get more than half their energy from hydropower, wood, and alcohol fuel. Israel, Japan, the Philippines, and Sweden plan to rely on renewable and perpetual sources for most of their energy. California has become the world's showcase for solar and wind power. What are you, your local community, and your state doing to save energy and money, use renewable and perpetual energy, and help sustain the earth?

Nuclear fission energy is safe only if a number of critical devices work as they should, if a number of people in key positions follow all their instructions, if there is no sabotage, no hijacking of the transport, if no reactor fuel processing plant or repository anywhere in the world is situated in a region of riots or guerrilla activity, and no revolution or war — even a "conventional" one — takes place in these regions. No acts of God can be permitted.

HANNES ALFVEN (NOBEL LAUREATE IN PHYSICS)

GUEST ESSAY Nuclear Power: A Faustian Bargain We Should Accept

Alvin M. Weinberg

Alvin M. Weinberg was a member of the group of scientists that developed the first experimental fission reactors at the University of Chicago in 1941. Since then, he has been a leading figure in the development of commercial nuclear power. From 1948 to 1973, he served as director of the Oak Ridge National Laboratory. In 1974, he was director of the Office of Energy Research and Development in the Federal Energy Administration (now the Department of Energy). From 1975 to 1985, he was director of the Institute for Energy Analysis of the Oak Ridge Associated Universities, where he is now a Distinguished Fellow. He has written numerous articles and books on nuclear energy (see Further Readings) and has received many awards for his contributions to the development of nuclear energy.

There are two basically different views of the world's future. The one most popular in recent years holds that the earth's resources are limited. According to this view, nothing except drastic reduction in population, affluence, and certain types of technology can prevent severe environmental degradation [Figure 1-16].

The other view holds that as scarce materials are exhausted, there will always be new, more expensive ones to take their place. According to this view, Spaceship Earth has practically infinite supplies of resources, but it will cost more and more to stay where we are as we use up those resources that are readily available.

The latter view seems to me to be the more reasonable, especially since all of our past experience has shown that as one resource becomes scarce, another takes its place. We do not use whale oil for lighting anymore; yet, we have better lighting than our ancestors who burned this oil in lamps.

In the long run, humankind will have to depend on the most abundant and almost infinitely abundant elements in the earth's crust: iron, sodium, carbon, nitrogen, aluminum, oxygen, silicon, and a few others [Figure 7-2]. Glass, cement, and plastics will perform many more functions than they do now. Our average standard of living will be diminished, but probably no more than by a factor of two.

Thus, in contrast to what seems to be the prevailing mood, I retain a certain basic optimism about the future. My optimism, however, is predicated on certain assumptions.

1. Technology can indeed deal with most of the effluents of this future society. Here I think I am on firm ground, for, on the whole, where technology has been given the task and been given the necessary time and funding, it has come through with very important improvements, such as reducing air pollution emissions by cars. On the other hand, carbon dioxide, which is the major greenhouse gas, cannot be controlled; this may place a limit on the rate at which we burn fossil fuels.

2. Phosphorus, though essentially infinite in supply in the earth's crust at various locations, has no substitute. Will we be able to so revolutionize agriculture that we can eventually use the "infinite" supply of phosphorus at acceptable cost? This technological and economic question is presently unresolved, although I cannot believe it to be unresolvable.

(continued)

3. All of this presupposes that we have at our disposal an inexhaustible, relatively cheap source of energy. As I and others now see the technological possibilities, there is only one energy resource we can count on — and that is *nuclear fission*, based on *breeder reactors* to extend the world's supply of fissionable uranium far into the future. That is not to say that nuclear fusion, geothermal energy, or solar energy will never be economically available. We simply do not know now that any of these will ever be available in sufficient quantity and at affordable prices. We know, however, that conventional nuclear fission and breeder reactors are already technologically feasible and that standardized, improved, and inherently safer reactor designs already being tested or on the drawing boards should bring costs down in the future.

In opting for nuclear fission breeders — and we hardly have a choice in the matter — we assume a moral and technological burden of serious proportion. A properly operating nuclear reactor and its subsystems are environmentally a very benign energy source. In particular, a reactor emits no carbon dioxide.

The issue hangs around the words *properly operating*. Can we ensure that henceforth we shall be able to maintain the degree of intellectual responsibility, social commitment, and stability necessary to maintain this energy form so as not to cause serious harm? This is basically a moral and social question, though it does have strong technological components.

It is a Faustian bargain that we strike: In return for this essentially inexhaustible energy source, which we must have if we are to maintain ourselves at anything like our present numbers and our present state of affluence, we must commit ourselves and generations to come — essentially forever — to exercising the vigilance and discipline necessary to keep our nuclear fires well behaved.

As a nuclear technologist who has devoted his career to this quest for an essentially infinite energy source, I believe the bargain is a good one, and it may even be an inevitable one, especially if our concerns about the greenhouse effects are justified. It is essential that the full dimension and implication of this Faustian bargain be recognized, especially by the young people who will have to live with the choices that are being made on this vital issue.

Guest Essay Discussion

1. The author bases his optimism on three assumptions. Do you believe that those assumptions are reasonable? Explain. Are there any other assumptions that should be added?

2. Do you agree that we should accept the Faustian bargain of conventional and breeder nuclear fission? Explain.

3. Do you agree with the author that "we hardly have any choice" in opting for nuclear fission breeder reactors? Explain.

DISCUSSION TOPICS

1. Explain why you agree or disagree with the ideas that the United States can get (a) all of the oil it needs by extracting and processing heavy oil left in known oil wells, (b) all of the oil it needs by extracting and processing heavy oil from oil shale deposits, (c) all of the oil it needs by extracting heavy oil from tar sands, (d) all the natural gas it needs from unconventional sources.

2. Coal-fired power plants in the United States cause an estimated 5,000 deaths a year, mostly from atmospheric emissions of sulfur oxides, nitrogen oxides, and particulate matter. These emissions also damage many buildings and some forests and aquatic systems.
   a. Should air pollution emission standards for *all* new and existing coal-burning plants be tightened significantly? Explain.
   b. Do you favor a U.S. energy strategy based on greatly increased use of coal-burning plants to produce electricity? Explain. What are the alternatives?

3. Explain why you agree or disagree with each of the following proposals made by the nuclear power industry and currently supported by the Bush administration:
   a. The licensing time of new nuclear power plants in the United States should be halved (from an average of 12 years) so they can be built at less cost and compete more effectively with coal and other energy alternatives.
   b. A large number of new, better-designed nuclear fission power plants should be built in the United States to reduce dependence on imported oil and slow down projected global warming.
   c. Large federal subsidies (already totalling $1 trillion) should continue to be given to the commercial nuclear power industry so it does not have to compete in the open marketplace with other energy alternatives receiving no, or smaller, federal subsidies.
   d. A comprehensive program for developing the nuclear breeder fission reactor should be developed and funded largely by the federal government to conserve uranium resources and keep the United States from being dependent on other countries for uranium supplies.

4. Explain why you agree or disagree with the following propositions suggested by various energy analysts:
   a. Federal subsidies for all energy alternatives should be eliminated so that all energy choices can compete in a true free-enterprise market system.
   b. All government tax breaks and other subsidies for conventional fuels (oil, natural gas, coal), synthetic natural gas and oil, and nuclear power should be removed and replaced with subsidies and tax breaks for improving energy efficiency and developing solar, wind, geothermal, and biomass energy alternatives.
   c. Development of solar and wind energy should be left to private enterprise with little or no help from the federal government, but nuclear energy and fossil fuels should continue to receive large federal subsidies (present U.S. policy).
   d. To solve present and future U.S. energy problems, all we need to do is find and develop more domestic supplies of conventional and unconventional oil, natural gas, and coal and increase our dependence on nuclear power (present U.S. policy).
   e. The United States should not worry about heavy dependence on foreign oil imports because they improve international relations and help prevent depletion of domestic supplies (the "don't drain America first" approach).
   f. A heavy federal tax should be placed on gasoline and imported oil used in the United States.
   g. Between 2000 and 2020, the United States should phase out all nuclear power plants.

*5. Throughout the United States, there are 42 nuclear reactors operating on college campuses. Does your campus have a nuclear reactor? If so, has it had any safety problems? Do you believe that nuclear reactors should be allowed on college campuses? Explain.

*6. How is electricity used in your community produced? How has the cost of electricity in your community changed since 1970? Do your community and your campus have an energy conservation plan? If so, what is this plan and how much money has it saved during the past ten years? If there is no plan, develop an energy plan for your school and community and present it to the appropriate officials.

CHAPTER 19

NONRENEWABLE MINERAL RESOURCES AND SOLID WASTE

General Questions and Issues

1. What are the harmful environmental impacts from mining, processing, and using minerals and other crustal resources?

2. How long will affordable supplies of key minerals last for the world and the United States?

3. How can we increase the supplies of key minerals?

4. How can we make supplies of key minerals last longer by reducing the production of solid waste?

Mineral resources are the building blocks on which modern society depends. Knowledge of their physical nature and origins and the web they weave between all aspects of human society and the physical earth can lay the foundations for a sustainable society.

ANN DORR

ONFUEL AND FUEL MINERALS are the foundations of modern civilization. Countries not having such minerals either are doomed to stay at a fairly low standard of living or must have enough money or other goods to get these resources in raw or finished form by purchase or trade. A key issue is how the world can provide adequate and affordable supplies of finite nonfuel mineral resources in environmentally sound ways to meet the needs of a growing world population whose per capita mineral demands are increasing.

19-1 Locating and Extracting Crustal Resources

FINDING AND MINING CRUSTAL RESOURCES
We know how to find and extract more than 100 nonrenewable minerals from the earth's crust (Figure 7-2). We convert these mineral raw materials into many everyday items we use and then discard, reuse, or recycle them.

Mining companies use several methods to find promising mineral deposits. Geological information about plate tectonics (Figure 7-4) and mineral formation helps mining companies find areas for closer study. Photos taken from airplanes or images relayed by satellites sometimes reveal geological features, such as rock formations, often associated with deposits of certain minerals (Figure 7-19). Other instruments on aircraft and satellites can detect deposits of minerals by effects on Earth's magnetic or gravitational fields.

Deposits of nonfuel minerals and rock and coal near the earth's surface are removed by **surface mining**. Mechanized equipment strips away the overlying layer of soil and rock, known as **overburden**, and vegetation. Surface mining is used to extract about 90% by weight of the mineral and rock resources and more than 60% by weight of the coal in the United States (Figure 7-17).

The type of surface mining used depends on the type of crustal resource and the local topography. In **open-pit mining**, machines dig holes and remove ore deposits, such as iron and copper (Figure 19-1). This method is also used to remove sand and gravel and building stone such as limestone, sandstone, slate, granite (Figure 7-13), and marble.

Strip mining is surface mining in which bulldozers, power shovels, or stripping wheels remove large chunks of Earth's surface in strips. It is used mostly for removing coal (Figures 18-9 and 18-11) and some phosphate rock (Figure 4-32), especially in Florida, North Carolina, and Idaho. Another form of surface mining is **dredging**, in which chain buckets and draglines scrape up sand, gravel containing placer deposits, and other surface deposits covered with water.

Some crustal resources deposits lie so deep that surface mining is impractical. These deposits of metal ores and coal are removed by **subsurface mining** (Figure 7-17).

ENVIRONMENTAL IMPACTS The mining, processing, and use of any nonfuel or fuel crustal resource has numerous environmental impacts (Figure 7-21), as discussed in Section 7-3. These include land disturbance (Figures 19-1, 18-10, and 18-11), erosion (Figure 10-12), air pollution, water pollution (Figure 18-13), and solid waste (see Section 19-4).

The greatest danger from high levels of resource consumption may not be the exhaustion of resources but the damage that their extraction and processing impose on the environment. Much of this environmental damage is not seen, thus most people know little about it.

Mining is one of the most environmentally damaging activities carried out by humans. In the United States, nonfuel mining produces at least six times more solid waste material than the total amount of garbage produced by all U.S. towns and cities. Abandoned and unrestored metal and coal surface mines in the United States cover an estimated 90,000 square kilometers (34,700 square miles)—an area about the size of Indiana. That figure does not include the probably larger area of abandoned quarries, pits, and mines used for extracting sand, gravel, and stone. Extracting the materials needed in the construction of a typical building requires excavating a hole equal to the size of the building.

Figure 19-1 The open-pit copper mine in Bingham, Utah, is the largest human-made hole in the world. It is 4.0 kilometers (2.5 miles) in diameter and 0.8 kilometer (0.5 mile) deep. This mine produces 227,000 metric tons (250,000 tons) of copper a year, along with fairly large amounts of gold, silver, and molybdenum.

Don Green/Kennecott Copper Corporation (now owned by British Petroleum)

19-2 Will There Be Enough Mineral Resources?

HOW FAST ARE SUPPLIES BEING DEPLETED?
Worldwide, demand for mineral commodities is increasing exponentially because of increasing population and rising per capita consumption (Figure 1-16). Economically attractive concentrations of nonrenewable mineral resources formed millions of years ago are now being depleted in only decades. The future supply of a nonrenewable mineral resource depends on two factors: its actual or potential supply and how rapidly the supply is being depleted.

We never completely run out of any mineral. Instead of becoming physically depleted, a mineral becomes *economically depleted* when finding, extracting, transporting, and processing the remaining lower-quality deposits cost more than the minerals in those deposits are currently worth. When that economic limit is reached, we have four choices: recycle or reuse what has already been extracted, cut down on unnecessary waste of the resource, find a substitute, or do without.

Most published estimates of the available supply of a particular crustal resource refer to *reserves*: identified resources from which a usable mineral can be extracted profitably at present prices with current mining technology (Figure 7-18). **Depletion time** is the time it takes to use a certain portion—usually 80%—of the known reserves of a mineral at an assumed rate of use. Resource experts project depletion times and plot them on a graph by making certain assumptions about the resource supply and its rate of use (Figure 19-2).

We get one estimate of depletion time by assuming that the resource is not recycled or reused, that its estimated reserves will not increase, and that its price increases over time (curve A, Figure 19-2). A longer depletion time estimate is obtained by assuming that recycling will extend the life of existing reserves and that improved mining technology, price rises, and new discoveries will expand present reserves by some factor, say two (curve B, Figure 19-2). An even longer depletion time estimate is obtained by assuming that new discoveries will expand reserves even more, perhaps five or ten times, and that recycling, reuse, and reduced consumption will extend supplies (curve C, Figure 19-2).

Finding a substitute for a resource cancels all these curves and requires a new set of depletion curves for the new resource. Figure 19-2 shows why experts disagree over projected supplies of nonrenewable nonfuel and fuel resources. We get optimistic or pessimistic projections of the depletion time for a nonrenewable resource by making different assumptions.

Generally, we use the more accessible and higher-grade mineral and energy resources first. As they are depleted, it takes more money, energy, water, and other materials to get resources of lower quality. That means that oil wells must be drilled deeper and larger quantities of rock must be processed to meet increased mineral demands from rising population and affluence (Figure 1-16). That increases the environmental impacts from mineral extraction, processing, and use (Figure 7-21).

Some minerals are more important than others, although that can change as new technologies and substitutes are developed. Minerals essential to the economy of a country are called **critical minerals**, and those necessary for national defense are called **strategic minerals**.

WHO HAS THE WORLD'S NONFUEL MINERAL RESOURCES? Nonfuel mineral resources are very unevenly distributed in the earth's crust. Five countries—the Soviet Union, the United States, Canada, Australia, and South Africa—supply most of the 20 minerals that make up 98% by weight of all nonfuel minerals consumed in the world today.

No industrialized country is self-sufficient in fuel and nonfuel mineral resources, although the Soviet Union comes close and is a principal exporter of critical and strategic minerals. Most western European countries are heavily dependent on oil from the Persian Gulf and nonfuel mineral resources from central and southern Africa. Japan lives by imports, which it upgrades to finished products and then exports to get enough money to buy the resources it needs to sustain its economy. It is nearly 100% dependent on imported oil, has little coal, has virtually no metals, and is the world's largest importer of tropical hardwoods (see Case Study on p. 266). Whether Japan can sustain its current economic miracle depends on the continuance of free trade and Japan's ability to use the money it makes to buy up resources and resource companies throughout the world. It was largely the lack of energy and mineral resources and the cutting off of foreign supplies of oil that caused Japan to go to war in 1941.

THE U.S. SITUATION Each year, the U.S. economy needs more than 4.8 billion metric tons (5.2 billion tons) of new nonfuel and fuel minerals. That means that *each 12 months, another 19 metric tons (21 tons) of mineral resources per American must be obtained just to maintain the present standard of living, unless the country begins changing from its wasteful, throwaway economy (Figure 3-20) to a sustainable-Earth economy (Figure 3-21).*

Because of its rich diversity of mineral and energy resources, the United States became the richest and most powerful nation in the world in less than 200 years—an event unequalled in history. However, the United States achieved this swift and remarkable rise in its standard of living by the rapid exploitation and depletion of many of its energy (especially oil) and nonfuel mineral resources (such as lead, aluminum ore, and iron

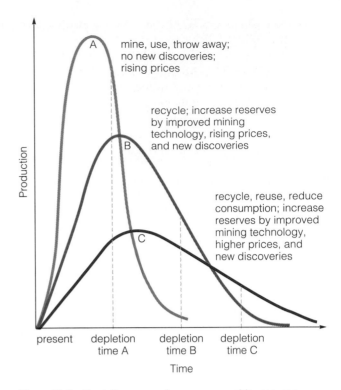

Figure 19-2 Depletion curves for a nonrenewable resource, such as aluminum or copper, using three sets of assumptions. Dashed vertical lines show when 80% depletion occurs.

ore). It has lived high by depleting its rich inheritance of Earth capital.

Now the United States must face up to some harsh realities that affect the vulnerability of its economy, its international monetary position, and the nature of its economic, military, domestic, and foreign policies. *The United States will never again be self-sufficient in oil, and the situation is the same for many of the key metals important to an industrialized country.* Yet, many people do not realize, or they deny the reality, that the era of abundant high-grade energy and mineral resources in the United States is gone forever.

In 1988, minerals produced in the United States were worth about $300 billion, and U.S. exports of minerals were worth about $35 billion. Yet, the United States had a nonfuel mineral trade deficit of $9 billion in 1988—a situation most mineral experts expect to worsen.

Even though the United States is the world's largest producer of nonfuel mineral resources, it is highly dependent on imports from 25 other countries for 50% or more of 24 of its 42 most critical and strategic nonfuel minerals, while the Soviet Union is dependent on imports for 50% or more of only 3 of these minerals. Some of these minerals are imported into the United States because they are consumed more rapidly than they can be produced from domestic supplies. Others are imported because other countries have higher-grade ore

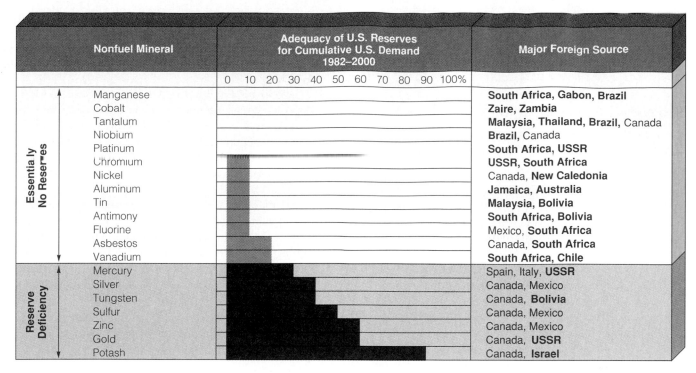

Figure 19-3 Estimated deficiencies of selected nonfuel mineral elements in the United States, 1982–2000, and major foreign sources of these minerals. Foreign sources subject to interruption of supply by political, economic, or military disruption are shown in boldface print. (Data from U.S. Geological Survey)

deposits that are cheaper to extract than the remaining lower-grade U.S. reserves.

Figure 19-3 shows the projected deficiency in U.S. reserves for 20 critical nonfuel minerals to the year 2000 and the major foreign sources of these minerals. Most U.S. mineral imports come from reliable and politically stable countries. There is particular concern, however, over embargoes or sudden cutoffs of supplies of four strategic minerals—manganese, cobalt, platinum, and chromium—for which the United States has essentially no reserves and depends on imports from the Soviet Union or potentially unstable African countries (South Africa, Zambia, Zaire). As the American Geological Institute has stated: "Without manganese, chromium, platinum, and cobalt, there can be no automobiles, no airplanes, no jet engines, no satellites, and no sophisticated weapons—not even home appliances."

The United States has stockpiles of most of its critical and strategic minerals to cushion against short-term supply interruptions and sharp price rises. These stockpiles are supposed to be large enough to last through a three-year conventional war, after subtracting the amounts available from domestic sources and secure foreign sources, but stockpiles for most of these minerals are far below that level.

The American public is only dimly aware of the fact that as more and more fuel and nonfuel mineral resources have to be imported, industries and jobs related to those resources are lost. If income from exports does not exceed what is paid out for imports (which is not the case), the United States faces an increasing balance-of-payments problem, a rising national debt, and an erosion in the international value of its currency.

This cannot be solved by continuing to print more money to pay for material things. Sooner or later, the suppliers and investors will lose confidence in the ability of the United States to pay its debts. Then, the destiny of the United States will be a decline in economic might, world prestige, and the standard of living.

WILL THERE BE ENOUGH? Experts disagree about whether there will be enough affordable supplies of key nonfuel minerals to meet the projected needs of the world's MDCs and LDCs. Geologists and environmentalists tend to view Earth's supply of minerals as finite because of the uneven concentrations of key minerals in the earth's crust and the two laws of energy (Section 3-6), which impose lower limits on the grades of ore that can be processed without spending more money than they are worth and causing unacceptable environmental damage.

Economists, by contrast, tend to view the supply of minerals as essentially infinite because of our ability to develop improved technologies for finding and processing minerals or for finding substitutes (see Guest Essay on p. 29).

Many LDCs fear that most of the world's resources will continue to be used to sustain increasingly greater economic growth by the MDCs, thus preventing many LDCs from becoming developed countries (see Pro/Con on p. 515).

19-3 Increasing Mineral Resource Supplies: The Supply-Side Approach

ECONOMICS AND RESOURCE SUPPLY Geologic processes determine how and where a mineral resource is concentrated in the earth (Sections 7-2 and 7-3). Economics determines what part of the total supply will be used (Figure 7-18).

According to standard economic theory, a competitive free market should control the supply and demand of goods and services. If a resource becomes scarce, its price rises. If there is an oversupply, the price falls. Some analysts believe that increased demand will raise mineral prices and stimulate new discoveries and development of more-efficient mining technology. Rising prices will also make it profitable to mine ores of increasingly lower grades and stimulate the search for substitutes.

Many economists argue that this theory does not apply to nonfuel mineral resources in most MDCs. In the United States and many other MDCs, industry and government have gained so much control over supply, demand, and prices of mineral raw materials and mineral products that a competitive free market does not exist.

Another problem is that the costs of nonfuel mineral resources are only a small part of the total cost of most final goods. Thus, scarcities of nonfuel minerals do not raise the market price of products very much.

Because market prices of products don't reflect dwindling mineral supplies, industries and consumers have no incentive to reduce demand soon enough to avoid economic depletion of the minerals. Low mineral prices, caused by failure to include the external costs of mining and processing them (Figure 7-21), also encourage resource waste, faster depletion, and more pollution and environmental degradation.

Another economic factor that can limit production of nonfuel minerals is lack of investment capital. In today's fluctuating mineral markets and because of rising costs, it is increasingly difficult to attract investors who are willing to have large amounts of their money tied up for long periods of time with no assurance of a reasonable return.

FINDING NEW LAND-BASED MINERAL DEPOSITS Geologic exploration guided by better geologic knowledge and satellite surveys and other new techniques will increase present reserves of most minerals.

In MDCs and many LDCs, however, most of the easily accessible, high-grade deposits have already been discovered. Thus, geologists believe that most new concentrated deposits will be found in unexplored areas in LDCs.

Some believe that the Antarctic may contain large deposits of fuel and nonfuel resources. Exploration and development of this hostile wilderness, however, may be too expensive and is opposed by conservationists who believe we should protect this only remaining large wilderness area on the planet from development (see Pro/Con on p. 516).

Exploration for new resources requires a large capital investment and is a risky financial venture. Typically, if geologic research identifies 10,000 sites where a deposit of a particular resource might be found, only 1,000 sites are worth costly exploration; only 100 justify even more costly drilling, trenching, or tunnelling; and only 1 out of the 10,000 will probably be a producing mine. Even if large new supplies are found, no nonrenewable mineral supply can stand up to continued exponential growth in its use.

IMPROVING MINING TECHNOLOGY AND MINING LOW-GRADE ORE Some analysts assume that all we have to do to increase supplies of any mineral is to mine increasingly lower grades of ore. They point to the development of large earth-moving equipment, techniques for removing impurities, and other advances in mining and processing technology during the past few decades.

For example, these and other technological changes have allowed the average grade of copper ore mined in the United States to fall from about 5% copper by weight in 1900 to 0.4% today, with a drop in the inflation-adjusted copper price. Technological improvements also led to a 500% increase in world copper reserves between 1950 and 1980. Future advances may increase our ability to extract metals from even lower-grade ores (see Spotlight at top of p. 520).

Other analysts point out that several factors limit the mining of lower-grade ores. As increasingly poorer ores are mined, energy costs increase sharply. We eventually reach a point where it costs more to mine and process such resources than they are currently worth, unless we have a virtually inexhaustible source of cheap energy. Most energy experts believe that in the future, energy will neither be unlimited nor cheap and will become the limiting factor in mining increasingly lower grades of ore.

Available supplies of fresh water also may limit the supply of some mineral resources, because large amounts of water are needed to extract and process most minerals. Many areas with significant mineral deposits are poorly supplied with fresh water.

Finally, exploitation of lower grades of ore may be limited by the environmental impact of waste material

To LDCs and some resource analysts, asking whether we will have enough affordable supplies of nonrenewable minerals means asking whether the world's MDCs, with 22% of the world's population, have enough of these resources. They believe there is little concern over meeting the mineral resource needs of the LDCs, which contain 78% of the world's people but now use only about 20% of the world's mineral resources.

MDCs argue that when they buy nonfuel minerals from LDCs, they provide funds that the LDCs need for their own economic development. Multinational companies point out that mines they develop in LDCs are a source of jobs and income for those countries. It is also argued that when MDCs depend on LDCs for critical minerals, the rich countries have an interest in helping preserve economic and political stability in the LDCs.

LDCs agree that selling their resources at any price helps stimulate their economic development. However, for short-term economic survival, they feel they have little choice but to sell their resources at prices they believe to be too low and thus hinder their long-term development.

Companies based in MDCs end up with most of the profits and, in the process, often cause severe environmental degradation and pollution in LDCs. Economic growth in mineral-exporting LDCs is stunted when they borrow money from MDCs to buy expensive imported finished products made from minerals they feel they had to sell too cheaply. The low mineral prices also encourage unnecessary resource waste in MDCs and rapidly deplete supplies of key resources that both LDCs and MDCs will need for their future economic growth.

Geologist Eugene Cameron points out that, contrary to popular opinion, the United States has not developed its industrial economy using the nonfuel mineral resources of the rest of the world. Data show that as late as 1979, the United States was still producing about 97% of its mineral consumption from domestic supplies. Today, mineral imports have increased, but about 62% of these imports come from other MDCs (Figure 19-3).

However, critics counter that U.S. mineral use is so high that the 38% of its imports from LDCs amounts to huge quantities. This gives the U.S. or other large volume buyers, such as Japan and western European countries, considerable influence over the market price of such resources. As the United States increases its dependence on imports (Figure 19-3), LDCs fear U.S. influence over mineral prices will grow.

Politics also plays a key role in mineral prices. If an LDC fails to go along with foreign policy decisions of a mineral-importing MDC, the MDC may stop importing resources from that LDC (assuming other sources are available) or reduce or cut off foreign aid. Then the LDC can face economic ruin. Such countries feel they are victims of economic blackmail by importing MDCs.

Currently, LDCs owe MDCs over $1 trillion. Each year, LDCs pay MDCs $43 billion for interest on this debt. To correct this situation, LDCs have called for a new international economic order, in which a larger and fairer share of the world's wealth would be shifted from MDCs to LDCs. This proposal calls for

- a substantial increase in aid from industrialized countries to LDCs
- relieving LDCs of some of their heavy indebtedness to MDCs
- removal of trade barriers that restrict LDCs from selling some of their products to MDCs
- increasing the prices paid for minerals, timber, and other resources exported from LDCs to MDCs
- giving LDCs greater influence in the decision making of international lending institutions, such as the World Bank and the International Monetary Fund

So far, MDCs have generally opposed this program. What do you think should be done?

---

produced during mining and processing (Figure 7-21). At some point, the costs of land restoration and pollution control exceed the current value of the minerals.

GETTING MORE MINERALS FROM SEAWATER AND THE OCEAN FLOOR Ocean resources are found in three areas: seawater, sediments and deposits on the shallow continental shelf, and sediments and nodules on the deep-ocean floor. Most of the chemical elements found in seawater occur in such low concentrations that recovering them takes more energy and money than they are worth. Only magnesium, bro-

mine, and sodium chloride are abundant enough in seawater to be extracted profitably at present prices with current technology.

Continental shelf deposits and placer deposits are already significant sources of sand, gravel, phosphates, and nine other nonfuel mineral resources. Offshore wells also supply large amounts of oil and natural gas (Figure 7-17).

The deep-ocean floor at various sites may be a future source of manganese and other metallic minerals. There are also deposits of metal sulfides of iron, manganese, copper, and zinc around hydrothermal vents

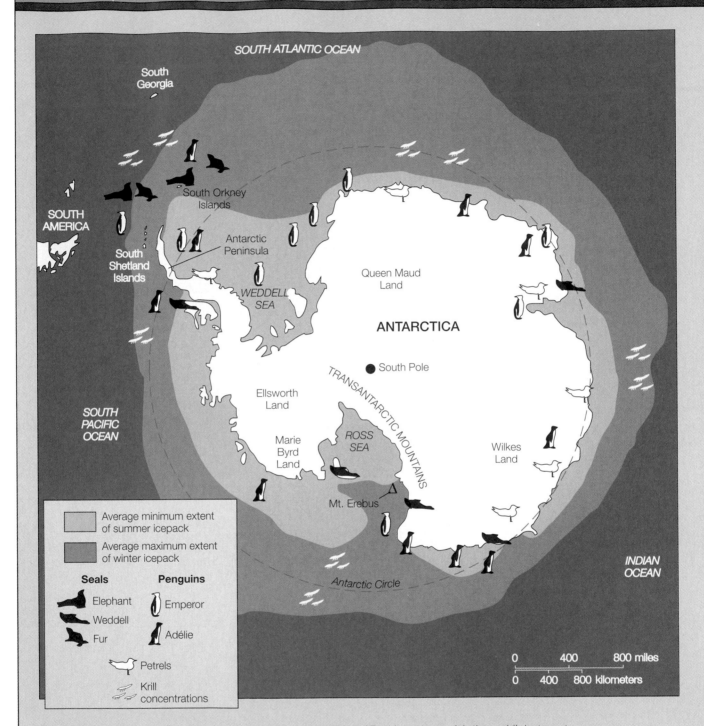

Figure 19-4 The ice-covered continent of Antarctica makes up 10% of Earth's landmass. It is the world's last great wilderness. Now there is a struggle between countries wanting to develop the continent's resources in a controlled manner and those wanting to declare Antarctica a permanent World Park, free from mineral development, in which only scientific research and carefully controlled tourism would be allowed.

Antarctica is an island continent the size of the United States and Mexico combined (Figure 19-4). It is the coldest, driest, windiest, highest, iciest, most remote, least developed, and generally most unpleasant of Earth's seven continents. Drier than the Sahara, its landmass has stored up 20 million to 25 million years of light snowfall as ice (Figure 19-5), which covers 98% of the continent's land area. This makes up 90% of Earth's ice and 70% of its fresh water.

In winter, parts of the sea freeze and the size of the continent doubles (Figure 19-4). In the summer, it contracts, when some of the ice pack melts and huge, mostly submerged icebergs break off from edges of the ice shelf.

Antarctica has not always been a frozen wilderness formed around the South Pole. About 250 million years ago, Antarctica formed the core of a vast supercontinent named Gondwana or Gondwanaland (Figure 7-27), which also contained what we now call Australia, New Zealand, Africa, India, and South America. Fossil remains retrieved from ice cores drilled into Antarctica show that it once had temperate forests.

About 160 million years ago, Gondwana began breaking up because of movement of some of Earth's tectonic plates (Figure 7-4). While most of its pieces stayed in warm regions, the part we know today as Antarctica drifted toward the South Pole, where its major glaciers and ice caps began forming about 20 to 25 million years ago.

Antarctica serves as a regulator of the world's climate and the level of its seas. This frozen ice mass draws heat out of the tropics and sends cold air and water north as part of Earth's global air circulation (Figure 5-4), while its cold waters help drive the circulation of world's oceans (Figure 5-7).

Antarctica's cold ocean waters dissolve enormous amounts of car-

Figure 19-5 About 98% of Antarctica's land area is covered with ice, which contains 70% of the world's fresh water. The average thickness of its ice sheets is 2.4 kilometers (1.5 miles), and in some places the ice is twice that thick. Although its land contains relatively little life, Antarctica is surrounded by nutrient-rich seas that contain a dazzling variety of life-forms. Here, adult and young Weddell seals rest on the ice while a group of cape pigeons feed offshore.

bon dioxide from the atmosphere as part of the global carbon cycle (Figure 4-28). This helps regulate Earth's average temperatures. Were large amounts of antarctic ice to melt because of an enhanced greenhouse effect (Section 11-1), global average sea levels would rise significantly.

The 2% of the continent that remains ice-free is so cold and dry that only a few forms of vegetation, mainly mosses and lichens (Figure 6-9), can survive. This vegetation is quite vulnerable to disruption—a human footprint on a bed of moss remains visible for several years.

Antarctica's cold, coastal waters, however, are teeming with marine life, because of an abundant supply of dissolved oxygen and continuous sunlight during the summer months. Also, the water is rich in nutrients brought up from the ocean (continued) by currents and released as sediment when ice and snow melt during the summer. These nutrients support an abundance of microscopic sea-dwelling phytoplankton, which are food for huge numbers of shrimplike krill, which in turn support many other forms of life (Figure 4-20).

That explains why Antarctica is home to 85 million penguins (Figure 19-6), 80 million seabirds (the world's largest gathering), 12 species of the world's remaining whales (Figure 16-30), half of Earth's seal populations, and 200 types of fish. Some of its aquatic life may be susceptible to the effects of greatly increased UV-radiation because of the extensive loss of stratospheric ozone that occurs over much of this continent during part of the year because of our activities (Figure 11-6). Another big threat to its aquatic life is overfishing of slowly reproducing krill, which support many other species.

The greatest threat to Antarctica's wildlife and pristine beauty comes from increasing pressure to develop the continent's huge estimated supplies of fuel and nonfuel minerals. No one knows what minerals are

there, but many geologists believe that the continent and its offshore waters may contain significant amounts of oil, natural gas, coal, and a wide variety of metals, including strategic minerals such as cobalt, chromium, and manganese. No one knows, however, whether it would be physically possible and economically profitable to exploit such resources.

For decades, 7 countries have staked out unresolved ownership claims to portions of Antarctica and its offshore waters, and 26 countries maintain a presence there by operating scientific research stations (Figure 19-4). This entitles them to vote on treaties governing how the continent is to be used.

By studying cores drilled out of the ice, scientists can detect changes in the temperature and composition of the atmosphere over the centuries. Analysis of this ice also reveals changes in the concentrations of air pollutants such as lead, radioisotopes, DDT, and other chemicals since 1945.

Since 1959, a treaty among these and other nations has declared Antarctica a demilitarized, nuclear-free zone dedicated to the peaceful pur-

suit of knowledge and the free exchange of scientific information. Today, 26 countries are voting members of the Antarctic Treaty System, and 13 others are nonvoting members. Together, these countries contain three-fourths of the world's population.

In 1977, the countries involved in the Antarctic Treaty System agreed not to carry out mineral exploration and development until they could develop a treaty regulating such activities and review the original 1959 treaty after 1991. In 1988, after six years of negotiations, these 39 nations completed an international treaty called the Convention on the Regulation of Antarctic Mineral Resources (CRAMR). By 1990, no countries had ratified this treaty and there was disagreement over whether it should be ratified.

Proponents say that the stringent environmental safeguards in the treaty will protect the area's wildlife and prevent uncontrolled development, but many environmentalists see the treaty as the first step toward potentially harmful exploitation of Antarctica's minerals. They argue that there is no way to enforce the treaty's environmental regula-

found at certain locations on the deep-ocean floor. However, concentrations of metals in most of these deposits are too low to be valuable mineral resources.

Environmentalists recognize that seabed mining would probably cause less harm than mining on land. They are concerned, however, that removing seabed mineral deposits and dumping back unwanted material will stir up ocean sediments. That could destroy seafloor organisms and have unknown effects on poorly understood ocean food webs. Surface waters might also be polluted by the discharge of sediments from mining ships and rigs.

At a few sites on the deep-ocean floor, manganese-rich nodules have been found in large quantities. These cherry- to potato-size rocks contain by weight 30% to 40% manganese, used in certain steel alloys. They also contain small amounts of other strategically important

metals, such as nickel, copper, and cobalt. These nodules could be sucked up from the muds of the ocean floor by pipe or scooped up by a continuous cable with buckets and be transported to a mining ship above.

However, most of these nodules are found in seabed sites in international waters. Development of these resources has been put off indefinitely because of squabbles between countries over who owns them.

FINDING SUBSTITUTES Some analysts believe that even if supplies of key minerals become very expensive or scarce, human ingenuity will find substitutes. They point out that new developments by scientists are already leading to a materials revolution in which materials made of silicon and other abundant elements (Figure 7-2) are being substituted for most scarce metals (see Spotlight at bottom of p. 520). In 1980, Japan's

tions, pointing out that treaty nations have failed to enforce existing regulations for protecting Antarctica's environment. Greenpeace, an international environmental organization, documented such abuses when it set up a base there in 1987.

Environmentalists call for the continent to be declared a permanent World Park, or International Wilderness Reserve, in which only scientific research and limited and carefully controlled tourism would be permitted. They argue that Antarctica is the only area on Earth that humans have not seriously despoiled and believe we have an ethical obligation to keep it that way.

In 1989, France and Australia, two countries with veto power over the treaty, announced that they backed the World Park idea and would not ratify the treaty. Other countries, such as Great Britain, the United States, Germany, and Japan, oppose a permanent ban on mineral development in Antarctica. In 1991, the 39 nations involved with Antarctica worked out a compromise in the treaty that would ban mining there for 50 years.

Figure 19-6 A huge colony of king penguins on an island near Antarctica. The adults have colorful markings, and their fuzzy offspring are brown. Each year, huge colonies of this and other penguin species return to the same islands to breed. This is only one of 35 species of penguins found in this region of the world.

government saw the development of new materials as a key technology of the future and launched a ten-year, $400-million program of research.

Substitutes can probably be found for many scarce mineral resources, but finding or developing a substitute is costly, and phasing it into a complex manufacturing process requires a long lead time. While an increasingly scarce mineral is being replaced, people and businesses dependent on it may suffer economic hardships as the price rises sharply.

Finding substitutes for some key materials may be extremely difficult, if not impossible. Examples are helium, phosphorus for phosphate fertilizers (Figure 4-32), manganese for making steel, and copper for wiring motors and generators.

Another problem is that some substitutes are inferior to the minerals they replace. For example, alumi-num could replace copper in electrical wiring, but the energy cost of producing aluminum is much higher than that of producing copper. Aluminum wiring is also more of a fire hazard than copper wiring.

19-4 Wasting Resources: The Throwaway Approach

SOLID WASTE With only 4.5% of the the world's population, the United States produces 33% of the world's **solid waste:** any unwanted or discarded material that is not a liquid or a gas. Americans generate about 10 billion metric tons (11 billion tons) of solid waste a year. That means that annual per capita production of solid

SPOTLIGHT Mining with Microbes

One emerging prospect for improving mining technology is the use of microorganisms for in-place (*in situ*) mining, which would remove desired metals from ores while leaving the surrounding environment relatively undisturbed. That would reduce land disturbance and the air pollution associated with the smelting of metal ores (Figure 7-22) and the water pollution often associated with using hazardous chemicals such as cyanides to extract gold.

With biotechnology extraction and processing, once an ore body had been identified and deemed economic to develop, wells would be drilled into it and the ore fractured. Then the ore would be inoculated with either naturally occurring bacteria or genetically engineered bacteria to extract the desired metal from the ore.

Once that had been done, the ore would be flooded with water, which would be collected and pumped to the surface, where the desired metals would be removed. Thus, metal production would become essentially biological, with little energy input compared with current extraction technologies.

In 1990, a gold-mining plant using microbes went into operation in Colorado. It uses *Thiobacillus ferrooxidans*, a naturally occurring bacterium, to extract gold that is embedded in iron sulfide ores and that is uneconomical to extract by conventional methods. The bacteria consume the sulfur and iron in the iron sulfide gold ores, leaving gold in a form that is easily extracted by current technology. The plant is expected to produce about 1,400 kilograms (50,000 ounces) of gold a year at about $240 an ounce, well below gold's price of about $375 an ounce.

One problem with microbiological processing of ores is that it is slow. It can take decades to remove the same amount of material that conventional methods can remove within months or years. So far, biological methods are economically feasible only with low-grade ore (such as gold), for which conventional techniques are too expensive.

There is also concern about the potential side effects of genetically engineered organisms (see Pro/Con on p. 161). However, proponents of mining biotechnology point out that these organisms get their energy from chemical sources, not from living or formerly living organisms as do genetically engineered organisms used in agriculture and medicine. Consequently, they argue, the risks to humans beings, other animals, or plants are several orders of magnitude lower than those from other uses of genetically engineered organisms.

SPOTLIGHT The Materials Revolution

Scientists and engineers are rapidly developing new materials that can replace many of the metals we now rely on. Ceramic materials are being used in engines, knives, scissors, batteries, fishhooks, and artificial limbs.

Ceramics are harder, stronger, lighter, and longer-lasting than many metals. They withstand enormous temperatures, and they do not corrode. Because they can burn fuel at higher temperatures than metal engines, ceramic engines can boost fuel efficiency by 30% to 40%. The cutting edge of ceramic technology is found in Japan.

Within a few decades, we may have high-temperature ceramic superconductors in which electricity flows without resistance. That may lead to faster computers, more efficient power transmission, and inexpensive electromagnets for propelling magnetic levitation trains. So far, Japanese scientists have filed more patent applications for such superconductors than the rest of the world combined.

High-strength plastics and composite materials strengthened by carbon and glass fibers are likely to transform the automobile (Figure 17-4) and aerospace industries. Many of these new materials are stronger and lighter than metals. They cost less to produce because they require less energy, don't need painting, and can easily be molded into any shape.

Many cars now have plastic body parts, which reduce weight and boost fuel economy. Planes and cars made almost entirely of plastics — held together by new superglues — may be common in the next century.

New plastic materials and gels are also being developed to provide superinsulation without taking up much space.

The materials revolution is also transforming medicine. So-called biomaterials, made of new plastics, ceramics, glass composites, and alloys, are being used in artificial skin, arteries, organs, and joints.

The keys to developing and taking advantage of the materials revolution is a highly educated citizenry — a country's most important resource — and a willingness of government and industry to make long-term investments in research and development. Any country that does not have the foresight and will to do these things is destined to be left behind in a sea of debt and environmental and social decay.

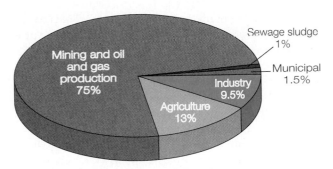

Figure 19-7 Sources of the 10 billion metric tons (11 billion tons) of solid waste produced each year in the United States. The indirect per capita production of solid waste by mining and industrial activities in the United States is 62 times the amount produced directly as household garbage. Although individuals don't generate this waste directly, they generate it indirectly through the products they consume. We face a garbage crisis, but it is only a small, visible tip of the iceberg of solid waste that is produced. Reducing this indirectly produced solid waste, rarely seen by the public, is the real waste crisis caused by a throwaway society. So far, reduction of this waste has received little public attention. (Data from Environmental Protection Agency and U.S. Bureau of Mines)

waste in the United States is 40 metric tons (44 tons) — two to five times that in other MDCs.

While garbage produced directly by households and businesses is a significant problem, about 98.5% of the solid waste in the United States comes from mining, oil and natural gas production, and industrial and agricultural activities (Figure 19-7). Most mining waste is left piled near mine sites and can pollute the air, surface water, and groundwater. Most industrial solid waste, such as scrap metal, plastics, paper, fly ash removed by air pollution control equipment in industrial and electrical power plants, and sludge from industrial waste treatment plants, is disposed of at the plant site where it is produced. Most of it is buried or incinerated. Dealing with this waste will require much greater emphasis on recycling, reuse, and waste reduction by redesigning processes and products to use the minimum amount of materials, while also reducing pollution and environmental impacts.

MUNICIPAL SOLID WASTE The remaining 1.5% of the mass of solid waste produced in the United States is **municipal solid waste** from homes and businesses in or near urban areas. The estimated 168 million metric tons (185 million tons) of municipal solid waste — often referred to as garbage — produced in the United States in 1990 would fill a bumper-to-bumper convoy of garbage trucks that would encircle the earth almost six times. That amounts to 670 kilograms (1,470 pounds) per American, and the EPA projects that the figure will rise to 806 kilograms (1,770 pounds) per person by the year 2010. Over a 70-year lifetime, a typical U.S. citizen throws away 46 metric tons (51 tons) of garbage (see Spotlight above).

About 59% of the total weight the typical American throws away as garbage and rubbish is paper, paperboard, and yard waste from potentially renewable resources (Figure 19-8). Most of the rest is products made from glass, plastic, aluminum, iron, steel, tin, and other nonrenewable mineral resources. Only about 13% of these potentially renewable resources is recycled or composted (a form of recycling) (Figure 19-9). The other 87% is hauled away and dumped or burned at a cost of about $6 billion a year.

Litter is also a source of solid waste. One example is helium-filled balloons that are released into the atmosphere at sporting events and celebrations. When the helium escapes or the balloons burst, the balloons fall back to Earth as long-lasting litter. Fish, turtles, seals, whales, and other aquatic animals die when they ingest balloons falling into oceans and lakes.

This practice also suggests to children and adults that it is acceptable to litter, waste helium (a scarce resource) and energy used to separate helium from air, and kill wildlife (even if we switched to balloons that

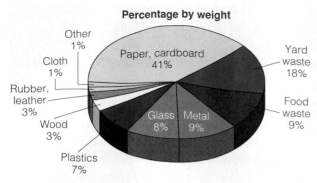

Percentage by weight

- Other 1%
- Cloth 1%
- Rubber, leather 3%
- Wood 3%
- Plastics 7%
- Paper, cardboard 41%
- Glass 8%
- Metal 9%
- Yard waste 18%
- Food waste 9%

Figure 19-8 Composition by weight of urban solid waste thrown away in the United States in 1989. Because plastic containers are replacing many glass containers, plastics are expected to make up 10% by weight of urban solid waste by the year 2000. However, by volume, the largest and fastest-growing source of solid waste is paper and cardboard. (Data from Environmental Protection Agency and Franklin Associates)

biodegraded within six weeks). The National Park Service has restricted the sale and use of helium balloons within the park system. Such frivolous uses of helium-filled balloons are a glaring example of an unnecessary and Earth-degrading product.

WAYS TO DEAL WITH SOLID WASTE There are two basic approaches to dealing with the mountains of solid waste we produce in mining, processing, manufacturing, and using resources: *waste management* and *waste prevention*. The first is a *throwaway*, or *high-waste, approach*, in which solid wastes are left where they are produced, are buried, or are burned (Figure 3-20). It is an output approach based on using the economic system to encourage waste production and then attempting to manage the wastes in ways that will reduce environmental harm.

Burning or burying wasted resources instead of not producing them or recycling and reusing them encourages us to continue producing more waste, removing it from one part of the environment, and putting it in another part. Sooner or later, even the best-designed landfills leak wastes into water supplies and we also run out of affordable or politically acceptable land for landfills. Even the best-designed waste incinerators release some toxic substances into the atmosphere and leave a toxic residue that must be disposed of — usually in landfills that ultimately leak toxic chemicals into underground water supplies.

The basic problem is that we use economic systems to reward those who produce waste instead of those who try to use resources more efficiently. We give timber, mining, and energy companies tax write-offs and other subsidies to cut trees and to find and extract copper, oil, coal, and uranium from Earth's crust. At the same time, we give few, if any, such subsidies to companies and businesses that recycle copper or paper, use oil or coal more efficiently, or develop renewable alter-

natives to using nonrenewable fossil fuels. That creates an uneven economic playing field that favors waste production over waste reduction.

In a world where more and more people are rapidly converting the world's resources into trash and waste heat, waste production is an outmoded and dangerous concept. It is not based on the way the natural processes that sustain life on Earth work.

The second method for dealing with solid waste is a *prevention*, or *low-waste, approach*, based on greatly increasing recycling, reuse, and waste reduction (Figure 3-21). It is an input approach that views solid wastes as wasted solids that we should be recycling, reusing, or, best of all, not producing. With this approach, the economic system is used to discourage waste production. While a mixture of waste management and waste prevention is needed, there has been much talk but little action on waste prevention so far.

BURYING SOLID WASTE IN LANDFILLS About 73% by weight of the municipal solid waste in the United States is buried in sanitary landfills, compared with 100% in Ireland, 98% in Australia, 93% in Canada, 90% in Great Britain, 54% in France, 44% in Sweden, 18% in Switzerland, and 16% in Japan (Figure 19-9). A **sanitary landfill** is a garbage graveyard in which wastes are spread out in thin layers, compacted, and covered with a fresh layer of clay or a plastic foam each day (Figure 19-10). Basically, it involves digging a hole in the ground and dumping trash in it. More-modern landfills are lined with clay and plastic before being filled with garbage.

No open burning is allowed, odor is seldom a problem, and rodents and insects cannot thrive. Sanitary landfills should be located so as to reduce water pollution from leaching, but that is not always done. Also, many older landfills in the United States did not have to meet the more stringent standards imposed on those put into operation since 1976.

A sanitary landfill can be put into operation quickly, has low operating costs, and can handle a huge amount of solid waste. After a landfill has been filled, the land can be graded, planted with grass and used as a park, a golf course, a ski hill, an athletic field, a wildlife area, or some other recreation area.

While landfills are in operation, there is much traffic, noise, and dust. Wind can scatter litter and dust before each day's load of trash is covered with clay. That is why most people do not want a landfill nearby. Another reason is that a 1990 study by the California state government found that 67% of the 356 landfills tested emitted one or more of ten toxic gases tested for.

Paper and other biodegradable wastes break down very slowly in today's compacted and water-deficient landfills. Newspapers dug up from some landfills are still readable after 30 or 40 years. After 10 years, hot dogs, carrots, and chickens that have been dug up have

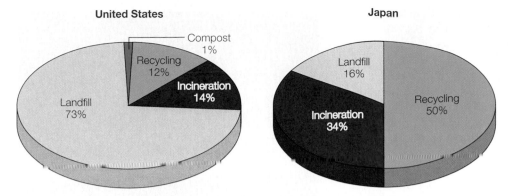

Figure 19-9 Fate of solid waste in the United States and Japan. Japan has been a pioneer in developing an integrated waste management program that emphasizes recycling. Typically, it recycles 50% of its wastepaper, 55% of its glass bottles, and 66% of its beverage and food cans. From their earliest school years on, Japanese children are taught about recycling and waste management and to view wastes as potential resources. They often tour local recycling centers and incinerators. Japan could probably recycle 70% to 80% of its municipal solid waste by instituting municipal and household composting programs for much of the yard and food waste it now burns. Recently, Japan has begun a national campaign to reduce production of solid waste. EPA's goals for the United States in 1992 are for 55% of the municipal solid waste to be buried in landfills, 20% to be incinerated, and 25% to be recycled. (Data from Environmental Protection Agency and INFORM)

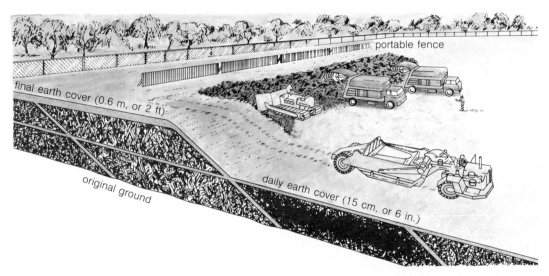

Figure 19-10 A sanitary landfill. Wastes are spread in a thin layer and then compacted with a bulldozer. A scraper (foreground) covers the wastes with a fresh layer of clay or plastic foam at the end of each day. Portable fences catch and hold windblown debris. The world's largest landfill is in Fresh Kills on Staten Island. It is as big as 16,000 baseball diamonds and is the final resting place for 80% of New York City's trash. It is as tall as a 15-story building. When it reaches its capacity, probably around the year 2005, it will be as tall as a 50-story building and will be the highest point on the East Coast between Maine and Florida. Fresh Kills opened in the early 1970s, before the EPA required stricter standards for new sanitary landfills. As a result, it has no liner, and each day 3.8 million liters (1 million gallons) of contaminated leachate oozes into groundwater beneath Fresh Kills. Fortunately, Staten Island residents do not rely on groundwater for their water supply. There are about 7,600 sanitary landfills in the United States. Careful analysis shows that 86% of those studied have contaminated groundwater.

not been degraded (Figure 19-11). New, expensive biodegradable plastics will take decades to degrade in landfills, are largely a waste of money, and discourage recycling of plastics and reduction in the use of plastics.

The underground anaerobic decomposition of organic wastes at landfills produces explosive methane gas, toxic hydrogen sulfide gas, and smog-forming volatile organic compounds, which are emitted into the atmosphere. This problem can be prevented by equipping landfills with vent pipes to collect these gases. Collected methane can be burned to produce steam or electricity (Figure 19-12). If all methane produced in existing and abandoned landfills in the United States were collected and burned to produce electricity or steam, it could account for up to 5% of all U.S. natural gas consumption. A single large landfill can provide enough methane to meet the energy needs of 10,000 homes.

Besides saving energy, collecting and burning methane gas from all large landfills worldwide would lower atmospheric emissions of methane 6% to 18% and help reduce projected global warming from greenhouse gases (Figure 11-2). So far, methane is collected at only about 125 of the more than 17,000 operating and filled and abandoned landfills in the United States.

Another problem with landfills is pollution of groundwater and surface water. When rain filters through a landfill, it leaches out inks, water-soluble metal compounds, and other toxic materials. This produces a contaminated leachate that seeps from the bottom of unlined landfills or cracks in the lining of lined landfills. Contamination of groundwater and nearby surface water is a serious problem, especially for thousands of older filled and abandoned landfills that did not have liners. Eventually, landfills with liners also leak because of liner failure. Landfills also deprive present and future generations of valuable resources and are output approaches that encourage waste production instead of waste reduction.

In 1990, 249 (21%) of the 1,177 worst Superfund hazardous-waste sites to be cleaned up by the EPA were unlined landfills, with 207 of these landfills closed and 42 still operating. Until 1980, it was perfectly legal to dump any amount of hazardous waste into a municipal landfill in the United States. After 1980, only households or companies generating less than 1.2 metric tons (1.3 tons) of hazardous waste a year could dump it into municipal landfills. Those generating more hazardous waste than that must send it to a federally approved landfill designed to accept hazardous wastes.

This provision is very difficult to enforce and can still allow large quantities of hazardous waste in conventional landfills. According to the General Accounting Office, the EPA does not know how much hazardous waste is produced by "small" generators each year, and they don't know how much of that ends up in municipal landfills.

Within the next five to ten years, half the existing U.S. landfills, especially in the East and the Midwest, will be filled and closed. Few new landfills are being built. Either there are no acceptable sites or else construction is prevented by citizens who want their trash hauled away but don't want a landfill anywhere near them.

Modern state-of-the-art landfills can handle municipal waste with little environmental impact if they are designed and located properly (Figure 19-12). However, only a small percentage of the 5,500 operating municipal landfills in the United States are state-of-the-art facilities. Only about 15% of existing landfills are lined, only 5% collect leachate, and only 25% monitor ground-

Figure 19-11 Hot dogs after ten years in a sanitary landfill. The idea that a landfill is a large compost pile in which things biodegrade fairly rapidly is a myth. Decomposition in modern landfills is quite slow because the garbage is tightly packed and exposed to little moisture and essentially no light. The biggest component in U.S. landfills is paper, which makes up 38% of the volume of waste. That is followed by plastic (18%), metals (14%), yard waste (11%), food (4%), glass (2%), and other materials (13%).

water. Places such as Long Island, New York, where the water table is high, should never have another landfill.

Some cities without enough landfill space are shipping their trash to other states or other countries, especially LDCs. Philadelphia, the fourth most populated U.S. city, has no active landfill and ships its wastes to seven other states. New York and New Jersey are also running out of landfill space and ship many of their solid wastes elsewhere.

However, some states and LDCs are rebelling against becoming the dumping grounds for other people's wastes (Figure 19-13). Increasingly, people, businesses, and communities will have to accept responsibility for the wastes they produce instead of trying to make them somebody else's problem. This will lead to increased recycling, reuse, and waste reduction because there is no away for the wastes we produce.

BURNING SOLID WASTE Incinerating solid waste has several advantages. It kills disease-carrying organisms (pathogens), reduces the volume of waste going to landfills by about 60% (not the 90% reduction usually cited), reduces the need for landfill space, and does not require changes in the throwaway habits of consumers, manufacturers, or waste haulers. Building incinerators is the biggest boost to construction engineering companies since the boom in nuclear power plant building in the 1960s. Also, once the waste is burned, the original producer of the waste escapes liability.

Proponents call incineration a form of waste reduction. However, instead of reducing the total amount of waste, it puts some of it into the air as gaseous pollutants and produces toxic fly ash and bottom ash that

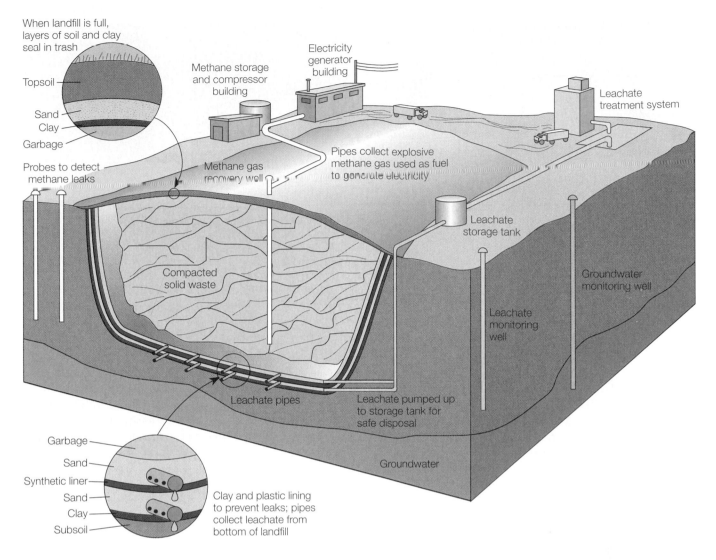

When landfill is full, layers of soil and clay seal in trash

Topsoil
Sand
Clay
Garbage

Probes to detect methane leaks

Methane storage and compressor building

Electricity generator building

Methane gas recovery well

Pipes collect explosive methane gas used as fuel to generate electricity

Leachate treatment system

Leachate storage tank

Compacted solid waste

Groundwater monitoring well

Leachate monitoring well

Leachate pipes

Leachate pumped up to storage tank for safe disposal

Groundwater

Garbage
Sand
Synthetic liner
Sand
Clay
Subsoil

Clay and plastic lining to prevent leaks; pipes collect leachate from bottom of landfill

Figure 19-12 A modern state-of-the art sanitary landfill is designed to eliminate or minimize environmental problems that plague older landfills. Siting is restricted to geologically suitable areas. Rainwater seeping into the landfill dissolves materials from the solid waste and forms a contaminated liquid called leachate. To collect leachate and prevent it from leaving the landfill and leaking into groundwater, the bottom is covered with an impermeable liner usually made of several layers of clay, thick plastic, and an asphalt membrane. Collected leachate is pumped from the bottom of the landfill and stored in tanks. It is then sent either to a regular sewage treatment plant or to an on-site treatment plant. When the landfill is full, it is covered with clay, sand, gravel, and topsoil to prevent water from seeping into its contents. Several wells are drilled around the landfill to monitor any leakage of leachate into nearby groundwater. Methane gas produced by anaerobic decomposition in the sealed landfill is collected and burned as a fuel to produce steam or electricity. Unfortunately, only a few of the municipal landfills in the United States have such state-of-the art design. Furthermore, even those landfills will leak, passing on contamination and cleanup costs to the next generation.

must be landfilled. Although the amount of material to be buried is greatly reduced, its toxicity is increased.

In *trash-to-energy incinerators*, trash is burned and the energy released is used to produce steam or electricity that can be sold or used to run the incinerator. Most are *mass-burn incinerators*, which burn mixed trash without separating out hazardous materials (such as batteries) and noncombustible materials that can interfere with combustion conditions and cause excessive air pollution. Denmark and Sweden burn 50% of their

solid waste to produce energy, compared with 10% in the United States.

Incineration has a number of drawbacks. In the United States, many existing municipal incinerators have been shut down because of numerous air pollution violations and excessive costs. In 1990, there were 128 trash-to-energy incinerators in operation in the United States and 19 under construction. Since 1985, about 64 new incinerator projects have been blocked, delayed, or cancelled because of citizen opposition and high costs.

Figure 19-13 There is no away. In 1987, the barge *Mobro* tried to dump 2,900 metric tons (3,190 tons) of garbage picked up from Islip, Long Island. It was refused permission to unload its cargo in North Carolina, Florida, Louisiana, the Bahamas, Mexico, and Honduras. After 164 days and a 9,700-kilometer (6,000-mile) journey, it came back to New York City, where it was barred from docking. After remaining in the harbor for three months, its garbage was incinerated in Brooklyn, leaving 364 metric tons (400 tons) of ash, which was shipped back to Islip for burial in a local landfill. The publicity from this event catalyzed Islip into developing a recycling program, and by 1989, it was recycling 35% of its solid waste. This has saved the community $2 million a year and has extended the life of the town landfill.

Of the 70 plants still in the planning stage, most face stiff opposition and may not be built as communities are discovering that recycling and waste reduction are cheaper, safer, and more politically acceptable alternatives. Recycling paper, for example, can save up to five times as much energy as can be recovered through incineration, which generated only about 0.2% of the country's energy production in 1990.

Incinerators are very expensive to build, operate, and maintain, and they create very few long-term jobs once they are built. Even with advanced air pollution control devices, incinerators emit small amounts of hydrochloric acid, highly toxic dioxins and furans, and tiny particles of lead, cadmium, mercury, and other toxic substances into the atmosphere. Without continuous maintenance and good operator training and supervision (see Spotlight on p. 527), the air pollution control equipment on incinerators often fails and exceeds emission standards.

Incinerators produce a residue of toxic ash, consisting of toxic *fly ash* (lightweight particles removed from smokestack emissions by air pollution control devices) and less toxic *bottom ash*. Usually, the two types of ash are mixed and disposed of in leak-prone ordinary landfills. The degree of toxicity of the ash varies with the composition of the trash burned, but in the United States the ash is usually contaminated with hazardous substances such as dioxins and lead, cadmium, mercury, and other toxic metals which can cause cancers and disorders of the nervous system. In the United States, the EPA does not classify such ash as hazardous waste, something biologist Barry Commoner calls "linguistic detoxification."

Because incinerator ash is in the form of a powder with a large surface area, toxic materials left after the

solid waste is burned can be leached into groundwater much faster than can bulkier toxic materials in conventional solid waste placed in a landfill. For the same reason, you get much stronger coffee by grinding up coffee beans in a drip coffee maker than if you used the larger raw beans. While many wastes can be viewed as a potential resource, that is not the case with toxic ash produced by incinerators.

Environmentalists have pushed the EPA to classify incinerator ash as hazardous waste and allow it to be disposed of only in landfills designed to handle hazardous waste, as is done in Japan. This has not been done, largely because waste management companies say it would make incineration too expensive and put them out of the incineration business. Environmentalists counter that if they aren't willing to properly dispose of the toxic ash they produce, they shouldn't be in the incineration business.

Environmentalists oppose heavy dependence on incinerators because it encourages people to continue tossing away paper, plastics, and other burnable materials rather than looking for ways to conserve, recycle, and reuse those resources and to reduce waste production. Once they are built, incinerators hinder recycling, reuse, and waste reduction because to be profitable, they must be fueled with a large volume of trash every day. According to biologist Barry Commoner, Director of the Center for the Biology of Natural Systems:

The proposed nationwide investment of $30 billion to be made over the next two decades by state, county, and municipal authorities in garbage incineration represents a monumental commitment to a technology which is fast becoming obsolete. If a similar investment were made in setting up and enforcing recycling programs, we would be much closer to solving the solid waste problem, ecologically and economically.

Incinerators, especially trash-to-energy incinerators, will play a role in a waste management system, because not everything can be recycled. However, environmentalists believe that no new incinerators should be built until a community is recycling *at least 60%* of its municipal solid waste. This allows a much smaller incinerator to be built and saves the community money.

Environmentalists also believe that incinerator operators should be required to have much better training, as is done in Japan (see Spotlight at right). Incineration in the United States is littered with faulty controls and errors by human operators that have exposed workers and people in surrounding areas to dangerous levels of air pollution.

Incinerator and landfill sites are hard to find because of citizen opposition. Indeed, one of the biggest environmental struggles in the 1990s is between citizens and environmentalists demanding pollution prevention and waste reduction, and the EPA and waste management companies pushing large-scale incinerators and landfills. The small number of large companies that dominate the multibillion-dollar waste hauling and disposal business in the United States are seeking ways to counter opposition to landfills and incinerators (see Spotlight on p. 528).

19-5 Extending Resource Supplies: Recycle, Reuse, Reduce

THE LOW-WASTE APPROACH Environmentalists and conservationists believe we should begin shifting from the high-waste, throwaway approach (Figure 3-20) to a low-waste, sustainable-Earth approach to dealing with nonfuel solid resources (Figure 3-21). This would require much greater emphasis on composting, recycling, reuse, and waste reduction, and much less emphasis on dumping, burying, and burning.

It involves teaching small children and adults to view trash cans and dumpsters as *resource containers* and trash as concentrated *urban ore* that needs to be separated into useful materials for recycling. Schools can be collection points for recycled materials as they were during World War II. Profits from school and university recycling centers run by students could be used to fund school activities. Students should also take field trips to recycling centers to see how the resources they collect are put back into use, as is done in Japan.

A pilot study of 100 families in East Hampton, New York, revealed that they achieved a recycling rate of 84% for their household trash. This shows that a 60% recycling rate—excluding yard waste which should be collected and composted—is achievable and should be the goal of all communities. Environmentalists believe that until that goal is achieved, communities should not

build new incinerators or open new landfills, which discourage recycling, reuse, and waste reduction and prevent reaching the 60% recycling goal.

Seattle, Washington, has the goal of recycling 60% of its municipal solid waste by 1998. With a 1989 recycling rate of 39%—the highest of any U.S. city its size—Seattle is well on its way. By comparison, New York City recycles only 6% of its garbage and Tucson, Arizona, only 0.02%.

Over half of the waste hauling and disposal business in the United States is dominated by two companies—Waste Management and Browning-Ferris Industries. In 1989, they took in $3.6 billion and $2.1 billion in revenues, respectively. With that sort of income, the $31 million in fines Waste Management was assessed for illegal dumping and spilling between 1981 and 1986 was paid off with just six days income as a minor cost of doing business.

However, their output approach to the country's waste problems is threatened by widespread citizen opposition to landfills and incinerators. Fighting these battles in every community is difficult and costly and has the effect of making recycling, reuse, and waste reduction cheaper in comparison. That, plus mounting legal costs and low profits, caused Browning-Ferris to an-

nounce in 1990 that it was getting out of the waste management business.

To help avoid these costly fights, large waste management companies have formed an alliance with the nation's railroads to develop a few giant landfills, which can accept wastes from cities thousands of kilometers away. That way, they have to fight only a few site battles. If these are state-of-the-art landfills (Figure 19-12), they reduce the number of potentially dangerous waste storage sites. These companies have also bought up old landfills and have offered to sell or lease the land as incinerator sites.

Environmentalists charge that these large waste management companies have enough economic and political power to keep the country too dependent on end-of-pipe, output approaches to waste manage-

ment, which hinders the shift to reuse, recycling, and waste reduction.

As evidence, environmentalists point to the revolving-door relationship between the waste industry and the EPA. The agency's former prosecutor, general counsel, and former director of enforcement now work for Waste Management. William Ruckelshaus, head of the EPA during most of Ronald Reagan's last term as president, is now head of Browning-Ferris Industries. In 1989, after a breakfast meeting with the head of Waste Management, the current EPA head, William Reilly, announced he would challenge a North Carolina law giving the state the power to prevent the siting of hazardous-waste facilities. After the story came out he backed down.

At least ten smaller U.S. communities have done even better than Seattle. Berlin Township, New Jersey, with a population of 6,000, recycled 57% of its solid waste in 1989. In that same year, Wellesley, Massachusetts, a town of 27,000, had a 41% recycling rate.

Twenty-nine states have set recycling goals ranging from 15% to 46%. Five states—Maine, Washington, New York, California, and Iowa—have plans to recycle 50% of their municipal solid waste by the year 2000 and New Jersey has set a 60% recycling goal. In 1986, Oregon passed a Recycling Opportunity Act designed to reduce the amount of waste generated by making recycling available to all citizens (see Individuals Matter on p. 529). However, more than half the states currently recycle less than 5% of the mass of their municipal solid waste.

COMPOSTING Biodegradable solid waste from slaughterhouses, food-processing plants, and kitchens, and yard waste, manure from animal feedlots (Figure 14-3), and municipal sewage sludge can be mixed with soil and decomposed by aerobic bacteria to produce **compost**, a sweet-smelling, dark brown humus material that is rich in organic matter and soil nutrients. It can be used as an organic soil fertilizer or conditioner, as topsoil, and as a landfill cover.

Compost can be produced from biodegradable solid waste in large plants, bagged, and sold. This ap-

proach is used in many European countries, including the Netherlands, the former West Germany, France, Sweden, and Italy, and in a large plant near Miami, Florida. Odor problems can be reduced by enclosing the facilities and using filters to deodorize the air inside.

Households can use backyard compost bins (Figure 12-19) to compost food and yard wastes. Seattle promotes backyard composting by using a network of volunteer composter experts to help people set up the process. Composting household yard waste would reduce the amount of solid waste in the United States by about 20%. Apartment dwellers can compost by using indoor bins in which a special type of earthworm converts food waste into humus.

Currently, only 1% of the mass of solid waste in the United States is composted. This could change because of a lack of landfill space, mandatory composting programs, and use of economic incentives to encourage composting. For example, locating a city compost heap next to a landfill would reduce the waste going to the landfill and extend its life. The compost can then be applied as landfill cover and used for fertilizing golf courses, parks, forests, roadway medians, and the grounds around public buildings. Compost can also be sold to the nursery and landscaping industries and commercial flower growers and can be used to help reclaim degraded rangeland (Figure 15-11).

In 1983, Lorie Parker, a long-time environmental activist, wrote an idealized recycling law based on voluntary participation for a college class project. She persuaded a legislator to introduce her proposed law as a state bill. To her surprise, it became Oregon's 1986 Recycling Opportunity Act.

Two years later, she was invited to administer the law as state manager of waste reduction. The first priority of the program she created and administers is to reduce the amount of waste generated, then to reuse material for its original purpose. The next priority is to recycle what cannot be reused. That is followed by energy recovery only from materials that cannot be reused or recycled, as long as incineration does not degrade the quality of air, water, or land resources. Only after those steps have been taken is landfilling used.

HIGH-TECH RESOURCE RECOVERY The salvaging of usable metals, paper, plastic, and glass from municipal solid waste and selling them to manufacturing industries for recycling or reuse is called **resource recovery**. This extends the supply of minerals by reducing the amount of virgin materials that must be extracted from Earth's crust to meet demand. Recycling and reuse usually require less energy and cause less pollution and land disruption than use of virgin resources. They also cut waste disposal costs and prolong the life of landfills by reducing the volume of solid waste.

Resources can be recycled by using high- or low-technology approaches. In *high-technology resource recovery plants*, machines shred and automatically separate mixed urban waste to recover glass, iron, aluminum, and other valuable materials (Figure 19-14). These materials are then sold to manufacturing industries as raw materials for recycling. The remaining paper, plastics, and other combustible wastes are recycled or incinerated. The heat given off is used to produce steam or

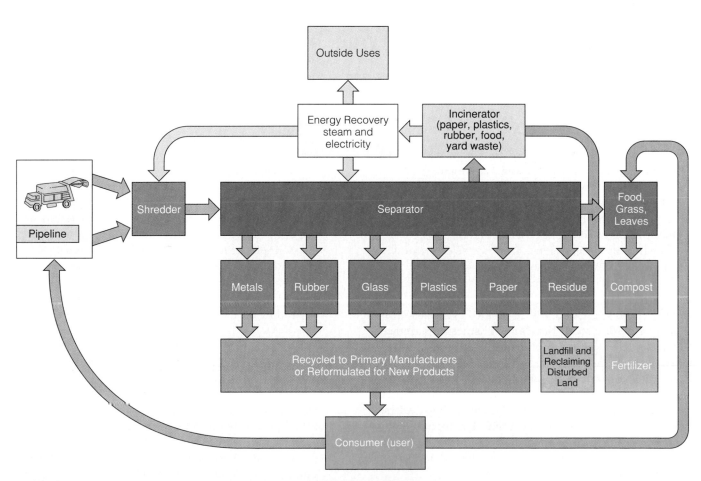

Figure 19-14 Generalized urban resource recovery system used to separate mixed wastes for recycling and burning to produce energy. Very few resource recovery plants of this type exist today. This high-tech approach is much more expensive and wasteful of energy than having consumers separate garbage into categories for recycling. Because resource recovery plants depend on high inputs of trash to be economical, they discourage reuse and waste reduction. For the same reason, trash-to-energy incinerators discourage the recycling of paper, plastics, and other combustible items.

Figure 19-15 Cart for separation of paper, plastics, glass, and cans in household waste to be picked up and recycled. This low-tech approach saves more energy and money than high-tech resource recovery plants and trash-to-energy incinerators. It also does more to sensitize consumers to the need to recycle and reuse and to reduce the amount of waste they produce.

electricity to run the recovery plant and for sale to nearby industries or residential developments.

Currently, the United States has only a few plants that recover some iron, aluminum, and glass for recycling. The plants are expensive to build and maintain. Once trash is mixed, it takes a lot of money and energy to separate it. It makes much more sense economically to have consumers separate trash into recyclable categories before it is picked up.

LOW-TECH RESOURCE RECOVERY With *low-technology resource recovery*, homes and businesses place various kinds of waste materials—usually glass, paper, metals, and plastics—into separate containers (Figure 19-15). Compartmentalized city collection trucks, private haulers, or volunteer recycling organizations pick up the segregated wastes and sell them to scrap dealers, compost plants, and manufacturers. The higher population density in large apartment and office buildings makes them better targets for recycling than single-household collection.

A comprehensive low-technology recycling program could save 5% of annual U.S. energy use—more than the energy generated by all U.S. nuclear power plants at perhaps one-hundredth of the capital and op-

erating costs. By contrast, burning all combustible urban solid waste in trash-to-energy plants would supply only 1% of the country's annual energy use.

The low-technology approach produces little air and water pollution, reduces litter, and has low start-up costs and moderate operating costs. It also saves more energy and provides more jobs for unskilled workers than high-technology resource recovery plants. This approach to recycling also creates three to six times more jobs per unit of material than landfilling or incineration. Another advantage is that collecting and selling aluminum cans (see Case Study on p. 531), paper, plastics (see Case Study on p. 533), and other materials for recycling is an important source of income for volunteer service organizations and for many people, especially the homeless and the poor in MDCs and LDCs (Figure 19-16).

Many communities are switching to low-tech recycling programs because it saves them money. Ideally, a community should set up one or more materials recovery centers. Each center would have a reuse and repair center, a place for consumers to take household toxic wastes and used motor oil, a composting area, a section for handling commercial waste, and a section in which separated household paper, aluminum, plastics, and iron and other metallic wastes are upgraded and marketed as sources of income for the community.

There are two types of recycling. The most desirable type is *primary*, or *closed-loop, recycling*, in which a product such as an aluminum can or a glass bottle is recycled to produce new products of the same type—newspaper into newspaper and cans into cans, for example.

The second and less desirable type, called *secondary*, or *open-loop, recycling*, occurs when waste materials such as plastics are converted into different products for which uses must be found. This does not reduce the use of resources as much as the first type of recycling. For example, primary recycling reduces the use of virgin materials in making a product by 20% to 90%, while the reduction with secondary recycling is 0% to 25%. Paper recycling involves a mix of these two methods, depending on the type of paper product produced.

BEVERAGE CONTAINER DEPOSIT BILLS Beverage container deposit laws can be used to decrease litter and encourage recycling of nonrefillable glass, metal, and plastic containers. Consumers pay a deposit (usually five or ten cents) on each beverage container they buy. The deposits are refunded when empty containers are turned in to retailers, redemption centers, or reverse vending machines, which return cash when consumers put in empty beverage cans and bottles.

Container deposit laws have been adopted in Sweden, Norway, the Netherlands, the Soviet Union, Ecuador, and parts of Australia, Canada, and Japan. Such laws have been proposed in almost every state in the

CASE STUDY Recycling Aluminum

Recycling aluminum produces 95% less air pollution and 97% less water pollution and requires 95% less energy than mining and processing aluminum ore. In the United States, the recycling rate for all aluminum in 1989 was 29%.

In 1990, about 62% of the new aluminum beverage cans used in the United States were recycled at more than 5,000 recycling centers set up by the aluminum industry, other private interests, and local governments.

People who returned the cans got about a penny a can, earning about $900 million. Within six weeks, the average recycled aluminum can has been melted down and is back on the market as a new can. Makers of aluminum cans saved $566 million and the energy equivalent of 20 million barrels of oil.

Despite this progress, about 38% of the 83 billion aluminum cans produced in 1990 in the United States

were still thrown away; more aluminum is in discarded cans than most countries use for all purposes. If the aluminum cans Americans throw away in one year were laid end-to-end, the cans would wrap around the earth more than 120 times. Each discarded aluminum can is almost indestructible solid waste.

The electricity needed to produce one aluminum can from virgin ore would keep a 100-watt light bulb burning for 100 hours. Recycling a can takes only 5% as much energy and saves the energy equivalent of six fluid ounces of gasoline.

Recycling aluminum cans is great, but many environmentalists see the aluminum can as a glaring example of an unnecessary and harmful product, regardless of how many are recycled. They believe that all aluminum cans could be replaced by reusable glass bottles that would be collected, washed, and filled by a nationwide network of local bottlers.

That would keep money and jobs in local communities, rather than in a few centralized production plants and distributors, and would reduce transportation and energy processing costs.

In 1964, 87% of beer and soda beverage containers in the United States were refillable glass bottles, but most local bottling companies were bought up or driven out of business by aluminum and large soft-drink companies. Refillable glass bottles now make up only 11% of the market, with nonrefillable aluminum and plastic containers making up the rest. Placing a heavy tax on each aluminum can and no tax on reusable glass bottles would help correct this situation. Meanwhile, consumers can refuse to buy anything packaged in aluminum cans (or plastic bottles, which are also an unnecessary item) and can buy reusable glass containers when they are available.

United States but have been enacted in only ten, affecting about one-fourth of the U.S. population. Maine has the toughest law. Studies by state and federal agencies show that such laws decrease litter, reduce the use of mineral resources, extend the life of landfills, increase recycling, save energy, reduce air and water pollution, and create jobs.

Environmentalists believe a nationwide deposit law should be passed by Congress. Surveys have also shown that a national container deposit law is supported by 73% of the Americans polled. So far, such a law has been effectively opposed in all but the ten states by a well-funded lobby of steel, aluminum, and glass companies, metalworkers' unions, supermarket chains, and most major brewers and soft-drink bottlers.

Ad campaigns financed by Keep America Beautiful and other groups opposing deposit laws have helped prevent passage of such laws in a number of states. These groups favor litter-recycling laws, which levy a tax on industries whose products may end up as litter or in landfills. Revenues from the tax are used to set up and maintain statewide recycling centers. By 1990, seven states, containing about 14% of the U.S. population, had this type of law.

Environmentalists point out that litter laws are waste management (output) approaches that provide

some money to clean up litter. By contrast, container deposit laws are waste reduction (input) approaches that reward consumers who return containers and that can make people aware of the need to shift to refillable containers. This is a main reason that companies making nonrefillable containers oppose such laws. Denmark has led the way by banning throwaway containers for soft drinks in 1977, and for beer in 1981.

TIRES There are now over 2 billion used tires heaped in landfills (Figure 19-18) and dump sites throughout the United States, and the pile grows by about 250 million tires a year. These tire dumps are fire hazards and breeding grounds for mosquitoes.

In recent years, several large dumps containing tires have caught fire and burned for weeks or months, polluting the air with soot, carbon dioxide, and particles of toxic metals such as cadmium, lead, zinc, and arsenic. In 1989, for example, there were at least 87 large tire fires in the United States. Each burning tire melts into crude oil and must be extinguished separately. Water sprayed onto the burning tires can carry the oil and other toxic substances with it and pollute nearby surface water and groundwater.

Some paper and cement companies are shredding tires and mixing the rubber with coal to burn in their

Figure 19-16 In many cities in LDCs, as much as 25% of the collected municipal waste is recycled by scavengers removing useful and salable materials from dump sites. Here, Philippine slum dwellers are scavenging for useful materials in Manila's main dump.

SIPA-Press

boilers. In Modesto, California, a power plant burns tires to generate enough electricity for 15,000 homes, using state-of-the-art air pollution controls. Next to the plant sits the world's largest pile of tires, 40 million of them.

Other companies are using pulverized tires to make resins for a number of products. Examples include car bumpers, garbage cans, doormats, road-building materials, and coverings for playgrounds. A Canadian firm and a Wisconsin firm have developed a process that converts used tires into heating oil and high-octane compounds that can substitute for lead in gasoline by heating the tires in the absence of oxygen in a sealed reactor (pyrolysis). Used tires have also been used to build artificial reefs to attract fish.

Used tires can be stacked up and filled with dirt to build the foundation and walls for passively heated solar homes at a low cost. The thick walls are finished with a cover of adobe mud and provide good insulation and thermal mass.

So far, however, only a tiny fraction of the tires thrown away each year are recycled. Even better, at least 20% of the tires thrown away could be retreaded to extend their life for almost as long as that of the original tires. Retreads are usually much cheaper than new tires. Also, tire companies could be required to make only tires that last for an average of 130,000 to 161,500 kilometers (80,000 to 100,000 miles) instead of 48,500 to 64,800 kilometers (30,000 to 40,000 miles).

OBSTACLES TO RECYCLING IN THE UNITED STATES Several factors hinder recycling in the United States. One is that Americans have been conditioned by advertising and example to accept a throwaway lifestyle. Another is that many of the environmental and health costs of items are not reflected in their market prices, so consumers have little incentive to recycle, reuse, or reduce their use of throwaway products.

The growth of the recycling, or secondary-materials, industry in the United States is hindered by several factors. One is that primary mining and energy industries get huge tax breaks, depletion allowances, and other tax-supported federal subsidies to encourage them to get virgin resources out of the ground as fast as possible. In contrast, recycling industries get few tax breaks and other subsidies, so there is an uneven economic playing field. The lack of large, steady markets for recycled materials also makes recycling a risky business. It is typically a boom-and-bust financial venture that attracts little investment capital.

Outdated laws also make mineral or timber resources on public lands available at low or no cost to private firms to encourage extraction of virgin materials. A glaring example is the U.S. General Mining Act of 1972, which environmentalists have been unable to persuade Congress to eliminate. This law allows anyone who finds metallic minerals on public land open for mineral exploration to buy the land for $12 per hectare ($4.86 per acre) or less, and does not require the miner to pay the government anything for the minerals extracted. In 1988, U.S. taxpayers received nothing for $4 billion worth of metallic minerals extracted from former public lands.

OVERCOMING THE OBSTACLES In 1988, the EPA set a goal of recycling 25% by weight of municipal solid waste by 1992—a step in the right direction but not enough to reach the 60% recycling level that would bring about a nationwide shift from waste management to waste reduction. By the year 2000, the United States

CASE STUDY What Should We Do About Plastics?

Plastics are synthesized from petrochemicals (chemicals produced from oil) to create long, repeating chains of molecules called polymers. The weight of plastics used in packaging in the United States more than doubled between 1974 and 1990 and is expected to triple by 1995. In 1990, about 25 million barrels of oil were used to produce plastic packaging in the United States. The plastics industry is among the leading producers of hazardous waste.

Plastics now account for about 8% of the weight and 20% of the volume of municipal solid wastes in the United States. Most plastics used today are nondegradable or take 200 to 400 years to degrade. In landfills, toxic cadmium and lead compounds used as binders and for other purposes can leach out of plastics and ooze into groundwater and surface water in unlined landfills or ones in which the liners have failed.

When plastics are thrown away as litter, they can harm wildlife (Figure 19-17). Plastics account for about 60% of the debris found on U.S. beaches.

Scientists have developed *photodegradable plastics* that disintegrate after a few weeks of exposure to sunlight. *Partially biodegradable plastics* are made with a combination of plastic and cornstarch. The cornstarch can be broken down in the soil by aerobic bacteria and moisture, leaving behind a fine powder of plastic. Instead of being biodegraded, the plastic in these products is merely converted into a plastic dust.

Photodegradable and biodegradable plastics make sense for products and containers likely to end up as outdoor litter but could also encourage people to throw away plastics. Without sunlight, photodegradable plastics take decades to hundreds of years to break down when covered in landfills. Even biodegradable plastics take decades to partially decompose in landfills because of a lack of oxygen and moisture.

Figure 19-17 Each year, plastic waste dumped from ships and left as litter on beaches threatens the lives of millions of marine animals and seabirds when they ingest such debris, wrap it around their mouth or beak, or choke on it. This Hawaii monk seal was slowly being choked to death by a discarded yoke before he was saved when the yoke was removed. Before disposing of such yokes, cut each of the holes. Maine has led the way by banning plastic yokes.

Doris Alcorn/National Marine Fisheries

We also need to know more about what degradable plastics degrade to. The residues from the breakdown of many plastics could contaminate groundwater supplies. They also may be hazardous to animals that ingest them.

To environmentalists it makes good sense to recycle plastics instead of burying slowly degradable plastics in landfills, and even better sense to reduce the amount of plastic we use. In theory, nearly all plastics could be recycled, but currently, less than 2% by weight of all plastic wastes and 5% of plastic packaging used in the United States are recycled.

When the label says that a plastic product is degradable or recyclable, this statement is true, but it is also highly misleading. Plastics degrade very slowly in landfills, and 98% of all plastic waste is not recycled.

One problem is that plastics rarely can be recycled to make the same products because of health and manufacturing problems, although some manufacturers are developing processes to correct this. Another problem is that trash contains several types of plastic, and some plastic products contain several types of plastic, which makes recycling difficult and costly.

With proper economic and political incentives, about 43% by weight of the plastic wastes produced in the United States could be recycled by

the year 2000. Since most of the raw materials used to make plastics come from petroleum and natural gas, recycling would help reduce unnecessary waste of these energy resources.

The $140-billion-a-year U.S. plastics industry has set up the Council for Solid Waste Solutions, which runs ads promoting plastics recycling. The main purpose of this organization is to keep us buying more plastics.

To environmentalists, the best solution is simply to use much less plastic in the first place, especially in throwaway items, and to pressure elected officials to ban the use of plastics in products for which other, less-harmful alternatives are available.

In 1991, McDonald's, whose 8,600 restaurants produce about 910 metric tons (1,000 tons) of trash a day, announced a 40-point plan to reduce its trash output by 80%. This plan, worked out with help from the Environmental Defense Fund, includes recycling, reusable packaging, and composting of garbage and an end to cutlery wrapped in plastic.

However, switching away from plastics to some other products is not always a clear environmental improvement. Problems and confusion over which products are the most environmentally benign could
(continued)

be dealt with by having standardized ecolabelling for all products, much like the Good Housekeeping Seal of Approval.

To be effective, such labelling programs must use a "cradle-to-grave" or life-cycle approach, in which the cumulative environmental impacts of products at the extraction, production, use, and disposal stages are taken into account (Figure 7-21). Labels awarded on narrower criteria, such as whether a product is made from recycled materials or is recyclable or biodegradable, can re-sult in use of products that cause considerable damage at other stages of their life cycle.

In the United States, a Green Seal, life-cycle labelling system is being set up by a coalition of environmental and consumer groups. In Canada, a government agency has established an Environmental Choice labelling system using cradle-to-grave analysis. Japan and several other countries have eco-labelling systems, but so far, they are not based on life-cycle analysis.

Meanwhile, when you go to a fast-food restaurant, why not take your own Earth-care kit consisting of a reusable cup, eating utensils, and dish? Ask the employees to fill your cup and put the food you order on your own plate. Before fast-food places arrived, all restaurants, school cafeterias, and other places serving food had dishes and silver-ware that were washed for reuse. No one's quality of life suffered from that approach. The price of packaging was not added to the food, and taxes used for waste disposal were lower.

Figure 19-18 Tires at a landfill in North Carolina illustrate the throwaway mentality prevalent in the United States and other affluent countries. The volume of waste tires could be reduced by recapping and requiring that all new tires last for at least 161,500 kilometers (100,000 miles). Tires could also be recycled or ground up and mixed with asphalt for road construction. With proper air pollution controls, used tires can also be burned in a power plant to produce electricity.

R. Calentine/Visuals Unlimited

could recycle and reuse 60% by weight of the municipal solid waste resources it now throws away.

Greatly increased recycling and reuse in the United States could be accomplished through the following measures:

- Enact a national beverage container law.

- Require that all beverage containers have several standardized sizes, forms, and colors, so that any bottler can refill bottles produced by other manufacturers.

- Ban use of disposable plastic items and disposable metal, glass, and plastic beverage containers.

- Establish a virgin materials tax.

- Tax manufacturers on the amount of waste they generate. In most countries, this could probably cut solid waste by at least a third.

- Include a waste disposal fee in the price of all disposable items (especially batteries, tires, cars, and appliances) rather than raising local taxes to pay for waste disposal, so market prices of items directly reflect what it costs to dispose of those items. This is now done in Florida, Massachusetts, and Minnesota.

- Provide economic incentives for recycling waste oil, plastics, tires, and CFCs used as coolants in refrigerators and air conditioners.

- Require labelling of products made with recycled materials and show the percentages used.

- Require manufacturers to design products to facilitate reuse and primary recycling.

- Provide federal and state subsidies and tax credits for secondary-materials industries and for municipal recycling and waste reduction programs. New York, North Carolina, Florida, Oregon, and Wisconsin give tax breaks to businesses that use secondary materials or buy recycling equipment.

- Decrease federal and state subsidies for primary-materials industries.

- Give sales tax exemptions or reductions for products made with recycled materials.

- Guarantee a large market for recycled items and stimulate the recycling industry by encouraging federal, state, and local governments to require the highest feasible percentage of recycled materials in all products they purchase. Twenty-two states have such laws, but their effectiveness varies widely.

- Use advertising and education to discourage the throwaway mentality.

- Require consumers to sort household wastes for recycling, or give them financial incentives for recycling. For example, trash separated for recycling can be picked up free, while people who don't separate their trash are charged a fee per bag or kilogram. Also, households can be provided with free reusable containers for separating recyclable trash. Ten states and many communities have laws making trash separation mandatory.

- Establish national standards for calculating and comparing municipal recycling rates.

- Encourage municipal composting and backyard composting by banning the disposal of yard wastes in landfills.

- Issue no permits for landfills or incinerators until a community or state has achieved a 60% recycling rate and established a program for waste reduction that reduces waste output per person by 20%.

REUSE Recycling is an important first step, but a much more important step is reuse, in which a product is used again and again in its original form. An example is glass beverage bottles that can be collected, washed, and refilled by local bottling companies (often as many as 50 or more times), a system that has now been largely dismantled in the United States (see Case Study on p. 531). This saves enormous amounts of energy compared with the other alternatives. It can also save consumers money in both product costs and in taxes and fees for waste management. Studies by Coca-Cola and Pepsi-Cola of Canada show that 0.5 liter (16-ounce) bottles of their soft drinks cost one-third less in refillable bottles.

All but one of Anheuser-Busch's 12 breweries in the United States still use refillable containers. According to company officials, the company has enough refilling capacity to provide the entire country with refillable bottles.

To encourage use of refillable bottles, Ecuador has a beverage container deposit fee that is 50% higher than the cost of the drink. This has been so successful that bottles as old as ten years continue to circulate. Sorting is not a problem because there are only two sizes of glass bottles allowed. In Finland, 95% of the soft drink, beer, wine, and spirits containers are refillable, and in Germany 73% are refillable.

Another reusable container is the metal or plastic lunchbox that most workers and school children once used. Today, many people carry their lunches in paper or plastic bags that are thrown away. At work, people can

SPOTLIGHT The Diaper Dilemma

Disposable diapers made from paper and coated with plastic may make life easier, but they are also messing up life in a throwaway society that has run out of places to throw things. The 18 billion disposable diapers used each year in the United States take up about 2% of the volume of solid waste dumped into landfills and take more than 200 years to degrade. Production of disposable diapers uses trees and creates air and water pollution.

Using cloth diapers, which can be washed and reused from 80 to 200 times and retired into lint-free rags, keeps about 8,000 to 10,000 disposable diapers weighing about 1 metric ton (1.1 ton) per baby from reaching landfills. This also saves trees and money. For example, using disposable diapers during the typical time a baby needs diapers costs about $1,533. A cloth diaper service costs about $975, and washing cloth diapers at home costs about $283.

The $3.3-billion-a-year disposable diaper industry hopes to keep its business by developing biodegradable diapers, but this is not a solution. Biodegradable diapers take decades to 100 years to break down in landfills, are still a throwaway item, and cost consumers more money than reusable cloth diapers.

The choice between disposable diapers and reusable cloth diapers is not clear-cut, illustrating the complexity of making environmentally sound decisions and the need to rate products on their entire life cycle. Disposable diapers consume paper and plastic resources, end up in landfills, and produce 90 times as much solid waste as cloth diapers, but laundering cloth diapers produces 9 times as much air pollution and 10 times as much water pollution as disposable diapers do in their lifetime. Over their lifetime, cloth diapers also consume 6 times more water and 3 times more energy than disposables.

From an environmental standpoint, neither product has a clear edge, but from a financial standpoint, cloth diapers have a distinct advantage. The best way to reduce use of any type of diaper is to encourage early toilet training, which will save money and time and also reduce the environmental impact of diaper use.

have their own Earth-care kit consisting of a reusable glass, coffee cup, plate, knife, fork, spoon, cloth napkin, and cloth towel, and they can encourage others to do this. These kits can also be taken to fast-food restaurants. Reusable cloth diapers can be used to replace disposable diapers, but this decision is not clear-cut (see Spotlight above).

Another example is reusable plastic or metal garbage cans and wastebaskets, which we should teach everyone to start calling *resource containers*. Using these containers to separate wastes for recycling (Figure 19-15) and rinsing them out as needed would eliminate the need to throw any garbage away in plastic bags, which waste oil and are themselves an unnecessary form of waste. Lining these containers with throwaway plastic bags is an expensive, unnecessary waste of matter and energy resources.

You can carry reusable baskets, canvas or plastic grocery bags, or string containers (Figure 19-19) when you shop for groceries or other items. Several can be folded up and kept in your handbag, pocket, or car. They eliminate the need to use either plastic or paper bags. This saves trees and oil and reduces pollution and environmental degradation.

Reuse extends resource supplies and reduces energy use and pollution even more than recycling. Refillable glass bottles are the most energy-efficient beverage container on the market. If reusable glass bottles replaced the 80 billion throwaway beverage cans produced annually in the United States, enough energy would be saved to supply the annual electricity needs of 13 million people. Denmark has led the way by banning all beverage containers that can't be reused.

Reuse is much easier if containers for products that can be packaged in reusable glass are available in only a few sizes. In Norway and Denmark, fewer than 20 sizes of reusable containers for beer and soft drinks are allowed. A popular bumper sticker reads: "Recyclers do it more than once." A much better version would be "Recyclers do it more than once, but reusers do it the most."

WASTE REDUCTION Reducing unnecessary waste of nonrenewable mineral resources, plastics, and paper can extend supplies even more dramatically than recycling and reuse. Reducing waste generally saves more energy and virgin resources than recycling and reduces the environmental impacts of extracting, processing, and using resources (Figure 7-21). Table 19-1 compares the throwaway resource system of the United States, a resource recovery and recycling system, and a sustainable-Earth, or low-waste, resource system. Ultimately, a sustainable-Earth resource system is based on this principle: "If you can't recycle or reuse something, don't make it."

Manufacturers can conserve resources by using less material per product and by redesigning manufacturing processes to use fewer resources and produce less waste. Lighter cars, for example, save nonfuel mineral resources as well as energy and can still meet, or exceed, the safety standards required for all cars (Figure 17-4). Solid-state electronic devices and microwave transmissions greatly reduce materials requirements. Optical fibers drastically reduce the demand for copper

Seventh Generation

Figure 19-19 An example of good Earthkeeping. A reusable string bag can be used to carry groceries and other purchases and avoid the use of throwaway paper and plastic bags, both of which are environmentally harmful even if they are recycled. Cloth or canvas bags can also be used.

wire in telephone transmission lines. Manufacturers have reduced the weight of some of their packaging bottles and cartons by 10% to 30%.

Unnecessary packaging, which makes up 50% of the volume and 32% of the weight of U.S. garbage, can be eliminated, which saves manufacturers and consumers money. One dollar out of every $11 spent for groceries in the United States pays for packaging, and U.S. consumers spend more on food packaging annually than all the revenue received by farmers. Many products in hardware, grocery, and clothing stores need no packaging. We should be asking for and buying products available "in the nude." Packaging should be minimal and where possible should be returnable, refillable, reusable. If that is not feasible, then the packaging should be recyclable and made from the greatest possible amount of recycled materials. Waste reduction in packaging could easily reduce the mass of solid waste produced by 10%; with vigorous standards, the reduction could be 20%.

Another low-waste approach is to make products that last longer. The economies of the United States and most industrial countries are built on the principle of planned obsolescence so people will buy more things to stimulate the economy and raise short-term profits, even though that can eventually lead to economic and environmental grief. Many consumers can empathize with Willy Loman in Arthur Miller's *Death of a Salesman*: "Once in my life I would like to own something outright before it's broken! I'm always in a race with the junkyard."

Table 19-1 Three Systems for Handling Discarded Materials

Item	For a High-Waste Throwaway System	For a Moderate-Waste Resource Recovery and Recycling System	For a Low-Waste Sustainable-Earth System
Glass bottles	Dump or bury	Grind and remelt; remanufacture; convert into building materials	Ban all nonreturnable bottles. Reuse bottles
Bimetallic "tin" cans	Dump or bury	Sort, remelt	Limit or ban production. Use returnable bottles
Aluminum cans	Dump or bury	Sort, remelt	Limit or ban production. Use returnable bottles
Cars	Dump	Sort, remelt	Sort, remelt. Tax cars lasting less than 15 years and getting less than 17 kilometers per liter (40 miles per gallon)
Metal objects	Dump or bury	Sort, remelt	Sort, remelt. Tax items lasting less than 10 years
Tires	Dump, burn, or bury	Grind and revulcanize or use in road construction; incinerate to generate heat and electricity	Recap usable tires. Tax or ban all tires not usable for at least 96,000 kilometers (60,000 miles)
Paper	Dump, burn, or bury	Incinerate to generate heat	Compost or recycle. Tax all throwaway items. Eliminate overpackaging
Plastics	Dump, burn, or bury	Incinerate to generate heat or electricity	Limit production; use returnable glass bottles instead of plastic containers; tax throwaway items and packaging
Yard wastes	Dump, burn, or bury	Incinerate to generate heat or electricity	Compost; return to soil as fertilizer; use as animal feed

Manufacturers should design products that are easy to reuse, recycle (primary), and repair. All engineering and design students should be taught how to do this as a major part of their education. Today, many items are intentionally designed to make repair, reuse, or recycling impossible or too expensive. Manufacturers should adopt the principle of modular design, which allows circuits in computers, television sets, and other electronic devices to be replaced easily and quickly without replacing the entire item. We also need to develop remanufacturing industries that would disassemble, repair, and reassemble used and broken items.

One of the best ways to reduce municipal solid waste is to cut down on unnecessary packaging, which makes up about 50% of the volume and 30% of the weight of municipal waste. Packaging accounts for 50% of all paper produced in the United States, 90% of all glass, and 11% of all aluminum.

Adopt the three Rs of Earth care: Reduce, Reuse, Recycle. Think of recycling as a first and important baby step in helping sustain the earth. Then move to reuse as part of environmental adolescence, and reach environmental maturity by sharply reducing the amount of waste you produce (see Individuals Matter on p. 538).

This means that making and using throwaway items should be considered anti-Earth activities.

We will always produce some wastes, but the amount we produce can be greatly reduced by not using wasteful or hazardous products and by redesigning manufacturing processes. To do that, we must force elected officials to get serious about using input approaches to prevent most waste (especially hazardous waste) from being produced or from reaching the environment. So far, less than 1% of the U.S. government's environmental spending goes for pollution prevention and waste reduction.

The end-of-pipe or output methods for managing wastes that we now depend on merely move potential pollutants from one part of the environment to another and are eventually overwhelmed by more people producing more wastes. This was summarized over a century ago by Chief Seattle: "Contaminate your bed, and you will one night suffocate in your own waste." To prevent pollution and waste we must understand and live by three key principles: Everything is interconnected; there is no away for the wastes we produce; and dilution is not the solution to most pollution.

In the 1980s, President Ronald Reagan said that "no country ever conserved its way into greatness." This

- As your top priority, make a conscious effort to produce less waste, mostly by not using disposable paper, plastic, or metal products when other alternatives are available. Before you buy anything, ask yourself whether you really need that product.

- If they are available, buy refillable glass containers for beverages instead of cans or throwaway bottles.

- Use plastic or metal lunchboxes and metal or plastic garbage containers without plastic throwaway bags as liners. Wrap sandwiches in biodegradable wax paper, or, better, put them in small reusable plastic containers. Use reusable containers to store food in refrigerators instead of wrapping food in aluminum foil or plastic wrap.

- Use pens that take refills or new cartridges instead of disposable pens.

- Use computer-paper and other cardboard boxes as storage files.

- Use unbleached paper coffee filters to reduce your exposure to toxic dioxins leached out of bleached paper filters. A much better and cheaper solution is cloth filters that can be reused. After use, they should be rinsed and stored in a glass of water in a refrigerator to prevent buildup of rancid coffee oils.

- Use rechargeable batteries. Manufacturing a standard disposable battery uses 50 times more electricity than the battery generates. The 2.5 billion disposable batteries thrown away each year in the United States are a significant source of toxic metals, such as lead and cadmium, that can leak from landfills.

- Carry groceries and other items in a reusable basket, a canvas or string bag (Figure 19-19), or a small cart. You could also save and reuse plastic bags from grocery and other stores. BYOC (bring your own container) is one reason why Europeans, Africans, and Asians produce so much less solid waste per person than most people in the United States. Tell store clerks and managers why you are doing this and increase their sensitivity to unnecessary waste. Ideally, all stores would not provide paper or plastic bags, or would charge for them.

- Skip the bag when you buy only a quart of milk, a loaf of bread, or anything you can carry out with your hands. Tell store clerks and managers why you are doing this.

- Use washable cloth napkins and dish towels and sponges instead of paper ones.

- Don't use throwaway paper and plastic plates and cups, eating utensils, razors, pens, lighters, and other disposable items when reusable or refillable versions are available.

- Avoid red or yellow packaging. Such packaging is the kind most likely to contain toxic cadmium and lead.

- Buy recycled goods, especially those made by primary, or closed-loop, recycling, and then recycle them. This is very important, because without a sufficient demand, products from recycled materials will not be profitable and will not be made in large quantities. Cardboard containers that are gray inside usually contain recycled paper fibers, while those with white interiors don't. A wide variety of items made from recycled paper can be ordered by catalog from Earth Care Paper, P.O. Box 335, Madison, WI 53704. A wide range of recycled and other environmentally sound items can also be bought by catalog from Seventh Generation, 10 Farell St., South Burlington, VT 05403, (800) 441-2358.

frontier view is no longer valid. Instead, the primary way the United States can maintain its economy and prestige is through resource conservation. This will require it to use its brainpower (based on greatly strengthening its educational system) and the money it can make from its remaining resources to help itself and the world make the transition from a high-waste, throwaway society to a low-waste, sustainable-Earth society over the next few decades. Denying the need to do this and waiting too long to begin this cultural change can lead to economic and environmental decline.

If consumers continue to buy products that are disposable, unessential, hard to repair, and short-lived, they are voting with their pocketbooks—the most powerful force they have—to continue depleting Earth's capital. We can send a powerful message by refusing to buy high-waste, Earth-degrading products and emphasizing purchase of things we truly need. This will catalyze companies into making low-waste, longer-lasting, Earth-sustaining products. This is using the buying power you have to help change the world.

Solid wastes are only raw materials we're too stupid to use.

ARTHUR C. CLARKE

- Recycle all newspapers, glass, and aluminum and any other items accepted for recycling in your community.

- Buy repairable items and ones that last for a long time.

- Just say no to throwaway plastic items. They are made from petrochemicals, take decades to degrade in today's landfills, can release toxics into the environment during production and when burned or degraded, hinder efforts to reduce and recycle plastics, and pose a threat to wildlife (Figure 19-17).

- Reduce the amount of junk mail you get by writing to Mail Preference Service, Direct Marketing Association, 11 West 42nd St., P.O. Box 3681, New York, NY 10163-3861, or by calling (212) 768-7277, asking that your name not be sold to large mailing-list companies. Write companies that send solicited or paid subscriptions, and ask that your name not be sold to mailing-list companies. Write shopping lists, notes, and phone messages on the backs of junk-mail paper and cut-up cereal cartons. Recycle as much of the paper from junk mail as possible.

- Cover used phone books with oilcloth, adhesive-backed plastic, or a heavy-duty plastic bag, and use them as a step stool, a footrest, or a child's booster chair and give them to friends.

- Push for mandatory trash-separation and recycling programs in your community and schools.

- Push for use of washable, reusable dishes and silverware in school and business cafeterias.

- Ask stores, communities, and colleges to install reverse vending machines that give you cash for each reusable or recyclable container you put in.

- Buy food items in large cans or in bulk to reduce packaging. Also, buy concentrates whenever possible.

- Avoid excessive packaged goods. For instance, buy fresh fruit and vegetables loose, not in plastic bags or wrapped in plastic on trays.

- Choose items that have the least packaging or, better yet, no packaging ("nude products"). When enough people do this, producers of packaged materials will get the message.

- Don't buy helium-filled balloons, and urge elected officials and university administrators to ban balloon releases except for atmospheric research and monitoring.

- Compost your yard and food wastes (Figure 12-19), and pressure local officials to set up a community composting program. Currently, an average of 15% of the solid food bought for use in U.S. households is thrown out.

- Cut up old carpet or carpet remnants into strips to make paths between garden rows or in other areas.

- Share, barter, trade, or donate items you no longer need.

- Pressure managers of businesses and schools to recycle computer and other office paper and to set up an easy system to encourage in-office recycling.

- Ask heads of companies to switch their letterhead and paper stock to recycled products.

- Copy and write on both sides of the page.

- Join a local environmental group and urge it to identify suppliers of recycled products in your area.

- Consider going into the recycling business as a way to make money.

- Don't litter.

DISCUSSION TOPICS

1. Debate each of the following propositions:
   a. The competitive free market will control the supply and demand of mineral resources.
   b. New discoveries will provide all the raw materials we need.
   c. The ocean will supply all the mineral resources we need.
   d. We will not run out of key mineral resources because we can always mine lower-grade deposits.
   e. When a mineral resource becomes scarce, we can always find a substitute.
   f. When a nonrenewable resource becomes scarce, all we have to do is recycle it.

2. Use the second law of energy (thermodynamics) to show why the following options are usually not profitable without subsidies:
   a. extracting most minerals dissolved in seawater
   b. recycling minerals that are widely dispersed
   c. mining increasingly lower-grade deposits of minerals
   d. using inexhaustible solar energy to mine minerals
   e. continuing to mine, use, and recycle minerals at increasing rates
   f. building high-tech resource recovery plants (Figure 19-14) to separate mixed wastes for recycling

3. Explain why you support or oppose the following:
   a. eliminating all tax breaks and depletion allowances for extraction of virgin resources by mining industries

b. passing a national beverage container deposit law

c. requiring that all beverage containers be reusable

4. Would you favor requiring all households and businesses to sort recyclable materials for curbside pickup in separate containers? Explain.

5. Compare the throwaway, recycling, and sustainable-Earth (or low-waste) approaches to waste disposal and resource recovery and conservation for **(a)** glass bottles, **(b)** "tin" cans, **(c)** aluminum cans, **(d)** plastics, **(e)** yard wastes, and **(f)** food wastes (see Table 19-1). Which approach do you favor? Which approach do you use in your own lifestyle?

*6. What mineral resources are mined in your local area? What mining methods are used? Do local, state, or federal laws require restoration of the landscape after mining is completed? If so, how well are those laws enforced?

*7. Keep a list for a week of the solid waste materials you dispose of. What percentage is composed of materials that could be recycled, reused, or burned as a source of energy?

*8. Determine whether **(a)** your school and your city have recycling programs; **(b)** your school sells soft drinks in throwaway cans or bottles; **(c)** your school bans release of helium-filled balloons at sporting events and other activities, and **(d)** your state has, or is contemplating, a law requiring deposits on all beverage containers.

*9. What happens to solid waste in your community? How much is landfilled? Incinerated? Composted? Recycled? What technology is used in local landfills and incinerators? What leakage and pollution problems have local landfills or incinerators had? Does your community have a recycling program? Is it voluntary or mandatory? Does it have curbside collection? Drop-off centers? Buy-back centers? What is the annual cost of the recycling program, and how much money has it saved?

*10. As a class project, develop an improved solid waste management program for your community and submit your plan to local officials.

PART SIX

POLLUTION

I am utterly convinced that most of the great environmental struggles will be either won or lost in the 1990s, and that by the next century it will be too late to act

THOMAS E. LOVEJOY

North America's largest copper smelter and the world's tallest smokestack in Sudbury, Ontario, Canada. The tallest stack is higher than the length of four football fields.

CHAPTER 20

RISK, HUMAN HEALTH, AND HAZARDOUS WASTE

General Questions and Issues

1. What are common hazards that people face, and what are their effects?

2. What are the biggest health risks for people living in LDCs and in MDCs?

3. How can the risks and benefits associated with using a particular technology or product be estimated and managed?

4. What risks can lead to cancer, and how can they be reduced?

5. What are the principal types, sources, and effects of hazardous waste, and how can hazardous wastes be managed and reduced?

Though their health needs differ drastically, the rich and the poor do have one thing in common: both die unnecessarily. The rich die of heart disease and cancer, the poor of diarrhea, pneumonia, and measles. Scientific medicine could vastly reduce the mortality caused by these illnesses. Yet, half the developing world lacks medical care of any kind.

WILLIAM U. CHANDLER

 VERY FORM OF TECHNOLOGY and everything we make or consume result in some pollution and degradation of the environment and involve some degree of risk to our health and the health of other species. Thus, there are no environmentally friendly products or processes, only ones that are more or less environmentally harmful than others. In evaluating the many risks we face, the key questions are whether the risks of damage from each hazard outweigh the benefits and how we can reduce the hazards and minimize the risks.

20-1 Hazards: Types and Effects

COMMON HAZARDS **Risk** is the possibility of suffering harm from a hazard. A **hazard** is a substance or an action that can cause injury, disease, economic loss, or environmental damage. Most hazards come from exposure to various factors in the environment.

- *Physical hazards*: ionizing radiation (see Spotlight on p. 543), noise (Table 9-2), fires, floods (see Case Study on p. 342), drought, tornadoes, hurricanes, landslides, earthquakes, and volcanoes (Section 7-4)

- *Chemical hazards*: harmful chemicals in air (Chapter 21), water (Chapter 22), and food (see Spotlight on p. 371 and Chapter 23)

- *Biological hazards*: disease-causing bacteria and viruses (Figure 20-2), pollen, and parasites

- *Cultural hazards*: working and living conditions, smoking, diet, drugs, drinking, driving, criminal assault, unsafe sex, and poverty (see Spotlight on p. 8)

CHEMICAL HAZARDS The principal types of chemical hazards (see Spotlight on p. 545) are

- **Toxic substances**: chemicals that are fatal to humans in low doses or fatal to over 50% of test animals at stated concentrations. Most are *neurotoxins*, which attack nerve cells. Examples are nerve gases, botulism toxin, potassium cyanide, heroin, chlorinated hydrocarbons (DDT, PCBs, dioxins), organophosphate pesticides (Malathion, Parathion), carbamate pesticides (Sevin, Zeneb), and various compounds of arsenic, mercury, lead, and cadmium. Most toxic substances are discharged into the environment by industry (Figure 20-3).

- **Hazardous substances**: chemicals that can cause harm because they are flammable or explosive, irritate or damage the skin or lungs (such as strong

Ionizing radiation, a form of electromagnetic radiation (Figure 3-4), has enough energy to damage body tissues. Examples of ionizing radiation are ultraviolet radiation from the sun and sunlamps (see Spotlight on p. 300), X rays, neutrons emitted by nuclear fission (Figure 3-10) and nuclear fusion (Figure 3-12), and alpha, beta, and gamma radiation emitted by radioactive isotopes (Figure 3-9).

Exposure to ionizing radiation can result in two kinds of damage to cells in the human body. One is *genetic damage*, which alters genes and chromosomes. This can show up as a genetic defect in immediate offspring or several generations later. The second type is *somatic damage*, which can cause harm during the victim's lifetime. Examples are burns, some types of leukemia, miscarriages, eye cataracts, and cancers (bone, thyroid, breast, skin, and lung).

The effects of ionizing radiation depend on the amount and frequency of exposure, the type of ionizing radiation, its penetrating power (Figure 3-9), and whether it comes from outside or inside the body. Rapidly growing tissues of the developing embryo are extremely sensitive, so pregnant women especially should avoid all unnecessary exposure to radioactivity and X rays unless they are essential for health or diagnostic purposes.

Exposure to a large dose of ionizing radiation over a short time can be fatal within a few minutes to a few months, depending on the dose. Small doses of ionizing radiation over a long period of time cause less damage than the same total dosage given all at once. However, a 1990 study by the National Academy of Sciences concludes that the likelihood of getting cancer from exposure to a low dose of radiation is three to four times higher than previously thought.

Some scientists believe that the current limit on occupational exposure to low-level radiation needs to be reduced by a factor of 10, and perhaps by as much as a factor of 1000. Evidence for this was provided by a 1991 study revealing that workers at Tennessee's Oak Ridge National Laboratory exposed to radiation well below permissible levels were more likely to die from leukemia than the rest of the American population. When two other researchers published data in the early 1970s showing a higher-than-suspected risk of cancer among workers at the Department of Energy's Hanford Nuclear Reservation, the DOE funding for their research was discontinued.

Each year, Americans are exposed to a fairly small amount of ionizing radiation from natural, or background, sources and from human activities (Figure 20-1). Sources of natural, or background, ionizing include cosmic rays (a high-energy form of ionizing electromagnetic radiation) from outer space; radioactive radon-222 in soil and rock (see Case Study on p. 580), and natural radioactivity in our bodies from intakes of air, water, and food.

We get additional exposure to ionizing radiation as a result of various human activities (Figure 20-1). The lowest level of exposure from human activities is from nuclear power plants and other nuclear facilities, as long as they are operating properly.

Most ionizing radiation from human activities comes from medical X rays and from diagnostic tests and treatment using radioactive isotopes. The federal government estimates that one-third of the 600 million X rays taken each year in the United States are unnecessary. If

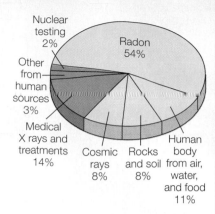

Natural background radiation (81%)
Human sources of radiation (19%)

Figure 20-1 Contribution of natural sources and human activities to the average annual dose of ionizing radiation received by the population of the United States. Most studies indicate that there is no safe dose of ionizing radiation. We can do little to avoid natural ionizing radiation, but we can minimize our exposure to ionizing radiation from human sources. (Data from National Council on Radiation Protection and Measurements)

your doctor or dentist proposes an X ray or a diagnostic test involving radioisotopes, ask why it is necessary, how it will help find what is wrong and influence possible treatment, and what alternative tests are available with less risk.

According to the National Academy of Sciences, exposure over an average lifetime to average levels of ionizing radiation from natural and human sources causes about 1% of all fatal cancers and 5% to 6% of all normally encountered genetic defects in the U.S. population. That explains why any unnecessary increase in emissions of or exposure to ionizing radiation from human activities should be avoided.

Figure 20-2 Unsafe water supply in Nigeria, Africa. Transmissible disease from drinking contaminated water is the leading killer, especially of young children, in LDCs.

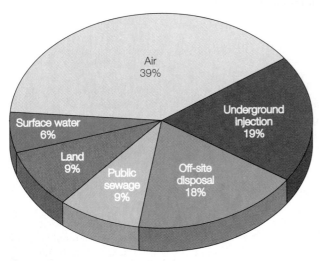

Figure 20-3 Legal toxic discharges by industry in the United States. In 1988, 19,762 industrial plants released at least 2.8 billion kilograms (6.24 billion pounds) of toxic chemicals into the environment. (Data from Environmental Protection Agency)

acidic or alkaline substances, Figure 12-6), or induce allergic reactions of the immune system (allergens).

- **Carcinogens**: chemicals, ionizing radiation, and viruses that cause or promote the growth of a malignant tumor, or **cancer**, in which cells in a certain type of tissue multiply and invade the surrounding tissue. If not detected and treated in time, many cancerous tumors undergo **metastasis**; that is, they release malignant (cancerous) cells that travel in body fluids to various parts of the body, making treatment much more difficult. Typically,

10 to 40 years may elapse before a cancer reaches detectable size.

- **Mutagens**: chemicals, ionizing radiation, and heat that cause **mutations** (inheritable changes in the DNA molecules in the genes found in chromosomes). The altered genes transmit these traits from parent to offspring. Some mutations are beneficial, but most are harmful. The harmful ones can cause some types of cancer or various inheritable diseases such as manic depression, cystic fibrosis, hemophilia, sickle-cell anemia, and Down's syndrome.

- **Teratogens**: chemicals, ionizing agents, and viruses that cause birth defects. Examples of chemicals known to cause birth defects in laboratory animals are caffeine, PCBs, and heavy metals such as arsenic, cadmium, lead, and mercury.

DETERMINING TOXICITY LEVELS Determining the toxicity levels of chemicals or ionizing radiation and the harmful effects of biological organisms is difficult, costly, and controversial. Because it is neither ethical nor practical to use people to test toxicity, it is usually determined by carrying out tests on live (*in vivo*) laboratory animals (mostly mice and rats for testing carcinogens and guinea pigs, mice, and some primates for testing harmful microorganisms), bacteria, and cell and tissue cultures.

Tests are run to develop a *dose-response curve*, which shows the effects of high doses of a toxic agent on a group of test organisms, with the results extrapolated by the use of mathematical models to project possible effects on test animals at low doses. Then the results on

Whether or not a chemical is harmful to us depends mostly on how much we are exposed to during a certain amount of time and how well our bodies' detoxification systems (especially the liver, lungs, and kidneys) work

Some people have the mistaken idea that all natural chemicals are safe and all synthetic chemicals are harmful. Many synthetic chemicals are quite safe for their intended uses, and a great many natural chemicals are quite deadly. Over millions of years of natural selection, plant species have survived by making natural chemicals to keep away or kill the animals or insects that eat them. Soil, water, and food often contain some of these natural chemicals that are potentially harmful. Thus, the problem with natural and synthetic chemicals is trying to take in enough of the ones we need to keep us alive and avoiding exposure to too much of the chemicals that can harm us.

We cannot live in a risk-free or pollution-free environment, but we don't want to take unnecessary risks. Therefore, we must have some understandable estimate of the risks and benefits involved in the use of a given chemical or technology (such as a car or nuclear power). However, there are several problems involved in getting such information.

- Estimating the risks and benefits for just one chemical or one technology is a difficult, expensive, time-consuming, and controversial activity.

- We are introducing new technologies and synthetic organic chemicals at such rapid exponential rates that our ability to estimate the risks and benefits of even a few of them has been overwhelmed. According to the National Academy of Sciences, only about 10% of the 70,000 chemicals in commercial use have been subjected to thorough toxicity testing, and only 2% have been adequately tested to determine whether they are carcinogens, teratogens, or mutagens. Thorough toxicity testing has been carried out for only 2% of cosmetic ingredients, 5% of food additives, 10% of pesticides, and 18% of drugs used in medicines. Each year, about 1,000 new chemicals are introduced into the marketplace, with little knowledge about their potentially harmful effects. In effect, we are playing an increasingly rapid game of chemical and technological Russian roulette with ourselves, other species, and Earth's life-support systems.

- Even if we could determine the biggest risks associated with a particular technology or chemical, we would know little about its possible interactions with other technologies, chemicals, and social systems and the effects of such interactions

- Some chemicals and radioactive isotopes bioaccumulate or become biologically magnified in certain parts of the body (Figure 16-18). Because such chemicals remain in the body for long periods, prolonged exposure to even small amounts can eventually exceed threshold levels of toxicity and cause serious harm or premature death.

We face a serious dilemma. We are adding more and more largely unknown and unpredictable risks to our lives, hoping that their benefits, mostly unknown, will outweigh their harm. Some call that progress and urge us to speed up the treadmill of economic production and growth (see Guest Essay on p. 29). Others call it madness and ask us to slow down the treadmill to a more manageable pace, with emphasis on pollution prevention and risk reduction rather than trying to manage a rapidly growing output of wastes (see Guest Essays on pp. 46 and 572).

---

test animals are extrapolated to humans. The **lethal dose** is the amount of material per unit of body weight of the test animals that kills all of the test population in a certain time. Then the dose is reduced until an exposure level is found that kills half the test population in a certain time. This is the **median lethal dose** or **LD$_{50}$**. Using high dose levels reduces the number of test animals needed, cuts the time needed for results to show up, and lowers costs.

There are several problems with animal tests. Extrapolating test animal data from high dose to low dose levels is uncertain and controversial. According to the *linear dose-response model*, any dose of ionizing radiation or some toxic chemical is harmful and the harm rises as the dose increases. With the *threshold dose-response model*, there is a threshold dose below which no detectable harmful effects occur. It is very difficult to establish whether these or other models apply at low doses. Many scientists also question the validity of extrapolating data from test animals to humans because human physiology and metabolism are different from those of the test animals. Also, animal tests take two to five years and cost from $200,000 to $1 million per substance and are coming under increasing fire from animal rights groups (see Pro/Con on p. 413).

There is also controversy over the effectiveness of using bacteria and cell and tissue cultures for determining harmful effects of toxic agents on humans. One of the most widely used bacterial tests, the Ames test, is considered to be an accurate predictor of substances that cause genetic mutations (mutagens) and is also quick (two weeks) and cheap ($1,000 to $1,500 per substance). However, evidence indicates that this test is not a reliable predictor of substances that cause or promote cancer (carcinogens). Cell and tissue culture tests have similar uncertainties, take several weeks to months, and cost about $18,000 per substance.

Another approach to toxicity testing and determining the agents causing diseases such as cancer is **epidemiology**—an attempt to find out why some people get sick and some do not. Typically, the effects on people exposed to a particular toxic chemical or other agent from an industrial accident, people working under high exposure levels, or people in certain geographic areas are compared with groups of people not exposed to those conditions to see if there are statistically significant differences.

This approach also has limitations. For many toxic agents, not enough people have been exposed to high enough levels to detect statistically significant differences. Because people are exposed to many different toxic agents and disease-causing factors throughout their lives, it is not possible to say with much certainty that an observed epidemiological effect is caused only by exposure to a particular toxic agent or to another hazardous condition. Because epidemiology can be used only to evaluate hazards to which people have already been exposed, it is rarely useful for predicting the effects of new technologies or substances.

Thus, all the methods we use to estimate toxicity levels have serious limitations. However, they are all we have.

20-2 Biological Hazards: Disease, Economics, and Geography

TYPES OF DISEASE Human diseases can be broadly classified as transmissible and nontransmissible. A **transmissible disease** is caused by living organisms, such as bacteria, viruses, and parasitic worms, and can be spread from one person to another by air, water (Figure 20-1), food, body fluids, and, in some cases, insects and other nonhuman transmitters (called *vectors*). Examples are sexually transmitted diseases (see Case Study on p. 547), malaria (see Case Study on p. 548), schistosomiasis, elephantiasis, sleeping sickness, and measles.

A **nontransmissible disease** is not caused by living organisms and does not spread from one person to another. Examples include cardiovascular (heart and blood vessel) disorders, cancer, diabetes, chronic respiratory diseases (bronchitis and emphysema), and mal-

nutrition (see Figure 1-3 and Spotlight on p. 370). Many of these diseases have several, often unknown, causes and tend to develop slowly and progressively over time.

DISEASE IN LDCs Poverty is by far the greatest risk to human health and is the underlying cause of lowered average life expectancy and increased infant mortality (Figure 8-10) in LDCs and for poor people in MDCs. It increases the spread of transmissible diseases, which account for about 40% of all deaths in LDCs, compared with only 8% of all deaths in MDCs. This occurs mostly because of overcrowding, unsafe drinking water (Figure 20-1), poor sanitation, and malnutrition (see Spotlight on p. 370), which are often associated with living in poverty. The hot, wet climates of tropical and subtropical countries also increase the chances of infection, because organisms that cause or carry disease can thrive year-round.

Fortunately, significant improvements in human health in LDCs can be made with primary preventive health care measures at a relatively low cost. These include providing

- Contraceptive supplies (Figure 8-7), sex education, and family planning counseling.

- Better nutrition, prenatal care, and birth assistance for pregnant women. At least 500,000 women in LDCs die each year of mostly preventable pregnancy-related causes, compared with only 6,000 in MDCs.

- Greatly improved postnatal care (including the promotion of breastfeeding) to reduce infant mortality.

- Immunization against tetanus, measles, diphtheria, typhoid, and tuberculosis.

- Oral rehydration for diarrhea victims by feeding them a simple solution of water, salt, and sugar.

- Antibiotics for infections.

- Clean drinking water and sanitation facilities to the third of the world's population that lacks them.

Extending such primary health care to all the world's people would cost an additional $10 billion a year, one twenty-fifth as much as the world spends each year on cigarettes. Relatively small expenditures on research and control of tropical diseases by governments of MDCs and LDCs would greatly reduce death rates and suffering from tropical diseases.

DISEASES IN MDCs As a country industrializes and makes the *demographic transition* (Figure 8-15), it also makes an *epidemiologic transition*, in which the infectious diseases of childhood become less important and the chronic diseases of adulthood (heart disease and

Major Sexually Transmitted Diseases

Sexually transmitted diseases (STDs) are caused mostly when certain bacteria or viruses are transmitted from infected to uninfected persons during sexual activity. In the United States, the number of new reported cases of most STDs has been rising each year since 1981. Each year, one out of every seven sexually active teenagers in the United States on average contracts a sexually transmitted disease.

Major STDs caused by bacteria are *chlamydia* (which affects as many as 45% of sexually active U.S. teenagers and college students), *gonorrhea*, and *syphilis*. These diseases can be treated with antibiotics if caught in time before damage occurs.

Major diseases caused by viruses are *genital warts* (which may have infected 10 million to 12 million Americans), *genital herpes* (which may have infected 20% of sexually active persons in the United States), and *Acquired Immune Deficiency Syndrome* or *AIDS* (which is spreading rapidly). All these virus-caused diseases are incurable.

The AIDS Epidemic As the incidence of this incurable and fatal disease rounds the bend of the J-curve of exponential growth, its visibility should convince almost everyone that it is one of the world's most serious health threats.

By April 1991, officials of the World Health Organization estimated that almost 1 million people worldwide had AIDS (700,000 of them in Africa), with 60% of those infections linked to heterosexual transmission. An additional 8 million to 10 million people are believed to be infected with the HIV virus, two-thirds of them in LDCs.

By the year 2000, the number of people infected with the AIDs virus is expected to be 40 million (80% of them in LDCs and 10 million of them children), and the number of people with full-blown AIDS is expected to reach at least 6 million. The World Health Organization projects that by then up to 90% of all HIV infections worldwide will be transmitted heterosexually, with this also becoming the primary transmission method in MDCs. If present trends continue, by the year 2010, 1.5 million to 2 million people will have died from AIDS.

By April 1991, about 1 million HIV infections (some estimate 3 million), 172,000 AIDS cases, and 84,000 deaths had occurred in the United States. About 2 of every 1,000 college students tested are infected with the AIDS virus. The crack cocaine epidemic has created a new group of high-risk heterosexual women who trade sex for the drug.

Preventing Sexually Transmitted Diseases

The risk of getting an STD can be greatly reduced in several ways by

- not having sex with another person

- not having sex with anyone known to be or suspected of being an intravenous (IV) drug user

- having sex only with one mutually faithful, uninfected partner

- having sex using a good-quality latex condom plus the spermicide nonoxynol-9 smeared on the outside and inside of the condom tip

- not shooting drugs; if drugs are shot, always using a clean needle that has not been used by anyone else and that is never reused

---

stroke, cancer, and respiratory infections) become more important in determining mortality. Generally, people in countries making this transition have a longer life expectancy at birth and a lower average infant mortality rate (Figure 8-10), although that usually does not hold true for the poorest people in such MDCs.

In MDCs, most deaths are a result of environmental and lifestyle factors rather than infectious agents invading the body. Except for auto accidents (see Pro/Con on p. 240), these deaths result from chronic diseases that take a long time to develop, have multiple causes, and are largely related to the area in which people live (urban or rural), their work environment, their diet, whether they smoke, how much exercise they get, their sexual habits (see Case Study above), and whether they abuse alcohol or other harmful drugs.

Changing these harmful lifestyle factors could prevent 40% to 70% of all premature deaths, one-third of all cases of acute disability, and two-thirds of all cases of chronic disability. So far, about 95% of the money spent on health care in the United States (amounting to about 11% of the GNP) is used to treat rather than prevent disease—a severe and tragic imbalance that needs to be corrected.

More than half the world's population live in malaria-prone regions in about 100 countries in tropical and subtropical regions, especially West Africa and Central and Southeast Asia (Figure 20-4). Malaria is spread by various species of the water-breeding *Anopheles* mosquito and afflicts up to 500 million people worldwide. Each year, it kills at least 2.5 million (some sources say 5 million) people. At least half of its victims are children under the age of five.

There are at least 100 million new cases each year, with the largest number of infections occurring in sub-Saharan Africa. Even in the United States, an average of four people discover they have malaria each day. Malaria's symptoms come and go; they include fever and chills, anemia, an enlarged spleen, severe abdominal pain and headaches, extreme weakness, and greater susceptibility to other diseases.

Malaria is caused by one or more of four species of protozoa of the genus *Plasmodium*. Most cases of the disease are transmitted when an uninfected female of about 60 of the 400 different species of *Anopheles* mosquito bites an infected person and then bites an uninfected person (Figure 20-5). When this happens, *Plasmodium* parasites move from the mosquito into the bloodstream, multiply in the liver, and then enter blood cells to continue multiplying (Figure 20-5). Malaria can also be transmitted when a person receives the blood of an infected donor or when a drug user shares a needle with an infected user. This cycle repeats itself until immunity develops, treatment is given, or the victim dies.

During the 1950s and 1960s, the

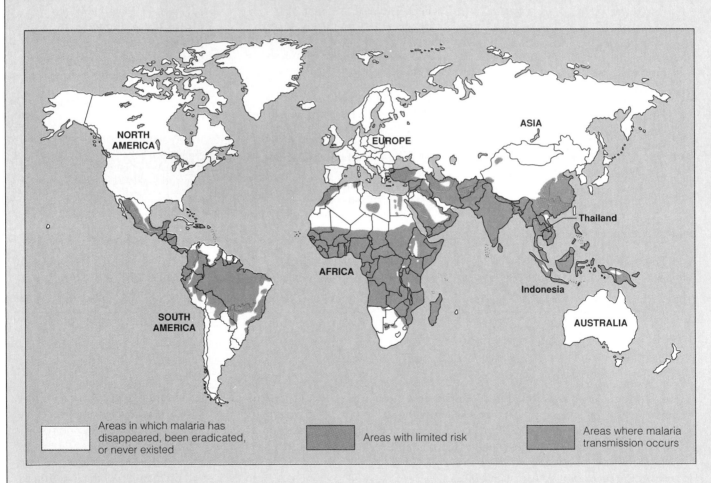

Figure 20-4 Malaria threatens half the world's population. (Data from the World Health Organization)

Legend:
- Areas in which malaria has disappeared, been eradicated, or never existed
- Areas with limited risk
- Areas where malaria transmission occurs

spread of malaria was sharply reduced by draining swamplands and marshes; by spraying breeding areas with DDT, dieldrin, and other pesticides; and by using drugs to kill the *Plasmodium* parasites in the bloodstream.

That strategy worked for two decades, but since 1970 malaria has made a dramatic comeback in many parts of the world, for several reasons. Because of repeated spraying, most of the malaria-carrying species of *Anopheles* mosquitoes have become genetically resistant to most of the insecticides used. The protozoa

have become genetically resistant to widely used antimalarial drugs. Irrigation ditches, which provide breeding grounds for mosquitoes, have increased in number, and budgets for malaria control have been reduced because of the mistaken belief that the disease was under control.

Researchers are working to develop new antimalarial drugs and vaccines and biological controls for *Anopheles* mosquitoes, but such approaches are in the early stages of development, have proved to be more difficult than originally

thought, and lack adequate funding. The World Health Organization estimates that only 3% of the money spent worldwide each year on biomedical research is devoted to malaria and other tropical diseases, even though more people suffer and die worldwide from these diseases than from all others combined.

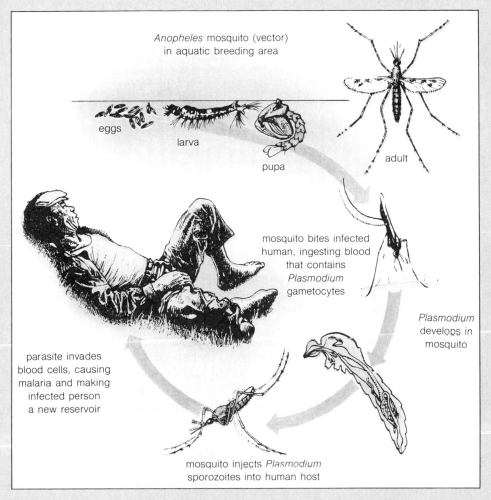

Figure 20-5 The life cycle of malaria.

Anopheles mosquito (vector) in aquatic breeding area

eggs

larva

pupa

adult

mosquito bites infected human, ingesting blood that contains *Plasmodium* gametocytes

Plasmodium develops in mosquito

parasite invades blood cells, causing malaria and making infected person a new reservoir

mosquito injects *Plasmodium* sporozoites into human host

Risk Assessment and Risk Management

RISK ANALYSIS AND ESTIMATING RISKS **Risk analysis** involves identifying hazards (Table 6-1), evaluating the nature and severity of risks (*risk assessment*), using that and other information to determine options and make decisions about reducing or eliminating risks (*risk management*), and communicating information about risks to decision makers and the public (*risk communication*).

Formal risk assessment is difficult, imprecise, and controversial. It involves determining the types of hazards involved, estimating the number of people likely to be exposed to the hazard and the number likely to suffer serious consequences, and estimating the probability of each hazard occurring. Probabilities based on past experience, animal and other tests, and epidemiological studies are used to estimate risks from older technologies and products. For new technologies and products, much more uncertain statistical probabilities, based on models rather than actual experience, must be calculated. Table 20-1 summarizes the greatest ecological and health risks identified by a panel of scientists acting as advisers to the U.S. Environmental Protection Agency.

The more complex a technological system, the more difficult it is to make realistic calculations of risks based on statistical probabilities of the failure of equipment and people. The total reliability of any technological system is the product of two factors:

$$\frac{\text{system}}{\text{reliability (\%)}} = \frac{\text{technology}}{\text{reliability}} \times \frac{\text{human}}{\text{reliability}} \times 100$$

With careful design, quality control, maintenance, and monitoring, a high degree of technology reliability can usually be obtained in complex systems such as a nuclear power plant, the space shuttle, or an early warning system for nuclear attack. However, human reliability is almost always much lower than technology reliability and is virtually impossible to predict; to be human is to err.

For example, suppose that the technology reliability of a system such as a nuclear power plant is 95% (0.95) and the human reliability is 65% (0.65). Then the overall system reliability is only 62% (0.95 × 0.65 = 0.62 × 100 = 62%). Even if we could increase the technology reliability to 100% (1.0), the overall system reliability would still be only 65% (1.0 × 0.65 = 0.65 × 100 = 65%).

This crucial dependence of even the most carefully designed systems on unpredictable human reliability helps explain the occurrence of events that risk analysts consider almost impossible. Examples are the Three Mile Island and Chernobyl nuclear power plant acci-

Table 20-1 Greatest Ecological and Health Risks

High-Risk Ecological Problems

Global climate change
Stratospheric ozone depletion
Wildlife habitat alteration and destruction
Species extinction and loss of biodiversity

Medium-Risk Ecological Problems

Acid deposition
Pesticides
Airborne toxic chemicals
Toxic chemicals, nutrients, and turbidity in surface waters

Low-Risk Ecological Problems

Oil spills
Groundwater pollution
Radioactive isotopes
Acid runoff to surface waters
Thermal pollution

High-Risk Health Problems

Indoor air pollution
Outdoor air pollution
Worker exposure to industrial or farm chemicals
Pollutants in drinking water
Pesticide residues on food
Toxic chemicals in consumer products

Data from Science Advisory Board, *Reducing Risks*. (Washington, DC: Environmental Protection Agency, 1990. Items in each category are not listed in rank order.

dents (see Spotlight on p. 490), the tragic (and unnecessary) explosion of the space shuttle *Challenger*, and the far too frequent false alarms given by early warning defense systems on which the fate of the entire world depends.

Poor management, poor training, and poor supervision increase the chances of human errors. Maintenance workers or people who monitor warning panels in complex systems such as the control rooms of nuclear power plants (Figure 20-6) become bored and inattentive because nothing goes wrong most of the time. They may fall asleep while on duty (as has happened at several U.S. nuclear plant control rooms); they may falsify maintenance records because they believe that the system is safe without their help; they may be distracted by personal problems or illness; or they may be told by managers to take shortcuts to increase short-term profits or to make the managers look more efficient and productive.

One way to improve system reliability is to move more of the potentially fallible elements from the human side to the technical side, making the system more foolproof or "fail-safe." However, chance events, such as a lightning bolt, can knock out automatic control systems. No machine or computer program can replace all the skillful human actions and decisions involved in

Figure 20-6 Control room of a nuclear power plant. Watching these indicators is such a boring job that government investigators have found some operators asleep, and in one case, they found no one in the control room. Most accidents at nuclear power plants have resulted primarily from human errors.

seeing that a complex system operates properly and safely. Also, the parts in any automated control system are manufactured, assembled, tested, certified, and maintained by fallible human beings.

RISK-BENEFIT ANALYSIS The key question is whether the estimated short- and long-term benefits of using a particular technology or product outweigh the estimated short- and long-term risks compared with other alternatives. One method for making such evaluations is **risk-benefit analysis**. It involves estimating the short- and long-term societal benefits and risks involved and then dividing the benefits by the risks to find a **desirability quotient**:

$$\text{desirability quotient} = \frac{\text{societal benefits}}{\text{societal risks}}$$

Assuming that accurate calculations of benefits and risks can be made (a big assumption), here are several possibilities

1. large desirability quotient = $\dfrac{\text{large societal benefits}}{\text{small societal risks}}$

Example: *X rays*. Use of ionizing radiation in the form of X rays to detect bone fractures and other medical problems has a large desirability quotient. This is true, however, only if X rays are not overused to protect doctors from liability suits, the dose is no larger than needed, and less harmful alternatives are not available. Other examples in this category are mining, most dams, and airplane travel. Proponents of nuclear power plants place that technology in this category.

2. very small desirability quotient = $\dfrac{\text{very small societal benefits}}{\text{very large societal risks}}$

Example: *Nuclear war*. Global nuclear war has no societal benefits (except the short-term profits made by companies making weapons and weapons defense systems) and involves totally unacceptable risks to the human species and Earth's life-support systems for all species, as discussed in Section 11-5.

3. small desirability quotient = $\dfrac{\text{large societal benefits}}{\text{much larger societal risks}}$

Example: *Coal-burning power plants* (Section 18-2) *and nuclear power plants* (Section 18-3). Nuclear and coal-burning power plants provide society with electricity—a highly desirable benefit—but many analysts contend that the short- and long-term societal risks from widespread use of these technologies outweigh the benefits. They believe that other, more economically and environmentally acceptable alternatives exist for producing electricity with less severe societal risks (see Chapter 17 and Guest Essay on p. 75).

4. uncertain desirability quotient = $\dfrac{\text{large benefits}}{\text{large risks}}$

Example: *Genetic engineering* (see Pro/Con on p. 161). Some see this new biotechnology as a way to increase food supplies, degrade toxic wastes, eliminate certain genetic diseases and afflictions, and make enormous amounts of money. Others fear that its use, without strict controls, could cause many unpredictable, possibly harmful effects, as have many other forms of technology.

According to the National Academy of Sciences, pesticides account for 2.1% of all U.S. cancer deaths each year. That means that pesticides licensed for use in the United States legally kill about 10,000 real, but nameless, Americans a year prematurely from cancer, without the informed consent of the victims.

Some environmentalists point out that if you or I put a poison in a supply of public drinking water or in food bought in a grocery or a restaurant and kill a number of people, we are committing premeditated murder. However, if the government allows companies to put enough poisonous chemicals in our water or food supply to kill a certain number of people, that is acceptable and not punishable by law. A 1991 study by researchers at the Oak Ridge National Laboratory concluded that the background environmental cancer risk from just 11 chemicals is 1 in 1,000—about 1,000 times more risk than the EPA would allow any individual to create.

These environmentalists argue that if the names of the victims were published, then most people would probably consider these actions that expose people to dangerous chemicals to be premeditated murder, and the public would demand that regulators concentrate on maximizing risk reduction by emphasizing pollution prevention instead of pollution control. Former EPA policy analyst Ken Bogen calls risk assessment that trades lives for dollars "probabilistic cannibalism."

While risk analysis attempts to find some politically or economically acceptable level of pollution or other risk, pollution prevention aims at reducing the risk to health to the lowest possible level. If a pollutant or a risky technology is eliminated or reduced to a very low level of risk, the elaborate and uncertain system of risk assessment, standard setting, and the resulting controversy and legal challenges become irrelevant.

Proponents of risk analysis argue that anything we do has some risk and that formal risk analysis helps regulators evaluate and reduce risks. Just because risk analysis is difficult and uncertain does not mean that it should not be done or that it is not useful.

Despite the inevitable uncertainties involved, proponents argue that risk analysis is a useful way to organize available information, identify significant hazards, focus on areas that need more research, and stimulate people to make decisions about health and environmental goals and priorities. What do you think?

PROBLEMS WITH RISK ASSESSMENT Calculation of desirability quotients and other ways of evaluating or expressing risk is extremely difficult, filled with uncertainty, and controversial. Listed here are some of the problems and issues.

- Some technologies benefit one group of people (population A) while imposing a risk on another (population B). Who should decide which groups benefit and which ones are harmed?

- Some people making the estimates emphasize short-term risks, while others put more weight on long-term risks. Which type of risk should get more emphasis and who decides this?

- Who should carry out a particular risk-benefit analysis or risk assessment? Should it be the corporation or government agency involved in developing or managing the technology, or some independent laboratory or panel of scientists? If it involves outside evaluation, who chooses the persons to do the study? Who pays the bill and thus has the potential to influence the outcome by refusing to give the lab, agency, or experts future business? How do we prevent risk assessors from selecting the goal that their assessment is supposed to achieve (such as killing no more than 1 in 1 million people) and then manipulating the data and assumptions to come up with the "right" answer?

- Once a risk-assessment study is done, who reviews the results—a government agency, independent scientists, the general public—and what influence will outside criticism have on the final decisions?

- Should the cumulative impacts of various risks be considered, or should risks be considered separately as is usually done? For example, a pesticide might be found to have a risk of killing 1 in 1 million Americans, the acceptable death limit set by the EPA. However, the cumulative effects from 40 such pesticides may kill 40 of every 1 million Americans, far beyond the officially acceptable limit.

- Is risk analysis a useful and much-needed tool, or is it, as some critics charge, a way to justify premeditated murder in the name of profit (see Pro/Con above)?

Scientists, politicians, and the general public who must make decisions based on risk assessments should be aware of their serious limitations. They should rec-

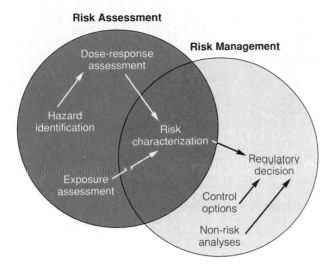

Risk Assessment

Risk Management

Dose-response assessment

Hazard identification

Risk characterization

Exposure assessment

Regulatory decision

Control options

Non-risk analyses

Figure 20-7 Summary of risk assessment and risk management. (Environmental Protection Agency)

ognize that politics, economics, and value judgments that can be biased in either direction are involved at every step of the risk analysis process. At best, risk assessments can be expressed only as a range of probabilities and uncertainties based on different assumptions—not the precise bottom-line numbers that decision makers want.

MANAGING RISK **Risk management** includes the administrative, political, and economic actions taken to decide how, and if, a particular societal risk is to be reduced to a certain level, and at what cost. It is integrated with risk assessment (Figure 20-7). Risk management involves trying to answer the following questions:

- Which of the vast number of risks facing society should be evaluated and managed with the limited funds available?

- In what sequence or priority should the risks be evaluated and managed?

- How reliable is the risk-benefit analysis or risk assessment carried out for each risk?

- How much risk is acceptable? How safe is safe enough?

- How much money will it take to reduce each risk to an acceptable level?

- How much will each risk be reduced if limited funds are available, as is usually the case?

- How will the risk management plan be communicated to the public, monitored, and enforced?

Risk managers must make difficult decisions involving inadequate and uncertain scientific data, potentially grave consequences for human health and the environment, and large economic effects on industry

and consumers. Thus, each step in this process involves value judgments and trade-offs to find some reasonable compromise between conflicting political and economic interests.

So far, most risk reduction from pollutants has focused on output or end-of-pipe pollution control techniques. Beginning with and emphasizing front-of-pipe pollution prevention instead of end-of-pipe pollution control is the key to risk reduction (Figure 20-8), but so far, efforts to do this have been mostly talk, not serious action.

RISK PERCEPTION AND COMMUNICATION

Most of us are bad at assessing the risks from the hazards that surround us. We are risk-illiterate and full of contradictions. On the one hand, we deny and shrug off high-risk activities such as driving or riding in a car, not wearing seat belts, hang gliding, and exposing ourselves to the cancer-causing rays of the sun or tanning lamps to get a tan (see Spotlight on p. 300).

On the other hand, we insist on zero or near-zero risk from things that are quite unlikely to kill us, mostly because of dramatized and well-publicized events. Some of us become almost paranoid about eating apples that might bear a trace of a pesticide, riding in a commercial airplane, or being killed by a burglar, a mugger, a shark, a snake, or a spider.

Being bombarded with news about people killed or harmed by various hazards distorts our sense of risk. The real news each year is that 99% of the people on Earth didn't die, but that is not considered dramatic news by the media and most of the public. Changing our concept of what news is means each day's leading story would be that 99% or more of the people in a community, a country, or the world did not get murdered, did not die in an automobile or airplane accident, and did not die from exposure to a certain chemical or ionizing radiation.

The public generally perceives that a technology or a product has a greater risk than the risk estimated by experts when it

- Is relatively new or complex (genetic engineering, nuclear power) rather than familiar (dams, automobiles).

- Is mostly involuntary (nuclear power plants, nuclear weapons, industrial pollution, food additives) instead of voluntary (smoking, drinking alcohol, driving).

- Is viewed as beneficial and necessary (cars and firearms) rather than unnecessary (CFCs and hydrocarbons as propellants in aerosol spray cans, food additives used to increase sales appeal).

- Involves a well-publicized large number of deaths and injuries from a single catastrophic accident (severe nuclear power plant accident, industrial explosion, or plane crash) rather than the same or a

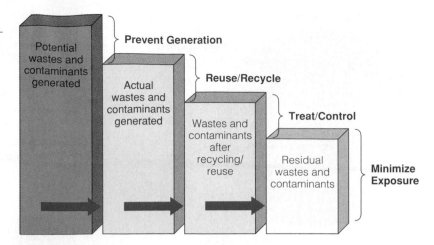

Figure 20-8 Priorities for reducing the risks from harmful wastes and contaminants. (Environmental Protection Agency)

Potential wastes and contaminants generated

Prevent Generation

Actual wastes and contaminants generated

Reuse/Recycle

Wastes and contaminants after recycling/reuse

Treat/Control

Residual wastes and contaminants

Minimize Exposure

Figure 20-9 The stretch along the Mississippi River between Baton Rouge and New Orleans, Louisiana, is lined with oil refineries and petrochemical plants. Along this corridor, known as "Cancer Alley" because of its abnormally high cancer rates, enormous amounts of carcinogenic and mutagenic chemicals leak into groundwater or are discharged into the river. In 1988, an environmental alliance of residents protested chemical dumping in their communities and groundwater by marching the 137 kilometers (85 miles) from Baton Rouge to New Orleans.

Sam Kittner/Greenpeace

larger number of deaths spread out over a longer time (coal-burning power plants, automobiles, malnutrition in LDCs). For example, U.S. citizens tolerate 45,000 deaths from automobile accidents each year — equivalent to a fully loaded passenger jet crashing with no survivors every day — because those deaths are distributed in space and time. If those deaths occurred at one place and at the same time, as in a plane crash, they would be considered a monstrous catastrophe and would not be tolerated, and safety standards for cars would be increased drastically.

■ Involves unfair distribution of the risks. Citizens are outraged when government officials decide to put a hazardous-waste landfill or incinerator in or near their neighborhood under the guise of scientific analysis. This is usually viewed as politics, not science.

■ Is poorly communicated. Does the decision-making agency or company come across as trust-worthy and concerned or as dishonest, unconcerned, and arrogant (as Exxon was viewed after the Valdez oil spill, and the Nuclear Regulatory Agency and the nuclear industry have been viewed since the Three Mile Island accident)? Does it involve the community in the decision-making process from start to finish and tell it what's going on before the real decisions are made? Does it understand, listen to, and respond to community concerns? Does it mostly let the public blow off steam at a few public meetings while decisions are made behind closed doors without serious public participation or consultation?

■ Does not take into account ethical and moral concerns. Spewing out numbers and talking about cost-risk trade-offs seem very callous when the risk involves moral issues such as the health of people and other species and environmental quality.

People who believe their lives and the lives of their children are being threatened because they live near an actual or proposed chemical plant (Figure 20-9), toxic waste dump, or waste incinerator couldn't care less that experts say the chemical is likely to kill only 1 out of 1 million people in the general population. Only a small number of those million people live or will live near the plant, dump, or incinerator as they do. To those on the front lines of risk, often the poor and middle class, risk is a personal threat, not a statistical abstraction.

Unless risk-analysis communicators understand and take into account the perceptions, concerns, fears, interests, values, priorities, and preferences of individuals and public groups, the information they provide is likely to be ignored (see Guest Essay on p. 572). Risk communicators also need to point out clearly the assumptions and uncertainties in their estimates and risk comparisons. They also must acknowledge that risk analysis is a way to help make political and economic decisions based on useful but incomplete and often controversial statistical and scientific evidence.

Some observers contend that when it comes to evaluation of large-scale, complex technologies, the public often is better at seeing the big picture than the risk-benefit specialists, who look primarily at the details. This commonsense wisdom does not usually depend on understanding or even caring about the details of risk-benefit analysis. Instead, it is based on the average person's understanding that science and technology have limits and that the people responsible for making and managing potentially hazardous technological systems and products are fallible just like everyone else.

20-4 Risk Factors and Cancer

CANCER INCIDENCE AND CURE RATES Cancer will strike about 1 million Americans this year, and one of every three Americans now living will eventually have some type of cancer (see Spotlight on p. 300). On the average, one person dies from cancer every 66 seconds in the United States. Worldwide, one of every ten deaths is due to cancer.

The good news is that almost 50% of Americans (under age 75) who get cancer can now be cured (defined as being alive and cancer-free five or more years after treatment), compared with only 38% in 1960. Survival rates for some types of cancers now range from 66% to 88%. This has happened mostly because of a combination of early detection and improved use of surgery, radiation, and drug treatments.

CANCER RISK FACTORS According to the World Health Organization, environmental and lifestyle factors play a key role in causing or promoting 80% to 90%

SPOTLIGHT Working Can Be Hazardous to Your Health

Roughly one-fourth of U.S. workers run the risk of some type of illness from routine exposure to one or more toxic compounds. The National Institute for Occupational Safety and Health estimates that as many as 100,000 deaths a year—at least half from cancer—are linked to worker exposure to toxic agents in the United States. In the United States, the most dangerous occupation is farming, followed by construction, mining, and factory work.

Most work-related illnesses and premature deaths could be prevented by stricter laws and enforcement of existing laws governing exposure of workers to ionizing radiation and dangerous chemicals. However, political pressure by industry officials has hindered effective enforcement of these laws.

Farmers, construction workers, miners, and factory workers should be at the forefront of the environmental movement because they face unusually high environmental risks, which could be greatly reduced. They and their families have more to lose than most people from poorly enforced or weak environmental and occupational safety laws. These workers are frontline guinea pigs who feel they must take high health risks to feed themselves and their families.

---

of cancers. Major sources of carcinogens are cigarette smoke (40% of cancers), dietary factors (25% to 30%), occupational exposure (10% to 15%; see Spotlight above), and environmental pollutants (5% to 10%). About 10% to 20% of cancers are believed to be caused by inherited genetic factors and some viruses.

The risks of developing cancer can be greatly reduced by working and living in a less hazardous environment, not smoking or being around smokers (see Case Study on p. 556), drinking in moderation (no more than two beers or drinks a day) or not at all, adhering to a healthful diet (see Spotlight on p. 558), and shielding oneself from the sun (see Spotlight on p. 300). According to experts, 60% of all cancers could be prevented by such lifestyle changes.

Many people don't make such changes, and the poor often have little choice but to work in hazardous jobs and live in hazardous areas. One problem is that usually 10 to 40 years elapse between the initial cause or causes of a cancer and the appearance of detectable symptoms. For instance, healthy high school and college students and young adults have difficulty accepting the fact that their smoking, drinking, eating, and other lifestyle habits today will be significant influences on whether they will die prematurely from cancer before they reach age 50. Denial can be deadly.

Smoking tobacco causes more death and suffering by far among adults than any other environmental factor. Each cigarette smoked reduces one's average life span by about 10 minutes.

Worldwide, at least 2.5 million smokers die prematurely each year from heart disease, lung cancer, other cancers, bronchitis, emphysema, and stroke—all related to smoking. Recent research indicates that about 27% of lung cancers are from an inherited gene alone, 42% are from smoking plus having the gene, and 27% are from smoking alone.

In 1989, smoking killed about 434,000 Americans—an average of 1,190 a day (Figure 20-10). This annual death toll is equal to three fully loaded jumbo jets crashing every day with no survivors, almost nine times the number of Americans killed in traffic accidents each year, and eight times the number of American soldiers killed in the nine-year Vietnam War.

Nicotine is not classified as an illegal drug; yet, it kills and harms more people each year in the United States than all illegal drugs and alcohol (the second most harmful drug), automobile accidents, suicide, and homicide combined (Figure 20-10).

Numerous studies have shown that the nicotine in tobacco is a highly addictive drug that, like her-

oin and cocaine, can quickly and strongly hook its victims. A British government study showed that adolescents who smoke more than one cigarette have an 85% chance of becoming smokers. The typical smoker has a 200- to 400-hit-a-day legalized habit, which costs about $26,000 for a person smoking 1 pack a day for 40 years.

Smokers develop tolerance to nicotine and experience withdrawal symptoms when they try to stop. Some recovering heroin addicts report they had a much harder time quitting smoking than quitting heroin. About 75% of smokers who quit start smoking again within six months, about the same relapse rate as recovering alcoholics and heroin addicts.

Several studies indicate that passive smoke inhaled by nonsmokers causes at least 3,800 premature deaths of Americans a year from lung cancer and an estimated 53,000 deaths from all diseases related to smoking. According to a 1986 study by the National Research Council, nonsmoking spouses of smokers have a 30% greater chance of getting lung cancer than spouses of nonsmokers. Women exposed to passive smoke three hours or more a day appear to have a threefold increased risk for cervical cancer. A 1990 study concluded that children raised in homes where two adults

smoke double their risk of lung cancer in adulthood, even though they may never smoke.

There is some good news, however. In the United States, the percentage of the adult population that smokes dropped from 42% in 1966 to 27% in 1990 (although that still means that one of every four American adults smokes). After about one year, an ex-smoker's chances of developing heart disease are about the same as a nonsmoker's, assuming all other heart disease risk factors are equal. Studies also show that 10 to 15 years after smokers quit, they have about the same risk of dying from lung cancer as those who never smoked.

Tobacco's harmful costs to American society exceed its economic benefits to tobacco farmers and employees and stockholders of tobacco companies by more than two to one. In the United States, smoking costs society at least $52 billion (some estimate $95 billion) a year in premature death, disability, medical treatment, increased insurance costs, and lost productivity because of illness (accounting for 19% of all absenteeism in industry). These external costs amount to an average cost to society of at least $2.20 per pack of cigarettes sold.

The American Medical Association and numerous health experts have called for

20-5 Risks from Hazardous Waste

WHAT IS HAZARDOUS WASTE? According to the Environmental Protection Agency, **hazardous waste** is any discarded chemicals that can cause harm because they are any of the following:

- *Flammable* (waste oils, used organic solvents, and PCBs).

- *Unstable* enough to explode or release toxic fumes (cyanide solvents).

- *Corrosive* to materials such as metals or human tissue (strong acids, strong bases, Figure 12-6).

- *Toxic* if handled in ways that release them into the environment. Examples are DDT, dioxins, PCBs (used to dissipate heat in electrical capacitors and transformers), and various compounds of arsenic, mercury, and lead (see Case Study on p. 559). In 1984, Congress ordered the EPA to include chemicals that can cause cancer, genetic mutations, and birth defects in humans and test animals in the toxic category, but that has not been done.

This definition does not include many major types of hazardous waste. Omitted categories include

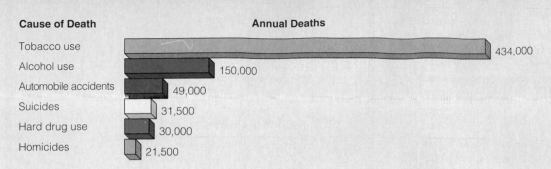

Cause of Death

Annual Deaths

Tobacco use	434,000
Alcohol use	150,000
Automobile accidents	49,000
Suicides	31,500
Hard drug use	30,000
Homicides	21,500

Figure 20-10 Annual deaths in the United States in 1989 related to tobacco use and other causes. Smoking is by far the nation's leading cause of preventable death, causing almost twice as many premature deaths each year as all the other categories shown in this figure combined. (Data from National Center for Health Statistics)

- A total ban on cigarette advertising in the United States.

- Prohibition of the sale of cigarettes and other tobacco products to anyone under 21, with strict penalties for violations.

- A ban on all cigarette vending machines.

- Classifying nicotine as a drug and placing the manufacture, distribution, sale, and promotion of tobacco products under the jurisdiction of the Food and Drug Administration.

- Eliminating all federal subsidies to U.S. tobacco farmers and tobacco companies.

- Taxing cigarettes at about $2.20 a pack to discourage smoking and to make smokers pay for the harmful effects of smoking now borne by society as a whole.

- Prohibiting elected and appointed government officials from exerting any influence on other governments to enhance the export of tobacco from the United States to other countries. Since 1985, the federal government has threatened to impose trade sanctions against foreign countries that do not lift tariffs and other restrictions on American tobacco products. That means that the U.S. government is coercing other governments into allowing imports of a very hazardous, addictive drug from America while trying to halt the flow of illicit drugs from other countries into the United States.

Enacting such restrictions is very difficult because of the immense political clout of the $36-billion-a-year U.S. tobacco industry. The American tobacco industry's response to the drop in the percentage of Americans who smoke is to sell more of its products overseas ($3 billion in sales for 1990) primarily to LDCs—especially those in Asia. Because of increased tobacco use, the World Health Organization predicts that LDCs will face a cancer epidemic by the year 2000. If current trends continue, the American Cancer Society projects that the worldwide death toll from smoking-related diseases will rise to 12 million annually by the year 2050.

- Radioactive wastes (Section 18-3), including reclassifying at least one-third of the nation's low-level radioactive wastes as nonradioactive and allowing them to be recycled, buried in municipal landfills, or burned in municipal incinerators.

- Hazardous materials discarded by households (Table 20-2).

- Mining wastes.

- Oil and gas drilling wastes.

- Eighty percent of all liquid hazardous waste the EPA allows to be burned as fuel with little regulation in cement kilns and industrial furnaces (which the EPA calls "recycling" these wastes).

- Cement kiln dust.

- Municipal incinerator ash. If the EPA classified this ash as hazardous waste, the increased cost of shipping and burning it in special landfills would make incineration of municipal garbage too expensive, and the whole industry would collapse. This would sharply reduce the profits of the big waste management companies (the largest of which are run by former EPA officials) and the large construction companies that build incinerators.

- Wastes from thousands of small businesses and factories that generate less than 100 kilograms (220 pounds) of hazardous waste per month.

Improper diet plays a key role in an estimated 25% to 30% of all cancer deaths. The National Academy of Sciences and the American Heart Association advise that the risk of certain types of cancer — lung, stomach, colon, breast, and esophagus cancer — heart disease, and diabetes can be significantly reduced by a daily diet that cuts down on certain foods and includes others. Such a diet limits

- total fat intake to 30% or less of total calories, with no more than 10% from saturated fats and the remaining 20% divided about equally between polyunsaturated fats (such as safflower oil and corn oil) and monosaturated fats (such as olive oil)

- protein (particularly meat protein) to 15% of total calories, or about 171 grams (6 ounces) a day (about the amount in one hamburger)

- alcohol consumption to 15% of total caloric intake — no more than two drinks, glasses of wine, or beers a day

- cholesterol consumption to no more than 300 milligrams a day, the goal being to keep blood cholesterol levels below 200 milligrams per deciliter

- sodium intake to no more than 6 grams (about 1 teaspoon of salt) a day to help lower blood pressure, which should not exceed 140 over 90

We should eat more poultry, fish, beans, peas, whole grains, cereals, fruits, and vegetables and much less red meat (which recently was linked to a higher risk of colon cancer) and processed foods. Also, each of us should achieve and maintain the ideal body weight for his or her frame size and age by a combination of diet and 20 minutes of exercise a day at least three days a week.

Table 20-2 Common Toxic and Hazardous Materials Found in Homes

Cleaning Products

Disinfectants
Drain, toilet, and window cleaners
Oven cleaners
Bleach and ammonia
Cleaning solvents and spot removers
Septic tank cleaners

Paint and Building Products

Latex and oil-based paints
Paint thinners, solvents, and strippers
Stains, varnishes, lacquers
Wood preservatives
Acids for etching and rust removal
Asphalt and roof tar

Gardening and Pest Control Products

Pesticide sprays and dusts
Old banned pesticides
Weed killers
Ant and rodent killers
Flea powder

Automotive Products

Gasoline
Used motor oil
Antifreeze
Battery acid
Solvents
Brake and transmission fluid
Rust inhibitor and rust remover

General Products

Dry cell batteries (mercury and cadmium)
Artist paints and inks
Glues and cements

- Waste generated by the military except at 116 sites so toxic that they are on the EPA's list of priority sites to be cleaned up. U.S. military installations produce more metric tons of hazardous waste each year than the top five U.S. chemical companies combined. Studies by the Department of Defense have identified over 17,482 contaminated sites at 1,855 military bases in every state.

Environmentalists call these omissions a form of "linguistic detoxification" designed to fool the public, and they urge that all excluded categories be designated as forms of hazardous waste so as to be identified and controlled under existing hazardous-waste laws. They contend that these types of hazardous wastes have not been included mostly because of lobbying of elected officials and EPA regulators by the industries involved and by the Department of Defense.

GROWING CONCERN There was little concern over hazardous waste in the United States and most parts of the world until 1977. Then it was discovered that hazardous chemicals leaking from an abandoned waste dump had contaminated a suburban development known as Love Canal, located in Niagara Falls, New York (see Case Study on p. 561). The publicity surrounding that event made the public and elected officials aware of dangers from the large amounts of hazardous waste we produce each day, as well as from wastes buried in the past.

HAZARDOUS-WASTE PRODUCTION: PRESENT AND PAST The total quantity of hazardous wastes produced throughout the world, or even in one country,

Lead is one of about 35 toxic metals that tend to accumulate in the brain, liver, and kidneys and can pose health risks to humans. Lead does not degrade, so after it is mined and put into commercial use, it becomes a permanent part of the environment.

Worldwide emissions of lead into the atmosphere from leaded gasoline, coal burning, mining, smelting and refining, waste incineration, and manufacturing processes are 28 times the amount emitted from natural sources such as volcanoes, windblown soil particles, sea salt spray, and forest fires. We take in small amounts of lead in the air we breathe, the food we eat, and the water we drink. Because it does not degrade, lead is a cumulative poison.

Once lead enters the blood, about 10% is excreted and the rest is stored in the bones. Children up to about age 9 are particularly vulnerable to lead poisoning, because their bodies absorb lead more readily than adults. Pregnant women can also transfer dangerous levels of lead to unborn children.

A 1986 EPA study revealed that 88% of all children under age 6 have lead levels in their blood (equal to or greater than 10 micrograms per 0.1 liter of blood) that may retard their mental, physical, and emotional development. Fairly low levels of lead in the blood of children under age 6 can damage the brain and central nervous system, lower IQ scores, lower the ability to absorb iron and calcium and metabolize vitamin D, and cause high blood pressure, partial hearing loss, hyperactivity, irritability, and behavior problems.

Each year, 12,000 to 16,000 American children (mostly poor and nonwhite) are treated for acute lead poisoning (caused mostly by ingesting chips of lead-based paint), and about 200 die. About 30% of those who survive suffer from palsy, partial paralysis, blindness, and mental retardation.

In other words, we have threatened an estimated 88% of American children with a lowered IQ from lead poisoning, sometimes called the "silent epidemic." According to the Public Health Service: "Lead-induced reductions in IQ not only place the individual at a disadvantage, but also eventually place the nation at a collective disadvantage in an increasingly competitive, technical, and cognitive-intensive world economy." Officials at the Center for Disease Control recommend that all preschool children be tested for lead as early as age 1.

The greatest sources of lead in the United States are

- Paint in 57 million houses built before 1978, when use of lead compounds in interior and exterior paint was banned. These houses are a major source of lead poisoning for children between ages 1 and 3, who crawl around the floor and inhale lead dust from cracking and peeling paint or ingest it by sucking their thumbs, putting toys in their mouths, or gnawing on window sills or furniture. Dust in yards and streets around such houses where children play also contains particles of chipped lead paint. People living in houses or apartments built before 1980 should chip off samples of paint and have them analyzed for lead by the local health department or by a private testing laboratory (cost $100 to $450).*

- Drinking water. According to the EPA, nearly 1 in 5 Americans (including 7 million children under age 7) drinks tap water containing excess levels of lead. This lead contamination occurs when

*If you find lead in your home, send a postcard to U.S. Consumer Product Safety Commission, Washington, DC 20207 and ask for the free pamphlet *What You Should Know About Lead-Based Paint in Your Home*. Two home kits for testing for lead in paint are sold by HybriVet Systems (800-262-LEAD) and Frandon Enterprises (800-359-9000).

acidic or soft water leaches lead from copper pipes that contain lead solder and lead connectors found in most plumbing systems and drinking fountains, or when individuals or communities get drinking water from 3,000 sources of groundwater suspected of being contaminated with lead, mercury, and cadmium leached from municipal landfills. Since 1987, the use of pipes and solder containing lead in public water systems has been banned, but a large percentage of existing houses, buildings, and drinking fountains have pipes and solder joints containing lead. Homeowners with copper pipes or joints should have the local water department or a private laboratory (cost $20 to $100) test their tap water for lead. Running tap water and drinking fountains 2 to 3 minutes before drinking may help, but that wastes water. Most home water filtration systems (except those using aluminum filters) don't remove lead or other toxic metals. An alternative is to drink bottled spring water, but be sure that it is regularly tested for lead content (and other pollutants) by the bottler. In building or remodeling, homeowners should use plastic or galvanized pipes or should ask plumbers to use lead-free solder on copper pipes. Before buying an existing house, have its water (that has been standing in pipes for at least 12 hours) and its paint tested for lead.

- Lead particles in air, dust, and soil in areas with heavy traffic and where lead has been, and continues to be, released into the atmosphere by municipal solid waste incinerators and various industrial plants. Since 1975, atmospheric emissions of lead have dropped sharply because of the gradual reduction by 91% of the lead allowed in gasoline in the

(continued)

United States, but burning leaded gasoline still releases over 205,000 metric tons (225,000 tons) of lead into the atmosphere each year. Since 1972, environmentalists and many health officials have been pushing unsuccessfully for a complete ban on lead in gasoline. Contamination of soil by emissions and toxic ash from municipal trash incinerators is now the fastest-growing source of lead (and other toxic metals such as mercury and cadmium) in the environment.

- Lead solder used to seal the seams on food cans, especially in acidic foods such as tomatoes and citric juices. This type of solder has been sharply reduced in U.S. food cans but may be found in cans of imported foods.

- Imported cups, plates, pitchers, and other types of ceramicware used to cook, store, or serve food, especially acidic foods and hot liquids and foods. Lead can be leached or chipped from the glaze of imported ceramicware (which makes up 60% of U.S. ceramic dinnerware sales) and older items made in the United States. Lead glass decanters used to hold wine and other alcoholic beverages are also sources of lead poisoning. Before using such items, consumers should test them for lead content.*

*A simple home test for lead content of up to 100 items of dishware is available for $24.50 from Frandon Enterprises, 511 N. 48th St., Seattle, WA 98103. Commercial testing costs about $60 per item. Contact American Council of Independent Laboratories, 1725 K Street N.W., Washington, DC 20006, (202) 887-5872, for a testing lab near you.

- Vegetables and fruits grown on soil contaminated for many years by lead, especially cropland or home gardens near highways, incinerators, and smelters. Careful washing should remove at least half of this lead.

- Burning certain types of paper in wood stoves and fireplaces. Homeowners should not burn comic strips, Christmas wrapping paper, or painted wood, which can be a source of lead contamination indoors and outdoors.

- Groundwater contaminated by lead leached from landfills. Lead-containing products often discarded in municipal landfills include lead-acid car batteries, T.V. picture tubes, electronic circuitry, and lead glass.

is impossible to determine accurately. According to the EPA, about 240 million metric tons (264 million tons) of federally defined hazardous waste is produced by U.S. industry each year, but the American Chemical Society says the true amount is two to ten times the EPA estimate. Using the EPA estimate, at least 0.9 metric ton (1 ton) to 9 metric tons (10 tons) of hazardous wastes are generated per American each year, and this amount is growing (see Spotlight on p. 562).

Those estimates do not include the many categories of hazardous waste not covered under the government's narrow definition or the vast quantities of toxic chemicals legally spewed into the atmosphere or discharged into waterways, the oceans, and municipal wastewater treatment facilities by U.S. industries (Figure 20-3).

By any of those estimates, the United States leads the world in total and per capita hazardous-waste production. If we use the EPA's narrow definition and estimate, then the hazardous wastes produced each year in the United States, stacked end-to-end in 55-gallon drums, would stretch to the moon.

About 93% by weight of this waste is produced by chemical, petroleum-refining (Figure 20-9), and metal-processing industries (see photo on p. 541). About 95% of the waste generated by large industries in the United States is treated on-site or stored on-site at a cost of about $16 billion a year. The remaining 5% is handled off-site by commercial facilities (mostly landfills, Figure 19-12) that take care of hazardous waste generated by others at an annual cost of about $7 billion.

A serious problem facing the United States and most industrialized countries is what to do with thousands of dumps, like the one at Love Canal, where in the past, large quantities of hazardous wastes were disposed of in an unregulated manner (Figure 20-11). Even with adequate funding, effective cleanup is difficult because officials don't know what chemicals have been dumped and where all the sites are located. It is estimated that eight out of ten Americans live near an active or abandoned hazardous-waste site, and half of all U.S. residents live in counties containing a hazardous-waste site classified among the most dangerous in the country.

Most LDCs have few, if any, regulations on the dumping of hazardous waste. For example, the dumping of hazardous waste by hundreds of metallurgical and other factories located along the 400-kilometer (248-mile) stretch between Rio de Janeiro and Saõ Paulo, Brazil (Figure 9-3) is unregulated. In Mexico City (Figure 9-4), industries discharge wastewater contaminated with toxic metals and organic compounds into the city sewer system. Hardly any of these wastes are removed by sewage treatment, and the contaminated water is then used to irrigate crops. As a result, traces of toxic

In 1977, residents of a suburb of Niagara Falls, New York, discovered that "out of sight, out of mind" did not apply to them. Hazardous industrial waste buried decades earlier bubbled to the surface, found its way into groundwater, and ended up in backyards and basements.

Between 1942 and 1953, Hooker Chemicals and Plastics Corporation dumped almost 20,000 metric tons (22,000 tons) of toxic and cancer-causing chemical wastes (mostly in steel drums) into an old canal excavation known as the Love Canal, named for its builder, William Love. In 1953, Hooker Chemicals covered the dump site with clay and topsoil and sold the site to the Niagara Falls school board for one dollar. The deed specified that the company would have no future liability for any injury or property damage caused by the dump's contents.

An elementary school, playing fields, and a housing project, eventually containing 949 homes, were built in the 10-square-block Love Canal area. Residents began complaining to city officials in 1976 about chemical smells and chemical burns received by children playing in the canal, but their complaints were ignored. In 1977, chemicals began leaking from the badly corroded steel drums into storm sewers, gardens, and basements of homes next to the canal.

Informal health surveys conducted by alarmed residents, led by Lois Gibbs (see Individuals Matter on p. 567 and Guest Essay on p. 572), revealed an unusually high incidence of birth defects, miscarriages, assorted cancers, and nerve, respiratory, and kidney disorders among people who lived near the canal. Complaints to local officials had little effect.

Continued pressure from residents and unfavorable publicity eventually led state officials to conduct a preliminary health survey and tests. They found that pregnant women in one area near the canal had a miscarriage rate four times higher than normal. They also found that the air, water, and soil of the canal area and the basements of nearby houses were contaminated with a number of toxic and carcinogenic chemicals.

In 1978, the state closed the school, permanently relocated the 238 families whose homes were closest to the dump, and fenced off the area around the canal. On May 21,1980, after protests from the outraged 711 families still living fairly close to the landfill, President Jimmy Carter declared Love Canal a federal disaster area and had the families relocated. Federal and New York state funds were then used to buy the homes of those who wanted to move permanently.

Since that time, the school and 239 homes within a block and a half of the canal have been torn down, and the state has purchased 570 of the remaining homes. About 45 families have remained in the desolate neighborhood, unwilling or unable to sell their houses to New York State and move.

The dump site has been covered with a clay cap and surrounded by a drain system that pumps leaking wastes to a new treatment plant. By 1990, the total cost for cleanup and relocation had reached $250 million. In June 1990, the EPA renamed the area Black Creek Village and proposed a sale of 236 remaining dilapidated and boarded-up houses at 20% below market value. However, several environmental groups have filed a federal complaint against the EPA for failing to conduct a health risk survey before moving people back into the Love Canal area.

Lois Gibbs says it would be "criminal to send people back in there" and has filed a lawsuit to prevent the sale. She and other environmentalists point out that the dump has not been cleaned up but only capped and fitted with a drainage system. According to Gibbs, "It isn't a matter of if the dump will leak again, but when." To her and other environmentalists, selling the houses in Love Canal sends a message from the government that "Chemical Dumps Make Good Homes for Poor and Middle Class Americans Who Can't Afford to Buy Homes in Safer Neighborhoods."

No conclusive study has been made to determine the long-term effects of exposure to hazardous chemicals on former Love Canal residents. All studies made so far have been criticized on scientific grounds. In 1988, an informal survey was made of families that once lived in a group of ten houses next to the canal. All but one had some cancer cases; there were also two suicides and three cases of birth defects among grandchildren.

The psychological damage to evacuated families is enormous. For the rest of their lives, they will wonder whether a disorder will strike and will worry about the possible effects of the chemicals on their children and grandchildren.

In 1985, former Love Canal residents received payments from a 1983 out-of-court settlement from Occidental Chemical Corporation (which bought Hooker Chemicals in 1968), the city of Niagara Falls, and the Niagara Falls school board. The payments ranged from $2,000 to $400,000 for claims of injuries ranging from persistent rashes and migraine headaches to cancers and severe mental retardation.

In 1988, a U.S. district court ruled that Occidental Chemical must pay the cleanup costs, but the company is appealing that ruling. In 1990, a trial began in which New York State is seeking $250 million in punitive damages from Occidental Chemical.

The Love Canal incident is a vivid reminder that we can never really throw anything away, that wastes don't stay put, and that preventing pollution is much safer and cheaper than trying to clean it up.

Nobody wants a waste dump, a deep-disposal well, or an incinerator nearby. At the local level, citizens who oppose dumps, deep-disposal wells, and incinerators in their communities are called NIMBYs — "Not in My Backyard" — by the industries they oppose.

The law of conservation of matter (Section 3-4) and the fact that hazardous chemicals we place in the ground or air don't stay put mean that we need to redefine our backyard. It is everywhere. Once we understand that, we will shift from waste production and management to waste prevention and recycling and reuse. Then, when it comes to particularly hazardous substances, we will become NOPEs — "Nowhere on Planet Earth."

The need to begin making such a shift now is illustrated by the exponential growth in the production of synthetic organic chemicals, many of which are hazardous to our health and to other species. Between 1945 and 1991, the U.S. chemical industry produced 5 trillion kilograms (11 trillion pounds) of synthetic organic chemicals, all of which have gone somewhere.

If the annual production of these chemicals continues to grow at its current exponential rate of 6.5%, in only 11 years we will produce another 5 trillion kilograms of them. If that rate of growth keeps up for a typical lifetime of 70 years, the quantity of these chemicals produced in the United States will increase 90-fold. That is why J-curves of exponentially growing quantities of chemicals can literally bury us.

On a weight basis, only 1% by weight of the estimated toxic chemicals released annually into the environment by the chemical industry in the United States is converted into harmless chemicals. To destroy the other 99% of these chemical industry wastes would cost about $20 billion a year. In recent years, the annual profits of the entire U.S. chemical industry have been only about $2 billion, so obviously the chemical industry cannot afford to destroy its own wastes. That is why the government, under intense pressure from the chemical industry, continues to allow the industry to release 99% of its toxic chemicals into the environment.

So what is the way out of this di-

lemma? Stopping all or most production of synthetic organic chemicals is not the answer because many of them are very important to our health and lifestyles. However, we can require manufacturers to greatly reduce or eliminate their inputs of particularly hazardous organic chemicals into the environment.

Two methods can be used to stimulate industry to redesign their processes to reduce, reuse, and recycle most of their toxic wastes over the next decade. One involves a carrot in the form of tax incentives for industries that do this. The other involves a phased withdrawal of all government subsidies, tax breaks, and other incentives that directly or indirectly encourage resource waste and waste production and phasing in emissions taxes on all toxic waste. To be effective, both the carrot and the stick methods are needed. Within a decade, this would result in a substantial reduction of toxic and hazardous waste and would save energy, nonfuel mineral resources, money, and lives.

---

metals and some organic compounds have begun to appear in vegetables and other crops, some of which are exported to the United States.

HOW IS HAZARDOUS WASTE CONTROLLED AND MANAGED?

There are five basic options for hazardous wastes: **(1)** hide them by putting them into a deep well, pond, pit, or landfill, or by dumping them in the ocean; **(2)** burn them in an incinerator or a cement kiln on land or on an incinerator ship at sea; **(3)** detoxify them; **(4)** recycle or reuse them; and **(5)** don't make them in the first place.

Most hazardous waste produced in the United States is disposed of in the land by deep-well injection, surface impoundments, and landfills (Figure 20-12). With deep-well disposal, wells are used to inject liquid wastes into geologic formations far beneath aquifers tapped for drinking water and irrigation (see Figure 22-12), as well as into fracture zones of rock where the wastes are expected to stay (see Pro/Con on p. 563).

Much of the country's hazardous waste is deposited into ponds, pits, or lagoons (see Figure 20-12) whose bottoms are supposed to be sealed with a plastic liner. The solids in these wastes settle to the bottom and accumulate, while water and other volatile compounds evaporate into the atmosphere.

According to the EPA, 70% of the pits, ponds, and lagoons used to store hazardous wastes have no liners, and as many as 90% may threaten groundwater. Pond liners can develop holes, and inadequate seals can allow wastes to percolate into groundwater. Most experts consider it only a matter of time before the liners leak. Major storms or hurricanes can cause overflows. Volatile compounds, such as hazardous organic solvents, can evaporate into the atmosphere and eventually return to Earth and contaminate surface and groundwater in other locations.

About 5% by weight of hazardous wastes produced in the United States are concentrated, put into drums, and buried in specially designed and monitored *secured*

Figure 20-11 Leaking barrels in a toxic waste dump near Washington, D.C. Most of the barrels are unlabelled, so that we have little knowledge of what chemicals are being released into the environment. Such dumps are now illegal in the United States and many MDCs. But there are tens of thousands of older dumps, and some illegal dumping still occurs.

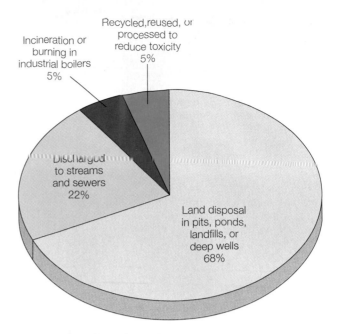

Incineration or burning in industrial boilers 5%

Recycled, reused, or processed to reduce toxicity 5%

Discharged to streams and sewers 22%

Land disposal in pits, ponds, landfills, or deep wells 68%

Figure 20-12 Management of hazardous waste in the United States. Even the best-designed landfills (Figures 19-12 and 20-13) eventually leak. Relying on landfills, deep wells, and incinerators for solid and hazardous wastes lets politicians off the hook today by passing on contamination and cleanup costs to the next generation—a repeat of the Love Canal tragedy (see Case Study on p. 561). (Data from Worldwatch Institute)

PRO/CON Is Deep-Well Disposal of Hazardous Waste a Good Idea?

Deep-well disposal of hazardous waste is widely used because it is simple, cheap, and not as visible (usually done on company-owned land) and not as carefully regulated as other disposal methods. Its use is increasing rapidly as other methods are restricted or become too expensive. As the public learns more about this method, it is expected to generate one of the biggest waste disposal fights of the 1990s.

If sites are selected carefully on the basis of geological data and evaluation of seismic data, deep wells may be an appropriate and reasonably safe way of disposing of fairly dilute organic and inorganic waste that is mostly water or that has been treated to reduce toxicity. It is also much cheaper and, with proper site selection and care, may be safer

than incineration. Also, if at some future date, some use should be found for the waste, it can be pumped back to the surface for reuse or recycling.

However, the Office of Technology Assessment and many environmentalists feel that current regulations for geologic evaluation, long-term monitoring of deep-well sites, and long-term liability if wells contaminate groundwater are inadequate to protect groundwater supplies from becoming contaminated by injected wastes (see Figure 22-12). Many companies are using such wells to inject fairly concentrated wastes, which is considered an unsafe practice.

Wastes can spill or leak at the surface and leach into groundwater, and well pipe casings can corrode

and allow wastes to escape into groundwater. Inadequate or leaking seals where the well casing passes through the impervious layer of rock can allow wastes to reach aquifers. Wastes can also migrate from the porous layer of rock where they are deposited to aquifers through existing fractures or new ones caused by earthquakes. There is also concern over the possibility that injection of wastes into deep wells can give rise to small earthquakes that can release the waste into aquifers.

Until this method is more carefully evaluated and regulated, environmentalists believe that its use should not be allowed to increase. What do you think?

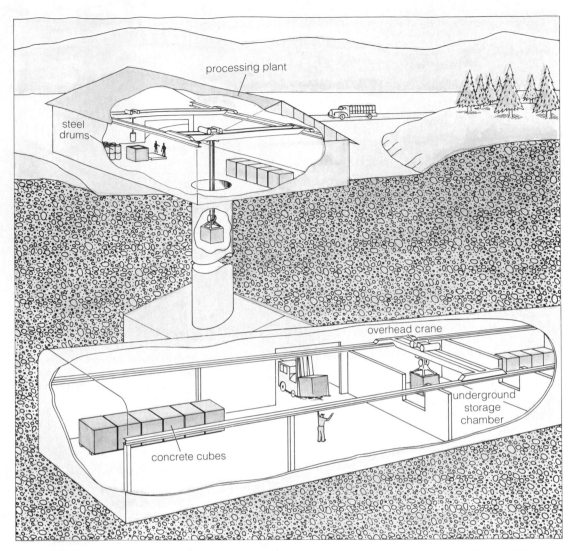

Figure 20-13 Swedish method for handling hazardous waste. Hazardous materials are placed in drums, which are stored in concrete cubes. The cubes are then placed in an underground vault.

landfills (Figure 19-12). Sweden goes further and buries its concentrated hazardous wastes in underground vaults (Figure 20-13).

Ideally, such landfills should be located in a geologically and environmentally secure place that is carefully monitored for leaks. In 1983, the Office of Technology Assessment concluded that sooner or later, even the best-designed, secured landfill will leak hazardous chemicals into nearby surface water and groundwater. Three-fourths of the hazardous-waste landfills in the southeastern United States are in low-income, nonwhite neighborhoods. Only 5% by weight of the hazardous waste produced in the United States is detoxified, recycled, or reused.

HOW SHOULD HAZARDOUS WASTE BE CONTROLLED AND MANAGED? There are three basic ways of dealing with hazardous waste, as outlined by the National Academy of Sciences: **(1)** waste prevention by waste reduction, recycling, and reuse; **(2)** conversion into less hazardous or nonhazardous material; and **(3)** perpetual storage (Figure 20-14). The first and most desirable method is an input, or waste prevention, approach. Its goal is to reduce the amount of hazardous waste produced by modifying industrial or other processes and by reusing or recycling the hazardous wastes that are produced.

Despite talk about waste reduction, the order of priorities for dealing with hazardous waste in the United States (Figure 20-12) is the reverse of what prominent scientists say it should be (Figures 20-8 and 20-14). So far, no country has implemented an effective hazardous-waste reduction program, but countries like Denmark, the Netherlands, the former West Germany, and Sweden are far ahead of the United States in starting to follow the priorities shown in Figure 20-14.

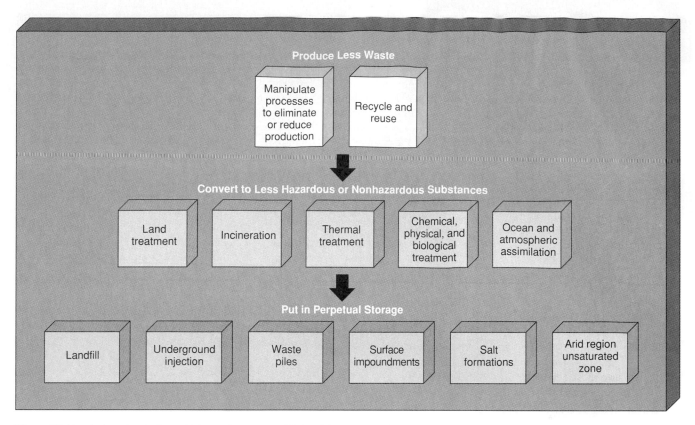

Figure 20-14 Options for dealing with hazardous waste. (National Academy of Sciences)

RECYCLING, REUSE, AND WASTE REDUCTION
The EPA estimates that 15% to 30% of the hazardous waste produced by industry in the United States could be recycled, reused, or exchanged so that one industry's waste becomes another's raw material, by using existing technology (see Spotlight on p. 566). Currently, however, only about 5% of such materials are managed in this manner, and the EPA devotes only a small portion of its waste management budget to waste reduction, reuse, and recycling.

WASTE TREATMENT AND INCINERATION The second phase of a hazardous-waste management program is to convert any waste remaining after waste reduction, recycling, and reuse into less-hazardous or nonhazardous materials (Figure 20-14). Conversion methods include spreading degradable wastes on the land, burning them on land or at sea in specially designed incinerators, thermally decomposing them, using natural or bioengineered microorganisms to degrade specific chemicals, or treating them chemically or physically.

The Netherlands incinerates about half its hazardous waste. The EPA estimates that 60% of all U.S. hazardous waste could be incinerated. With proper air pollution controls and highly trained personnel, incineration is potentially a safe method of disposal for most

types of hazardous waste, but it is also the most expensive method. The ash that is left and must be disposed of often contains toxic metals, and the gaseous and particulate combustion products emitted can be health hazards if not controlled. Another problem is that not all hazardous wastes are combustible.

According to environmentalists, required pollution controls and operator training in the United States for hazardous waste and municipal trash incinerators are not nearly enough to protect the public from potential harm. Increasingly, citizens are successfully opposing the location of hazardous-waste incinerators, landfills, or treatment plants near their communities, with the goal of protecting their health and forcing elected officials to get serious about waste reduction and pollution prevention (see Individuals Matter on p. 567).

Denmark, which relies almost exclusively on groundwater for drinking water, has the most comprehensive and effective program for detoxifying most of its hazardous waste. Each municipality has at least one facility that accepts paints, solvents, and other hazardous wastes from households. Toxic waste from industries is delivered to 21 transfer stations scattered throughout the country. All waste is then transferred to a large treatment facility in the town of Nyborg on the island of Fyn near the country's geographic center. There, about 75% of the waste is detoxified and the rest

Some firms have found that waste reduction and pollution prevention save them money. In 1974, the Minnesota Mining and Manufacturing Company (3M) produced enormous amounts of hazardous waste and accounted for 2% of all industrial emissions of air pollutants in the United States.

Since 1975, the company, which makes 60,000 products in 100 manufacturing plants, has had a program that by 1990 had cut its hazardous-waste production by two-thirds and its emissions of air pollutants by 90%, and had saved over $500 million. This was done by redesigning equipment and processes, using less-hazardous raw materials, identifying hazardous chemical outputs and recycling these chemicals or selling them as raw materials to other companies, and making products that don't pollute.

An EPA study of 28 firms engaged in waste reduction found that 93% of the companies got their investment back within three years and 54% within a year or less. The key is to get everyone in a company thinking about ways to reduce waste and pollution by making it a top corporate priority.

However, most firms have little incentive to reduce their output of waste because waste management makes up only about 0.1% of the total value of the products they ship. Placing a tax on each unit of hazardous waste generated would provide enough money to support a strong program for reducing, recycling, and reusing hazardous waste.

North Carolina has taken the lead in encouraging waste reduction. The state's $650,000-a-year Pollution Prevention Pays Program offers technical assistance, a database of information, and matching grants to small and large companies and communities wanting to implement waste reduction and recycling projects. In 1987, savings documented in 60 case studies were $16 million. California, New York, Pennsylvania, Illinois, Wisconsin, Minnesota, and Tennessee also have waste reduction programs. Developing such programs in all states would be an important step in waste prevention.

---

is buried in a carefully designed and monitored landfill. The German state of Bavaria has a similar system in operation, and South Korea is developing a system based on the Danish approach.

Biological treatment of hazardous waste by natural or genetically engineered microorganisms, called bioremediation, may increase in the future. It can cost less than half the cost of disposal in landfills, and only one-third the cost of on-site incineration. However, its effectiveness is unknown, and releasing genetically engineered microorganisms into the environment is controversial (see Pro/Con on p. 161).

BURIAL The third phase of waste management involves concentrating and placing any waste left after detoxification in containers and storing them in specially designed *secured landfills* (Figure 19-12) or *underground vaults* (Figure 20-13). However, according to the Office of Technology Assessment, eventually even the best-designed landfill or vault will leak and can threaten groundwater supplies.

There is also growing concern about accidents during some of the more than 500,000 shipments of hazardous wastes in the United States each year. Between 1980 and 1988, there were 11,048 toxic-chemical accidents, causing 309 deaths, 11,000 injuries, and evacuation of 500,000 people. Most communities do not have the equipment and trained personnel to deal adequately with most types of hazardous-waste spills.

SHIPPING WASTES ELSEWHERE As the costs of hazardous-waste disposal have risen, waste disposal firms in the United States and several other industrialized nations have shipped hazardous wastes to other countries, especially LDCs in Asia, Africa, and Latin America (see Spotlight on p. 568).

THE RESOURCE CONSERVATION AND RECOVERY ACT In 1976, the U.S. Congress passed the Resource Conservation and Recovery Act (RCRA, pronounced "rick-ra"), amending it in 1984. This law requires the EPA to identify hazardous wastes and set standards for their management, and provides guidelines and financial aid to establish state waste management programs. The law also requires all firms that store, treat, or dispose of more than 100 kilograms (220 pounds) of hazardous wastes per month to have a permit stating how such wastes are to be managed.

To reduce illegal dumping, hazardous-waste producers granted disposal permits by the EPA must use a "cradle-to-grave" manifest system to keep track of waste transferred from point of origin to approved off-site disposal facilities. EPA administrators, however, point out that this requirement is impossible to enforce

One highly effective frontline activist is Lois Gibbs (see Guest Essay on p. 572), who organized residents of the Love Canal development near Niagara Falls, New York, when they discovered they were living near a leaking toxic waste dump (see Case Study on p. 561). She then went on to form the Citizens' Clearing House for Hazardous Waste. This organization provides information and help for citizens' groups organizing to prevent hazardous-waste dumps, landfills, waste-injection wells, and incinerators from being located in their areas, and to monitor and demand reduction of pollution and hazardous waste produced by existing waste management facilities and chemical and industrial plants.

She and other grassroots activists are not swayed by the highly profitable waste management industry's technical risk-assessment and cost-benefit studies, slick glossy publications, promises to use state-of-the-art technology, expressions of their concern for the environment, and arguments that protesting citizens are holding up progress. Based on her experience, Lois Gibbs says, "Don't listen to them. It's all BS. The simple truth is, they're trying to kill you, to sacrifice you and your family just so they can make money."

Here are her guidelines for Earth citizens.

- Don't compromise our children's futures by cutting deals with polluters and regulators. Environmental justice cannot be bought or sold.

- Hold polluters and elected officials who go along with polluters directly and personally accountable. What they are doing is wrong and they must be held accountable for their actions.

- Don't fall for the argument voiced by industry that protesters against hazardous-waste landfills, incinerators, and injection wells are holding up progress because we have to deal with the hazardous wastes we produce. Instead, recognize that the best way to deal with waste and pollution is not to produce so much of it. After that has been done, we can decide what to do with what is left as recommended by the National Academy of Sciences (Figure 20-14).

- Oppose all hazardous waste landfills, deep-disposal wells, and incinerators to sharply raise the cost of dealing with hazardous materials. Only in this way will waste producers and elected officials get serious about waste reduction and pollution prevention instead of talking about it while spending little money or effort to do it. The goal of politically powerful waste management companies is to have us produce even larger amounts of hazardous (and nonhazardous) waste so they can make higher profits. Our goal should be to drastically reduce the production of wastes, and for especially hazardous materials, the goal should be: Not in Anyone's Backyard (NIABY) or Not on Planet Earth (NOPE).

---

effectively. The EPA and state regulatory agencies do not have enough personnel to review the documentation of more than 750,000 hazardous-waste generators and 15,000 haulers each year, let alone to verify them and prosecute offenders. If caught, however, violators are subject to large fines.

Environmentalists argue that fines for violators are too low and fail to recover amounts larger than the profits earned by illegal activity—sending polluters the clear message that crime pays. They believe that people who deliberately or through negligence illegally release harmful chemicals into the environment should be subject to jail terms because such environmental crimes kill or damage the health of many people for decades.

Facilities that treat, store, or dispose of hazardous waste must have EPA permits and follow EPA procedures for handling the waste. By 1990, there were 21 commercial hazardous-waste landfills that take wastes from anyone for a fee. There were also 35 noncommercial landfills run by individual companies to handle their own hazardous wastes.

Operators of EPA-licensed hazardous-waste landfills must prevent leakage, continually monitor the quality of groundwater around the sites, and report any contamination to the EPA. When a landfill reaches its capacity and is closed, the operators must cover it with a leakproof cap, monitor the nearby groundwater for 30 years, and be financially responsible for cleanup and damages from leaks for 30 years. Environmentalists consider that a serious weakness in the law because most landfills will probably begin leaking after 30 years, passing on the hazardous costs to the next generation.

Another loophole exempts "recycled" chemical wastes from control. This includes hazardous chemical wastes burned in industrial boilers, industrial furnaces, and cement kilns, which are not required to meet the stringent permit requirements and emission standards required for EPA-licensed hazardous-waste incinera-

To save money and avoid regulatory hurdles and local opposition, cities and waste disposal companies in the United States and other MDCs legally ship vast quantities of hazardous waste to other countries. Most legal U.S. exports of hazardous wastes go to Canada and Mexico.

All that U.S. firms have to do to ship hazardous wastes to other countries is notify the EPA of their intent to ship, get written permission from the recipient country, and file an annual report with the EPA. Between 1980 and 1989, notifications by U.S. companies for overseas shipments of hazardous waste jumped from 30 to 626.

There is evidence of a growing trade in illegal shipments of hazardous wastes across international borders. This is fairly easy to do because customs officials in the United States and other countries are not trained to detect illegal shipments and don't have enough inspectors to examine most shipments. Sometimes, exported wastes are labelled as materials to be recycled and then are dumped after reaching their destination. Hazardous wastes have also been mixed with wood chips or sawdust and shipped legally as burnable material.

Waste disposal firms can charge high prices for picking up hazardous wastes. If they can then dispose of them legally or illegally in other countries at low costs, they pocket huge profits. Officials of poor LDCs find it hard to resist the income

(often in the form of bribes) from receiving these wastes.

In 1986, a cargo ship named *Khian Sea* left Philadelphia carrying a load of the city's municipal incinerator ash. For the next two years, the ship wandered from country to country trying, without success, to find a country that would accept its hazardous cargo (except for a small portion that was dumped illegally in Haiti). After touring five continents and changing its name three times, the ship returned empty of its cargo in 1988. Its owners and crew members would not reveal where its cargo was dumped. Greenpeace claims it was dumped illegally in the Indian Ocean.

In 1987, an Italian businessman worked out a scheme to make a $4.3-million profit in the illegal toxic waste trade. He paid a retired timber worker $100 a month to store thousands of barrels of PCBs and other hazardous wastes in his backyard in Koko, Nigeria, a remote port town with about 5,000 inhabitants. Since then, 19 people have died from rice contaminated by chemicals from leaking barrels. In 1988, outraged Nigerian officials arrested 54 people and made Italy take back the wastes. This incident prompted the country to pass a law that requires life imprisonment for anyone found guilty of dumping or aiding the dumping of hazardous waste in Nigeria.

More countries are beginning to realize how importing hazardous waste can threaten their environ-

ment and the health of their people and weaken their long-term economic growth. Some countries are beginning to adopt the slogan Not in Our Country (NIOC) and a "return to sender" policy when illegal waste shipments are discovered.

In 1989, representatives from 116 countries drafted a treaty on the export and disposal of hazardous waste. It would ban such exports (excluding radioactive waste) unless the government of a receiving country gives prior written permission to receive the wastes. By 1991, the treaty had been signed by 53 countries but ratified by only 4. It will not become international law until ratified by 20 countries.

Environmentalists and some members of Congress call for the United States to ban all exports of hazardous waste and all pesticides and drugs not approved for use in the United States. They believe that it is wrong to export Love Canals or banned pesticides and drugs to other countries and that each country and state should be responsible for the wastes it produces. Being able to export wastes also discourages waste reduction. Such a ban on exports is opposed by the Bush administration and the majority of members of Congress.

A U.S. or worldwide ban on hazardous-waste exports would help but would not end illegal trade of these wastes. The profits to be earned are simply too great. What do you think should be done?

tors. This rapidly growing practice of "sham recycling" pollutes the air with toxic metals and other hazardous chemicals. It also produces toxic fly ash that does not have to be disposed of in EPA-licensed hazardous-waste landfills.

In 1984, Congress amended the 1976 Resource Conservation and Recovery Act to make it national policy to minimize or eliminate land disposal of 450 regulated hazardous wastes by May 1990 unless the EPA has determined that it is an acceptable approach or the only feasible approach for a particular hazardous material. Even then, each chemical is to be treated to the fullest

extent possible to reduce its toxicity before land disposal of any type is allowed.

If enforced, this policy represents a much more ecologically sound approach to dealing with hazardous wastes. However, phasing out land disposal is hampered by a shortage of facilities to treat and handle hazardous wastes in safer ways, an inexperienced EPA staff with rapid turnover (many leave for jobs in the waste management industry), lack of funds, and too little emphasis on waste reduction, recycling, and reuse.

Instead of requiring treatment, EPA regulations issued in 1990 would allow industries to dilute hazardous

Under RCRA, the EPA gives states control over their hazardous-waste programs, but the EPA also has the right to take over those programs—presumably to bring them up to federal standards. In 1987, the North Carolina legislature passed a law requiring waste dilution standards that in effect prohibited GSX Chemical Services from building a hazardous-waste treatment plant along a river that is used as a drinking water supply for a downstream community populated mostly by Native Americans (Lumbee Indians).

The waste management industry, fearing this type of action would spread to other states and hurt their business, pressured the Reagan administration and EPA officials to prevent the action. They argued that the EPA should exercise its right to take over North Carolina's hazardous-waste program. That would send a message to North Carolina and other states contemplating similar action or attempting to refuse to accept out-of-state shipments of hazardous wastes to landfills, incinerators, or treatment plants in their states. Such laws could cripple the waste management business.

EPA administrator Lee Thomas initially leaned toward suspending North Carolina's right to run their hazardous-waste program. However, after several months of study

and vigorous opposition from Congress and environmental groups, he issued a finding in December 1988 that North Carolina's law did not violate RCRA.

In February 1989, President George Bush appointed William Reilly, former head of the Conservation Foundation, to head the EPA. In April 1989, Reilly announced that he was reopening the North Carolina case.

In May 1989, two EPA staff members, William Sanjour and Hugh B. Kaufman (see Guest Essay on p. 703), both known as whistleblowers, filed a formal complaint with the EPA's Inspector General charging Reilly with possible criminal conspiracy and ethical violations. They charged that Reilly reversed this EPA policy because he was unduly influenced by lobbying at a breakfast he had in March 1989 with top officials of the waste management industry, including Dean Buntrock, head of Waste Management, Inc., the nation's largest hazardous-waste management company.

The breakfast was hosted by Jay Hair, president of the National Wildlife Foundation, which has Buntrock on its board of directors. Waste Management, Inc. is a big donor to the National Wildlife Foundation and was also a big donor to the Conservation Foundation, which Reilly headed before he took over the EPA.

Sanjour and Kaufman found no apparent study or open discussion of this reversal of the finding by former EPA administrator Lee Thomas. They pointed out that this reversal took place one month after the breakfast meeting. The Inspector General's office waited 39 days to officially open the investigation and consulted with Reilly about how the investigation should take place. Reilly and the other participants at the breakfast denied the charges, and Reilly was cleared of all charges.

Environmentalists charge that the investigation was a whitewash. They contend that Reilly should not have been involved in the planning of an investigation of himself and that the long delay in starting the investigation allowed the participants to get their stories straight. They also point out that investigators did not interview a reporter who talked to Reilly before the charges were made. According to the reporter's notes, Reilly volunteered that at the breakfast, he was lobbied by Buntrock to reverse EPA's decision on the North Carolina case.

In April 1990, a U.S. administrative law judge reviewed EPA's proposed policy and recommended that it drop its effort to block North Carolina's tough hazardous-waste law. Later, Reilly agreed to do so.

---

wastes by mixing them with other wastes and then injecting the mixture into deep wells. According to environmentalists, this violates the 1984 RCRA amendments by allowing dilution to replace treatment of hazardous wastes before land disposal is allowed. In 1990, several environmental groups filed a lawsuit against the EPA, charging it with not carrying out the 1984 amendments to RCRA. There is also controversy over whether states have a right to have stronger hazardous-waste control laws than the federal government (see Case Study above).

SUPERFUND LEGISLATION The 1980 Comprehensive Environmental Response, Compensation and Lia-

bility Act is known as the Superfund program. This law (plus amendments in 1986 and 1990) established a $16.3-billion fund, financed jointly by federal and state governments and taxes on chemical and petrochemical industries. The money is to be used for the cleanup of abandoned or inactive hazardous-waste dump sites and leaking underground tanks that are threats to human health and the environment. The EPA is authorized to collect fines and sue the owners of abandoned sites and tanks (if they can be found and held responsible) to recover up to three times the cleanup costs.

In 1989, the EPA estimated that there are more than 32,000 sites in the United States containing potentially hazardous wastes, but it has stopped looking for new

Here are some ways you can reduce your inputs of hazardous waste into the environment.

- Use pesticides and other hazardous chemicals (Table 20-2) only when absolutely necessary, and in the smallest amount possible.

- Use rechargeable batteries. Although they contain toxic nickel and cadmium, they last longer than alkaline batteries (which contain toxic mercury) and thus contribute less to the hazardous-waste problem. When their usable life is up (after being recharged about 1,000 times), however, they — like all batteries — should be treated as hazardous waste and separated from normal household trash.

- Use less-hazardous (and usually cheaper) cleaning products (see Individuals Matter inside the back cover). Three cheap chemicals — baking soda, vinegar, and borax — can be used as an Earthcare chemical kit for most cleaning and clothes bleaching and as a deodorant and a toothpaste (baking soda).

- Don't mix household chemicals, because many of them react and produce deadly chemicals. For example, when ammonia and household bleach are combined or even get near one another, they react to produce deadly poisonous chloramine gas.

- Do not flush hazardous chemicals down the toilet, pour them down the drain, bury them, throw them away in the garbage, or dump them down storm drains.* Consult your local health department or environmental agency for safe disposal methods. Find out if they have set up hazardous-waste collection days or a center that accepts these wastes. If not, organize efforts to develop a safe disposal system.

- Take used motor oil, transmission fluid, brake fluid, and car batteries to a local auto service center or to a hazardous-waste collection center for recycling. Just 0.9 liter (1 quart) of motor oil can pollute 94,340 liters (250,000 gallons) of drinking water.

- Insist that local, state, and federal elected officials establish and strictly enforce laws and policies that emphasize pollution prevention and waste reduction.

*See the *Household Hazardous Waste Wheel*, Environmental Hazards Management Institute, 10 Newmarket Road, P.O. Box 932, Durham, NH 03824 ($3.75), and *Earth Wise Household Inventory Sheet*, P.O. Box 682, Belmar, NJ 07719

($2.00). You can make a household inventory of hazardous and wasteful items by using the *Household Inventory Worksheet: A Blueprint for Safer Homes*, available for $2.00 from EarthWays, P.O. Box 682, Belmar, NJ 07719.

---

sites. The General Accounting Office estimates that there are between 103,000 and 425,000 sites.

None of these estimates includes hazardous wastes deposited in the 17,000 sites at military bases throughout the United States (called 17,000 "points of blight" by scientist Peter Montague, see Guest Essay on p. 46) or radioactive wastes at government nuclear weapons facilities (see Spotlight on p. 494). The Department of Defense has never evaluated the health effects of hazardous wastes deposited at military bases on military personnel or civilians living near contaminated bases.

By September 1991, the EPA had placed 1,211 sites on a National Priority List for cleanup because of their threat to nearby populations; the list is expected to reach 2,000 sites by the year 2000. Many of the sites are located over major aquifers and pose a serious threat to groundwater. In order, states with the largest number of priority sites are New Jersey, Pennsylvania, California, Michigan, and New York.

By 1991, after spending $7 billion of taxpayers' money, the EPA had declared only 64 sites clean and had removed only 24 from the priority list. Each site cost an average of $26 million to clean up. According to a 1989 report by the Office of Technology Assessment, about 75% of the cleanups are unlikely to work over the long term. Only $2.4 billion was spent on site-specific activities, with the rest used for administrative, management, and litigation costs and for outside consultants. Because of personnel freezes, much of Superfund spending has gone to outside consultants and experts, who make more money by dragging the process out. The EPA estimates the cost of cleaning up today's Superfund sites at $77 billion.

In 1985, the Office of Technology Assessment estimated that the final list may include at least 10,000 sites, with cleanup costs amounting to as much as $500 billion over the next 50 years, perhaps rivaling the cost of the nation's savings and loan bailout. Cleanup funds provided by taxes on industries that generate waste have amounted to about $1 billion a year — far short of the need.

Each of us has a role to play in reducing the input of hazardous waste into the environment (see Individuals Matter above).

For the first time in the history of the world, every human being is now subjected to dangerous chemicals, from the moment of conception until death.

RACHEL CARSON

Vincent T. Covello

Vincent T. Covello is Professor of Environmental Sciences in the School of Public Health at Columbia University and Director of Columbia University's Center for Risk Communication in New York City. Before these appointments, he was Director of the Risk Assessment Program at the National Science Foundation and a senior scientist at the White House Council on Environmental Quality. He is on the editorial board of several scientific journals and is the past president of the Society for Risk Analysis. He has written or edited over 25 books and 75 articles on environmental risk management. Two of his most recent books are Effective Risk Communication *(Plenum, 1989) and* Principles and Methods for Analyzing Health and Environmental Risks *(Council on Environmental Quality, 1988).*

Obtaining reliable scientific information about environmental risk is a matter of intense concern to the public. In the United States, the majority of people view industry and government as the most knowledgeable sources of information about those risks. Yet, at the same time, public confidence in industry and government as trusted sources of risk information has declined precipitously over the last two decades. Today, most Americans view industry and government as two of the least trusted sources of information about the risks of chemicals, radiation, and potential environmental hazards.

Several factors have contributed to a crisis in communication between industry and government on the one side and concerned citizens on the other. They include

- *Disagreements among scientific experts.* Because of different assumptions, data, and methods, experts in industry and government often engage in highly visible debates about the reliability, validity, and interpretation of risk-assessment results. In many cases, equally prominent experts have taken diametrically opposed positions. While such debates may be constructive to the development of scientific knowledge, they often undermine confidence in industry and government, which are perceived to be incapable of resolving critical questions.

- *Lack of resources for risk assessment and management.* Technical and organizational resources are seldom adequate to meet demands by citizens and public interest groups for definitive findings and actions. Explanations that the generation of health and environmental data about risks can be prohibitively expensive — or that risk assessment and management activities are constrained by resource, technical, statutory, legal, or other limitations — are seldom perceived as satisfactory. Individuals facing what they believe is a new and significant health and environmental risk are especially reluctant to accept such claims.

- *Lack of adequate coordination among responsible authorities.* Few requirements exist for regulatory agencies to develop coherent, coordinated, consistent, and interrelated plans, programs, and guidelines for assessing and managing risks. As a result, regulatory systems tend to be highly fragmented. This fragmentation often leads to jurisdictional conflicts about which agency and which level of government has the ultimate responsibility for assessing and managing the risk in question. Different mandates and confusion about responsibility and authority also lead, in many cases, to the production of multiple and competing estimates of risk.

- *Lack of attention to and priority for risk communication.* Many industry and government officials lack the understanding and skills needed to be effective in communicating risk information to the public. For example, officials often use complex language and jargon in communicating with the media and the public about risks. Technical jargon is difficult to comprehend, and its use can also create a perception that the official is being unresponsive, dishonest, or evasive. Aggravating this problem is the lack of attention paid by officials to the many pitfalls of risk communication, including the inappropriate use of quantitative risk numbers in public presentations, attacks upon the credibility of environmental or consumer activists, the inappropriate use of risk/cost/benefit arguments, and comparisons of the risks of activities that are perceived by the public to be dissimilar.

- *Insensitivity to the information needs and concerns of the public.* Experts in risk analysis often operate on the assumption that they and their audience share a common framework for evaluating and interpreting risk information. However, that is often not the case. Experts and laypersons frequently differ in how they evaluate and interpret risks. For example, experts tend to focus on the risk numbers themselves, while laypeople take into consideration a complex array of qualitative and quantitative factors in defining, evaluating, and acting on risk issues. Such factors include voluntariness, familiarity, effects on children, effects on future generations, benefits, origin (natural or from human activities), and fairness.

(continued)

Public perceptions of trust and confidence in industry and government will be restored only when the public is convinced that industry and government officials share the concerns of citizens about environmental risks; that they are scientifically, technologically, and managerially competent; that they are honest, fair, frank, and open; and that they are personally dedicated and committed to eliminating risks or reducing them to an absolute minimum. At a more fundamental level, trust and credibility will be restored only when industry and government officials recognize, accept, and involve the public as a legitimate partner in making decisions about risk.

Such a partnership also places demands on citizens, who must be open-minded and willing to take the time to learn about issues. A guiding principle of risk communication in a democracy is that people and communities have a right to participate in decisions that affect their lives, their property, and the things they value. The goal of risk communication in a democracy should be to produce an informed public that is involved, interested, reasonable, thoughtful, solution oriented, and collaborative. It should not be to defuse public concerns or to act as a substitute for needed action.

Guest Essay Discussion

1. In general, do you trust information provided by government or industry officials about environmental risks? Explain why you do or don't. Whom do you trust as sources of such information? Why?

2. What things would have to be done before you put more trust in government and industry officials about environmental risks?

3. Are you willing to learn about and participate in making decisions about environmental risks? Explain. Have you ever done this? Why or why not?

GUEST ESSAY We Have Been Asking the Wrong Questions About Wastes

Lois Marie Gibbs

Lois Marie Gibbs was once a housewife living nearing the Love Canal toxic dump site (see Case Study on p. 561) who had never engaged in any sort of political action. Alarmed at what she saw happening to the health of her own children and those of neighbors, she organized her neighborhood and became the president and major strategist for the Love Canal Homeowners Association in their successful fight against a multimillion dollar corporation and the New York State and federal governments to provide relief for their endangered community. This dedicated grassroots political action by "amateurs" brought hazardous-waste issues to national prominence and was a major factor leading to the development and passage of the federal Superfund legislation. Lois Gibbs then moved to Washington, D.C., and formed Citizens' Clearinghouse for Hazardous Wastes, an orga-nization that has helped ordinary citizens in over 7,000 community grassroots organizations protect themselves from hazardous wastes. Her story is told in her autobiography, Love Canal: My Story *(State University of New York Press, 1982), and was also the subject of a CBS movie,* Lois Gibbs: The Love Canal, *which aired in 1982. She is an inspiring example of what an ordinary citizen can do to change the world.*

Just about everyone knows our environment is in danger. One of the most serious threats to our environment is the millions of metric tons of waste put into the air, water, and ground every year. All across the United States and around the world, there are thousands of places that have been, and continue to be, polluted by toxic chemicals, radioactive waste, and just plain garbage.

For generations, the main question people have asked is, "Where do we put all this waste? It's got to go somewhere." That is the wrong question, as is shown by the long series of experiments in waste disposal we have carried out to try to answer it and by the simple fact that there is no away [Section 3-4].

We tried dumping our waste into the oceans. That was wrong. We tried injecting it into deep, underground wells. That was wrong. We've been trying to build landfills that don't leak. That doesn't work. We've been trying to get rid of waste by burning it in high-tech incinerators. That only produces different types of pollution, such as air pollution and toxic ash. We've tried a broad range of "pollution" controls. But all that does is allow legalized, high-tech pollution. Even recycling, which is a very good thing to do, suffers from the same problem as all the other methods: It addresses waste *after* it has been produced.

For many years, people have been assuming that "it's got to go somewhere," but now many people, especially young people, are starting to ask, "Why?" Why do we produce so much waste? Why do we need products and services that have so many toxic by-products? Why can't industry change the way it makes things so that it stops producing so much waste?

These are the *right* questions. When you start asking them, you start getting answers that lead to *pollution prevention* and *waste reduction* instead of simply *pollution control* and *waste management*. People, young and old, who care about pollution prevention begin challenging our use and disposal of enormous amounts of polystyrene (Styrofoam) plastic each year. They begin challenging companies to stop making products with gases that destroy the ozone layer [Section 11-3] and contribute to the threatening possibility of global warming [Section 11-1]. They begin to ask why so many goods are wrapped in excessive, throwaway packaging. They begin challenging companies that sell pesticides, cleaning fluids, batteries, and other hazardous products to either take the toxics out of those products or begin taking them back for recovery or recycling, rather than disposing of them in the environment. They begin demanding alternatives to throwaway materials in general.

Starting in 1988, hundreds of student groups have contacted my organization to get help and advice in taking these effective types of actions. Many of these groups begin by working to get polystyrene food packaging out of their school cafeterias and out of local fast food restaurants.

Oregon students even took legal action to get rid of cups and plates made from bleached paper, because the paper contains the deadly poison dioxin. They were asking the right questions and gave the right answer when they demanded the school systems switch to nondisposable, reusable cups, plates, and utensils.

Dozens of student groups have joined with local environmental and grassroots organizations in their communities to get toxic-waste sites cleaned up or to stop new toxic-waste sites, radioactive-waste sites, or waste incinerators from being built.

Waste issues are not simply environmental issues. They are issues that are all tied up with economics. Our economy is geared to producing and getting rid of waste. *Somebody* is making money from every scrap of waste and has a vested interest in leaving things the way they are. Environmentalists and industry officials constantly argue about what's called "cost-benefit analysis" [Section 24-4]. Simply stated, this poses the question of whether the benefit of controlling pollution or waste will be greater than the cost. I think this is another example of the wrong question. Instead, I think the right question is, "Who will benefit and who will pay the cost?"

Waste issues are also issues of *justice* and *fairness*. Again, there's a lot of debate between industry officials and environmentalists, especially those in federal and state environmental agencies, about what they call "acceptable risk." Simply stated, that means that industry officials and environmentalists will decide how much people will be exposed to toxic chemicals. Unfortunately, they hardly ever ask the people who are actually going to be exposed how they feel about it. Instead, industry officials debate and ask each other how much exposure other people will be allowed to get. Again, I think this is the wrong question. I believe it's not fair to expose people to chemical poisons without their consent and, in fact, without even being asked.

Risk analysts often say, "But there's only a one in a million chance of increased death from this toxic chemical." That may be true. But suppose I took a pistol and went to the edge of your neighborhood and began shooting. There's probably only a one in a million chance that I'll hit somebody. But would you give me permission, would you give me a license, to do that? As long as we don't stand up for our rights and demand that "bullets" in the form of hazardous chemicals not be "fired" in our neighborhoods, we are giving environmental regulators and waste producers a license to kill a certain number of us without even being consulted.

When you study the issues of the environment, remember that they are not abstract issues that only happen somewhere else. We *all* have to live, breathe, and survive in this environment. We have all learned that decisions made for us or by us in the past have come back to haunt us. Likewise, today's decisions will affect all of us tomorrow and far into the future.

From my personal experience, I know that decisions made to dump wastes at Love Canal and in thousands of other places in the past were not made simply on the basis of the best available scientific knowledge. The same holds true for decisions made about how to manage the wastes we produce today.

Instead, the real world we live in is shaped by decisions based on money and power. If you really want to understand what's behind any given environmental issue, the first question you should ask is, "Who stands to profit from this?" Then ask, "Who is going to pay the price?" You will then be able to identify both sides of the issue, and you can decide whether you want to be part of the problem or part of the solution.

Guest Essay Questions

1. What changes would you be willing to make in your own lifestyle to prevent pollution and reduce waste?

2. What political and economic changes do you believe need to be made so that we shift from a waste production and waste management society to a pollution prevention and waste reduction society? What things are you doing to help bring about such social changes?

DISCUSSION TOPICS

1. Should standards for allowed pollution levels be set to protect the most sensitive or the average person in a population? Explain. Should we have zero pollution levels for all hazardous chemicals? Explain.

2. Explain why you agree or disagree with each of the following proposals:
    a. All advertising of cigarettes and other tobacco products should be banned.
    b. All smoking should be banned in public buildings and commercial airplanes, buses, subways, and trains.
    c. All government subsidies to tobacco farmers and the tobacco industry should be eliminated.
    d. Cigarettes should be taxed at about $2.20 a pack so that smokers — not nonsmokers — pay for the health and productivity losses now borne by society as a whole.

3. Assume you have been appointed to a technology risk-benefit assessment board. Explain why you approve or disapprove of widespread use of each of the following: **(a)** abortion pills (now used in France and China); **(b)** effective sex stimulants; **(c)** drugs that would retard the aging process; **(d)** drugs that would enable people to get high but are physiologically and psychologically harmless; **(e)** electrical or chemical methods that would stimulate the brain to eliminate anxiety, fear, unhappiness, and aggression; **(f)** genetic engineering that would produce people with superior intelligence, strength, and other traits.

4. Would you oppose locating a hazardous-waste landfill, treatment plant, deep-injection well, or incinerator in your community? Explain. If you oppose these alternatives, how would you propose that the hazardous waste generated in your community and state be managed?

5. Give your reasons for agreeing or disagreeing with each of the following proposals for dealing with hazardous waste:
    a. Reduce the production of hazardous waste and encourage this and recycling and reuse of hazardous materials by levying a tax or fee on producers for each unit of waste generated.
    b. Ban all land disposal of hazardous waste to encourage recycling, reuse, and treatment and to protect groundwater from contamination.
    c. Provide low-interest loans, tax breaks, and other financial incentives to encourage industries that produce hazardous waste to recycle, reuse, treat, destroy, and reduce generation of such waste.
    d. Ban the shipment of hazardous waste from the United States to any other country.
    e. Ban the shipment of hazardous waste from one state to another.

*6. What hazardous wastes are produced at your school? What happens to them?

*7. Are there any active or abandoned hazardous-waste dumps in your community? Where are they located? What has been dumped there? Do they have one or more liners? Has there been any testing to determine whether wastes have leaked from the sites? What were the results of the tests? Who owns the sites now?

CHAPTER 21

AIR POLLUTION

General Questions and Issues

1. What are the principal types and sources of air pollutants?

2. What is smog? What is acid deposition?

3. What undesirable effects can air pollutants have on people, other species, and materials?

4. What legal and technological methods can be used to reduce air pollution?

I thought I saw a blue jay this morning. But the smog was so bad that it turned out to be a cardinal holding its breath.

MICHAEL J. COHEN

AKE A DEEP BREATH. About 99% of the volume of air you inhaled is gaseous nitrogen and oxygen. You also inhaled trace amounts of other gases, minute droplets of various liquids, and tiny particles of various solids. Many of these chemicals are classified as air pollutants. Most come from cars, trucks, power plants, factories, cigarettes, cleaning solvents, and other sources related to our activities. Most are related to the burning of fossil fuels, with motor vehicles responsible for at least half of the air pollution in urban areas.

You are exposed to air pollutants outdoors and indoors. Repeated exposure to trace amounts of many of these chemicals can damage lung tissue, plants, fish and other animals, buildings, metals, and other materials, as discussed in this chapter. Air pollutants emitted by our activities are also increasing the amount of the sun's harmful ultraviolet radiation reaching Earth's surface and are projected to alter local, regional, and global climates from an enhanced greenhouse effect, as discussed in Chapter 11.

21-1 Outdoor and Indoor Air Pollution

PRINCIPAL TYPES OF OUTDOOR AIR POLLUTION The atmosphere is divided into several spherical layers, much like the successive layers of skin on an onion (Figure 4-3). About 95% of the mass of Earth's air is found in the innermost layer, known as the troposphere, extending only about 17 kilometers (11 miles) above Earth's surface. If Earth were an apple, this lower layer that contains the air we breathe would be no thicker than the apple's skin.

As clean air moves across Earth's surface, it collects various chemicals produced by natural events and human activities. Once in the troposphere, these potential air pollutants mix vertically and horizontally, often reacting chemically with each other or with natural components of the atmosphere. Air movements and turbulence help dilute potential pollutants, but long-lived pollutants are transported great distances before they return to Earth's surface as solid particles, liquid droplets, or chemicals dissolved in precipitation.

Hundreds of air pollutants are found in the troposphere. However, trace amounts of nine classes of pollutants cause most outdoor (ambient) air pollution:

1. *Carbon oxides*—carbon monoxide (CO) and carbon dioxide (CO_2) (Section 11-1)

2. *Sulfur oxides*—sulfur dioxide (SO_2) and sulfur trioxide (SO_3)

3. *Nitrogen oxides*—nitric oxide (NO), nitrogen dioxide (NO_2), and nitrous oxide (N_2O)

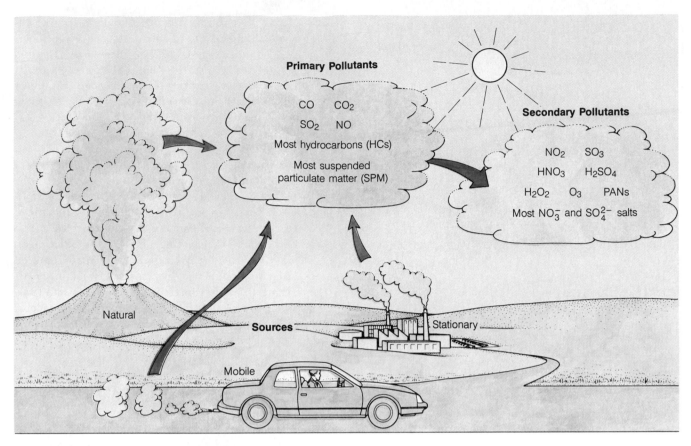

Figure 21-1 Primary and secondary air pollutants.

4. *Volatile organic compounds (VOCs)* — hundreds of compounds such as methane (CH_4), benzene (C_6H_6), formaldehyde (CH_2O), chlorofluorocarbons (CFCs), and bromine-containing halons

5. *Suspended particulate matter (SPM)* — thousands of different types of *solid particles* such as dust, soot (carbon), pollen, asbestos, and lead (see Case Study on p. 559), arsenic, cadmium, and nitrate (NO_3^-) and sulfate (SO_4^{2-}) salts, and *liquid droplets* of chemicals such as sulfuric acid (H_2SO_4), oil, PCBs, dioxins, and various pesticides

6. *Photochemical oxidants* — ozone (O_3), PANs (peroxyacyl nitrates), hydrogen peroxide (H_2O_2), hydroxyl radicals (OH), and aldehydes, such as formaldehyde (CH_2O), formed in the atmosphere by the reaction of oxygen, nitrogen oxides, and volatile hydrocarbons under the influence of sunlight

7. *Radioactive substances* — radon-222, iodine-131, strontium-90, plutonium-239, and other radioisotopes that enter the atmosphere as gases or suspended particulate matter

8. *Heat* — produced when any kind of energy is transformed from one form to another, especially when fossil fuels are burned in cars, factories, homes, and power plants (Figure 9-12)

9. *Noise* — produced by motor vehicles, airplanes, trains, industrial machinery, construction machinery, lawn mowers, vacuum cleaners, food, sirens, earphones, radios, cassette players, and live concerts (Table 9-2)

A **primary air pollutant**, such as sulfur dioxide, directly enters the air as a result of natural events or human activities. A **secondary air pollutant**, such as sulfuric acid, is formed in the air through a chemical reaction between a primary pollutant and one or more air components (Figure 21-1).

Pollutants, such as suspended particulate matter, remain in the atmosphere for different lengths of time depending mostly on the relative size of the particles (Figure 21-2) and the amount of precipitation in various areas. Large particles, with diameters greater than 10 micrometers (about 0.0004 inch), normally remain in the troposphere only a day or two before being brought to Earth by gravity or precipitation. Medium-size particles, with diameters between 1 and 10 micrometers, are lighter and tend to remain suspended in the air for several days.

Fine particles, with diameters less than 1 micrometer, may remain suspended in the troposphere for one to two weeks and in the stratosphere for one to five

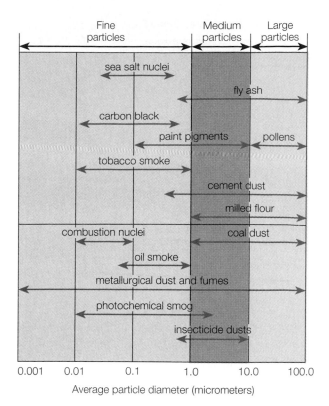

Fine particles | Medium particles | Large particles

sea salt nuclei

fly ash

carbon black

paint pigments   pollens

tobacco smoke

cement dust

milled flour

combustion nuclei   coal dust

oil smoke

metallurgical dust and fumes

photochemical smog

insecticide dusts

0.001   0.01   0.1   1.0   10.0   100.0

Average particle diameter (micrometers)

Figure 21-2 Suspended particulate matter is found in a wide variety of types and sizes. (1 micrometer = 0.001 millimeter = 0.00004 in.)

years—long enough to be transported all over the world. These fine particles are the most hazardous to human health because they are small enough to penetrate the lungs' natural defenses; they can also bring with them droplets or other particles of toxic or cancer-causing pollutants that become attached to their surfaces.

Recently, it has been recognized that trace amounts of hundreds of *toxic outdoor air pollutants* may be a threat to human health when inhaled over several years. According to the EPA, at least 1.1 billion kilograms (2.43 billion pounds) of 320 toxic compounds, 60 of them known carcinogens, were released by industries into American skies in 1988. That does not cover perhaps an equal amount of toxic chemicals released from 198 million motor vehicles, thousands of toxic-waste dumps, and tens of thousands of small businesses such as dry cleaners and gas stations.

The EPA estimates that these toxic pollutants are responsible for 2,000 excess cancer deaths a year in the United States. People who work in or who live near or downwind from chemical plants, metal smelters, paper plants, oil refineries and petrochemical plants (Figure 20-9), coal-burning electric power plants, and hazardous-waste and municipal trash incinerators have the highest risk from exposure to these chemicals.

Humans probably first experienced harm from air pollution when they built fires in poorly ventilated caves. As cities grew during the Agricultural Revolution, air pollution from the burning of wood and later of coal became an increasingly serious problem. In 1273, King Edward I of England banned the burning of coal in order to reduce air pollution.

In 1911, at least 1,150 Londoners died from the effects of coal smoke. The author of a report on this disaster coined the word *smog* for the mixture of smoke and fog that often hung over London. An even worse air pollution incident in London killed 4,000 people in 1952, and further disasters in 1956, 1957, and 1962 killed a total of about 2,500 people. As a result, London has taken strong measures against air pollution and has much cleaner air today.

In the United States, the Industrial Revolution brought air pollution as coal-burning industries and homes filled the air with soot and fumes. In the 1940s, air in industrial centers like Pittsburgh and St. Louis became so thick with coal smoke that automobile drivers sometimes had to use their headlights at midday. The rapid rise of the automobile, especially since 1940, brought new forms of pollution such as photochemical smog, which causes the eyes to sting, and toxic lead compounds from the burning of leaded gasoline.

The first known U.S. air pollution disaster occurred in 1948, when fog laden with sulfur dioxide vapor and suspended particulate matter stagnated for five days over the town of Donora in Pennsylvania's Monongahela Valley south of Pittsburgh. About 6,000 of the town's 14,000 inhabitants fell ill, and 20 of them died. This killer fog resulted from a combination of mountainous terrain surrounding the valley and stable weather conditions that trapped and concentrated deadly pollutants emitted by the community's steel mill, zinc smelter, and sulfuric acid plant.

In 1963, high concentrations of air pollutants accumulated in the air over New York City, killing about 300 people and injuring thousands. Other episodes during the 1960s in New York City, Los Angeles, and other large cities led to much stronger air pollution control programs in the 1970s.

SOURCES OF OUTDOOR AIR POLLUTION Air pollution is not new (see Spotlight above), but the types and quantities of air pollutants have increased since the Industrial Revolution. Most of the widely recognized outdoor air pollution in the United States (and other industrialized countries) comes from five groups of primary pollutants: carbon monoxide, nitrogen oxides,

What They Are

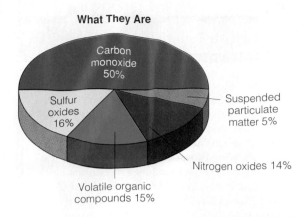

Carbon monoxide 50%

Sulfur oxides 16%

Suspended particulate matter 5%

Nitrogen oxides 14%

Volatile organic compounds 15%

Where They Come From

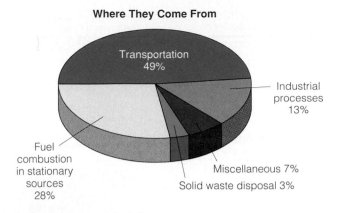

Transportation 49%

Industrial processes 13%

Fuel combustion in stationary sources 28%

Miscellaneous 7%

Solid waste disposal 3%

Figure 21-3 Emissions of key outdoor air pollutants in the United States. Emission percentages on the left are on a per weight basis. Each of the 198 million motor vehicles in the United States spews out an average of 0.9 metric ton (1 ton) of air pollutants a year. (Data from Environmental Protection Agency)

sulfur oxides, volatile organic compounds (mostly hydrocarbons), and suspended particulate matter (Figure 21-3). Other key pollutants are ozone (a secondary pollutant) and lead (mostly from burning leaded gasoline, metal smelters—see photo on p. 541), and municipal waste incinerators (see Spotlight on p. 527).

In MDCs, most of these pollutants are emitted into the atmosphere from the burning of fossil fuels in power and industrial plants (*stationary sources*) and in motor vehicles (*mobile sources*) (see Pro/Con on p. 240). Thus, most air pollution is a result of our addiction to oil and other fossil fuels.

In LDCs, especially in rural areas where over half of the world's people live, most air pollution is produced by the burning of wood, dung, and crop residues in inefficient crude stoves and open fires. This adds carbon dioxide and soot to the atmosphere and causes the desperately poor to deplete forests for enough fuelwood to survive (Section 10-4).

The burning of forests and savanna grasslands in tropical and subtropical regions to create cropland and pastures injects large quantities of carbon dioxide, carbon monoxide, nitrogen oxides, and methane into the atmosphere. When forests are cleared, the exposed soil emits nitrous oxide (Figure 11-2). Nitrous oxide is also emitted when nitrogen-rich fertilizers are spread on cropland. Significant amounts of methane are emitted into the atmosphere from the stomachs of livestock and by anaerobic decomposition from wet rice paddies (Figure 11-2).

War is also a major source of pollution and environmental degradation (Section 11-5). According to the Worldwatch Institute, the combination of the 600 oil well fires in Kuwait, the deliberate spill of huge quantities of oil into the Persian Gulf (see Spotlight on p. 618), and the direct destruction of the desert ecology in Kuwait and Iraq by bombs, shells, and tanks during

the 1990–1991 war in the Persian Gulf was the greatest environmental disaster in modern history. Some of the carbon soot from the burning oil wells was distributed to spots around the globe, including Hawaii 12,900 kilometers (8,000 miles) away.

TYPES AND SOURCES OF INDOOR AIR POLLUTION Assuming you are reading this book indoors, take a deep breath. Chances are that you inhaled more air pollutants than if you had been outside. As many as 20 to 150 hazardous chemicals in concentrations 10 to 40 times those outdoors can be found in the typical American home (Table 20-2 and Figure 21-4).

Since we spend 70% to 98% of our time indoors, the EPA has called indoor air quality "the most significant environmental issue we have to face." It poses an especially high health risk for the elderly, young children, the sick, pregnant women, people with existing respiratory or heart problems, and factory and office workers who spend a large amount of time indoors.

The EPA estimates that indoor air pollutants in U.S. homes and offices cause as many as 6,000 cancer deaths each year and up to 20,000 more deaths from indoor inhalation of the decay products of radioactive radon gas (see Case Study on p. 580). Other air pollutants found in buildings produce dizziness, headaches, coughing, sneezing, nausea, burning eyes, upper respiratory problems, and flulike symptoms in many people—a health problem called the "sick building syndrome."

An estimated one-fifth to one-third of all U.S. buildings, including the EPA headquarters, are considered "sick." Each year, exposure to pollutants inside factories and businesses in the United States kills from 100,000 to 210,000 workers prematurely. According to the EPA and public health officials, cigarette smoke (see Case Study on p. 556), radioactive radon-222 gas (see

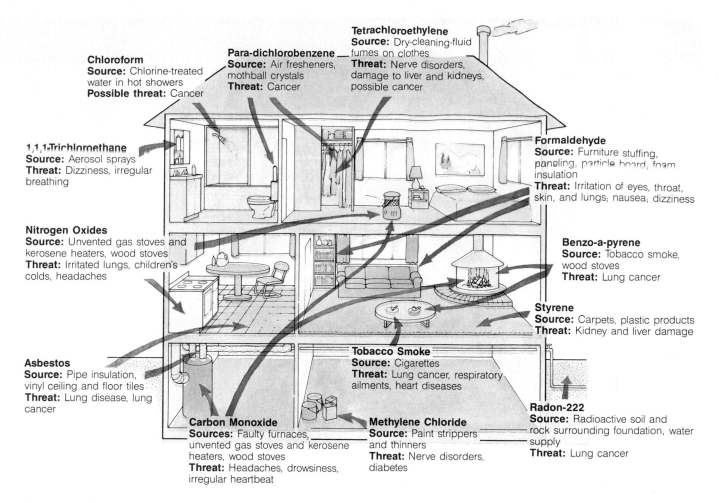

Chloroform
Source: Chlorine-treated water in hot showers
Possible threat: Cancer

Para-dichlorobenzene
Source: Air fresheners, mothball crystals
Threat: Cancer

Tetrachloroethylene
Source: Dry-cleaning-fluid fumes on clothes
Threat: Nerve disorders, damage to liver and kidneys, possible cancer

1,1,1-Trichloroethane
Source: Aerosol sprays
Threat: Dizziness, irregular breathing

Formaldehyde
Source: Furniture stuffing, paneling, particle board, foam insulation
Threat: Irritation of eyes, throat, skin, and lungs; nausea; dizziness

Nitrogen Oxides
Source: Unvented gas stoves and kerosene heaters, wood stoves
Threat: Irritated lungs, children's colds, headaches

Benzo-a-pyrene
Source: Tobacco smoke, wood stoves
Threat: Lung cancer

Styrene
Source: Carpets, plastic products
Threat: Kidney and liver damage

Asbestos
Source: Pipe insulation, vinyl ceiling and floor tiles
Threat: Lung disease, lung cancer

Tobacco Smoke
Source: Cigarettes
Threat: Lung cancer, respiratory ailments, heart diseases

Carbon Monoxide
Sources: Faulty furnaces, unvented gas stoves and kerosene heaters, wood stoves
Threat: Headaches, drowsiness, irregular heartbeat

Methylene Chloride
Source: Paint strippers and thinners
Threat: Nerve disorders, diabetes

Radon-222
Source: Radioactive soil and rock surrounding foundation, water supply
Threat: Lung cancer

Figure 21-4 Some important indoor air pollutants. (Data from Environmental Protection Agency)

Case Study on p. 580), asbestos (see Pro/Con on p. 582), and formaldehyde are the four most dangerous indoor air pollutants.

As many as 10 million to 20 million Americans have chronic respiratory problems, dizziness, rash, lethargy, headaches, sore throat, sinus and eye irritation, and nausea caused by daily exposure to low levels of formaldehyde emitted (outgassed) from common building materials and household items (Figure 21-4). Chronic exposure to low levels of formaldehyde for years can cause cancer.

Formaldehyde is widely used in pressed and veneered wood products such as plywood, particleboard, panelling, and medium-density fiberboard (the worst of the bunch). These materials are widely used to build countertops, kitchen cabinets, subflooring, and furniture (about 90% of the furniture sold in the United States). Other products containing formaldehyde include drapes, upholstery, urea-formaldehyde foam insulation (now banned), adhesives in carpeting and wallpaper, and permanent-press clothing.

Most mobile homes have large quantities of formaldehyde-emitting materials. According to the EPA, at least half the mobile homes in America have formaldehyde levels high enough to cause harmful symptoms. The EPA estimates that as many as 2 out of every 10,000 persons who live in mobile homes for more than 10 years will probably develop cancer because of exposure to formaldehyde. Many new condos, town houses, and tract development houses also contain large quantities of formaldehyde-emitting materials.

While MDCs have serious indoor air pollution problems, the most severe exposure to indoor air pollution, especially particulate matter, occurs inside the dwellings of poor rural people in LDCs. In those dwellings, the burning of wood, dung, and crop residues in unvented or poorly vented stoves for cooking and heating (in temperate and cold areas) exposes the people, especially women and young children, to very high levels of indoor air pollution. This helps explain why respiratory illnesses are the chief cause of death and illness in most LDCs. By contrast, wood stoves and fireplaces used by most people in MDCs have chimneys or flues.

Radon-222 is a colorless, odorless, tasteless, naturally occurring radioactive gas produced by the radioactive decay of uranium-238. Small amounts of radon-producing uranium-238 are found in most soil and rock, but this isotope is much more concentrated in underground deposits of uranium, phosphate (Figure 4-32), granite (Figure 7-13) and shale.

When radon gas from such deposits seeps upward to the soil and is released outdoors, it disperses quickly in the atmosphere and decays to harmless levels. However, when the gas seeps into or is drawn into buildings through cracks, drains, hollow concrete blocks, and drains in basements, or into water in underground wells over such deposits, it can build up to high levels (Figure 21-5). Stone and other building materials obtained from radon-rich deposits can also be a source of indoor radon contamination.

Radon-222 gas quickly decays into solid particles of other radioactive elements that can be inhaled, exposing lung tissue to a large amount of ionizing radiation from alpha particles (Figure 3-9). Smokers are especially vulnerable because the inhaled radioactive particles contained in smoke tend to adhere to tobacco tar deposits in the lungs and upper respiratory tract (see Case Study on p. 556). Repeated exposure to radioactive particles over 20 to 30 years can cause lung cancer.

According to the EPA, average indoor radon levels in a closed house above 4 picocuries per liter are considered unsafe (Figure 21-5). However, some researchers think this level is too low and recommend that corrective action needs to be taken only if radon levels exceed 10 to 20 picocuries per liter — claims disputed by EPA scientists. EPA indoor radon surveys indicate that there may be several million U.S. homes with annual radon levels above 4 picocuries per liter, and more than 100,000 homes with levels above 20 picocuries per liter. In Pennsylvania, radon levels in the home of one family created a cancer risk equal to having 455,000 chest X rays a year.

In 1989, the EPA reported that about 54% of 130 schools tested had unsafe levels of radon.

According to studies by the EPA and the National Research Council, prolonged exposure to high levels of radon over a 70-year lifetime is estimated to cause up to 20,000 of the 136,000 lung cancer deaths each year in the United States. About 85% of these deaths are due to a combination of radon and smoking.

Radon released from water obtained from groundwater near radon-laden rock and then heated and used for showers and washing clothes and dishes may be responsible for 50 to 400 of these premature deaths. However, some recent research indicates that the risk from waterborne radon may be even higher than from airborne radon.

Because radon "hot spots" can occur almost anywhere, it is impossible to know which buildings have unsafe levels of radon without carrying out tests. In 1988, the EPA and the U.S. Surgeon General's Office recommended that everyone living in a detached house, a town house, or a mobile home or on the first three floors of an apartment building test for radon. By 1990, however, less than 3% of U.S. households had conducted such tests, even though radon is one of the most controllable environmental hazards we face today. Apparently, most people are reluctant to test for radon because they fear they will find high levels of the gas and will have to bear the costs of radon-proofing their houses and will worry about the possible effects of past exposure. They would rather not know — a potentially deadly form of denial.

Unsafe levels can build up easily in a superinsulated or airtight home unless the building has an air-to-air heat exchanger to change indoor air without losing much heat. Some tests also indicate higher levels of radon in houses with electric heat. Homeowners with wells should also have their water tested for radon.

Individuals can measure radon levels in their homes or other buildings with radon detection kits that can be bought in many hardware

stores and supermarkets or from mail-order firms for $10 to $20. Pick one that is EPA-approved and, after testing, mail the device to an EPA-certified testing laboratory to get the test result.*

If testing reveals an unacceptable level (more than 4 picocuries of radiation per liter of air), the EPA recommends several ways to reduce radon levels and health risks.[†] The first is to stop all indoor smoking, or at least confine it to a well-ventilated room, and do not allow people to live or sleep in basement rooms with unsafe radon levels. The next corrective measure is natural ventilation, especially leaving basement windows partially open or crawl-space vents open. Typically, this reduces radon levels by a factor of about 2.5.

Cracks in basement walls and floors and around pipes and joints between floors and walls should be sealed. However, that does little good if foundation or basement walls are constructed of porous, hollow-core concrete blocks, unless the interior surfaces of the blocks are liberally coated with latex paint or a concrete topcoat.

Air-to-air heat exchangers ($1,200 to $2,500 installed) can be installed to remove radon if radiation levels are not above 10 picocuries per liter of air.[‡] These devices also remove most other indoor air pollutants, but intake and outlet vents must be well balanced or the house can become depressurized and take in even more radon. Large positive-ion generators costing about $400 can also help in a house with low to moderate levels.

*For information, see "Radon Detectors: How to Find Out if Your House Has a Radon Problem," *Consumer Reports*, July 1987.

[†]A free copy of *Radon Reduction Methods* can be obtained from the Environmental Protection Agency, 401 M St. S.W., Washington, DC 20460. A free copy of *Radon Reduction in New Construction* is available from state radiation-protection offices or the National Association of Home Builders, Attention: William Young, 15th and M Streets N.W., Washington, DC 20005.

[‡]Before buying such a device, consult the Department of Energy's fact sheet *Air-to-Air Heat Exchangers* (available free from Renewable Energy Information, P.O. Box 8900, Silver Spring, MD 20907).

Figure 21-5 Sources of indoor radon-222 gas and comparable risks of exposure to various levels of this radioactive gas for a lifetime of 70 years. Levels are those in an actual living area, not a basement or crawl space where levels are much higher. Smokers have the highest risk of getting lung cancer from a combination of prolonged exposure to cigarette smoke and radon-222 gas. (Data from Environmental Protection Agency)

For houses with serious radon gas problems, special venting systems usually have to be installed below the foundations at a cost of $700 to $2,500. To remove radon from contaminated well water (more than 2,500 picocuries per liter), a special type of activated carbon filter can be added to holding tanks at a cost of about $1,000. Contact the state radiological health office or regional EPA office to get a list of approved contractors, and avoid unscrupulous radon testing and repair firms.

In Sweden, no house can be built until the lot has been tested for radon. If the reading is high, the builder must follow government-mandated construction procedures to ensure that the house won't be contaminated.

Environmentalists urge enactment of a similar building-code program for all new construction in the United States. They also suggest that before buying a lot to build a new house, individuals have the soil and the water tested for radon.

Similarly, no one should buy an existing house unless its indoor air and its water have been tested for radon by certified personnel, just as houses must now be inspected for termites. People building a new house should insist that the contractor use the relatively simple construction practices that prevent harmful buildup of radon and add only $100 to $1,000 to the construction cost. This includes using foundation materials such as solid concrete blocks or poured concrete walls and installing a heat-bonded nylon mat (called Enkavent and costing $450 to $650) under the slab of a house during construction.

Has the building where you live or work been tested for radon?

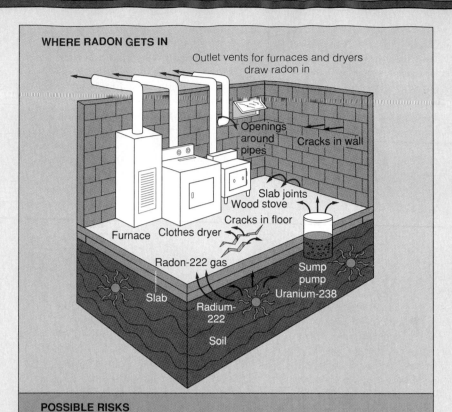

WHERE RADON GETS IN

Outlet vents for furnaces and dryers draw radon in

Openings around pipes
Cracks in wall
Slab joints
Wood stove
Cracks in floor
Furnace
Clothes dryer
Radon-222 gas
Slab
Sump pump
Uranium-238
Radium-222
Soil

POSSIBLE RISKS

Exposure (picocuries per liter of air)*	Lung-Cancer Deaths Per 1,000 People Exposed (for a lifetime of 70 years)	Comparable Lifetime Risk (70 years)	Recommended Action
200	440–470	Smoking 4 packs of cigarettes a day	**20–200 picocuries** Lower levels within several months. If higher than 200, remedy within a few weeks or move out until levels are reduced.
100	270–630	2,000 chest X rays a year	
40	120–380	Smoking 2 packs of cigarettes a day	
20	60–210	Smoking 1 pack of cigarettes a day	**4–20 picocuries** You've got a few years to make changes, but do it sooner if you're at the top of the scale.
10	30–120	5 times the lung-cancer risk of a nonsmoker	
4	13–50		
2	7–30	200 chest X rays a year	**Below 4 picocuries** Once you get around 4, it's nearly impossible to bring levels lower.
1	3–13	Same lung-cancer risk as a nonsmoker	
0.2	1–3	20 chest X rays a year	

* A picocurie is a trillionth of a curie, a standard measure of ionizing radiation.

Asbestos is the name given to a group of natural minerals made up of tiny fibers. Unless completely sealed in a product, asbestos can easily crumble into a dust of tiny fibers small enough to become suspended in the air and inhaled into the lungs, where they remain for many years.

Prolonged exposure to asbestos fibers can cause lung cancer, mesothelioma (a cancer of the lung and abdominal lining), or asbestosis (a chronic lung condition that eventually makes breathing nearly impossible) 15 to 40 years later. Most of these diseases occur in industrial workers exposed for years to high levels of asbestos fibers. Such workers include insulators, pipe fitters, shipyard employees, auto mechanics (from brake linings), and workers in asbestos-producing factories.

In 1991, an estimated 10,000 people — mostly industrial and construction workers exposed to asbestos fibers for years — died prematurely from asbestos-related disease. Workers who smoke and are exposed to asbestos have a much

greater chance of dying from lung cancer than those who don't smoke.

Experts project that exposure to asbestos — mostly in the workplace — could cause 2 million deaths between 1990 and 2020. Asbestos manufacturing companies in the United States have been swamped with, and in some cases driven into bankruptcy by, health claims from more than 350,000 former workers who have come down with asbestos-caused disease. The number filing claims grows by at least 20,000 each year.

Between 1900 and 1986, over 28 million metric tons (31 million tons) of asbestos were used in the United States for hundreds of purposes. Much of it was sprayed on ceilings and other parts of schools and public and private buildings for fireproofing, sound deadening, insulating heaters and pipes, and decorating walls and ceilings, until those uses were banned in 1974.

In 1989, the EPA ordered a ban on almost all other uses of asbestos such as brake linings, roofing shingles, and water pipes, by 1997. This

ban will eliminate 94% of the asbestos used in the United States. Higher costs for products made with asbestos substitutes would cost each consumer, on the average, a total of $10 during this period.

Representatives of the asbestos industry in the United States and Canada (which produces most of the asbestos used in the United States) oppose the EPA ban and may challenge it in court. They contend that with proper precautions, asbestos products can be used safely and that the costs of the ban outweigh the benefits.

Some researchers argue that about 95% of all asbestos used inside buildings contains chrysotile fibers, which are not as dangerous as fibers — especially amphibole fibers — from other types of asbestos. Some health scientists estimate that the risk of cancer from inhaling asbestos fibers in homes, offices, and schools is 0.25 death per million people exposed and that the typical levels of asbestos in such buildings is about the same as the natural background level of asbestos in out-

21-2   Smog and Acid Deposition

SMOG: CARS + SUNLIGHT = TEARS A mixture of dozens of primary pollutants and secondary pollutants formed when some of the primary pollutants interact under the influence of sunlight is called **photochemical smog** (Figure 21-6). Virtually all modern cities have photochemical smog, but it is much more common in those with sunny, warm, dry climates and lots of motor vehicles. Cities with serious photochemical smog include Los Angeles, Denver, Salt Lake City, Sydney, Mexico City (Figure 9-5), and Buenos Aires. The worst episodes of photochemical smog tend to occur in summer.

Thirty years ago, cities like London, Chicago, and Pittsburgh burned large amounts of coal and heavy oil, which contain sulfur impurities, in power and industrial plants and for space heating. During winter, such

cities suffered from **industrial smog** consisting mostly of a mixture of sulfur dioxide, suspended droplets of sulfuric acid formed from some of the sulfur dioxide, and a variety of suspended solid particles.

Today, coal and heavy oil are burned only in large boilers and with reasonably good control or tall smokestacks (see photo p. 541), so industrial smog, sometimes called gray-air smog, is rarely a problem. However, that is not the case in China and in some eastern European countries, such as Poland (see Case Study on p. 20) and Czechoslovakia, where large quantities of coal are burned with inadequate controls.

LOCAL CLIMATE, TOPOGRAPHY, AND SMOG
The frequency and severity of smog in an area depend on the local climate and topography; the density of population and industry; and the principal fuels used in industry, heating, and transportation. In areas with high average annual precipitation, rain and snow help cleanse the air of pollutants. Winds also help sweep

door air. However, other health scientists dispute the evidence and reasoning upon which these claims are made.

Asbestos is dangerous only if the fibers escape into the air. An asbestos object is *friable* and can release asbestos fibers if it can be crumbled with the hand. Products containing asbestos that were sprayed for fireproofing, insulating, and ceiling decoration are usually friable. Other products, such as vinyl flooring and roof shingles, are unlikely to lose their asbestos fibers unless they are cut or sanded.

In 1988, the EPA estimated that one of every seven commercial and public buildings in the United States contains friable asbestos. These buildings include Manhattan's World Trade Center, Chicago's John Hancock Building, Houston's Astrodome, and possibly a building you live or work in. In two-thirds of these buildings, the asbestos has been so damaged that it is likely to become airborne and be inhaled.

In 1986, Congress passed the Asbestos Hazards Emergency Response Act. It required all schools to have a qualified inspector check for asbestos and submit plans for containment or removal by May 8, 1989.* It is estimated that removing asbestos from schools will cost $6 billion and cleanup of all buildings will cost $51 billion. Financially strapped schools cannot afford such expenditures without increased local taxes or help from state and federal governments.

Some analysts argue that the benefits of asbestos removal from schools, homes, and other buildings are not worth the costs, except in cases where ceilings and walls are deteriorating and releasing enough amphibole asbestos fibers to cause high airborne levels of asbestos fibers, determined by measurement,

*For information on the control or removal of asbestos, call the EPA's Toxic Substances Control Hotline at (202) 554-1404, or write the EPA. You can also get a copy of EPA's booklets *Asbestos in the Home, Asbestos Fact Book, Guidance for Controlling Asbestos-Containing Materials in Buildings,* and *Asbestos Waste Management Guide* from the U.S. Government Printing Office, Washington, DC 20402.

not just visual inspection. They call for sealing, wrapping, and other forms of containment instead of removal of most asbestos, and point out that improper removal can release more hazardous fibers than sealing off asbestos that is not crumbling.

A number of asbestos-removal contractors have done shoddy work, overcharged home and building owners, and have increased the indoor levels of asbestos fibers. The EPA estimates that half of all asbestos-removal projects and three-fourths of those carried out in schools have been done improperly. Unnecessary asbestos removal can also increase deaths from exposure by asbestos-removal workers who do not follow stringent safety precautions.

However, some leading U.S. health experts, such as Dr. Irving Selikoff, contend that even the best available containment methods leave an unacceptable margin of risk for those exposed to asbestos fibers. What do you think should be done?

---

pollutants away and bring in fresh air but may transfer some pollutants to distant areas.

Hills and mountains tend to reduce the flow of air in valleys below and allow pollutant levels to build up at ground level. Buildings in cities also slow wind speed and reduce dilution and removal of pollutants.

During the day, the sun warms the air near Earth's surface. Normally, this heated air expands and rises, carrying low-lying pollutants higher into the troposphere. Colder, denser air from surrounding high-pressure areas then sinks into the low-pressure area created when the hot air rises (Figure 21-7, left). This continual mixing of warm and cold air helps keep pollutants from reaching dangerous levels in the air near the ground.

Sometimes, however, weather conditions trap a layer of dense, cool air beneath a layer of less dense, warm air in an urban basin or valley. This is called a **temperature inversion** or a **thermal inversion** (Figure 21-7, right). In effect, a lid of warm air covers the region and prevents upward-flowing air currents from developing, which would disperse pollutants. Usually, these inversions last for only a few hours, but sometimes, when a high-pressure air mass stalls over an area they last for several days. Then air pollutants at ground level build up to harmful and even lethal levels (see Spotlight on p. 577). Thermal inversions also enhance the harmful effects of urban heat islands and dust domes that build up over urban areas (Figure 9-12).

A city with several million people and automobiles in an area with a sunny climate, light winds, mountains on three sides and the ocean on the other has the ideal conditions for photochemical smog worsened by frequent thermal inversions. This describes the Los Angeles basin (Figure 21-8). It has almost daily inversions—many of them prolonged during the summer months—13.8 million people, 8.5 million cars, and thousands of factories. Despite having the world's toughest air pollution control program, Los Angeles is the air pollution capital of the United States.

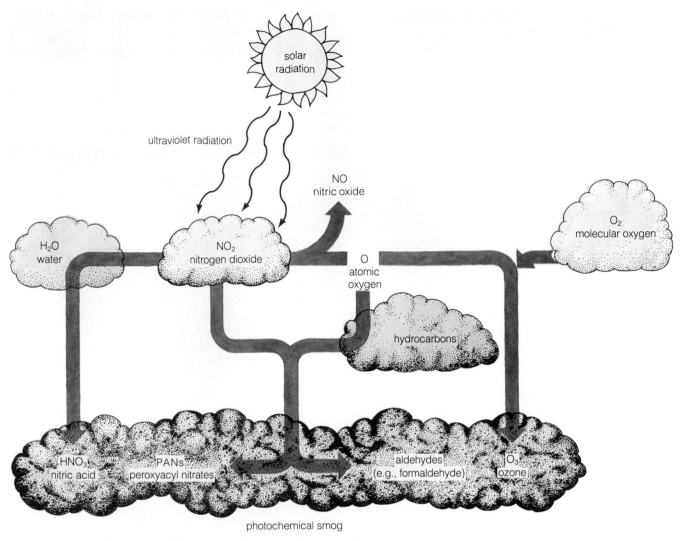

Figure 21-6 Simplified scheme of the formation of photochemical smog. The severity of smog is generally associated with atmospheric concentrations of ozone at ground level. Other harmful compounds in photochemical smog are aldehydes, peroxyacyl nitrates (PANs), and nitric acid. Traces of the secondary pollutants in photochemical smog build up to peak levels by early afternoon on a sunny day, irritating people's eyes and respiratory tracts. People with asthma and other respiratory problems, and healthy people who exercise outdoors between 11 A.M. and 4 P.M., are especially vulnerable. The hotter the day, the higher the levels of ozone and other components of photochemical smog.

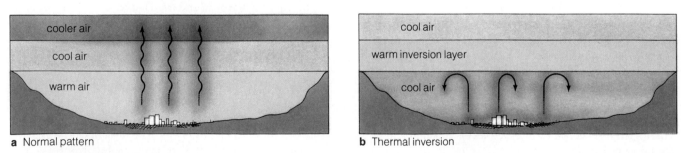

a Normal pattern   **b** Thermal inversion

Figure 21-7 Thermal inversion traps pollutants in a layer of cool air that cannot rise to carry the pollutants away.

Figure 21-8 Buildup of photochemical smog in Los Angeles during a weekday with a thermal inversion.

National Archives

ACID DEPOSITION When electric power plants and industrial plants burn coal or oil, their smokestacks emit large amounts of sulfur dioxide, suspended particulate matter, and nitrogen oxides. To reduce local air pollution and meet government standards without having to add expensive air pollution control devices, power plants and industries began using tall smokestacks (see photo on p. 541) to spew pollutants above the inversion layer (Figure 21-7). As more power plants and industries began using this fairly cheap output approach to controlling local pollution in the 1960s and 1970s, pollution in downwind areas began to rise. Since 1950, global emissions of sulfur dioxide and nitrogen oxides have tripled.

As emissions of sulfur dioxide and nitric oxide from stationary sources are transported long distances by winds, they form secondary pollutants such as nitrogen dioxide, nitric acid vapor, and droplets containing solutions of sulfuric acid and sulfate and nitrate salts (Figure 21-1). These chemicals descend to Earth's surface in wet form as acid rain or snow and in dry form as gases, fog, dew, or solid particles. The combination of dry deposition and wet deposition of acids and acid-forming compounds onto the surface of the earth is known as **acid deposition**, commonly called *acid rain* (Figure 21-9). Other contributions to acid deposition come from emissions of nitric oxide from great numbers of automobiles in large urban areas. Because water droplets and most solid particles are removed from the atmosphere fairly quickly, acid deposition is a regional or continental problem rather than a global problem.

Different levels of acidity and basicity of water solutions of substances are commonly expressed in terms of pH (Figure 12-6). A neutral solution has a pH of 7; a solution with a pH greater than 7 is basic, or alkaline; and one with a pH less than 7 is acidic. The lower the pH below 7, the more acidic the solution. Each whole-number decrease in pH represents a tenfold increase in acidity.

Natural precipitation varies in acidity, with an average pH of 5.0 to 5.6, but the average rain in the eastern United States is as acidic as tomato juice, with a pH of 4.3. Precipitation in some areas is more than ten times as acidic, with a pH of 3—as acidic as vinegar (Figure 12-6). Some cities and mountaintops downwind from cities are bathed in acid fog as acidic as lemon juice, with a pH of 2.3.

Acid deposition has a number of harmful effects, especially when the pH falls below 5.1 and below 5.5 for aquatic systems:

- It damages statues, buildings, metals, and car finishes.

- It kills fish, aquatic plants, and microorganisms in lakes and streams. Like the canary that miners used to carry into a coal mine to warn them of hazardous air pollution, fish can tell us when something is wrong with their environment. When the pH falls below 6, many species of fish can't reproduce. Brown trout need water with a pH of 5.5 or higher to survive, and rainbow trout need a pH of 6 or higher. Water with a pH below 4.3 is generally fishless.

- It contaminates fish eaten by humans with highly toxic methylmercury which, like DDT (Figure 16-18), can be biologically amplified to high concentrations in food chains and webs. Apparently, increased acidity of lakes converts naturally occurring and human-deposited inorganic mercury compounds in lake-bottom sediments into more toxic methylmercury, which is more soluble in the fatty tissue of animals than inorganic forms of mercury.

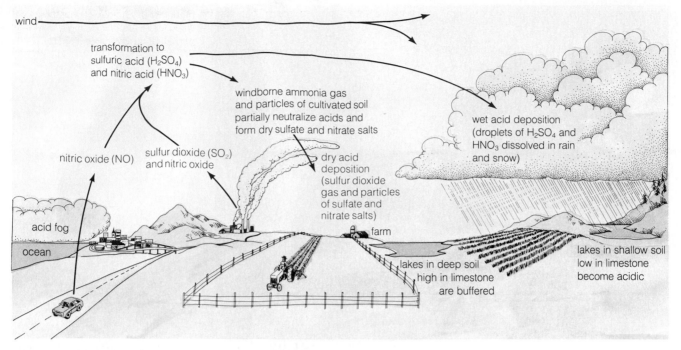

Figure 21-9 Acid deposition. It consists of acidified rain, snow, dust, or gas with a pH lower than 5.6. The lower the pH level, the greater the acidity of this wet and dry deposition, commonly called acid rain.

■ It is a major contributor to regional haze in the East and parts of the West, mostly from fine particles of sulfate salts in the atmosphere. At times the sulfate pollution is so great that people can't see to the bottom of the Grand Canyon or across Virginia's Shenandoah Valley.

■ It weakens or kills trees, especially conifers at high elevations (bathed almost continuously in very acidic fog and clouds), by leaching calcium, potassium, and other plant nutrients from soil (Figure 21-10).

■ It damages tree roots and kills many kinds of fish by releasing ions of aluminum, lead, mercury, and cadmium from soil and bottom sediments (Figure 21-10).

■ It weakens trees and makes them more susceptible to diseases, insects, drought, and fungi and mosses that thrive under acidic conditions (Figure 21-10).

■ It stunts the growth of crops such as tomatoes, soybeans, spinach, carrots, broccoli, and cotton.

■ It leaches toxic metals such as copper and lead from city and home water pipes into drinking water.

■ It causes and aggravates many human respiratory diseases and leads to premature death. Dr. Philip Landrigan at New York's Mt. Sinai School of Medicine estimates that acid deposition is the third largest cause of lung disease in the United States, after smoking (see Figure 20-10) and indoor radon (see Case Study on p. 580).

Soils and bedrock in some areas contain limestone and other alkaline substances, which easily dissolve in water and can neutralize acids. Soils in other areas are acidic and thin or contain rocks like granite (Figure 7-13), shale, and sandstone, which do not readily dissolve and have little ability to neutralize acids. Soils, vegetation, and aquatic life in lakes in such areas are especially sensitive to acid deposition (Figure 21-11).

Acid deposition illustrates the threshold, or straw-that-broke-the-camel's-back, effect. Most soils, lakes, and streams contain alkaline (or basic) chemicals that can react with a certain amount of acids and thus neutralize them, but repeated exposure to acids year after year can deplete most of these acid-buffering chemicals. Then, suddenly, large numbers of trees start dying and most fish in a lake or stream die when exposed to the next year's input of acids. By that time, it is 10 to 20 years too late to prevent serious damage.

Acid deposition is already a serious problem in many areas (Figure 21-11). The acidity of the precipitation falling over much of eastern North America has a pH of 4.0 to 4.2. That is 30 to 40 times greater than the acidity of the normal precipitation that fell on those areas several decades ago.

Estimated damage from acid deposition already costs the United States at least $6 billion a year and perhaps $10 billion a year, and costs are expected to rise sharply unless action is taken now. A 1990 study by Resources for the Future, a leading research organization, indicated that the benefits of controlling acid deposition will be worth roughly $5 billion a year,

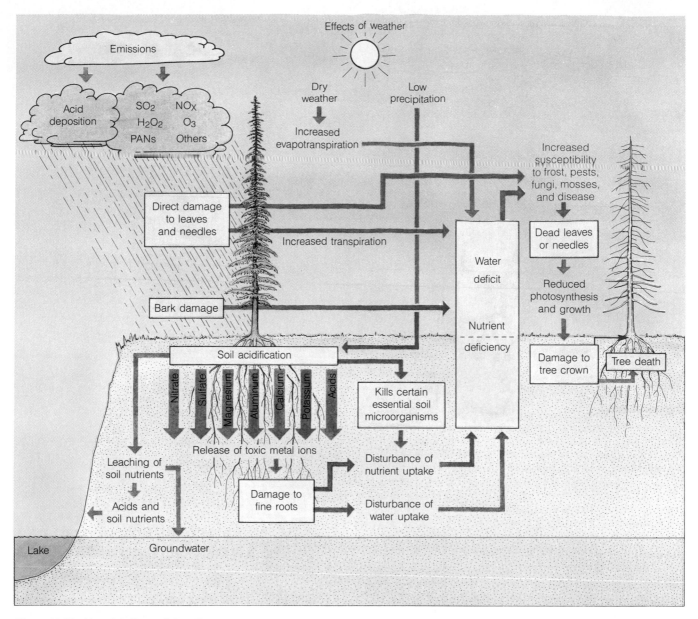

Figure 21-10   Harmful effects of air pollutants on trees.

about 50% greater than the costs of controlling acid deposition.

A large portion of the acid-producing chemicals produced in one country is exported to others by prevailing surface winds. For example, over three-fourths of the acid deposition in Norway, Switzerland, Austria, Sweden, the Netherlands, and Finland is blown to those countries from industrialized areas of western and eastern Europe (Figure 21-11).

More than half the acid deposition in heavily populated southeastern Canada and in the eastern United States originates from emissions from the heavy concentration of coal- and oil-burning power and industrial plants in seven central and upper midwestern states —

Ohio, Indiana, Pennsylvania, Illinois, Missouri, West Virginia, and Tennessee. Canada produces almost twice as much sulfur dioxide per person and per unit of energy consumed as the United States and thus exports some acid deposition to the northeastern United States (see photo on p. 541). However, total U.S. production of sulfur dioxide and nitrogen oxides is five to six times that of Canada. Thus, Canada receives much more acid deposition from the United States than it exports across the border.

The large net flow of acid deposition from the United States to Canada has been straining relations between the two countries for over a decade. During the 1980s, the United States refused to do much about

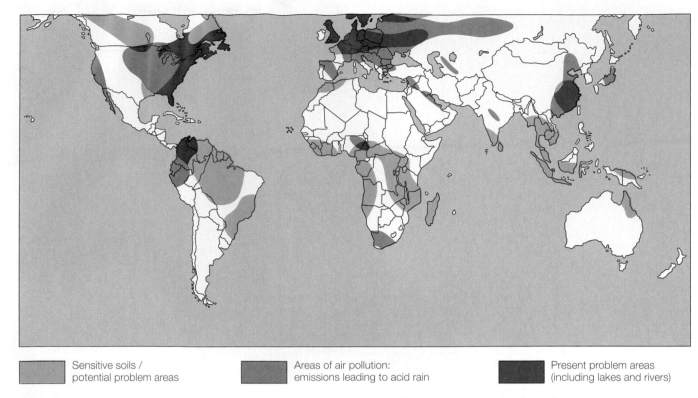

| Sensitive soils / potential problem areas | Areas of air pollution: emissions leading to acid rain | Present problem areas (including lakes and rivers) |

Figure 21-11 Areas of the world suffering from acid deposition, areas where air pollution emissions may lead to acid deposition, and areas with soils sensitive to acid deposition because the soils do not contain enough of the chemicals that neutralize acids. Often pollutants leading to acid deposition are produced in one area but transported by wind to other areas, where they are removed from the atmosphere as wet or dry deposition. (Data from World Resource Institute and Environmental Protection Agency)

this chemical assault on its neighbor and on its own people, citing the need for more research.

A large-scale, government-sponsored research study on acid deposition in the United States in the 1980s concluded that the problem was serious but not yet at a crisis stage. Its basic scientific findings were that acid rain has severely affected aquatic life in about 10% of eastern lakes and streams, has contributed to the decline of the red spruce at high elevations by reducing that species' tolerance to cold, has contributed to erosion and corrosion of buildings and materials, and has reduced visibility (mostly from fine sulfate particles) throughout the Northeast and in parts of the West. Critics claim that this $50 million, 10-year study was used mostly by the Reagan administration to justify its denial and delay policy on controlling acid deposition during the 1980s.

Tensions between the United States and Canada were eased by the Clean Air Act of 1990, which calls for a significant reduction in U.S. emissions of sulfur dioxide and a modest reduction in emissions of nitrogen oxides by the year 2000. Canada has agreed to make comparable reductions in its emissions of these air pollutants. In 1991, these agreements were formalized in a transboundary air pollution agreement between the two countries.

 21-3 **Effects of Air Pollution on Living Organisms and Materials**

DAMAGE TO HUMAN HEALTH Your respiratory system has a number of mechanisms that help protect you from air pollution. Hairs in your nose filter out large particles. Sticky mucus in the lining of your upper respiratory tract captures small particles and dissolves some gaseous pollutants. Automatic sneezing and coughing mechanisms expel contaminated air and mucus when your respiratory system is irritated by pollutants. Your upper respiratory tract is lined with hundreds of thousands of tiny, mucus-coated hairlike cell structures, called cilia. They continually wave back and forth, transporting mucus and the pollutants they trap to your mouth, where they are either swallowed or expelled.

Years of smoking (see Case Study on p. 556) and exposure to air pollutants can overload or deteriorate these natural defenses, causing or contributing to a number of respiratory diseases such as lung cancer, chronic bronchitis, and emphysema. Elderly people, infants, pregnant women, and people with heart disease, asthma, or other respiratory diseases are especially vul-

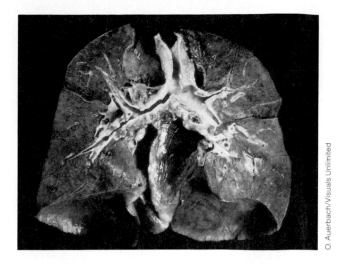

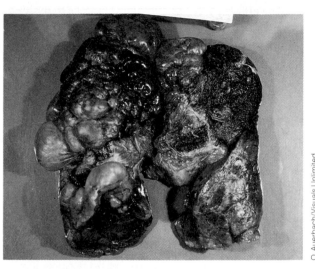

Figure 21-12 Normal appearance of the human lung (top) and appearance of a lung taken from a person who died from emphysema (bottom).

O. Auerbach/Visuals Unlimited

The air pollution capital of the world may be Cubatao, an hour's drive south of São Paulo, Brazil (Figure 9-3). This city of 100,000 people lies in a coastal valley that has frequent thermal inversions. Residents call the area "the valley of death."

In this heavily industrialized city, scores of plants spew thousands of tons of pollutants a day into the frequently stagnant air. More babies are born deformed there than anywhere else in Latin America.

In one recent year, 13,000 of the 40,000 people living in the downtown core area suffered from respiratory disease. One resident says, "On some days, if you go outside, you will vomit." The mayor refuses to live in the city.

Most residents would like to live somewhere else, but they need the jobs available in the city and cannot afford to move. The government has begun some long overdue efforts to control air pollution, but it has far to go. Meanwhile, the poor continue to pay the price of this form of economic progress: bad health and premature death.

nerable to air pollution. Recent evidence on test animals indicates that nitrogen dioxide—a common pollutant from automobile exhaust—may encourage the spread of cancer, especially deadly melanoma (Figure 11-8c), throughout the body.

Fine particles (Figure 21-2) are particularly hazardous to human health because they are small enough to penetrate the lung's natural defenses. Smoking is considered the leading cause of lung cancer, but the disease has also been linked to inhalation of a number of other air pollutants, such as asbestos fibers (see Pro/Con on p. 582).

Inhaling the ozone found in photochemical smog (Figure 21-6) causes coughing, shortness of breath, nose and throat irritation, and discomfort and aggravates chronic diseases such as asthma, bronchitis, emphysema, and heart trouble. Outdoor exercise in areas where ozone exceeds safe levels (0.12 part per million

per hour) amplifies these effects. Many U.S. cities frequently exceed safe levels, especially during warm weather.

Emphysema is an incurable condition that reduces the ability of the lungs to transfer oxygen to the blood, so the slightest exertion causes acute shortness of breath (Figure 21-12). Prolonged smoking and exposure to air pollutants can cause emphysema in anyone, but about 2% of emphysema cases are caused by a defective gene that reduces the elasticity of the air sacs of the lungs. Anyone with this hereditary condition, for which testing is available, should certainly not smoke and should not live or work in a highly polluted area.

The World Health Organization (WHO) estimates that worldwide nearly 1 billion urban dwellers—almost one of every five people on Earth—are being exposed to health hazards from air pollutants (see Spotlight above). An estimated 60% of the people living in Calcutta, India, suffer from respiratory diseases related to air pollution, and breathing the polluted air in Bombay, India, is equivalent to smoking ten cigarettes a day. In New Delhi, India, levels of suspended particulate matter are five times higher than World Health Organization standards 294 days a year, and in Beijing, China, they are five times higher for 272 days a year.

In Mexico City (Figure 9-5), smog levels exceeded WHO standards on 312 days in 1988—and in January 1989, it was so bad that schoolchildren were given the entire month off. Sulfur dioxide concentrations in Shenyang, China, are three times higher than WHO standards about half the year.

The congressional Office of Technology Assessment estimates that 50,000 premature deaths occur in the United States each year from respiratory or cardiac problems caused or aggravated by current air pollution levels. The American Lung Association estimates that up to 120,000 Americans die each year as a result of air pollution.

According to the EPA and the American Lung Association, air pollution costs the United States at least $150 billion annually in health care and lost work productivity. About $100 billion of that is caused by indoor air pollution—the problem we have focused on the least—and $40 billion is caused by air pollution from motor vehicles.

DAMAGE TO PLANTS Until recently, most damage to plants was believed to be caused by ozone and acid deposition. Recent research, however, indicates that such damage is caused by prolonged exposure to a complex and poorly understood mix of these and other air pollutants. Some of the damage is direct, but much of it is indirect, and this indirect damage is believed to be much more threatening than the direct damage from air pollution.

Some gaseous pollutants, such as sulfur dioxide, nitrogen oxides, ozone, and PANs, cause direct damage to leaves of crop plants and trees when they enter leaf pores (stomata) (Figure 21-10). Chronic exposure of leaves and needles to air pollutants can break down the waxy coating that helps prevent excessive water loss and damage from diseases, pests, drought, and frost. Such exposure also interferes with photosynthesis and plant growth, reduces nutrient uptake, and causes leaves or needles to turn yellow or brown and drop off (Figure 21-13). Spruce, fir, and other coniferous trees, especially at high elevations, are highly vulnerable to the effects of air pollution because of their long life spans and the year-round exposure of their needles to polluted air, often in the form of clouds and fog containing high concentrations of ozone, acidic compounds, and other pollutants.

In addition to causing direct leaf and needle damage, acid deposition can leach vital plant nutrients, such as calcium, magnesium, and potassium, from the soil and kill essential soil microorganisms (Figure 21-10). It also releases aluminum ions, which are normally bound to soil particles, into soil water. There, they may damage fine root hairs, disrupt the ability of roots to absorb water from the soil, kill decomposers that break down organic matter and make nutrients available to plants, and make plants more vulnerable to damage or death from drought, frost, insects, fungi, mosses, and disease (Figure 21-10). Recent research indicates that a syner-

gistic interaction between sulfur dioxide and ammonia amplifies tree damage from nutrient loss caused by each pollutant acting alone.

Prolonged exposure to high levels of multiple air pollutants can kill all trees and most other vegetation in an area (Figure 7-22). In Canada's Ontario province, sulfur and nitrogen oxide emissions from International Nickel's Sudbury smelting plant (see photo on p. 541) have killed all vegetation, caused severe soil erosion, and killed most aquatic life in lakes in a 32-kilometer (20-mile) area downwind from the plant. Under Canadian air pollution control laws, the plant had reduced its weight of air pollution emissions 75% between 1979 and 1989 and is supposed to achieve a 90% reduction by 1994. If that reduction is achieved, the plant will still emit 455 metric tons (500 tons) of sulfur dioxide *per day* into the atmosphere.

The effects of chronic exposure of trees to multiple air pollutants may not be visible for several decades. Then, suddenly, large numbers begin dying off because of depletion of soil nutrients and increased susceptibility to pests, diseases, fungi, mosses, and drought.

That is what is happening to about 35% of the forested area in 28 European countries. The phenomenon, known as *Waldsterben* (forest death), turns whole forests of spruce, fir, and beech into stump-studded meadows. The four European countries with the highest percentages of their conifer forests damaged are Czechoslovakia (71%), Greece (64%), the United Kingdom (64%), and the former West Germany (52%). It is estimated that such forest damage could cost Europe at least $30 billion per year over the next 100 years.

Similar diebacks in the United States have occurred in mostly coniferous forests on high-elevation slopes facing moving air masses. The most seriously affected areas are the Appalachian Mountains from Georgia to New England. By 1988, most spruce, fir, and other conifers atop North Carolina's Mt. Mitchell, the highest peak in the East, were dead from being bathed in ozone and acid fog for years (Figure 21-14). The soil was so acidic that new seedlings could not survive.

Plant pathologist Robert Bruck warns that damage to mountaintop forests is an early warning that many tree species at lower elevations may soon die or be damaged by prolonged exposure to air pollution. Many scientists fear that elected officials in the United States will continue to delay establishing stricter controls on the worst forms of air pollution until it is too late to prevent a severe loss of valuable forest resources, as is happening in Europe.

Air pollution, mostly by ozone, also threatens some types of crops—especially corn, wheat, soybeans, and peanuts and is reducing U.S. crop production by 5% to 10%. In the United States, estimates of economic losses from reduced crop yields as a result of air pollution range from $1.9 billion to $5.4 billion a year.

DAMAGE TO AQUATIC LIFE Acid deposition has a severe harmful impact on the aquatic life of freshwater lakes with low alkaline content or in areas where surrounding soils have little acid-buffering capacity (Figure 21-11). Much of the damage to aquatic life in the Northern Hemisphere is a result of *acid shock*. It is caused by the sudden runoff of large amounts of highly acidic water (along with toxic aluminum leached from the soil) into lakes and streams when snow melts in the spring or when heavy rains follow a period of drought.

Unfortunately, this sudden increase in acidity comes at a time when most fish and amphibians (Figure 4-35) breed. The aluminum leached from the soil and lake sediment suffocates fish by causing them to release mucus, which clogs their gills and prevents the exchange of oxygen and carbon dioxide across the gill membrane. The crystal clear water of a highly acidic lake is a clear sign that it contains few fish or other forms of aquatic life.

In Norway and Sweden, at least 16,000 lakes contain no fish and an additional 52,000 have lost most of their acid-neutralizing capacity because of excess acidity. In Canada, some 14,000 lakes are almost fishless, and 150,000 more are in peril because of excess acidity.

In the United States, about 9,000 lakes are threatened with excess acidity, one-third of them seriously. Most are concentrated in the Northeast and the Upper Midwest (mostly in parts of Minnesota, Wisconsin, and the upper Great Lakes), where 80% of the lakes and streams are threatened by excess acidity. Over 200 lakes in New York's Adirondack Mountains are too acidic to support fish. About 2.7% of the nation's streams are acidified. In California, pollution from automobile exhaust and industries is threatening life in lakes in the Sierra Nevada.

Acidified lakes can be neutralized by treating them or the surrounding soil with large amounts of limestone. Such liming prevents declines in aquatic life or allows a comeback of life and can buy some time until pollution controls reduce acid deposition. However, it is expensive, is only a temporary Band-Aid approach that must be repeated, and its long-term effects are unknown. More than 4,000 of Sweden's lakes are being limed at an annual cost of about $45 million.

DAMAGE TO MATERIALS Each year, air pollutants cause billions of dollars in damage to various materials (Table 21-1). The fallout of soot and grit on buildings, cars, and clothing requires costly cleaning. Air pollutants break down exterior paint on cars and houses and deteriorate roofing materials. Irreplaceable marble statues, historic buildings, and stained-glass windows throughout the world have been pitted and discolored by air pollutants (Figure 21-15). Damage to buildings in the United States from acid deposition alone is estimated at $5 billion a year.

Figure 21-13 Injury to ponderosa pine needles from exposure to ozone and other pollutants in photochemical smog.

Figure 21-14 Tree death and damage to coniferous trees near the top of Mt. Mitchell, North Carolina — the highest peak in the East — is believed to have been the result of long-term exposure to multiple air pollutants, which made the trees more vulnerable to disease, insects, and drought.

21-4 Controlling Air Pollution

U.S. AIR POLLUTION LEGISLATION Air pollution or any other type of pollution can be controlled by laws to establish desired standards and by technology to achieve the standards. The type of pollution control technology can be mandated by government regulators or pollution standards, and deadlines can be set, with polluters allowed to determine how to meet those standards and goals.

In the United States, Congress passed the Clean Air acts of 1970, 1977, and 1990 (see Spotlight on p. 594), which gave the federal government considerable power to control air pollution. Each state is required to develop and enforce an implementation plan for attainment of these standards.

Table 21-1 Harmful Effects of Air Pollution on Materials

Material	Effects	Principal Air Pollutants
Stone and concrete	Surface erosion, discoloration, soiling	Sulfur dioxide, sulfuric acid, nitric acid, particulate matter
Metals	Corrosion, tarnishing, loss of strength	Sulfur dioxide, sulfuric acid, nitric acid, particulate matter, hydrogen sulfide
Ceramics and glass	Surface erosion	Hydrogen fluoride, particulate matter
Paints	Surface erosion, discoloration, soiling	Sulfur dioxide, hydrogen sulfide, ozone, particulate matter
Paper	Embrittlement, discoloration	Sulfur dioxide
Rubber	Cracking, loss of strength	Ozone
Leather	Surface deterioration, loss of strength	Sulfur dioxide
Textile fabrics	Deterioration, fading, soiling	Sulfur dioxide, nitrogen dioxide, ozone, particulate matter

Adrian P. Davies/Bruce Coleman Ltd.

Figure 21-15 This marble monument on a church in Surrey, England, has been damaged by exposure to acidic air pollutants.

These laws required the EPA to establish **national ambient air quality standards (NAAQS)** for seven outdoor pollutants: suspended particulate matter, sulfur oxides, carbon monoxide, nitrogen oxides, ozone, hydrocarbons, and lead. Each standard specifies the max-imum allowable level, averaged over a specific time period, for a certain pollutant in outdoor (ambient) air.

The EPA was required to set two types of NAAQS without taking into consideration the cost of meeting them. *Primary ambient air quality standards* were set to protect human health, with a margin of safety for the elderly, infants, and other vulnerable persons, and deadlines were set for their attainment. Each of the 247 air quality control regions established by the EPA across the country was supposed to meet all primary standards by 1982, with some extensions possible to 1987, but many areas failed to meet the deadlines. *Secondary ambient air quality standards* were set to maintain visibility and to protect crops, buildings, and water supplies. No deadlines were set for their attainment.

The EPA has also established a policy of *prevention of significant deterioration (PSD)*. It is designed to prevent a decrease in air quality in regions where the air is cleaner than required by the NAAQS for suspended particulate matter and sulfur dioxide. Otherwise, industries would move into those areas and gradually degrade air quality to the national standards for these two pollutants.

The EPA is also required to establish *national emission standards* for less-common air pollutants capable of causing serious harm to human health at low concentrations. Scientists have identified at least 600 potentially toxic air pollutants. By 1991, the EPA had established emission standards for only seven toxic air pollutants: arsenic, asbestos, benzene, beryllium, mercury, vinyl chloride, and radioactive isotopes. Part of the problem is the difficulty of getting accurate scientific data on the effects of specific pollutants on human health (Section

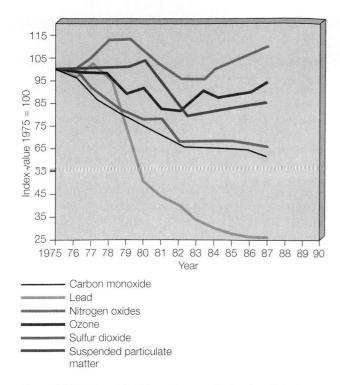

Index value 1975 = 100

—— Carbon monoxide
—— Lead
—— Nitrogen oxides
—— Ozone
—— Sulfur dioxide
—— Suspended particulate
matter

Figure 21-16 Trends in U.S. outdoor quality for six pollutants, 1975–87. (Data from Environmental Protection Agency)

20-1). Economic and political pressures also hamper the EPA's work. During the 1980s, Congress slashed the EPA budgets, and the Reagan administration reduced enforcement of air pollution laws. The Clean Air Act of 1990 uses a different approach for reducing the levels of such pollutants (see Spotlight on p. 594)

Congress also set a timetable for achieving certain percentage reductions in emissions of carbon monoxide, hydrocarbons, and nitrogen oxides from motor vehicles. These standards forced automakers to build cars that emit six to eight times less pollutants than the cars of the late 1960s. Although significant progress has been made, a series of legally allowed extensions has pushed deadlines for complete attainment of most of these goals into the future.

TRENDS IN U.S. OUTDOOR AIR QUALITY There is still a long way to go, but since 1975 the United States has achieved significant progress in reducing outdoor air pollution from outdoor pollutants: lead, carbon monoxide, ozone, sulfur dioxide, and suspended particulate matter (Figure 21-16). Lead made the sharpest drop because of the 91% reduction in the amount of lead allowed in leaded gasoline.

According to the Council on Environmental Quality, the Clean Air Act of 1970 has saved 14,000 lives and $21 billion in health, property, and other damages each year since 1970. Without the 1970 standards, emissions of the outdoor air pollutants shown in Figure 21-16 would be 130% to 315% higher today.

Except for Sweden, the United States has made more progress in reducing or maintaining levels of the outdoor pollutants (except nitrogen oxides) shown in Figure 21-16 than other countries. However, most U.S. air pollution control laws are based on pollution cleanup rather than pollution prevention. Pollution control is better than doing nothing, but the increase in new vehicles and other emission sources gradually overwhelms pollution control efforts. This, plus relaxing fuel efficiency standards (Figure 17-2) and decreasing budgets for enforcement of air pollution laws during the 1980s, explains why levels of ozone and suspended particulate matter increased and nitrogen dioxide levels stayed the same between the years 1986 and 1988.

The only air pollutant with a sharp drop in its atmospheric level was lead, which was virtually banned in gasoline. This shows the effectiveness of the pollution prevention approach.

The EPA uses a pollution standards index (PSI) to indicate how frequently and to what degree the air quality in a particular city exceeds one or more of the primary health standards. Daily PSI indexes are reported by the media in many areas to alert the public to air pollution levels.

Despite this progress, in 1990, more than 84 million Americans — 1 out of 3 — were breathing outdoor air that violated at least one federal standard and more than half the people in the United States lived in communities polluted by too much smog.

In the 1970s, most western European countries, Canada, Australia, Japan, and South Korea established automobile emissions standards similar to those in the United States, although some European countries lag behind. Brazil will have similar standards by 1997. Little, if any, attempt is made to control vehicle emissions in India, Mexico (Figure 9-5), Argentina, China, the Soviet Union, and eastern European countries. Switzerland and Austria have the world's toughest air pollution control laws.

METHODS OF POLLUTION CONTROL Once a pollution control standard has been adopted, two general approaches can be used to prevent levels from exceeding the standard. One is *pollution prevention* or *input control*, which prevents or reduces the severity of the problem. The other is *pollution cleanup* or *output control*, which treats the symptoms. Output methods such as scrubbers on smokestacks can reduce emissions dramatically, but they are not ultimate solutions. Eventually they are overwhelmed by increases in population and industrialization (Figure 1-16). In addition, they also create environmental problems of their own, such as the need to dispose of scrubber ash, a hazardous waste.

Pollution prevention is usually easier and cheaper in the long run than pollution cleanup methods. The best methods for preventing or reducing the total

The Clean Air Act of 1977 was supposed to be updated in the early 1980s, but debates between industry officials, environmentalists, members of Congress, and members of the executive branch prevented passage of a new clean air act until 1990. The most important provisions of the Clean Air Act of 1990 include

- Reducing the mass of 1988 CFC emissions 20% by 1993 and 50% by mid-1999.

- Requiring industries to use the best available technology to reduce the mass of industrial emissions of 189 toxic chemicals by 90% between 1995 and 2003. Companies not entering into legally enforceable agreements with the EPA to do this voluntarily by methods the companies choose will be told by the EPA what technologies they must use to achieve the reduction goals.

- Requiring 87 cities not meeting federal emissions standards for ozone to meet such standards between 1993 and 1999 and giving 8 severely polluted cities until between 2005 and 2007 to meet those standards. Los Angeles has

until 2010, although it must meet even tougher state standards.

- Reducing auto emissions of hydrocarbons 35% and nitrogen oxides 60% for all new cars by 1994. By 1998 all new cars must have emission control systems good for 10 years or 161,000 kilometers (100,000 miles) instead of the current 5 years or 80,500 kilometers (50,000 miles). Stricter emission standards for new cars will go into effect in 2003.

- Requiring large diesel trucks to cut emissions of particulate matter 90% by 1998 compared to uncontrolled levels. Buses in urban areas must do even better than trucks in controlling harmful emissions.

- Requiring oil companies to sell cleaner-burning gasoline and other fuels in the nine dirtiest cities — Los Angeles, Baltimore, Chicago, Houston, Milwaukee, Muskegon, New York, Philadelphia, and San Diego — by 1995 and to sell at least 150,000 electric or other clean-fuel vehicles in California by 1996.

- Requiring coal-burning power plants to cut their annual sulfur

dioxide emissions by 9 million metric tons (10 million tons) — about half the current levels — by the year 2000 or by 2005 if they switch to low-sulfur coal or other clean-coal technologies. During the same period, emissions of nitrogen oxides must be cut to 1.8 million metric tons (2 million tons) below 1980 levels. In 2003, stricter emission standards go into effect.

- Using market forces to help reduce pollution by allowing companies to buy and sell pollution rights for sulfur dioxide emissions from one another. With this *emissions trading policy*, specific air pollution control emissions would be established for each company. Companies that reduce their emissions below their limit would receive credit in the form of permits. They could then use those credits to avoid emission reductions in some of their existing or new facilities, or they could sell the permits to other companies. Companies wishing to expand would have to buy credits to be allowed to produce more air pollution. Thus, all companies would have a finan-

amount of pollution of any type from reaching the environment are

- regulating population growth (Section 8-3)

- reducing unnecessary waste of metals, paper, and other matter resources through increased recycling and reuse and by designing products that last longer and are easy to repair (Section 19-5)

- reducing energy use (Section 18-5)

- using energy more efficiently (Sections 17-2 and 18-5)

- switching from coal to natural gas, which produces less pollution when burned (Section 18-1)

- switching from fossil fuels and nuclear power (Chapter 18) to energy from the sun, wind, and flowing water (Chapter 17)

- identifying the source of pollution in a production process, eliminating it from that process, and finding a more environmentally benign substitute (Figure 20-8)

So far, these methods for preventing pollution have rarely been given serious consideration in national and international strategies for pollution control and energy use (Section 18-5).

CONTROL OF SULFUR DIOXIDE EMISSIONS FROM STATIONARY SOURCES

In the United States, about 66% by weight of SO_2 emissions come from burning fossil fuels (mostly coal) in power plants. An additional 30% comes from burning fossil fuels in factories and other stationary sources and 4% comes from motor vehicles. In addition to the general prevention methods

cial incentive to cut their emissions: profit from the sale of their surplus permits. Instead of the government dictating how each company should meet its emissions target, this approach would let the marketplace determine the cheapest, most efficient way to get the job done. If this approach works for reducing SO_2 emissions, it could be applied to other air and water pollutants.

Environmentalists praise the Bush administration for pushing Congress to pass a new Clean Air Act after years of delay. However, they point to several serious deficiencies in the new law. They include

- Failing to sharply increase the fuel efficiency standards for cars and light trucks, which would cut oil imports and air pollution more quickly and effectively than any other method and would also save consumers enormous amounts of money.

- Failing to classify the ash from municipal trash incinerators as hazardous waste, thus encouraging the building of incinerators instead of pollution prevention as

a solution to solid- and hazardous-waste reduction.

- Giving trash incinerators 30-year permits, which locks us into hazardous air pollution emissions and toxic waste from incinerators well into the twenty-first century and undermines waste reduction, recycling, and reuse.

- Setting weak standards for air emissions from incinerators, thus allowing unnecessary emissions of mercury, lead, dioxins, and other toxic pollutants.

- Setting municipal recycling goals at a token 25% (which can easily be waived by the EPA and states) instead of the achievable 60%. This undermines source reduction, recycling, and reuse and encourages us to continue to bury and burn solid and hazardous wastes.

- Doing essentially nothing to reduce emissions of carbon dioxide and other greenhouse gases (Figure 11-2). That means that the United States has failed to assume a global leadership role in dealing with projected climate change at a time when such leadership is urgently needed and

there is little time to waste (Section 11-2).

- Failing to recognize the seriousness of ozone depletion in the stratosphere by not banning all emissions of CFCs and other ozone-depleting chemicals by 1995 and certainly no later than the year 2000 (Section 11-4).

- Continuing to rely almost entirely on temporary pollution cleanup methods instead of on methods that prevent pollution. In other words, the new law is mostly a new Band-Aid that will eventually be overwhelmed by increased pollution and in the long-run will cost consumers and taxpayers much more than pollution prevention and waste reduction.

By 2015, when this act is fully implemented, it will have cost about $25 billion a year. However, on a per person basis, this amounts to only about 24 cents a day — a small price to pay for cleaner air.

just mentioned, the following approaches can lower sulfur dioxide emissions or reduce their effects.

Prevention

1. *Burn low-sulfur coal.* Especially useful for new power and industrial plants located near deposits of such coal.

2. *Remove sulfur from coal.* Fairly inexpensive; present methods remove only 20% to 50%; scientists hope to eventually use natural or genetically engineered bacteria to remove sulfur in coal more efficiently and cheaply than present physical and chemical methods do; bacteria used so far remove only about 40% of the organic sulfur and take four to six weeks to do it.

3. *Convert coal to a gas (Figure 18-15) or liquid fuel.* Low net energy yield (Figure 3-19).

4. *Remove sulfur during combustion by fluidized bed combustion (FBC) of coal (Figure 18-14). Removes up to 90% of the SO_2, reduces CO_2 by 20%, and increases energy efficiency by 5%; should be commercially available for small to medium plants in the mid-1990s.*

5. *Remove sulfur during combustion by limestone injection multiple burning (LIMB). (Figure 21-17). Still in the development and testing stage.*

Dispersion or Cleanup

1. *Use smokestacks tall enough (see photo on p. 541) to pierce the thermal inversion layer (Figure 21-7). Can decrease pollution near power or industrial plants, but increases pollution levels in downwind areas.*

2. *Remove pollutants after combustion by using flue gas scrubbers (Figure 21-18d). Removes up to 95% of*

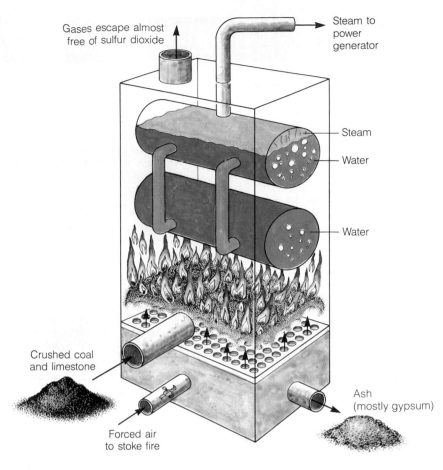

Figure 21-17 Limestone injection multiple burning (LIMB). Crushed limestone is injected into a boiler burning powdered coal at a lower temperature than normal burners. The limestone combines with sulfur dioxide to produce a solid material (gypsum).

Gases escape almost free of sulfur dioxide

Steam to power generator

Steam

Water

Water

Crushed coal and limestone

Forced air to stoke fire

Ash (mostly gypsum)

SO_2 and 99.9% of suspended particulate matter (but not the more harmful fine particles); can be used in new plants and added to most existing large plants, but is expensive. Presently, most of the resulting slurry or sludge is deposited in landfills or holding ponds, but 90% of it could be converted into useful chemicals for use as fertilizers, catalysts, and construction materials.

3. *Add a tax on each unit emitted.* Encourages development of more efficient and cost-effective methods of emissions control; opposed by industry because it costs more than tall smokestacks and requires polluters to bear more of the harmful costs now passed on to society.

By 1985, the Soviet Union and 21 European countries had signed a treaty agreeing to reduce their annual emissions of sulfur dioxide from 1980 levels by at least 30% by 1993; 4 countries agreed to 70% cuts. While that is an important step, ecologists believe that SO_2 emissions must be cut by about 90% to prevent continuing serious ecological damage. Between 1983 and 1989, the former West Germany cut power plant emissions of sulfur dioxide by 90%, and Switzerland and Austria reduced their emissions by more than 90%.

The United States and Great Britain refused to participate in this historic but moderate agreement, citing the need for more research on the harmful effects of sulfur dioxide. U.S. air pollution control laws encourage emissions of SO_2 and suspended particulate matter by allowing tall smokestacks and by not requiring coal-burning power and industrial plants built before 1972 to install effective pollution control devices. This has given corporations an incentive to keep old, polluting plants in operation rather than build new, advanced plants. The Clean Air Act of 1990, however, requires these older plants to meet stricter emissions standards for sulfur dioxide (and nitrogen oxides) by the year 2000.

CONTROL OF EMISSIONS OF NITROGEN OXIDES FROM STATIONARY SOURCES About half the mass of emissions of nitrogen oxides in the United States comes from the burning of fossil fuels at stationary sources, primarily electric power and industrial plants. The rest comes mostly from motor vehicles.

So far, little emphasis has been placed on reducing emissions of nitrogen oxides from stationary sources because control of sulfur dioxide and particulates was considered more important. Now it is clear that nitrogen oxides are a major contributor to acid deposition and that they increase tropospheric levels of ozone and other photochemical oxidants that can damage crops, trees, and materials. The following approaches can be used to decrease emissions of nitrogen oxides from stationary sources:

Prevention

1. *Remove nitrogen oxides during fluidized bed combustion* (Figure 18-14). Removes 50% to 75%.

2. *Remove during combustion by limestone injection multiple burning (LIMB)* (Figure 21-17). Removes 50% to 60%, but is still being developed.

3. *Reduce by decreasing combustion temperatures.* Well-established technology that reduces production of these gases by 50% to 60%.

Dispersion or Cleanup

1. *Use tall smokestacks.*

2. *Add a tax for each unit emitted.*

3. *Remove after combustion by reburning.* Removes 50% or more, but is still under development for large plants.

4. *Remove after burning by reacting with isocyanic acid (HCNO).* Removes up to 99% and breaks down into harmless nitrogen and water; will not be available commercially for at least ten years.

5. *Remove after combustion in flue gas scrubbers* (Figure 21-18d) by adding phosphorus, which reacts with oxygen in flue gas to form ozone. This in turn reacts with NO to form water-soluble nitrogen dioxide, which can be removed in the same way as SO_2. Currently, the effectiveness of this new technology is being evaluated.

In 1988, representatives from 24 countries, including the United States, signed an agreement that would freeze emissions of nitrogen oxides at 1987 levels by 1995. Twelve western European countries agreed to cut emissions of nitrogen oxides by 30% between 1987 and 1997. Environmentalists applaud these efforts but believe that a 90% reduction in these emissions is needed to prevent continuing serious ecological damage.

CONTROL OF PARTICULATE MATTER EMISSIONS FROM STATIONARY SOURCES The only way to prevent emissions of suspended particulate matter is to convert coal into a gas (Figure 18-15) or a liquid, a method that is expensive and low in net energy yield (Figure 3-19). The following cleanup approaches can be used to decrease emissions of suspended particulate matter from stationary sources:

Dispersion or Cleanup

1. *Use tall smokestacks.*

2. *Add a tax on each unit emitted.*

3. *Remove particulates from stack exhaust gases.* The most widely used method in electric power and industrial plants. Several methods are in use: **(a)** electrostatic precipitators (Figure 21-18a); **(b)** baghouse filters (Figure 21-18b); **(c)** cyclone

separators (Figure 21-18c); and **(d)** wet scrubbers (Figure 21-18d). Except for baghouse filters, none of these methods removes many of the more hazardous fine particles (Figure 21-2); all produce hazardous solid waste or sludge that must be disposed of safely; and except for cyclone separators, all are expensive.

CONTROL OF EMISSIONS FROM MOTOR VEHICLES The following are methods for decreasing emissions from motor vehicles:

Prevention

1. *Rely more on mass transit, bicycles, and walking* (Section 9-3).

2. *Shift to less-polluting automobile engines.* Examples are the stratified charge engine, engines that run on hydrogen gas (Section 17-8), or electric motors (if the additional electricity needed to charge batteries is not produced by fossil-fuel burning power plants or by expensive and potentially dangerous nuclear power plants). The government could overcome the auto industry's resistance to producing such engines by specifying smog-free engines on the $5 billion worth of vehicles it buys each year.

3. *Shift to less-polluting fuels.* Examples are natural gas (Section 18-1), alcohols (Section 17-6), and hydrogen gas (Section 17-8).

4. *Improve fuel efficiency.* The quickest and most cost-effective approach (Section 17-2), which unfortunately is not being used (Section 18-5).

5. *Modify the internal combustion engine to reduce emissions.* Burning gasoline using a lean, or more air-rich, mixture reduces carbon monoxide and hydrocarbon emissions but increases emissions of nitrogen oxides; a new lean-burn engine that reduces emissions of nitrogen oxides by 75% to 90% may be available in about ten years.

6. *Raise annual registration fees on older, more-polluting, gas-guzzling (petro-pig) cars, or offer owners an incentive to retire such cars.*

7. *Add a charge on all new cars based on the amount of the key pollutants emitted by the engine according to EPA tests.* This would prod manufacturers to reduce emissions and encourage consumers to buy less-polluting cars.

8. *Give subsidies to carmakers for each low-polluting, energy-efficient car they sell.* This would allow consumers to pay less for this type of vehicle and much more for polluting gas guzzlers.

9. *Give buyers federally subsidized rebates when they buy low-polluting, energy-efficient cars and charge them fees when they buy more-polluting, energy-inefficient cars.* Revenues from the fees would be used to provide the rebates.

10. *Restrict driving in downtown areas.*

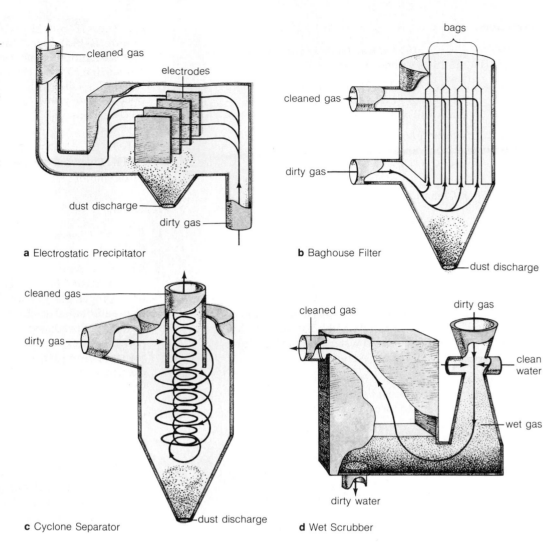

Figure 21-18 Four commonly used methods for removing particulates from the exhaust gases of electric power and industrial plants. The wet scrubber is also used to reduce sulfur dioxide emissions.

a Electrostatic Precipitator

b Baghouse Filter

c Cyclone Separator

d Wet Scrubber

Cleanup

1. *Use emission control devices.* Most widely used approach. A new car with an emission control device emits 95% less pollutants than a car without such a device. Engines must be kept well tuned for such devices to work effectively; current catalytic converters increase carbon dioxide emissions, which can enhance global warming; three-way catalytic converters now being developed can decrease pollutants further and should be available within a few years.

2. *Require car inspections twice a year and have drivers exceeding the standards pay an emission charge based on the grams of pollutants emitted per kilometer and the number of kilometers driven since the last inspection.* This would encourage drivers not to tamper with emission control devices and to keep them in good working order. Currently, the emission control systems on about 60% of the U.S. car fleet have been disconnected or are not working properly.

3. *Establish emission standards for light-duty trucks* (presently not effectively regulated by U.S. air pollution control laws).

CONTROL OF TROPOSPHERE OZONE LEVELS

Ozone levels in the troposphere are mostly the result of photochemical smog, which forms when nitrogen oxides and hydrocarbons interact with sunlight (Figure 21-6). Thus, decreasing ozone levels involves combining the prevention and cleanup methods already discussed for nitrogen oxides and for motor vehicles.

It also involves decreasing hydrocarbon emissions from cars, which produce half of the pollutants that cause smog, and from a variety of hard-to-control sources, such as oil-based paints, aerosol propellants, dry-cleaning plants, and gas stations, that emit the other half.

In 1989, California's South Coast Air Quality Management District Council proposed a drastic program to reduce ozone and photochemical smog in the Los Angeles area. If approved by the state environmental agency and the EPA, this plan would require

- outlawing drive-through facilities to keep vehicles from idling in lines

- substantially raising parking fees and assessing high fees for families owning more than one car to discourage automobile use and encourage car and van pooling and use of mass transit

- strictly controlling or relocating petroleum refining, dry-cleaning, auto-painting, printing, baking, and trash-burning plants and other industries that release large quantities of hydrocarbons and other pollutants

- finding substitutes for or banning use of aerosol propellants, paints, household cleaners, barbecue starter fluids, and other consumer products that release hydrocarbons

- gradually eliminating gasoline-burning engines over two decades by converting trucks, buses, and lawnmowers to run on electricity or on alternative fuels such as methanol, ethanol, or natural gas (Section 17-6)

- requiring gas stations to use a hydrocarbon vapor recovery system on gas pumps and sell alternative fuels

- banning 70% of any fleet's trucks from streets during weekday morning and evening rush hours

The plan may be defeated by public opinion when residents begin to feel the economic pinch from such drastic changes. However, proponents argue that the economic costs in health and other external costs of not carrying out such a program will cost consumers and businesses much more.

Such measures are a glimpse of what most cities will have to do as people, cars, and industries proliferate. Without such changes, scientists estimate that ground level ozone pollution in U.S. urban areas could increase as much as 50% between 1990 and 2020.

CONTROL OF INDOOR AIR POLLUTION For most people, indoor air pollution poses a much greater threat to their health than outdoor air pollution. Yet, the EPA spends $200 million a year trying to reduce outdoor air pollution and only $2 million a year on indoor air pollution.

To sharply reduce indoor air pollution, it is not necessary to establish mandatory indoor air quality standards and then monitor the more than 100 million homes and buildings in the United States. Instead, reduction can be done by

- modifying building codes to prevent radon infiltration or requiring use of air-to-air heat exchangers or other devices to change indoor air at certain intervals

- removing some of the hazardous materials in furniture and building materials in new and older homes, apartments, and workplaces by moving people out, baking these structures out at 38°C (100°F) for three to four days, and then using a fan to exhaust and replace the contaminated air several times

- requiring exhaust hoods or vent pipes for stoves, refrigerators, dryers, kerosene heaters, or other appliances burning natural gas or other fossil fuels

- setting emission standards for building materials that emit formaldehyde, such as particleboard, plywood, some types of insulation, and materials used in furniture, carpets, and carpet backing

- finding substitutes for potentially harmful chemicals in aerosols, cleaning compounds, paints, and other products used indoors (see Individuals Matter inside the back cover) and requiring all such products to have labels listing their ingredients

- requiring employers to provide safe indoor air for employees

In LDCs, significant reductions in respiratory illnesses would occur if governments gave rural residents and poor people in cities simple stoves that burn biofuels more efficiently (which would also reduce deforestation) and that are vented outside.

PROTECTING THE ATMOSPHERE Considerable progress has been made in reducing the levels of several outdoor air pollutants in the United States and many other MDCs, but much more needs to be done. And few LDCs have begun to tackle their air pollution problems, which are increasing as these countries become more urbanized and more industrialized.

As long as MDCs and LDCs rely mostly on end-of-pipe output methods for controlling air pollution, the air we breathe will eventually be overwhelmed by potentially harmful chemicals emitted into the atmosphere by the consumption of more energy and other resources by increasing numbers of people. Protecting this commonly shared resource will require the following significant changes:

- emphasizing pollution prevention rather than pollution control in both MDCs and LDCs

- recognizing that the burning of fossil fuels is the primary cause of air pollution, reducing use of these fuels (especially coal), and reducing unnecessary waste of these fuels (Section 17-2)

- integrating air pollution and energy policies with primary emphasis on improving energy efficiency, shifting from fossil fuels to perpetual and renewable energy resources (Chapter 17 and Section 18-5), discouraging automobile use, boosting the use of public transportation, revamping transportation systems and urban design, increasing recycling and reuse, and reducing the production of all forms of waste

- developing air quality strategies based on the air flows and pollution sources for an entire region instead of the current piecemeal, city-by-city approach

- controlling population growth (Section 8-3)

The most important thing you can do to reduce air pollution and ozone depletion, slow projected global climate change, and save money is to improve energy efficiency (see Individuals Matter inside the back cover and Section 17-2).

Recycle newspapers, aluminum, and other materials (see Individuals Matter on p. 538). Decrease your emissions of ozone-depleting chlorofluorocarbons (see Individuals Matter on p. 303) and greenhouse gases (see Individuals Matter on p. 297). Lobby for much stricter national clean air laws and enforcement and for development of international treaties to slow projected global warming (Section 11-2) and reduce depletion of ozone in the stratosphere (Section 11-4).

Protect yourself from most indoor air pollutants by

- Testing for radon and taking corrective measures as needed (see Case Study on p. 580).

- Installing air-to-air heat exchangers or regularly ventilating your house by opening windows.

- Avoiding the purchase of formaldehyde products or using "low-emitting formaldehyde" or non-formaldehyde building materials. If plywood is used for inside construction, use exterior-grade plywood, which has a formaldehyde resin that outgases less formaldehyde than that in most interior-grade plywood. Seal all plywood, particleboard, and medium-density fiberboard with one coat of Valspar formaldehyde sealer or, as a second choice, two coats of nitrocellulose-based varnish.

- Testing indoor air for formaldehyde at the beginning of the winter heating season when the house is closed up. Cost is about $200 to $300. To locate a testing

laboratory in your area, call or write Consumer Product Safety Commission, Washington, DC 20207, (301) 492-6800.

- Not using synthetic wall-to-wall carpeting, which emits a variety of potential harmfully organic compounds, including formaldehyde. Use natural fiber rugs (colored with nontoxic dyes) that can be cleaned by being taken outside and beaten, or use natural wood floors. Seal natural wood floors with penetrating oils followed by waxing instead of using polyurethane and other finishes that contain toxic ingredients.

- Reducing indoor levels of formaldehyde and several other toxic gases by using houseplants such as the spider or airplane plant (the most effective), golden pothos, syngonium, philodendron (especially the elephant-ear species), chrysanthemum, and Gerbera daisy. About 20 plants can help clean the air in a typical home. Plants should be potted with a mixture of soil and granular charcoal (which absorbs organic air pollutants).

- Baking unoccupied houses (especially mobile homes) out at 38°C (100°F) for three to four days and then changing the air several times.

- Testing your house or workplace for asbestos fiber levels if it was built before 1980. To get a free list of certified asbestos laboratories that charge $25 to $50 to test a sample, send a self-addressed mailing label to NIST/NVLAP, Building 411, Room A124, Gaithersburg, MD 20899, or call the EPA's Toxic Substances Control Hotline at (202) 554-1404. If asbestos levels are too high, hire an independent consultant — not an asbestos-removal firm — to ad-

vise you on what to do. (The typical charge is $500 or more, but this could save you asbestos-removal costs of $10,000 to $100,000.) Don't buy a pre-1980 house without having its indoor air tested for asbestos.

- Changing air filters regularly, cleaning air-conditioning systems, emptying humidifier water trays frequently, and not storing gasoline, solvents, or other volatile hazardous chemicals inside a home or attached garage.

- Not using commercial room deodorizers or air fresheners (see Individuals Matter inside the back cover for safe alternatives).

- Not using any aerosol spray products.

- Not smoking or smoking outside or in a closed room vented to the outside.

- Having everyone take off his or her shoes when entering a house. This greatly reduces indoor levels of toxic lead dust (see Case Study on p. 559) and pesticides picked up by shoe bottoms and transferred to floors and especially to indoor carpets.

- Attaching whole-house electrostatic air cleaners and charcoal filters to central heating and air conditioning equipment. Humidifiers, however, can load indoor air with bacteria, mildew, and viruses.

- Making sure that wood-burning stoves and fireplaces are properly installed, vented, and maintained. If you use a wood stove for heating, buy one of the newer, more energy-efficient models that greatly reduce indoor and outdoor pollution.

Making these changes will require major modifications in our economic systems. As long as most of the social costs of air pollution and other forms of pollution are not included in the market prices of goods and services, industries, utilities, and individuals will have little incentive to reduce the amount of pollution they generate.

Making this fundamental shift in our economic priorities will require political involvement by individuals to overcome the built-in resistance to such changes. Bringing about the needed political and economic changes from the bottom up and changing our polluting and Earth-degrading lifestyles will require that we shift from our current unsustainable, throwaway worldview to a sustainable-Earth worldview (Sections 1-5 and 26-2). It is not too late, if we act now.

Turning the corner on air pollution requires moving beyond patchwork, end-of-pipe approaches to confront pollution at its sources. This will mean reorienting energy, transportation, and industrial structures toward prevention.

HILARY F. FRENCH

DISCUSSION TOPICS

1. Evaluate the pros and cons of this statement: "Since we have not proven absolutely that anyone has died or suffered serious disease from nitrogen oxides, present federal emission standards for this pollutant should be relaxed."

2. Why is air pollution from fine particulate matter a serious problem? What should be done about it?

3. What topographical and climate factors either increase or help decrease air pollution in your community?

4. Should all tall smokestacks be banned? Explain.

5. Should standards be set and enforced for key indoor air pollutants? Explain.

*6. Do buildings in your school contain asbestos? If so, what is being done about this potential health hazard?

*7. Have dormitories and other buildings on your campus been tested for radon? If so, what were the results and what has been done about areas with unacceptable levels? If this testing has not been done, talk with school officials about having it done.

CHAPTER 22

WATER POLLUTION

General Questions and Issues

1. What are the principal types, sources, and effects of water pollutants?

2. What are the biggest pollution problems of streams and lakes?

3. What are the biggest pollution problems of the world's oceans?

4. What are the biggest pollution problems of groundwater aquifers, and how can those problems be reduced?

5. What legal and technological methods can be used to reduce surface water pollution?

6. What can you do to reduce your contribution to water pollution?

Brush your teeth with the best toothpaste. Then rinse your mouth with industrial waste.

TOM LEHRER

RESH WATER IS A RENEWABLE resource (Figure 4-34). However, it can become so contaminated by human activities that it is no longer useful for many purposes and can be harmful to living organisms using the water.

Water pollution is a local, regional, and global environmental problem and is connected with air pollution and how we use the land. As long as we emphasize pollution control instead of an integrated approach to pollution prevention, we will continue to shift potential pollutants from one part of the ecosphere to another.

22-1 Principal Forms of Water Pollution

PRINCIPAL TYPES AND EFFECTS OF WATER POLLUTANTS The following are eight common types of water pollutants:

- *Disease-causing agents* — bacteria, viruses, protozoa, and parasitic worms that enter water from domestic sewage and animal wastes (Table 22-1). In LDCs, they are the biggest cause of sickness and death, prematurely killing an average of 25,000 people each day — half of them children under five. A good indicator of the quality of water for drinking or swimming is the number of colonies of *coliform bacteria* present in a 100-milliliter sample of water. The World Health Organization recommends a coliform bacteria count of 0 colonies per 100 milliliters for drinking water, and the EPA-recommended maximum level for swimming water is 200 colonies per 100 milliliters.

- *Oxygen-demanding wastes* — organic wastes, which can be decomposed by aerobic bacteria, which use oxygen to biodegrade organic wastes. Large populations of bacteria supported by these wastes can deplete water of dissolved oxygen gas (Figure 22-1). Without enough oxygen, fish and other forms of oxygen-consuming aquatic life die. The quantity of oxygen-demanding wastes in water can be determined by measuring the **dissolved oxygen (DO) content** (Figure 22-1) or the **biological oxygen demand (BOD):** the amount of dissolved oxygen needed by aerobic decomposers to break down the organic materials in a certain volume of water over a five-day incubation period at 20°C (68°F).

- *Water-soluble inorganic chemicals* — acids, salts, and compounds of toxic metals such as mercury and lead (see Case Study on p. 559). High levels of such dissolved solids can make water unfit to drink, harm fish and other aquatic life, depress crop yields, and accelerate corrosion of equipment that uses water.

- *Inorganic plant nutrients* — water-soluble nitrate and phosphate compounds that can cause excessive

Table 22-1 Common Diseases Transmitted to Humans Through Contaminated Drinking Water

Type of Organism	Disease	Effects
Bacteria	Typhoid fever	Diarrhea, severe vomiting, enlarged spleen, inflamed intestine; often fatal if untreated
	Cholera	Diarrhea, severe vomiting, dehydration; often fatal if untreated
	Bacterial dysentery	Diarrhea; rarely fatal except in infants without proper treatment
	Enteritis	Severe stomach pain, nausea, vomiting; rarely fatal
Viruses	Infectious hepatitis	Fever, severe headache, loss of appetite, abdominal pain, jaundice, enlarged liver; rarely fatal but may cause permanent liver damage
	Polio	High fever, severe headache, sore throat, stiff neck, deep muscle pain, severe weakness, tremors, paralysis in legs, arms, and body; can be fatal
Parasitic protozoa	Amoebic dysentery	Severe diarrhea, headache, abdominal pain, chills, fever; if not treated can cause liver abscess, bowel perforation, and death
	Giardia	Diarrhea, abdominal cramps, flatulence, belching, fatigue
Parasitic worms	Schistosomiasis	Abdominal pain, skin rash, anemia, chronic fatigue, and chronic general ill health

growth of algae and other aquatic plants, which then die and decay, depleting water of dissolved oxygen and killing fish. Excessive levels of nitrates in drinking water can reduce the oxygen-carrying capacity of the blood and kill unborn children and infants, especially those under three months old.

- *Organic chemicals* — oil, gasoline, plastics, pesticides, cleaning solvents, detergents, and many other water-soluble and insoluble chemicals that threaten human health and harm fish and other aquatic life. Some of the more than 700 synthetic organic chemicals found in trace amounts in surface and underground drinking-water supplies in the United States can cause kidney disorders, birth defects, and various types of cancer in laboratory test animals (Section 20-1).

- *Sediment or suspended matter* — insoluble particles of soil and other solid inorganic and organic materials that become suspended in water and that in terms of total mass are the largest source of water pollution (Figure 10-8). Suspended particulate matter clouds the water, reduces the ability of some organisms to find food, reduces photosynthesis by aquatic plants, disrupts aquatic food webs, and carries pesticides, bacteria, and other harmful substances. Bottom sediment destroys feeding and spawning grounds of fish and clogs and fills lakes, artificial reservoirs, stream channels, and harbors.

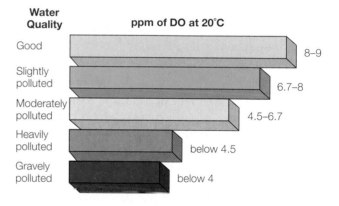

Figure 22-1 Water quality and dissolved oxygen (DO) content in parts per million (ppm). Dissolved oxygen enters water by diffusion from the atmosphere. Only a few species of fish can survive in water with fewer than 4 ppm of dissolved oxygen. The solubility of oxygen (and other dissolved gases, such as carbon dioxide) decreases as the temperature of water increases. For example, at 15°C (59°F), water can dissolve no more than 10.1 ppm of oxygen. At 30°C (86°F), it can hold no more than 7.5 ppm of dissolved oxygen.

- *Radioactive substances* — radioisotopes that are water soluble or capable of being biologically amplified to higher concentrations as they pass through food chains and webs. Ionizing radiation from such isotopes can cause birth defects, cancer, and genetic damage (see Spotlight on p. 543).

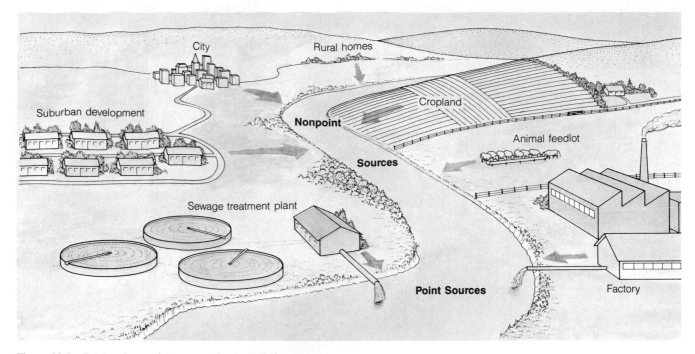

Figure 22-2 Point and nonpoint sources of water pollution.

■ *Heat* — excessive inputs of water that is heated when it is used mostly to cool electric power plants. The resulting increases in water temperatures lower dissolved oxygen content and make aquatic organisms more vulnerable to disease, parasites, and toxic chemicals.

POINT AND NONPOINT SOURCES The largest sources of water pollution are domestic wastewater, industrial effluents, land-use runoff, atmospheric deposition (Figure 21-9), and leaching from mine operations (Figure 18-13) and landfills (Figure 19-10). Damage from all types of water pollution in the United States is estimated to be $20 billion annually.

Point sources discharge pollutants at specific locations through pipes, ditches, or sewers into bodies of surface water (Figure 22-2). Examples include factories, sewage treatment plants (which remove some but not all pollutants), active and abandoned underground coal mines (Figure 18-13), gold mines (Figure 10-12), offshore oil wells (Figure 7-17), and oil tankers.

Although only about 9% of the mass of surface water pollution in the United States comes from point sources by industry, much of this pollution consists of synthetic organic chemicals and heavy metals that are toxic even in small quantities. In 1988, U.S. industries discharged 425 million kilograms (935 million pounds) of toxic chemicals directly into surface waters or municipal sewers (Figure 20-3). Industries emitted an additional 2.4 billion kilograms (5.3 billion pounds) of toxic

chemicals into the air (where some can fall back to Earth and cause water pollution), stored such chemicals in surface impoundments, or injected them into deep wells, with the possibility that some of these substances can contaminate groundwater.

Because point sources are at specific places (mostly in urban areas), they are fairly easy to identify, monitor, and regulate. In MDCs, many industrial discharges are strictly controlled, while in LDCs, such discharges are largely uncontrolled.

Nonpoint sources are big land areas that discharge pollutants into surface and underground water over a large area and parts of the atmosphere where pollutants are deposited on surface waters (Figure 22-2). Examples include runoff of chemicals into surface water and seepage into the ground from croplands, livestock feedlots (Figure 14-3), logged forests, urban and suburban lands, septic tanks, construction areas, parking lots, roadways, and acid deposition (Figure 21-9).

In the United States, nonpoint pollution from agriculture — mostly in the form of sediment, commercial inorganic fertilizer, manure, salts dissolved in irrigation water, and pesticides — is responsible for an estimated 64% of the total mass of pollutants entering streams and 57% of those entering lakes. Livestock in the United States produce five times as much organic waste as humans and twice as much as industry. Little progress has been made in the control of nonpoint water pollution because of the difficulty and expense of identifying and controlling discharges from so many diffuse sources.

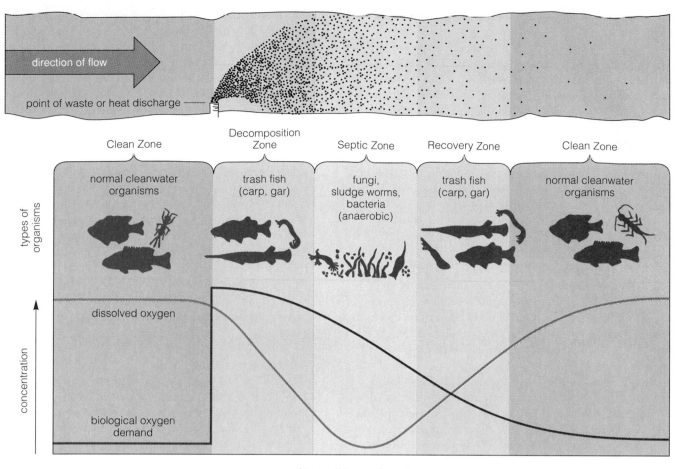

Figure 22-3 The oxygen sag curve (orange) versus oxygen demand (blue). Depending on flow rates and the amount of pollutants, streams recover from oxygen-demanding wastes and heat if given enough time and if they are not overloaded.

22-2 Pollution of Streams and Lakes

STREAMS AND OXYGEN-CONSUMING WASTES

Because they flow, most streams recover rapidly from some forms of pollution, especially excess heat and degradable oxygen-demanding wastes (Figure 22-3). This works only as long as they are not overloaded with degradable pollutants or heat and their flow is not reduced by drought, damming, or diversion for agriculture and industries. Slowly degradable and nondegradable pollutants are not eliminated by these natural dilution and degradation processes.

The depth and width of the *oxygen sag curve*, and thus the time and distance a stream takes to recover, depend on the stream's volume, flow rate, temperature, and pH and on the volume of incoming degradable wastes. Similar oxygen sag curves occur when heated water from power plants is discharged into streams.

Along many streams, water for drinking is removed *upstream* from a city, and the city's industrial and sewage wastes are discharged *downstream*. The stream can then become overloaded with pollutants as this pattern is repeated hundreds of times along the stream as it flows toward the sea.

Requiring each city to withdraw its drinking water downstream rather than upstream would dramatically improve the quality of stream water. Each city would be forced to clean up its own waste outputs rather than passing them on to downstream areas. However, this pollution prevention approach is fought by upstream users, who have the use of fairly clean water without high cleanup costs.

STREAM WATER QUALITY IN THE UNITED STATES
Water pollution control laws enacted in the 1970s have greatly increased the number and quality of wastewater treatment plants in the United States and in many other MDCs. Laws have also required industries

to reduce or eliminate point source discharges into surface waters.

Since 1972, these efforts have enabled the United States to hold the line against increased pollution of most of its streams by disease-causing agents and oxygen-demanding wastes. That is an impressive accomplishment, considering the rise in economic activity and population since 1972.

One success story is the cleanup of Ohio's Cuyahoga River, which was so polluted that in 1969 it caught fire as it flowed through the city of Cleveland. That prompted city and state officials to pass laws limiting the discharge of wastes by industries into the river and sewage systems and to upgrade sewage treatment facilities. Today, the river has made a comeback and is widely used by boaters and anglers.

However, there is still much to be done in improving the water quality of many U.S. streams. A 1988 survey by the Environmental Protection Agency showed that more than 17,000, or 10%, of the nation's streams and bays are significantly polluted, mostly by nitrates, phosphates, pesticides, and other toxic chemicals.

Further improvements in the quality of U.S. streams will require stricter monitoring and enforcement of existing standards for discharges from point sources and extensive efforts to reduce inputs from nonpoint sources. This, however, can lead to social and economic conflicts.

STREAM WATER QUALITY IN OTHER COUNTRIES
Pollution control laws have also led to improvements in dissolved oxygen content in many streams in Canada, Japan, and most western European countries since 1970. Numerous streams in the Soviet Union and in eastern Europe, however, have become more polluted with industrial wastes as industries have expanded without adequate pollution controls.

A spectacular cleanup has occurred in Great Britain. In the 1950s, the river Thames was little more than a flowing anaerobic sewer, but after more than 30 years of effort, $250 million of British taxpayers' money, and millions more spent by industry, the Thames has made a remarkable recovery. Commercial fishing is thriving, and many species of waterfowl and wading birds have returned to their former feeding grounds.

Despite progress in improving stream quality in most MDCs, large fish kills and contamination of drinking water still occur. Most of these disasters are caused by accidental or deliberate releases of toxic inorganic and organic chemicals by industries, malfunctioning sewage treatment plants, and nonpoint runoff of pesticides from cropland.

For example, in 1986, a fire at a Sandoz chemical warehouse in Switzerland released large quantities of toxic chemicals into the Rhine River, which flows through Switzerland, France, the former West Germany, and the Netherlands before emptying into the North Sea. The chemicals killed large numbers of aquatic life, forced temporary shutdowns of drinking-water plants and commercial fishing, and set back improvements in the river's water quality that had taken place between 1970 and 1986. The river is now making a slow comeback.

Available data indicate that pollution of streams from large discharges of sewage and industrial wastes is a serious and growing problem in most LDCs, where waste treatment is practically nonexistent. Most of Poland's streams are severely polluted (see Case Study on p. 20). Of India's 3,119 towns and cities, only 218 have any type of sewage treatment facilities. India's Ganges River receives untreated sewage and industrial wastes from millions of people in 114 cities along with pesticide and fertilizer runoff. It has even caught fire twice. Of the 78 streams monitored in China, 54 are seriously polluted. In Latin America and Africa, most streams passing through urban or industrial areas are severely polluted.

POLLUTION PROBLEMS OF LAKES AND ARTIFICIAL RESERVOIRS In lakes, reservoirs, estuaries, and oceans, dilution is often less effective than in streams, because these bodies of water frequently contain stratified layers that undergo little vertical mixing (Figures 5-28 and 5-38). Stratification also reduces the levels of dissolved oxygen, especially in the bottom layer. In addition, lakes and reservoirs have little flow, further reducing dilution and replenishment of dissolved oxygen. The flushing and changing of water in lakes and large artificial reservoirs can take from 1 to 100 years, compared with several days to several weeks for streams.

Thus, lakes are more vulnerable than streams to contamination by plant nutrients, oil, pesticides, and toxic substances that can destroy bottom life and kill fish. Atmospheric fallout and runoff of acids into lakes is a serious problem in lakes vulnerable to acid deposition (Figure 21-9). In the Soviet Union, Lake Baikal — the world's largest and deepest body of fresh water — is threatened with pollution (see Guest Essay on p. 631).

In any body of water, some synthetic organic compounds and toxic metals such as lead and mercury are not biodegraded, and other synthetic organic compounds are biodegraded very slowly. Some chemicals, such as DDT (Figure 16-18), PCBs (Figure 22-4), some radioactive isotopes, and some mercury compounds, can be biologically amplified to higher concentrations as they pass through food webs.

Cultural eutrophication from the stepped-up addition of phosphates and nitrates as a result of human activities is a serious pollution problem for shallow lakes and reservoirs, especially near urban or agricultural centers (Figure 22-5). During warm weather, this nutrient overload produces dense growths of plants such

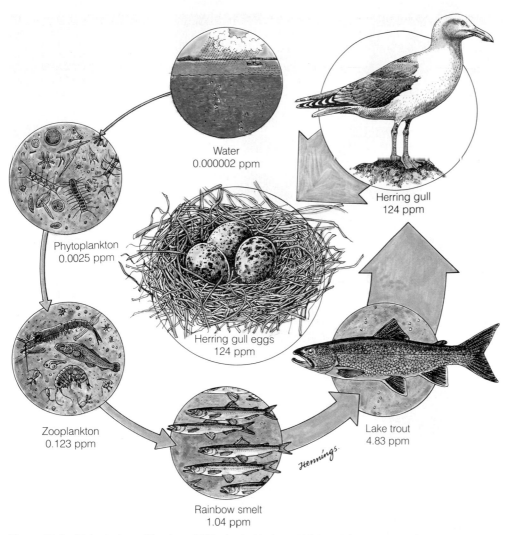

Figure 22-4 Biological amplification of PCBs (polychlorinated biphenyls) in an aquatic food chain in the Great Lakes. Most of these 209 different oily, synthetic chlorinated hydrocarbon compounds are insoluble in water, soluble in fats, and resistant to biological and chemical degradation—properties that result in their bioaccumulation in the tissues of organisms and their biological amplification in food chains and webs. The long-term health effects on people exposed to low levels of PCBs and their more toxic furan impurities are unknown. However, in laboratory animals, high doses of PCBs produce liver and kidney damage, gastric disorders, birth defects, bronchitis, miscarriages, skin lesions, hormonal changes, and tumors. Some studies indicate that most of these harmful effects are caused by polychlorinated dibenzofurans (commonly called furans) found as contaminants in some PCBs. In the United States and Canada, PCBs have been banned since 1976. However, before those bans, millions of metric tons of these chemicals were released into the environment, many of them ending up in bottom sediments of lakes, streams, and oceans.

as algae, cyanobacteria, water hyacinths, and duckweed (Figure 22-6). Dissolved oxygen in the surface layer of water near the shore, and in the bottom layer, is depleted when large masses of algae die, fall to the bottom, and are decomposed by aerobic bacteria. This can kill fish and other oxygen-consuming aquatic animals. If excess nutrients continue to flow into a lake, the bottom water becomes foul and almost devoid of animals, as anaerobic bacteria take over and produce smelly decomposition products such as hydrogen sulfide and methane.

About one-third of the 100,000 medium to large lakes and about 85% of the large lakes near major population centers in the United States suffer from some degree of cultural eutrophication (see Case Study on p. 609).

CONTROL OF CULTURAL EUTROPHICATION The solution to cultural eutrophication is the use of prevention methods to reduce the flow of nutrients into lakes and reservoirs and pollution control methods to clean up lakes suffering from excessive eutrophication.

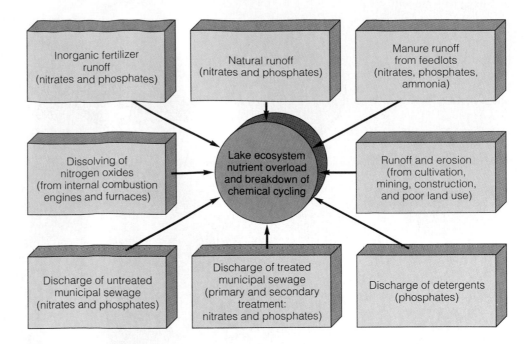

Figure 22-5 Principal sources of nutrient overload, or cultural eutrophication, in lakes, ponds, slow-flowing streams, and estuaries. The amount of nutrients from each source varies, depending on the types of human activities taking place in each airshed and watershed.

W. A. Banaszweski/Visuals Unlimited

Figure 22-6 Cultural eutrophication. Plant nutrients from agriculture and domestic sources have stimulated growth of algae and aquatic plants in this lake in the northeastern United States. Levels of dissolved oxygen (Figure 22-1) are decreased when these excess algae and plants die and are decomposed by aerobic bacteria. This can kill fish and other oxygen-requiring forms of aquatic life and lower the aesthetic and recreational value of the lake.

Prevention Methods

- Use advanced waste treatment (Section 22-5) to remove 90% of phosphates from effluents of sewage treatment and industrial plants before they reach a lake.

- Ban or set low limits on phosphates in household detergents and other cleaning agents to reduce the amount of phosphate reaching sewage treatment plants.

- Control land use (Section 9-4), use sound soil conservation practices (Section 12-3), and clean streets regularly to reduce runoff of fertilizers, manure, and soil from nonpoint sources. Farmers can be required to plant buffer areas of trees or other vegetation between their fields and nearby lakes or other surface waters.

- Protect coastal and inland wetlands that filter and retain nutrients flowing off the land (see Case Study on p. 137 and Spotlight on p. 143).

Cleanup Methods

- Dredge bottom sediments to remove excess nutrient buildup. Impractical in large, deep lakes and not very effective in shallow lakes; often reduces water quality by resuspending toxic pollutants and can increase water salinity; dredged material must go somewhere and is often dumped into the ocean; changes wildlife habitats.

- Remove or harvest excess weeds. Disrupts some forms of aquatic life and is difficult and expensive in large lakes.

- Control nuisance plant growth with herbicides and algicides. Can pollute water and kill off animals and other plants (Section 23-3).

- Pump air through lakes and reservoirs to avoid oxygen depletion. Expensive.

As with other forms of pollution, prevention approaches are the most effective and usually the cheapest in the long run, but prevention methods have to be tailored to each situation based on the limiting factor principle (Section 4-2). For example, because phosphorus is the limiting factor in most freshwater lakes, its

The five interconnected Great Lakes contain at least 95% of the surface fresh water in the United States and 20% of the world's fresh water (Figure 22-7). The Great Lakes basin is home for about 37 million people, making up one-third of Canada's population and one-tenth of the U.S. population. The lakes supply drinking water for 26 million people. About 40% of U.S. industry and half of Canada's industry are located in this watershed. Great Lakes tourism generates $16 billion annually, with $2 billion of that from sport fishing.

Despite their enormous size, these lakes are vulnerable to pollution from point and nonpoint sources because less than 1% of the water entering the Great Lakes flows out to the St. Lawrence River each year. The Great Lakes also receive large quantities of acids, pesticides, and other toxic chemicals by deposition from the atmosphere — often blown in from hundreds or thousands of kilometers away.

By the 1960s, many areas of the Great Lakes were suffering from severe cultural eutrophication, huge fish kills, and contamination from bacteria and other wastes. The impact on Lake Erie was particularly

(continued)

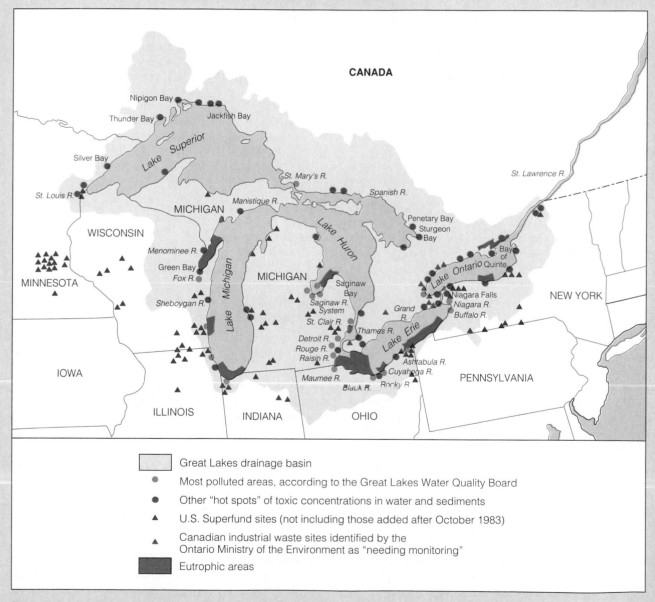

Figure 22-7 The Great Lakes basin. (Data from Environmental Protection Agency)

intense because it is the shallowest of the Great Lakes and has the smallest volume of water. Its drainage basin is heavily industrialized and has the largest human population of any of the lakes. Many bathing beaches had to be closed, and by 1970, the lake had lost nearly all its native fish.

Since 1972, a joint $19 billion pollution control program, carried out by Canada and the United States, has led to significant decreases in levels of phosphates, coliform bacteria, and many toxic industrial chemicals in the Great Lakes. Algal blooms have also decreased, and dissolved oxygen levels and sport and commercial fishing have increased. By 1988, only 8 of 516 swimming beaches around Lake Erie remained closed because of pollution.

These improvements were mainly the result of decreased point source discharges, brought about by new or upgraded sewage treatment plants and improved treatment of industrial wastes. Also, phosphate detergents, household cleaners, and water conditioners were banned or their phosphate levels were lowered in many areas of the Great Lakes drainage basin.

The most serious problem today is contamination from toxic wastes flowing into the lakes (especially Lake Erie and Lake Ontario) from land runoff, streams, and atmospheric deposition (Figure 22-7). For example, there are 164 toxic-waste disposal sites in a 4.8-kilometer (3-mile) strip along the U.S. side of the Niagara River. Sores and liver cancers are common in fish in these areas.

Toxic chemicals such as PCBs have built up in food chains and webs and contaminated many types of fish caught by anglers (Figure 22-4). These and other toxic chemicals have caused birth defects, reproductive problems, and brain, liver, and kidney damage in birds, river otters, and other animals feeding on contaminated fish.

According to U.S. and Canadian researchers, people who live around the Great Lakes generally have 20% higher levels of PCBs and several other toxic chemicals in their bodies than other North Americans. Children under age 16 and pregnant women are advised not to eat any salmon, trout, or other fatty fish from many areas of the Great Lakes. Other people are advised not to eat such fish more than once a week.

In 1978, the United States and Canada signed a new agreement with the goal of virtual elimination of discharges of about 360 toxic chemicals, but implementation of the agreement has been delayed by a sharp drop in federal funds for the cleanup since 1980. Also, recent studies indicate that much of the input of toxic chemicals — more than 50% in Lake Superior — comes from the atmosphere, a source not covered by the agreement.

Environmentalists are calling for a ban on the use of chlorine in the pulp and paper industry around the Great Lakes, for a ban on all new incinerators in the area, and for existing discharge permits to be modified to specify fixed dates for phasing out *all* toxic discharges. Solving these problems will be quite expensive and will take many years, but failure to deal with the problems will cost far more.

---

control should be emphasized. It is also easier to control than nitrogen.

There is disagreement, however, over whether phosphorus inputs should be lowered by banning or limiting phosphates in laundry detergents and other cleaning agents, by removing phosphates from wastewater at sewage treatment plants, or both. Studies of over 400 bodies of water indicate that a reduction of 20% in the total phosphate load must be achieved to produce a detectable effect on water quality.

Currently, eight states — Indiana, Maryland, Michigan, Minnesota, New York, Vermont, Virginia, and Wisconsin — many cities, and many parts of Canada have banned the use of phosphate detergents. Such bans have made a great contribution to reducing cultural eutrophication in the Great Lakes and other areas and have saved consumers and taxpayers money.

In some lakes and in coastal waters and estuaries, emphasis should be on reducing inputs of nitrogen because it is the limiting factor. Fortunately, if excessive inputs of limiting plant nutrients stop, the lake will usually return to its previous state. However, it is much harder to control nitrogen than phosphorus because nitrates are more water soluble and run off from large areas of land.

THERMAL POLLUTION OF STREAMS AND LAKES Almost half of all water withdrawn in the United States each year is for cooling electric power plants. The cheapest and easiest method is to withdraw cool water from a nearby body of surface water, pass it through the plant, and return the heated water to the same body of water (Figure 18-16).

Large inputs of heated water from a single plant or a number of plants using the same lake or slow-moving stream can have harmful effects on aquatic life. This is called **thermal pollution**.

Warmer temperatures lower dissolved oxygen content by decreasing the solubility of oxygen in water. Warmer water also causes aquatic organisms to increase their respiration rates and consume oxygen faster, and it increases their susceptibility to disease, parasites, and toxic chemicals. Discharge of heated water into shallow water near the shore of a lake also may disrupt spawning and kill young fish.

Fish and other organisms adapted to a particular temperature range can also be killed from **thermal shock:** the effect of sharp changes in water temperature when new power plants open up or when plants shut down for repair. Many fish die on intake screens used to prevent fish and debris from clogging the heat exchanger pipes.

While some scientists call the addition of excess heat to aquatic systems thermal pollution, others talk about using heated water for beneficial purposes, calling it **thermal enrichment**. They point out that heated water results in longer commercial fishing seasons and reduction of winter ice cover in cold areas.

Warm water from power plants can also be used for irrigation to extend the growing season in frost-prone areas and cycled through aquaculture pens to speed the growth of commercially valuable fish and shellfish. For example, waste hot water is used to cultivate oysters in aquaculture lagoons in Japan and in New York's Long Island Sound and to cultivate catfish and redfish in Texas.

Heated water could also be used to heat nearby buildings and greenhouses, desalinate ocean water, and run under sidewalks to melt snow. However, because of dangers from air pollution and release of radioactivity, most coal-burning and nuclear electric power plants and heat-producing factories are usually not located near enough to aquaculture operations, buildings, and industries to make thermal enrichment economically feasible.

REDUCTION OF THERMAL WATER POLLUTION

There are a number of ways to minimize the harmful effects of excess heat on aquatic ecosystems:

- Use and waste less electricity (Section 17-2).

- Limit the number of power and industrial plants discharging heated water into the same body of water.

- Return the heated water at a point away from the ecologically vulnerable shore zone.

- Transfer the heat from the water to the atmosphere by means of wet or dry cooling towers (Figure 22-8).

- Discharge the heated water into shallow cooling ponds or canals, allow the water to cool, and withdraw it for reuse as cooling water. This method is useful where enough affordable land is available.

22-3 Ocean Pollution

THE ULTIMATE SINK The oceans are the ultimate sink for much of the waste matter we produce. This is summarized in the African proverb: "Water may flow in a thousand channels, but it all returns to the sea."

Oceans can dilute, disperse, and degrade large amounts of sewage, sludge, oil, and some types of industrial waste, especially in deep-water areas. Marine life has also proved to be more resilient than some scientists had expected, leading these experts to suggest that it is much safer to dump much of the sewage sludge and various toxic and radioactive wastes into the deep ocean than to bury them on land (Figure 19-9) or burn them in incinerators.

Other scientists dispute this idea, pointing out that we know less about the deep ocean than we do about outer space. They add that using the ocean as the last large place to support our throwaway lifestyles will eventually overwhelm its dilution and renewal capacity. To advocate dumping waste in the ocean would delay urgently needed pollution prevention and resource reduction and promote further degradation of this vital part of Earth's life-support system. Marine explorer Jacques Cousteau has warned that "the very survival of the human species depends upon the maintenance of an ocean clean and alive, spreading all around the world. The ocean is our planet's life belt."

OVERWHELMING COASTAL AREAS Coastal areas, especially wetlands and estuaries (see Case Study on p. 613), mangrove swamps (Figure 5-31), and coral reefs (Figure 5-32), bear the brunt of our enormous inputs of wastes into the ocean and coastal development (Figures 5-35 and 5-36). A 1986 study by the United Nations concluded that most of the world's coastal areas are polluted, with the most widespread and serious pollution coming from sewage disposal and sediment from land clearing and erosion (Figures 10-8 and 5-29).

In most coastal LDCs and in some MDCs, municipal sewage and industrial wastes are often discarded into the sea without treatment. The most polluted seas are off the densely populated coasts of Bangladesh (Figure 13-10), India (Figure 8-17), Pakistan, Indonesia (Figure 8-16), Malaysia, Thailand, and the Philippines.

In Latin America, 98% of the volume of the urban sewage is not treated. About 85% of the volume of the sewage from large cities in the Mediterranean basin, which has a coastal population of 200 million people during the tourist season, is discharged into the sea untreated, causing extensive beach pollution and shellfish contamination. In the United States, about 35% of all municipal sewage ends up with little or no treatment in marine waters. Most of America's harbors and bays

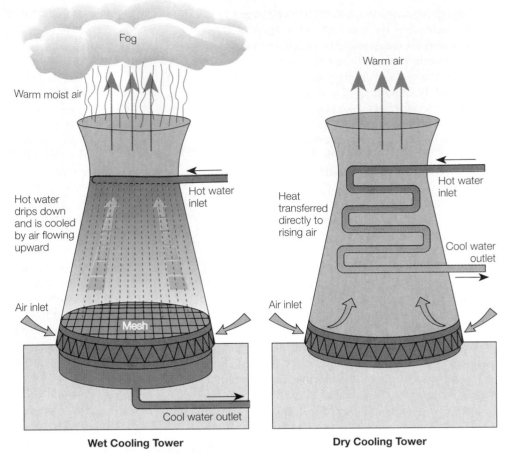

Figure 22-8 Wet and dry cooling towers transfer heat from cooling water to the atmosphere. Most new power plants use wet cooling towers, but they have several drawbacks: larger withdrawals of surface water to replace water lost by evaporation, visual pollution from the gigantic cooling towers, high construction and operating costs, and excessive fog and mist in nearby areas. Dry towers are seldom used because they cost two to four times more to build than wet towers.

are badly polluted from municipal sewage and industrial wastes. Nearly half the oil reaching marine waters comes from urban runoff.

Runoff of sewage and agricultural wastes into coastal waters introduces large quantities of nitrogen and phosphorus, which can cause explosive growth of algae. When the algae die and are decomposed, coastal waters are depleted of oxygen, fish and other species die, and what is called a "dead zone" is created. Currently, a 7,800-square-kilometer (3,000-square-mile) dead zone exists in the Gulf of Mexico, near the mouth of the Mississippi River (Figure 5-29).

TOXIC CHEMICALS AND PLASTICS There is little life in ocean areas where large amounts of toxic sewage sludge is dumped. Lobsters and crabs caught in some areas have mysterious burn holes, and fish caught in some areas have tumors and lesions, mostly from exposure to toxic chemicals. By 1990, about one-third of

the area of U.S. coastal waters around the lower 48 states was closed to shellfish harvesters because of pollution and habitat disruption.

Studies indicate that each year, as many as 2 million seabirds and more than 100,000 marine mammals, including whales, seals (Figure 19-17), dolphins, sea lions, and sea turtles, die when they ingest or become entangled in plastic cups, bags, six-pack yokes, drift nets (Figure 14-22), ropes, and other forms of trash thrown into the ocean from boats or washed into the ocean from rivers and from coastal land areas. The United States is responsible for approximately one-third of all the trash thrown or washed into the world's oceans.

OCEAN DUMPING Dumping of industrial waste off U.S. coasts has stopped, although it is still dumped in coastal waters by a number of other MDCs and LDCs. Pollution from industrial and other wastes is a serious

The Chesapeake Bay (Figure 22-9) on the East Coast is the largest estuary in the United States and one of the world's most productive. It is the largest source of oysters in the United States and the largest producer of blue crabs in the world. The bay is also important for shipping, recreational boating, and sport fishing. Between 1940 and 1990, the number of people living close to the

bay grew from 3.7 million to 13.7 million. The number is projected to reach 15 million by 2000.

The estuary receives wastes from point and nonpoint sources scattered throughout a huge drainage basin that includes 9 large rivers and 141 smaller streams and creeks in parts of six states. The bay has become a huge pollution sink because it is quite shallow — with an average

depth less than 7 meters (22 feet) — and only 1% of the waste entering it is flushed into the Atlantic Ocean.

Levels of phosphate and nitrate plant nutrients have risen sharply in many parts of the bay, causing algal blooms and oxygen depletion. Studies have shown that point sources, primarily sewage treatment plants, contribute about 60% by weight of the phosphates. Nonpoint sources,

(continued)

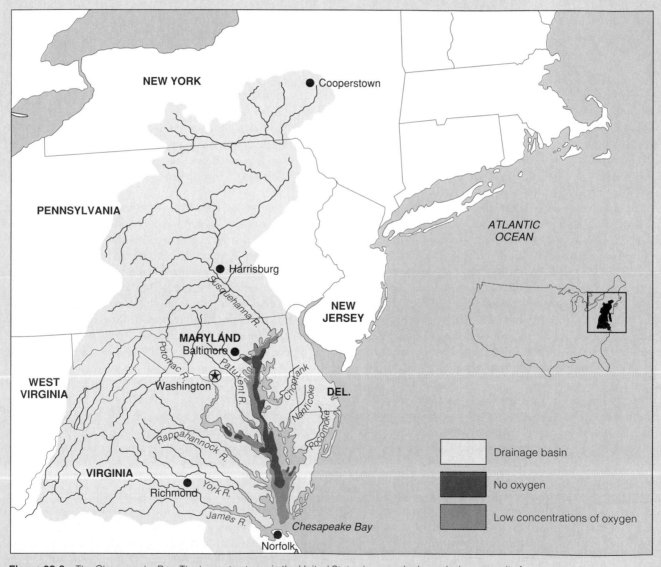

Figure 22-9 The Chesapeake Bay. The largest estuary in the United States is severely degraded as a result of water pollution from point and nonpoint sources in six states and deposition of pollutants from the atmosphere.

mostly runoff from urban and suburban areas and agricultural activities and deposition from the atmosphere, constitute about 60% by weight of the inputs of nitrates.

Additional pollution comes from nonpoint runoff of large quantities of pesticides from cropland and urban lawns. Point source discharge of numerous toxic wastes by industries, often in violation of their discharge permits, is also a problem.

Commercial harvests of oysters, crabs, and several commercially important fish have fallen sharply since 1960 because of a combination of overfishing and pollution. Populations of bluefish, menhaden, and other species that spawn in salt water and feed around algal blooms have increased.

Since 1983, over $700 million in federal and state funds have been spent on a Chesapeake Bay cleanup program that will ultimately cost several billion dollars. Between 1980 and 1987, discharges of phosphates from point sources dropped by about 20%, but there is a long way to go to reverse severe eutrophication and oxygen depletion in many areas (Figure 22-9).

Bans on phosphate-containing detergents and cleaning agents will probably have to be enacted throughout the six-state drainage basin. Forests and wetlands around the bay must also be protected from development. Halting the deterioration of this vital estuary will require the prolonged, cooperative efforts of citizens, officials, and industries.

---

problem in the North Sea, the Black Sea, the Persian Gulf, the Mediterranean Sea, the Adriatic Sea, and the Arabian Sea.

Every year, barges and ships legally dump more than 172 million metric tons (189 million tons) of solid waste off the Atlantic, Pacific, and Gulf coasts at 109 sites. About 80% of these wastes are **dredge spoils**, materials scraped from the bottoms of harbors and rivers to maintain shipping channels.

Most of the remaining 20% of the wastes barged out and dumped into the ocean is **sewage sludge**, a gooey mixture of toxic chemicals, infectious agents, and settled solids removed from wastewater at sewage treatment plants. Only the United States and Great Britain currently dump large quantities of sewage sludge at sea. Some politicians and environmentalists believe there should be a ban on using the ocean as a dumping ground for sludge, but others believe that ocean disposal is safer than other alternatives (see Pro/Con on p. 615).

Ships also dump large amounts of garbage at sea. Countries could ban such dumping in waters under their control, and an international treaty could ban garbage dumping in international waters, but such bans would be hard to enforce. Garbage that can be dumped at sea free of charge can cost 25 cents to 50 cents a pound to dispose of at a port—costing a typical ship $500 to $1,000 each time it docks. Most shipowners would continue dumping at sea and risk getting caught and paying small fines to avoid such costs.

Since 1985, ocean dumping of radioactive waste in the open sea beyond the limits of national jurisdiction has been banned by an international agreement. Although the United States has not dumped radioactive material into the sea since 1970, it did not sign this agreement because Energy and Defense Department officials wanted to retain the option of dumping such wastes at sea. For more than 40 years, the British government has allowed the nuclear industry to discharge radioactive water into coastal areas under government jurisdiction with little monitoring of radioactive levels in these seas.

OIL POLLUTION Crude petroleum (oil as it comes out of the ground) and refined petroleum (fuel oil, gasoline, and other products obtained by distillation and chemical processing of crude petroleum; Figure 18-1) are accidentally or deliberately released into the environment from a number of sources. Tanker accidents and blowouts (oil escaping under high pressure from a borehole in the ocean floor) at offshore drilling rigs (Figure 7-17) receive most of the publicity. However, almost half (some experts estimate 90%) of the oil reaching the oceans comes from the land when waste oil dumped onto the land by cities, individuals, and industries ends up in streams that flow into the ocean.

In 1979, the largest blowout occurred at the *Ixtoc I* oil well in the southern Gulf of Mexico. During the eight months it took to cap the borehole, over 694 million liters (184 million gallons) of oil leaked into the gulf. However, releases of oil from offshore wells during normal operations and during transport of oil in tankers add a much larger volume of oil to the oceans than occasional blowouts. The bulk of this oil results from washing tankers out with seawater and releasing oily ballast water into the ocean. Natural oil seeps also release large amounts of oil into the ocean at some sites.

Tanker accidents account for only 10% to 15% of the annual input of oil into the world's oceans, but concentrated spills can have severe ecological and economic

During the summer of 1988, hypodermic needles, IV tubing, blood sample vials, and other medical wastes washed ashore on beaches from Maine to North Carolina. Beaches in several states, especially New York and New Jersey, had to be closed.

In an election year, the resulting public outcry prompted Congress to pass the Ocean Dumping Ban Act of 1988, banning all dumping of sludge in the ocean by 1992. In 1988, New Jersey ordered an end to all ocean dumping of sludge by 1991, with the goal of protecting its $7-billion coastal tourism industry and its $100-million-a-year fishing industry.

Some elected officials and scientists oppose this ban. They argue that ocean disposal is safer and cheaper than land dumping and incineration, especially for areas like New York City where there are not enough suitable sites for landfills or incinerators.

It is also argued that banning ocean dumping of sludge will do little to prevent pollution of beaches, because sewage sludge and the floatable solid waste that fouls beaches are two different things.

Proponents of ocean dumping of sludge argue that debris found on beaches comes from

- combined sewers that mix storm runoff with municipal wastewater and overflow during periods of heavy rain
- sewage treatment plants that occasionally malfunction
- illegal dumping of medical and other wastes
- floatable material that collects in streets and drains and is washed out by big storms or high tides
- garbage dumped at sea by commercial and pleasure boats
- debris thrown away by beach users

Potentially harmful medical waste represents less than 1% of beach litter. Most of the rest is plastic and paper debris dropped by beachgoers. Thus, if we want clean and safe beaches, we will have to change our throwaway lifestyles.

There is general agreement that the deep ocean is better equipped than land to handle sewage and some forms of industrial waste.

However, most scientists believe that the ocean should not be used for the dumping of slowly degradable or nondegradable pollutants like PCBs (Figure 22-4), some pesticides and radioactive isotopes, and toxic mercury compounds that can be biologically amplified in ocean food webs. Unfortunately, many of these materials are mixed with some types of sewage sludge, dredge spoils, and industrial waste being dumped into the ocean in large quantities.

Environmentalists favor requiring that sludge be treated to remove PCBs, toxic metals, and other hazardous substances. Then the sludge would be safer to dispose of on the land or at sea, or, better yet, it could be used as a soil conditioner for forests, parks, and other areas not used to grow food. The small volume of highly toxic chemicals removed from the sludge could be disposed of in landfills designed for such wastes (Figure 19-12). What do you think should be done with sewage sludge?

---

impacts on coastal areas (see Case Study on p. 616). The largest accident took place in 1983 when the tanker *Castillow de Bellver* caught fire and released 296 million liters (78.5 million gallons) of oil into the ocean off the coast of Capetown, South Africa. Oil can also be released as an act of environmental terrorism or as a result of war (see Spotlight on p. 618).

EFFECTS OF OIL POLLUTION The effects of oil on ocean ecosystems depend on a number of factors: type of oil (crude or refined), amount released, distance of release from shore, time of year, weather conditions, average water temperature, and currents. Oil reaching the ocean evaporates or is slowly degraded by bacteria.

Volatile organic hydrocarbons in oil immediately kill a number of aquatic organisms, especially in their more vulnerable larval forms. In warm waters, most of these toxic chemicals evaporate into the atmosphere within a day or two, but in cold waters, this may take up to a week.

Some other chemicals remain on the surface and form floating tarlike globs or mousse. This floating oil coats the feathers of birds (Figure 22-11), especially diving birds, and the fur of marine mammals such as seals and sea otters. This oily coating destroys the animals' natural insulation and buoyancy, and many drown or die of exposure from loss of body heat. These globs of oil are broken down by bacteria over several weeks or months, although they persist much longer in cold polar waters. Heavy oil components that sink to the ocean floor or wash into estuaries can kill bottom-dwelling organisms such as crabs, oysters, mussels, and clams or make them unfit for human consumption because of their oily taste and smell.

Most forms of marine life recover from exposure to large amounts of crude oil within three years. However, recovery of marine life from exposure to refined oil, especially in estuaries, may take ten years or longer. The world's most thoroughly studied oil spill occurred when the *Barge Florida* ran aground off Cape Cod in

Crude oil extracted from fields in Alaska's North Slope near Prudhoe Bay is carried by pipeline to the port of Valdez and then shipped by tanker to the West Coast (Figure 22-10). Just after midnight on March 24, 1989, the *Exxon Valdez*, a tanker more than three football fields long, went off course in a 16-kilometer (10-mile) wide channel in Prince William Sound near Valdez and hit submerged rocks on a reef. About 42 million liters (11 million gallons) of oil—22% of its cargo—gushed from several gashes in the hull, creating the worst oil spill ever in U.S. waters.

In 1990, an administrative judge and the National Transportation Safety Board found the captain of the tanker guilty of drinking before sailing and of leaving the bridge and turning over the ship to an inexperienced and fatigued third mate. Since 1984, the captain had been arrested for drunk driving three times and had lost his license to drive a car, but Exxon officials still kept him in charge of one of their largest tankers, carrying a $20-million cargo. The National Transportation Safety Board ruled that the accident was the result of drinking by the captain, a fatigued and overworked crew, and inadequate traffic control by the Coast Guard.

The rapidly spreading oil slick is known to have killed 580,000 birds (including 144 bald eagles), up to 5,500 sea otters, 30 seals, 22 whales, and unknown numbers of fish. It also oiled more than 5,100 kilometers (3,200 miles) of shoreline. The final toll on wildlife will never be known because most of the animals killed sank and decomposed without being counted. The good news is that these animal populations are expected to recover.

Knowledge of the true damage and projections about the rate and extent of recovery are not available to the public. Data has been collected by hundreds of scientists, but lawyers have forced them to keep this information secret because of pending lawsuits that may take years to resolve.

In the early 1970s, conservationists predicted that a large, damaging spill might occur in these treacherous waters containing submerged reefs and frequented by icebergs and violent storms. Conservationists urged that Alaskan oil be brought to the lower 48 states by pipeline over land to reduce potential damage.

Officials of Alyeska, a company formed by the seven oil companies extracting oil from Alaska's North Slope, said that a pipeline would take too long to build and that a large spill was "highly unlikely." They assured Congress that they would be at the scene of any accident within five hours and have enough equipment and trained people to clean up any spill. The oil companies won when the 49-to-49 tie vote in the U.S. Senate was broken by Vice President Spiro Agnew under orders from President Richard M. Nixon.

When the Valdez spill occurred, Alyeska and Exxon officials did not have enough equipment and personnel and did too little too late. To its credit, Exxon mounted a $2-billion cleanup program (including $125 million spent by the U.S. government) and promptly established a claims process, which no law required. Cleanup and legal settlements could raise the total cost of the spill to $4 billion.

A 1991 agreement in which Exxon was to pay a criminal misdemeanor fine of $100 million and an additional $1 billion fine in civil damages over ten years was rejected by the courts as being inadequate. After tax write-offs and inflation adjustments, Exxon would have actually paid only about $400 million in fines, with the rest being absorbed by taxpayers through lost tax revenue.

This $4-billion accident might have been prevented if the *Exxon Valdez* had had a double hull, which would have added $22.5 million to its initial cost. In the early 1970s, Interior Secretary Rogers Morton told Congress that all oil tankers using Alaskan waters would have double hulls, now on virtually all merchant ships—except oil tankers. Later, under pressure from oil companies, the requirement was dropped.

According to Jay Hair, president of the National Wildlife Federation: "This is a classic example of corporate greed. Big oil, big lies. Big lie number one was, 'Don't worry, be happy; nothing's going to happen at Valdez.' Big lie number two was, 'We're doing such a good job with the environment at the North Slope we ought to be allowed into the Arctic National Wildlife Refuge'" (Figure 16-24).

Others must also share the blame for this tragedy. State officials had been lax in monitoring Alyeska, and

1969. Data show that even after 20 years, traces of oil are still present in marsh sediments and in the tissues of some marine life. The effects of spills in cold waters (such as Alaska's Prince William Sound and antarctic waters, Figure 19-5) generally last longer.

Oil slicks that wash onto beaches can have serious economic effects on coastal residents, who lose income from fishing and tourist activities. Oil-polluted beaches washed by strong waves or currents are cleaned up after about a year, but beaches in sheltered areas remain contaminated for several years. Estuaries and salt marshes suffer the most damage and cannot effectively be cleaned up.

CONTROLLING OCEAN OIL POLLUTION The Valdez disaster and other oil spills dramatize the need for

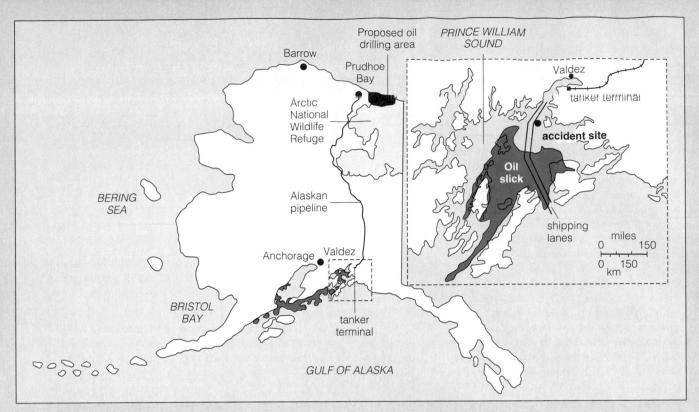

Figure 22-10 Site of the oil spill in Alaska's Prince William Sound from the tanker *Exxon Valdez* on March 24, 1989.

the Coast Guard did not effectively monitor tanker traffic because of inadequate radar equipment and personnel.

American consumers must also share some of the blame. Their unnecessarily wasteful use of oil and gasoline (Section 17-2) is the driving force behind the search for more domestic oil but without adequate environmental safeguards. For example, insisting that Congress raise the fuel-economy standards for new automobiles and light trucks from 12 kilometers per liter to 17 kilometers per liter (28.5 miles per gallon to 40 miles per gallon) by the year 2000 would *daily* save twice as much oil as was spilled in Prince William Sound. It would also save more oil than is expected to be found in new searches for oil in Alaska and in U.S. coastal waters.

Even after the most expensive cleanup in history, the Congressional Office of Technology assessment estimates that only 3% to 4% of the volume of oil spilled by the *Exxon Valdez* was recovered. Also, use of high-pressure water to clean beaches did more harm than good by killing coastal plants and animals. Beach-cleaning crews and their equipment consumed more than three times the amount of oil spilled by the tanker. Exxon also shipped 27,000 metric tons (30,000 tons) of oil-contaminated solid waste to an Oregon landfill.

pollution prevention because no large oil spill can be contained or effectively cleaned up.

Prevention Methods

- Use and waste less oil (Section 17-2).

- Collect used oils and greases from service stations and other sources and reprocess them for reuse.

- Prohibit oil drilling in ecologically sensitive offshore and nearshore areas (see Pro/Con on p. 428).

- Strictly regulate the construction and operation of oil tankers, offshore oil rigs, and oil refineries.

- Greatly increase the financial liability of oil companies for cleaning up oil spills to encourage pollu-

Figure 22-11 A seabird coated with crude oil from an oil spill. Most of these birds die unless the oil is removed with a detergent solution, and many die even when the oil is removed.

- Require all existing tankers to have double hulls by 1998. The Oil Pollution Act of 1990 requires this but allows up to 25 years for it to take place.

- Require oil companies to routinely test employees for drug and alcohol abuse, and ban convicted drunk drivers from tanker commands and from management positions on offshore drilling rigs.

- Require the Coast Guard to have state-of-the art radar equipment linked to tankers using harbors and sounds, and sound an alarm automatically if a tanker goes off course.

- Require updated and stringent oil-spill cleanup plans, with large and strict penalties for noncompliance.

- Ban the rinsing of sludge from empty oil tankers and the dumping of sludge into the sea.

- Require oil tankers to load and unload oil on platforms far offshore to keep tankers out of sensitive coastal areas. Oil would be piped to and from the platforms.

- Strictly regulate safety, operation, and disposal procedures for oil refineries and industrial plants.

Cleanup Methods

- Treat spilled oil with chemical dispersants sprayed from aircraft within a day after a spill so that the oil will disperse, dissolve, or sink; not effective after one or two days; some biologists contend that the dispersants kill more marine life than the oil does.

- Use helicopters equipped with lasers to ignite and burn off much of the oil, especially the more toxic volatile components; cheaper and more effective than dispersants for small spills and the only effective method in ice-congested seas; must be done very soon after the spill; creates air pollution, and the ashes may be toxic to fish.

tion prevention. The Oil Pollution Act of 1990 substantially raised liability and compensation limits for tanker oil spills in U.S. waters. It also placed a five-cent fee on each barrel of oil to create a $1-billion trust fund to pay for cleanup and damages beyond the spiller's $10-million liability limit.

- Route oil tankers as far as possible from sensitive coastal areas, and have Coast Guard vessels guide tankers out of all harbors and enclosed sounds and bays.

- Require all new tankers to have double hulls to lessen chances of severe leaks. This is required for new U.S. tankers by the Oil Pollution Act of 1990, but oil companies can get around this provision by operating tankers under the flags of other countries.

- Use mechanical barriers (inflatable booms) to prevent oil from reaching the shore; ineffective in high seas and bad weather conditions, in ice-congested water, or for large spills.

- Pump the oil-water mixture into small boats called skimmers, where special machines separate the oil from the water and pump the oil into storage tanks; pillows containing chicken feathers can also be used to absorb oil from small spills; ineffective in high seas and for large spills.

- Use genetic engineering techniques to develop bacterial strains that can degrade compounds in oil faster and more efficiently than natural bacterial strains; possible ecological side effects of such "superbugs" should be carefully investigated before widespread use (see Pro/Con on p. 161); not effective for large spills.

- Clean up polluted beaches with straw, detergents, and high-pressure hoses, by spreading nitrogen and phosphorus fertilizers to accelerate growth of natural bacteria that break down oil, and by other methods; time-consuming; too expensive for cleaning up large areas; detergents and high-pressure hoses are harmful to wildlife.

- Greatly increase government and oil company research on methods for containing and cleaning up oil spills. The Valdez spill revealed how little research the oil companies have done in this area since the mid-1970s, mostly because it wasn't required by law.

22-4 Groundwater Pollution and Its Control

GROUNDWATER CONTAMINATION Groundwater (Figure 13-3) is a vital source of water for drinking and irrigation in the United States and other parts of the world. However, this vital form of Earth capital is easy to deplete because it is renewed so slowly; on a human time scale, groundwater contamination can be considered permanent.

Laws protecting groundwater are weak in the United States and nonexistent in most countries. By 1990, only 38 of the several hundred chemicals found in U.S. groundwater were covered by federal water quality standards and routinely tested for in municipal drinking-water supplies.

Results of limited testing of groundwater in the United States are alarming. In a 1982 survey, the EPA found that 45% of the large public water systems served by groundwater were contaminated with synthetic organic chemicals that posed potential health threats (see Case Study above). Another EPA survey in 1984 found that two-thirds of the rural household wells tested vio-

CASE STUDY Groundwater Contamination in Woburn, Massachusetts

Woburn, Massachusetts, like many American cities, relies on wells to supply drinking water for its 37,000 inhabitants. For decades, this industrial town has been home to a number of factories and chemical plants making pesticides, glues, dry-cleaning fluids, leather, and other products.

For years, these companies dumped much of their wastes at a site that was less than 0.8 kilometer (0.5 mile) from two of the town's wells. In the late 1970s, tests showed that water from those two wells contained hazardous levels of a number of toxic synthetic organic chemicals.

The wells were closed, but people's health had already been affected. The rates of childhood leukemia in Woburn are two to three times the national average, and 19 children have died from the disease. A study by the Harvard School of Medicine linked the deaths to two industrial solvents, trichloroethylene and perchloroethylene, which had leaked into community wells.

lated at least one federal health standard for drinking water. A 1990 EPA survey found that 1.2% of the community wells and 2.4% of the rural wells used for domestic drinking water had nitrate concentrations—which cause a life-threatening blood disorder in infants—above the safe level.

The EPA has documented groundwater contamination by 74 pesticides in 38 states. In a 1990 national survey, the EPA found that 1% of the wells tested contained water with pesticide residues at levels that might cause health problems. The most frequently detected pesticide was a breakdown product of DCPA, a herbicide used mostly on lawns.

Crude estimates indicate that while only 2% of the volume of all U.S. groundwater is contaminated, up to 25% by volume of the usable groundwater is contaminated. In some areas, up to 75% by volume is contaminated.

In New Jersey, every major aquifer is contaminated. In California, pesticides contaminate the drinking water of more than 1 million people. In Florida, where 92% of the residents rely on groundwater for drinking, over 1,000 wells have been closed, and state officials and environmentalists are worried about the increasing number of sites contaminated with pesticides used by many citrus growers. Between 1985 and 1990, more than 1.3 million liters (340,000 gallons) of oil have been spilled under the tarmac at Miami airport.

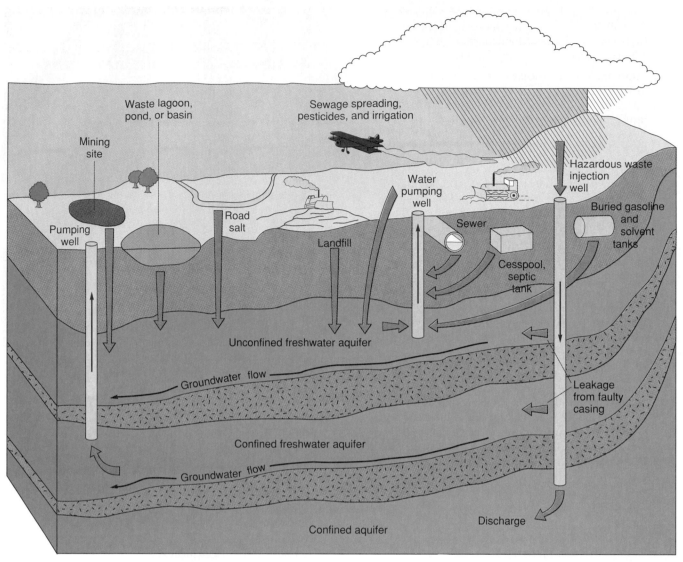

Figure 22-12   Principal sources of groundwater contamination in the United States.

**VULNERABILITY OF GROUNDWATER TO POLLU-
TION**   Some bacteria and most suspended solid pollutants are removed as contaminated surface water
percolates through the soil into aquifers. This process,
however, can be overloaded by large volumes of wastes,
and its effectiveness varies with the type of soil. No soil
is effective in filtering out viruses and many synthetic
organic chemicals.

When groundwater becomes contaminated, it
does not cleanse itself, as surface water tends to (Figure
22-3). Because groundwater flows are slow and not turbulent, contaminants are not effectively diluted and dispersed. Also, there is little decomposition by aerobic
bacteria, because groundwater is cut off from the atmosphere's oxygen supply and has fairly small populations
of aerobic and anaerobic decomposing bacteria. The
cold temperature of groundwater also slows down
decomposition reactions. That means it can take hundreds to thousands of years for contaminated groundwater to cleanse itself of degradable wastes.

Because groundwater is not visible, there is little
awareness of it and little public outcry against its contamination — "out of sight, out of mind" — until wells
and public water supplies must be shut down. By then,
slowly building pollution thresholds have been exceeded and it is too late (see Case Study on p. 619). That
explains why a number of environmentalists believe
that long-lasting groundwater contamination will soon
emerge as one of our most serious water resource problems as more and more threshold levels of contamination are crossed.

SOURCES OF GROUNDWATER CONTAMINATION
Groundwater can be contaminated from a number of
point and nonpoint sources (Figure 22-12). Principal
sources of groundwater contamination are leaks of hazardous organic chemicals from underground storage
tanks (see Pro/Con on p. 621) and seepage of hazardous
organic chemicals and toxic heavy metal compounds
from landfills, abandoned hazardous-waste dumps,

The EPA estimates that at least 1 million of the estimated 6 million (some say 7 million to 15 million) underground tanks used to store petroleum, gasoline, solvents, and other hazardous chemicals throughout the United States are leaking their contents into groundwater. Of these, 2 million are large commercial tanks used by refineries, airports, and gasoline stations; the remainder are small tanks, such as home-heating fuel tanks. Leaks occur from improper installation, corrosion (most are bare steel tanks designed to last only 20 to 40 years), cracking (fiberglass tanks), and overfilling. Just as all landfills will eventually leak, so too will all underground storage tanks.

According to the EPA, 300,000 to 500,000 of the nation's 2 million large commercial tanks are leaking. The estimated amount of gasoline and other solvents leaking from these underground tanks each year equals the volume of oil spilled by the *Exxon Valdez* tanker (see Case Study on p. 616). A slow gasoline leak of just 4 liters (1 gallon) a day can seriously contaminate the water supply for 50,000 people. Such slow leaks usually remain undetected until someone discovers that a well is contaminated.

Determining the extent of a leak can cost $25,000 to $250,000. Cleanup costs from $10,000 for a small spill to $250,000 and up if the chemical reaches an aquifer. Replacing a leaking tank adds an additional $10,000 to $60,000, and damages to injured parties and legal fees can run into the millions.

Most gasoline tanks are owned by independent operators or local petroleum suppliers and distributors, who tend not to report leaks for fear of going bankrupt. In 1986, Congress passed legislation placing a tax on motor fuel to create a $500-million fund for cleaning up leaking underground tanks.

The EPA requires that all tanks installed after 1993 have a leak detection system and that discovered leaks must be stopped right away. New tanks must also be made of noncorrosive material (such as fiberglass, which is likely to degrade more slowly than most metals). By 1998, tanks that contain petroleum products or any of 701 hazardous chemicals listed under the Superfund law must have overfill and spill prevention devices and doublewall or concrete vaults to help prevent leaks into groundwater (already required in 13 states for some or all tanks). Also, each owner of a commercial underground tank must carry at least $1 million in liability insurance—a requirement that has driven many independent gasoline stations out of business.

Even with the new regulations, the EPA projects that 62,000 private water wells and 4,700 public water wells have been or will be contaminated by leaks from underground tanks. Estimated costs of only partial cleanup of such spills are as high as $32 billion—another glaring example of short-term economic gain leading to long-term economic and environmental grief.

Environmentalists believe these regulations are too little too late and do little to deal with the millions of older tanks that are "toxic time bombs." Some tanks, especially near large refineries, have been leaking for years but have received little publicity. The largest known oil spill beneath a tank is at Chevron's facility in El Segundo, California. This 755-million-liter (200-million-gallon) leak, which has not been cleaned up, is 18 times larger than the Valdez spill and is 1.4 times as large as the amount of oil released in the Persian Gulf. A Tosco Corporation tank near San Francisco has leaked 1 billion liters (28 million gallons) of oil—2.5 times more than the oil spilled by the *Exxon Valdez*. In Brooklyn, New York, a Mobil Oil tank has leaked 642 million liters (17 million gallons) of oil—1.5 times more oil than was spilled by the *Exxon Valdez*.

Environmentalists call for faster phasing in of EPA regulations and requiring much stricter training and certification for tank installers, as is done in Maine and Massachusetts. They also believe that monitoring systems should be required for all underground tanks, not just new ones. Operators of older tanks should also be required to carry enough liability insurance to cover cleanup and damage costs and be liable for leaks from abandoned tanks. Aboveground steel tanks encased in thick concrete can also be used.

In the former West Germany, such a program has been quite successful in reducing leaks from underground tanks for 20 years. Most business owners in the United States oppose such regulations, believing they are too costly. What do you think should be done?

and industrial-waste storage lagoons located above or near aquifers (Section 20-5).

A survey by the EPA found that a third of 26,000 industrial-waste ponds and lagoons have no liners to prevent toxic liquid wastes from seeping into aquifers. One-third of those sites are within 1.6 kilometers (1 mile) of one or more water supply wells.

Another concern is accidental leaks into aquifers from wells used to inject much of the country's hazardous wastes deep underground (Figure 22-12). Environmentalists believe that deep-well disposal of hazardous waste in the United States should be banned, since there are other, safer ways to deal with such wastes (Section 20-5).

CONTROL OF GROUNDWATER POLLUTION

Groundwater pollution is much more difficult to detect and control than surface water pollution. Monitoring groundwater pollution is expensive (up to $10,000 per monitoring well), and many monitoring wells must be sunk.

Because of its location underground, pumping polluted groundwater to the surface, cleaning it up, and returning it to the aquifer is usually too expensive — $5 million to $10 million or more for a single aquifer. Recent attempts to pump and treat slow-flowing contaminated aquifers show that it may take decades, even hundreds of years, of pumping before all of the contamination is forced to the surface.

Thus, *preventing contamination is the only effective way to protect groundwater resources*. This will require

- banning virtually all disposal of hazardous wastes in sanitary landfills and deep injection wells (Figure 22-12)

- monitoring aquifers near existing sanitary and hazardous-waste landfills, underground tanks, and other potential sources of groundwater contamination (Figure 22-12)

- placing much stricter controls on the application of pesticides and fertilizers by millions of farmers and homeowners

- requiring people using private wells for drinking water to have their water tested once a year

- establishing nationwide standards for groundwater contaminants

22-5 Controlling Surface-Water Pollution

NONPOINT SOURCE POLLUTION Although most U.S. surface waters have not declined in quality since 1970, they also have not improved. The primary reason has been the absence until recently of any national strategy for controlling water pollution from nonpoint sources.

The leading nonpoint source of water pollution is agriculture (see Spotlight on p. 372). Farmers can sharply reduce fertilizer runoff into surface waters and leaching into aquifers by not using excessive amounts of fertilizer and by using none on steeply sloped land. They can use slow-release fertilizers and alternate between planting fields with row crops and soybeans or other nitrogen-fixing plants to reduce the need for fertilizer. Farmers should also be required to have buffer zones of permanent vegetation between cultivated fields and nearby surface water.

Similarly, farmers can reduce pesticide runoff and leaching by applying no more pesticide than is needed and by applying it only when needed. They can reduce the need for pesticides by using biological methods of pest control or integrated pest management (Section 23-5). Use of commercial inorganic fertilizers and pesticides on golf courses, yards, and public lands would also have to be sharply reduced.

Livestock growers can control runoff and infiltration by animal wastes from feedlots and barnyards by controlling animal density, planting buffers, and not locating feedlots on land sloping toward nearby surface water. Diverting runoff of animal wastes into detention basins would allow this nutrient-rich water to be pumped and applied as fertilizer to cropland or forestland.

Critical watersheds should also be reforested. In addition to reducing water pollution from sediment, this would reduce soil erosion and the severity of flooding (see Case Study on p. 342) and help slow projected global warming (Section 11-1) and loss of Earth's precious biodiversity (Chapter 16).

POINT SOURCE POLLUTION: WASTEWATER TREATMENT In many LDCs and in some parts of MDCs, sewage and waterborne industrial wastes from point sources are not treated. Instead, most are discharged into the nearest waterway or into **wastewater lagoons** — large ponds where air, sunlight, and microorganisms break down wastes, allow solids to settle out, and kill some disease-causing bacteria. Water typically remains in a lagoon for 30 days. Then, it is treated with chlorine and pumped out for use by a city or farms.

In MDCs, most wastes from point sources are purified to varying degrees. In rural and suburban areas with suitable soils, sewage from each house is usually discharged into a **septic tank** (Figure 22-13). About 24% of all homes in the United States are served by septic tanks.

In urban areas in MDCs, most waterborne wastes from homes, businesses, factories, and storm runoff flow through a network of sewer pipes to wastewater treatment plants. Some cities have separate lines for storm water runoff, but in 1,200 U.S. cities, the lines for these two systems are combined because it is cheaper (Figure 22-14). When rains cause combined sewer lines to overflow, they discharge untreated sewage directly into surface waters.

When sewage reaches a treatment plant, it can undergo up to three levels of purification, depending on the type of plant and the degree of purity desired. **Primary sewage treatment** is a mechanical process that uses screens to filter out debris such as sticks, stones, and rags. Then suspended solids settle out as sludge in a settling tank (Figure 22-15). Improved primary treatment using chemically treated polymers does a better job of removing suspended solids.

Secondary sewage treatment is a biological process that uses aerobic bacteria as a first step to remove up to 90% of biodegradable, oxygen-demanding organic wastes (Figure 22-16). Some plants use *trickling filters*, where aerobic bacteria degrade sewage as it seeps through a large vat bed filled with crushed stones cov-

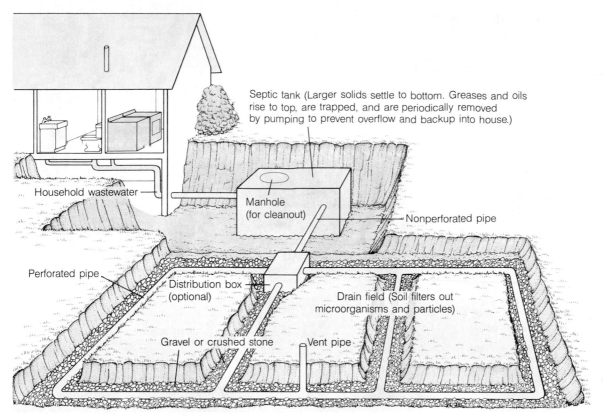

Figure 22-13 Septic tank system used for disposal of domestic sewage and wastewater in rural and suburban areas. This system traps greases and large solids and discharges the remaining wastes over a large drainage field. As these wastes percolate downward, the soil filters out some potential pollutants, and soil bacteria decompose biodegradable materials. To be effective, septic tanks must be installed in soils with adequate drainage, not placed too close together or too near well sites, installed properly, and pumped out when the settling tank becomes full.

ered with bacteria and protozoa. Others use an *activated sludge process*, in which the sewage is pumped into a large tank and mixed for several hours with bacteria-rich sludge and air bubbles to increase degradation by microorganisms. The water then goes to a sedimentation tank, where most of the suspended solids and microorganisms settle out as sludge. The sludge is removed and then is broken down in an anaerobic digestor, disposed of by incineration, dumped in the ocean or a landfill, or applied to land as fertilizer.

In the United States, combined primary and secondary treatment must be used in all communities served by wastewater treatment plants. Combined primary and secondary treatment, however, still leaves about 3% to 5% by weight of the oxygen-demanding wastes, 3% of the suspended solids, 50% of the nitrogen (mostly as nitrates), 70% of the phosphorus (mostly as phosphates), and 30% of most toxic metal compounds and synthetic organic chemicals in the wastewater discharged from the plant. Virtually none of any long-lived radioactive isotopes and persistent organic substances such as pesticides is removed by these two processes.

Advanced sewage treatment is a series of specialized chemical and physical processes that lower the quantity of specific pollutants still left after primary and secondary treatment (Figure 22-17). Types of advanced treatment vary depending on the contaminants in specific communities and industries. Except in Sweden, Denmark, and Norway, advanced treatment is rarely used because the plants cost twice as much to build and four times as much to operate as secondary plants.

Before water is discharged from a sewage treatment plant, it is disinfected to remove water coloration and kill disease carrying bacteria and some, but not all, viruses. The usual method is chlorination. However, chlorine reacts with organic materials in the wastewater or in surface water to form small amounts of chlorinated hydrocarbons, some of which cause cancers in test animals. Several other disinfectants, such as ozone, hydrogen peroxide, and UV light, are being used in some places but are more expensive than chlorination.

Without expensive advanced treatment, effluents from primary and secondary sewage treatment plants contain enough nitrates and phosphates to contribute to accelerated eutrophication of lakes, slow-moving streams, and coastal waters (Figure 22-5). Conventional sewage treatment has helped reduce pollution of surface water, but environmentalists point out that it is a limited and flawed output approach that is eventually overwhelmed by more people producing more wastes.

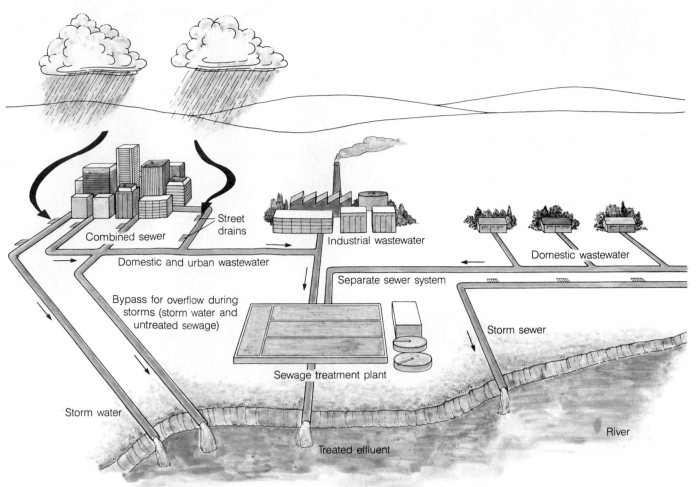

Figure 22-14 Separated and combined storm and sewer systems used in cities. When combined storm and sewer lines are used, even a light rain can overload the systems and cause untreated sewage to be discharged into nearby surface waters.

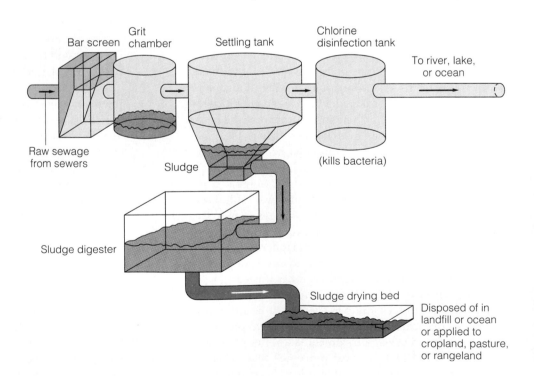

Figure 22-15 Primary sewage treatment. If a combination of primary and secondary (or advanced) treatment is used, the wastewater is not disinfected until the last step.

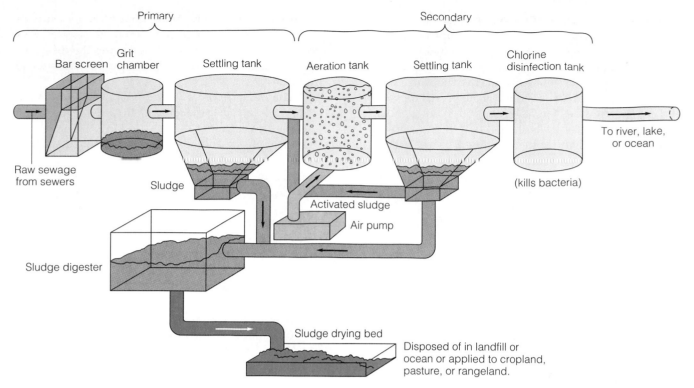

Figure 22-16   Secondary sewage treatment.

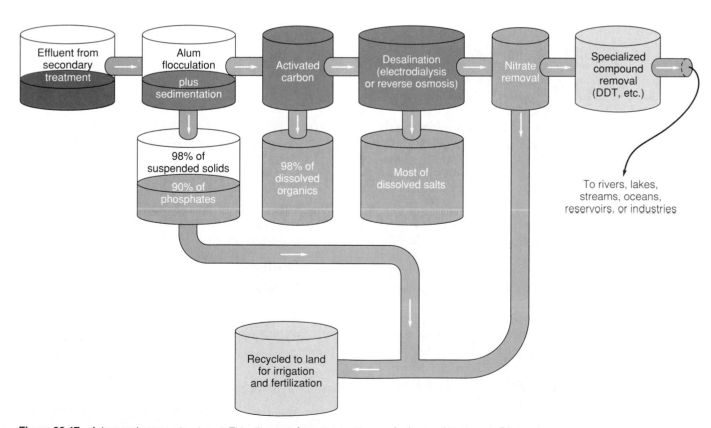

Figure 22-17   Advanced sewage treatment. This diagram shows several types of advanced treatment. Often only one or two of these processes are used to remove specific pollutants in a particular area.

ALTERNATIVES TO LARGE-SCALE TREATMENT PLANTS Small-scale, *package wastewater treatment plants* are sometimes used for secondary treatment of small quantities of wastes from shopping centers, apartment complexes, villages, and small housing subdivisions. However, many of these do not work properly and require considerable attention and maintenance. Often, they are put in by developers and then are abandoned or are poorly run and maintained.

Some small rural villages and suburban developments where groundwater used for drinking is being polluted by large numbers of septic tanks (Figure 22-13) have installed a small-diameter, gravity flow sewer system to link the septic tanks of all residences and carry wastewater to large soil-absorption drainage fields or beds of sand. Such systems cost about one-third to one-half as much as conventional sewage treatment plants used in larger cities, but sufficient land must be available for the drainage fields.

In LDCs and in many areas in MDCs, using low-tech, natural or created ecosystems may be the cheapest and best way to purify wastewater (see Case Study on p. 627).

LAND DISPOSAL OF SEWAGE EFFLUENT AND SLUDGE Sewage treatment produces a toxic gooey sludge that must be disposed of or recycled as fertilizer to the land. About 42% by weight of the sludge produced in the United States is dumped in conventional landfills where it can contaminate groundwater. Another 6% is dumped into the ocean, which transfers water pollution from one part of the hydrosphere to another. The 21% of the sludge that is incinerated can pollute the air with traces of toxic chemicals, and the resulting toxic ash must be disposed of, usually in landfills where it can pollute groundwater.

A better alternative is to return the nitrate and phosphate plant nutrients in sewage plant effluent and sludge to the land directly as fertilizer or to compost it and use it as a soil conditioner. In Denmark, 48% of the weight of sludge produced is used to fertilize land. In the United States, about 16% is used directly as a fertilizer and 9% is composted to produce a soil conditioner.

Before it is applied, sludge can be heated to kill harmful bacteria, as is done in the former West Germany and Switzerland, or composted. Sludge and effluents can also be treated to remove toxic metals and organic chemicals before application, but that can be expensive.

Untreated sludge can be applied to land not used for crops or livestock or to land where groundwater is already contaminated or is not used as a source of drinking water. Examples include forests, surface-mined land, golf courses, lawns, cemeteries, and highway medians.

PURIFICATION OF DRINKING WATER Treatment of water for drinking by urban residents is much like wastewater treatment. Areas depending on surface water usually store it in a reservoir for several days to improve clarity and taste by allowing the dissolved oxygen content to increase and suspended matter to settle out.

The water is then pumped to a purification plant. There it is given the degree of treatment needed to meet federal drinking-water standards. Usually, it is run through sand filters, then through activated charcoal, and then disinfected. In areas with very pure sources of groundwater, little, if any, treatment is necessary.

PROTECTING COASTAL WATERS The most important suggestions for preventing excessive pollution of coastal waters include the following:

Prevention Methods

- Eliminate the discharge of toxic pollutants into coastal waters from both industrial facilities and municipal sewage treatment plants.

- Eliminate all discharges of raw sewage from sewer-line overflows by requiring separate storm and sewer lines in cities (Figure 22-14).

- Promote water conservation in homes and industries to reduce the flow to sewage treatment plants and hence the danger of overflow (see Individuals Matter inside the back cover).

- Ban all ocean dumping of sewage sludge and hazardous dredged materials.

- Enact and enforce laws and land-use practices to sharply reduce runoff from nonpoint sources in coastal areas.

- Protect coastal waters that are already clean by not allowing harmful forms of development.

- Protect sensitive marine areas from all forms of development by designating them as ocean sanctuaries, much like protected wilderness areas on land.

- Regulate the types and density of coastal development to minimize its environmental impact, and eliminate subsidies and tax incentives that encourage harmful coastal development (see Case Study on p. 137).

- Institute a national energy policy based on energy efficiency and renewable energy resources to reduce dependence on oil (Section 18-5).

- Prohibit oil drilling in ecologically sensitive offshore and nearshore areas (see Pro/Con on p. 428).

- Use the methods for preventing oil pollution given on pp. 617–618.

- Ban discharge of plastic items and garbage from ocean vessels.

- Sharply reduce the use of disposable plastic items (Section 19-5 and Figure 19-17).

In Lima, Peru, most of the sewage produced by its 7 million, mostly poor, people, is discharged untreated into the Pacific Ocean. In poor areas, this sewage runs to the ocean through a series of open ditches in which children often swim, despite warnings from their parents.

The country cannot afford to build expensive waste treatment plants. However, there are now experiments in which the sewage in some areas is channelled into holding ponds, where solids fall to the bottom. Bacteria then decompose many of the wastes. After 20 to 30 days, the water is safe to use. Some of it is used to irrigate corn fed to cattle, and some is pumped to other ponds where the remaining nutrients are used to raise fish.

Natural wetlands can also be used effectively to treat sewage, but many have been destroyed or overwhelmed by pollution (see Case Study on p. 137). An alternative is to create artificial wetlands outdoors in warm climates. Artificial wetlands are now being used to treat sewage in at least 31 towns in North America.

One of these systems is used in Arcata, California (Figure 9-16). In this coastal northern California town of 15,000, some 63 hectares (155 acres) of wetlands have been created between the town and the adjacent bay in an area that was once a dump. The newly created marshes act as an inexpensive, low-tech waste treatment plant by removing nitrogen and phosphorous plant nutrients, degrading organic wastes, and filtering out toxic materials.

Instead of using expensive, high-tech waste treatment plants that only partially clean up wastewater, Arcata's beautifully simple approach is based on working with nature. First, the city's wastewater passes through oxidation ponds, where wastes settle out and are partially broken down. Then, the water moves on to be further filtered and

Figure 22-18 At the Providence, Rhode Island, Solar Sewage Plant, biologist John Todd is demonstrating how ecological waste engineering taking place in a greenhouse can be used to purify wastewater in urban and rural areas.

cleansed in marshes. The water then moves on to irrigate and nourish other wetlands, and some is pumped into the nearby bay. The marshes are also an Audubon bird sanctuary and provide habitats for thousands of animals, including otters, seabirds, and marine animals.

Compared with sewage treatment plants, this highly effective approach is cheap and easy to maintain. However, it does require more land than the conventional approach. In colder climates, wastewater can be purified in greenhouses containing rows of large tanks containing aquatic plants (Figure 22-18). Sewage flows into a greenhouse room containing rows of large aquarium tanks covered

with plants such as water hyacinths, cattails, and bulrushes. In these tanks, algae and microorganisms decompose wastes into nutrients absorbed by the plants. Toxic metals are absorbed into the tissues of trees to be transplanted outside. Then, the water passes through an artificial marsh filter and enters other aquariums, where snails and zooplankton consume microorganisms and are themselves consumed by small fish that can be sold for bait. The water then flows into a second artificial marsh filter. When working properly, such systems have produced water fit for drinking. John Todd (Figure 22-18) and others are carrying out research to perfect such systems.

- Institute a nationwide program to collect and safely dispose of household hazardous wastes (Section 20-5), and educate consumers to use cheaper and safer alternatives to most common household chemicals (see Individuals Matter inside the back cover).

- Adopt a nationwide tracking program to ensure that medical waste is safely disposed of.

Cleanup Methods

- Greatly improve oil-spill cleanup capabilities. However, according to a 1990 report by the Office of Technology Assessment, there is little chance that large spills can be effectively contained or cleaned up.

- Upgrade all coastal sewage treatment plants to at least the degree required for inland waters (secondary treatment), or develop alternative methods for sewage treatment (see Case Study on p. 627).

22-6 U.S. Water Pollution Control Laws

PROTECTING DRINKING WATER Only about 54 of the world's 164 countries have safe drinking water. Most of them are in North America and Europe. Currently, about 89% of the U.S. population get their drinking water from approximately 200,000 public water supply systems. The other 11%, mainly in rural areas, get their drinking water from private wells.

The Safe Drinking Water Act of 1974 requires the EPA to establish national drinking-water standards, called *maximum contaminant levels*, for any pollutants that "may" have adverse effects on human health. Environmentalists and health officials, however, have criticized the EPA for being slow in implementing this law. By 1990, the EPA had set maximum contaminant levels for only 65 of the at least 700 potential pollutants found in municipal drinking-water supplies. Of the chemicals found in U.S. drinking water that have been tested, 97 cause cancers, 82 cause mutations, 28 are toxic, and 23 promote tumors in test animals. By 1995, the EPA is required by Congress to set new standards for 108 drinking-water contaminants.

Privately owned wells for millions of individual homes in suburban and rural areas are not required to meet federal drinking water standards. The biggest reasons are the cost of testing each well regularly (at least $1,000) and political opposition to mandatory testing and compliance by some homeowners.

Since 1974, the Safe Drinking Water Act has helped improve drinking water in much of the United States, but there is still a long way to go. A survey by the National Wildlife Federation found that only 2% of the

roughly 100,000 violations of federal drinking-water standards and of water testing and reporting requirements, which affected 40 million people, were subject to enforcement action and fines. In 94% of the cases, people were not notified when their drinking water either was contaminated or had not been adequately tested. The EPA's inspector general also reported that the agency has been failing to enforce regulations covering 140,000 noncommunity water systems such as those in restaurants and hospitals, serving 36 million people.

Contaminated wells and concern about possible contamination of public drinking-water supplies has created a boom in the number of Americans drinking bottled water or adding water purification devices to their home systems. This has created enormous profits for legitimate companies and for con artists in these businesses (see Spotlight on p. 629).

CONTROLLING SURFACE-WATER POLLUTION The Federal Water Pollution Act of 1972, renamed the Clean Water Act of 1977 when it was amended (along with amendments in 1981 and 1987), and the 1987 Water Quality Act form the basis of U.S. efforts to control pollution of the country's surface waters. The goal of these laws is to make all U.S. surface waters safe for fishing and swimming.

These acts require the EPA to establish *national effluent standards* and to set up a nationwide system for monitoring water quality. These effluent standards limit the amounts of certain conventional and toxic water pollutants that can be discharged into surface waters from factories, sewage treatment plants, and other point sources. Each point source discharger must get a permit specifying the amount of each pollutant that a facility can discharge.

As a result of the Clean Water Act, most U.S. cities have secondary sewage treatment, made possible by over $50 billion in federal grants for building sewage treatment plants. By 1988, 87% of the country's publicly owned sewage treatment plants complied with effluent limits set by the Clean Water Act, and about 80% of all industrial dischargers were officially in compliance with their discharge permits.

In 1989, however, the EPA found that more than 66% of the nation's sewage treatment plants have water quality or public health problems, and studies by the General Accounting Office have shown that most industries sometimes violate their permits. Five hundred cities ranging from Boston to Key West, Florida, have failed to meet federal standards for sewage treatment plants. In 1989, 34 cities on the East Coast were not doing anything more to their sewage than screening out large floating objects and discharging the rest into coastal waters. According to the EPA, an additional $88 billion is needed for new wastewater-treatment facilities.

In 1990, about 1 in 17 Americans spent more than $2 billion to buy bottled water, at an average price 700 times that of tap water. Sales of bottled water in the United States are expected to exceed $4 billion by 1993.

Water-bottling companies can legally get their water from springs, wells, or public water from the tap. More than one-third of the bottled water sold in the United States comes from the same groundwater and surface water sources that provide tap water. Sellers are not required to identify on their labels the source of their water or the type of purifying equipment, if any, used.

Bottled water is regulated by the Food and Drug Administration (FDA), not the EPA, and the FDA requires bottlers to check for only 22 of the 30 chemicals tested for in tap water provided by municipalities. Only bottled water marketed over state lines must meet all federal drinking-water standards, and testing is required every one to four years, depending on the contaminant, except for bacteria, which are tested for weekly. Bottlers are not required to submit their test results to the EPA. FDA inspectors check bottling plants only every two to three years. Mineral water is not regulated by the FDA or any other agency.

To be safe, you should purchase bottled water only from companies that have their water frequently tested and certified, ideally by EPA-certified laboratories. Obtain copies of their past year's tests, and ask them to give you the source of their water in writing. Compare this with test results from your source of public drinking water to determine whether you need to buy bottled water. *Consumer Reports* magazine tested 50 brands of bottled water and reported the results in their January 1987 issue.

Before buying bottled water, determine whether the bottler belongs to the International Bottled Water Association (IBWA) and adheres to its testing requirements. The IBWA requires its members to test for 181 contaminants and sends an inspector from the National Sanitation Foundation, a private lab, to bottling plants annually to check all pertinent records and make sure the plant is run cleanly. By 1991, IBWA water-testing standards were required in 15 states.

Several processes can be used in devices for treating home drinking water, each with certain advantages and disadvantages:*

- *Activated-carbon filters* ($200 to $2,500). Remove most synthetic organic chemicals, chlorine, and radon if filter is changed regularly; not effective in removing bacteria, viruses, nitrates and other dissolved salts, and toxic metals such as lead and mercury; unless the filter is changed regularly and kept scrupulously clean, there is a risk of bacterial contamination.

- *Reverse-osmosis* ($600 to $1,000). Effective for removing particulates and dissolved solids and some volatile synthetic organic chemicals; does not remove radon, and some models don't do well in removing bacteria and viruses; not effective against arsenic, chloroform, and phenol; 75% to 95% of the water flowing into the unit is wasted and goes down the drain with the contaminants; filters must be changed regularly; calcium must be removed by a water softener, and water must have a pH below 8.

- *Distillation* ($200 to $700). Removes toxic metals, radioactive contamination, and nonvolatile organic compounds, and kills bacteria; does not remove volatile organic chemicals (like chloroform) or radon; expensive to operate; produces flat-tasting water; slow process with low output; must be cleaned and serviced regularly.

- *Ultraviolet light*. Kills most bacteria and some viruses, but does not remove other pollutants.

- *Water softeners* ($1,000). Remove dissolved minerals and prevent scales in water pipes and equipment; do not remove bacteria, viruses, and most other toxic substances.

Machines that combine several approaches can remove most pollutants if they are properly maintained at a cost of at least $100 a year. Before buying expensive purifiers, consumers should have their water tested by local health authorities or private labs to find out what contaminants, if any, need to be removed, and then buy a unit that does the job.

Buyers should be suspicious of door-to-door salespeople, telephone appeals, and scare tactics. They should carefully check out companies selling such equipment and demand a copy of purifying claims by EPA-certified laboratories.

*See *Consumer Reports*, January 1990, pp. 27–43, for an evaluation of water treatment equipment.

FUTURE WATER QUALITY GOALS Serious pollution of the hydrosphere is preventable and potentially reversible, but this requires that we shift from pollution cleanup to pollution prevention. Otherwise, even the best cleanup approaches are eventually overwhelmed by increases in population and industrialization.

To make such a shift, we must truly accept the fact that the environment that we now treat as separate parts — air, water, soil, life — is an interconnected whole. Without an integrated approach to all forms of pollution, we will continue to shift environmental problems from one part of the environment to another. Ultimately, this form of environmental musical chairs will fail as population and industrialization continue to grow.

We must organize our efforts to sustain the earth on the basis of its watersheds, airsheds, and ecosystems instead of the neat geopolitical lines we draw on maps. This will require unprecedented cooperation between communities, states, and countries. Aquatic systems can't recover until we stop overloading their natural cleansing and renewal processes, but once we do, recovery is amazingly fast.

Individuals can contribute to bringing about this drastic change in the way we view and act in the world by reducing their contributions to water pollution (see Individuals Matter below).

The reason we have water pollution is not basically the paper or pulp mills. It is, rather, the social side of humans — our unwillingness to support reform government, to place into office the best-qualified candidates, to keep in office the best talent, and to see to it that legislation both evolves from and inspires wise social planning with a human orientation.

Stewart L. Udall

INDIVIDUALS MATTER What You Can Do

- Use commercial inorganic fertilizers, pesticides, detergents, bleaches, and other chemicals only if necessary and then in the smallest amounts possible.

- Use less-harmful substances for most household cleaners (see Individuals Matter inside the back cover).

- Use low-phosphate, phosphate-free, or biodegradable dishwashing liquid, laundry detergent, and shampoo.

- Don't use water fresheners in toilets.

- Contact your local Health Department about how to dispose of household hazardous and medical wastes. Don't pour products containing harmful chemicals, such as pesticides, paints, solvents, oil, and cleaning agents, down the drain or on the ground.

- Join with others to encourage your local Health Department or other agency to organize communitywide Household Hazardous-Waste Collection Days.

- Recycle old motor oil and antifreeze at an auto service center or auto parts center that has an oil recycling program.* If such a program is not available, pressure local officials or businesses

to start one. If disposed of improperly, the oil from one oil change can pollute 3.8 million liters (1 million gallons) of water. The amount of used motor oil improperly disposed of *each year* by Americans who change the oil in their cars themselves is 11 times the oil spilled by the *Exxon Valdez*.

- Use manure or compost instead of commercial inorganic fertilizers (Section 14-6) to fertilize garden and yard plants.

- Use biological methods or integrated pest management (Section 23-5) instead of commercial pesticides to control garden, yard, and household pests.

- Use and waste less water (see Individuals Matter inside the back cover).

- If you get water from a private well or suspect that municipally supplied water is contaminated, have it tested by an EPA-certified laboratory for lead, nitrates, trihalomethanes, radon, volatile organic compounds, and pesticides.[†]

- If you have a septic tank, monitor it yearly and have it cleaned out every three to five years by a reputable contractor so that it won't contribute to groundwater pollution. Do not use septic tank cleaners. They contain toxic chemicals that can kill bacteria important to sewage decomposition in the septic system and that can contaminate groundwater if the system malfunctions.

- If you are a boater, don't dump trash overboard and discharge boat sewage only into regulated onshore facilities.

- Support ecological land-use planning (see Spotlight on p. 245) in your local community.

- Get to know your local bodies of water, and form community watchdog groups to help monitor, protect, and restore them.

- Support tougher water pollution control laws and their enforcement at the local, state, and federal levels, with emphasis on pollution prevention.

[†]Check with local health officials, state environmental agencies, or the EPA for a list of certified laboratories. The following labs will send you a kit to collect tap water that you mail back for analysis: National Testing Laboratories (6151 Wilson Mills Rd., Cleveland, OH 44143, 800-458-3330); Suburban Water Testing Laboratories (4600 Kutztown Rd., Temple, PA 19560, 800-433-6595); and Water Test, 33 South Commercial St., Manchester, NH 03101, 800-426-8378.

*You can take used motor oil to auto service centers and auto parts centers operated by Jiffy Lube, Valvoline Instant Oil Change, Pep Boys stores, and Sears Auto Centers.

Philip R. Pryde

Philip R. Pryde is a specialist in land-use planning, water re-sources, energy resources, and environmental impact analysis in the Department of Geography at San Diego State University. He is also a leading U.S. expert on environmental problems and resource conservation in the USSR. He has served on the San Diego County Planning Commission and San Diego's Growth Management Review Task Force, and he is a director of the San Diego County Water Authority. In addition to numerous arti-cles, he is the author of Nonconventional Energy Resources *(Wiley, 1983) and* Environmental Management in the So-viet Union *(Cambridge University Press, 1991).*

Lake Baikal is perhaps the most remarkable lake in the world. It is located in the Soviet Union just north of the border with Mongolia and contains the world's largest volume of fresh water. At 1,620 meters (5,315 feet), it is also the world's deepest body of fresh water. It stretches for about 700 kilometers (434 miles) between steep moun-tain ranges, in a geological depression called a *graben*. The geological faults that produced the graben also subject the entire region to severe earthquakes.

However, the lake's uniqueness is not limited to its size. In Lake Baikal's unusually clear waters can be found about 1,700 species of plants and animals, 1,200 of which are not found anywhere else on Earth. Because of its uniqueness and scientific value, controversy over the po-tential pollution of Lake Baikal has drawn considerable interest, not just within the Soviet Union, but throughout the world.

Timber cutting and small industrial facilities have existed in the Lake Baikal basin for decades. But in the 1960s, plans were prepared for two new wood-processing plants to be built on its shores. To keep them supplied with timber, large increases were planned in the logging activities on the surrounding mountain slopes. That not only would be an eyesore but also could result in consid-erable erosion of soil into the lake.

Wood-processing plants of the type proposed produce large amounts of potential water pollutants. A debate be-gan almost immediately over whether the proposed waste-water treatment plants at the two factories would be adequate to preserve the quality of Lake Baikal's waters. This debate was noteworthy because it was the first major

environmental issue to be widely publicized in the Soviet press.

Despite the pleas of many leading Soviet scientists, artists, and writers, there was at that time little likelihood that the plans for the factories would be abandoned. The most feasible goal of the protestors was to ensure that the highest possible degree of protection would be provided for the lake. And indeed, in addition to more advanced wastewater treatment plants, several other safeguards to protect the lake were adopted.

A special decree was passed on the need to protect Lake Baikal, and a commission was appointed to monitor water quality in the lake. A later decision required that the wood pulp manufactured by the plants be trans-ported to other industrial centers for processing to pre-vent further addition of pollutants to Lake Baikal. Finally, natural reserves and other types of protected areas have been established around the lake.

As a result of all that controversy, planning, and re-planning, could people feel confident that Lake Baikal had been saved from pollution? Unfortunately, the differ-ences of opinion went on. The industrial planners contin-ued to defend their operations, claiming that no serious harm had come to the lake, that the treatment facilities were adequate, and that the lake itself could act as a puri-fier of pollutants.

But in the early 1980s, the chief Soviet scientist in charge of protecting the lake stated that he still had seri-ous doubts that the steps taken were sufficient. The prob-lem is that even a small amount of pollution, an amount that might be acceptable in an ordinary lake or river, could do irreversible harm in this unique body of water. Not all the pollutants discharged into the lake are degrad-able, and some are highly toxic. Further, it is known that wastewater purification facilities at the wood-processing plants have been closed down on more than one occasion for improvements.

Finally, in 1987, another decree was enacted that will convert one pulp mill by 1993 to furniture manufactur-ing, which involves much less pollution. A closed cycle water system will be built at the other pulp mill. Further reductions in timber cutting were also ordered. Thus, after decades of controversy, Lake Baikal's amazing store-house of biotic treasures, including many that are quite rare, may soon be in somewhat less jeopardy.

The Lake Baikal saga shows clearly that environmental pollution is a worldwide phenomenon inherent in any country experiencing large-scale industrial development. Its cure involves a combination of increased funding for improved pollution abatement facilities and the political determination to see that they are used effectively.

Guest Essay Discussion

1. Do you think that Soviet officials have done enough to protect Lake Baikal? Explain.

2. Compare these efforts with those to protect the Great Lakes in the United States (see Case Study on p. 609).

DISCUSSION TOPICS

1. Explain why dilution is not always the solution to water pollution. Give examples and conditions for which this solution is, and is not, applicable.

2. Explain how a stream can cleanse itself of oxygen-demanding wastes. Under what conditions will this natural cleansing system fail?

3. Explain why you agree or disagree with the idea that we should deliberately dump most of our wastes in the ocean because it is a vast sink for diluting, dispersing, and degrading wastes, and if it becomes polluted, we can get food from other sources.

4. Should all dumping of wastes in the ocean be banned? Explain. If so, where would you put those wastes? What exceptions, if any, would you permit? Under what circumstances? Explain why banning ocean dumping alone will not stop ocean pollution.

5. Should the injection of hazardous wastes into deep underground wells be banned? Explain. What would you do with these wastes?

*6. In your community:
   a. What are the principal nonpoint sources of contamination of surface water and groundwater?
   b. What is the source of drinking water?
   c. How is drinking water treated?
   d. What contaminants are tested for?
   e. Has drinking water been analyzed recently for the presence of synthetic organic chemicals, especially chlorinated hydrocarbons? If so, were any found and are they being removed?
   f. How many times during each of the past five years have levels of tested contaminants violated federal standards, and was the public notified about the violations?

CHAPTER 23

PESTICIDES AND

PEST CONTROL

General Questions and Issues

1. What principal types of pesticides are being used?

2. What are the advantages of using insecticides and herbicides?

3. What are the disadvantages of using insecticides and herbicides?

4. How is pesticide usage regulated in the United States?

5. What alternatives are there to using pesticides?

A weed is a plant whose virtues have not yet been discovered.

RALPH WALDO EMERSON

PEST IS ANY UNWANTED organism that directly or indirectly interferes with human activity. **Pests** compete with people for food, and some spread disease. Only about 100 of the at least 1 million cataloged insect species cause about 90% of damage to food crops. In diverse ecosystems, their populations are kept in control by a variety of natural enemies.

Since 1945, vast fields planted with only one crop or only a few crops, as well as homes, home gardens, and lawns, have been treated with a variety of chemicals called **pesticides** (or *biocides*): substances that can kill organisms that we consider to be undesirable. The most widely used types of pesticides are **insecticides** (insect killers), **herbicides** (weed killers), **fungicides** (fungus killers), **nematocides** (nematode killers), and **rodenticides** (rodent killers).

There is controversy over whether the harmful effects of these chemicals outweigh their benefits compared with other alternatives, as discussed in this chapter.

23-1 Pesticides: Types and Uses

THE IDEAL PESTICIDE The ideal pest-killing chemical would

- kill only the target pest
- have no short- or long-term health effects on nontarget organisms, including people
- be broken down into harmless chemicals in a fairly short time
- prevent the development of genetic resistance in target organisms
- save money compared with making no effort to control pest species

Unfortunately, no known pest control method meets all those criteria.

FIRST-GENERATION PESTICIDES Pesticides are not a modern invention. So-called *first-generation pesticides* included mostly persistent inorganic chemicals and nonpersistent organic compounds made or extracted from insect poisons produced by plants to ward off herbivores.

Sulfur was used as an insecticide well before 500 B.C. By the fifteenth century, inorganic compounds made from toxic metals such as arsenic, lead, and mercury were being applied to crops as insecticides. Use of those compounds continued until the late 1920s, when

633

there were enough poisonings and fatalities to encourage a search for less-toxic substitutes. Also, such toxic-metal insecticides contaminate the soil for 100 years or more. Traces of some of them are still being taken up by tobacco, vegetable, and other crops grown on soil that received heavy doses of toxic-metal pesticides decades ago.

In the seventeenth century, nicotine sulfate, extracted from tobacco leaves, was used as an insecticide. In the mid-1800s, two additional natural pesticides were introduced. One was rotenone, extracted from the root of the derris plant and other legumes that grow in tropical forests. It was first used by natives to paralyze fish. Later, it was used as an insecticide on crops and to control parasites on cattle, sheep, and humans. Today, chemists have modified the rotenone molecule to produce a variety of synthetic rotenoids used as insecticides.

The other natural pesticide was pyrethrum, which was obtained from the heads of chrysanthemum flowers (Figure 23-1). Other natural insecticides include red pepper (for ant control) and garlic oil and lemon oil (for use against fleas, mosquito larvae, houseflies, and other insects).

SECOND-GENERATION PESTICIDES A major revolution in insect pest control occurred in 1939 when entomologist Paul Mueller discovered that DDT (dichlorodiphenyltrichloroethane), a chemical known since 1874, was a potent insecticide. DDT soon became the most widely used pesticide in the world, and Paul Mueller received the Nobel Prize for Medicine in 1948 for his discovery. Worldwide, more than 1.8 million metric tons (2 million tons) of DDT have been used to control insects and insect-transmitted diseases since its discovery.

Since 1945, chemists have developed many synthetic organic chemicals for use as pesticides. Collectively, these chemicals are known as *second-generation pesticides*.

Worldwide, about 2.3 million metric tons (2.5 million tons) of these pesticides are used each year — an average of 0.45 kilogram (1 pound) for each person on Earth. About 85% of all pesticides are used in MDCs, but use in LDCs is growing rapidly and is projected to increase at least fourfold between 1985 and 2000. Nearly half of India's cropland is treated with pesticides, and pesticides are also widely used in Brazil and Mexico. Global sales of pesticides have risen from $3 billion in 1970 to $20 billion in 1990.

In the United States, about 600 biologically active ingredients and 1,475 inert (presumably biologically inactive) ingredients are mixed to make some 55,000 pesticide products. Between 1964 and 1981, pesticide use in the United States almost tripled, but since then, annual use has levelled off at around 500 million kilograms (1.1 billion pounds). At that rate, an average of 2.0 kilo-

Figure 23-1 The heads of these chrysanthemum flowers being grown in Kenya, Africa, contain a natural insecticide called pyrethrum. The flower heads are harvested and ground into a powder, which is used as a commercial insecticide. Natural pyrethrum was once widely used as a household insecticide because of its "knockdown" effect on flying insects and its low toxicity for mammals. However, it did not necessarily kill the insects it knocked down. Also, it is not suitable for use on crops because it is rapidly destroyed by sunlight. Since 1949, chemists have modified the natural pyrethrum molecule to produce a variety of more stable *synthetic pyrethroids*, which are used as insecticides in homes and on crops.

grams (4.4 pounds) of these products is used for each American each year. Pesticide sales in the United States in 1990 were about $5 billion, with half of that spent on herbicides.

Herbicides account for 69% of all pesticides used by American farmers, insecticides 19%, and fungicides 12%. Four crops — corn, cotton, wheat, and soybeans — account for about 70% of the insecticides and 80% of the herbicides used on crops in the United States. Fungicides are used primarily to treat seeds and to protect fruits and vegetables during growth and after harvest from fungal diseases.

About 20% of the pesticides used each year in the United States are applied to lawns, gardens, parks, golf courses, and cemeteries. The average homeowner in the United States applies about five times more pesticide per unit of land area than do farmers. Each year, Americans spend $1.5 billion on indoor pesticides and another $1.5 billion on pesticides used for lawn control.

PRINCIPAL TYPES OF INSECTICIDES AND HERBICIDES Most of the thousands of insecticides used today fall into one of four classes of compounds: chlorinated hydrocarbons, organophosphates, carbamates, or pyrethroids (Table 23-1). Most of these chemicals kill target and nontarget insects in the sprayed area by disrupting their nervous systems. These chemicals vary widely in their persistence, the length of time they remain active in killing insects (Table 23-1).

Table 23-1 Principal Types of Insecticides

Type	Examples	Persistence
Chlorinated hydrocarbons	DDT, aldrin, dieldrin, endrin, heptachlor, toxaphene, lindane, chlordane, kepone, mirex	High (2–15 years)
Organophosphates	Malathion, parathion, monocrotophos, methamidophos, methyl parathion, DDVP	Low to moderate (normally 1–12 weeks, but some can last several years)
Carbamates	Carbaryl, maneb, priopoxor, mexica-bate, aldicarb, aminocarb	Usually low (days to weeks)
Pyrethroids	Pemethrin, decamethrin	Usually low (days to weeks)

Table 23-2 Principal Types of Herbicides

Type	Examples	Effects
Contact	Triazines such as atrazine and paraquat	Kills foliage by interfering with photosynthesis
Systemic	Phenoxy compounds such as 2,4-D, 2,4,5-T, and Silvex; substituted ureas such as diuron, norea, fenuron, and other nitrogen-containing compounds such as daminozide (Alar), glyphosate	Absorption creates excess growth hormones; plants die because they cannot obtain enough nutrients to sustain their greatly accelerated growth
Soil sterilants	Trifluralin, diphenamid, dalapon, butylate	Kills soil microorganisms essential to plant growth; most also act as systemic herbicides.

By the mid-1970s, DDT and most other slowly degradable, chlorinated hydrocarbon insecticides shown in Table 23-1 (except lindane) were banned or severely restricted in the United States and most MDCs. However, many of these compounds are still produced in the United States and exported to other countries, mostly LDCs, where they have not been banned.

In the United States and most MDCs, chlorinated hydrocarbon insecticides have been replaced by a number of more rapidly degradable pesticides, especially organophosphates and carbamates (Table 23-1). Organophosphate insecticides resulted from research on developing extremely toxic nerve gases for use during wartime.

However, some of these compounds, especially organophosphates such as parathion, are more toxic to birds, people, and other mammals than the chlorinated hydrocarbon insecticides they replaced. They are also more likely to contaminate surface water and groundwater because they are water soluble, whereas chlorinated hydrocarbon insecticides are insoluble in water but soluble in fats. Furthermore, to compensate for their fairly rapid breakdown, farmers usually apply nonper-

sistent insecticides at regular intervals to ensure more effective insect control. That means they are often present in the environment almost continuously, like the slowly degradable pesticides they replaced. However, malathion, another organophosphate insecticide, has a low mammalian toxicity and is widely used on crops and in homes.

Other insecticides resulted from learning how wild plants, especially tropical species, produce chemical compounds that repel insects or inhibit their feeding. Today, synthetic pyrethroids (Figure 23-1) and synthetic rotenoids made by altering the natural insecticide molecules in chrysanthemum flowers (Figure 23-1) and the roots of certain legumes are widely used as insecticides in homes and on crops. Both types of compounds are biodegradable, are effective at low doses, and cause little harm to birds and mammals, including humans.

Herbicides can be placed into three classes, based on their effect on plants: contact herbicides, systemic herbicides, and soil sterilants (Table 23-2). Most herbicides are active for only a short time. In the United States and most MDCs, the use of 2,4,5-T and Silvex has been banned.

23-2 The Case for Pesticides

Proponents of pesticides believe that the benefits of pesticides outweigh their harmful effects. They point out the following benefits:

- *Pesticides save lives.* Since World War II, DDT and other chlorinated hydrocarbon and organophosphate insecticides have probably prevented the premature deaths of at least 7 million people from insect-transmitted diseases such as malaria (carried by the *Anopheles* mosquito, Figure 20-5), bubonic plague (rat fleas), typhus (body lice and fleas), and sleeping sickness (tsetse fly).

- *They increase food supplies and lower food costs.* Each year, about 55% of the world's potential food supply is lost to pests before (35%) and after (20%) harvest. Proponents argue that without pesticides, those losses would be much higher and food prices would increase (perhaps by 30% to 50% in the United States).

- *They increase profits for farmers.* In the United States, 42% of the annual potential food supply is destroyed by pests before and after harvest. Pesticide companies estimate that every $1 spent on pesticides leads to an increase in crop yield worth $3 to $5 to farmers.

- *They work faster and better than other alternatives.* Compared with alternative methods of pest control, pesticides can control most pests quickly and at a reasonable cost, have a relatively long shelf life, are easily shipped and applied, and are safe when handled properly. When genetic resistance occurs in pest insects and weeds, farmers can usually keep them under control by using stronger doses or switching to other pesticides.

- *The health risks of pesticides are insignificant compared with their health and other benefits.* According to Elizabeth Whelan, director of the American Council on Science and Health (ACSH), which presents the position of the pesticide industry, "The reality is that pesticides, when used in the approved regulatory manner, pose no risk to either farm workers or consumers." Will Carpenter, president of Monsanto Agricultural Company, claims that "pesticides are safe and the food supply in the United States is safer than it has ever been." ACSH and pesticide industry scientists argue that most consumers do not realize that the health risk studies carried out by the pesticide industry (as required by law) and by independent researchers are highly unlikely worst-case scenarios. They also point out that the EPA sets maximum allowable levels of pesticide residues in food many times below the levels at which harmful health effects in people are likely to occur. They call the pesticide health-scare stories often appearing in the media examples of scientific distortion and irresponsible reporting.

- *Safer and more effective products are continually being developed.* Pesticide company scientists are continually developing pesticides, such as pyrethroids (Table 23-1), that are safer to use and that cause less ecological damage. New herbicides are being developed that are effective at very low dosage rates. Genetic engineering also holds promise (see Pro/Con on p. 161). However, the costs for research and development and government approval for a single pesticide have risen from $6 million in 1976 to more than $40 million today, explaining why pesticide prices have risen sharply.

23-3 The Case Against Pesticides

DEVELOPMENT OF GENETIC RESISTANCE The most serious drawback to using chemicals to control pests is that most pest species, especially insects, can develop genetic resistance to a chemical poison through natural selection (Section 6-3). When an area is sprayed with a pesticide, most of the pest organisms are killed. However, a few organisms in a large population of a particular species usually survive because they have genes that make them resistant or immune to a specific pesticide.

Most pest species—especially insects and disease organisms—can produce a large number of similarly resistant offspring in a short time. For example, the boll weevil (Figure 23-2), a major cotton pest, can produce a new generation every 21 days.

When populations of offspring of resistant parents are repeatedly sprayed with the same pesticide, each succeeding generation contains a higher percentage of resistant organisms. Thus, eventually, widely used pesticides (especially insecticides) fail because of genetic resistance and usually lead to even larger populations of pest species, especially insects with large numbers of offspring and short generation times. In temperate regions, most insects develop genetic resistance to a chemical poison within five to ten years and much sooner in tropical areas. Weeds and plant disease organisms also develop genetic resistance, but not as quickly as most insects.

Since 1950, at least 440 major insect pest species have developed genetic resistance to one or more insecticides, and at least 20 insect species are now apparently immune to all widely used insecticides. It is estimated that by the year 2000, virtually all major insect pest species will show some form of genetic resistance. About 80 species of the more than 500 major weed species are resistant to one or more herbicides. Because half of all pesticides applied worldwide are herbicides, genetic resistance in weeds is expected to increase significantly. Genetic resistance has also appeared in 70 species of fungi treated with fungicides and in 10 species of rodents (mostly rats) treated with rodenticides.

Because of genetic resistance, most widely used insecticides no longer protect people from insect-transmitted diseases in many parts of the world , leading to even more serious outbreaks of disease. That is the primary reason for the almost 10 fold increase in malaria between 1970 and 1988 in 84 tropical and subtropical countries (see Case Study on p. 548).

KILLING OF NATURAL PEST ENEMIES AND CONVERSION OF MINOR PESTS INTO MAJOR PESTS

Most insecticides are broad-spectrum poisons that kill not only the target pest species but also a number of natural predators and parasites that may have been maintaining the pest species at a reasonable level. Without sufficient natural enemies, and with much food available, a rapidly reproducing insect pest species can make a strong comeback a few days or weeks after initially being controlled.

The use of broad-spectrum insecticides also kills off the natural enemies of many minor pests. Then their numbers can increase greatly and they become major pests. That was the case with the boll worm. As cotton farmers used huge and repeated doses of insecticides to control the boll weevil (Figure 23-2), they also destroyed the natural predators of the boll worm. Without predators, the boll worm became a major pest. This is an example of harmful runaway feedback.

THE PESTICIDE TREADMILL

When genetic resistance develops, pesticide sales representatives usually recommend more frequent applications, stronger doses, or a switch to new (usually more expensive) chemicals to keep the resistant species under control, rather than suggesting nonchemical alternatives. That puts farmers on an accelerating **pesticide treadmill**, in which they pay more and more for a pest control program that becomes less and less effective.

A 1989 study by David Pimentel (see Guest Essay on p. 330), an expert in insect ecology, revealed that increased pesticide use in the United States has not led to a corresponding reduction in pests. That study, based on data from more than 300 agricultural scientists and economists, concluded that

- Although the amount of synthetic pesticides used in the United States has increased 33-fold since the 1940s, U.S. crop losses to pests have increased from about 31% in the 1940s to about 37% today.

- Since the 1940s, losses to insects have nearly doubled, from 7.1% to 13%, despite a more than 10-fold increase in the amount and toxicity of synthetic insecticides.

Figure 23-2   In the cotton fields of the southern United States, there may be as many as six generations of cotton boll weevils in one growing season. Controlling the cotton boll weevil accounts for at least 25% of the pesticides used in the United States. However, farmers are now increasing their use of natural predators and other biological methods to control this major pest.

- Losses to plant pathogens increased slightly, from 10% to 12%, since the 1940s, and losses to weeds declined slightly, from 13.8% to 12%.

- The estimated environmental, health, and social costs of pesticide use in the United States range from $4 billion to $10 billion a year.

- Use of alternative pest control practices (Section 23-5) could cut the use of chemical pesticides in the United States in half without any reduction in crop yields.

- A 50% cut in pesticide use in the United States would cause food prices to rise by only 0.6%. This rise would cost consumers $1 billion a year, but it would be more than offset by an estimated $2-billion to $5-billion reduction in environmental, health, and social costs.

MOBILITY AND BIOLOGICAL AMPLIFICATION OF PERSISTENT PESTICIDES

Pesticides don't stay put. According to the U.S. Department of Agriculture, only 1% to 2% (and often less than 0.1%) of the insecticides applied to crops by aerial spraying (Figure 23-3) or ground spraying reach the target pests. Less than 5% of herbicides applied to crops reach the target weeds.

The 95% to 99% of pesticides not reaching target pests end up in the soil, air, surface water, groundwater, bottom sediment, food, and nontarget organisms, including people and even penguins in the Antarctic (Figure 19-6). Concentrations of fat-soluble, slowly degradable insecticides such as DDT, PCBs, and other chlorinated hydrocarbons (Table 23-1) can be biologically amplified thousands to millions of times in food chains and webs (Figures 16-18 and 22-4).

Figure 23-3 Crop duster spraying a pesticide on grapevines south of Fresno, California. Typically, no more than 2%, and often as little as 0.1%, of the chemical being applied reaches the target organisms. Aircraft are used to apply 60% of the pesticides used on croplands in the United States.

National Archives/EPA Documerica

Pesticide waste can be reduced by using recirculating sprayers that catch pesticides that miss their targets the first time, placing shrouds around spray booms to reduce drift, and using rope-wick applicators, which deliver herbicides directly to weeds and reduce herbicide use by 90%. Substituting such methods for aerial spraying increases the amount of pesticide reaching target organisms by 75%.

THREATS TO WILDLIFE Each year, an estimated 20% of all honeybee colonies in the U.S. are killed by pesticides, and an additional 15% of the colonies are damaged, causing annual losses of at least $206 million from reduced pollination of vital crops. Pesticide runoff from cropland is a leading cause of fish kills in the United States and in other countries.

During the 1950s and 1960s, there were drastic declines in populations of fish-eating birds such as the osprey, cormorant, brown pelican (Figure 2-7), and bald eagle (Figure 2-10). There were also sharp declines in populations of predatory birds such as the prairie falcon, sparrow hawk, and peregrine falcon (Figure 16-13); these birds help control populations of rabbits,

ground squirrels, and other crop-damaging small mammals (see Spotlight on p. 420).

SHORT-TERM THREATS TO HUMAN HEALTH FROM PESTICIDE USE AND MANUFACTURE The World Health Organization estimates that each year, between 500,000 and 1 million people are poisoned by pesticides and 5,000 to 20,600 of them die. At least half of those poisoned, and 75% of those killed, are farm workers in LDCs, where educational levels are low, warnings are few, and pesticide regulation and control methods are often lax or nonexistent. The actual number of pesticide-related illnesses among farm workers in the United States and throughout the world is probably greatly underestimated because of poor records, lack of doctors and reporting in rural areas, and faulty diagnoses.

Each year, about 45,000 cases of pesticide poisoning, most involving children, are reported in the United States, including 3,000 hospital admissions and 200 deaths. The majority of the poisonings occur because of unsafe use or storage of pesticides in and around the home. In the United States, pesticides are the second most frequent cause of poisoning in young children, following medicines.

Each year, an estimated 10,000 Americans get some form of cancer, mostly from the handling of pesticides by farmers, pesticide plant workers, pesticide applicators, crop pickers, and home gardeners, all of whom are repeatedly exposed directly to much higher levels of pesticides than the rest of society. Accidents and unsafe practices in pesticide plants can expose workers, their families, and sometimes the general public to harmful levels of pesticides or chemicals used in their manufacture (see Case Study on p. 639).

LONG-TERM THREATS TO HUMAN HEALTH According to the Food and Drug Administration, about 40% of the food bought in supermarkets contains detectable residues of one or more of the active ingredients used in pesticides in the United States. Approximately 3% of this food has levels of one or more pesticides above the legal limit. Pesticide residues are especially likely to be found in tomatoes, grapes, apples, lettuce, oranges, potatoes, beef, and dairy products. The results of this long-term worldwide experiment, with people involuntarily playing the role of guinea pigs, may never be known because it is almost impossible to determine that a certain level of specific chemical caused a particular cancer or some other harmful effect (Section 20-1).

In 1987, the National Academy of Sciences reported that the active ingredients in 90% of all fungicides, 60% of all herbicides, and 30% of all insecticides in use in the United States may cause cancer in humans. According to the *worst-case estimate* in this study, exposure to pesticides in food causes 4,000 to 20,000 cases of cancer a year in the United States. In 1987, the EPA ranked

In 1984, the world's worst industrial accident occurred at a Union Carbide pesticide plant in Bhopal, India. An estimated 3,700 people were killed and 300,000 more were injured when about 36 metric tons (40 tons) of highly toxic methyl isocyanate gas, used in the manufacture of carbamate pesticides, leaked from a storage tank. About 2,800 people lost their jobs when the plant was permanently closed.

The Indian Supreme Court ordered Union Carbide to pay a $470-million settlement and dropped criminal charges against the company. The Indian government has challenged the ruling, arguing that the settlement is inadequate and that the court had no constitutional right to drop the criminal charges.

Union Carbide probably could have prevented this tragedy, which cost at least $570 million, by spending no more than $1 million to improve plant safety.

---

pesticide residues in foods as the third most serious environmental health threat in the United States (after worker exposure and indoor radon) in terms of cancer risk.

Cancer is only one possible harmful effect of long-term exposure to low levels of pesticides. Some scientists are becoming increasingly concerned about possible genetic mutations, birth defects, disorders of the nervous system, and effects on the immune and endocrine systems from long-term exposure to low levels of pesticides. The EPA requires studies of some of these effects on new pesticides, but critics argue that these effects are not studied sufficiently for new pesticides and have been poorly evaluated for most of 600 older chemicals still in widespread use in pesticides.

Critics also argue that the health effects of low-level pesticide residues on children are not given enough weight in risk analysis, although EPA officials deny the charge. It is also argued that the long-term health risks from pesticides are too narrowly focused on pesticide exposure from food. While this is important, many people can be exposed to much higher levels of pesticides from community spraying programs used to control mosquitoes or other insect pests; pesticide-sprayed lawns, parks, golf courses, and roadsides; and living near sprayed croplands, rangelands, and forests. There is also controversy over the effects on American soldiers who were exposed to herbicides sprayed as defoliants during the Vietnam War (see Spotlight at right).

Between 1962 and 1970, large amounts of Agent Orange, a 50-50 mixture of the herbicides 2,4-D and 2,4,5-T, were sprayed to defoliate swamps and forests in Southeast Asia during the Vietnam War. Since 1985, 2,4,5-T has been banned by the EPA for use in the United States. However, 2,4-D is the third most widely used pesticide in the United States.

Some 35,000 Vietnam veterans have filed claims with the Veterans Administration for disabilities allegedly caused by exposure to Agent Orange. The Veterans Administration and chemical manufacturers of Agent Orange, however, continue to deny any connection between the medical disorders and Agent Orange, and attribute the problems to the post-Vietnam stress syndrome. In 1984, the companies making Agent Orange agreed to a $180-million out-of-court settlement with about 9,300 Vietnam veterans, without admitting any guilt or connection between the disorders and the use of the herbicide.

In 1988, an epidemiologic study provided evidence strongly linking many of the health problems of military veterans with exposure to TCDD, a highly toxic dioxin, formed in minute quantities as a contaminant during the manufacture of 2,4,5-T. In 1989, a federal court ordered the Veterans Administration to reconsider the claims of the veterans exposed to Agent Orange.

In 1990, a study by the Centers for Disease Control (CDC) found no evidence linking Agent Orange to an increased risk of getting a rare, fatal cancer called non-Hodgkin's lymphoma. Other scientists have criticized this study for being incomplete because of refusal of the Defense Department to provide all of its records and for suppressing reports from the National Academy of Sciences that challenged CDC conclusions. In 1991, two new studies by the Air Force and the Veterans Affairs Department found little, if any, health impact on Vietnam veterans exposed to Agent Orange and its TCDD contaminant.

In 1989, National Cancer Institute scientists reported as much as a three-fold increase in non-Hodgkin's lymphoma in Nebraska farmers who mixed or applied 2,4-D. In 1990, an independent scientific review of 285 studies of the effects of Agent Orange on humans concluded that there is a significant statistical association between exposure to the herbicide Agent Orange and various cancers (non-Hodgkin's lymphoma and soft-tissue sarcomas), serious skin disorders (chloracne), and liver disorders.

23-4 Pesticide Regulation in the United States

IS THE PUBLIC ADEQUATELY PROTECTED? Because of the potentially harmful effects of pesticides on wildlife and people, Congress passed the Federal Insecticide, Fungicide, and Rodenticide Act (FIFRA) in 1972. This law, which was amended in 1975, 1978, and 1988, requires that all commercial pesticides be approved for general or restricted use by the Environmental Protection Agency.

Approval is based mostly on an evaluation of the safety of the chemicals that pesticide companies designate as biologically active ingredients in their pesticide products. These data are submitted to the EPA by the companies seeking approval and must include test data on the potential to cause adverse short- and long-term effects in humans, fish, wildlife, and endangered species. Data must also be included on the environmental fate of the active ingredients so that the EPA can evaluate, among other things, whether these chemicals pose a threat to surface water or groundwater.

Since 1972, the EPA has used this law to ban the use, except for emergencies, of over 50 pesticides because of their potential hazards to human health. The banned chemicals include most chlorinated hydrocarbon insecticides, several carbamates and organophosphates (Table 23-1), and several herbicides, such as 2,4,5-T and Silvex (Table 23-2).

However, according to a 1988 report by the National Academy of Sciences, federal laws regulating the use of pesticides in the United States are inadequate and poorly enforced by the Food and Drug Administration (FDA) and the EPA (see Spotlight on p. 641).

23-5 Alternative Methods of Insect Control

MODIFYING CULTIVATION PROCEDURES Opponents of the widespread use of pesticides argue that there are many safer, and in the long-run cheaper and more effective, alternatives to the use of pesticides by farmers and homeowners. For centuries, farmers have used cultivation methods that discourage or inhibit pests. Examples are

- *Crop rotation*, in which the types of crops planted in fields are changed from year to year so that populations of pests that attack a particular crop don't have time to multiply to uncontrollable sizes.

- *Planting rows of hedges or trees in and around crop fields* to act as barriers to invasions by insect pests, provide habitats for their natural enemies, and serve as windbreaks to reduce soil erosion (Figure 12-17).

- *Adjusting planting times* to ensure that most major insect pests either starve to death before the crop is available or are consumed by their natural predators.

- *Gowing crops in areas where their major pests do not exist*. This would be aided by removal of government price-support programs that encourage growing of crops in certain regions. With such changes, farmers would find it more profitable to grow cotton in areas with fewer cotton pests than the Southeast, such as Texas, Arizona, and California.

- *Switching from monocultures to modernized versions of intercropping, agroforestry, and polyculture* that use plant diversity to help control pests (Section 14-6).

- *Removing diseased or infected plants and stalks and other crop residues that harbor pests*.

- *Using photodegradable plastic to prevent growth of weeds between rows of some crops*.

- *Using denser planting patterns to crowd out weeds among some crops and mowing weeds around other crops instead of using herbicides*.

- *Using vacuum machines that gently remove bugs from plants*.

Unfortunately, to increase profits, qualify for government subsidies, and, in some cases, avoid bankruptcy, many farmers in MDCs such as the United States have abandoned these cultivation methods.

ARTIFICIAL SELECTION, CROSSBREEDING, AND GENETIC ENGINEERING Varieties of plants and animals that are genetically resistant to certain pest insects, fungi, and diseases can be developed. New varieties usually take a long time (10 to 20 years) to develop by conventional methods and are costly.

However, insect pests and plant diseases can develop new strains that attack the once-resistant varieties, forcing scientists to continually develop new resistant strains. Genetic engineering techniques are now being used to develop resistant crops (Figure 23-4) and animals more rapidly (see Pro/Con on p. 161).

BIOLOGICAL CONTROL Various natural predators (Figure 23-5), parasites, and pathogens (disease-causing bacteria and viruses) can be introduced or imported to regulate the populations of specific pests. Worldwide, more than 300 biological pest control projects have been successful, especially in China and the Soviet Union. In Nigeria, crop-spraying planes release parasitic wasps instead of pesticides in a biological assault on the cassava mealybug. Farmers get a $178 return for

Numerous studies by the National Academy of Sciences and the General Accounting Office have shown that the weakest and most poorly enforced U.S. environmental law in the United States is the Federal Insecticide, Fungicide, and Rodenticide Act (FIFRA) of 1972 and its subsequent amendments.

This act required the EPA to reevaluate the 600 active ingredients approved for use in pesticide products before 1972 to determine whether any of them caused cancer, birth defects, or other health risks. The EPA was supposed to complete its analysis by 1975 using data submitted by pesticide manufacturers, but it failed to do so.

In 1987, Congress extended the deadline for completing the review to 1997, but many observers believe that this deadline will not be met. By 1989, the EPA had carried out preliminary assessment of only 139 of these chemicals and had completed its review on only 2 of them. The EPA claims that Congress has not appropriated enough money for it to do the job.

According to the National Academy of Sciences, up to 98% of the potential risk of developing cancer from pesticide residues on food grown in the United States would be eliminated if the EPA set the same stricter standards for pesticides registered for use before 1972 as it has for those registered after 1972.

It has also become clear that many of the 1,475 so-called inert or biologically inactive ingredients in pesticide products are in fact biologically active and can cause harm to people and some forms of wildlife. So far, most of these chemicals have not been tested and none of them has been banned, mostly because they are not covered by the present pesticide law.

This law also allows the EPA to leave inadequately tested pesticides on the market and to license new chemicals without full health and safety data. It also gives the EPA unlimited time to remove a chemical when its health and environmental effects are shown to outweigh its economic benefits. The appeals and other procedures built into the law often allow a dangerous chemical to remain on the market for up to ten years.

The EPA can immediately cancel the use of a chemical on an emergency basis. Until 1990, however, the law required the EPA to use its already severely limited funds to compensate pesticide manufacturers for their remaining inventory and for all the costs of storing and disposing of the banned pesticide. This provision made it very difficult for the EPA to cancel a chemical quickly. For only one chemical, compensation costs could amount to more than the agency's pesticide budget for one year. Usually, therefore, the only economically feasible solution has been for the EPA to allow existing stocks of a chemical that should be banned immediately to be sold.

After 20 years of pressure from environmentalists, Congress passed several new amendments to the federal pesticide law in 1988. One of those amendments shifts some, but not all, of the costs of banning and disposing of banned pesticides from the EPA to companies making the chemicals.

Environmentalists consider the 1988 amendments better than nothing, but they point out that the law still has numerous weaknesses and loopholes. One loophole allows the sale in the United States of a number of insecticide products containing as much as 15% DDT by weight, classified as an impurity. These products, along with others illegally smuggled into the United States (mostly from Mexico), are believed to be responsible for increases in DDT levels in some vulnerable forms of wildlife and on some fruits and vegetables grown and sold in the United States (especially in California).

Also, this law is the only major environmental statute that does not provide for citizen lawsuits against the EPA for violations in enforcing the law, an essential tool to assure government compliance with a law.

Environmentalists consider it a human tragedy that the U.S. pesticide control statute is the nation's weakest and most poorly enforced environmental law when the EPA ranks pesticide residues in food as the third most serious environmental health threat in the country in terms of cancer risk. This is a testimony to the economic and political power of pesticide producers and the unwillingness of citizens to elect people who will protect their health.

Each year, the Food and Drug Administration inspectors check less than 1% (about 12,000 samples) of domestic and imported food for pesticide contamination. Furthermore, the FDA's turnaround time for food analysis is so long that about half of contaminated foods have been sold and eaten by the time the contamination is detected. Even when contaminated food is found, the growers and importers are rarely penalized.

Pesticide companies can make and export to other countries pesticides that have been banned in the United States or that have not been submitted to the EPA for approval. The United States leads the world in pesticide exports, followed by the former West Germany and the United Kingdom.

About one-fourth of the 455,000 metric tons (500,000 tons) of pesticides exported by U.S. companies each year are banned for use in the United States. That means that on average, 5.5 metric tons (6 tons) of pesticides banned for use in the United States are shipped to other countries *each hour*.

In what environmentalists call a *circle of poison*, residues of some of these banned chemicals return to the United States as pesticide resi-

(continued)

dues on imported coffee, fruits, and vegetables. One-fourth of the produce sold in the United States is imported, and an estimated 10% of that is contaminated with pesticides banned for use in the United States.

Environmentalists have pressured Congress to halt all export of pesticides banned or not approved for use in the United States and to bar imports of food treated with such chemicals. They believe that it is morally wrong for the United States to export pesticides that we have determined to be a serious risk to human health to other countries and to allow food with residues of those pesticides to be imported for use by U.S. consumers.

President Bush opposes such a ban. He argues that such a decision should be a two-way one between the United States and the importing country, that unilateral bans will not work, and that since the chemicals can be purchased from other countries, the United States shouldn't lose this business.

If the newest version of the General Agreement on Tariffs and Trade (GATT) treaty on international trade goes into effect, no country or state would be able to have stricter regulations on pesticide residues on imported goods than international standards unless it paid importers a fee to make up for their extra costs. Although many U.S. pesticide residue standards are higher than international standards, the Bush administration, backed by the food and pesticide industries, favors this international levelling of health and pollution standards.

Environmentalists charge that this law deters a country from imposing higher health and pollution standards for its citizens, prevents any state from passing laws that are stricter than federal regulations, and severely limits the ability of the public to participate in the development of pesticide and pollution regulations (which would be developed mostly behind closed doors by international commissions).

The outward goal of this harmonization of international standards is to prevent countries from imposing protectionist measures in the guise of health and safety regulations. However, environmentalists fear that it is a way for food and other industries to weaken food and pollution control laws, or at least prevent them from being strengthened. The U.S. delegation to the international commission to evaluate standards for food products included numerous executives from the food and pesticide industries but no representatives from environmental, consumer, or farm interests. Environmentalists believe that unfair trade sanctions should be investigated and treated on a case-by-case basis instead of by imposing international standards that some countries and states may consider too weak.

What, if anything, do you think should be done to provide more protection for the public from contamination of food and drinking water by traces of numerous pesticides?

Figure 23-4 Use of genetic engineering to reduce pest damage. Both of these tomato plants were exposed to destructive caterpillars. The foliage on the normal tomato plant on the left has been almost completely eaten, while the genetically engineered plant on the right shows few signs of damage.

every $1 they spend on the wasps. In the United States, natural enemies (pathogens, predators, and insect pathogens) have been used to control about 70 insect pests, and the use of biological control is increasing rapidly as more farmers seek alternatives to conventional chemical pesticides.

Bacillus thuringiensis, a bacterial agent, is a registered pesticide sold commercially as a dry powder. By choosing which of the thousands of strains of this microorganism to use, companies selling this biological agent can tailor their products to combat a variety of pests. Sales are soaring, and by 1990, there were 42 of these and other biological pesticides on the market.

A gene from *Bacillus thuringiensis* has been transferred to cotton plants. These plants then produce a protein that disrupts the digestive system of pests. Insects that bite the plant die within a few hours. Other applications of genetic engineering are expanding the effectiveness of this bacterial agent.

Researchers have also sealed insect nematodes, parasitic worms that kill many household and agricultural insect pests, in a gelatinous capsule that also con-

Figure 23-5 Biological control of pests. An adult convergent ladybug is consuming an aphid (left). The wolf spider, like most spiders, is harmless to humans and plays an important role in keeping insects in check (right).

tains a specific insect attractant, a feeding stimulant, and food for the nematodes. When a target insect eats the tiny capsule, the nematodes enter its body, feed on its tissues, and kill it within two days.

Other examples of biological control include the use of

- *Guard dogs* to protect livestock from predators. Guard dogs are more effective and cost less than erecting fences and shooting, trapping, and poisoning predators (see Pro/Con on p. 403), methods that sometimes kill nontarget organisms, including people.

- *Ducks* to devour insects and slugs. However, ducks sometimes damage vegetables, especially leafy greens, and should be kept out of those parts of gardens.

- *Geese* for weeding orchards, eating fallen and rotting fruit (often a source of pest problems), and controlling grass in gardens and nurseries. Geese also warn of approaching predators or people by honking loudly.

- *Chickens* to control insects and weeds and to increase the nitrogen content of the soil in orchards or in gardens after plants have become well established.

- *Birds* to eat insects. Farmers and homeowners can provide habitats and nesting sites that attract woodpeckers, purple martins, chickadees, barn swallows, nuthatches, and other insect-eating species.

- *Spiders* to eat insects (Figure 23-5). Spiders are insects' worst enemies, devouring enough bugs worldwide in a single day to outweigh the entire human population. Leaving strips of weeds around soybean and cotton fields provides habitats for wolf spiders (Figure 23-5), which devour most insect pests for free. One type of banana spider, harmless to humans, can keep a house clear of cockroaches. Most spiders, except the brown

recluse and the black widow, are harmless to humans.

- *Allelopathic plants* that naturally produce chemicals that are toxic to their weed competitors or that repel or poison their insect pests. For example, certain varieties of barley, wheat, rye, sorghum, and Sudan grass can be grown in gardens or orchard trees to suppress weeds. Plant combinations that help protect against various insect pests include cassavas and beans, potatoes and mustard greens, and a mixture of sunflowers, maize, oats, and sesame. Peppermint can be planted around houses to repel ants and to be used as a natural mouth freshener (pull off a leaf, wash it, and chew it) and a cooking spice.

Biological control has a number of advantages. Normally, it affects only the target species and is nontoxic to other species, including people. Once a population of natural predators or parasites is established, control of pest species is often self-perpetuating. Development of genetic resistance is minimized because both pest and predator species usually undergo natural selection to maintain a stable interaction (coevolution). In the United States, biological control has saved farmers an average of $25 for every $1 invested in pesticides.

No method of pest control, however, is perfect. Typically, 10 to 20 years of research may be required to understand how a particular pest interacts with its various enemies and to determine the best biological control agent. Mass production of biological agents is often difficult, and farmers find that they are slower to act and harder to apply than pesticides.

Biological agents must be protected from pesticides sprayed in nearby fields, and there is a chance that some can later also become pests; others (such as praying mantises) may also devour other beneficial insects. In addition, some pest organisms can develop genetic resistance to viruses and bacterial agents used for biological control.

INSECT STERILIZATION Males of some insect pest species can be raised in the laboratory and sterilized by radiation or chemicals, then released in large numbers in an infested area to mate unsuccessfully with fertile wild females. If sterile males outnumber fertile males by ten to one, a pest species in a given area can be eradicated in about four generations, provided reinfestation does not occur.

This technique works best if the females mate only once, if the infested area is isolated so that it can't be periodically repopulated with nonsterilized males, and if the insect pest population has already been reduced to a fairly low level by weather, pesticides, or other factors. Success is also increased if only the sexiest—the loudest, fastest, and largest—males are sterilized.

The screwworm fly is a major livestock pest in South America, Central America, and the southeastern and southwestern United States. This metallic blue-green insect, about two to three times the size of the common housefly, deposits its eggs in open wounds of warm-blooded animals such as cattle and deer. Within a few hours the eggs hatch into parasitic larvae that feed on the flesh of the host animal (Figure 23-6). A severe infestation of this pest can kill a mature steer within ten days.

The Department of Agriculture used the sterile-male approach to essentially eliminate the screwworm fly from the southeastern states between 1962 and 1971. In 1972, however, the pest made a dramatic comeback, infesting 100,000 cattle and causing serious losses until 1976, when a new strain of the males was developed, sterilized, and released to bring the situation under temporary control. To prevent resurgences of this pest, new strains of sterile male flies have to be developed, sterilized, and released every few years. This approach is also being used in an attempt to reduce populations of fruit flies in Florida.

Serious problems with this approach include ensuring that sterile males are not overwhelmed numerically by nonsterile males, needing to know the mating times and behavior of each target insect, preventing reinfestation by new nonsterilized males, and high costs.

INSECT SEX ATTRACTANTS In many insect species, when a virgin female is ready to mate, she releases a minute amount (typically about one-millionth of a gram) of a species-specific chemical sex attractant called a *pheromone*. Pheromones can be extracted from an insect pest species or synthesized in the laboratory. They are then used in minute amounts to lure pests into traps containing toxic chemicals or to attract natural predators of insect pests into crop fields. In 1991, Cornell University scientists announced development of a pheromone that confuses male grape berry moths. Its use could take the place of half the pesticides sprayed over vineyards throughout the eastern United States and Canada.

Figure 23-6 Infestation of a steer by screwworm fly larvae. A fully grown steer can be killed in ten days from thousands of maggots feeding on a single wound.

Figure 23-7 A lemon infested with red scale mites. Pheromones are now being used to help control red scale mites.

Research indicates that instead of using pheromones to trap pests, it is more effective to use them to lure the pests' natural predators into fields and gardens. Scientists have identified sex-attractant pheromones for more than 436 insect species. Worldwide, more than 50 companies sell about 250 of these pheromones to control pests (Figure 23-7).

These chemicals work on only one species, are effective in trace amounts, have little chance of causing genetic resistance, and are not harmful to nontarget species. However, it is costly and time-consuming to identify, isolate, and produce the specific sex attractant for each pest or natural predator species. Pheromones have also failed for some pests because only adults are drawn to the traps; for most species, the juvenile forms—such as caterpillars—do most of the damage.

INSECT HORMONES Hormones are chemicals, produced in an organism's cells, that travel through the bloodstream and control various aspects of the organ-

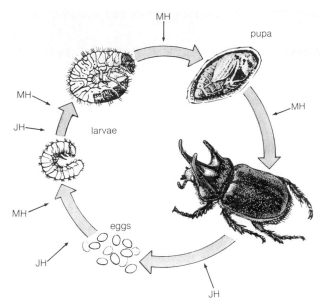

Figure 23-8 For normal growth, development, and reproduction, certain juvenile hormones (JH) and molting hormones (MH) must be present at genetically determined stages in the typical life cycle of an insect. If applied at the right time, synthetic hormones can be used to disrupt the life cycle of insect pests.

ism's growth and development. Each step in the life cycle of a typical insect is regulated by the timely release of juvenile hormones (JH) and molting hormones (MH) (Figure 23-8).

These chemicals can be extracted from insects or synthesized in the laboratory. When applied at certain stages in an insect's life cycle (Figure 23-8), they produce abnormalities that cause the insect to die before it can reach maturity and reproduce (Figure 23-9).

Insect hormones have the same advantages as sex attractants, but they take weeks to kill an insect, are often ineffective with a large infestation, and sometimes break down before they can act. Also, they must be applied at exactly the right time in the life cycle of the target insect. They sometimes affect natural predators of the target insect species and other nonpest species and can kill crustaceans if they get into aquatic ecosystems. Like sex attractants, they are difficult and costly to produce.

IRRADIATION OF FOODS Exposing certain foods to various levels of ionizing radiation is being touted by the nuclear industry and the food industry as a means of killing insects and preventing them from reproducing in certain foods after harvest, extending the shelf life of some perishable foods, and destroying parasitic worms (such as trichinae) and bacteria (such as salmonellae, which infect 51,000 Americans and kill 2,000 of them each year).

In 1986, the FDA approved the use of low doses of ionizing radiation on spices, fruits, vegetables, wheat

Figure 23-9 Chemical hormones can prevent insects from maturing completely and make it impossible for them to reproduce. Comparison of a stunted (left) and a normal (right) tobacco hornworm. The stunted hornworm was fed a compound that prevents its larvae from producing molting hormones (MH).

and wheat flour, pork, nuts, seeds, teas, and spices. In 1990, it was approved for use on poultry and may soon be approved for use on seafood. Irradiated foods are already sold in 33 countries, including the Soviet Union, Japan, Canada, Brazil, Israel, and many western European countries.

Because tests show that consumers will not buy food labelled as being irradiated, foods exposed to radiation sold in the United States bear a characteristic logo and a label stating that the product has been *picowaved*. Food does not become radioactive when it is irradiated, just as being exposed to X rays does not make the body radioactive. There is controversy, however, over irradiating food (see Pro/Con on p. 646).

INTEGRATED PEST MANAGEMENT Pest control is basically an ecological problem, not a chemical problem. That is why using large quantities of broad-spectrum chemical poisons to kill and control pest populations eventually fails and ends up costing more than it is worth. As biologist Thomas Eisner puts it: "Bugs are

According to the FDA and the World Health Organization, over 1,000 studies show that foods exposed to low doses of ionizing radiation are safe for human consumption. However, critics of irradiation argue that not enough animal studies have been done and that evaluations of the effects of irradiated foods on people have been too few and brief to turn up any long-term effects, which typically require 30 to 40 years to be evaluated.

Opponents also point to studies suggesting that consuming irradiated food may be harmful. For example, a USDA study carried out between 1976 and 1989 and a later study carried out by Soviet scientists showed an increase in testicular tumors and kidney disease in rats and other test animals fed irradiated chicken. A 1984 EPA study ties food irradiation to increased production of aflatoxin, a deadly carcinogen. Irradiating food also destroys some of its vitamins and other nutrients.

Opponents also fear that more people might die of deadly botulism in irradiated foods. Present levels of irradiation do not destroy the spore-enclosed bacteria that cause this disease, but they do destroy the microbes that give off the rotten odor that warns of the presence of botulism bacteria. Also, some microorganisms can mutate when exposed to radiation, possibly creating new and more dangerous species.

Most commercial facilities use ionizing radiation released by radioactive cesium-137 to irradiate food and sterilize medical supplies, cosmetics, and consumer products such as disposable diapers. The same safety problems apply to irradiation facilities as to nuclear power plants and nuclear weapons facilities (Section 18-3). However, regulations governing the design, construction, operation, and safety of irradiation facilities are far less strict than those applied to nuclear power plants.

In June 1988, a leak at an irradiation facility in Decatur, Georgia, exposed workers and their families to radiation and contaminated several products that had been shipped before the leak was discovered. By 1991, federal and state officials had not determined the cause of the accident. The cleanup, which is not complete, has already cost over $18 million.

Because the food-irradiation market is potentially enormous, the Department of Energy and the food and irradiation industry have proposed increasing the number of irradiation facilities in the United States from 40 to 1,000. The Department of Energy actively supports greatly increased food irradiation as an attempt to find a less strictly regulated use of cesium-137, one of the most abundant isotopes in nuclear waste produced by nuclear power plants and nuclear weapons facilities.

Environmentalists and consumer advocates consider food irradiation a giant step backward. What Americans want and need is fresh, wholesome food, not old food made to appear fresh and healthy by irradiation or food that has reduced nutritional value. They call for consumers to pressure elected officials to halt food irradiation, strictly regulate all irradiation facilities, and require that any food product that is irradiated, or that contains irradiated ingredients, be clearly labelled.

Proponents respond that irradiation of food is likely to reduce health hazards to people by decreasing the use of some potentially damaging pesticides and that its potential benefits greatly exceed the risks. What do you think?

---

not going to inherit the earth. They own it now. So we might as well make peace with the landlord."

The solution is to replace this ecologically and economically unsustainable chemical approach with an ecological approach. An increasing number of pest control experts believe that in most cases, the best way to control crop pests is a carefully designed **integrated pest management (IPM)** program. In this approach, each crop and its pests are evaluated as an ecological system. Then, a pest control program is developed that uses a variety of cultivation, biological, and chemical methods in proper sequence and timing.

The overall aim of integrated pest management is not eradication but keeping pest populations just below the size at which they cause economic loss (Figure 23-10). Fields are carefully monitored to check whether pests have reached an economically damaging level. When such a level is reached, farmers first use biological and cultivation controls, including vacuuming up harmful bugs. Small amounts of pesticides are applied only when absolutely necessary, and a variety of chemicals are used to retard development of genetic resistance. This approach allows farmers to escape from the pesticide treadmill and to minimize the hazards to human health, wildlife, and the environment from the widespread use of chemical pesticides.

China, Brazil, Indonesia, and the United States have led the world in the use of this approach, especially to protect cotton (China, Nicaragua, and Texas), soybeans (Brazil), cassava (equatorial Africa), and rice (Indonesia). Their experiences have shown that a well-designed integrated pest management program can

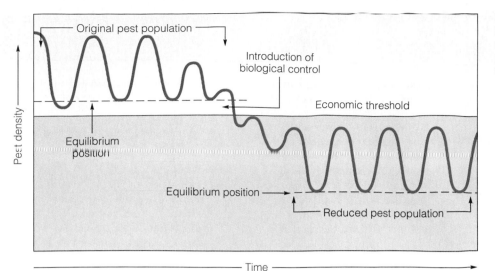

Figure 23-10 The goal of biological control and integrated pest management is to keep each pest population just below the size at which it causes economic loss.

- reduce inputs of fertilizer and irrigation water
- reduce preharvest pest-induced crop losses by 50%
- reduce pesticide use and control costs by 50% to 90%
- increase crop yields and reduce crop production costs

However, there are some drawbacks to integrated pest management. It requires expert knowledge about each pest-crop situation and is slower acting and more labor-intensive (but this creates jobs) than the use of conventional pesticides. Methods developed for a given crop in one area may not be applicable to another area with slightly different growing conditions. Although long-term costs are typically lower than the costs of using conventional pesticides, initial costs may be higher. To date, the primary focus has been on insects and pathogens, with weeds being neglected.

Use of IPM is hindered by government subsidies of conventional chemical pesticides. In Egypt, for example, the government spends more on chemical pesticide subsidies than it spends on health.

Switching to integrated pest management on a large scale in the United States is very difficult. First, it is strongly opposed by the politically and economically powerful agricultural chemical companies, who would suffer from a sharp drop in pesticide sales. They see little profit to be made from most alternative pest control methods, except insect sex attractants, hormones, and patented genetically engineered strains of plants and animals that have increased resistance to pests.

Second, farmers get most of their information about pest control from pesticide salespeople. They also get information from U.S. Department of Agriculture county farm agents, who have supported pesticide use

for decades and rarely have adequate training in the design and use of integrated pest management. The small number of integrated pest management advisers and consultants is overwhelmed by the army of pesticide sales representatives.

Third, integrated pest management methods will have to be developed and introduced to farmers by federal and state agencies because pesticide companies see little profit in this approach. Currently, however, only about 2% of the Department of Agriculture's budget is spent on integrated pest management.

Environmentalists urge the USDA to promote integrated pest management by

- adding a 2% sales tax on pesticides and using all of these revenues to greatly expand the federal budget for integrated pest management
- setting up a federally supported demonstration project on at least one farm in every county
- training Department of Agriculture field personnel and all county farm agents in integrated pest management so they can help farmers use this alternative
- revising federal government policies, such as the commodity and price-support programs, which deter farmers from using crop rotations and other agricultural practices that would reduce pesticide use, waste of irrigation water, and soil erosion
- providing federal and state subsidies and perhaps government-backed crop-loss insurance to farmers who use integrated pest management or other approved alternatives to pesticides
- gradually phasing out federal and state subsidies to farmers who depend almost entirely on pesticides once effective integrated pest management methods have been developed for major pest species

- Pressure elected officials to significantly strengthen the Federal Insecticide, Fungicide, and Rodenticide Act to better protect human health and the environment from the harmful effects of pesticides.

- Pressure elected officials to ban exports of pesticides not approved for use in the United States.

- Pressure elected officials to ban food irradiation or require all food that is irradiated or contains irradiated projects to be clearly labelled to show that it has been irradiated (not picowaved). Also, require much stricter regulation of irradiation facilities.

- Use pesticides in your home and on your yard or garden only when absolutely necessary, and use them in the smallest amount possible.

- Dispose of any unused pesticides in a safe manner (contact your local health department or environmental agency for safe disposal methods).

- Fix all leaking pipes and faucets, because they provide moisture that attracts ants and roaches. This also saves water and money.

- Allow plants native to an area to grow on all or most of the land around a house site not used for gardening. These plants can be supplemented by a mix of wildflowers, herbs (for cooking), low-growing ground cover, small bushes, and other vegetation natural to the area. This type of yard reduces infestations by mosquitoes and other insects by providing a diversity of habitats for their natural predators. It also saves time, energy, and money (no lawn mower, gasoline, or mower repairs).

- Don't cut grass below 8 centimeters (3 inches). Taller grass provides more habitats for natural predators of many pest species, shades weeds out, and holds moisture in the soil.

- If you fertilize your lawn, reduce insect and plant disease problems by using compost (Figure 12-19) instead of commercial inorganic fertilizers, and don't use any synthetic pesticides.

- If you hire a company to take care of your lawn, use one that relies only on organic methods.*

*For names of lawn companies that don't use toxic chemicals, write Lorens Tronet, Executive Director of Lake Country Defenders, Box 911, Lake Zanich, IL 60047, and the Bio-Integral Resource Center, Box 7414, Berkeley, CA 94707. Also consult *Success with Lawns Starts with Soil*, Ringer Research Corp., 6860 Flying Cloud Drive, Eden Prairie, MN 55344.

If a company claims to use only organic methods, get its claims in writing.

Use the following natural alternatives to pesticides for controlling common household pests:[†]

- *Ants*. Make sure firewood and tree branches are not in contact with the house; caulk common entry points, such as windowsills, door thresholds, and baseboards (also saves energy and money). Keep ants out by planting mint or onion around the outside of a house and by putting coffee grounds or crushed mint leaves around doors and windows; sprinkle cayenne, red pepper, or boric acid (with an anticaking agent) along ant trails inside your house, and wipe off countertops with vinegar. After about four days of such treatments, ants usually go somewhere else.

- *Mosquitoes*. Establish nests and houses for insect-eating birds; eliminate sources of stagnant water in or near your yard; plant basil outside windows and doors; use screens on all doors and win-

[†]For further information on safe control of insect pests, contact the National Coalition Against the Misuse of Pesticides, 530 7th St. N.E., Washington, DC 20003.

Environmentalists call for a 50% reduction in the use of chemical pesticides in the United States by 2000. Indonesia (Figure 8-16) has led the way in the pest management revolution. In 1986, the Indonesian government banned the use of 57 pesticides on rice and launched a nationwide program to switch to integrated pest management. Denmark, Sweden, the Netherlands, and the Canadian province of Ontario have passed legislation to reduce pesticide use by 50% over the next 5 to 15 years. Between 1985 and 1990, there was a 50% drop in pesticide use in Sweden with no decline in crop yields.

CHANGING THE ATTITUDES OF CONSUMERS AND FARMERS Three attitudes tend to support the widespread use of pesticides and lock us into the pesticide treadmill:

- Many people believe that the only good bug is a dead bug.

- Most consumers insist on buying only perfect, unblemished fruits and vegetables, even though a few holes or frayed leaves do not significantly affect the taste, nutrition, or shelf life of such produce.

dows; and use a yellow light bulb outside entryways. Reduce bites by not using scented soaps and not wearing perfumes, colognes, and other scented products outdoors during mosquito season. Repel mosquitoes by rubbing a bit of vinegar on exposed skin. Don't use No-Pest strips for control of flying insects, especially in bedrooms or areas where food is prepared or eaten, because most contain DDVP, an organophosphate that some environmentalists have been trying to have banned. Don't use electric zappers to kill mosquitoes and other flying insects. These devices are noisy and waste electricity, and the light attracts insects rather than repelling them.

- *Roaches*. Caulk or otherwise plug small cracks around wall shelves, cupboards, baseboards, pipes, sinks, and bathroom fixtures (also saves energy); eliminate folded grocery sacks and newspapers, which are favorite hiding places for roaches; and don't leave out dirty dishes, food spills, dog or other indoor pet food, or uncovered food or garbage overnight. Kill roaches by sprinkling boric acid (or a mixture of boric acid and flour, cornmeal, or

sugar) under sinks and ranges, behind refrigerators, and in cabinets, closets, and other dark, warm places. Repel roaches by sprinkling a mixture of bay leaves and cucumbers or a mixture of 1 cup borax, 1/2 cup flour, 1/4 cup confectioners' sugar, and 1 cup cornmeal. Establish populations of banana spiders.

- *Mice*. Seal holes and keep areas free of food, as with roaches and ants. Use glass, metal, or sturdy plastic containers to store food. Trap mice remaining in the house by using spring-loaded traps baited with a small amount of peanut butter. Put traps in an out-of-the-way place to protect children and pets. Check traps daily and remove dead mice.

- *Flies*. Dispose of garbage, and clean garbage cans regularly; eat or remove overripened fruit; and don't leave moist, uneaten pet food out for more than an hour. Clean up dog manure and cat litter boxes daily. Repel flies by planting sweet basil and tansy near doorways and patios and hanging a series of polyethylene strips in front of entry doors (like the ones you see on some grocery store coolers); put a blend of equal amounts of bay leaf pieces, coarsely ground cloves, clover

blossoms, and eucalyptus leaves in several small bags, mosquito netting, or other mesh material, and hang the bags just inside entrance doors; grow sweet basil in the kitchen; place sweet clover in small bags made of mosquito netting and hang the bags around the room; make flypaper by applying honey to strips of yellow paper, and hang it from the ceiling in the center of rooms.

- *Termites*. Make sure that soil around and under your home is well drained and that crawl spaces are dry and well ventilated; remove scrap wood, stumps, sawdust, cardboard, firewood, and other sources of cellulose close to your house; replace heavily damaged or rotted sills, joists, or flooring; fill voids in concrete or masonry with mortar grout. In new construction, install a termite shield between the foundation and floor joists, and don't let untreated wood touch soil. Inspect for damage each year, and if infestation is discovered, apply a heat lamp for ten minutes to any infested area; nematodes (tiny parasitic worms) can also be used; for a large infestation, have your house treated by a professional

(continued)

- Most people accept the argument of pesticide makers that without these chemicals, there wouldn't be enough to eat and food prices would soar. However, studies show that cutting pesticide use in half in the United States by using alternative forms of pest management would not decrease crop yields, would raise food prices only slightly, and would reduce the health, environmental, and social costs of pesticides to consumers by $2 billion to $5 billion a year.

Educating farmers and consumers to change their attitudes and pressuring elected officials to change U.S. agricultural and pesticide policies would help reduce unnecessary pesticide use and economic loss and the resulting risks to human health and wildlife (see Individuals Matter on p. 648).

We need to recognize that pest control is basically an ecological, not a chemical, problem.

ROBERT L. RUDD

using one of the new termicides such as Dursban, Torpedo, or Dragnet. Safer treatments that may soon be available are freezing termites to death by pouring liquid nitrogen into walls and infested areas, a growth regulator that transforms young termites into soldiers instead of workers needed to feed a colony, and antibiotics that eliminate the wood-digesting microorganisms that live inside termites.

- *Fleas.* Keep fleas off you by bathing in soaps that contain certain green dyes that repel fleas. Vacuum frequently, and toss a couple of mothballs into the vacuum cleaner bag to kill fleas sucked into the bag. Dust your pet with flea powders made from eucalyptus, sage, tobacco, wormwood, bay leaf, or vetiver. Mix essential oils such as citronella, cedarwood, eucalyptus, pennyroyal, orange, sassafras, geranium, clove, or mint with water and use for dips and shampoos for pets. Some people contend that fleas can be repelled by adding cedar shavings to pet pillows and by

adding a small amount of either brewer's yeast or onion to pets' food. Do not use flea collars or flea preparations containing synthetic insecticides, which contain chemicals that can cause cancer, nerve damage, and mutations in pets and may be a hazard to humans (especially small children).

You can reduce potential health risks from pesticide residues in food by

- Buying organically grown produce that has not been treated with synthetic fertilizers, pesticides, or growth regulators. Purchase only organic produce that is certified to be free of pesticide residues by independent testing laboratories, and urge your supermarket manager to carry only organic produce that meets those standards.*

*For a list of more than 100 sources of organically grown and processed fruits, vegetables, grains, and meats, send a self-addressed business envelope with 50 cents postage to Mail-Order Organic, The Center for Science in the Public Interest, 1501 16th St. N.W., Washington, DC 20036.

- Not buying imported produce, which generally contains more pesticide residues than domestic fruits and vegetables. Show your concern and influence supermarket buying decisions by asking managers where their produce comes from.

- Not buying perfect-looking fruits and vegetables, which are more likely to contain higher levels of pesticide residues.

- Buying produce in season, because it is less likely to be treated with fungicides and other chemicals to preserve its appearance during storage.

- Carefully washing and scrubbing all fresh produce in soapy water.

- Removing and not using the outer leaves of lettuce and cabbage and peeling fruits that have thick skins.

- Growing your own fruits and vegetables using organic methods.

DISCUSSION TOPICS

1. Should DDT and other pesticides be banned from use in malaria control throughout the world? Explain. What are the alternatives?

2. Environmentalists argue that because essentially all pesticides eventually fail, their use should be phased out and farmers should be given economic incentives for switching to integrated pest management. Explain why you agree or disagree with this proposal.

3. Explain how the use of insecticides can increase the number of insect pest problems.

4. Debate the following resolution: Because DDT and the other banned chlorinated hydrocarbon pesticides pose no demonstrable threat to human health and have saved millions of lives, they should again be approved for use in the United States.

5. Should certain types of foods used in the United States be irradiated? Explain.

6. What changes, if any, do you believe should be made in the Federal Insecticide, Fungicide, and Rodenticide Act regulating pesticide use in the United States?

7. Should U.S. companies continue to be allowed to export to other countries pesticides, medicines, and other chemicals that have been banned or severely restricted in the United States? Explain.

*8. How are bugs and weeds controlled on your yard and garden and on the grounds of your school and the public schools, parks, and playgrounds where you live? Consider mounting efforts to have integrated pest management and organic fertilizers used on school and public grounds. Do the same thing for your yard and garden.

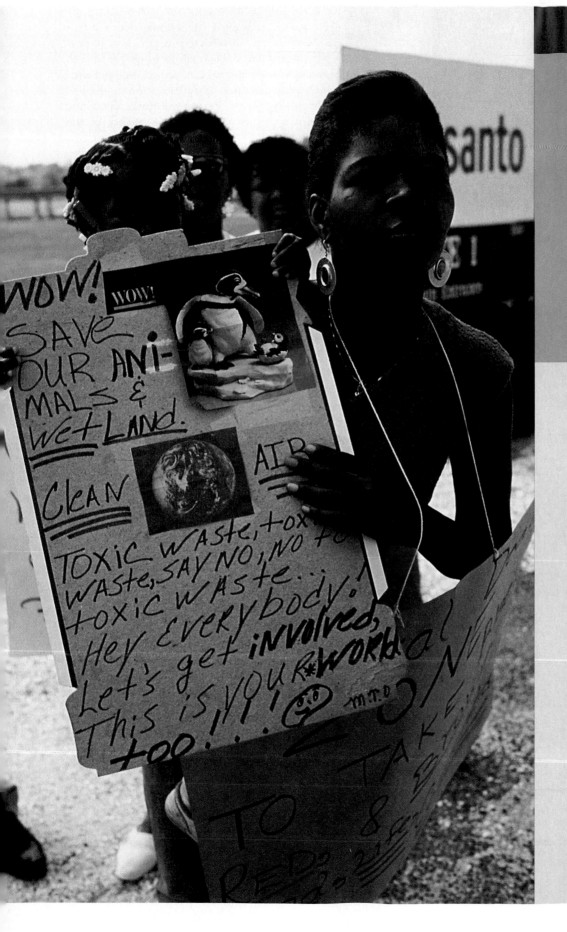

PART SEVEN

ENVIRONMENT AND SOCIETY

When it is asked how much it will cost to protect the environment, one more question should be asked: How much will it cost our civilization if we do not?

GAYLORD NELSON

We do not have generations, we only have years, in which to turn things around.

LESTER BROWN

Antipollution demonstration in Louisiana against Monsanto Chemical Company.

CHAPTER 24

ECONOMICS AND ENVIRONMENT

General Questions and Issues

1. What are the principal types of economic goods and resources?

2. What types of economic systems are found throughout the world?

3. What is economic growth? How can it and economic systems be redirected and managed to sustain Earth's life-support systems?

4. How can economics be used to regulate resource use and reduce environmental degradation and pollution?

5. What are the main causes of poverty, and what can be done to help people escape from the poverty trap?

6. How can we shift from an Earth-plundering economy to an Earth-sustaining economy?

As important as technology, politics, law, and ethics are to the pollution question, all such approaches are bound to have disappointing results, for they ignore the primary fact that pollution is primarily an economic problem, which must be understood in economic terms.

LARRY E. RUFF

NDIVIDUALS, BUSINESSES, AND SOCIETIES make **economic decisions** about what goods and services to produce, how to produce them, how much to produce, how to distribute them, and what to buy and sell. Because producing and using anything requires resources and has some harmful impact on the environment, economic decisions affect resource use and the quality of the environment.

As the number of people and their use of resources increase, the environmental impacts of their economic activities increase (Figure 1-16 and Table 1-1). The basic problem is how economic systems can be used to produce economic goods to meet human needs and wants and at the same time sustain, rather than degrade, Earth's finite capital, which supports all economic activities (see Spotlight on p. 3).

24-1 Economic Goods and Resources

ECONOMIC GOODS, NEEDS, AND WANTS An **economic good** is any material item or service that gives people satisfaction. Some of these goods are *material items*, such as food, gasoline, cars, and TV sets. Others are *services*—intangible things such as medical care, education, defense, insurance, and cleaning. An **economy** is a system of production, distribution, and consumption of economic goods.

The types and amounts of certain economic goods—food, clothing, water, oxygen, shelter, health care, education—that you must have to survive and to stay healthy are your **economic needs**. Anything beyond those is an **economic want**. What you believe you need and want is influenced by the customs and conventions of the society in which you live, your level of affluence, and advertising. Worldwide, over $250 billion a year ($100 billion in the United States) is spent on advertising and sales promotion, largely to increase economic wants.

PRIVATE AND PUBLIC GOODS Any economic good that can be produced and sold in units and enjoyed on a private, or exclusive, basis is a **private good**. Most things you buy in the marketplace are private goods.

An economic good that cannot be divided and sold in units and that can be enjoyed by anybody is a **public good**. National defense is an example. Once provided for any citizen by a given level of expenditure, it is available to all. Other examples are police forces, fire departments, courts of law, public parks, public education, and clean air.

Private producers have little incentive, sometimes none, to provide public goods because once they are produced, anyone can enjoy them without having to pay the producers. Thus, governments step in and use tax revenues to provide public goods or to pay others to supply them. With limited tax revenues, the government can't satisfy all needs and wants for public goods.

ECONOMIC RESOURCES The things used in an economy to produce material goods and services are called **economic resources** or **factors of production**. They are usually divided into three groups:

1. **Natural resources**: resources produced by Earth's natural processes. These include the actual area of Earth's solid surface, nutrients and minerals in the soil and deeper portions of Earth's crust, wild and domesticated plants and animals (biodiversity), water, air, and nature's dilution, waste disposal, pest control, and recycling services.

2. **Capital or intermediate goods**: manufactured items made from natural resources and used as inputs to produce and distribute economic goods and services bought by consumers. These include tools, machinery, equipment, factory buildings, and transportation and distribution facilities.

3. **Labor**: the physical and mental talents of people. *Workers* sell their time and talents for *wages*. *Managers* take responsibility for combining natural resources, capital goods, and workers to produce an economic good. *Entrepreneurs* and *investors* put up and risk the capital needed to produce an economic good in the hope of making a *profit* on their investment.

PRIVATE-, COMMON-, AND PUBLIC-PROPERTY RESOURCES Any resource owned by individuals or groups of individuals is a **private-property resource**. Others can be excluded from the use of such a resource. People tend to maintain and improve resources they own.

A **common-property resource** is one to which people have virtually free and unmanaged access and in which each user can subtract from or degrade the supply available to other users. Most are potentially renewable resources. Examples are air in the troposphere, fish and whales in international waters, migratory birds, groundwater, and the ozone content of the stratosphere.

Because it is difficult, and in some cases impossible, to restrict access to common-property resources, they can easily be polluted (air, international waters) or overharvested (whales, migratory birds) and converted from renewable into slowly renewable or nonrenewable resources. This is sometimes referred to as the tragedy of the commons (see Spotlight on p. 14).

Laws can be passed to restrict access to or overexploitation of such resources, but the laws are difficult, and often impossible, to enforce. Another approach is for users to get together and agree voluntarily to limit their use of common-property resources so they are used on a sustainable basis. Evidence suggests that this is the most effective approach.

Other resources, called **public-property resources**, fall somewhere between private- and common-property resources. Such resources are owned jointly by all people of a country, state, or locality but are managed for them by the government. Examples are public lands such as national and state forests, wildlife refuges, parks, and areas protected from most uses except hiking and camping in the national wilderness preservation system (see Spotlight on p. 390). There is continual pressure on governments to sell these resources to private individuals or to give private enterprise access to timber, grazing land, minerals, and energy resources on such lands at below normal market prices (Section 2-4).

24-2 Economic Systems

TRADITIONAL ECONOMIC SYSTEM: CUSTOM DECIDES In a **traditional economic system**, people use past customs and traditions to answer the basic economic questions. Often, these systems are **subsistence economies**, in which families, tribes, or other groups produce only enough goods to meet their basic survival needs, with little or no surplus for sale or trade.

PURE MARKET ECONOMIC SYSTEM: THE MARKET DECIDES In a **pure market economic system**, also known as **pure capitalism**, all economic decisions are made in *markets*, where buyers (demanders) and sellers (suppliers) of economic goods freely interact without government or other interference.

In its pure form, this is a *produce-or-die distribution system*. Those who don't produce anything have no income, can't buy anything, and starve to death.

All economic resources are owned by private individuals and private institutions, rather than by the government. All buying and selling is based on **pure competition**, in which many small buyers and many small sellers act independently. No seller or buyer is large enough to control the supply, demand, or price of a good. Anyone is allowed to produce a product and attempt to sell it to others, but to participate, sellers and buyers must accept the going market price.

In a pure free enterprise system, a company has no legal obligation to a particular nation and no obligation to produce steel, energy, timber, or any particular good or service. Instead, a company's obligation is to produce the highest possible short-term economic return (profit) for the owners or stockholders who have provided and risked the capital that the company uses to do business. Unless instructed otherwise by its owners, a company

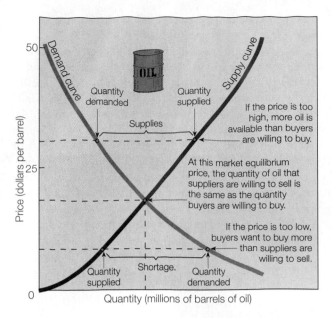

Figure 24-1 Monthly supply, demand, and market equilibrium for gasoline in a pure market system. If price, supply, and demand are the only factors involved, the market equilibrium point occurs where the demand and supply curves intersect.

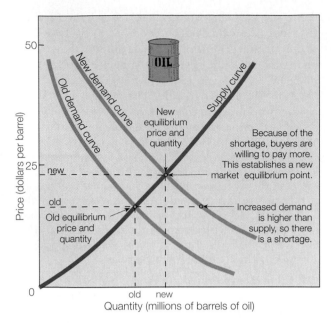

Figure 24-2 Short-term effects of an increase in demand for gasoline. Demand can increase because of more drivers, a switch to bigger cars with lower fuel efficiency, more spendable income for travel, or decreased use of mass transit. Here, the original demand curve shown in Figure 24-1 shifts to the right. The increased demand creates a temporary shortage. Buyers are then willing to pay more. This establishes a new market equilibrium point. A different situation occurs if the demand for gasoline decreases because of fewer drivers, a switch to more fuel-efficient cars, less spendable income for travel, or increased use of mass transit. In that case, the original demand curve shifts to the left. Decreased demand creates a temporary surplus. Then competition stimulates sellers to charge less, until the price reaches a new market equilibrium point.

must meet its obligation regardless of the environmental consequences.

SUPPLY, DEMAND, AND MARKET EQUILIBRIUM IN THE PURE MARKET SYSTEM

Economic decisions in the pure market system are governed by interactions of demand, supply, and price. In a pure market system, buyers want to pay as little as possible for an economic good and sellers want to get as high a price as possible. **Market equilibrium** occurs when the quantity supplied equals the quantity demanded and the price is no higher than buyers are willing to pay and no lower than sellers are willing to accept. If price, supply, and demand are the only factors involved, the demand and supply curves for an economic good intersect at the *market equilibrium point* (Figure 24-1).

However, things are not that simple. Factors other than price can shift the original supply and demand curves to the right or to the left, upsetting the market equilibrium and establishing new equilibrium points.

Factors that increase demand shift the demand curve to the right (Figure 24-2), and those that decrease demand shift it to the left. Examples are changes in the number of buyers, in buyer taste, in average income, and in prices of related goods. The supply curve for an economic good like gasoline can be shifted to the right or to the left by changes in technology, in production costs, in taxes, in prices of related goods, and in the number of suppliers (Figure 24-3).

ECONOMIC AND ECOLOGICAL VIEWS OF ECONOMIC SYSTEMS

The general operation of a pure market economy can be represented by a **circular flow model** (Figure 24-4). It shows how the factors of production and the economic goods produced flow between households and businesses, and how money flows between households and businesses to produce and buy economic goods.

Most economies show only the top portion of this diagram, implying that a market economy is isolated from and not dependent on the ecosphere. The environment is viewed as an infinite source of raw materials and an infinite sink for wastes, with no economic value put on ecosphere processes. This view of the economy as essentially a perpetual motion machine (which violates the second law of energy) is used to justify the goal of increased economic growth found in virtually all economies.

By contrast, environmentalists view economic systems as human-created subsystems of the ecosphere that are totally dependent on resources and services provided by the sun and by Earth's natural processes (Figure 24-4). To them, a throwaway or frontier eco-

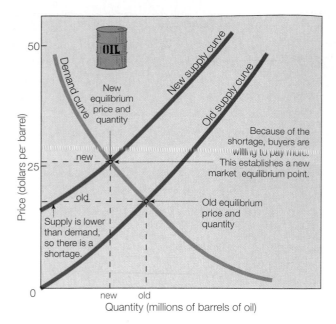

Figure 24-3 Short-term effects of a decrease in the supply of gasoline. A decrease can occur if the cost of finding, extracting, and refining oil increases or if existing oil deposits are economically depleted and not replaced by new discoveries. Also, if oil producers expect higher prices in the future, they may lower present production with the hope of making larger profits later. The original supply curve shown in Figure 24-1 shifts to the left. During the temporary shortage, buyers are willing to pay more for gasoline. Thus, the price reaches a higher market equilibrium point. A similar situation occurs if the supply increases. In that case, the original supply curve shifts to the right, reflecting a temporary surplus. Then competition stimulates sellers to charge less, and the price moves down to a new market equilibrium point.

nomic system based on unlimited growth is outdated, impossible, and dangerous in a world with no frontiers and with 5.4 billion people whose numbers and resource consumption are increasing exponentially (see Pro/Con on p. 657).

PURE COMMAND ECONOMIC SYSTEM: THE GOVERNMENT DECIDES In a **pure command economic system**, or **totally planned economy**, all economic decisions are made by the government. It determines what economic goods are produced, how they are produced, how much of each is produced, how much each will cost, and how they are distributed.

The pure command economy is based on the belief that government control and ownership of the means of production is the most efficient way to produce, use, and distribute scarce resources. Socialism and its purer form, communism, are types of command economic systems.

MIXED ECONOMIC SYSTEMS: THE REAL WORLD
None of the world's countries has a pure market economy or a pure command economy. Instead, they have mixed economic systems that fall somewhere between the pure market and pure command systems and have some elements of tradition (Figure 24-5).

Pure market economies don't exist because they have weaknesses that can be controlled only by government intervention in the marketplace. Government intervention in the marketplace is used to

- prevent one seller (a *monopoly*) or a group of sellers (*oligopoly* or *cartel*) from dominating the supply and thus being able to set the price of a desired good

- provide national security, education, and other public goods

- promote fairness (equity) through the redistribution of income and wealth, especially to people unable to meet their basic needs

- protect people from fraud, trespass, theft, and bodily harm

- ensure economic stability by preventing cycles of boom and depression that commonly occur in a pure market system

- help compensate owners for large-scale destruction of assets by floods, earthquakes, hurricanes, and other natural disasters (Section 7-4)

- prevent or reduce pollution

- prevent or reduce depletion of natural resources that are undervalued in market economies because it is assumed that such resources are infinite or that we can always find substitutes

- manage public land resources (Chapter 15)

Pure market economies also don't exist because businesses lobby government to give them special breaks that shield them from free-market forces. Business leaders talk about the virtues free-market competition, but what they want is free-market competition for everyone but themselves.

Almost every business lobbyist in Washington and in other capitals of market-economy countries is there to subvert free-market competition. Their goal is to get a subsidy or a tax break that will increase the profits of the businesses they represent at the expense of one of their competitors or other businesses. In some countries, bribery of public officials to get special breaks is part of doing business.

Most western countries have mixed economies that blend socialism and capitalism with an emphasis on capitalism. In most MDCs, government is the biggest industry and thus exerts considerable influence on the marketplace by both regulation and purchasing power. In 1987, government spent 47% of the GNP in the former West Germany, 37% in the United States, and 33% in Japan.

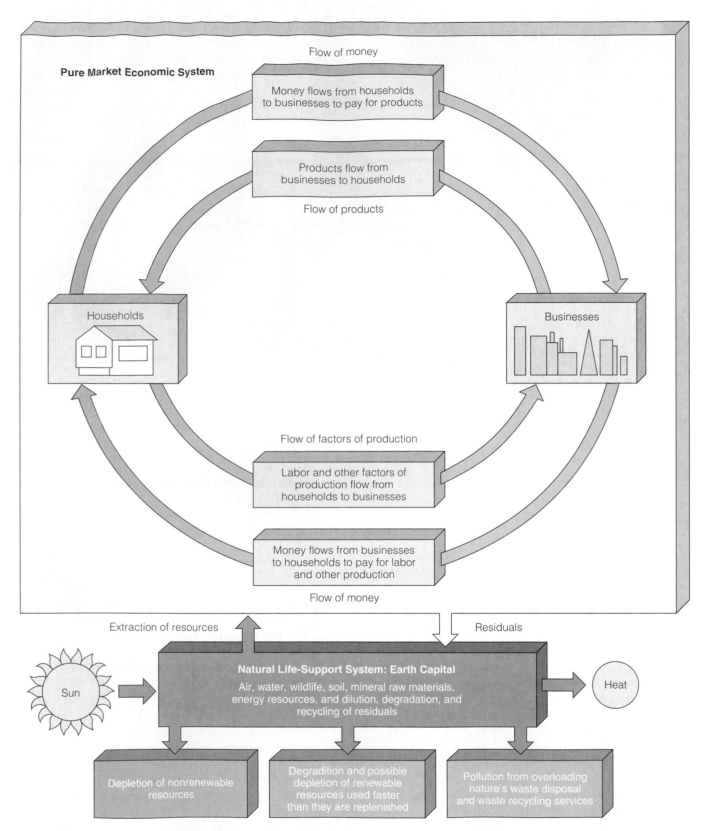

Figure 24-4 Economists view a pure market economy as operating through a circular flow of economic goods and money between households and businesses. People in households spend money to buy goods that firms produce, and firms spend money to buy factors of production (natural resources, capital goods, and labor) owned by people in households. Most economics textbooks show only the top portion of this diagram, implying that the economy is isolated from and not dependent on the ecosphere. The entire diagram represents how environmentalists view the operation of a pure market economy. It shows that a pure market economy, or any type of economy, operates as a human-created subsystem within the ecosphere and is totally dependent upon resources and services provided by the sun and the ecosphere. Real wealth is, and always has been, based on the sun and the resources and ecological integrity of the earth.

It is not surprising that economists who have been taught that the economy is essentially a perpetual motion machine operating virtually independent of the ecosphere believe that

- unlimited economic growth is possible and desirable
- resources are infinite in supply or we can always find substitutes
- the environment has an essentially infinite capacity to absorb, dilute, or degrade the wastes produced by the world's economies

Those economists justify such beliefs by pointing to the rapid economic growth that has taken place since the Industrial Revolution (especially since 1950), using increases in the GNP and GNP per capita as the primary measures of human welfare and environmental health, and believing that technology based on human ingenuity can overcome any limits on economic growth (see Guest Essay on p. 29). They also justify unlimited economic growth by holding out the hope that the lives of the poor will be better from the economic crumbs that trickle down to them without sacrifices from the rich.

Most economists see economic growth in terms of unlimited J-shaped curves. Environmentalists see such growth in terms of S-shaped curves, or overshoots and diebacks caused when a species reaches, or temporarily exceeds, the carrying capacity of its environment (Figure 6-3). Progrowth economists see unlimited economic growth as the cure for our social and environmental problems.

To environmentalists and some economists (see Guest Essay on p. 671), our current economic system, based on maximizing unlimited economic growth, is madness. They see such growth as the disease causing or at least intensifying most of our social and environmental problems. To them, maximizing economic growth is like driving a car at an accelerating rate toward an infinitely thick and infinitely high concrete wall (the limits imposed by the ecosphere) while saying that

- the wall doesn't exist, and the best thing for the economy and for us is to eat the golden eggs (Earth income) laid by a goose (Earth capital) and then eat the goose because we can invest the money we make in finding a substitute for the goose (the economy is not dependent on the ecosphere)
- driving faster and faster will solve our social ills (why worry about controlling population growth and redistributing some of the wealth to the poor and the middle class when the economic pie is growing and they can live adequately off the crumbs provided by the rich and powerful who are doing the driving and getting most of the benefits (Figure 1-7)
- driving faster and faster will provide enough money to control pollution and prevent serious disruption of the environment without having to build the economy around waste reduction and pollution prevention (producing more and more waste and pollution is so good for business that it will provide enough money for us to keep us from hitting the wall even if we keep accelerating straight toward it)
- the ride is fantastic (or will soon be fantastic for those who survive on crumbs) and we haven't hit the wall yet (don't worry, be happy, shop till you drop, don't think about the wall, and let us do the driving)
- even if we hit the wall, it won't happen in our lifetime (eat, drink, and consume, and let our children and grandchildren and other species hit the wall)
- somehow we will figure out a way for the car to jump over or go through the wall (we are such a clever and powerful species that we are not limited by how the ecosphere works)

When there is a fairly small number of people using relatively few resources, rapid growth in numbers of people and resource consumption is possible and desirable, and the environmental impacts of these economic activities is not significant. This is similar to the rapid growth in numbers and resource use when pioneer species invade a new environment with ample resources at an early stage of ecological succession (Figure 6-10).

Environmentalists believe that we now have so many people using high levels of resources, or hoping to use resources at a high rate, that the once-useful frontier economic model (Figures 3-20 and 24-4), based on rapid and uncontrolled economic growth, is both obsolete and dangerous. As Kirkpatrick Sale put it: "If economics is the science of the distribution and use of the earth's resources, every single one of which without exception is derived from a finite ecosphere, why has it come up with nothing but systems that will use these resources all up?"

Environmentalists believe we must develop and implement new economic models or modify existing ones based on how more-mature ecosystems sustain themselves. For example, when a simple field matures to a complex forest, the forest is sustained by decreased population growth, putting biological productivity into increases in quality instead of quantity, efficient recycling of nutrients, and efficient use of energy (Table 6-4).

Environmentalists call on us to learn this lesson of sustainabilty from nature by acting as a mature species. That means we must face the ecological reality that there are no substitutes for Earth capital and ecosphere processes and that the primary goal of any economic system must be the health of the ecosphere. Without environmental security, economic security, military security, and individual security cannot be sustained.

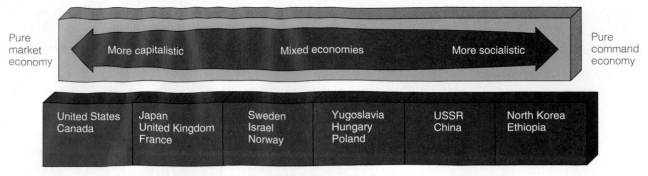

Pure market economy

More capitalistic   Mixed economies   More socialistic

Pure command economy

| United States Canada | Japan United Kingdom France | Sweden Israel Norway | Yugoslavia Hungary Poland | USSR China | North Korea Ethiopia |

Figure 24-5   Countries throughout the world have mixed economic systems that fall somewhere between the extremes of a pure market system and a pure command system.

The Soviet Union, China, Cuba, and most eastern European countries have mixed economies that blend socialism and capitalism with emphasis on socialism (Figure 24-5). Recently, the economies of most eastern European countries, and to a lesser degree the Soviet Union, have increased their reliance on capitalism.

24-3   Economic Growth and External Costs

ECONOMIC GROWTH AND GROSS NATIONAL PRODUCT   Virtually all economies in the world today seek to increase their **economic growth**: an increase in the capacity of the economy to provide goods and services for final use. Such growth is accomplished by maximizing the flow of matter and energy resources (throughput) through society as fast as possible (Figure 3-20). Economic growth is seen as good, limitless, and necessary to maximize wealth and power over people and the rest of nature.

Economic growth is usually measured by an increase in a country's **gross national product (GNP)**: the market value in current dollars of all goods and services produced by an economy for final use during a year. To get a better idea of how much economic output is actually growing or declining, economists use the **real GNP**: the gross national product adjusted for *inflation* — any increase in the average price level of final goods and services.

To show how the average person's slice of the economic pie is changing, economists often calculate the **real GNP per capita**: the real GNP divided by the total population. If population expands faster than economic growth, the real GNP per capita falls. The pie has grown, but the slice per person has shrunk. This is useful, but the size of the per capita slice may hide the fact that the wealthy few have an enormous slice and the many poor have only a few crumbs.

GNP, QUALITY OF LIFE, AND ENVIRONMENTAL DEGRADATION   Since 1942, most governments have used real GNP and real GNP indicators as if they were measures of Gross National Quality of Life, when in fact they measure only the speed at which an economy is producing economic goods of any type. GNP and GNP per capita are poor indicators of social well-being, environmental health, and even economic health because

- They hide the harmful effects of an economy by including the production of harmful goods and services. For example, producing more cigarettes raises GNP and GNP per capita, but it also causes more cancer and heart disease (Figure 20-10), which also increase GNP and GNP per capita by increasing health and insurance costs and decreasing life quality through poor health and premature death. The $2.2 billion that Exxon spent trying to clean up the oil spill from the tanker *Exxon Valdez* (see Case Study on p. 616) helped push up the U.S. GNP, as did the $1 billion spent because of the Three Mile Island nuclear accident (see Spotlight on p. 490). The more waste and pollution we produce, the higher the GNP, a form of runaway or positive feedback (Section 6-1) that explains why some think the GNP should be renamed gross national pollution or gross national waste.

- They don't tell us how resources and income are distributed among the people in a country — how many people have a large slice and how many have only a few crumbs of the economic pie.

- They are used to stimulate economic growth that favors the production of wants (created or stimulated by advertising). This puts people on an accelerating consumption treadmill where they are driven to make enough money to keep buying things as status symbols and to fulfill artificially created wants that add little to their life quality. Psychological studies show that for people above the poverty level, the main elements of happiness are not related to consumption.

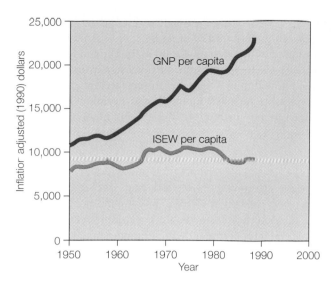

Figure 24-6 Comparison of GNP per person and the Daly–Cobb index of sustainable economic welfare (ISEW) per person in the United States between 1950 and 1988. This index is the most comprehensive indicator of well-being available. It includes average per capita GNP adjusted for inequalities in income distribution, depletion of nonrenewable resources, loss of wetlands, loss of farmland from soil erosion and urbanization, the cost of air and water pollution, and estimates of long-term environmental damage from global changes such as ozone depletion and projected global warming. Note that after rising between 1950 and 1976, the ISEW for the United States declined between 1977 and 1988. (Data from Herman E. Daly, John B. Cobb, Jr., and Clifford W. Cobb)

■ Depletion and degradation of natural resources, upon which all economies ultimately depend (Figure 24-4), are not subtracted from the GNP. That means that a country can exhaust its mineral resources, erode its soils, pollute its aquifers, cut down its forests, and deplete its wildlife and fisheries and none of it shows up as a loss in the country's GNP while it is being done. That means that a country can have a rapidly rising GNP while it is headed toward ecological bankruptcy from permanent loss of its true wealth in the form of Earth capital.

SOCIAL AND ENVIRONMENTAL INDICATORS

What we really need are widely used indicators of net national product or net national welfare. Economists William Nordhaus and James Tobin have developed an indicator called **net economic welfare (NEW)** to estimate the annual change in quality of life in a country. They calculate the NEW by putting a price tag on pollution and other "negative" goods and services included in the GNP—those that do not improve the quality of life. The costs of these negative factors are then subtracted from the GNP to give the NEW.

The net economic welfare can then be divided by a country's population to estimate the **net economic welfare per capita.** This indicator and net economic welfare can then be adjusted for inflation. Applying these indi-

cators to the United States shows that since 1940, the real NEW per capita has risen at about half the rate of the real GNP per person and that since 1968, the gap between these two indicators has been widening.

The net economic welfare indicator was developed in 1972, but it is still not widely used. One reason is that putting a price tag on the "bads" is difficult and controversial. Another reason is that some elected officials prefer using the real GNP per capita because it can make people think they are better off than they are and prevent them from recognizing the need for significant economic and political change.

Social factors can also be used to evaluate average quality of life in a country or part of a country. Recently, the United Nations has developed a *human development index (HDI)* as a estimate of average quality of life in different countries. This index, measured on a scale of 0 to 1, is an aggregate of three indicators: life expectancy at birth (Figure 8-10), literacy rates, and real GNP per person. In 1988, 18 other countries (including Australia, Canada, Sweden, and Spain) had a higher HDI than the United States.

Another indicator, called the *human suffering index (HSI)*, has been developed by the Population Crisis Committee. It adds together ratings on ten scales—GNP per capita, inflation, job growth, urban population growth, access to clean drinking water, infant mortality, adult literacy, food sufficiency, energy sufficiency, and personal freedom.

In 1989, economist Robert Repetto and other researchers at the World Resources Institute proposed that the depletion of natural resources be included as a factor in the GNP to calculate a country's *net national product (NNP)*. They have developed a fairly simple model for doing this and have successfully applied it to Indonesia. Between 1970 and 1984, Indonesia's GNP grew by 7% a year, but if the depleted values of its forests, soils, and oil are subtracted, its net national product grew by only 4% a year. If the country's depletion of coal, mineral ores, and other nonrenewable resources had been included, its NNP would have grown at an even lower annual rate.

Recently, Herman E. Daly (see Guest Essay on p. 671) and John B. Cobb, Jr., have developed an index of sustainable economic welfare (ISEW) and applied it to the United States (Figure 24-6). This index, the most comprehensive indicator of well-being available, shows that between 1950 and 1976, the average welfare or well-being per person in the United States rose by 46%. Since 1976, however, the ISEW has been decreasing, and it declined 12% between 1977 and 1988. The biggest problems with this indicator are that it has been calculated only for the United States and that it depends on information available for only a few countries. In LDCs, where such information is not available, grain consumption per person provides a rough estimate of life quality.

These social and environmental indicators are not perfect. Without such indicators, however, we know too little about what is happening to people, the environment, and the planet's natural resource base, what needs to be done, and what types of policies work. We have blindfolded ourselves so that we cannot see what we are doing at a time when we have immense power to harm ourselves and other living things.

INTERNAL AND EXTERNAL COSTS The price you pay for a car reflects the costs of building and operating the factory, raw materials, labor, marketing, shipping, and company and dealer profits. After you buy the car, you also have to pay for gasoline, maintenance, and repair. All these direct costs, paid for by the seller and the buyer of an economic good, are called **internal costs**.

Making, distributing, and using any economic good also involve what economists call **externalities**. These are social benefits ("goods") and social costs ("bads") not included in the market price of an economic good or service. For example, if a car dealer builds an aesthetically pleasing sales building, that is an **external benefit** to other people who enjoy the sight at no cost to them.

On the other hand, when a car factory and the cars sold emit pollutants into the environment, their harmful effects are an **external cost** passed on to society, and in some cases to future generations. Pollution from making cars and driving them harms people and kills some of them. That means that car insurance, health insurance, and medical bills go up for everyone. Air pollution from cars also kills or weakens some types of trees (Figure 21-10), raising the price of lumber, paper, and this textbook. Taxes may also go up, because the public may demand that the government spend money to regulate the land, air, and water pollution and degradation caused by producing and using cars and by mining and processing the raw materials used to make them.

Because these harmful costs are external and, hence, aren't included in the market price, you don't connect them with the car or type of car you are driving. As a consumer and taxpayer, however, you pay these hidden costs sooner or later.

If you use a car, you can pass other external costs on to society. You increase those costs when you throw trash out of a car, drive a car that gets poor gas mileage and thus adds more air pollution per kilometer than a more efficient car, dismantle or don't maintain a car's air pollution control devices, drive with a noisy muffler or faulty brakes, and don't keep your motor tuned. You don't pay directly for these harmful activities, but you and others pay indirectly in the form of higher taxes, higher health costs, higher health insurance, and higher cleaning and maintenance bills.

To environmentalists, the increasing number of harmful externalities (Table 1-1) is a warning sign that our economic systems are stressing the ecosphere (Figure 24-4). To progrowth economists, externalities (as the name implies) are minor imperfections in the circular flow of production and consumption (Figure 24-4) that can be cured from the profits made from more economic growth.

INTERNALIZING EXTERNAL COSTS As long as people are rewarded for polluting, depleting, degrading, and wasting resources, few are going to volunteer to change; doing so would be committing economic suicide. Suppose you own a company and believe it is wrong to pollute the environment any more than can be handled by Earth's natural processes. If you voluntarily install expensive pollution controls and your competitors don't, your product will cost more and you will be at a competitive disadvantage. Your profits will decline, and sooner or later, you will probably go bankrupt and your employees will lose their jobs.

A general way to deal with the problem of external costs is for the government to add taxes, pass laws, or use other devices to force producers to include all or most of this expense in the market price of all economic goods. Then the market price of an economic good would be its **true cost**: its internal costs plus its short- and long-term external costs. This is what economists call *internalizing the external costs*. Internalizing external costs requires government action because few people are going to increase their cost of doing business unless their competitors have to do it.

What would happen if we internalized enough of the external costs of pollution and resource waste to help prevent pollution and to use resources more efficiently? Economic growth would be redirected. We would increase the beneficial parts of the GNP, decrease the harmful parts, increase production of beneficial goods, raise the net economic welfare, and help sustain the earth. Pollution prevention would be more profitable than pollution control, and waste reduction, recycling, and reuse would be more profitable than waste management.

On the other hand, some things you like would not be available any more because they would cost producers so much to make that few people could afford to buy them. You would pay more for most things because their market prices would be closer to their true costs, but everything would be "up front." External costs would no longer be hidden. You would have the information you need to make informed economic decisions about the effects of your lifestyle on the planet's life-support systems.

Moreover, real market prices wouldn't always be higher. Some things could even get cheaper. Internalizing external costs stimulates producers to find ways to cut costs by inventing more resource-efficient and less-harmful ways do produce things.

Internalizing external costs makes so much sense you might be wondering why it's not more widely done. One reason is that many producers of harmful and wasteful goods fear they would have to charge so much they couldn't stay in business, or would have to give up government subsidies that have helped hide the external costs. Their philosophy is: "If it isn't broken and we are making money, why fix it?" By contrast, environmentalists believe that our throwaway economic system is broken and we don't have much time to fix it.

Another problem is that it's not easy to put a price tag on all the harmful effects of making and using an economic good. People disagree on the values they attach to various costs and benefits, but making difficult choices about resource use is what economics and politics are all about.

24-4 Economic Approaches to Improving Environmental Quality and Conserving Resources

HOW FAR SHOULD WE GO? Shouldn't our goal always be zero pollution? For most pollutants, economists say, the answer is no. First, because nature can handle some of our wastes, as long as we don't destroy, degrade, or overload these natural processes. Exceptions are toxic products that cannot be degraded by natural processes or that break down very slowly in the environment. They should be neither produced nor used, except in small amounts with special permits.

Second, we can't afford to have zero pollution for any but the most harmful substances. Removing a small percentage of the pollutants in air, water, or soil is not too costly, but when we remove more, the price per unit multiplies. The cost of removing pollutants follows a J-shaped curve of exponential growth (Figure 24-7).

If we go too far in cleaning up, the costs of pollution control will be greater than the harmful effects of pollution. That may cause some businesses to go bankrupt. You and others may lose jobs, homes, and savings (see Case Study on p. 18). If we don't go far enough, the harmful external effects will cost us more than it would cost to reduce the pollution to a lower level. Then, you and others may get sick or even die. Getting the right balance is crucial.

How do we do this? Theoretically, we begin by plotting a curve of the estimated social costs of cleaning up pollution and a curve of the estimated social costs of pollution. Adding the two curves together, we get a third curve showing the total costs. The lowest point on this third curve is the optimal level of pollution (Figure 24-8).

On a graph, this looks neat and simple, but environmentalists and business leaders often disagree in their estimates of the social costs of pollution. Furthermore, the optimal level of pollution is not the same in different areas. Soils and lakes in some areas are more sensitive to acids and other pollutants than those in other places (Figure 21-11). Some believe we should go much further than merely establishing optimal pollution levels (see Spotlight on p. 663).

Figure 24-7 The cost of removing each additional unit of pollution rises exponentially.

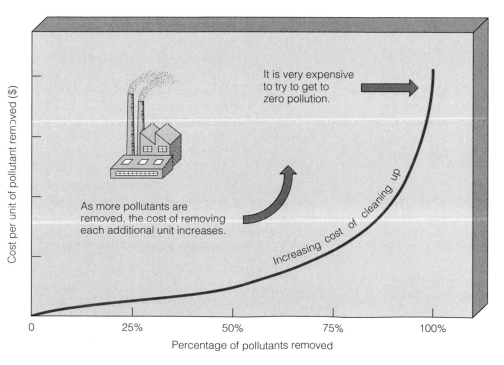

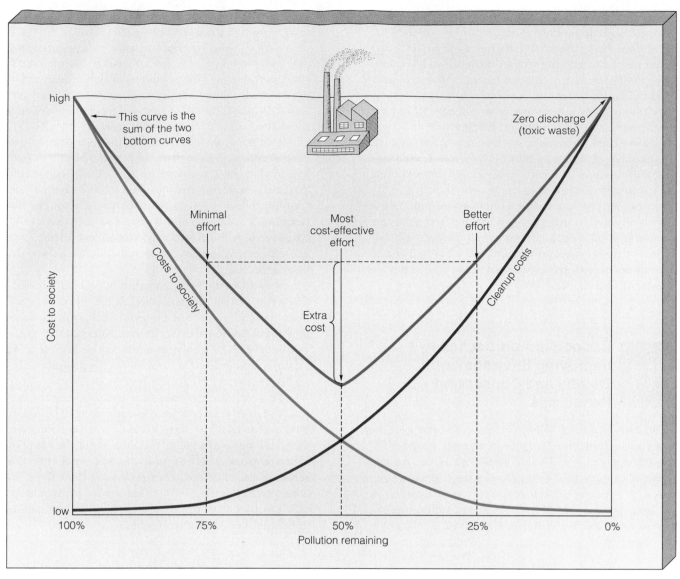

Figure 24-8 Finding the optimal level of pollution.

IMPROVING ENVIRONMENTAL QUALITY AND REDUCING RESOURCE WASTE Controlling or preventing pollution and reducing unnecessary resource use and waste require government intervention in the marketplace. There are four ways local, state, and federal governments can intervene.

1. *Make harmful actions illegal.* Pass and enforce laws that set pollution standards, regulate harmful activities, ban the release of toxic chemicals into the environment (see Spotlight on p. 663), and require that certain resources be conserved.

2. *Penalize harmful actions.* Levy taxes on each unit of pollution discharged into the air or water and each unit of unnecessary resource waste; require polluters to carry high levels of liability insurance; and have pollution control laws carry large automatic fines and automatic jail sentences.

3. *Market pollution rights and resource use rights.* Sell rights that allow pollution up to the estimated optimal level; sell the right to harvest or extract a sustainable amount of resources from public lands or common-property resources.

4. *Reward beneficial actions.* Use tax dollars to pay subsidies to businesses and individuals that install pollution control equipment or prevent pollution and reduce unnecessary resource use and waste by recycling and reusing resources and by inventing more-efficient processes and devices.

The first three are *consumer-pays* approaches that internalize some or most external costs of pollution and resource waste. Approaches 2 and 3 produce tax or other revenue that can be used to help prevent and control pollution and environmental degradation and promote sustainable use of energy and other resources.

Some analysts argue that setting optimal or politically acceptable levels of pollutants based on using pollution cleanup is a legalized way of justifying the killing or harming of an "acceptable" number of people (Section 20-3). To them, that approach is ethically unacceptable.

They say that instead of spending a lot of money and time cleaning up chemicals we release into the environment, we shouldn't produce or release harmful chemicals into the environment in the first place. Use the economic system to reward those who prevent pollution and punish those who don't. Then most of the expensive time- and talent-consuming apparatus of setting standards and arguing over optimal levels would no longer be needed.

These environmentalists also call for reversing the present legal principle by which a chemical is assumed innocent until it is proved to have caused harm. They point out that by then it is too late, and the people who have been harmed usually don't have the money and other resources needed to establish their claims in the courts.

Instead, these environmentalists believe that a chemical should be assumed to be guilty until proven otherwise by the people proposing to make or use it. Why should chemicals be given the same legal rights as people, they ask? This standard is already applied to pharmaceutical chemicals, so why shouldn't it be expanded to cover all potentially harmful chemicals?

Critics of this proposal and the idea of zero discharge argue that these changes would bring the production of most things to a halt, wreck the economy, and put large numbers of people out of work. Proponents counter that not making these changes will eventually wreck the environment and thus the economy, eventually put more people out of work, kill large numbers of workers and citizens, and reduce Earth's biodiversity. What do you think?

The first three approaches share several disadvantages. Because pollution costs are internalized, the initial cost of products may be higher unless new, more cost-effective and productive technologies are developed. This can put a country's products at a competitive disadvantage in the international marketplace. Higher initial costs also mean that the poor are penalized unless they are given tax relief or other subsidies from public funds. Also, fines and other punishments must be severe enough and enforced quickly enough to deter violations.

The fourth approach is a *taxpayer-pays* approach that does little to internalize external costs. It leads to higher-than-optimal levels of pollution and resource waste. It is not surprising that polluting industries and resource wasters usually prefer this approach, which has taxpayers pay them not to pollute or waste resources.

Another problem with subsidies is that often they go to those with the most political power and influence regardless of need. They reward the greedy rather than the needy. Also, it is difficult to lower or withdraw a subsidy when it is no longer needed because companies with subsidies use their influence to keep them.

COST-BENEFIT ANALYSIS One method used to help make economic decisions is **cost-benefit analysis**. It involves comparing the estimated short-term and long-term costs (losses) and benefits (gains) of an economic decision. If the estimated benefits exceed the estimated costs, the decision to produce or buy an economic good or provide a public good is considered worthwhile. You intuitively make such evaluations when you decide to buy a particular economic good or service.

More formal cost-benefit analysis is often used in evaluating whether to build a large hydroelectric dam, to clean up a polluted river, or to reduce air pollution emissions to an optimal level (Figure 24-8). In 1981, President Reagan issued an executive order that requires all executive departments and agencies to use cost-benefit analysis to justify every new regulation by showing that its estimated benefits exceed it estimated costs. The Office of Management and Budget is directed to review these cost-benefit analyses and has the power to block funding for any project in which estimated costs exceed benefits.

Environmental, consumer, and labor groups have charged the Reagan and Bush administrations with manipulating the results of cost-benefit analyses and using them as a political device to slow down, and in some cases halt, the implementation of environmental protection, consumer protection, and worker safety laws (see Pro/Con on p. 664).

24-5 Poverty: A Human and Environmental Tragedy

THE GLOBAL POVERTY TRAP **Poverty** is usually defined as not being able to meet one's basic economic needs. Most of the world's 1.2 billion desperately poor

The two main arguments for using cost-benefit analysis are that it is a useful way to gather and analyze data on a proposed project or course of action and that it can be used to find the cheapest way to do something. However, unless decision makers and citizens are also aware of its severe limitations, cost-benefit analysis can be used as a device for justifying something that should not be done or that could be done in a less harmful and a cheaper way.

A great source of disagreement between environmentalists and business people is the **discount rate**: how much economic value a resource will have in the future compared with its present value. Because the future is unknown, all we can do is make educated guesses based on various assumptions about what the future value of a resource might be.

Suppose a stand of redwood trees has a current market value of $1 million. At a zero discount rate, it will still be worth $1 million 50 years from now, while at a 10% discount rate, it would be worth only $10,000. Thus, the choice of discount rate is a primary factor affecting the outcome of any cost-benefit analysis.

Businesses and the Office of Management and Budget generally use a discount rate of 10%, which gives much more weight to immediate profits and resource values than to possible future profits and resource values. Proponents of high discount rates argue that inflation will make the value of their earnings less in the future than now. They also fear that innovation or changed consumer preferences will make a product or service obsolete.

Proponents also assume that economic growth through technological progress will automatically raise average living standards in the future. Why, then, should the current generation pay higher prices and taxes to benefit future generations who will be better off anyway? Environmentalists believe that this is not a reasonable assumption as long as our economic systems are based upon depleting the natural capital that supports them.

Environmentalists point out that high discount rates encourage rapid exploitation of resources and environmental quality for immediate payoffs. This makes sustainable management of most natural resources virtually impossible by loading the economic dice in favor of rapid exploitation.

Environmentalists charge that high discount rates are economic fudge factors designed to justify overexploitation of resources now, and they call for discount rates to be set much lower. Unique and scarce resources would be protected by having a 0% or a negative discount rate, and discount rates of 1% to 3% would be used to make it profitable to use other resources sustainably or slowly.

Another problem is determining who gets the benefits and who is harmed by the costs. For example, suppose a cost-benefit analysis concludes that it is too expensive to meet certain safety and environmental standards in a manufacturing plant. The owners of the company benefit by not having to spend money on making the plant less hazardous. Consumers may also benefit from lower prices. However, the workers are harmed by having to work under hazardous and unhealthful conditions. On the other hand, they may lose their jobs if the plant shuts down because its owners can't or won't spend the money to meet stricter safety and environmental standards (see Case Study on p. 18).

In the United States, for example, an estimated 100,000 Americans die each year from exposure to hazardous chemicals and other safety hazards at work. An additional 400,000 are seriously injured from such ex-

people live in LDCs (see Spotlight on p. 8). The gap between the rich and the poor has been widening, especially since 1980 (Figure 1-7).

Poverty is also found in MDCs. One in five Soviet citizens reportedly lives below the country's official poverty line. In the United States, 33 million people — one in eight Americans — are below the official poverty line. Some 13 million American children — one in five — now grow up in poverty. At least 12 million Americans (62% of them white), 5 million of them children, are "hyper-poor," trying to survive on cash incomes of less than half that of the official poverty level.

Most poverty in MDCs is not as serious as that for the desperately poor in LDCs, but poverty anywhere represents an unnecessary degradation of human life and a failure of the world's economic and political systems. At the local level, there are four parts of the poverty trap:

- Lack of access to enough land and income to meet basic needs.

- Physical weakness and poor health caused by not having enough land to grow or enough income to buy enough food for good health. This decreases the ability of the poor to work and plunges them deeper into poverty (Figure 14-12).

- Rapid population growth, which produces more workers than can be employed and forces wages down as the poor compete with each other for scarce work.

posure. Is that a necessary or an unnecessary (and unethical) cost of doing business?

The most serious limitation of cost-benefit analysis is that many things we value cannot be reduced to dollars and cents. Some of the costs of air pollution, such as extra laundry bills, house repainting, and ruined crops, are fairly easy to estimate. But how do we put meaningful price tags on human life, good health, clean air and water, beautiful scenery, a wilderness area, whooping cranes, and the ability of natural systems to degrade and recycle some of our wastes and replenish timber, fertile soil, and other vital potentially renewable resources?

The dollar values we assign to such items will vary widely because of different assumptions and value judgments, leading to a wide range of projected costs and benefits. For example, values assigned to a human life in various cost-benefit studies vary from nothing to about $7 million, with the most frequently assigned values ranging from $200,000 to $500,000. If you were asked to put a price tag on your life, you might say it is priceless, or you might contend that making such an estimate would be impossible or even immoral. Assigning fairly low economic value to human life today

and discounting this value at a high rate means that people in future generations are assigned little, if any, economic value.

Although you may not want others to place a low monetary value on your life, you do so if you choose to smoke cigarettes, not to eat properly, to drive without a seat belt, to drive while impaired by alcohol or some other drug, or not to pay more for a safer car. In each case, you decide that the benefits — pleasure, convenience, or a lower purchase price — outweigh the potential costs — poorer health, injury, or death.

Critics of cost-benefit analysis argue that because estimates of many costs and benefits are so uncertain, they can easily be weighted to achieve the desired outcome by proponents or opponents of a proposed project or action. The experts making or evaluating such analyses have to be paid by somebody, so they often represent the point of view of that somebody.

The difficulty in making cost-benefit analyses does not mean that they should not be made or that they are not useful. They can be useful if decision makers and the public are aware that they give only rough estimates and guidelines for resource use and management based on as-

sumptions and that they can easily be distorted.

To avoid some of the abuses, environmentalists and economists have suggested ways to improve cost-benefit analysis.

- Require all studies to use a uniform set of standards.
- Clearly state all assumptions.
- Show all projected costs, with their estimated range of values based on each set of assumptions.
- Estimate the short- and long-term benefits and costs to all affected population groups.
- Estimate the effectiveness of the project or form of regulation, instead of assuming (as is often done) that all projects and regulations will be executed with 100% efficiency and effectiveness.
- Open such evaluations to public review and challenge.
- Do not use cost-benefit analysis as the sole method of determining environmental, health, resource, or consumer protection policies.

- Powerlessness that can subject the poor to being tricked into signing away the little land or livestock they own, paying such high interest rates on loans that they lose their land and livestock, and having to pay bribes to get work.

These local parts of the poverty trap are reinforced by government policies at the national level. They include national budgets that favor urban and industrial over rural development and military over social expenditures.

Additional layers of the global poverty trap are added at the international level. They include

- the $1.3-trillion debt LDCs owe to MDC banks and governments (UNICEF blames the death of

500,000 children a year on the debt burden of the LDCs)

- sharp declines in the income of LDCs that depend on exports of cash crops such as coffee, sugar, and cotton and raw materials such as iron ore and copper because of drops in the market prices of those commodities since 1980

- rising trade barriers in rich countries that each year cost LDCs about $100 billion in lost sales and depressed prices

- decreased investment in LDCs by MDCs because of the economic turmoil and uncertainty in these poor countries

- loss of investment capital because wealthy elites in LDCs have invested or deposited much of their money abroad, where it is safe from taxation and political and economic disruptions

POVERTY AND ENVIRONMENTAL DEGRADA-
TION Poverty is the primary cause of environmental degradation in LDCs. For the rural poor, sustaining soil fertility, forest productivity, and wildlife populations is not just an idea, it is what keeps them alive. The poor are also the world's greatest recyclers and reusers. They can't afford to waste anything.

However, when the rural poor are faced with starvation, they are driven to knowingly overexploit their vital resource base. The result is increased deforestation, soil erosion and flooding, spreading deserts, and loss of biodiversity. They become locked into a downward spiral of increasing poverty, desperation and misery, and environmental degradation. This is a tragedy for the poor, the rich, and the earth.

In effect, LDCs are being coerced into depleting their resources to help support the wasteful, Earth-degrading lifestyles of people in MDCs and the rich in their own countries who refuse to share enough of their enormous wealth to eliminate poverty. If these LDCs don't sell off their resources at bargain basement prices they can't pay the interest on their debts and don't have enough income to prevent economic decline. However, by selling off and degrading their resource base, these LDCs face an even bleaker economic and environmental future.

Without radical shifts in policies by both MDCs and LDCs, perhaps 3 billion to 5 billion people—half of humanity—could be living in absolute poverty some time between 2050 and 2075. Another possibility is that pollution and environmental degradation by the rich and the poor will become so great that there will be a population crash (Figure 6-3), with 2 billion to 5 billion people dying prematurely.

WHAT CAN BE DONE? The solution to the global poverty–environmental degradation trap is to direct virtually all forms of aid from MDCs and from the governments of LDCs to the one out of five people on Earth without enough land or income to meet basic needs. This is based on Mahatma Gandhi's concept of *antyodaya*: putting the poor and their environment first, not last.

Instead of asking only experts and consultants what to do, we must also ask the poor. They must be actively involved as advisers, leaders, and participants in determining what they need and in the design and running of programs that enable them to help themselves. They know far more about poverty, survival, and environmental sustainability than bureaucrats or experts. How many of the world's experts could survive by growing food on a steeply sloping plot or could raise and keep a family of six alive on 80 cents a day?

The role of MDCs and the governments of LDCs is to give the poor enough land and job income to meet their basic needs, putting them in charge, getting out of their way, spotlighting what works, and transferring that information to others.

The layers of the poverty trap at the national level must be dismantled by drastic and difficult changes in government policies. They include

- shifting more of the national budget to the rural and urban poor

- seeing that the present trickle of aid to the poor becomes a healthy flow and that this flow is not diverted by the greedy before it reaches the needy

- giving villages, villagers, and the urban poor title to common lands and to crops and trees they plant on common lands

- redistributing some of the land owned by the wealthy to the poor, as has been done in South Korea and China

- allocating much more money for education, health care, and family planning, clean drinking water, and sanitation for the poor in rural villages and in urban slums, with these programs planned and run by local residents

- greatly increasing the rights of poor women, who grow and cook most of the food, collect most of the firewood, haul most of the water, and provide most of the health care for the poor with no pay and few human rights

The local poor and the governments of LDCs cannot escape the widening jaws of the poverty–environmental degradation trap unless MDCs and the rich in LDCs dismantle their layers of this trap. Ways to dismantle those layers include

- Forgiving much (at least 60%) of the present debt owed by LDCs to MDCs and recognizing that this is a vital investment in global environmental and economic security for the rich and the poor. Much of this debt can be forgiven in exchange for agreements by the governments of LDCs to increase expenditures for rural development, family planning, health care, education, and better land redistribution, protection of remaining wilderness areas, and sustainable use of other lands and renewable resources (see Case Study on p. 270).

- Increasing the nonmilitary aid given by MDCs to LDCs to 5% of the annual GNP of the MDCs. Currently, the United States contributes less than 0.25% of its GNP as nonmilitary aid to LDCs. This aid should be given directly to the poor to help them sustain themselves. All national and international lending agencies should not lend money for projects unless a favorable environmental impact assessment has been made and strict controls are used to see that environmental controls are fully implemented.

- Lifting trade barriers that hinder the export of commodities from LDCs to MDCs. Businesses in MDCs now being protected from cheaper foreign imports will oppose this. However, it is time for protected businesses to innovate and become more competitive instead of resisting change in the name of protecting short-term profits and keeping prices for consumers higher than they need be. They should practice the basic principle of free enterprise: If you can't compete, you shouldn't be in business. However, lifting these trade barriers should not be used by powerful multinational companies as an excuse for reducing environmental and consumer protection by reducing pollution and food safety standards to global standards decided by international bodies.

- Having governments throughout the world cooperate in tracking the flight and concealment of capital from LDCs to MDCs and requiring the owners of that capital to pay taxes on it and any income it generates to their national treasuries to help finance the economic recovery of their homelands.

- Recognizing that the greatest threat to the global environment for the rich and the poor and other species are the throwaway economic systems (Figure 3-20) in MDCs and replacing them with sustainable-Earth economic systems (Section 24-6).

- Aiding LDCs in developing new, diversified sustainable-Earth economies instead of using the throwaway economic systems of the MDCs that must now be modified and replaced because they threaten the life-support systems for everyone (Section 24-6).

24-6 Making the Transition to a Sustainable-Earth Economy

A SUSTAINABLE-EARTH ECONOMY Environmentalists and a few economists, including Herman Daly (see Guest Essay on p. 671), Kenneth Boulding (see Guest Essay on p. 306), Nicholas Georgescu-Roegen, Joseph Vogel, E. J. Mishan, E. F. Schumacher, and John Gowdy, have proposed that the world's countries make a transition to a **sustainable-Earth economy** (see Spotlight below).

They call for us to move from an Earth-plundering economy based on addiction to unlimited economic growth to an Earth-sustaining economy based on cooperating with the earth. They see the processes that sustain the earth as the best model for any human economy, a model based on recognizing that the wealth that truly sustains us is not money or property but nature.

SPOTLIGHT Characteristics of a Sustainable-Earth Economy

A sustainable-Earth economy discourages Earth-degrading types of economic growth and encourages Earth-sustaining activities to prevent overloading and degradation of Earth's life-support systems now and in the future.

Discourages

- Throwaway and nondegradable products, use of oil and coal, nuclear energy, deforestation, overgrazing, groundwater depletion, soil erosion, resource waste, and output pollution control.

- Creation and satisfaction of wants that cause high levels of pollution, environmental degradation, and resource waste.

Does This By

- Using taxes and marketable permits to internalize the external costs of goods and services so that market prices of all goods and services reflect their true costs.

- Removing government subsidies from highly pollution-producing, resource-depleting, and resource-wasting economic activities.

- Discouraging policies and practices that support current living standards by depleting Earth's natural resource capital for us, future generations, and other species.

- Requiring an environmental audit for all economic goods from "cradle to grave" and widely publishing the results.

Encourages

- A demographic transition to a stable world population of low birth and death rates (Figure 8-15).

- An energy transition with emphasis on high efficiency and increasing reliance on perpetual and renewable energy resources.

- An economic transition from a society devoted to satisfying the artificially created wants of a few to one committed to providing

(continued)

the basic needs of all. This includes making sure that taxes and other burdens of making this transition do not fall unfairly on the poor.

- Recycling, reuse, solar energy, improving energy efficiency, education, prevention of health problems, ecological restoration, pollution prevention, appropriate technology, waste reduction, and long-lasting, reusable, easily repaired products (durability instead of disposability).

- Sustainable development that emphasizes growth in the quality of life instead of the quantity of economic goods and that does not deplete or degrade Earth's natural capital for current and future generations. Proposals made under the name of sustainable development must be evaluated carefully to be sure that they are not sanitized versions of economic growth as usual.

- Preservation of biological diversity at local, national, and global levels by setting aside and controlling the use of forests, wetlands, grasslands, soil, wildlife, and representative aquatic ecosystems.

- Use of renewable resources at a sustainable rate.

- Limiting waste discharge into the environment to the rate at which wastes can be diluted, absorbed, and degraded by natural processes with no harm to humans, other species, or the functioning of natural processes.

- Sustainable agriculture (Section 14-6) that conserves soil (Section 12-3) and water (Section 13-4), emphasizes polyculture instead of monoculture, and emphasizes use of natural fertilizers and integrated pest management (Section 23-5).

- Use of locally available matter and energy resources to reduce the loss of capital, income, and jobs from the local economy (see Case Study on p. 506).

- Decentralization of some production facilities to reduce transportation costs, make better use of locally available resources, enhance national security by spreading out targets, increase employment, and keep money circulating in local economies.

- A transition from competitive nationalistic politics to cooperative planetary politics in which countries work together politically and economically to promote peace and sustain Earth's life-support systems for everyone now and in the future.

- A fairer distribution of the world's resources and wealth, with primary emphasis on meeting the basic needs of the poor and helping them sustain themselves (see Case Study on p. 669).

- Breaking down trade barriers between MDCs and LDCs (see Spotlight on p. 669).

- A broadened definition of national security to include resource, environmental, and economic security and consideration of demographic issues. In 1990, the U.S. federal government spent $330 billion on military security and only $14 billion on environmental security.

Does This By

- Recognizing that economics is a subsystem of the ecosphere (Figure 24-4) and integrating economics and ecology in decision making (the most important condition).

- Using government subsidies and taxes to encourage pollution prevention, resource conservation, and waste reduction, and selling marketable permits for resource extraction.

- Increasing aid from rich countries to poor countries that helps LDCs become more self-reliant rather than more dependent on MDCs. Since 1982, the traditional flow of capital from MDCs to LDCs has been reversed, with more than $50 billion annually transferred to MDCs from LDCs, mostly to pay interest on their enormous debt. This causes such countries to deplete their natural capital to pay the interest on their debt.

- Eliminating at least 60% of the $1.3-trillion debt that LDCs owe to MDCs and international lending agencies through debt forgiveness in exchange for agreements to improve environmental quality, education, and health care, reduce poverty, and use resources sustainably.

- Requiring all international lending institutions and governments to make only loans that enhance the transition to a sustainable-Earth economy.

Determines Progress with Indicators That Measure

- Changes in the quality of life.

- Sustainable use of renewable resources.

- Recycling and reuse of nonrenewable resources.

- Pollution prevention and waste reduction.

- Improvements in energy efficiency.

- The life-cycle environmental impacts of all goods and services.

The Kerala Experiment

The state of Kerala in southwest India (Figure 8-17) has shown how quality of life can be improved without emphasizing economic growth. Although this region suffers from tremendous poverty and is one of the world's most densely populated areas, it has achieved some of the highest scores in LDCs on key indicators of life quality.

Its life expectancy at birth of 68 years approaches the average of 74 years in MDCs and exceeds that of 61 years in LDCs and 57 years in India. Kerala's infant mortality rate is 27 per 1,000 births compared with 16 for MDCs, 81 for LDCs, and 95 for India. Its birth rate is 22 per 1,000 compared with 15 for MDCs, 31 for LDCs, and 32 per 1,000 for India. Almost 75% of Kerala's citizens can read or write compared with

less than 50% for the rest of India. Although Kerala's per capita income is lower than that of the rest of India, nutrition in this state is at least equal to and perhaps better than that of the rest of the country.

In Kerala, which has India's most extensive and accessible medical facilities, health care is a right. Its improved health is a result of better housing (including a homebuilding program for landless laborers), drinking water, sanitation, immunization, funding, food distribution (including a school lunch program, feeding programs for infants and pregnant and lactating women, and ration cards for all households that allow them to buy rice and certain basic commodities at subsidized prices) than in the rest of India.

In Kerala, these quality of life

benefits are fairly evenly distributed among men and women, urban and rural areas, and low and high castes. Its remarkably high levels of health, education, and social justice are the results of decades of political struggles, which have led to distribution of land ownership and fairly even distribution of its rich resources.

That does not mean that Kerala does not have problems. Its economy suffers from serious unemployment for about 25% of its potential work force. However, the Kerala experiment shows that fairer distribution of land, food, and health care and widespread education can improve the quality of life for the poor even when per capita income is low.

Using Free Trade as an Excuse to Restrict Environmental Protection and Sustainable Use of Resources

Reducing unfair trade barriers between countries, especially between MDCs and LDCs, is important. However, this should not be done by establishing global standards that would prevent any country from having higher standards than other countries for pollution control, soil conservation, food safety, use of recycled materials, and export or import of hazardous chemicals or wastes, as is being proposed in the latest version of the international General Agreement on Tariffs and Trade (GATT).

If these proposals are adopted, communities, states, and countries would no longer be able to decide how to use their resources and protect their environment. This power would be turned over to an international commission dominated by multinational corporations and the

governments of MDCs, which represent the interests of those businesses. Decisions on legally enforceable international standards would be made behind closed doors with little, if any, public participation. According to consumer advocate Ralph Nader, GATT will impose "a mega-corporate view of the world on the world. It is designed to circumvent democratic institutions and override local, state, and national government efforts to protect consumers and the environment."

Precedents for what is expected to happen can be seen from enforcement of regional free-trade agreements. In 1987, the European Commission took Denmark to the European Court of Justice and won because it charged that Denmark's requirement of only refillable bottles was a restraint on free trade. After

being pushed by the Bush administration, British Columbia ended a government-funded tree-planting program because the United States (with pressure from U.S. timber companies) argued that it was an unfair subsidy to Canada's timber industry.

If there is not a quick and effective public outcry against this portion of GATT, environmental protection and sustainable use of resources could be set back at a time when they should be significantly increased. Allowed levels of DDT and other pesticides on foods imported by the United States may have to be raised, U.S. efforts to label tuna fish products as dolphin-safe may be banned, and the former West Germany's law requiring beverage containers to be recycled could be overturned because they

(continued)

could be viewed as nontariff trade barriers.

Government bans on the export of raw logs to slow the destruction of rain forests or ancient forests could also be overturned. Proposed GATT standards could also prevent countries from restricting the import of goods, such as hazardous wastes or medicines or pesticides, they consider too risky, because they could not apply higher environmental standards than other countries.

GATT would also make it difficult for any nation to protect local and small businesses. Instead, it would pit small and fledgling business against large multinational companies in the name of free trade, somewhat like putting Arnold Schwarzenegger in the ring with a five-year old.

Environmentalists believe that the primary purpose of any international trade agreement should be to greatly increase environmental protection and sustainable resource use, and eliminate poverty by making poor nations richer and making the distribution of wealth within countries more equitable. Environmentalists charge that the current GATT proposals not only fail to do this, they also hinder such goals.

MAKING SUSTAINING THE EARTH PROFITABLE

Making the transition to a sustainable-Earth economy will cost about $500 billion a year (including $130 billion a year for retiring the debt of LDCs) for ten years or more. This involves spending only about half as much per year for environmental and economic security as the world now spends each year on military security.

The exciting news is that there is a way to shift from our current Earth-degrading economy to a sustainable-Earth economy within 10 to 20 years by using the profit motive that drives the world's market-based economic systems. Money can be made by working with the earth or by working against the earth.

The basic problem is that over the years, governments have used taxpayers' money mostly to reward Earth-degrading businesses. The way out of this self-destructive behavior is to switch the rewards from Earth-degrading to Earth-sustaining businesses, and do this over a time period that allows companies to make the shift.

To do this, elected officials, prodded by voters, would have to announce that over the next decade, all federal, state, and local subsidies that encourage resource depletion and waste, and environmental degradation would be phased out and replaced with taxes on such activities. During that same period, new government subsidies would be phased in for businesses built around resource conservation, waste reduction, recycling, reuse, and pollution prevention.

Because this shift would be well publicized and would take place over ten years, businesses would have time to shift into these new ways to make a profit. This would also provide jobs because most Earth-sustaining businesses are more labor intensive than Earth-degrading businesses. Also, managers, workers, and stockholders in these businesses would be able to feel better about what they were making and doing.

Those with vision and creativity are busy creating the Earth-sustaining businesses of the future. Those scared of change and risk taking will be left behind to remain part of the problem instead of part of the solution until they are forced to change or go out of business.

Making this transition will not be easy. Powerful economic interests making profits from the present system of rewards will vigorously oppose such changes, but if voters eliminate those who cave in to those interests, politicians will get the message loud and clear. Consumers and investors will have to exercise the enormous power they have over corporate behavior, what products are produced, and how they are produced (see Individuals Matter on p. 671).

There is something fundamentally wrong in treating the earth as if it were a business in liquidation.

HERMAN E. DALY

Individual consumers are the catalyst for making the shift to an Earth-sustaining economy. By choosing what to buy and what companies to invest in, American and other consumers can also force companies and elected leaders to become more environmentally responsible.

Here are some guidelines for green consuming.

1. Begin by asking yourself if you really need this product. Recognize that green consuming is still consuming, much of it devoted to meeting harmful and unsatisfying wants.

2. When possible, buy products that are durable and reusable and used rather than new.

3. When that is not possible, buy products that are made from recycled materials or renewable resources and that are recyclable. Just because something is recyclable doesn't mean that it will be recycled unless you see that it gets to a recycling center and unless you buy recycled products to create a demand for such products.

4. Buy the product with the least packaging.

5. Boycott harmful products.*

6. Buy products whose products have been evaluated from cradle to grave and given the Green Seal of approval.

7. Help elect people to local, state, and national offices who make sustaining the earth their top priority.

Buying green and recycling a little bit (25% instead of at least 60%) may make us feel good and may buy a little time. But if that is all we do, sooner or later we will be overwhelmed by the diseases of rapid population growth, overconsumption of resources, and resource waste and by failure to modify the economic and political systems that promote those afflictions.

*For information on boycotted products, subscribe to *National Boycott News*, 6506 28th Avenue N.E., Seattle, WA 98115 ($10.00 a year).

If you invest in money market funds or in stocks, invest in green funds and companies.† Try to work for or start green companies. Each year, the Council on Economic Priorities publishes a small book rating companies on their social and environmental responsibility. To reduce the hemorrhage of capital, energy, resources, and jobs from local economies, participate in, invest in, and support environmentally responsible production by locally owned, operated, and controlled enterprises.

On Earth Day 1990, millions of people signed the Earth Day Pledge, promising to honor the environment when they vote, purchase, consume, and invest. Honoring this pledge is a way of exercising the most important economic and political power we have to help sustain the earth.

†For information on green investing, contact The Social Investment Forum, 711 Atlantic Avenue, Boston, MA 02111.

GUEST ESSAY The Steady State Economy in Outline

Herman E. Daly

Herman E. Daly is Senior Environmental Economist at the World Bank. Until 1988, he was Alumni Professor of Economics at Louisiana State University. He has been a member of the Committee on Mineral Resources and Environment of the National Academy of Sciences and has served on the boards of advisers of numerous environmental organizations. He is also coeditor of the journal Ecological Economics *(Elsevier). His interest in economic development, population, resources, and environment has resulted in some 75 professional articles, as well as four books including* Steady-State Economics *(Island Press, 1991),* Economics, Ecology, Ethics *(Freeman, 1980), and* For the Common Good: Redirecting the Economy Towards Community, the Environment, and a Sustainable Future *(with John Cobb, Beacon Press, 1989). He is one of a small number of economists seriously thinking about sustainable-Earth economics.*

The steady state economy is basically a physical concept with important social and moral implications. It is defined as a constant stock of physical wealth and people. This wealth and population size is maintained at some desirable, chosen level by a low rate of throughput of matter

(continued)

and energy resources so the longevity of people and goods is high.

Throughput is roughly equivalent to GNP, the annual flow of new production. It is the cost of maintaining the stocks of final goods and services by continually importing high-quality matter and energy resources from the environment and exporting waste matter and low-quality heat energy back to the environment [Figure 3-20].

Currently, we attempt to maximize the growth of the GNP, but the reasoning just given suggests that we should relabel it gross national cost or GNC. We should minimize it, subject to maintenance of a chosen level of stocks of essential items. For example, if we can maintain a desired, sufficient stock of items such as cars with a lower throughput of iron, coal, petroleum, and other resources, we are better off, not worse off.

To maximize GNP throughput for its own sake is absurd. Physical and ecological limits to the volume of throughput imply the eventual necessity of a steady state economy. Less recognizable but probably more stringent social and moral limits imply the desirability of a steady state economy long before it becomes a physical necessity.

For example, the development and use of nuclear reactors to produce electricity is heavily subsidized by the government. Since the mid-1970s, the growth of this technology has declined sharply. The decline is not due to a shortage of uranium fuel. Instead, it is due to social and economic limits. Poor management, excessive costs, and serious accidents such as the one at the Chernobyl nuclear plant have seriously undermined public support of this technology.

These plants exist only because of huge government subsidies. If the nuclear power industry was forced to operate in an open market without government subsidies, it would probably not be developed because of too low an economic return on the investment. Attempts to revive the nuclear industry by providing more subsidies based on the argument that nuclear power is needed to reduce the rate of global warming will further waste enormous amounts of limited economic and human resources and will do little to slow global warming compared with other, more cost-effective alternatives [see Pro/Con on p. 500].

Once we have attained a steady state economy at some level of stocks, we are not forever frozen at that level. Moral and technological changes may make it both possible and desirable to grow (or decline) to a different level. Growth, however, will be seen as a temporary process necessary to move from one steady state level to another, not as an economic norm. This requires a substantial shift in present economic thought. It will require that most current economic ideas and models be replaced or drastically modified. Most economists strongly resist this radical change in the way they think and act.

The greatest challenges facing us today are

- for physical and biological scientists to define more clearly the limits and interactions within ecosystems

and the ecosphere (which determine the feasible levels of the steady state) and to develop technologies more in conformity with such limits

- for social scientists to design the institutions that will bring about the transition to a steady state and permit its continuance

- for philosophers, theologians, and educators to stress the neglected traditions of stewardship and distributive justice that exist in our cultural and religious heritage

The last item is of paramount importance because the problem of sharing a fixed amount of resources and goods is much greater than that of sharing a growing amount. Indeed, this has been the primary reason for giving top priority to growth. If the pie is always growing, it is said, there will be crumbs for the poor. This avoids the moral question of a more equitable distribution of the world's resources and wealth.

The kinds of economic institutions needed to make this transition follow directly from the definition of a steady state economy. We need an institution for maintaining a constant population size within the limits of available resources. For example, economic incentives can be used to encourage each woman or couple to have no more than a certain number of children, or each woman or couple could be given a marketable license to have a certain number of children, as economist Kenneth Boulding has suggested.

We also need an institution for maintaining a constant stock of physical wealth and limiting resource throughput. For example, the government could set and auction off transferable annual depletion quotas for key resources. Finally, there must be an institution to limit inequalities in the distribution of the constant physical wealth among the constant population in a steady state economy. For example, there might be minimum and maximum limits on personal income and maximum limits on personal wealth.

Many such institutions could be imagined. The problem is to achieve the necessary global and societal (macro) control with the least sacrifice of freedom at the individual (micro) level.

Guest Essay Discussion

1. Does a steady state economy imply the end of technological growth? Explain.

2. Why does the concept of the steady state economy force us to face up to the moral issue of the distribution of wealth?

3. Should minimum and maximum limits on personal income and wealth be established? Explain.

DISCUSSION TOPICS

1. Some economists argue that only through unlimited economic growth will we have enough money to eliminate poverty and protect the environment. Explain why you agree or disagree with that view. If you disagree, how should we deal with these problems? For example, do you agree or disagree with the proposals for dismantling the global poverty trap listed on pages 666–667? Explain.

2. The primary goal of all current economic systems is to maximize growth by maximizing the production and consumption of economic goods. Do you agree with that goal? Explain. What are the alternatives?

3. Do you believe that cost-benefit analysis should be used to make all decisions about how limited federal, state, and local government funds are to be used? Explain. If not, what decisions should not be made in this way?

4. What are the biggest advantages and disadvantages of the present mixed economic system in the United States? What substantial changes, if any, would you make in this system?

5. Do you favor internalizing the external costs of pollution and unnecessary resource waste? Explain. How might it affect your lifestyle? The lifestyle of the poor? Wildlife?

6. If a particular investment in resource exploitation will cause the relatively well-off to get richer and the poor and the middle class to become more impoverished, should the investment be made? Explain.

7. Are jobs and profits more important than the health of the ecosphere? Explain. How can we have jobs, profits, and environmental security?

8. **a.** Do you believe that we should establish optimal levels or zero discharge levels for most of the chemicals we release into the environment? Explain. What effects would adopting zero discharge levels have on your life and lifestyle?

   b. Do you believe that all chemicals we release or propose to release into the environment should be assumed to be guilty of causing harm until proven otherwise? Explain. What effects would adopting this legal principle have on your life and lifestyle?

9. Do you favor making a shift to a sustainable-Earth economy? Explain. How might this affect your lifestyle? The lifestyle of the poor? Wildlife?

*10. Make a list of all the economic goods you use, and then identify those that meet your basic needs and those that satisfy your wants. Identify any economic wants you would be willing to give up. Identify those you believe you should give up but are unwilling to give up. Identify wants that you hope to satisfy in the future. List what you believe will make you happy and improve the quality of your life. Compare these items with your list of currently satisfied wants and those you hope to satisfy in the future. Relate the results of this analysis to your personal impact on the environment. Compare your results with those of your classmates.

CHAPTER 25

POLITICS AND ENVIRONMENT

General Questions and Issues

1. How do political decisions affect resource use and environmental quality?

2. How are environmental and resource laws and policies made in the United States?

3. What are some of the outstanding achievements of environmental law in the United States?

4. How can we bring about change?

A technological society has two choices. First, it can wait until catastrophic failures expose systemic deficiencies, distortions, and self-deceptions. . . . Second, a culture can provide social checks and balances to correct for systemic distortions prior to catastrophic failures.

MAHATMA GANDHI

OLITICS IS THE PROCESS by which individuals and groups try to influence or control the policies and actions of governments of the local, state, national, or international community. **Politics** is concerned with the distribution of resources and benefits—who gets what, when, and how. Thus, it plays a significant role in regulating the world's economic systems and influencing economic decisions (Chapter 24).

Solving the environmental and resource problems we face is fundamentally a political problem because it requires the public to unite and force elected officials at the local, state, and national levels to make substantial changes in the rewards (subsidies) and penalties (taxes and regulations) that rich and powerful corporations receive for using Earth's resources in certain ways. This involves restructuring the way business is done by shifting production and profits from Earth-degrading to Earth-sustaining businesses (see Spotlight on p. 667).

While this shift will benefit everyone in the long run, in the short run it is seen as a serious threat to entrenched economic and political interests. However, we have come to the point where the old ways of doing business are so threatening to our environmental, economic, and military security and to the ecosphere processes upon which all life depends that we must have the wisdom and courage to make drastic political and economic changes.

We are at a turning point. We can reshape our economic and political systems based on how nature works, or nature will do the job for us with an unprecedented and unnecessary increase in human misery and loss of life.

25-1 Influencing Public Environmental and Resource Policy

GROUPS INVOLVED IN INFLUENCING PUBLIC POLICY Decisions about environmental and resource use policies are influenced by a mixture of governmental and nongovernmental organizations (NGOs) operating at the global, regional, national, and subnational (state and local) levels (Table 25-1).

Elites, the relatively few people who have power, govern all societies, but governments differ in the way elites carry out the major functions of government. There are two broad types of government:

- *Constitutional democracy*, in which an effective constitution provides the basis of governmental authority and puts restraints on governmental power through free elections and freely expressed public opinion. A democracy is government "by the peo-

Table 25-1 Groups Influencing Environmental and Resource Use Public Policy

Levels	Governmental	Nongovernmental	
		Nonprofit	**Profit Making**
Global	Intergovernmental organizations such as the UN Food and Agriculture Organization, UN Environment Programme, International Atomic Energy Agency	International Union for the Conservation of Nature and Natural Resources, Friends of the Earth, Greenpeace (see Appendix 1)	Multinational businesses such as Dole, Mobil Oil, Mitsubishi
Regional	European Economic Community, Joint Commission on the Great Lakes (Canada and the United States)	European League for Economic Cooperation	Businesses operating in a region such as North America or the Mediterranean basin
National	National governments, agencies such as the U.S. Environmental Protection Agency and the U.S. Forest Service (see Appendix 1)	American Forestry Association, Sierra Club, Natural Resources Defense Council (see Appendix 1)	Businesses operating within a country
Subnational	State and local governments and agencies	State and local citizen groups	Businesses operating within a state or local area

ple" through elected elites who are supposed to follow a constitution. Countries that are constitutional democracies include the United States, Canada, Venezuela, and most western European countries.

- *Autocracy*, in which governmental power is concentrated in a self-authorized, self-directing, self-perpetuating elite. In an *authoritarian autocracy*, the ruling elite allow individuals and societal groups significant independent activity as long as such activity does not threaten the power or policies of the ruling elite. Examples are China, Syria, the former USSR, Kuwait, Saudi Arabia, and Chile. In a *totalitarian autocracy*, little independent activity is permitted unless it is specifically authorized by the ruling elite. Examples are Cuba, Ethiopia, and Iraq (under Saddam Hussein).

The primary mechanism for change in autocratic governments is the overthrow of the ruling elite by the people, or by some portion of the government (often military leaders), and the establishment of a new governing elite.

Constitutional democracies are run by elected elites drawn largely from the upper socioeconomic strata of society. These government officials are strongly influenced by other elites who run corporations, the media, educational institutions, and other organized special-interest groups. Individuals and organized groups influence and change government policies in constitutional democracies mainly by

- voting
- contributing money and time to candidates running for office
- lobbying and writing elected representatives to pass certain laws, establish certain policies, and fund various programs (see Individuals Matter on p. 676)
- using the formal education system and the media to influence public opinion
- filing lawsuits asking the courts to overturn, enforce, or interpret the meaning of existing laws
- carrying out grassroots activities such as marches, mass meetings, sit-ins, hugging trees to prevent them from being cut (see Individuals Matter on p. 280), protesting the location of waste landfills and incinerators, organizing product boycotts, and using consumer buying power (see Individuals Matter on p. 671)

REACTION-TO-CRISIS PUBLIC POLITICS IN DEMOCRACIES Political systems in constitutional democracies are designed to bring about gradual or incremental change, not revolutionary change. Rapid change is difficult because of distribution of power among different branches of government, conflicts among interest groups, conflicting information from experts, and lack of money.

Decision makers in democratic governments must deal with an array of conflicting groups. Each special-

It is very important to write or call elected officials to ask them to oppose or support specific environmental legislation or to compliment them for a particular stand. You may be thinking, "What can my one letter or call do?" If done correctly, letters or calls supporting or opposing a particular position can accumulate. When that happens, elected officials are forced to recognize that if they don't vote a certain way for the people they represent, they may not be reelected.

The following are guidelines for communicating with elected officials effectively:*

1. Address the letter properly:
    a. The President
        The White House
        1600 Pennsylvania Ave.,N.W.
        Washington, DC 20500
        Dear Mr. President:
    b. Your senators:
        The Honorable _____
        Senate Office Building
        Washington, DC 20510
        Dear Senator _____:
    c. Your representative:
        The Honorable _____
        House Office Building
        Washington, DC 20515
        Dear Representative _____:

2. Concentrate on your own representatives.

3. Be brief (a page or less) and cover only one subject. Write the letter in your own words and express your own views — don't sign and send a form or photocopied letter.

4. If possible, identify the bill by number (for example, "H.R.

123" or "S. 313") or name, and ask the representative or senator to do something specific (cosponsor, support, or oppose it). You can get a free copy of any bill or committee report by writing to the House Document Room, U.S. House of Representatives, Washington, DC 20515, or the Senate Document Room, U.S. Senate, Washington, DC 20510.

5. Give specific reasons for your position, and give the impact of the legislation on you and your district.

6. If you have expert knowledge, share it with your elected representatives.

7. Be courteous and reasonable. Don't threaten or berate.

8. Be constructive. If you believe the bill takes the wrong approach, offer an alternative.

9. Ask for a response and include your name and return address.

10. Use positive reinforcement. After the vote supporting your position, write your representative a short note of thanks. A general rule here (as well as for life in general) is to give at least two earned compliments for every criticism. Also, write and thank other elected representatives who supported your position. Each year, the League of Conservation Voters, P.O. Box 500, Washington, DC 20077, (202) 785-VOTE, publishes an *Environmental Scorecard* (cost $5.00), which rates all members of Congress on how they voted on environmental issues. This list is not only useful in determining whom to thank, but is also a way to identify proenvironment legislators whose election campaigns should be supported.

11. If you are going to Washington, D.C., consider visiting your representative to lobby for your position. Go prepared, or you risk destroying your credibility and effectiveness. It helps to call or write ahead to ask for an appointment, but you can probably get an appointment (at least with a staff member) by calling after you arrive in Washington. You can also talk with your elected congressional representative when he or she is in your district. Phone the field office for an appointment.

12. Getting a bill passed is only the first step. Follow up by writing the president to be sure that the bill isn't vetoed and to the chairperson and members of the appropriations committee to request that enough money be appropriated to implement the law. Finally, write the federal agency (see addresses in Appendix 1) charged with carrying out the program, asking it to establish effective regulations promptly or to be more active in enforcing the law. It is even more important to monitor and influence action at the state and local levels, where all federal and state laws are either ignored or enforced. As Thomas Jefferson once said, "The execution of laws is more important than the making of them."

13. If you don't have time to write a letter, make a phone call and ask to speak to a staff member who works on the issue you are concerned about. The president: (202) 456-1414; U.S. Senate: (202) 224-3121; House of Representatives (202) 456-1414.

14. Get others to write or call.

15. These same rules apply to influencing elected officials at the local and state levels.

*A list of the elected federal officials for your state and district is usually available at the local post office. Each year, the League of Women Voters publishes a pamphlet, "When You Write to Washington," which lists all elected officials and includes a list of all committee members and chairpersons. This pamphlet can be obtained from the League of Women Voters, 1730 M St. N.W., Washington, DC 20036.

interest group is asking for resources or money or relief from taxes to help purchase or control more of certain resources. Interest groups that are highly organized and well funded usually have the most influence.

Because tax income is limited, developing and adopting a budget is the most important thing decision makers do. This involves answering two key questions: What resource use and distribution problems will be addressed? How much of limited tax income will be used to address each problem? Someone once said that the way to understand human history is to study budgets.

Most political decisions are made by bargaining, accommodation, and compromise between leaders of competing elites or power groups within a society. Most politicians who remain in power become good at finding compromises and making trade-offs that give a little to each side. They play an important role in holding society together, preventing chaos and disorder, and making incremental changes, but these same processes hinder substantial changes and dealing with long-range problems.

Politicians who call for the public to make short-term sacrifices in the interests of projected long-term gains often find it hard to win or hold office. For example, suppose a presidential candidate ran on a platform calling for the federal tax on gasoline to be raised to the point where gasoline would cost about three dollars a gallon. The candidate argues that this tax increase (with rebates or other aid to the poor, who would be hardest hit by such a consumption tax) is necessary to encourage conservation of oil and gasoline (see Spotlight on p. 441), to reduce air pollution, and to enhance future economic, environmental, and military security. Would you vote for a candidate who promises to triple the price of gasoline?

In the United States, the term of a representative is only 2 years, the president 4, and a senator 6. Those hoping to get reelected must devote much of their time and energy during the last year of their term to this task. Thus, the time horizon is only about 1 year for a representative, 3 years for a president, and 5 years for a senator. Yet, preventing or dealing with most of the environmental, economic, and social problems we face today requires a time horizon of 10 to 50 years.

Most business leaders also take a short-term view because their salaries, bonuses, and jobs are usually tied to the profits made during the past year (and in some cases, every three months). The quarterly and annual profit-and-loss statements submitted to owners and stockholders summarize management's short-term success or failure. However, all bottom lines are irrelevant if we don't build our actions around Earth's bottom line of sustaining the natural capital that supports all life and economic activity (Figure 24-4 and Spotlight on p. 667).

25-2 Environmental and Resource Policy in the United States

IMPORTANT FACTORS IN ENVIRONMENTAL POLICY MAKING The writers of the U.S. Constitution wanted to develop a political system strong enough to provide security and order and to protect liberty and property, but without giving too much power to the federal government. That was done by dividing political power between the federal and state governments and within the three branches of the federal government — legislative, executive, and judicial (Figure 25-1). Political power at the state level is also divided between executive, legislative, and judicial branches. Figure 25-2 summarizes the primary forces involved in environmental policy-making at the federal level. Similar factors are found at the state level.

The first step in establishing environmental or other policies is to persuade lawmakers that a problem exists and that the government has a responsibility to find solutions to the problem. This must be accomplished by a combination of public concern, media coverage, and scientific and economic judgments (Figure 25-2).

Once that hurdle is passed, lawmakers try to pass laws to deal with the problem (Figure 25-3). Most proposed environmental laws are evaluated by as many as ten committees in each chamber, because no single committee has complete responsibility for all environmental issues. Effective proposals are inevitably weakened by this fragmentation and the accompanying intense pressure and lobbying from groups supporting or opposing the law.

The end result is usually a compromise that satisfies no one but muddles through, mostly by making short-term incremental changes. Even if a tough environmental law is passed, the next hurdle is to see that Congress appropriates enough funds to adequately enforce the law.

The Environmental Protection Agency, created by administrative reorganization in 1970, has the responsibility for enforcing most federal environmental laws, for administering the Superfund to clean up abandoned toxic-waste sites, and for awarding grants for local sewage treatment plants. Laws governing the use of national forests, wilderness areas, wildlife refuges, and other public lands (see Spotlight on p. 390) are enforced by the appropriate managing department (Interior or Agriculture) working through the Department of Justice.

U.S. ENVIRONMENTAL LEGISLATION Environmentalists, with backing from many other citizens and members of Congress, have pressured Congress to

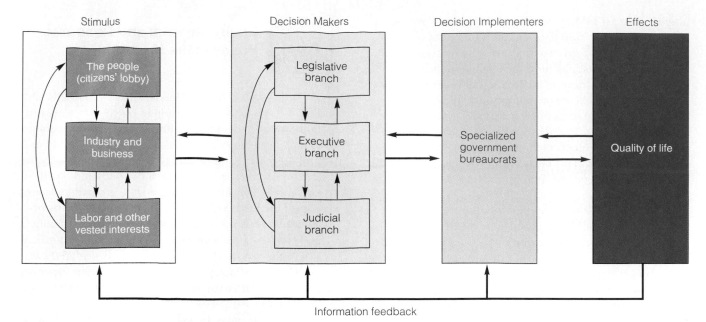

Figure 25-1 Simplified model of the U.S. political system.

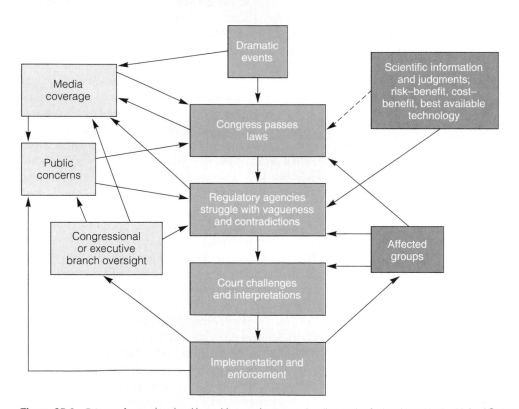

Figure 25-2 Primary forces involved in making environmental policy at the federal level in the United States.

enact a number of important federal environmental and resource protection laws, as discussed throughout this text and listed on the page before the inside of the back cover. Similar laws, and in some cases even stronger laws, have been passed by most states.

These laws attempt to provide environmental protection using mainly these five approaches:

1. setting standards for pollution levels or limiting emissions or effluents for various classes of pollutants (Federal Water Pollution Control Act and the Clean Air Act)

2. screening new substances before they are widely used in order to determine their safety (Toxic Substances Control Act of 1976)

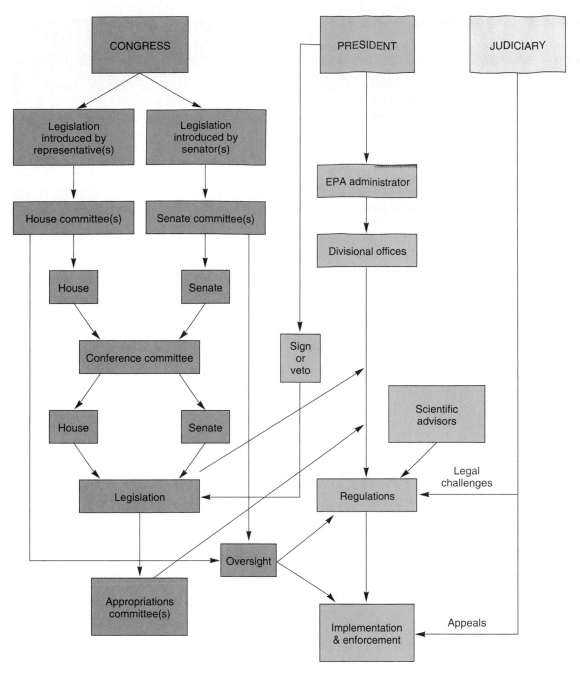

Figure 25-3 Interaction of the branches of the federal government involved in environmental laws and regulations.

3. requiring a comprehensive evaluation of the environmental impact of an activity before it is undertaken (National Environmental Policy Act, see Case Study on p. 680)

4. setting aside or protecting various ecosystems, resources, or species from harm (Wilderness Act and Endangered Species Act)

5. encouraging resource conservation (Resource Conservation and Recovery Act and National Energy Act)

Most states have modelled their environmental and resource conservation laws after federal laws and have established environmental and state agencies similar to those at the federal level. Some states, such as California, have adopted air pollution laws and standards that are more stringent than those at the federal level. Each year, an environmental organization, *Renew America* (see Appendix 1), publishes a report summarizing and rating the states on various aspects of environmental protection and resource conservation.

One important environmental law is the National Environmental Policy Act of 1969 (NEPA). This landmark legislation declared that the federal government has a responsibility to restore and maintain environmental quality.

One section of the law, designed to put this policy into action, requires that all federal agencies (except the EPA) file an *environmental impact statement (EIS)* or an *Environmental Assessment (EA)* for any proposed legislation or project having a significant effect on environmental quality.

Environmental assessments are prepared for projects with minimal environmental impacts. More comprehensive environmental impact statements are prepared for those that an agency views as having significant environmental impacts. Each year, about 10,000 environmental assessments and several hundred environmental impact statements are prepared by federal agencies and submitted to the EPA for review.

Each environmental impact statement must include

1. The purpose and need for the proposed action.

2. The probable environmental impacts (positive, negative, direct, and indirect) of the proposed action and of possible alternatives, including doing nothing.

3. Any adverse environmental effects that could not be avoided should the project be implemented.

4. Relationships between the probable short-term and long-term impacts of the proposal on environmental quality.

5. Irreversible and irretrievable commitments of resources that would be involved should the project be implemented.

6. Objections raised by reviewers of the preliminary draft of the statement.

7. The names and qualifications of the people primarily responsible for preparing the EIS.

8. References to back up all statements and conclusions.

Having to prepare EAs or EISs has forced government agencies to think more seriously about the effects of proposed projects and, in many cases, to consider and develop alternatives more carefully. Despite its many successes, the EIS process has been abused in some cases. Problems include

- using an EIS to justify a decision that has already been made rather than to make it a key part of the decision-making process

- trying to avoid the process by filing a Finding of Insignificant Impact statement denying that a

given project will have a significant environmental impact

- reporting impacts in such general terms (for example, "loss of wildlife," "elimination of vegetation," "increase in turbidity") that they are meaningless

- filling documents with great amounts of irrelevant or technical information to obscure serious impacts, overwhelm reviewers, and absorb the limited time and funds of the EPA and environmental groups

- inaccurate EISs produced by persons who specialize in preparing such documents but who do most (if not all) of their "research" in the literature instead of doing actual on-site studies

- using the process to delay and raise the costs of legitimate projects

Today, 36 states also have laws or executive orders requiring environmental impact statements for state projects. Australia, Canada, France, Ireland, New Zealand, Sweden, and several other countries also require environmental impact statements for projects carried out by government agencies.

IMPLEMENTING ENVIRONMENTAL LAWS The interpretation and implementation of laws passed by federal and state legislatures are turned over to bureaucracies and the courts (Figure 25-2). Some environmental laws contain glowing rhetoric about goals, but only vague, unrealistic, or indirect guidance about how those goals are to be achieved. In other cases, the laws specify general mechanisms for setting regulations. Examples are

- *no unreasonable risk*: food regulations in the Food, Drug, and Cosmetic Act

- *no-risk*: the Delaney clause, which prohibits the deliberate use of any food additive shown to cause

cancer in test animals or in people, and the zero discharge goals of the Safe Drinking Water Act and the Clean Water Act

- *risk-benefit balancing* (Section 20-3): pesticide regulations (see Spotlight on p. 641)

- *standards based on best available technology*: Clean Air Act, Clean Water Act, and Safe Drinking Water Act

- *cost-benefit balancing* (Section 24-4): Toxic Substances Control Act and Executive Order 12291, which gives the Office of Management and Budget the power to delay indefinitely, and in some cases veto, any federal regulation that is not proved to have the least cost to society (see Pro/Con on p. 664)

In its early pioneer stages, a vigorous, small bureaucratic agency with dynamic leadership can make progress. However, as a bureaucratic agency ages and grows in size, it can become complex, rigid, and more concerned with its own survival and getting an increasing share of the federal budget than with its mission.

Also, an agency's policies can become increasingly influenced by the industries it is supposed to regulate. Industries influence the president to appoint people to head and manage bureaucracies who favor industry positions and reward regulators who support industry positions with jobs when they leave the agency (see Pro/Con on p. 682).

Another problem is that responsibility for managing the nation's environmental and resource policy is widely fragmented among many agencies within the executive branch of the federal government and among state agencies. This often leads to contradictory policies, duplicated efforts, and wasted funds, while prohibiting an effective integrated approach to interrelated problems.

Almost every major environmental regulation is challenged in court by industry, environmental organizations, or both.

25-3 Environmental Law

SOME PRINCIPLES OF ENVIRONMENTAL LAW

There are two types of laws: statutory and common. A **statutory law** is one passed by a state legislature or Congress. Environmental laws (see page before inside the back cover pages) govern how the environment and human health should be protected and how resources are to be managed. Many of these laws have been discussed throughout this book. **Common law** is a large body of unwritten principles and rules based on thousands of past legal decisions. It is used by judges to resolve disputes in the absence of applicable statutory law.

In any court case, the **plaintiff** is the individual, group of individuals, corporation, or government agency bringing the charges, and the **defendant** is the individual, group of individuals, corporation, or government agency being charged. Civil and class action suits are the principal types of lawsuits used in environmental law.

In a **civil suit**, the plaintiff seeks to collect damages for injuries to health or for economic loss, to have the court issue a permanent injunction against any further wrongful action, or both. Such suits may be brought by an individual plaintiff or a group of clearly identified plaintiffs. Another type of civil suit is the **class action suit**, in which a group, often a public interest or environmental group, files a suit on behalf of a larger number of citizens who allege similar damages but who need not be listed and represented individually.

PROBLEMS WITH ENVIRONMENTAL LAWSUITS

The effectiveness of environmental lawsuits is limited by several factors.

- Permission to file a damage suit is granted only if it is clear that the harm to an individual plaintiff is unique and different enough to be distinguished from that to the general public. For example, you could not sue the Department of the Interior for actions leading to the commercialization of a wilderness area on the grounds that you do not want your taxes used to bring about environmental harm. The harm to you could not be distinguished from that to the general public. However, if the government damaged property you own, you would have standing to sue.

- Bringing any suit is expensive. Often, the defendant in an environmental suit is a large corporation or a government agency with ample funds for legal and scientific advice. In contrast, the plaintiffs in such cases usually use volunteer legal and scientific talent and rely on donations. According to EPA employee and whistle-blower, Hugh Kaufman (see Guest Essay on p. 703), "The citizens are armed with rubber bands and chewing gum against major polluters armed with the best-paid engineers and lawyers in the country. It ain't a fair fight."

- Public interest law firms cannot recover attorneys' fees unless Congress has specifically authorized such recovery in the law they have sued to enforce.

- It is often difficult for the plaintiff to prove that the accused is liable and responsible for a harmful action. Generally, the plaintiff must be able to (1) identify the harmful substance, (2) prove that identifiable damages occurred because of the presence of that substance, and (3) demonstrate that the substance came from the defendant. For example, suppose that one company is charged with bringing harm to individuals by polluting a river. If hundreds of other industries and cities dump waste into that river, establishing that the defendant company is the culprit will be very difficult, requiring extensive, costly scientific testing, research, and expert testimony.

- The court, or series of courts if the case is appealed, may take years to reach a decision. During that time, the defendant may continue the alleged damage unless the court issues a temporary injunction forbidding the allegedly harmful actions until the case is decided.

- A plaintiff may win the case but not be able to collect awarded damages because the company may have gone into bankruptcy.

Every decision the EPA makes is loaded with economic and political importance and intense controversy. That is not surprising, since each decision the agency makes has a tremendous impact on the short-term profits of corporations and the long-term sustainability of our life-support system.

Given its mission, its limited resources, and the volatile political arena within which it must operate, some view the EPA's performance as a qualified success. Without this agency, these analysts argue, the country's environmental problems would be much worse than they were in 1970 when the EPA was created.

Critics argue that the EPA has failed to carry out the goal stated in the National Environmental Policy Act of 1969: "to prevent and eliminate damage to the environment and the biosphere." They charge that after a vigorous start, the agency has become less bold and forceful, has not adequately implemented and enforced environmental laws, has had to be forced by legal suits brought by environmental organizations to enforce environmental laws and establish environmental priorities, does not adequately consult with and represent the environmental community and the general public, and has increasingly come under the influence of the industries it is supposed to regulate.

These critics point out that most of the EPA's efforts have been directed at negotiating and working out compromises with corporations about how much pollution is acceptable and what loss of human life is acceptable. In other words, the EPA has taken, or has been forced to take, the political "soft path" of pollution control (dealing with symptoms by applying bandages) instead of the more difficult, controversial, and confrontational "hard path" of pollution prevention (dealing with the diseases that cause pollution and environmental degradation).

Long-time EPA employee and whistle-blower William Sanjour has summarized why he believes the EPA has failed in its mission.* According to Sanjour, the problem starts at the White House because the president has a small number of top-priority programs, such as defense, the budget, economic growth, and reelection. The president wants real performance from these high-priority programs but wants only peace and quiet from all other programs. Thus, an EPA administrator can make tough-talking speeches about improving environmental quality and emphasizing pollution prevention but must not push policies or make decisions that cause political waves.

According to Sanjour, that means that the people who get ahead in the EPA (and in other low-priority bureaucracies) are those who don't try to get much done and don't make waves. Many EPA employees who have tried to do what the the law re-

*See William Sanjour, "Why the EPA Is Like It Is" (1990), 13 pages available from the author, EPA Mail Code WH-562B, 401 M St. S.W., Washington, DC 20460; 202-382-4502.

quires of them and what they are being paid for have ruined their careers in the EPA. Many others who have failed to do what the law required have not lost their jobs or suffered any career setbacks, and many have been rewarded with lucrative jobs in the corporations they were supposed to regulate. As Hugh Kaufman, another EPA whistle-blower (see Guest Essay on p. 703), puts it, "No good deed will go unpunished."

While EPA officials and lobbyists for industry and environmental groups are fighting over improved pollution standards, citizens whose health is threatened by polluted air and water are fighting for no exposure at all. Sanjour's advice is for individuals to fight for pollution prevention at the local level and expand such local grassroots efforts to the state level. Once enough pressure is received from the state level, the EPA and Congress begins listening and taking action.

It is encouraging that after 20 years, the EPA has discovered pollution prevention and its administrator and some of its staff are calling for prevention to become the agency's top priority. Because this approach will make waves for the president and industry, it won't become a priority until people demand that it become the basis of all EPA policy and insist that Congress provide the agency with enough funding and staffing to accomplish its incredibly difficult and important job.

- Plaintiffs sometimes abuse the system by bringing frivolous suits that delay and run up the costs of projects.

Despite these handicaps, proponents of environmental law have accomplished a great deal since the 1960s. Now there are more than 100 public interest law firms and groups (see Appendix 1) specializing partially or totally in environmental and consumer law, and hundreds of other lawyers and scientific experts participate in environmental and consumer law cases as needed (see Case Study on p. 684).

STRATEGIES OF POLLUTERS AND RESOURCE DEPLETERS It is natural that producers of pollution and resource degradation resist government regulations or taxes that require them to reduce or eliminate pollution and use resources more efficiently. Being forced to internalize some of the external costs they pass on to society (Section 24-3) costs them money and can reduce their profits.

Corporate elites use several basic strategies to ensure that government laws and regulations do little to damage corporate profit margins. They

- Make donations to the election campaigns of politicians favoring their positions.

- Establish groups of lobbyists and lawyers in national and state capitals. The corporate representatives oppose restrictive legislation, weaken proposed laws and standards, inject loopholes and opportunities for delays and legal challenges into laws, divert attention from important issues such as pollution prevention and waste reduction, make penalties for violations trivial compared with the profits to be made by not complying with the law, and make laws so complex and full of unnecessary technical jargon that they cannot be understood by even well-educated citizens.

- Lobby elected officials to reduce the budgets of the EPA, Department of the Interior, and other agencies so they do not have enough money or personnel to effectively monitor, implement, and enforce the laws passed by federal or state legislatures.

- Pressure elected officials to appoint agency heads and middle- and upper-level managers who support the position of industries threatened with environmental regulation — the "put the fox in the henhouse" approach. This is part of the revolving-door strategy in which members of the corporate elite temporarily accept government positions of power and government officials move into corporations.

- Make donations or give research grants to environmental and resource conservation organizations with the goal of diluting or influencing how far they go and withdrawing support if they go too far.

- Influence media by directly or implicitly threatening to withdraw vital advertising income if those organizations probe too deeply. If necessary, buy up media businesses.

- Mount well-funded advertising and political campaigns to encourage support for industry positions (see Pro/Con on p. 500), to scare and divide people by saying that certain laws and environmental regulations will put them out of work (see Case Study on p. 18), and to oppose tougher environmental and resource laws.

- Set up and highly publicize showcase environmental and resource conservation projects while continuing to do most of their business as usual.

- Adopt the latest environmental slogans, such as sustainable development, pollution prevention, recycling, reuse, resource reduction, and biodegradable products, and use them to give the appearance of change while continuing to do business as usual. Use this superficial adoption of environmental goals to convince the public that corporate elites will look out for them and the environment.

- Decide what is most profitable to manufacture, use advertising to create a demand for mostly throwaway products, and tell people that they are the problem because businesses are merely responding to consumer demands for a throwaway society. The goal of this strategy is to shift blame for environmental problems from corporate elites to the general public — a blame-the-victim strategy.

- Brand environmentalists as radical, anti-American terrorists who are a threat to environmental health and safety, jobs, the economy, and national security. Use propaganda and scare tactics to get the public to think of environmentalists as the Green Menace instead of people who are trying to make the planet a safer, better, and more just place to live.

- Intimidate and disrupt environmental activists and groups, using the tactics employed against labor, civil rights, women's, and antiwar movements. Fire whistle-blowers in industries and government service. Sue individuals and environmental groups to intimidate them and deplete their funds. Use smear campaigns to pit one activist group against another and divert attention from the real issues (the divide-and-conquer strategy). Persuade government officials to use the FBI and police to infiltrate environmental groups, to put activists under surveillance and collect dossiers on them, and to arrest or harass effective environmental activists (see Pro/Con on p. 689). Urge judges to set high bail for arrested environmental activists. In Texas, for example, a local magistrate demanded $100,000 bail for a Greenpeace activist who blocked a railroad track, roughly ten times the bond set for drug dealers and murderers in the same jurisdiction. Use of these tactics is a clear signal that a social-change movement is beginning to threaten the power of elites. Because of its growth in numbers and impact, the environmental movement in the United States and other countries is increasingly being subjected to such tactics.

- Centralize waste dumps and incinerators to avoid having to fight expensive and often unsuccessful battles with grassroots organizations of angry citizens (see Individuals Matter on p. 528).

- Defuse the importance of the environmental crisis by disconnecting it from the problems of economic recession and unemployment (which would be lessened by investing in Earth-sustaining businesses), health care (which would be greatly reduced by pollution prevention), worker safety

The Natural Resources Defense Council (NRDC) was founded in 1970. It now has 150 staff members working out of five offices in New York City, Washington, D.C., San Francisco, Los Angeles, and Honolulu. These staff members coordinate a nationwide network of scientists, lawyers, resource specialists, and activists working on critical environmental and resource problems.

These efforts are supported by membership fees and contributions from about 65,000 individuals and more than 100 foundations. NRDC's new central headquarters building in New York City has been designed to be the most energy-efficient office space in the United States.

The following are some of the many accomplishments of the NRDC:

- 1972—won a precedent-setting case requiring government environmental impact statements to consider all practical alternatives to and all potential effects of offshore oil leases; filed the first suit in federal court against the use of tall smokestacks as a substitute for controlling pollution from power plants.

- 1973—compelled the EPA to establish regulations reducing the use of toxic lead additives in gasoline; launched the National Clean Air Coalition.

- 1974—won a suit against the use of tall smokestacks in the U.S. Court of Appeals; launched an effort to ban use of chlorofluorocarbons (CFCs) in spray cans.

- 1975—forced the Nuclear Regulatory Commission to adopt tougher regulations for storage and disposal of radioactive wastes from uranium mining and processing.

- 1976—won a court case that required the EPA to set an ambient air quality standard for airborne lead.

- 1978—won the fight to have the EPA ban the use of CFCs in aerosol products.

- 1979—helped shape EPA regulations that require installation of pollution controls to cut sulfur dioxide emissions on all new coal-fired power plants.

- 1980—filed a petition with EPA to regulate emissions of fine particulates.

- 1981—joined with the National Clean Air Coalition in a successful effort to stop the Reagan administration's attempt to weaken the Clean Air Act in Congress.

- 1982—led a nationwide effort that defeated EPA plans to rescind rules to phase out lead in gasoline.

- 1983—filed a lawsuit that forced the National Steel Company to comply with air pollution control laws and pay $2.5 million in back penalties; spearheaded a successful campaign to protect fragile coastal areas in Florida, California, and Massachusetts from an offshore oil leasing program pushed by oil companies and the Reagan administration.

- 1984—filed a lawsuit compelling oil refineries to tighten pollution

(with worker safety and health being sacrificed for larger profit margins), and military security (which is meaningless without environmental security and is more vulnerable in a country with centralized power plants and manufacturing facilities than in a country where facilities are decentralized).

- Urge the federal government to prevent localities and states from passing stronger environmental laws than those at the federal level (see Case Study on p. 569).

- Circumvent local, state, and national environmental and resource use laws and regulations by having them established by international commissions dominated by multinational companies and elites under the guise of promoting free trade (see Spotlight on p. 669).

Not all corporations follow this model, but too many do. According to a study by Amitai Etzioni of the Harvard Business School, two-thirds of the Fortune 500 companies have been charged with serious crimes, from price fixing to illegal dumping of hazardous wastes.

Some businesses, recognizing the growing political and economic power of the national and global environmental movement, are changing their ways. They realize that producing green products that help sustain the earth is an important source of future economic growth and profit. Instead of digging in their heals and adopting the philosophy that "if it isn't broken, don't fix it," innovative business leaders say "If it isn't broken, break it and fix it better." These are the companies of the future. Invest in or work for this type of Earth-sustaining company, or start one of your own.

control and reduce toxic discharges; won a Supreme Court case giving the public the right to obtain chemical industry data on the health effects of pesticides.

- 1985—led a coalition of citizen groups in successful negotiations with the chemical industry to strengthen safety provisions of the federal pesticide law; won a suit in which the court ordered the EPA to issue emissions standards for diesel-powered trucks and buses.

- 1986—launched a history-making agreement with the Soviet Academy of Sciences that will allow scientists to monitor nuclear test sites in both countries; won a court case mandating a schedule for the EPA to begin withdrawal of other uses of CFCs.

- 1987—won an environmental penalty of $1.5 million against the Bethlehem Steel Company for polluting the Chesapeake Bay; played a key role in promoting the International Ozone Treaty, designed to cut worldwide use of CFCs at least 35% by the end of this century; years of lobbying led to new federal appliance energy efficiency standards; won a suit requiring that EPA standards for toxic air pollutants be based on protecting health and not on cost-benefit analyses.

- 1988—launched the Atmospheric Protection Initiative.

- 1989—published a research study projecting increased cancer rates among preschool children from exposure to pesticides in their food; filed a lawsuit to force the EPA to phase out all production and use of CFCs in the United States; petitioned the president to convene an international summit meeting of world leaders on global warming; lobbied Congress for legislation that would cut U.S. fossil-fuel use by 50% by 2015, increase the use of renewable energy resources (Chapter 17), sharply reduce sulfur dioxide emissions, and set new deadlines for cities to control smog (Section 21-4); filed suit against the Department of the Interior for failure to comply with the nation's environmental laws in recommending that oil and natural gas be developed in Alaska's Arctic National Wildlife Refuge (see Pro/Con on p. 428); filed suit against the EPA to enforce existing water pollution laws; filed the first case in federal court challenging the government's failure to address global warming.

- 1990—culmination of a decade-long effort to amend the Clean Air Act; joined with other groups in filing a federal complaint against the EPA for failing to conduct a health risk assessment before allowing people to move back into the Love Canal area.

- 1991—launched the National Energy Efficiency Initiative to reduce the nation's dangerous addiction to oil and replace it with policies and laws recognizing that improving energy efficiency must be the foundation of environmental and national security.

25-4 Bringing About Change

ANTICIPATORY PUBLIC POLITICS We are usually driven to action only by dramatic events or sudden crises that have actually been building for a long time. However, such short-term, reaction-to-crisis politics is like putting a bandage on a gaping wound and hoping it will hold. *Perhaps the greatest challenge we face is that of using or modifing existing national political and economic systems to anticipate and prevent serious long-term problems, many of them global.*

The motivation for making significant change may come from a rare type of political leader who has the vision and the ability to inspire and mobilize people to see and take new paths. To paraphrase George Bernard Shaw, "Some see things as they are and say why? I dream of things that never were and say why not?" These rare individuals practice *anticipatory public politics*. They try to change our institutions and individual actions to prevent anticipated crises, or they react to crises in ways that may keep them from recurring. Instead of saying something can't be done because it's too idealistic, they say, "Let's do it!"

Such leaders challenge and prod us to do more than we think we can. They bring out the best in us. That is also what a good teacher does.

Writer Kurt Vonnegut has suggested a prescription for choosing leaders:

I hope you have stopped choosing abysmally ignorant optimists for positions of leadership. . . . The sort of leaders we need now are not those who promise ultimate victory over Nature, but those with the courage and intelligence to present what appear to be Nature's stern, but reasonable surrender terms:

1. *Reduce and stabilize your population.*
2. *Stop poisoning the air, the water, and the topsoil.*
3. *Stop preparing for war and start dealing with your real problems.*
4. *Teach your kids, and yourselves too, while you're at it, how to inhabit a small planet without killing it.*
5. *Stop thinking science can fix anything, if you give it a trillion dollars.*
6. *Stop thinking your grandchildren will be OK no matter how wasteful or destructive you may be, since they can go to a nice new planet on a spaceship. That is really mean and stupid.*

THE AMERICAN POLITICAL SYSTEM: MUDDLING THROUGH The government established by the U.S. Constitution was designed for consensus and accommodation to promote survival and adaptation through gradual change. By staying as close to the middle of the road as possible, the government attempts to steer or muddle its way through crises. Ralph Waldo Emerson once said, "Democracy is a raft which will never sink, but then your feet are always in the water."

Some analysts believe that the U.S. political-economic system is working reasonably well and no fundamental changes need to be made. Others think that the system must undergo changes that will improve its ability to deal with, anticipate, or prevent the growing number of regional, national, and global environmental and resource problems we face today.

We face an interlocking set of environmental, economic, and social problems that must be dealt with using integrated, comprehensive approaches. Yet most of our political institutions are compartmentalized and fragmented into specialized, narrowly focused cells that bear little relationship to the real world.

J. M. Stycos has observed that significant social changes go through four stages:

- Phase 1: No Talk–No Do
- Phase 2: Talk–No Do
- Phase 3: Talk–Do
- Phase 4: No Talk–Do

We have reached the Talk–Do phase in some areas, but mostly we are still stuck in the Talk–No Do phase, despite over 25 years of effort. We must now shift to phases 3 and 4.

THE ROLE OF INDIVIDUALS A principal theme of this book is that individuals matter. History shows that significant change comes from the bottom up, not the top down. Leaders with vision can lead only when they have the support of the people. Leaders without vision or courage must be pushed to lead by the people. The earth is too vital and under too much stress to be left in the hands of politicians and corporate elites alone.

Without the grassroots political actions of millions of individual citizens and organized groups, the air you breathe and the water you drink today would be much more polluted. Leading leaders is not easy, but history shows that it can be done. You can make a difference.

There are three types of environmental leadership:

- *Leading by working within the system* — bringing about environmental improvement by using existing economic and political systems, often in new, creative ways

- *Leading by example* — using your own life and life-style to show others that change is possible and beneficial

- *Leading by challenging the system* — raising public awareness and building political support for far-reaching changes by challenging existing political and economic systems

All three types of leadership are needed to sustain the earth. Many lawyers, lobbyists, and technical experts are playing important roles in sustaining the earth by working within the system (see Case Study on p. 684). They are supported, pushed, and challenged by grassroots activists who are leading by example and by challenging the system. Find the type of leadership you are most comfortable with and become such a leader or work with such leaders. Also, consider an environmental career (see Spotlight on p. 687).

REDEFINING NATIONAL SECURITY Many people call for the United States and other countries to expand the concept of national security to include economic and environmental security rather than defining it only in military terms. They agree with President and General Dwight D. Eisenhower's warning in the 1960s:

Every gun that is made, every warship launched, every rocket fired, signifies in the final sense a theft from those who are hungry and are not fed, those who are cold and not clothed. This world in arms is not spending money alone. It is spending the sweat of its laborers, the genius of its scientists, and the hopes of its children.

Providing environmental security will require political action by Earth citizens and the expenditure of about $500 billion a year — money that could be obtained by cutting world military expenditures in half. Such a cut would also free one-fourth of the world's scientists and engineers to work on environmental rather than military security, free capital for investments in environmental and economic security, and

In addition to dedicated Earth citizens, the environmental movement needs dedicated professionals working to help sustain the earth. There is an incredible variety of jobs in the environmental field.

Examples are careers in sustainable forestry and range management, parks and recreation, environmental planning, air and water quality control, solid waste management, hazardous-waste management, urban and rural land-use planning, soil conservation, water conservation, fishery and wildlife conservation and management, environmental education, environmental health and toxicology, environmental geology, ecology, conservation biology, environmental chemistry, climatology, population dynamics and regulation (demography), environmental law, environ-

mental journalism and communication, environmental engineering, environmental design and architecture, energy conservation, energy analysis, environmental consulting, environmental activism and lobbying, environmental economics, the development and marketing of Earth-sustaining products, environmental law enforcement (pollution detection and enforcement teams), and running for an elected office on an environmental platform.

For details on these careers, consult The CEIP Fund, *The Complete Guide to Environmental Careers* (Covelo, Calif.: Island Press, 1989). The CEIP Fund (68 Harrison Ave., Boston, MA 02111, 617-426-4375) places college students and recent college graduates as interns in short-term, paid professional positions with corporations, consultants, govern-

ment agencies, and nonprofit organizations. For a superb guide to career planning and job searches in any field, see Richard Nelson Bolles, *What Color is Your Parachute?* (Berkeley, Calif.: Ten Speed Press, published annually).

Other sources of information on jobs in the environmental field are

- *Job Scan*, published monthly ($22.00 for six months or $39.00 for one year) by the Student Conservation Association, P.O. Box 550, Charlestown, NH 03603.

- *Environmental Job Opportunities*, published ten times a year (subscription $10.00) by the Institute for Environmental Studies, 550 North Park St., 15 Science Hall, Madison, WI 53706.

create several times more jobs than using the money for military expenditures.

Numerous government studies have shown that in the United States, at least half of the money spent on military security is wasted because of cost overruns and corporate greed. Thus, the United States, and presumably other countries, could have the same degree of military security for half the cost by requiring cost-effective expenditure of these public funds. Some of the funds currently devoted to maintaining military forces could be shifted to development of an Earth Conservation Corps (ECC) at global, national, state, and local levels. By 1991, more than 60 youth Conservation Corps, involving 52,000 individuals, has been established in the United States.

Worldwide, citizens must let their leaders know that they will no longer tolerate a world in which there are enough nuclear weapons to kill everyone on the planet 60 times, where there are 556 soldiers but only 85 doctors for every 100,000 people, and where we spend $20,000 a year for every soldier and only $380 for every school-age child. Biologist Barry Commoner has summarized what we must do:

Now that the people of the world have begun to understand that survival depends equally on ending our ultimately suicidal war with nature and on ending the wars among ourselves, the path to

peace on both fronts becomes clear. To make peace with the planet, we must make peace among the people who live in it.

THE GRASSROOTS ACTION LEVEL OF THE ENVIRONMENTAL MOVEMENT Practicing green politics means working from the bottom up to protect the earth. The base of the environmental movement in the United States and in other countries consists of thousands of grassroots groups of citizens who have organized to protect themselves from pollution and environmental degradation at the local level (see Individuals Matter on p. 688). In the United States alone, there are almost 7,000 such groups. Their motto is *think globally and act locally*.

Some Earth citizens work within the existing system to bring about change while others often risk their lives to protect various patches of the earth and various species from being devastated (see Pro/Con on p. 689). Others work to restore or rehabilitate degraded areas.

It is encouraging that members of minority groups, who often bear the brunt of pollution and environmental degradation, are becoming involved in improving environmental security (Figure 20-9). Many are heeding Jesse Jackson's call to become environmental activists. Recalling his participation in many demonstrations for civil rights and improved housing, he said, "Unless

Writing letters to elected officials is essential (see Individuals Matter on p. 676), but we also need to support national lobbying environmental organizations (see Appendix 1) to counteract the powerful lobbying activities of industry and other vested interests.

We also need to join or form local organizations or temporary task forces on particular issues. The late John W. Gardner, former cabinet official and founder of Common Cause (see *In Common Cause*, 1972), summarized the basic rules for effective political action by grassroots organizations:

1. Have a full-time continuing organization.

2. Limit the number of targets and hit them hard. Most groups dilute their efforts by taking on too many issues.

3. Get professional advisers to provide you with accurate, effective information and arguments.

4. Form alliances with other organizations on a particular issue.

5. Have effective communication that will state your position in an accurate, concise, and moving way.

6. Persuade and use positive reinforcement—don't attack. Confine your remarks to the issue; do not make personal attacks on individuals. Try to find allies within the institution, and compliment individuals and organizations when they do something you like. Do your homework, and then privately approach public officials whose support you need, without lecturing them or using high-pressure tactics. In most cases, it is best not to bring up something at a public meeting unless you have the votes lined up ahead of time. Most political influence is carried on behind the scenes through one-on-one conversations. This is the basis of "Akido politics." Instead of fighting with opponents, you respect their beliefs and work with them to achieve your goals.

7. Organize for action, not just for study, discussion, or education. Minimize regular meetings, titles, and minutes. Have a group coordinator, a series of task forces with a project leader, a press and communications contact, legal and professional advisers, and a small group of

dedicated workers. A small cadre can accomplish more than a large, unwieldy group. Work in groups, but always keep in mind that people in groups can tend to act collectively in ways they individually know to be stupid.

8. Concentrate much of your efforts at the state and particularly at the local level (see Further Readings for guidelines).

9. Be honest with, accessible to, and on good terms with your local press.

The largest student environmental group in the United States is the Student Environmental Action Coalition (SEAC), established in 1988 at the University of North Carolina, Chapel Hill (SEAC, 217 A Carolina Union, University of North Carolina, Chapel Hill, NC 27599, 919-962-0888). It has members on over 650 campuses in all 50 states. Its goal is to forge a student movement to protect and restore the earth and build a sustainable and just society.

I have the right to breathe clean air and drink good water, no other right can be realized."

Unlike environmental organizations at the national and state levels, most grassroots organizations are unwilling to compromise or negotiate. Instead of dealing with environmental goals and abstractions, they are fighting immediate threats to their lives and the lives of their children and grandchildren and to the value of any property they own. They are inspired by the words of ecoactivist Edward Abbey: "At some point we must draw a line across the ground of our home and our being, drive a spear into the land, and say to the bulldozers, earthmovers, and corporations, 'this far and no further.'"

YOU CAN MAKE A DIFFERENCE Can we sustain the earth at the local, regional, and global levels? Yes—if we care enough to make the necessary commitment and in the process discover that understanding and caring for the earth is a never-ending source of joy and inner peace. We must become *Earth conservers*, not *Earth degraders*.

No goal is more important, more urgent, and more worthy of our time, energy, creativity, and money. In sustaining the earth, we should be guided by historian Arnold Toynbee's observation: "If you make the world ever so little better, you will have done splendidly, and your life will have been worthwhile," and by George Bernard Shaw's reminder that "indifference is the essence of inhumanity."

The ultimate test of our conscience is our willingness to sacrifice something today for future generations whose words of thanks will never be heard.

GAYLORD NELSON

The world's largest environmental group is Greenpeace. Between 1980 and 1990, membership in this organization increased from 240,000 to 1.6 million in the United States, and worldwide the group has 2.5 million members.

Greenpeace members have risked their lives by placing themselves in small boats between whales and the harpoon guns of Icelandic and Soviet whaling ships. Its members have dangled from a New York bridge to stop traffic and protest a garbage barge heading to sea; protested the dumping of toxic wastes into rivers by industries and sewage treatment plants (Figure 25-4); skydived from the smokestacks of coal-burning power plants to protest acid rain; sneaked into plants to document illegal pollution and dumping; led countless demonstrations; established a base in Antarctica (see Pro/Con on p. 516) to monitor environmental abuse; and helped organize local activist organizations.

Two environmental groups that are more activist than Greenpeace are Earth First!, led by Dave Foreman until 1990, and the Sea Shepherd Conservation Society, headed by Paul Watson. In 1981, Dave Foreman left his job as a Washington, D.C., lobbyist for the Wilderness Society and formed Earth First! because he had become fed up with what he considered to be political compromising. His first law of government is that the purpose of State is the defense of an entrenched economic elite. Paul Shepherd was one of the founders of Greenpeace but left in 1977 to form the Sea Shepherd Conservation Society because Greenpeace objected to his calls for bolder tactics.

These two organizations use aggressive tactics because its members believe that the earth can't wait for the beneficial, but much too slow, pace of change accomplished by working only within the system. Their goals are to prevent environ-

Figure 25-4 Greenpeace activists protesting discharge of toxic wastes from the "Pig's Eye" sewage treatment plant in St. Paul, Minnesota. This plant is the largest discharger of toxic chemicals into the Mississippi River north of St. Louis.

mental destruction, increase citizen awareness, and raise the costs of business for loggers, whalers, and others practicing planet wrecking.

They practice civil disobedience and aggressive nonviolence. This means *absolute nonviolence* against humans and other living things and *strategic violence* against inanimate objects such as bulldozers, power lines, and whaling ships. Tactics include chaining themselves to the tops of trees to keep loggers from cutting them down; driving spikes into trees and labelling these trees (the spikes don't hurt the trees, but they shatter sawblades, which could hurt loggers or millworkers, so the trees are labelled to keep them from being cut down); blocking bulldozers with their bodies (Figure 25-5); blocking or sinking illegal whaling ships; taking photos and videos of illegal or brutal commercial fishing and hunting activities; pulling up survey stakes; felling high-voltage towers; dying the fur of harp seals to prevent them from being killed for their furs; and sabotaging bulldozers, road graders, power shovels, and backhoes.

In May 1989, Dave Foreman was arrested by FBI agents and charged

with conspiracy for allegedly helping finance the destruction of an electric power tower near Phoenix, Arizona. The FBI spent three years and $2 million infiltrating Earth First!, monitoring personal calls and conversations, and recording over 500 hours of the group's meetings. The FBI informant who had infiltrated the group drove the three men to the tower. According to Foreman, the whole escapade was largely the infiltrator's idea, and the infiltrator was the one talking about using explosives to knock down the tower.

Foreman has charged that the government was attempting to intimidate and destroy the group just as it did in the 1960s with civil rights and antiwar groups that opposed what they considered unjust government policies. He cites a memo issued to all FBI field offices in the 1970s. It tells agents trying to break up a dissident group not to worry if they don't have enough evidence to hold up in the courts. Just go in, make a big arrest, make wild charges, and hold a press conference that gets widespread media coverage. The damage to the group is done by labelling it as a bunch of

(continued)

Figure 25-5 Earth First! activists blocking a logging road in the Siskiyou National Forest in Oregon.

David Cross

dangerous terrorists. Charges can always be dropped later, which gets little press coverage. According to long-time conservationist David Brower, "I think the Fortune 500 companies are the radicals, considering what they're doing to the earth as opposed to what Earth First! is doing."

Members of more-militant environmental groups point to the long history of civil disobedience against laws believed to be unjust—the American Revolution, the fight to allow women to vote, the civil rights movement, the antiwar movement, and now the environmental movement. Benjamin White, Jr., Atlantic Director of the Sea Shepherd Conservation Society, summarizes why we must all become environmental activists:

We must begin by declaring a state of planetary emergency. . . . We must stop compromising our basic right to clean air, water, soil, and bloodstreams, and a future with wild animals and wilderness. . . . We must also be willing to take risks. If your family were threatened, would you put your life on the line? Would you go to jail if necessary? Your family is threatened. It's time to take direct action.

As Ralph Nader has said, "Pollution is violence with a seriousness of harm exceeding that of crime in the streets. . . . The first priority is to deprive the polluters of their unfounded legitimacy. Too often they assume a conservative, patriotic posture when in reality they are radical destroyers of the nation's resources and the most fundamental rights of people."

An increasing number of ordinary citizens are directly or indirectly supporting more-militant grassroots environmental groups because they fear for their children's environmental future. They are fed up with presidents and other politicians who make nice speeches about protecting the environment, support a few symbolic projects, and behind the scenes allow the continuing rape of the earth in the name of short-term economic growth.

In 1988, a Kansas woman who lived near Wichita's Vulcan Chemical plant and whose family had been beset with health problems handcuffed herself to a chair outside the governor's office until he saw her. In 1989, protesters of Conoco, Inc., a refinery in Ponca City, Oklahoma, set up a tent city on the

grounds of the state capitol in 1989. In 1990, Conoco offered the families who lived near the refinery up to $27 million to relocate.

In 1989, a social studies class at a New Jersey high school persuaded the school board to switch from Styrofoam lunch trays to old-fashioned washable dishes. Since then, these students have protested McDonald's recycling practices and are raising money to buy and protect 121 hectares (300 acres) of rain forest in Belize.

Environmentalists disagree over the use of such tactics. Some applaud, and join or financially support, such activist groups. Some point out that leaders of mainstream environmental groups need to have more-militant groups nipping at their heels to make them take stronger positions.

Other environmentalists fear that activist groups, especially if they begin using illegal or violent actions, could cause a public backlash against other environmental efforts and groups. Some worry that if environmentalists alienate the public and Congress, industry will be able to successfully lobby Congress to rewrite and weaken environmental laws. What do you think?

Claudine Schneider

U.S. Representative Claudine Schneider is a five-term Congresswoman representing Rhode Island. She has been at the forefront of national efforts to protect and promote environmental quality and has championed a wide range of legislation to protect the environment, preserve endangered species, and promote balanced use of natural resources. She was one of the leaders in the fight to stop the Clinch River breeder nuclear fission reactor. She was lead sponsor of both the Ocean Dumping Act of 1989 and the Wolpe-Schneider Hazardous Waste Reduction Act. She has been especially active in promoting improvements in energy efficiency, promoting least-cost energy planning, and developing a comprehensive plan to deal with projected global warming. These efforts include being the author and primary sponsor of the Global Warming Prevention Act of 1989.

In recent years, we have witnessed record heat waves, droughts, forest fires, hurricanes, floods, and urban pollution. These are all warnings that Mother Earth is sending us. We ignore these warnings at our own peril. The gaping annual hole in the planet's protective ozone shield [Figure 11-6] and the rapid destruction of vast regions of tropical rain forests [Section 10-2] threaten humanity's well-being, just as if someone ripped off the skin protecting our bodies.

Each of us can help heal the planet. Choked by the smog of gridlocked autos, we can buy more-efficient and less-polluting cars, or carpool and remove two or three vehicles from the road; we can take the bus or subway; or even better, we can emulate Dutch and Danish communities, where half the people bicycle to and from work, preventing the release of tons of pollutants.

The food we grow or eat, the homes and appliances we buy, the packaging we avoid, reuse, or recycle — in short, the lifestyles we lead — offer endless opportunities for healing the planet. A healthy future depends on the degree to which we practice a stewardship ethic by living as if Mother Earth mattered.

Individual changes of habit constitute an essential first step we all must take, but not a sufficient one. In an ideal world, the good stewardship actions willingly taken by each person would add up to an ecologically sustainable world economy. Unfortunately, we are far from that ideal world. Whether because of ignorance, slothful indifference, outright greed, or callous disregard, the collective actions of humans now wreak havoc on the planet. We need to alter society's habits.

The production of greenhouse gases from burning fossil fuels [Figure 11-2] has brought us numerous economic goods and services, but the benefits from producing those gases are being surpassed by their costs and risks. It is time to stop the growth of greenhouse gases and substitute safer alternatives. This will require a broad range of changes at all levels of decision making — at home, at work, through community, state, and federal governments, and by international agreements.

Individuals have a responsibility here, as well, to lobby for changing the focus of these various institutions, especially those involved in producing legislation. Just as physical exercise maintains a healthy body, so the exercise of citizen advocacy maintains a healthy politic.

The healthy politic is a potent metaphor that emerged in the 1800s. At that time, individuals mobilized to remove the scourge of diseases afflicting society that were spread from contaminated water, due in part to the lack of sanitary waste disposal options. We need to galvanize public support for sustaining this noble tradition in the face of new environmental challenges.

Any review of history shows that it takes years, decades, sometimes centuries, to effect change in monumental problems. This has been the case with democracies overthrowing dictators, with abolishing slavery, and with protecting human rights. These struggles continue in our day, and they all turn on the concern and commitment of individuals working to effect change.

Grappling with environmental problems like projected global climate change poses a no less daunting task. It is too easy for policymakers elected for two- to six-year terms to evade action by pushing the problem far into the future. Some have referred to this unconscionable behavior as the NIMLT syndrome: "Not in My Life Time."

Without strong, ongoing citizen advocacy for change, most policymakers will continue to support environmental deficit spending, just as they have budget deficit spending. That is to say, current policies encourage squandering the natural endowment of future generations, who will be faced with paying off our environmental debts (pollutants) with fewer capital resources (forests, topsoil, watersheds, extinct species, and so forth).

We must refuse to submit to the gloom-and-doom future implicit in the policies and practices of our time. Decades of scientific research, technical advancements, and ecological insights show us that humans can thrive on Earth in an ecologically sustainable manner. The key insight of our time is that environmental quality and economic well-being are compatible. By acting on that

(continued)

insight, we can eliminate the seemingly intractable problems of hunger and poverty and maintain a thriving economy for generations to come.

The greatest barrier to recognizing this insight is the way policymakers make decisions. Issues get quickly compartmentalized. Transportation, housing, health, security, energy, and the environment are dealt with separately by specialized bureaucracies, few of whom exchange ideas with their fellow specialists. So we build more highways for polluting cars instead of designing land uses to minimize the need for cars. We operate highly polluting power plants instead of installing lower-cost, energy-efficient lights, motors, and appliances in homes and factories. We contaminate soil and groundwater instead of reducing, reusing, and recycling wastes.

This fragmentary approach must be replaced by an integrated, holistic approach. This is where citizens can gain considerable leverage from their efforts. There are numerous examples of how cities and states have established advisory commissions to look at the future shape of their regions and recommend changes in public policies. When that happens, trends become more apparent, problems are more readily identified, and concerned citizens can voice alternative visions that could be further studied and duly incorporated.

Analytic tools have been developed and are available for helping citizens ensure that comprehensive planning is performed. Often, for example, half or more of the food, energy, and water services could be produced locally, saving millions of dollars for the local economy and cutting pollutants and solid wastes in half. With that kind of information base, a powerful tool is available for accelerating public policy.

A citizens' commission can serve a tremendous education function for voters in helping them identify ecologically sustainable ways to spur economic growth. Perhaps never in history are individual actions so greatly influencing the course of planetary change.

Prevention pays, and it is incumbent on all of us to capitalize upon these abundant opportunities. A healthy environment is the basis for a healthy economy. In promoting ecologically sound economic practices, we will not only slow global climate change but also greatly alleviate urban smog, acid rain, tropical deforestation, and a host of other social and environmental problems.

Guest Essay Discussion

1. How would you go about getting elected officials and government agencies to deal with the problems we face in an integrated, holistic manner?

2. What economically sound ecological policies would you propose for dealing with the problem of projected global warming?

DISCUSSION TOPICS

1. What prominent trends do you see in society today? Which ones are desirable and which are undesirable? Use various combinations of these trends to construct three scenarios of what the world might be like in 2020. Identify the scenario you favor and outline a program for achieving this alternative future.

2. What do you believe are the greatest strengths and weaknesses of the form of government in the United States (or in any country where you live) in protecting the environment and sustaining the earth? What substantial changes, if any, would you make in this system?

3. Explain why you agree or disagree with the idea that the most important form of patriotism is primary loyalty to sustaining the earth, and any action that harms the earth is unpatriotic and wrong.

4. Do you believe that activist environmental groups such as Earth First! and the Sea Shepherd Conservation Society serve a useful role? Explain.

5. List ten things that you plan to do during the 1990s to help sustain the earth. Which of them are you already doing?

*6. A 1990 national survey by the Roper Organization found that while 78% of Americans believe that a major national effort is required for environmental improvement (ranking it fourth among national priorities), only 22% were making significant efforts to improve the environment. The poll identified five categories of citizens: (1) *true-blue greens* (11%), involved in a wide range of environmental activities; (2) *greenback greens* (11%), who don't have time to be involved but will pay more for a cleaner environment; (3) *grousers* (24%), who aren't involved in environmental action mainly because they don't see why they should if everybody else isn't; (4) *sprouts* (26%), who are concerned but don't believe individual action will make much difference; and (5) *basic browns* (28%), who are the most apathetic and the least involved, and who also tend to be the poorest. Which category do you belong to? As a class, conduct a similar poll on your campus.

*7. Conduct a survey of how environmental education is presented at your school and in your community. Develop a plan for making environmental education a priority at your school and in your community. Present your plan to school officials and the local school board, and call for a public meeting to discuss this issue.

CHAPTER 26

WORLDVIEWS, ETHICS, AND ENVIRONMENT

General Questions and Issues

1. What worldview leads to the throwaway societies found in most of today's industrialized countries?

2. What worldview leads to a sustainable-Earth society, and how can we achieve such a worldview?

3. What can you do to help sustain the earth?

So long as we are under the illusion that we know best what is good for the earth and for ourselves, then we will continue our present course, with its devastating consequences on the entire earth community. . . . We need not a human answer to an earth problem, but an earth answer to an earth problem. . . . We need only listen to what the earth is telling us. . . . The time has come when we will listen, or we will die.

THOMAS BERRY

OUR DECISIONS AND ACTIONS are built around your **worldview**—how you think the world works and what you think your role in the world should be—and your **ethics**—what you believe to be right or wrong behavior. Regardless of what you say you believe, how you act in the world reveals your true beliefs.

Worldviews are based on the cultures in which people are raised and educated and on their progress through various levels of environmental awareness, summarized on the page after the list of principles found inside the front cover of this book. Conflicts about how serious the world's present and projected environmental and resource problems are and what should be done about them arise mostly out of differing worldviews.

The real question is what worldview will lead to a high quality of life for the maximum number of people. People with a high quality of life have a long-term sense of joy in living, a sense of physical well-being, a belief that they have been or can be successful human beings, and a passionate desire to participate in life's unfolding drama. People with a low quality of life have a sense of hopelessness and despair, a belief that their life has been a failure, a sense of poor physical well-being, and a pervading sense of unhappiness.

We are living at an incredibly exciting time—the most important turning point since the Agricultural Revolution. For several decades, we have used our brains to degrade Earth's life-support systems at an accelerating pace. Our power to destroy life, including our own species, is now so great that we must use our brains and our hearts to protect and heal the earth. Making this crucial transition requires that we change our human-centered view of the world to an Earth-centered or life-centered one.

26-1 The Throwaway and Spaceship-Earth Worldviews in Industrial Societies

THE THROWAWAY WORLDVIEW According to E. F. Schumacher, "Environmental deterioration does not stem from science or technology, or from a lack of information, trained people, or money for research. It stems from the lifestyle of the modern world, which in turn arises from its basic beliefs."

Most people in today's industrialized societies have a **throwaway worldview**, also known as a **frontier worldview**, which is based on several beliefs:

- We are apart from nature.

- We are superior to other species.

- Our role is to conquer and subdue wild nature and use nature for our purposes.

- Resources are unlimited because of our ingenuity in making them available or in finding substitutes — there is always more.

- The more we produce and consume, the better off we are. Unlimited material progress can be achieved through economic and technological growth. All growth is good, and more growth is better.

- The most important individual or nation is the one that can command and use the largest fraction of the world's resources.

You may not accept all these statements, but most people in today's industrialized societies act as if they did, and that's what counts.

If there is always more, why go to the trouble and expense of picking up, recycling, or reusing what we dump into the environment? If Earth's resources, coupled with our ingenuity, are unlimited, why attempt to regulate population growth, discourage the production and consumption of anything people are willing to buy, and face up to the problem of a fairer distribution of wealth built upon exploiting the earth's resources? If life will always get better because of our ingenuity, why should we make sacrifices now for future generations whose lives will be better anyway?

If the air, water, and soil can handle all the wastes we dump into them, why worry about pollution? Even if we do pollute an area, we can invent a technology to clean it up or we can move somewhere else. So don't worry, don't get involved, be happy. We will always be able to use technology to save us from ourselves.

As a world species, we have become the planet's most successful predators, with the entire earth as our prey. We seek out the planet's resources, devour them, and move on. Some argue that because of this strategy, we are now at the pinnacle of civilization. They believe continuing to expand our domination of the earth will lead to an even more glorious future — the belief that more and bigger consumption of resources is better because there are no limits to economic growth.

This view is based on the idea that we are entering a new age of communication and technological progress in which information is the greatest source of wealth and power. In an information age, information is the most important resource in allowing us to dominate the planet.

Those who say there are limits to economic growth are sometimes derided as gloom-and-doom pessimists, but many analysts fear that continuing devotion to the seductive throwaway, or there-will-always-be-more, worldview will turn out to be a fatal attraction. Catholic theologian Thomas Berry calls the industrial-consumer society built upon the throwaway worldview the "supreme pathology of all history."

We can break the mountains apart; we can drain the rivers and flood the valleys. We can turn the most luxuriant forests into throwaway paper products. We can tear apart the great grass cover of the western plains, and pour toxic chemicals into the soil and pesticides onto the fields, until the soil is dead and blows away in the wind. We can pollute the air with acids, the rivers with sewage, the seas with oil — all this in a kind of intoxication with our power for devastation. . . . We can invent computers capable of processing ten million calculations per second. And why? To increase the volume and speed with which we move natural resources through the consumer economy to the junk pile or the waste heap. Our managerial skills are measured by our ability to accelerate this process. If, in these activities, the topography of the planet is damaged, if the environment is made inhospitable for a multitude of living species, then so be it. We are, supposedly, creating a technological wonderworld. . . . But our supposed progress toward an ever-improving human situation is bringing us to a wasteworld instead of a wonderworld.

THE SPACESHIP-EARTH WORLDVIEW Pictures of the earth taken from space have provided us with a powerful image: This beautiful and endangered planet is the only one we have.

Some have likened the earth to a large spaceship whose life-support systems we must protect. While this Spaceship-Earth worldview is useful, it is a mechanistic, human-centered worldview. It views the earth as a spaceship — a machine that we have the capacity and the duty to control and dominate by using advanced technology. This view is a sophisticated expression of the basic idea found in the throwaway worldview — that through technology and human ingenuity we can control nature and create artificial environments and lifeforms to avoid environmental overload.

If resources become scarce or a substitute can't be found, we can get materials from the moon, asteroids, or other planets in the "new frontier" of space. We can use genetic engineering to control the evolution of lifeforms and develop organisms that produce more food, clean up oil spills and toxic wastes, and satisfy more of our unlimited wants. We can also use space as the ultimate waste dump. Already, we have left wastes on the moon and cluttered space with tens of thousands of fragments from burned-out satellites. A comedian remarked that soon we will need windshield wipers on spaceships to see where we are going and to find our way back to Earth.

If Earth becomes too crowded or too polluted, we will build stations in space for the excess population. Never mind that to do that, we would have to send off 2.6 million people a day — 11,000 an hour — just to keep Earth's current population of 5.4 billion from rising. Assuming that each spaceship could carry 500 people (compared with about 6 people on today's spaceships),

22 much larger ships would have to be launched every hour, without stop. Never mind that the pollution from these ships would worsen conditions and deplete the ozone layer for the 5.4 billion people left behind on a dying planet. Never mind that we don't know how to build a space station that could sustain even 5 people indefinitely, much less 95 million more people each year. Never mind that the materials used to build these stations would deplete resources for the billions of people left behind on Earth.

This outlook is an upside-down view of reality. It thinks of Earth as a spaceship—a simple, unsustainable, human creation. This is a simplified, arrogant, and dangerous view for a species that doesn't even understand what is going on in a pond or in the first few millimeters of topsoil. This worldview, like the throwaway worldview, can lead to environmental overload and resource depletion because it is based on two false ideas—that we understand how nature works and that there are no limits to Earth's resources and our ability to overcome any problem with technological innovations.

Thinking of Earth as a spaceship is also a great threat to individual freedom. Astronauts on a spaceship are very vulnerable and have virtually no individual freedom. Instead of being free of the earth, they are totally dependent on life-support systems and limited supplies produced by Earth materials. Virtually everything they do is dictated by a central command (ground control). Staying alive requires adhering to a rigid and monotonous daily schedule of maintenance and repair. Living in a spaceship or a space station may be an exciting adventure at first, but only because the astronauts believe, or hope, they can return to Earth before their supplies run out and regain some control over their lives.

Very few people could, or would want to, tolerate living on a spaceship—a high-tech prison—where survival is totally dependent on fallible human technology and social regimentation. The Spaceship-Earth worldview is inadequate for dealing with an overpopulated, environmentally stressed, and globally interconnected world based on living by depleting and degrading Earth's natural capital.

Many people in MDCs have an uneasy feeling that things are not right, that the old ways of thinking and acting no longer work. Wendell Berry, farmer and author, has summarized this dilemma:

[A typical American] is probably the most unhappy citizen in the history of the world. He has not the power to provide himself with anything but money, and his money is inflating like a balloon and drifting away. . . . From morning to night he does not touch anything that he has produced himself, in which he can take pride. . . . His air, water, and food are all known to contain poisons. . . . He suspects that his love life is not as fulfilling as other people's. He wishes he had been born sooner, or later. . . .

He does not care much and does not know why he does not care. . . . He feels that all his possessions are under threat of great pillage.

We live in a disintegrating culture, as summarized by Ron Miller:

Our culture does not nourish that which is best or noblest in the human spirit. It does not cultivate vision, imagination, or aesthetic or spiritual sensitivity. It does not encourage gentleness, generosity, caring, or compassion. Increasingly in the late twentieth century, the economic-technocratic worldview has become a monstrous destroyer of what is loving and life-affirming in the human soul.

In other words, we are caught in a transition between worldviews. We suspect or know deep down that our old worldview is no longer valid, but we are unwilling or afraid to give it up completely and adopt a new way of viewing and acting in the world. Change is threatening, but so is not changing in a world we are changing at an accelerating pace.

26-2 A Sustainable-Earth Worldview

SUSTAINABLE-EARTH SOCIETIES The view of Earth from space as a blue and white ball floating in the dark void of space has led some to think of the planet as a nonliving, mechanistic spaceship whose life-support systems we must dominate, manage, and control. This view sees us as apart from and in charge of the rest of nature.

Others see Earth as a single living, holistic system (Gaia), with no political boundaries. They see our species as a part of, not apart from, the rest of nature—one member of a global community of interacting and interdependent species. To people with this view, sustaining the earth does not involve trying to manage and control Earth as a spaceship. Instead, it calls for us to cooperate with the complex and poorly understood feedback mechanisms, symbiotic and synergistic interactions, biogeochemical cycles, biodiversity, and evolutionary processes that sustain life on Earth.

We now have a series of nationalistic societies devoted to gaining power over other people and the earth through excessive competition, military might, and economic domination. A growing number of people see this arrangement as unsustainable. They call for us to make a new cultural change by transforming our present societies into a diverse network of interacting and interdependent societies that provide environmental and economic security for everyone and that are sustainable, safe, equitable, not oppressive, and flexible. Such societies would be built around a healthy balance of competition and cooperation with one another and the rest of the earth.

People in such societies see holistic wisdom, not information, as the key to sustainability. They believe that we are like a rudderless ship sinking in a rising sea of information that hampers our ability to seek precious nuggets of knowledge and wisdom that can be used to keep the ship from sinking.

What we need is more wisdom, not more information—a *wisdom revolution*, not an information revolution. Why should we continue to grow in numbers and in the production of more and more material objects? What value does such growth have? As a powerful species, what should our role on Earth be? The answers to such questions require knowledge and wisdom based on understanding Earth as a holistic, interacting, interdependent system.

Instead of a single sustainable-Earth global society, we need to give birth to a variety of such societies adapted to different physical, biological, and cultural conditions. Each culture provides different experiences, wisdom, and insights that can be used to develop a variety of sustainable-Earth economies (see Spotlight on p. 667), political systems, and individual lifestyles. That is why we need to preserve both biological diversity and cultural diversity.

SUSTAINABLE-EARTH WORLDVIEW Despite variations in the nature of sustainable-Earth societies, they are based primarily on the following general beliefs and guidelines that make up the **sustainable-Earth worldview**.

- We can never completely "do our own thing"; everything we do has mostly unpredictable present and future effects on other people and other species (*first law of ecology*).

- We are part of nature; all living species are interconnected and interdependent (*second law of ecology, or principle of interdependence*).

- Nature is not only more complex than we think but also more complex than we can ever think (*principle of complexity*).

- The earth does not belong to us; we belong to the earth; we are just one particular strand in the web of life; in the words of Aldo Leopold, each of us is "to be a plain member and citizen of nature" (*principle of humility*).

- Our role is to understand and work with the rest of nature, not to conquer it (*principle of cooperation*).

- Every living species has a right to live, or at least to struggle to live, simply because it exists; this right is not dependent on its actual or potential use to us (*respect-for-nature principle*).

- Something is right when it tends to maintain the ecological integrity, sustainability, and diversity of Earth's life-support systems for us and other species and wrong when it tends otherwise; the bottom line is that Earth is the bottom line (*principle of sustainability and ecocentrism*).

- The best things in life aren't things (*principle of love, caring, and joy*).

- It is wrong for humans to cause the premature extinction of any wild species and the elimination and degradation of their habitats (*preservation of wildlife and biodiversity principle*).

- When we alter nature to meet what we consider to be basic needs or nonbasic wants, we should choose the method that does the least possible harm to other living things; in minimizing harm, it is in general worse to harm a species than an individual organism, and still worse to harm a community of living organisms; when damage cannot be avoided, it should be minimized and repaired (*principle of minimum wrong*).

- When we alter nature we should make such changes at nature's rates and in nature's ways (*principle of sustainable change*).

- Resources are limited and must not be wasted (*principle of limits*).

- No individual, corporation, or nation has a right to an ever-increasing share of Earth's finite resources. As the Indian philosopher and social activist Mahatma Gandhi said, "The earth provides enough to satisfy every person's need but not every person's greed" (*principle of enoughness*).

- It is wrong to treat people and other living things primarily as factors of production, whose value is expressed only in economic terms (*economics-is-not-everything principle*).

- Everything we have or will have comes from the sun and the earth; the earth can get along without us, but we can't get along without the earth; an exhausted planet is an exhausted economy (*respect-your-roots*, or *Earth-first, principle*).

- Don't do anything that depletes Earth's physical, chemical, and biological capital which supports all life and human economic activities; the Earth deficit is the ultimate deficit; short-term greed leads to long-term economic and environmental grief (*balanced-Earth-budget principle*).

- We should leave the earth in as good a shape as we found it, if not better (*rights-of-the-unborn principle*).

- All people should be held responsible for their own pollution and environmental degradation; dumping our wastes in another area or country is the equivalent of using chemical warfare on the people or other species receiving our wastes (*responsibility-of-the-born principle*).

- We must protect Earth's remaining wild systems from our activities, rehabilitate or restore natural systems we have degraded, use natural systems only on a sustainable basis, and allow many of the systems we have occupied and abused to return to a wild state; as David Brower said, "The wild places are where we began. When they end so do we" (*principle of Earth protection and healing*).

■ In protecting and sustaining nature, go farther than the law requires (*ethics-often-exceeds-legality principle*).

■ To prevent excessive deaths of people and other species, people must prevent excessive births (*birth-control-is-better-than-death-control principle*).

■ Put the poor and their environment first, not last; help the poor sustain themselves and their local environment, and do this with love, not condescension; we cannot have peace, environmental justice, or a sense of pride about our accomplishments as a species as long as anyone still lives in poverty (*eliminate-the-poverty-trap principle*).

■ To love, cherish, celebrate, and understand the earth and yourself, take time to experience and sense the air, water, soil, trees, animals, bacteria, and other parts and rhythms of the earth directly (*direct-experience-is-the-best-teacher principle*).

■ Learn about, love, and care for your local environment and live gently within that place; walk lightly on the earth (*love-your-neighborhood principle*).

Most of the ethical principles listed as part of the sustainable-Earth worldview are found in the world's religions. Some critics of this worldview claim that it is idealistic and impractical, the same criticisms that have been made of the beliefs of the world's major religions. All religions and ethical systems call for us to believe and act in certain ways because it is wrong to do otherwise. Dismissing them because they are "impractical" is merely an excuse for not taking them seriously and not facing up to what kind of persons and societies we should and can be.

Social and political change can take place much faster than most people think. No one predicted or expected the rapid political changes that recently took place in eastern Europe and the former Soviet Union. Anyone who had called for such rapid change would have been labelled an impractical dreamer.

People with a sustainable-Earth worldview believe that societies that emphasize cooperation, justice, compassion, love, and empathy for humans and other creatures are more sustainable and lead to a higher quality of life than those that emphasize selfishness, competition, aggression, maximization of material wealth, and domination of the earth, other humans, and other creatures.

A sustainable-Earth worldview does not reject technology. Instead, it insists that technology be used in appropriate, just, and humane ways to protect — not to degrade and destroy — forms of life on Earth. It in-

sists that technology be used to help us make the transition from a high-entropy culture to a low-entropy culture by reducing the flow and unnecessary waste of energy and matter resources to sustainable levels. It also rejects the idea that a technology should be developed and encouraged just because it is possible.

A sustainable-Earth view does not call for everyone to move to the countryside and grow his or her own food or become a modern hunter-gatherer. The world is much too populated and developed for that to happen, even if people thought it was desirable. Instead, it calls for each of us to learn how to live more sustainably in the places we occupy.

That means we must distinguish between our unnecessary wants and our true needs. Some affluent people in MDCs are adopting a lifestyle of *voluntary simplicity*, based on doing and enjoying more with less by learning to live more simply but richly. They are learning that buying more products and luxuries to satisfy artificially created wants doesn't provide security, freedom, or joy.

Instead, it can lead to insecurity and reduced freedom because *the more things you own, the more you are owned by things* (principle of overconsumption, or thing-tyranny). You have to spend a lot of time and money buying, protecting, repairing, or replacing them. However, voluntary simplicity by those who have more than they really need should not be confused with the forced simplicity of the poor, who do not have enough to meet their most basic needs for food, clothing, shelter, clean water, clean air, and health.

Voluntary simplicity does not mean deprivation and hardship. Quite the opposite, it gives one a sense of joy and purpose, as I have found in struggling to find ways to walk more lightly on the earth (see Spotlight on p. 470). I have learned the meaning of Aldo Leopold's wisdom when he said, "One of the penalties of an ecological education is that one lives alone in a world of wounds." At the same time, I have learned the joy of experiencing nature and of trying to make the world a better place to live. The trick is to keep our excitement, joy, and thankfulness for the privilege of living on this wondrous planet slightly ahead of our frustration about what we are doing to our only home and to ourselves, our children, and our grandchildren.

Some believe that male domination, which has existed since the beginning of the Agricultural Revolution, is a major threat to sustaining the earth. Males are culturally conditioned to believe that they must conquer nature, women, and other men. Polls show that 15% more women than men support environmental protection. Analysts believe that women have a much better chance than men of leading humanity into sustaining the earth and the human species. Many of the most successful efforts to help sustain the earth have been accomplished mostly by women (see Individuals Matter on pp. 280 and 567).

No one can heal the entire planet. Planetary healing will occur only through people working together to heal each human and natural neighborhood we have wounded. Once you have a personal commitment to a place, you can apply that understanding and those feelings to other parts of your life, to other places, and to other forms of life. As Aldo Leopold pointed out, "All ethics rest upon a single premise that the individual is a member of a community of interdependent parts."

ACHIEVING A SUSTAINABLE-EARTH WORLD-VIEW Achieving a sustainable-Earth worldview involves working our way through four levels of environmental awareness summarized inside the front cover, opposite the title page. It also means distinguishing between fallacy and reality about how the world works (see Guest Essay on p. 703).

However, we cannot achieve a sustainable-Earth worldview merely by reading and thinking about it. According to Aldo Leopold, "We can be ethical only in relation to something we can see, feel, understand, love, or otherwise have faith in." Thus, sustaining the earth requires not only a new way of thinking but also a new way of feeling based on listening to and experiencing the earth and ourselves with our senses and our hearts (see Spotlight on p. 699).

Rich nations and individuals must set an example by curbing their enormous use and waste of Earth's resources, reducing their tremendous environmental impact, and curbing their population growth (Figure 1-16). They must change from a high entropy-producing culture to a much lower entropy-producing culture. They must dedicate their financial resources and talents to using known ways and discovering new ways for people in developed and developing societies to live more sustainably. Environmental and economic justice require that we use and redistribute the world's wealth more equitably so everyone's basic needs are met.

Another aid to achieving a sustainable-Earth worldview is to view the geographic area where you live as part of a natural region or **bioregion**, a unique life-place with its own soils, landforms, watersheds, climates, native plants and animals, and many other distinct natural characteristics. A bioregion is a life-territory—a region ultimately governed by nature, not by laws we pass. The diffuse and changing boundaries of bioregions have little to do with the artificial city, county, state, and national boundaries we draw on maps.

To live sustainably requires that we understand our bioregion in ecological terms, not merely in economic or political terms. That means we must become dwellers in the land who establish an ecologically and socially sustainable pattern of existence within it. The first step is to learn as much as we can about how our bioregion works, the network of symbiotic and synergistic relationships that sustain its human and nonhuman inhabitants, and what we have done to disrupt those relationships through past exploitation. Then we must reinhabit this place and begin healing its wounds by cooperating with the natural processes that shape and sustain this bioregion.

Many people now see themselves as members of a global community with ultimate loyalty to the planet, not merely to a particular country (Figure 26-1). They see themselves as common citizens of One Earth who represent every culture, every race, every species, and every living creature in this and future generations.

Sustaining the earth means that all of us, especially those with an affluent lifestyle, must adopt a simpler, less consumptive, Earth-caring lifestyle. Helen and Scott Nearing offer the following ten tips for doing this:

1. Do the best you can, whatever arises.
2. Be at peace with yourself.
3. Find a job you enjoy.
4. Simplify your life. Live in simple conditions: housing, food, clothing.
5. Contact nature every day. Feel the earth under your feet.
6. Exercise physically through hard work, gardening, or walking.
7. Don't worry. Live one day at a time.
8. Share something every day with someone.
9. Take time to wonder at life and the world. See some humor in life where you can.
10. Be kind to all creatures, and observe the one life in all things.

26-3 Achieving a Sustainable-Earth Society

AVOIDING SOME COMMON TRAPS Sustaining the earth requires each of us to make a personal commitment to live an environmentally ethical life. We must do this not because it is required by law but because it is right. It is our responsibility to ourselves, our children and grandchildren, our neighbors, and the earth.

Start by being sure you have not fallen into some common traps or excuses that lead to indifference and inaction.

- *Gloom-and-doom pessimism*: the belief that the world is doomed by nuclear war or environmental catastrophe, so we should enjoy life while we can.

- *Blind faith in experts and leaders*: the belief that someone is in charge who knows what to do and will do it without continual pressure and help from ordinary citizens. Usually, the people are far

The essence, rhythms, and pulse of the earth within and around us can only be experienced at the deepest level by our senses and feelings — our emotions. We must tune in our senses to the flow of air and water into our bodies — nature providing the air and water, absolute needs, for us at no charge.

We must listen to the soft, magnificent symphony of billions of organisms expressing their interdependency. We must pick up a handful of soil and try to sense the teeming microscopic life-forms in it that keep us alive. We must look at a tree, a mountain, a rock, a bee and try to sense how they are a part of us and we are a part of them.

We must learn to cherish and listen to the gentle sounds of silence within and around us instead of identifying any lack of frantic activity as boredom and loneliness. We must tune in to our urgent yearning to understand and experience ourselves and the rest of nature. Instead, we often cover up that need by seeking a frantic life of motion and artificial things and sensations that only deepen our emotional separation from our inner selves and from the rest of the earth.

Michael J. Cohen urges each of us to recognize who we really are by saying,

I am a desire for water, air, food, love, warmth, beauty, freedom, sensations, life, community, place, and spirit in the natural world. These pulsating feelings are the Planet Earth, alive and well within me. I have two mothers: my human mother and my planet mother, Earth. The planet is my womb of life.

We need to stop attaching more feelings of survival and happiness to dollars that we can't eat, breathe, and drink than to the sun, land, air, water, plants, bacteria, and other organisms that really keep us alive. We need to recognize that our technological cocoon and our feeling of self importance as a species has given us an incredibly distorted picture of what is really important and joyful.

If we think of nature as separate from us and made up of disjointed parts to be manipulated by us, then we will tend to become people whose main motivation with regard to each other and to nature is also manipulation and control. That is an unsatisfying, empty, and joyless way to live.

We need to understand that although formal education is important, it is not enough. Much of it is designed to socialize and homogenize us so that we will accept and participate in the worldview that our role is to conquer nature and to suppress and deny the deep feelings of guilt we have about doing so. We can no longer wage a war against nature and ourselves while telling ourselves that that is progress.

The way to break out of this mental straitjacket is to experience nature directly, so that you truly feel that you are part of nature and it is part of you. As philosopher Simone Weil observed, "To be rooted is perhaps the most important and least recognized need of the human soul."

To be rooted, you need to find a *sense of place* — a stream, a mountain, a yard, a neighborhood lot, or any piece of the earth you feel truly at one with. It can be a place where you live or a place you occasionally visit and experience in your inner being. When you become part of a place, it becomes a part of you. Then you are driven to defend it against damage and to heal its wounds.

Experiencing nature allows you to get in touch with your deepest self that has sensed from birth that when you destroy and degrade the natural systems that support you, you are attacking yourself. Then you will love the earth as an inseparable part of yourself and live your life in ways that sustain and replenish the earth and thus yourself and other living things. We must experience the earth as a gift to be cherished and sustained, not as an object to be dominated and controlled as summarized in the quote from Thomas Berry found at the beginning of this chapter.

Thus, the most important frontier that we must explore and understand is ourselves. Discovering and understanding our true selves means experiencing and understanding the earth with our heart. This is true progress. This is living life at its fullest.

We can begin by embracing the Pledge to the Earth developed by Peter Barnes and Chellis Glendinning:

I pledge my kinship with the Earth, with its oceans and clouds, and forests, and all its precious inhabitants. And this kinship I shall show each day, when I speak and act, when I work and play, when I gather, and when I throw away. We are one planet, interconnected, ever dedicated to the flowering of life to come.

---

ahead of their political and economic leaders in understanding what must be done and must organize and lead the leaders.

- *Blind technological optimism*: the belief that human ingenuity will always be able to come up with technological advances that will solve our problems. This is the most seductive and dangerous trap. It is something that we would like to believe.

- *Fatalism*: the belief that whatever will be will be, and we have no control over our actions and the future.

Figure 26-1 A growing number of people are pledging allegiance to the planet that keeps them alive. Some display the Earth Flag as a symbol of their commitment to sustaining the earth. (Courtesy of Earth Flag Co., 33 Roberts Road, Cambridge, MA 02138)

- *Why-bother syndrome*: the belief that even if I do my share, nobody else will, so why should I waste my time and energy trying to make the world a better place.

- *Extrapolation to infinity*: the belief that "if I can't change the entire world quickly, I won't try to change any of it." This rationalization is reinforced by modern society's emphasis on instant gratification and quick results with as little effort as possible.

All of these traps represent various forms of *denial* to enable us to avoid facing up to problems and the need for change. With our present power to destroy ourselves and most other species, denial is a recipe for disaster. It is like jumping off the top of a tall skyscraper and as we hurtle past the twentieth floor proclaiming, "So far, so good. Some new technological breakthrough will save me before I hit the ground."

GROWING UP AS A SPECIES Our species is still in its adolescent phase of development. We can no longer remain at this stage. We must face reality, accept our responsibility to sustain and heal the earth, and become a mature species. That means we can no longer view the world in terms of "we" and "they." Instead, there is only "us"—a diverse, global community of interacting and interdependent individuals and species.

We must recognize that we exist at an incredibly exciting time in human history—a unique window of opportunity to grow up as a species by making a cultural change. Instead of succumbing despair and denial, we should rejoice that this generation has the opportunity to make a planetary transformation that can avoid environmental disaster by abandoning our aggression against each other and the planet. No future generation will have this chance, because if we don't do the job now future humans and other species will have to exist on an earth that we have impoverished.

This is an incredible time to be alive. We are members of a fortunate generation who have the power and responsibility to give birth to new, mature ways of thinking and acting. If I had a choice of when to exist, I would pick the hinge of history we now live in. Get involved in the sustainable-Earth revolution.

BECOMING EARTH CITIZENS: THE EARTH-SUSTAINING DOZEN The good news is that we can sustain the earth and lead more meaningful and joyful lives. To do this, begin with yourself by doing 12 things.

1. **Evaluate the way you think the world works and sensitize yourself to your local environment.** Look around, experience what is going on in the environment around you, compare what is with what could and should be. Where do the water you drink and the air you breathe come from? What kind of soil is around your home? Where does your garbage go? What forms of wild plants and animals live around you? Which species have become extinct in your area, and which ones are threatened with extinction? What is the past history of land use in your area, and what are the projected future uses of this land? What are your environmental bad habits? What is your worldview? How does your worldview influence the way you act?

2. **Become ecologically informed.** Immerse yourself in sustainable-Earth thinking by looking for connections between everything we do and Earth's ecological health and sustainability for us and other species. Specialize in one particular area of environmental knowledge and awareness, relate it to sustainable-Earth thinking, and share your knowledge and understanding with others (networking). Consider going into an environmental profession (see Spotlight on p. 687) or starting or working in an environmentally responsible business, buy green products (see Individuals Matter on p. 538), and invest only in green companies. Not everyone should be an ecologist or a professional environmentalist, but you do need to "ecologize" your lifestyle. Keep in mind Norman Cousins's statement: "The first aim of education should not be to prepare young people for careers, but to enable them to develop respect for life."

3. **Become emotionally involved in caring for the earth by experiencing nature directly and by trying to find a place that you love and must defend because you are part of it and it is part of you.** Intellectual ecological knowledge of how the world works is vitally important. However, it will not be enough to bring about a change in the way you live unless it is combined with a sense of place—a feeling of oneness and rootedness with, and thankfulness for, some piece of the earth that you experience, love, and respect. Care for one piece of land—a yard, a neighborhood lot or park, a stream. Poet-philosopher Gary Snyder urges us to "find our place on the planet, dig in, and take responsibility from there."

4. **Choose a simpler lifestyle by reducing resource consumption and waste and pollution production.** Do this by distinguishing between your true needs and your wants and by using trade-offs to develop a lifestyle that reduces the entropy (disorder) you add to the environment. For every high-energy, high-waste, or highly polluting thing you do (buying a car, living or working in an air-conditioned building), give up a number of other things. Such a lower entropy-producing lifestyle will be less expensive and should bring you joy as you learn how to walk more gently on the earth.

5. **Focus especially on energy use and energy waste.** Recognize that energy—the integrating theme of this book—is the currency of life for us and other species. People in MDCs have achieved their higher standards of living primarily by increasing their use of energy (Figure 2-1). At the same time, our rapid depletion of Earth's one-time deposit of fossil fuels is the primary cause of most air pollution, water pollution, land degradation, and international tension over control of dwindling oil supplies. Fossil fuels also give us more energy to rapidly clear forests and degrade other ecosystems that are homes for Earth's vital biodiversity. These fuels are also used to produce petrochemicals that in turn are used to produce the plastics, pesticides, solvents, chlorofluorocarbons, and thousands of other hazardous, and often slowly degradable, chemicals and products we are dumping into the environment.

    The second law of energy tells us that the more high-quality energy each of us uses, the less is available for other life now and in the future. Thus, any effective efforts to sustain and heal the earth must be built around two things that must be carried out at the individual, local, national, and global levels within your lifetime. First, we must waste as little energy as possible. By adhering to this moral imperative, we are expressing our love of current and future life on Earth. One of the most serious threats to the earth is that American society unnecessarily wastes at least half of the energy it uses. Second, we must shift from lifestyles and economies built around the use of nonrenewable fossil and nuclear fuels to ones built around perpetual and renewable energy from the sun, wind, falling and flowing water, sustainable burning of biomass, and Earth's interior heat.

6. **Become more self-sustaining by trying to unhook yourself from dependence on large, centralized systems for your water, energy, food, and livelihood.** You can do this in the country or in the city. Use organic, intensive gardening techniques to grow some of your own food in a small plot, roof garden, or window-box planter. Get as much of your energy as possible from renewable sources, such as the sun, wind, water, or biomass. Move closer to work or try to work at home.

7. **Remember that environment begins at home.** Before you start trying to convert others, begin by changing your own living patterns. If you become an Earth citizen, be prepared to have everyone looking for, and pointing out, your own environmental sins. Your actions force people to look at what they are doing—a threatening process that disrupts the denial syndrome. People are most influenced by what we do, not by what we say.

8. **Become politically involved on local and national levels.** Start or join a local environmental group, and also join and financially support national and global environmental and conservation organizations whose causes you believe in (see Appendix 1). Work to elect sustainable-Earth leaders and to influence officials once they are elected to public office. Remember that change takes place from the bottom up based on actions by ordinary citizens.

9. **Do the little things based on thinking globally and acting locally.** Environmental problems are caused by quadrillions of small, unthinking actions by billions of people. They'll be cured by quadrillions of small, environmentally beneficial actions that you and others substitute for the thoughtless and wasteful ones. Recycle and, better yet, reuse things; don't waste energy (see Individuals Matter inside the back cover); improve the energy efficiency of your house; don't use electricity to heat space or household water; drive a car that gets at least 17 kilometers per liter (40 miles per gallon); join a car pool; use mass transit; ride a bicycle to work; replace incandescent lights with energy-efficient fluorescent lights; turn off unnecessary lights; plant trees; have a compost pile; help restore a damaged part of the earth; eat lower on the food chain by reducing or eliminating your consumption of meat (especially beef); grow food organically; don't waste water (see Individuals Matter inside the back cover); choose to have no more than one, or at most, two children, and teach any child you have to sustain the earth; write on both sides of a piece of paper; don't discard useful clothing and other items and buy new ones just to be fashionable; don't buy overpackaged products; distinguish between your needs and your wants before you buy anything; reduce use of, recycle, and reuse matter resources; buy products from, or work for and invest in, companies that are working to sustain the earth.

    Each of these small measures sensitizes you to Earth-sustaining acts and leads to more such acts. Each of these individual actions is also a small-scale economic and political decision that, when coupled with actions of others, leads to larger-scale political and economic changes.

10. **Work on the big polluters and big problems, primarily through political action, economic boycotts, and selective consumption.** Individual actions help reduce pollution and environmental degradation, give us a sense of involvement, and help us develop a badly needed Earth consciousness. Our awareness must then expand to recognize that large-scale pollution and environmental degradation are caused by industries, governments, and big agriculture driven by overemphasis on short-term economic gain that eventually leads to economic and environmental grief for us and premature extinction for many other spe-

cies. Recognize that Love Canal, Bhopal, Chernobyl, the *Exxon Valdez* spill, and all other preventable forms of pollution and environmental degradation are peacetime acts of aggression against the earth and ultimately ourselves. The ethic of the international Greenpeace movement is "not only to personally bear witness to atrocities against life; it is to take direct nonviolent action to prevent them."

11. **Start a movement of awareness and action.** You can change the world by changing the two people next to you. For everything, big or little, that you decide to do to help sustain the earth, try to persuade two others to do the same thing, and encourage them in turn to persuade two others. Carrying out this doubling or exponential process only 24.5 times would persuade everyone in the United States, and doing it 28.5 times would persuade everyone in the world. However, it is necessary to have only about 5% to 10% of the people in a community, a state, a country, or the world actively involved to bring about change. Get involved and become a part of the solution instead of a part of the problem.

12. **Don't make people feel guilty.** If you know people who are overconsuming or carrying out environmentally harmful acts, don't make them feel bad. Instead, lead by example and find the things that others are willing to do to sustain the earth. There is plenty to do, and no one can do everything. Use positive rather than negative reinforcement. We need to nurture, reassure, understand, and love, rather than to threaten, one another.

Make a difference by caring. Care about the air, water, soil. Care about wild plants, wild animals, wild places. Care about people—young, old, handicapped, black, white, brown—in this generation and generations to come. Let this caring be your guide for doing. Live your life caring about the earth and you will be fulfilled.

Envision the world as made up of all kinds of matter cycles and energy flows. See these life-sustaining processes as a beautiful and diverse web of interrelationships—a kaleidoscope of patterns and rhythms whose very complexity and multitude of potentials remind us that cooperation, honesty, humility, and love must be the guidelines for our behavior toward one another and the earth.

The main ingredients of an environmental ethic are caring about the planet and all of its inhabitants, allowing unselfishness to control the immediate self-interest that harms others, and living each day so as to leave the lightest possible footprints on the planet.

ROBERT CAHN

Hugh Kaufman

Lynn Moorer

Hugh Kaufman, a former Captain in the United States Air Force, has been an engineer in the U.S. Environmental Protection Agency since its inception in 1970. In the 1970s, he was the agency's chief investigator of hazardous-waste sites. He helped develop all federal laws for the EPA in the waste disposal field, including the Resource, Conservation, and Recovery Act and the Superfund Law (Section 20-5). He is known as the agency's whistle-blower because of his congressional testimony exposing Love Canal and thousands of other hazardous sites in the U.S. and because of his testimony that led to the removal of former EPA Administrator Anne Burford and the incarceration of the former EPA Assistant Administrator Rita Lavelle. In addition to his official duties in EPA's superfund program, he uses his spare time to help grassroots groups and state officials around the country "fight environmental battles." He is an inspiring public servant and planetary citizen.

Lynn Moorer, a former journalist, is a grassroots leader in Nebraska dealing with an array of environmental problems, including nuclear, hazardous, and solid waste issues. She heads Citizens for Nebraska, working with grassroots citizens statewide in the environmental field. She is an inspiring example of an Earth citizen working on the environmental frontlines.

No environmental problem provides clearer examples of false general assumptions held by the public as to how the system works than waste (air, water, and land pollution) issues. For those wanting to make a difference in protecting the financial and environmental health of their communities, the following practical advice is offered about key fallacies and realities as to how the world works.

Fallacy: Industry has an incentive to prevent pollution.

Reality: As long as industry can continue to transfer the costs and liabilities of pollution to citizens and the waste business can continue to reap its phenomenally high rate of return on investment, current national policies do not provide any incentive to industry to prevent pollution.

While labelling citizens who oppose projects "NIMBY's" (Not in My Backyard), the industries are anxious to transfer the projects' liabilities out of their own backyards.

Fallacy: Industry spends the majority of its pollution control budgets on engineering and technical research and development to reduce pollution and waste.

Reality: The majority of industry expenditures in pollution control are directed toward attorneys, lobbying, and PR efforts to kill proposals that reduce waste. In fact, more times than not, the business of pollution control has almost no science or technology to it. Instead, industry officials engage in word games, or "semantic detoxification," to obscure the real problems of pollution, sanitize risks, and conceal their inability to control and reduce risks.

Fallacy: The industrial sector wields the greatest influence in the governmental decision-making process because its positions are based upon scientifically and technically derived data and rigorous independent analysis.

Reality: As our nation's preeminent and best-financed lobbying power, the industrial sector has the greatest influence on environmental policy, on who is elected and reelected as the citizens' representatives, and on the decisions of elected officials. As the largest election campaign contributor in U.S. society, industry has the most control of the governmental mechanisms that permit pollution. (Thus, the fox has the most influence on how the chicken coop is guarded.)

As an example of a political directive from a proindustry group overriding federal environmental policy, the President's Council on Competitiveness instructed the EPA Administrator in 1990 to delete the agency's recycling requirement for incinerators. That was done because of complaints from the incinerator industry that since recycling would limit the burning of high-Btu, low-cost paper in incinerators, their profits would be hurt. Reducing waste is not good for the waste management business.

Fallacy: Environmental protection costs jobs and drains the economy.

Reality: Once projects are reviewed carefully, implementation of environmental protection strategies usually creates jobs. For example, the system of mandatory deposits on reusable beverage containers, in place in America through the end of World War II, was more labor-intensive and created less pollution than the throwaway beverage container system in use throughout the country today.

Fallacy: The driving force in the siting of waste dumps, incinerators, deep wells, and other projects that have the

(continued)

potential to cause significant environmental impacts, or in decisions made about correcting problems (such as abandoned waste dumps) that have significant environmental impact, is based on technology, meteorology, hydrology, and geology.

Reality: The driving force in siting projects and correcting hazardous situations is the sociology of the potentially affected area.

For example, Nebraska ranchers and farmers, who exhibit little stamina for continuing substantive participation in the political process, are currently targeted to receive a national dump for low-level radioactive waste, even though, comparatively, the state does not produce large amounts of nuclear waste. Despite highly productive farmland, groundwater around one's ankles, and wide seasonal temperature changes, Nebraska has been targeted to "host" one of the nation's first regional dumps for low-level radioactive waste (vulnerable to receiving the entire nation's output of such waste). Consideration of technical factors ranks Nebraska toward the bottom of the list as a nuclear dump site. Nebraska's sociological characteristics, however, put it at the top of the list for a dump that is difficult to site nationally. These sociological characteristics include a unicameral (single house) legislature in which only 25 votes are needed to pass legislative measures and its unsophisticated rural people with limited access to information and national media outlets.

Fallacy: Government's scientific conclusions can be trusted to be derived from analysis that is objectively developed and authentically reported.

Reality: Significant factors have been ignored in scientifically peer-reviewed studies that are used as a foundation for national environmental policy. An EPA risk-assessment study released in 1991, for example, "loaded the dice" by ignoring groundwater contamination as an environmental risk; thus, one of the most significant environmental impacts of waste disposal was dismissed. As a result, the EPA environmental model concluded that waste disposal presents a low environmental risk for the nation.

Fallacy: Government environmental officials have environmental protection as their goal.

Reality: Avoiding pain and perpetuating or increasing their position and power drive government officials. Those who can wield the greatest clout in delivering pain to officials have the greatest power in directing the government bureaucracy. On balance, the incentive that proves most powerful is to keep polluters polluting.

Fallacy: There is little citizens can do to influence significantly or to prevent projects and policies that cause major environmental problems.

Reality: Grassroots coercion or pressure has been demonstrated to be an effective way to affect both government and industry. One important lever is exerted through the ballot box (other levers are discussed in the following paragraphs). An organized cadre of citizens can effectively influence elections for local and county officials, state legislators, and members of the U.S. Congress. Citizen organizations statewide can influence state officials and members of Congress.

In Nebraska, for example, Republican Governor Kay Orr lost a tight race for reelection in 1990 by losing the key support of conservative Republican farmers and ranchers opposing her promotion of a nuclear waste dump and other waste disposal projects in the state. Grassroots political action by concerned citizens played a key role in this political defeat.

DISCUSSION TOPICS

1. What obligations, if any, concerning the environment do you have to future generations? List the most important environmental benefits and harmful conditions passed on to you by the last two generations.

2. What is your worldview? Has taking this course changed your worldview? How?

3. Do you feel that you are alienated from the earth and without a sense of place? If not, describe the place you love and feel a part of to other members of your class. If you do not have a sense of place, try to explain why, and identify changes in your lifestyle that might enable you to have a sense of place.

4. Do you agree with the cartoon character Pogo that "we have met the enemy and he is us"? Explain. Criticize this statement from the viewpoint of the poor. From the viewpoint that large corporations and government are the really big polluters and resource depleters and degraders.

5. Do you agree with the principles and guidelines of the sustainable-Earth worldview given in Section 26-2? Explain. Can you add others? Which ones do you try to follow?

6. If you won $10 million in a sweepstakes, how would you live your life differently? Why?

Fallacy: Government regulators are the only ones with any real, sustained leverage on industry through permitting and enforcement. At best, citizens can testify at permitting hearings and hope they receive adequate and unbiased coverage of their views.

Reality: Citizens can exert significant leverage by using several tactics. They include **(1)** concentrating leverage and activities on strategic projects; **(2)** actively and continuously watchdogging policymakers (elected and unelected) and industrial representatives; **(3)** knowing the fine print of relevant laws; **(4)** seeking direct, "in-the-face" accountability of officials; **(5)** making face-to-face contact with policymakers through personal visits (including unannounced ones) to their offices; **(6)** corresponding with elected and unelected officials, sharing information, formulating proposed policies, and requesting information, data, and records using Freedom of Information laws; **(7)** participating in public meetings and hearings of governmental bodies and, in so doing, exercising all rights belonging to the public as provided in state public meeting laws; and **(8)** encouraging volunteer participation on task forces and committees created to advise policymaking bodies.

Fallacy: Since you can trust your government officials to do the right thing, there is no reason to watch their actions carefully.

Reality: Democracy is not a spectator sport. Officials' feet must be held to the fire by continuous citizen monitoring and involvement. The most effective citizen involvement in government begins after an election or at the passage of a new law. The potential leverage citizens can exert is severely diminished if their activity is evident only at election time. Continuous monitoring and involvement, however, consume a formidable amount of citizen time and stamina — a commodity that is often in short supply. Government and industry officials are aware of this reality and often defuse citizen action by a wear-them-down-and-they'll-go-away strategy.

Fallacy: Stopping an environmentally or financially ruinous project in your community will not positively affect policy because the promoters will just move down the road and force the project on your neighbors.

Reality: Empowered citizens who "plug the toilets" by blocking big polluting projects and refusing to be patsies exert significant leverage in forcing government to pursue better environmental policies. Strong opposition everywhere also costs polluting industries money and time and wears them down, and can eventually make pollution prevention and waste reduction more economically attractive than having to fight thousands of individual political and legal battles. Thus, once enough monkey wrenches are successfully embedded in the policy mechanism, the system is forced to address pollution prevention and waste reduction head-on.

Guest Essay Discussion

1. As a class, use the fallacy–reality items given in this essay to develop a political strategy for opposing an environmentally harmful pollution, waste management, or land-use project in your local community, and put this plan into action.

2. Do you disagree with any of the fallacy–reality items in this essay? If so, list them and explain why you disagree. Can you add any other fallacy–reality items to this list?

7. Would you work on a project that you knew would kill or harm people? Degrade or destroy a wild habitat? Explain.

8. Do you believe that women have a better chance than men of leading us in making the transition to a sustainable-Earth society? Explain. How would you nurture a shift to societies based on more balanced, symbiotic, and synergistic cooperation between men and women?

9. Explain the fallacies in the following statements:
   a. We have always had wars and we will always have them.
   b. People are naturally aggressive and competitive.
   c. Aggression and competition, not cooperation, is the best way to get what you want.
   d. Men will always dominate women.
   e. The system is so big and powerful that it can't be changed.
   f. If we don't continue to vigorously exploit natural resources to grow economically, we will go back to the horse-and-buggy days, freeze in the dark, go hungry, and lead a miserable life.

10. In general, the higher one's level of affluence, the more one benefits from environmental injustice for other people and other living organisms. What benefits do you receive from the world's environmental injustices?

EPILOGUE

Where there is no dream, the people perish.
PROVERBS 29:18

THIS BOOK IS BASED on several simple theses:

1. The ecosphere is not only more complex than we think but also more complex than we can ever think.

2. In Garrett Hardin's terms, the basic principle of ecology is "that everything and everyone are all interconnected." Because we can never completely know how everything is connected, we must function in the ecosphere with a sense of humility and cooperation instead of arrogance and domination. Accepting this will require that our patterns of living become life-centered or Earth-centered instead of merely human-centered.

3. Everything we have, or will have, ultimately comes directly or indirectly from the sun and the earth. To accept this dependence is to recognize that we cannot sustain ourselves by depleting the Earth capital that supports us and other species. To deny this dependence is a recipe for disaster.

4. Because of the law of conservation of matter, we can never really throw anything away. Because of the first law of thermodynamics, we can't get anything for nothing, and because of the second law of thermodynamics, virtually every action we take has some undesirable present or future impact on the environment (the entropy trap). That means that any society built upon a rapidly growing population attempting to maximize resource use is unsustainable. Resources are depleted and wasted matter resources (pollution) are transferred from one part of the environment (air, water, or land) to another until the environment's capacity to dilute, absorb, degrade, and recycle matter resources is overwhelmed.

5. Because we have rounded the bend on the J-shaped curves of exponentially increasing population, resource use, pollution, and environmental degradation, we now have the power to disrupt Earth's life-support systems for us and many other species. There is increasing evidence that we have already surpassed the planet's carrying capacity for humans in various parts of the world (Table 1-1).

6. Without environmental security, there can be no lasting or meaningful economic or military security. That means that using funds and human talent to provide environmental security on a cooperative basis must be the number one priority of all nations.

7. The greatest threats to the human species and many other species are unsustainable throwaway societies built around population growth (more consumers), unlimited economic growth (produce more regardless of the consequences), a widening gap between the haves and the have-nots (economic and environmental injustice), pollution cleanup, resource waste, waste management, and decreases in biological and cultural diversity. The way out of this crisis is to shift to sustainable-Earth societies built around population stabilization, sustainable economic growth (quality, not quantity), a decreasing gap between the haves and the have-nots (economic and environmental justice), pollution prevention, efficient use of resources, waste reduction, and preservation of biological and cultural diversity.

8. We live during incredibly exciting times because we have a unique opportunity and responsibility to make a cultural change that far surpasses the Agricultural and Industrial revolutions. The human species is now in its adolescence, and we will either grow up and become a mature species or suffer severe consequences. The choice of which path to take is ours, but the time to choose and act is running out. Not to decide is to decide.

9. It is not too late. There is time to deal with the complex, interacting problems we face and to make an orderly rather than a catastrophic transition to a variety of dynamic, sustainable-Earth societies if enough of us really care. It's not up to "them," it's up to "us." Don't wait.

Publications

The following publications can help you keep well informed and up to date on environmental and resource problems. Subscription prices, which tend to change, are not given.

Ambio: A Journal of the Human Environment Royal Swedish Academy of Sciences, Box 50005, S-104 05 Stockholm, Sweden.

American Forests American Forestry Association, 1516 P St. NW, Washington, DC 20005.

American Journal of Alternative Agriculture 9200 Edmonston Rd., Suite 117, Greenbelt, MD 20770.

Amicus Journal Natural Resources Defense Council, 122 E. 42nd St., New York, NY 10168.

Annual Review of Energy Department of Energy, Forroctal Building, 1000 Independence Ave. SW, Washington, DC 20585.

Audubon National Audubon Society, 950 Third Ave., New York, NY 10022.

Audubon Wildlife Report National Audubon Society, 950 Third Ave., New York, NY 10022. Published every two years.

Biologue National Wood Energy Association, 1730 N. Lynn St., Suite 610, Arlington, VA 22209.

BioScience American Institute of Biological Sciences, 730 11th St. NW, Washington, DC 20001.

Buzzworm P.O. Box 6853, Syracuse, NY 13217-7930.

The CoEvolution Quarterly P.O. Box 428, Sausalito, CA 94965.

Conservation Biology Blackwell Scientific Publications, Inc., 52 Beacon St., Boston, MA 02108.

Demographic Yearbook Department of International Economic and Social Affairs, Statistical Office, United Nations Publishing Service, United Nations, NY 10017.

Earth Island Journal Earth Island Institute, 300 Broadway, Suite 28, San Francisco, CA 94133.

The Ecologist MIT Press Journals, 55 Hayward St., Cambridge, MA 02142.

Ecology Ecological Society of America, Dr. Duncan T. Patten, Center for Environmental Studies, Arizona State University, Tempe, AZ 85281.

E Magazine P.O. Box 5098, Westport, CT 06881.

Environment Heldref Publications, 4000 Albemarle St. NW, Washington, DC 20016.

Environment Abstracts Bowker A & I Publishing, 245 W. 17th St., New York, NY 10011. In most libraries.

Environmental Action 6930 Carroll Ave., 6th floor, Tacoma Park, MD 20912

Environmental Engineering News School of Civil Engineering, Purdue University, West Lafayette, IN 47907.

Environmental Ethics Department of Philosophy, The University of Georgia, Athens, GA 30602.

Environmental Opportunities (Jobs) Sanford Berry, P.O. Box 969, Stowe, VT 05672.

The Environmental Professional Editorial Office, Department of Geography, University of Iowa, Iowa City, IA 52242.

EPA Journal Environmental Protection Agency. Order from Government Printing Office, Washington, DC 20402.

Everyone's Backyard Citizens' Clearinghouse for Hazardous Waste, P.O. Box 926, Arlington, VA 22216.

The Futurist World Future Society, P.O. Box 19285, Twentieth Street Station, Washington, DC 20036.

Garbage: The Practical Journal for the Environment P.O. Box 56520, Boulder, CO 80321-6520.

Greenpeace Magazine Greenpeace USA, 1436 U St. NW, Washington, DC 20009.

International Environmental Affairs University Press of New England, 17½ Lebanon St., Hanover, NH 03755.

Issues in Science and Technology National Academy of Sciences, 2101 Constitution Ave. NW, Washington, DC 20077-5576.

Journal of Environmental Education Heldref Publications, 4000 Albemarle St. NW, Suite 504, Washington, DC 20016.

Journal of Environmental Health National Environmental Health Association, 720 S. Colorado Blvd., Suite 970, Denver, CO 80222.

Journal of Pesticide Reform P.O. Box 1393, Eugene, OR 97440.

National Geographic National Geographic Society, P.O. Box 2805, Washington, DC 20077-9960.

National Parks and Conservation Magazine National Parks and Conservation Association, 1015 31st St. NW, Washington, DC 20007.

National Wildlife National Wildlife Federation, 1400 16th St. NW, Washington, DC 20036.

Natural Resources Journal University of New Mexico School of Law, 1117 Stanford NE, Albuquerque, NM 87131.

Nature 711 National Press Building, Washington, DC 20045.

The New Farm Rodale Research Center, Emmaus, PA 18049.

New Scientist 128 Long Acre, London, WC 2, England.

Newsline Natural Resources Defense Council, 122 E. 42nd St., New York, NY 10168.

Not Man Apart Friends of the Earth, 530 Seventh St. SE, Washington, DC 20003.

One Person's Impact P.O. Box 751, Westborough, MA 01581

Organic Gardening & Farming Magazine Rodale Press, Inc., 33 E. Minor St., Emmaus, PA 18049.

Orion Nature Quarterly P.O. Box 2130, Knoxville, IA 50198-7130.

Pollution Abstracts Cambridge Scientific Abstracts, 7200 Wisconsin Ave., Bethesda, MD 20814. Found in many libraries.

Population Bulletin Population Reference Bureau, 1875 Connecticut Ave. NW, Washington, DC 20009.

Rachel's Hazardous Waste News Environmental Research Foundation, P.O. Box 73700, Washington, DC 20056-3700.

Renewable Energy News Solar Vision, Inc., 7 Church Hill, Harrisville, NH 03450.

Renewable Resources 5430 Grosvenor Lane, Bethesda, MD 20814.

Rocky Mountain Institute Newsletter 1739 Snowmass Creek Rd., Snowmass, CO 81654.

Science American Association for the Advancement of Science, 1333 H St. NW, Washington, DC 20005.

Science News Science Service, Inc., 1719 N St. NW, Washington, DC 20036.

Scientific American 415 Madison Ave., New York, NY 10017.

Sierra 730 Polk St., San Francisco, CA 94108.

State of the States Renew America, 1001 Connecticut Ave. NW, Suite 719, Washington, DC 20036. Published annually.

State of the World Worldwatch Institute, 1776 Massachusetts Ave. NW, Washington, DC 20036. Published annually.

Statistical Yearbook Department of International Economic and Social Affairs, Statistical Office, United Nations Publishing Service, United Nations, NY 10017.

Technology Review Room E219-430, Massachusetts Institute of Technology, Cambridge, MA 02139.

Transition Laurence G. Wolf, ed., Department of Geography, University of Cincinnati, Cincinnati, OH 45221.

The Trumpeter Journal of Ecosophy P.O. Box 5883 Stn. B, Victoria, B.C., Canada V8R 6S8.

Vegetarian Journal P.O. Box 1463, Baltimore, MD 21203

Wilderness The Wilderness Society, 1400 I St. NW, 10th Floor, Washington, DC 20005.

Wildlife Conservation New York Zoological Society, 185th St. and Southern Boulevard, Bronx, NY 10460.

World Rainforest Report Rainforest Action Network, 300 Broadway, Suite 298, San Francisco, CA 94133.

World Resources World Resources Institute, 1735 New York Ave. NW, Washington, DC 20006. Published every two years.

World Watch Worldwatch Institute, 1776 Massachusetts Ave. NW, Washington, DC 20036.

Worldwatch Papers Worldwatch Institute, 1776 Massachusetts Ave. NW, Washington, DC 20036.

Yearbook of World Energy Statistics Department of International Economic and Social Affairs, Statistical Office, United Nations Publishing Service, United Nations, NY 10017.

Environmental and Resource Organizations

For a more detailed list of national, state, and local organizations, see Conservation Directory, *published annually by the National Wildlife Federation, 1400 16th St. NW, Washington, DC 20036,* Your Resource Guide to Environmental Organizations *(Irvine, CA: Smiling Dolphins Press, 1991), and* World Directory of Environmental Organizations *published by the California Institute of Public Affairs, P.O. Box 10, Claremont, CA 91711.*

Acid Rain Foundation 1410 Varsity Dr., Raleigh, NC 27606.

African Wildlife Foundation 1717 Massachusetts Ave. NW, Washington, DC 20036.

Alan Guttmacher Institute 2010 Massachusetts Ave. NW, 5th Floor, Washington, DC 20036.

Alliance for Chesapeake Bay 6600 York Rd., Baltimore, MD 21212.

Alliance to Save Energy 1925 K St. NW, Washington, DC 20006-1401.

American Cetacean Society P.O. Box 2639, San Pedro, CA 90731-0943.

American Council for an Energy Efficient Economy 1001 Connecticut Ave. NW, Suite 535, Washington, DC 20013.

American Forestry Association 1516 P St. NW, Washington, DC 20005.

American Geographical Society 156 Fifth Ave., Suite 600, New York, NY 10010.

American Institute of Biological Sciences, Inc. 730 11th St. NW, Washington, DC 20001.

American Rivers 801 Pennsylvania Ave. SE, Suite 303, Washington, DC 20003.

American Society for the Prevention of Cruelty to Animals (ASPCA) 441 E. 92nd St., New York, NY 10128.

American Solar Energy Society 859 W. Morgan St., Raleigh, NC 27603.

American Water Resources Association 5410 Grosvenor Lane, Suite 220, Bethesda, MD 20814.

American Wilderness Alliance 7500 E. Arapahoe Rd., Suite 114, Englewood, CO 80112.

American Wildlife Association 1717 Massachusetts Ave. NW, Washington, DC 20036.

American Wind Energy Association 1730 N. Lynn St., Suite 610, Arlington, VA 22209.

Appropriate Technology International 1331 H St. NW, Washington, DC 20005.

Bat Conservation International P.O. Box 162603, Austin, TX 78716.

Bio-Integral Resource Center P.O. Box 8267, Berkeley, CA 94707.

Bioregional Project (North American Bioregional Congress) Turtle Island Office, 1333 Overhulse Rd. NE, Olympia, WA 98502.

Carrying Capacity 1325 G St. NW, Washington, DC 20005.

Center for Conservation Biology Department of Biological Sciences, Stanford University, Stanford, CA 94305.

Center for Marine Conservation 1725 DeSales St. NW, Suite 500, Washington, DC 20036.

Center for Science in the Public Interest 1501 16th St. NW, Washington, DC 20036.

Chipko P.O. Silyara via Ghansale, Tehri-Garwhal, Uttar Pradesh, 249155, India.

Citizens' Clearinghouse for Hazardous Waste P.O. Box 926, Arlington, VA 22216.

Clean Water Action 317 Pennsylvania Ave. SE, Washington, DC 20003.

Conservation Foundation 1250 24th St. NW, Suite 500, Washington, DC 20037.

Council for Economic Priorities 30 Irving Pl., New York, NY 10003.

Council for Solid Waste Solutions 275 K St. NW, Suite 400, Washington, DC 20005.

Cousteau Society 930 W. 21st St., Norfolk, VA 23517.

Critical Mass Energy Project 215 Pennsylvania Ave. SE, Washington, DC 20003.

Cultural Survival 11 Divinity Ave., Cambridge, MA 02138.

Defenders of Wildlife 1244 19th St. NW, Washington, DC 20036.

Ducks Unlimited One Waterfowl Way, Long Grove, IL 60047.

Earth First! 305 N. Sixth St., Madison, WI 53704.

Earth Island Institute 300 Broadway, Suite 28, San Francisco, CA 94133.

EarthSave 706 Frederick St., Santa Cruz, CA 95062-2205.

Earthscan 1717 Massachusetts Ave. NW, Washington, DC 20036.

Earthwatch 680 Mt. Auburn St., Box 403N, Watertown, MA 02272.

Elmwood Institute P.O. Box 5805, Berkeley, CA 94705.

Energy Conservation Coalition 1525 New Hampshire Ave. NW, Washington, DC 20036.

Environmental Action, Inc. 6930 Carroll Ave., 6th floor, Takoma Park, MD 20912

Environmental Defense Fund, Inc. 257 Park Ave. South, New York, NY 10010.

Environmental Law Institute 1616 P St. NW, Suite 200, Washington, DC 20036.

Environmental Policy Institute 218 D St. SE, Washington, DC 20003.

Food First (Institute for Food and Development Policy) 145 Ninth St., San Francisco, CA 94103.

Friends of Animals P.O. Box 1244, Norwalk, CT 06856.

Friends of the Earth 218 D St. SE, Washington, DC 20003.

Friends of the Trees P.O. Box 1466, Chelan, WA 98816.

Fund for Animals 200 W. 57th St., New York, NY 10019.

Global Greenhouse Network 1130 17th St. NW, Suite 530, Washington, DC 20036.

Global Tomorrow Coalition 1325 G St. NW, Suite 915, Washington, DC 20005.

Greenhouse Crisis Foundation 1130 17th St. NW, Suite 630, Washington, DC 20036.

Greenpeace, USA, Inc. 1436 U St. NW, Washington, DC 20009.

Humane Society of the United States, Inc. 2100 L St. NW, Washington, DC 20037.

INFORM 381 Park Ave. South, New York, NY 10016.

Institute for Alternative Agriculture 9200 Edmonston Rd., Suite 117, Greenbelt, MD 20770.

Institute for Local Self-Reliance 2425 18th St. NW, Washington, DC 20009.

International Alliance for Sustainable Agriculture 1201 University Ave. SE, Suite 202, Minneapolis, MN 55414.

International Planned Parenthood Federation 105 Madison Ave., 7th Floor, New York, NY 10016.

Izaak Walton League of America 1401 Wilson Blvd., Level B, Arlington, VA 22209.

Land Institute Route 3, Salina, KS 67401.

League of Conservation Voters 2000 L St. NW, Suite 804, Washington, DC 20036.

League of Women Voters of the U.S. 1730 M St. NW, Washington, DC 20036.

National Audubon Society 950 Third Ave., New York, NY 10022.

National Clean Air Coalition 801 Pennsylvania Ave. SE, Washington, DC 20003.

National Coalition Against the Misuse of Pesticides 530 Seventh St. SE, Washington, DC 20001.

National Environmental Health Association 720 S. Colorado Blvd., Suite 970, Denver, CO 80222.

National Geographic Society 17th and M Sts. NW, Washington, DC 20036.

National Parks and Conservation Association 1015 31st St. NW, 4th Floor, Washington, DC 20007.

National Recreation and Park Association 3101 Park Center Dr., 12th Floor, Alexandria, VA 22302.

National Recycling Coalition 1101 30th St. NW, Suite 304, Washington, DC 20007.

National Solid Waste Management Association 1730 Rhode Island Ave. NW, Suite 100, Washington, DC 20036.

National Toxics Campaign 29 Temple Pl., 5th Floor, Boston, MA 02111.

National Wildlife Federation 1400 16th St. NW, Washington, DC 20036.

National Wood Energy Association 1730 N. Lynn St., Suite 610, Arlington, VA 22209.

Natural Resources Defense Council 40 W. 20th St., New York, NY 10011, and 1350 New York Ave. NW, Suite 300, Washington, DC 20005.

Nature Conservancy 1814 N. Lynn St., Arlington, VA 22209.

New Alchemy Institute 237 Hatchville Rd., East Falmouth, MA 02536.

Nuclear Information and Resource Service 1424 16th St. NW, Suite 601, Washington, DC 20036.

The Oceanic Society 218 D St. SE, Washington, DC 20003.

Permaculture Association P.O. Box 202, Orange, MA 01364.

Permaculture Institute of North America 4649 Sunnyside Ave. N, Seattle, WA 98103.

Planetary Citizens 325 Ninth St., San Francisco, CA 94103.

Planet/Drum Foundation P.O. Box 31251, San Francisco, CA 94131.

Planned Parenthood Federation of America 810 Seventh Ave., New York, NY 10019.

Population Crisis Committee 1120 19th St. NW, Suite 530, Washington, DC 20036-3605.

Population-Environment Balance 1325 G St. NW, Washington, DC 20005

Population Institute 110 Maryland Ave. NE, Suite 207, Washington, DC 20036.

Population Reference Bureau 1875 Connecticut Ave. NW, Suite 520, Washington, DC 20009.

Public Citizen 215 Pennsylvania Ave. SE, Washington, DC 20003.

Rainforest Action Network 300 Broadway, Suite 29A, San Francisco, CA 94133.

Rainforest Alliance 295 Madison Ave., Suite 1804, New York, NY 10017.

Renewable Natural Resources Foundation 5430 Grosvenor Lane, Bethesda, MD 20814.

Renew America 1001 Connecticut Ave. NW, Suite 719, Washington, DC 20036.

Resources for the Future 1616 P St. NW, Washington, DC 20036.

Rocky Mountain Institute 1739 Snowmass Creek Rd., Snowmass, CO 81654.

Rodale Research Center 222 Main St., Emmaus, PA 18098.

Scientists' Institute for Public Information 355 Lexington Ave., New York, NY 10017.

Sea Shepherd Conservation Society P.O. Box 7000-S, Redondo Beach, CA 90277.

Sierra Club 730 Polk St., San Francisco, CA 94109, and 408 C St. NE, Washington, DC 20002.

Smithsonian Institution 1000 Jefferson Dr. SW, Washington, DC 20560.

Social Investment Forum C.E.R.E.S. Project, 711 Atlantic Ave., Boston, MA 02111.

Society of American Foresters 5400 Grosvenor Lane, Bethesda, MD 20814.

Soil and Water Conservation Society 7515 N.E. Ankeny Rd., Ankeny, IA 50021.

Student Conservation Association, Inc. P.O. Box 550, Charlestown, NH 03603.

Student Environmental Action Coalition (SEAC) 217 A Carolina Union, University of North Carolina, Chapel Hill, NC 27599.

Tree People 12601 Mulholland Dr., Beverly Hills, CA 90210.

Union of Concerned Scientists 26 Church St., Cambridge, MA 02238.

U.S. Public Interest Research Group 215 Pennsylvania Ave. SE, Washington, DC 20003.

The Wilderness Society 900 17th St. NW, Washington, DC 20006.

Windstar Foundation 2317 Snowmass Creek Rd., Snowmass, CO 81654.

Work on Waste 82 Judson St., Canton, NY 13617.

World Future Society 4916 St. Elmo Ave., Bethesda, MD 20814.

World Resources Institute 1735 New York Ave. NW, Washington, DC 20006.

Worldwatch Institute 1776 Massachusetts Ave. NW, Washington, DC 20036.

World Wildlife Fund 1250 24th St. NW, Suite 500, Washington, DC 20037.

Zero Population Growth 1400 16th St. NW, 3rd Floor, Washington, DC 20036.

Addresses of Federal and International Agencies

Agency for International Development State Building, 320 21st St. NW, Washington, DC 20523.

Bureau of Land Management U.S. Department of Interior, 18th and C Sts., Room 3619, Washington, DC 20240.

Bureau of Mines 2401 E St. NW, Washington, DC 20241.

Bureau of Reclamation Washington, DC 20240.

Congressional Research Service 101 Independence Ave. SW, Washington, DC 20540.

Conservation and Renewable Energy Inquiry and Referral Service P. O. Box 8900, Silver Spring, MD 20907, (800) 523-2929.

Consumer Product Safety Commission Washington, DC 20207.

Council on Environmental Quality 722 Jackson Pl. NW, Washington, DC 20006.

Department of Agriculture 14th St. and Jefferson Dr. SW, Washington, DC 20250.

Department of Commerce 14th St. between Constitution Ave. and E St. NW, Washington, DC 20230.

Department of Energy Forrestal Building, 1000 Independence Ave. SW, Washington, DC 20585.

Department of Health and Human Services 200 Independence Ave. SW, Washington, DC 20585.

Department of Housing and Urban Development 451 Seventh St. SW, Washington, DC 20410.

Department of the Interior 18th and C Sts. NW, Washington, DC 20240.

Department of Transportation 400 Seventh St. SW, Washington, DC 20590.

Environmental Protection Agency 401 M St. SW, Washington, DC 20460.

Federal Energy Regulatory Commission 825 N. Capitol St. NE, Washington, DC 20426.

Fish and Wildlife Service Department of the Interior, 18th and C Sts. NW, Washington, DC 20240.

Food and Agriculture Organization (FAO) of the United Nations 101 22nd St. NW, Suite 300, Washington, DC 20437.

Food and Drug Administration Department of Health and Human Services, 5600 Fishers Lane, Rockville, MD 20852.

Forest Service P.O. Box 96090, Washington, DC 20013.

Government Printing Office Washington, DC 20402.

Inter-American Development Bank 1300 New York Ave. NW, Washington, DC 20577.

International Whaling Commission The Red House, 135 Station Rd., Histon, Cambridge CB4 4NP England 02203 3971.

Marine Mammal Commission 1625 I St. NW, Washington, DC 20006.

National Academy of Sciences Washington, DC 20550.

National Aeronautics and Space Administration 400 Maryland Ave. SW, Washington, DC 20546.

National Cancer Institute 9000 Rockville Pike, Bethesda, MD 20892.

National Center for Appropriate Technology 3040 Continental Dr., Butte, MT 59701.

National Center for Atmospheric Research P.O. Box 3000, Boulder, CO 80307.

National Marine Fisheries Service U.S. Dept. of Commerce, NOAA, 1335 East-West Highway, Silver Spring, MD 20910.

National Oceanic and Atmospheric Administration Rockville, MD 20852.

National Park Service Department of the Interior, P.O. Box 37127, Washington, DC 20013.

National Science Foundation 1800 G St. NW, Washington, DC 20550.

National Solar Heating and Cooling Information Center P.O. Box 1607, Rockville, MD 20850.

National Technical Information Service U.S. Department of Commerce, 5285 Port Royal Rd., Springfield, VA 22161.

Nuclear Regulatory Commission 1717 H St. NW, Washington, DC 20555.

Occupational Safety and Health Administration Department of Labor, 200 Constitution Ave. NW, Washington, DC 20210.

Office of Ocean and Coastal Resource Management 1825 Connecticut Ave., Suite 700, Washington, DC 20235.

Office of Surface Mining Reclamation and Enforcement 1951 Constitution Ave. NW, Washington, DC 20240.

Office of Technology Assessment U.S. Congress, 600 Pennsylvania Ave. SW, Washington, DC 20510.

Organization for Economic Cooperation and Development (U.S. Office) 2001 L St. NW, Suite 700, Washington, DC 20036.

Soil Conservation Service P.O. Box 2890, Washington, DC 20013.

Solar Energy Research Institute 1617 Cole Blvd., Golden, CO 80401.

United Nations 1 United Nations Plaza, New York, NY 10017.

United Nations Environment Programme Regional North American Office, United Nations Room DC2-0803, New York, NY 10017, and 1889 F St. NW, Washington, DC 20006.

U.S. Geological Survey 12201 Sunrise Valley Dr., Reston, VA 22092.

World Bank 1818 H St. NW, Washington, DC 20433.

APPENDIX 2

UNITS OF
MEASUREMENT

Length

Metric
1 kilometer (km) = 1,000 meters (m)
1 meter (m) = 100 centimeters (cm)
1 meter (m) = 1,000 millimeters (mm)
1 centimeter (cm) = 0.01 meter (m)
1 millimeter (mm) = 0.001 meter (m)

English
1 foot (ft) = 12 inches (in)
1 yard (yd) = 3 feet (ft)
1 mile (mi) = 5,280 feet (ft)
1 nautical mile = 1.15 miles

Metric-English
1 kilometer (km) = 0.621 mile (mi)
1 meter (m) = 39.4 inches (in)
1 inch (in) = 2.54 centimeters (cm)
1 foot (ft) = 0.305 meter (m)
1 yard (yd) = 0.914 meter (m)
1 nautical mile = 1.85 kilometers (km)

Area

Metric
1 square kilometer (km^2) = 1,000,000 square meters (m^2)
1 square meter (m^2) = 1,000,000 square millimeters (mm^2)
1 hectare (ha) = 10,000 square meters (m^2)
1 hectare (ha) = 0.01 square kilometer (km^2)

English
1 square foot (ft^2) = 144 square inches (in^2)
1 square yard (yd^2) = 9 square feet (ft^2)
1 square mile (mi^2) = 27,880,000 square feet (ft^2)
1 acre (ac) = 43,560 square feet (ft^2)

Metric-English
1 hectare (ha) = 2.471 acres (ac)
1 square kilometer (km^2) = 0.386 square mile (mi^2)
1 square meter (m^2) = 1.196 square yards (yd^2)
1 square meter (m^2) = 10.76 square feet (ft^2)
1 square centimeter (cm^2) = 0.155 square inch (in^2)

Volume

Metric
1 cubic kilometer (km^3) = 1,000,000,000 cubic meters (m^3)
1 cubic meter (m^3) = 1,000,000 cubic centimeters (cm^3)
1 liter (L) = 1,000 milliliters (mL) = 1,000 cubic centimeters (cm^3)
1 milliliter (mL) = 0.001 liter (L)
1 milliliter (mL) = 1 cubic centimeter (cm^3)

English
1 gallon (gal) = 4 quarts (qt)
1 quart (qt) = 2 pints (pt)

Metric-English
1 liter (L) = 0.265 gallon (gal)
1 liter (L) = 1.06 quarts (qt)
1 liter (L) = 0.0353 cubic foot (ft^3)
1 cubic meter (m^3) = 35.3 cubic feet (ft^3)
1 cubic meter (m^3) = 1.30 cubic yard (yd^3)
1 cubic kilometer (km^3) = 0.24 cubic mile (mi^3)
1 barrel (bbl) = 159 liters (L)
1 barrel (bbl) = 42 U.S. gallons (gal)

Mass

Metric
1 kilogram (kg) = 1,000 grams (g)
1 gram (g) = 1,000 milligrams (mg)
1 gram (g) = 1,000,000 micrograms (μg)
1 milligram (mg) = 0.001 gram (g)
1 microgram (μg) = 0.000001 gram (g)
1 metric ton (mt) = 1,000 kilograms (kg)

English
1 ton (t) = 2,000 pounds (lb)
1 pound (lb) = 16 ounces (oz)

Metric-English
1 metric ton = 2,200 pounds (lb) = 1.1 tons
1 kilogram (kg) = 2.20 pounds (lb)
1 pound (lb) = 454 grams (g)
1 gram (g) = 0.035 ounce (oz)

Energy and Power

Metric
1 kilojoule (kJ) = 1,000 joules (J)
1 kilocalorie (kcal) = 1,000 calories (cal)
1 calorie (cal) = 4.184 joules (J)

Metric-English
1 kilojoule (kJ) = 0.949 British thermal unit (Btu)
1 kilojoule (kJ) = 0.000278 kilowatt-hour (kW-h)
1 kilocalorie (kcal) = 3.97 British thermal units (Btu)
1 kilocalorie (kcal) = 0.00116 kilowatt-hour (kW-h)
1 kilowatt-hour (kW-h) = 860 kilocalories (kcal)
1 kilowatt-hour (kW-h) = 3,400 British thermal units (Btu)
1 quad (Q) = 1,050,000,000,000,000 kilojoules (kJ)
1 quad (Q) = 2,930,000,000,000 kilowatt-hours (kW-h)

Temperature Conversions

Fahrenheit ($°F$) to Celsius ($°C$): $°C = \dfrac{(°F - 32.0)}{1.80}$

Celsius ($°C$) to Fahrenheit ($°F$): $°F = (°C \times 1.80) + 32.0$

FURTHER READINGS

Chapter 1 Population, Resources, Environmental Degradation, and Pollution

Bender, David L., and Bruno Leone, eds. 1990. *Environment: Opposing Viewpoints*, vol. I. San Diego: Greenhaven.

Brown, Lester R., et al. Annual. *State of the World*. New York: W. W. Norton.

Brundtland, G. H., et al. 1987. *Our Common Future: World Commission on Environment and Development*. New York: Oxford University Press.

Catton, William R. 1980. *Overshoot: The Ecological Basis of Revolutionary Change*. Urbana: University of Illinois Press.

Commoner, Barry. 1990. *Making Peace with the Planet*. New York: Pantheon.

Council on Environmental Quality. *Annual Report*. Washington, D.C.: Government Printing Office.

Council on Environmental Quality and U.S. Department of State. 1980. *The Global 2000 Report to the President*, Vols. I–3. Washington, D.C.: Government Printing Office.

Dahlberg, Kenneth A., et al. 1985. *Environment and the Global Arena*. Durham, N.C.: Duke University Press.

Ehrlich, Anne H., and Paul R. Ehrlich. 1987. *Earth*. New York: Franklin Watts.

Ehrlich, Paul R., and Anne H. Ehrlich. 1990. *The Population Explosion*. New York: Doubleday.

Ehrlich, Paul R., and John P. Holdren, eds. 1988. *The Cassandra Conference: Resources and the Human Predicament*. College Station: Texas A & M University Press.

Ember, Lois R. 1990. "Pollution Chokes East-Bloc Nations." *Chemistry & Engineering News*, 16 April, 7–16.

Global Tomorrow Coalition. 1990. *The Global Ecology Handbook: What You Can Do About the Environmental Crisis*. Boston: Beacon Press.

Goldfarb, Theodore D. 1989. *Taking Sides: Clashing Views on Controversial Environmental Issues*. Guilford, Conn.: Dushkin Publishing Group.

Goldsmith, Edward, et al. 1990. *Imperiled Planet: Restoring Our Endangered Ecosystems*. Cambridge, Mass.: MIT Press.

Gordon, Anita, and David Suzuki. 1991. *It's a Matter of Survival*. Cambridge, Mass.: Harvard University Press.

Hardin, Garrett. 1968. "The Tragedy of the Commons." *Science*, vol. 162, 1243–1248.

Hardin, Garrett. 1985. *Filters Against Folly*. New York: Viking Press.

Henning, Daniel H., and William R. Mangun. 1989. *Managing the Environmental Crisis: Incorporating Competing Values in Natural Resource Management*. Durham, N.C.: Duke University Press.

Kirdon, Michael, and Ronald Segal. 1990. *The New State of the World Atlas*. New York: Simon & Schuster.

Lapp, Ralph. 1973. *The Logarithmic Century*. Englewood Cliffs, N.J.: Prentice Hall.

Lean, Geoffrey, et al. 1990. *Atlas of the Environment*. Englewood Cliffs, N.J.: Prentice Hall.

Meadows, Donella H., et al. 1992. *The Limits to Growth*. 2nd ed. New York: Universe Books.

Meadows, Donella H., et al. 1991. *The Global Citizen*. Covelo, Calif.: Island Press.

Myers, Norman, ed. 1984. *Gaia: An Atlas of Planet Management*. New York: Anchor/Doubleday.

Myers, Norman. 1990. *The Gaia Atlas of Future Worlds*. New York: Anchor/Doubleday.

Office of Technology Assessment. 1987. *U.S. Oil Production: The Effect of Low Oil Prices*. Washington, D.C.: Government Printing Office.

Seager, Joni, ed. 1990. *The State of the Earth Atlas*. New York: Simon & Schuster.

Silver, Cheryl S., and Ruth S. Defries. 1990. *One Earth, One Future: Our Changing Global Environment*. Washington, D.C.: National Academy Press.

Simon, Julian L. 1981. *The Ultimate Resource*. Princeton, N.J.: Princeton University Press.

Simon, Julian L., and Herman Kahn, eds. 1984. *The Resourceful Earth*. Cambridge, Mass.: Basil Blackwell.

Weiner, Jonathan. 1990. *The Next One Hundred Years: Shaping the Fate of Our Living Earth*. New York: Bantam Books.

World Resources Institute and International Institute for Environment and Development. Published every two years. *World Resources*. New York: Basic Books.

Chapter 2 Brief History of Resource Use, Resource Conservation, and Environmental Protection

Arrandale, Thomas. 1983. *The Battle for Natural Resources*. Washington, D.C.: Congressional Quarterly Books.

Axelrod, Robert. 1984. *The Evolution of Cooperation*. New York: Basic Books.

Borrelli, Peter, ed. 1988. *Crossroads: Environmental Priorities for the Future*. Covelo, Calif.: Island Press.

Bramwell, Anna. 1989. *Ecology in the 20th Century*. New Haven, Conn.: Yale University Press.

Bronowski, Jacob, Jr. 1974. *The Ascent of Man*. Boston: Little, Brown.

Burger, J. 1990. *The Gaia Atlas of First Peoples: A Future for the Indigenous World*. New York: Doubleday.

Cahn, Robert, ed. 1985. *An Environmental Agenda for the Future*. Covelo, Calif.: Island Press.

Callicott, J. Baird. 1989. "American Indian Land Wisdom? Sorting Out the Issues." *Journal of Forest History*, vol. 33, no. 1, 35–42.

Calvin, William H. 1990. *The Ascent of Mind*. New York: Bantam Books.

Carson, Rachel. 1962. *Silent Spring*. Boston: Houghton Mifflin.

Carter, V. G., and T. Dale. 1974. *Topsoil and Civilization*. Norman: University of Oklahoma Press.

Clawson, Marion. 1983. *The Federal Lands Revisited*. Washington, D.C.: Resources for the Future.

Coalition of Environmental Groups. 1989. *Blueprint for the Environment*. Salt Lake City: Howe Brothers Press.

Cohen, Mark N. 1989. *Health and the Rise of Civilization*. New Haven, Conn.: Yale University Press.

Cohen, Michael P. 1984. *The Pathless Way: John Muir and American Wilderness*. Madison: University of Wisconsin Press.

Culhane, Paul J. 1981. *Public Land Politics: Interest Group Influences on the Forest Service and the Bureau of Land Management*. Washington, D.C.: Resources for the Future.

Dunlap, Thomas. 1988. *Saving America's Wildlife*. Princeton, N.J.: Princeton University Press.

Eisler, Riabe. 1987. *The Chalice and the Blade: Our History, Our Future*. San Francisco: Harper & Row.

Fagan, Brian M. 1990. *The Journey from Eden: The Peopling of Our World*. London: Thames & Hudson.

Ferguson, Denzel, and Nancy Ferguson. 1983. *Sacred Cows at the Public Trough*. Bend, Oreg.: Maverick Publications.

Fox, Stephen. 1981. *John Muir and His Legacy: The American Conservation Movement*. Boston: Little, Brown.

Friends of the Earth et al. 1982. *Reagan and Environment*. San Francisco: Friends of the Earth.

Goudie, Andrew. 1990. *The Human Impact on the Natural Environment*. 3rd ed. Cambridge, Mass.: MIT Press.

Graham, Frank. 1971. *Man's Dominion: The Story of Conservation in America*. New York: M. Evans.

Hartzog, George B., Jr. 1988. *Battling for the National Parks*. Mt. Kisco, N.Y.: Moyer Bell.

Hays, Samuel. 1987. *Beauty, Health, and Permanence: Environmental Politics in the United States: 1955–1985*. New York: Cambridge University Press.

High Country News. 1989. *Reforming the Western Frontier*. Covelo, Calif.: Island Press.

Hughes, J. Donald. 1975. *The Ecology of Ancient Civilizations*. Albuquerque: University of New Mexico Press.

Hughes, J. Donald. 1983. *American Indian Ecology*. El Paso: Texas Western Press.

Hyams, Edward. 1976. *Soils and Civilization*. New York: Harper & Row.

Jacks, G. W., and R. O. Whyte. 1939. *The Rape of the Earth*. New York: Faber & Faber.

Lash, Jonathan, et al. 1984. *A Season of Spoils*. New York: Pantheon.

Leopold, Aldo. 1949. *A Sand County Almanac*. New York: Oxford University Press.

Livingston, John. 1973. *One Cosmic Instant: Man's Fleeting Supremacy*. Boston: Houghton Mifflin.

Marsh, George Perkins. 1864. *Man and Nature*. New York: Charles Scribner's.

McCormick, John. 1989. *Reclaiming Paradise: The Global Environmental Movement*. Bloomington: Indiana University Press.

Meine, Curt. 1988. *Aldo Leopold: His Life and Work*. Madison: University of Wisconsin Press.

Mumford, Lewis. 1962. *The Transformations of Man*. New York: Collier.

Nash, Roderick. 1982. *Wilderness and the American Mind*. 3rd ed. New Haven, Conn.: Yale University Press.

Nash, Roderick. 1988. *The Rights of Nature: A History of Environmental Ethics*. Madison: University of Wisconsin Press.

Nicholson, Max. 1987. *The New Environmental Age*. New York: Cambridge University Press.

Odell, Rice. 1980. *Environmental Awakening: The New Revolution to Protect the Earth*. Cambridge, Mass.: Ballinger.

Osborn, Fairfield. 1948. *Our Plundered Planet*. Boston: Little, Brown.

Petulla, Joseph M. 1988. *American Environmental History*. 2nd ed. Columbus, Ohio: Charles E. Merrill.

Repetto, Robert, ed. 1986. *The Global Possible: Resources, Development, and the New Century*. New Haven, Conn.: Yale University Press.

Repetto, Robert. 1986. *World Enough and Time*. New Haven, Conn.: Yale University Press.

Roe, Frank G. 1970. *The North American Buffalo*. Toronto: University of Toronto Press.

Sabaloff, Jeremy A., and C. C. Lamberg-Karlovsky. 1975. *The Rise and Fall of Civilizations*. Menlo Park, Calif.: Benjamin/Cummings.

Sears, Paul B. 1980. *Deserts on the March*. Norman: University of Oklahoma Press.

Shanks, Bernard. 1984. *This Land Is Your Land*. San Francisco: Sierra Club Books.

Short, C. Brant. 1989. *Ronald Reagan and the Public Lands: America's Conservation Debate: 1979–1984*. College Station: Texas A & M University Press.

Simmons, I. G. 1989. *Changing the Face of the Earth: Culture, Environment, and History*. London: Basil Blackwell.

Stroup, Richard L., and John A. Baden. 1986. *Natural Resources: Bureaucratic Myths and Environmental Management*. San Francisco: Institute for Public Policy Research.

Tanner, Thomas, ed. 1987. *Aldo Leopold: The Man and His Legacy*. Ankeny, Iowa: Soil Conservation Society of America.

Toynbee, Arnold. 1972. *A Study of History*. New York: Oxford University Press.

Turner, R. L., ed. 1990. *The Earth as Transformed By Human Actions*. New York: Cambridge University Press.

Udall, Stewart L. 1963. *The Quiet Crisis*. New York: Holt, Rinehart & Winston. Reprint, with updating, Salt Lake City: Gibbs Smith.

U.S. Department of Agriculture, Forest Service. 1976. *Highlights in the History of Forest Conservation*. Washington, D.C.: Government Printing Office.

Vecsey, Christopher, and Robert W. Veneables, eds. 1980. *American Indian Environments: Ecological Issues in Native American History*. Syracuse, N.Y.: University of Syracuse Press.

Vig, Norman J., and Michael J. Craft. 1984. *Environmental Policy in the 1980s*. Washington, D.C.: Congressional Quarterly Press.

Vig, Norman J., and Michael J. Craft. 1990. *Environmental Policy in the 1990s*. Washington, D.C.: Congressional Quarterly Press.

Vogt, William. 1948. *The Road to Survival*. New York: Sloane.

Williams, Michael. 1989. *Americans and Their Forests: A Historical Account*. New York: Cambridge University Press.

World Resources Institute. 1989. *The Crucial Decade: The 1990s and the Global Environmental Challenge*. Washington, D.C.: World Resources Institute.

Worster, Donald, ed. 1988. *The Ends of the Earth: Perspectives on Modern Environmental History*. Cambridge: Cambridge University Press.

Zaslowsky, Dyan, and Wilderness Society. 1986. *These American Lands*. New York: Henry Holt & Co.

Chapter 3 Matter and Energy Resources: Types and Concepts

American Physical Society. 1975. *Efficient Use of Energy*. New York: American Institute of Physics.

Bent, Henry A. 1977. "Entropy and the Energy Crisis." *Journal of Science Teaching*, vol. 44, no. 4, 25–29.

Berry, R. Stephen. 1972. "Recycling, Thermodynamics, and Environmental Thrift." *Bulletin of Atomic Scientists*, May, 28–31.

Carrying Capacity, Inc. 1987. *Beyond Oil*. Cambridge, Mass.: Ballinger.

Christensen, John W. 1990. *Global Science: Energy, Resources, and Environment*. 3rd ed. Dubuque, Iowa: Kendall/Hunt.

Colorado Energy Research Institute. 1976. *Net Energy Analysis: An Energy Balance Study of Fossil Fuel Resources*. Golden, Colo.: Colorado Energy Research Institute.

Fowler, John M. 1984. *Energy and the Environment*. 2nd ed. New York: McGraw-Hill.

Glasby, G. P. 1988. "Entropy, Pollution, and Environmental Degradation." *Ambio*, vol. 17, no. 5, 330–335.

Hirsch, Robert L. 1987. "Impending United States Energy Crisis." *Science*, vol. 235, 1467–1473.

Kuhn, Thomas S. 1970. *The Structure of Scientific Revolutions*. 2nd ed. Chicago: University of Chicago Press.

Lovins, Amory B. 1977. *Soft Energy Paths*. Cambridge, Mass.: Ballinger.

Lovins, Amory B., and L. Hunter Lovins. 1986. *Energy Unbound: Your Invitation to Energy Abundance*. San Francisco: Sierra Club Books.

Miller, G. Tyler, Jr. 1971. *Energetics, Kinetics, and Life: An Ecological Approach*. Belmont, Calif.: Wadsworth.

Nash, Hugh, ed. 1979. *The Energy Controversy: Soft Path Questions and Answers*. San Francisco: Friends of the Earth.

Odum, Howard T., and Elisabeth C. Odum. 1980. *Energy Basis for Man and Nature*. New York: McGraw-Hill.

Rifkin, Jeremy. 1989. *Entropy: Into the Greenhouse World: A New World View*. New York: Bantam Books.

Rose, David. 1986. *Learning About Energy*. New York: Plenum.

Smil, Vaclar. 1991. *General Energetics: Energy in the Biosphere and Civilization*. New York: John Wiley.

Chapter 4 Ecosystems: What Are They and How Do They Work?

Ahmadjian, V., and S. Paracer. 1986. *Symbiosis: An Introduction to Biological Associations*. New Haven, Conn.: University Press of New England.

Andrewartha, H. G., and L. C. Birch. 1986. *The Ecological Web: More on the Distribution and Abundance of Animals*. Chicago: University of Chicago Press.

Bolin, B., and R. B. Cook. 1983. *The Major Biogeochemical Cycles and Their Interactions*. New York: John Wiley.

Colinvaux, Paul A. 1986. *Ecology*. New York: John Wiley.

DiSilvestro, Roger L. 1990. *Fight for Survival*. New York: John Wiley.

Ehrlich, Anne H., and Paul R. Ehrlich. 1987. *Earth*. New York: Franklin Watts.

Ehrlich, Paul R. 1986. *The Machinery of Life: The Living World Around Us and How It Works*. New York: Simon & Schuster.

Ehrlich, Paul R., Anne H. Ehrlich, and John P. Holdren. 1977. *Ecoscience: Population, Resources and Environment*. New York: W. H. Freeman.

Gates, David M. 1985. *Energy and Ecology*. Sunderland, Mass.: Sinauer.

Kormondy, Edward J. 1984. *Concepts of Ecology*. 3rd ed. Englewood Cliffs, N.J.: Prentice Hall.

Krebs, Charles J. 1985. *Ecology*. 3rd ed. New York: Harper & Row.

Odum, Eugene P. 1989. *Ecology and Our Endangered Life-Support Systems*. Sunderland, Mass.: Sinauer.

Post, Wilfred M., et al. 1990. "The Global Carbon Cycle." *American Scientist*, vol. 78, 310–326.

Ramadé, Francois. 1984. *Ecology of Natural Resources*. New York: John Wiley.

Rickleffs, Robert E. 1990. *Ecology*. 3rd ed. New York: W. H. Freeman.

Smith, Robert L. 1990. *Elements of Ecology*. 4th ed. New York: Harper & Row.

Springer, Victor G., and Joy P. Gold. 1989. *Sharks in Question: The Smithsonian Answer Book*. Washington D.C.: Smithsonian Institution.

Tudge, Colin. 1988. *The Environment of Life*. New York: Oxford University Press.

Watt, Kenneth E. F. 1982. *Understanding the Environment*. Boston: Allyn & Bacon.

Worster, Donald. 1985. *Nature's Economy: A History of Ecological Ideas*. New York: Cambridge University Press.

Chapter 5 Climate, Terrestrial Life, and Aquatic Life

See also the readings for Chapter 4.

Aber, John, and Jerry Melito. 1991. *Terrestrial Ecosystems*. Philadelphia, Pa.: Saunders.

Akin, Wallace E. 1991. *Global Patterns: Climate, Vegetation, and Soils*. Norman: University of Oklahoma Press.

Attenborough, David. 1984. *The Living Planet*. Boston: Little, Brown.

Attenborough, David, et al. 1989. *The Atlas of the Living World*. Boston: Houghton Mifflin.

Brown, J. H., and A. C. Gibson. 1983. *Biogeography*. St. Louis: C. V. Mosby.

Brown, Lauren. 1985. *Grasslands*. New York: Random House.

Burke, David G., et al. 1989. *Protecting Nontidal Wetlands*. Washington, D.C.: American Planning Association.

Carson, Rachel. 1955. *The Edge of the Sea*. Boston: Houghton Mifflin.

Clapham, W. B., Jr. 1984. *Natural Ecosystems*. 2nd ed. New York: Macmillan.

Couper, Alastair, ed. 1990. *The Times Atlas and Encyclopedia of the Sea*. Hagerstown, Md.: Lippincott Books.

Cousteau, Jacques-Yves. 1981. *The Cousteau Almanac: An Inventory of Life on Our Water Planet*. New York: Doubleday.

Culliny, John L. 1976. *The Forest of the Sea*. San Francisco: Sierra Club Books.

Daiber, Franklin C. 1986. *Conservation of Tidal Marshes*. New York: Van Nostrand Reinhold.

Environmental Protection Agency. 1989. *Marine and Estuarine Protection: Programs and Activities*. Washington, D.C.: EPA.

Goldman, C., and A. Horne. 1983. *Limnology*. New York: McGraw-Hill.

Goldman-Carter, Jan. 1989. *A Citizen's Guide to Protecting Wetlands*. Washington, D.C.: National Wildlife Federation.

Goldsmith, Edward, et al. 1990. *Imperiled Planet: Restoring Our Endangered Ecosystems*. Cambridge, Mass.: MIT Press.

Golley, Frank B., ed. 1983. *Tropical Rain Forest Ecosystems: Structure and Function*. New York: Elsevier.

Graham, N. E., and W. B. White. 1988. "The El Niño Cycle: A Natural Oscillator of the Pacific Ocean-Atmosphere System." *Science*, vol. 240, 1293–1302.

Greenland, David. 1983. *Guidelines for Modern Resource Management: Soil, Land, Water, Air*. Columbus, Ohio: Charles E. Merrill.

Kaufman, Wallace, and Orin Pilkey. 1979. *The Beaches Are Moving*. New York: Anchor /Doubleday.

Lauw, G. N., and M. K. Seely. 1982. *Ecology of Desert Organisms*. New York: Longman.

Mabberly, D. J. 1983. *Tropical Rain Forest Ecology*. London: Blackie.

MacMahon, James A. 1985. *Deserts*. New York: Random House.

Maltby, Edward. 1986. *Waterlogged Wealth*. East Haven, Conn.: Earthscan.

McArthur, R. H. 1972. *Geographical Ecology*. New York: Harper & Row.

Mitsch, William J., and James G. Gosselink. 1986. *Wetlands*. New York: Van Nostrand Reinhold.

Myers, Norman. 1984. *The Primary Source: Tropical Forests and Our Future*. New York: W. W. Norton.

National Wildlife Federation. 1987. *Status Report of Our Nation's Wetlands*. Washington, D.C.: National Wildlife Federation.

Niering, William A. 1985. *Wetlands*. New York: Random House.

Office of Technology Assessment. 1984. *Wetlands: Their Use and Regulation*. Washington, D.C.: Government Printing Office.

Pilkey, Orin H., Jr., et al. 1984. *Coastal Design: A Guide for Builders, Planners, & Homeowners*. New York: Van Nostrand Reinhold.

Pilkey, Orin H., Jr, and William J. Neal, eds. 1987. *Living with the Shore*. Durham, N.C.: Duke University Press.

Simon, Anne W. 1978. *The Thin Edge: Coast and Man in Crisis*. New York: Harper & Row.

Teal, John, and Mildred Teal. 1969. *Life and Death of a Salt Marsh*. New York: Ballantine.

Thorne-Miller, Boyce, and John Catena. 1990. *The Living Ocean: Understanding and Protecting Marine Diversity*. Covelo, Calif.: Island Press.

Tudge, Colin. 1988. *The Environment of Life*. New York: Oxford University Press.

Urban Land Institute. 1990. *Wetlands: Mitigating and Regulating Development Impacts*. Washington, D.C.: Urban Land Institute.

Wallace, David. 1987. *Life in the Balance*. New York: Harcourt Brace Jovanovich.

Whittaker, R. H. 1975. *Communities and Ecosystems*. 2nd ed. New York: Macmillan.

Yates, Steve. 1988. *Adopting a Stream*. Seattle: University of Washington Press.

Yates, Steve. 1989. *Adopting a Wetland*. Everett, Wash.: Adopt-A-Stream Foundation.

Chapter 6 Changes in Populations, Communities, and Ecosystems

See also the readings for Chapters 4 and 5.

Anderson, Walter T. 1987. *To Govern Evolution*. New York: Harcourt Brace Jovanovich.

Berger, John J. 1986. *Restoring the Earth*. New York: Alfred A. Knopf.

Berger, John J., ed. 1990. *Environmental Restoration*. Covelo, Calif.: Island Press.

Boulding, Kenneth E. 1985. *The World as a Total System*. Beverly Hills: Sage Publications.

Busch, Lawrence, et al. 1990. *Plants, Power, and Profit: Social, Economic, and Ethical Consequences of the New Biotechnologies*. Cambridge, Mass.: Basil Blackwell.

Ehrlich, Paul R. 1980. "Variety Is the Key to Life." *Technology Review*, March/April, 599–608.

Endler, John A. 1986. *Natural Selection in the Wild*. Princeton, N.J.: Princeton University Press.

Farvar, M. Tagi, and John Milton, eds. 1972. *The Careless Technology*. Garden City, N.Y.: Natural History Press.

Freedman, Bill. 1989. *Environmental Ecology: The Impacts of Pollution and Other Stresses on Ecosystem Structure and Function*. San Diego: Academic Press.

Gould, Stephen Jay. 1977. *Ever Since Darwin*. New York: W. W. Norton.

Gould, Stephen Jay. 1980. *The Panda's Thumb*. New York: W. W. Norton.

Hardin, Garrett. 1985. "Human Ecology: The Subversive, Conservative Science." *American Zoologist*, vol. 25, 469–476.

Joseph, Lawrence E. 1990. *Gaia: The Growth of an Idea*. New York: St. Martin's Press.

Lovelock, James E. 1979. *Gaia: A New Look at Life on Earth*. New York: Oxford University Press.

Lovelock, James E. 1988. *The Ages of Gaia: A Biography of Our Living Earth*. New York: W. W. Norton.

Margulis, Lynn, and Dorion Sagan. 1986. *Microcosmos: Four Billion Years of Evolution from Our Microbiological Ancestors*. New York: Summit Books.

McArthur, Robert H., and E. O. Wilson. 1967. *The Theory of Island Biogeography*. Princeton, N.J.: Princeton University Press.

National Academy of Sciences. 1986. *Ecological Knowledge and Environmental Problem-Solving*. Washington, D.C.: National Academy Press.

Odum, Eugene P. 1969. "The Strategy of Ecosystem Development." *Science*, vol. 164, 262–270.

Olson, Steve. 1989. *Shaping the Future: Biology and Human Values*. Washington, D.C.: National Academy Press.

Pimentel, David, et al. 1989. "Benefits and Risks of Genetic Engineering in Agriculture." *Bioscience*, vol. 39, no. 9, 606–614.

Power, J. F., and R. F. Follett. 1987. "Monoculture." *Scientific American*, January, 30–36.

Rifkin, Jeremy. 1983. *Algeny*. New York: Viking/Penguin.

Rifkin, Jeremy. 1985. *Declaration of a Heretic*. Boston: Routledge & Kegan Paul.

Schneider, S. H., and R. S. Londer. 1984. *The Coevolution of Climate and Life*. San Francisco: Sierra Club Books.

Schneider, Stephen H., and Penelope J. Boston, eds. 1991. *Scientists on Gaia*. Cambridge, Mass.: MIT Press.

Slobodkin, Laurence B. 1980. *Growth and Regulation of Animal Populations*. New York: Dover.

Suzuki, David, and Peter Knudtson. 1989. *Genethics: The Clash Between the New Genetics and Human Values*. Cambridge, Mass.: Harvard University Press.

Wilson, E. O. 1984. *Biophilia*. Cambridge, Mass.: Harvard University Press.

Wilson, E. O., ed. 1988. *Biodiversity*. Washington, D.C.: National Academy Press.

Woodwell, G. M. 1970. "Effects of Pollution on the Structure and Physiology of Ecosystems." *Science*, vol. 168, 429–433.

Chapter 7 Geologic Processes: The Dynamic Earth

Bolt, Bruce A. 1987. *Earthquakes*. Rev. ed. Berkeley and Los Angeles: University of California Press.

Brown, Bruce, and Lane Morgan. 1990. *The Miracle Planet*. Edison, N.J.: W. H. Smith.

Bullard, Fred. 1984. *Volcanoes of the Earth*. 2nd ed. Austin: University of Texas Press.

Craig, James R., et al. 1988. *Resources of the Earth*. Englewood Cliffs, N.J.: Prentice Hall.

Erickson, Jon. 1989. *The Living Earth: The Coevolution of the Planet and Life*. Blue Ridge Summit, Pa.: TAB Books.

Ernst, W. G. 1990. *The Dynamic Planet*. New York: Columbia University Press.

Hamblin, W. Kenneth. 1989. *The Earth's Dynamic Systems: A Textbook in Physical Geology*. 5th ed. New York: Macmillan.

Hansen, Gladys, and Emmet Condon. 1989. *Denial of Disaster*. San Francisco: Cameron.

Harris, Stephen L. 1990. *Agents of Chaos: Earthquakes, Volcanoes, and Other Natural Disasters*. Missoula, Mont.: Mountain Press Publishing Co.

Keller, Edward A. 1988. *Environmental Geology*. 5th ed. Columbus, Ohio: Charles E. Merrill.

McAlester, R. A., et al. 1984. *The History of the Earth's Crust*. Englewood Cliffs, N.J.: Prentice Hall.

Montgomery, Carla W. 1989. *Environmental Geology*. Dubuque, Iowa: Wm. C. Brown.

Plummer, C. C., and D. McGeary. 1985. *Physical Geography*. 3rd ed. Dubuque, Iowa: Wm. C. Brown.

Redfern, Ron. 1983. *The Making of a Continent*. New York: Times Books.

Tilling, Robert I. 1982. *Eruptions of Mount St. Helens: Past, Present, and Future*. Washington, D.C.: U.S. Geological Survey, Government Printing Office.

Tilling, Robert I. 1989. *Volcanic Hazards: Short Course in Geology*, vol. 1. Washington, D.C.: American Geophysical Union.

Westbrook, Peter. 1991. *Life as a Geological Force: Dynamics of the Earth*. New York: W. W. Norton.

Youngquist, Walter. 1990. *Mineral Resources and the Destinies of Nations*. Portland, Oreg.: National Book Company.

Chapter 8 Population Dynamics and Population Regulation

Brown, Lester R., and Edward C. Wolf. 1985. *Reversing Africa's Decline*. Washington, D.C.: Worldwatch Institute.

Brown, Lester R., and Jodi Jacobson. 1986. *Our Demographically Divided World*. Washington, D.C.: Worldwatch Institute.

Callahan, Daniel. 1972. "Ethics and Population Limitation." *Science*, vol. 175, 487–494.

Commission on Population Growth and the American Future. 1972. *Population and the American Future*. Washington, D.C.: Government Printing Office.

Crewdson, John. 1983. *The Tarnished Door*. New York: Times Books.

Croll, Elisabeth, et al. 1985. *China's One-Child Family Policy*. New York: St. Martin's Press.

Dankelman, Irene, and Joan Davidson. 1988. *Women and the Environment in the Third World*. East Haven, Conn.: Earthscan.

Davis, Kingsley, et al., eds. 1989. *Population and Resources in a Changing World*. Stanford, Calif.: Morrison Institute for Population and Resource Studies.

Djerassi, Carl. 1989. "The Bitter Pill." *Science*, vol. 245, 356–361.

Donaldson, Peter J., and Amy Ong Tsui. 1990. "The International Family Planning Movement." *Population Bulletin*, vol. 43, no. 3, 1–42.

Dychtwald, Ken. 1989. *Age Wave: The Challenges and Opportunities of an Aging America*. New York: Jeremy Tarcher.

Ehrlich, Paul, et al. 1981. *The Golden Door: International Migration, Mexico, and the United States*. New York: Wideview Books.

Ehrlich, Paul R., and Anne H. Ehrlich. 1990. *The Population Explosion*. New York: Doubleday.

Formos, Werner. 1987. *Gaining People, Losing Ground: A Blueprint for Stabilizing World Population*. Washington, D.C.: Population Institute.

Goliber, Thomas J. 1985. "Sub-Saharan Africa: Population Pressures on Development." *Population Bulletin*, vol. 40, no. 1, 1–45.

Grant, James P. 1991. *The State of the World's Children 1991*. New York: Oxford University Press.

Gupte, Pranay. 1984. *The Crowded Earth: People and the Politics of Population*. New York: W. W. Norton.

Hardin, Garrett. 1982. *Naked Emperors, Essays of a Taboo Stalker*. Los Altos, Calif.: William Kaufmann.

Hartmann, Betsy. 1987. *Reproductive Rights and Wrongs: The Global Politics of Population Control and Contraceptive Choice*. New York: Harper & Row.

Haub, Carl. 1987. "Understanding Population Projections." *Population Bulletin*, vol. 42, no. 4, 1–41.

Haupt, Arthur, and Thomas T. Kane. 1985. *The Population Handbook: International*. 2nd ed. Washington, D.C.: Population Reference Bureau.

Hernandez, Donald J. 1985. *Success or Failure? Family Planning Programs in the Third World*. Westport, Conn.: Greenwood Press.

International Union for Conservation of Nature and Natural Resources and Planned Parenthood Federation. 1984. *Population and Natural Resources*. Gland, Switzerland: IUCN.

Jacobson, Jodi. 1987. *Planning the Global Family*. Washington, D.C.: Worldwatch Institute.

Jacobson, Jodi. 1990. *The Global Politics of Abortion*. Washington, D.C.: Worldwatch Institute.

Jacobson, Jodi. 1991. *Women's Reproductive Health: The Silent Emergency*. Washington, D.C.: Worldwatch Institute.

Jaffe, Frederick S., et al. 1980. *Abortion Politics*. New York: Alan Guttmacher Institute.

Jones, Elsie F., et al. 1986. *Teenage Pregnancy in Industrialized Countries*. New Haven, Conn.: Yale University Press.

Keyfitz, Nathan. 1989. "The Growing Human Population." *Scientific American*, September, 119–126.

Lamm, Richard D., and Gary Imhoff. 1985. *The Immigration Time Bomb*. New York: Dutton.

Loup, Jacques. 1983. *Can the Third World Survive?* Baltimore: Johns Hopkins University Press.

Menken, Jane, ed. 1986. *World Population and U.S. Policy: The Choices Ahead*. New York: W. W. Norton.

Merrick, Thomas W. 1986. "World Population in Transition." *Population Bulletin*, vol. 41, no. 2, 1–51.

Merrick, Thomas W., and Stephen J. Tordella. 1988. "Demographics: People and Markets." *Population Bulletin*, vol. 43, no. 1, 1–46.

Morgan, Robin. 1984. *Sisterhood Is Global*. New York: Doubleday.

National Academy of Sciences. 1990. *Developing New Contraceptives: Obstacles and Opportunities*. Washington, D.C.: National Academy Press.

Peters, Gary L., and Robert P. Larkin. 1989. *Population Geography*. 3rd ed. Dubuque, Iowa: Kendall/Hunt.

Population Reference Bureau. 1986. *Women in the World: The Women's Decade and Beyond*. Washington, D.C.: Population Reference Bureau.

Population Reference Bureau. 1990. *World Population: Fundamentals of Growth*. Washington, D.C.: Population Reference Bureau.

Population Reference Bureau. Annual. *World Population Data Sheet*. Washington, D.C.: Population Reference Bureau.

Russell, Cheryl. 1987. *100 Predictions for the Baby Boom: The Next 50 Years*. New York: Plenum.

Saunders, John. 1988. *Basic Demographic Measures: A Practical Guide for Users*. Lanham, Md.: University Press of America.

Simon, Julian L. 1989. *Population Matters: People, Resources, Environment, and Immigration*. New Brunswick, N.J.: Transaction.

Simon, Julian L. 1990. *The Economic Consequences of Immigration*. Cambridge, Mass.: Basil Blackwell.

Soldo, Beth J., and Emily M. Agree. 1988. "America's Elderly." *Population Bulletin*, vol. 43, no. 3, 1–51.

Teitelbaum, Michael, and Jay M. Winter. 1985. *The Fear of Population Decline*. San Diego: Academic Press.

United Nations. Annual. *Demographic Yearbook*. New York: United Nations.

Wattenberg, Ben J. 1987. *The Birth Dearth*. New York: Pharos Books.

Weber, Susan, ed. 1988. *USA by Numbers: A Statistical Portrait of the United States*. Washington, D.C.: Zero Population Growth.

Weeks, John R. 1989. *Population: An Introduction to Concepts and Issues*. 4th ed. Belmont, Calif.: Wadsworth.

Zero Population Growth. 1990. *Planning the Ideal Family: The Small Family Option*. Washington, D.C.: Zero Population Growth.

Chapter 9 Population Distribution: Urbanization, Urban Problems, and Urban Land Use

American Public Transit System. 1989. *Mass Transit—The Clean Air Alternative*. Washington, D.C.: American Public Transit Association.

Berg, Peter, et al. 1989. *A Green City Program*. San Francisco: Planet/Drum Foundation.

Bookchin, Murray. 1986. *The Limits of City*. New York: Black Rose.

Brenneman, Russell L., and Sarah M. Bates, eds. 1984. *Land-Saving Action*. Covelo, Calif.: Island Press.

Brown, Lester R., and Jodi Jacobson. 1987. *The Future of Urbanization: Facing the Ecological and Economic Restraints*. Washington, D.C.: Worldwatch Institute.

Cadman, D., and G. Payne, eds. 1990. *The Living City: Towards a Sustainable Future*. London: Routledge.

Canfield, Christopher, ed. 1990. *Ecocity Conference*. Berkeley, Calif.: Urban Ecology.

Cassidy, Robert. 1980. *Livable Cities: A Grass-Roots Guide to Rebuilding Urban America*. New York: Holt, Rinehart & Winston.

Choate, Pat, and Susan Walter. 1981. *America in Ruins: Beyond the Public Works Pork Barrel*. Washington, D.C.: Council on State Planning Agencies.

Coates, Gary. 1981. *Resettling America: Energy, Ecology, and Community*. Andover, Mass.: Brick House.

Corbett, Michael. 1990. *A Better Place to Live*. Davis, Calif.: agAccess.

Dantzig, George B., and Thomas L. Saaty. 1973. *Compact City: A Plan for a Liveable Environment*. New York: W. H. Freeman.

Environmental Action. 1989. *Clean Motion*. Washington, D.C.: Environmental Action.

Fabos, Julius Gy. 1985. *Land-Use Planning: From Global to Local Challenge*. New York: Chapman and Hall.

Farallones Institute. 1979. *The Integral Urban House: Self-Reliant Living in the City*. San Francisco: Sierra Club Books.

Frey, William H. 1990. "Metropolitan America: Beyond the Transition." *Population Bulletin*, vol. 45, no. 2, 1–49.

Gottman, Jean, and Robert A. Harper, eds. 1990. *Since Megalopolis: The Urban Writings of Jean Gottman*. Baltimore: Johns Hopkins University Press.

Gratz, Roberta B. 1989. *The Living City*. New York: Simon & Schuster.

Hardoy, Jorge, and David Satterwaite. 1989. *Squatter Citizen: Life in the Third World*. East Haven, Conn.: Earthscan.

Herbes, J. 1986. *The New Heartlands: America's Flight Beyond the Suburbs*. New York: Time-Life Books.

Jacobs, Jane. 1984. *Cities and the Wealth of Nations*. New York: Random House.

Johnson, William C. 1989. *The Politics of Urban Planning*. New York: Paragon.

Kaplan, Marshall. 1989. *The Future of National Urban Policy*. Durham, N.C.: Duke University Press.

Kelbaugh, Doug, ed. 1989. *The Pedestrian Pocketbook: A New Suburban Design Strategy*. New York: Princeton Architectural Press.

Kemp, Roger L., ed. 1988. *America's Cities: Strategic Planning for the Future*. New York: Interstate Printers and Publishers.

Kozol, Jonathan. 1988. *Rachel and Her Children*. New York: Crown.

Leckie, Jim, et al. 1975. *Other Homes and Garbage: Designs for Self-Sufficient Living*. San Francisco: Sierra Club Books.

Lowe, Marcia D. 1989. *The Bicycle: Vehicle for a Small Planet*. Washington, D.C.: Worldwatch Institute.

Lowe, Marcia D. 1990. *Alternatives to the Automobile: Transport for Living Cities*. Washington, D.C.: Worldwatch Institute.

Luten, Daniel B. 1986. *Progress Against Growth*. New York: Guilford Press.

Mantrell, Michael L., et al. 1989. *Creating Successful Communities: A Guidebook to Growth Management Strategies*. Covelo, Calif.: Island Press.

Marcus, Clare C., and Wendy Sarkissian. 1986. *Housing as if People Mattered*. Berkeley and Los Angeles: University of California Press.

May, Richard, Jr., ed. 1989. *The Urbanization Revolution: Planning a New Agenda for Human Settlements*. New York: Plenum.

McHarg, Ian L. 1969. *Design with Nature*. Garden City, N.Y.: Natural History Press.

Morehouse, Ward, ed. 1989. *Building Sustainable Communities*. New York: Bootstrap Press.

Morris, David. 1982. *Energy and the Transformation of Urban America*. San Francisco: Sierra Club Books.

Mumford, Lewis. 1968. *The Urban Prospect*. New York: Harcourt Brace Jovanovich.

Register, Richard. 1987. *Ecocity Berkeley: Building Cities for a Healthy Future*. Berkeley, Calif.: North Atlantic Books.

Renner, Michael. 1988. *Rethinking the Role of the Automobile*. Washington, D.C.: Worldwatch Institute.

Replogle, Michael L. 1988. *Bicycles and Public Transportation: New Links to Suburban Transit*. 2nd ed. Washington, D.C.: The Bicycle Federation.

Ryn, Sin van der, and Peter Calthorpe. 1986. *Sustainable Communities: A New Design Synthesis for Cities, Suburbs, and Towns*. San Francisco: Sierra Club Books.

Stokes, Samuel N., et al. 1989. *Saving America's Countryside: A Guide to Rural Conservation*. Baltimore: Johns Hopkins University Press.

Thornton, Richard D. 1991. "Why the U.S. Needs a Maglev System." *Technology Review*, April, 31–42.

Todd, John, and George Tukel. 1990. *Reinhabiting Cities and Towns: Designing for Sustainability*. San Francisco: Planet/Drum Foundation.

Todd, Nancy Jack, and John Todd. 1984. *Bioshelters, Ocean Arks, City Farming: Ecology as the Basis of Design*. San Francisco: Sierra Club Books.

Tolley, Rodney, ed. 1991. *The Greening of Urban Transport: Planning for Walking and Cycling in Western Cities*. New York: Pinter.

Wachs, Martin. 1989. "U.S. Transit Subsidy Policy: In Need of Reform." *Science*, vol. 244, 1545–1549.

Westman, Walter E. 1985. *Ecology, Impact Assessment and Environmental Planning*. New York: John Wiley.

Whyte, William. 1988. *City: Discovering the Center*. New York: Doubleday.

Yang, Linda. 1990. *The City Gardener's Handbook: From Balcony to Backyard*. New York: Random House.

Chapter 10 Deforestation and Loss of Biodiversity

Anderson, Anthony B., et al., eds. 1990. *Alternatives to Deforestation: Steps Toward Sustainable Use of the Amazon Rain Forest*. Irvington, N.Y.: Columbia University Press.

Anderson, Patrick. 1989. "The Myth of Sustainable Logging: The Case for a Ban on Tropical Timber Imports." *The Ecologist*, vol. 19, no. 5, 166–168.

Barber, Chip. 1991. *Cutting Our Losses: Policy Reform to Sustain Tropical Forest Resources*. Washington, D.C.: World Resources Institute.

Caufield, Catherine. 1985. *In the Rainforest*. New York: Alfred A. Knopf.

Clay, Jason W. 1988. *Indigenous Peoples and Tropical Forests*. Cambridge, Mass.: Cultural Survival.

Colchester, Marcus. 1990. "The International Tropical Timber Organization: Kill or Cure for the Rainforests." *The Ecologist*, vol. 20, no. 5, 166–181.

Collins, Mark, ed. 1990. *The Last Rainforests: A World Conservation Atlas*. Emmaus, Pa.: Rodale Press.

Cowell, Adrian. 1990. *The Decade of Destruction: The Crusade to Save the Amazon Rain Forest*. New York: Henry Holt & Co.

Eckholm, Erik, et al. 1984. *Fuelwood: The Energy Crisis That Won't Go Away*. East Haven, Conn.: Earthscan.

Ervin, Keith. 1989. *Fragile Majesty: The Battle for North America's Last Great Forest*. Seattle: The Mountaineers.

Friends of the Trees. 1988. *Green Front Report*. Chelan, Wash.: Friends of the Trees.

Gomez-Pumpa, A. 1990. *Rain Forest Regeneration and Management*. New York: Parthenon.

Goodland, Robert, ed. 1990. *Race to Save the Tropics: Ecology and Economics for a Sustainable Future*. Covelo, Calif.: Island Press.

Gradwohl, Judith, and Russell Greenberg. 1988. *Saving the Tropical Forests*. Covelo, Calif.: Island Press.

Head, Suzanne, and Robert Heinzman. 1990. *Lessons of the Rainforest*. San Francisco: Sierra Club Books.

Hecht, Susanna, and Alexander Cockburn. 1989. *The Fate of the Forest: Developers, Destroyers, and Defenders of the Amazon*. New York: Verso (Routledge, Chapman and Hall).

Jacobs, Marius. 1988. *The Tropical Rain Forest: A First Encounter*. New York: Springer-Verlag.

Jolly, Alison, and Frans Lanting. 1990. *Madagascar: A World Out of Time*. New York: Aperture.

Kelly, David, and Gary Braasch. 1988. *Secrets of the Old Growth Forest*. Salt Lake City: Peregrine Smith.

Living Earth Foundation. 1990. *The Rainforests: A Celebration*. San Francisco: Chronicle Books.

Maser, Chris. 1988. *The Redesigned Forest*. San Pedro, Calif.: R. & E. Miles.

Maser, Chris. 1989. *Forest Primeval*. San Francisco: Sierra Club Books.

Miller, Kenton, and Laura Tangley. 1991. *Trees of Life: Protecting Tropical Forests and Their Biological Wealth*. Washington, D.C.: World Resources Institute.

Morgan, F., and J. R. Vincent. 1987. *Natural Management of Tropical Moist Forests: Silvicultural and Management Prospects of Sustained Utilization*. New Haven, Conn.: Yale School of Forestry.

Myers, Norman. 1984. *The Primary Source: Tropical Forests and Our Future*. New York: W. W. Norton.

Myers, Norman. 1989. *Deforestation Rates in Tropical Forests and Their Climatic Implications*. London: Friends of the Earth.

Newman, Arnold. 1990. *The Tropical Rainforest: A World Survey of Our Most Valuable Endangered Habitats*. New York: Facts on File.

Nichol, John. 1990. *The Mighty Rainforest*. London: David & Charles.

Norse, Elliot A. 1990. *Ancient Forests of the Pacific Northwest*. Covelo, Calif.: Island Press.

Patterson, Alan. 1990. "Debt-for-Nature Swaps and the Need for Alternatives." *Environment*, vol. 32, no. 10, 5–13, 31–32.

Postel, Sandra, and Lori Heise. 1988. *Reforesting the Earth*. Washington, D.C.: Worldwatch Institute.

Reid, Walter V. C., and Kenton R. Miller. 1989. *Keeping Options Alive: The Scientific Basis for Conserving Biodiversity*. Washington, D.C.: World Resources Institute.

Repetto, Robert. 1990. "Deforestation in the Tropics." *Scientific American*, vol. 262, no. 4, 36–42.

Revkin, Andrew. 1990. *The Burning Season: The Murder of Chico Mendes and the Fight for the Amazon*. Boston: Houghton Mifflin.

Rice, R. E. 1990. "Old-Growth Logging Myths." *The Ecologist*, vol. 20, no. 4, 141–146.

Roselle, Mike, and Tracy Katelman. 1989. *Tropical Hardwoods: A Report*. San Francisco: Rainforest Action Network.

Shoumatoff, Alex. 1990. *The World of Burning: The Tragedy of Chico Mendes*. Boston: Little, Brown.

Tree People. 1990. *The Simple Act of Planting a Tree*. Los Angeles, Calif.: Jeremy Tarcher.

Wilderness Society. 1988. *Ancient Forests: A Threatened Heritage*. Washington, D.C.:The Wilderness Society.

Wilderness Society. 1989. *Old Growth in the Pacific Northwest: A Status Report*. Washington, D.C.: Wilderness Society.

Wilson, E. O., ed. 1988. *Biodiversity*. Washington, D.C.: National Academy Press.

Wilson, Edward O. 1989. "Threats to Biodiversity." *Scientific American*, September, 108–116.

Winterbottom, Robert. 1990. *Taking Stock: The Tropical Forestry Action Plan Five Years Later*. Washington, D.C.: World Resources Institute.

World Resources Institute, World Bank, and United Nations Development Program. 1985. *Tropical Forests: A Call for Action*. Washington, D.C.: World Resources Institute.

Zuckerman, Seth. 1991. *Saving Our Ancient Forests*. Federalsburg, Md.: Living Planet Press.

Chapter 11 Climate Change, Ozone Depletion, and Nuclear War

Bates, Albert K. 1990. *Climate in Crisis: The Greenhouse Effect and What We Can Do*. Summertown, Tenn.: Book Publishing Co.

Blair, Bruce G., and Henry W. Kendall. 1990. "Accidental Nuclear War." *Scientific American*, vol. 263, no. 6, 53–58.

California Energy Commission. 1989. *The Impacts of Global Warming on California*. Sacramento, Calif.: California Energy Commission.

Cogan, Douglas G. 1988. *Stones in a Glass House: CFCs and Ozone Depletion*. Washington, D.C.: Investor Responsibility Research Center.

Crutzen, Paul J. 1985. "The Global Environment After Nuclear War." *Environment*, vol. 27, no. 8, 6–11, 34–37.

Department of Energy Multi-Laboratory Climate Change Committee. 1990. *Energy and Climate Change*. New York: Lewis Publishers.

Dotto, Lydia. 1986. *Planet Earth in Jeopardy: Environmental Consequences of Nuclear War*. New York: John Wiley.

Dotto, Lydia. 1990. *Thinking the Unthinkable: Civilization and Rapid Climate Change*. Waterloo, Ontario: Wilfrid Lanier University Press.

Dudek, Daniel J. 1988. *Offsetting New CO_2 Emissions*. New York: Environmental Defense Fund.

Edgerton, Lynne T. 1990. *The Rising Tide: Global Warming and World Sea Levels*. Covelo, Calif.: Island Press.

Ehrlich, Anne H., and John Birks, eds. 1991. *Hidden Dangers: Environmental Consequences of Preparing for War*. San Francisco: Sierra Club Books.

Environmental Defense Fund. 1988. *Protecting the Ozone Layer: What You Can Do*. New York: Environmental Defense Fund.

Environmental Protection Agency. 1988. *The Potential Effects of Global Climate Change on the United States*. Washington, D.C.: EPA.

Environmental Protection Agency. 1989. *Policy Options for Stabilizing Global Climate*. Washington, D.C.: EPA.

Erikson, Jon. 1990. *Greenhouse Earth: Tomorrow's Disaster Today*. New York: TAB Books.

Fisher, David E. 1990. *Fire and Ice: The Greenhouse Effect, Ozone Depletion, and Nuclear Winter*. New York: Harper & Row.

Fishman, Albert, and Robert Kalish. 1990. *Global Alert: The Ozone Pollution Crisis*. New York: Plenum.

Flavin, Christopher. 1989. *Slowing Global Warming: A Worldwide Strategy*. Washington, D.C.: Worldwatch Institute.

Graedel, Thomas E., and Paul J. Crutzen. 1989. "The Changing Atmosphere." *Scientific American*, September, 58–68.

Graham, Robert L., et al. 1990. "How Increasing CO_2 and Climate Change Affect Forests." *BioScience*, vol. 40, no. 8, 575–586.

Greenhouse Crisis Foundation. 1990. *The Greenhouse Crisis: 101 Ways to Save the Earth*. Washington, D.C.: Greenhouse Crisis Foundation.

Gribbin, John. 1990. *Hothouse Earth: The Greenhouse Effect and Gaia*. London: Grove Weidenfeld.

Hammond, Allen L., et al. 1991. "Calculating National Accountability for Climate Change." *Environment*, vol. 33, no. 1, 11–15, 33–34.

Houghton, J. T., et al., eds. 1990. *Climate Change: The IPCC Scientific Assessment*. New York: Cambridge University Press.

Houghton, Richard A., and George M. Woodwell. 1989. "Global Climatic Change." *Scientific American*, vol. 260, no. 4, 36–44.

Idso, Sherwood B. 1989. *Carbon Dioxide and Global Change: Earth in Transition*. Tempe, Ariz.: Institute for Biospheric Research.

Ince, Martin. 1990. *The Rising Seas*. East Haven, Conn.: Earthscan.

Jones, Philip D., and Tom M. L. Wiglet. 1990. "Global Warming Trends." *Scientific American*, August, 84–91.

Kimball, Norman J., et al. 1990. *Impact of Carbon Dioxide, Trace Gases, and Climate Change on Global Agriculture*. Madison, Wis.: Soil Science Society of America.

Kome, Penny, and Patrick Crean. 1986. *Peace: An Unfolding Dream*. San Francisco, Calif.: Sierra Club Books.

Lamb, H. H. 1982. *Climate, History, and the Modern World*. New York: Methuen.

Leggett, Jeremy, ed. 1990. *Global Warming: The Greenpeace Report*. New York: Oxford University Press.

Levenson, Thomas. 1990. *Ice Time: Climate, Science, and Life on Earth*. New York: Harper & Row.

Lovins, Amory B., et al. 1989. *Least-Cost Energy: Solving the CO_2 Problem*. 2nd ed. Andover, Mass.: Brick House.

Lyman, Francesca, et al. 1990. *The Greenhouse Trap: What We're Doing to the Atmosphere and How We Can Slow Global Warming*. Washington, D.C.: World Resources Institute.

MacKenzie, James J., and Michael P. Walsh. 1990. *Driving Forces: Motor Vehicle Trends and Their Implications for Global Warming, Energy Strategies, and Transportation Planning*. Washington, D.C.: World Resources Institute.

Makhijani, Arjon, et al. 1990. "Beyond the Montreal Protocol: Still Working on the Ozone Hole." *Technology Review*. May/June, 53–59.

Mathews, Jessica Tuchman, ed. 1991. *Greenhouse Warming: Negotiating a Global Regime*. Washington, D.C.: World Resources Institute.

McKibben, Bill. 1989. *The End of Nature*. New York: Random House.

Mintzer, Irving, and William R. Moomaw. 1990. *Escaping the Heat Trap: Probing the Prospects for a Stable Environment*. Washington, D.C.: World Resources Institute.

Mintzer, Irving, et al. 1990. *Protecting the Ozone Shield: Strategies for Phasing Out CFCs During the 1990s*. Washington, D.C.: World Resources Institute.

National Academy of Sciences. 1985. *The Effects on the Atmosphere of a Major Nuclear War*. Washington, D.C.: National Academy Press.

National Academy of Sciences. 1989. *Global Environmental Change*. Washington, D.C.: National Academy Press.

National Academy of Sciences. 1989. *Ozone Depletion, Greenhouse Gases, and Climate Change*. Washington, D.C.: National Academy Press.

National Academy of Sciences. 1990. *Confronting Climate Change*. Washington, D.C.: National Academy Press.

National Academy of Sciences. 1990. *Sea Level Change*. Washington, D.C.: National Academy Press.

National Academy of Sciences. 1991. *Policy Implications of Greenhouse Warming*. Washington, D.C.: National Academy Press.

National Audubon Society. 1990. *CO_2 Diet for a Greenhouse Planet: A Citizen's Guide to Slowing Global Warming*. New York: National Audubon Society.

Office of Technology Assessment. 1991. *Changing by Degrees: Steps to Reduce Greenhouse Gases*. Washington, D.C.: Government Printing Office.

Oppenheimer, Michael, and Robert H. Boyle. 1990. *Dead Heat: The Race Against the Greenhouse Effect*. New York: Basic Books.

Public Citizen. 1989. *Turning Down the Heat: Solutions to Global Warming*. Washington, D.C.: Public Citizen.

Ray, Dixie Lee, and Lou Guzzo. 1990. *Trashing the Planet: How Science Can Help Us Deal with Acid Rain, Depletion of the Ozone, and Nuclear War (Among Other Things)*. Washington, D.C.: Regnery Gateway.

Roan, Sharon L. 1989. *Ozone Crisis: The 15-Year Evolution of a Sudden Global Emergency*. New York: John Wiley.

Rowland, F. Sherwood. 1989. "Chlorofluorocarbons and the Depletion of Stratospheric Ozone." *American Scientist*, vol. 77, 36–45.

Schell, Jonathan. 1982. *The Fate of the Earth*. New York: Alfred A. Knopf.

Schneider, Stephen H. 1987. "Climate Modelling." *Scientific American*, vol. 256, no. 5, 72–80.

Schneider, Stephen H. 1989. *Global Warming: Are We Entering the Greenhouse Century?* New York: Random House.

Schneider, Stephen. H., and R. S. Londer. 1984. *The Coevolution of Climate and Life*. San Francisco: Sierra Club Books.

Shea, Cynthia Pollack. 1988. *Protecting Life on Earth: Steps to Save the Ozone Layer*. Washington, D.C.: Worldwatch Institute.

Thompson, Staley L., and Stephen H. Schneider. 1986. "Nuclear Winter Reappraised." *Foreign Affairs*, Summer.

Turco, R. P., et al. 1990. "Climate and Smoke: An Appraisal of Nuclear Winter." *Science*, vol. 247, 166–176.

Waggoner, Paul E., ed. 1990. *Climate Change and U.S. Water Resources*. New York: John Wiley.

Weiner, Jonathan. 1990. *The Next One Hundred Years: Shaping the Fate of Our Living Earth*. New York: Bantam Books.

Westing, Arthur, ed. 1991. *Environmental Hazards of War*. Newbury Park, Calif.: Sage Publications.

White, Robert M. 1990. "The Great Climate Debate." *Scientific American*, July, 36–43.

Young, Louise B. 1990. *Sowing the Wind: Reflections on Earth's Atmosphere*. Englewood Cliffs, N.J.: Prentice Hall.

Chapter 12 Soil Resources

Brady, Nyle C. 1989. *The Nature and Properties of Soils*. 10th ed. New York: Macmillan.

Brown, Lester R., and Edward C. Wolf. 1984. *Soil Erosion: Quiet Crisis in the World Economy*. Washington, D.C.: Worldwatch Institute.

Donahue, Roy, et al. 1990. *Soils and Their Management*. 5th ed. Petaluma, Calif.: Inter Print.

Dregnue, Harold. E. 1983. *Desertification of Arid Lands*. San Diego: Academic Press.

Dregnue, Harold E. 1985. "Aridity and Land Degradation." *Environment*, vol. 27, no. 8, 33–39.

Gorse, Jean E., and David R. Steeds. 1987. *Desertification in the Sahelian and Sudanian Zones of West Africa*. Washington, D.C.: World Bank.

Grainger, Alan. 1983. *Desertification: How People Make Deserts, How People Can Stop, and Why They Don't*. East Haven, Conn.: Earthscan.

Lal, Rattan. 1990. *Soil Erosion in the Tropics: Principles and Management*. New York: McGraw-Hill.

Little, Charles E. 1987. *Green Fields Forever: The Conservation Tillage Revolution in America*. Covelo, Calif.: Island Press.

Mollison, Bill. 1990. *Permaculture*. Covelo, Calif.: Island Press.

Myers, Norman, ed. 1984. *Gaia: An Atlas of Planet Management*. New York: Anchor/Doubleday.

National Academy of Sciences. 1986. *Soil Conservation*. 2 vols. Washington, D.C.: National Academy Press.

Paddock, Joe, et al. 1987. *Soil and Survival: Land Stewardship and the Future of American Agriculture*. San Francisco: Sierra Club Books.

Rodale Press. 1990. *Five Steps to Quick Composting*. Emmaus, Pa.: Rodale Press.

Sheridan, David. 1981. *Desertification of the United States*. Washington, D.C.: Resources for the Future.

Tompkins, Peter, and Christopher Bird. 1988. *Secrets of the Soil*. New York: Harper & Row.

Wilson, G. F., et al. 1986. *The Soul of the Soil: A Guide to Ecological Soil Management*. 2nd ed. Montreal, Quebec: Gaia Services.

Chapter 13 Water Resources

Ashworth, William. 1982. *Nor Any Drop to Drink*. New York: Summit Books.

Briscoe, John, and David de Ferrani. 1988. *Water for Rural Communities: Helping People Help Themselves*. Washington, D.C.: World Bank.

Cousteau, Jacques-Yves, et al. 1981. *The Cousteau Almanac: An Inventory of Life on Our Water Planet*. New York: Doubleday.

Echeverria, John D., et al. 1990. *Rivers at Risk: The Concerned Citizen's Guide to Hydropower*. Covelo, Calif.: Island Press.

El-Ashry, Mohamed, and Diana C. Gibbons, eds. 1988. *Water and the Arid Lands of the Western United States*. New York: Cambridge University Press.

Falkenmark, M. 1986. "Fresh Water—Time for a Modified Approach." *Ambio*, vol. 15, 192–200.

Franco, David A., and Robert G. Wetel. 1983. *To Quench Our Thirst: The Present and Future Status of Freshwater Resources of the United States*. Ann Arbor: University of Michigan Press.

Goldsmith, Edward, and Nicholas Hidyard, eds. 1986. *The Social and Environmental Effects of Large Dams*. 3 vols. New York: John Wiley.

Golubev, G. N., and A. K. Biswas. 1985. *Large Scale Water Transfers: Emerging Environmental and Social Experiences*. Oxford, England: Tycooly.

Gottlieb, Robert. 1989. *A Life of Its Own: The Politics and Power of Water*. New York: Harcourt Brace Jovanovich.

Ingram, Helen. 1990. *Water Politics: Continuity and Change*. Albuquerque: University of New Mexico Press.

Ives, J. D., and B. Messeric. 1989. *The Himalayan Dilemma: Reconciling Development and Conservation*. London: Routledge.

Kotlyakov, V. M. 1991. "The Aral Sea Basin: A Critical Environmental Zone." *Environment*, vol. 33, no. 1, 4–9, 36–39.

Kourik, Robert. 1988. *Gray Water Use in the Landscape*. Santa Rosa, Calif.: Edible Publications.

Mather, J. R. 1984. *Water Resources Distribution, Use, and Management*. New York: John Wiley.

Meybeck, Michael, et al., eds. 1990. *Global Freshwater Quality*. Cambridge, Mass.: Basil Blackwell.

Myers, Norman, ed. 1984. *Gaia: An Atlas of Planet Management*. New York: Anchor/Doubleday.

Okun, Daniel L. 1975. "Water Management in England: A Regional Model." *Environmental Science and Technology*, vol. 9, no. 10, 918–923.

Pimentel, David, et al. 1982. "Water Resources in Food and Energy Production." *BioScience*, vol. 32, no. 11, 861–867.

Postel, Sandra. 1985. *Conserving Water: The Untapped Alternative*. Washington, D.C.: Worldwatch Institute.

Postel, Sandra. 1989. *Water for Agriculture: Facing the Limits*. Washington, D.C.: Worldwatch Institute.

Pringle, Laurence. 1982. *Water—The Next Great Resource Battle*. New York: Macmillan.

Reisner, Marc. 1986. *Cadillac Desert: The American West and Its Disappearing Water*. New York: Viking Press.

Reisner, Marc, and Sara Bates. 1990. *Overtapped Oasis: Reform or Revolution for Western Water*. Covelo, Calif.: Island Press.

Rocky Mountain Institute. 1990. *Catalog of Water-Efficient Technologies for the Urban/Residential Sector*. Old Snowmass, Colo.: Rocky Mountain Institute.

Sloggett, Gordon, and Clifford Dickason. 1986. *Groundwater Mining in the United States*. Washington, D.C.: Government Printing Office.

Waggoner, Paul E., ed. 1990. *Climate Change and U.S. Water Resources*. New York: John Wiley.

Waller, Roger M. 1988. *Ground Water and the Rural Homeowner*. Denver: U. S. Geological Survey.

Watson, Lyall. 1988. *The Water Planet*. New York: Crown.

Wijkman, Anders, and Lloyd Timberlake. 1984. *Natural Disasters: Acts of God or Acts of Man?* East Haven, Conn.: Earthscan.

Worster, Donald. 1985. *Rivers of Empire: Water, Aridity, and the Growth of the American West*. New York: Pantheon.

Chapter 14 Food Resources

Aliteri, Miguel A., and Susanna B. Hecht. 1990. *Agroecology and Small Farm Development*. New York: CRC Press.

Amato, Paul R., and Sonia A. Partridge. 1989. *The New Vegetarians: Promoting Health and Protecting Life*. New York: Plenum.

Bardach, John. 1988. "Aquaculture: Moving from Craft to Industry." *Environment*, vol. 30, no. 2, 7–40.

Bartholomew, Mel. 1987. *Square Foot Gardening*. Emmaus, Pa.: Rodale Press.

Bennett, Jon. 1987. *The Hunger Machine: The Politics of Food*. Cambridge, Mass.: Basil Blackwell.

Berry, Wendell. 1990. *Nature as Measure*. Berkeley, Calif.: North Point Press.

Berstein, Henry, et al., eds. 1990. *The Food Question: Profits Versus People*. East Haven, Conn.: Earthscan.

Bezdicek, D. F., ed. 1984. *Organic Farming: Current Technology and Its Role in a Sustainable Agriculture*. Washington, D.C.: American Society of Agronomy.

Brown, Larry. 1987. "Hunger in America." *Scientific American*, vol. 256, no. 2, 37–41.

Brown, Lester R. 1988. *The Changing World Food Prospect: The Nineties and Beyond*. Washington, D.C.: Worldwatch Institute.

Brown, Lester R. 1988. "The Vulnerability of Oil-Based Farming." *World Watch*, March/April, 24–29.

Brown, Lester R., and John E. Young. 1990. "Feeding the World in the Nineties." In *State of the World 1990*, Lester R. Brown et al., 59–78. Washington, D.C.: Worldwatch Institute.

Carroll, C. Ronald, et al. 1990. *Agroecology*. New York: McGraw-Hill.

Clawson, David L. 1985. "Small-Scale Polyculture: An Alternative Development Model." *Philippines Geographical Journal*, vol. 29, nos. 3, 4, 1–12.

Coleman, Elliot. 1989. *The New Organic Grower*. Post Mills, Vt.: Chelsea Green.

Crosson, Pierre R., and Norman J. Rosenberg. 1989. "Strategies for Agriculture." *Scientific American*, September, 128–135.

Dover, Michael J., and Lee M. Talbot. 1988. "Feeding the Earth: An Agroecological Solution." *Technology Review*, February/March, 27–35.

Doyle, Jack. 1985. *Altered Harvest: Agriculture, Genetics, and the Fate of the World's Food Supply*. New York: Viking Press.

Dunning, Alan B., and Holly W. Brough. 1991. *Taking Stock: Animal Farming and the Environment*. Washington, D.C.: Worldwatch Society.

The Ecologist, vol. 21, no. 2. 1991. Entire issue devoted to world hunger.

Editorial Research Reports. 1988. *How the U.S. Got into Agriculture and Why It Can't Get Out*. Washington, D.C.: Congressional Quarterly.

Editors of *Organic Gardening and Farming Magazine*. 1987. *The Encyclopedia of Organic Gardening*. Emmaus, Pa.: Rodale Press.

Edwards, Clive A., et al., eds. 1990. *Sustainable Agricultural Systems*. Ankeny, Iowa: Soil and Water Conservation Society.

Fowler, Cary, and Pat Mooney. 1990. *Shattering: Food, Politics, and the Loss of Genetic Diversity*. Tucson: University of Arizona Press.

Francis, Charles A., and Richard Hardwood. 1985. *Enough Food: Achieving Food Security Through Regenerative Agriculture*. Emmaus, Pa.: Rodale Press.

Francis, Charles A., et al., eds. 1990. *Sustainable Agriculture in Temperate Zones*. New York: John Wiley.

Fukuoka, Masanobu. 1985. *The Natural Way of Farming: The Theory and Practice of Green Philosophy*. Japan Publications.

Gabel, Medard. 1986. *Empty Breadbasket: The Coming Challenge to America's Food Supply and What We Can Do About It*. Emmaus, Pa.: Rodale Press.

Gips, Terry. 1987. *Breaking the Pesticide Habit*. Minneapolis: IASA.

Gordon, R. Conway, and Edward R. Barbier. 1990. *After the Green Revolution: Sustainable Agriculture for Development*. East Haven, Conn.: Earthscan.

Granatstein, David. 1988. *Reshaping the Bottom Line: On-Farm Strategies for a Sustainable Agriculture*. Stillwater, Minn.: Land Stewardship Project.

Grant, James P. 1991. *The State of the World's Children 1991*. New York: Oxford University Press.

Hamilton, Geoff. 1987. *The Complete Guide to Growing Flowers, Fruits, and Vegetables Naturally*. New York: Crown.

Harrison, Paul. 1987. *The Greening of Africa*. New York: Viking/Penguin.

Hellinger, Stephen, et al. 1988. *Aid for Just Development*. Boulder, Colo.: Lynne Rienner.

Hendry, Peter. 1988. "Food and Population: Beyond Five Billion." *Population Bulletin*, April, 1–55.

Huessy, Peter. 1978. *The Food First Debate*. San Francisco: Institute for Food and Development Policy.

Hunger Project. 1985. *Ending Hunger: An Idea Whose Time Has Come*. New York: Praeger.

International Rice Institute. 1988. *Science, Ethics, and Food*. Manila, Philippines: International Rice Institute.

Jackson, Wes. 1980. *New Roots for Agriculture*. San Francisco: Friends of the Earth.

Jackson, Wes. 1986. *The Unsettling of America*. San Francisco: Sierra Club Books.

Jackson, Wes. 1987. *Altars of Unhewn Stone: Science and the Earth*. Berkeley, Calif: North Point Press.

Jackson, Wes, et al., eds. 1985. *Meeting the Expectations of Land: Essays in Sustainable Agriculture and Stewardship*. Berkeley, Calif.: North Point Press.

Jacobson, Michael, et al. 1991. *Safe Food: Eating Wisely in a Risky World*. Washington, D.C.: Living Planet Press.

Jeavons, John. 1982. *How to Grow More Vegetables*. Berkeley, Calif.: Ten Speed Press.

Jones, Byron. 1988. *The Farming Game*. Lincoln: University of Nebraska Press.

Juma, Calestous. 1989. *The Gene Hunters: Biotechnology and the Scramble for Seeds*. Princeton, N.J.: Princeton University Press.

Klopenburg, Jack R., ed. 1988. *Seeds and Sovereignty*. Durham, N.C.: Duke University Press.

Kourik, Robert. 1986. *Designing and Maintaining Your Edible Landscape*. Santa Rosa, Calif.: Edible Landscape.

Lal, Rattan. 1987. "Managing the Soils of Sub-Saharan Africa." *Science*, vol. 236, 1069–1076.

Lambert, T. A. 1980. "Energy, Entropy, and Agriculture." *Cornell Journal of Social Relations*, vol. 15, no. 1, 84–97.

Lappé, Francis M., and Joseph Collins. 1977. *Food First*. Boston: Houghton Mifflin.

Lappé, Francis M., et al. 1988. *Betraying the National Interest*. San Francisco: Food First.

League of Women Voters, 1991. *U.S. Farm Policy: Who Benefits? Who Pays? Who Decides?* Washington, D.C.: League of Women Voters.

LeMay, Brian, ed. 1988. *Science, Ethics, and Food*. Washington, D.C.: Smithsonian Institution Press.

Lockeretz, William G., ed. 1987. *Sustaining Agriculture Near Cities*. Ankeny, Iowa: Soil and Water Conservation Society.

Lowrance, Richard, ed. 1984. *Agricultural Ecosystems: Unifying Concepts*. New York: John Wiley.

McKinney, Tom. 1987. *The Sustainable Farm of the Future*. Old Snowmass, Colo.: Rocky Mountain Institute.

Mollison, Bill. 1990. *Permaculture: A Practical Guide for a Sustainable Future*. Covelo, Calif.: Island Press.

Molnar, Joseph J., and Henry Kinnucan. ed. 1989. *Biotechnology and the New Agricultural Revolution*. Boulder, Colo.: Westview Press.

Morrimore, Michael. 1989. *Adapting to Drought: Farmers, Famines, and Desertification in West Africa*. New York: Cambridge University Press.

National Academy of Sciences. 1989. *Alternative Agriculture*. Washington, D.C.: National Academy Press.

National Academy of Sciences. 1989. *Triticale: A Promising Addition to the World's Cereal Grains*. Washington, D.C.: National Academy Press.

National Academy of Sciences. 1990. *Saline Agriculture: Salt-Tolerant Plants for Developing Countries*. Washington, D.C.: National Academy Press.

Office of Technology Assessment. 1988. *Enhancing Agriculture in Africa*. Washington, D.C.: Office of Technology Assessment.

Phipps, Tim T., Pierre R. Crosson, and Kent A. Price, eds. 1986. *Agriculture and the Environment*. Washington, D.C.: Resources for the Future.

Pierce, John T. 1990. *Food Resources*. New York: John Wiley.

Pimentel, David, and Carl W. Hall. 1989. *Food and Natural Resources*. San Diego: Academic Press.

Pimentel, David, et al. 1989. "Benefits and Risks of Genetic Engineering and Agriculture." *BioScience*, vol. 39, no. 9, 606–614.

Poincelot, Raymond P. 1986. *Toward a Sustainable Agriculture*. Westport, Conn.: AVI Publishing.

Reaganold, John P., et al. 1990. "Sustainable Agriculture." *Scientific American*, June, 112–120.

Ritchie, Mark. 1990. "GATT, Agriculture, and the Environment." *The Ecologist*, vol. 20, no. 6, 214–220.

Robbins, John. 1987. *Diet for a New America*. Waldpole, N.H.: Stillpoint Publishing.

Sanchez, Pedro A., and Jose R. Benites. 1987. "Low-Input Cropping for Acid Soils of the Humid Tropics." *Science*, vol. 238, 1521–1527.

Schell, Orville. 1984. *Modern Meat: Antibiotics, Hormones, and the Pharmaceutical Farm*. New York: Random House.

Schriefer, Donald L. 1984. *From the Soil Up*. Des Moines: Wallace-Homestead Printing Co.

Soil and Water Conservation Society. 1990. *Sustainable Agricultural Systems*. Ankeny, Iowa: Soil and Water Conservation Society.

Steinman, David. 1990. *Diet for a Poisoned Planet: How to Choose Safe Foods for You and Your Family*. New York: Harmony Books.

Todd, Nancy J., and John Todd. 1984. *Bioshelters, Ocean Arks, City Farming: Ecology as a Basis for Design*. San Francisco: Sierra Club Books.

Tudge, Colin. 1988. *Food Crops for the Future: Development of Plant Resources*. Oxford, UK: Blackwell.

United Nations World Food Commission. 1989. *The Global State of Hunger and Malnutrition*. New York: United Nations.

U.S. Department of Agriculture. Annual. *Fact Book of Agriculture*.

Vietmeyer, Noel D. 1986. "Lesser-Known Plants of Potential Use in Agriculture." *Science*, vol. 232, 1379–1384.

Whelan, Elizabeth M., and Frederick J. Stare. 1983. *The 100% Natural, Purely Organic, Cholesterol-Free, Megavitamin, Low-Carbohydrate Nutrition Hoax*. New York: Atheneum.

Widdowson, R. W. 1987. *Toward Holistic Agriculture*. New York: Pergamon Press.

Witter, Sylvan, et al. 1987. *Feeding a Billion: Frontiers of Chinese Agriculture*. East Lansing: Michigan State University Press.

Wojcik, Jan. 1989. *The Arguments of Agriculture: A Casebook in Contemporary Agricultural Controversy*. West Lafayette, Ind.: Purdue University Press.

Wolf, Edward C. 1986. *Beyond the Green Revolution: New Approaches for Third World Agriculture*. Washington, D.C.: Worldwatch Institute.

Yang, Linda. 1990. *The City Gardener's Handbook: From Balcony to Backyard*. New York: Random House.

Chapter 15 Land Resources: Forests, Rangelands, Parks, and Wilderness

See also the readings for Chapter 2.

Allin, Craig W. 1982. *The Politics of Wilderness Preservation*. Westport, Conn.: Greenwood Press.

Beattie, Mollie, et al. 1983. *Working with Your Woodland*. Hanover, N. H.: University Press of New England.

Cairns, John, Jr., and Todd V. Crawford. 1990. *Integrated Environmental Management*. New York: Lewis Publishers.

Camp, Orville. 1984. *The Forest Farmer's Handbook: A Guide to Natural Selection Forest Management*. Berkeley, Calif.: Sky River Press.

Chase, Alston. 1986. *Playing God in Yellowstone: The Destruction of America's First National Park*. New York: Atlantic Monthly Press.

Clary, David. 1986. *Timber and the Forest Service*. Lawrence: University of Kansas Press.

Collard, Andree, and Joyce Contrucci. 1989. *Rape of the Wild: Man's Violence Against Animals and the Earth*. Bloomington: Indiana University Press.

Conservation Foundation. 1989. *State Parks in a New Era*. 3 vols. Washington, D.C.: Conservation Foundation.

Deacon, Robert T., and M. Bruce Johnson, eds. 1986. *Forestlands: Public and Private*. San Francisco: Pacific Institute for Public Policy.

Defenders of Wildlife. 1982. *1080: The Case Against Poisoning Our Wildlife*. Washington, D.C.: Government Printing Office.

Dysart, Benjamin, III, and Marion Clawson. 1988. *Managing Public Lands in the Public Interest*. New York: Praeger.

Eckholm, Erik. 1982. *Down to Earth: Environment and Human Needs*. New York: W. W. Norton.

Foreman, Dave, and Howie Wolke. 1989. *The Big Outside*. Tucson: Nedd Ludd Books.

Friends of the Trees. 1989. *1988 International Green Front Report*. Whelan, Wash.: Friends of the Trees.

Fritz, Edward. 1983. *Sterile Forest: The Case Against Clearcutting*. Austin, Tex.: Eakin Press.

Frome, Michael. 1974. *The Battle for the Wilderness*. New York: Praeger.

Frome, Michael. 1983. *The Forest Service*. Boulder, Colo.: Westview Press.

Gamlin, L. 1989. "Sweden's Factory Forests." *New Scientist*, 26 January, 41–44.

Greenpeace. 1990. *The Greenpeace Guide to Paper*. Washington, D.C.: Greenpeace USA.

Harris, L. D. 1984. *The Fragmented Forest*. Chicago: University of Chicago Press.

Hartzog, George B., Jr. 1988. *Battling for the National Parks*. New York: Moyer Bell.

Hendee, John, et al., eds. 1991. *Principles of Wilderness Management*. 2nd ed. Golden, Colo.: Fulerum.

Hunter, Malcolm L., Jr. 1990. *Wildlife, Forests, and Forestry: Managing Forests for Biological Diversity*. New York: Prentice Hall.

Krippendorf, J. 1987. *The Holiday Makers*. London: Heinmann.

Land Trust Alliance. 1990. *Starting a Land Trust: A Guide to Forming a Land Conservation Organization*. Washington, D.C.: Land Trust Alliance.

Ledec, George, and Robert Goodland. 1988. *Wildlands: Their Protection and Management in Economic Development*. Washington, D.C.: World Bank.

Leopold, Aldo. 1949. *A Sand County Almanac*. New York: Oxford University Press.

Libecap, Gary D. 1986. *Locking Up the Range: Federal Land Control and Grazing*. San Francisco: Pacific Institute for Public Policy Research.

Lopez, Barry. 1989. *Crossing Open Ground*. New York: Vintage (Random House).

McNeely, Jeffery A., and Kenton R. Miller, eds. 1984. *National Parks, Conservation, and Development*. Washington, D.C.: Smithsonian Institution Press.

Mello, Robert A. 1987. *Last Stand of the Red Spruce*. Covelo, Calif.: Island Press.

Minckler, Leon S. 1980. *Woodland Ecology*. 2nd ed. Syracuse, N.Y.: Syracuse University Press.

Moll, Gary, and Sara Ebenreck. 1989. *Shading Our Cities: A Resource Guide for Urban and Community Forests*. Covelo, Calif.: Island Press.

Nash, Roderick. 1982. *Wilderness and the American Mind*. 3rd ed. New Haven, Conn.: Yale University Press.

National Parks and Conservation Association. 1988. *Blueprint for National Parks*. 9 vols. Washington, D.C.: National Parks and Conservation Association.

National Wildlife Federation and Natural Resources Defense Council. 1989. *Our Ailing Public Rangelands: Condition Report — 1989*. Washington, D.C.: Natural Resources Defense Council.

Oelschlager, Max. 1991. *The Idea of Wilderness from Prehistory to the Age of Ecology*. New Haven, Conn.: Yale University Press.

O'Toole, Randal. 1987. *Reforming the Forest Service*. Covelo, Calif.: Island Press.

Perlin, John. 1989. *A Forest Journey: The Role of Wood in the Development of Civilization*. New York: W. W. Norton.

Postel, Sandra. 1984. *Air Pollution, Acid Rain, and the Future of Forests*. Washington, D.C.: Worldwatch Institute.

Ramadé, Francois. 1984. *Ecology of Natural Resources*. New York: John Wiley.

Repetto, Robert, and Malcolm Gillis, eds. 1988. *Public Policy and the Misuse of Forest Resources*. New York: Cambridge University Press.

Robinson, Gordon. 1987. *The Forest and the Trees: A Guide to Excellent Forestry*. Covelo, Calif.: Island Press.

Romme, William H., and Don G. Despain. 1989. "The Yellowstone Fires." *Scientific American*, vol. 261, no. 5, 37–46.

Runte, Alfred. 1987. *National Parks: The American Experience*. 2nd ed. Lincoln: University of Nebraska Press.

Sampson, Neil, and Dwight Hair, eds. 1989. *Natural Resources for the 21st Century*. Covelo, Calif.: Island Press.

Sierra Club. 1982. *Our Public Lands: An Introduction to the Agencies and Issues*. San Francisco: Sierra Club Books.

Simon, David J., ed. 1988. *Our Common Lands: Defending the National Parks*. Covelo, Calif.: Island Press.

Smith, D. M. 1982. *The Practice of Silviculture*. New York: John Wiley.

Society of American Foresters. 1981. *Choices in Silviculture for American Forests*. Washington, D.C.: Society of American Foresters.

Spurr, Stephen H., and Buron V. Barnes. 1980. *Forest Ecology*. 3rd ed. New York: Ronald Press.

Stoddard, Charles H., and Glenn M. Stoddard. 1987. *Essentials of Forestry Practice*. 4th ed. New York: John Wiley.

Valentine, John E., ed. 1990. *Grazing Management*. San Diego: Academic Press.

Waring, R. H., and W. R. Schlesinger. 1985. *Forest Ecosystems: Concepts and Management*. San Diego: Academic Press.

Weber, Thomas. 1990. *Hugging the Trees: The Story of the Chipko Movement*. New York: Penguin.

Westoby, Jack. 1989. *Introduction to World Forestry*. Cambridge, Mass.: Basil Blackwell.

Wilcove, David S. 1988. *National Forests: Policies for the Future*, vols. 1, 2. Washington, D.C.: Wilderness Society.

Wright, Henry A., and Arthur W. Bailey. 1983. *Fire Ecology*. New York: John Wiley.

Wuerthner, George. 1989. *Yellowstone and the Fires of Change*. Salt Lake City: Dream Garden Press.

Chapter 16 Wild Plant and Animal Resources

Abbey, Edward. 1988. *One Life at a Time Please*. New York: Henry Holt & Co.

Bailey, J. A. 1984. *Principles of Wildlife Management*. New York: John Wiley.

Baker, Ron. 1985. *The American Hunting Myth*. New York: Vantage Press.

Bonner, Nigel. 1989. *Whales of the World*. New York: Facts on File.

Boo, Elizabeth. 1990. *Ecotourism: The Potential and the Pitfalls*, vols. 1, 2. Washington, D.C.: World Wildlife Fund.

Causey, Ann S. 1989. "On the Morality of Hunting." *Environmental Ethics*, Winter, 327–343.

Cohn, Jeffery P. 1990. "Elephants: Remarkable and Endangered." *BioScience*, vol. 40, no. 1, 10–14.

Credlund, Arthur G. 1983. *Whales and Whaling*. New York: Seven Hills Books.

Dasmann, Raymond F. 1981. *Wildlife Biology*. 2nd ed. New York: John Wiley.

Decker, Daniel J., and Gary R. Goff, eds. 1987. *Valuing Wildlife: Economic and Social Perspectives*. Boulder, Colo.: Westview Press.

DiSilvestro, Roger L. 1989. *The Endangered Kingdom: The Struggle to Save America's Wildlife*. New York: John Wiley.

DiSilvestro, Roger L. 1990. *Fight for Survival*. New York: John Wiley.

Dixon, John A., and Paul B. Sherman. 1990. *Economics of Protected Areas*. Covelo, Calif.: Island Press.

Dunlap, Thomas R. 1988. *Saving America's Wildlife*. Princeton, N.J.: Princeton University Press.

Durrell, Lee. 1986. *State of the Ark: An Atlas of Conservation in Action*. New York: Doubleday.

Ehrlich, Paul, and Anne Ehrlich. 1981. *Extinction*. New York: Random House.

Elliot, David K. 1986. *Dynamics of Extinction*. New York: John Wiley.

Elton, Charles S. 1958. *The Ecology of Invasions by Plants and Animals*. London: Methuen.

Evernden, N. 1985. *The Natural Alien*. Toronto: University of Toronto Press.

Gaskin, D. E. 1982. *The Ecology of Whales and Dolphins*. London: Heinemann.

Gilbert, Frederick F., and Donald G. Dodds. 1987. *The Philosophy and Practice of Wildlife Management*. Malabar, Fla.: Robert E. Krieger.

Graf, William L. 1990. *Wilderness Preservation and the Sagebrush Rebellion*. Savage, Md.: Rowman & Littlefield.

Harrison, R., and M. M. Bryden, eds. 1988. *Whales, Dolphins, and Porpoises*. New York: Facts on File.

Huxley, Anthony. 1984. *Green Inheritance*. New York: Anchor/Doubleday.

International Union for Conservation of Nature and Natural Resources. 1980. *World Conservation Strategy*. New York: Unipub.

International Union for Conservation of Nature and Natural Resources. 1985. *Implementing the World Conservation Strategy*. Gland, Switzerland: IUCN.

Kohm, Kathryn A., ed. 1990. *Balancing on the Brink of Extinction: The Endangered Species Act and Lessons for the Future*. Covelo, Calif.: Island Press.

Koopowitz, Harold, and Hilary Kaye. 1983. *Plant Extinctions: A Global Crisis*. Washington, D.C.: Stone Wall Press.

Leopold, Aldo. 1933. *Game Management*. New York: Charles Scribner's.

Livingston, John A. 1981. *The Fallacy of Wildlife Conservation*. Toronto: McClelland and Stewart.

Luoma, Jon. 1987. *A Crowded Ark: The Role of Zoos in Wildlife Conservation*. Boston: Houghton Mifflin.

McNeely, Jeffery A., et al. 1989. *Conserving the World's Biological Resources: A Primer on Principles and Practice for Development Action*. Washington, D.C.: World Resources Institute.

Miller, Debbie. 1989. *Midnight Wilderness: Journeys in Alaska's Arctic National Wildlife Refuge*. San Francisco: Sierra Club Books.

Myers, Norman. 1983. *A Wealth of Wild Species: Storehouse for Human Welfare*. Boulder, Colo.: Westview Press.

Myers, Norman. 1987. "The Impending Extinction Spasm: Synergisms at Work." *Conservation Biology*, vol. 14, 15–22.

Nash, Roderick F. 1988. *The Rights of Nature: A History of Environmental Ethics*. Madison: University of Wisconsin Press.

National Academy of Sciences. 1988. *Use of Laboratory Animals in Biomedical Research*. Washington, D.C.: National Academy Press.

National Audubon Society. Published every two years. *Audubon Wildlife Report*. New York: National Audubon Society.

National Wildlife Federation. 1987. *The Arctic National Wildlife Refuge Coastal Plain: A Perspective for the Future*. Washington, D.C.: National Wildlife Federation.

Norton, B. G., ed. 1986. *Why Preserve Natural Variety?* Princeton, N.J.: Princeton University Press.

Office of Technology Assessment. 1986. *Alternatives to Animal Use in Research, Teaching, and Education*. Washington, D.C.: Government Printing Office.

Office of Technology Assessment. 1987. *Technologies to Maintain Biological Diversity*. Washington, D.C.: Government Printing Office.

Office of Technology Assessment. 1989. *Oil Production in the Arctic National Wildlife Refuge*. Washington, D.C.: Government Printing Office.

Oldfield, Margery. 1984. *The Value of Conserving Genetic Resources*. Washington, D.C.: National Park Service.

Orians, Gordon H. 1990. "Ecological Concepts of Sustainability." *Environment*, November, 10–39.

Passmore, John. 1974. *Man's Responsibility for Nature*. New York: Charles Scribner's.

Prescott-Allen, Robert, and Christine Prescott-Allen. 1982. *What's Wildlife Worth?* East Haven, Conn.: Earthscan.

Pringle, Laurence. 1989. *The Animal Rights Controversy*. New York: Harcourt Brace Jovanovich.

Reagan, Tom. 1983. *The Case for Animal Rights*. Berkeley and Los Angeles: University of California Press.

Reid, Walter V. C., and Kenton R. Miller. 1989. *Keeping Options Alive: The Scientific Basis for Conserving Biodiversity*. Washington, D.C.: World Resources Institute.

Reisner, Marc. 1991. *Game Wars*. New York: Viking.

Rolston, Holmes, III. 1988. *Environmental Ethics: Duties to and Values in the Natural World*. Philadelphia: Temple University Press.

Runte, Alfred. 1989. *The Embattled Wilderness*. Lincoln: University of Nebraska Press.

Schweitzer, Albert. 1949. *Out of My Life and Thought: An Autobiography*. New York: Holt, Rinehart & Winston.

Shaw, J. H. 1985. *Introduction to Wildlife Management*. New York: McGraw-Hill.

Singer, Peter. 1975. *Animal Liberation: A New Ethics for Our Treatment of Animals*. New York: New York Review of Books.

Soulé, Michael E., ed. 1987. *Viable Populations for Conservation*. New York: Cambridge University Press.

Soulé, Michael E., and Bruce Wilcox, eds. 1980. *Conservation Biology*. Sunderland, Mass.: Sinauer.

Sperling, Susan. 1988. *Animal Liberators: Research and Morality*. Berkeley and Los Angeles: University of California Press.

Terborgh, John. 1989. *Where Have All the Birds Gone?* Princeton, N.J.: Princeton University Press.

Tobin, Richard J. 1990. *The Expendable Future: U.S. Politics and the Protection of Biodiversity*. Durham, N.C.: Duke University Press.

Tudge, Colin. 1988. *The Environment of Life*. New York: Oxford University Press.

Tuttle, Merlin D. 1988. *America's Neighborhood Bats: Understanding and Learning to Live in Harmony with Them*. Austin: University of Texas Press.

Vitali, Theodore. 1990. "Sport Hunting: Moral or Immoral?" *Environmental Ethics*, Spring, 69–81.

Wallace, David Rains. 1987. *Life in the Balance*. New York: Harcourt Brace Jovanovich.

Watkins, T. H. 1988. *Vanishing Arctic: Alaska's National Wildlife Refuge*. New York: Aperture.

Western, David, and Mary C. Pearly. 1989. *Conservation in the Twenty-First Century*. New York: Oxford University Press.

Wilson, E. O. 1984. *Biophilia*. Cambridge, Mass.: Harvard University Press.

Wilson, E. O., ed. 1988. *Biodiversity*. Washington, D.C.: National Academy Press.

Wolf, Edward C. 1987. *On the Brink of Extinction: Conserving the Diversity of Life.* Washington, D.C.: Worldwatch Institute.

World Wildlife Fund. 1990. *The Official World Wildlife Fund Guide to Endangered Species of North America.* Washington, D.C.: Beacham.

Yalden, D. W., and P. A. Morris. 1975. *The Lives of Bats.* New York: Quadrangle/New York Times.

Chapter 17 Perpetual and Renewable Energy Resources

See also the readings for Chapter 3.

American Council for an Energy Efficient Economy. 1988. *Energy Efficiency: A New Agenda.* Washington, D.C.: American Council for an Energy Efficient Economy.

American Institute of Physics. 1985. *Energy Efficiency and Renewable Resources.* New York: American Institute of Physics.

American Solar Energy Society. 1990. *Assessment of Solar Energy Technologies.* Boulder, Colo.: American Solar Energy Society.

Anderson, Bruce. 1990. *Solar Building Architecture.* Cambridge, Mass.: MIT Press.

Blackburn, John O. 1987. *The Renewable Energy Alternative: How the United States and the World Can Prosper Without Nuclear Energy or Coal.* Durham, N.C.: Duke University Press.

Bleviss, Deborah Lynn. 1988. *The New Oil Crisis and Fuel Economy Technologies.* Westport, Conn.: Quorum.

Bockris, J. O. 1980. *Energy Options: Real Economics and the Solar-Hydrogen System.* London: Taylor & Francis.

Brower, Michael. 1990. *Cool Energy: The Renewable Solution to Global Warming.* Cambridge, Mass.: Union of Concerned Scientists.

Butti, Ken, and John Perlin. 1980. *A Golden Thread—2500 Years of Solar Architecture.* Palo Alto, Calif.: Cheshire Press.

Davidson, Joel. 1987. *The New Solar Electric Home.* Ann Arbor, Mich.: Aatec Publications.

Dinga, Gustav P. 1988. "Hydrogen: The Ultimate Fuel and Energy Carrier." *Journal of Chemical Education,* vol. 65, no. 8, 688–691.

Dostrovsky, I. 1989. *Energy and the Missing Resource.* New York: Cambridge University Press.

Echeverria, John, et al. 1989. *Rivers at Risk: The Concerned Citizen's Guide to Hydropower.* Covelo, Calif.: Island Press.

Energy Conservation Coalition. 1990. *Building a Brighter Future.* Washington, D.C.: Energy Conservation Coalition.

Flavin, Christopher, and Alan B. Durning. 1988. *Building on Success: The Age of Energy Efficiency.* Washington, D.C.: Worldwatch Institute.

Flavin, Christopher, and Nicholas Lenssen. 1990. *Beyond the Petroleum Age: Designing a Solar Economy.* Washington, D.C.: Worldwatch Institute.

Flavin, Christopher, and Rock Piltz. 1990. *Sustainable Energy.* Washington, D.C.: Renew America.

Gever, John, et al. 1986. *Beyond Oil.* Cambridge, Mass.: Ballinger.

Goldenberg, Jose, et al. 1988. *Energy for a Sustainable World.* New York: John Wiley.

Heede, H. Richard, et al. 1985. *The Hidden Costs of Energy.* Washington, D.C.: Center for Renewable Resources.

Helm, John L., ed. 1990. *Energy: Production, Consumption, and Consequences.* Washington, D.C.: National Academy Press.

Hinkel, Kenneth M. 1990. "Wood Burning for Residential Space Heating in the United States: An Energy Efficiency Analysis." *Applied Geography,* vol. 9, 259–272.

Hohmeyer, O. 1988. *Social Costs of Energy Consumption.* New York: Springer-Verlag.

Krupnick, Alan. 1990. *The Environmental Costs of Energy: A Framework for Estimation.* Washington, D.C.: Resources for the Future.

Lovins, Amory B. 1989. *Energy, People, and Industrialization.* Old Snowmass, Colo.: Rocky Mountain Institute.

Lovins, Amory B. 1990. *The Negawatt Revolution.* Old Snowmass, Colo.: Rocky Mountain Institute.

Mackenzie, James L., and Michael P. Walsh. 1990. *Driving Forces: Motor Vehicle Trends and Their Implications for Global Warming, Energy Strategies, and Transportation Planning.* Washington, D.C.: World Resources Institute.

McKeown, Walter. 1991. *Death of the Oil Age and the Birth of Hydrogen America.* San Francisco: Wild Bamboo Press.

National Academy of Sciences. 1988. *Geothermal Energy Technology.* Washington, D.C.: National Academy Press.

Nussbaum, Bruce. 1985. *The World After Oil: The Shifting Axis of Power and Wealth.* New York: Simon & Schuster.

Office of Technology Assessment. 1990. *Replacing Gasoline: Alternative Fuels for Light-Duty Vehicles.* Washington, D.C.: Government Printing Office.

Ogden, Joan M., and Robert H. Williams. 1989. *Solar Hydrogen: Moving Beyond Fossil Fuels.* Washington, D.C.: World Resources Institute.

Oppenheimer, Michael, and Robert H. Boyle. 1990. *Dead Heat: The Race Against the Greenhouse Effect.* New York: Basic Books.

Penny, Terry R., and Desikan Bharathan. 1987. "Power from the Sea." *Scientific American,* vol. 286, no. 1, 86–92.

Pimentel, David, et al. 1984. "Environmental and Social Costs of Biomass Energy." *BioScience,* February, 89–93.

Rader, Nancy, et al. 1989. *Power Surge: The Status and Near-Term Potential of Renewable Energy Technologies.* Washington, D.C.: Public Citizen.

Real Goods. 1991. *Alternative Energy Sourcebook 1991.* Ukiah, Calif.: Real Goods Trading Co.

Rocky Mountain Institute. 1988. *An Energy Security Reader.* 2nd ed. Old Snowmass, Colo.: Rocky Mountain Institute.

Rocky Mountain Institute. 1991. *Resource-Efficient Housing.* Old Snowmass, Colo.: Rocky Mountain Institute.

Scientific American. 1990. *Energy for Planet Earth,* entire September issue.

Shea, Cynthia Pollack. 1988. *Renewable Energy: Today's Contribution, Tomorrow's Promise.* Washington, D.C.: Worldwatch Institute.

Skelton, Luther W. 1984. *The Solar-Hydrogen Economy: Beyond the Age of Fire.* New York: Van Nostrand Reinhold.

Smith, Ralph Lee. 1988. *Smart House: The Coming Revolution.* New York: C. P. Publishing.

Solar Energy Research Institute. 1981. *A New Prosperity: Building a Sustainable Energy Future.* Andover, Mass.: Brick House.

Sperling, Daniel. 1989. *New Transportation Fuels.* Berkeley and Los Angeles: University of California Press.

Starr, Gary. 1987. *The Solar Electric Book.* Lower Lake, Calif.: Integral Publishing.

Swan, Christopher C. 1986. *Suncell: Energy, Economy, Photovoltaics.* New York: Random House.

Tapp, B. A., and J. R. Watkins. 1989. *Energy and Mineral Resource Systems: An Introduction.* Cambridge, Mass.: Cambridge University Press.

Tester, Jefferson, ed. 1991. *Energy and the Environment in the 21st Century.* Cambridge, Mass.: MIT Press.

Underground Space Center, University of Minnesota. 1979. *Earth-Sheltered Housing Design.* New York: Van Nostrand Reinhold.

Union of Concerned Scientists. 1990. *Motor-Vehicle Efficiency and Global Warming.* Cambridge, Mass.: Union of Concerned Scientists.

Wade, Herb. 1983. *Building Underground: The Design and Construction Handbook for Earth-Sheltered Houses.* Emmaus, Pa.: Rodale Press.

Wells, Malcolm. 1990. *Underground Buildings.* Brewester, Mass.: Malcolm Wells.

Wilson, Alex. 1991. *Consumer Guide to Home Energy Savings.* Washington, D.C.: American Council for an Energy Efficient Economy.

Zweibel, Ken. 1990. *Harnessing Solar Power: The Challenge of Photovoltaics.* New York: Plenum.

Chapter 18 Nonrenewable Energy Resources

See also the readings for Chapter 3.

American Physical Society. 1985. *Radionuclide Release from Severe Accidents at Nuclear Power Plants.* New York: American Physical Society.

American Solar Energy Society. 1989. *Societal Costs of Energy: A Roundtable.* Boulder, Colo.: American Solar Energy Society.

Atomic Industrial Forum. 1985. *Nuclear Power Plant Response to Severe Accidents.* Bethesda, Md.: Atomic Industrial Forum.

Bartlett, Donald L., and James B. Steele. 1985. *Forevermore: Nuclear Waste in America.* New York: W. W. Norton.

Browning, William, and L. Hunter Lovins. 1989. *The Energy Casebook.* Old Snowmass, Colo.: Rocky Mountain Institute.

Burnett, W. M., and S. D. Ban. 1989. "Changing Prospects for Natural Gas in the United States." *Science,* vol. 244, 305–310.

Campbell, John L. 1988. *Collapse of an Industry: Nuclear Power and the Contradictions of U.S. Policy.* Ithaca, N.Y.: Cornell University Press.

Carter, Luther J. 1987. *Nuclear Imperatives and Public Trust: Dealing with Radioactive Waste.* Baltimore: Resources for the Future.

Clark, Wilson, and Jake Page. 1983. *Energy, Vulnerability, and War.* New York: W. W. Norton.

Close, Frank. 1991. *Too Hot to Handle: The Race for Cold Fusion.* Princeton, N.J.: Princeton University Press.

Cohen, Bernard L. 1990. *The Nuclear Energy Option: An Alternative For the 90s.* New York: Plenum.

Energy Conservation Coalition. 1990. *Building a Brighter Future: State Experiences in Least-Cost Electrical Planning.* Washington, D.C.: Environmental Action Foundation.

Flavin, Christopher. 1985. *World Oil: Coping with the Dangers of Success.* Washington, D.C.: Worldwatch Institute.

Flavin, Christopher. 1987. *Reassessing Nuclear Power: The Fallout from Chernobyl.* Washington, D.C.: Worldwatch Institute.

Flavin, Christopher. 1988. "The Case Against Reviving Nuclear Power." *World Watch,* July/August, 27–35.

Ford, Daniel F. 1986. *Meltdown.* New York: Simon & Schuster.

Fund for Renewable Energy and the Environment. 1987. *The Oil Rollercoaster.* Washington, D.C.: Fund for Renewable Energy and the Environment.

Golay, Michael W., and Neil E. Todreas. 1990. "Advanced Light-Water Reactors." *Scientific American,* April, 82–89.

Herman, Robin. 1990. *Fusion: The Search for Endless Energy.* New York: Cambridge University Press.

Holdren, John. 1982. "Energy Hazards: What to Measure, What to Compare." *Technology Review,* April, 32–38.

Hubbard, Harold H. 1991. "The Real Costs of Energy." *Scientific American,* vol. 264, no. 4, 36–41.

Hughes, Barry B., et al. 1985. *Energy in the Global Arena: Actors, Values, Policies, and Futures.* Durham, N.C.: Duke University Press.

Humphrey, Craig R., and Frederick R. Buttel. 1982. *Environment, Energy, and Society.* Belmont, Calif.: Wadsworth.

Jacop, Gerald. 1990. *Sight Unseen: The Politics of Siting a Nuclear Waste Repository.* Pittsburgh: University of Pittsburgh Press.

Jasper, James M. 1990. *Nuclear Politics: Energy and the State in the United States, Sweden, and France.* Princeton, N.J.: Princeton University Press.

Kaku, Michio, and Jennifer Trainer. 1982. *Nuclear Power: Both Sides.* New York: W. W. Norton.

League of Women Voters Education Fund. 1985. *The Nuclear Waste Primer.* Washington, D.C.: League of Women Voters.

Lidsky, Lawrence M. 1983. "The Trouble with Fusion." *Technology Review,* October, 32–44.

Lidsky, Lawrence M. 1984. "The Reactor of the Future." *Technology Review,* February/March, 52–56.

Lovins, Amory B. 1986. "The Origins of the Nuclear Power Fiasco." *Energy Policy Studies,* vol. 3, 7–34.

Lovins, Amory B., and L. Hunter Lovins. 1982. *Brittle Power: Energy Strategy for National Security.* Andover, Mass.: Brick House.

Marples, David R. 1986. *Chernobyl and Nuclear Power in the USSR.* New York: St. Martin's Press.

May, John. 1990. *The Greenpeace Book of the Nuclear Age.* New York: Pantheon.

McCracken, Samuel. 1982. *The War Against the Atom.* New York: Basic Books.

Medvedev, Grigori. 1990. *The Truth About Chernobyl.* New York: Basic Books.

Medvedev, Zhores. 1990. *The Legacy of Chernobyl.* New York: W. W. Norton.

Morone, Joseph G., and Edward J. Woodhouse. 1989. *The Demise of Nuclear Energy?* New Haven, Conn.: Yale University Press.

Murray, Raymond L. 1989. *Understanding Radioactive Waste.* 3rd ed. Columbus, Ohio: Battelle Press.

National Academy of Sciences. 1990. *Energy: Production, Consumption, and Consequences*. Washington, D.C.: National Academy Press.

National Academy of Sciences. 1991. *Nuclear Power: Technical and Institutional Options for the Future*. Washington, D.C.: National Academy Press.

Office of Technology Assessment. 1984. *Managing the Nation's Commercial High-Level Radioactive Waste*. Washington, D.C.: Government Printing Office.

Office of Technology Assessment. 1991. *Complex Cleanup: The Environmental Legacy of Nuclear Weapons Production*. Washington, D.C.: U.S. Government Printing Office.

O'Hefferman, Patrick, Amory Lovins, and L. Hunter Lovins. 1984. *The First Nuclear World War*. New York: Morrow Books.

Oppenheimer, Ernest J. 1990. *Natural Gas, the Best Energy Choice*. New York: Pen & Podium.

Park, Chris C. 1989. *Chernobyl: The Long Shadow*. New York: Routledge & Kegan Paul.

Pasqualetti, M. J. 1990. *Nuclear Decommissioning and Society: Public Links to a Technical Task*. New York: Routledge & Kegan Paul.

Patterson, Walter C. 1984. *The Plutonium Business and the Spread of the Bomb*. San Francisco: Sierra Club Books.

Pollock, Cynthia. 1986. *Decommissioning: Nuclear Power's Missing Link*. Washington, D.C.: Worldwatch Institute.

President's Commission on the Accident at Three Mile Island. 1979. *Report of the President's Commission on the Accident at Three Mile Island*. Washington, D.C.: Government Printing Office.

Public Citizen. 1987. *Nuclear Legacy: Too Costly to Continue*. Washington, D.C.: Public Citizen.

Public Citizen. 1987. *The Price-Anderson Act: Multi-Billion Dollar Nuclear Subsidy*. Washington, D.C.: Public Citizen.

Public Citizen. 1988. *Consequences of a Nuclear Accident*. Washington, D.C.: Public Citizen.

Public Citizen. 1989. *Forever Is the Debt*. Washington, D.C.: Public Citizen.

Public Citizen. 1989. *Nuclear Lemons: An Assessment of America's Worst Nuclear Reactors*. Washington, D.C.: Public Citizen.

Public Citizen. 1989. *Nuclear Power Safety: 1979–1989*. Washington, D.C.: Public Citizen.

Public Citizen. 1989. *On Again, Off Again: The Unreliability of U.S. Nuclear Power Plants*. Washington, D.C.: Public Citizen.

Public Citizen. 1989. *Runaway Costs: Rising Operating and Maintenance Expenses at U.S. Nuclear Plants*. Washington, D.C.: Public Citizen.

Reddy, Amulya K. N., and Jose Goldenberg. 1990. "Energy for the Developing World." *Scientific American*, September, 111–118.

Resnikoff, Marvin. 1983. *The Next Nuclear Gamble: Transportation and Storage of Nuclear Waste*. Washington, D.C.: Council on Economic Priorities.

Resnikoff, Marvin. 1987. *Living Without Landfills*. New York: Radioactive Waste Campaign.

Resnikoff, Marvin. 1988. *Deadly Defense: Military Radioactive Landfills*. New York: Radioactive Waste Campaign.

Rocky Mountain Institute. 1988. *An Energy Security Reader*. 2nd ed. Old Snowmass, Colo.: Rocky Mountain Institute.

Rosenbaum, Walter A. 1987. *Energy, Politics, and Public Policy*. 2nd ed. Washington, D.C.: Congressional Quarterly.

Saleska, Scott. 1989. *Nuclear Legacy: An Overview of the Places, Problems, and Politics of Radioactive Waste in the United States*. Washington, D.C.: Public Citizen.

Schobert, Harold H. 1987. *Coal: The Energy Source of the Past and Future*. Washington, D.C.: American Chemical Society.

Shea, Cynthia Pollock. 1989. "Decommissioning Nuclear Plants: Breaking Up Is Hard to Do." *World Watch*, July/August, 10–16.

Squillace, Mark. 1990. *Strip Mining Handbook*. Washington, D.C.: Friends of the Earth.

Taylor, John J. 1989. "Improved and Safer Nuclear Power." *Science*, vol. 244, 318–325.

Union of Concerned Scientists. 1990. *Safety Second: The NRC and America's Nuclear Power Plants*. Bloomington: Indiana University Press.

U.S. Department of Energy. 1988. *An Analysis of Nuclear Power Operating Costs*. Washington, D.C.: Government Printing Office.

Watson, Robert K. 1988. *Fact Sheet on Oil and Conservation Resources*. New York: Natural Resources Defense Council.

Weinberg, Alvin M. 1985. *Continuing the Nuclear Dialogue*. La Grange Park, Ill.: American Nuclear Society.

Weinberg, Alvin M., et al. 1985. *The Second Nuclear Era: A New Start for Nuclear Power*. New York: Praeger.

Yergin, Daniel. 1988. "Energy Security in the 1990s." *Foreign Affairs*, Autumn, 93–116.

Yergin, Daniel. 1990. *The Prize: The Epic Quest for Oil, Money, and Power*. New York: Simon & Schuster.

Chapter 19 Nonrenewable Mineral Resources and Solid Waste

Blumberg, Louis, and Robert Grottlieb. 1988. *War on Waste—Can America Win Its Battle with Garbage?* Covelo, Calif.: Island Press.

Borgese, Elisabeth Mann. 1985. *The Mines of Neptune: Minerals and Metals from the Sea*. New York: Abrams.

Boyd, Susan, et al., eds. 1988. *Waste: Choices for Communities*. Washington, D.C.: CONCERN.

Cameron, Eugene N. 1986. *At the Crossroads—The Mineral Problems of the United States*. New York: John Wiley.

Canby, Thomas Y., and Charles O'Rear. 1989. "Reshaping Our Lives: Advanced Materials." *National Geographic*, December, 746–781.

Clark, Joel P., and Frank R. Field III. 1985. "How Critical Are Critical Materials?" *Technology Review*, August/September, 38–46.

Cohen, Levin, et al. 1988. *Coming Full Circle: Successful Recycling Today*. New York: Environmental Defense Fund.

Connett, Paul. 1989. *Waste Management as if the Future Mattered*. Canton, N.Y.: Work on Waste.

Debus, Keith H. 1990. "Mining with Microbes." *Technology Review*, August/September, 50–57.

Denison, Richard A., and John Ruston. 1990. *Recycling and Incineration: Evaluating the Choices*. Covelo, Calif.: Island Press.

Dorr, Ann. 1984. *Minerals—Foundations of Society*. Montgomery County, Md.: League of Women Voters of Montgomery County Maryland.

Earth Works Group. 1990. *The Recycler's Handbook: Simple Things You Can Do*. Berkeley, Calif.: Earth Works Press.

Environmental Protection Agency. 1989. *Solid Waste Disposal in the United States*. Washington, D.C.: Government Printing Office.

Forrester, Tom. 1988. *The Materials Revolution: Superconductors, New Materials, and the Japanese Challenge*. Cambridge, Mass.: MIT Press.

Frosch, Robert A., and Nicholas E. Gallopoulos. 1989. "Strategies for Manufacturing." *Scientific American*, September, 144–152.

Gordon, Robert B., et al. 1988. *World Mineral Exploration: Trends and Issues*. Washington, D.C.: Resources for the Future.

Hershkowitz, Allen. 1987. "Burning Trash: How It Could Work." *Technology Review*, July, 26–34.

Hershkowitz, Allen, and Eugene Salermi. 1987. *Garbage Management in Japan: Leading the Way*. New York: INFORM.

Holdgate, Martin W. 1990. "Antarctica: Ice Under Pressure." *Environment*, vol. 32, no. 8, 4–9, 30–35.

Huls, Jon, and Neil Seldman. 1985. *Waste to Wealth*. Washington, D.C.: Institute for Local Self-Reliance.

Husingh, Donald, et al. 1986. *Proven Profits from Pollution Prevention*. Washington, D.C.: Institute for Local Self-Reliance.

Institute for Local Self-Reliance. 1988. *Recycling Goals and Strategies*. Washington, D.C.:Institute for Local Self-Reliance.

Kharbanda, O. P., and E. A. Stallworthy. 1990. *Waste Management: Toward a Sustainable Society*. New York: Auburn House.

Kimball, Lee A. 1990. *Southern Exposure: Deciding Antarctica's Future*. Washington, D.C.: World Resources Institute.

Kirshner, Dan, et al. 1988. *To Burn or Not to Burn*. New York: Environmental Defense Fund.

Leontief, Wassily, et al. 1983. *The Future of Nonfuel Minerals in the U.S. and World Economy: 1980–2030*. Lexington, Mass.: Lexington (Heath).

Lester, Stephen, and Brian Lipsett. 1988. *Incineration: The Burning Issue—A Manual on the Science and Politics of Hazardous Waste Incinerators*. Arlington, Va.: Citizen's Clearinghouse for Hazardous Waste.

Lester, Stephen, and Brian Lipsett. 1989. *Track Record of the Hazardous Waste Incineration Industry*. Arlington, Va.: Citizen's Clearinghouse for Hazardous Waste.

Maurice, Charles, and Charles W. Smithson. 1984. *The Doomsday Myth*. Stanford, Calif.: Hoover Institution Press.

May, John. 1989. *The Greenpeace Book of Antarctica*. New York: Doubleday.

McLaren, Digby J., and Brian J. Skinner, eds. 1987. *Resources and World Development*. New York: John Wiley.

National Academy of Sciences. 1990. *Our Seabed Frontier: Challenges and Choices*. Washington, D.C.: National Academy Press.

Neal, Homer A., and J. R. Schubel. 1987. *Solid Waste Management and the Environment: The Mounting Garbage and Trash Crisis*. Englewood Cliffs, N.J.: Prentice Hall.

Newsday. 1989. *Rush to Burn: Solving America's Garbage Crisis?* Covelo, Calif.: Island Press.

Office of Solid Waste. 1989. *Recycling Works! State and Local Solutions to Solid Waste Management*. Washington, D.C.: EPA.

Office of Technology Assessment. 1985. *Strategic Materials: Technologies to Reduce U.S. Import Vulnerability*. Washington, D.C.: Government Printing Office.

Office of Technology Assessment. 1987. *Marine Minerals: Exploring Our New Ocean Frontier*. Washington, D.C.: Government Printing Office.

Office of Technology Assessment. 1988. *Advanced Materials by Design: New Structural Materials Technologies*. Washington, D.C.: Government Printing Office.

Office of Technology Assessment. 1989. *Facing America's Trash: What's Next for Municipal Solid Waste*. Washington, D.C.: Government Printing Office.

Office of Technology Assessment. 1989. *Polar Prospects: A Minerals Treaty for Antarctica*. Washington, D.C.: Government Printing Office.

Platt, Brenda, et al. 1991. *Beyond 40 Percent: Record-Setting Recycling and Composting Programs*. Covelo, Calif.: Island Press.

Pollock, Cynthia. 1987. *Mining Urban Wastes: The Potential for Recycling*. Washington, D.C.: Worldwatch Institute.

Polprasert, Chongrak. 1989. *Organic Waste Recycling*. New York: John Wiley.

Seldman, Neil, and Bill Perkins. 1988. *Designing the Waste Stream*. Washington, D.C.: Institute for Local Self-Reliance.

Tapp, B. A., and J. R. Watkins. 1989. *Energy and Mineral Resource Systems: An Introduction*. New York: Cambridge University Press.

Underwood, Joanna D., and Allen Hershkowitz. 1989. *Facts About U.S. Garbage Management: Problems and Practices*. New York: INFORM.

Westing, Arthur H. 1986. *Global Resources and International Conflict*. New York: Oxford University Press.

Wolf, Nancy, and Ellen Feldman. 1990. *America's Packaging Dilemma*. Covelo, Calif.: Island Press.

Young, John E. 1991. *Discarding the Throwaway Society*. Washington, D.C.: Worldwatch Institute.

Youngquist, Walter. 1990. *Mineral Resources and the Destinies of Nations*. Portland, Oreg.: National Book.

Chapter 20 Risk, Human Health, and Hazardous Waste

Agency for Toxic Substances and Disease Registry. 1988. *The Nature and Extent of Lead Poisoning in Children in the United States*. Atlanta: U.S. Department of Health and Human Services.

Amato, Paul R., and Sonia A. Partridge. 1989. *The New Vegetarians: Promoting Health and Protecting Life*. New York: Plenum.

Ames, Bruce N., et al. 1987. "Ranking Possible Carcinogenic Hazards." *Science*, vol. 236, 271–279.

Aral, Sevgi O., and King K. Holmes. 1991. "Sexually Transmitted Diseases in the AIDS Era." *Scientific American*, vol. 264, no. 2, 62–69.

Armstrong, David. 1984. *The Insider's Guide to Health Foods*. New York: Bantam Books.

Bergin, Edward J., and Ronald Grandon. 1984. *The American Survival Guide: How to Survive Your Toxic Environment*. New York: Avon.

Bernarde, Melvin A. 1989. *Our Precarious Habitat: Fifteen Years Later*. New York: John Wiley.

Bertell, Rosalie. 1986. *No Immediate Danger*. New York: Women's Press.

Block, Alan A., and Frank R. Scarpitti. 1984. *Poisoning for Profit: The Mafia and Toxic Waste in America.* New York: Morrow.

Bowen, Otis R., and Robert E. Windom. 1988. *Understanding AIDS.* Washington, D.C.: Government Printing Office.

Bower, John. 1989. *The Healthy House.* New York: Lyle Stuart.

Brill, Bertrand, ed. 1985. *Low-Level Radiation Effects: A Fact Book.* New York: New York Society for Nuclear Medicine.

Brodeur, Paul. 1989. *Currents of Death: Power Lines, Computer Terminals, and the Attempt to Cover Up Their Threat to Your Health.* New York: Simon & Schuster.

Brown, Phil, and Edwin J. Mikkelsen. 1990. *No Safe Place: Toxic Waste, Leukemia, and Community Action.* Berkeley and Los Angeles: University of California Press.

Caufield, Catherine. 1989. *Multiple Exposures: Chronicles of the Nuclear Age.* New York: Harper & Row.

Chandler, William U. 1986. *Banishing Tobacco.* Washington, D.C.: Worldwatch Institute.

Citizen's Clearinghouse for Toxic Waste. 1987. *Dealing with Military Toxics: What You Can Do.* Falls Church, Va.: Citizen's Clearinghouse for Toxic Waste.

Clarke, Lee. 1989. *Acceptable Risk? Making Decisions in a Toxic Environment.* Berkeley and Los Angeles: University of California Press.

Cohen, Gary, and John O'Connor. 1990. *Fighting Toxics: A Manual for Protecting Family, Community, and Workplace.* Covelo, Calif.: Island Press.

Cohen, Mark N. 1989. *Health and the Rise of Civilization.* New Haven, Conn.: Yale University Press.

Cohrssen, John J., and Vincent T. Covello. 1989. *Risk Analysis: A Guide to Principles and Methods for Analyzing Health and Environmental Risks.* Springfield, Va.: National Technical Information Service.

Commoner, Barry. 1990. *Making Peace with the Planet.* New York: Pantheon.

Council on Environmental Quality. 1988. *Risk Analysis: Guide to Principles and Methods for Analyzing Health and Environmental Risks.* Springfield, Va.: National Technical Information Service.

Covello, V. T., et al., eds. 1989. *Effective Risk Communication.* New York: Plenum.

Crone, Hugh D. 1986. *Chemicals and Society.* Cambridge, Mass.: Cambridge University Press.

Dadd, Debra Lynn. 1990. *Nontoxic, Natural & Earthwise.* Los Angeles: Jeremy Tarcher.

Davis, Charles E., and James P. Lester, eds. 1988. *Dimensions of Hazardous Waste Politics and Policies.* Westport, Conn.: Greenwood Press.

Douglas, Mary, and Aaron Wildavsky. 1982. *Risk and Culture.* Berkeley and Los Angeles: University of California Press.

Efron, Edith. 1984. *The Apocalyptics: Cancer and the Big Lie.* New York: Simon & Schuster.

Enterprise for Education. 1989. *Hazardous Wastes from Homes.* Santa Monica, Calif.: Enterprise for Education.

Environmental Health Watch and Housing Resource Center. 1988. *The 1988 Healthy House Catalog.* Cleveland: Environmental Health Watch and Housing Resource Center.

Environmental Protection Agency. 1984. *Risk Assessment and Risk Management: Framework for Decision Making.* Washington, D.C.: Government Printing Office.

Environmental Protection Agency. 1987. *The Hazardous Waste System.* Washington, D.C.: EPA.

Environmental Protection Agency. 1987. *Unfinished Business: A Comparative Assessment of Environmental Problems.* Washington, D.C.: EPA.

Environmental Protection Agency. 1988. *Future Risk: Research Strategies for the 1990s.* Washington, D.C.: EPA.

Environmental Protection Agency. 1990. *Reducing Risk: Setting Priorities and Strategies for Environmental Protection.* Washington, D.C.: EPA.

Epstein, Samuel S., et al. 1982. *Hazardous Waste in America.* San Francisco: Sierra Club Books.

Fischoff, Baruch, et al. 1984. *Acceptable Risk: Science and Determination of Safety.* New York: Cambridge University Press.

Freudenburg, William R. 1988. "Perceived Risk, Real Risk: Social Science and the Art of Probabilistic Risk Assessment." *Science,* vol. 242, 44–49.

Freudenthal, Ralph I., and Susan L. Freudenthal. 1989. *What You Need to Know to Live with Chemicals.* Greens Farms, Conn.: Hill & Garnett.

Gibbs, Lois. 1982. *The Love Canal: My Story.* Albany: State University of New York Press.

Gibbs, Lois, and Will Collette. 1987. *Solid Waste Action Project Guidebook.* Arlington, Va.: Citizen's Clearinghouse for Hazardous Waste.

Gofman, John W. 1981. *Radiation and Human Health.* San Francisco: Sierra Club Books.

Goldman, Benjamin A., et al. 1986. *Hazardous Waste Management: Reducing the Risk.* Covelo, Calif.: Island Press.

Gordon, Ben, and Peter Montague. 1989. *Zero Discharge: A Citizen's Toxic Waste Manual.* Washington, D.C.: Greenpeace.

Gordon, Wendy, and Jane Bloom. 1985. *Deeper Problems: Limits to Underground Injection as a Hazardous Waste Disposal Method.* New York: Natural Resources Defense Council.

Gough, Michael. 1989. "Estimating Cancer Mortality." *Environmental Science and Technology,* vol. 23, no. 8, 925–930.

Gould, Jay, and Benjamin Goldman. 1990. *Deadly Deceit: Low-Level Radiation—High-Level Cover-Up.* New York: Four Walls Eight Windows.

Graham, J. D., et al., eds. 1988. *In Search of Safety: Chemicals and Cancer Risk.* Cambridge, Mass.: Harvard University Press.

Greenberg, M. R. 1987. *Public Health and Environment: The United States Experience.* New York: Guilford Publications.

Hadden, Susan G. 1989. *A Citizen's Right to Know: Risk Communication and Public Policy.* Boulder, Colo.: Westview Press.

Hall, Bob, and Mary L. Kerr. 1991. *1991–1992 Green Index: A State-by-State Guide to the Nation's Environmental Health.* Covelo, Calif.: Island Press.

Hirschorn, Joel S. 1988. "Cutting Production of Hazardous Waste." *Technology Review,* April, 52–61.

Holleb, Arthur I., ed. 1990. *The American Cancer Society Cancer Book.* New York: Doubleday.

Hunter, Linda Mason. 1989. *The Healthy House: An Attic-to-Basement Guide to Toxin-Free Living.* Emmaus, Pa.: Rodale Press.

Imperato, P. J., and Greg Mitchell. 1985. *Acceptable Risks.* New York: Viking Press.

Jones, K., and G. Moon. 1987. *Health, Disease, and Society: An Introduction to Medical Geography.* San Diego: Academic Press.

Kenworthy, Lauren, and Eric Schaeffer. 1990. *A Citizen's Guide to Promoting Toxic Waste Reduction.* New York: INFORM.

Krimsky, Sheldon, and Alonzo Plough. 1988. *Environmental Hazards: Communicating Risks as a Social Process.* Dover, Mass.: Auburn House.

Kupchella, Charles E. 1987. *Dimensions of Cancer.* Belmont, Calif.: Wadsworth.

Lave, Lester B. 1987. *Risk Assessment and Management.* New York: Plenum.

Lewis, H. W. 1990. *Technological Risk.* New York: W. W. Norton.

Love Canal Homeowners Association. 1984. *Love Canal: A Chronology of Events That Shaped a Movement.* Arlington, Va.: Citizen's Clearinghouse for Hazardous Wastes.

Merrell, Paul, and Carol Van Strum. 1990. "Negligible Risk or Premeditated Murder?" *Journal of Pesticide Reform,* vol. 10, Spring, 20–22.

Minnesota Mining and Manufacturing. 1988. *Low- or Non-Pollution Technology Through Pollution Prevention.* St. Paul, Minn.: 3M Company.

Montague, Peter. 1989. "What We Must Do—A Grass-Roots Offensive Against Toxics in the 90s." *The Workbook,* vol. 14, no. 3, 90–113.

Morone, Edward J., and Edward J. Woodhouse. 1986. *Averting Catastrophe: Strategies for Regulating Risky Technologies.* Berkeley and Los Angeles: University of California Press.

Moyers, Bill. 1990. *Global Dumping Ground: The International Traffic in Hazardous Waste.* Cabin John, Md.: Seven Locks Press.

Muir, Warren, and Joanna Underwood. 1987. *Promoting Hazardous Waste Reduction.* New York: INFORM.

National Academy of Sciences. 1983. *Transportation of Hazardous Materials: Toward a National Strategy.* Washington, D.C.: National Academy Press.

National Academy of Sciences. 1984. *Toxicity Testing: Strategies to Determine Needs and Priorities.* Washington, D.C.: National Academy Press.

National Academy of Sciences. 1986. *Environment Tobacco Smoke: Measuring Exposures and Assessing Health Effects.* Washington, D.C.: National Academy Press.

National Academy of Sciences. 1988. *Use of Laboratory Animals in Biomedical Research.* Washington, D.C.: National Academy Press.

National Academy of Sciences. 1989. *AIDS: The Second Decade.* Washington, D.C.: National Academy Press.

National Academy of Sciences. 1989. *Diet and Health: Implications for Reducing Chronic Disease Risk.* Washington, D.C.: National Academy Press.

National Academy of Sciences. 1989. *Improving Risk Communication.* Washington, D.C.: National Academy Press.

National Academy of Sciences. 1990. *Health Effects of Exposure to Low Levels of Ionizing Radiation.* Washington, D.C.: National Academy Press.

National Council on Radiation Protection and Measurements. 1987. *Ionizing Radiation Exposure of the Population of the United States.* Bethesda, Md.: NCRP Publications.

National Toxics Campaign Fund. 1990. *Fighting Toxics: A Manual for Protecting Your Family, Community, and Workplace.* Covelo, Calif.: Island Press.

National Toxics Campaign Fund. 1991. *The U.S. Military's Toxic Legacy: America's Worst Environmental Enemy.* Boston: National Toxics Campaign Fund.

Nelkin, M. M., and M. S. Brown. 1984. *Workers at Risk: Voices from the Workplace.* Chicago: University of Chicago Press.

North Carolina Pollution Prevention Pays Program. 1986. *Accomplishments of North Carolina Industries.* Raleigh: North Carolina Department of Natural Resources and Community Development.

Nriagu, Jerome O. 1990. "Global Metal Pollution: Poisoning the Biosphere." *Environment,* vol. 32, no. 7, 7–32.

Office of Technology Assessment. 1985. *Status of Biomedical Research and Related Technology for Tropical Diseases.* Washington, D.C.: Government Printing Office.

Office of Technology Assessment. 1986. *Alternatives to Animal Use in Research, Testing, and Education.* Washington, D.C.: Government Printing Office.

Office of Technology Assessment. 1986. *Serious Reduction of Hazardous Waste.* Washington, D.C.: Government Printing Office.

Office of Technology Assessment. 1986. *Transportation of Hazardous Materials.* Washington, D.C.: Government Printing Office.

Office of Technology Assessment. 1987. *From Pollution to Prevention: A Progress Report on Waste Reduction.* Washington, D.C.: Government Printing Office.

Office of Technology Assessment. 1988. *Are We Cleaning Up? 10 Superfund Case Studies.* Washington, D.C.: Government Printing Office.

Office of Technology Assessment. 1989. *Biological Effects of Power Frequency Electric and Magnetic Fields.* Washington, D.C.: Government Printing Office.

Office of Technology Assessment. 1989. *Cleaning Up: Superfund's Problems Can Be Solved.* Washington, D.C.: Government Printing Office.

Padock, Todd. 1989. *Dioxins and Furans: Questions and Answers.* Philadelphia: Academy of Natural Sciences.

Pearson, David. 1989. *The Natural House Book.* New York: Simon & Schuster.

Perrow, Charles. 1985. *Normal Accidents: Living with High-Risk Technologies.* New York: Basic Books.

Piasecki, Bruce, and Gary Davis. 1987. *America's Future in Toxic Waste Management: Lessons from Europe.* Westport, Conn.: Quorum.

Pochin, Edward. 1985. *Nuclear Radiation: Risks and Benefits.* New York: Oxford University Press.

Pollack, Stephanie. 1989. "Solving the Lead Dilemma." *Technology Review,* October, 22–31.

Postel, Sandra. 1987. *Defusing the Toxics Threat: Controlling Pesticides and Industrial Waste.* Washington, D.C.: Worldwatch Institute.

Regenstein, Lewis. 1982. *America the Poisoned.* Washington, D.C.: Acropolis Books.

Robbins, Anthony, and Phyllis Freeman. 1988. "Obstacles to Developing Vaccines for the Third World." *Scientific American,* November, 126–133.

Sandman, Peter M. 1986. *Explaining Environmental Risk.* Washington, D.C.: EPA, Office of Toxic Substances.

Scott, Ronald M.. 1989. *Chemical Hazards in the Workplace.* New York: Lewis Publishers.

Segel, Edward, et al. 1985. *The Toxic Substances Dilemma: A Plan for Citizen Action.* Washington, D.C.: National Wildlife Federation.

Sternglass, Ernest J. 1981. *Secret Fallout: Low-Level Radiation from Hiroshima to Three Mile Island.* New York: McGraw-Hill.

United Nations. 1990. *Radiation: Doses, Effects, and Risks*. New York: United Nations Publications.

U.S. Department of Health and Human Services. 1986. *The Health Consequences of Involuntary Smoking: A Report of the Surgeon General*. Rockville, Md.: U.S. Department of Health and Human Services.

U.S. Department of Health and Human Services. 1988. *The Surgeon General's Report on Nutrition and Health*. Washington, D.C.: Government Printing Office.

U.S. Department of Health and Human Services. Annual. *The Health Consequences of Smoking*. Rockville, Md.: U.S. Department of Health and Human Services.

Water Pollution Control Federation. 1989. *Household Hazardous Waste: What You Should and Shouldn't Do*. Alexandria, Va.: Water Pollution Control Federation.

Whelan, Elisabeth M. 1985. *Toxic Terror*. Ottawa, Ill.: Jameson Books.

Chapter 21 Air Pollution

See also the readings for Chapter 20.

Borman, F. H. 1985. "Air Pollution and Forests: An Ecosystem Perspective." *BioScience*, vol. 35, no. 7, 434–441.

Brenner, David J. 1989. *Radon: Risk and Remedy*. New York: W. H. Freeman.

Brookins, Douglas G. 1990. *The Indoor Radon Problem*. Irvington, N.Y.: Columbia University Press.

Brouder, Paul. 1985. *Outrageous Misconduct: The Asbestos Industry on Trial*. New York: Pantheon.

Brown, Michael. 1987. *The Toxic Cloud*. New York: Harper & Row.

Cohen, Bernie. 1988. *Radon: A Homeowner's Guide to Detection and Control*. Mt. Vernon, N.Y.: Consumer Reports Books.

Elson, Derek. 1987. *Atmospheric Pollution: Causes, Effects, and Control Policies*. Cambridge, Mass.: Basil Blackwell.

Environmental Protection Agency. 1988. *The Inside Story: A Guide to Indoor Air Quality*. Washington, D.C.: EPA.

EPA Journal, vol. 17, no 1. 1991. Entire issue devoted to 1990 Clean Air Act.

French, Hilary F. 1990. *Clearing the Air: A Global Agenda*. Washington, D.C.: Worldwatch Institute.

Lafavore, Michael. 1987. *Radon: The Invisible Threat*. Emmaus, Pa.: Rodale Press.

MacKenzie, James J., and Mohamed T. El-Ashry. 1990. *Air Pollution's Toll on Forests and Crops*. New Haven, Conn.: Yale University Press.

McKormick, John. 1985. *Acid Earth: The Global Threat of Acid Pollution*. East Haven, Conn.: Earthscan.

Mello, Robert A. 1987. *Last Stand of the Red Spruce*. Covelo, Calif.: Island Press.

Mohnen, Volker A. 1988. "The Challenge of Acid Rain." *Scientific American*, vol. 259, no. 2, 30–38.

Mossman, B. T., et al. 1990. "Asbestos: Scientific Developments and Implications for Public Policy." *Science*, vol. 251, 247–300.

National Academy of Sciences. 1988. *Air Pollution, the Automobile, and Human Health*. Washington, D.C.: National Academy Press.

Nero, Anthony V. 1988. "Controlling Indoor Air Pollution." *Scientific American*, vol. 258, no. 5, 42–48.

Office of Technology Assessment. 1985. *Acid Rain and Transported Air Pollutants: Implications for Public Policy*. New York: Unipub.

Office of Technology Assessment. 1989. *Catching Our Breath: Next Steps for Reducing Urban Ozone*. Washington, D.C.: Government Printing Office.

Pawlick, Thomas. 1986. *A Killing Rain: The Global Threat of Acid Precipitation*. San Francisco: Sierra Club Books.

Postel, Sandra. 1984. *Air Pollution, Acid Rain, and the Future of Forests*. Washington, D.C.: Worldwatch Institute.

Public Citizen. 1989. *Electricity Conservation: A Legislative Solution to Acid Rain*. Washington, D.C.: Public Citizen.

Public Citizen. 1989. *Radon: What You Don't Know Can Hurt You*. Washington, D.C.: Public Citizen.

Regens, James L., and Robert W. Rycroft. 1988. *The Acid Rain Controversy*. Pittsburgh: University of Pittsburgh Press.

Schmandt, Jurgen, et al., eds. 1989. *Acid Rain and Friendly Neighbors: The Policy Dispute Between Canada and the United States*. Durham, N.C.: Duke University Press.

Smith, Kirk R. 1987. *Biofuels, Air Pollution, and Health: A Global Review*. New York: Plenum.

Wark, K., and C. F. Warner. 1986. *Air Pollution: Its Origin and Control*. 3rd. ed New York: Harper & Row.

Wellburn, Alan. 1988. *Air Pollution and Acid Rain: The Biological Impact*. New York: John Wiley.

Chapter 22 Water Pollution

See also the readings for Chapters 5 and 20.

Ashworth, William. 1986. *The Late, Great Lakes: An Environmental History*. New York: Alfred A. Knopf.

Borgese, Elisabeth Mann. 1986. *The Future of the Oceans*. New York: Harvest House.

Bullock, David K. 1989. *The Wasted Ocean*. New York: Lyons & Burford.

Center for Marine Conservation. 1989. *The Exxon Valdez Oil Spill: A Management Analysis*. Washington, D.C.: Center for Marine Conservation.

Colborn, Theodora E., et al. 1989. *Great Lakes, Great Legacy?* Washington, D.C.: Conservation Foundation.

Costner, Pat, and Glenna Booth. 1986. *We All Live Downstream: A Guide to Waste Treatment That Stops Water Pollution*. Berkeley, Calif.: Bookpeople.

Davidson, Art. 1990. *In the Wake of the Exxon Valdez*. San Francisco: Sierra Club Books.

Environmental Protection Agency. 1987. *Lead and Your Drinking Water*. Washington, D.C.: Environmental Protection Agency.

Environmental Protection Agency. 1990. *Citizen's Guide to Ground-Water Protection*. Washington, D.C.: Environmental Protection Agency.

Gabler, Raymond. 1988. *Is Your Water Safe to Drink?* Mt. Vernon, N.Y.: Consumer Reports Books.

Hansen, Nancy R., et al. 1988. *Controlling Nonpoint-Source Water Pollution*. New York: National Audubon Society and The Conservation Society.

Harleman, Donald R. F. 1990. "Cutting the Waste in Wastewater Cleanups." *Technology Review*, April, 60–68.

Hitteman, Bette. 1988. "The Great Lakes Cleanup Effort." *Chemistry & Engineering News*, 8 February, 22–39.

Hodgson, Bryan. 1990. "Alaska's Big Spill—Can the Wilderness Heal?" *National Geographic*, January, 5–43.

Holing, Dwight. 1990. *Coastal Alert: Energy, Ecosystems, and Offshore Oil Drilling*. Covelo, Calif.: Island Press.

Horton, Tom, and William Eichbaum. 1991. *Turning the Tide: Saving the Chesapeake Bay*. Covelo, Calif.: Island Press.

Irwin, Frances H. 1989. "Integrated Pollution Control." *International Environmental Affairs*, vol. 1, no. 4, 255–274.

Jorgensen, Eric P., ed. 1989. *The Poisoned Well: New Strategies for Groundwater Protection*. Covelo, Calif.: Island Press.

Keeble, John. 1991. *Out of the Channel: The Exxon Valdez Oil Spill in Prince William Sound*. New York: Harper-Collins.

King, Jonathan. 1985. *Troubled Water: The Poisoning of America's Drinking Water*. Emmaus, Pa.: Rodale Press.

Lahey, William, and Michael Connor. 1983. "The Case for Ocean Waste Disposal." *Technology Review*, August/September, 61–68.

Loer, Raymond C. 1984. *Pollution Control for Agriculture*. 2nd ed. San Diego: Academic Press.

Loveland, David G., and Beth Reichfield. 1987. *Safety on Tap: A Citizen's Drinking Water Handbook*. Washington, D.C.: League of Women Voters Education Fund.

Lowe, Marcia D. 1989. "Down the Tubes: Human Excrement Is Full of Valuable Nutrients." *World Watch*, March/April, 22–29.

Marquardt, Sandra, et al. 1989. *Bottled Water: Sparkling Hype at a Premium Price*. Washington, D.C.: Environmental Policy Institute.

Marx, Wesley. 1981. *The Oceans: Our Last Resource*. San Francisco: Sierra Club Books.

Montgomery, Ted. 1990. *On-Site Wastewater Treatment Systems*. East Falmouth, Mass.: New Alchemy Institute.

National Academy of Sciences. 1984. *Disposal of Industrial and Domestic Wastes: Land and Sea Alternatives*. Washington, D.C.: National Academy Press.

National Academy of Sciences. 1984. *Groundwater Contamination*. Washington, D.C.: National Academy Press.

National Academy of Sciences. 1985. *Ocean Disposal Systems for Sewage Sludge and Effluent*. Washington, D.C.: National Academy Press.

National Academy of Sciences. 1985. *Oil in the Sea*. Washington, D.C.: National Academy Press.

National Academy of Sciences. 1986. *Drinking Water and Health*. Washington, D.C.: National Academy Press.

Natural Resources Defense Council. 1989. *Ebb Tide for Pollution: Actions for Cleaning Up Coastal Waters*. New York: Natural Resources Defense Council.

Office of Technology Assessment. 1984. *Protecting the Nation's Groundwater from Contamination*. Washington, D.C.: Government Printing Office.

Office of Technology Assessment. 1987. *Wastes in Marine Environments*. Washington, D.C.: Government Printing Office.

Office of Technology Assessment. 1989. *Coping with Oiled Environments*. Washington, D.C.: Government Printing Office.

Patrick, R., E. Ford, and J. Quarles, eds. 1987. *Groundwater Contamination in the United States*. Philadelphia: University of Pennsylvania Press.

Pryde, Philip R. 1991. *Environmental Management in the Soviet Union*. New York: Cambridge University Press.

Rail, Chester D. 1989. *Groundwater Contamination: Sources, Control, and Preventive Measures*. Lancaster, Pa.: Technomic Publishing.

Rice, Rip G. 1985. *Safe Drinking Water: The Impact of Chemicals on a Limited Resource*. New York: Lewis Publishers.

Sierra Club Defense Fund. 1989. *The Poisoned Well: New Strategies for Groundwater Protection*. Covelo, Calif.: Island Press.

Simon, Anne W. 1985. *Neptune's Revenge: The Ocean of Tomorrow*. New York: Franklin Watts.

U.S. Geological Survey. 1988. *Groundwater and the Rural Homeowner*. Denver: U.S. Geological Survey.

Chapter 23 Pesticides and Pest Control

See also the readings for Chapters 12, 14, and 20.

Bogard, William. 1989. *The Bhopal Tragedy: Language, Logic, and Politics in the Production of a Hazard*. Boulder, Colo.: Westview Press.

Bosso, Christopher. 1987. *Pesticides and Politics*. Pittsburgh: University of Pittsburgh Press.

Brown, Joseph E. 1983. *The Return of the Brown Pelican*. Baton Rouge: Louisiana State University Press.

Bull, David. 1982. *A Growing Problem: Pesticides and the Third World Poor*. London: Oxfam.

Carr, Anna. 1985. *Good Neighbors: Companion Planting for Gardeners*. Emmaus, Pa.: Rodale Press.

Carson, Rachel. 1962. *Silent Spring*. Boston: Houghton Mifflin.

Dover, Michael J. 1985. *A Better Mousetrap: Improving Pest Management for Agriculture*. Washington, D.C.: World Resources Institute.

Dunlap, Thomas R. 1981. *DDT: Scientists, Citizens, and Public Policy*. Princeton, N.J.: Princeton University Press.

Environmental Protection Agency. 1989. *Pesticides Fact Book*. Washington, D.C.: Environmental Protection Agency.

Flint, Mary Louise. 1990. *Pests of the Garden & a Small Farm: A Grower's Guide to Using Less Pesticide*. Oakland, Calif.: ANR Publications.

Foundation for Advancements in Science and Education. 1990. *Pesticide Export: Trafficking Biocides*. Los Angeles: Foundation for Advancements in Science and Education.

Friends of the Earth. 1990. *How to Get Your Lawn and Garden Off Drugs*. Ottawa, Ontario: Friends of the Earth.

Fukuoka, Masanobu. 1985. *The Natural Way of Farming: The Theory and Practice of Green Philosophy*. New York: Japan Publications.

Garland, Ann W. 1989. *For Our Kids' Sake: How to Protect Your Child Against Pesticides*. San Francisco: Sierra Club Books.

Gips, Terry. 1987. *Breaking the Pesticide Habit*. Minneapolis: IASA.

Goldstein, Joan. 1990. *Demanding Clean Food and Water*. New York: Plenum.

Gough, Michael. 1986. *Dioxin, Agent Orange: The Facts*. New York: Plenum.

Heylin, Michael, ed. 1991. "Pesticides: Costs Versus Benefits." *Chemistry & Engineering News*, 7 January, 5, 27–56.

Horn, D. J. 1988. *Ecological Approach to Pest Management*. New York: Guilford Publications.

Hussey, N. W., and N. Scopes. 1986. *Biological Pest Control*. Ithaca, N.Y.: Cornell University Press.

Hynes, Patricia. 1989. *The Recurring Silent Spring*. New York: Pergamon Press.

Kourik, Robert. 1990. "Combatting Household Pests Without Chemical Warfare." *Garbage*, March/April, 22–29.

Kurzman, Dan. 1987. *A Killing Wind: Inside Union Carbide and the Bhopal Catastrophe*. New York: McGraw-Hill.

League of Women Voters. 1989. *America's Growing Dilemma: Pesticides in Food and Water*. Washington, D.C.: League of Women Voters.

Marco, G. J., et al. 1987. *Silent Spring Revisited*. Washington, D.C.: American Chemical Society.

Marquardt, Sandra. 1989. *Exporting Banned Pesticides: Fueling the Circle of Poison*. Washington, D.C.: Greenpeace.

Mollison, Bill. 1990. *Permaculture*. Covelo, Calif.: Island Press.

Mott, Lawrie, and Karen Snyder. 1988. *Pesticide Alert: A Guide to Pesticides in Fruits and Vegetables*. San Francisco: Sierra Club Books.

National Academy of Sciences. 1986. *Pesticide Resistance: Strategies and Tactics for Management*. Washington, D.C.: National Academy Press.

National Academy of Sciences. 1987. *Regulating Pesticides in Food: The Delaney Paradox*. Washington, D.C.: National Academy Press.

Natural Resources Defense Council. 1989. *Intolerable Risk: Pesticides in Our Children's Food*. New York: Natural Resources Defense Council.

Natural Veterans Legal Services Project. 1990. *Human Health Effects Associated with Exposure to Herbicides and/or Their Associated Contaminants — Chlorinated Dioxins*. Washington, D.C.: Natural Veterans Legal Services Project.

Pimentel, David, and Lois Levitan. 1986. "Pesticides: Amounts Applied and Amounts Reaching Pests." *BioScience*, vol. 36, no. 2, 86–91.

Postel, Sandra. 1987. *Defusing the Toxics Threat: Controlling Pesticides and Industrial Waste*. Washington, D.C.: Worldwatch Institute.

Schultz, Warren. 1989. *The Chemical-Free Lawn*. Emmaus, Pa.: Rodale Press.

Shrivastava, Paul. 1987. *Bhopal: Anatomy of a Crisis*. New York: Harper & Row.

van den Bosch, Robert. 1978. *The Pesticide Conspiracy*. New York: Doubleday.

van den Bosch, Robert, and Mary L. Flint. 1981. *Introduction to Integrated Pest Management*. New York: Plenum.

Webb, Tony, et al. 1987. *Food Irradiation: Who Wants It?* Rochester, Vt.: Thorsons.

Weir, David. 1987. *The Bhopal Syndrome: Pesticides, Environment, and Health*. San Francisco: Sierra Club Books.

Yepsen, Roger B., Jr. 1987. *The Encyclopedia of Natural Insect and Pest Control*. Emmaus, Pa.: Rodale Press.

Chapter 24 Economics and Environment

Adams, P., and L. Solomon. 1985. *In the Name of Progress*. Toronto: Energy Probe.

Anderson, Bruce, ed. 1990. *Ecologue: The Environmental Catalogue and Consumer's Guide for a Safe Earth*. Englewood Cliffs, N.J.: Prentice Hall.

Anderson, Terry, and Donald Leal. 1990. *Free Market Environmentalism*. San Francisco: Pacific Research Institute for Public Policy.

Banks, Ronald, ed. 1990. *Costing the Earth*. New York: Robert Schalkenbach Foundation.

Berry, Wendell. 1987. *Home Economics*. Berkeley, Calif.: North Point Press.

Bhaskara, H., et al. 1989. *Against All Odds: Breaking the Poverty Trap*. London: Panos.

Binder, Alan. 1990. *Hard Heads, Soft Hearts: Tough Minded Economics for a Just Society*. Reading, Mass.: Addison-Wesley.

Boulding, Kenneth E. 1985. *The World as a Total System*. Beverly Hills: Sage Publications.

Bowden, Elbert V. 1990. *Principles of Economics: Theory, Problems, Policies*. 5th ed. Cincinnati: South-Western.

Brundtland, G. H., et al. 1987. *Our Common Future: World Commission on Environment and Development*. New York: Oxford University Press.

Butlin, John A. 1981. *The Economics of Environmental and Natural Resources Policy*. Boulder, Colo.: Westview Press.

Campbell, Monica E., and William M. Glenn. 1982. *Profit from Pollution Prevention*. Willowdale, Ontario: Firefly Books.

Clark, William C., and R. E. Munn, eds. 1986. *Sustainable Development of the Biosphere*. New York: Cambridge University Press.

Collard, David, et al., eds. 1988. *Economics, Growth, and Sustainable Environments*. New York: St. Martin's Press.

Conroy, Czech, et al. 1988. *The Greening of Aid: Sustainable Livelihood in Action*. East Haven, Conn.: Earthscan.

Corson, Ben, et al. Annual. *Shopping for a Better World*. New York: Council on Economic Priorities.

Daly, Herman E., ed. 1980. *Economics, Ecology, and Ethics*. New York: W. H. Freeman.

Daly, Herman E. 1991. *Steady-State Economics*. Covelo, Calif.: Island Press.

Daly, Herman E., and John B. Cobb, Jr. 1989. *For the Common Good: Redirecting the Economy Toward Community, the Environment, and a Sustainable Future*. Boston: Beacon Press.

Dixon, John A., and Paul B. Sherman. 1990. *Economics of Protected Areas: A New Look at Benefits and Costs*. Covelo, Calif.: Island Press.

Dixon, John A., et al. 1988. *Economic Analysis of the Environmental Impacts of Development Projects*. East Haven, Conn.: Earthscan.

Durning, Alan B. 1989. *Poverty and the Environment: Reversing the Downward Spiral*. Washington, D.C.: Worldwatch Institute.

Elkington, John, et al. 1990. *The Green Consumer*. New York: Penguin.

Etizoni, A. 1988. *The Moral Dimension: Toward A New Economics*. New York: The Free Press.

Finkelstein, J., ed. 1989. *Windows on a New World: The Third Industrial Revolution*. Westport, Conn.: Greenwood Press.

Fisher, Anthony C. 1981. *Resource and Environmental Economics*. New York: Cambridge University Press.

Freeman, A. Myrick, III. 1982. *Air and Water Pollution Control: A Benefit-Cost Assessment*. New York: John Wiley.

Galbraith, John Kenneth. 1988. *Economics in Perspective: A Critical History*. Boston: Houghton Mifflin.

Georgescu-Roegen, Nicholas. 1971. *The Entropy Law and the Economic Process*. Cambridge, Mass.: Harvard University Press.

Georgescu-Roegen, Nicholas. 1977. "Inequality, Limits, and Growth from a Bioeconomic Point of View." *Review of Social Economics*, vol. 35, 361–376.

Georgescu-Roegen, Nicholas. 1977. "The Steady State and Ecological Salvation: A Thermodynamic Analysis." *BioScience*, vol. 27, no. 4, 266–270.

Global Tomorrow Coalition. 1989. *Sustainable Development: A Guide to Our Common Future*. Washington, D.C.: Global Tomorrow Coalition.

Gupta, Avijit. 1988. *Ecology and Development in the Third World*. New York: Routledge, Chapman and Hall.

Hamrin, Robert D. 1983. *A Renewable Resource Economy*. New York: Praeger.

Hamrin, Robert D. 1988. *America's New Economy: A Basic Guide*. New York: Franklin Watts.

Hare, W. L., ed. 1990. *Ecologically Sustainable Development*. Fitzroy, Victoria, Australia: Australian Conservation Foundation.

Harrison, Bennett, and Barry Bluestone. 1988. *The Great U-Turn: Corporate Restructuring and the Polarizing of America*. New York: Basic Books.

Hawken, Paul. 1983. *The Next Economy*. New York: Random House.

Heaton, George, et al. 1991. *Transforming Technology: An Agenda for Environmentally Sustainable Growth in the Twenty-First Century*. Washington, D.C.: World Resources Institute.

Hirschhorn, Joel S., and Kirsten U. Oldenburg. 1990. *Prosperity Without Pollution: The Prevention Strategy for Industry and Consumers*. New York: Van Nostrand Reinhold.

Institute for Local Self-Reliance. 1990. *Proven Profits from Pollution Prevention*. Washington, D.C.: Institute for Local Self-Reliance.

Kassiola, Joel Jay. 1990. *The Death of Industrial Civilization*. Albany: State University of New York Press.

Kolko, Joyce. 1988. *Restructuring the World Economy*. New York: Pantheon.

Krutilla, John V., and Anthony C. Fisher. 1985. *The Economics of Natural Environments*. Washington, D.C.: Resources for the Future.

Leonard, H. Jeffrey. 1988. *Pollution and the Struggle for the World Product: Multinational Corporations, Environment, and International Comparative Advantage*. New York: Cambridge University Press.

Lydenberg, Steven D., et al. 1989. *Rating America's Corporate Conscience*. Reading, Mass.: Addison-Wesley.

Makower, Joel. 1991. *The Green Consumer Supermarket Guide*. New York: Penguin.

Maurice, Charles, and Charles W. Smithsonian. 1984. *The Doomsday Myth*. Stanford, Calif.: Hoover Institution Press.

McConnell, Campbell R. 1990. *Economics: Principles, Problems, and Policies*. 11th ed. New York: McGraw-Hill.

Meeker-Lowry, Susan. 1988. *Economics as if the Earth Mattered: A Catalyst Guide to Socially Conscious Investing*. Philadelphia: New Society Publishers.

Mishan, E. J. 1977. *The Economic Growth Debate: An Assessment*. London: Allen & Unwin.

Neber, Philip A. 1990. *Natural Resource Economics: Conservation and Exploitation*. New York: Cambridge University Press.

Pearce, David, et al. 1989. *Blueprint for a Green Economy*. East Haven, Conn.: Earthscan.

Pearce, David, et al. 1989. *Sustainable Development: Economics and Environment in the Third World*. London: Edward Elgar.

Population Crisis Committee. 1987. *The International Human Suffering Index*. Washington, D.C.: Population Crisis Committee.

Portney, Paul, ed. 1990. *Public Policies for Environmental Protection*. Washington, D.C.: Resources for the Future.

Redclift, Michael. 1987. *Sustainable Development: Exploring the Contradictions*. New York: Methuen.

Rees, B. 1990. "The Ecology of Sustainable Development." *The Ecologist*, vol. 20, no. 1, 18–23.

Repetto, Robert. 1990. *Promoting Environmentally Sound Economic Progress: What the North Can Do*. Washington, D.C.: World Resources Institute.

Repetto, Robert, et al. 1989. *Wasting Assets: Natural Resources in the National Income Accounts*. Washington, D.C.: World Resources Institute.

Riddel, Robert. 1981. *Ecodevelopment: An Alternative to Growth Imperative Models*. Hampshire, England: Gower Publishing.

Robertson, J. 1990. *Future Wealth: New Economics for the Twenty-First Century*. London: Cassell.

Sargoff, Mark. 1988. *The Economy of the Earth: Philosophy, Law, and the Environment*. New York: Cambridge University Press.

Schramm, Gunther, and Jeremy J. Warford. 1989. *Environmental Management and Economic Development*. Baltimore: Johns Hopkins University Press.

Schumacher, E. F. 1973. *Small Is Beautiful: Economics as if People Mattered*. New York: Harper & Row.

Smith, V. Kerry. 1979. *Scarcity and Growth Reconsidered*. Baltimore: Johns Hopkins University Press.

Theobald, Robert. 1987. *The Rapids of Change: Entrepreneurship in Turbulent Times*. Chicago: Knowledge Systems.

Thurow, Lester. 1980. *The Zero Sum Society*. New York: Basic Books.

Tietenberg, Tom. 1988. *Environmental and Resource Economics*. 2nd ed. Glenview, Ill.: Scott, Foresman.

Toffler, Alvin, and Heidi Toffler. 1990. *Powershift*. New York: Bantam Books.

Turner, Kerry, ed. 1988. *Sustainable Environmental Management: Principles and Practice*. Boulder, Colo.: Westview Press.

Wachtel, Paul. 1988. *The Poverty of Affluence*. Santa Cruz, Calif.: New Society.

Ward, Barbara. 1979. *Progress for a Small Planet*. New York: W. W. Norton.

Watt, K. E. F. 1982. *Understanding the Environment*. Boston: Allyn & Bacon.

Chapter 25 Politics and Environment

Abbey, Edward. 1986. *The Monkey Wrench Gang*. New York: Avon.

Bahro, Rudolf. 1986. *Building the Green Movement*. London: Heretic Books.

Barnaby, Frank, ed. 1988. *The Gaia Peace Atlas: Survival into the Third Millennium*. New York: Doubleday.

Benjamin, Medea, and Andrea Freeman. 1989. *Bridging the Global Gap: A Handbook to Linking Citizens of the First and Third Worlds*. Santa Fe: Seven Locks Press.

Borrelli, Peter, ed. 1988. *Crossroads: Environmental Priorities for the Future*. Covelo, Calif.: Island Press.

Boulding, Kenneth E. 1989. *Three Faces of Power*. Beverly Hills: Sage Publications.

Branch, Melville C. 1990. *Planning: Universal Process*. New York: Praeger.

Brown, Janet W., ed. 1990. *In the U.S. Interest: Resources, Growth, and Security in the Developing World*. Washington, D.C.: World Resources Institute.

Caldwell, Lynton K. 1990. *Between Two Worlds: Science, the Environmental Movement, and Policy Choice*. New York: Cambridge University Press.

Caldwell, Lynton K. 1990. *International Environmental Policy*, 2nd ed. Durham, N.C.: Duke University Press.

Cappo, J. *FutureScope: Success Stories for the 1990s and Beyond*. New York: Longman.

Capra, Fritjof, and Charlene Spretnak. 1984. *Green Politics*. New York: Dutton.

CEIP Fund. 1989. *The Complete Guide to Environmental Careers*. Covelo, Calif.: Island Press.

Chomsky, Noam, and Edward Herman. 1988. *Manufacturing Consent: The Political Economy of the Mass Media*. New York: Pantheon.

Choucri, Nazli. 1991. "The Global Environment and Multinational Corporations." *Technology Review*, April, 52–59.

Chubb, John E., and Paul E. Peterson, eds. 1988. *Can the Government Govern?* Washington, D.C.: Brookings Institute.

Clark, John, ed. 1990. *Renewing the Earth: The Promise of Social Ecology: A Celebration of the Work of Murray Bookchin*. London: Green Print.

Cleveland, Harlan. 1990. *The Global Commons: Policy for the Planet*. Aspen, Colo.: Aspen Institute.

Cornish, Edward, ed. 1984. *Global Solutions: Innovative Approaches to World Problems*. Bethesda, Md.: World Future Society.

Costanza, Robert. 1987. "Social Traps and Environmental Policy." *BioScience*, vol. 37, no. 6, 407–412.

Cousins, Norman. 1987. *The Pathology of Power*. New York: W. W. Norton.

Dahlberg, Kenneth A., et al. 1985. *Environment and the Global Arena*. Durham, N.C.: Duke University Press.

Day, David. 1990. *The Environmental Wars: Reports from the First Line*. New York: St. Martin's Press.

Durning, Alan B. 1989. *Action at the Grassroots: Fighting Poverty and Environmental Decline*. Washington, D.C.: Worldwatch Institute.

Dye, Thomas R., and Harmon Zeigler. 1987. *The Irony of Democracy: An Uncommon Introduction to American Politics*. 7th ed. Pacific Grove, Calif.: Brooks/Cole.

Erickson, Brad, ed. 1990. *Call to Action: Handbook for Ecology, Peace, and Justice*. San Francisco: Sierra Club Books.

Firestone, David B., and Frank C. Reed. 1983. *Environmental Law for Non-Lawyers*. Salem. N.H.: Butterworths.

Florio, James, et al. 1990. *The Rebellion of the Planet: Environmental Policy in the 1990s*. New York: Pharos Books.

Foreman, Dave. 1990. *Confessions of an Eco-Warrior*. New York: Crown.

Foreman, Dave, and Bill Haywood, eds. 1988. *Ecodefense: A Field Guide to Monkeywrenching*. 2nd ed. Tucson: Ned Ludd Books.

Freedman, Leonard, and Roger A. Riske. 1987. *Power and Politics in America*. 5th ed. Pacific Grove, Calif.: Brooks/Cole.

Hall, Bob. 1990. *Environmental Politics: Lessons from the Grassroots*. Durham, N.C.: Institute for Southern Studies.

Hall, Bob, and Mary L. Kerr. 1991. *1991–92 Green Index: A State-by-State Report Card on the Nation's Environmental Health*. Durham, N.C.: Institute for Southern Studies.

Harvey, H., M. Shuman, and D. Arbess. 1989. *Alternative Security: Beyond the Controlled Arms Race*. Old Snowmass, Colo.: Rocky Mountain Institute.

Henderson, Hazel. 1978. *Creating Alternative Futures*. New York: G. P. Putnam's.

Henderson, Hazel. 1981. *The Politics of the Solar Age*. New York: Anchor/Doubleday.

Henning, Daniel H., and William R. Manguin. 1989. *Managing the Environmental Crisis*. Durham, N.C.: Duke University Press.

Hirsch, F. 1978. *The Social Limits to Growth*. London: RKP.

Irvine, Sandy, and A. Ponton. 1988. *A Green Manifesto*. London: Optima.

Kahn, Si. 1982. *A Guidebook for Grassroots Leaders*. New York: McGraw-Hill.

Kennedy, Paul. 1989. *The Rise and Fall of Great Powers: Economic Change and Military Conflict from 1500 to 2000*. New York: Vintage Books.

Korten, David C. 1990. *Getting to the 21st Century: Voluntary Action and the Global Arena*. West Hartford, Conn.: Kumarian Press.

Krannich, R. L. 1988. *Careering and Re-Careering for the 1990s: The Complete Guide to Planning the Future*. Manassas, Va.: Impact Publications.

Landy, Marc K., et al. 1990. *The Environmental Protection Agency: Asking the Wrong Questions*. New York: Oxford University Press.

Manes, Christopher. 1990. *Green Rage: Radical Environmentalism and the Unmaking of Civilization*. Boston: Little, Brown.

Mathews, Christopher. 1988. *Hardball: How Politics Is Played — Told by One Who Knows the Game*. New York: Summit Books.

Mathews, Jessica Tuchman, ed. 1989. "Redefining Security." *Foreign Affairs*, Spring, 162–177.

Mathews, Jessica Tuchman, ed. 1990. *Preserving the Global Environment: The Challenge of Shared Leadership*. Washington, D.C.: World Resources Institute.

Meadows, Donella H. 1991. *Global Citizen*. Covelo, Calif.: Island Press.

Myers, Norman. 1988. "Environment and Security." *Foreign Policy*, vol. 74, 23–41.

Nadler, G., and Hibino, S. 1990. *Breakthrough Thinking*. New York: Prima (St. Martin's Press).

Nanus, B. 1989. *The Leader's Edge: The Seven Keys to Leadership in Turbulent Times*. Los Angeles: Contemporary Books.

Ophuls, William. 1977. *Ecology and the Politics of Scarcity*. New York: W. H. Freeman.

Paehlke, Robert C. 1989. *Environmentalism and the Future of Progressive Politics*. New Haven, Conn.: Yale University Press.

Parkin, S. 1989. *Green Parties*. London: Heretic Books/GMP Publications.

Peavey, Fran, Myra Levey, and Charles Varon. 1986. *Heart Politics*. Santa Cruz, Calif.: New Society.

Petulla, Joseph M. 1987. *Environmental Protection in the United States: Industry, Agencies, Environmentalists*. San Francisco: San Francisco Study Center.

Piasecki, Bruce, and Peter Asmus. 1990. *In Search of Environmental Excellence: Moving Beyond Blame*. New York: Simon & Schuster.

Porritt, Jonathan. 1984. *Seeing Green: The Politics of Ecology Explained*. Oxford, England: Blackwell.

Renner, Michael. 1989. *National Security: The Economic and Environmental Dimensions*. Washington, D.C.: Worldwatch Institute.

Renner, Michael. 1990. *Swords into Plowshares: Converting to a Peace Economy*. Washington, D.C.: Worldwatch Institute.

Rosenbaum, Walter A. 1990. *Environment, Politics, and Policy*. 2nd. ed. Washington, D.C.: Congressional Quarterly.

Ross, Donald K. 1973. *A Public Citizen's Action Manual*. Washington, D.C.: Public Citizen.

Scarce, Rick. 1990. *Eco-Warriors*. Chicago, Ill.: Noble Press.

Schlesinger, Arthur M., Jr. 1986. *The Cycles of American History*. Boston: Houghton Mifflin.

Schneider, Bertrand. 1988. *The Barefoot Revolution: A Report to the Club of Rome*. London: Intermediate Technologies Publications.

Shephard, Mark. 1987. *Gandhi Today: A Report on Mahatma Gandhi's Successors*. Arcata, Calif.: Simple Productions.

Sierra Club. 1987. *Conservation Action Handbook*. San Francisco: Sierra Club Books.

Sivard, Ruth. 1991. *World Military and Social Expenditures*. Cambridge, Mass.: World Priorities, Inc.

Spretnak, Charlene, and Fritjof Capra. 1986. *Green Politics: The Green Promise*. Santa Fe, N.M.: Bear and Company.

Timberlake, Lloyd. 1987. *Only One Earth: Living for the Future*. New York: Sterling.

Tokar, Michael. 1988. *The Green Alternative: Creating an Alternative Future*. San Pedro, Calif.: R. & E. Miles.

Vig, Norman, and Michael Kraft. 1990. *Environmental Policy in the 1990s*. Washington, D.C.: Congressional Quarterly.

Watt, K.E.F. 1982. *Understanding the Environment*. Boston: Allyn & Bacon.

Westman, Walter E. 1985. *Ecology, Impact Assessment and Environmental Planning*. New York: John Wiley.

Willhoite, Fred H. 1988. *Power and Governments: An Introduction to Politics*. Pacific Grove, Calif.: Brooks/Cole.

Yandle, Bruce. 1989. *The Political Limits of Environmental Regulation*. Westport, Conn.: Quorum.

Chapter 26 Worldviews, Ethics, and Environment

See also the readings for Chapters 2 and 16.

Anderson, Bruce, ed. 1990. *Ecologue: The Environmental Catalogue and Consumer's Guide for a Safe Earth*. Englewood Cliffs, N.J.: Prentice Hall.

Baldwin, J., ed. 1990. *Whole Earth Ecologue*. New York: Harmony Books.

Barbour, Ian G., ed. 1973. *Western Man and Environmental Ethics*. Reading, Mass.: Addison-Wesley.

Barbour, Ian G. 1980. *Technology, Environment, and Human Values*. New York: Praeger.

Beckwith, B. P. 1986. *Beyond Tomorrow: A National Utopia*. Palo Alto, Calif.: B. P. Beckwith.

Berman, Morris. 1981. *The Reenchantment of the World*. Ithaca, N.Y.: Cornell University Press.

Berry, Thomas. 1988. *The Dream of the Earth*. San Francisco: Sierra Club Books.

Berry, Wendell. 1990. *What Are People For?* Berkeley, Calif.: North Point Press.

Bobo, Kim, et al. 1991. *Organizing for Social Change*. Cabin John, Md.: Seven Locks Press.

Bookchin, Murray. 1990. *Remaking Society: Pathways to a Green Future*. San Francisco: South End Press.

Botkin, Daniel. 1990. *Discordant Harmonies: A New Ecology for the Twenty-First Century*. New York: Oxford University Press.

Bowles, Samuel, et al. 1983. *Beyond the Wasteland*. New York: Anchor Books.

Boyer, William H. 1984. *America's Future: Transition to the 21st Century*. New York: Praeger.

Brennan, Andrew. 1988. *Thinking About Nature: An Investigation of Nature, Value, and Ecology*. Athens: University of Georgia Press.

Brown, Lester R. 1981. *Building a Sustainable Society*. New York: W. W. Norton.

Cahn, Robert. 1978. *Footprints on the Planet: A Search for an Environmental Ethic*. New York: Universe Books.

Cahn, Robert, and Patricia Cahn. 1990. "Did Earth Day 1990 Change the World?" *Environment*, vol. 32, no. 7, 16–20, 36–42.

Callahan, Daniel. 1973. *The Tyranny of Survival*. New York: Macmillan.

Callenbach, Ernest. 1975. *Ecotopia*. New York: Bantam Books.

Callenbach, Ernest. 1981. *Ecotopia Emerging*. New York: Bantam Books.

Callicott, J. Baird. 1988. *In Defense of the Land Ethic: Essays in Environmental Philosophy*. Albany: State University of New York Press.

Capra, Fritjof. 1983. *The Turning Point: Science, Society, and the Rising Culture*. New York: Bantam Books.

Capra, Fritjof. 1988. *Uncommon Wisdom*. London: Century Hutchinson.

Capra, Fritjof, and Charlene Spretnak. 1986. *The Spiritual Dimensions of Green Politics*. Berkeley and Los Angeles: University of California Press.

Catton, William R. 1989. *Overshoot: The Ecological Basis of Revolutionary Change*. Urbana: University of Illinois Press.

Christensen, Karen. 1990. *Home Ecology: Simple and Practical Ways to Green Your Home*. Golden, Colo.: Fulcrum Publishing.

Clark, M. E. 1989. *Ariadne's Thread: The Search for New Models of Thinking*. New York: St. Martin's Press.

Cohen, Michael J. 1988. *How Nature Works: Regenerating Kinship with Planet Earth*. Waldpole, N.H.: Stillpoint Publishing.

Cohen, Michael J. 1989. *Connecting with Nature: Creating Moments That Let Earth Teach*. Eugene, Oreg.: World Peace University.

Cook, Stephen, and Donella H. Meadows. 1990. *Coming of Age in the Global Village: The Science and Technology, Politics, Economics, and Ethics Literacy Book*. Russellville, Ark.: Parthenon.

Cornell, Joseph. 1989. *Sharing the Joy of Nature*. Nevada City, Calif.: Dawn Publications.

Council on Economic Priorities. Annual. *Shopping for a Better World*. Washington, D.C.: Council on Economic Priorities.

Court, T. de la. 1990. *Beyond Bruntland: Green Development in the 1990s*. London: Zed Books.

Daly, Herman E., ed. 1980. *Economics, Ecology, and Ethics*. New York: W. H. Freeman.

de Haes, C. 1986. *The Assisi Declarations: Messages on Man and Nature from Buddhism, Christianity, Hinduism, Islam, and Judaism.* Gland, Switzerland: World Wildlife Fund.

Devall, Bill. 1988. *Simple in Means, Rich in Ends: Practicing Deep Ecology.* Salt Lake City: Peregrine Smith.

Devall, Bill, and George Sessions. 1985. *Deep Ecology: Living as if Nature Mattered.* Salt Lake City: Gibbs Smith.

Diamond, Irene, and Gloria F. Orenstein, eds. 1990. *Reweaving the World: The Emergence of Ecofeminism.* San Francisco: Sierra Club Books.

Drengson, Alan. 1989. *Beyond the Environmental Crisis: From Technology to Planetary Person.* New York: Peter Lang.

Earth Works Group. 1990. *50 Simple Things You Can Do to Save the Earth.* Berkeley, Calif.: Earth Works Press.

Earth Works Group. 1991. *The Next Step: 50 More Things You Can Do to Save the Earth.* Kansas City, Mo.: Andrews & McMeel.

Earth Works Group. 1991. *The Student Environmental Action Guide: 25 Simple Things We Can Do.* Berkeley, Calif.: Earth Works Press.

Ehrenfeld, David. 1978. *The Arrogance of Humanism.* New York: Oxford University Press.

Elder, Frederick. 1970. *Crisis in Eden: A Religious Study of Man and Environment.* Nashville, Tenn.: Abingdon Press.

Elgin, Duane. 1981. *Voluntary Simplicity: Toward a Way of Life That Is Outwardly Simple, Inwardly Rich.* New York: Morrow.

Elkington, John, et al. 1990. *The Green Consumer.* New York: Penguin.

Engel, J. Ronald., and Joan G. Engel, eds. 1990. *The Ethics of Environment and Development.* Tucson: University of Arizona Press.

Evernden, Neil. 1985. *The Natural Alien: Humankind and Environment.* Toronto: University of Toronto Press.

Fox, Stephen. 1981. *John Muir and His Legacy: The American Conservation Movement.* Boston: Little, Brown.

Fritsch, Albert J. 1980. *Environmental Ethics: Choices for Concerned Citizens.* New York: Anchor Press.

Garbarino, J. 1988. *The Future as if It Really Mattered.* Longmont, Colo.: Bookmakers Guild.

Glacken, Clarence. 1967. *Traces on the Rhodian Shore: Nature and Culture in Western Thought.* Berkeley and Los Angeles: University of California Press.

Goldsmith, Edward. 1978. *The Stable Society.* Cornwall, England: Wadebridge Press.

Goldsmith, Edward. 1988. *The Great U-Turn: De-Industrializing Society.* London: Green Books.

Goldsmith, Edward, et al. 1990. *5000 Days to Save the World.* London: Hamlyn.

Granberg-Michaelson, Wesley. 1984. *A Worldly Spirituality.* New York: Harper & Row.

Gray, Elizabeth. 1982. *Green Paradise Lost.* Wellesley, Mass.: Roundtable Press.

Griffin, Susan. 1978. *Woman and Nature: The Roaring Inside Her.* New York: Harper & Row.

Hardin, Garrett. 1977. *The Limits of Altruism: An Ecologist's View of Survival.* Bloomington: Indiana University Press.

Hardin, Garrett. 1978. *Exploring New Ethics for Survival.* 2nd ed. New York: Viking Press.

Hardin, Garrett. 1986. *Filters Against Folly.* New York: Penguin.

Hargrove, Eugene C., ed. 1986. *Religion and Environmental Crisis.* Athens: University of Georgia Press.

Hargrove, Eugene C. 1989. *Foundations of Environmental Ethics.* Englewood Cliffs, N.J.: Prentice Hall.

Harmon, Willis. 1988. *Global Mind Change: The Promise of the Last Years of the Twentieth Century.* Indianapolis: Knowledge Systems.

Heilbroner, Robert. 1974. *An Inquiry into the Human Prospect.* New York: W. W. Norton.

Henderson, Hazel. 1978. *Creating Alternative Futures.* New York: Berkley Publishing.

Hiss, Tony. 1990. *The Experience of Place.* New York: Random House.

Hollander, Jeffrey. 1990. *How to Make the World a Better Place.* New York: Quill.

Hynes, H. Patricia. 1990. *Earth Right: Every Citizen's Guide.* New York: Prima (St. Martins Press).

Irvine, Sandy. 1989. *Beyond Green Consumerism.* London: Friends of the Earth.

Johnson, Warren. 1978. *Muddling Toward Frugality.* San Francisco: Sierra Club Books.

Johnson, Warren. 1985. *The Future Is Not What It Used to Be: Returning to Traditional Values in an Age of Scarcity.* New York: Dodd, Mead.

Kidder, Rushworth M. 1989. *Reinventing the Future: Global Goals for the 21st Century.* Cambridge, Mass.: MIT Press.

LaChapelle, Dolores. 1989. *Sacred Land, Sacred Sex, Rapture of the Deep: Concerning Deep Ecology and Celebrating Life.* Silverton, Colo.: Finn Hill Arts.

Lamb, Marjorie. 1990. *2 Minutes a Day for a Greener Planet.* New York: Harper & Row.

Lappé, Francis Moore. 1989. *Rediscovering America's Values.* New York: Ballantine.

Laszlo, E. 1989. *The Inner Limits of Mankind.* London: Oneworld Publications.

Leopold, Aldo. 1949. *A Sand County Almanac.* New York: Oxford University Press.

Livingston, John A. 1981. *The Fallacy of Wildlife Conservation.* Toronto: McClelland and Stewart.

Livingston, John A. 1985. *"Moral Concerns and the Biosphere."* Alternatives, vol. 12, 3–9.

MacEachern, Diane. 1990. *Save Our Planet: 750 Everyday Ways You Can Help Clean Up the Earth.* New York: Dell Pub. Co., Inc.

McGaa, Ed. 1990. *Mother Earth Spirituality.* New York: Harper & Row.

Meeker, Joseph W. 1972. *The Comedy of Survival: Studies in Literary Ecology.* New York: Charles Scribner's.

Meeker, Joseph W. 1988. *Minding the Earth: Thinly Disguised Essays on Human Ecology.* Berkeley, Calif.: Latham Foundation.

Merchant, Carolyn. 1980. *The Death of Nature: Women, Ecology, and the Scientific Revolution.* New York: Harper & Row.

Merchant, Carolyn. 1981. *"Earthcare: Women and the Environmental Movement."* Environment, vol. 23, no. 5, 6–13, 38–42.

Milbrath, Lester W. 1989. *Envisioning a Sustainable Society.* Albany: State University of New York Press.

Molesworth, C. 1983. *Gary Snyder's Vision.* Columbia: University of Missouri Press.

Myers, Norman. 1990. *The Gaia Atlas of Future Worlds.* New York: Doubleday.

Naar, Jon. 1990. *Design for a Liveable Planet.* New York: Harper & Row.

Naess, Arne. 1989. *Ecology, Community, and Lifestyle.* New York: Cambridge University Press.

Nash, Roderick. 1988. *The Rights of Nature: A History of Environmental Ethics.* Madison: University of Wisconsin Press.

Nearing, Helen and Scott. 1970. *Living the Good Life.* New York: Schocken.

Newman, Peter, et al. 1990. *Case Studies in Environmental Hope.* Perth: Australia: E.P.A. Support Services.

Null, Gary. 1990. *Clearer, Cleaner, Safer, Greener: A Blueprint for Detoxifying Your Environment.* New York: Villard Books.

Ornstein, Robert, and Paul Ehrlich. 1989. *New World, New Mind.* New York: Doubleday.

Passmore, John. 1980. *Man's Responsibility for Nature: Ecological Problems and Western Traditions.* New York: Charles Scribner's.

Peccei, Aurelio, and Daisaku Ikeda. 1984. *Before It Is Too Late.* Tokyo: Kodansha International.

Physicians for Social Responsibility. 1989. *Our Common Future: Healing the Planet: A Resource Guide for Individual Action.* Los Angeles: Physicians for Social Responsibility.

Piltz, Rick, and Shelia Machado. 1990. *Searching for Success.* Washington, D.C.: Renew America.

Plant, Judith, and Christopher Plant, eds. 1990. *Turtle Talk: Fifteen Voices for a Sustainable Future.* Santa Cruz, Calif.: New Society Publishers.

Potter, Van Rensselaer. 1988. *Global Bioethics: Building on the Leopold Legacy.* Rensselaer: Michigan State University Press.

Regan, Tom. 1984. *Earthbound: New Introductory Essays in Environmental Ethics.* New York: Random House.

Rifkin, Jeremy. 1983. *Algeny.* New York: Viking/Penguin.

Rifkin, Jeremy. 1985. *Declaration of a Heretic.* Boston: Routledge & Kegan Paul.

Rifkin, Jeremy. 1989. *Into the Greenhouse World.* New York: Bantam Books.

Rifkin, Jeremy, ed. 1990. *The Green Lifestyle Handbook: 1001 Ways You Can Heal the Earth.* New York: Henry Holt & Co.

Rolston, Holmes, III. 1988. *Environmental Ethics: Duties to and Values in the Natural World.* Philadelphia: Temple University Press.

Roszak, Theodore. 1978. *Person/Planet.* New York: Doubleday.

Roszak, Theodore. 1988. *The Cult of Information.* London: Paladin.

Rothburg, Paul, and Robert L. Olson, eds. 1990. *Mending the Earth: A World for Our Grandchildren.* Berkeley, Calif.: North Atlantic Books.

Rothenberg, D. 1987. *"A Platform of Deep Ecology."* The Environmentalist, vol. 7, no. 3, 185–190.

Rowe, Stan. 1990. *Home Places: Essays on Ecology.* Edmonton, Alberta: NeWest Publishing.

Sale, Kirkpatrick. 1985. *Dwellers in the Land: The Bioregional Vision.* San Francisco: Sierra Club Books.

Sale, Kirkpatrick. 1990. *Conquest of Paradise.* New York: Alfred A. Knopf.

Santmire, H. Paul. 1985. *The Travail of Nature: The Ambiguous Ecological Promise of Christian Theology.* Philadelphia: Temple University Press.

Schumacher, E. F. 1973. *Small Is Beautiful: Economics as if People Mattered.* New York: Harper & Row.

Seed, John, et al. 1988. *Thinking Like a Mountain.* Madison, Wis.: Madison Rainforest Group.

Sessions, George. 1989. *"Ecocentrism, Wilderness, and Global Ecosystem Protection."* Paper prepared for conference on "The Wilderness Condition," Estes Park, Colorado, August 17–23.

Seymour, John, and Herbert Giradet. 1987. *Blueprint for a Green Planet: Your Practical Guide to Restoring the World's Environment.* Englewood Cliffs, N.J.: Prentice Hall.

Sheldrake, Rupert. 1991. *The Rebirth of Nature: The Greening of Science and God.* New York: Bantam Books.

Snyder, Gary. 1980. *The Real Work: Interviews and Talks, 1964–1977.* New York: New Directions.

Soloman, Lawrence. 1978. *The Conserver Society.* New York: Doubleday.

Sombke, Laurence. 1990. *The Solution to Pollution: 101 Things You Can Do to Clean Up.* New York: MasterMedia.

Starke, Linda. 1990. *Signs of Hope: Working Towards Our Common Future.* New York: Oxford University Press.

Steger, Will, and Jon Bowermaster. 1990. *Saving the Earth.* New York: Alfred A. Knopf.

Stivers, Robert L. 1976. *The Sustainable Society.* Philadelphia: Westminster.

Stone, Christopher. 1987. *Earth, and Other Ethics: The Case for Moral Pluralism.* New York: Harper & Row.

Swan, James A. 1990. *Sacred Places: How the Living Earth Seeks Our Friendship.* Santa Fe, N.M.: Bear and Company.

Taylor, Paul W. 1986. *Respect For Nature: A Theory of Environmental Ethics.* Princeton, N.J.: Princeton University Press.

Theobald, Robert. 1987. *The Rapids of Change.* Indianapolis: Knowledge Systems.

Tobias, Michael, ed. 1985. *Deep Ecology.* San Diego: Avant Books.

Todd, John, and George Tukel. 1990. *Reinhabiting Cities and Towns: Designing for Sustainability.* San Francisco: Planet/Drum Foundation.

Todd, Nancy Jack, and John Todd. 1984. *Bioshelters, Ocean Arks, City Farming: Ecology as the Basis of Design.* San Francisco: Sierra Club Books.

Van Andruss, Christopher, et al. 1990. *Home! A Bioregional Reader.* Santa Cruz, Calif.: New Society Publishers.

Van Matre, Steve. 1990. *Earth Education.* Warrenville, Ill.: The Institute for Earth Education.

Wenz, Peter. 1988. *Environmental Justice.* Albany: State University of New York Press.

White, Lynn, Jr. 1967. *"The Historical Roots of Our Ecologic Crisis."* Science, vol. 155, 1203–1207.

Wilkinson, Loren, ed. 1980. *Earthkeeping: Christian Stewardship of Natural Resources.* Grand Rapids, Mich.: Eerdmans.

Williams, Rosalind. 1990. *Notes on the Underground: An Essay on Technology, Society, and the Imagination.* Cambridge, Mass.: MIT Press.

World Resources Institute. 1989. *The Crucial Decade: The 1990s and the Global Environmental Challenge.* Washington, D.C.: World Resources Institute.

Zerzan, John, and Alice Carnes, eds. 1988. *Questioning Technology.* Seattle: Left Bank Distributors.

GLOSSARY

abiotic   Nonliving. Compare *biotic*.

absolute resource scarcity   Situation in which there are not enough actual or affordable supplies of a resource left to meet present or future demand. Compare *relative resource scarcity*.

acclimation   Adjustment to slowly changing new conditions. Compare *threshold effect*.

acid deposition   The falling of acids and acid-forming compounds from the atmosphere to Earth's surface. Acid deposition is commonly known as *acid rain*, a term that refers to only wet deposition of droplets of acids and acid-forming compounds.

acid rain   See *acid deposition*.

acid solution   Any water solution that has more hydrogen ions (H^+) than hydroxide ions (OH^-); any water solution with a pH less than 7. Compare *basic solution, neutral solution*.

active solar heating system   System that uses solar collectors to capture energy from the sun and store it as heat for space heating and heating water. A liquid or air pumped through the collectors transfers the captured heat to a storage system such as an insulated water tank or rock bed. Pumps or fans then distribute the stored heat or hot water throughout a dwelling as needed. Compare *passive solar heating system*.

advanced sewage treatment   Specialized chemical and physical processes that reduce the amount of specific pollutants left in wastewater after primary and secondary sewage treatment. This type of treatment is usually expensive. See also *primary sewage treatment, secondary sewage treatment*.

aerobic organism   Organism that needs oxygen to stay alive. Compare *anaerobic organism*.

aerobic respiration   Complex process that occurs in the cells of most living organisms in which nutrient organic molecules such as glucose ($C_6H_{12}O_6$) combine with oxygen (O_2) and produce carbon dioxide (CO_2), water (H_2O), and energy. Compare *photosynthesis*.

age structure (age distribution)   Percentage of the population, or the number of people of each sex, at each age level in a population.

Agricultural Revolution   Gradual shift from small, mobile hunting-and-gathering bands to settled agricultural communities, where people survived by learning how to breed and raise wild animals and to cultivate wild plants near where they lived. It began 10,000 to 12,000 years ago. Compare *Industrial Revolution*.

agroforestry   Planting trees and crops together.

air pollution   One or more chemicals in high enough concentrations in the air to harm humans, other animals, vegetation, or materials. Excess heat or noise can also be considered forms of air pollution. Such chemicals or physical conditions are called air pollutants. See *primary air pollutant, secondary air pollutant*.

algae   One-celled or many-celled plants that usually carry out photosynthesis in streams, lakes, ponds, oceans, and other surface waters.

algal bloom   Population explosion of algae in surface waters due to an increase in plant nutrients (such as nitrates and phosphates), temperature, or both.

alien species   See *immigrant species*.

alley cropping   Planting of crops in strips with rows of trees or shrubs on each side.

alpha particle   Positively charged matter, consisting of two neutrons and two protons, that is emitted as a form of radioactivity from the nuclei of some radioisotopes. See also *beta particle, gamma rays*.

altitude   Height above sea level. Compare *latitude*.

ambient   Outdoor.

anaerobic organism   Organism that does not need oxygen to stay alive. Compare *aerobic organism*.

ancient forest   Uncut virgin forest or old, secondary forest. See *old-growth forest, secondary forest*.

animal manure   Dung and urine of animals that can be used as a form of organic fertilizer. Compare *green manure*.

animals   Eukaryotic, multicelled organisms such as sponges, jellyfishes, arthropods (insects, shrimp, lobsters), mollusks (snails, clams, oysters, octopuses), fishes, amphibians (frogs, toads, salamanders), reptiles (turtles, lizards, alligators, crocodiles, snakes), birds, mammals (kangaroos, bats, cats, rabbits, elephants, whales, porpoises, monkeys, apes, humans). See *carnivores, herbivores, omnivores*.

annual   Plant that grows, sets seed, and dies in a single year. Compare *perennial*.

aquaculture   Growing and harvesting of fish and shellfish for human use in freshwater ponds, irrigation ditches, and lakes, or in cages or fenced-in areas of coastal lagoons and estuaries. See *fish farming, fish ranching*.

aquatic   Pertaining to water. Compare *terrestrial*.

aquatic ecosystem   Any water-based ecosystem, such as a stream, a pond, a lake, or an ocean.

aquifer   Porous, water-saturated layers of sand, gravel, or bedrock that can yield an economically significant amount of water. See *confined aquifer, unconfined aquifer*.

arable land   Land that can be cultivated to grow crops.

area strip mining   Cutting deep trenches to remove minerals such as coal and phosphate found near the earth's surface in fairly flat terrain. Compare *contour strip mining, open-pit mining*.

arid   Dry. A desert or other area with an arid climate has little precipitation.

artificial reservoir   Human-created body of standing fresh water; often built behind a dam. Compare *lake*.

asthenosphere   Portion of the earth's mantle that is capable of solid flow. See *crust, lithosphere, mantle*.

atmosphere   The whole mass of air surrounding the earth. See *stratosphere, troposphere*.

atomic number   Number of protons in the nucleus of an atom. Compare *mass number*.

atoms   Minute units made of subatomic particles that are the basic building blocks of all chemical elements and thus all matter; the smallest unit of an element that can exist and still have the unique characteristics of that element. Compare *ion, molecule*.

autotroph   See *producer*.

average life expectancy at birth   See *life expectancy*.

bacteria   Prokaryotic, one-celled organisms. Some transmit diseases. Most act as decomposers and get the nutrients they need by breaking down complex organic compounds in the tissues of living or dead organisms into simpler inorganic nutrient compounds.

basic   See *basic solution*.

basic solution   Water solution with more hydroxide ions (OH^-) than hydrogen ions (H^+); water solution with a pH greater than 7. Compare *acid solution, neutral solution*.

beneficiation   Separation of an ore mineral from the waste mineral material (gangue). See *tailings*.

benign tumor   A growth of cells that are reproducing at abnormal rates but remain within the tissue where the growth develops. Compare *cancer*.

beta particle   Swiftly moving electron emitted by the nucleus of a radioactive isotope. See also *alpha particle, gamma rays*.

bioaccumulation   See *biological amplification*.

bioconcentration   Accumulation of a harmful chemical in a particular part of the body. Compare *biological amplification*.

biodegradable pollutant   Material that can be broken down into simpler substances (elements and compounds) by bacteria or other decomposers. Paper and most organic wastes such as animal manure are biodegradable but can take decades to biodegrade in modern landfills. Compare *degradable pollutant, nondegradable pollutant, slowly degradable pollutant*.

biodiversity   See *biological diversity*.

biofuel   Gas or liquid fuel (such as ethyl alcohol) made from plant material (biomass).

biogeochemical cycle   Natural processes that recycle nutrients in various chemical forms from the nonliving environment, to living organisms, and then back to the nonliving environment. Examples are the carbon, oxygen, nitrogen, phosphorus, sulfur, and hydrologic cycles.

biological amplification   Increase in concentration of DDT, PCBs, and other slowly degradable, fat-soluble chemicals in organisms at successively higher trophic levels of a food chain or web.

biological community   See *community*.

biological control   See *biological pest control*.

biological diversity   Variety of different species (*species diversity*), genetic variability among individuals within each species (*genetic diversity*), and variety of ecosystems (*ecological diversity*). Compare *ecological diversity, genetic diversity, species diversity*.

biological evolution   See *evolution*.

biological magnification   See *biological amplification*.

biological oxygen demand (BOD)   Amount of dissolved oxygen needed by aerobic decomposers to break down the organic materials in a given volume of water at a certain temperature over a specified time period.

biological pest control   Control of pest populations by natural predators, parasites, or disease-causing bacteria and viruses (pathogens).

biomass   Organic matter produced by plants and other photosynthetic producers; total dry weight of all living organisms that can be supported at each trophic level in a food chain; dry weight of all organic matter in plants and animals in an ecosystem; plant materials and animal wastes used as fuel.

biome   Terrestrial regions inhabited by certain types of life, especially vegetation. Examples of these vegetational zones are various types of deserts, grasslands, and forests.

bioregion   A unique life-place with its own soils, landforms, watersheds, climates, native plants and animals, and many other distinct natural characteristics.

biosphere   Zone of Earth where life is found. It consists of parts of the atmosphere (the troposphere), hydrosphere (mostly surface water and groundwater), and lithosphere (mostly soil and surface rocks and sediments on the bottoms of oceans and other bodies of water) where life is found. See also *ecosphere*.

biotic   Living. Living organisms make up the biotic parts of ecosystems. Compare *abiotic*.

biotic potential Maximum rate (r_{max}) at which the population of a given species can increase when there are no limits of any sort on its rate of growth. See *environmental resistance*.

birth rate See *crude birth rate*.

bitumen Gooey, black, high-sulfur, heavy oil extracted from tar sand and then upgraded to synthetic fuel oil. See *tar sand*.

breeder nuclear fission reactor Nuclear fission reactor that produces more nuclear fuel than it consumes, by converting nonfissionable uranium-238 into fissionable plutonium-239.

calorie Unit of energy; amount of energy needed to raise the temperature of 1 gram of water 1°C. See also *kilocalorie*.

cancer Group of more than 120 different diseases — one for each type of cell in the human body. Each type of cancer produces a tumor in which cells multiply uncontrollably and invade surrounding tissue. Compare *benign tumor*.

capital goods Tools, machinery, equipment, factory buildings, transportation facilities, and other manufactured items made from natural resources and used to produce and distribute consumer goods and services. Compare *labor, natural resources*.

capitalism See *pure market economic system*.

carbon cycle Cyclic movement of carbon in different chemical forms from the environment, to organisms, and then back to the environment.

carcinogen Chemical, ionizing radiation, and viruses, that cause or promote the growth of a malignant tumor, or cancer, in which cells in a certain type of tissue multiply and invade the surrounding tissue. See *mutagen, teratogen*.

carnivore Animal that feeds on other animals. Compare *herbivore, omnivore*.

carrying capacity (K) Maximum population of a particular species that a given habitat can support over a given period of time. See *consumption overpopulation, people overpopulation*.

cell Smallest living unit of an organism. See *eukaryotic cell, prokaryotic cell*.

cellular aerobic respiration See *aerobic respiration*.

CFCs See *chlorofluorocarbons*.

chain reaction Multiple nuclear fissions taking place within a certain mass of a fissionable isotope that release an enormous amount of energy in a short time.

chemical One of the millions of different elements and compounds found naturally and synthesized by humans. See *compound, element*.

chemical change Interaction between chemicals in which there is a change in the chemical composition of the elements or compounds involved. Compare *physical change*.

chemical reaction See *chemical change*.

chemosynthesis Process in which certain organisms (mostly specialized bacteria) extract inorganic compounds from their environment and convert them into organic nutrient compounds without the presence of sunlight. Compare *photosynthesis*.

chlorinated hydrocarbon Organic compound made up of atoms of carbon, hydrogen, and chlorine. Examples are DDT and PCBs.

chlorofluorocarbons (CFCs) Organic compounds made up of atoms of carbon, chlorine, and fluorine. An example is Freon-12 (CCl_2F_2), used as a refrigerant in refrigerators and air conditioners and in making plastics such as Styrofoam. Gaseous CFCs can deplete the ozone layer when they slowly rise into the stratosphere and their chlorine atoms react with ozone molecules.

chromosome A grouping of various genes and associated proteins in plant and animal cells that carry certain types of genetic information. See *genes*.

circular flow model Model of the general operation of a pure market economy that shows how the factors of production and economic goods flow between household, businesses, and the environment and how money flows between households and businesses that buy economic goods.

civil suit Lawsuit in which an individual plaintiff seeks to collect damages for injuries to health or for economic loss, to have the court issue a permanent injunction against any further wrongful action, or both. Compare *class action suit*.

class action suit Civil lawsuit in which a group files a suit on behalf of a larger number of citizens who allege similar damages but who need not be listed and represented individually. Compare *civil suit*.

clear-cutting Method of timber harvesting in which all trees in a forested area are removed in a single cutting. Compare *seed-tree cutting, selective cutting, shelterwood cutting, whole-tree harvesting*.

climate General pattern of atmospheric or weather conditions, seasonal variations, and weather extremes in a region over a long period — at least 30 years; average weather of an area. Compare *weather*.

climax community See *mature community*.

closed forest Forest where the crowns of trees touch and form a closed canopy during all or part of a year. Compare *open forest*.

coal Solid, combustible mixture of organic compounds with 30% to 98% carbon by weight, mixed with varying amounts of water and small amounts of sulfur and nitrogen. It is formed in several stages as the remains of plants are subjected to heat and pressure over millions of years.

coal gasification Conversion of solid coal to synthetic natural gas (SNG).

coal liquefaction Conversion of solid coal to a liquid hydrocarbon fuel such as synthetic gasoline or methanol.

coastal wetland Land along a coastline, extending inland from an estuary that is covered with salt water all or part of the year. Examples are marshes, bays, lagoons, tidal flats, and mangrove swamps. Compare *inland wetland*.

coastal zone Relatively warm, nutrient-rich, shallow part of the ocean that extends from the high-tide mark on land to the edge of a shelflike extension of continental land masses known as the continental shelf. Compare *open sea*.

coevolution Evolution when two or more species interact and exert selective pressures on one another that can lead each species to undergo various adaptations. See *evolution, natural selection*.

cogeneration Production of two useful forms of energy such as high-temperature heat or steam and electricity from the same fuel source.

commensalism An interaction between organisms of different species in which one type of organism benefits, while the other type is neither helped nor harmed to any great degree. Compare *mutualism*.

commercial extinction Depletion of the population of a wild species used as a resource to a level where it is no longer profitable to harvest the species.

commercial fishing Finding and catching fish for sale. See *poaching*. Compare *sport fishing, subsistence fishing*.

commercial hunting Killing of wild animals for profit from sale of their furs, meat, or other parts. See *poaching*. Compare *sport hunting, subsistence hunting*.

commercial inorganic fertilizer Commercially prepared mixtures of plant nutrients such as nitrates, phosphates, and potassium applied to the soil to restore fertility and increase crop yields. Compare *organic fertilizer*.

common law Large body of legal principles and rules based on past legal decisions; judgemade law. Compare *statutory law*.

common-property resource Resource that is difficult to exclude people from using; each user depletes or degrades the available supply. Most are potentially renewable and are owned by no one. Examples are clean air, fish in parts of the ocean not under the control of a coastal country, migratory birds, gases of the lower atmosphere (troposphere), and the ozone content of the stratosphere. See *tragedy of the commons*. Compare *private-property resource, public-property resource*.

community Populations of all species living and interacting in an area at a particular time.

community development See *ecological succession*.

competition Two or more individual organisms of a single species (*intraspecific competition*), or two or more individuals of different species (*interspecific competition*), attempting to use the same scarce resources in the same ecosystem.

competitive exclusion principle No two species can occupy exactly the same fundamental niche indefinitely in a habitat where there is not enough of a particular resource to meet the needs of both species. See *ecological niche, fundamental niche, realized niche*.

compost Partially decomposed organic plant and animal matter that can be used as a soil conditioner or fertilizer.

compound Combination of atoms, or oppositely charged ions, of two or more different elements held together by attractive forces called chemical bonds. See *inorganic compound, organic compound*. Compare *element*.

concentration Amount of a chemical in a particular volume or weight of air, water, soil, or other medium.

confined aquifer Aquifer between two layers of relatively impermeable Earth materials, such as clay or shale. Compare *unconfined aquifer*.

conifer See *coniferous trees*.

coniferous trees Cone-bearing trees, mostly evergreens, that have needle-shaped or scalelike leaves. They produce wood known commercially as softwood. Compare *deciduous plants*.

conservationists People who believe resources should be used, managed, and protected so they will not be degraded and wasted and will be available to present and future generations.

conservation-tillage farming Crop cultivation in which the soil is disturbed little (*minimum-tillage farming*) or not at all (*no-till farming*) to reduce soil erosion, lower labor costs, and save energy. Compare *conventional-tillage farming*.

constancy Ability of a living system, such as a population, to maintain a certain size. See *homeostasis*. Compare *inertia, resilience*.

consumer Organism that cannot synthesize the organic nutrients it needs and gets its organic nutrients by feeding on the tissues of producers or of other consumers; generally divided into *primary consumers* (herbivores), *secondary consumers* (carnivores), *tertiary and higher consumers*, omnivores, and *detritivores* (decomposers and detritus feeders). In economics, one who uses economic goods.

consumption overpopulation Situation in which people in a given area use resources at such a high rate and without sufficient pollution prevention and control that significant pollution, resource depletion, and environmental degradation occur. Compare *people overpopulation*.

consumptive water use See *water consumption*.

continental shelf Submerged part of a continent.

contour farming Plowing and planting across the changing slope of land, rather than in straight lines, to help retain water and reduce soil erosion.

contour strip mining Cutting a series of shelves or terraces along the side of a hill or mountain to remove a mineral such as coal from a deposit found near the earth's surface. Compare *area strip mining, open-pit surface mining*.

contraceptive Physical, chemical, or biological method used to prevent pregnancy.

conventional-tillage farming Making a planting surface by plowing land, disking it several times to break up the soil, and then smoothing the surface. Compare *conservation-tillage farming*.

convergent plate boundary Area where Earth's lithospheric plates are pushed together. See *subduction zone*. Compare *divergent plate boundary, transform fault*.

core Inner zone of the earth. It consists of a solid *inner core* and a liquid *outer core*. Compare *crust, mantle*.

cost-benefit analysis Estimates and comparison of short-term and long-term costs (losses) and benefits (gains) from an economic decision. If the estimated benefits exceed the estimated costs, the decision to buy an economic good or provide a public good is considered worthwhile.

critical mass Amount of fissionable nuclei needed to sustain a branching nuclear fission chain reaction.

critical mineral A mineral necessary to the economy of a country. Compare *strategic mineral*.

crop rotation Planting a field, or an area of a field, with different crops from year to year to reduce depletion of soil nutrients. A plant such as corn, tobacco, or cotton, which removes large amounts of nitrogen from the soil, is planted one year. The next year a legume such as soybeans, which add nitrogen to the soil, is planted.

crown fire Extremely hot forest fire that burns ground vegetation and tree tops. Compare *ground fire, surface fire*.

crude birth rate Annual number of live births per 1,000 persons in the population of a geographical area at the midpoint of a given year. Compare *crude death rate*.

crude death rate Annual number of deaths per 1,000 persons in the population of a geographical area at the midpoint of a given year. Compare *crude birth rate*.

crude oil Gooey liquid consisting mostly of hydrocarbon compounds and small amounts of compounds containing oxygen, sulfur, and nitrogen. Extracted from underground accumulations, it is sent to oil refineries, where it is converted into heating oil, diesel fuel, gasoline, tar, and other materials.

crust Solid outer zone of the earth. It consists of *oceanic crust* and *continental crust*. Compare *core, mantle*.

cultural eutrophication Overnourishment of aquatic ecosystems with plant nutrients (mostly nitrates and phosphates) because of human activities such as agriculture, urbanization, and discharges from industrial plants and sewage treatment plants. See *eutrophication*.

DDT Dichlorodiphenyltrichloroethane, a chlorinated hydrocarbon that has been widely used as a pesticide.

death rate See *crude death rate*.

debt-for-nature swap Agreement in which a certain amount of foreign debt is cancelled in exchange for local currency investments that will improve natural resource management or protect certain areas from harmful development in the debtor country.

deciduous plants Trees, such as oaks and maples, and other plants that survive during dry seasons or cold seasons by shedding their leaves. Compare *coniferous trees, succulent plants*.

decomposer Organism that digests parts of dead organisms and cast-off fragments and wastes of living organisms by breaking down the complex organic molecules in those materials into simpler inorganic compounds and absorbing the soluble nutrients. Most of these chemicals are returned to the soil and water for reuse by producers. Decomposers consist of various bacteria and fungi. Compare *consumer, detritivore, producer*.

deep ecology See *sustainable-Earth worldview*.

defendant The individual, group of individuals, corporation, or government agency being charged in a lawsuit. Compare *plaintiff*.

deforestation Removal of trees from a forested area without adequate replanting.

degradable pollutant Potentially polluting chemical that is broken down completely or reduced to acceptable levels by natural physical, chemical, and biological processes. Compare *biodegradable pollutant, nondegradable pollutant, slowly degradable pollutant*.

degree of urbanization Percentage of the population in the world, or a country, living in areas with a population of more than 2,500 people (significantly more in some countries). Compare *urban growth*.

delta Buildup deposit of river-borne sediments at the mouth of a river.

demographic transition Hypothesis that countries, as they become industrialized, have declines in death rates followed by declines in birth rates.

demography Study of characteristics and changes in the size and structure of the human population in the world or other geographical area.

depletion time How long it takes to use a certain fraction — usually 80% — of the known or estimated supply of a nonrenewable resource at an assumed rate of use. Finding and extracting the remaining 20% usually costs more than it is worth.

desalination Purification of salt water or brackish (slightly salty) water by removing dissolved salts.

desert Biome where evaporation exceeds precipitation and the average amount of precipitation is less than 25 centimeters (10 inches) a year. Such areas have little vegetation or have widely spaced, mostly low vegetation. Compare *forest, grassland*.

desertification Conversion of rangeland, rain-fed cropland, or irrigated cropland to desertlike land, with a drop in agricultural productivity of 10% or more. It is usually caused by a combination of overgrazing, soil erosion, prolonged drought, and climate change.

desirability quotient A number expressing the results of risk-benefit analysis by dividing the estimate of the benefits to society of using a particular product or technology by its estimated risks. See *risk-benefit analysis*. Compare *cost-benefit analysis*.

detritivore Consumer organism that feeds on detritus, parts of dead organisms and cast-off fragments and wastes of living organisms. The two principal types are *detritus feeders* and *decomposers*.

detritus Parts of dead organisms and cast-off fragments and wastes of living organisms.

detritus feeder Organism that extracts nutrients from fragments of dead organisms and cast-off parts and organic wastes of living organisms. Examples are earthworms, termites, and crabs. Compare *decomposer*.

deuterium (D: hydrogen-2) Isotope of the element hydrogen, with a nucleus containing one proton and one neutron, and a mass number of 2. Compare *tritium*.

developed country See *more developed country*.

dieback Sharp reduction in the population of a species when its numbers exceed the carrying capacity of its habitat. See *carrying capacity, consumption overpopulation, overshoot, people overpopulation*.

differential reproduction Ability of individuals with adaptive genetic traits to produce more living offspring than individuals without such traits. See also *natural selection*.

discount rate How much economic value a resource will have in the future compared with its present value.

dissolved oxygen (DO) content (level) Amount of oxygen gas (O_2) dissolved in a given volume of water at a particular temperature and pressure, often expressed as a concentration in parts of oxygen per million parts of water.

divergent plate boundary Area where Earth's lithospheric plates move apart in opposite directions. Compare *convergent plate boundary, transform fault*.

diversity Variety. See *biological diversity*.

DNA (deoxyribonucleic acid) Large molecules that carry genetic information in living organisms. They are found in the cells of organisms.

doubling time The time it takes (usually in years) for the quantity of something growing exponentially to double. It can be calculated by dividing the annual percentage growth rate into 70. See *rule of 70*.

drainage basin See *watershed*.

dredge spoils Materials scraped from the bottoms of harbors and streams to maintain shipping channels. They are often contaminated with high levels of toxic substances that have settled out of the water. See *dredging*.

dredging Type of surface mining, in which chain buckets and draglines scrape up sand, gravel, and other surface deposits covered with water. It is also used to remove sediment from streams and harbors to maintain shipping channels. See *dredge spoils*.

drift-net fishing Catching fish in huge nets that drift in the water.

drip irrigation Using small tubes or pipes to deliver small amounts of irrigation water to the roots of plants.

drought Condition in which an area does not get enough water because of lower than normal precipitation, higher than normal temperatures that increase evaporation, or both.

dust dome Dome of heated air that surrounds an urban area and traps and keeps pollutants, especially particulate matter in suspension. See also *urban heat island*.

Earth capital Earth's natural resources and processes that sustain us and other species.

earthquake Shaking of the ground resulting from the fracturing and displacement of rock, producing a fault, or from subsequent movement along the fault.

ecological diversity The variety of forests, deserts, grasslands, oceans, streams, lakes, and other biological communities interacting with one another and with their nonliving environment. See *biological diversity*. Compare *genetic diversity, species diversity*.

ecological niche Total way of life or role of a species in an ecosystem. It includes all physical, chemical, and biological conditions a species needs to live and reproduce in an ecosystem. See *fundamental niche, realized niche*.

ecological succession Process in which communities of plant and animal species in a particular area are replaced over time by a series of different and usually more complex communities. See *primary ecological succession, secondary ecological succession*.

ecology Study of the interactions of living organisms with one another and with their nonliving environment of matter and energy; study of the structure and functions of nature.

economic decision Choosing what to do with scarce resources; deciding what goods and services to produce, how to produce them, how much to produce, and how to distribute them to people.

economic depletion Exhaustion of 80% of the estimated supply of a nonrenewable resource. Finding, extracting, and processing the remaining 20% usually costs more than it is worth; may also apply to the depletion of a potentially renewable resource, such as a species of fish or trees.

economic good Any service or material item that gives people satisfaction.

economic growth Increase in the real value of all final goods and services produced by an economy; an increase in real GNP. Compare *productivity*.

economic needs Types and amounts of certain economic goods — food, clothing, water, oxygen, shelter — that each of us must have to survive and to stay healthy. Compare *economic wants*. See also *poverty*.

economic resources Natural resources, capital goods, and labor used in an economy to produce material goods and services. See *capital goods, labor, natural resources*.

economics Study of how individuals and groups make decisions about what to do with economic resources to meet their needs and wants.

economic system Method that a group of people uses to choose *what* goods and services to produce, *how* to produce them, *how much* to produce, and *how* to distribute them to people. See *mixed economic system, pure command economic system, pure market economic system, traditional economic system*.

economic wants Economic goods that go beyond our basic economic needs. These wants are influenced by the customs and conventions of the society we live in and by our level of affluence. Compare *economic needs*.

economy System of production, distribution, and consumption of economic goods.

ecosphere Earth's collection of living organisms (found in the biosphere) interacting with one another and their nonliving environment (energy and matter) throughout the world; all of Earth's ecosystems. See also *biosphere*.

ecosystem Community of different species interacting with one another and with the chemical and physical factors making up its nonliving environment.

efficiency Measure of how much output of energy or of a product is produced by a certain input of energy, materials, or labor. See *energy efficiency*.

electromagnetic radiation Forms of kinetic energy travelling as electromagnetic waves. Examples are radio waves, TV waves, microwaves, infrared radiation, visible light, ultraviolet radiation, X rays, and gamma rays. Compare *ionizing radiation, nonionizing radiation*.

electron Tiny particle moving around outside the nucleus of an atom. Each electron has one unit of negative charge (−) and almost no mass.

element Chemical, such as hydrogen (H), iron (Fe), sodium (Na), carbon (C), nitrogen (N), or oxygen (O), whose distinctly different atoms serve as the basic building blocks of all matter. There are 92 naturally occurring elements. Another 15 have been made in laboratories. Two or more elements combine to form compounds that make up most of the world's matter. Compare *compound*.

El Niño–Southern Oscillation (ENSO)
Recurrent fluctuation in the atmospheric pressures and surface water temperature in the tropical Pacific Ocean.

emigration Migration of people out of one country or area to take up permanent residence in another country or area. Compare *immigration*.

endangered species Wild species with so few individual survivors that the species could soon become extinct in all or most of its natural range. Compare *threatened species*.

energy Capacity to do work by performing mechanical, physical, chemical, or electrical tasks or to cause a heat transfer between two objects at different temperatures.

energy conservation Reduction or elimination of unnecessary energy use and waste. See *energy efficiency*.

energy efficiency Percentage of the total energy input that does useful work and is not converted into low-quality, usually useless, heat in an energy conversion system or process. See *net useful energy*.

energy quality Ability of a form of energy to do useful work. High-temperature heat and the chemical energy in fossil fuels and nuclear fuels is concentrated high-quality energy. Low-quality energy, such as low-temperature heat, is dispersed or diluted and cannot do much useful work. See *high-quality energy, low-quality energy*.

enhanced oil recovery Removal of some of the heavy oil left in an oil well after primary and secondary recovery. Compare *primary oil recovery, secondary oil recovery*.

entropy A measure of disorder or randomness of a system. The higher the entropy of a system, the greater its disorder. See *high-quality energy, high-quality matter, low-quality energy, low-quality matter*.

environment All external conditions and factors, living and nonliving (chemicals and energy), that affect an organism or other specified system during its lifetime.

environmental degradation Depletion or destruction of a potentially renewable resource such as soil, grassland, forest, or wildlife by using it at a faster rate than it is naturally replenished. If such use continues, the resource can become nonrenewable on a human time scale or nonexistent (extinct). See also *sustainable yield*.

environmentalists People who are primarily concerned with preventing pollution and degradation of the air, water, soil, and Earth's biodiversity. See *conservationists*.

environmental resistance All the limiting factors jointly acting to limit the growth of a population. See *biotic potential, limiting factor*.

environmental science Study of how we and other species interact with each other and with the nonliving environment of matter and energy. It is a holistic science that uses and integrates knowledge from physics, chemistry, biology (especially ecology), geology, resource technology and engineering, resource conservation and management, demography (the study of population dynamics), economics, politics, and ethics.

EPA Environmental Protection Agency. It is responsible for managing federal efforts in the United States to control air and water pollution, radiation and pesticide hazards, environmental research, and solid waste disposal.

epidemiology Study of the patterns of disease or other harmful effects from toxic exposure within defined groups of people to find out why some people get sick and some do not.

epiphytes Plants that use their roots to attach themselves to branches high in trees, especially in tropical forests.

erosion Process or group of processes by which earth materials, loose or consolidated, are dissolved, loosened, and worn away, removed from one place and deposited in another. See *weathering*.

estuarine zone Area near the coastline that consists of estuaries and coastal saltwater wetlands, extending to the edge of the continental shelf.

estuary Partially enclosed coastal area at the mouth of a river where its fresh water, carrying fertile silt and runoff from the land, mixes with salty seawater.

ethics What we believe to be right or wrong behavior.

eukaryotic cell Cell containing a *nucleus*, a region of genetic material surrounded by a membrane. Membranes also enclose several of the other internal parts found in a eukaryotic cell. Compare *prokaryotic cell*.

eutrophication Physical, chemical, and biological changes that take place after a lake, an estuary, or a slow-flowing stream receives inputs of plant nutrients — mostly nitrates and phosphates — from natural erosion and runoff from the surrounding land basin. See also *cultural eutrophication*.

eutrophic lake Lake with a large or excessive supply of plant nutrients — mostly nitrates and phosphates. Compare *mesotrophic lake, oligotrophic lake*.

evaporation Physical change in which a liquid changes into a vapor or gas.

even-aged management Method of forest management in which trees, usually of a single species in a given stand, are maintained at about the same age and size and are harvested all at once so a new stand may grow. Compare *uneven-aged management*.

even-aged stand Forest area where all trees are about the same age. Usually, such stands contain trees of only one or two species. See *even-aged management, tree farm*. Compare *uneven-aged management, uneven-aged stand*.

evergreen plants Plants that keep some of their leaves or needles throughout the year. Examples are ferns, and cone-bearing trees (conifers) such as firs, spruces, pines, redwoods, and sequoias. Compare *deciduous plants, succulent plants*.

evolution Changes in the genetic composition (gene pool) of a population exposed to new environmental conditions as a result of differential reproduction. Evolution can lead to the splitting of a single species into two or more different species. See also *differential reproduction, natural selection, speciation*.

exhaustible resources See *nonrenewable resources*.

exponential growth Growth in which some quantity, such as population size or economic output, increases by a fixed percentage of the whole in a given time period; when the increase in quantity over time is plotted, this type of growth yields a curve shaped like the letter *J*. Compare *linear growth*.

external benefit Beneficial social effect of producing and using an economic good that is not included in the market price of the good. Compare *external cost, internal cost, true cost*.

external cost Harmful social effect of producing and using an economic good that is not included in the market price of the good. Compare *external benefit, internal cost, true cost*.

externalities Social benefits ("goods") and social costs ("bads") not included in the market price of an economic good. See *external benefit, external cost*. Compare *internal cost, true cost*.

extinction Complete disappearance of a species from the earth. This happens when a species cannot adapt and successfully reproduce under new environmental conditions or evolves into one or more new species. See also *endangered species, threatened species*. Compare *speciation*.

factors of production See *economic resources*.

family planning Providing information, clinical services, and contraceptives to help individuals or couples choose the number and spacing of children they want to have.

famine Widespread malnutrition and starvation in a particular area because of a shortage of food, usually caused by drought, war, flood, earthquake, or other catastrophic event that disrupts food production and distribution.

feedback loop Circuit of sensing, evaluating, and reacting to changes in environmental conditions as a result of information fed back into a system. See *information feedback, negative feedback, positive feedback*.

feedlot Confined outdoor or indoor space used to raise hundreds to thousands of domesticated livestock. Compare *rangeland*.

fertilizer Substance that adds inorganic or organic plant nutrients to soil and improves its ability to grow crops, trees, or other vegetation. See *commercial inorganic fertilizer, organic fertilizer*.

first law of ecology We can never do merely one thing. Any intrusion into nature has numerous effects, many of which are unpredictable.

first law of energy See *first law of thermodynamics*.

first law of thermodynamics (energy) In any physical or chemical change, no detectable amount of energy is created or destroyed, but in these processes, energy can be changed from one form to another; you can't get more energy out of something than you put in; in terms of energy quantity, you can't get something for nothing (there is no free lunch). This law does not apply to nuclear changes, where energy can be produced from small amounts of matter. See also *second law of thermodynamics*.

fishery Concentrations of particular aquatic species suitable for commercial harvesting in a given ocean area or inland body of water.

fish farming Form of aquaculture in which fish are cultivated in a controlled pond or other environment and harvested when they reach the desired size. See also *fish ranching*.

fish ranching Form of aquaculture in which members of a fish species such as salmon are held in captivity for the first few years of their lives, released, and then harvested as adults when they return from the ocean to their freshwater birthplace to spawn. See also *fish farming*.

fissionable isotope Isotope that can split apart when hit by a neutron at the right speed and thus undergo nuclear fission. Examples are uranium-235 and plutonium-239.

floodplain Flat valley floor next to a stream channel. For legal purposes, the term is often applied to any low area that has the potential for flooding, including certain coastal areas.

flyway Generally fixed route along which waterfowl migrate from one area to another at certain seasons of the year.

food additive A natural or synthetic chemical deliberately added to processed foods to retard spoilage, to provide missing amino acids and vitamins, or to enhance flavor, color, and texture.

food chain Series of organisms, each eating or decomposing the preceding one. Compare *food web*.

food web Complex network of many interconnected food chains and feeding relationships. Compare *food chain*.

forage Vegetation eaten by animals, especially grazing and browsing animals.

forest Biome with enough average annual precipitation (at least 76 centimeters, or 30 inches) to support growth of various species of trees and smaller forms of vegetation. See also *closed forest, open forest*. Compare *desert, grassland*.

fossil fuel Products of partial or complete decomposition of plants and animals that occur as crude oil, coal, natural gas, or heavy oils as a result of exposure to heat and pressure in Earth's crust over millions of years. See *coal, crude oil, natural gas*.

Freons See *chlorofluorocarbons*.

frontier worldview See *throwaway worldview*.

fundamental niche The full potential range of the physical, chemical, and biological factors a species could use, if there is no competition from other species. See *ecological niche*. Compare *realized niche*.

fungi Eukaryotic, mostly multicelled organisms such as mushrooms, molds, and yeasts. They are decomposers that get the nutrients they need by secreting enzymes that break down the organic matter in the tissue of other living or dead organisms. Then they absorb the resulting nutrients.

fungicide Chemical that kills fungi.

Gaia hypothesis Proposal that Earth is alive and can be considered a system that operates and changes by feedbacks of information between its living and nonliving components.

game species Type of wild animal that people hunt or fish for sport and recreation, and sometimes for food.

gamma rays A form of ionizing, electromagnetic radiation with a high energy content emitted by some radioisotopes. They readily penetrate body tissues.

gangue Waste or undesired material in an ore. See *ore*.

gasohol Vehicle fuel consisting of a mixture of gasoline and ethyl or methyl alcohol—typically 10% to 23% ethanol or methanol by volume.

gene pool All genetic (hereditary) information contained in a reproducing population of a particular species.

generalists See *generalist species*.

generalist species Species with a broad ecological niche. They can live in many different places, eat a variety of foods, and tolerate a wide range of environmental conditions. Examples are flies, cockroaches, mice, rats, and human beings. Compare *specialist species*.

genes Segments of various DNA molecules that control hereditary characteristics in organisms.

genetic adaptation Changes in the genetic makeup of organisms of a species that allow the species to reproduce and gain a competitive advantage under changed environmental conditions. See *differential reproduction, evolution, natural selection*.

genetic diversity Variability in the genetic makeup among individuals within a single species. See *biodiversity*. Compare *ecological diversity, species diversity*.

geosphere Earth's interior core, mantle, and crust (containing soil and rock). Compare *atmosphere, biosphere, ecosphere, hydrosphere, lithosphere*.

geothermal energy Heat transferred from the earth's interior to underground concentrations of dry steam (steam with no water droplets), wet steam (a mixture of steam and water droplets), or hot water trapped in fractured or porous rock.

glacier A flowing body of ice, formed in a region where snowfall exceeds melting.

GNP See *gross national product*.

grassland Biome found in regions where moderate annual average precipitation (25 to 76 centimeters, or 10 to 30 inches) is enough to support the growth of grass and small plants but not enough to support large stands of trees. Compare *desert, forest*.

greenhouse effect A natural effect that traps heat in the atmosphere (troposphere) near Earth's surface. Some of the heat flowing back toward space from Earth's surface is absorbed by water vapor, carbon dioxide, ozone, and several other gases in the atmosphere and then reradiated back toward the earth's surface. If the atmospheric concentrations of these greenhouse gases rise, the average temperature of the lower atmosphere will gradually increase.

greenhouse gases Gases in Earth's lower atmosphere (troposphere) that cause the greenhouse effect. Examples are carbon dioxide, chlorofluorocarbons, ozone, methane, water vapor, and nitrous oxide.

green manure Freshly cut or still-growing green vegetation that is plowed into the soil to increase the organic matter and humus available to support crop growth. Compare *animal manure*.

green revolution Popular term for introduction of scientifically bred or selected varieties of grain (rice, wheat, maize) that, with high enough inputs of fertilizer and water, can greatly increase crop yields.

gross national product (GNP) Total market value in current dollars of all goods and services produced by an economy for final use during a year. Compare *per capita GNP, per capita real NEW, real GNP*.

ground fire Fire that burns decayed leaves or peat deep below the ground surface. Compare *crown fire, surface fire*.

groundwater Water that sinks into the soil and is stored in slowly flowing and slowly renewed underground reservoirs called aquifers; underground water in the zone of saturation, below the water table. See *confined aquifer, unconfined aquifer*. Compare *runoff, surface water*.

growth rate (r) Increase in the size of a population per unit of time (such as a year).

gully erosion Severe soil erosion caused when high-velocity water flow removes enough soil to form large ditches or gullies. Compare *rill erosion, sheet erosion*.

gully reclamation Restoring land suffering from gully erosion by seeding gullies with quick-growing plants, building small dams to collect silt and gradually fill in the channels, and building channels to divert water from the gully.

habitat Place or type of place where an organism or a population of organisms lives. Compare *niche*.

hardwood Tree species with wood that has a high density (mass per unit of volume) and that is hard to saw, plane, or carve. Compare *softwood*.

hazard Something that can cause injury, disease, economic loss, or environmental damage.

hazardous substance Chemical that can cause harm because it is flammable or explosive, or that can irritate or damage the skin or lungs (such as strong acidic or alkaline substances) or cause allergic reactions of the immune system (allergens).

hazardous waste Any solid, liquid, or containerized gas that can catch fire easily, is corrosive to skin tissue or metals, is unstable and can explode or release toxic fumes, or has harmful concentrations of one or more toxic materials that can leach out. See also *toxic waste*.

heat Total kinetic energy of all the randomly moving atoms, ions, or molecules within a given substance, excluding the overall motion of the whole object. This form of kinetic energy flows from one body to another when there is a temperature difference between the two bodies. Heat always flows spontaneously from a hot sample of matter to a colder sample of matter. This is one way to state the second law of thermodynamics. Compare *temperature*.

heavy oil Black, high-sulfur, tarlike oil found in deposits of crude oil, tar sands, and oil shale.

herbicide Chemical that kills a plant or inhibits its growth.

herbivore Plant-eating organism. Examples are deer, sheep, grasshoppers, and zooplankton. Compare *carnivore, omnivore*.

heterotroph See *consumer*.

high-quality energy Energy that is organized or concentrated (low entropy) and has great ability to perform useful work. Examples are high-temperature heat and the energy in electricity, coal, oil, gasoline, sunlight, and nuclei of uranium-235. Compare *low-quality energy*.

high-quality matter Matter that is organized (low entropy), concentrated, and contains a high concentration of a useful resource. Compare *low-quality matter*.

homeostasis A dynamic steady state in which internal processes change in response to changes in external conditions to maintain constant internal conditions. See *constancy, inertia, resilience*.

host Plant or animal upon which a parasite feeds.

humification Process in which organic matter in the upper soil layers is reduced to finely divided pieces of humus or partially decomposed organic matter.

humus Slightly soluble residue of undigested or partially decomposed organic material in topsoil. This material helps retain water and water-soluble nutrients, which can be taken up by plant roots. See *humification*.

hunter-gatherers People who get their food by gathering edible wild plants and other materials and by hunting wild animals and fish.

hydrocarbon Organic compound of hydrogen and carbon atoms.

hydroelectric power plant Structure in which the energy of falling or flowing water spins a turbine generator to produce electricity.

hydrologic cycle Biogeochemical cycle that collects, purifies, and distributes the earth's fixed supply of water from the environment, to living organisms, and back to the environment.

hydropower Electrical energy produced by falling or flowing water. See *hydroelectric power plant*.

hydrosphere Earth's liquid water (oceans, lakes and other bodies of surface water, and underground water), Earth's frozen water (polar ice caps, floating ice caps, and ice in soil known as permafrost), and small amounts of water vapor in the atmosphere.

identified resources Deposits of a particular mineral-bearing material of which the location, quantity, and quality are known or have been estimated from direct geological evidence and measurements. Compare *total resources, undiscovered resources*.

igneous rock Rock formed when molten rock material (magma) wells up from Earth's interior, cools, and solidifies into rock masses called igneous intrusions. Compare *metamorphic rock, sedimentary rock*. See *rock cycle*.

immature community Community at an early stage of ecological succession. It usually has a low number of species and ecological niches, and cannot capture and use energy and cycle critical nutrients as efficiently as more complex, mature ecosystems. Compare *mature community*.

immigrant species Species that migrate into an ecosystem or that are deliberately or accidently introduced into an ecosystem by humans. Some of these species are beneficial, while others can take over and eliminate many native species. Compare *indicator species, keystone species, native species*.

immigration Migration of people into a country or area to take up permanent residence. Compare *emigration*.

indicator species Species that serve as early warnings that a community or an ecosystem is being degraded. Compare *immigrant species, keystone species, native species*.

industrialized agriculture Using large inputs of energy from fossil fuels (especially oil and natural gas), water, fertilizers, and pesticides to produce large quantities of crops and livestock for domestic and foreign sale. Compare *subsistence agriculture*.

Industrial Revolution Uses of new sources of energy from fossil fuels and later nuclear fuels and use of new technologies to grow food and manufacture products.

industrial smog Type of air pollution consisting mostly of a mixture of sulfur dioxide, suspended droplets of sulfuric acid formed from some of the sulfur dioxide, and a variety of suspended solid particles. Compare *photochemical smog*.

inertia Ability of a living system to resist being disturbed or altered. Compare *constancy, resilience*.

infant mortality rate Number of babies out of every 1,000 born each year that die before their first birthday.

infiltration Downward movement of water through soil.

information feedback Process by which information is fed back into a system, causing it to change. See *negative feedback, positive feedback*.

inland wetland Land away from the coast, such as a swamp, marsh, or bog, that is covered all or part of the year with fresh water. Compare *coastal wetland*.

inorganic compound Any compound not classified as an organic compound. Compare *organic compound*.

inorganic fertilizer See *commercial inorganic fertilizer*.

input pollution control See *pollution prevention*.

insecticide Chemical that kills insects.

intangible resource See *nonmaterial resource*.

integrated pest management (IPM) Combined use of biological, chemical, and cultivation methods in proper sequence and timing to keep the size of a pest population below the size that causes economically unacceptable loss of a crop or livestock animal.

intercropping Growing two or more different crops at the same time on a plot. For example, a carbohydrate-rich grain that depletes soil nitrogen and a protein-rich legume that adds nitrogen to the soil may be intercropped. Compare *monoculture, polyculture, polyvarietal cultivation*.

intermediate goods See *capital goods*.

internal cost Direct cost paid by the producer and the buyer of an economic good. Compare *external cost*.

interplanting Simultaneously growing a variety of crops on the same plot. See *agroforestry, intercropping, polyculture, polyvarietal cultivation*.

interspecific competition Members of two or more species trying to use the same limited resources in an ecosystem. See *competition, competitive exclusion principle, intraspecific competition*.

intraspecific competition Two or more individual organisms of a single species trying to use the same limited resources in an ecosystem. See *competition, interspecific competition*.

inversion See *thermal inversion*.

invertebrates Animals that have no backbones. Compare *vertebrates*.

ion Atom or group of atoms with one or more positive (+) or negative (−) electrical charges. Compare *atom, molecule*.

ionizing radiation Fast-moving alpha or beta particles or high-energy radiation (gamma rays) emitted by radioisotopes. They have enough energy to dislodge one or more electrons from atoms they hit, forming charged ions in tissue that can react with and damage living tissue.

isotopes Two or more forms of a chemical element that have the same number of protons but different mass numbers due to different numbers of neutrons in their nuclei.

J-shaped curve Curve with a shape similar to that of the letter *J* that represents exponential growth.

kerogen Solid, waxy mixture of hydrocarbons found in oil shale rock. When the rock is heated to high temperatures, the kerogen is vaporized. The vapor is condensed and purified and then sent to a refinery to produce gasoline, heating oil, and other products. See also *oil shale, shale oil*.

keystone species Species that play roles affecting many other organisms in an ecosystem. Compare *immigrant species, indicator species, native species*.

kilocalorie (kcal) Unit of energy equal to 1,000 calories. See *calorie*.

kilowatt (kw) Unit of electrical power equal to 1,000 watts. See *watt*.

kinetic energy Energy that matter has because of its motion and mass. Compare *potential energy*.

K-strategists Species that produce a few, often fairly large, offspring but invest a great deal of time and energy to ensure that most of the offspring will reach reproductive age. Compare *r-strategists*.

kwashiorkor Type of malnutrition that occurs in infants and very young children when they are weaned from mother's milk to a starchy diet low in protein. See also *marasmus*.

labor Physical and mental talents of people used to produce, distribute, and sell an economic good. Labor includes entrepreneurs, who assume the risk and responsibility of combining the resources of land, capital goods, and workers who produce an economic good. Compare *capital goods, natural resources*.

lake Large natural body of standing fresh water formed when water from precipitation, land runoff, or groundwater flow fills a depression in the earth created by glaciation, earth movement, volcanic activity, or a giant meteorite. See *eutrophic lake, mesotrophic lake, oligotrophic lake*. Compare *reservoir*.

landfill See *sanitary landfill*.

land-use planning Process for deciding the best present and future use of each parcel of land in an area.

latitude Distance from the equator. Compare *altitude*.

lava Magma that has been extruded onto Earth's surface; also a general name for igneous rocks that form from it.

law of conservation of energy See *first law of thermodynamics*.

law of conservation of matter In any physical or chemical change, matter is neither created nor destroyed, but merely changed from one form to another; in physical and chemical changes, existing atoms are rearranged into either different spatial patterns (physical changes) or different combinations (chemical changes).

law of conservation of matter and energy In any nuclear change, the total amount of matter and energy involved remains the same. Compare *law of conservation of energy, law of conservation of matter*.

law of energy degradation See *second law of thermodynamics*.

law of pollution prevention If you don't put something into the environment, it isn't there.

law of tolerance The existence, abundance, and distribution of a species in an ecosystem are determined by whether the levels of one or more physical or chemical factors fall within the range tolerated by the species. See *threshold effect, tolerance*.

LD₅₀ See *median lethal dose*.

LDC See *less developed country*.

leaching Process in which various chemicals in upper layers of soil are dissolved and carried to lower layers, and in some cases to groundwater.

less developed country (LDC) Country that has low to moderate industrialization and low to moderate GNP per person. Most are located in the

Southern Hemisphere in Africa, Asia, and Latin America. Compare *more developed country*.

lethal dose Amount of a toxic material per unit of body weight of the test animals that kills all of the test population in a certain time. See *median lethal dose*.

life-cycle cost Initial cost plus lifetime operating costs of an economic good.

life expectancy Average number of years a newborn infant can be expected to live.

limiting factor Single factor that limits the growth, abundance, or distribution of the population of a species in an ecosystem. See *limiting factor principle*.

limiting factor principle Too much or too little of any abiotic factor can limit or prevent growth of a population of a species in an ecosystem, even if all other factors are at or near the optimum range of tolerance for the species.

linear growth Growth in which a quantity increases by some fixed amount during each unit of time. Compare *exponential growth*.

liquefied natural gas (LNG) Natural gas converted to liquid form by cooling to a very low temperature.

liquefied petroleum gas (LPG) Mixture of liquefied propane and butane gas removed from natural gas.

lithosphere Outer shell of the earth, composed of the crust and the rigid, outermost part of the mantle outside of the asthenosphere; material found in Earth's plates. See *crust, geosphere, mantle, plates, plate tectonics*.

loams Soils containing a mixture of clay, sand, silt, and humus. Good for growing most crops.

low-quality energy Energy that is disorganized or dispersed (high entropy) and has little ability to do useful work. An example is low-temperature heat. Compare *high-quality energy*.

low-quality matter Matter that is disorganized (high entropy), dilute or dispersed, or contains a low concentration of a useful resource. Compare *high-quality matter*.

LPG See *liquefied petroleum gas*.

macronutrient Element that a plant or an animal needs in large amounts to stay alive and healthy. Examples are carbon, oxygen, hydrogen, nitrogen, phosphorus, sulfur, calcium, magnesium, and potassium. Compare *micronutrient*.

magma Molten rock below the earth's surface.

magnitude Measure of the amount of energy released in an earthquake; usually reported in terms of the Richter scale.

malignant tumor See *cancer*.

malnutrition Faulty nutrition. Caused by a diet that does not supply an individual with enough proteins, essential fats, vitamins, minerals, and other nutrients needed for good health. See *kwashiorkor, marasmus*. Compare *overnutrition, undernutrition*.

mantle Zone of the earth's interior between its core and its crust. Compare *core, crust*. See *lithosphere*.

manure See *animal manure, green manure*.

marasmus Nutritional-deficiency disease caused by a diet that does not have enough calories and protein to maintain good health. See *kwashiorkor, malnutrition*.

market equilibrium State in which sellers and buyers of an economic good agree on the quantity to be produced and the price to be paid.

mass The amount of material in an object.

mass number Sum of the number of neutrons and the number of protons in the nucleus of an atom. It gives the approximate mass of that atom. Compare *atomic number*.

material resource A resource whose quantity can be measured and whose supply is limited. Examples are oil and iron. Compare *nonmaterial resource*.

matter Anything that has mass (the amount of material in an object) and takes up space. On Earth, where gravity is present, we weigh an object to determine its mass.

matter quality Measure of how useful a matter resource is based on its availability and concentration. See *high-quality matter, low-quality matter*.

matter-recycling society Society that emphasizes recycling the maximum amount of all resources that can be recycled. The goal is to allow economic growth to continue without depleting matter resources and without producing excessive pollution and environmental degradation. Compare *sustainable-Earth society, throwaway society*.

mature community Fairly stable, self-sustaining community in an advanced stage of ecological succession. It usually has a diverse array of species and ecological niches, and captures and uses energy and cycles critical chemicals more efficiently than simpler, immature communities. Compare *immature community*.

maximum sustainable yield See *sustainable yield*.

MDC See *more developed country*.

median lethal dose (LD$_{50}$) Amount of a toxic material per unit of body weight of test animals that kills half the test population in a certain time. Compare *lethal dose*.

meltdown The melting of the core of a nuclear reactor.

mesotrophic lake Lake with a moderate supply of plant nutrients. Compare *eutrophic lake, oligotrophic lake*.

metabolic reserve Lower half of rangeland grass plants; these plants can grow back as long as this part is not consumed by herbivores.

metamorphic rock Rock produced when a preexisting rock is subjected to high temperatures (which may cause it to melt partially), high pressures, chemically active fluids, or a combination of these agents. See *rock cycle*. Compare *igneous rock, sedimentary rock*.

metastasis Spread of malignant (cancerous) cells from a cancer to other parts of the body.

microconsumer See *decomposer*.

micronutrient Element that a plant or an animal needs in small, or trace, amounts to stay alive and healthy. Examples are iron, copper, zinc, chlorine, and iodine. Compare *macronutrient*.

mineral Any naturally occurring inorganic substance found in the earth's crust as a crystalline solid. See *mineral resource*.

mineralization Process taking place in soil in which decomposers turn organic materials into inorganic ones.

mineral resource Concentration of naturally occurring solid, liquid, or gaseous material, in or on Earth's crust, in such form and amount that its extraction and conversion into useful materials or items is currently or potentially profitable. Mineral resources are classified as metallic (such as iron and tin ores) or nonmetallic (such as fossil fuels, sand, and salt).

minimum-tillage farming See *conservation-tillage farming*.

mixed economic system Economic system that falls somewhere between pure market and pure command economic systems. Virtually all the world's economic systems fall into this category, with some closer to a pure market system and some closer to a pure command system. Compare *pure command economic system, pure market economic system, traditional economic system*.

mixture Combination of one or more elements and compounds.

molecule Combination of two or more atoms of the same chemical element (such as O_2) or different chemical elements (such as H_2O) held together by chemical bonds.

monoculture Cultivation of a single crop, usually on a large area of land. Compare *polyculture*.

more developed country (MDC) Country that is highly industrialized and has a high GNP per person. Compare *less developed country*.

multiple use Principle of managing public land, such as a national forest, so it is used for a variety of purposes, such as timbering, mining, recreation, grazing, wildlife preservation, and soil and water conservation. See also *sustainable yield*.

municipal solid waste Solid materials discarded by homes and businesses in or near urban areas. See *solid waste*.

mutagen Chemical, or form of ionizing radiation, that causes inheritable changes in the DNA molecules in the genes found in chromosomes. See *carcinogen, mutation, teratogen*.

mutation An inheritable change in the DNA molecules in the genes found in the chromosomes. See *mutagen*.

mutualism Type of species interaction in which both participating species generally benefit. Compare *commensalism*.

national ambient air quality standards (NAAQS) Maximum allowable level, averaged over a specific time period, for a certain pollutant in outdoor (ambient) air.

native species Species that normally live and thrive in a particular ecosystem. Compare *immigrant species, indicator species, keystone species*.

natural capital See *Earth capital*.

natural gas Underground deposits of gases consisting of 50% to 90% by weight methane gas (CH_4) and small amounts of heavier gaseous hydrocarbon compounds such as propane (C_3H_8) and butane (C_4H_{10}).

natural hazard Event that destroys or damages wildlife habitats, kills or harms humans, and damages property. Examples are earthquakes, volcanoes, floods, and mass wasting.

natural ionizing radiation Ionizing radiation in the environment from natural sources.

natural radioactivity Nuclear change in which unstable nuclei of atoms spontaneously shoot out particles (usually alpha or beta particles), energy (gamma rays), or both at a fixed rate.

natural recharge Natural replenishment of an aquifer by precipitation, which percolates downward through soil and rock. See *recharge area*.

natural resources Area of the earth's solid surface, nutrients and minerals in the soil and deeper layers of the earth's crust, water, wild and domesticated plants and animals, air, and other resources produced by the earth's natural processes. See *Earth capital*. Compare *capital goods, labor*.

natural selection Process by which some genes and gene combinations in a population of a species are reproduced more than others when the population is exposed to an environmental change or stress. When individual organisms in a population die off over time because they cannot tolerate a new stress, they are replaced by individuals whose genetic traits allow them to cope better with the stress. When these better-adapted individuals reproduce, they pass their adaptive traits on to their offspring. See also *differential reproduction, evolution*.

negative feedback Flow of information into a system that counteracts the effects of a change in external conditions on the system. Compare *positive feedback*.

nematocide Chemical that kills nematodes.

neritic zone See *coastal zone.*

net economic welfare (NEW) Measure of annual change in quality of life in a country. It is obtained by subtracting the value of all final products and services that decrease the quality of life from a country's GNP. See *per capita NEW.*

net economic welfare per capita See *per capita NEW.*

net energy See *net useful energy.*

net primary productivity Rate at which all the plants in an ecosystem produce net useful chemical energy. It is equal to the difference between the rate at which the plants in an ecosystem produce useful chemical energy (primary productivity) and the rate at which they use some of that energy through cellular respiration. Compare *primary productivity.*

net useful energy Total amount of useful energy available from an energy resource or energy system over its lifetime minus the amount of energy used (the first energy law), automatically wasted (the second energy law), and unnecessarily wasted in finding, processing, concentrating, and transporting it to users.

neutral solution Water solution containing an equal number of hydrogen ions (H^+) and hydroxide ions (OH^-); water solution with a pH of 7. Compare *acid solution, basic solution.*

neutron (n) Elementary particle in the nuclei of all atoms (except hydrogen-1). It has a relative mass of 1 and no electric charge.

NEW See *net economic welfare.*

niche See *ecological niche.*

nitrogen cycle Cyclic movement of nitrogen in different chemical forms from the environment, to organisms, and then back to the environment.

nitrogen fixation Conversion of atmospheric nitrogen gas into forms useful to plants, by lightning, bacteria, and cyanobacteria; it is part of the nitrogen cycle.

noise pollution Any unwanted, disturbing, or harmful sound that impairs or interferes with hearing, causes stress, hampers concentration and work efficiency, or causes accidents.

nondegradable pollutant Material that is not broken down by natural processes. Examples are the toxic elements lead and mercury. Compare *biodegradable pollutant, degradable pollutant, slowly degradable pollutant.*

nonionizing radiation Forms of radiant energy such as radio waves, microwaves, infrared light, and ordinary light that do not have enough energy to cause ionization of atoms in living tissue. Compare *ionizing radiation.*

nonmaterial resource A resource whose quantity cannot be measured. Examples are solitude, beauty, knowledge, security, joy, and love. Compare *material resource.*

nonpersistent pollutant See *degradable pollutant.*

nonpoint source Large or dispersed land areas such as crop fields, streets, and lawns that discharge pollutants into the environment over a large area. Compare *point source.*

nonrenewable resource Resource that exists in a fixed amount (stock) in various places in the earth's crust and has the potential for renewal only by geological, physical, and chemical processes taking place over hundreds of millions to billions of years. Examples are copper, aluminum, coal, and oil. We classify these resources as exhaustible because we are extracting and using them at a much faster rate than the geological time scale on which they were formed. Compare *perpetual resource, potentially renewable resource.*

nontransmissible disease A disease that is not caused by living organisms and that does not spread from one person to another. Examples are most cancer, diabetes, cardiovascular disease, and malnutrition. Compare *transmissible disease.*

no-till farming See *conservation-tillage farming.*

nuclear change Process in which nuclei of certain isotopes spontaneously change, or are forced to change, into one or more different isotopes. The three principal types of nuclear change are natural radioactivity, nuclear fission, and nuclear fusion. Compare *chemical change.*

nuclear energy Energy released when atomic nuclei undergo a nuclear reaction such as the spontaneous emission of radioactivity, nuclear fission, or nuclear fusion.

nuclear fission Nuclear change in which the nuclei of certain isotopes with large mass numbers (such as uranium-235 and plutonium-239) are split apart into lighter nuclei when struck by a neutron. This process releases more neutrons and a large amount of energy. Compare *nuclear fusion.*

nuclear fusion Nuclear change in which two nuclei of isotopes of elements with a low mass number (such as hydrogen-2 and hydrogen-3) are forced together at extremely high temperatures until they fuse to form a heavier nucleus (such as helium-4). This process releases a large amount of energy. Compare *nuclear fission.*

nucleus Extremely tiny center of an atom, making up most of the atom's mass. It contains one or more positively charged protons and one or more neutrons with no electrical charge (except for a hydrogen-1 atom, which has one proton and no neutrons in its nucleus).

nutrient Any element an organism needs to live, grow, and reproduce. See *macronutrient, micronutrient.*

oil See *crude oil.*

oil shale Underground formation of a fine-grained rock containing varying amounts of kerogen, a solid, waxy mixture of hydrocarbon compounds. Heating the rock to high temperatures converts the kerogen into a vapor that can be condensed to form a slow-flowing heavy oil called shale oil. See *kerogen, shale oil.*

old-growth forest Uncut, virgin forest containing trees that are often hundreds, sometimes thousands, of years old. Examples include forests of Douglas fir, western hemlock, giant sequoia, and coastal redwoods in the western United States. Compare *ancient forest, secondary forest, tree farm.*

oligotrophic lake Lake with a low supply of plant nutrients. Compare *eutrophic lake, mesotrophic lake.*

omnivore Animal organism that can use both plants and other animals as food sources. Examples are pigs, rats, cockroaches, and people. Compare *carnivore, herbivore.*

open forest (woodland) An area where trees are abundant but their crowns do not form a closed canopy. Compare *closed forest.*

open-pit mining Removal of materials such as iron and copper by digging them out of the earth's surface and leaving a large depression or pit. See also *area strip mining, contour strip mining.*

open sea The part of an ocean that is beyond the continental shelf. Compare *coastal zone.*

ore Part of a metal-yielding material that can be economically and legally extracted at a given time. An ore typically contains two parts: the ore mineral, which contains the desired metal, and waste mineral material (gangue). See *beneficiation.*

organic compound Molecule that contains atoms of the element carbon, usually combined with each other and with atoms of one or more other elements such as hydrogen, oxygen, nitrogen, sulfur, phosphorus, chlorine, and fluorine. Compare *inorganic compound.*

organic farming Producing crops and livestock naturally by using organic fertilizer (manure, legumes, compost) and natural pest control (bugs that eat harmful bugs, plants that repel bugs, and environmental controls such as crop rotation) instead of using commercial inorganic fertilizers and synthetic pesticides and herbicides.

organic fertilizer Organic material, such as animal manure, green manure, and compost, applied to cropland as a source of plant nutrients. Compare *commercial inorganic fertilizer.*

organism Any form of life.

output pollution control See *pollution cleanup.*

overburden Layer of soil and rock overlying a mineral deposit that is removed during surface mining.

overconsumption Situation where some people consume much more than they need at the expense of those who cannot meet their basic needs and at the expense of Earth's present and future life-support systems.

overfishing Harvesting so many fish of a species, especially immature ones, that there is not enough breeding stock left to replenish the species so it is not profitable to harvest them.

overgrazing Destruction of vegetation when too many grazing animals feed too long and exceed the carrying capacity of a rangeland area.

overnutrition Diet so high in calories, saturated (animal) fats, salt, sugar, and processed foods, and so low in vegetables and fruits, that the consumer runs high risks of diabetes, hypertension, heart disease, and other health hazards. Compare *malnutrition, undernutrition.*

overpopulation State in which there are more people than can live on Earth or in a geographic region in comfort, happiness, and health and still leave the planet or region a fit place for future generations. It is a result of growing numbers of people, growing affluence (resource consumption), or both. See *carrying capacity, consumption overpopulation, dieback, overshoot, people overpopulation.*

overshoot Condition in which population size of a species temporarily exceeds the carrying capacity of its habitat. This leads to a sharp reduction in its population. See *carrying capacity, consumption overpopulation, dieback, people overpopulation.*

oxygen cycle Cyclic movement of oxygen in different chemical forms from the environment, to organisms, and then back to the environment.

oxygen-demanding wastes Organic materials that are usually biodegraded by aerobic (oxygen-consuming) bacteria, if there is enough dissolved oxygen in the water. See also *biological oxygen demand.*

ozone layer Layer of gaseous ozone (O_3) in the stratosphere that protects life on Earth by filtering out harmful ultraviolet radiation from the sun.

PANs Peroxyacyl nitrates. Group of chemicals found in photochemical smog.

parasite Consumer organism that lives on or in and feeds on a living plant or animal, known as the host, over an extended period of time. The parasite draws nourishment from and gradually weakens its host. This may or may not kill the host.

particulate matter Solid particles or liquid droplets suspended or carried in the air.

parts per billion (ppb) Number of parts of a chemical found in one billion parts of a particular gas, liquid, or solid.

parts per million (ppm) Number of parts of a chemical found in one million parts of a particular gas, liquid, or solid.

passive solar heating system System that captures sunlight directly within a structure and converts it into low-temperature heat for space heating or for heating water for domestic use without the use of mechanical devices. Compare *active solar heating system.*

pathogen Organism that produces disease.

PCBs See *polychlorinated biphenyls.*

people overpopulation Situation in which there are more people in the world or a geographic region than available supplies of food, water, and other vital resources can support. It can also occur where the rate of population growth so exceeds the rate of economic growth, or the distribution of wealth is so inequitable, that a number of people are too poor to grow or buy enough food, fuel, and other important resources. Compare *consumption overpopulation*.

per capita GNP   Annual gross national product (GNP) of a country divided by its total population. See *gross national product, per capita real GNP*.

per capita NEW   Annual net economic welfare (NEW) of a country divided by its total population. See *net economic welfare, per capita real NEW*.

per capita real GNP   Per capita GNP adjusted for inflation. See *per capita GNP*.

per capita real NEW   Per capita NEW adjusted for inflation. See *net economic welfare, per capita NEW*.

perennial   Plant that grows from the root stock each year and that does not need to be replanted. Compare *annual*.

permafrost   Permanently frozen underground layers of soil in tundra.

permeability   The degree to which underground rock and soil pores are interconnected and thus a measure of the degree to which water can flow freely from one pore to another. Compare *porosity*.

perpetual resource   Resource, such as solar energy, that is virtually inexhaustible on a human time scale. Compare *nonrenewable resource, potentially renewable resource*.

persistence   See *inertia*.

persistent pollutant   See *slowly degradable pollutant*.

pest   Unwanted organism that directly or indirectly interferes with human activities.

pesticide   Any chemical designed to kill or inhibit the growth of an organism that people consider to be undesirable. See *fungicide, herbicide, insecticide*.

pesticide treadmill   Situation in which the cost of using pesticides increases while their effectiveness decreases, mostly because the pest species develop genetic resistance to the pesticides.

petrochemicals   Chemicals obtained by refining (distilling) crude oil. They are used as raw materials in the manufacture of most industrial chemicals, fertilizers, pesticides, plastics, synthetic fibers, paints, medicines, and many other products.

petroleum   See *crude oil*.

pH   Numeric value that indicates the relative acidity or alkalinity of a substance on a scale of 0 to 14, with the neutral point at 7. Acid solutions have pH values lower than 7, and basic or alkaline solutions have pH values greater than 7.

phosphorus cycle   Cyclic movement of phosphorus in different chemical forms from the environment, to organisms, and then back to the environment.

photochemical smog   Complex mixture of air pollutants produced in the atmosphere by the reaction of hydrocarbons and nitrogen oxides under the influence of sunlight. Especially harmful components include ozone, peroxyacyl nitrates (PANs), and various aldehydes. Compare *industrial smog*.

photosynthesis   Complex process that takes place in cells of green plants. Radiant energy from the sun is used to combine carbon dioxide (CO_2) and water (H_2O) to produce oxygen (O_2) and carbohydrates (such as glucose, $C_6H_{12}O_6$), and other nutrient molecules. Compare *aerobic respiration, chemosynthesis*.

photovoltaic cell (solar cell)   Device in which radiant (solar) energy is converted directly into electrical energy.

physical change   Process that alters one or more physical properties of an element or a compound without altering its chemical composition. Examples are changing the size and shape of a sample

of matter (crushing ice and cutting aluminum foil) and changing a sample of matter from one physical state to another (boiling and freezing water). Compare *chemical change*.

phytoplankton   Small, drifting plants, mostly algae and bacteria, found in aquatic ecosystems. Compare *plankton, zooplankton*.

pioneer community   First integrated set of plants, animals, and decomposers found in an area undergoing primary ecological succession. See *immature community, mature community*.

pioneer species   First hardy species (often microbes, mosses, and lichens) that begin colonizing a site as the first stage of ecological succession. See *ecological succession, pioneer community*.

plaintiff   The individual, group of individuals, corporation, or government agency bringing the charges in a lawsuit. Compare *defendant*.

plankton   Small plant organisms (phytoplankton) and animal organisms (zooplankton) that float in aquatic ecosystems.

plantation agriculture   Growing specialized crops such as bananas, coffee, and cacao in tropical LDCs, primarily for sale to MDCs.

plants   Eukaryotic, mostly multicelled organisms such as algae (red, blue, and green), mosses, ferns, flowers, cacti, grasses, beans, wheat, trees. They use photosynthesis to produce organic nutrients for themselves and for other organisms feeding on them. Water and other inorganic nutrients are obtained from the soil for terrestrial plants and from the water for aquatic plants.

plates   Various-sized areas of Earth's lithosphere that move slowly around on the mantle's flowing asthenosphere. Earthquakes and volcanoes occur around the boundaries of these plates. See *asthenosphere, lithosphere, plate tectonics*.

plate tectonics   Theory of geophysical processes that explains the movements of Earth's plates and the processes that occur at their boundaries. See *lithosphere, plates*.

poaching   Illegal commercial hunting or fishing.

point source   A single identifiable source that discharges pollutants into the environment. Examples are the smokestack of a power plant or an industrial plant, the drainpipe of a meat-packing plant, the chimney of a house, or the exhaust pipe of an automobile. Compare *nonpoint source*.

politics   Process through which individuals and groups try to influence or control the policies and actions of governments that affect the local, state, national, and international communities.

pollution   An undesirable change in the physical, chemical, or biological characteristics of air, water, soil, or food that can adversely affect the health, survival, or activities of humans or other living organisms.

pollution cleanup   Device or process that removes or reduces the level of a pollutant after it has been produced or has entered the environment. Examples are automobile emission control devices and sewage treatment plants. Compare *pollution prevention*.

pollution prevention   Device or process that prevents a potential pollutant from forming or from entering the environment or that sharply reduces the amounts entering the environment. Compare *pollution cleanup*.

polychlorinated biphenyls (PCBs)   Group of 209 different toxic, oily, synthetic chlorinated hydrocarbon compounds that can be biologically amplified in food chains and webs.

polyculture   Complex form of intercropping in which a large number of different plants maturing at different times are planted together. See also *intercropping*. Compare *monoculture, polyvarietal cultivation*.

polyvarietal cultivation   Planting a plot of land with several varieties of the same crop. Compare *intercropping, monoculture, polyculture*.

population   Group of individual organisms of the same species living within a particular area.

population crash   Large number of deaths over a fairly short time, brought about when the number of individuals in a population is too large to be supported by available environmental resources.

population density   Number of organisms in a particular population found in a specified area.

population dispersion   General pattern in which the members of a population are arranged throughout its habitat.

population distribution   Variation of population density over a particular geographical area. For example, a country has a high population density in its urban areas and a much lower population density in rural areas.

population dynamics   Major abiotic and biotic factors that tend to increase or decrease the population size, and age and sex composition of a species.

population size   Number of individuals making up a population's gene pool.

porosity   The pores (crack and spaces) in rocks or soil, or the percentage of the rock's or soil's volume not occupied by the rock or soil itself. Compare *permeability*.

positive feedback   Situation in which a change in a system in one direction provides information that causes the system to change farther in the same direction. Compare *negative feedback*.

potential energy   Energy stored in an object because of its position or the position of its parts. Compare *kinetic energy*.

potentially renewable resource   Resource that theoretically can last indefinitely without reducing the available supply because it is replaced more rapidly through natural processes than are nonrenewable resources. Examples are trees in forests, grasses in grasslands, wild animals, fresh surface water in lakes and streams, most groundwater, fresh air, and fertile soil. If such a resource is used faster than it is replenished, it can be depleted and converted into a nonrenewable resource. See also *environmental degradation*. Compare *nonrenewable resource, perpetual resource*.

poverty   Inability to meet basic needs for food, clothing, and shelter.

ppb   See *parts per billion*.

ppm   See *parts per million*.

precipitation   Water in the form of rain, sleet, hail, and snow that falls from the atmosphere onto the land and bodies of water.

predation   Situation in which an organism of one species (the predator) captures and feeds on parts or all of an organism of another species (the prey).

predator   Organism that captures and feeds on parts or all of an organism of another species (the prey).

predator-prey relationship   Interaction between two organisms of different species in which one organism called the predator captures and feeds on parts or all of another organism called the prey.

prescribed burning   Deliberate setting and careful control of surface fires in forests to help prevent more destructive crown fires and to kill off unwanted plants that compete with commercial species for plant nutrients; may also be used on grasslands. See *crown fire, ground fire, surface fire*.

prey   Organism that is captured and serves as a source of food for an organism of another species (the predator).

primary air pollutant   Chemical that has been added directly to the air by natural events or human activities and occurs in a harmful concentration. Compare *secondary air pollutant*.

primary consumer   Organism that feeds directly on all or part of plants (*herbivore*) or other producers. Compare *detritivore, omnivore, secondary consumer*.

primary ecological succession Sequential development of communities in a bare area that has never been occupied by a community of organisms. Compare *secondary ecological succession*.

primary oil recovery Pumping out the crude oil that flows by gravity or under gas pressure into the bottom of an oil well. Compare *enhanced oil recovery, secondary oil recovery*.

primary productivity The *rate* at which an ecosystem's producers capture and store a given amount of chemical energy as biomass in a given length of time. Compare *net primary productivity*.

primary sewage treatment Mechanical treatment of sewage in which large solids are filtered out by screens and suspended solids settle out as sludge in a sedimentation tank. Compare *advanced sewage treatment, secondary sewage treatment*.

primary succession See *primary ecological succession*.

prime reproductive age Years between ages 20 and 29, during which most women have most of their children. Compare *reproductive age*.

principle of multiple use See *multiple use*.

prior appropriation Legal principle by which the first user of water from a stream establishes a legal right to continued use of the amount originally withdrawn. See also *riparian rights*.

private good Economic good that can be owned and enjoyed on a private, or exclusive, basis. It can be produced and sold in units. Compare *public good*.

private-property resource Resource owned by an individual or a group of individuals other than the government. Compare *common-property resource, public-land resource*.

producer Organism that uses solar energy (green plant) or chemical energy (some bacteria) to manufacture the organic compounds it needs as nutrients from simple inorganic compounds obtained from its environment. Compare *consumer, decomposer*.

productivity Measure of the output of economic goods and services produced by the input of the factors of production (natural resources, capital goods, labor). Increasing economic productivity means getting more output from less input. Compare *economic growth*.

profundal zone Deep, open-water region of a lake, a region not penetrated by sunlight. Compare *benthic zone, limnetic zone, littoral zone*.

prokaryotic cell Cell that doesn't have a distinct nucleus. Other internal parts are also not enclosed by membranes. Compare *eukaryotic cell*.

protists Eukaryotic, mostly single-cell organisms such as diatoms, amoebas, some algae (golden brown and yellow-green), protozoans, and slime molds. Some protists produce their own organic nutrients through photosynthesis. Others are decomposers and some feed on bacteria, other protists, or cells of multicellular organisms.

proton (p) Positively charged particle in the nuclei of all atoms. Each proton has a relative mass of 1 and a single positive charge.

public good Economic good that cannot be divided and sold in units, is owned by nobody in particular, and can be enjoyed by anybody. Examples are national defense, clean air, clean water, beautiful scenery, and wild plants and animals (biological diversity). Compare *private good*.

public-land resources Land that is owned jointly by all citizens, but is managed for them by an agency of the local, state, or federal government. Examples are state and national parks, forests, wildlife refuges, and wilderness areas. Compare *common-property resource, private-property resource*.

public-property resource See *public-land resource*.

pure capitalism See *pure market economic system*.

pure command economic system System in which all economic decisions are made by the government or some other central authority. Compare *mixed economic system, pure market economic system, traditional economic system*.

pure competition State in which there are large numbers of independently acting buyers and sellers for each economic good in a pure market economic system. No buyer or seller is able to control the supply, demand, or price of a good. All buyers and sellers are free to enter or leave the market as they please but must accept the going market price.

pure market economic system System in which all economic decisions are made in the *market*, where buyers and sellers of economic goods freely interact, with no government or other interference. Compare *mixed economic system, pure command economic system, traditional economic system*.

pyramid of biomass Diagram representing the biomass, or total dry weight of all living organisms, that can be supported at each trophic level in a food chain or food web. See also *pyramid of energy flow, pyramid of numbers*.

pyramid of energy flow Diagram representing the flow of energy through each trophic level in a food chain or food web. With each energy transfer, only a small part (typically 10%) of the usable energy entering one trophic level is transferred to the organisms at the next trophic level. Compare *pyramid of biomass, pyramid of numbers*.

pyramid of numbers Diagram representing the number of organisms of a particular type that can be supported at each trophic level from a given input of solar energy at the producer trophic level in a food chain or food web. Compare *pyramid of biomass, pyramid of energy flow*.

radiation Fast-moving particles (particulate radiation) or waves of energy (electromagnetic radiation). See *ionizing radiation, nonionizing radiation*.

radioactive decay Change of a radioisotope to a different isotope by the emission of radioactivity.

radioactive isotope See *radioisotope*.

radioactive waste Radioactive waste products of nuclear power plants, research, medicine, weapons production, or other processes involving nuclear reactions. See *radioactivity*.

radioactivity Nuclear change in which unstable nuclei of atoms spontaneously shoot out "chunks" of mass, energy, or both, at a fixed rate. The three principal types of radioactivity are gamma rays and fast-moving alpha particles and beta particles.

radioisotope Isotope of an atom that spontaneously emits one or more types of radioactivity (alpha particles, beta particles, gamma rays).

rain shadow effect Low precipitation on the far side (leeward side) of a mountain when prevailing winds flow up and over a high mountain or range of high mountains. This creates semiarid and arid conditions on the leeward side of a high mountain range.

range See *rangeland*.

range condition Estimate of how close a particular area of rangeland is to its potential for producing vegetation that can be consumed by grazing or browsing animals.

rangeland Land that supplies forage or vegetation (grasses, grasslike plants, and shrubs) for grazing and browsing animals and that is not intensively managed. Compare *feedlot*.

range of tolerance Range of chemical and physical conditions that must be maintained for populations of a particular species to stay alive and grow, develop, and function normally. See *law of tolerance*.

real GNP Gross national product adjusted for inflation. Compare *gross national product, per capita GNP, per capita real GNP*.

realized niche Parts of the fundamental niche of a species that is actually used by a species. See *ecological niche, fundamental niche*.

recharge area Any area of land allowing water to pass through it and into an aquifer. See *aquifer, natural recharge*.

recycling Collecting and reprocessing a resource so it can be made into new products. An example is collecting aluminum cans, melting them down, and using the aluminum to make new cans or other aluminum products. Compare *reuse*.

reforestation Renewal of trees and other types of vegetation on land where trees have been removed. This can be done naturally by seeds from nearby trees or artificially by planting seeds or seedlings.

relative resource scarcity Situation in which a resource has not been depleted but there is not enough available to meet the demand because of unbalanced distribution. This can be caused by a war, a natural disaster, or other events that disrupt the production and distribution of a resource, or by deliberate attempts of its producers to lower production to drive prices up. Compare *absolute resource scarcity*.

renewable resource See *potentially renewable resource*.

replacement-level fertility Number of children a couple must have to replace themselves. The average for a country or the world is usually slightly higher than 2 children per couple (2.1 in the United States and 2.5 in some LDCs) because some children die before reaching their reproductive years. See also *total fertility rate*.

reproductive age Ages 15 to 44, when most women have all their children. Compare *prime reproductive age*.

reproductive isolation Long-term geographic separation of members of a particular sexually reproducing species.

reserves (economic resources) Resources that have been identified and from which a usable mineral can be extracted profitably at present prices with current mining technology. Compare *resources*.

reservoir See *artificial reservoir*.

resilience Ability of a living system to restore itself to its original condition after being exposed to an outside disturbance that is not too drastic. See also *constancy, inertia*.

resource Anything obtained from the living and nonliving environment to meet human needs and wants.

resource partitioning Process of dividing up resources in an ecosystem so species with similar requirements (overlapping ecological niches) use the same scarce resources at different times, in different ways, or in different places. See *ecological niche, fundamental niche, realized niche*.

resource recovery Salvaging usable metals, paper, and glass from solid waste and selling them to manufacturing industries for recycling or reuse.

resources All undiscovered resources and the portion of identified resources that can't be recovered profitably with present prices and technology. Some of these materials may be converted into reserves when prices rise or mining technology improves. Compare *reserves*.

respiration See *aerobic respiration*.

reuse To use a product over and over again in the same form. An example is collecting, washing, and refilling glass beverage bottles. Compare *recycling*.

rill erosion Soil erosion caused when small streams (rivulets) of surface water flow at high velocities over the ground and cut small channels or ditches in the soil. Compare *gully erosion, sheet erosion*.

riparian rights System of water law that gives anyone whose land adjoins a flowing stream the right to use water from the stream as long as some is left for downstream users. Compare *prior appropriation*.

risk The probability that something undesirable will happen from deliberate or accidental exposure to a hazard. See *risk assessment, risk-benefit analysis, risk management*.

risk analysis Identifying hazards, evaluating the nature and severity of risks (*risk assessment*), using this and other information to determine options and make decisions about reducing or eliminating risks (*risk management*), and communicating information about risks to decision makers and the public (*risk communication*).

risk assessment Process of gathering data and making assumptions to estimate short- and long-term harmful effects on human health or the environment from exposure to hazards associated with the use of a particular product or technology. See *risk, risk-benefit analysis*.

risk-benefit analysis Estimate of the short- and long-term risks and benefits of using a particular product or technology. See *desirability quotient, risk*. Compare *cost-benefit analysis*.

risk communication Communicating information about risks to decision makers and the public. See *risk, risk analysis, risk-benefit analysis*.

risk management Using risk assessment and other information to determine options and make decisions about reducing or eliminating risks. See *risk, risk analysis, risk-benefit analysis, risk communication*.

river See *stream*.

river runoff Water flowing in rivers to the ocean. Compare *surface runoff*.

rock Any material that makes up a large, natural, continuous part of Earth's crust. See *mineral*.

rock cycle Largest and slowest of the earth's cycles, consisting of geologic, physical, and chemical processes that form and modify rocks and soil in the earth's crust over millions of years.

rodenticide Chemical that kills rodents.

r-strategists Species that reproduce early in their life span and that produce large numbers of usually small and short-lived offspring in a short period of time. Compare *K-strategists*.

rule of 70 Method for calculating the doubling time in years for a quantity that is growing exponentially. This involves dividing the annual percentage growth rate of a quantity into 70 (70 ÷ percentage growth rate = doubling time in years).

ruminant animals Grazing and browsing herbivores such as cattle, sheep, goats, and buffalo that have a three- or four-chambered stomach that digests the cellulose in grasses and vegetation they eat.

runoff Fresh water from precipitation and melting ice that flows on the earth's surface into nearby streams, lakes, wetlands, and reservoirs. See *river runoff, surface runoff, surface water*. Compare *groundwater*.

rural area Geographical area in the United States with a population of less than 2,500 people per unit of area. The number of people used in this definition may vary in different countries. Compare *urban area*.

salinity Amount of various salts dissolved in a given volume of water.

salinization Accumulation of salts in soil that can eventually make the soil unable to support plant growth.

saltwater intrusion Movement of salt water into freshwater aquifers in coastal and inland areas as groundwater is withdrawn faster than it is recharged by precipitation.

sanitary landfill Land waste disposal site in which waste is spread in thin layers, compacted, and covered with a fresh layer of clay or plastic foam each day.

scavenger Organism that feeds on dead organisms that either were killed by other organisms or died naturally. Examples are vultures, flies, and crows. Compare *detritivore*.

science Attempts to discover order in nature and then use that knowledge to make predictions about what will happen in nature. See *scientific data, scientific hypothesis, scientific law, scientific methods, scientific theory*.

scientific data Facts obtained by making observations and measurements. Compare *scientific hypothesis, scientific law, scientific theory*.

scientific hypothesis An educated guess that attempts to explain a scientific law or certain scientific observations. Compare *scientific data, scientific law, scientific theory*.

scientific law Summary of what scientists find happening in nature over and over in the same way. See *first law of thermodynamics, law of conservation of matter, second law of thermodynamics*. Compare *scientific data, scientific hypothesis, scientific theory*.

scientific methods The ways scientists gather data and formulate and test scientific laws and theories. See *scientific data, scientific hypothesis, scientific law, scientific theory*.

scientific theory A well-tested and widely accepted scientific hypothesis. Compare *scientific data, scientific hypothesis, scientific law*.

secondary air pollutant Harmful chemical formed in the atmosphere when a primary air pollutant reacts with normal air components or with other air pollutants. Compare *primary air pollutant*.

secondary consumer Organism that feeds only on primary consumers. Most secondary consumers are animals, but some are plants. Compare *detritivore, omnivore, primary consumer*.

secondary ecological succession Sequential development of communities in an area in which natural vegetation has been removed or destroyed but the soil is not destroyed. Compare *primary ecological succession*.

secondary forest Stands of trees resulting from secondary ecological succession. Compare *ancient forest, old growth forest, tree farm*.

secondary oil recovery Injection of water into an oil well after primary oil recovery to force out some of the remaining, usually thicker, crude oil. Compare *enhanced oil recovery, primary oil recovery*.

secondary sewage treatment Second step in most waste treatment systems, in which aerobic bacteria break down up to 90% of degradable, oxygen-demanding organic wastes in wastewater. This is usually done by bringing sewage and bacteria together in trickling filters or in the activated sludge process. Compare *advanced sewage treatment, primary sewage treatment*.

secondary succession See *secondary ecological succession*.

second law of ecology Everything is connected to and intermingled with everything else.

second law of energy See *second law of thermodynamics*.

second law of thermodynamics In any conversion of heat energy to useful work, some of the initial energy input is always degraded to a lower-quality, more-dispersed (higher entropy), less useful energy, usually low-temperature heat that flows into the environment; you can't break even in terms of energy quality. See *first law of thermodynamics*.

sedimentary rock Rock that forms from the accumulated products of erosion and in some cases from the compacted shells, skeletons, and other remains of dead organisms. Compare *igneous rock, metamorphic rock*. See *rock cycle*.

seed-tree cutting Removal of nearly all trees on a site in one cutting, with a few seed-producing trees left uniformly distributed to regenerate the forest. Compare *clear-cutting, selective cutting, shelterwood cutting, whole-tree harvesting*.

selective cutting Cutting of intermediate-aged, mature, or diseased trees in an uneven-aged

forest stand, either singly or in small groups. This encourages the growth of younger trees and maintains an uneven-aged stand. Compare *clear-cutting, seed-tree cutting, shelterwood cutting, whole-tree harvesting*.

septic tank Underground tank for treatment of wastewater from a home in rural and suburban areas. Bacteria in the tank decompose organic wastes and the sludge settles to the bottom of the tank. The effluent flows out of the tank into the ground through a field of drain pipes.

sewage sludge See *sludge*.

shale oil Slow-flowing, dark brown, heavy oil obtained when kerogen in oil shale is vaporized at high temperatures and then condensed. Shale oil can be refined to yield gasoline, heating oil, and other petroleum products. See *kerogen, oil shale*.

sheet erosion Soil erosion caused by surface water moving down a slope or across a field in a wide flow. Because it removes topsoil evenly, it may not be noticeable until much damage has been done. Compare *gully erosion, rill erosion*.

shelterbelt See *windbreak*.

shelterwood cutting Removal of mature, marketable trees in an area in a series of partial cuttings to allow regeneration of a new stand under the partial shade of older trees, which are later removed. Typically, this is done by making two or three cuts over a decade. Compare *clear-cutting, seed-tree cutting, selective cutting, whole-tree harvesting*.

shifting cultivation Clearing a plot of ground in a forest, especially in tropical areas, and planting crops on it for a few years (typically 2 to 5 years) until the soil is depleted of nutrients or until the plot has been invaded by a dense growth of vegetation from the surrounding forest. Then a new plot is cleared and the process is repeated. The abandoned plot cannot successfully grow crops for 10 to 30 years. See also *slash-and-burn cultivation*.

silviculture Science and art of cultivating and managing forests to produce a renewable supply of timber.

slash-and-burn cultivation Cutting down trees and other vegetation in a patch of forest, leaving the cut vegetation on the ground to dry, and then burning it. The ashes that are left add nutrients to the nutrient-poor soils found in most tropical forest areas. Crops are planted between tree stumps. Plots must be abandoned after a few years (typically two to five years) because of loss of soil fertility or invasion of vegetation from the surrounding forest. See also *shifting cultivation*.

slowly degradable pollutant Material that is slowly broken down into simpler chemicals or reduced to acceptable levels by natural physical, chemical, and biological processes. Compare *biodegradable pollutant, degradable pollutant, nondegradable pollutant*.

sludge Gooey mixture of toxic chemicals, infectious agents, and settled solids, removed from wastewater at sewage treatment plants.

smelting Process in which a desired metal is separated from the other elements in an ore mineral.

smog Originally a combination of smoke and fog, but now used to describe other mixtures of pollutants in the atmosphere. See *industrial smog, photochemical smog*.

softwood A tree species with wood that usually has a lower density and generally is easier to saw, plane, or carve than that from a hardwood. Compare *hardwood*.

soil Complex mixture of inorganic minerals (clay, silt, pebbles, and sand), decaying organic matter, water, air, and living organisms.

soil conservation Methods used to reduce soil erosion, to prevent depletion of soil nutrients, and to restore nutrients already lost by erosion, leaching, and excessive crop harvesting.

soil erosion Movement of soil components, especially topsoil, from one place to another, usually by exposure to wind, flowing water, or both. This natural process can be greatly accelerated by human activities that remove vegetation from soil. See *gully erosion, rill erosion, sheet erosion*.

soil horizons Horizontal zones that make up a particular mature soil. Each horizon has a distinct texture and composition that vary with different types of soils.

soil permeability Rate at which water and air move from upper to lower soil layers.

soil porosity See *porosity*.

soil profile Cross-sectional view of the horizons in a soil.

soil structure How the particles that make up a soil are organized and clumped together. See also *soil permeability, soil texture*.

soil texture Relative amounts of the different types and sizes of mineral particles in a sample of soil.

soil water Underground water that partially fills pores between soil particles and rocks within the upper soil and rock layers of the earth's crust, above the water table. Compare *groundwater*.

solar cell See *photovoltaic cell*.

solar collector Device for collecting radiant energy from the sun and converting it into heat. See *active solar heating system, passive solar heating system*.

solar energy Direct radiant energy from the sun and a number of *indirect* forms of energy produced by the direct input. Principal indirect forms of solar energy include wind, falling and flowing water (hydropower), and biomass (solar energy converted into chemical energy stored in the chemical bonds of organic compounds in trees and other plants).

solar pond Fairly small body of fresh water or salt water from which stored solar energy can be extracted, because of temperature difference between the hot surface layer exposed to the sun during daylight and the cooler layer beneath it.

solid waste Any unwanted or discarded material that is not a liquid or a gas. See *municipal solid waste*.

Spaceship-Earth worldview Earth is viewed as a spaceship—a machine that we can understand, control, and change at will by using advanced technology. Compare *sustainable-Earth worldview, throwaway worldview*.

specialists See *specialist species*.

specialist species Species with a narrow ecological niche. They may be able to live in only one type of habitat, tolerate only a narrow range of climatic and other environmental conditions, or use only one or a few types of food. Compare *generalist species*.

speciation Formation of new species from existing ones through natural selection, in response to changes in environmental conditions; usually takes thousands of years. Compare *extinction*.

species Group of organisms that resemble one another in appearance, behavior, chemical makeup and processes, and genetic structure. Organisms that reproduce sexually are classified as members of the same species only if they can actually or potentially interbreed with one another and produce fertile offspring.

species diversity Number of different species and their relative abundances in a given area. See *biological diversity*. Compare *ecological diversity, genetic diversity*.

spoils Unwanted rock and other waste materials produced when a material is removed from the earth's surface or subsurface by mining, dredging, quarrying, and excavation.

sport fishing Finding and catching fish, mostly for recreation. Compare *commercial fishing, subsistence fishing*.

sport hunting Finding and killing animals, mostly for recreation. Compare *commercial hunting, subsistence hunting*.

spreading center See *divergent plate boundary*.

S-shaped curve Levelling off of an exponential, J-shaped curve when a rapidly growing population exceeds the carrying capacity of its environment and ceases to grow in numbers. See also *overshoot, population crash*.

stability Ability of a living system to withstand or recover from externally imposed changes or stresses. See *constancy, inertia, resilience*.

statutory law Law passed by a state or national legislature or other governing body. Compare *common law*.

stocking rate Number of a particular kind of animal grazing on a given area of grassland.

strategic mineral A fuel or a nonfuel mineral vital to the industry and defense of a country. Ideally, supplies are stockpiled to cushion against supply interruptions and sharp price rises.

stratosphere Second layer of the atmosphere, extending from about 17 to 48 kilometers (11 to 30 miles) above the earth's surface. It contains small amounts of gaseous ozone (O_3), which filters out about 99% of the incoming harmful ultraviolet (UV) radiation emitted by the sun. Compare *troposphere*.

stream Flowing body of surface water. Examples are creeks and rivers.

strip cropping Planting regular crops and close-growing plants, such as hay or nitrogen-fixing legumes, in alternating rows or bands to help reduce depletion of soil nutrients.

strip mining Form of surface mining in which bulldozers, power shovels, or stripping wheels remove large chunks of the earth's surface in strips. See *surface mining*. Compare *subsurface mining*.

subatomic particles Extremely small particles—electrons, protons, and neutrons—that make up the internal structure of atoms.

subduction zone Area in which oceanic lithosphere is carried downward (subducted) under the island arc or continent at a convergent plate boundary. A trench ordinarily forms at the boundary between the two converging plates. See *convergent plate boundary*.

subsidence Slow or rapid sinking down of part of Earth's crust that is not slope related.

subsistence agriculture Supplementing solar energy with energy from human labor and draft animals to produce enough food to feed oneself and family members; in good years, there may be enough food left over to sell or put aside for hard times. Compare *industrialized agriculture*.

subsistence economy Economic system where the primary goal is to produce enough goods to meet basic survival needs, with little or no surplus for sale or trade. It is often a traditional economic system. See *traditional economic system*. Compare *mixed economic system, pure command economic system, pure market economic system*.

subsistence farming See *subsistence agriculture*.

subsistence fishing Finding and catching fish to get food for survival. Compare *commercial fishing, sport fishing*.

subsistence hunting Finding and killing wild animals to get enough food and other animal material for survival. Compare *commercial hunting, sport hunting*.

subsurface mining Extraction of a metal ore or fuel resource such as coal from a deep underground deposit. Compare *surface mining*.

succession See *ecological succession*.

succulent plants Plants, such as desert cacti, that survive in dry climates by having no leaves, thus reducing the loss of scarce water. They store water and use sunlight to produce the food they need in the thick fleshy tissue of their green stems and branches. Compare *deciduous plants, evergreen plants*.

sulfur cycle Cyclic movement of sulfur in different chemical forms from the environment, to organisms, and then back to the environment.

superinsulated house House that is heavily insulated and extremely airtight. Typically, active or passive solar collectors are used to heat water and an air-to-air heat exchanger is used to prevent buildup of excessive moisture and indoor air pollutants.

surface fire Forest fire that burns only undergrowth and leaf litter on the forest floor. Compare *crown fire, ground fire*.

surface mining Removal of soil, subsoil, and other strata, and then extracting a mineral deposit found fairly close to the earth's surface. See *area strip mining, contour strip mining, open-pit surface mining*. Compare *subsurface mining*.

surface runoff Water flowing off the land into bodies of surface water. Compare *river runoff*.

surface water Precipitation that does not infiltrate the ground or return to the atmosphere by evaporation or transpiration. See *river runoff, runoff, surface runoff*. Compare *groundwater*.

sustainable agriculture See *sustainable-Earth agricultural system*.

sustainable development See *sustainable economic development*.

sustainable-Earth agricultural system Method of growing crops and raising livestock based on organic fertilizers, soil conservation, water conservation, biological control of pests, and minimal use of nonrenewable fossil fuel energy.

sustainable-Earth economy Economic system in which the number of people and the quantity of goods are maintained at some constant level. This level is ecologically sustainable over time and meets at least the basic needs of all members of the population.

sustainable-Earth society Society based on working with nature by recycling and reusing discarded matter, by preventing pollution, by not unnecessarily wasting matter and energy resources, by preserving biodiversity, and by not allowing population size to exceed the carrying capacity of the environment. See *sustainable-Earth worldview*. Compare *matter-recycling society, throwaway society*.

sustainable-Earth worldview Belief that Earth is a place with finite room and resources, so continuing population growth, production, and consumption inevitably put severe stress on natural processes that renew and maintain the resource base of air, water, and soil that support all life. To prevent environmental overload, environmental degradation, and resource depletion, people should work with nature by controlling population growth, reducing unnecessary use and waste of matter and energy resources, and not causing the premature extinction of any other species. Compare *Spaceship-Earth worldview, throwaway worldview*.

sustainable economic development Forms of economic growth and activities that do not deplete or degrade natural resources upon which present and future economic growth depend.

sustainable yield (sustained yield) Highest rate at which a potentially renewable resource can be used without reducing its available supply throughout the world or in a particular area. See also *environmental degradation*.

sustained yield See *sustainable yield*.

symbiotic relationship Species interaction in which two kinds of organisms live together in an intimate association, with members of one or both species benefiting from the association. See *commensalism, mutualism*.

synergistic interaction Interaction of two or more factors so the net effect is greater than that expected from adding together the independent effects of each factor.

synfuels Synthetic gaseous and liquid fuels produced from solid coal or sources other than natural gas or crude oil.

synthetic natural gas (SNG) Gaseous fuel containing mostly methane produced from solid coal.

tailings Rock and other waste materials removed as impurities when waste mineral material is separated from the metal in an ore. See *beneficiation*.

tangible resource See *material resource*.

tar sand Deposit of a mixture of clay, sand, water, and varying amounts of a tarlike heavy oil known as bitumen. Bitumen can be extracted from tar sand by heating. It is then purified and upgraded to synthetic crude oil. See *bitumen*.

technology Creation of new products and processes that are supposed to improve our survival, comfort, and quality of life. Compare *science*.

temperature Measure of the average speed of motion of the atoms, ions, or molecules in a substance or combination of substances at a given moment. Compare *heat*.

temperature inversion See *thermal inversion*.

teratogen Chemical, ionizing agent, or virus, that causes birth defects. See *carcinogen, mutagen*.

terracing Planting crops on a long, steep slope that has been converted into a series of broad, nearly level terraces with short vertical drops from one to another that run along the contour of the land to retain water and reduce soil erosion.

terrestrial Pertaining to land. Compare *aquatic*.

tertiary (and higher) consumers Animals that feed on animal-eating animals. They feed at high trophic levels in food chains and webs. Examples are hawks, lions, bass, and sharks. Compare *detritivore, primary consumer, secondary consumer*.

tertiary oil recovery See *enhanced oil recovery*.

tertiary sewage treatment See *advanced sewage treatment*.

thermal enrichment Beneficial effects in an aquatic ecosystem from a rise in water temperature. Compare *thermal pollution*.

thermal inversion Layer of dense, cool air trapped under a layer of less dense warm air. This prevents upward-flowing air currents from developing. In a prolonged inversion, air pollution in the trapped layer may build up to harmful levels.

thermal pollution Increase in water temperature that has harmful effects on aquatic life. See *thermal shock*. Compare *thermal enrichment*.

thermal shock A sharp change in water temperature that can kill or harm fish and other aquatic organisms. See *thermal pollution*. Compare *thermal enrichment*.

thermocline Zone of gradual temperature decrease between warm surface water and colder deep water in a lake, a reservoir, or an ocean.

third law of ecology Any substance we produce should not interfere with any of Earth's natural biogeochemical cycles.

threatened species Wild species that is still abundant in its natural range but is likely to become endangered because of a decline in numbers. Compare *endangered species*.

threshold effect The harmful or fatal effect of a small change in environmental conditions that exceeds the limit of tolerance of an organism or population of a species. See *law of tolerance*.

throwaway society Society found in most advanced industrialized countries, in which ever-increasing economic growth is sustained by maximizing the rate at which matter and energy resources are used, with little emphasis on recycling, reuse, reduction of unnecessary waste, pollution prevention, and other forms of resource conservation. Compare *matter-recycling society, sustainable-Earth society*.

throwaway worldview Belief that Earth is a place of unlimited resources. Any type of resource conservation that hampers short-term economic growth is unnecessary because if we pollute or deplete resources in one area, we will find substitutes, control the pollution through technology, and, if necessary, get resources from the moon and asteroids in the "new frontier" of space. Compare *Spaceship-Earth worldview, sustainable-Earth worldview*.

time delay Lapse between the time when a system receives a stimulus and the time when the system makes a corrective action.

total fertility rate (TFR) Estimate of the average number of children that will be born alive to a woman during her lifetime if she passes through all her childbearing years (ages 15–44) conforming to age-specific fertility rates of a given year. In simpler terms, it is an estimate of the average number of children a woman will have during her childbearing years.

totally planned economy See *pure command economic system*.

total resources Total amount of a particular resource material that exists on Earth. Compare *identified resources, reserves, resources*.

toxic substance Chemical that is fatal to humans in low doses, or fatal to over 50% of test animals at stated concentrations. Most are neurotoxins, which attack nerve cells. See *carcinogen, hazardous substance, mutagen, teratogen*.

toxic waste Form of hazardous waste that causes death or serious injury (such as burns, respiratory diseases, cancers, or genetic mutations). See *hazardous waste*.

traditional economic system System in which past customs and traditions are used to make economic decisions. This system is found in most remaining tribal communities and is often a subsistence economic system. Compare *mixed economic system, pure command economic system, pure market economic system*.

traditional intensive agriculture Producing enough food for a farm family's survival and, perhaps, a surplus that can be sold. This type of agriculture requires higher inputs of labor, fertilizer, and water than traditional subsistence agriculture. See *traditional subsistence agriculture*.

traditional subsistence agriculture Production of enough crops or livestock for a farm family's survival, and in good years, a surplus to sell or put aside for hard times. Compare *traditional intensive agriculture*.

tragedy of the commons Depletion or degradation of a resource to which people have free and unmanaged access. An example is the depletion of commercially desirable species of fish in the open ocean beyond areas controlled by coastal countries. See *common-property resource*.

transform fault Area where Earth's lithospheric plates move in opposite but parallel directions along a fracture (fault) in the lithosphere. Compare *convergent plate boundary, divergent plate boundary*.

transmissible disease A disease that is caused by living organisms such as bacteria, viruses, and parasitic worms and that can spread from one person to another by air, water, food, body fluids, or, in some cases, insects or other organisms. Compare *nontransmissible disease*.

transpiration Process in which water is absorbed by the root systems of plants, moves up through the plant, passes through pores (stomata) in their leaves or other parts, and then evaporates into the atmosphere as water vapor.

tree farm Site planted with one or only a few tree species in an even-aged stand. When the stand matures, it is usually harvested by clear-cutting and is then replanted. Normally used to grow rapidly growing tree species for fuelwood, timber, or pulpwood. See *even-aged management*. Compare *uneven-aged management, uneven-aged stand*.

tritium (T: hydrogen-3) Isotope of hydrogen with a nucleus containing one proton and two neutrons, thus having a mass number of 3. Compare *deuterium*.

trophic level All organisms that are the same number of energy transfers away from the original source of energy (e.g., sunlight) that enters an ecosystem. For example, all producers belong to the first trophic level and all herbivores belong to the second trophic level in a food chain or a food web.

troposphere Innermost layer of the atmosphere. It contains about 95% of the mass of Earth's air and extends about 17 kilometers (11 miles) above sea level. Compare *stratosphere*.

true cost Cost of a good when its internal costs and its short- and long-term external costs are included in its market price. Compare *external cost, internal cost*.

unconfined aquifer Collection of groundwater above a layer of Earth material (usually rock or clay) through which water flows very slowly (low permeability). Compare *confined aquifer*.

undernutrition Consuming insufficient food to meet one's minimum daily energy requirement, for a long enough time to cause harmful effects. Compare *malnutrition, overnutrition*.

undiscovered resources Potential supplies of a particular mineral resource, believed to exist because of geologic knowledge and theory, though specific locations, quality, and amounts are unknown. Compare *resources, reserves*.

uneven-aged management Method of forest management in which trees of different species in a given stand are maintained at many ages and sizes to permit continuous natural regeneration. Compare *even-aged management*.

uneven-aged stand Stand of trees in which there are considerable differences in the ages of individual trees. Usually, such stands have a variety of tree species. See *uneven-aged management*. Compare *even-aged stand, tree farm*.

upwelling Movement of nutrient-rich bottom water to the ocean's surface. This occurs along certain steep coastal areas where the surface layer of ocean water is pushed away from shore and replaced by cold, nutrient-rich bottom water.

urban area Geographic area with a population of 2,500 or more people. The number of people used in this definition may vary, with some countries setting the minimum number of people at 10,000 to 50,000.

urban growth Rate of growth of an urban population. Compare *degree of urbanization*.

urban heat island Buildup of heat in the atmosphere above an urban area. This heat is produced by the large concentration of cars, buildings, factories, and other heat producing activities. See also *dust dome*.

urbanization See *degree of urbanization*.

vertebrates Animals with backbones. Compare *invertebrates*.

wastewater lagoon Large pond where air, sunlight, and microorganisms break down wastes, allow solids to settle out, and kill some disease-causing bacteria. Water typically remains in a lagoon for 30 days. Then it is treated with chlorine and pumped out for use by a city or spread over cropland.

wastewater pond See *wastewater lagoon*.

water consumption Water that is not returned to the surface water or groundwater from which it came, mostly because of evaporation and transpiration. As a result, this water is not available for use again in the area from which it came. See *water withdrawal*.

water cycle See *hydrologic cycle*.

waterlogging Saturation of soil with irrigation water or excessive precipitation, so the water table rises close to the surface.

water pollution Any physical or chemical change in surface water or groundwater that can harm living organisms or make water unfit for certain uses.

watershed Land area that delivers the water, sediment, and dissolved substances via small streams to a major stream (river).

water table Upper surface of the zone of saturation in which all available pores in the soil and rock in the earth's crust are filled with water.

water table aquifer See *unconfined aquifer*.

water withdrawal Removing water from a groundwater or surface water source and transporting it to a place of use. Compare *water consumption*.

watt Unit of power, or rate at which electrical work is done. See *kilowatt*.

weather Short-term changes in the temperature, barometric pressure, humidity, precipitation, sunshine (solar radiation), cloud cover, wind direction and speed, and other conditions in the troposphere at a given place and time. Compare *climate*.

weathering Physical and chemical processes in which solid rock exposed at Earth's surface is changed to separate solid particles and dissolved material, which can then be moved to another place as sediment. See *erosion*.

wetland Land that is covered all or part of the year with salt water or fresh water, excluding streams, lakes, and the open ocean. See *coastal wetland, inland wetland*.

whole-tree harvesting Use of machines to cut trees off at ground level, or to pull entire trees from the ground, and then reduce the trunks and branches to small wood chips.

wilderness Area where the earth and its community of life have not been seriously disturbed by humans and where humans are only temporary visitors.

wildlife All free, undomesticated species. Sometimes the term is used to describe only free, undomesticated species of animals.

wildlife management Manipulation of populations of wild species (especially game species) and their habitats for human benefit, the welfare of other species, and the preservation of threatened and endangered wildlife species.

wildlife resources Species of wildlife that have actual or potential economic value to people. See also *game species*.

wild species See *wildlife*.

windbreak Row of trees or hedges planted to partially block wind flow and reduce soil erosion on cultivated land.

wind farm Cluster of small to medium-sized wind turbines in a windy area, to capture wind energy and convert it into electrical energy.

woodland See *open forest*.

work What happens when a force is used to move a sample of matter over some distance or to raise its temperature. Energy is defined as the capacity to do such work.

worldview How individuals think the world works and what they think their role in the world should be. See *Spaceship-Earth worldview, sustainable-Earth worldview, throwaway worldview*.

zero population growth (ZPG) State in which the birth rate (plus immigration) equals the death rate (plus emigration) so the population of a geographical area is no longer increasing.

zone of saturation Area where all available pores in soil and rock in the earth's crust are filled by water. See *water table*.

zoning Regulating how various parcels of land can be used.

zooplankton Animal plankton. Small floating herbivores that feed on plant plankton (phytoplankton). Compare *phytoplankton*.

INDEX

MAJOR U.S. RESOURCE CONSERVATION AND ENVIRONMENTAL LEGISLATION

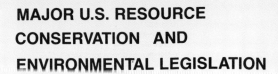

General

National Environmental Policy Act of 1969 (NEPA)
International Environmental Protection Act of 1983

Energy

National Energy Act of 1978, 1980
National Appliance Energy Conservation Act of 1987

Water Quality

Water Quality Act of 1965
Water Resources Planning Act of 1965
Federal Water Pollution Control Acts of 1965, 1972
Ocean Dumping Act of 1972
Ocean Dumping Ban Act of 1988
Safe Drinking Water Act of 1974, 1984
Water Resources Development Act of 1986
Clean Water Act of 1977, 1987

Air Quality

Clean Air Act of 1963, 1965, 1970, 1977, 1990

Noise Control

Noise Control Act of 1965
Quiet Communities Act of 1978

Resources and Solid Waste Management

Solid Waste Disposal Act of 1965
Resource Recovery Act of 1970
Resource Conservation and Recovery Act of 1976
Marine Plastic Pollution Research and Control Act of 1987

Toxic Substances

Hazardous Materials Transportation Act of 1975
Toxic Substances Control Act of 1976
Resource Conservation and Recovery Act of 1976
Comprehensive Environmental Response, Compensation, and Liability (Superfund) Act of 1980, 1986
Nuclear Waste Policy Act of 1982

Pesticides

Federal Insecticide, Fungicide, and Rodenticide Control Act of 1972, 1988

Wildlife Conservation

Anadromous Fish Conservation Act of 1965
Fur Seal Act of 1966
National Wildlife Refuge System Act of 1966, 1976, 1978
Species Conservation Act of 1966, 1969
Marine Mammal Protection Act of 1972
Marine Protection, Research, and Sanctuaries Act of 1972
Endangered Species Act of 1973, 1982, 1985, 1988
Fishery Conservation and Management Act of 1976, 1978, 1982
Whale Conservation and Protection Study Act of 1976
Fish and Wildlife Improvement Act of 1978
Fish and Wildlife Conservation Act of 1980 (Nongame Act)

Land Use and Conservation

Taylor Grazing Act of 1934
Wilderness Act of 1964
Multiple Use Sustained Yield Act of 1968
Wild and Scenic Rivers Act of 1968
National Trails System Act of 1968
National Coastal Zone Management Act of 1972, 1980
Forest Reserves Management Act of 1974, 1976
Forest and Rangeland Renewable Resources Act of 1974, 1978
Federal Land Policy and Management Act of 1976
National Forest Management Act of 1976
Soil and Water Conservation Act of 1977
Surface Mining Control and Reclamation Act of 1977
Antarctic Conservation Act of 1978
Endangered American Wilderness Act of 1978
Alaskan National Interests Lands Conservation Act of 1980
Coastal Barrier Resources Act of 1982
Food Security Act of 1985

WITHDRAWN

Bathroom (65% of typical residential water use; 40% for toilet flushing)

- For existing toilets, reduce the amount of water used per flush by putting a tall plastic container weighted with a few stones into each tank, or buy and insert a toilet dam. Ask school officials to install toilet dams.

- In new houses, install water-saving toilets that use no more than 6 liters (1.6 gallons) per flush (now required for all new residences in Massachusetts and in Phoenix, Arizona).

- Flush toilets only when necessary, using the advice found on a bathroom wall in a drought-stricken area: "If it's yellow, let it mellow—if it's brown, flush it down."

- Take short showers (less than five minutes) instead of baths. Shower by wetting down, turning off the water while soaping up, and then rinsing off.

- Install water-saving shower heads and flow restrictors on all faucets. Ask school officials to install these devices.

- Check frequently for water leaks, and repair them promptly. A pinhole-sized leak can waste up to 640 liters (170 gallons) per month. A toilet must be leaking more than 940 liters (250 gallons) *a day* before you can hear the leak. To test for toilet leaks, add some water-soluble dye to the water in the tank but don't flush. If you have a leak, some color will show up in the bowl's water within a few minutes.

- Don't keep water running while brushing teeth, shaving, or washing.

Laundry Room (15%)

- Wash only full loads; use the short cycle and fill the machine to the lowest possible water level. Use a dryer powered by natural gas, not energy- and money-wasting electricity. Better yet, let the sun dry your clothes or use the dryer's unheated air or fluff cycle for drying.

- When buying a new washer, choose one that uses the least amount of water and fills up to different levels for loads of different sizes. Front-loading clothes washers use less water and energy than comparable top-loading models.

- Check for leaks frequently, and repair all leaks promptly.

Kitchen (10%)

- Use an automatic dishwasher only for full loads; use the short cycle and let dishes air-dry to save energy and money.

- When washing many dishes by hand, don't let the faucet run. Instead, use one filled dishpan for washing and another for rinsing.

- Keep a reusable jug of water in the refrigerator rather than running water from a tap until it gets cold enough to drink.

- Check for leaks frequently, and repair all leaks promptly.

- Don't use a garbage disposal system—a large user of water. Instead, compost your food wastes (Figure 12-18).

Outdoors (10%, higher in arid and semiarid areas)

- Don't wash your car, or wash it less frequently. Wash the car from a bucket of soapy water; use the hose only for rinsing. Use a commercial car wash that recycles its water.

- Sweep walks and driveways instead of hosing them off.

- Reduce evaporation losses by watering lawns and gardens in the early morning or in the evening, rather than in the heat of midday or when windy. Better yet, landscape with native plants adapted to local average annual precipitation so that watering is unnecessary. Think of a conventional grass lawn, which must be frequently watered, fertilized, and protected with pesticides, as a glaring example of unnecessary Earth degradation. Botanists in Florida are experimenting with a disease-resistant hybrid grass that remains lush with just four waterings a year and also repels chinch bugs and several other types of insects.

- Use drip irrigation systems and mulch on home gardens to improve irrigation efficiency and reduce evaporation.

- To irrigate plants, install a system to capture rainwater or collect, filter, and reuse normally wasted gray water from bathtubs, showers, sinks, and the clothes washer.

Chemical	Alternative
Deodorant	Sprinkle baking soda on a damp wash cloth and wipe skin.
Oven cleaner	Baking soda and water paste, scouring pad.
Toothpaste	Baking soda.
Drain cleaner	Pour ½ cup salt down drain, followed by boiling water; or pour 1 handful baking soda and ½ cup white vinegar and cover tightly for one minute.
Window cleaner	Add 2 teaspoons white vinegar to 1 quart warm water.
Toilet bowl, tub, and tile cleaner	Mix a paste of borax and water; rub on and let set one hour before scrubbing. Can also scrub with baking soda and a brush.
Floor cleaner	Add ½ cup vinegar to a bucket of hot water; sprinkle a sponge with borax for tough spots.
Shoe polish	Polish with inside of a banana peel, then buff.
Silver polish	Clean with baking soda and warm water.
Air freshener	Set vinegar out in an open dish. Use an opened box of baking soda in close areas such as refrigerators and closets. To scent the air, use pine boughs or make sachets of herbs and flowers.

Chemical	Alternative
General surface cleaner	Mixture of vinegar, salt, and water.
Bleach	Baking soda or borax.
Mildew remover	Mix ½ cup vinegar, ½ cup borax, and warm water.
Disinfectant and general cleaner	Mix ½ cup borax in 1 gallon of hot water.
Furniture or floor polish	Mix ½ cup lemon juice and 1 cup vegetable or olive oil.
Carpet and rug shampoos	Sprinkle on cornstarch, baking soda, or borax and vacuum.
Detergents and detergent boosters	Washing soda or borax and soap powder.
Spray starch	In a spray bottle, mix 1 tablespoon cornstarch in a pint of water.
Fabric softener	Add 1 cup white vinegar or ¼ cup baking soda to final rinse.
Dishwasher soap	1 part borax and 1 part washing soda.
Pesticides (indoor and outdoor)	Use natural biological controls.